INDUSTRIAL ENGINEERING AND MANAGEMENT

SOME FAMOUS BOOKS BY THE SAME AUTHOR

Construction Equipment & Management	**ISBN:** 978-93-82609-05-6	**Pages:** 492
Construction Engineering & Management	**ISBN:** 978-93-91505-35-6	**Pages:** 472
Total Quality Management and Reliability	**ISBN:** 978-93-91505-22-6	**Pages:** 456
Industrial Safety & Health Management	**ISBN:** 978-93-86173-18-8	**Pages:** 456
Disaster Management	**ISBN:** 978-93-55383-96-9	**Pages:** 248
Basic Mechanical Engineering	**ISBN:** 978-93-86173-33-1	**Pages :** 792
Environmental Studies	**ISBN:** 978-93-90779-02-4	**Pages :** 536
Environmental Engineering	**ISBN:** 978-93-90779-07-9	**Pages :** 500
Automobile Mechanics	**ISBN:** 978-93-86173-01-0	**Pages :** 512

INDUSTRIAL ENGINEERING AND MANAGEMENT

S.C. SHARMA
Formerly General Manager,
THDC India Limited Govt.

T.R. BANGA
Formerly Principal,
Polytechnic, Alwar (Raj.)

KHANNA BOOK PUBLISHING CO. (P) LTD.

Publisher of Engineering and Computer Books

4C/4344, Ansari Road, Darya Ganj, New Delhi-110002
Phone : 011-23244447-48 **Mobile:** +91-9910909320
E-mail : contact@khannabooks.com
Website : www.khannabooks.com

Dear Readers,

To prevent the piracy, this book is secured with HIGH SECURITY HOLOGRAM on the front title cover. In case you don't find the hologram on the front cover title, please write us to at contact@khannabooks.com or whatsapp us at +91-99109 09320 and avail special gift voucher for yourself.

Specimen of Hologram on front Cover title:

Moreover, there is a SPECIAL DISCOUNT COUPON for you with EVERY HOLOGRAM.

How to avail this SPECIAL DISCOUNT:

Step 1: Scratch the hologram
Step 2: Under the scratch area, your "coupon code" is available
Step 3: Logon to www.khannabooks.com
Step 4: Use your "coupon code" in the shopping cart and get your copy at a special discount
Step 5: Enjoy your reading!

Price: ₹ 550.00

ISBN: 978-93-5538-009-8

Industrial Engineering and Management *by* S.C.Sharma & T.R. Banga

First Edition: 2017
Second Edition: 2022
Reprint Edition: 2025

To view complete list of books, Please scan the QR Code:

Published by:
Khanna Book Publishing Co. (P) Ltd.
CIN: U22110DL1998PTC095547

Visit us at: **www.khannabooks.com**
Write us at: **contact@khannabooks.com**

Printed in Bharat.

PREFACE

The book "Industrial Engineering and Management" covers the syllabus of the subjects Industrial Engineering, Industrial Management, Production Planning and Control, Production Management, Engineering Economics and Costing, Industrial Organisation, Principles of Management prescribed by different Indian Universities.

The book is also useful for the students of management courses, section B of AMIE, and U.P.S.C. Engineering services examination.

Efforts have been made to present the subject-matter in concise, compact and simple language. The theoretical concepts have been supported by large number of numerical illustrations to provide clarity.

Although extreme care has been taken to remove all the mistakes and misprints, yet some of them might have been creeped in. The authors shall feel highly obliged if the errors are pointed out by the readers. The suggestions will be gratefully appreciated by the authors for enhancing the utility of this book.

We are highly thankful to the publishers for taking keen interest in bringing out this edition well in time.

S.C. Sharma

T.R. Banga

CONTENTS

PART 4: PRODUCTION

Introduction to Industrial Engineering and Industrial Management

1.1. HISTORY AND DEVELOPMENT OF INDUSTRIAL ENGINEERING

Starting from the days of Frederick W. Taylor and his contemporaries, notably H.L. Gantt and the F.W. Gilberth (1882 to 1912), Industrial Engineering has been considered a dynamic profession. In the engineering field, Industrial Engineering is one of the fastest growing profession. In the beginning, industrial engineering was closely associated with the Time and Motion Study. This position continued from 1903; the year of main pioneer work of F.W. Taylor through his paper on "shop management", till 1933 when the term "method engineering" or "method study" developed by H.B. Maymard and his associates was added.

Significant era in the development of industrial engineering began after World War II, when many new activities developed and application of principles and techniques was vastly broadened. These activities were

(*i*) Industrial engineering and computer.

(*ii*) Development of system analysis and design.

(*iii*) Application of mathematical and statistical tools.

(*iv*) Network planning techniques and their application.

(*v*) Value engineering.

(*vi*) Behavioural science and human factors.

(*vii*) Human engineering or Ergonomics.

Details about the pioneers and developments made by them have been dicussed in detail in the chapter on "Management Concept".

Definition

In the year 1943, the work standardization committee of the management division of the American Society of Mechanical Engineering (A.S.M.E.) attempted to define the limits of the field of industrial engineering. One appealing definition described by the American Institute of Industrial Engineers is given hereunder :

"Industrial engineering is concerned with the design, improvement and installation of integrated system of man, materials and equipments drawing upon specialized knowledge and skill in the mathematical, physical and social sciences either with the principles or methods of engineering analysis and design to specify, predict and evaluate the results to be obtained from such system."

The above definition shows that the field of Industrial engineering is quite broad and all the high productivity techniques are well within its purview. Industrially advanced nations have been greatly benefited by the application of the Industrial Engineering techniques in raising their productivity and consequently, their standard of living.

1.2. SCOPE OF INDUSTRIAL ENGINEERING

A wide area is covered under the Industrial Engineering. Following are the main branches of Industrial Engineering:

1. Work study
   (*a*) Method study. (*b*) Work measurement
2. Plant layout and Material handling.
3. Inventory control.
4. Operation research.
5. Production Planning and Control.
6. System Engineering.
7. C.P.M. and P.E.R.T.
8. Value Engineering.
9. Cybernetics.

1. **Work Study.** It deals with the problems :
   (*a*) as to how should a job be done, and
   (*b*) how much time a job should take for completion ?

   Answer for the first question is found by the Method Study, while for the second question by work measurement.

   (*a*) **Method Study.** The aim of this study is to find a scheme of least wastage.

   (*b*) **Work Measurement.** This technique is used to find the correct manufacturing time for a product. In this, the time required to do each detailed element of an industrial operation (including manual, mental and machining operations) is observed and recorded.

2. **Plant Layout and Material Handling**

   (*a*) **Plant Layout.** This is a technique of locating different machines and plant services within the factory, so that each operation is performed at the point of greatest convenience and greatest possible output of high quality at the lowest possible total cost can be achieved.

   (*b*) **Material Handling.** As lot of production time is consumed in handling materials before, during and after the manufacture, therefore, by proper selection, operation and maintenance of material handling devices, we can increase the output, improve quality, speed up the deliveries and, therefore, reduce the cost of production.

3. **Inventory Control.** It is the systematic location, storage and recording of goods in such a way that desired degree of service can be made to the operating shops at minimum ultimate cost.

4. **Operation Research.** This is a research technique, which offers alternative plans for a problem, to the management for making decisions. The scientific and quantitative analysis of the problem (done by the team of statisticians, psychologists, labour

specialists, mathematicians, Industrial Engineers etc.) is presented before the management, to enable it to make sounder decisions.This deals with the complicated problems like, queuing theory, linear programming, transportation problems, inventory control, sequential decisions, equipment replacement policy etc.

5. **Production Planning and Control.** It is the process of planning the production in advance, setting the exact route for each item to give production orders to shops and lastly to follow up the progress of products according to the production orders.
6. **System Engineering.** System engineering is the process of a successfully developing large scale complex man-machine systems within cost, time and performance targets. System Engineer is a combination of Engineer, Scientist and Administrator. He must make use of new and unfamiliar disciplines also to achieve its objectives.
7. **C.P.M. and P.E.R.T.** These are the modern net-work techni-ques used by the management for programming.
8. **Value Engineering.** It is used for reducing the cost of a product by making changes in design, specifications of material used, source of supply, tool design, machinability, tolerances, aesthetics etc.
9. **Cybernatics.** It has been observed that there is marked similarity between the structures of classical control system and various biological and other physical systems. Thus cybernatics is a new engineering discipline in which biological and other physical systems are studied and,then applied to engineering problems.

1.3. APPLICATIONS (ACTIVITIES) OF INDUSTRIAL ENGINEERING

The field of Industrial Engineering represents an area that is today undergoing rapid expansion and diversification. For example, among the many activities that an Industrial Engineering specialist might be called upon to engage in, we find the following :

1. Locate new plants and design their physical layout.
2. Analyze and plan production schedules and inventories.
3. Devise ways to improve the productivity and moral of people at work.
4. Study equipment replacement feasibility.
5. Conduct the effective work measurement and set the time standards for effective wage payment.
6. Diagnose and correct causes of poor quality.
7. Conduct the study for methods improvement.
8. Measure the effectiveness of marketing, advertising and other distribution policies.
9. Design, develop and evaluate complex man-machine systems.
10. Utilization of digital computers to receive tremendous quantities of information to digest, process and store information, and then to display this information for appropriate decision making.
11. Evolve better production methods by applying operation research techniques.
12. Analyze and schedule big projects by using C.P.M. and P.E.R.T. network techniques.
13. Develop and maintain standards governing administrative and sales budget, including the summarizing of the slates forecasting function and the responsibility for the market analysis function.

14. Analyze, establish and control of all office routines and procedure from a functional stand point, including their simplification, development and control and the design of management information systems.
15. Aid in establishing cost controls, performance rating charts, budgetary controls, and the like designed to fit his actual needs.
16. Assist in the development of training programmes and aid in training supervisors and workers in the proper performance of their duties.

1.4. PRODUCTIVITY IMPROVEMENT THROUGH INDUSTRIAL ENGINEERING

All these activities of Industrial Engineering, if used properly, leads to increase in productivity. As every one knows, that productivity is of very much importance to a nation, as it creates the wealth of the nation. To improve the economic position in comparison to other countries, we must improve our productivity and performance. Productivity is the key to the important problem of inflation. In recent years, there had been regular pay increases, but we have forgotten that without improving the productivity, prices will be sky rocketing and we will lose competition in the world market. To compensate wage increase, we must increase the productivity.

To fight against inflation, we must increase the productivity. The battle fields of this fight are every place where resources (men, material, equipment, money, time, efforts etc.) are used. The factory and the agriculture are most important places where we must emphasise for productivity improvement. Other places like offices, hospitals, teaching institutions etc., also need productivity improvement if the society and the country is to move forward.

Thus, our aim must be to make people more productivity conscious if we want to improve their standard of living. Productivity holds the key to the prosperity of the individual, a company and of a nation.

Increase in productivity results in :

1. Increase in production and hence higher profits.
2. Products produced will be cheaper.
3. Higher wages and bonus can be allowed to workers because of larger profits.
4. Improvement in living standards of workers.
5. Brings prosperity in the country.

Thus, we have seen that "Industrial Engineering is an organised continuous effort to improve productivity and quality and to reduce costs within an organisation." For this purpose an industrial engineer must continue to lead the way in "Resource utilization" and he can play a vital role in increasing the productivity based on various factors stated earlier.

1.5. PLACE OF INDUSTRIAL ENGINEERING DEPARTMENT IN THE ORGANISATION

Industrial Engineering Department must be given a high position in the organisation of a factory, so that the persons working in this department cannot be influenced by the officers working on the shop floor and their suggestions can be accepted with respect and acted upon. Since the Industrial Engineering Department is for the service of the management of an enterprise, therefore, it must be a staff and not a line activity.

The position of the head of the Industrial Engineering Department in relation to his fellow members of the staff depends upon following important factors:

(*i*) Size of the Organisation.

(*ii*) Type of organisation and whether managed by owner himself or by professionals.

(*iii*) Nature of work carried out in the factory.

(*iv*) Qualifications, experience, personality etc. of the Chief Industrial Engineer and those of other Department Heads.

Looking to the above factors, there cannot be any standard chart for organisational structure. A typical organisation chart showing the position of Industrial Engineering Department is given hereunder:

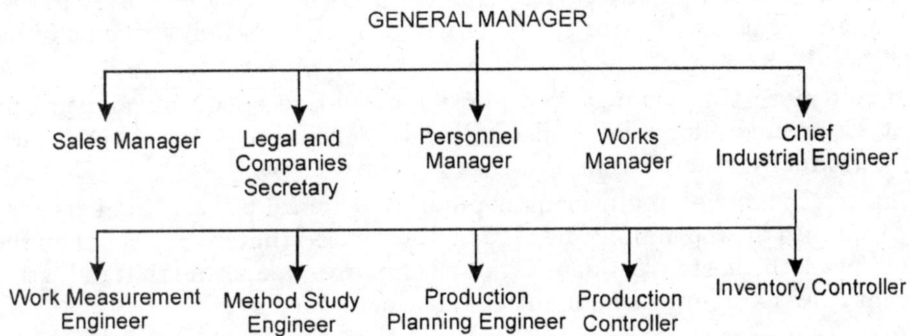

Sometimes Chief Industrial Engineer is given a place under works Manager. It is due to the reason that Works Manager is responsible to increase the overall productivity and by putting the Industrial Engineering Department under him, he can give more importance to the suggestions or advices placed before him. In such cases the organisational structure will be similar to that shown in the chart below:

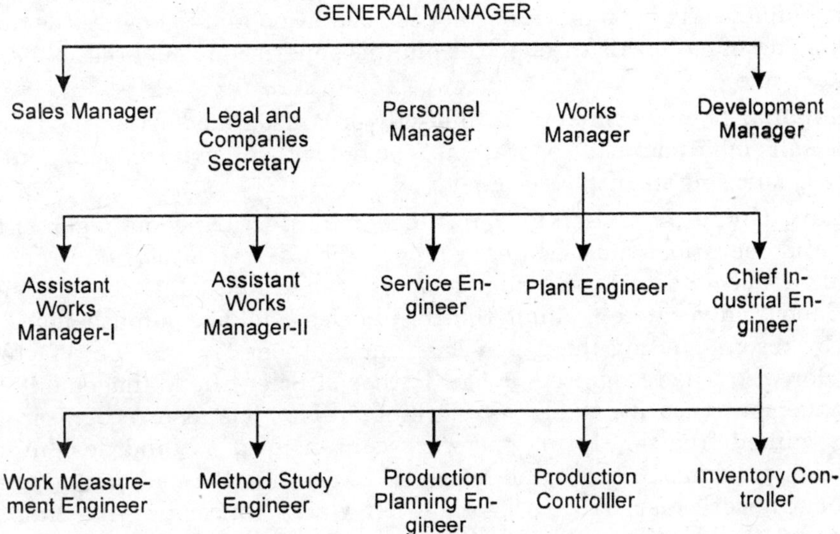

1.6. FUTURE OF INDUSTRIAL ENGINEERING

For the rapid development of our country in economic field, we must be cost conscious and productivity conscious and which is possible by giving due consideration to industrial engineering. If industrial engineering is to take root in the country, our immediate aim should be to provide education facilities in the universities at the graduate and post graduate levels and they must also run special courses of short duration in collaboration with industries for :

(*i*) existing industrial engineers to make them familiar with the latest'development in the field, and

(*ii*) other staff members to impart basic knowledge of the activities of industrial engineering.

There is also a need for the massive and continuous research and development to get facts which we do not yet have. Productivity measurement methods must be evolved in the production field as well as in the service sector specially where it is extremely difficult to measure the work.

We must put more time, money and effort for positive encouragement of productivity improvement. Concerted efforts must also be made to remove many of the road blocks and restrictions to productivity improvement which presently exist.

In making the industrial engineering popular, it is moral duty of the existing Industrial Engineers to convince the top management (with their work) that money spent on their salaries and projects is one of the best investment which a company makes, and that industrial engineering department is an excellent investment and not just added overhead.

To justify their existence, they must give a high return of the investment made on them.

1.7. INDUSTRIAL (PRODUCTION) MANAGEMENT

Concept and Background

Industrial management involves studying the performance of machines as well as people. Specialists are employed to keep machines in good condition and to ensure the quality of their production. The flow of materials through the plant is superised to ensure that neither workers nor machines are idle.

Industrial management term applies to highly organised modern methods of carrying on industrial especially manufacturing operations. The field of industrial (production) management has been evolved since eighteenth century.

Progressing through a series of names—manufacturing management, production management, and operations management - all of which describe the same general principle. The traditional view of *manufacturing management*began in eighteenth century with the concept of 'division of labour' advocated by Adam Smith. Charles Babbage, a mathematician extended Smith's work by recommending the use of scientific methods for analysing factory problems. Then F.W. Taylor who was recognised as the 'Father of Scientific Management' extended the scientific management theories to factory working. Taylor has also recognised the potential improvements gained from analysing the work content of a job and designing the job for maximum efficiency. Frank Gilbreth and his wife Lillion Gilbreth contributed to motion study in 1911. Lillion Gilbreth also wrote a book on her works concerning the human factors in organisation. In 1913, Henry Ford developed the concept of mass production, and work stations into an assembly line with moving belt. "In 1913 also, Henry Gantt contributed in charting the production schedule. Harrington suggested the use of experts in organisation to improve efficiency.

In 1928, Wilson developed the concept of Economic Ordering Quantity (EOQ). Elton Mayo contributed towards human relations. Till 1930, traditional view on manufacturing management prevailed.

Production Management then became more widely accepted term from 1930s through the 1950s. During this period use of statistics was recognised in quality control, and operation research techniques were applied in production problems, techniques were developed on economic efficiency in manufacturing. Studies were also conducted to eliminate wasteful efforts of works and achieve greater efficiency. At this time other needs of workers were also realised, and social scientists started studying human behaviour in the work environment. Economists, mathematicians, and computer scientists also contributed newer, and more sophisticated analytical approaches. During this period value engineering technique, and concepts of CPM and PERT were also developed.

Around 1970s, two distinct changes emerged, which reflected the new name — *Operations Management* and was a clear shift in the service and manufacturing sector. As the service sector became more prominent, the change from 'production' to 'operations' emphasized the broadening of field to service organisations. Now-a-days, organisational goals are better focussed to meet consumers' needs. Systems approach is taking an integrated look at the problems of operating systems. Computer applications to manufacturing, scheduling, and control, materials requirement planning, applications of Japanese theories like 'Just in Time (JIT) system', Quality circles are being adopted. Other notable developments in recent past have been group technology (GT), computer-aided design/manufacturing (CAD/GAM) etc.

Thus the term operations management includes the number of non-manufacturing sectors of economy such as transport, energy, health, agriculture, warehousing, banking etc. Therefore, the terms *production and operation management* or *operations management* have been suggested to indicate the general applications of the techniques of management of machines and materials. However, by generalizing the concept of production as the 'process through which goods and sendees are created' we can include both manufacturing and service organisations within the purview of production management.

Definitions

Production Management is a branch of general management which is concerned with production activities. It can also be defined as 'Production management deals with decision-making related to production process so that the resulting goods or services are produced according to specifications in amounts and by the schedules demanded, and at a minimum cost'.

Operations Management can be defined as the management of the conversion process, which converts land, labour, capital, and management inputs into desired outputs of goods and services.

Production is an organised activity of converting raw materials into useful products, by organised utilisation of natural resources, men, money, materials and machines. Whereas in the input-conversion-output sequence, the smallest unit of productive activity, is termed as *operation*. Therefore, an operation is some step in the overall process of producing a product or service that leads to the final output.

Production can also be defined as follows :

(*i*) Production is a sequence of technical processes, requiring either directly or indirectly the mental and physical skill of craftsman and consists of changing the shape, size and properties of materials and ultimately converting them into more useful articles.

(*ii*) Production is a process developed to transform a set of inputs like men, materials, money, machinery, and energy into a specified set of outputs like finished products and services in desired quantity and quality in order to achieve the objectives of the enterprise.

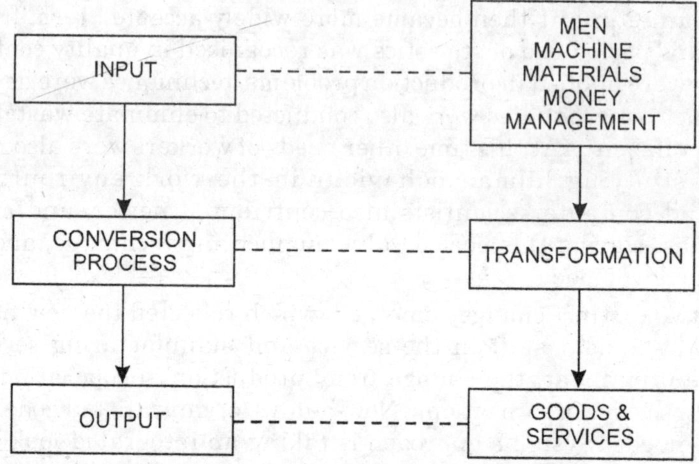

Fig. 1.1. Production system.

Production includes Manufacture of Goods and Services, which has four recognised factors, namely (*i*) natural resources including land, (*ii*) labour, (*iii*) capital *i.e.* factory building, machinery, tools, raw materials etc, (*iv*) organisation. Production involves wide range of activities starting from selection of site to packing of products for distribution.

1.8. SCOPE OF PRODUCTION MANAGEMENT

1. **Relating to Designing of Production System:** These activities concern the production engineering, and include design of tools and jigs ; design, development and installation of equipment, and selection and optimisation of the size of the firm. Selection of plant location, plant layout, materials handling systems are functions of production engineering. The problems of human factor, and research and development are also considered.
2. **Relating to Analysis and Control of Production Operations:** These activities include production planning, production control. Production control activities are looked after at three levels : control of inventory, control of flow of materials, and control of work-in-progress. Other controls to be looked into are quality control, cost control and labour control.

1.9. MANAGEMENT SCIENCE

Management Science is a problem solving process used by interdisciplinary team for decision-making and may use quantitative analysis and other scientific approach. The management science is that application of the scientific methods to the study of the operations of large and complex organisations.

Management Science has following Characteristics

(*i*) Uses inter-disciplinary approach.

(*ii*) Identifies all important functional interactions and determine their impact on the company as a whole.

(*iii*) Uncovers new problems to light for study.

(*iv*) Uses systematic approach including mathematic modes.

(*v*) Primary focus is on managerial decision-making.

Management Science uses following important **tools for solving managerial problems:**

1. Mathematical Programming.
2. Network Techniques.
3. Dynamic Programming.
4. Markov chains.
5. Simulation Models.
6. Game Theory.
7. Inventory Models.
8. Waiting line Models.
9. Decision Matrices.
10. Decision Trees.
11. Linear Programming.

QUESTIONS

1. Define the following :

(*i*) Cybernatics,

(*ii*) Inventory control,

(*iii*) System engineering,

(*iv*) Work measurement,

(*v*) Operation research.

2. List the various activities of Industrial Engineering.

3. How Productivity can be improved by the aid of Industrial engineering?

4. Describe the place of Industrial Engineering department in the organisation.

5. Write a note on the future of Industrial Engineering.

6. What are the main branches of Industrial Engineering? Write a paragraph on each of them.

7. What is Management Science? List the tools of Management Science for solving managerial problems.

8. Define industrial management. Discuss functions of production manager of a modern factory.

9. Write short notes on:

(*a*) Scope of production management.

(*b*) Evolution of industrial management.

(*c*) History and development of industrial engineering.

10. Explain the scope of industrial engineering.

11. Mention different applications of industrial engineering.

12. Explain as to how productivity can be improved through the application of industrial engineering.

Part–1 **Basic Management**

2

MANAGEMENT CONCEPT

2.1. INTRODUCTION

Management is concerned with direction and control over the various activities and work for the attainment of the objectives laid by the administration. As per W.R. Spriegal, management is an executive function, which is mainly concerned with carrying out the policies laid by the administration.

Management is an executive function which actively directs human efforts towards common goal.

Management can also be defined as, the art of getting things done through the people, this concept of management is old and often not liked as it ignores the needs of workers and does not offer them human treatment.

Harold Koontz defined, "the management as, the art of getting things done through and with people in formally organised groups. Thus it is an art of creating an environment in which people can perform as individuals and yet cooperate towards attainment of group goals. It is the art of removing blocks to such performance, a way of optimising efficiency in reaching goals,".

This definition covers the following aspects of management, namely.

(*i*) Management as a process.

(*ii*) Management as an activity.

(*iii*) Management as a group of management personnel.

(*iv*) Management as a discipline of knowledge.

(*v*) Management as a science.

Characteristics of Management

Following are some of the characteristics of good management:

1. To maintain discipline and to keep control over the employees of various sections.
2. To distribute work and machines among the workers in such a way as to secure maximum output.
3. To keep co-ordination among the staff at various levels.
4. To improve efficiency, management keeps sufficient watch and strict inspection.
5. To suggest new ideas and improvements.
6. To arrange for the efficient storing and recording.
7. To make the arrangement of payments and their records etc.

8. To provide good training to staff for attaining high skill in all fields.
9. To impart the instruction timely and to provide consistent guidance
10. By adhering to high standards of performance it must be able to provide facilities and wages to the workers and reduce the prices.

Importance of Management

A scientific management is most essential as it fulfils the following necessities:

1. It maintains discipline by keeping proper control over the employees of various departments.
2. It distributes the work and machines among the workers in such a way so as to secure maximum output.
3. It keeps co-ordination among the staff at various levels.
4. It improves efficiencies, as it keeps sufficient watch and strict inspection.
5. It suggests new idea and improvements.
6. It arranges for the efficient storing and recording.
7. It makes arrangement for payment on scientific basis and to keep their records properly.
8. It develops means of marketing and publicity.
9. It gives due importance to labour grievances and study their psychology of the purpose of maintaining the good human relations and for achieving the goals.

2.2. DEVELOPMENT OF MANAGEMENT THOUGHTS

The diagram given under represents the most important contribution to the modern management thoughts. Only few important pioneers have been listed. Vertical columns represent the broad divisions. Some pioneers of management thoughts made the contribution in more than one field *e.g.* Taylor). Here we are dealing only some of those ideas that have made important role to the management thought.

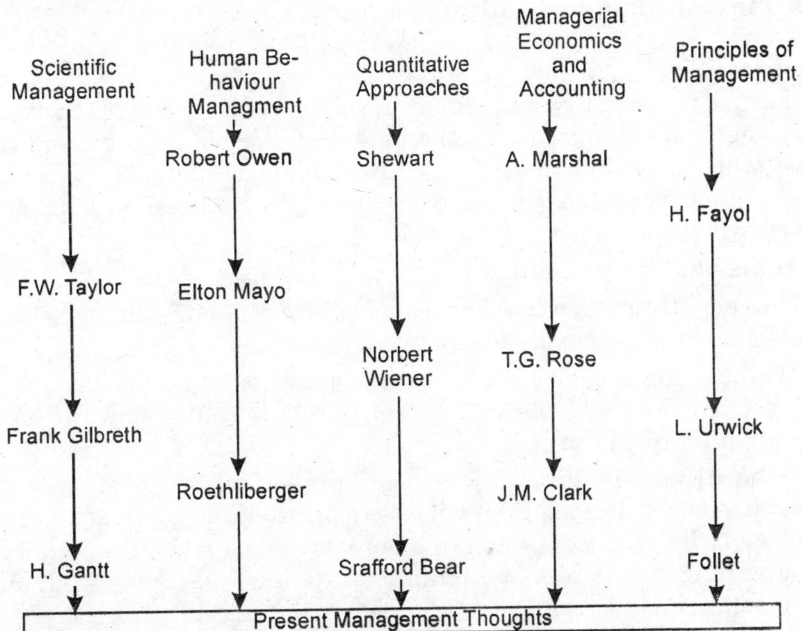

Management being very wide and comprehensive subject, developed since civilisation, and the present state has been achieved gradually. Management thoughts have been developed very slowly and managers are working since centuries. But the actual development in the field of management have taken place in last one hundred years only.

With the increasing growth and size of organisations, there is need for more efficient managers. Depending upon the efficiency of the management some companies have grown, whereas others have stagnated or even been eliminated.

It is very difficult to write detailed description on the development of management thoughts, since much work has gone unnoticed and unrecorded. Whereas, writers on management have been very few. Here only the most important thoughts are covered.

Field of Management	*Functional Approach*	*Scientific Management*	*Human Behaviour Management*
Pioneers	Henry Fayol (1841-1925)	F.W. Taylor (1856-1912) ↓ Gilbreth (1868-1924) ↓ Henry Gantt (1861-1919)	Robert Owen (1771-1855) ↓ G.Elton Mayo (1880-1949) ↓ Mary Parker Follet (1880-1933)

These pioneers laid the foundation of modern management. Development of management Science can be studied in 3 categories (1) Functional Approach, which includes work of Fayol, (2) Scientific Management approach, which includes the work of Taylor, Gilbreth and Gantt. (3) Human Relations approach, which includes the work of Mayo, Owen and Follet.

2.2.1. Functional Approach to Management

Henry Fayol (1841-1925)

Henry Fayol, a French industrialist and Manager, was one of the first writers who developed his theory of management. He is regarded as the Father of modern management theory, because he was the first who suggested the functions of management. These functions have been recognised as the main task of manager in modern management theories. Management Thoughts of Fayol can be classified into following three categories.

1. **Functions of Management**

   (i) **Forecasting.** As soon as an idea comes in the mind for manufacturing, an attempt is made to assess possible quantities, price etc.

   Forecasting is concerned with the estimation of quantities, the sales forecast, cost, finance problems, capital expenditure, profit or loss alternatives available and planning is started.

   (ii) **Planning.** Planning means "thinking before doing". Before actual work is started, it is decided that, what is to be produced, how much is to be produced, how to be produced, when to be produced and who are to produce it, etc. The planning should aim at eliminating the wastage of material, idleness of men, machinery and capital.

(*iii*) **Organizing.** When complete planning is done, next step is to arrange the men, money and material, for actual execution of manufacture.

(*iv*) **Directing.** It means the system of directing the plan to operation. The person who directs must have dynamic leadership and must guide the subordinates. The instruction must be simple, clear, complete and as far as possible in writing.

(*v*) **Motivating.** Suppose a person is a highly capable, physically strong and technically qualified, but if he is not willing to work hard his output will be much less. So the function of the motivating is to find out the motives of work in a man and then he should be encouraged to do work by keeping his moral high.

(*vi*) **Co-ordinating.** In an enterprise, there may be large number of workers, all engaged with the object of producing particular product. This is the task of co-ordination to integrate and harmonise them to achieve a common object.

(*vii*) **Controlling.** It's function of the management to see that other functions are being done perfectly alright. Controlling means to watch actual performance with the plans and to point out defective work, to rectify them and to prevent recurrence. Some of the controls are Quality Control, Cost Control, Material Control and Production Control etc.

(*viii*) **Communication.** This function transmits the informations and instructions to all concerned parties, *i.e.* to employees, customers, suppliers, shareholders and to general public. Without this there are chances of mistrust, fears etc. and therefore, management must stress on better communication system.

Communication must include the acceptance of good ideas coming from the persons who are direct in touch with practical use. Therefore, for sound communication, joint consultations and works committees must be formed for free exchange of views.

(*ix*) **Leadership.** All the managers are supposed to have the quality of leadership as they are leaders of concern.

(*x*) **Decision Making.** As managers are required to take decisions very frequently, and the efficiency of the concern, loss or profit etc. are affected by these decisions, great amount of attention is required to be paid to this function.

2. Principles of Organisation

Fayol, the founder of the movement for better organisation, in 1916 gave the following principles of organisation:

(*i*) **Division of Work.** It promotes efficiency, because it permits the work to be executed in limited space or area. Division of work permits all the work to be performed more effectively.

(*ii*) **Authority and Responsibility.** Authority and Responsibility always go together. Authority means "right to act, decide and command". Hence, whenever a task is assigned to a manager, he must be given sufficient powers (*i.e.*, authority) to exercise control to achieve the task.

Responsibility is the obligations of a subordinate for the performance of any job allotted by the superior.

(*iii*) **Discipline.** It means obedience, application, energy and respect. There are many examples that poor performance is due to the lack of these four mentioned factors or say discipline.

(*iv*) **Unity of Command.** A subordinate should take orders from only one superior. If not, then according to Fayol, authority is undetermined, discipline is in jeopardy, orders disturbed and stability threatened".

(*v*) **Unity of Direction.** According to Fayol, each management objective should have only one plan.

(*vi*) **Subordination of Individual Interest to General Interest.** This means that the interest of the organisation is much before the interests of individual.

(*vii*) **Remuneration of Personnel.** Payment to workers should be fair, and some proper method should be adopted.

(*viii*) **Centralisation.** According to this principle, there should be one central point in the organisation which have power to control overall work.

(*ix*) **Equity.** Kindness and justice on the part of management to create loyalty and devotion among employees.

(*x*) **Stability.** Efficiency can be achieved by having stable work force.

(*xi*) **Initiative.** To have success, plans should be well made before starting the actual work.

3. Activities of Managers

Concept developed by Fayol in General and Industrial Management are identified into following six activities. Managers must have ability to perform these activities well to give good results.

(*i*) **Managerial.** Managerial activity means to follow management functions like, planning, organising, commanding, co-ordinating and controlling etc.

(*ii*) **Technical.** Technical know how and production work.

(*iii*) **Commercial.** Buying, selling and exchange functions.

(*iv*) **Financial.** Utilisation of capital in an optimum way.

(*v*) **Security.** Property and interests of the organisation must be secured.

(*vi*) **Accounting.** To keep accounts properly so as to determine financial position of the organisation.

2.2.2. Scientific Management Approach

Frederick Winslow Taylor (1856-1912)

F.W.Taylor is a most significant figure in the history of management thoughts. He is known as founder of "Scientific management". He reformed the management through a thoughtful and systematic approach to its problems. Taylor found that much of waste (man, long time, energy, efficiency etc.) is due to the lack of order and system in the management. He emphasized that usually management was ignorant about the amount of work performed by a worker in a day, and also about the best way of doing the job. Hence it remained at the mercy of the workers. Taylor, therefore, suggested that management should adopt scientific methods for achieving higher efficiency.

Some significant achievements of Taylor are listed below :

(*i*) **Work Study.** This is a work measurement and work improvement technique. Taylor scientifically conducted Time and Motion Studies, Method Study and Fatigue Studies. Work-study is used to determine the standard time, that a qualified worker should take to perform the operation when working at a normal pace. Work study also determines the best method of performing each operation and to eliminate wastage so that production increases with less fatigue.

(*ii*) **Standardisation of Tools and Equipment of Workman and Working Conditions.** Taylor carried out several experiments, out of which following is the famous shovelling experiment of Taylor:

In 1898, at the works of the Bethlehem Steel Corporation, Taylor gave his attention to the best size of shovel for different types of materials. After several experiments he selected $21\frac{1}{2}$ *lb* as being the optimum shovel load and then he designed shovel of such a size sufficient to hold this quantity of material. He designed small shovel for heavier material and larger shovel for lighter materials so that each man can lift $21\frac{1}{2}$ lb of material so as to achieve maximum output.

(*iii*) **Incentive Scheme.** The Taylor differential Piece Rate scheme provides an incentive for a worker to achieve high level of optimum output.

(*iv*) **Principles of Management.** Taylor introduced the idea of functional management. He recommended that greater productivity and improved efficiency is possible through the use of specialised knowledge and skill.

(*v*) **Application of Scientific Methods.** Taylor introduced the scientific method in management to solve various problems. He observed, recorded the facts, applied knowledge and avoided mistakes, and thus was able to solve problems. Thus he was able to apply his thought to improve the efficiency of workers and increased productivity, and higher wages were also possible for workers.

Frank B. Gilbreth and Lilian M. Gilbreth

Frank Bunker Gilbreth (1868-1924) did work with his wife Lilian M.Gilbreth (1878-1972) regarding modern management. Frank B. Gilbreth started his career from the apprenticeship as a bricklayer and rose to the position of having his own contracting business. His wife Lilian was a trained psychologist. She helped Mr. Gilbreth in the matters related to the fatigue and monotony.

Some of the important works of Gilbreth are:

(*i*) **Development of Motion Study.** Gilbreth did development of motion study as part of the work study. His thought was to find "one best way of doing a work".

(*ii*) **Development of New Techniques.** They invented several techniques, out of which following are important:

(*a*) **Micromotion Study.** Motions are taken on picture films with the help of picture camera, which helps in measuring the time of a motion up to 0.0005 min. This procedure of motion study is known as Micromotion Study.

(*b*) **Therbligs.** For the purpose of recording motions, he split up different motions of a process into fundamental events made by various members of human body and each event was allotted a symbol and letter abbreviation. These, are 17 therbligs are :

Search, Hold, Select, Grasp, Release Load, Transport loaded, Transport empty, Position, Preposition, Assemble, Disassemble, Use, Inspect, Avoidable delay, Unavoidable delay, Rest to overcome fatigue, Plan.

(*c*) **Cronocycle Graph.** This is an improvement over cycle-graph. Cyclegraph and crononcyclegraph both invented by Gilbreth, are explained as under.

A small electric bulb is attached to the finger, hand or other part of the body of the operator, and it is photographed to record the path of motion. With a still camera, the path of light so photographed is called cyclegraph.

If an interrupter is placed in the electric circuit with the bulb and the light is flashed quickly and off slowly, then the path of bulb shall appear as a dotted line with pear-shaped dots indicating the direction of motions. The space between the dots will be according to the speed of the hand or finger. The number of dots will give the time taken by that motion. Such a record is called chronocyclegraph.

(*d*) **Study of Fatigue.** Gilbreth suggested that fatigue can be reduced by allowing rest periods, planning seating arrangements and working conditions.

Henry Gantt (1861-1919)

Gantt made many improvements in production planning and control. He is mainly remembered for the production control chart, known as Gantt chart or Bar chart. Gantt also suggested an incentive scheme.

2.2.3. Human Relations Approach

Elton Mayo (1880-1949)

Elton Mayo, the director of Hawthrone studies is considered as the father of the human relations management thought. Mayo headed a team of researchers from the Harvard University, who conducted experiments at the Hawthrone plant of the Western Electric Company, between 1927 to 1936. He recognised emotional factors in determining production efficiency.

Robert Owen (1771-1858)

Robert Owen played an important role in the field of Personnel management. He being a social reformer helped in the development of the management thoughts. He gave an idea that workers should be treated as human beings. He emphasized that good results can be obtained through "positive motivation". Positive Motivation means that employees should be given a fair treatment and they should also feel that they are being given fair treatment. Owen is mainly responsible for getting Factory Act introduced for the first time in 1891.

Mary Parker Follet (1868-1933)

Mary Parker Follet, an American philosopher, had her approach to the study of management essentially psychological. Her main contributions are:

1. Mary Follet rejected the remedies during conflict through :

   (*i*) domination and

   (*ii*) compromise, on the plea that domination leaves the feeling of having been dominated and compromise gives a feeling of loss and surrender to both sides. She was for the integration of desires of both the sides as a solution during conflict since this gives a more stable solution of problem of conflict.

2. She was of the view that for achieving good results, various parts of the organisation should be well coordinated and closely knitted so that they work as a single entity. She also pleaded for integrating the interests of the workers, investors and consumers. She pleaded for the application of scientific method to the solution of personnel problems.

Latest Management Thoughts

Latest techniques for management are quantitative techniques. Many writers have used mathematical models for solving management problems. These techniques are Operation research, Linear programming, use of statistics in quality control: work sampling, study for work measurement, Queuing or Waiting line theory, Simulation and Monte Carlo techniques, Game theory, Dynamic programming.

Use of Management Theories

Management theories provide special attention to the motivation for establishing the correct social relationship, to develop the moral. These also recognise that management must concern itself with human problems and conflicts by employing work study, operation research and psychological aspects etc. The management theories are also applied on productivity and efficiencies with the help of quantitative approach.

2.3. PRINCIPLES OF MANAGEMENT

Large efforts have been made in the later nineteenth and in the twentieth century to establish universal generalised principles of management. Examples of these principles are- "no man should work under two bosses". Henry Fayol a French industrialist, has large contribution to this school of thought. Some of the important concepts developed by Fayol in this school are mentioned below in brief:

1. **Division of work.** It promotes efficiency, because it permits the work to be executed in limited space of area. Division of work permits all the work to be performed more effectively.
2. **Authority and responsibility.** Authority and responsibility always go together. The right and power to give other cause a good performance.
3. **Discipline.** It means obedience, application, energy and respect. There are many examples that poor performance is due to the lack of these four mentioned factors or say Discipline.
4. **Unity of common.** A subordinate should take orders from only one superior. If not, then according to Fayol "authority is undermined, discipline is in jeopardy, order disturbed and stability threatened".
5. **Unity of direction.** According to Fayol "each management objective should have only one head and one plan".
6. **Subordination of individual interest to general interest** means that the interest of the organisation is much before the interest of individual.
7. **Remuneration of personnel.** Payment to workers should be fair and some proper method should be adopted.
8. **Centralization.** According to this principle, there should be one central point in the organisation which have power to control overall work.
9. **Order means** "a place for everyone and everyone in his place".
10. **Equity.** Kindness and justice on the part of management create loyalty and devotion among employees.
11. **Stability.** Efficiency can be achieved by having stable work force.
12. **Initiative.** To have success, plans should be well made before starting the actual work.

2.4. MANAGEMENT CLASSIFICATION

The term of management have three classifications :

1. **Top level management.** It consists of Managing Director or General Manager and other high rank officers such as Deputy General Manager etc. They are the chiefmen or heads in the concern.
2. **Middle level management.** Different departmental heads such a Purchase Officer, Production Superintendent, Chief Store Officer, Works Manager etc. come under middle level. They are responsible for top management on one hand and on the other side they have to control and supervise over the lower level management staff.
3. **Lower level management.** It consists of Foremen, Supervisors, Inspectors, Chargemen and Office Superintendent and such other staff. They are just above the operational staff and their function is to get the work done from operational staff according to the instructions of middle management issued by the top level management.

2.5. MANAGEMENT OBJECTIVES

Organizations are created by their members as a means for satisfying their personal objectives, but organizations also have objectives, other than the members' objectives. An organization can also exist when it achieves both types of objectives, first its own and then of members. Thus organizational or management objectives give purpose and meaning of the organization.

Importance of Management Objectives:

The importance of well-defined objectives are well recognized, such as :

1. Objectives serve as reference points for the efforts of management.
2. Objectives are needed for co-ordinating effort.
3. For co-ordination the first step is to state the objectives, the organization desires to achieve.
4. The organization that wishes to complete effectively and grow, must continually renew its objectives.
5. Management objectives are the ends towards which all organizational action is directed.
6. Management objectives define the destination of the organisation, they move forward as rapidly as they are attained.
7. Well-defined management objectives are similar to a star which can be used for navigation by ships and airplanes.

2.5.1. Setting the Objectives

For the determination of the objectives of a concern, large number of complex questions are to be decided. What is to be produced and how is to be produced are very simple matters. Other questions may either be related to the internal structure of the concern. Following are some of the factors which must be considered for establishing the company's objectives:

1. Government rules and regulations and other government controls like, taxes, restrictions, price control etc.
2. Political atmosphere.

3. Personnels available.
4. Level of productivity.
5. Total expected demand.

Objectives of a concern are determined by Board of directors. Main object of management is to secure the 'maximum prosperity of the employer' means a state of highest productivity. While for the employees it means the development of each person to his highest state of efficiency through proper training and taking proper work from him. Objectives determination is concerned with establishing the targets for all level of staff.

Objectives are needed in every area where performance and results directly and vitally affect the survival and prosperity of the business. The areas in which objectives of performance and results have to be set are market standing, innovation, productivity, financial and physical resources, profitability, managerial performance and attitude, public responsibility etc.

As per latest thinking objectives for the management are set in order to increase managerial efficiency by following logical techniques, the existing rating system, which use rating for measuring objectives such as good, better, normal, outstanding, describe manager's personality rather than measure for his productivity. The objectives for managers, uses quantitative approach to deal actual results than traditional rating system.

Management by objectives places great importance on defining of responsibilities and thereby establishing targets. For this purpose, managerial performance is measured objectively and quantitatively by using statements of responsibility which have a very specific targets. The way individual manager becomes familiar with the expectations from him by contributing to the achievement of company goals.

The objectives set for the managers are useful when the interest of both the manager and the company are taken into account. For the company, objectives should measure performance in terms of contribution to profits and other significant goods. For the managers, objectives must be such that they can be understood by the manager, and they are attainable with in the authority he exercises.

Performance objective programmes must be designed in such a way so that they can easily be adaptable to changing conditions.

Performance Objectives are Realistic

There had been a disappointment in the past because none of the techniques for performance measurement was fool-proof. For deciding performance objectives some thought should be given to the relationship between the company and manager and the authority of manager.

Performance objective is a statement describing the conditions that will exist when a job is being done. The statement includes measure to determine clearly the extent to which the objective is to be achieved. An example of an objective is "scrap loss will not be more than 4 percent of the total value of the material used."

Important aspect of performance objectives is that this should have clear relation with company goals. Some of the concepts which are of significance for the manager and company as well, and should be incorporated in the objective are- savings, costs, over-heads, profits, sales etc.

Normally a rating of objectives are fixed to provide suitable coverage of managers responsibilities. To assess his overall achievements, relative values are assigned for each objective, depending upon their importance over each other. Hence if a manager has done very well in objectives having a high value but not too well in objectives of lesser importance, his assessment for overall achievement would be considered quite good.

Basic idea of performance objectives is, therefore, to provide a systematic method of measurement to indicate how well or how poorly each manager is doing. To know his role, a manager should have objectives which he and his boss understand and agree and which the manager can relate to company goals. These objectives will provide, a manager, with the greatest satisfaction.

The performance objective also provide satisfaction to the manager's boss. Manager's boss also does not want uncertainty as to what his subordinates are supposed to do or how well they are doing it.

Principles For Setting Objectives

Following are the principles for objectives :

1. Manager and his boss determines the objectives jointly.
2. Objectives set must be able to be modified if conditions change substantially.
3. Appraisal of performance is done by comparing results attained with agreed upon objectives.
4. Results depending upon the unpredictable circumstances, which affect the ability of manager to attain any objective may also be considered.
5. Get good coverage of the manager's job to avoid loop holes.
6. Objectives set should be meaningful and realistic in terms of company goals, and important results expected from manager's job.
7. Number of objectives must be limited.
8. Objectives must focus on the job, not the man.
9. Objectives must be set at high level, so as to get better results than that achieved last year. But the level must not be such high which is impossible to achieve.
10. Objectives must be stated in a language that managers will understand.
11. Give more weightage to the most important objectives.

Some Typical Examples for Objectives.

1. Decrease the hours required for producing the item by *X* percent
2. To increase the efficiency for productive labour (ratio of actual hours to standard hours) by *X* percent.
3. Overtime should not exceed *X* percent of total hours.
4. More than *X* % of total productive hours should not be spent on rework.
5. Total scrap loss must be under *X* percent of total material.
6. Items rejected must be under *X* percent of total acceptable units produced.
7. Keep hours of absentee with pay below *X* percent of total productive hours.
8. There will be no lost time by accident.
9. The new business of Rs. *X* shall be obtained in the year in the Zone 'A'.
10. (*a*) Sales overheads, including sales efforts, market research, advertisement, training etc. not to exceed *X* percent of the volume of new business.
    (*b*) Increase over all sales volume by *X* percent.
11. No procurement of items having more than 6 months stock on hand.
12. Increase production of 'A' units by *X* percent.
13. Find dependable, stable and economical sources of raw material.

14. Increase production of export quality and promote sales in foreign market by X percent.
15. Reduce operating cost by X percent, through mechanisation of operations.

Minimum Number of Objectives Must be Set

A good performance objective programme for managers must include minimum number of objectives but with more specific targets. This makes the programme easy to administer, easy for the manager to have a better grasp over the objectives, and eliminate the vagueness and unreality.

Selection of Objectives

Objectives are selected by the boss of the manager, in advance of discussions with the manager. This helps the manager in having prior knowledge of his position and the position of manager with respect to authority and responsibilities. He also studies the company goals and decides the objectives as per this guiding. He then talks to the manager with an awareness of what targets he should like the manager to accept during their discussion.

Objectives for the manager are set in the following stages :

1. **Analyse the Manager's Authority and Responsibility.** After knowing goals for the company, division or department, next step for the boss is to determine basic important functional responsibilities of the manager. The boss then writes down the statements describing the function, covering all major areas of the responsibility. These statements should be limited in numbers and compared with the company goals. Boss must also keep in his mind about the authority vested in the position of the manager.
2. **Compare Goals with Managers Job.** The boss then compares the goals with the functional relationship of the manager, in order to see whether any relationship exists between the goals and the functions or not. If some degree of relationship is found to be existing, the boss then writes down in simple and direct language the nature of relationship and its importance. This list of statement thus prepared becomes the raw data for initial definition of objectives.
3. **Initial Definition of Objectives.** At this stage the boss is ready to make preliminary list of objectives for the manager. This list is tentative and forms the background for the discussions with the manager to finalise these objectives.
4. **Determining the Units of Measure.** After having an idea about the tentative list of objectives, boss then decides on the yard stick or units of measure. These units of measure must be selected by thinking of the terms; word of expressions frequently used. Examples of such units are:

   Volume of sale for sales promotion; man weeks for production department for measuring strike period, work period for production, number of customers for increasing sales, rupees for reducing the cost, earning profits; percentage for rejects in products and scraps which become waste, number of accidents for safety measures etc.
5. **Select specific Targets.** The final step in the preliminary analysis of objectives is to decide the specific point of the yard stick which shall be quoted as the degree of achievement expected from the manager. In the example of an objective "Increase overall sales by 20 percent", this 20 percent is the specific target, he selects for this tentative objective. The boss has to decide the quantum of target the change desired be expressed either in percentage or in units. This is actually answered on the basis of the opinion of the boss, that what degree of achievement is possible and what are the goals with in the responsibility and authority and with respect to activities of the company.

This step of selecting the specific target is very crucial one for the boss. In this target, boss reflects that what he wants from the manager? The targets are fixed based on two type of tendencies "hard" and the "soft". In first case, too high targets are fixed and while in the later too low targets are fixed. Obviously, there are many intermediate points between these two philosophies at which targets can be fixed.

6. **Discussion with the Manager.** Since the manager is a key man in the successful use of managerial performance objectives, only he can ensure attainment of the objectives set for him. For this purpose, he must understand these objectives, believe in them and through this he increases his contribution to the company.

   Before discussions with the manager, the boss must have in mind tentative set of objectives. If the use of performance objective is completely new to the managers, the boss must prepare a written explanation of the concept and give it to the manager ahead of time. This also gives him an opportunity to think about any suggestions he may want to put forward.

   The main object of the discussion is to arrive at better mutual understanding about the manager's job and then to set performance objectives. During discussions, boss explains about the concept of performance objectives and then about company or departmental goals. After clarifying the goals and his views about the objective, he can ask the manager about his views. The discussions must be then centered on these objectives with reference to the goals and the functions of the manager. These discussions are concluded with a joint agreement regarding the areas the objectives should cover. These objectives are decided for a definite period in the future, preferably 6 months to a year ahead.

Aims for Discussions

Boss must achieve the following in the discussion with the manager:

(*i*) To finalise the objectives, enable to fulfil the goals.

(*ii*) To help the manager for better understanding of his responsibilities.

(*iii*) To show the managers as to how their livelihood is closely related to the success of the company.

(*iv*) Make the managers understand that they can act independently their jobs.

2.5.2. Types of Objectives

There are many ways to categorise performance objectives, but most meaningful and useful categories which can be made are:

(*i*) Direct objectives.

(*ii*) Indirect objectives.

Direct Objectives. These are those objectives which pertain to tasks in which performance can be measured directly and quantitatively. These are measured in terms of results. Manager's performance in respect of quality and quantity of output, which can be measured directly are dealt in this category. Examples of this category are reduction of cost, improvement in sales and profits, increase in turnover.

Indirect Objectives. These objectives pertain to the characteristics of the manager himself. These are related to his technical or administrative skills, his personal traits and behaviour. Indirect objectives include his attitudes, his motivation, his leadership qualities, his health and his stamina. These are the qualities which are not possible to measure although they are of importance while setting of objectives for complete measurement of managers objectives. These indirect objectives are graded in terms of objective rating system, rather than measuring in terms of results.

For complete coverage of managerial objectives generally a balance between direct and indirect objectives is taken.

As already explained, direct objectives measure results, while indirect objectives measure managerial skill required for discharging his duties. Following are some of the indirect objectives regarding managerial abilities:

Managerial Abilities. Some of the most important and frequently used indirect objectives about managerial abilities are :

(*i*) Leadership ability
(*ii*) Integrity
(*iii*) Technical skill
(*iv*) Administrative ability
(*v*) Intelligence
(*vi*) Initiative
(*vii*) Resourcefulness
(*viii*) Judgement
(*ix*) Ability to organise
(*x*) Tactfulness
(*xi*) Physical health and stamina
(*xii*) Ability to develop other man and motivate subordinates
(*xiii*) Spirit of co-operation
(*xiv*) Ability to plan
(*xv*) Reliability,

How to Measure Indirect Objectives

Till recently rating system was used to measure these indirect objectives. In the rating system these objectives are rated in terms of excellent, very good, good, average, poor, very poor etc. Now-a-days the technique of measurement for these indirect objectives is based on a numerical scale. In this technique a value of 100 is assigned for excellent performance of that ability. This excellent performance is defined clearly in words as performance objectives are agreed to by the manager and his boss. When the 100 point level of performance is clearly defined, there is no difficulty in driving a series of definitions for several other levels of work above and below excellent. The values are then assigned with reference to this value of 100 point for the defined excellent performance.

Value Objectives

The values are assigned to each objective on the basis of the importance of the related company goals, the degree of difficulty of achieving the various objectives. This method is a refinement of the performance objectives and is a new approach. Thus this is a method of modifying adjusting and updating objectives by reviewing or revising the objectives quarterly or monthly. The annual objectives retain their importance as a guideline, but relative values of these objectives may be changed during monthly or quarterly review from the point of view of relative importance. This helps the boss to communicate his manager as to what degree of efforts should be made for each objective.

In the value objectives methods, the boss and manager jointly determine and assigns the value for each target, considering the relative importance of each objective for the entire year. Thereafter every month or every quarter the boss and the manager jointly determine if the values previously decided are appropriate, otherwise if felt necessary the values are changed but the total of values for all the objectives, must always be equal to 100.

2.5.3. Harmony of Objectives

Harmony of objectives means to harmonise the 'primary' and 'collateral' objectives. Management is to put this theory into practice for attaining two goals. Primary objectives are the producting and selling of products or services, thus these are in the interest of the business. While collateral objectives are the financial rewards and job satisfaction for the individuals.

These two types of objectives must have positive link, *e.g.*, status of individual, satisfaction in the work performed, pride in belonging to a particular concern, feeling of justice from the management, are all cases of harmonisation of objectives. Thus each manager is required to understand the requirements of each individual and the group as a whole.

Harmony of objectives reconciles the objectives of the business and those of the employees, so that they both aim for a common goal. Thus it inspires the persons to work hard. For knowing the individual objectives, it is essential to understand their basic needs from psychological aspects. These basic needs are following :

1. **Physiological Needs.** These are the necessities of food, cloth and shelter. These needs must be fulfillled so as to keep worker worryless. Worker also desires a guarantee that these needs will also be met in future.
2. **Safety Needs.** An employee also wants security for his job and protection against danger and threat.
3. **Social Needs.** Main social desires of a man are reputation, confidence, appreciation, status, independence and strength. These needs can be recognised by providing the participation of employees in the organisation.
4. **Self-realisation Needs.** Man desires that he should be put to such job for which he is fit. A person will not remain happy on the post which is lower than that for which he is suited.

Factors for the Achievement of Harmony of Objectives

Following are some of the important factors which affect the harmonisation of objectives :

1. **Leadership.** For the harmonisation of objectives, a manager and a foreman must have all the properties of a good leader, *i.e.*, intelligence, good technical knowledge, managerial skills, maturity, loyalty and drive. A manager, who is very successful in the plant having no union may find himself in difficulty in the plant having one or more unions. To overcome these difficulties, he must possess the properties of a good leader.
2. **Sound Organisation.** Workers who are working together tend to form their own groups and it leads to the formation of variety of relationships. It is very essential to recognise these informal relationship as well as the formal organisation. Therefore, a manager or a forman must learn this informal relationship for effective management and he has to take the two together and harmonise them to work for the common goal. For knowing informal relation it is necessary to recognise the unofficial leader (as official leaders are managers or foreman), who commands the labour. A good communication system helps in understanding the views and attitude of each other.

2.6. MANAGEMENT BY OBJECTIVES

Management by objectives is a style of managing an organisation which emphasises the achievements of result expressed in terms of objectives. The objectives must be specific, time bound, realistic and qualitative or measurable. This concept is gaining importance since last two decades as a style of management to improve business results. Management objectives have already been discussed earlier in this chapter.

Advantages of Management by Objectives

(*i*) M.B.O. keeps a constant watch over company objectives/targets.

(*ii*) It is easy to understand by the persons who are to perform the task.

(*iii*) It motivates the people because they work on the objectives decided with their own consent.

(*iv*) It provides a better co-ordination among various departments of the organisation.

(*v*) It identifies the point where more emphasis is to be given.

(*vi*) It leads to a better understanding between the superiors and the subordinates.

Reviews

At the end of each quarter or any other period mutually decided upon, a review meeting is held between the job holder and his boss to assess the performance towards the targets agreed mutually. Thus the manager reviews his own performance along with his boss to measure the progress towards the results. The meeting helps *(i)* in ascertaining the areas where boss should provide additional facilities or helps him in solving his problems, and *(ii)* to analyse the causes which had been responsible for managers not achieving the target and remedial actions to be taken.

Annual review meetings are held to consider overall performance of the manager and to prepare the objectives for next year. The reviews thus provide the opportunity to judge manager's strength and weakness and also his potential for further progress, thus the training and development needs are worked out.

Problems in the Approach of Management by Objectives

Although it is an integral approach for the fulfilment of the overall objectives, but there are many difficulties in formulating and implementing management by objectives. Some of these problems are listed below :

1. **Mis-direction by the Boss.** The whole process of management by objectives is based on pleasing the boss, therefore, sometimes the interest of the enterprise and the self-interest of the boss pull in opposite directions.
2. **Different Angle of Vision.** Some business is seen from different angles of vision by various levels of management. Each discipline of management (production, finance, marketing, personnel etc.) will view the business in the perspective of its own activities.
3. **Decentralisation of Decision Making Powers and Delegation of Authority.** Management by objectives necessitates decentralisation of decision making powers and delegation of authority so as to fulfil the objectives. Too much decentralisation is also problematic.
4. **Professional Specialisation.** More and more specialisation is leading towards more and more departmentalisation, and creates problems of integration of various efforts. Hence functional manager measures his performance by his own professional criteria, instead of measuring his contribution to the enterprise.
5. **Lack of Financial Benefits.** If the reward, promotion or increments are not allowed for good performance then with the passage of time consistent good performance cannot be maintained.

6. **Self-control Through Management.** In the system of management by objectives, Manager controls his own performance. This self-control means desire to do the best then that prescribed. But difficulty is that the managers may put up the datas and other informations in distorted way to show good performance on papers only. This abuse may harm the enterprise by demoralising management and by seriously lowering the effectiveness of managers.

2.7. MANAGEMENT BY EXCEPTION

It is a system of identification and communication that signals the manager as to when and where his attention is needed. The main subject of this system is to enable the manager to identify and isolate the problems that call for decision and action, and avoid or ignore or pay less attention to less critical problems which are better handled by his subordinates.

Under this system, the manager should receive only condensed, summarised and invariable comparative reports covering all the elements, and he should have all the exceptions to the part averages or standards pointed out, both the specially good and the specially bad exceptions. This gives him a full view of the progress in a few minutes of time. Thus by using the experience in a systematic way (*i.e.* having the knowledge of past attainments) a careful ayalysis is made with reference to existing records and standards of performances.

Advantages of Management By Exception

1. It saves time, Manager attends to real problems at a particular point of time.
2. Concerted efforts are possible, as this system enables the manager to decide when and where he should pay his attention. As it identifies crisis and critical problems.
3. Lesser number of decisions are required to be taken, which enables the manager to go into detail.
4. This enables to increase span of control and increase the activities for a manager.
5. Use of past trends, history and available data can be made fully.
6. It alarms the management about the good opportunities as well as difficulties.
7. Qualitative and quantitative yard sticks are provided for judging the current position.
8. It prevents management from over managing.

Limitations

Management By Exception is not a solution to all management problems, it has its limitations as well. Some of them are :

1. It requires comprehensive observing and reporting system.
2. It increases paper work.
3. The system is silent till the problem becomes critical.
4. Some important factors, like human behaviour are difficult to measure.

System of Management By Exception

The system of management By Exception can be evolved in following phases:

I Phase: Measurement Phase. In this phase facts of operational situation are collected and assessed, *i.e.*, use of performance of its whole range inputs such as efforts contributing to the goals of the organisation; its productivity, money flow, effectiveness of financial resources being used to produce goods, services and profits, availability and wastage of material and its economy from its purchase through processing and storing to delivery of finished products, utilisation, capability and productivity of the machine.

The information about all these factors are utilised by way of qualitative measurements, like using time standards, balance sheet data, inventory data, inspection results of finished products, inventory accumulation for sales, current assets, equipment utilisation data.

II Phase : Projection Phase. In this phase, analysis of those measurements which are meaningful to the objectives of the organisation for future outlook of expectations, is carried out. Past and present data are projected by using the statistical concept, like, probability, standard variation, confidence, correlation, sample size, significance etc. Then examine the potential effect of changes expected as per forecast. The projections are then modified by the forecasts to decide the 'goals'. At this stage complete planning is thoroughly looked at from the angle of existing policies and procedures, organisation structure, adequacy and capability of the existing staff and equipments. If need arises necessary changes are made.

III Phase : Selection Phase. In this phase, those vital and economical available measures are selected, which will indicate the best progress towards its objectives. Thus, those criteria are selected, which the management would like to use to follow the progress or performance towards produced objectives.

IV Phase : Observation Phase. In this phase, one periodically observes and measures the current status of performance. The system should be reliable, automatic and adequate. Adequate means the observations should neither be too less nor too more, and only necessary information at desired frequency.

V Phase : Comparison Phase. In this phase, comparisons are made between the actuals and expected performance or progress in order to identify the exceptions, analyse causes and report the need for action to the appropriate authority to the exception that required priority of attention.

VI Phase: Action Phase. This is the phase, where decisions are taken and implemented with a view to bring performance to desired level or adjusting anticipations to reflect changing conditions or take full advantage of better performance or opportunity.

Thus management by Exception compromises a systematic approach of handling the management problems and free the manager from the demands of routine work, which enables him to devote more time for creative efforts directed towards "improving the overall efficiency of the organisation". This also provide necessary information readily available, for taking timely and qualitative decisions, which would otherwise requires lot of time.

QUESTIONS

1. Relate the difference between "policy" and 'objectives' of management.
2. F.W.Taylor originated the idea of scientific management, comment on this statement.
3. Write short note on :
   (*a*) Management for results.
   (*b*) Span of control.
4. Why management is necessary and what are its functions ?
5. "Objectives" are, what management tries to achieve. How can you utilise objectives to manage an organisation? Discuss.
6. Discuss some of the reasons for the failure of management by objectives programmes.

7. Discuss various principles for setting managerial objectives.
8. Describe the procedure for setting the managerial objectives.
9. Discuss Direct objectives and Indirect objectives for the management. Also explain as to how these are measured.
10. Write short notes on the following:
    (*i*) Value objectives.
    (*ii*) Managerial objectives
    (*iii*) Hierarchy
11. What are the principles of management? Explain them.
12. How the management thoughts were developed? Explain various approaches of management thoughts.
13. Explain functional approach to management, in detail.
14. Discuss scientific management approach.
15. What is human relations approach? Explain in detail.

3

Functions of Management

3.1 INTRODUCTION

For attainment of objectives, every organisation has a group of persons for managing its affairs. This group directs the activities of the organisation for effective utilisation of the resources. It is concerned with productivity, effectiveness and efficiency by performing various managerial functions.

Henry Fayol, the father of principles of management described the various functions of management as :

(*i*) Forecasting and planning
(*ii*) Organising
(*iii*) Commanding
(*iv*) Coordinating, and
(*v*) Controlling.

Various pioneers in the field listed different functions of management. A comprehensive list of all such functions is given hereunder :

1. Planning
2. Organising
3. Staffing
4. Directing
    - Leadership
    - Communication,
    - Motivation
    - Supervision
5. Controlling
6. Coordinating

Ralph Davis has divided managerial functions in only three categories, namely planning, organising and controlling. He considered commanding/directing and coordination as a part of controlling, while staffing as part of organising. Some authors have classified these functions as planning, organising, leading and controlling. They considered staffing as a part of organising, whereas leading included motivation, communication and supervision. Some authors have considered decision-making also a separate category of function.

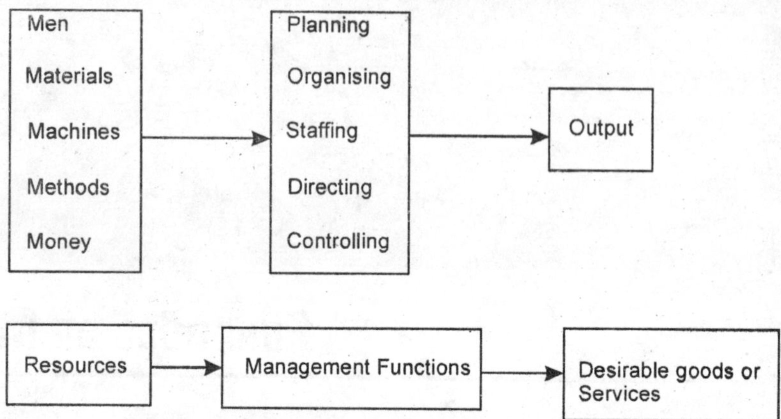

3.2. PLANNING

Planning is the process of establishing goals and suitable courses of action for achieving those goals. Planning involves setting the 'right' goals and then choosing the 'right' means for attaining those goals. Planning is necessary to ensure proper utilisation of resources (*i.e.*, men, materials, machines, time and money) to achieve the objectives of the enterprise. In planning, a manager searches for the alternative courses open to him, and then selects from these alternatives to determine general and specific objectives and detailed means for achieving them.

Planning is a mental process requiring the use of intellectual facilities imagination, foresight, sound judgement etc. to decide in advance as to what is to be done, how and where it is to be done, who will do it and how the results are to be evaluated. In other words, planning is the process of thinking before doing. Planning is performed by the managers at all levels. The managers at the top level spend more time on planning as compared to those at lower levels. The managers at low level are supposed to follow the policies, programmes and procedures laid down by higher level managers.

Steps in Planning

Following steps are taken by the planning manager for the purpose of planning.

1. Recognition of the need for planning
2. Establishing objectives
3. Building the premises for planning. Forecast is based on the inferences drawn from the known facts and figures. The forecasts are used for formulating plans for future.
4. Identifying alternative courses of action.
5. Evaluating alternatives courses.
6. Selecting a course of action.

Nature of Planning

1. Planning is an intellectual process.
2. Planning is goal oriented
3. Planning is a primary function of management.
4. Planning spreads to all managerial activities.
5. Planning is directed towards efficiency.

Principles of Effective Planning

An effective plan must conform to the following principles :

1. *Principles of limitations.* As limitations stand in the way of attainment of goals, planners are required to recognize these limitations and confine their search for alternatives which can overcome these limitations.
2. *Commitment Principle.* The commitment principles imply long range planning for future decisions. These decisions are commitment, normally of funds, direction of action or reputation.
3. *Flexibility Principle.* Flexibility means ability to change a plan without undue costs, to keep moving towards a goal, even if changes are there in environment or there is a failure of plan. The more the flexibility can be built into plans, the less the danger of losses incurred by unexpected events.
4. *Principle of Navigational Changes.* The planners, like a navigator must continuously check his course and redraw plan to meet desired goals.
5. *Principle of Open System Approach.* Manager must consider interactions of economical, technical, social, political and other elements of enterprise with their total environment.
6. *SWOT Principle.* While planning one should know strengths, weaknesses, opportunities, and threats. These factors should be analysed in the light of the market, competitions, customers requirements, etc.

Advantages of Planning

1. Planning gives direction.
2. Planning helps to offset changes and uncertainty.
3. Planning helps in economic operation
4. Planning focuses attention on important activities in order to fulfil its objectives
5. Planning helps in controlling.
6. Planning helps in growth.

3.2.1. Types of Plans

Plans can be classified in following categories :

1. Standing or Repeated use Plans:
   (*a*) Objectives
   (*b*) Policies
   (*c*) Procedures
   (*d*) Rules
   (*e*) Strategy
2. Single-use Plans:
   (*a*) Budget
   (*b*) Programmes
   (*c*) Projects
3. Kinds of Enterprise Plans:
   (*a*) Divisional Plans
   (*b*) Functional Plans

(*c*) Regional Plans

(*d*) Corporate Plans

4. Time Plans:

(*a*) Short Range Plan

(*b*) Medium Range Plan

(*c*) Long Range Plan.

1. Standing or Repeated-use Plans

These plans are used again and again and are repetitive in nature. These are formulated by managers at different levels meant for repeated use as and when the situation demands. Such plans are :

(*a*) **Objectives.** These are the goals established to guide the efforts of the enterprise, its each department and each section. Every organisation is required to set its objectives in respect of market standing, innovation, physical and financial resources, productivity, performance, attitude and public relations etc. The objectives must be both for long term and short term. Objectives may be treated as goals or targets.

(*b*) **Policies.** Policies are the statements that guide the decision maker. Policies are adopted by the management, and the employees are expected to follow them to attain the goals. Policies must be clear, definite, and reasonably stable. These provide guidelines for action and helps the subordinate in their day-to-day working.

(*c*) **Procedures.** Procedures are more specific than a policy statement, as it enumerates the sequences of steps to be taken in order to achieve an objective. It ensures uniformity of action and decision-making as simple and easy.

(*d*) **Rules.** A rule is definite and rigid and do not allow any deviation of or diserection to subordinates. Generally breach of rules invite a penalty.

(*e*) **Strategies.** It is a special kind of plan, prepared to meet the challenges of the policies of the competitors. These are generally formulated by the top management.

2. Single-Use Plans

Single-use plans are drafted to meet a particular situation. These include the following:

(*a*) **Budget.** A budget is an estimate of revenue and expenditure and as a plan it is a statement of expected results expressed in numerical terms. These are mostly prepared in terms of money units. Budget preparation is a part of planning, as it is a compilation of all relevant facts and figures like any plan. Budgets are also used as a tool for control. Budgets may be : sales budget, materials budget, production budget, personnel budget, cash budget, etc.

(*b*) **Programmes.** A programme is a specific plan drawn for a specific purpose for which the programme was drawn is achieved. This programme is not likely to be used again in the same form.

(*c*) **Projects.** Planning of a project is a single use plan. While planning a project, special task force and ad-hoc administrative set up is also envisaged for its implementation.

3. Kinds of Enterprise Plans.

(*a*) **Divisional Plans.** These are the plans for individual division in an enterprise.

(*b*) **Functional Plans.** Separate plans are drawn for each of the functional departments. These should match with the organisation plan.

(c) **Regional Plans.** These are the plans concerning to the activities of each region or zone.

(d) **Corporate Plans.** These are the plans prepared for the enterprise as a whole.

4. **Time Plans**

(a) **Short Range Plans.** Short range plans are generally for a period upto one year. In some cases planning for a week in advance is also sufficient. These plans must contribute towards long term plans. Being for a shorter period these are more realistic, as in this case it is easy to predict resource availability.

(b) **Medium Range Plans.** Medium-range plans are generally for a period between 1 to 5 years.

(c) **Long Range Plans.** Long-range plans generally extend for more than 5 years. In large organisations, because of the complexibility, long-range planning has acquired considerable significance. These plans are drawn considering the strengths, weaknesses, opportunities and threats concerning the organisation.

3.2.2. Strategic Planning

Strategic planning establishes long term goals considering the current environmental conditions. Strategic planning process consists of following steps :

1. *Analyse the environment* to identify new opportunities for existing and new products and services. Environment includes political, social, economical technological and internal environment.
2. Identify company strengths and weaknesses,
3. Identify opportunities and risks.
4. Define product scope
5. Define the competitive edge
6. Established objectives and measures of performance
7. Determine deployment of resources.

3.3. POLICIES, OBJECTIVES, GOALS AND MISSION

Policies

Policies are the guidelines set by the management for action. These provide broad guide for achieving the objectives of the firm. Problems are handled by the lower management by following these policies without going to the top management for a decision every time.

Objectives

These are the end results towards which the activities of the firm are aimed. Objectives may be classified as external or internal; short term, long term or medium term; economic or non-economic; major or minor objectives. A firm can have number of objectives and sets the priorities. Objectives may be set for different levels, i.e., for the corporate level, business level, divisional level and individual level.

Goals

A goal is an achievement of an end point and stated in quantitative terms. Goal represent the desired future condition, which organization strives to achieve, e.g., manufacture of 10,000 items in a given time period. The goals are the relatively long term targets, and provide an index or standard for measuring progress and performance.

Mission

This is a general term to describe the company's overall reason for existence. Mission refers to the broad purpose that society expects the organisation to serve.

Thus goals are derived from the organizations mission, and its objectives are derived from the goals, mission must be clear enough so that it leads to action. A firm exists and fuctions only in relation to the customer whose need(s) it satisfies. Thus the starting point for defining the mission of any business is its customer. The mission should be so described that it remains valid for at least some years.

The formulation of mission, objectives and strategy imply interaction with the environment and concern with improving the effectiveness, while policies, programmes and procedures affect the internal structure and operational effectiveness of the firm.

Mission, objectives and strategy are mainly the concern of top management while policies, programmes and procedures are concerned primarily with the middle and operating management level.

The mission, objectives and strategy are for long-term and their formulation have ar-reaching consequences on the firm while policies, programmes and procedures have a shorter time horizon and are easier to change.

3.4. ORGANISING

Organising is that part of managing that involves establishing an intentional structure of role for people to fill in an organisation. Intentional means to assign the tasks, to accomplish the goals, to people who can do them best.

Organising involves the following :

(*a*) Identification and classification of required activities,

(*b*) Grouping of activities necessary to attain objectives,

(*c*) Assignment of each group to a manager with the authority necessary for its supervision, and

(*d*) making provision for coordination horizontally and vertically in the organisation structure.

Organising is providing everything essential for proper functioning and combining the human power with other resources to give desired output.

Organisation is a large group of persons united to achieve any task. Organisational structure deals with the overall organisational arrangement in an enterprise.

Organisation is concerned with the building, developing and maintaining a structure of the working relationship in order to accomplish the objectives of the enterprise.

Organisation structure means the systematic arrangement of the people working for the organisation, their positions, and the relationships between positions. The structure provides an appropriate authority and responsibility relationships. The organisation structure varies with the organisation and the functions to be performed and depends upon the goals and objectives established, the resources availability, the communications, and the working relationships of the individuals, motivational other factors.

Effectiveness in Organising

1. Plan properly
2. Clarify relationships
3. Proper authority delegation
4. Avoid confusion of lines of authority and lines of information.
5. Sufficient flexibility
6. Avoid conflict by clear instruction
7. Promoting an appropriate organisation culture.

3.4.1 Principles of Good Organisation

Efficiency of an enterprise depends on the organisational structure. A good organisation should have the following main principles :

(*i*) Allotment of work,

(*ii*) Grant of necessary authority.

(*iii*) Flexibility to permit slight alternatives and expansions whenever needed.

(*iv*) Distribution of work in different departments.

(*v*) Coordination among different departments.

(*vi*) Able to avoid wastage of labour, money and materials.

Principles of organisation assist in arriving at the final structure of an organisation. Major common principles of organisation are :

1. **Consideration of Objectives:** Objectives decide the functions to be performed in the organisation and have direct bearing on the organisation structure.
2. **Responsibility and Authority:** Refer chapter on "Organisation-Structure".
3. **Span of Control:** Span of control is a number of subordinates which are directly under their supervisors. This number should be reasonable, as too small number will lead to non utilisation of full time and energy of the superior while large number will lead to difficulty in exercising control. An ideal number is 4, and at the lowest level 12 to 16. Thus a manager may have 4 deputy managers, and a foreman may have 16 workers.

   For details refer chapter on 'Organisation-Structure'.
4. **Delegation:** Delegation is a process a manager follows, in dividing the work assigned to him so that he can perform that part which only he, because of his unique organisational placement, can perform effectively and so he can get others to help him with that remains.

   Guidelines for Delegation

   (*i*) Establish the goals

   (*ii*) Define the Authority and Responsibility

   (*iii*) Motivate the subordinates

   (*iv*) Provide proper check and control

   (*v*) Chain of command. It has been felt that for efficient working, employee should receive the orders only from his superior boss. If he has more bosses, work may suffer and it creates discipline problem difficult.

   (*vi*) Specialisation

(*vii*) Balance stability and flexibility

(*viii*) Discipline

(*ix*) Unity of command. This means that employees should get orders and instructions from one boss only.

3.4.2. Division of Labour

It means division of work into different parts or processes which are performed by one group of workers according to their ability and aptitude. A good example of division of labour is found in mass scale production factory, where workers are classified according to the nature of work performed by them, *e.g.*, electrician, welder, blacksmith, carpenter etc.

In this system every worker specialises in a particular type of work, therefore, it improves the efficiency and results in economy.

3.4.3. Types of Organisations

According to different methods of distribution of authorities and responsibilities, the organisational structures are of following types :

1. **Line or Scalar organisation.** In this type of organisation, also known as departmental or military type of organisation, the flow of authority moves from top to bottom in vertical lines.
2. **Functional Organisation.** In this type, specialised people are employed under the production superintendent and everybody is supposed to give his functionalised advice to all other foreman and workers. Every specialised boss will go to individual worker for his related function.
3. **Line and Staff Organisation.** In a firm of large size, managers cannot give full attention to every function of management, they can not give time to think and plan. They are busy with routine tasks. Hence 'some staff' is deputed to do their work of investigation, research, recording, planning and advising the managers. Thus line maintains the discipline and stability, and staff provides expertise and helps to improve the overall efficiency. In other words, staff are 'thinkers' while line are 'doers'. A staff man usually controls one function of which he is an expert.

3.5. STAFFING

Staffing, now-a-days also termed as 'human resource management', is defined as filling, and keeping filled, positions in the organisation structure. Thus staffing function comprises, the activities essential to manage and keep manned the positions created by the organisation structure. Staffing function involves recruiting, selecting, placing, promoting, appraising, career planning, training, compensating etc. so that they can accomplish their tasks effectively and efficiently.

Various staffing functions have been discussed separately in the book.

3.6. DIRECTING

Directing is the inter-personnel aspect of managing by which subordinates are led to understand and contribute effectively and efficiently to attainment of enterprise objectives. Directing is a dynamic function of management because it infuses life into organisation. Directing can also be defined as a function which includes all those activities which are designed to encourage subordinates to work effectively both in short and long run.

Directing is telling people that what to do and seeing that they do it to the best of their ability. It includes making assignments, corresponding procedures, seeing that mistakes are corrected, providing on-the-job instructions and, of course, issuing orders.

Directing process involves :

1. Leadership
2. Communication
3. Motivation
4. Supervision

Principles of Direction

(*i*) Harmony of objectives
(*ii*) Unity of command
(*iii*) Direct supervision
(*iv*) Effective communication
(*v*) Effective leadership

3.6.1. Leadership

Leadership is the process of influencing other members of the organisation or the group to co-operate in achieving the organisational goals. **Leadership means to inspire confidence and trust so that there is maximum co-operation from the employees within the control of a manager. Leadership can also be defined as the ability to persuade others to seek defined objectives enthusiastically.** Leadership is the ability to get desirable action, voluntarily and without force from the followers.

Success of leader depends upon his qualities and characteristics. These characteristics are natural in some cases but there are many cases where these have been developed by constant efforts. Thus it can be said that leaders are both born and self-made. Leadership can also be defined as "the quality of the behaviour of the individual in the guidance of the people on the desired activities". *Living-stone* has described it as **"the quality to awaken in others the desire to follow a common objective".** It can also be defined as "the relation between an individual and a group for some common interest and behaving in a manner directed or determined by him".

Leadership is the process of directing and influencing the task-related activities of group members. This definition includes three implications : (*i*) Leadership involves other people may be subordinates or followers, who willingly accept direction from the leader. Group members help to define the status of leader (*ii*) Leadership involves unequal distribution of power between leaders and followers. Here *power* means the ability to exert influence, *i.e.*, to change the attitudes or behaviour of individuals or groups (*iii*) Leadership involves the ability to use the different forms of power to influence the behaviour of followers.

Weber said that in a leader oriented organisation there are followers and a leader to whom the followers allow some special strength or powers. When followers lose confidence in the leader then his leadership position can fall. He is the manager of the organisation. Leader makes decisions and centralizes delegation of authority. Personal devotion and obedience to the leader is necessary, while qualification, professional competency or training etc. is of less consideration. Working depends on the decisions of the leader and his wishes are taken as commands.

To be more clear a leader's role in an organisation can be compared with the role of an electrons entering an atom. An electrons with low energy will generally be absorbed without substantially changing the atom. In the same way, a low energy 'leader' will have small effect on the organisation and a high energy leader will be largely beneficial to the organisation.

Leadership of Dynamic Organisation

In the previous chapters it has been explained as to how managers perform the important functions of creating, planning, organising, motivating, communicating and controlling the organisations. These show the manager's job. Still there are few more additional functions that do not fit nearly into the six managerial functions mentioned above. The additional functions are very critical to the success or failure of enterprise.

These functions of a leader may be :

1. Arbitrating
2. Suggesting
3. Supplying objectives.
4. Catalyzing
5. Providing Security
6. Representing
7. Inspiring
8. Praising

1. **Arbitrating.** A leader has to make several decisions to set the organisation moving. Generally other members sometime may disagree even on the best decision of the leader. So an effective leader should be able to resolve the conflict or disagreement by arbitrating.
2. **Suggesting.** Suggesting allows the subordinate to maintain his dignity and sense of participation more than if he is given a direct order. In the long run, the power of suggestions is a powerful tool in the manager's hand. Suggestions should often be given by a leader. The leader may say, "I think it will be best done in this way".
3. **Supplying Objectives.** A manager frames and then defines the organisational objectives to their members. These objectives will allow members to work together collectively. The leader must, therefore, see that the organisation is always supplied with suitable objectives.
4. **Catalyzing.** Some force is essentially needed to begin or accelerate movement. A leader can provide this force. When he provides this force, he is acting like a catalyst. In this way, leader initiates the subordinates to work.
5. **Providing Security.** In organisations, personal security is an important factor. A leader can develop a large measures of security by developing a positive optimistic attitude.
6. **Representing.** A leader is said to be the symbol of the organisation. He is the representative of his organisation. He has to speak on behalf of the organisation stating the organisation's position on matters with which it is concerned. Whenever a leader makes contact with outsiders, they think of the entire organisation in terms of the impression of the leader. If the impression of the leader is favourable, they may think of the entire organisation. On the other hand, if the leader leaves a poor impression, the reputation of the entire organisation will suffer.

7. **Inspiring.** If the leader lets workers know that the work they are doing is worthwhile and important, then certain workers will atleast do them more efficiently. Thus they can be more inspired to achieve organisational goals, and will enthusiastically accept organisational objectives and work more effectively.
8. **Praising.** Praising is necessary for the good and hard work done. It increases the interest in work and sincerity at heart. Leader should satisfy these needs by sincere praise. Workers need to know that they are important and their good work is praised. It is to note that empty flatterıng will fail, while a sincere pat on the back for good job done will make a person pleased and help him to become involved with his job.

Types of Leaders

Different types of leaders in an industry can be classified as under :

A-According to Style of Leadership :

1. **Authoritarian or Autocratic Leaders.** This type of leaders drive their gang through command and by developing fear in their followers. Such leaders give orders, assign duties and responsibilities without consulting the employees or caring for their opinions. Such leaders never like to delegate their powers.
2. **Democratic or Consultative Leaders.** These leaders always work according to the wishes of their followers. They frame the policies and procedures in consultation with them but sometimes such leaders also work as a moderator of the ideas and suggestions of the gang.
3. **Persuasive Leaders.** Such leaders influence their followers due to his personal contacts, to join with him in getting things done. He gives directions personally and whole of the gang responds to his call, because they love and respect him and have full confidence in him.
4. **Functional Leaders.** Such leaders lead because of their expert knowledge and win the confidence of their followers by their superior knowledge.
5. **Free-rein Leaders.** Such leaders use very little power and give a high degree of independence in their working. These leaders are dependent on subordinates to set their own goals.

Practical experience has shown that the authoritarian leadership produces hostility towards their leaders and whenever the leader is out, the production drops to a minimum. But in the democratic leadership the difference in production in the absence of leader is very less. It tends to increase the production because it wins the confidence, co-operation, loyalty and initiative from his followers.

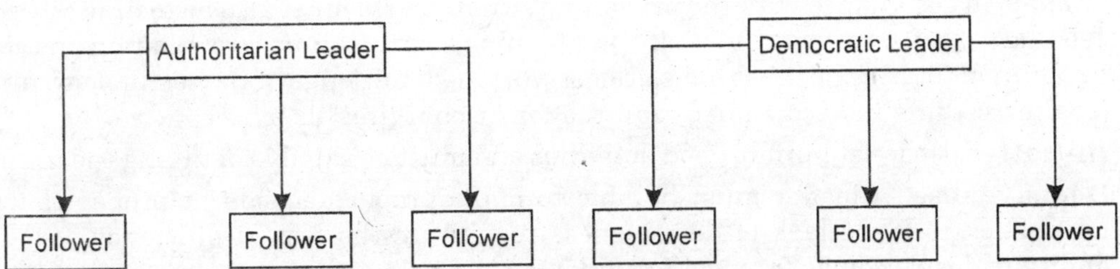

Fig. 3.1. Flow of influence of leaders.

B-According to Field

1. **Labour Leaders.** These leaders come to prominence due to their qualities of speech,

behaviour and action. They are capable to convince the people and bring them round their view point. They then organise themselves into trade unions.

2. **Administrative Leaders.** By administrative leadership we mean leaders or bosses in the administration. These leaders obtain this position by virtue of their ability, experience and association with the organisation. These persons are responsible for formulation of policies, programmes and plans of the industry and also responsible for their execution. Administrative leadership must work in close co-operation with the workers' leadership for smooth working.

In an industry, general manager or managing director works as administrative leader. But in big industries he alone cannot direct all the activities of the concern. Hence, he is assisted by subleaders (managers) and deputy leaders like the sectional managers, foremen and supervisors etc. Each one works as a leader of certain group of men, although the number of such persons under each leader depends upon the responsibility and post held by each.

Acceptance of Administrative Leadership

Following are some of the factors, because of which a worker accepts the administrative leadership :

1. **Fear of Losing Jobs.** Generally workers obey their boss because of the fear of losing jobs. This factor is more important in the society where unemployment problem is more.
2. **Thankfulness and Faithfulness.** Workers also obey their bosses because of their thankfulness and faithfulness. Generally this factor holds good where approach is positive rather than negative. The workers look to their leader and obey him because they feel indebted to him.
3. **Bargaining.** Sometimes workers obey their leaders as a result of bargain and leaders provide certain benefits or facilities to the workers. Management enters into agreement with the union and a mutual obligation is created.
4. **Common Object.** Sometimes management convinces the workers that there is something common, which both of them wanted to achieve, and then get the confidence of the workers. However, it is very difficult to convince the workers.

Qualities of Leaders

Following are some of the qualities, which a good administrative leader must possess :

1. **Intelligence and Technical Knowledge.** A good leader must have an intelligence which is more than that of his followers. He must be able to understand and solve the problem in accordance with the prevailing situation. He must also be technically sound. Technically soundness includes skill in planning, organisation, coordination and control. In addition to these he must have atleast working knowledge of the technology, finance, legal procedure and economies required for discharging his job.
2. **Initiative.** He must initiate good activities and must be capable of taking the initiative.
3. **Decisiveness.** A leader must be able to make proper decision at proper time and must stick to it, as lack of decisiveness results in .the loss of efficiency. Generally ability to decide comes from self-confidence.
4. **Persuasiveness.** Persuance is also a good quality of a leader. It also **helps him** in implementing his decisions, orders etc.
5. **Responsibility.** A leader must be able to know and feel his responsibilities. **He must not** shirk his responsibilities and must be in a position to take the burden of **decisions on** his shoulders.

6. **Ability to Inspire.** A leader cannot do whole of the work himself. He **has to inspire his** men so as to get the work done from them. Generally best inspiration is from **the conduct and** personality of the leader and the standards set by him.
7. **Social Consciousness.** He must always realise that he is dealing with human **beings,** who are also having feelings of social status and sense of respect.
8. **Positive Attitude.** He should always have a positive attitude towards the **problems of the** industry or workers.
9. **Energy.** Good health and physical as well as mental energy.
10. **Knowledge of Human Relations.** He should feel for individuals and **recognise their** problems and should be considerate towards them. Such leaders can motivate and get people **to work** together.
11. **Communication Skills.** He should be able to talk and write clearly and forcefully.
12. **Teaching Ability.** He should help, develop and inspire his subordinates.
13. **Maturity.** He should be emotionally stable and do not breakdown with frustration and able to take decision in any situation.
14. **Attitude.** He should have enthusiastic, optimistic, and loyalist attitude towards the organisation.
15. Creative and independent thinking.
16. Open mindedness.
17. Self-confidence.
18. Foresightedness.
19. Faith and respect from followers.
20. Vigilant.

3.6.2. Communication

It is the process of conveying information so that thoughts or opinions are interchanged. It is two way media for transmitting ideas, plans, commands, reports and suggestions that influence attitudes towards the organisation objectives. A good communication can play important role in motivating people and stimulating them to put extra effort. Success of the leader and the organisation depends upon adequacy of communication. Communication determines the quality and climate of human relationships.

Communication Flow

There are three basic directions in which communications can be sent within an organisation:

(*i*) Downward Communication, (*ii*) Upward Communication, and (*iii*) Crosswise Communication.

(*i*) **Downward Communication.** This type of flow begins **from** superior to subordinates. It is closely associated with the exercise of authority generally concerned with the introduction of new decisions, the clarification and interpretation of previous decisions and requests from higher officers for some specific information.

(*ii*) **Upward Communication.** In this, information moves from subordinates to superior officers. It is associated with the response **to** order from officers and requests from subordinates for higher level **decisions** on operating problems. Also flowing upwards are opinions, **attitudes,** ideas, suggestions, complaints, grievances and rumours etc.

(*iii*) **Crosswise Communication.** This type of communication is found between individuals working at the same level and under one officer, when advice related to organisational activity is sought from fellow workers.

Types of Communication

There are usually two means for sending communication:

(*i*) Oral

(*ii*) Written.

(*i*) **Oral.** Oral instructions may be given to the individual when they are face to face or can be communicated through the telephone or messengers.

(*ii*) **Written.** It means sending the messages, instructions, orders or information in writing. Written communication carries more authority and leaves a record.

In any organisation both types of communication are employed. If an individual has difficulty in hearing, there is an increased chances that he will misunderstand or even fail to hear some of the verbal communications. Students of foreign countries are required to be better acquainted with the language in which the course work is being presented. In such cases written instructions may be given.

Factors for Effective Communication

The following are the guiding principles of effective communication:

(*a*) Clarity. The message must be simple and very clear so that the recipient can understand it fully.

(*b*) Consistency. It means that message should be consistent with one another and with known objective of the organisation.

(*c*) Adequacy. The purpose of communication is to transmit optimum flow of information. It should also be noted that not all informations need be communicated. Some officers think that, if subordinates are informed about everything, they can be highly motivated and, therefore, they sent very heavy downward flow of information but it is found that with such a heavy information recipients become confused.

(*d*) Timing and Timeliness. The different individuals should receive a particular message at the same time, and proper time should be allowed for the action to be taken on the message.

(*e*) Distribution. A communication from top to bottom should pass through every stage of the line of authority. It is also seen that sometimes informations do not reach to the right person. It must be born in mind that who is to be told is as important as what is to be told.

(*f*) Balance Between Adaptability and Uniformity. The smooth working of any organisation also depends upon uniformity. Yet adaptability should be resorted to when different situations and individuals are involved. Orders and reports should be transmitted through a system that provides opportunity for adoption to specific situations.

(*g*) Interest and Acceptance. The purpose of communication is to secure positive response. Therefore, the receiver of message must be capable and interested in accepting the message. Downward communication is more effective, if moral is high and upward communication gets through when the higher officer is a good listener.

3.6.3. Motivation and Morale

Motivation. All administrative actions are of no use if the workers are not willing to contribute efforts towards the completion of the assigned task. By any way each worker must desire to do his duties effectively. Motivation is the means of increasing this desire among the individuals. Motivation is a powerful tool in the hands of managers for getting work done.

Each individual has variety of desires and belief that shape his reactions. It is the task of manager to arrange the total work situation and group attitudes in such a way so that each of his subordinates find greater satisfaction in carrying out his duties. In fact, every worker should have a positive desire to do the work effectively and efficiently.

In building such an attitude in his subordinate, a manager should consider a variety of measures such as higher financial income, social status and respect, attractive work, security, opportunity, personal power and influence, treatment as in individual person, voice in own affairs and fair supervision etc. Some of these measures provide general background of co-operative efforts while others can be related directly to performance of particular instructions.

In fact leadership and motivation go together. Managers must motivate every employee so that they can act with enthusiasm and vigour.

Morale. It means the prevailing mood or spirit which is conducive to willing and dependable performance of task. This mood is a large measure of the degree of faith for the ultimate success of group effort. Morale presumably determines the extent of co-operation in achievement of goal leading in exceptional cases necessarily synonymous with relation, cheerfulness or what is sometimes called good fellowship. Good morale means much more being in a good mood.

In increasing efficiency, good motivation and morale are essentially required.

For details refer seprate chapter.

3.6.4. Supervision

Supervising and over-seeing his subordinates is an important part of direction function of every manager. Supervision means observing the subordinates at work, to see that they are working according to plans and policies of the organisation and keeping the time schedule, and to help them in solving their work problems.

The lowest level managers have, as their primary duty, to supervise workers in basic operations. Therefore, the managers at the lowest level are known as supervisors. They are directly in touch with their operative employees or the workers. In a plant or factory, supervisors may be called as foreman, gangman, chargeman or a section officer.

Functions of a Supervisor

(*i*) Planning the work
(*ii*) Issuing orders
(*iii*) Providing guidance or leadership
(*iv*) Controlling output
(*v*) Controlling schedule
(*vi*) Motivate
(*vii*) Maintaining records
(*viii*) Liaison between management and workers.

Requisites of Effective Supervision

1. Technical and Managerial knowledge
2. Position and Authority
3. Knowledge of rules and regulations
4. Skill in leading
5. Human orientation
6. Issuing clear instructions

Qualities of a Supervisor

1. Technical competence.
2. Social skills.
3. Tact and discretion
4. Communication skills.
5. Honesty.
6. Empathy
7. Courage to take right decision
8. Teaching and guiding ability.
9. Self confidence.
10. Strong common sense.

3.7. CONTROLLING

Controlling function of management can be defined as :

1. Controlling is a continuous process of measuring actual results in relation to those planned.
2. Controlling is that managerial activity whereby the manager compares actual performance against the planned one, finds out the deviation, and takes corrective actions.
3. Controlling is a process which sets standards, measures job performance and takes corrective action, if required.

Controlling consists of verifying whether everything occurs in conformity with the plans adopted; the instructions issued and the. principles established. The object is to point out the weaknesses and errors in order to rectify them and prevent recurrence.

Controlling is the checking current performance against predetermined standards contained in the plans, with a view to ensuring adequate progress and satisfactory performance.

Control Process

The control process in all the situations have following steps :

(*a*) **Establishment of Standards:** A standard is a criterion against which results can be measured. These standards refer to goal, plan, objectives, targets, norms or a yard stick.

(*b*) **Measurement of Performance:** Second step in the process of control is to measure performance for the purpose of comparison with standards. This step in the control process includes the setting up of methods of observation, inspection and reporting. Reports at regular intervals, audits, test checks etc. are generally done to control the performance at various levels in the organisation.

(c) **Comparing the Activity:** Results obtained are then compared with the standards. Returns received at regular intervals, audits etc. provide feed back for performance which is then compared to find out if there is any deviation. Negative deviation means a loss and needs remedial action, whereas positive deviation means a gain and does not warrant any control function, and as such the feedback informations are ignored.

(d) **Remedial Action:** In the last step in the process of control, manager initiates action for correction of deviation from standards. For such action, a review is promptly done to make control function more effective. In good organisations, a system is made for automatic and self-regulating control process.

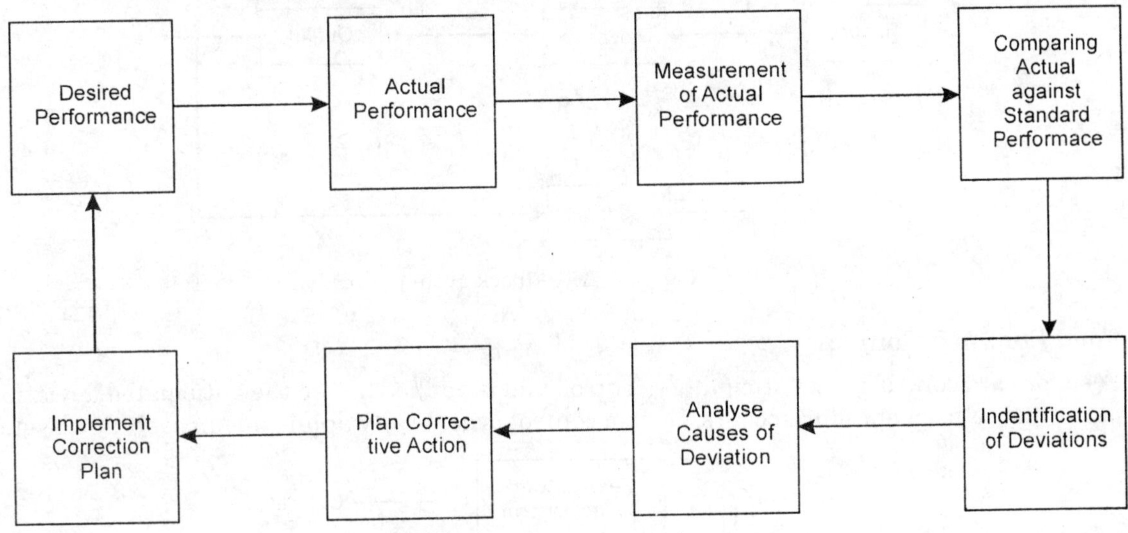

Fig. 3.2. Management control system.

Open and Closed Loops Control Systems

An open loop control system has inputs, processes, and outputs and do not have any information flow from process or outputs back to the inputs. In this system, control depends on the inputs and the processes being corrected. In closed loop systems, information about process and/or about the outputs is fed back to adjust the inputs and systems as per requirement. These systems are also known as information feedback systems.

Input, Processor and Output In a System

The basic elements (functionally or operationally) are same for all the systems regardless to their complexity. Input is the start up component on which the system operates. An input to a system is the output of some other system. Output is the result of an operation and is the purpose or objective for which the system was designed. The processor is the activity that makes possible the transformation of input into output. Men, machines, operations, organisation or their combinations are the processors.

Control and Feedback

Systems are dynamic, where it is necessary to review periodically or continuously the state of output, which may necessitate alterations due to changes which might occur.

The purpose of feedback is control. Control is defined as the system function that compares output to a predetermined standard. Feedback is the function that provides information on the deviation between output and control standard, and delivers this information as input into the process from which the output was derived.

The positions of feedback and control are indicated in the Fig. 3.3.

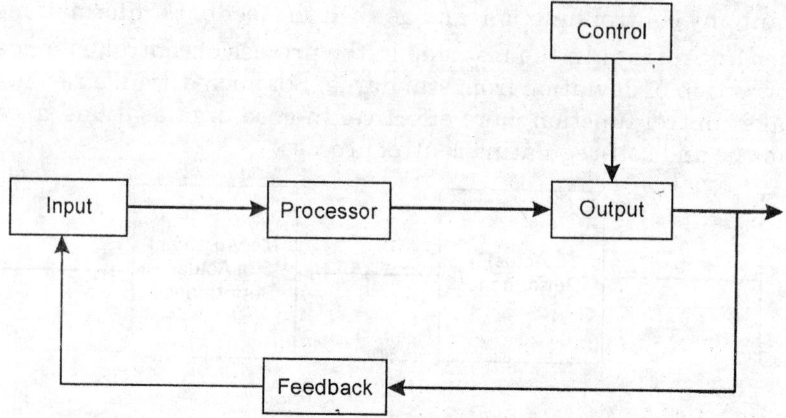

Fig. 3.3. A feedback system.

Feed Forward Control

Feed forward control is an anticipatory control, and is applied before the anticipated deviation of performance from standard occurs. Such a control is generally applicable in cash flow system,

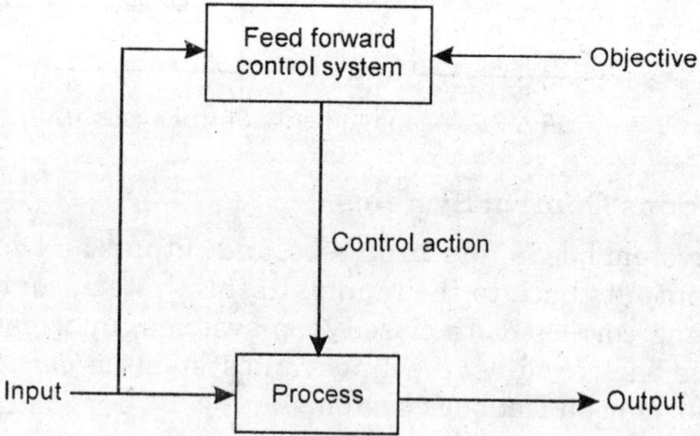

Fig. 3.4. Feed forward control system.

Essentials of an Effective Control System

While designing a control system for an enterprise following considerations should be kept in mind:

(*i*) **Suitability.** Controlling system should be so devised that it must fulfil the objectives sought from it.

(*ii*) **Responsibility for Control.** Main responsibility for exercising the control rests with the person who is assigned with the task of implementation of a plan.

(*iii*) **Objective.** Control system should be objective and not to be influenced by any other criteria. Objective standards must be quantitative (say, quantity produced per unit time, quantity of raw material consumed per unit of item produced).

(*iv*) **Flexibility.** Control system should be such that it remains effective even if the plan is changed. Thus it should be flexible and responsive to the changing conditions.

(*v*) **Prompt Reporting.** A control system should be such that an immediate report is sent whenever there is any deviation from the plans and targets.

(*vi*) **Focus on Strategic Points.** A good control system pin points the important or strategic points, in addition to reporting the deviations.

(*vii*) **Understandable.** The system should be clear and easy to understand by both, who are reporting and who are taking corrective steps.

(*viii*) **Economical.** A control system should be economical, *i.e.*, the expenditure incurred on its maintenance should be less than the benefits derived from it.

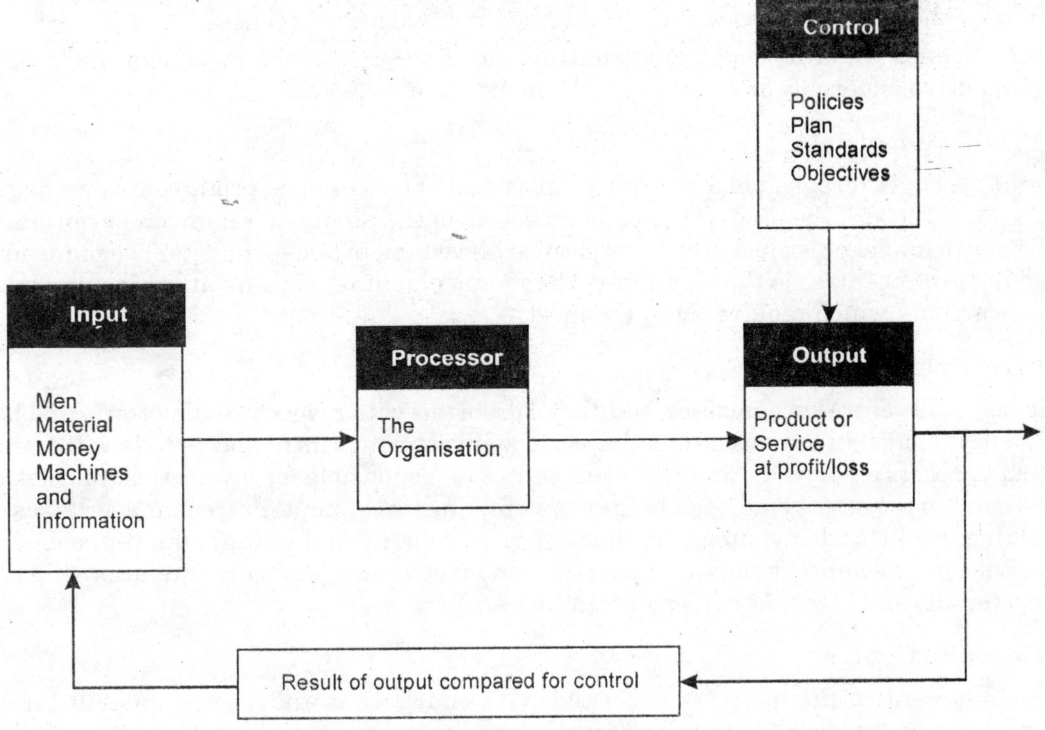

Fig. 3.5. A business system

3.7.1. Responsibility Centres

A responsibility centre enables to measure a manager's financial performance. **Any business organisation is concerned with four major elements, known as responsibility** centres **namely expenses, revenue, profit and investment.** All these elements are inter-related and have mutually interactive relationship. If the manager incharge of a responsibility centre has control over expenses, his sphere of control can be termed an expense centre. Similarly manager who has control over revenue, and profits, those areas of responsibility are termed as revenue centre and profit centres respectively.

A company has one or more profit centres and each profit centre will have one or more expense responsibility centres. An effective responsibility centre should have following characteristics:

(*i*) It is a clearly defined segment of an organisation.
(*ii*) A designated individual is responsible for its performance.
(*iii*) The designated individual has the necessary authority to discharge the assigned responsibilities.

(*a*) Expense Centres

Manager of this responsibility centre is basically responsible for production of a product or service. His decision authority relates to how human resources, machinery and materials should be used to the product or service. The expense centre manager has no control over revenues, profits or investments. An appropriate reporting system is used to report effectiveness. Efficiency is normally judged in terms of financial performance. Usually his performance is evaluated by comparing the actual expenses of the centre against budgeted expenses.

An expense could be considered controllable if the centre manager can make decisions which could considerably or significantly influence that expense.

(*b*) Profit Centres

A profit centre is responsible for both revenues and expenses. The profit centre managers are concerned with both the production and marketing of the products. Financial performance of a profit centre manager is measured in terms of achievement of budget profits. The main advantage of having profit centres is that it enables the management to focus its attention and advice on those segments which require them the most.

(*c*) Investment Centres

An investment centre encompasses, additional problems with respect to what assets and liabilities should be included in the investment base of the investment centre and as to how the profits be related to assets employed. An investment centre is responsible for production, marketing and investment in the assets employed in the segment. The investment centre manager takes decision regarding credit and inventory, equipment requirement and equipment replacement. For measuring performance it employs the return on investment (ROI), *i.e.*, a relationship between return (profit) and investment as a percentage.

(*d*) Revenue Centres

A revenue centre manager is concerned with marketing and is responsible for all the revenues of the division. The performance of the revenue centre is evaluated on the basis of achievement of the budgeted targets.

Performance Evaluation of Various Centres

Type of centre	*Control variables of the Centre*	*Objective*	*Variable pre-determined by top management*
1. Expense Centre	Prices and quantities of inputs.	Minimum cost	Prices and quantities of output/budget
2. Profit centre	Prices and quantities of inputs and outputs.	Maximum profit.	Investment
3. Investment centre	Prices and quantities of inputs and outputs and investment.	Maximum return on investment.	None
4. Revenue Centre of inputs	Prices and quantities of inputs	Maximum sales revenue	Quantities to be sold/budget

Designing Performance Evaluation Report

For the purpose of designing a performance evaluation reporting system, following steps are taken:

1. Establish desired segmentation like product line, geographic divisions, classes of customers, production units or departments etc.
2. Identify separable and controllable costs.
3. Select performance indicators. These indicators may be :
   (*a*) Results achieved: sales, units produced, orders booked etc.
   (*b*) Efforts in terms of inputs : machine hours, men hours, customers contacted etc.
   (*c*) Costs incurred : to support efforts and future capabilities.
   (*d*) Resources employed.
4. Compare performance achieved with expectations.

Designing Control Systems

- A control system must provide accurate feedback in a timely and economical way, and acceptable to organisation members.
- It should be carefully decided as to what needs to be controlled, and how often progress needs to be measured.
- Too much control of too many elements too strictly can waste valuable time, energy and money, annoy and demoralise employees.

Identifying Strategic Control Points: It is important to identify the critical points in the system where monitoring is essential. Such areas and points may be as follows :

(*a*) *Production* – quantity, quality, cost, job performance by individuals.
(*b*) *Marketing* – sales volume, expense, advertising expenses, performance of individuals.
(*c*) *Finance and Accounting* – Capital expenditure, flow of capital, inventory.
(*d*) *Personnel Management* – labour relations, labour turnover, labour absenteeism.

3.7.2. Techniques of Management Control

Following are the important techniques used by managers to help them to secure effective control of engineering systems :

- Budget and budgetary control
- Cost control and cost accounting
- Inventory control
- Quality control
- Network techniques
- Production control
- Special reports.

Here, in this chapter we shall discuss only introduction of these techniques. However, each of them has been described separately in detail.

1. **Budget and Budgetory Control**

   Budget is a tool of management for planning its future activities including estimate of sales, production, expenditure etc. Budget estimates are based on past experiences, present business conditions and expected future trends. Expected results are projected in financial terms or in numerical terms, like units of products, man-hours, machine-hours etc.

Budget provides predetermined standards of performance for the guidance of the efforts and activities in the business. As budgets provide standards of performance, they become the basis for control. Control used for the execution of budgets is what is called, "budgetory control".

Budgetory control means application of control in relation to budgets. This is a process of comparing the actual result with the corresponding budget data to know the actual cause of differences. Budgetory control can also be defined as **"the process which keeps the actual standard as nearly as possible to the predetermined standard by strict supervision and control."**

2. **Cost Accounting and Cost Control**

Cost accounting is the application of costing and cost accounting principles, methods and techniques as the science, art and practice of cost control and the ascertainment of profitability. It includes the presentation of information derived therefrom for the purpose of managerial decision-making. **Cost accounting completely analyses the financial records and tries to allocate and a proportion expenses incurred to the departments, processes, jobs or contracts to which they apply and thus builds up the total cost of each activity.**

Cost control is a technique which involves the determination of standards in respect of each item of cost and determining the actual cost of those very items, detection of variations of actuals from the standards laid down, analysing these variances in order to find out the real cause and then taking necessary corrective steps for future.

3. **Inventory Control**

Inventory control may be defined as, the systematic location, storage and recording of goods in such a way that desired degree of service can be made at the minimum cost. The necessity of inventory control is to maintain a reserve (store) of goods that will ensure manufacturing according to a production plan with the lowest possible ultimate cost. This topic is explained in detail in the chapter on "Materials Management".

4. **Quality Control**

In simplest term, quality control is the control of quality during manufacturing. Whereas, quality of any product is regarded as the degree to which it fulfils the requirements of the customer. Quality can be determined by some characteristics namely design, size, material, chemical composition, mechanical functioning, workmanship, finish and other properties. Quality of a product depends upon the application of materials, men, machines and manufacturing conditions. Systematic control of all these factors is the quality control.

In the words of Alford and Beatly, "quality control" may be broadly defined as that, **"industrial management technique by means of which products of uniform acceptable quality are manufactured".** Quality control is concerned with the making things right rather than discovering and rejecting those made wrong.

Now-a-days Statistical Quality Control technique is used as a means for quality control in the industries. Statistical quality control involves the statistical analysis of the inspection data obtained from samples. The quality in statistical quality control is usually related to measurements made of the items manufactured. A good quality item is an item which conforms to specified standards, and does not mean having highest standards of manufacture. Most desirable situation is which represents consistency in quality standards rather than the absolute standards. Quality control has been described in a separate chapter in the book.

5. **Network Techniques. (For Progress Monitoring).**

Network technique is a technique for planning, scheduling (programming) and controlling the progress of projects. This technique provides an effective management, determines project duration more accurately, identifies the activities which are critical at different stages of project completion to enable to pay more attention on these activities, analyse the scheduling at regular intervals for taking corrective action well in advance, facilitates in optimising resources, helps management for taking timely and better decisions for effective monitoring and control during execution of the project.

Network technique is basically a synthesis of two techniques namely, Programme Evaluation and Review Technique (PERT) and Critical Path Method (C.P.M.). Both these methods have many common features and are combined together and are called network technique. Network techniques are increasingly being used for planning and management of complex, inter-related projects. Network technique also helps in resource allocation. For details, refer chapter on "Network Techniques".

6. **Production Control**

Production control is the design and use of a systematic procedure to establish planning and controlling all the elements of an activity. Production control can also be defined as **(the process of planning the production in advance, setting the exact route of each item, fixing the starting and finishing dates for each item, to give production orders to shops and lastly to follow-up, the progress according to the production orders)**. The aim of production control is to produce the products of right quality, in the right quantity, at the right time, by using the best and least expensive methods.

Henry Fayol defines production control as, "ensuring that all which occurs is in accordance with the rules established and the instructions issued". Production control rests on mechanism by means of which observations of current happenings are recorded and continuously compared with the planned production programme. Production control includes the control of activities, control over material movement, control over time, control of tool availability, control of quantity produced, control over workers efficiency.

For the purpose of effective production control, it is necessary to properly implement : routing, scheduling, dispatching, and follow-up, as described separately in the book.

7. **Reports and Returns**

As we know that during the process of production, delays may creep up either due to material receipts, work in progress, assembly or errection etc. In order to know the point of delay and time of delay so that the follow-up can be done, certain reporting system should be introduced. The reporting system and returns should be so designed that the manager must not only take corrective action after a delay has occured, but also anticipate and prevent it before it actually develops, as we all know that, 'prevention is better than cure', and also that, 'a stitch in time saves nine'.

A report in the form of tabular statements, charts, comparing side by side is always preferred. Columns of the statement, axes of charts and other factors to be reported alongwith the frequency should be designed considering the purpose for which reports are required. The speed with which information is produced is important where short-term decisions have to be made.

3.7.3. Reporting

Reporting is a part of management information system, and reports are helpful for the management to take necessary decisions. Reports may be written or verbal. Written reports are treated as formal and authentic. The reports should be clear, concise and **well presented.** Report should serve following main functions:

(*i*) To help the writer to assess his work.
(*ii*) To convey correct information to others.
(*iii*) To provide a record for future references.

Principles of Reporting

Following are the main principles which determine the effective reporting:

(*i*) Cost of producing the information should be less as compared to the cost of not producing the information.
(*ii*) The information should contribute to decision-making.
(*iii*) Information should be able to provide meaningful conclusion.
(*iv*) Information should be accurate only upto desired degree, as higher degree of accuracy, where not required, may result in avoidable expenditure.
(*v*) Information should be furnished at desired frequency. As too frequent information may result in extra expenditure, while infrequent information may lead to delay in decision and delayed decision may result in avoidable expenditure.
(*vi*) Speed of the information is determined by the importance of decisions and their effect due to delay.

Principles of Designing Monitoring Reports.

1. Report should be need based. Report should be tailor made, *i.e.*, not same for similar organisations. Even in the same organisation, these should be amended according to priorities from time to time.
2. Report should be control and action oriented. It should be able to highlight variances, problems and corrective action.
3. Report should be based on 'Management by Exception', in order to focus attention on major items and critical problems.
4. Report should be forward looking and predictive to alert in advance and not to alarm.
5. Format should be able to be understood by the person who is filling it up and those who will use or interpret.
6. Only needed information be included.
7. It should indicate correct status.
8. Periodicity of the report should be decided on the basis of:
   - User level
   - Criticality of items
   - Scheme size and complexity.
   - Time required for processing the information for action.
   - Type of report : Detailed/analytical reports, control reports, routine reports, summary reports.

The task of monitoring and control is simplified, if suitable formats are designed for each purpose. Principle of designing a format is that, it should be related to time, cost and other resources like manpower, equipment and material, and should be properly presented so that it can be understood properly and quick decisions can be taken.

Generally, the reports are obtained for monitoring and control with following objects :

- Comparing progress achieved with targets.
- Cost incurred on each unit of production is to be compared with that of budget.
- To review the targets and time schedules for future, if necessary.
- Identifying the deviations and short fall and determining the causes for initiating corrective action.
- Record keeping. Information so received are recorded so as to use them in future, if so required.

3.8. COORDINATION

Coordination means achieving harmony of individual effort towards the accomplishment of company objectives. Coordination implies joint efforts, and as such it may be described as the orderly arrangement of group efforts to provide unity of action in pursuit of a common purpose. Coordination can also be defined as the orderly synchronisation of efforts of the subordinates to provide the proper quantity, timing and quality of execution so that their unified efforts lead to the common purpose of the enterprise.

Objectives of Coordination

Following objectives are sought through coordinations :

(*i*) Reconciliation of goals

(*ii*) Total accomplishment

(*iii*) Economy and efficiency

(*iv*) Good Personnel relations

(*v*) Helps in keeping high moral of employees.

Techniques of Effective Coordination

1. Clearly defined goals.
2. Clear lines of authority and responsibility
3. Precise and comprehensive programmes and policies
4. Cooperation
5. Effective communication
6. Effective leadership and supervision.

3.9. MANAGERIAL SKILLS

Managerial skills are the skills required of a successful manager. These can be viewed from the differing emphasis placed by various management thoughts. According to management science group, he is a decision maker and should use mathematical models and computers to help in arriving at optimum decisions. Behavioural scientists emphasise on the leadership and motivational skills.

Managerial skills can be classified as follows :

1. **Technical Skills.** He should have proficiency in handling methods, processes and techniques required for his job.

2. **Conceptual Skills.** He should be able to see the entire organisation, and recognise inter-relationship among different functions and should be able to guide effectively to his subordinates for organisational goals. Technical skills are required more for lower level managers, while conceptual skills are required more for top management, as shown in the Fig. 3.6.

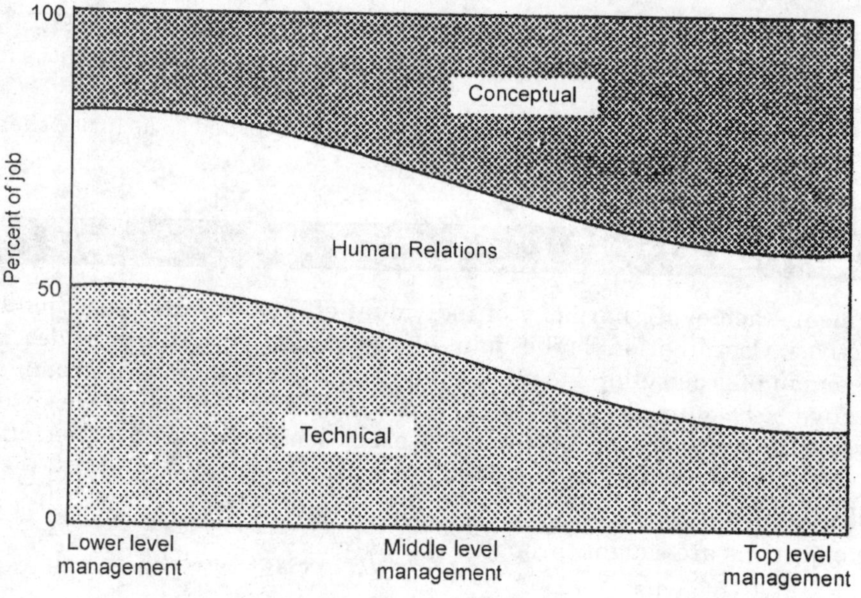

Fig. 3.6. Managerial Skills.

Conceptual skills are decision making skills and organisational skills. Decision making skill is the ability of a person to take timely and accurate decisions, while organisational skills help to select and post different people at work best suited for them.

Top Management		Strategic planning and decision-making
Middle Management	Conceptual skills / Human skills / Technical skills	Coordinating and planning for implementation
Lower level Management		Implementation

Fig. 3.7. Relative significance of managerial skills with the level of management.

3. **Human Relations Skills.** This is the ability of a manager to work effectively with others and build cooperation in his team so as to achieve organisational goals. For this purpose, he should have communicating skills, motivating skills, and leadership skills.

3.10. TASKS OF A MANAGER

A professional manager is expected to fulfil various tasks, for which he must have following characteristics:

(i) A professional manager must learn the necessary skills and gain competence from his experience.

(ii) His primary concern must be organisation for the company in which he works.

(iii) He must be responsible for performance, managing resources (men, money, materials and machines) in the most optimal manner for achievement of some pre-deteremined objectives.

Following tasks are expected to be fulfilled by a professional manager :

1. Providing purposeful direction.
2. Managing survival and growth.
3. Maintaining firm's efficiency for profit generation.
4. Meeting the challenge of competition.
5. Managing for innovation.
6. Building human organisation.
7. Retaining talent.
8. Substaining leadership effectiveness.
9. Inculcating sense of loyalty.
10. Meeting the challenge of change.
11. Coping with level of aspiration, public criticism.
12. Coping with growing technological sophistication.
13. Maintaining relations with various segments of society.

3.11. RESPONSIBILITIES OF A MANAGER

A manager is expected to discharge his responsibilities towards :

(i) customers by fulfilling his needs, ensuring the desired quality of product and keep the right price of product,

(ii) shareholder so that they can earn profit on their capital,

(iii) employees by providing good wages, safe and healthy environment which is conducive to work,

(iv) supplies by providing correct design of product for adhering quality as per schedule at a fixed price and timely payment,

(v) distributors and retailers by providing products of specified quality as per schedule at reasonable price,

(vi) industry by discharging its obligations towards industry by registering the firm as a member of the industry association,

(vii) union by handling them sensibly and tactfully,

(viii) government by paying all taxes fairly and regularly, and operating the firm well within the legal framework,

(ix) society by keeping the pollution free environment.

3.12. INTER-RELATIONSHIP OF FUNCTIONS

In actual practice the functions of management are interrelated. As explained earlier, planning is done in organising, staffing, motivating, leading and controlling. Similarly controlling is done while planning, directing, and staffing and also while decision theory is used in the organisation, communication and M.I.S. Thus each function affects the others, and all are intimately interrelated in a system to form the major components of the system of management.

QUESTIONS

1. Describe the management approach to planning.
2. Describe different types of plans.
3. Write short notes on :
   (*a*) Rules (*b*) Strategy
   (*c*) Single use plan (*d*) Strategic planning
   (*e*) Policy (*f*) Objectives
   (*g*) Repetitive use plans.
4. Describe in detail the planning of engineering systems.
5. Describe the term organising. Explain the procedure for organising.
6. Explain, as to how various Management functions are interrelated.
7. Write short notes on :
   (*a*) Staffing (*b*) Directing
   (*c*) Communication (*d*) Leadership
   (*e*) Controlling (*f*) Controlling-aids
   (*g*) Coordination (*h*) Managerial skills.
8. Name the type of leaders. Explain them in brief.
9. What are the qualities expected from a good leader?
10. What are the requisites of an effective controlling?
11. Why management is necessary, and what are its functions?
12. Describe various functions of management.
13. Discuss planning as a major activity of management.
14. Discuss the importance of planning in implementation of a programme.
15. Discuss the main features of a good plan.
16. Comment on the following types of plans:
    (*i*) Objectives, (*ii*) Policies,
    (*iii*) Procedure, and (*iv*) Programmes

4

ORGANISATION

4.1. INTRODUCTION

An organisation is a large group of persons united to achieve any task. It may also be defined as pooling of human physical and spiritual resources in order to achieve any predetermined task.

Organisation structure deals with the overall organisational arrangements in an enterprise. A clear understanding of organisation structure is helpful in making the more frequent detailed adjustments in organisational arrangements. Organisation structure is similar to the architectural plan of a building and the larger and more complicated the building, the more important a central architectural plan becomes.

An administrator, while designing an organisation structure must take into consideration the advantages of specialization, the limitations of authority, problems of communication and a variety of other specialized aspects of organisation. In designing an organisation structure, one should start with the objectives and activities of the enterprise.

Organisation can also be defined as under:

- Organisation is a mechanism or structure that enables living things to work effectively together.
- Organisation is the process of
  - (*i*) *identifying* and grouping the work to be performed,
  - (*ii*) defining and delegating the *responsibility* and authority, and
  - (*iii*) establishing *relationships* for the purpose of enabling the people to work most effectively together in accomplishing objectives.

Necessity of Organisation

An organisation is necessary with the increase in size of the manufacturig plant, intoduction of most complex methods of production, tough competitions between the enterprises, and labour problems for every industry so as to produce required quantity of products of required quality, at required time with minimum production cost.

A well designed organisation structure with qualified personnel in all key positions achieves execution, coordination and control of all functions and policies of the company.

A good organisation is necessary due to following reasons:

1. It enables the use of large size industrial units, introduction of modern techniques and modern machines.

2. It ensures the success in competitive market due to production of quality products economically.
3. By having good organisation structure, it is possible to have optimum utilisation of resources.
4. With clearly defined responsibilities and authorities the individuals strive hard to achieve results.
5. A well organised enterprise is able to maintain good employer employee relations.
6. A good organisation makes it possible to direct and coordinate the efforts of individuals, departments etc.

4.2. CHARACTERISTICS OF ORGANISATION

As we have already discussed that an organisation comes into existance when there are number of persons in communication and relationship to each other and are willing to contribute towards a common endeavour and in order to achieve this common purpose, these persons pool their efforts by defining and dividing the various activities, responsibility and authority. Therefore, a good organisation must have following characteristics so as to fulfil the organisational objectives:

1. Organisation is group of persons and represents cooperative relationship between them.
2. The group members are in a position to communicate with each other.
3. The group works under an executive leadership.
4. The organisation leads to division of work and responsibility.
5. Designed to achieve specific objectives and goals.
6. It clearly establishes the authority.
7. This helps in fixing the responsibilities, may it be department, or a section or a group or an individual, which avoids confusion, duplication or inefficiency.
8. It helps in achieving the desired level of coordination.
9. It is based on the division of work, which helps in adopting specialised skills and techniques.
10. It enables in deciding flow of information and decision-making.

An ideal Hierarchy is one which has unbroken line of authority and chain of command through all levels (from General manager to the lowest employee). Every undertaking has some kind of hierarchy (*i.e.*, treating the orders of superiors, like the order of angels), involving superior subordinate relationships.

4.3. ELEMENTS (COMPONENTS) OF ORGANISATION

Essential elements of a good organisation are:

1. Well defined objectives of the firm.
2. Clear and well defined policies and procedures.
3. Harmonious grouping of activities.
4. Well organised and coordinated group of people.
5. Proper division of work and labour.
6. Proper division of authority and responsibility.

7. An effective system of communication.
8. The span of control should be reasonable.
9. Adequate facility for necessary changes according to the need.
10. Satisfy the employees, increase their moral and motivate them to work for the success of the enterprise.

4.4. PRINCIPLES OF ORGANISATION

A few common principles of organisation are listed hereunder. These assist in arriving at the final structure of an organisation.

1. Consideration of objectives.
2. Responsibility and authority.
3. Span of control.
4. Dividing and grouping of work.
5. Effective delegation
6. Specialization
7. Coordination
8. Unity of Command
9. Simplicity
10. Balance
11. Continuity
12. Communication
13. Line and staff relationship
14. Stability and flexbility

4.5. DEPARTMENTALISM

When two or more people contribute their efforts together then an understanding as to "who does what" is necessary. The activities and objectives must be arranged in the form of duties that can be allotted to specific individuals and relationship be framed between these individuals so that their efforts are coordinated towards a predetermined goal. In other words, team must be organized.

The administrative process of organising the team consists of:

(*i*) dividing and grouping the work

(*ii*) defining the established relationship between individuals filling these jobs. Departmentalism is the process of grouping activities into units for the purposes of administration. This process takes place at all levels in an industry. For examples in an industry, there may be sales department, production department, service department and so on. Further, the sales department manager may divide his work among market research department, statistics department, advertising department, selling department and servicing department etc. This process of partitioning is generally called departmentalism.

Methods of Departmentalism

There are large number of primary basic methods of departmentalism in an organisation structure, namely:

1. Grouping by products or services
2. Grouping by locations
3. Grouping by time
4. Grouping by customers
5. Grouping by processes
6. Grouping by functions.

1. **Grouping by Products or Services.** In this method, the main activities associated with a given product are organised under a single head and are largely used as the basis of departmentalism. For example, the work of the purchasing department may be divided according to different types of products to be served. This method takes advantage of specialised product knowledge, promotes co-ordination of the various activities connected with the product (such as purchase, production, storage, sales and the tool) generally make it easier to place responsibility for the results achieved.
2. **Grouping by Locations.** If the factory is a huge one in area then departmentalism can be done by divisional basis with a divisional manager incharge of each division.
3. **Grouping by Time.** It means the organisation can keep more than one shift. In this system, although the operations may be same as in the first shift but additional supervisory staff is required. The more difficult questions are : how fully served and self-contained each shift should be and what relationships should be set up between managers who work only in normal hours and the men who perform similar duties in the off hours.
4. **Grouping by Customers.** This type of departmentalism can be found in sales activities. For example a big restaurant can serve regular meals in a big hall and maintain an espresso bar separately.
5. **Grouping by Processes.** Departmentalism on a process basis can be found both in manufacturing and in distribution activities. For example, a Hosiery Mill may have separate departments of knitting, steaming, cutting, sewing, trimming, pressing, inspection, packing and shipment. This method has the advantage of expertness that comes with concentration on the single process and when the process is performed at one place, the improvement in supervision occurs.
6. **Grouping by Functions.** Today, due to much advancement there is growing complexity of administration in all types of business. In such industries, functional departmentalism has become increasingly popular and the organisation structure may be built by setting up departments by functions, such as sales, accounting, personnel, inspection, purchasing, production etc.

Factors of Departmentalism

While framing various departments, following main factors are taken into consideration :

1. Specialisation
2. Control
3. Co-ordination
4. Securing attention
5. Recognition of local conditions
6. Economy.

1. **Specialisation.** It means breaking up the work into simple process and sub-process. Specialisation is a necessity to have economic growth in the industry and to increase the production power of labour. Department should be framed in such a way so as to

secure the advantage of specialisation. Specialisation may be functional as in establishment of separate departments for sales, finance, production and accounts etc. or by-products, as the work within the purchasing department is mostly specialized by products rather than functions.

2. **Control.** It is the most important job of administration. Control means to assume that performance conforms as nearly as possible to plans. Departmentalism can simplify the manager's work of control. As a general rule, one activity intended to serve as a check on another should be under a separate manager. For example, the inspection should not be under the indirect control of a person who is responsible for output, unless the quality is of average importance.

3. **Co-ordination.** Departmentalism is only one of the ways for achieving co-ordination. Co-ordination means to combine activity into a consistent and harmonious action, sometimes different activities need to be grouped under a single manager, as the activities need to be closely co-ordinated. For example, a trained cricket team, the members of which willingly respond to their instructor and captain demonstrates good examples of the highest form of co-ordination. Similarly, in manufacturing industry, often raw material inventory control and purchasing are under the same officer, even though the nature of work is quite different. Here a knowledge of stock on hand and quantity of consumption must be related to the ordering of new supplies.

4. **Securing Attention.** If there is a very important activity which requires special attention then it may be placed in a separate division and also at a higher level in the administrative hierarchy. For example, in a Chalk Industry, the production foreman himself can do the inspection while in a precision instrument factory, where the quality control is more important, the inspection will be done by separate independent department. Similarly, in an aircraft plant, where reliable quality is vital for the success of the enterprise, the inspection should be under the General Manager.

5. **Recognition of Local Condition.** The departmentalism should take into consideration the local conditions at the place concerned.

   Here three aspects are considered :

   (*a*) Adjustment should be made according to the availability of personalities.

   (*b*) To recognise normal groups, and

   (*c*) To provide full-time jobs.

6. **Economy.** The additional expenditure is needed in creating various departments. Each separate department will require executives, separate staff and such other aspects, therefore, proper consideration must be paid to this aspect.

   It is to note that the least expensive arrangement is not necessarily be the best one, as sometimes it becomes ineffective but if a more elaborate arrangement is adopted, then additional benefits should clearly exceed the additional expenses.

Compatibility to Management Objectives

It means the individual objectives are compatible with the objectives of the organisation or management. Both individual and organisational objectives can be fulfilled without undue sacrifice to either. The individual keeps his identity within the organisation but at the same time he respects the organisation need for co-ordination.

If the individual is a member of the organisation he will be benefitted from the efforts of the organisation and the organisation will be benefitted from his efforts. The majority of successful organisations are due to the existence of individual and organisational objectives that are compatible.

For example, the objectives of scientist in Atomic Energy Department and the research laboratory are compatible. The scientist applies his knowledge and skill and enquiring mind while in return he gets research facilities and monetary rewards from the management. The management does not necessarily provide him with unlimited facilities or allow him to do whatever experiment he desires. The scientist recognises the right of the management to assign projects that lead to the fulfilment of the organisation' task. Scientist has the option of voicing objection and having those objections heard and he also has the option of striving to become a member of the group that determines priorities and assignments. If his proposals are not approved he will abide by organisational demands as long as he can continue to achieve his own objectives within the framework of the organisational objectives.

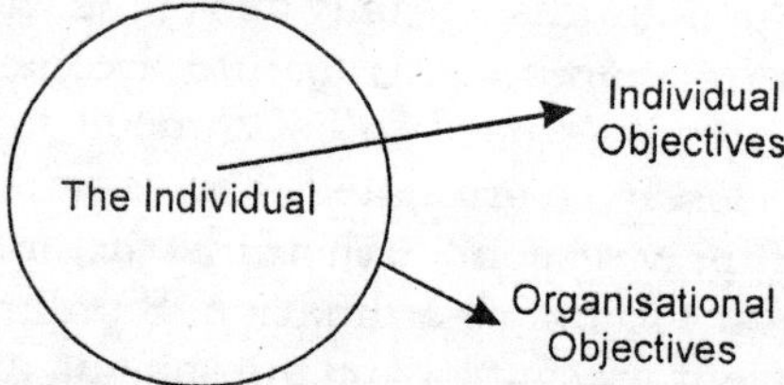

Fig. 4.1. Compatible individual and organisation objectives.

Fig.4.1. shows how individual and organisational objectives can exist compatibly. The individual objectives move in the same general direction as the objectives of the organisation.

4.6. AUTHORITY AND DELEGATION

Authority means the right of one man to require another man to do certain duties and obligations. Unless a man is given necessary authority to perform certain duties and obligations, he cannot be held responsible. Authority means "right to act, decide and command".

Delegation of Authority

It means giving someone permission to do certain things. For example, the supervisor gives a worker permission to run a machine and to use materials; the sales manager gives a salesman permission to call on customers in a given area and to enter into contracts for the delivery of products. It means the supervisor and the sales manager have authority to take such action and they simply extend this permission to people working for him.

Problem of delegation of authority. Delegation takes place even in the smallest of administrative organisations. For example, as soon as the manager of a firm finds that he cannot perform all of the activities of his firm and hires an assistant, delegation takes place. In a large firm not only are delegations made from the Board of Directors to Managing Director, but also redelegations are made by the Managing Director to managers, managers to supervisors and so on down the executive pyramid.

When the manager of a small firm first employs an assistant, he probably assigns to the assistant a number of more routine duties, explaining in some detail just what he wants to be done. The manager continues to make decisions regarding method, schedules and other phases of the operation, but he has relieved himself of at least part of the actual performance that is required. This is not all net gain, however, because the manager now has additional duties of directing and controlling the activities of his assistant. But as the size of the firm increases, this process of delegation is repeated. Each new assistant is assigned a certain part of the doings and part of the planning related to his activity. Some of the activities that the original assistant performed will probably be reassigned to new man and the manager will delegate more of the duties that he himself formerly performed. Note that as the manager increases the number of his subordinates, he spends as smaller proportion of his time in actually doing and a large proportion in supervision.

In a big firm, of course, a whole series of redelegations down to the point where the duties can be performed by the subordinate without further assistance. Where this occurs, a whole series of assignments and authorizations run down the channel of command, and a corresponding series of responsibilities run up the channel.

Relationship Created by Delegation. The process of delegation has three aspects:

(*i*) The assignment of'duties' by an executive to his immediate subordinates.

(*ii*) The granting of authority to his immediate subordinate to make commitment, use resources and take other actions necessary to perform the duties.

(*iii*) The creation of responsibility on the part of each subordinate to the executive for the satisfactory performance of the duties.

Recognised Principles Related to Delegation

The following three basic principles are related to delegation :

1. Responsibility cannot be delegated
2. Avoid dual subordination
3. Coequality of authority and responsibility.

1. **Responsibility Cannot be Delegated.** An executive may think that once he has delegated a duty to a subordinate, he has responsibility for its proper performance. Similarly a subordinate may feel that once his boss has delegated a duty to him, the boss should not be concerned with it. This is a false notion.

   This can be explained by the following:

   Suppose top official *A* assigns duties to executive *B* and the executive *B* makes in turn to subordinate *C*. The redelegation by executive *B* does not relieve him of his responsibility to his senior A. *A* has still the same authority, he had before, although he may voluntarily restrict his actions so as to keep the work going to C, and he still is accountable for the result achieved.

   The redelegations, it is true, has created an additional set of relationships between executive *B* and his subordinate C. The flow of obligation then becomes *C* to *B* to A, but executive *B* can not duck out.

2. **Avoid Dual Subordination.** It is a recognised fact that a man cannot serve two masters well and this idea leads to condemnation of dual subordination in modern administration. Therefore, in an organization, a subordinate should always report to one boss only. Passing of instructions may lead to dual subordination. Dual subordination decreases the moral of workers.

3. **Coequality of Authority and Responsibility.** Coequality of authority and responsibility is the most widely recognised principle of organisation. In any organisation 'authority and responsibility' both go together, unless a man is given necessary authority to perform certain duties he cannot be held responsible.

   'Responsibility' may be defined as the obligation of a subordinate for the performance of any job allotted by the superior. As the superior officer cannot perform all the activities of a bussiness alone, therefore, some men must be there to assist him and to whom certain responsibilities and authority may be delegated.

   Suppose, if you are given authority to act in disciplinary cases including suspension or discharge, you will also be that responsible for the avoidance of strikes and consequent shutdowns that may occur from certain mistakes on your part. So in this way we can say that authority can never be completely delegated but it can only be shared. So, the authority and responsibility both go together.

Therefore, the rule that authority and responsibility be equal, is sound, provided that—The authority that can and should be delegated is often limited and consequently, an individual can be held strictly responsible to the extent that actions are really subject to his control and a person can be expected to feel a sense of responsibility even though his authority is confined.

4.7. SPAN OF CONTROL

Principle of Span of Control

It is the number of subordinates which are directly under their superiors. The number of subordinates, over whom control is to be exercised, should be reasonable. As, too small number will lead to not-utilisation of full time and energy of the manager, while large number will lead to difficulty in exercising proper control. An ideal number of subordinates for superior authority is 4; and at the lowest level the ideal number is 12 to 16. Thus a manager may have 4 deputy managers and a foreman may have 16 workers. In practice the ratio is, therefore, kept between 3 to 5 and in exceptional cases 6. Generally, where the work is of routine nature the number is more.

For example, a General Manager has 5 Managers in a factory of 3000 employees. Then he will however be a boss of 3000 but he will have a direct contact with 5 only. Hence for him, span of control is 5 and not 3000.

Factors Determining Span of Control

Proper span of control is determined on the basis of circumstances. Some of the circumstances affecting the span are as follows :

(*i*) *Nature of work.* When the work is of routine and standardised nature, greater span of control can be kept. Such jobs require general instructions and will need very rare changes and additions. But for the posts having works of frequently changing nature, instructions need be given each time and in such cases span of control must be kept low.

(*ii*) *Define responsibility.* In organisations where responsibilities of supervisors are definite and clear, and the plans and policies are clear and easily understandable at different levels, officers can control a wide span. But where the policies and responsibilities are not clear officers need more time for giving the clarifications to their subordinates and will also require more time in discussions and in deciding the problems. Hence in such cases span of control is required to be kept smaller.

(*iii*) *Capacity of person involved.* While deciding the span of control for an organisation, it is necessary to consider the capacity and ability to control their subordinates, ability to make decisions, tactfulness, experience, quality of leadership, grasping power and power of command.

It has been generally experienced that larger the number of such subordinates reporting directly to an executive, the more difficult it is for him to supervise and co-ordinate their activities effectively. Mr. V.A. Graicunas, a management consultant, made an original study of organisation structure and published it in the form of a paper entitled *Relationship in Organisation in 1933.*

In his paper he analysed the nature of relationship, *direct group* relationships and other relationships. Thus in his own words, "if Tom supervises two persons, Dick and Harry, he can speak to each one of them individually or he can speak to them as a pair. The behaviour of Dick in the presence of Harry and of Harry in the presence of Dick will vary from their behaviour when with Tom alone. Further, what Dick thinks of Harry and what Harry thinks of Dick constitute two cross relationships which Tom must collaborate in his absence." Thus even in this extremely simple unit of organisation, when Tom is supervising only two persons, he will have four to six relationships within his span of control : two direct single relationships, two direct group relationship and two cross-relationships.

Thus he found that when an executive supervises two persons, there are six relationships, with four subordinates it increases to 44; when fifth subordinate is added it rises to 100, to 222 for a sixth and to 900 for the seventh subordinate added. By the time, tenth subordinate is reached the number of relationships jumps to 5,210 and with the addition of the twelfth, it reaches to 24,708. From this he concluded that as the number of subordinates increases, there is more than proportionate increase in the total number of relationships and this imposes a heavier load on the mental capacity of the superior executive. This conclusion of Graicunas follows from the well known psychological principle that for the average run of people, the span of attention is strictly limited and so the number of relationships with which an individual can be expected to control must be limited. According to Graicunas, 222 relationships arising out of six subordinate are about the maximum that an average individual can supervise effectively.

According to F.L. Brech, however, the mental factor of span of attention is not the only factor which limits the number of subordinates. There are five other factors, namely, (*i*) emotional stability, (*ii*) time, (*iii*) moral, (*iv*) geographical distribution, and (*v*) the nature and diversity of responsibilities which tend to further limit this number.

1. *Emotional stability.* The emotional aspect of attention refers to the ability of an individual to deal with interruptions that emerge when he has a variety of individuals coming to him for consultation, discussion and decision. An individual who has an average span of attention but less emotional stability will not be able to adjust so readily to the impect on his personal attitudes and behaviour of a variety of matters of persons coming to him. He will, therefore, be able to supervise a smaller number of subordinates than another executive who has a greater span of emotional stability.
2. *Time.* As regards the time factor, it is obvious that an executive has to give time to his subordinates so that he can consider their problems and give them the necessary advice and direction. If the number of subordinates become large, he would not physically be able to find the necessary time to meet their needs. Moreover, it leads to a considerable waste of expensive time of the subordinates who have to wait on the doorsteps of a manager to get an audience with him.
3. *Moral.* Contact with subordinates has also a morale aspect which no superior can afford to overlook. If a superior has such a large number of subordinates that he is unable to find time to consult and discuss with them in an atmosphere of reasonable calm and leisure, he is likely to find serious deterioration setting in the morale of his team.
4. *Geographical Distribution.* The geographical distribution of subordinates allocated to an executive is another factor which affects the number supervised. If several subordinates are in different localities, travelling time is involved and this imposes a further limitation of the number that an average executive can have reporting to him.
5. *Nature of diversity of responsibility:* If the responsibilities are widely varied, complex

and heavy, a more serious limitation on the number will be imposed than when they are relatively simple straight forward and confined to one or a few areas.

6. *Capacity of persons involved.* While deciding the span of control for an organisation, it is necessary to consider the capacity and ability to control their subordinates, ability to make decisions, tactfulness, experience, quality of leadership, grasping power and power of command.

'Matrix' Type of Organisation

It is a form of organisation which constitute both the project structure and the traditional functional structure. Matrix management provides for specialised knowledge for carrying on a number of specific projects. The difficulties may arise because of the dual accountability of personnel involved in the project.

4.8. MATCHING OF JOB

It may also be called as men specifications. It means the kind of individuals who can satisfactorily fill the positions. In an organisation, a large number of activities are to be carried out by different persons. The man employed for a particular task can be effective and efficient only if he is allotted the work according to his ability, experience, skill and interest. Therefore, matching of job is an important factor for any organisation.

Vocational guidance is a scientific method of matching jobs. Guidance aims at finding out what type of job will suit a particular worker and then jobs are assigned to them.

We know that all workers differ in physical abilities, inclination and intelligence etc. and if a worker is not suitable for a certain job, it does not mean that he is not suitable for any other job. The purpose of Vocational Guidance is to match a worker with suitable job so that his efficiency should be very high and he may have job satisfaction.

The various techniques and methods used for vocational guidance are

(*a*) Interview (*b*) Psychological test
(*c*) Aptitude test (*d*) Trade test
(*e*) Medical test

In matching jobs, following requirements in any individual must be seen :

(*a*) Performance requirements.
(*b*) Personal qualities required for the job.

(*a*) Performance requirements. In this, qualification, age, experience, mental skill, level of intelligence, physical ability, etc., needed in a job are seen.

(*b*) Personal qualities required in job. In this, list of qualities needed for a particular job is prepared such as honesty, sincerity, hardwork, loyalty and obedience etc.

Man-Power Requirements

It means how many various categories of individuals are required by an organisation, and this is a vital problem. The success of any industry depends very much on this. While planning this requirement, the quantity of production with the help of sales forecasting is decided, so as to enable to know the capacity of the machines and plants and then the number of individuals required to meet plan is decided. In this respect, time and motion study and other standard data will be of much use.

4.9. CHAIN OF COMMAND

For efficient working, employee should receive the orders only from his superior boss. If he has more bosses, work may suffer and it makes discipline problem difficult. Chain of command shows that under which boss an employee should be, so that he may obey the orders and instructions of his boss.

Organisation charts clearly define the line of position of each individual. Each employee, therefore, knows his relative position in the organisation. He also knows that who is his superior boss and who is his subordinate. The chart also indicates the delegation of authority (*i,e.,* right to command) and the person to whom each employee is responsible. To maintain this line of authority, employee should not by pass the lines of authority mentioned in the chart.

4.10. HIERARCHY (THE SCALAR PRINCIPLE)

The Scalar Principle states that there should be unbroken line of authority and chain of command through all levels from General manager to the lowest employee. This principle means that every undertaking should have some kind of hierarchy, *i.e.,* treating the orders of superiors, like the order of angels involving superior-subordinate relationships.

This principle has the importance only in planning the organisation, *i.e.,* recognising the formal authority in the organisation but this does not help in determining the extent of that authority.

Employees are expected to obey the orders of the superior or to suffer penalties (may be even dismissal or loss of promotion etc.) But in actual practice a good manager will not always be interested in taking the help of these penalties, he should try that the orders must be obeyed willingly. Although, legally an employer can dismiss for disobedience of an order, but the award of penalties is not always suitable as looked from psychological point of view, which will not help in maintaining the good relations. Thus scalar principle has controversy in this regard, *i.e.,* on the point of extent of authority.

4.11. ORGANISING (PROCESS OF ORGANISATION)

Steps involved in organising are listed hereunder.

1. Determination of Objectives
2. Indetification and classification of required activities.
3. Grouping of activities necessary to attain objectives.
4. Assignment of duties.
5. Assigning each group to a manager with necessary authority.
6. Developing authority, responsibility relationship.
7. To establish inter-relationships. This means providing matrix *i.e.,* coordination requirements horizontally and vertically with other groups.
8. Providing physical facilities and proper environment.
9. Preparation of organisation chart.

4.12. ORGANISATION STRUCTURES

Organisation structure provides an appropriate framework of authority and responsibility relationship between various positions. It is concerned with the establishment of positions of persons and the relationship between them. Thus an organisation structure greatly affect the people of a concern, and a proper structure facilitates the effective use of the manpower and their technical expertise.

Organisation structure can also be defined as the systematic arrangement of the people working in the enterprise in order to achieve predecided goals. Organisation structures of a concern is shown on an organisation chart with horizontal and vertical relationship. Horizontal dimensions define the basic departmentation while vertical one relate to the hierarchy of superiors and subordinates.

Sound organisation structure helps in organising to achieve mosteffective utilisation of resources, may it be human, material, machinery or monetary so as to accomplish specific objectives. Organisation structures vary from organisation to organisation mainly depending upon the functions to be performed. Organisation structure decided after following a detailed conscious planning process and is designed to achieve specific objectives.

4.12.1. Formal and Informal Organisation

Formal organisation means the intentional structure of roles in a formally organised enterprise. Informal organisation is joint personal activity without conscious joint purpose, even though contributing to joint results. The idea behind this is that it is easier to ask for help on an organisational problem from some one you know personally, even if he is in differentdepartment.

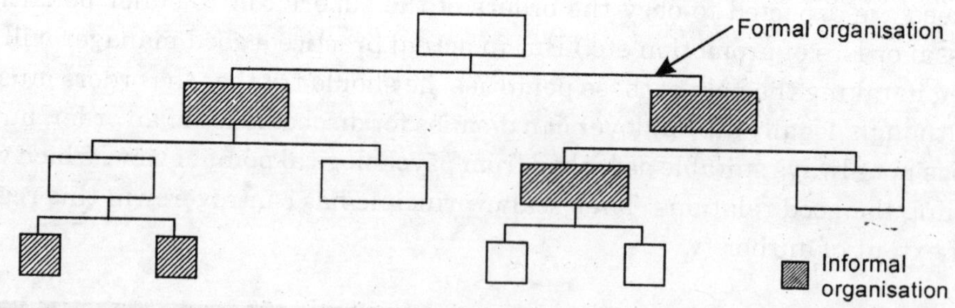

Fig. 4.2. Formal and Informal Organisation

4.12.2. Structuring the Organisation

As we know that an organisation is a large group of persons united to achieve any task. It may also be defined as pooling of human and physical resources in order to achieve predetermined goals and objectives. Organisation structure deals with the overall organisational arrangements in an enterprise. The classical hierarchical organisation structure is the most influential structural rationale of the modern corporation.

While designing an organisational structure, different factors considered are: specialisation of work (departmentation), span of control, chain of command, authority delegation (authority is delegated down the hierarchy), other principles of organisation as discussed earlier for a particular type of industry.

While preparing the structure, it is first drawn roughly considering different aspects and then attempted to weld various systems into a unified concept. This designed structure is refined until it takes final shape for implementation. The structure should be able to fulfil the objectives and achieve the coordination and decision making. Integrated organisational system is shown in Fig. 5.7.

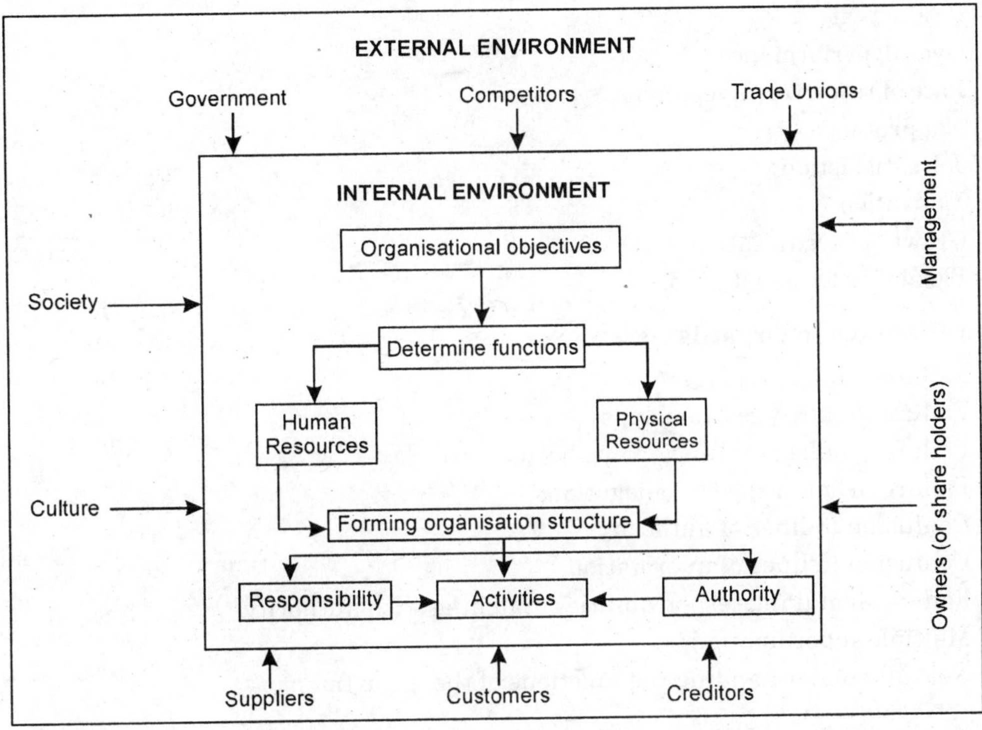

Fig. 4.3. Structuring the organisation

During organisational structure designing following precautions be taken :

1. Develop a technical organisation structure based on the traditional methods of departmentation.
2. Start with total company objectives, develop a hierarchy or network of systems required.
3. Examine all the related functions like Production planning and control, Quality control, Inventory control etc. and outline the various positions to be filled to take up these functions.
4. Involve key managers and experts in developing a matrix, team or one system. A detailed analysis of decision process, and information requirement will help in reviewing and refining the organisational structure.

Introducing behavioural, decision and information concept helps in giving final shape to the structure. Matrix between project managers and functional managers be drawn for better coordination. Project managers are responsible for planning, scheduling, and cost control, whereas functional managers are responsible for the functional activities for all the products. Fulfilling information needs through organisation structure is also necessary.

Factors Influencing the Choice of Structure

1. Impact of environment.
2. Impact of technology.
3. Impact of psychological factors

4.12.3. Organisational Effectiveness

Organisational effectiveness is the degree by which operational goals have been attained. It has following criteria for its evaluation :

1. Productivity
2. Overall performance
3. Rate of return on investment
4. Net profit
5. Job satisfaction
6. Motivation
7. Growth of organisation
8. Flexibility for adoptation.

Common Mistakes in Organising

1. Failure to plan properly.
2. Failure to clarify relationships.
3. Failure to delegate sufficient authority.
4. Failure in balancing the delegations.
5. Confusion in lines of authority.
6. Confusion in lines of information.
7. Failure in making responsibilities matching with authority.
8. Multiple subordination.
9. Not fully understanding the functions of the department.

4.13. ORGANISATION THEORIES

Organisation theory may be defined as the study of (*i*) structure, (*ii*) functioning, (*iii*) performance of organisation, (*iv*) behaviour of groups, and (*v*) individuals working in organisation. Organisation theory also explains as to how organisations are actually designed so as to improve organisational effectiveness. It helps the people to understand, diagnose and respond to organisational needs and problems.

The main objective of organisation theory is to;

(*i*) furnish a general frame of reference for understanding and explaining behaviour of patterns in organisation, and

(*ii*) for providing scientific basis for managerial actions concerned with predicting, controlling and influencing these behaviours with a view to improve organisational effectiveness.

Thus organisation theory can make a manager more competent and more influential.

Different Organisation Theories

For the purpose of convenience, William G. Scott has grouped these theories into following three broad categories:

1. Classical organisation theory
2. Neo-Classical organisation theory
3. System (Modern Classical) theory

4.13.1. Classical Organisation Theory

According to this theory, the efficiency of the organisation can be increased by making each individual efficient in it. The emphasis is more on specialisation of performance and coordination of various activities. This theory ignores the human aspects of organisation and deals exclusively with the formal structure of the organisation.

This theory is based on the principles of division of labour, scalar and functional processes, structure (*i.e.*, line/staff function), and span of control.

• This theory of organisation emphasises on economics, man, rationality and specialisation. Classical theory holds that an individual is motivated almost solely by financial incentive. Classical theory has been developed in following three streams :

(*a*) **Scientific Management.** This includes the science of work study, work measurement and other scientific views in the work process.

(*b*) **Administrative Theory.** This theory was developed by the people for overall improvement in organisational performance so as to get prescribed objectives. The administrative theory defines an organisation as a structure of relationship, powers, objectives, roles, activities, communications and other factors that exist when persons work together.

(*c*) **Bureaucratic Theory.** The Bureaucracy is found in all large systems and can be indentified by the following characters :

(*i*) An impersonal routinized structure.

(*ii*) A hierarchical build up.

(*iii*) Activities governed by well defined rules and decisions demand precedence.

Bureaucracy is found everywhere in government, business, military, political or religious or any other organisation grown too big for work by personal contact.

4.13.2. Neo-Classical Organisation Theory

This theory has introduced the human relations approach in the classical theory of organisation. This theory views the organisation as a combination of formal and informal forms of organisation. The informal form was missing in classical theory.

This theory focusses on the individual and adds the psychological and social aspects of the individual into organisation design. Neoclassical theory is developed by human relationship movement and is build upon the classical theory by giving due consideration to psychological and social needs of individual and work groups.

Main aspects of Neo-classical theory are as under.

1. The organisation, in general, is a social system composed of several other interacting parts.
2. Organisational and indvidual goals must be integrated.
3. The people are interdependent and their behaviour can be predicted in terms of social factors.
4. Money is only one of the motivators but not the sole. Men are diversely motivated and socio-psychological factors are also important.
5. Both way communication is necessary for sound functioning of the organisation.
6. Man's approach is not always rational. He behaves irrationally as far as rewards from the job are concerned.

7. Team work is essential for higher productivity.

4.13.3. System (Modern Classical) Theory

This theory has an analytical base. The organisation being a system has the following 5 parts:

1. Individual
2. Formal organisation
3. Informal organisation
4. Status and roles the individuals play
5. Physical conditions environment

These 5 parts of the system work unitedly, cooperatively and in callaboration with each other they interact within and between themselves. No part of the system works in isolation. They are interdependent and interlinked. The linking is achieved by communication, decision-making by joint efforts, and maintaining various parts of the system in a harmoniously structured relationship to one another.

It is multi-disciplinary approach to organisational development and it is natural consequence of the growth of large multinational organisations and also development of new disciplines like operations research, Cybernetic etc. Systems theory defines organisation as a dynamic process of interaction in which individuals react for objectives.

4.14. TYPES OF ORGANISATION STRUCTURES

Organisational structure is the network of relationship between various positions in an organisation. In this structure different tasks and authorities are distributed. According to different methods of distribution of authorities and responsibilities, the organisation structures are of following types.

1. Line or Scalar (or military type) organisation.
2. Functional organisation.
3. Line and staff organisation.
4. Line, staff and functional organisation.
5. Committee organisation.

4.14.1. Line or Scalar (or Military type) Organisation

In this type of organisation business activities are divided into three groups, namely; finance and accounts, production and sales. Each of these departments is sub-divided into certain self-contained sections. Each departmental head has sole control over his section and has full authority to select his labours, staff, purchase of raw materials, stores and to set the standards of output etc. Foreman of each shop trains new men and supervises the quality of output.

In such a system superior exercises a direct authority over his subordinates who become entirely responsible for their performance to the commanding superior. No operation is under two bosses.

Following is an example of line organisation chart:

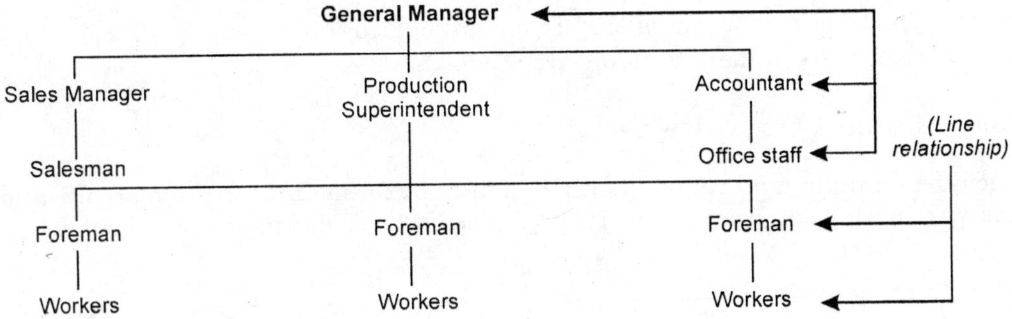

Fig. 4.4. Chart of Line Organisation

This is known as military type organisation, because in military discipline is of high order. Orders and instructions issued from the top have to be followed by the lowers. Similarly in this type of organisation, order of General Manager are to be carried out, without any say by subordinates and hence no chances of shifting of responsibility as in military and hence known as military type organisation.

As in this organisation, the flow of authority moves from top to bottom in vertical lines, therefore, this is also called line or scalar organisation.

Advantages

1. A clear-cut division of authority and responsibility, hence no scope of shifting the responsibility.
2. Strong in discipline.
3. It permits quick decisions.
4. As responsibility of each individual is fixed, hence faults can be easily and quickly known.
5. Everybody from top to bottom remains busy like a machine and hence total cost of product will be less.
6. It is simple to understand.
7. Flexible and able to extend or contract.

Disadvantages

1. It requires different departmental heads to be expert in their respective functions, hence lack of specialisation.
2. Departmental heads are over-burdened with various routine jobs, hence no time for further expansion and planning.
3. Certain people become key points and they are loaded maximum with work.
4. Chances of accidents, wastage of material and labour are more because of insufficient knowledge of all the works by one man.
5. Chances of delay in reaching the orders nf General Manager or any other departmental head upto the workers and, therefore, possibility of distortion, due to long channel.
6. Over-burdened foreman may not be able to give sufficient time for each job and will cause wastage and error.
7. It has no means of rewarding good workers.

Applications

1. Such organisations are suitable for factories of small and medium size, in which subordinate and operational staff is not too much.

2. Suitable for continuous process such as sugar, paper, oil refining, spinning and weaving industries etc.
3. Suitable where labour problems are not difficult to solve.
4. Suitable where automatic plants are used.

4.14.2. Functional Organisation

The difficulties in finding all round qualified man to be foreman in the line organisation are overcome with this type of organisation. He is replaced by various functionalised people.

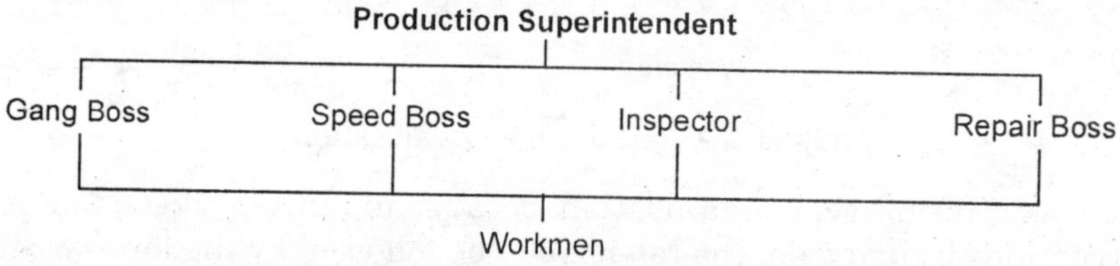

Fig. 4.5. Simplified Chart of Functional Organisation

This system is advantageous because each supervisor is specialised in a particular field and he attends to one factor in all the departments. Below is its layout:

In chart at Fig. 4.5 these different bosses are just like foreman. In some factory, they are called foreman and in another factory they may be designated as gang boss, speed boss etc. Each boss goes to individual workman for instructing and guiding about his activity.

Fig. 4.5 is a short and simplified form showing the structure of functional type of organisaion, Fig. 4.6 shows the order of authority and the stages in the organisation.

In this, specialised people like chemists, purchasers, engineers, designers etc. are employed under the production superintendent and everybody is supposed to give his functionalised advice to all other foremen (bosses) and workers. Every foreman (boss) will go to individual worker for his related function. This type of organisation is sometimes called "Taylor's organisation" as it was for the first time introduced by F.W.Taylor. Taylor said that the well qualified foreman required brain, education (special or technical knowledge), manual strength, tact, energy, honesty, judgement or common sense and good health. He believed that a man with three of these qualities could be hired at any time. If four were required, it was necessary to secure a higher priced man. The man combining five of the qualities was hard to find and the one with six, seven or eight almost impossible to discover. Therefore, Taylor employed functionalised bosses and as far as the workman was concerned, instead of coming in contact with the management at one point, only he was to receive his daily orders and help directly from eight different bosses. Four of these were located in the planning room and four in the shop as shown in Fig. 4.6.

Advantages

1. Due to specialisation quality of work is better.
2. This system provides more specialised knowledge and guidance to individual workers through experts.
3. It helps mass production by standardisation and specialisation.
4. If any operation needs improvement, it can be improved even upto the last moment.
5. Considerable expansion of the factory is possible.
6. Since for every operation expert guidance is there, hence wastage of material will be minimum which will reduce prime cost.

7. Unnecessary overloading of responsibilities will not be there, as was in the case of line organisation.
8. No special knowledge of workers is required as the instructions are supplied by drawing and experts.

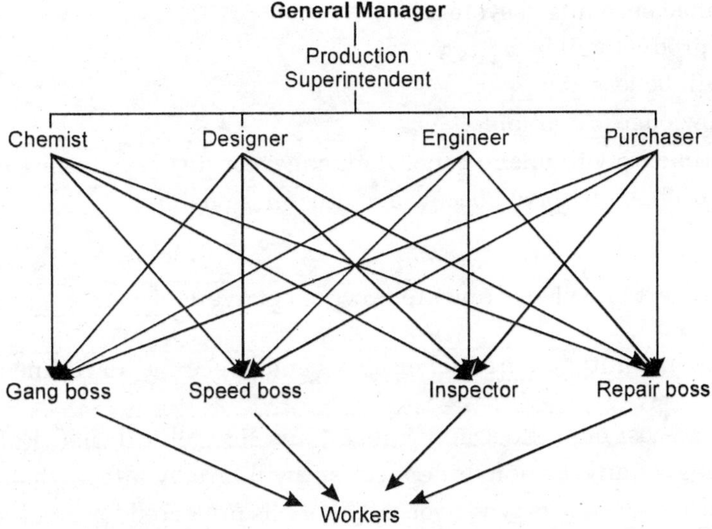

Fig. 4.6. Detailed Chart of Functional Organisation

Disadvantages

1. It is complicated from control point of view as every functionalized expert feels himself to be superior than the other and there is no one-man control over the workers. Therefore, it makes discipline problem difficult to solve among lower level.
2. By employing high waged experts, the total cost of job may become high.
3. As line workers will not be using their skill, their initiative cannot be utilised.
4. Shifting of responsibility is possible.
5. The failure of any of the expert will largely affect the production because, if any expert tells wrong operation, there is no other body to correct him. This will result in large wastage of material.
6. Proper co-ordination of the work of different departments is required but it is difficult to maintain as everybody is working individually.

Application. In practice a pure functionalised system is rarely found. In fact, a factory where responsibilities are divided on a functional basis, line relationship may also exist. This is suitable for large manufacturing concerns which are capable of expansion in future.

4.14.3. Line and Staff Organisation

In a firm of large size operating on big scale, managers can not give careful attention to every part of management. They are unable to think and plan. They are busy with ordinary task of production and selling. Hence 'Some Staff' is deputed to do other works like investigation,research, recording, planning and advising to managers.

Thus staff brings specialisation by assisting the line officers. The line maintains discipline and stability. Staff provides expert information and helps to improve the overall efficiency. Thus the staff are 'thinkers' while line are 'doers'.

A staff man usually controls one function of business of which he is an expert. Usually the staff has no administrative authority, but an expert in some phase of operation. He reports to the executive and gives the advice on the subject of his speciality.

Advantages

1. It is a planned specialised system.
2. Quality of product will be better.
3. Wastage will be less.
4. Expert knowledge is available.
5. Sufficient time is available to general manager for future planning and expansion.
6. Discipline problem is solved because of line relationship.

Disadvantages

1. Sufficient expert knowledge and guidance is not available as compared with functional type.
2. Lack of responsibility among higher levels and hence the discipline as a whole will be poor.
3. The overhead cost of product may rise, because of high salaried staff.
4. The slackness of any section or department will largely affect whole working.

Application. Now-a-days this type of organisation is preferred for medium and large scale industries, depending upon internal structure, nature of productive activities and span of business area. It is applied in automobile industries and other intermittent nature of industries.

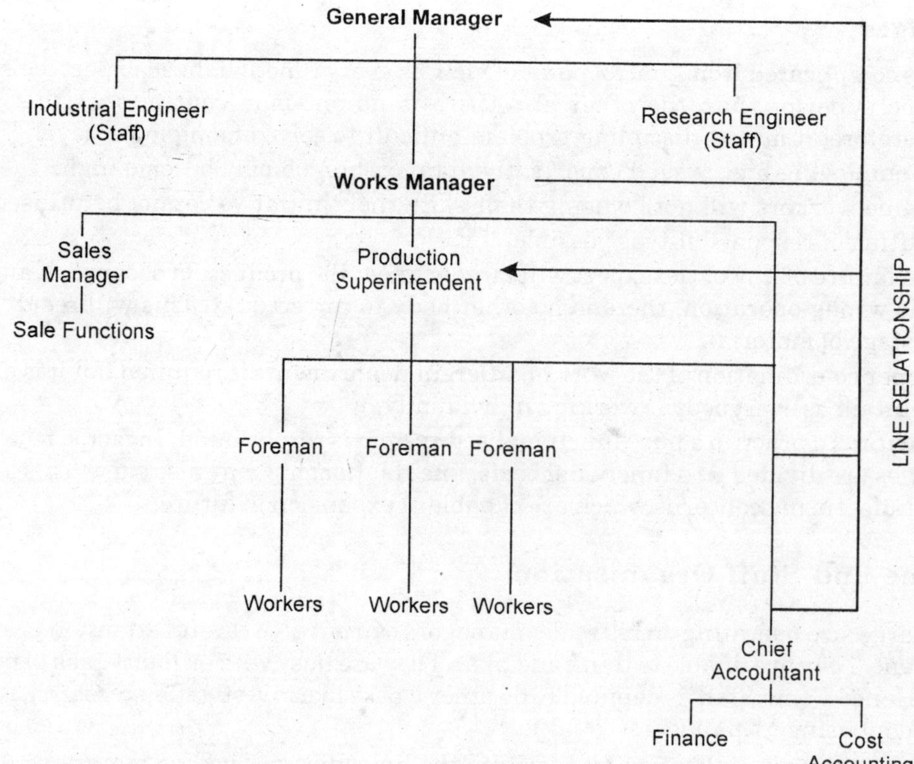

Fig. 4.7. Chart of a Line and Staff Organisation

4.14.4. Line, Staff and Functional Organisation

Because of scientific methods, enough market competition and complications in the business, to obtain a sound system, the combination of line, staff and functional type of organisation is required.

In this system, as regards the discipline and output are concerned, the workers are kept under the direct control of foreman.

As regards quality, the inspector will have the proper authority to control the quality and he can directly order the workman as in the functional organisation.

In the staff relationship, there may be research department for the analysis of raw materials, semi-finished and finished products to withstand market competition.

In this way all the three are combined together and as this is complicated in nature, therefore, also called complicated type of organisation.

Application. Now-a-days this pattern is followed by all government and private concerns, in which much complicated processes or operations are involved, i.e., in big chemical plants, electricity boards, steel plants and other huge undertakings.

4.14.5. Committee Organisation

A committee is a group of persons formed for the purpose of giving advice on certain important problems, which cannot usually be solved by an individual. It helps by pooling the thoughts of several persons on problems involving several functions and offered for criticism. Therefore, now-a-days many large companies add a network of committees to the line and staff organisation.

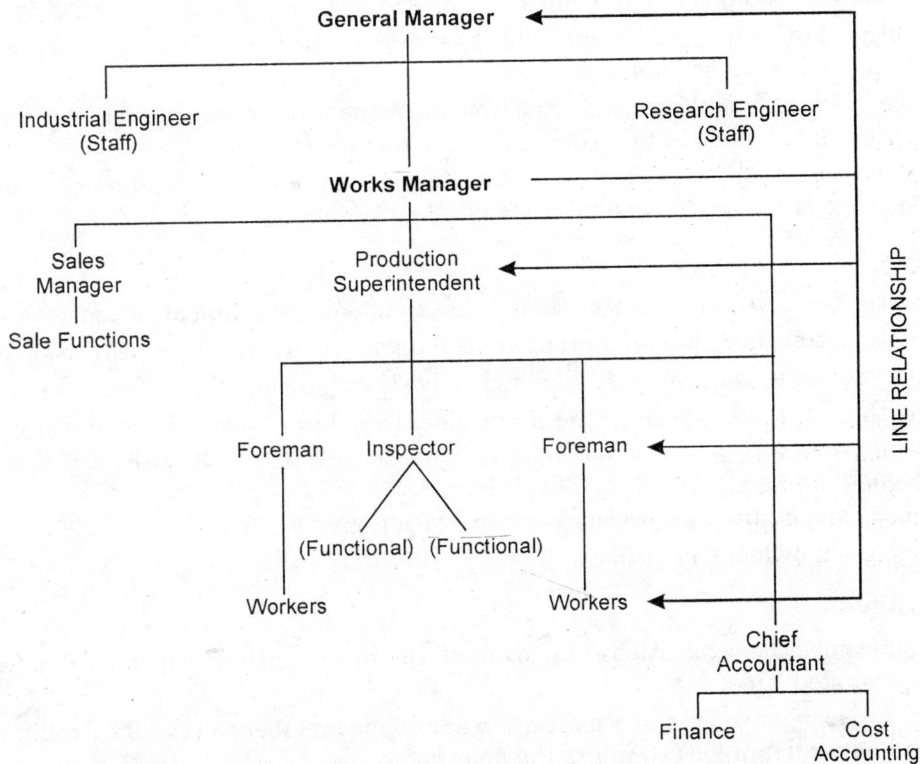

Fig. 4.8. Chart of Line, stall and Functional Organisation

These committees may be either "Permanent" sometimes referred to as standing committees or they may be organised to serve a temporary function only. Examples of committees are Research Committee, Co-ordination and Advisory Committee, Purchase Committee, Education Committee etc.

A committee is a tool for the development of ideas and recommendations of policy and procedure. It brings better plans and policies for operations and results in better co-operation in their execution. The final decision to put committee recommendations into action rests with the line. The committee simply performs advisory function.

Actually, the committee is similar to the staff and several owners think it a costly substitute for staff but it is found that no other method is so effective in solving common problems or in getting new ideas as committee organisation of collective judgement.

Fundamental Principles

Committee like other forms of organisation should be varied according to the needs of a given organisation. However, there are certain basic principles given below, which must be considered:

1. In this, members should be minimum, i.e., generally 3 to 5. This is found by experience that too many members result in much wasted time by lengthy discussions and delayed decisions.
2. The chairman of the committee must prepare the agenda to be discussed much in advance of the meeting and circulate among the members so that they can get sufficient time to think over the problems to be discussed.
3. The chairman must control the behaviour and discipline among the members when the meeting is held so that there is least wasted time and thought.
4. Meetings should begin and end at fixed time.
5. Duties, authorities and responsibilities must be clearly defined and owing to circumstances they can be subject to changes.
6. The meetings should be conducted from an agenda containing those things which require attention arranged in the order of their importance.
7. All the members must realise that more time can be wasted unless each member co-operates sincerely to save the time of other members.

Advantages

1. Since "two" heads are better than "one", quick and valuable decisions can be taken.
2. By this, time schedule and proper follow up are instituted which cause speedy action.
3. Decision taken are impersonal which leave the chairman free from personal criticism.
4. As the members are from the plant side, they know better what is going on in the shops and can give the correct suggestions and team up with other persons and departments.
5. There is a stimulus towards co-operative action.
6. Expert knowledge is utilised.

Disadvantages

1. Sometimes the committees may be too large in strength which cause delayed actions and wasted time.
2. It is an expensive form of organisation as outside members are paid travelling allowance and honorarium for attending the meetings.

3. As members are from different departments, they may not reach to a final conclusion at all.
4. It functions very slowly.
5. As there is joint responsibility of members hence, it amounts to irresponsibility, as "every body's business is no body's business."

4.15. TYPES OF BUSINESS ORGANISATIONS (OWNER SHIP)

Several types of business organisations are existing in order to satisfy various social, economic and human requirements. Following are the main types of business organisations:

(A) Private Sector

1. Individual ownership or Sole proprietorship.
2. Partnership organisation
3. Joint stock companies
4. Cooperative organisation
5. Joint Hindu family firm

(B) Public Sector (State Ownership)

1. Departmental organisations
2. Public corporations
3. Government Companies

(C) Joint Sector

Ownership and control shared by private enterpreneur, state and public.

4.16. PRIVATE SECTOR

4.16.1 Private Companies (Individual Ownership)

As the name suggests, such type of business is owned by one man. This is the oldest simplest form of business organisation. The businessman invests capital, employs labour and machines. In such business owner supplies all the capital needed to run the organisation.

Hence the owner alone enjoys the profits and suffers the losses in his business. Therefore, he is the supreme authority to decide into different matters concerning to his business and has unlimited freedom of action within legal jurisdiction.

Overall control in single hand helps him in quick decision, efficient administation and working. In this type of organisation, owner must be anxious to obtain valuable advice and guidance from other sources.

In such organisations owner himself is responsible for all the liabilities. Hence creditor can collect the money even from the personal property. Therefore, to have this type of business it is not the money alone of the debtor that is necessary to start but also the zeal, enthusiasm, courage and faith of the person.

Applications. This form of organisation is most satisfactory in the following cases :

1. In small enterprises requiring small capital which can be spared by the one man (owner).
2. Where risk required is not too heavy. Because in this system risk involved is very high.
3. Where management by one man is possible.

Advantages.

Following are the advantages of this form of organisation :

1. Such individual enterprises can easily be formed and simple to run and at the same time owner is free from all legal restrictions.
2. His (owner's) interest, care and efficiency directly affects the profit in the business. Hence efforts and rewards are directly related.
3. In this system owner himself is in touch with customers and hence can know their likings.
4. Since it is supervised by the proprietor himself, the overheads are very less and products can be sold cheaply.
5. Most of the business have their monopoly because of certain secrecy in their functioning. In this form of organisation such secret functions are performed by the owner himself and he does not disclose it to any body else. Therefore, he has the greatest possibility of running business well. In other forms of organisation, there are little chances of keeping such activities secret for a longer period.
6. It offers full freedom for work and hence such persons who do not want to serve under or with any body can get the chance to work independently and can show their talent. Thus they can enjoy free life.
7. As he has not to seek direction for any decision to be taken, he can act promptly. If at any time he feels some benefit in doing some work, he can act quickly without any body's advice and can avail the benefit.

Disadvantages

This type of organisation has the following disadvantages :

1. Amount of capital that can be invested is limited, therefore, modern factory cannot be run with this system of organisation.
2. Owner cannot be the master of all techniques like management, sales, engineering processes etc. Hence work suffers.
3. Due to unlimited liability owner cannot take risk to start a big industry.

4.16.2. Partnership Organisations

Some of the above mentioned drawbacks of private companies are removed in the partnership organisation upto some extent.

Partnership is the relationship between the persons desirous of starting a business and they combine or invite together to incease their resources, i.e., capital, labour, skill and ability. The success of partnership depends upon mutual confidence, understanding, co-operation and adjustment of the members to accommodate and appreciate each other's view. Each of the partner should realise that it is his business and he should work hard to earn greater and greater profit.

Partnership has been defined by the Indian Partnership Act 1932. As "the relationship between persons who have agreed to share profit of a business concern carried on by all or any one of them acting for all". When two and upto twenty persons in case of nonbanking business and upto ten in case of banking business enter into a contract to carry on a business allowed by law, with the object of making profit, a partnership is said to be formed.

Every partner is liable and responsible for the acts of other partners in that business. To avoid any complication at a later stage the constitution of the company may be written in an agreement form. For the best partnership the number of partners should not be more than six, the lesser the better. It generally happens that persons with a good idea and experience of a business make partnership with moneyed people. Thus money and knowledge both are combined to earn profit.

Advantages.

This type of organisation has the following important advantages :

1. It can be formed without much legal formalities and without heavy expenditure of organisation and stamp duty.
2. This type of organisation enjoys more freedom and is not subject to strict government supervision.
3. Due to more number of owners the amount of capital that can be collected is more than that in the case of sole trade organisation.
4. In this type of organisation persons possessing different abilities and skills are chosen and brought together. Therefore, the managerial ability of the firm as a whole would be much greater than in case of a sole trader.
5. The affairs of firm can easily be kept secret.

Disadvantages.

Following are the disadvantages or limitations of the partnership organisation:

1. Due to unlimited liability risk involved is more.
2. After the death or retirement of any one partner, the partnership organisation may come to an end.
3. It can raise much less capital in comparison to the joint stock company. It is, therefore, unsuitable for modern industries, because they require huge capital and a large number of managerial abilities.
4. Sometimes, due to some misunderstanding, friction may arise between the partners, which affect adversely on the efficiency and expansion of business.
5. All the partners are jointly and severally liable for the acts of the partner, who is placed incharge of management. Thus sometimes mistakes of one partner may cause a big loss to all the partners.

In conclusion, though partnership firm can reduce the limitations of sole trade organisation to some extent, yet it has more or less all the limitations of a sole-trade organisation and, therefore, suffers the same fate.

Types of Partners

Members of this type of organisation may be associated in different ways and their extent of involvement may be also different, although their interest is common. These members can be classified in the following ways :

(a) *General Partners.* All the partners who are in the partnership known as general partners.

(b) *Active Partners.* These are those partners who take active part in the management and help in the formulation of policies. These are also known as working or managing partners.

(c) *Sleeping and Silent Partners.* Partners, who just invest money and do not take any part in the management are known as sleeping or silent partners. Such members after contributing their share of capital, wake up only either to share the profits or to liquidate the business.

(d) *Nominal Partners*. Partners, who do not invest money and do not take part in the management, but they lend their reputed name for the company's reputation are known as nominal partners. The nominal partners may, however, associate themselves only after ascertaining the soundness of the business.

(e) *Secret Partners*. These partners take part in the management secretly but nowhere their names appear.

(f) *Minor Partners*. A person who has not attained the age of 18 years and associated with the business is known as a minor partner. Such partner can be allowed only with the consent of other members. His liability is limited to investment only (i.e., limited liability).

Formation of Partnership

Partnership can be formed either verbally or by written agreement but to avoid the possibility of misunderstanding and further troubles which can arise at a later stage, it is desirable to enter into a written agreement. This written agreement is known as "Partnership Deed".

4.16.3. Joint Stock Companies

Limited financial resources and heavy burden of risk involved in both of the previous forms of organisations has led to the formation of joint stock companies. These have limited liability.

In this system capital is contributed by a large number of persons. It is voluntary association of individuals for profit, having a capital divided into transferable shares of different values.

The capital is raised by selling shares of different values. Persons who purchase the shares are called shareholders. The managing body known as "Board of Directors" is elected by these shareholders. The board of directors is responsible for policy making, important financial and technical decisions and efficient working of an enterprise.

In this form of organisation liability of a shareholder is limited to the extent of the amount of shares held by him and he is free from the responsibility of the debts and claims on the company beyond the value of shares. Because of this advantage all sections of people are encouraged to contribute for the company. These shares are transferable.

Characteristics of Joint Stock Company

Some of the important characteristics of joint stock company are :

1. A joint stock company can be created by registering or incorporating an association of persons under the Company Act.
2. A very stable existence.
3. A company has a separate legal existence as distinct from its members.
4. A company has a common seal and acts as its signature. It is affixed on all important legal documents and contracts.
5. There is a complete separation of an ownership from management.
6. Liability of share holders is limited.
7. Lower tax liability.
8. Easy transferability of shares.
9. Risk of loss is widely distributed.
10. Large number of members.

Types of Joint Stock Companies

There are two main types of joint stock companies :

(*a*) Private Limited Company. (*b*) Public Limited Company.

(*a*) **Private Limited Company.** This type of company can be formed by two or more persons. The maximum number of membership is limited to 50. In this, transfer of shares is limited to members only and general public cannot be invited to subscribe the shares. Normally the members of such a company are friends and relatives.

A private limited company need not make the prospectus, accounts and other particulars open to the public. The members only are entitled to receive a copy of the balance sheet, and auditors' report. The government also does not interfere in the working of the company. In this system persons who want to take advantage of limited liability and at the same time to keep the business as private as possible, can-subscribe.

(*b*) **Public Limited Company.** It is one whose membership is open to general public as its name indicates. The minimum number required to form such a company is seven, but there is no upper limit.

Such companies can advertise to offer its shares to general public through a prospectus. These public limited companies are subjected to greater control and supervision of the government. This control is necessary to protect the interest of the shareholders and the members of the public. Shares are transferable in part or full without requiring any prior approval. The affairs of the company are managed by an elected body, known as 'Board of Directors'. The number of members in the board of directors is limited to seven.

Liquidation

It becomes difficult to run the company if liability becomes much more than assets and when creditors press for payments of loan etc. At this time the company has to be dissolved or wind up. This is known as liquidation.

Liquidation may be compulsory or voluntary or under the supervision of court. If the resources do not permit the payment, then the assets of the company have to be sold and then the amount is paid to the creditors in proportion. If some amount is left after payments then it is distributed among the shareholders.

Amalgamation

An Amalgamation is a joining together of two businesses. It usually results in more efficient operation because of economics of large sales, administrative, and marketing etc.

Clearly both parties in a proposed amalgamation will have some existing assets and liabilities which could be set out in a balance sheet or statement of affairs at the date of amalgamation. The existing conditions may or may not be acceptable to the proposed partner. Usually some adjustments will be made to one or both of the balance sheets to take account of objections raised by the other party.

Raising Finance for Joint Stock Companies

Money is necessary to start and to keep the business running. It is also needed to meet expansion, replacement and alterations. The required capital is supplied by individuals, societies and associations. Funds can also be taken from banks, finance corporations etc., in the form of loan. Following are the sources from where money can be taken for an enterprise :

1. *Issue of Shares.* A portion of the money required for enterprise is collected in the form of shares.

2. *Issue of Debentures.* When company desires to raise the required finance through loans instead of sale of shares, then debentures are issued. In this way it is advantageous because debenture holder cannot claim for ownership and he is to be paid interest only. Debentures may be issued either for initial needs of enterprise or for development and extension.
3. Loan advances from banks, and other financial institutions, like L.I.C. and U.T.I.
4. State loans from Industrial Corporations, State Finance Corporation or through Industrial Development Corporation.

Advantages

Following are the advantages of the joint stock company over the previous two forms of business organisation :

1. The liability being limited, the shareholder bears no risk and, therefore, more and more persons are encouraged to invest capital. Thus more amount of capital can be collected to run modern industries.
2. Because of large number of investors, the risk of loss is divided. Therefore, even an average person can contribute capital without much hesitation.
3. In the joint stock companies the work is divided among different groups of persons ; hence better work can be done.
4. It can bear the high salaries of the good managing agents, chief manager and other managers etc. Thus administration is better.
5. Joint stock companies are not affected by the death or retirement of the shareholders.
6. It has great potentialities for expansion.

Disadvantages

Following are the main disadvantages of the joint stock company :

1. Lack of personal interest on the part of the salaried managers because there is no relation between effort and income for them and this leads to inefficiency and waste.
2. This form of organisation offers sufficient scope to the directors and other members of the management for their personal profits. Because they have intimate knowledge of the financial position of the company, therefore, they can purchase or sell the shares accordingly.
3. In this form of business there are hundreds of investors from different parts of the country who invest their savings but very rarely come to atttend the general body meetings or exercise any effective check. Such persons offer unlimited scope for cautious persons to secure control over companies and deceive the innocent shareholders.
4. It requires a large number of legal formalities to be observed.
5. It is difficult to preserve secrecy in these companies.

4.16.4. Co-operative Societies

With the study of individual ownership, partnership and joint stock companies we have seen that they neglect the interest of consumers and employees in the concern. This is the most democratic form of business organisation for the betterment of general public. These co-operative societies help to protect the interests of the consumers, small and independent producers, and of the workers while fighting against the monopolists and capitalists. Members supply the capital, manage the business and share all its profits and losses. These have been developed in agriculture to a large extent. In economic field, these do not have the idea of earning profits but to benefit the members.

Co-operative society is an association of individuals formed for the purpose of obtaining goods, specially the articles of daily use at rates lower than that of market. Thus, it is a means to level the inequality of wealth which had come into existence as a result of private individual form of ownership. The idea of co-operative society is to benefit the shareholders who are the consumers or producers.

Mr. N. Barow defined co-operative society, as "voluntary organisation" of persons with unrestricted membership and collectively owned fund, consisting of wage earners and small producers, united on a democratic basis for the establishment of enterprises under joint management for the purpose of improving their household or business economy.

The main object of co-operative society is to promote self help and mutual assistance among men of moderate means and incomes having needs and interests in common. Such men are industrial workers, small artisans, agriculturists and members of the middle class. In this system liability of shareholders is limited.

To start a co-operative society an application is submitted to the registrar of co-operative societies. The officials of this department will attend the first general body meeting in which bye-laws are framed to govern the society and the directors are elected by the shareholders. Then if the authorities are satisfied about its soundness, a licence will be issued by the registrar and thus the company is formed. Board of Directors meet at least once in every three months.

The Indian Government to protect the interests of small consumers, is encouraging the co-operative movement and provides loans through financial corporations, banks etc. The accounts of the enterprise are audited by state government. It can be formed by minimum of 10 members and should be registered with the registrar of co-operatives. The government of India has tried to introduce co-operative societies in many fields since long but it has not met with much success. Although co-operative movement is very conducive for Indian economy but has failed to achieve the objectives.

Main Objectives

Main objectives of the co-operative societies are following :

1. It is a voluntary organisation. A member can continue his membership as long as he desires, and can, by giving a notice, withdraw his capital and cease to be a member.
2. There is no limit to its membership. Face value of one share is generally kept as Rs. 10. Thus small value of share makes it possible to enroll a large number of persons because even a poor man can afford this much amount.
3. Its management is based on democratic basis of equality. Therefore, every member can cast only one vote, whatsoever the number of shares he has.
4. Its object is to serve the members and to earn profit.

Types

The various types of co-operative societies in our country are :

(*a*) Producers' or Manufacturers' co-operative society.

(*b*) Consumers' co-operative society.

(*c*) Housing co-operative society.

(*d*) Co-operative farming.

(*e*) Co-operative credit society.

Consumers' and housing co-operative societies are gaining popularity in our country.

(*a*) **Producers' Co-operative Society.** This is the form of association in which persons combine together to form a society for the purpose of manufacturing goods. Although it is a democratic management of industrial production, this is useful where neither large capital is necessary nor much technical and expert knowledge of management isneeded. In India, this is applied to agricultural and cottage industries. This has largely succeeded in countries like Denmark, United State of America, Sweden, Israel etc. In India some of the Sugar mills, Rice mills and Ginning mills are running under this formation.

(*b*) **Consumers' Co-operative Society.** This type has got some popularity. Its object is to eliminate the middleman's profit by directly purchasing things from manufacturers and distributing among the members and non-members at reasonable prices. This can be of retail or whole-sale type.

These are also named as "co-operatives". Super Bazars in all the important cities have been established so as to make available the things at cheaper rates. These co-operatives achieved good success in the very beginning but later on it was found that due to mismanagement, corruption and lack of experience some of them were functioning satisfactorily.

(*c*) **Housing Co-operative Societies.** These societies are formed for the purpose of getting plots or houses for the needy persons. For such purpose government provides great facilities.

(*d*) **Co-operative Farming.** This type is not popular in India. The object is to enlarge the size of agriculture land by forming the co-operative group of cultivators. It will thus make possible the use of modern implements, science and technology in agriculture which in turn increase the yield.

(*e*) **Co-operative Credit Society.** Its object is to finance the poor cultivators by advancing loans for the development of land and purchase of machinery etc.

Advantages.

Following are the advantages of co-operative organisations :

1. It sells the products cheaper; as money required to spend on advertisement and publicity is not needed.
2. Expenses for book keeping, auditing and management task are kept minimum, as members provide honorary service for such tasks.
3. It offers to its employees better wages and reasonable conditions of service.
4. There is no question of profiteering, hoarding and black marketing type of evils as the aim is to serve the community.
5. Middleman's profit is eliminated as purchasing is directly made from manufacturer.
6. It suits well to Indian cultivators in improving the problems of mechanised farming, warehousing and credit etc.
7. Profits are shared equally and, the balance goes for social causes and development of locality such as medical aid, education, playgrounds and children gardens etc.
8. It tries to equalise money distribution.
9. It benefits general public.
10. It promotes a sense of co-operation among the members.
11. It is possible to take large amount of capital in the form of loans (say upto 8 times the subscribed capital) from the government.

Limitations.

It has its own limitations, some of them are listed below :

1. As its members come mostly from the working class and middle class, its capacity to raise capital is limited. Therefore, it is suitable for small and medium sized undertakings only.
2. Due to limited financial resources services of highly qualified persons cannot be utilized.
3. Although it trades for the benefit of members only but at the same time it is not possible to refuse to trade with non members.
4. Mostly inefficient management and sometimes found that management is inexperienced and corrupt.
5. Members usually try to make undue advantage.
6. It requires better and strict supervision.
7. There are chances of excess officialization.

4.16.5. Joint Hindu Family Firms

Ancestral property inherited by a Hindu from his great grandfather to grandfather, by grandfather to father and by father to him. Therefore after the death of a Hindu, his business is jointly owned by the living male issues. Such firm is known as Joint Hindu Family Firm. The female members or their relatives do not have any claim in the firm.

Advantages

(*i*) These are not dissolved on the death of a member.

(*ii*) It has no binding of Company's Act 1956.

Drawbacks

(*i*) Continuity of the firm depends upon the continuity of the joint family itself.

(*ii*) Resources are limited compared to joint stock company.

(*iii*) Since the management of this type of firm is in the hands of eldest male member, there is generally lack of management skill or adequate business knowledge.

(*iv*) Business is looked after by the active member(s), but the profit is shared by all. This affects his interest and efforts for the growth and efficient running of the firm.

Joint Hindu Family Firm v/s Partnership Firms

(*i*) This is a creation of Hindu law, hence there is no contract. Partnership firm is formed under the contract.

(*ii*) This is a continuous firm and do not dissolve on the death of a member, but ceases if the joint family breaks down, whereas partnership firm gets dissolved in the event of death of a partner.

(*iii*) This does not have female as members, whereas partnership firm can have female partners.

4.17. STATE OWNERSHIP (PUBLIC SECTOR ORGANISATIONS)

Such ownership is only serious competitor to the joint stock companies. This form is most suitable for the establishment and development of modern industries, because facilities like power, transport, credit, insurance etc. are easily available to them.

The private ownership and the joint stock company gave rise to exploitation of labour and of the cunsumers. This gave idea of state ownership. The former system of ownership neglected the well-being of workers and the welfare of the community, as a whole.

Government either starts or nationalises (acquires) certain industries to prevent the economic imbalance in the country. It serves as a means to obstruct the monopolistic tendencies. It helps for the betterment of the community and for the welfare of the people.

The railways, post and telegraph are completely state owned. Ship-building, steel industry, . electricity generation, fertiliser production, railway engine manufacture etc. are owned by the government and also by joint stock companies.

Main drawbacks in above mentioned state ownership is that they cannot be handled like private enterprises. In private enterprises, the employees are believed and certain confidence is placed in them, therefore, they try to achieve the maximum benefit for the undertaking. The employers do not tolerate any bad workmanship or inefficiency or indiscipline, etc.

Forms pf Public Sector Organisations

1. Departmental Organisations.
2. Public Corporations.
3. Government Companies.

4.17.1. Government Departmental Organisations

The organisations are organised like any other Government departments. These are managed in two ways :

1. *Management through the concerned ministry.* It is managed by the officials of the government under the charge of the secretary of the ministry concerned. The examples are Posts and Telegraphs, Railways, Defence, Industries, Broadcasting etc.
2. *Management by Inter-department Committee or Board.* In certain organisations co-operation is required from several ministries. Therefore, a board or committee of representatives from concerning ministries is formed so that co-operation, consultation and quick decisions may be taken. Bhakra Control Board, Hirakund Control Board, Chambal Control Board, All India Handloom Board are few examples of organisations managed by interdepartmental committee or board.

All the governmental organisations have following essential characteristics :

(*a*) Financed out of government budget.

(*b*) Revenue goes to public exchequer.

(*c*) All the rules and regulations of government are applicable.

(*d*) Direct control of the concerned ministry.

(*e*) Employees are government servants.

Merits

1. Because of the government control, it is easy to achieve its economical, political, and social objectives

2. Such organisations are suitable for public utility services and defence industries.
3. Because of the government control, complete secrecy is possible as in ordnancefactories etc.

Demerits

1. Because of bureaucratic control, generally timely decisions are not taken.
2. Government officials prefer to work according to certain rules and regulations and thus it becomes difficult to bring about major modifications and innovation etc.
3. Because of red-tapism, officers are discouraged from taking quick and independent decisions.
4. Lack of initiative because promotions are seniority based rather than merit based.

4.17.2. Public Corporations

A Public Corporation is wholly owned by the Government—Centre or State. It is established usually by a Special Act of the Parliament with internal autonomy. Special statute also prescribes its management pattern, powers, duties and jurisdictions. Though the total capital is provided by the Government, they have separate entity and enjoy independence in matters related to appointments, promotions etc. These corporations have no profit motive and work for maximisation of social welfare.

Merits

1. These are supposed to be better managed. These are expected to provide better working conditions to the employees and cheaper and better products to the consumers.
2. Quick decision can be possible, because of absence of red-tapism and bureaucratic control.
3. More flexibility as compared to departmental organisations.
4. Because of the absence of profit motive, these are most suitable for managing public utilities at a reasonable cost to the people.
5. Since the management is in the hands of experienced and capable directors and managers, these are managed more efficiently than that of government departments.

Demerits

1. Any alteration in the power and constitution of corporation requires an amendment in the particular Act, which is difficult and time consuming.
2. The autonomy of the corporations are only on papers whereas in reality, there are lot of interference by the political leaders and government officers. Therefore, they do not enjoy real freedom in their working.
3. Public corporations possess monopoly and in the absence of competition, these are not interested in adopting new techniques and in making improvement in their working.

4.17.3. Government Companies

A state enterprise can also be organised in the form of a Joint Stock Company under Companies Act. A government company, according to Indian Companies Act 1956, is any company in which not less than 50% of the share capital is held by the central government, or by any state government or governments or partly by the central government and partly by one or more state governments. This form of organization is becoming very popular in recent times. It is created by an executive and not a legislative decision and is managed by nominated board of directors which may include private individuals. These are accountable for its working to the concerned ministry or department and its annual report is required to be placed every year on the table of the parliament or state legislature alongwith comments of the government or concerned department. Auditors are appointed on the recommendations of the Comptroller and Auditor General of India. The employees, excluding deputationists are not civil servants. In its day-to-day working it is free from government interference, however, Bureau of Public Enterprises can issue guidance and directions.

Merits

1. It is easy to form.
2. The directors of a government company are free to take decisions and are not bound by certain rigid rules and regulations.
3. They always try to satisfy their customers because otherwise they might lose to their competitors
4. More efficiency.

Demerits

1. Misuse of excessive freedom cannot be ruled out.
2. Inadequate-accountability.
3. The directors are appointed by the government, so they spend more time in pleasing their political masters and top government officials, which results in inefficient management.

Some Problems

1. *Price Policy.* As the state undertakings have a monopoly they may charge a price higher than what would have been under competition. Of course, it may be for covering the inefficiency of the management and not to make the profit.
2. *Excessive centralization.*'Because of the nationalisation of the industries, each of the organisation is bigger than the biggest organisation in the private sector. Practical results show that it results in poor management, poor labour relations and higher inefficiency.

4.18. THE JOINT SECTOR MANAGEMENT

It is a known fact that today in government organisations whether it is a public limited company or state enterprise management is a big headache. This is one of the main causes of today's unrest' high rise in prices, strikes and lock-outs etc. To overcome this great trouble, recently in political and governmental circles considerable stress is being given to the future growth of industry on the line of joint sector.

Concept of the Joint Sector

Joint sector means participation by the government and private industry in the share capital and the general management of the unit to be set up. It aims at achieving the task of social justice through efficient use of resources. The government finances and private enterprise maintains the efficient working of the industry. In our country a large number of industrial units have come up under this concept. Examples are : The Indian Oil, the Cochin Refineries ; The Madras Refineries, the Madras Fertilizers Limited etc.

Contribution

In regard to the individual ventures already functioning under the joint sector principle the participation has not generally been on an equal footing and it has been ensured that the government would be the senior partner. With the exception of the Indian Oil, in which share participation is on a 50 : 50 basis, the contribution to the share capital is usually in the ratio of 51 : 49 and in all cases the government holds 51% of the shares.

Participation

In this set-up chairman is a government nominee but managing director is nominated by the collaborating private industry. The government also has a large representation in the board of directors. On account of this and the large share holding, its view is more likely to prevail on matters of importance. The salaries and other service conditions of both officers and workers in these are higher than those enjoyed by their counterparts in the public sector plants and in conservative enterprises.

Advantages

1. Promotion of social objectives.
2. Mobilisation of resources.
3. Controlling the business malpractices.
4. Antidose to monopoly and concentration of economic power.
5. Acceleration of industrial growth.
6. Making nationalisation unnecessary.

Limitations

1. Lack of confidence between two sectors.
2. Managerial autonomy.
3. Joint sector is facing the problems of (*a*) pattern of management and powers of the management (*b*) salary structure (*c*) accountability (*d*) performance appraisal etc.

4.19. LIABILITIES

Liability of a business means what it owns to others. Loans taken in the form of cash or in the form of credit purchases are known as liabilities. Payments due for services like electricity, water supply, insurance premium and salary of staff are also considered as liabilities of a business. Owners of the busines are legally responsible for the payment of these liabilities.

Liabilities on owners are of two types :

1. Unlimited Liability, and
2. Limited Liability.

Unlimited Liability

In this system, there is no maximum limit of capital which can be collected from debtors in the case of failure of business. The creditors may collect money even from the personal property of the owner. Because the risk involved in this system is very high, it provides a most serious limitation for those business in which unlimited liabilities are involved.

Therefore, if unluckily the business runs into heavy loss or fails, the owner and his family will suffer seriously and even may be reduced to poverty.

Effect of unlimited liability on :

(*a*) **Sole Trade Organisation.** In this type of organisation if the business goes into loss, the whole amount has to be paid by a single person (owner) upto the last paisa of his personal property. Therefore, due to the risk of heavy losses to be borne by the individual, this type of organisation is confined to small scale manufacturing or works of small nature.

(*b*) **Partnership Organisation.** In this type of organisation all the partners have unlimited liability. This means that if property of the firm is insufficient to clear the debts of the firm, then the creditor can collect the money from the personal property of the individual partner. In this way, as risk involved in this system is less than that of the sole trade organisation, the partners will not hesitate even to start medium size concerns.

Limited Liability

In case of limited liability the maximum limit of amount that can be collected from an owner or share holder is upto the capital invested by him in the industry. Thus the risk in-volved is limited to the amount of shares only and their private property cannot be sold.

Effect of limited liability on :

(*a*) **Joint Stock Company.** In this system liability of a member is limited to the face value of the shares he purchases. Thus shareholder is responsible to the extent of amount of shares purchased by him. This type of organisation has unique feature in this respect, therefore, now-a-days big industries are being run with this form of organisation.

(*b*) **Co-operative Society.** In this system also shareholder is responsible upto the extent of the face value of the shares purchased by him. As regards liability is concerned it is similar to those of Joint Stock Company as explained earlier.

4.20. JOINT STOCK COMPANY V/S PARTNERSHIP ORGANISATION

A joint stock company and partnership form of'organisation can be compared as under :

Joint Stock Company	*Partnership*
1. It has a separate legal entity, having its existence separate from its shareholders.,	1. It has no separate legal existence apart from its partners.
2. It may consist of any number of members.	2. It may consist of maximum 20 members for nonbanking and 10 for banking business.
3. Shares can.be transferred to others without the consent of any body.	3. Shares cannot be transferred on sweet will without the consent of other partners.
4. It invests according to memorandum and can't do any other business activities.	4. It can do any business activities on the sweet will of partners.
5. Liability is limited.	5. Generally unlimited liability.
6. The property of the firm is the property of the company.	6. The property is that of the individual partners.
7. Management is done by directors which are elected by shareholders.	7. Every partner is entitled to perform managerial activities.
8. It has got certain obligations such as maintenance of accounts, preparing balance sheets, returns, registers and other informa-tions desired by the government, and on failure to do so are penalised.	8. No such obligations in this form of organisation.
9. Death or retirement of any of the share-holders does not affect the business.	9. Business may suffer and sometimes may come to standstill.
10. Large capital can be collected.	10. Large capital can't be collected.
11. Management is smooth and efficient.	11. Here control is divided between different partners and there may be difficulty and disagreement in management.

4.21. SOLE PROPRIETORSHIP V/S PARTNERSHIP

Basis of Distinction	Sole Proprietorship	Partnership
1. Membership	One man's business	Minimum....2 Maximum....20
2. Agreement	No agreement	An agreement is required
3. Capital	Fully by the owner	Contributed by the partners
4. Registration	No provision	Required under the Partnership Act 1932
5. Risk	Entire risk	Joint risk
6. Management	Owner is supreme	Division of work subject to agreement
7. Secrecy	Ensured	Known to all partners, difficult to maintain.

4.22. PRIVATE COMPANY V/S PUBLIC COMPANY

Basis of Distinction	Private Company	Public Company
1. Minimum number of members	Two	Seven
2. Maximum number of members	Fifty	Unlimited
3. Invitation of public for capital	No	Yes
4. Transferability of shares	Restricted to members	Free
5. Secrecy	Possible	Not possible
6. Prospectus	Not necessary	Yes, necessary
7. Minimum number of Directors	Two	Three
8. Exemption from legal restrictions	Yes	No
9. Quick decisions	Possible	Not possible
10. Credit and Resources	Small	Large
11. Protection to members	Less	More

4.23. CO-OPERATIVE SOCIETY V/S JOINT STOCK COMPANY

Basis of Distinction	Co-operative Society	Joint Stock Company
1. Basic object	Service	Profiteering
2. Membership	Limited to a particular group	Open to all
3. Minimum number of members	Ten	2 for Private company and 7 for Public company
4. Transferability of shares	No	Free
5. Voting right	One man one vote	One share one vote
6. Privileges	Exemption under stamp duty, taxes, cheaper finance	No such benefits
7. Disposal of profit	Fixed return on capital, surplus distributed either as bonus or spent for the welfare of the members	Divided without any limit

4.24. PRIVATE LIMITED V/S PUBLIC LIMITED JOINT STOCK COMPANIES

S.No.	Particulars	Private Limited	Public Limited Joint Stock Company
1.	Membership	Membership is confined to the close friends and relatives of the promoters. Cannot invite public to share capital	Membership is open to the general public. Any person can contribute and become share holder.
2.	Limits to Membership	Minimum members-2. Maximum members-50	Minimum members -7 Maximum members-No Limit
3.	Election of Directors	No need for holding statutory meeting	Shareholders elect the directors in the statuatory meeting.
4.	Resale of shares	Shares cannot be resold or transferred without the consent of the company	Shares can be resold or transferred without the consent of the company.
5.	Audit of accounts	No legal provision of the audit	Audit of accounts is mandatory and circulated among the members of the company.
6.	Name	The words "Private Limited" are used at the end of its name	The word "Limited" is used at the end of its name.
7.	Number of directors	Minimum two directors	Minimum 3 directors
8.	Legal controls	Less legal controls	Strict legal controls

4.25. ORGANISATION CHARTS

An organisation chart helps in understanding the organisational relationships. These show the grouping of major activities in the departments and the main lines of authority and responsibilities among these departments. These draw graphically the structural relationships among the different functions (departments) and the positions (persons) of those who are responsible for these functions in the organisation.

Since organisation structure is represented by organisation charts, it should be designed considering various aspects discussed in the chapter. It should also consider internal and external environment of the organisation. Internal environment include workers, managers, working conditions, culture etc., while external environment include suppliers, customers, competitors, government agencies etc.

Organisation structure is designed in following steps :

(*i*) Understand and formulate the objectives and goals of the organisation.

(*ii*) Determine necessary functions for achieving the objectives and goals.

(*iii*) Functions related to each other be grouped together.

(*iv*) Positions for each group be decided.

(*v*) Job descriptions, duties and responsibilities of each position be prepared.

(*vi*) Relative positions and their relationship be determined so as to form the organisation chart.

Since we know that organisation structure means the systematic arrangement of the people working for the organisation, their positions, and the relationship between positions, the structure provides an appropriate authority and responsibility relationships. The organisation structure is generally shown on an organisation chart. The organisation structure varies with the organisation and the functions to be performed, and depends upon the goals and objectives established, the resources availability, the communications, and the working relationships of the individual participants, motivation and other factors.

Considering these principles, and the type of organisation structures, the chart is drawn. Types of organisation structures are :

(*a*) Line or Scalar organisation,

(*b*) Line and staff organisation.

(*c*) Functional organisation.

(*d*) Line, staff and functional organisation.

A sample organisation chart is drawn hereunder :

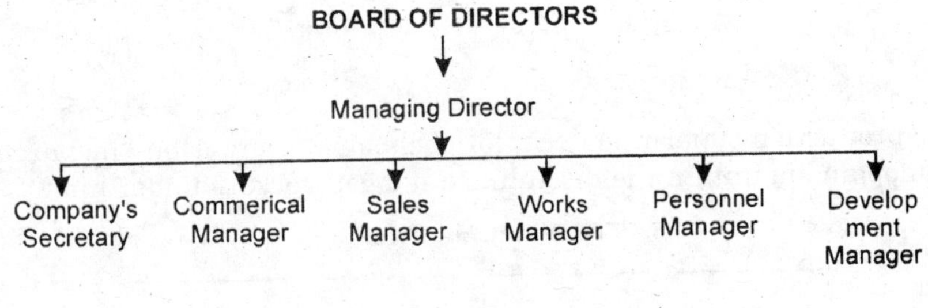

Note. The duties of the company's secretary are ; to arrange board's meeting, legal matters, business considerations.

2. COMMERCIAL MANAGER

Office Manager
(a) Correspondence
(b) Typing
(c) Maintaining record
(d) Other official works

Chief Manager
(a) Accounts
(b) Sales and wages
(c) Cost accounting

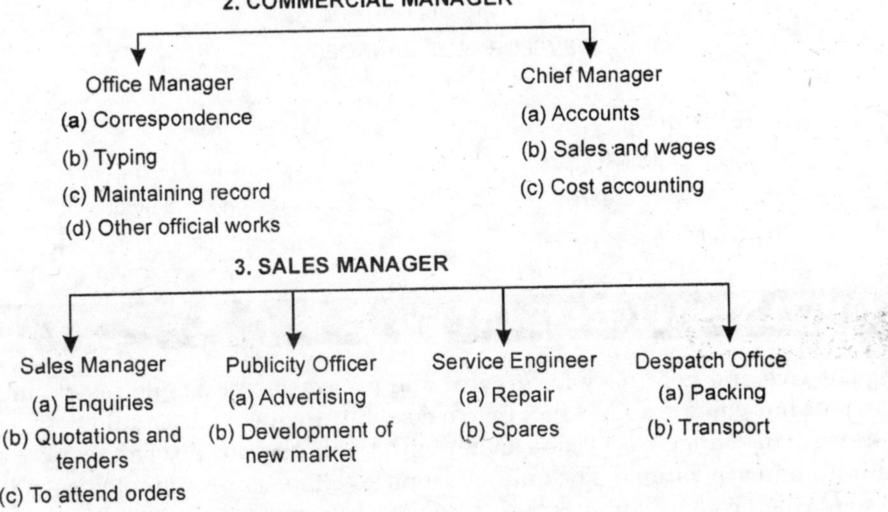

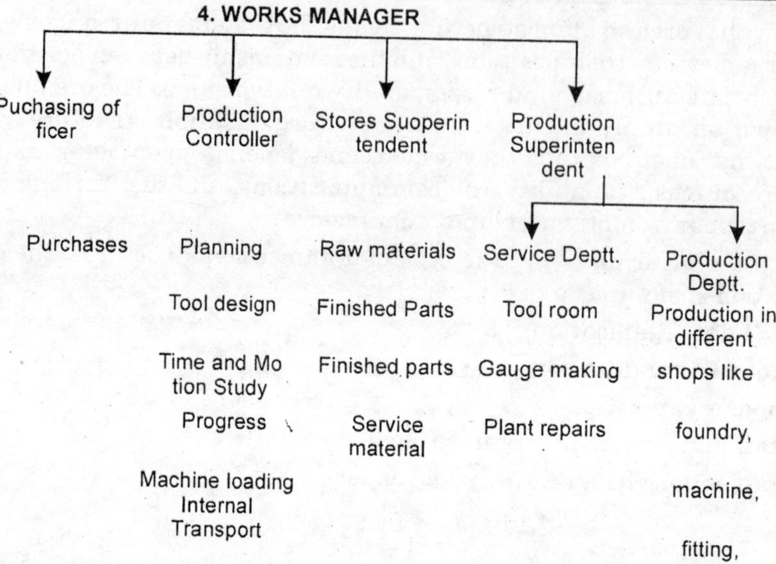

Note. Under-production superintendent, for each shop, there is one incharge to look after the work in his shop and maintain the discipline amongst workers under him.

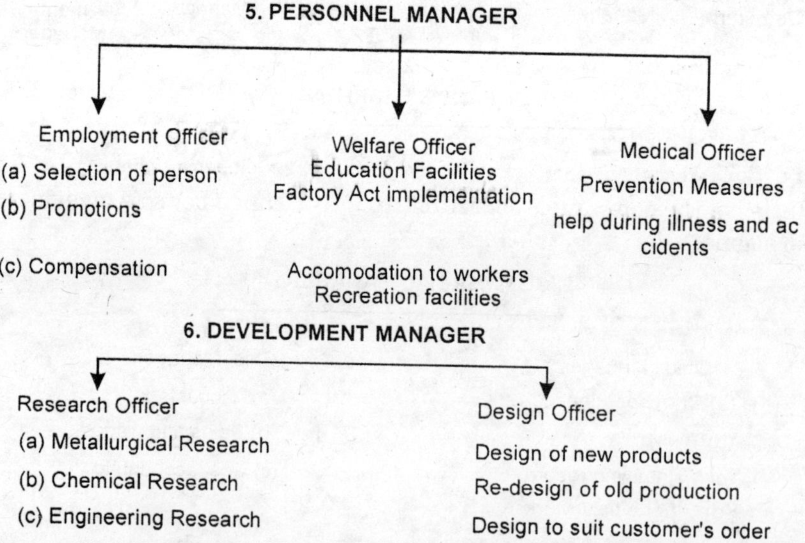

4.26. ORGANISATIONAL CHANGE

Change is positive and necessary for growth and progress, but people resist change because it is easier to do what you are doing than to learn something new and mould yourself accordingly. The requirement of change has become faster with the higher levels of education, communication and greater human aspirations. The main reasons for change are technological advances, changes in government rules, competitors strategies, habits and preferences of people based on internal and external factors.

The process of changing the people are—training, orientation, guidance etc, but these are more to 'educate to change' the people rather than to 'change them'.

Necessity for a Change

Organisational change becomes necessary to adopt changes in the external environment or to achieve new goals. Change is a part of life and provides opportunity for growth. Management of an organisation takes a conscious decision in favour of a change after taking a stock of the overall situation for optimisation, organisations must adopt themselves to changing conditions, corporate objectives and priorities. This is necessary for its growth and survival.

Change must be carried out in a planned and systematic manner. An organisation consists of inter-related and interacting systems to perform the required tasks. Principal systems affected by change are :

(*a*) System of work flow and process or system of authority and power needs to be amended.

(*b*) Changes in the tools and techniques used, and provision of better equipments.

(*c*) Change in attitude, behaviour and inter personnel relationship of people working in the organisation.

Since the change is complex, expensive and painstaking, it is necessary to plan the change with the aim to prepare the entire organisation or a major part of it. In order to carry out a change employees are asked to leave the familiar work habits for a new organisation with new policies, procedures and expectations.

The changes become necessary due to following main reasons :

1. Environmental changes threaten the organisation's survival. An organisation must regularly interact with their external environment.
2. Environmental changes offer new opportunities, and an organisation must take advantage of the opportunity for its growth.
3. One organisation structure is suitable for particular environment and it is slow in adaptation to the complex and changing external environment. The organisations which are more flexible, creative and innovative in reacting to environmental changes are preferred.

Resistance to Change

The members of the organisation resist changes because of the social and economical fears. In order to understand the real cause, it is necessary to understand socio-psychological and socio-economic factors. Some of the reasons for resistance to change are :

(*i*) Fear of being out of job

(*ii*) Fear of reduced earnings or chances of promotion

(*iii*) Inconvenience

(*iv*) Traditional customs

(*v*) Fear of uncertainties

(*vi*) Fear of losing special privileges

(*vii*) Increased control

(*viii*) Attitude of the union

(*ix*) Personality related factors, like habit, ego, vested interests.

Dealing with the Resistance to Change

Management can expect cooperation from the members of the organisation, only when it is able to convince them that their fears are baseless and that the change is advantageous for them. A systematic process must be followed for reducing resistance.

(*a*) Two-way communication provides opportunity for feed back, *i.e.*, suggestions and criticism etc. It encourages effective participation and involvement of the people.

(*b*) Group decision making. It involves subordinate's active participation and is necessary for support from every body in the group.

(*c*) Collective Bargaining. In order to get the proposed change acceptable, discussions and making a compromise, *i.e.*, negotiation and agreement in writing with unions are very helpful.

(*d*) Education and training.

(*e*) Persuation, and providing sufficient time for mental change to take place.

(*f*) Introducing changes slowly and gradually.

(*g*) Treat people with dignity.

(*h*) Manipulation and cooperation. This means giving key persons a desirable role in designing or implementing the changed process.

Implementing the Change

There are three types of changes, namely changing the structure, changing the technology and changing the people.

1. **Changing the Structure.** Changing the organisation's structure means rearranging its internal systems, like, change in hierarchy, work flow and information flow. This includes authority, responsibility, division of labour etc.
2. **Changing the Technology.** This change includes changing the equipment, engineering process, production methods etc. for improving the performance.
3. **Changing the people.** This tries to change the behaviour of employees by focussing on their attitudes, skills, perceptions and expectations.

Forces in Favour and Against a Change

Forces in favour of a change and against it decide the state of equilibrium. If more force than that required is applied, it may result in hostility, distrust and greater resistance, which may ultimately lead to lower performance.

A. Forces in favour of change

(*i*) New technology

(*ii*) Better raw material

(*iii*) Competition

(*iv*) Pressure from supervisors.

B. Forces against change

1. Change of performance norms
2. Fear of change
3. Change in traditional customs and skills
4. Other factors resisting the change.

Planning the Organisation Change

The organisation is required to be redesigned systematically so that it may adapt to changes in external environment or to achieve new goals or to implement new policy. The change in the organisation needs to be carried out considering the following aspects :

(*i*) Environmental changes which threaten the organisation's survival.

(*ii*) Environmental changes which offer new opportunities.

(*iii*) Existing structure not matching with the pace of adaptation to environmental changes.

QUESTIONS

1. What factors should be considered while forming various departments in an organisation?
2. Explain the term "organisation structure". What are the characteristics of a sound organisation structure?
3. How the organisational structure is designed? Explain.
4. Explain the organisational theories.
5. Explain the term "Division of Labour". Give its advantages and disadvantages.
6. Describe departmentalism in an industry.
7. What factors must be considered while deciding "span of cotrol"?
8. What do you understand by "Authority" and "Responsibility"?
9. Write an essay on "Delegation of Authority".
10. Define the terms "organisation, co-ordination, authority and responsibilities. How are these structured to the management objectives of a medium sized industry ?
11. How does Frederick Taylor's Scientific Management theory differ from Henry Fayol's process theory?
12. State the important assumptions and general contributions to management made by the following schools of management thoughts:
    (*i*) Human behaviour school.
    (*ii*) Decision theory school.
    (*iii*) Quantitative management school.
13. Define the terms: Business, Industry, and Trade.
14. How will you classify business? Describe various business characteristics.
15. Explain various factors, you would like to consider, for deciding the form of organisation.
16. Explain various objectives of a business.
17. What factors should be considered before deciding about the form of organisation to be started?
18. What are the different types of ownership?
19. How partnership organisation differs with sole trade organisation. Explain.
20. What are the advantages of a co-operative enterprise over a joint stock company.
21. Distinguish between Public Limited and Private Limited types of companies.
22. What is state ownership? What are its advantages?
23. Discuss the term "liability". Explain the different types of liabilities with example.
24. Explain different types of partners.

25. Write short note on:
   (*i*) Partnership
   (*ii*) Debenture
   (*iii*) Capital turnover
   (*iv*) Debenture and bonds
   (*v*) Share and debenture
26. (*i*) What is a government company ? (*ii*) Many government companies have, during recent years, been formed as joint stock companies. Why? (*iii*) Describe how capital shares are raised by a public limited company.
27. Discuss the characteristics of the joint stock company responsible for making it the most important type of ownership of industrial organisations.
28. Discuss the merits and demerits of raising capital by: (*a*) Preference shares; (*b*) Debentures and (c) Bank.
29. Name the different types of ownership of industrial organisation and indicate the significant features of each.
30. Detail the steps which a joint stock company has to follow in raising capital shares. Indicate the significant of each step and the considerations necessary to follow it properly.
31. How capital is raised in different types of owership of industrial organisation ? What types of ownership do you prefer ? Give reasons and state advantages and disadvantages.
32. Enumerate the various sources of financing for large scale industry in India. Discuss their relative importance.
33. What is a joint stock company ? Trace the history of Industrial Organisation from individual development to combinations and pools in the modern system.
34. (*a*) Show the important difference between state ownership and private ownership of industrial enterprises. (*b*) Why is it that one thinks of co-operative societies for smaller organisations and not for large ones?
35. Differentiate between private ownership and state ownership. Indicate with justification, their special fields of application with reference to Indian background.
36. (*i*) Distinguish between "Policies", "Procedures" and "Methods", (*ii*) Explain clearly the necessity of well defined policies for a business organisation.
37. (*a*) What are the different types of co-operative societies in India? Explain how they differ from joint stock enterprises, (*b*) State the main objective for consumer co-operative.

Part–2 Human Resource Management

5 PERSONNEL (HUMAN RESOURCE) MANAGEMENT

5.1. INTRODUCTION

Personnel Management (staffing function of management), also known as Human Resource Management, is concerned with the proper use of human factor, and may be defined as that part of the management process which is primarily concerned with the human constituents of an organisation.

It can also be defined as that field of management which is concerned with the planning, organising, directing, and controlling various operative functions of procurement, development, maintenance, and utilisation of a labour force in such a way that objectives of company, those of personnel of all levels and those of community are achieved.

Human Resource Management system is concerned primary with the five basic sub-systems, namely: recruitment, placement, training, compensation (pay, fringe benefits etc.) and maintenance.

Functions of Personnel Management

1. **Acquisition,** (*a*) Manpower Planning (*b*) Job Analysis (c) Recruitment and selection, placement, induction and orientation.
2. **Development,** (*a*) Training (*b*) Management Development (*c*) Career Development
3. **Motivation,** (*a*) Job design (*b*) Performance appraisals, (c) Rewards (*d*) Job Evaluation (*e*) Compensation (pay, fringe benefits etc.) (*f*) Benefits
4. **Maintenance** (*a*) Safety (*b*) Welfare (*c*) Industrial Relations (*d*) Discipline (*e*) Collective Bargaining

Principles of Personnel Management

1. Maximum individual development.
2. Scientific selection.
3. High moral.
4. Dignity of labour.
5. Team spirit.
6. Effective communication.
7. Participative management
8. Fair reward

9. Effective utilisation of human resources.
10. Contribution to national prosperity.

5.2. PERSONNEL POLICY

A personnel policy is a directive, usually written to help personnel department in accomplishing the objectives or functions effectively. A personnel policy contains the information regarding following:

1. Recruitment.
2. Employment conditions.
3. Financial help.
4. Promotions.
5. Discharge.
6. Safety practices, health and welfare.
7. Training.
8. Separation etc.

Need or Importance of Personnel Policy

1. Helps in achieving the objectives of organisation
2. Uniformity in decisions.
3. Helps in decentralisation
4. Helps in proper control.
5. Help in evaluation of performance.
6. Increases morale
7. Guarantee of security.
8. Guide to management.

5.3. HUMAN RESOURCE MANAGEMENT PROCESS

Human resource management (HRM) process includes following basic activities:

1. Human resource planning (Man power planning).
2. Recruitment.
3. Selection.
4. Socialization. This is to help the selected pesson to fit smoothly into the organisation.
5. Training and development.
6. Peformance appraisal.
7. Promotions, Transfers, demotions and separations
8. Compensation.
9. Benefits.
10. Counselling and other assistance.
11. Labour relations.
12. Organisation development.

5.4. MAN-POWER PLANNING

"Vetter" has defined the manpower planning as the process by which management determines how the organisation should move from its current manpower position to its desired manpower position. Through this planning, management strikes to have the right number and right kind of people at the right places at the right time, doing things which result in both the organisation and the individual receiving maximum long run benefits.

It deals with calculations of manpower requirements in future considering various factors such as internal and external economies, social and political pressures, organisation policy, availability and suitability of the manpower requirements etc.

It is a continuous dynamic process and manpower requirement should be done every year and revised periodically at fixed interval keeping in view the yearly manufacturing programme.

Requirements of Sound Manpower Planning

Following are the essential requirements for a sound manpower planning.

1. It should be done sufficiently in advance.
2. It should be reviewed periodically, so that modification or alterations, if any, can be incorporated.
3. The planning should have top management support.
4. It should be need based.
5. It should be economic in nature.
6. It should incorporate the elements of flexibility and elasticity.
7. It should be efficient and effective in nature.
8. It should be simple and easy to understand.
9. It should provide definite instructions and methods.
10. It should provide a suitable policy.
11. To be more effective, it should be rigid but the elements of flexibility and elasticity should not be ignored.

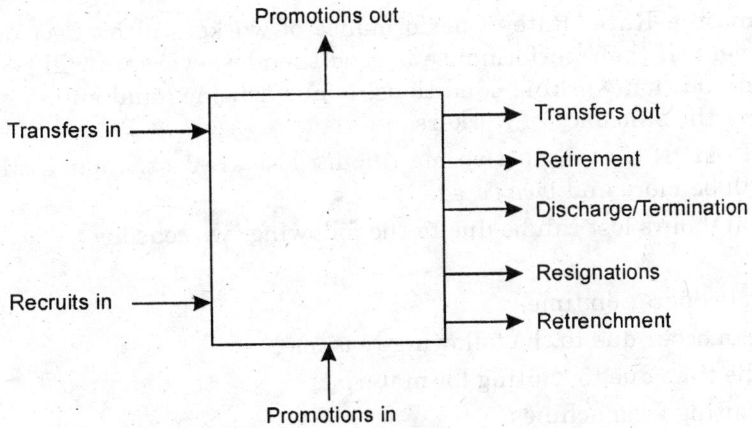

Fig. 5.1. Man-power flow in an organisation.

Factors Affecting Manpower Planning

This is very complex dynamic and complicated work. For an effective and efficient manpower planning a number of factors should be considered. These are:

(*i*) Working hours.
(*ii*) Number of shifts
(*iii*) Nature of production,
(*iv*) Product mix.
(*v*) Performance rate.
(*vi*) Hours lost.

1. **Working Hours.** Manpower requirement is directly related to the total hours worked per day by the employee in an industry. If number of hours for which a worker has to work is more, less man power will be needed and *vice versa*.

   For example, due to complexity in process and working conditions in a chemical plant, workers are asked to work for 6 hours instead of 8 hours shift while an another assembly industry workers are to work for 8 hours in a shift, so the manpower planning basis will differ in both the industries.

2. **Number of Shifts.** It is seen that production falls in the night shifts imparted to day shifts. This factor should be considered while running the factory in shifts and deciding manpower requirements.

3. **Nature of Production.** Nature of production means whether we are manufacturing some machine component or chemical product or some gas or assembly items etc. These affect the utilisation of the capacity which depends on machine or plant utilisation and all this affects manpower requirements.

   Idle time, setting time, cycle time etc. all vary greatly with the nature of production and therefore manpower requirement also vary.

4. **Product Mix.** "Product mix", means a production programme based on optimum productive capacity and sales forecast. In a mass production factory, once it is planned then remains almost fixed but in a jobbing factory, it always vary with the customer orders. Since this calls for a variety of products, hence it becomes difficult to forecast the volume and mix of the sales.

   Hence it is essential to be more selective while accepting the orders. This will result in maximum utilisation of manpower.

5. **Performance Rate.** Rate of performance of workers also affect on the manpower requirement. If their performance is good then less workers will be needed and *vice versa*. In addition working conditions, bonus schemes and suitable incentive plans also affect the efficiency of workers.

6. **Hours Lost.** If the productive man hours lost are less, their available productive hours will be more and *vice versa*.

Productive man-hours lost can be due to the following two reasons :

(*i*) Delays
(*ii*) Addition to operation time.

1. Delays can occur due to the following reasons :
   (*a*) Idle time due to waiting for material.
   (*b*) Waiting for machines.
   (*c*) Waiting for transporting equipment.

(*d*) Waiting for want of proper instructions.
(*e*) Waiting for power and services.
(*f*) Lack of preventive maintenance.

2. Addition to operation time may be due to the following reasons :
   (*a*) Change in design and specification.
   (*b*) Change in consumer needs.
   (*c*) Use of oversize material, tools and equipment.
   (*d*) Rectification and rework due to poor workmanship, poor material or tools and defective design etc.

5.4.1. DATA AND ALLOWANCES

Various data and allowances relating to the past performance of the workers are kept in the record and these are used as guidelines while calculating manpower requirements of the industry.

These may be :

(*i*) Machine utilisation
(*ii*) Operator's efficiency.
(*iii*) Extra time allowance.
(*iv*) Waiting time.

(*i*) **Machine Utilisation.** Production performance return is obtained from accounts department, which indicates the extent of machine tools and equipment being utilised in the past. This gives the percentage of idle time of the machines in a particular section or department.

(*ii*) **Operator's Efficiency.** The record of efficiency of workers is also obtained from accounts department. Normally following standard is considered as guidelines for measuring worker's efficiency.

(*a*) Operators having one year of job experience = 85%
(*b*) Newly appointed after apprenticeship = 60%

On the basis of these efficiencies and the utilisation factor the effective hours/man/year can be estimated as under :

1. Total days in a year	= 365
2. *Less*	
(*a*) Sundays	= 52
(*b*) General holidays	= 10
(*c*) Casual leaves	= 10
(*d*) Sick leaves	= 10
(*e*) Earned leaves	= 20
	102

Therefore working days will be (365 – 102) = 263 days.

Thus, total available working hours/worker/year at 100%, efficiency = 263 × (48/6) = 2104 hours.

∴ Effective working hours/worker/year at 95% machine tool utilisation and 85% operator's efficiency

= 2104 × 0.95 × 0.85 = **1700 hours**

(*iii*) **Extra Time Allowance.** Sometimes incomplete specifications are given on the manufacturing sheet or improper materials are being purchased, which consume unnecessary more time and worker is not able to proceed strictly according to planned process. For all such problems an extra time allowance has to be provided.

(*iv*) **Waiting Time.** Sometimes workers have to wait for obtaining proper instructions, material handling not available at the desired time, spares and repairs are not provided at the right time and alike factors. Allowance has to be allowed for this can be worked out from productive performance sheets.

In addition, following are other data needed for manpower requirements.

1. Availability of manpower.
2. Expected turn over rates, such as promotions, transfers and retirements etc.
3. Absenteeism rate of workers.
4. Forecasting of future sales and product mix.
5. Time standards for assessment of manpower requirements.
6. Industry, state and national indices on employment and labour productivity.
7. Wages and grades prevailing in the surrounding areas or industries.
8. Job analysis and job specifications given qualitative information on the manpower requirements.

Man-power Planning Involves Four Basic Steps

(*a*) Anticipating man power needs.

(*b*) Planning job requirements and descriptions.

(c) Analysing skills to determine the nature of needed manpower.

(*d*) Selecting adequate sources of recruitment.

5.4.2. Man-power Planning Techniques

There are following two main techniques of manpower planning :

1. Work measurement.
2. Work sampling.

1. **Work Measurement.** This technique is very popular now-a-days and almost all the industries adopt it. It may be defined as 'the art of observing and recording the time required to do each detailed element of an industrial operation'. With the help of this technique standard time required to complete the job is obtained and how many machines an operator can run. In this method analysis of the complete job is done and total output is obtained. Thus by dividing total output with the standard time to complete the job, total manpower requirements can be calculated. This method is very simple and accurate and is, therefore, commonly used by the industries. For detailed study readers are advised to read the chapter on "Time Study".
2. **Work Sampling.** Work sampling also called "Activity Sampling" is based on the statistical method first devised by L.H.S. Tippet in 1934. Though "work measurement" study proved to be very useful for repetitive operations but it cannot measure accurately and economically long and irregular work cycles. While most of the indirect activities are of irregular nature and, therefore, there must be some way to control the indirect labour activities. For such tasks "work sampling" has been well established and gained lot of popularity.

Theory of Work Sampling. It states that the percentage of observation recording an operation in any state is a reliable estimate of the percentage time the operation is in that state provided. "Sufficient number of observations are taken at random". Hence particular stress should be paid on the words "random" and "sufficient number of observations". In this method, some error is likely to occur but the error tends to diminish as the number of samples increases.

For example in the following table there are 36 working observations and 4 idle observations, *i.e.*, a total of 40 observations.

State	Total
Working	36
Idle	4

Table to show "working time" and "Idle time".

In this example, the percentage of idle time is $\frac{4}{40} \times 100 = 10\%$

$$\text{Working time is } \frac{36}{40} \times 100 = 90\ \%$$

This study is for one operator for an 8 hours a day and indicates that the operator was idle 10% or 48 minutes of the day while working 90% or 432 minutes of the day.

Now man power requirement can be calculated as follows :

Let working percentage is $W\%$.

To this working percentage various allowances such as fatigue and rest, extra time allowance etc. are added and say it is $A\%$ and if the existing "Man Power" is M, then over-utilisation or under-utilisation can be obtained accordingly.

Say, for example, average percent of working is 50% allowance for rest and fatigue, anticipated load and leave etc. is 20% then total utilisation = 50% + 20% = 70%.

Now, if existing employees are 10 men at present then actually need at 100% utilisation and 100% efficiency will be

$$\frac{70}{100} \times \frac{10}{1} = 7 \text{ employees.}$$

It means there would have been 7 employees instead of 10, *i.e.*, the existing staff is underutilised and therefore employees should be allotted more work load.

For detailed study of the topic, readers are advised to read chapter on "Work Sampling" in this book.

Problems and Limitations of Manpower Planning

(*i*) It suffers from inaccuracy since it is difficult to forecast long range requirements precisely.

(*ii*) Changes to economic conditions, technology, marketing situation and labour force lead to make long range forecasts unreliable. Still there is also greater danger in not forecasting at all.

(*iii*) It cannot be anticipated as to who will be replaced.

(*iv*) Top management does not support to those who are incharge of manpower planning.

(*v*) No action can be taken on general estimates of personnel needs.

5.4.3. Job Analysis

For the purpose of manpower planning, job is studied carefully regarding activities involved in the job. This study is known as 'job analysis', job analysis can be defined as the systematic exploration of the activities within a job.

Job analysis involves compiling a detailed description of tasks, determining the relationship of the job to technology and other jobs and examining the knowledge, qualifications or employment standards accountabilities and other incumbent requirements.

Job analysis is the careful study about the activities of an employee on a particular job to determine different operations involved and other facts, which are helpful for job description and job specification.

The terms related to this are described hereunder :

Job. It is regular assignment to individual employee including their duties, responsibilities, skill, knowledge etc.

Job Description. It is an abstract of information received from the job analysis. It gives the informations regarding the responsibilities , skill or training required, working conditions, type of person which should be employed for performing the job, qualifications and job knowledge.

Job Specifications. On the basis of details of a job, the capabilities and qualification necessary for performing the job are determined. This is known as job specifications. It is obtained from the job analysis and job description reports. Therefore job specifications can be defined as "the statement which specifies the type of employee required". It helps in the selection of employee.

Methods of Job Analysis

1. Observation Method
2. Individual interview method
3. Group interview method
4. Structured questionnaire method
5. Technical conference method

5.5. RECRUITMENT

Recruitment is the process by which prospective employees are identified and then encouraged to apply for a particular job or jobs in an organisation. The purpose of recruitment is to collect sufficient number of application for each job from whom proper selection of the most suitable person can be made.

Sources (Methods) of Recruitment

1. Schools and colleges
2. Employees contact with the public
3. From own application files
4. Use of outside agencies
5. Employment exchanges
6. Advertisement
7. Using present employees

8. Use of contractors for unskilled workers
9. On deputation from other organisation.

5.6. SELECTION

Selection is the process of examining the applicants with regard to their suitability for the given job or jobs, and choosing the best from them. Thus selection is essentially a process of picking out the man or man best suited for the organisation's requirements. Selection process involves rejection of unsuitable or less suitable applicants.

Selection can also be defined as the process of securing relevant information about an applicant to evaluate his qualifications, experience and other qualities with a view to matching these with the requirement of a job.

Selection Process

1. Initial Screening
2. Employment Tests.
   (*a*) Achievement or Intelligence Tests
   (*b*) Aptitude or Potential Ability Tests
   (*c*) Personality Tests, and
   (*d*) Interest Tests
3. Comprehensive Interviews including Group discussions.
4. Background Investigation
5. Physical Examination, and
6. Final Employment Decision.

5.7. PLACEMENT

Placement is the determination of the job for which a selected candidate is best suited and assigning that job for him. It means the right man for the right job. A proper placement reduces employee turnover, absenteeism and improves morale.

5.8. INDUCTION AND ORIENTATION

Induction is the introduction of an employee to the job and the organisation. The idea behind this is that the new employee must feel proud of his association with the company.

Orientation covers the activities involved in introducing a new employee to the organisation and to his work unit.

A good induction programme should cover the following :

1. Information about the company, products, manufacturing process and major tasks in his job.
2. Intricacies about the job including its hazards.
3. Organisational structure and functions of various departments.
4. Employees own position in the organisation and department.
5. Personnel policy of the organisation.

6. Service conditions, amenities and welfare facilities .
7. Policies, objectives and rules and regulations of the company.
8. Grievance and discipline handling procedures.
9. Promotions, transfers, suggestion schemes, job satisfaction etc.

5.9. TRAINING

To attain a very high standard, it is essential to impart training right from unskilled worker to the specialised executive in every concern. Today, due to modern advancement and mass production, a very high skill is required, which can only be developed by proper training. Training has become increasingly important as jobs have become more sophisticated and influenced by technological change.

If a systematic training is imparted to workers in the beginning, it helps in reduction in absenteeism, accidents, labour turnover, bad workmanship, spoilage of tools and plants etc., which ultimately reduces cost of product.

Training is an organised activity for increasing the knowledge and skills of the people for a definite purpose. The purpose of training is to achieve a change in the behaviour of trained personnel and to enable them to do their jobs in a better way.

Training can also be defined as a short-term process utilising a systematic and organised procedure by which people acquire technical knowledge and skills for a definite purpose.

Training is a bearing experience that seeks a relatively permanent change in an individual that will improve his ability to perform the job.

Training and Education

Training is a short-time process and is concerned with increasing knowledge and skill in doing a particular job, while education is concerned with increasing general knowledge and understanding of total enviornment. Burden of training lies with the employer, while educa-tion is gained generally in schools and colleges for the development of individuals.

Training and Development

As explained above, training is the act of increasing the knowledge and skill for doing a particular job, the development means growth of the individual in all respects. Development is a long term educational process utilising a systematic and organised procedure by which managerial personnel get conceptual and theoretical knowledge. An executive development programme aims at increasing the capacities of the individuals to achieve the desired objectives.

Training Needs

1. **For Top Management.** *(a)* Conceptual skill, Decision making; *(b)* Organisation and communication ; (*c*) Industrial relations.
2. **For Middle Management.** Specialised courses in various management and productivity techniques.
3. **For Lower Management.** (*a*) Social and administrative aspects; *(b)* Productive technique; (*c*) Production Engineering and Industrial Engineering ; *(d)* Company information.

Benefits of Training

1. **To organisation**
   (*a*) Improvement in performance
   (*b*) Improvement in working methods
   (*c*) Reduction in wastage and spoilage
   (*d*) Reduction in learning time
   (e) Reduction in supervisory burden
   (*f*) Improvement in moral and reduction in grievances
   (*g*) Reduction in accident rates
   (*h*) Reduction in machine breakdown and maintenance cost.
   (*i*) Improvement in quality of work.
2. **To Employees**
   (*a*) Improvement in knowledge and skills.
   (*b*) Increased productivity which results in enhanced earnings.
   (*c*) Lesser chances of accidents.
   (*d*) More opportunity for growth/promotions.
   (*e*) High Morale.
   (*f*) Increase in self confidence.

Types of Training Programmes

1. Induction Training
2. Job Training
3. Refresher Training
4. Apprenticeship Training
5. Internship Training

Principles of Learning

For developing an effective training programme, following principles are followed:

1. Every human being is capable of learning.
2. People learn faster by doing than by hearing alone.
3. Learning is active, and not passive.
4. People learn faster when they are informed of their achievements.
5. Learning is a cumulative process.
6. Learning is closely related to attention and concentration.

Training Methods

1. On-the-job training
2. Training-Centre Training
3. Demonstration
4. Apprenticeship
5. Lectures
6. Conferences
7. Seminar or Group discussions

8. Case discussions
9. Programmed Instructions
10. Films/slides presentation
11. Simulation exercises

5.10. MANAGEMENT DEVELOPMENT

Management Development is more future oriented, and more concerned with education. Education helps in sound reasoning processes, *i.e.*, to enhance the ability to understand and interpret knowledge. Therefore, development focuses more on the employee's personal growth.

Management Development is a systematic process of training and growth by which managerial personnel gain knowledges, skills, attitudes, and insights to manage the work effectively and efficiently.

Objectives of Management Development

As management development relates to all managers in the organisation, it leads to growth and self-development of the organisation. Its focus should be on future requirements. Management development programme must have following objectives :

(*a*) ensuring the availability of required number of managers with the required skills to meet the present and anticipated future needs.

(*b*) growing of managers in handling greater responsibility.

(*c*) improving the performance of managers in the jobs presently held by them.

(*d*) maintaining the performance level of the managers through out their careers.

Techniques of Management Development

1. Planned promotions
2. Job rotation
3. Creation of 'Assistant to' position
4. Training
5. Coaching counselling
6. Case discussions
7. Committee assignments
8. Simulation exercises.

5.11. CAREER DEVELOPMENT

Career is a sequence of positions occupied by a person during the course of a life time. Career development involves tracking career paths. Individuals career development focuses on assisting individuals to identify their major career goals and to determine what they need to do to achieve these goals. The career development looks at the long-term career effectiveness and success of organisational personnel.

A career can be defined as a sequence of positions occupied by a person during the course of a lifetime.

Objectives of Career Development

An effective organisational career development must have followingobjectives:

(a) Ensures that needed talent is available.

(b) Improves the organisation's ability to attract and retain personnel of high talent.

(c) Reduces the frustrations amongst the employees.

5.11.1. PROMOTIONS

A promotion is usually made to place employees in positions for which they can be better suited. Their they will develop high levels of abilities as it involves significant increase in income and responsibilities. Promotions are the form of awards which can be given for achievement and serves as a means of motivating individuals to increase their abilities.

Since promotion is a very sensitive and important issue for both the employee and the enterprise, each promotion should be made very carefully. Therefore each organisation must have its promotion programme and policy. The promotion programme must be developed, based on the promotion policy of the enterprise. Promotion policy should be such that a balance of new recruitment to infuse new blood and promotion system of existing competent employees. promotion should be based on correct assessemt rather than adhocism.

Promotion systems are of mainly two types, namely, promotion by seniority and promotion by merit. Each system has its own merits and demerits.

5.11.2. Transfers

Transfers are carried out for the following purposes:

1. So as to employees get more experience.
2. To fill up the vacancy.
3. To make employees fit for promotion and to discharge his job better after promotion.
4. To keep employee interested in the work. It also avoids monotony in work.

Career Stages

Most people begin to form their careers during elementary and secondary school years. The careers begin to wind down as they reach retirement age : Most people go through following five career stages during these years:

1. **Exploration.** Exploration period is the period when one passes from school to work and occurs prior to employment. It is a time when a number of expectations about one's career are developed. This is the result of career of our parents, their aspirations for the children and what one sees around them. In most cases, these may be unrealistic. These expectations may be dormant for years and then pop up later to frustrate both the employee and employer.
2. **Establishment.** This period begins with the search for work and includes getting first job, and learning the job.
3. **Mid Career.** This stage is beyond learning or apprenticeship stage. Those who make successful transition got greater responsibilities and rewards. Others think for reassessment and proceed for job changes, adjustment of priorities.
4. **Late Career.** Those who grow through mid-career stage, late career usually a pleasant time when one feels luxury to relax a bit and enjoy playing the part of the elder

statesman. It is a time when individuals recognize that they have decreased work mobility and may be locked into their current job.

5. **Decline.** In this stage, individuals are forced to step out of the limelight. This is the time when one prepares himself for retirement.

Effective Organisational Career Development Techniques

(*i*) Challenging job assignments early in the careers
(*ii*) Dissemination of career option information
(*iii*) Job postings
(*iv*) Assessment centres
(*v*) Career counseling
(*vi*) Career development workshops
(*vii*) Continuing education and training
(*viii*) Periodic job changes.

Individual Career Development

Following steps are necessary for self assessment for individual career development.

1. Identifying and organising skills, interests, work-related needs and values.
2. Converting these above mentioned inventories into general career fields and specific job goals.
3. Testing these against the realities.

5.12. JOB DESIGN

Job design is essential so that individuals feel good about their work. This requires an appropriate job structure in terms of content, function, and relationship. In designing jobs, enterprise requirements are taken into account. Thus job design is the division of an organisation's work among its employees.

Methods of Job Design

1. **Mechanistic Job Design.** In this method, each worker is required to do only one or two simple things, over and over again. Though it is fairly easy to learn and do these jobs, but are usually boring. The workers are generally dissatisfied and unmotivated and have high rate of absenteeism.
2. **Motivational Job Design.** It has been experienced that employees having responsible jobs are more motivated and satisfied with their position. A high level of autonomy makes workers more responsible and accountable for their acts. The jobs having characteristics of skill variety, task identity, task significance, autonomy and feed back highly motivate and satisfy the employee.
3. **Biological Job Design.** Jobs with lesser physical work are preferred as in such cases there is less chances of accidents. The branch of science which deals with this approach is known as 'Ergonomics'.
4. **Perceptual Job Design.** This approach seeks to ensure that the mental demands of their work do not exceed workers' mental capabilities.

Techniques for Making Job Design as Motivational

1. **Job Enlargement.** For breaking up the monotony of a routine work, job scope is increased. This is done by combining various operations at a similar level into one job to provide more variety and thus increase their motivation and satisfaction.
2. **Job Enrichment.** This deals with dissatisfied workers by increasing the depth of their jobs. It is the combining of several activities from a vertical cross section of the organisation into one job to provide the employee with more autonomy and responsibility.
3. **Empowerment.** It is the act of delegating power and authority to a subordinate so that the goals of the manager can be accomplished.
4. **Job Rotation.** It is done to broaden the knowledge of managers. It also helps in dealing with the problem of general dissatisfaction by allowing employees to diversify their activities and offset the occurrence of boredom.

5.13. PERFORMANCE APPRAISAL

Performance means doing a job effectively and efficiently, with a minimum degree of employee - created disruptions. A good worker is one who performs well in terms of productivity and also minimises problems for organisation by being to work on time, by not remaining absent, and by minimising work related problems.

Performance appraisal is the process through which an individual employee's behaviour and accomplishment for a fixed time period are measured and evaluated.

Purposes of Performance Appraisal

1. It can be used as a basis for reward allocations, *i.e.,* salary increases, promotions and other rewards.
2. It can be used for identifying areas where development efforts like training and development are needed. Performance appraisal helps in identifying those deficiencies where development is needed.
3. Selection process can be developed on the basis of a valid reliable, and Bias free performance appraisal system.

Performance Appraisal Process

The process consists of following steps.

1. Establish performance standards
2. Communicate performance expectations to employees.
3. Measure actual performance
4. Compare actual performance with standard
5. Discuss the appraisal with the employee
6. If necessary, initiate corrective action.

Types of Appraisals

1. **Informal Performance Appraisal.** This is a process of continually feeding back to subordinates information regarding their work performance.
2. **Formal Systematic Appraisal.** This is a formalised appraisal process for rating subordinate performance, to identify deserving subordinates for promotion, wage increase and other rewards, and to identify those who need further training.

Factors for Distorting Appraisals

In the performance appraisal system, it is assumed that evaluator is free from personal biases and prejudices and that all managers impartially interpret and standardise the criteria for the appraisal. Efforts should be made to utilise direct performance criteria for appraising individuals wherever possible. Following are the main factors which can affect the objective evaluation, and thereby validity and dependability of the performance appraisal system :

1. **Leniency Error.** Sometimes rater has his own value system which acts as a standard against which appraisals are made. When the subordinate is rated high than actual, it is referred to as positive leniency error, and when rated low, it is referred to as negative leniency error.
2. **Halo Error.** Halo error or effect is a tendency to evaluate on all factors due to the general impression.

QUESTIONS

1. Describe a procedure suitable for recruitment in a large scale manufacturing industry.
2. Discuss the procedure for 'selection and training' of skilled and semi-skilled workers in a factory.
3. Define 'Human resource management'. Describe its sub-systems briefly.
4. Explain functions and objectives of human resource management.
5. What is manpower planning? What are its requirements.
6. Explain the factors which affect the manpower planning.
7. Describe the techniques used for manpower planning.
8. Explain as to how selection, training and placement of skilled workers should be done in a new manufacturing concern of large size.
9. Write short notes on:
   (*i*) Promotions.
   (*ii*) Transfers.
   (*iii*) Management development
   (*iv*) Career development.

6 Motivation, Morale And Behavioural Science

6.1. MOTIVATION

Today management pays more attention towards motivation of employees. The main task of management is to direct the working force in such a way so that by their collective efforts objectives of the enterprise are achieved. This is only possible when the workers take interest in their work and have the desire to do good work. This depends on the fact that the worker is how much motivated. There is basic difference between the 'capability to work' and 'desire to work'.

Motivation is a psychological act which attracts the workers to do more work and instigates. If the workers are investigated, they will try to do more than the standard work and earn more for themselves which increases their living standard.

Instigation may be positive, *i.e.*, by encouraging to do work or negative, *i.e.*, by punishing for the wrong work. These both schemes tend to increase production and productivity. Motivation has got, in reality no definite source or plan, it is a coordination programme of all the different investigatory schemes organised in such a way so that every individual worker is instigated.

Definition of Motivation

Management is the art of taking work from other persons. Hence for taking proper work from the persons, to create interest in them for the work and to maintain that interest and instigate them to development is in reality 'motivaton'.

'Instigation' is an element on which organisation's whole performance depends. Work ability and desire to work are separate elements. It is possible that the person may have the work ability but he may not have the desire to accomplish the work and in this way he cannot accomplish the work so nicely as expected from him. Motivation is a psychological aspect which has relation with mental state and brain.

Motivation has derived from the word 'instigation'. Some instigation element is necessary to accomplish a job and the object of instigation for the accomplishment of the job is called 'motivation'.

Basis of Motivation

As put forth by 'Brech', Motivation is a general inspiration process which gets the members of the team to do their task effectively, to give their loyalty to the group, to carry out properly the tasks they have accepted and generally to play an effective part in the job that the group has undertaken.

According to 'Michael J. Jucius' 'Motivation is the act of stimulating someone or oneself to get a desired course of action, to push the right button to get desired action'.

As mentioned by 'Dalton E. McFarland', The concept of motivation is mainly psychological, it relates to those forces operating within the individual employee or subordinate which impels him to act or not active in certain ways'.

Characteristics of Motivation

(i) *Motivation is a psychological concept.* Motivation is a psychological concept which should be inherent in every person.

(ii) Man as a whole is motivated and not a part.

(iii) Motivation is created from aims.

(iv) *Motivation is an unending process.* Man is a social animal, his needs are unending. Needs instigate to motivation. Because after the completion of a need, commences the second need and hence act of motivation also is an unending process. Time, place, behaviour and circumstances uniting together prepare favourable and unfavourable atmosphere.

(v) *Motivation is the strength of work.* Motivation is that strength which leads to do or not to do a work and instigates to do work in the same specific direction.

(vi) *Motivation is different from mental strength.* There is difference between motivation and mental strength. Motivation is the strength that instigates a person to do an act while mental strength is the desire to do a work oneself which is strengthened by motivation.

Importance of Motivation

The aim of motivation is instigation to do work by all the employees working in any organisation so that more good results are attained through less efforts. Effects of motivation comes to all acts of the organisation. Any concern may have best instruments, raw materials in sufficient quantity and sufficient persons and finances but their proper use is not possible till the working persons do not use them properly. Importance of motivation could be seen under these heads :

(a) *Appropriate use of factors :* All factors can only be used appropriately through motivation. It satisfies the human needs of individual.

(b) *Kindling of desire to work :* Capacity to work and desire to work are different things. Any person may be efficient but in the absence of desire to work he cannot do appropriate work. By motivation, his desire to work is actuated and then only he works with full efficiency.

(c) *Lessening in labour turnover, attraction of new persons.* Labour does not try to go to another place due to motivation schemes as his gross wages increase. Not only this, in those institutions utilising motivation schemes, have the good efficient workers.

(d) *Increase in Production and Productivity.* It increases the desire to work and hence it leads to increase in production and there is increase in productivity per worker per machine per hour.

(e) *Basis of co-operation.* It increases job satisfaction, so the worker's interest for the organisation increases. This develops the sense of cooperation while in the absence of motivation co-operation is not possible.

Kinds of Motivation

There are two kinds :

(a) Positive Motivation

(b) Negative Motivation

(a) *Positive Motivation.* Positive motivation means workers may be instigated to work with some facilities or giving some prize so that they may do good or more work than was done previously and with less supervision. Prize or facilities may be financial or non financial. To give more wages for more work is the financial motivation, while appraisal of the worker's work, promotion, appreciation etc. are non-financial positive motivation.

(b) *Negative Motivation.* This is based on punishment or fines if the labour is not encouraged for work. For less work or for not doing work, he must be punished or fined. This is of two kinds : financial or non-financial.

In financial punishment, a cut is made in the wages of the labour. Non-financial punishment consists in giving less facilities such as to do work for more time, reduction in the facilities of leave, etc. Generally these are for improving him and the objective of this is to motivate him for more work.

Positive or negative motivation are the two ends of a rope. As motivation is a psychological aspect and its relation is concerned with the person's brain to his thoughts and behaviour, hence they should be motivated with different ways.

A good manager should use both the ways of motivation at times. At times good work should be prized but wrong work or no work should be punished. If there is no arrangement for punishment, worker becomes unrestrained and those who cannot do good work, will do less work as they will think that less work will have no punishment though doing more than prescribed work will fetch them award.

6.1.1 Benefits

In addition to pay, certain benefits are also provided to all the employees of organisation. These benefits when added together account for about 40 to 50% of direct wage bill. Benefits do not motivate the employees, as these are offered to all the employees. However these help in maintaining cordial atmosphere in the organisation. Benefits can be classified into following two categories:

1. Legally required benefits.
   (a) Social security : insurance, provident fund
   (b) Worker's compensation on accident, retrenchment etc.
   (c) Holidays and rest periods as per Factory act.
2. Voluntary Benefits provided by the employer
   (a) Additional rest periods and holidays with pay
   (b) Leave including sick leaves
   (c) Pension plans
   (d) Health insurance
   (e) Housing
   (f) Counseling
   (g) Cultural activities
   (h) Education facilities for children
   (i) Recreational activities.

6.2. THOUGHTS OF MANAGEMENT PHILOSOPHY

6.2.1. Douglass McGregore 'X' and 'Y' Theory

Douglass McGregore has divided the thoughts of management philosophy in two parts. These are:

(a) Traditional or X theory.

(b) Modern theory or Y theory.

(A) X Theory:

This theory is based on traditional view. In this theory, management or authority do not trust the labour and use restraining policies so that labour will be unable to act against him. Management is of the opinion that work could be extracted from labour through fear, strict discipline and rebukes, their cooperation should not be taken in management. Here authority or power is thought not to be superior. Management acts right or wrong labour cannot say anything and thus mentally, he is dependent on management.

Assumption of 'X theory'

This theory is based on the following assumptions :

1. A person is disinclined to work and hence he always shirks from work;
2. To get work from an employee, he is to be frightened, rebuked necessarily. Through fear, he becomes ready to do the work.
3. Workers try to shirk from responsibility hence they put off the work till the work is not urgent.
4. Workers are less ambitious. They do not try to do or improve the work through interest but wait for instructions and directions.
5. Workers care more for security hence they work slowly.
6. Workers act on the basis of financial greed if they are paid more wages, they will take more interest in work.
7. Management does not give any importance to labour, they think them to be an instrument of machines. Labour is not given opportunity to show workability or to develop it.
8. This theory has authority as superior. Labour has no right to give his suggestions, neither he can do any work without directions by his own will.

Suitability of X theory in Modern Times

Management extracts work from labour with its own will as management believes more in power and control. According to this theory, labour is thought to be a part of the machine who works according to instructions. He is not given a chance to use his own intellect. This theory presents a pessimistic view. With the above assumptions, the assumption can be right to some extent that labour works more due to financial greed but this is not possible always and in every circumstances. Besides financial greed, he cares for human values.

(B) Y Theory,

This theory is quite opposite to 'X theory'. In this, labour is assumed to be partner in the management and all they work, is with the cooperation of labour.

Assumptions of Y Theory

1. Every work is not disinteresting. Like a game, playing again and again gives satisfaction.
2. Workers are not instigated to work by fear, outer restraint, or strict discipline. They feel responsible for the work for which they are appointed.
3. For the execution of work, it is necessary that it should be recognized. Recognition of work is a great prize.
4. Tendency to escape from the responsibility is not natural but the reason is lack of ambition and more stress on security.
5. Generally workers are not instigated to do by financial greed but non-financial greed also instigates to work.
6. This is based on democratic principles, where everybody has equal chances.
7. Labour can also cooperate to solve the problems of enterprise.
8. This establishes coordination between basic personal objectives and the collective objectives of the organisation.
9. Manager works as a leader and gets more good and solid results by the advices of the personnel. Management thinks personnel on equal footing for advices.

Suitability of Y Theory in India

In our country, development of management thought is gaining popularity day-by-day. Previously employer was treating the labour just like servant. They were extracting work from the employees and their suggestions were not accepted and even today X theory is applied in most of the places. But now-a-days labour unions have become sufficient strong. Government have made sufficient provisions in labour acts for the security of workers. Not only this, employers have also realised that workers are human beings and they should be treated on humanitarian grounds. Although assumptions of Y theory are not fully accepted by employers but efforts are being made by government and labour unions in this direction.

6.2.2. Herzberg's Motivation—Hygiene Theory

Frederick Herzberg developed a theory of work motivation by indicating the way to better performance through increased job satisfaction. He conducted his study on a group of 200 Engineers and Accountants from eleven industries from the Pittsburg area in the U.S.A.

His hypothesis about job satisfaction and job dis-satisfaction suggests that:

(*a*) The factors that are present when job satisfaction is produced are separate and distinct from the factors that lead to job dis-satisfaction.

(*b*) The opposite of job-satisfaction is 'no job-satisfaction' and not job dissatisfaction'.

(*c*) The opposite of job dis-satisfaction is 'no Job-satisfaction' and not 'Job-satisfaction.'

Herzberg draws a distinction between what we called Motivator and Hygiene factors."

1. **Motivators.** Factors connected with satisfaction or motivation were called as 'Motivators' by the Herzberg. Motivators, have a positive power to satisfy and produce high performance, and are related to job contents. These factors are:
   - Achievement
   - Recognition
   - Challenging work
   - Increase responsibility; and
   - Advancement

2. **Hygiene Factors.** The factors related to the dissatisfaction were called as hygiene factors because these factors primarily prevent dissatisfaction like hygiene prevents sickness. These factors are related to the work environment. These factors are :
   — Company policies and administration
   — Supervision
   — Interpersonal relations
   — Salary
   — Working condition
   — Status, and
   — Security

These factors prevent losses in the performance of the workers. When these hygiene factors are inadequate in an industry, then these will significantly have negative effect on worker's attitude, but do not have any positive effect when all the factors are available in the concern.

6.3. HUMAN NEEDS

The behaviour or nature of individual is different. There are three things which require study for his behaviour :

(*i*) To study his behaviour 'Well'.
(*ii*) To understand his behaviour Well'.
(*iii*) His behaviour should be changed to a determined direction.

This third point is very important and requires thorough knowledge of the human needs.

When a machine goes out of order, we understand that it needs something like oil or repairs or replacement of certain parts etc. In the same way, human behaviour should have some reason and if his behaviour is not well, we suppose that some of his wants are not satisfied.

Needs create tension in worker. Needs are created by person's culture and for its fulfilment needs force him work. For example, a hungry man's primary motive is to satisfy his hunger. Through needs of meals he feels tension but what meals he will take, depends on his culture, *i.e.*, a Bengali will like to eat meat and fish while a Rajasthani will prefer vegetarian meals. To earn his meals, he will do some work which will fetch him wages and by that money he will satisfy his hunger. Series of needs go on. After the fulfilment of one need, another arises.

Classification of Needs

These can be classified under two heads:

(*i*) Primary needs
(*ii*) Secondary needs

1. **Primary needs.** These are the basic needs of an individual and are found in whole humanity but its intensity differs from man to man. These are essential for everybody otherwise he cannot remain alive, such as meals, air, water, sleep, rest and sexual desire etc.
2. **Secondary Needs.** This is proved by psychological investigations that man works not only for his primary needs but also for other needs which are related to his mind or soul. These needs are learnt by experience and atmosphere.

Secondary needs are of two kinds :

(*a*) Social needs.
(*b*) Egoistic needs.

(*a*) **Social Needs.** People want to live with respect in the society. He wants that he should have relations with different groups of people and they should help during difficulties. These are produced by the social desires existing in men and instigated to lead social life.

(*b*) **Egoistic Needs.** These are related to human self-thoughts which are mostly dependent on human nature. These are simulated from the people personal value and ideals. These instigate a person to : self-expression and self-accomplishment.

Fig. 6.1. Maslow's hierarchy of needs

Priority of Needs

Psychologists are of the opinion that priority of needs has a definite order. Famous scientist A.H. Maslow has given a definite order to the needs while developing his theory of motivation. He said that person first satisfies basic needs.

The definite order of the needs is :

(*a*) Basic physical needs
(*b*) Safety and security
(*c*) Belongingness and love
(*d*) Esteem and status
(*e*) Self realisation and self accomplishment

He said that a person satisfies his needs in this order. This conception of Maslow is known as Maslow's need priority model.

Above first two needs are called the 'low strata' needs while the rest are called 'high strata' needs.

Low Strata Needs

A person satisfies first all the necessities of the first kind, *i.e.,* bodily needs. A hungry person puts his full efforts for earning bread. After coping up the bodily needs, he tries to fulfil his second need of security and safety. This is the reason that he collects grains and some money for future use. He manages for pension and social security.

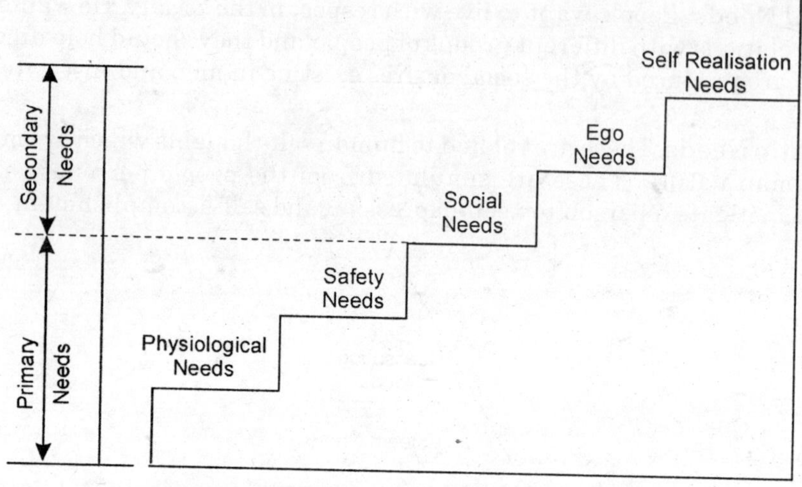

Fig. 6.2. Maslow's hierarchy of human needs

High Strata Needs

Bodily needs are limited but rest three needs are unlimited.

Every man wishes respect and fame. He thinks that he is able and other persons should also think him so and respect him. This is important in more industrially progressed countries as the people care more for esteem and status.

The fifth need is realisation and self-accomplishment. It means that a person should be what he desires. After the four needs are satisfied, he tries for achieving this.

Comparison of Three Theories

Hicks and Gullet compared these theories and had shown the similarity in three theories. This is illustrated in the following table:

Maslow	Herzberg	McGragore
1. Lower level needs 1. Social 2. Safety 3. Physiological	**Hygiene factors** 1. Company policy and administration 2. Supervision 3. Interpersonal relations 4. Salary 5. Working conditions 6. Status 7. Security	**Theory X:** 1. Security above all. 2. Directions preferable 3. Threats of punishment needed.
1. High level needs 1. Self actualisation 2. Esteem	**Motivation** 1. Achievement 2. Recognition 3. Challenging work 4. Increased responsibility 5. Advancement	**Theory Y** 1. Satisfaction of esteem 2. Self actualisation needs 3. Responsibility 4. Imagination and creativity 5. Self direction and self control.

6.4. INCENTIVE AS MOTIVATORS

Incentives are of two kinds :

(*i*) Financial incentives

(*ii*) Non-financial incentives

1. Financial Incentives

In the light of need hierarchy concept, in case of persons operating at the lower level, where the physiological needs are not fully satisfied, money can be very powerful motivator of human conduct.

It is necessary to have an adequate compensation programme that will attract and retain key people of superior calibre in the organisation. Such a programme would also stimulate such persons to improve their performance. Monetary compensation can be used to reward significant achievement made by them.

Some people suggest that besides compensation in monetary rewards geared directly to an employee's performance, fringe benefits including bonus motivate an employee.

2. Non-Financial Incentives

Money is not the only motivator of human behaviour in terms of need hierarchy, it can help to satisfy only the 'physiological' needs of the person. The psychological need for 'safety or security" can be satisfied by the psychological climate or environment of the work place.

The employee should be made to feel that owner has achieved something through his contributions. Such a feeling of achievement can motivate him to extra effort. Still, achievement should be followed by recognition. Human beings want others to know of their accomplishments.

Some of the important non-financial incentives are :

1. Providing responsibility through job enlargement
2. Providing participation
3. Creating a sense of achievement
4. Providing recognition for accomplishment
5. Offering inducement of promotion and growth as result of effective performance.

Promotion Policies as Motivators

Sufficient policies should be laid down regarding promotion to generate continued motivation of the employees. Promotion refers to assignment of a position of greater responsibility or increased authority to an individual. Normally, it involves ascending in the management hierarchy or at last an increase in the pay or status or both for the employee concerned.

An adequate promotion policy giving effective motivation would be one which offers the employee a career within the organisation itself. A climate is to be created that promotion is not only based on seniority but that merit also plays an important role.

Promotion Systems

1. Promotion by seniority.
2. Promotion by merit.
3. Promotion through Reports.

1. **Promotion by Seniority.** In this system, those who have put in specified years of service are considered for promotion in order of their seniority.
2. **Merit System.** In this, the organisation fixes job requirements for all the higher posts

as and when these fall vacant and all persons whether inside or outside the organisation are allowed to compete so that those who are the best should come forward and have their chance.

3. **Promotion Through Reports.** In this, the organisation is more concerned with results. All workers, senior or junior, with proper qualification and experience should be given promotion, if their work has been found satisfactory by their superiors.

Factors Affecting Motivation

Motivation can be achieved by directly motivating and also by avoiding dissatisfaction. Both these types are given hereunder:

- Satisfaction through achivements
- Growth
- Recognition
- Job security
- Salary including fringe benefits
- Inter-personal relations
- Personal life
- Advancement
- Responsibility and authority
- Company policies
- Company administration
- Working conditions

Motivational Techniques

1. **Positive Motivating Techniques**
   - Give due credit to workers for their work.
   - Fair wages, incentives and fringe benefits.
   - Promote healthy competition.
   - Improve working conditions.
   - Delegate reasonable responsibilities and authorities.
   - Promote interpersonal relationship.
   - Formulate fair, clear and consistent management policies.
   - Implement suitable suggestion system.
   - Provide opportunities for growth and promotions.
2. **Negative Motivating Techniques**
   - Reprimand
   - Demotions
   - Discharge
   - Fines
   - Lay off

6.5. WELFARE

Labour welfare is the voluntary efforts by the employers to provide best conditions of employment in their own industries.

The object of introducing labour welfare scheme is to secure on improved standards of living for the workers, which results in the increase in their productive efficiency.

Labour (Personnel) welfare schemes are aimed at:

1. making the employees healthier, sound thinking
2. to motivate people to carry out production in a better way,
3. to improve and maintain employees' morale and loyalty.
4. to keep workforce in competition with other organisations,
5. to maintain better employee-employer relations
6. to meet the social, recreational and cultural needs of the employees.
7. To reduce the labour turn over, absenteeism.

Welfare Measures

Welfare measures can be categorised as :

1. **Economic Welfare Measures**
   (*a*) Health services and first aid
   (*b*) Paid holidays, reduced hours of work
   (*c*) Profit sharing
   (*d*) Pension scheme
   (*e*) Insurance scheme, including group insurance
   (*f*) Subsidised lunch, water, electricity
   (*g*) Loans on reduced rate of interest.
2. **Facilitate Welfare Measures**
   (*a*) Housing
   (*b*) Transport
   (*c*) Canteen and lunch facility
   (*d*) Company stores for cheaper shopping
   (*e*) Sale of company products on discount to employees
   (*f*) Educational facilities
   (*g*) Rest rooms
   (*h*) Safety measures
   (*i*) Measures to reduce fatigue
3. **Recreational Measures**
   (*a*) Games and Sports
   (*b*) Recreational clubs
   (*c*) Cultural programmes
   (*d*) Social get-togethers

6.6. MORALE

Morale is a mental condition or attitude of employees, either individually or in a group which determines their willingness to cooperate. Morale can also be defined as the extent to which an individual's needs are satisfied and the extent to which he feels satisfaction.

Industrial morale may be defined as the possession of a feeling on the part of employee, of being accepted and belonging to a group of employees through adherence to common goals and confidence in the desirability of these goals.

Morale Determiners

(a) *Group Cohesiveness :* Ideal situation is one in which there is single group that indues all employees, representative of employer and the employer. This creates 'feeling of togetherness'.

(b) *Goals :* Group cooperation can be promoted easily if the group has a common goal to achieve.

(c) *Progress towards Goals:* In addition of having a goal, it must be possible for employees to make observable progress towards it.

(d) *Meaningful Tasks:* There should be specific meaningful task for the individual in the group to perform, and a sense of participating in the group's work towards the goal.

High Morale

High Morale is the spirit of whole-hearted cooperation. High Morale means :

(*a*) Loyalty to organisation and its leadership

(*b*) Good discipline

(*c*) High degree of interest in the job

(*d*) Reasonable initiative from employees

(*e*) Team spirit

(*f*) No frustration

(*g*) Pride in the organisation.

Low Morale

Low morale is the result of:

(*a*) Wrong or improper selection/placement of employees and supervisors.

(*b*) Too many supervisors

(*c*) Low motivating factors

(*d*) Improper authority and responsibility

Results of Low Morale

(*a*) Higher rate of absenteeism and labour turnover

(*b*) Friction, jealousy and frustration.

(*c*) More complaints and grievances.

(*d*) Enemity towards the management.

(*e*) Poor interpersonal relations.

How to Improve Morale

Following measures help in morale building :

(*a*) Sound wage structure

(*b*) Good incentives schemes

(*c*) Security of income and employment to competent and disciplined workers

(*d*) Sound promotion policy

(*e*) Grievance redressal system

(f) Consulting workers on matters related to their work
(g) An effective communication system
(h) Suggestions schemes
(i) Recreational facilities and social get-together.

6.7. JOB SATISFACTION

Satisfaction refers to the contentment experienced when a want is satisfied.

Need-Want-Satisfaction. Fair needs give rise to wants or goals sought, which cause tension and give rise to actions towards achieving goals, which finally result in satisfaction.

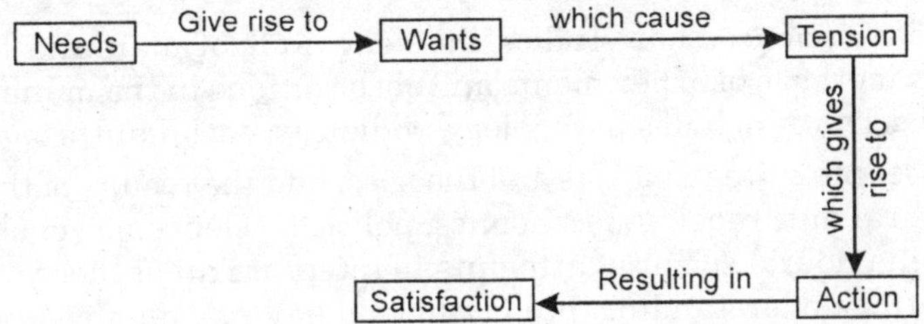

Fig. 6.3. Need-want-satisfaction chain.

Satisfaction Through Job Design. As discussed in earlier parts of this chapter, rational and scientific job design leads to job satisfaction amongst employees. It has been observed that employees having responsible jobs are more motivated and satisfied with their position. A high level of autonomy makes workers more responsible and accountable for their acts. The jobs having characteristics of skill variety, task identity, task significance, autonomy, and feed back highly motivate and satisfy the employees. Use of Ergonomics in job design also helps in job satisfaction to a great extent.

Job enrichment and job enlargement techniques also satisfy the individual employees. Some people who have higher growth need are satisfied with expanded and challenging jobs. Social dimensions are also important to job satisfaction.

Herzberg's Theory of Job Satisfaction and Dissatisfaction

Herzberg has suggested two classes of work variables, namely: satisfiers and dissatisfiers. Satisfiers are those things which lead to job satisfaction, they are generally job content factors or motivators. The satisfiers include achievement, recognition, challenging work, advancement, and growth in the job. Their existence yields feelings of satisfaction or no satisfaction (not dissatisfaction).

Dissatisfiers are those things which result in job dissatisfaction, they are generally job content or 'hygiene' factors. Their existence does not motivate in the sense of yielding satisfaction, their lack of existence would, however, result in dissatisfaction. These factors include company policy, supervision, working conditions, interpersonal relations, salary, status and job security.

Here it is necessary to clarify that reverse of Job satisfaction is 'no job satisfaction' and not job dissatisfaction.

Managing Dissatisfaction and Frustration

If an employee builds high expectations, and his expectations are not met, or if he does not get promised thing, he feels dissatisfied and frustrated. A disappointed employee may neglect his work, causes delays, makes errors etc. The frustrated employee may be annoyed with himself for such deterioration and he may continue in such a state, and then feels and gets isolated which leads to fantasies, exaggerations and distorted perception of the situation.

Effective managers are expected to take following sequential steps to manage employee's frustation:

1. Listen to feelings of the staff.
2. Help the employees to accept and confront reality.
3. Help the employee assess damage by frustration.
4. Develop alternatives to solve the problem.

6.8. BEHAVIOURAL SCIENCE

Behavioural Science is a science that studies the behaviour of man and their physical and social environment, by methods of experiments and observations in the manner of other natural sciences. Behavioural science includes psychology, radiology, social anthropology etc.

Behavioural science integrates concepts and theories, and the results of the empirical studies from the areas of cultural anthropology, economics, political science, psychology, sociology and social psychology. A behavioural scientist attempts to integrate all of those areas or disciplines which are useful in better understanding, predicting and having an impact on the behaviour of individuals and groups.

One's behaviour is generally motivated by a desiere to attain some goal. The specific goal may or may not be conscious but known by the individual. To predict a behaviour, manager must know which motives or needs of people evoke a certain action at a particular time. The "Goal" may be referred to as, hope for rewards towards which motives are directed. Psychologists call these goals as incentives.

As motives or needs are the reasons underlying behaviour, and all individuals have many needs. All these needs compete for the behaviour. The blocking of goal attainment is frustration. A person may be frustrated by an imaginary barrier to the goals.

6.9. INDIVIDUAL BEHAVIOUR

Following are the main features of individual behaviour:

(*a*) Performance of an individual is affected by his own characteristics, like brain, qualifications, abilities, motivation, nature etc.

(*b*) Every individual has unique behaviour

(*c*) Individuals collect and form groups within which they live.

(*d*) Individuals differ and therefore paid at different rates, assigneddifferent jobs.

(*e*) Differences in individuals can be classified as individual variables and situational variables. These affect the individuals behaviour and have major role in influencing the performance of an employee.

1. Individual Variables.

– Physical characteristics
– Intellectual factors
– Temperament
– Character
– Experience
– Age and sex

- Aptitude
- Personality characteristics

2. **Situational Variables:**
   - Physical environment
   - Workplace and its layout
   - Design and condition of work equipment
   - Method of work
   - Organisational set up
   - Kind and style of supervision
   - Types of incentives
   - Social environment

6.10. GROUP BEHAVIOUR

A group is any number of people who :

(*a*) have a common purpose or objective,
(*b*) interact with each other to accomplish their objective,
(*c*) are aware of one another,
(*d*) perceive themselves to be part of the group.

- An organisation has formal and informal groups. Formal groups are formed from functional requirements, while informal groups are formed by employees themselves due to social and security needs, common interests and other psychological factors.
- An employee behaves differently in a group. Group influences the attitude and behaviour of an individual.
- Each group has its own cultural pattern, and individual for stay in this group must conform to this culture, if he has to remain in the group.
- Group behaviour may be beneficial as well as detrimental for the organisation and management depending upon the attitude of the group. Generally chances are more for detrimental nature.
- Groups also differ in their degree of cohesiveness. Cohesiveness of any group depends upon status, size, location and nature of the group.
- A group is formed on the basis of the attraction of persons towards each other as they have similar attitudes towards common objects or goals. Common attitudes and values may be politics, religion, literature, language, work, aesthetics, traditions, authority etc.

Group Dynamics

Group behaviour is sometimes called as 'Group Dynamics' or 'Human behaviour under group influence'.

The word dynamics is a Greek word which means 'forced'. Therefore the term 'group dynamics' refers to the forces operating in groups. The study of this subject is necessary to investigate these forces and conditions modifying them. In order to fulfil their social needs, people form small groups on the job itself. They behave as members of the group and their membership in group helps to shape their work behaviour and attitude towards the organisation and the job. There is a significant change in the behaviour of a person who was acting as an individual when allowed to act as a member of some group. Groups generally exercise stronger control over their members than the management.

Group dynamics is a social process by which people interact face to face in small groups. Group dynamics focuses a team work, wherein the small member group are constantly in touch with each other and effectively contribute their ideas to accomplish a task. The group develops its goal clearly. Every member participates in discussions. The group has a common objective. The group creates leaders who can coordinate group efforts effectively towards the achievement of their objectives.

These groups may produce good or bad effects in the organisation. The groups are formed because every body wants companionship identification, job satisfaction and protection.

QUESTIONS

1. What is motivation? Define it. Explain different kinds of motivation.
2. What are the characteristics of motivation? What is its importance in industries?
3. What are the different theories of motivation? Explain them in brief.
4. "Motivation is a psychological concept". Discuss the statement.
5. Explain following theories as regards to motivation:
   (*i*) Douglass Mc Gregore's 'X' and 'Y' theory.
   (*ii*) Herzberg's Motivation—Hygiene theory.
   (*iii*) Maslow's theory of priority of needs.
6. Explain the statement, "Motivation satisfies the personal, social, and basic needs of personnel."
7. What do you understand by "capability to do and desire to do" in motivation?
8. What do you know by human needs? How will you classify needs? Explain them.
9. Write short notes on:
   (*a*) Hierarchy of needs
   (*b*) High strata and low strata needs
   (*c*) Incentives as motivators
   (*d*) Factors affecting motivation
   (*e*) Morale.
10. Write an essay on behavioural science.
11. Write a note on "Motivation and Job Satisfaction".
12. Discuss the "Maslow's theory" of hierarchy of human wants. How this theory helps us in motivating industrial workers?
13. Describe Maslow's need hierarchy and indicate how type and nature of incentive should vary with the level of needs.

7

Job Evaluation, Wages and Incentives

7.1. INTRODUCTION

For rewarding workers, there should be some systematic procedure. For this purpose, job is studied carefully as regards operations involved and other specific tasks are concerned. This study is known as **job analysis**. With the help of job analysis, job description is set down which gives details about the capacity and skill required for performing the job. After this, the value of the job is determined for the purpose of payment, which is known as **job evaluation**. It does not give the price of the job but gives relative values.

It is extremely important that the employees should be adequately paid for their services. An efficient system of compensation should be planned, developed, and administered. System of remuneration should be equitable from the viewpoint of both employer and employee. Compensation should be integrated with job worth, individual job performance and the external market forces. Therefore the compensation system should be internally equitable and externally competitive.

Definitions

Job. It is regular assignment to individual employees including their duties, responsibilities, skill and knowledge etc.

Job Analysis. It is careful study about the activities of an employee on a particular job to determine different operations in olved and other facts, which are helpful for description and job specification.

Thus, it is the procedure to discover the facts about each job requirement and personal qualities for satisfactory working.

The report of job analysis is helpful for motion and time study, job description, job specification and to determine existing hazards, which are helpful for avoiding accidents.

Job Description. It is an abstract of information received from the job analysis report. It gives information regarding the responsibilities, skill or training required, working conditions and type of persons employed for performing the job.

For example, the work of gate-keeper is analysed and his job description will be:

(*i*) To guard at the gate.

(*ii*) To keep watch on men coming in and going out of the factory.

(*iii*) To watch on goods entering and leaving the factory etc.

Job Specification. On the basis of details of a job, the capabilities and qualifications necessary for performing any job are calculated. This is known as job specification. It is obtained from the job analysis and job description reports. Therefore, job specification can be defined as "the statement which specifies the type of employees required". It helps in the selection of employees.

Job specification can be compared with the specification of material. As material specification helps in purchasing and procurement of material similarly job specification helps in the appointment of staff. It can be well understood by the previous examples of gate-keeper, whose job specification will be :

(*i*) Physical and mental alertness.
(*ii*) Honesty
(*iii*) Keen observation.

Job Design

As discussed above, job analysis helps in developing appropriate design of job to improve efficiency and satisfaction. Job design can be defined as follows:

– "Job design is a systematic attempt to structure the technical and social aspects of work so as to improve technical efficiency and job satisfaction."

– "Job design is an attempt to create a match between job requirement and human attribute. It involves both organising the components of the job and the interaction patterns among the members of a work group."

It is essential to design a job so as to meet organisational and individual needs. Organisational needs refer to high productivity, technical efficiency and quality of work. Needs of employees include job satisfaction in terms of interest, challenge, achievement and career growth.

7.2. JOB EVALUATION

Job evaluation is the process of comparing job with other jobs in terms of wages a worker should be paid for performing any task. Thus, it is rating of job. It can also be defined as "the procedure to determine the relative values of the job in a plant and to determine the basic wages for that job".

Objects

(*i*) Its main object is to estimate the correct wages for the work performed.
(*ii*) It is a means to reduce wages imbalance in the factories.
(*iii*) It can be used to resolve wage disputes.
(*iv*) It helps in standardisation.
(*v*) It helps to establish a method for future promotion of workers.

Principles of Job Evaluation.

Mr. A.L. Kress an authority in job evaluation underlines the following principles :

1. Rate the job not man, job requirements are definite and fixed. The man selected for doing the job may have some plus or minus points as regard to job, thus the payment should be made accordingly.
2. While doing ratings the elements selected should be minimum, but it should cover the requirement of jobs.
3. The success in job rating is totally dependent upon the uniformity of understanding with

regard to definitions assigned to each element and on the consistency in the selection of the degrees of those elements.

4. The job rating plan must be easily understandable, so that there may not be any difficulty to understand the plant by workers or supervisors.
5. Foremen or supervisors must be asked to participate in the rating plan.
6. Employees must be allowed to discuss the job rating plan.
7. While discussing with supervisors and workers, consider the points only, not the money aspect of plan.
8. Too many occupational wages should not be established.

Steps Required for Job Evaluation

As per Lytle, following steps are to be taken :

1. Most suitable method or technique must be selected.
2. First select the major job characteristics, then minor ones.
3. Proper information should be given to all concerned, *i.e.*, workers, foremen etc.
4. Build definitions and their measuring scale, for comparison purposes.
5. Prepare job rating performs and questionnaires, and collect initial description.
6. Sort out initial descriptions and establish grades or classes.
7. Identify and evaluate the key jobs.
8. Evaluate the remaining jobs and award the job title to them.
9. While job rating, make sure that representation of workers should be considered.
10. For key jobs only, make inter-company survey, but try to find at least one per grade.
11. Transfer the rating values in money values temporarily.
12. Plot a scatter diagram, for the more sure key jobs and end jobs.
13. Bargain on wage structure.
14. Decide the range limits and line of reference.
15. Re-adjust all rates relative to the line of reference, put into working forms and finally fix all operation procedures.

7.3. METHODS FOR JOB EVALUATION

As already stated that the purpose of job evaluation is to compare all demands made on each worker and, by means of this comparison to establish the relative worth of each job in a factory or company. The comparison is done by two methods.

(*a*) **Non-quantitative Method.** By simple ranking, classify the job from lowest to highest. This includes the following techniques :

(*i*) Ranking technique

(*ii*) Classification method.

(*b*) **Quantitative Method.** Here point values are assigned to the various demands of a job, and relative value is obtained by summing all such point values.

This includes the following techniques :

(*i*) Factor comparison

(*ii*) Point rating.

1. **Ranking Method.**

This is the simplest method and in this job description is arranged in the order of rank and according to the report of analysis. Job description is arranged in ascending order, beginning with the one of minimum requirements and ending up with the one of maximum requirement. While ranking, following facts are considered :

(*i*) Amount of work.
(*ii*) Supervision needed
(*iii*) Responsibility required
(*iv*) Difficulty in work
(*v*) Monotony of work
(*vi*) Working conditions.
(*vii*) Knowledge and experience needed.

Advantages

(*i*) It is very simple method.
(*ii*) With this method very quick results can be obtained.

Disadvantages

(*i*) It does not give actual information that how much one job differs from other. It only shows higher or lower.
(*ii*) It gives inaccurate results, as every time exactly same details cannot be followed for all the jobs.

This ranking methods is particularly suitable for use in small organisations in establishing the relative worth of jobs. The salaries based on the evaluation by ranking method are more reliable than that as based on guess and experience. Care must be taken that ranking must not be based on salary. This method is more suitable for supervisory or similar positions.

2. **Classification Method.**

In this method of job evaluation, several classes or classifications of job are determined for a particular organisation, and various jobs of the company are sorted out according to this classification. For example, in a factory for a section, there are three classifications (*i*) class 150 includes skilled workers doing precision and die work; (*i*) class 151 includes the workers working on lathe and milling machines; (*iii*) class 152 includes all other less skilled machine operators, such as drill, press operators, sanders etc. After this classification, the different jobs are fitted into the particular classification and relative positions can be determined.

3. **Factor Comparison**

In this method, job analysis is made by considering the following five main factors :

(*i*) Mental requirement
(*ii*) Skill requirement
(*iii*) Physical requirement
(*iv*) Responsibility
(*v*) Working conditions.

This plan starts out with the money value paid for several important jobs. In this, at a time one job is taken and is compared with the other job, with respect to the above five main factors. Each factor is compared separately and its money value is given. For example, working conditions as a factor for a key job is given money value equal to 50 paise. The same factor, *i.e.*, working condition for another job treated should be given same money value, now if the working conditions are much better than that for the key job, then money value to this job is less worth, may be 30 paise or so on. It should be remembered that first of all key jobs are rated. After rating key jobs, other are rated in between these.

When all the jobs have been rated by considering each of the above five factors separately, a wage rate for each job is fixed.

Advantages

(*i*) This can be used for the calculation of unlike jobs.

(*ii*) It can also be applied to combination of electrical, manual and supervisory staff.

(*iii*) It is not difficult to understand and use this method, even unions and workers can do the rating with some training.

Disadvantages:

(*i*) This is a complicated method.

(*ii*) It is costly to introduce.

(*iii*) Job evaluation staff must be highly qualified and competent.

(*iv*) Controversy on the selection of key job.

4. Point Rating

There are so many point methods, but all have a common characteristics, that is point values are assigned to each requirement.

Suppose a job is given 100 point values, then other jobs will be compared with it in all respects and they are given point values, which becomes the basis of job evaluation. In this, four job factors such as skill, effort, responsibility and job condition are taken as basis point values and in some cases these factors are further sub-divided for more accuracy. The following table explains the point method of job evaluation developed by the National Metal Traders Association, America.

Characteristics	*First Degree*	*Second Degree*	*Third Degree*	*Fourth Degree*	*Fifth Degree*
1. Skill					
(*a*) Education	14	28	42	56	70
(*b*) Experience	22	44	66	88	110
(*c*) Initiative and Ingenuity	14	28	42	56	70
2. Efforts					
(*a*) Physical demand	10	20	30	40	50
(*b*) Mental demand	5	10	15	20	25
3. Responsibility					
(*a*) Equipment or Process	5	10	15	20	25
(*b*) Material or product	5	10	15	20	25
(*c*) Safety of others	5	10	15	20	25
(*d*) Work of others	5	10	15	20	25
4. Job Conditions					
(*a*) Working conditions	10	20	30	40	50
(*b*) Unavoidable hazards	5	10	15	20	25
Total					500

If we again consider the example for the job, evaluation of a gate-keeper, the evaluation can be done as follows :

Factors	*Points*
Skill	10
Efforts	20
Responsibility	80
Working conditions	30
Total	140

140 points are equivalent to Rs. 1400 in money value, if it is assumed that 1 point is equal to Rs. 10.00. In this way, in point system evaluation is done.

Advantage. Evaluation is comparatively more accurate.

Disadvantage. Much complicated and costly method.

7.4. DEVELOPMENT OF WAGE STRUCTURE FOR BASE WAGES

There are three major steps in achieving the final wage structure for base wages. These are :

(*i*) Decision about range, i.e., maximum and minimum wages for the grade.

(*ii*) Decision about the number of grades for workers.

(*iii*) Decision about the overlap in between the different grades.

All the above mentioned steps are closely related, *i.e.*, if there is any change in one will cause some change in other.

There are so many theories about the decision of first two points but about the third point a wage curve is to be drawn. The wage curve is drawn in Fig. 7.1 and explained as under :

A wage curve is a graphic representation between job difficulty values (point, ranks or grade level) and wages paid for the jobs. When the curve obtained is a straight line then it is called as wage line. But in general, a curve as shown in the figure is obtained, which is a second degree curve.

As regards the overlap theoretically, it is clear that there should be no overlap because a worker near the top of lower grade could have higher wage than the person on a higher grade. It is recommended that for high accuracy number of grades should not be more than twelve while upto six grades the accuracy may be coarse. Thus number of grades between six to eleven, are generally taken into consideration. For number of grades lying between six to eleven the range is assumed @ 10% of average pay line. If there are more number of grades then overlapping must be more between the grades. The overlapping can be reduced by different methods such as by increasing the slope of the pay line, or by reducing wage or by reducing number of grades.

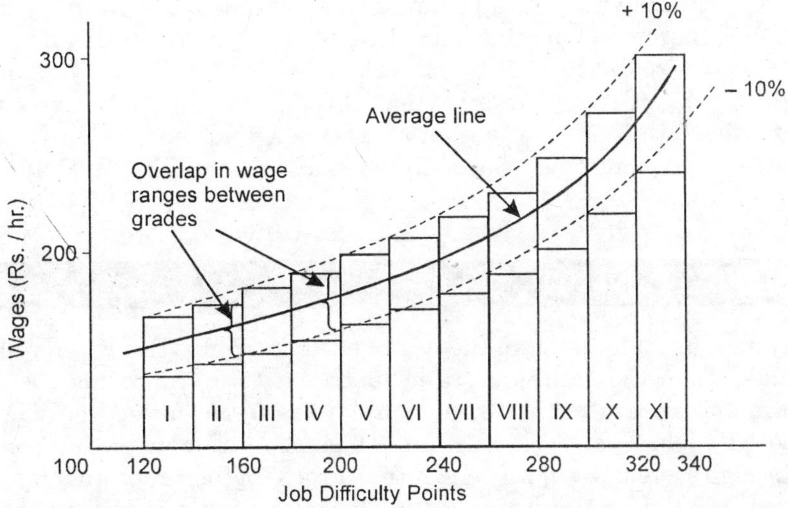

Fig. 7.1. Wage curve.

Though the overlapping should be avoided but it is a fact that there should be some overlapping between the grades so that workers under the lower grade should get more wages on excellent performance than to a worker working under higher grade having poor performance. Further, due to overlapping, the foreman can transfer workers temporarily to other jobs. Normally overlapping should be limited to within three adjacent grades.

7.5. JOB EVALUATION IN SUPERVISORY AND EXECUTIVE POSITIONS

The above methods are also used for the evaluation of these positions but the characteristics may differ, as they depend upon the nature of job and their importance.

For supervisory position characteristics are:

(*i*) Technical education
(*ii*) Length of service or experience
(*iii*) Judgement
(*iv*) Planning
(*v*) Condition of work
(*vi*) Number of employees under him
(*vii*) Responsibility

In the same way, characteristics for an executive may be :

(*i*) Planning
(*ii*) Policy formulation
(*iii*) Methods
(*iv*) Administration
(*v*) Personal relations
(*vi*) Executive contacts
(*vii*) Original thinking
(*viii*) Analysis of job
(*ix*) Influence upon profits.

Above are the requirements but importance for the same post may differ from organisation to organisation and, therefore, job rates may also change from organisation to organisation. For example, in factory where the cost of raw materials used is very high, by employing high rated purchasing officer, we can make large savings through purchases but on the other hand in another factory, where the cost of raw materials is low and, normally available at standard prices, a low rate can be paid to purchase officer because there is no much importance given to this job.

7.6. MERIT RATING

In job evaluation we are interested in the relative worth of jobs. But when relative worth of an employee is made, then the technique used is known as merit rating. Merit rating can be defined as a systematic evaluation of an employee's performance on the job in terms of requirements of the job. The merit rating enables the foreman to differentiate among his subordinates through systematic approach for the purpose of their recommendation for promotion, for wage increase ... or the special training etc. The employees are rated on certain factors such as attendance, co-operation, initiative, safety habits, judgment, creativeness, honesty, intelligence etc.

Objects of Merit Rating

Following are the important objects of merit rating :

1. It is commonly used to justify wage increase.
2. This is one of the methods for deciding whether employees engaged on production are to be confirmed or not.
3. It helps the supervisor in deciding, which person is to be given which task.
4. It helps in deciding which employee deserves promotion.
5. It can be used as a scale by the selection officers to judge whether their selections are successful.
6. It protects the employees from discrimination, favouritism etc.

Methods of Merit Rating.

Following are the important methods for merit-rating:

1. **Straight Ranking Method.** In this method, each worker is ranked in his group against each other. Comparison between employees is made, ranking them from poorest to best one.
2. **Description or Essay Type Merit Rating.** Generally this type of merit rating is used for the persons of supervisory cadre. In this, incharge writes a report on his subordinates. The report must cover the following factors :
   (*a*) Relation with subordinates and fellow persons.
   (*b*) Job knowledge and capacity to understand.
   (*c*) Knowledge about industrial engineering aspects.
   (*d*) Knowledge about safety precautions and first aid.
   (*e*) Organisational and planning ability.
   (*f*) Explanation power.
   (*g*) Physical aptitude.

3. **Forced Choice Method.** In this method, characteristics are printed on a sheet of paper and incharge is asked to tick them. The marks for the rating can be given on the basis of these characteristics.
4. **Graphic Rating Plan.** In this system, points in numerical values are given (generally rating from 1.2 for the poorest to 12.0 for the best worker) for various characteristics. The total of these points in them is used to compare the workers. The important characteristics generally considered for the rating of workers are :
   (*a*) Accuracy of work
   (*b*) Quantity of work
   (*c*) Co-ordination and co-operation
   (*d*) Safety
   (*e*) Initiative and effort
   (*f*) Responsibility
   (*g*) Care and use of equipment, tools and materials
   (*h*) Attendance and punctuality
   (*i*) Dependability
   (*j*) Integrity.

WAGES AND INCENTIVES

7.7. INTRODUCTION

Although the system of payment of wages in industry is as old as the industry itself, yet in the earlier days, when slavery was in vogue, the payment to slaves was in the form of kind rather than in cash. Work is done with a motive of earning money and proper compensation must be given for the industrial efforts. Wages constitute the principal source of income of workers for their labour or service. For employer these form a significant part of cost of production of products manufactured. Therefore, these have a direct influence on the price level and through it on the life of a community and its economic development.

Definitions

Wages. These are the payments made by the employer for the efforts put in by the worker in production. These are the payments made for the services rendered by labour.

As wages determine the standard of living of the worker and his dependents, it is necessary that they should represent a fair return for the efforts of the worker. But above all, wages should be sufficient to satisfy his ordinary needs and necessity. They should be enough to provide him some comforts of life and help him in maintaining his standard of living.

Nominal Wages. It is the amount of money paid to a worker in cash for the efforts put in by him in an industry and no other advantage to the worker is made. This is also called money wage. The rates of wages at different places may differ from each other as per the availability of the workers and necessities of life, the amount of payment is so calculated that every worker should get actual worth of his services.

Real wages. It refers to the amount of necessaries, comforts, luxuries and cash payment which a worker can get in return for this effort and work.

For example, uniforms, essential commodities, housing with free water and electric supplies, conveyance and together such facilities are generally provided by the factory, in addition to the money in cash. If all this amount as a whole is considered for wages, these become 'Real Wages'.

Living Wages. When the rates of wages are such that can meet some of the social requirements of a family like Education, Food, Clothes and some Insurance against the more important misfortunes along with prime necessities of life are called 'Living Wages'.

Fair Wages. It is actually the wage which must be fair for the work of a worker and should provide him with other necessities of life in addition to food for his family.

The rates for the fair wage range between the minimum wage and living wage but between these two ranges the actual wages will depend on :

(*i*) Production capacity of the worker,

(*ii*) Rates in the surrounding area.

(*iii*) The level of the national income and its distribution.

(*iv*) The place of industry in the economy of the country.

(*v*) the bargaining power of employer and employee.

Minimum Wages. Wages cannot be raised beyond the capacity of industry to pay. The productivity of an industry is the source from which wages are paid. At the same time it cannot be forgotten that labour is a human being, and from humanitarian point of view, he is to be protected. Hence there is the problem of fixing a minimum wage for the worker. This minimum should be sufficient for allowing the worker to maintain himself according to his needs.

Minimum wages may be deputed as the wages, which provide not only for bare subsistence but something more than this. It must be sufficient for the preservation of the efficiency of the worker. It must also provide for some measure of education, medical requirements and other amenities of life. Thus, in fixing a minimum wage, we have to take into consideration the cost of living. To ensure this, in India, Minimum Wages Act, 1948, has been in force where wages have been fixed for different parts of the country and this has forced employers to give not less than this fixed minimum wages to any of their workers.

The main object of minimum wages are :

1. To protect those sections of the working population whose wages are very low and whose conditions are materially unsatisfactory.
2. To prevent exploitation of workers and to secure a wage according to the values of the work done.
3. To promote peace in industry.
4. To improve the normal standard of living.

Wage Differentials

In any Industry or office, different workers or employees get different wages. Workers with same qualifications engaged in similar work in different industries get different wages or salaries. This difference in wages is called wage differentials.

Reasons for Wage Differentials

1. Difference in marginal productivity of the workers.
2. Difference in qualification, experience and training of the workers.
3. Difference in skill and specialisation of the workers.
4. Difference in hazards and risk involved in fulfilling the jobs.
5. Difference in degree of responsibility required for the jobs.
6. Difference in exploitation by the employer.
7. Availability of workers (This follows the rule of supply and demand).

Factors Which Influence Wages

The problem of a fair and adequate wage is very complicated. It is difficult to arrive at a wage which may be considered satisfactory both for the workers and for the management. Yet it is vital problem and so vital that the success of any industry largely rests upon its satisfactory solution. There are various factors which determine the wage level and some of them are as follows :

1. The condition of demand and supply.
2. The respective bargaining capacity of employers and employees.
3. Cost of living which may vary from time to time according to industrial situation of each industrial district.
4. The economic capacity of the industry to pay wages.
5. Level of wage rates ruling in each industrial area for the same class of industry and same grade of workers.
6. The workers' skill, training and experience.
7. The economic outlook of the employer.
8. The nature of task involved, *i.e.*, risky, noisy, requiring high concentration, heavy or light work and hot work, etc.
9. The regularity in service.
10. Extra earnings on the job.
11. Prospects of future promotions.

Characteristics of a Good Wage or Incentive System

A good wage or incentive system should have the following characteristics :

1. This should guarantee an adequate minimum day wage.
2. It must have the free consent of the workers.
3. It must reward the worker according to his capacity and merit.
4. It must be simple in its working so that it may be readily understood by the workers.
5. It must not involve heavy clerical work and theory which may increase the utlimate cost.
6. It should aim at increasing production without adversely affecting quality.
7. It should reduce wastage of material and careless use of plant, tools and equipment.
8. It should have effective supervision but it should not be too heavy.
9. Incentive, bonus etc., should be payable alongwith the wage and not put off for future.
10. The system should be fair both to the employees and the employers.

7.8. COMPONENTS OF PAY STRUCTURE

Pay packet in India consists of several elements such as:

1. Basic wage:
2. Dearness allowance
3. House rent allowance
4. City compensatory allowance
5. Leave travel concession
6. Education allowance
7. Transport subsidy
8. Provident fund

9. Gratuity
10. Group-linked insurance scheme
11. Pension fund
12. Medical benefits
13. Employees State Insurance Scheme
14. Leave with pay, etc

7.9. SALARY ADMINISTRATION

First step of salary administration is to determine salary levels by the process of job evaluation, which we have already discussed. After deciding salary levels, salary administration is concerned with the following:

1. Design and maintenance of salary structure.
2. Operation of salary progression system *i.e.*, relating salary increase to merit.
3. Administration and control of salary reviews.
4. Design and operation of other allowances.

Objectives of Salary Administration

A sound wage and salary administration seeks to achieve the following objectives:

1. To establise a fair and equitable remuneration. Here equity means similar pay for similar work.
2. To attract competent personnel.
3. To retain present employees.
4. To improve productivity.
5. To control costs.
6. To establish lines of promotion wherever applicable.
7. To improve image of company

Principles of Salary Administration.

1. Differences in pay should be based on differences of job requirements.
2. Wage and salary level should be in line with those prevailing in the job market.
3. Follow the principle of equal pay for equal work.
4. Recognise individual differences in ability and contribution.
5. The wages should be sufficient enough to ensure for the worker and his family reasonable standard of living.
6. There should be a system for hearing and removal of grievances related to the wages.
7. Employees and trade union should be informed about the procedure used to establish wage rates.
8. A wage committee should review and revise wages from time to time.

7.10. METHODS OF WAGE PAYMENT

Various methods of remunerating labour are :

(*a*) Time or Day Rate System.

(*b*) Straight Piece Work Rate System
(*c*) Combination of Time Rate and Piece Rate System
(*d*) Profit Sharing System.
(*e*) High Wage Plan.

1. Time or Day Rate System.

This is the most common system found in practice. Under this the worker is paid an hourly, daily or weekly rate of wages. Thus his remuneration depends upon the number of hours for which he is employed and not upon the amount of his production.

Advantages

(*i*) There is no dispute about the amount of payment, because it has been fixed from the very beginning and the worker knows in advance what he is going to get.

(*ii*) It possesses security from the stand point of the worker because they are sure to receive their wages irrespective of temporary reductions in personal efficiency, which may result from unavoidable accident or sickness or fatigue from outside activities.

(*iii*) The quality of the work can be achieved very easily, as there is no need of hurrying about the things to be done.

(*iv*) There is no rough handling of machinery due to "slow and steady" working of workers.

(*v*) The interruptions to work due to breakdown of machinery or some other part of the plant will not make workers to suffer from the loss of wages.

(*vi*) There are no difficult calculations to be made. If there are many calculations to be made to arrive at the remuneration of a worker, it is possible that an illiterate worker may doubt the exactness of his remuneration from time to time.

Disadvantages

(*i*) The employer bears the loss resulting from slow and sluggish workers as they are paid the same wages, irrespective of their output.

(*ii*) This system tends to reduce production, unless a strict supervision is managed. Therefore, a well-qualified and strict foreman is required for satisfactory production.

(*iii*) This system tends to give higher production cost.

(*iv*) This system is not suitable in the case of lazy workers.

(*v*) In this system, efficient workers may also become inefficient by working with inefficient workers.

Suitability. In this system several times, the minimum work becomes the maximum work. Everybody may try to do the minimum and no one may try to do above that because there is no immediate gain for hard and difficult work, hence this system leads to higher cost of production and hence is suitable to pay the factory workers such as Foremen, Supervisors, Time-keepers, Cleaners, Enginemen, Store-keepers and Gatemen etc., as the nature of their work is such that 'Time' alone can be taken as the basis on which to remunerate them.

2. Straight Piece Work Rate System

This is improvement on the Time Rate System. Under this, a fixed rate of wage is paid for each piece of unit produced.

Advantages

(*i*) It is simple in its working and the workmen can easily calculate their wages.

(*ii*) An inducement is given to the workers to increase their production and thus the overhead expenses per unit of production are reduced and hence the margin of profit increases and scope of reduction of selling price, therefore, increases.

(*iii*) The relations of the workers and employers improve and no dispute takes place for wages, as the workers get satisfactory reward for their work.

(*iv*) The employer is enable to know his labour cost per unit of job.

(*v*) Workers are paid on their merits.

(*vi*) The work and time spent on preparing pay roll and bills is eliminated.

(*vii*) Wasted time is not paid as done in time rate system.

(*viii*) There is no need of keeping strict supervision and workers aretough self-reliance and responsible.

(*ix*) In this method, production will improve as workers demand material and machinery free from defects and under perfect working condition.

Disadvantages

(*i*) It is difficult in certain cases to fix accurate piece-work rate.

(*ii*) When the wages earned by workers are high, the employer may be induced to reduce the rate, which will cause friction between the employer and employees.

(*iii*) The workers put maximum efforts to earn more and more, which results suffering of their health.

(*iv*) This causes displacement of labour as with increase in production, the number of workers engaged will be reduced.

(*v*) It will cause an increase in the waste of materials because the workers will always try to obtain the maximum output, which may lead to spoilage of work.

(*vi*) Accidents due to hasty work and improper use of machines and tools in order to give more production and machines become out of order frequently.

(*vii*) Mis-utilisation of costly machines and tools.

(*viii*) The quality of work may reduce. This can be checked, if a rigid system of inspection is enforced.

(*ix*) It may cause over-production and may result in losses, if there is only a limited demand for the products in the market.

(*x*) The entire benefit of the extra wages earned goes to the workman and do direct benefit to employer.

(*xi*) When a lazy worker takes unnecessary long time for completing a given job, the employer will suffer extra shop and machine charge, thus increasing the overhead cost of production.

Suitability. Hence this system is only suitable where the worker repeats regularly a definite operation or produce the same type of products continuously. Many employers in India have introduced this system and it has been found efficient, easy and economical. For the application of this system, a careful time study is conducted and different types of workmen are observed for the time they take in carrying out the job. Standard time for the completion of a job by workmen of different calibres is found out and the rates of the wages per job is decided so that every worker can get at least a minimum wage. The skilled and active workers are free to earn more by putting more efforts.

3. **Combination of Day Rate and Piece Work Rate System**

Under this system, minimum weekly wages are fixed for every worker, which shall be paid to him irrespective of his output during the week, provided he has worked for the full working hours required in a week. If a worker is absent for some length of time during a week, his wages will be deducted proportionately, *e.g.*, a week consists of 48 working hours and if a worker works for only 40 hours, then he will be paid 5/6 of his regular weekly wages. Thus the payment is based on time rate system. The piece-work system is combined with the above as follows :

A job card of each worker is maintained, which clearly shows number of pieces of job completed by the worker during a week. Piece-work rate of each job is fixed in advance. If the piece-work wages earned by a worker are in excess than the time wages, the balance is paid to the worker. On the other hand, if they are short of the time rate, the worker shall have to make good producing the next week, *i.e.*, suppose the worker is paid Rs. 24 a week according to time rate and the piece rate of a job which he is doing is Rs. 3 each. Again he has completed 10 jobs during a week, he will be paid Rs. 30 for that week. However, if he completes only seven jobs, he shall still be paid Rs. 24. During the next week, he shall only be paid in excess than time wage, if he completes more than nine jobs, *i.e.*, after compensating for last week's shortfall.

Advantages

(*i*) It provides incentive to the workers to produce more.

(*ii*) The overhead costs of production on quality.

Disadvantages

(*i*) It needs check on quality.

(*ii*) It needs careful piece rate fixing.

(*iii*) The entire benefit of extra payment goes to the worker.

4. **Profit Sharing System**

This system has been introduced by the employers in order to encourage their employees and by means of which the workers receive a share of the profits over and above their normal wages.

Advantages:

(*i*) Better co-operation may be easily expected.

(*ii*) There is reduction of supervision, which results in reduction of supervision cost.

(*iii*) Non-productive labour cost will be reduced.

(*iv*) As there is a community of interest of all the workers, they all work more harmoniously and honestly, resulting in better production.

Disadvantages:

(*i*) It is difficult to ascertain the share of profit to be given to each worker and unless the profits are large, the share of each worker may appear to him very insignificant.

(*ii*) Since the efficiency of individual worker is of no concern to the group, individual efficiency escapes from the notice of the management.

(*iii*) As the distribution will normally take place only once a year, workers may lose interest in it.

(*iv*) If the efficient workers are not selected as group leaders, the efficiency of the whole group suffers.

5. **High Wage Plan**

   In this system, to attract workers, wages are fixed at higher rate than those paid in the surrounding areas so as to attract more skilled workers and these higher wages are paid with the understanding that the workers shall put in their best efforts to attain the highest standard of efficiency and output.

7.11. INCENTIVES

It is something that encourages a worker to put in more productive efforts voluntarily. Mostly, workers are not willing to exert themselves to produce anywhere near their full capacity unless their interest in work is created by some kind of reward. This reward is called 'incentive'.

The incentive is a kind of monetary reward, which is closely related to the performance of a worker, resulting increase in wages corresponding to an increase in output.

Types of Incentives

(*a*) Financial Incentives.
(*b*) Non-financial Incentives

7.11.1. Financial Incentives

If an employer finds that he will be earning an extra profit of Rs. 5, if a particular work is finished in 5 hours less than the prescribed time. Now, if the workman is promised an extra payment of Rs. 2. This extra payment is known as incentive and is in the first instance calculated in term of time or hour of employment.

Methods of financial incentive payments :

(*i*) Piece rate system.
(*ii*) Cent per cent premium.
(*iii*) Halsey premium plan.
(*iv*) Weir premium plan,
(*v*) Beduax premium plan.
(*vi*) Rowan premium plan.
(*vii*) Emerson Efficiency plan.
(*viii*) Gantt's task and bonus system.
(*ix*) Taylor's multiple piece-rate system.
(*x*) Merric's multiple piece-rate system.

1. **Piece Rate System**

   Under this system, a piece rate for the completion of job is fixed. Now, if a worker completes the job earlier, he can save his time and in that saved time, he can make jobs and whatever the extra money he gets for the extra work, it wholly goes to him but the employer will also be benefited by the savings in overheads for the extra output.

   It will more clear by the following numerical example :

   Example 7.1. *Worker is employed for manufacture of M.S. pins at a piece rate of 15 paise. He has to prepare 40 pins in 8 hours of work, but he prepared 55 pins in 8 hours. Calculate his total daily earning by piece-rate system.*

   Also calculate extra earnings.

Solution. Rate per piece = 15 paise. He has to manufacture minimum 40 pins per day.

Then, his normal earning per day = 40 × 15 = Rs. 6.00

But he prepared 55 pins/day.

∴ Total earnings/day = 55 × 15 = Rs. 8.25

∴ His extra earning will be Rs. 8.25 - Rs. 6.00

Rs. 2.25

From this, it is clear that all the extra money earned by the worker goes to him only.

2. **Cent Percent Premium Plan**

In this system, the standard time for the completion of job is fixed and its rate of completion during this period is also fixed. Now the worker who completes the job in this standard time is not given any incentive but those who complete the job earlier, they get full payment for the time saved.

It will be made clear by the following solved numerical example :

Example 7.2. *The standard time for the completion of a job is 8 hours and the worker is paid Rs. 10.00 for it. If he completes it in 6 hours, calculate his earning by cent per cent premium system for the whole day (i.e. for 8 hours of work).*

Solution. Standard time for the job =8 hours.

Wages of 8 hours = Rs. 10.00

Time taken by worker to complete the job = 6 hours

In 6 hours, worker can earn Rs. 10.00

In 8 hours of a day he will earn Rs. $\frac{10}{6} \times 8 = \frac{40}{3}$ = Rs. 13.33

Therefore, worker gets cent per cent of his savings.

Actually, this is also a piece-rate system but adopted in the case of heavier jobs, in which a single job takes several days for completion, and if a number of small jobs can be completed in a day, then piece-rate system is used.

3. **Halsey Premium Plan**

In this system, an hourly rate or daily rate is guaranteed to the workers. A standard time is fixed for the performance of each job and the worker is paid the agreed rate per hour for the time spent thereon plus a fixed percentage (usually 33 1/3%) of the time he can save on the standard. This plan is easy to introduce.

It will be clear by the following solved example:

Example 7.3. *Standard time for a given job is 15 hours and hourly rate of wages 50 paise. If a worker completes the job in 10 hours and he is allowed $33\frac{1}{3}$% of the time saved as incentive. Calculate the earning of the worker and also direct saving of employer.*

Solution. Worker will receive wages for 10 hours plus 33 ***1/3%*** of the time saved as bonus, that is, its further 5/3 hours wages.

Hence total remuneration for 11 2/3 hours at the rate of 50 paise per hour is Rs. 5.83.

Thus, the employer has made a saving of Rs. 1.67 in direct wages where as the worker has gained Re. 0.83 extra in 10 hours.

Therefore, from this, it is clear that a part of saving goes to the worker and remaining part of the saving to the employer.

4. **Weir premium Plan**

   This is similar to Halsey premium plan but in this workers get upto 50% of his extra output along with standard day rate.

5. **Beduax Premium Plan**

   This is also like Halsey and Weir premium plans. But in this, workers are given at the rate of 75% of their extra output alongwith standard day rate.

6. **Rowan Premium Plan**

   In this, the worker is again guaranteed his daily or hourly rate. A standard time is fixed for each job and a premium is given in the ratio of the time saved to the standard time multiplied by the time taken on the job.

   Taking the numerical problem of Halsey premium plan, the workers' wages and premium under this plan would be as follows : Actual wages for the time taken (10 hours @ 50 paise) is Rs. 5.00. Time saved = 5 hours

   Proportion of time saved to standard time = $\frac{5}{15} = \frac{1}{3}$

   Premium $\frac{1}{3}$ of time taken = $\frac{10}{3}$ hours @ 50 paise = Rs. 1.65

   Therefore, total wages = Rs. 5 + 1.65 = Rs. 6.65

   It is observed that, in this system, the incentive increases upto certain output but decreases in the same ratio afterwards but in Halsey plan, incentive goes on increasing as the output increases.

   Example 7.4. *Prove that in Rowan bonus plan, the bonus hours cannot, in any circumstances exceed 25% of the allowed standard time. (A.M.I.E. Nov., 1976)*

   Solution. This can be proved by the following table. Let the standard time for the completion on a given task be 8 hours and an hourly rate of wages be Re. 1.00. The table for 7 different workers who finished the task of 8 hours in different hours is shown as under :

Workers	*Standard Time*	*Time Taken*	*Hourly Rate*	*Rated Income*	*Incentive by Rowan Method*	*Total Wages*	*Hourly Rate*
1	8	8	1.00	8.00	Nil	8.00	1.00
2	8	7	1.00	7.00	0.88	7.88	1.13
3	8	6	1.00	6.00	1.50	7.50	1.25
4	8	5	1.00	5.00	1.88	6.88	1.38
5	8	4	1.00	4.00	2.00	6.00	1.50
6	8	3	1.00	3.00	1.88	4.88	1.63
7	8	2	1.00	2.00	1.50	3.50	1.75

From this table, it is clear that under Rowan method, a worker cannot get more than a fixed amount even if he finishes his task too early. It is also seen that he can get maximum bonus, if he completes the task in half the standard time and at this time bonus hours are 25% of the allowed standard time as shown in table for worker No. 5

and if he saves more than half the time his bonus decreases as shown in table for worker 6 and 7.

Therefore, this method safeguards the management against the chances of paying big sums to the workers as bonus, if a mistake has been made in setting the standard time. The weak point in Halsey system is that in extreme cases the workers receive a very high rate of bonus, which is not possible under this system.

7. Emerson Efficiency Plan

In this method, standards are set and workers get additional incentive along with their basic day rate. A basic day rate is fixed irrespective of the workers capabilities and every worker gets atleast his minimum day wage.

Following are the rates at different efficiencies :

(*a*) If a worker performs upto 66.6% of the standard output, he gets no incentive.

(*b*) If a worker performs upto 80% of the standard output, he gets 10% of the day wages as incentive.

(*c*) If a worker performs upto 100% of the standard output, he gets 20% of the day wages as incentive.

(*d*) If a worker performs upto 120% of the standard output, he gets 40% of the day wages as incentive, and so on.

Example 7.5. *There are five workers, who are manufacturing electric switches. The standard day rate is Rs. 8.00 per worker and standard output is 40 switches. Calculate their daily earning by Emerson Efficiency Plan, if they are manufacturing 24, 32, 36, 40 and 48 switches respectively.*

Solution. It can be solved in the following table :

Workers	*Quantity Produced*	*Standard output*	*Standard Day rate Rs.*	*percentage standard output Rs.*	*Incentive Rs.*	*Total Wage Rs.*	*Hourly Rate Rs.*
1	24	40	8.00	$\frac{24}{40} \times 100 = 60\%$	0.00	8.00	1.00
2	32	40	8.00	$\frac{32}{40} \times 100 = 80\%$	0.80	8.80	1.10
3	36	40	8.00	$\frac{36}{40} \times 100 = 90\%$	1.20	9.20	1.15
4	40	40	8.00	$\frac{40}{40} \times 100 = 100\%$	1.60	9.60	1.20
5	48	40	8.00	$\frac{48}{40} \times 100 = 120\%$	3.20	11.20	1.40

It can be seen from the table above, that the wages of the workers go on increasing as the output increase.

8. Gantt's Task Bonus System

In this system, first careful study of the job is made from that study best conditions for the performance of the job are determined. On the basis of these performance, a standard output for a given time is set. Now, if a worker completes the job in given standard time, he receives wages for the standard time and bonus ranging from 20 to 50% of time taken. When a worker fails to produce the required output, he only gets his time rate without any bonus.

It will be more clear from the following solved example :

Example 7.6. Four workers have taken 7, 6, 5 and 3 hours respectively for the completion of a job. The time rate is Re. 1.00 per hour. A bonus of 25% on the time taken is fixed for those, who complete the job within 6 hours.

Calculate the earning of individuals and their hourly rates by Gantt's Task and Bonus system.

Solution. It can be solved in the following table :

Workers	Time Hours	Day rate Rs.	Bonus Rs.	Total earning Rs.	Hourly rate Rs.
1	7	7.00	Nil	7.00	1.00
2	6	6.00	1.50	7.00	1.25
3	5	6.00	1.25	7.25	1.45
4	3	6.00	0.75	6.75	2.25

In this method, foreman also receives bonus along with the workers and, therefore, the foreman of each department is thus directly interested to see that the men under his charge bring up their work to the bonus standard.

9. Taylor's Differential Piece Rate System

In this system, standard time is fixed for the performance of piece-work and those who complete the job in standard time or produce jobs earlier are paid at higher rates and those who do not complete the job in standard time are paid at lower rates.

This system, therefore, gives an encouragement to active worker but punishes lazy workers. In this system, it is difficult to determine the standard of higher and lower production and thus the system may prove to be unjust to the workers.

10. Merric's Multiple Piece Rate System

In this system, Merric divided the workers into three categories, namely, beginners, average and first class workers and three different rates for them. The higher rates are paid to those who reach the standard. The second rates are for those who reach at least 80% of standard and third rate is below the 80% output.

This system is very well suited for increasing efficiency and is modification of Taylor's system.

7.11.2 Non-Financial Incentives

The financial and non-financial type of incentives are complementary and must go together if satisfactory results are desired. The financial incentive must be supported by the non-financial incentives, since only case wages cannot help in solving the problems of industrial productivity. In order to create interest in a worker for greater and better output, non-financial incentives must also be enforced and workers will also enjoy richer and fuller life.

Some of the chief non-financial incentives are :

1. Personal interest and pride in work to be created in workmen.
2. Fair and sympathetic treatment with workers.
3. Opportunity for quick promotions.
4. Opportunity for technical training in other technical organisations as well as abroad.
5. Security of employment and hopes for reward.
6. Perfect confidence in the management.
7. Provisions of canteens, where cheap, wholesome and balanced food is available to workers.
8. Provisions of children welfare, maternity and other medical aid etc

Advantages of Incentive System

(*i*) Apart from the direct reduction of the cost of labour, there is indirect saving due to reduction of shop and machine charges as the time is saved.

(*ii*) Workers are encouraged to increase production to earn more.

(*iii*) Worker's day wages are guaranteed, even if they are not able to complete the job in standard time. In case the job completed in less than the specified time, incentive is earned.

(*iv*) This promotes relation between employers and employees.

The success of the incentive systems depends on efficient and sufficient machines and tools, avoidance of delay and interruptions. If the rate of incentive is too high, it will result in loss to employers and if too low, it will fail to induce workers.

7.12. BONUS SYSTEM

This system is used, where efforts of a number of workers are required to complete the job and, where, it is not practicable to measure the output of individual worker, there it is necessary to pay a collective or group bonus to retain the incentive payment idea.

Following are the methods of payment in this system :

(*a*) **Collective Bonus System.** In some big industrial concerns, a collective bonus in the form of an extra salary for one or more months is given to its employees, if the profits during the business year are handsome. If there are good profits, the bonus will be declared after about six months or at the end of year and will be payable to the workers in service at the time of declaration.

(*b*) **Group Bonus System.** In this system, each department or section is offered a separate fixed bonus per unit time or per unit job, if the standard time is saved or the production reaches or exceeds a predetermined quantity. Such bonus is divided between the foremen and workmen of the department or section in proportions agreed before hand. In this system, bonus is given to foremen also, as they are mainly responsible for increasing output and preventing wastage of material.

The Bonus Act September, 1965

It states that, "Every factory employing 20 or more workers must pay minimum of bonus of 8.33% of the annual wage inclusive of dearness allowances or Rs. 100 to all workers, whichever is higher, irrespective of whether it has made some profit or not (or Rs. 60 to child worker).

The Following are some of the most **essential features of this Act**:

(*i*) It ensures the worker of a definite minimum addition of his yearly wages.

(*ii*) It is applicable to all factories, employing 20 or more workers and once a factory is covered by this Act, it will continue to do so, even if there is reduction in the number of workers below 20.

(*iii*) This would enable the workers to maintain their health and efficiency and thereby reduce their discontent to some extent.

(*iv*) Workers in newly established organisations will not be eligible for bonus in the first 5 years.

(*v*) The minimum bonus is 8.33% of wages inclusive of dearness allowance or Rs. 100, whichever is greater and the maximum 20%.

(*vi*) Workers getting salary upto Rs. 3500 per month are covered by this Act.

[**Note.** Workers getting salary upto Rs. 10,000 per month are covered by this Act but for calculating the bonus their salary upto Rs. 3500/month are considered. Amended Nov. 1985].

(*vii*) A worker must have worked for a period of atleast 30 days to become eligible for bonus.

(*viii*) After deducting all the charges, 60% of the net profit (67% in the foreign companies) will be credited to the bonus fund.

If in any year net profit exceeds the maximum bonus (20%) payable, the excess amount will be carried forward to the next year's Bonus Fund. Similarly, when in any year there is no profit, the deficit will be set off in the following year. This facility will be allowed for four consecutive accounting years.

Advantage:

It ensures stability of workman as any worker leaving the job at any time in a year shall have to miss some of the bonus.

Disadvantages:

(*i*) No distinction is made between efficient and ordinary worker for the payment of bonus.

(*ii*) Bonus is paid much after the completion of work and there is no immediate incentive to the workers in their work.

(*iii*) Bonus being collective, an individual worker may not put his entire skill in the work.

(*iv*) Sometimes a good worker may receive only a small amount of bonus in comparison to his efforts.

7.13. TIME RATE V/S PIECE RATE

In the piece-rate system, worker is paid per piece of job and no consideration of time taken is made. Actualy this system is an improvement on the "time rate" system of payment. This system gives every workman an opportunity to earn more by putting more efforts and at the same time output also increases. In the time rate system, strict supervision is required, as now-a-day it has become difficult to extract more and more work from workers. Foremen are always found saying to workers, "you are wasting time" or you have not so far completed the job or do this or that by that time and so on. While in the piece-rate system workers believe that every second has its value and "work is worship". This system is applicable to productive workers, where they repeat regularly a definite operation or produce the same type of product constantly. Many employers in India have introduced this method and they found it more simple, easy, economical and efficient.

This system is not suitable for the workers such as Foremen, Supervisor, Time-keeper, Cleaner, Enginemen etc. and time rate system is used as the nature of their work is such that "Time" alone can be taken as the basis on which to remunerate them.

The other drawback of the piece rate system is that no incentive scheme can be introduced and worker's life is reduced because of hard labour involved to earn more and more. It also affects on the quality of product.

Advantages of Piece Rate

To Workers:

(*i*) It is simple in its working and they can easily calculate their wages.
(*ii*) An inducement is given to the workers to increase their production. i.e. greater earnings.
(*iii*) Workers are paid on their merits.
(*iv*) As supervision will be less, they feel more independence.

To Employer:

(*i*) The employer can know easily labour cost per unit produced.
(*ii*) Wasted time is not paid, as done in time rate system.
(*iii*) No strict supervision is required.
(*iv*) Output increases and higher profits can be earned.
(*v*) Labour turnover is reduced, as no dispute takes place for earnings.
(*vi*) The allotment of work and loading of machines etc. once decided, work satisfactorily.

Disadvantages of Piece Rate System

To Workers:

(*i*) As the workers put maximum efforts to earn more and more, their health is reduced.
(*ii*) Active and slow workers feel jealousy among each other.
(*iii*) When the wages earned by workmen are high, the employer may be induced to reduce the rates, which will cause friction between the employer and employee.

To Employer:

(*i*) It is difficult to fix an accurate piece-work rate.
(*ii*) This causes displacement of labour with increase in production, the number of workers engaged will be reduced.
(*iii*) It will cause an increase in the waste of material, because the worker will always try to obtain the maximum output.
(*iv*) The quality of work may be reduced.
(*v*) It may cause over-production and may result in losses, if there is a limited demand for the product in the market.
(*vi*) The entire benefit of the extra wages earned goes to the workmen.
(*vii*) When a sluggish worker takes unnecessary longer time for completing a given job, the employer will suffer extra shop and machine charges, thus increasing the overhead cost of production.

(*viii*) Accidents due to hasty work will be more.

(*ix*) Mis-utilisation of machinery.

QUESTIONS

1. Define 'Job Evaluation' and explain various job rating methods.
2. Write short notes on :
   (*a*) Job
   (*b*) Job description
   (*c*) Job specification
3. Enumerate the objectives of job evaluation.
4. What do you know about merit rating?
5. Explain different methods of merit rating. Which method do you prefer and why?
6. What is the purpose of evaluation ? Explain how the purpose is achieved. Enumerate the weaknesses of job evaluation and the difficulties in carrying it out.
7. Define job evaluation. Discuss principle types of job rating methods.
8. What is meant by job evaluation ? Describe briefly the procedure to be adopted for making quantitative evaluation of jobs at the operator's level. What are the essential factors to be considered for constructing job, evaluated job, evaluated wages structure?
9. (*i*) Define performance rating. What are the factors to be considered in evaluating the performance rating of an operator ?
   Do you consider rating to be a variable function dependent on the cycle time?
   (*ii*) Discuss briefly any suitable method of training a work study observed in the art of rating.
10. How does job-evaluation help in developing an equitable wage structure ? What precautions should be observed in installing an evaluation scheme ?
11. (*i*) Examine critically the different methods of job evaluation,
    (*ii*) Enumerate the advantages of job evaluation.
12. Describe briefly the factor comparison method of job evaluation. Indicate the limitations of this method.
13. Explain, how a normal operator specified for rate fixing purposes in a well-established factory having a recognized workers union.
14. (*i*) State the essential requirement of job evaluation programme,
    (*ii*) Explain, the "Point plan" method of job evaluation.
15. Discuss the various methods of wage payment.
16. Discuss the difference between the Time Rate and Piece Rate. Show their relative advantages and state which you would prefer for efficient and quick production.
17. What are incentives ? How these help the production ?
18. List the non-financial incentives that are generally provided to workers in a large industry.
19. Make a co-operative study of any two good systems of remunerating labour. Give your preference with justification.
20. Explain the various methods of remunerating labour in factories. Discuss their advantages and disadvantages.

21. "Both the Halsey and Rowan system" are for reduction in the labour cost of the articles manufactured. Discuss and give your opinion.
22. Define the following :
    Normal Wages, Real Wages, Minimum Wages and Fair Wages.
23. What are the essential features of Halsey Premium Plan ?
24. "Incentives are necessary for smooth and efficient running of a factory", discuss. State some important incentive schemes.
25. (*a*) Discuss the basis of industrial wages.
    (*b*) Describe briefly the different types of Wage Payment Plans, giving the salient features of each.
26. What is meant by non-financial incentives ? Name few non-financial incentive schemes.
27. Define base wages, wage rates, salary rates and incentive wages. Of the many wage Payment Plans, discuss clearly :
    (*a*) Halsey Premium Plan.
    (*b*) Taylor Differential Piece Rate Plan.
    (*c*) Gantt Task and Bonus Plan.
28. Name the different Wage Payment Plans commonly used in industry today. Explain why these plans, different from one another, should be in use at the same time.
29. What is meant by "Wage Structure" ? State the essentials of standard wage structure. Outline any one non-financial incentive scheme suitable for large industrial concern.
30. Define "wages" within the meaning of the Payment of Wages Act 1964. Who is responsible of payment of wages ? Discuss under what conditions the following deductions from wages are possible in accordance with the provisions of the said Act:
    (*a*) Fines, (*b*) for damages or loss of property, and (*c*) for recovery of advances.
31. What is understood by incentive wage systems ? State any three important incentive wage systems and show their individual characteristics.
32. (*a*) Discuss the important conditions which should be fulfilled before any incentive wage scheme could be installed.
    (*b*) How will you examine effectiveness of an incentive scheme in use?
33. (*a*) Define the terms "incentive" and "motivation". State the advantages of the non-financial incentive system.
    (*b*) Discuss the fundamental requirements of a good financial incentive system.
34. (*a*) State the different types of Incentive Plans used in industry.
    (*b*) Describe any incentive scheme commonly employed in Indian industries.
    (*c*) Some people think that "Profit Sharing Plans", have no incentive value. Do you agree?
35. (*i*) State the essentials of a good financial incentive plan.
    (*ii*) Outline a Plan suitable for a mass production shop in which outputs (Performances) are measured individual-wise in some cases and group wise in the others.
36. Propose a suitable wage system for each of the following industrial units. Describe the same and state reasons for your choice.
    (*a*) Industrial unit manufacturing 20,000 bicycles per year.
    (*b*) Industrial unit manufacturing four ships per year.

(*c*) Industrial unit manufacturing 100,000 pairs of shoes of all sizes and shapes per year.

(*d*) Ordnance unit manufacturing jet fighters.

37. State the merits of group bonus system, and indicate the characteristic of the group and its workers for which the system will be suitable.

38. Why is productivity desired as a basis of wages ? What type of incentive plan will you recommend for the following industrial units ? State reasons for your choice.

(*a*) Diesel locomotive plan in public sector

(*b*) Machine tool manufacturing plant in private sector.

39. (*a*) State the salient features of the Compulsory Bonus scheme for industrial workers.

(*b*) How far it helps in securing greater co-operation and higher efficiency, from the employees? Give reasons for your answer.

40. Discuss the application of group incentives *versus* the use of individual incentives.

41. (*a*) Explain the difference between minimum wage and fair wage.

(*b*) Discuss the relative merits and demerits of the piece rate system and the time system of wage payment.

(*c*) In case of Rowan Bonus Plan, prove that the bonus hours cannot under any circumstances exceed 25% of the time allowed.

8 Industrial Relations and Trade Union

8.1. INDUSTRIAL RELATIONS

Industrial relations, also called employee relations, labour relations, and personnel relations, represent the relationship that exist between the employer and employees in an industrial undertaking. If these relations are strained, industrial disputes occur and industrial progress suffers. The employer suffer losses, the workers do not get wages and there is shortage of goods and services.

Hence, it is in the interest of both the employers and employees as well as of the society in general that industrial relations should be cordial and harmonious.

Industrial relations is the management aspect which deals with the manpowers of the enterprise. It is essential that Industrial Relations between the employees and employer remain co-ordial and peaceful, as enterprise can advance only if industrial relations are good. Industrial Relations are the relations between the employees and the management that grows during the employment.

Goal of industrial relations system has been 'industrial peace', which means 'harmony or absence of conflict' between employers and employees in an industrial concern.

For any industrial relations programme following are the basic requirements.

(*i*) To have support of top management

(*ii*) To adopt proper practices

(*iii*) To adopt and follow sound personnel policies

Labour management relations problem can be solved easily when industrial relation system is understood and the problem is analysed after studying different components of the system. Industrial relation system can be understood in terms of interaction between two sets of organisations, namely;

(*i*) industrial organisation (management and workers), and

(*ii*) union organisation (union leaders and workers),

Interaction among persons within each of these two organisations can be understood with the help of following elements:

(*a*) Objectives about productivity, economy, efficiency welfare etc.

(*b*) Rules, regulations, and conventions.

(*c*) Distribution of authority and power, as it influences the attitude of employees.

(*d*) Values and beliefs.

(*e*) Motivation
(*f*) Culture
(*g*) Personalities

8.2. INDUSTRIAL DISPUTES (CONFLICTS)

Conflicts or dispute is a type of behaviour which occurs when two or more parties are in opposition or in battle. These disputes:

(*a*) Adversely affect the effectiveness of individuals or groups
(*b*) May break down the relationship between individuals or groups, and
(*c*) May result in acute neurosis of strike.

This makes difficult to achieve objectives of the organisation. Organisation conflict is disagreement between two or more members or groups of the organisation. The conflict may arise due to :

(*a*) Sharing of scarce resource or work activities
(*b*) Different statuses, goals, values or perceptions
(*c*) Disagreement over facts, methods
(*d*) Social economical and psychological reasons.

It is essential to eliminate disputes by :

(*a*) Adequate job definition
(*b*) Detailed specifications of relationship between various positions
(*c*) Careful selection of people to fill up various posts, and
(*d*) Thorough training of people for the job assigned to them.

Stages of Conflict

(*a*) **Latent Conflict.** It may be due to competition for scare resources, role conflict, drive for autonomy or ego problem.
(*b*) **Perceived Conflict.** This is due to misunderstandings, and can be sorted out by improving communications.
(*c*) **Felt Conflict.** When official differences become personalised, such conflicts arise.
(*d*) **Manifest Conflict.** At this stage, conflict takes the form of open agressions, sabotage, apathy or withdrawal etc.
(*e*) **Conflict aftermath.** If the conflict is suppressed, the latest condition conflict may be aggravated and explode in more serious or violent form at a later date.

Resolution of Conflict

(*a*) Find out full details of conflict, then
(*b*) Analyse the issues involved in the conflict, then
(*c*) Conflict may be solved by mediation, bargaining, politics etc.

Preventive Measures for Conflict Resolution

1. Develop effective leadership
2. Develop effective communication
3. Adopt participative decision-making
4. Improve interpersonal relationship
5. Review facilities etc.

Types of Conflicts

1. Conflict within an individual
2. Conflict between individuals
3. Conflict between an individual and a group
4. Conflict between groups within an organisation
5. Conflict between organisations

Impact of Conflict

1. **Changes that may occur within the groups:**
   (*i*) Group cohesiveness increases.
   (*ii*) The group becomes task-oriented.
   (*iii*) Organisational structure becomes more effective.
   (*iv*) Leadership becomes more effective.
2. **Prolonged group conflicts cause following changes between groups:**
   (*i*) Each group sees the other as an enemy who interferes with its goal-oriented behaviour.
   (*ii*) Develops positive perceptions about own group and negative perceptions towards the other.
   (*iii*) Communication ceases to exist.
   (*iv*) Each group clearly sees all the variuos acts of the other, while remains blind to the same acts performed by their own group.
3. **Potential benefits of inter-group conflicts are:**
   (*i*) Conflict clarifies the real issue.
   (*ii*) Conflict increases innovation.
   (*iii*) Strengthens the group and reduces the internal conflicts.
   (*iv*) Conflict can provide an outlet for ventilating their feelings.
   (*v*) Conflict resolution may strengthen inter-group relationship.

Sources of Conflict

In any organisation, large number of potential sources of conflict exist. Some of such sources of conflict are:

1. Competition for limited resources.
2. Diversity of goals.
3. Task interdependence.
4. Organisational ambiguities.
5. Differences in values and perception.
6. Poor communication.
7. Aggressive nature of people.
8. Introduction of change.

Perception

Visual perception or seeing, which plays an important role in our daily life is very complex phenomenon. People differ in the ways they perceive the things surrounding them. What we see is dependent upon the way the brain organises the nervous impules which come from the eye. Our perception is usually dependent upon the frame or background or the context in which we see things. People also differ in the 'rapidity' with which they perceive. Size of the visual also assumes the importance in perception. The perception can be improved by learning and training only upto some extent.

Attitudes

Attitudes may be defined as learned orientation or disposition towards an object, person, situation or issue which makes an individual to react to them in a favourable or unfavourable manner. Thus from the definition, we see that

(*i*) attitudes are learned as human being learn various other responses,

(*ii*) an attitude is an orientation or disposition we carry around with us just as we carry all our habits,

(*iii*) when the appropriate circumstances arise, the attitude makes the individual to react in a favourable, unfavourable or indifferent manner.

A person will react to a thing, person or situation depending upon the intensity of his attitude. Workers may acquire a feeling of hate or dislike towards their foreman or company or a particular department etc. that their behaviour on various company matters may become extreme resentment or even violent behaviour if the situation arises.

As we have seen that 'attitude' is a set of action with an emotion all over', it is a tendency to regard things with approval or disapproval. In case of approval, there is a feeling towards attraction for it, while in the case of disapproval, there is a feeling against or repulsion from it.

Inter-personal Relations

Every organisation exists either for doing a job for rendering the service with the help of human resource. In any organisation, 'task-oriented relationship', for combining 'task' with 'human relations' plays an important role.

Every inter-personal relationship is based on mutual and reciprocal initiating and responding behaviour pattern. It takes two parties to build it, and both are equally responsible.

Once a relationship is formed-negative, positive or neutral—any late behaviour is interpreted and responded to on its basis. For example, if the existing relationship is of hostility, then any behaviour of affection will be suspected and will be indifferently responded with.

Inter-personal relationship of any type can be developed or changed through consciously planned efforts. Although change may require series efforts.

8.3. RESULTS OF CONFLICTS

Following are some of the serious results which arise out of these disputes:

1. Strike
2. Lock-out

8.3.1. Strike

A common form of industrial dispute is the 'strike' which means abstaining from work until the demands are met or a compromise is affected. Reasons for the occurrence of strikes are:

1. Labour unions try to maximise the wage gains of their members.
2. To fight against exploitation at the hands of capitalists.
3. Recognition of unions, rivalries of the unions.

4. Lack of communication and understanding between the mangement and workers.
5. Desire of the workmen to protect the conditions of their work.

A strike is considered to be the last resort of the workers to express their discontent.

Forms of Strikes

Strikes may be in the following forms.

1. **Sit-down Strike.** In this, the workers go to the work place but refuse to work. They do not leave the premises of the workplace until the strike is over.
2. **Go Slow or Slow-down Strike.** In this, the workers continue to work but do so at much slow rate, since, they do not totally abstain from work, they are entitled to pay for the period of slow down.
3. **Picketing.** In order to call the attention of the public that a strike is going on, and disallow others from entering the plant (work premises) or doing business in the undertaking, the workers or their sympathizers place themselves at the entrance of the premises causing obstruction to people who want to go inside or come out. These persons are termed **'pickets'** and the method as a whole **'picketing'**.
4. **Gherao.** It is a form of dispute, in which workers do not allow the officer to leave his room or working place for a considerably long period so as to press for their demands. The officer can't even go for making off water.

Causes of Strikes

Whenever workers feel any grievance and if the same is not removed by the management, the workers unite together to fight it out and this causes the industrial unrest/conflict/dispute. The industrial disputes generally result in strikes, lockouts, picketing or gherao.

Common causes of strikes are:

1. Wage disputes (including bonus etc).
2. Working conditions.
3. Discipline and other rules
4. Dismissals, retrenchments, suspension etc.
5. Dispute over working hours/hours of work.
6. Trade union recognition.
7. Misbehaviour from supervisors or management.

Effects of Strikes

1. Strikes are costly to workers.
2. It causes mental strains
3. It causes mass unemployment.
4. It may result in violence and damage to property.
5. It results in loss of production and profits.
6. Public suffers from shortage of products of the striking industry.
7. If the strike fails, it brings misery, dismissal, withdrawal of already given privilages and degrades the morale of workers.

8.3.2. Lock-out

Lockout is just opposite procedure of strike and consists in the closing of factory by the employer because of a dispute with the employees and is the refusal of entry to them.

As strike is a weapon in the hands of workers to force employers to accept their demands; lockout is the weapon of employer to pressurize workers to come down in their demands.

A lock-out can also be defined as, "closing the place of employment or suspension of worker or the refusal by an employer to employ any number of persons employed by him."

8.4. SETTLEMENT OF INDUSTRIAL DISPUTES

Industrial disputes may be resolved by voluntary method or under compulsions by the State (Government). Nearly all industrial countries have passed laws and set-up machinery for their settlement. The methods adopted for the settlement of industrial disputes are:

1. Collective Bargaining
2. Conciliation and Mediation
3. Arbitration

8.4.1. Collective Bargaining

Collective Bargaining is the method of negotiation between the representatives of labour and management to solve some labour dispute and to enter some agreement to prevent a dispute. As we know that strike and lockouts go against the interests of the society, therefore genuine collective bargaining is important in promoting industrial harmony. Collective bargaining is a preventive method to prevent the situation arising for strikes and lockouts.

Collective bargaining can be defined in several ways, some of them are :

1. Collective bargaining can be described as a procedure whereby employers must reach an agreement about wage rates and basic conditions of labour with trade unions instead of individual workers.
2. It is the process of discussion and negotiation between the employer and union, culminating in a written agreement or contract adjustment of problems arising under the agreement.

Collective bargaining is basically a give-and-take process involving proposals and counter proposals.

Compulsory Collective Bargaining

If either union or management resists the voluntary collective bargaining (the one explained above), but the state (government) feels that collective bargaining will be useful, it may advise or direct for collective bargaining compulsorily on the two parties to settle their dispute through negotiations.

Importance of Collective Bargaining

Collective Bargaining is the most effective instrument in the hands of workers for improving their living conditions. Following are the main advantages through collective bargaining:

1. It ensures lasting industrial peace and avoid conflicts
2. It fastens responsibility on both the parties
3. It helps in achieving the important status for workers
4. It encourages the industrial democracy
5. It is best method to settle the dispute.

8.4.2. Conciliation and Mediation

1. **Conciliation**

   Conciliation is an important method for pervention and settlement of industrial disputes through third party intervention. It is an attempt to reconcile the views of the disputants and bring them to an agreement. Conciliation is generally understood as friendly intervention of a neutral person in a dispute to help the parties to settle their differences peacefully.

   Thus it is a process of peace-making in industrial relations, which tends to bring about a speedy settlement of disputes without resorting to strikes or lockouts. Its aim is to assist the parties to move towards a mutually acceptable compromise or solution.

2. **Mediation**

   Mediation is a process by which a third party brings together the opposing groups not only to eliminate differences between them but also to find an answer to problems and offer alternative suggestions. The mediator can be described as a confidential advisor. He neither imposes his will nor his judgement upon them, he gives each party, his evaluation of its position, and by doing so, he influences these parties. He helps the two parties to come to an argreement of their own accord rather than to render an award or decision of his own.

   The mediator should be an impartial and unprejudiced person, having influence on parties, and must infuse confidence in them.

   The difference between 'conciliation' and 'mediation' is of degree rather than kind. Conciliation is limited to encouraging the parties to discuss their differences and help them develop their own proposed solutions. 'Mediation' on the other hand, implies to a stronger form of intervention, and a mediator may be permitted to offer to the parties proposals for settlements.

8.4.3. Arbitration

Arbitration is a process in which a dispute is submitted to an impartial outsider who makes a decision which is usually binding on both the parties. It is a process where there is a hearing and determination of a cause between parties in controversy by a person (s) chosen by them, or appointed under a statutory provision. The parties are bound by the award of arbitrator.

8.5. TRADE UNIONS

The associations formed by workers are known as 'Trade Unions'. A trade union may be defined as an association or union of workers engaged in a particular trade and formed chiefly with the object of helping the members in times of distress and getting their grievances settled and legitimate rights established.

According to Webbs, Trade union is a continuous association of wage earners for the purpose of improving conditions of employment. Trade unions are also seen as moral institutions which will uplift the weak and downtrodden and render them the place, dignity and justice they deserve. Trade union generally raise demands for higher wages, better working conditions, fringe benefits, promotional opportunities and safeguards in most cases, demands are directed against the management.

Workers join trade unions in order to protect their various job interests. These job interests can be grouped into following categories:

1. Economic–to get livable wage
2. Job safety–job security and freedom from management's arbitrary actions
3. Social affiliations
4. Self-esteem–to have voice in the systems
5. Status and self-fulfilment.

Functions Trade Unions

- Social service
- Wage bargaining
- Safety of job
- Develop cooperation amongst employees
- Protect workers from delay in payments, poor working conditions etc.
- Bargain for share in profit and participation in management.

8.6. DISCIPLINE

Discipline means employees' self control to meet organisational standards of objectives. Discipline relates to employee's conduct and may be defined as the force that promotes employees to behave in accordance with the rules, regulations and orders. Discipline may be described as the force that promotes an individual or group to observe rules.

Discipline means orderliness, obedience and maintenance of proper subordination among employees and a check or restraint on the liberty of individuals. Discipline cannot be maintained merely with the help of legislative sanctions, it requires persuation on a moral plane. Discipline refers to one's efforts at self-control for the purpose of adjusting oneself to certain needs and demands.

Discipline encourages employees to behave sensibly at work to gain the objectives of organisation. Discipline helps in reducing the absenteeism, accidents, labour turnover, grievances and frustration and wastages, while it helps in increasing production, production quality and morale.

Discipline is of two types:

1. Positive
2. Negative

As explained above, generally discipline is thought of only as negative discipline but now it is being realised that positive discipline is more effective. Sound discipline helps in maintaining successful operation with full coordination.

Positive Discipline

It develops good habits among workers and establishes good tradition and customs. It improves the state of mind of the workers and performs the work in a better way with or without the general instructions.

Experiments have shown good results, if suitable incentives are given for accurate and better performances than to punish for mistakes because it develops proper attitude of the workers. Incentives may be in the form of better wages, reward in the form of money, certificates, medals, promotions etc. Positive discipline helps to build up favourable feelings.

Negative Discipline

Negative discipline means imposition of penalties and fear of penalties. To secure compliance at once, positive disciplines uses constructive forces, while the other negative discipline uses different forces.

Negative discipline helps to secure only minimum performance necessary to avoid punishment while positive discipline creates interest in the work. Negative discipline also encourages the worker to adopt unfavourable attitude towards foreman and the plant.

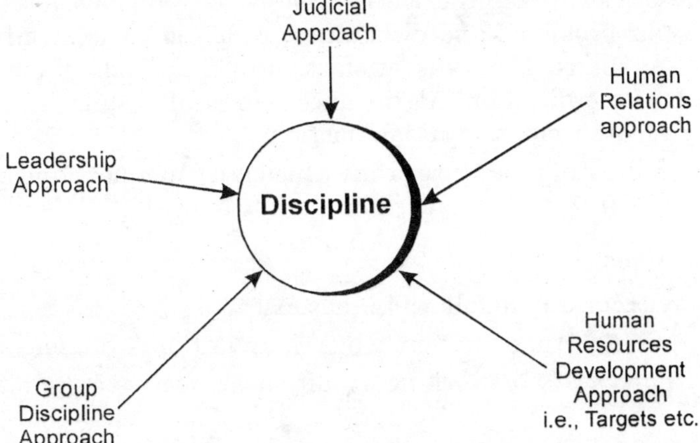

Fig. 8.1. Managerial approaches for discipline.

Common Discipline Problems

Most frequent discipline problems may be related to :

(*a*) Attendance
(*b*) On the job-behaviour
(*c*) Dishonesty
(*d*) Outside activities

Disciplinary Actions

(*a*) Oral warning
(*b*) Written warning
(*c*) Suspension
(*d*) Demotion
(*e*) Pay cut
(*f*) Dismissal

Disciplinary actions must be taken as per rules and procedures. Judicial approach is also necessary while taking disciplinary action. Severity of the action depends upon following :

1. Seriousness of the problem/offence
2. Duration of the offence
3. Frequency and nature of the offence
4. Employee's work history
5. History of organisation's discipline practices

6. Implication of other employees.
7. Management backing.

8.7. WORKERS GRIEVANCES

Individual employees many times, have some or the other complaints called grievances, against the working rules or decisions in an organisation. It is necessary that there should be same system to remove these grievances, otherwise the employees will have a feeling that management does not look into their problems and difficulties, which is very harmful for attaining good industrial relations. As distrust and dissatisfaction in the minds of employees will result in inefficiency and lack of coordination. A grievance redressal system is, therefore, essential to have the feeling of discontentment or dissatisfaction.

A good grievance redressal procedure is one which is (*i*) Adequate and effective, (*ii*) Simple to understand and operate, (*iii*) Prompt and (*iv*) Permit to appeal.

Reasons for Grievances

Grievances may occur due to following reasons:

(*a*) *Economic reasons:* Wage fixation, wage computation, overtime, bonus etc.

(*b*) *Work Environment:* Poor working conditions, defective equipments, tools, materials etc.

(*c*) *Supervision :* Behaviour of the boss, perceived notions of favouritism, nepotism, bias etc.

(*d*) *Workgroup:* Strained relations, feeling of neglect and victimisation.

(*e*) *Work organisation :* Rigid or unfair rules, too much or too less work responsibility, lack of recognition etc.

8.8. SUGGESTION SYSTEM

Use of suggestion system is most successful bridge between plant improvement efforts and good industrial relations. Suggestions system taps the tremendous store of ideas for the performance improvement, which otherwise lying in the minds of the employees. Most employees feel satisfied by volunteering their ideas but they feel reluctant. Therefore, it is necessary to set up a suitable suggestion system so that employees can give way to their feelings, ideas and valuable suggestions. Most companies give awards for valuable and useful suggestions.

This not only enables management to receive ideas for improving the efficiency, but reduces the complaints and enhances the morale of the employees also.

8.9. PARTICIPATIVE MANAGEMENT

Participative management concept is a powerful tool of industrial relation system.It is based on industrial democracy and develops team spirit with the employees and belongingness in them. This helps in realisation of common objectives.

Participative management may be defined as "a system of communication and consultation either formal or informal to keep employees of the organisation informed about the affairs of the concerns through which they can express their opinions and contribute to management decisions."

Employees participation in management is based on many considerations including political, economical, psychological, and social. Political and industrial democracy have to go hand in hand. In this endeavour, involvement of employees is must. The employee needs a sense of identity and by way of participation, he feels to have achieved it.

Advantages from Participation

1. **Advantages to the Employees.** These include a sense of identity and belongingness, and motivation to perform better. When an organisation perform better, he will have economic gains in terms of increased wages and incentives and better standard of living.
2. **Advantages to the Organisation.** These include, improved quality of decision-making, better implementation of the decisions, better quality performances, resulting in better profit, easier acceptability of change of technology etc. on the part of employees, better materialisation of creative ideas and suggestions.

Participative Forums

Following types of participative forums are common:

- Works committee
- Joint management council
- Joint Council
- Plant Council
- Shop Council

Other small group committees are:

- Production Committee
- Welfare committe
- Canteen Committee
- Quality Circle
- Waste Control Committee

Achievements Expected from Participative Forums

- Improvement of quality consciousness among the employees
- Improvement of team work
- Wastage control
- Better attendance
- Reduction in grievances
- Sense of belongingness on the part of employees
- Better Communication
- Improved work conditions and welfare
- Improved employee relations

QUESTIONS

1. Explain how industrial relations affect the efficiency.
2. What is an industrial dispute? What are the causes of dispute?

3. Explain how an industrial dispute can be settled.
4. What is trade union? What are its functions.
5. Write a short note on 'Collective bargaining?'
6. Discuss the impact of collective bargaining on the employee-employer relations in the industry.
7. What is 'participative management'? What are its advantages?
8. Discuss various participative forums and group committees.
9. What are the areas, which should be covered under participative management?
10. What is the difference between 'strike' and 'lock out'? Explain.

9 Industrial Legislation (Labour Laws)

9.1. INTRODUCTION

These has been struggle, conflict and clashes between the employes and the employer on the matters related to wages, allowances, safety, welfare and other facilities etc. This has resulted in increase in strikes, lockouts, picketings and gheraos.

In view of the above and to minimise employee-employer disputes, for the welfare of employees and their families, and in the interest of economy of the country, the government had to intervene. Since 1920s there has been a growing stream of protective labour laws regulating wages, compensation, safety, disputes, health, working conditions, welfare, social justice etc.

Importance (Necessity) of Labour Laws

1. These laws help in improving industrial relations.
2. Reduce conflicts, and thereby reduces national wastage.
3. Helps in payment of fair wages to workers.
4. Minimise unrest and maintain cordial relations.
5. Gives compensation to workers, victims etc in case of accidents and other hazards.
6. Helps in providing job security to workers.
7. Regulates hours of work, rest pauses etc.

Some of the Common Labour Laws are

1. Factories Act
2. Industrial Disputes Act
3. Workmen's Compensation Act
4. Payment of Wages Act
5. Minimum Wages Act
6. Mines Act
7. Employees State Insurance Act
8. Employees Provident Fund Act
9. Trade Union Act
10. Construction and Other Workers Act

Here in this chapter we shall discuss most common Acts (Srl 1 to 5)

9.2. THE FACTORIES ACT, 1948

9.2.1. Introduction

This Act safeguards the interest of the workers engaged in factories. The Act is now applicable in whole of India. It came first into force from 1st April, 1949 and was extended to the Union Territories of Goa, Daman and Diu in 1963, and to the State of Jammu and Kashmir in 1970. It has detailed provisions relating to the health, safety and welfare of workers as well as their working conditions, safety measures and other facilities to enhance their welfare. These include provisions such as prescribing the maximum number of hours a worker may be employed in a factory, facilities of interval, for rest, weakly off, earned and other leave etc. The Act also prescribes specific hours of work for women and children. It applies to every factory established in India, including the ones owned by the Government.

Thus the **main aim of enactment of Factories Act 1948, is to protect factory workers from the dangers to their health from machines and from adverse working conditions in the factories.**

The **Act is a labour welfare legislation**and was enacted with the prime object of protecting workmen employed in factories against industrial and occupational hazards and with this intention, it imposes upon the owners and occupiers certain obligations to protect the workers.

The Act is enforced by the State Governments through their Factory Inspectorates. It also empowers the State Governments to frame rules so that the local conditions prevailing in the State are appropriately reflected in the enforcement.

The object of the Act is

(*i*) to protect the workers from being subject to unduly long hours of bodily strain and manual labour,

(*ii*) to provide that employees should work in healthy and sanitary conditions and precautions should be taken for their safety and for prevention of accidents, and

(*iii*) to regulate the labour and protect the workers from being exploited.

9.2.2. Definitions

Following are some of the important definitions described in the Act:

1. *Adult.* A person who has completed the age of 18 years.
2. *Adolescent.* A person who has completed his 15th year of age, but has not completed 18th year of age.
3. *Child.* A person who has not completed his 15th year of age.
4. *Calendar Year.* A period of 12 months from 1st January.
5. *Young Person.* Either a child or an adolescent.
6. *Week.* A period of 7 days beginning at midnight on Saturday night.
7. *Power.* Electrical energy or any other form of energy, which is not generated by human or animal agency.
8. *Prime Mover.* Any engine, motor or other appliance, which generates or otherwise provides power.
9. *Transmission Machinery.* Any shaft, wheel, drum, pulley, system of pulleys, coupling, clutch, driving belt or any other device by which the motion of prime-mover is transmitted to or received by any machinery or appliance.

10. *Manufacturing Process.* Any process for :
    (*a*) making, altering, repairing, ornamenting, finishing, packing, oiling, washing, cleaning, breaking up, demolishing, treating or adopting any article or substance with a view to its use, sale, transport, delivery or disposal, or
    (*b*) pumping oil, water or sewerage, or any other substances or
    (*c*) generating, transforming or transmitting power, or
    (*d*) composing types for printing by letter press, lithography, photogravure or other similar process or book binding.
    (*e*) constructing, reconstructing, repairing, finishing, refitting or breaking up ships or vessels.
    (*g*) preserving or storing in cold storage.
11. *Worker.* A person employed directly or through any agency, whether for wages or not, in any manufacturing process or in cleaning any part of the machinery or premises used for manufacturing process or in any other kind of work incidental, to or connected with, the manufacturing process.
12. *Factory.* Any premises:
    (*i*) wherein 10 or more workers are working, or were working on any day of the preceeding 12 months, and in any part of which a manufacturing process is being carried on with the aid of power, or
    (*ii*) wherein 20 or more workers are working or were working on any day of the preceding 12 months, and in any part of which a manufacturing process is being carried out without the aid of power, but does not include a Mine *or* a Railway running shed.
13. *Occupier.* Occupier of factory means the person who has ultimate control over the affairs of the factory and where the said affairs are entrusted to a managing agent, such agent shall be deemed to be occupier of the factory.

9.2.3. Licence and Registration

1. The Act specifies that before a factory can be started,
    (*a*) Prior permission for the site of the factory construction or extension has to be obtained from the Chief Inspector ;
    (*b*) Plans and specifications should have been approved by the Factory Inspector; and
    (*c*) The factory has to be registered and the licence fee has to be paid.
2. If an application for permission referred at item (*a*) above accompanied by the plans and specifications required by rules referred at item (*b*) above sent to the State Government or the Chief Inspector by registered post, and no order is communicated to the applicant within 3 months from the date on which it is so sent; the permission applied for the said application shall be deemed to have been granted.
3. Where a State Government or a Chief Inspector refuses to grant permission to the site, construction or extension of factory or to the registration and licencing of a factory, the applicant may within 30 days of the date of such refusal appeal to the Central Government if the refusal is from the State Government and to the State Government in any other case.

9.2.4. Inspecting Staff

The act permits the State Government:

(a) To appoint Chief Inspector and other Inspectors to supervise the conditions in factories and to see that the provisions of the act are practised;

(b) To appoint qualified medical practitioners to be certifying surgeons to examine medically the young persons to examine the conditions in factory to find out whether any process or action in manufacturing is harmful to cause any injury to the health of workers.

9.2.5. Health Provisions

This act prescribes the following provisions for maintaining the health of the workers and reducing the possibilities of injuries to their bodies :

1. Cleanliness

Every factory shall be kept clean and free from gases arising from any drain or their nuisance. For this purpose, following steps should particularly be taken:

(a) The dirt and refuse shall be removed daily by sweeping from the floors, benches of workrooms, staircases and from passages.

(b) The floor of every workroom shall be cleaned at least once in every week by washing, using disinfectant where necessary.

(c) Effective means of drainage shall be provided and maintained.

(d) All inside walls, partitions, ceilings of rooms and passages ;

(i) where they are painted or varnished, shall be repainted or revarnished at least once in every five years ;

(ii) where they are whitewashed, or colourwashed, shall be whitewashed or colourwashed at least once in every period of 14 months.

2. Ventilation and Temperature

(a) Effective and suitable provisions shall be made for

(i) securing and maintaining adequate ventilation by the circulation of fresh air in the workroom, and

(ii) securing reasonable conditions of comfort and preventing injury to health of worker.

(b) Walls and roofs should be of such material and so designed that temperature shall not be exceeded but kept as low as practicable. Effective arrangement should also be made to protect the workers from processes producing excessively high temperature. Hot parts of the machinery shall be insulated.

3. Artificial Humidification

(a) If there is an artificial humidification, it shall be of prescribed standard and created by the prescribed methods.

(b) The water used for such humidification shall be clean and free from dirt.

4. Overcrowding

No room in the factory shall be overcrowded, for this at least 350 cu. ft. or 9.9 m^3 of space for every worker is necessary in the factories which were in existence before the date of the commencement of this Act and at least 500 cu. ft. or 14.2 m^3 of space for every worker shall be provided in the factories built after the commencement of this Act. For this purpose, any space which is more than 14. ft. or 4.2 m above the level of the floor of the room shall not be taken into account, i.e., height above 14 ft. or 4.2 m from floor shall not be taken into consideration.

5. Lighting

(*i*) Sufficient, and suitable lighting whether natural or artificial or both shall be maintained at the working place or passages.

(*ii*) All glazed windows and skylight shall be kept clean on both the inner and outer surfaces.

(*iii*) Glare and formation of shadows should be prevented to avoid eye strain or risk of accident.

6. Drinking Water

Drinking water should be made available to all workers at all working hours and should be provided and maintained at suitable points. All such points shall be marked "drinking water" in a language understood by a majority of workers. Such points shall not be situated within 20 ft or 6.0 m of any washing place, urinal or latrine or any other source of contamination.

In every factory employing more than 250 workers, provision shall be made for cooling drinking water during hot weather.

7. Bath Rooms

If the work in the factory is of such a nature which involves dirt, a sufficient number of bath rooms shall be provided.

8. Latrines and Urinals

(*a*) Sufficient number of prescribed type, separate enclosed accommodation for male and female workers shall be provided. The accommodation shall be adequately lighted and ventilated and shall be maintained in clean and sanitary conditions at all times.

(*b*) In the factories employing more than 250 workers, all the latrines and urinals shall be of prescribed sanitary types and the floors and internal walls upto a height of 3 ft or 0.90 m and the sanitary blocks shall be laid in glazed tiles or otherwise finished to provide a smooth polished impervious surface.

(*c*) (*i*) One latrine shall be provided for every 20 female workers; and one latrine shall be provided for 20 to 100 male workers and thereafter one additional for every 50 male workers.

(*ii*) There shall be one urinal for every 50 workers upto 500 workers and thereafter for every 100 workers.

9. Spittoons

Sufficient number of spittoons shall be provided at convenient places. These shall be washed regularly and kept clean.

9.2.6. Safety Provisions

Following important provisions for safety are provided in the Act:

1. **Fencing of Machinery.** Following items shall be fenced in every factory :

(*a*) Every moving part of a prime-mover, every flywheel;

(*b*) Head race and tail race of every water turbine ;

(*c*) Following items should be properly safeguarded; every part of an electric generator, a motor, or a rotary converter; every part of transmission machinery and dangerous parts of other machines.

2. **Work on or near machinery in motion.** The work on or near moving machinery shall be done by a specially trained adult male worker, wearing tight fitting clothing. No woman or young person shall be allowed to clean, lubricate or adjust any part of a prime-mover or of any transmission machinery when it is in motion.
3. Devices for cutting off power from running machines in emergency shall be provided.
4. **Casing of machinery.** In all the machines driven by power and installed in any factory after the commencement of this Act—every set screw, bolt or key on any revolving shaft, spindle, wheel or pinion shall be so sunk, encased or otherwise effectively guarded as to prevent danger, every toothed or friction gearing shall be completely encased.
5. **Hoists and lifts.** In every factory :

(*a*) Every hoist and lift shall be of good mechanical construction and of adequate strength. They shall be properly maintained and thoroughly examined regularly. It shall be marked with maximum safe working load.

(*b*) Every hoistway and liftway shall be sufficiently protected by an enclosure fitted with gates

(*c*) Hoists and lifts used for carrying persons shall have atleast 2 ropes or chains separately connected with the cage and balance weight and each rope or chain with its attachment shall be capable of carrying the whole weight of the cage together with its maximum load.

6. **Lifting machines, chains, ropes and lifting tackles.**All parts including the working gears, lifting machines, chains, ropes or lifting tackles shall be of good construction and of adequate strength; properly maintained and thoroughly examined at least once in every period of 12 months. Lifting machine means a crane, crab, winch, pulley block etc.
7. **Revolving machinery.** A notice shall be affixed to every grinder, indicating the maximum safe working peripheral speed of every grind stone or abrasive wheel, the speed of the shaft or spindle upon which the wheel is mounted.
8. **Excessive weights.** No person shall be employed in any factory to lift, carry or move any load so heavy as to be likely to cause him injury. State Government may make rules prescribing the maximum weight which may be lifted or carried by adult men, adult women, adolescent and childern.
9. **Protection of eyes.** To protect the eyes, screens or goggles shall be provided to the persons engaged in the following manufacturing processes :

(*a*) Welding or cutting the metals with electric or oxyacetylene flame or any other such process.

(*b*) Fettling, rivet cutting, removal of scales or dressing of metals or stones or any other such process involving risk of injury to the eyes from particles thrown off in the course of process.

10. **Precautions against dangerous fumes gases etc.**

(*i*) In any factory, no person shall enter or be permitted to enter any chamber, tank, pit, pipe, flue or other confined space in which dangerous fumes are likely to be present to such an extent as to involve risk to persons, unless it is provided with a manhole of adequate size.

(*ii*) Portable electric light above 24 volts shall not be permitted to such confined space.

(*iii*) Any person shall only be allowed to enter any confined space after the measures have been taken to remove fumes and a certificate in writing has been given by a competent person based on a test carried out himself, and the worker is wearing suitable breathing apparatus and a belt securely attached to a rope, the free end of which is held by a person standing outside the confined space.

11. Precautions against Fire

(*i*) Every factory shall be provided with means of escape in case of fire as may be prescribed.

(*ii*) Doors affording exit from any room shall not be locked or fastened so that they cannot be easily and immediately opened from the inside while any person is inside room.

(*iii*) Every window, door or other exit affording means of escape in case of fire, other than the means of exit in ordinary use shall be marked in language understood by majority of the workers.

(*iv*) Effective means of giving warning in case of fire to every person shall be provided.

(*v*) A free passage-way giving access to escape in case of fire shall be maintained.

9.2.7. Welfare Provisions

1. **Washing Facilities.** Adequate and suitable facilities for washing shall be provided separately for male and female workers and maintained for their use. Suitable place for keeping clothing not worn during working hours and for the drying of wet clothings should be marked.
2. **Sitting Facilities.** Suitable arrangements for sitting shall be provided and maintained for all workers, who work in standing position.
3. **First-Aid Appliances.** First-aid boxes or cup-boards equipped with the prescribed contents shall be provided and maintained so as to be readily accessible during all working hours. At least one such box shall be provided for every 150 workers.

   In every factory employing more than 500 workers, an ambulance room of the prescribed size with prescribed equipment shall be in the charge of medical and nursing staff.
4. **Canteens.** A canteen or canteens shall be provided in every factory wherein more than 250 workers are ordinarily employed.
5. **Shelter, Rest-rooms, Lunch-rooms.** In every factory where more than 150 workers are ordinarily employed, adequate and suitable shelter, rest rooms and lunch-rooms with provision of drinking water, where the workers can take the meals brought by them, shall be provided and maintained.
6. **Creches.** Every factory employing more than 30 female workers, shall provide and maintain a suitable room or rooms for the use of children under the age of 6 years of such women. Its incharge shall be a woman trained in this aspect.
7. **Welfare Facilities.** Welfare officers shall be employed in every factory employing more than 500 workers. The Government may prescribe the duties, the qualifications and conditions of service and number of such officers.

9.2.8. Working Hours

1. **Hours of Work.** No adult worker shall be required or allowed to work in factory for more than 48 hours in a week and for more than 9 hours in a day. No worker shall work for more than 5 hours before he has an interval of atleast half an hour. The period of work shall be so arranged that inclusive of rest intervals, it shall not spread over more than 10 1/2 hours in any day. Chief Inspector may, for reasons to be specified in writing, increase this spread-over time to 12 hours.
2. **Holidays.** No adult worker shall be required or allowed to work in a factory on Sunday, unless he has or will have a holiday for a whole day on one of the 3 days immediately before or after the Sunday. Thus no worker shall work for more than 10 days continuously without a holiday.
3. **Overtime Wages.** When a worker works for more than 9 hours in any day or for more than 48 hours in any week, he shall be entitled to wages at the rate of twice his ordinary rate of wages, in respect of overtime work. Here ordinary rate of wages means the basic wages plus such allowances as the worker is for the time being entitled to, but does not include a bonus.
4. **Restriction on double Employment.** No worker shall be required or allowed to work in any other factory.
5. **Employment of Women.** This provision provides a further restriction to female workers that no women shall be employed in any factory except between 6 A.M. and 7 P.M. State Government may vary this limit, but variation shall not authorise the employment of any woman between 10 P.M. and 5 A.M.

9.2.9. Employment of Young Persons

1. No child who has not completed his 14th year, shall be allowed to work in any factory.
2. A child who has completed his 14th year or an adolescence shall not be allowed to work unless a certificate of fitness is granted to him. This certificate shall be renewed every year.
3. An adolescent, who has been granted a certificate of fitness to work in a factory and who while at work in a factory carries a token giving reference to the certificate, shall be deemed to be an adult. Female-child shall not be permitted to work between 7 P.M. and 8 A.M.
4. No child shall be permitted to work for more than 4½ hours in a day and he will also not be allowed to work in the night.

9.2.10. Annual Leave with Wages

The Act provides a paid weekly holiday in a week. Besides the weekly holiday, every worker after completion of service of 240 days in a calendar year is entitled to get annual leave with wages in the subsequent year at the rate not less than :

(*a*) One day per 20 days of actual work for adults ;

(*b*) One day per 15 days of actual work for a child.

These are known as earned leaves, and can be accumulated upto 30 days in case of an adult and 40 days in case of a child.

For granting leave, the worker should apply 15 days before or immediately in case of illness. The Act further provides that the number of times for which leave may be taken during any year shall not exceed 3.

9.2.11. Dangerous Operations

If any operation carried on in the factory exposes any worker to a serious risk of bodily injury, poisoning or disease, the State Government may declare that operation to be dangerous and may ask for the provision of proper safeguard and if necessary, may prohibit or restrict the use of any material.

It also prohibits women, adolescent and children to be employed therein and to ask for the medical examination of workers employed.

9.2.12. Enforcing Authority

The State Governments, who administer and enforce this Act, may appoint a Chief Inspector and other officers for the purpose. An inspector may enter, alone or with assistants, the premises of a factory, may conduct examination of the premises, plant and machinery, require production of registers or other documents.

9.2.13. Accidents And Diseases

1. In a factory accident resulting in death or causing any bodily injury due to which the person induced is prevented from working for a period of 48 hours or more immediately following the accident, Manager of the factory shall send an intimation to the Factory Inspector within the prescribed time.
2. (*a*) Where any worker suffers from any disease specified in the schedule, the Manager of the factory shall send its intimation to Factory Inspector within the prescribed time.

   (*b*) If a medical practitioner attends to a person who has been employed in a factory and suffering from any disease specified in the schedule, he shall without delay send a report in writing to the Chief Inspector stating the name and address of the patient and the factory mentioning the name of disease.

9.2.14. Offences and Penalties

1. On any contravention of any of the provisions of this Act or any rules made thereunder or of any order in writing given thereunder, the occupier and the manager of the factory shall each be guilty of an offence, and punishable with imprisonment upto 2 years or with a fine upto Rupees one lakh or with both, if the contravention is continued after conviction, with a further fine upto Rs. 1000 per day.

   If he is again guilty of an offence involving in contravention of the same provision, he shall be punishable on a subsequent conviction with imprisonment upto 3 years or with fine from Rs 10,000 to Rs 2.0 lacs.
2. If any worker contravenes any provision of this Act or Rules or Orders made thereunder imposing any duty or liability on workers, he shall be punishable with fine upto Rs. 500.
3. If a child works in two factories on any day, his parent or guardian or the person having custody of or control over him or obtaining any direct benefit from his wages, shall be punishable with fine upto Rs. 1000.

9.2.15. Miscellaneous Provisions

1. **Appeals.** The manager of a factory on whom an order in writing has been served by Inspector under the provisions of this Act may within 30 days of the serving of the order, appeal against it to the prescribed authority.
2. **Obligations of Workers**
   (*a*) No worker in a factory :
      (*i*) Shall wilfully interfere with or misuse any appliance, convenience or other thing provided in a factory for the purpose of securing health, safety or welfare of the workers ;
      (*ii*) Shall wilfully and without reasonable cause do any thing likely to endanger himself or others :
      (*iii*) Shall wilfully neglect to make use of any appliance or other thing provided for the purposes of securing health or safety of the workers there in.
   (*b*) If any worker contravenes any of the provisions of this section or of any rule or order made thereunder, he shall be punishable with imprisonment upto 3 months or with line upto Rs. 100 or with both.

9.3. INDUSTRIAL DISPUTES ACT

9.3.1. Introduction

In the rapid, industrialisation scenerio, inter-personal relationships between employer and employee has changed, and direct contact between the employer and the employed has diminished. In these circumference, disputes and differences of opinion between the two need investigation and settlement by a third independent agency. And here government involvement is essential under the Industrial Disputes Act. The Industrial Disputes Act, 1947 is Government's effort to regulate industrial relations in India. It seeks to ensure progress of industry through harmony and coordial relations between employers and employees.

The objectives of the enactment of this Act are:-

(*i*) Promotion of measures for securing and preserving amity and good relations between employers and employees;
(*ii*) Investigation and settlement of industrial disputes between
   (*a*) employers and employers;
   (*b*) employers and employees; and
   (*c*) employees and employees;
(*iii*) Prevention of illegal strikes and lock-outs;
(*iv*) Payment of compensation to workmen in the event of Lay-off and Retrenchment; and
(*v*) Promotion and collective bargaining.

This Act thus ensures uninterrupted production and supply of services to society, and thereby contribute to growth and development of the national economy.

9.3.2. Definitions

This is an Act to make provision for the investigation and settlement of industrial disputes and for certain other purposes.

(*i*) *Average pay*. It is the average of the wages payable to the workmen :

(*a*) in 3 complete months for monthly paid workman ;

(*b*) in 4 complete weeks for weekly paid workman ;

(*c*) in 12 full working days for daily paid workman ;

preceding the date on which the average pay becomes payable. When the worker has worked for less than this period, then, the average pay is calculated as the average of the wages payable to a workman during the period he actually worked.

(*ii*) *Award*. "Award" means an interim or a final determination by any Labour Court, Industrial Tribunal or National Industrial Tibunal.

(*iii*) *Employer*. Employer means :

(*a*) in relation to an industry carried on by or under the authority of any department of the Central or State Government, the authority prescribed in this behalf or where no authority prescribed in this behalf or where no authority is prescribed, the head of the department.

(*b*) in relation to an industry carried on by or on behalf of a local authority, the chief executive officer of that authority.

(*iv*) *Industry*. "Industry" means any business, trade, undertaking, manufacturer or calling of employers. It includes any calling service, employment , handicraft or industrial occupation.

(*v*) *Industrial Dispute*. "Industrial Dispute" means any dispute or differences between ;

1. Employers and employers or
2. Employers and workman or
3. Workman and workman or which is connected with :

(*vi*) *Dismissal of Workers*. A worker dismissed after obtaining the written permission from the Regional Conciliation Officer by the employer does not validate the dismissal but only removes the ban on the right of the employer, his agent or manager to dismiss the worker, even then dismissal may be industrial dispute.

(*vii*) *Suspension of Workman*. A workman may be suspended pending enquiry and disciplinary action. If after enquiry misconduct is proved, the worker is dismissed and is not entitled to any wages of the suspension period. In case when a worker is fully exonerated after the enquiry, he would remain in service and would be entitled to his full wages of the suspension period.

(*viii*) *Closure*. In case of "Closure" employer closes the business, and thus closure means the final and irrevocable termination of the business itself.

(*ix*) *Lock-out*. "Lock-out" means (*a*) temporary closing of a place of employment, (*b*) suspension of work, or (*c*) refusal to continue to employ any number of persons employed. The lock-out indicates the closure of the place of business and not the closure of the business itself, as in "closure". Experience has shown the "Lock-out" is the weapon of employer to compel the employees to accept his proposals, just in the reply of the strike, the weapon of the employees, to compel the employer to accept their demands.

(*x*) *Retrenchment*. It is the termination of the service of a workman for any reason what so ever except as a punishment inflicted by way of disciplinary action. It does not involve retirement of worker or termination of the service of a worker on the ground of continued ill health.

(*xi*) *Settlement*. "Settlement" means a settlement, arrived at during the conciliation proceedings and includes a written agreement between the employer and workmen.

(*xii*) *Strike*. "Strike" is refusal under a common understanding of any number of workers to continue to work or to accept employment.

(*xiii*) *Workman*. "Workman" means any person (including an apprentice) employed in any industry to do any skilled or un-skilled, manual, supervisory, technical or electrical work for hire or reward.

9.3.3. Authorities Under the Act

(*a*) **Work Committees.** A Works Committee is constituted in any industrial establishment in which 100 or more workers are employed and have been employed on any in the preceding 12 months by an employer. This committee consists of representatives of employer and workers but the number of representatives of the employer should not be more than that of workers.

Main duty of Works Committee is to promote the measures for securing and preserving amity and good relations between the employers and workers.

(*b*) **Conciliation Officers.** Conciliation officers are appointed by the State Governments for the industries in a specified area permanently or for a limited period. Main duty of Conciliation officer is to mediate in the settlement of industrial disputes.

(*c*) **Board of Conciliation.** A Board of Conciliation is constituted by the State Government by notification in the Official Gazette. It consists of a Chairman and two or four other members. Chairman is an independent person and other members are persons appointed in equal numbers to represent the parties of the dispute. The duty of the board is to promote the settlement of an industrial dispute.

Power of the Board,

(*i*) A member of a board can enter the premises of the establishment for the purpose of enquiry into any industrial dispute after any reasonable notice.

(*ii*) Every Board has the same powers as vested as in a civil court.

(*iii*) Every enquiry by a Board is treated to be a judicial proceeding within the meaning of sections 193 and 228 of the Indian Penal Code.

(*d*) **Courts of Enquiry.** These courts of enquiry are also appointed by the State Government by notification in the Official Gazette, to inquire into any matter appearing to be connected with industrial dispute. After conducting the enquiry into the matters referred, they report to the Government within 6 months from the commencement of its enquiry.

(*e*) **Labour Courts.** State Governments constitute Labour Courts for the adjudication of industrial disputes for any matter specified in the second schedule.

The matters specified in the second schedule are :

(*i*) The legality of an order passed by an employer.

(*ii*) The application and interpretation of standing orders.

(*iii*) Discharge or dismissal of workers including reinstatement or, grants of relief to workmen wrongly dismissed.

(*iv*) Withdrawal of any customary privilege.

Labour court shall consist of one person only and who should have any of the following qualifications :

(*a*) he is, or has been a Judge of a High court, or

(*b*) he has been a District Judge for at least 3 years.

(f) **Industrial Tribunals.** State Governments may also constitute one or more Industrial Tribunals for the adjudication of industrial disputes. A tribunal shall consist of one person only to be appointed and he should have the minimum qualifications as required for that of labour courts.

The tribunal adjudicates of industrial disputes relating to any matter in the second schedule (jurisdiction of labour courts) or the third schedule. The third schedule mentions the following matters :

1. Wages, including the period and mode of payment.
2. Compensatory and other allowances.
3. Hours of work and rest intervals.
4. Leave with wages and holidays.
5. Bonus, profit-sharing, provident fund and gratuity.
6. Classification by grades.
7. Rules or discipline.
8. Rationalisation.
9. Retrenchment of workers and closure of establishment.

(g) **National Tribunals.** Central Government may constitute one or more National Industrial Tribunals for adjudication of industrial disputes involving question of national importance. It consists of only one person and who should have the qualifications as mentioned for that of Labour Courts. It can also take up the industrial disputes which are of such a nature that industrial establishments situated in more than one state are likely to be increased in or affected by such disputes.

No person can continue in the office of the presiding officer of a Labour Court, Tribunal or National Tribunal after he has attained the age of sixty five years.

9.3.4. Strikes and Lock–Outs

A strike or lockout is illegal in public utility services like railways, postal, telephone services, supplying power, light or water to public, transport for the carriage of goods or passengers or sanitation or any other industry specified in first schedule of the Act.

(a) **Strikes.** No person employed in a public utility service shall go on strike :

(i) without giving a notice of strike to the employer, within 6 weeks before striking; or

(ii) within 14 days of giving such notice ; or

(iii) before the date mentioned in the notice ; or

(iv) during the pendency of conciliation proceedings.

(b) **Lock–Outs.** No employer carrying on any public utility service shall lock out:

(i) without giving a notice of lock-out to the workers in a prescribed manner within 6 weeks before locking out;

(ii) within 14 days of giving such notice ;

(iii) before the date specified in the notice ;

(iv) during the pendency of any arbitrary conciliation proceedings.

A strike or lock-out in non-public utility services is illegal, if it is commenced

(i) during the pendency of conciliation proceedings and seven days after the conclusion of such proceedings; or (*ii*) during the pendency of proceedings before a labour court, tribunal or national tribunal or arbitrator, and two months after the conclusion of such proceedings; or

(*iii*) during the period of operation of a settlement of award.

Penalty of Illegal Strikes and Lock-Outs

Any worker, who commences or continues strike, which is illegal under this Act, shall be punishable with imprisonment upto one month or fine upto Rs. 1000 or both.

Any employer who commences, continues lockout, which is illegal under this act, shall be punishable with imprisonment upto one month or fine upto Rs. 1000 or both.

Penalty for Instigation. Any person who instigates other to take part in strike or lockout, which is illegal under this act, shall be punishable with imprisonment upto 6 months or a fine upto Rs. 1000 or both.

9.3.5. Lay-Off and Retrenchment

1. **Continuous Service.** As per section 25-B, a workman shall be deemed to be in continuous service under an employer, if during a period of twelve calender months preceding the date with reference to which calculation is to be made, actually worked for not less than :

   (*a*) 190 days in the case of a workman employed below the ground in a time ; and

   (*b*) 240 days in other cases.

   The number of days in which a workman has actually worked under an employer shall include the days on which :

   (*i*) he has been on leave with full wages earned in the previous years.

   (*ii*) he has been absent due to temporary disablement, caused by accident arising out of and in the course of his employment.

   (*iii*) in the case of a female, she has been on maternity leave upto 12 weeks.

2. **Lay-off.** "Lay-off" means the failure, refusal or inability of an employer on account of shortage of coal, power or raw materials of the accumulation of stock or the breakdown of machinery or for any other reasons to give employment to a workman and who has not been retrenched.

   (A) Right of Workmen laid off for Compensation

   (*i*) Whenever a workman who has completed more than one year of continuous service under an employer is laid off, he shall be paid by the employer for all days during which he is so laid off (for a maximum period of 45 days), compensation equal to 50% of the total of the basic wages and dearness allowance.

   Provided that if a person so laid off is retrenched, then the compensation paid to the workmen for having been laid off during the preceding 12 months may be set off against compensation payable for retrenchment.

   (B) Workmen not entitled to compensation in certain cases

   No compensation shall be payable to a workman who has been laid off in following conditions:

   (*i*) If he refuses to accept any alternative employment in the same establishment or in any other establishment belonging to the same employer situated within 5 miles (8 km) from the establishment to which he belongs.

(ii) If he does not present himself for work at the establishment at the appointed time during normal working hours at least once a day.

(iii) If such laying off is due to strike or slowing down of production on the part of workmen in another part of the establishment.

3. **Retrenchment.** As per section 25-F, no workman employed in an industry who had put in more than one year's continuous service under an employer shall be retrenched until:

   (i) The workman has been given one month's notice in writing indicating the reason for retrenchment and the period of notice has expired or the workman has been given in lieu of such notice, wages for the period of notice :
   Provided that no such notice shall be necessary if the retrenchment is under an agreement which specifies a date of the termination of service.

   (ii) The workman has been paid at the time of retrenchment, compensation which shall be equivalent to 15 day's average pay for every completed year of continuous service or any part thereof in excess of 6 months.

4. **Closure of an undertaking.** Where an undertaking is closed down for any reason whatsoever, every man who has completed the continuous service of at least one year in that undertaking is entitled to notice and compensation in accordance with the provisions of section 25-F (*i.e.*, as if the workman had been retrenched). This compensation shall be paid before such closure. He should also be served with a notice as mentioned earlier.

9.4. THE WORKMEN'S COMPENSATION ACT, 1923

9.4.1. Introduction

The growing complexity of industry in the country, with the increasing use of machinery and consequent danger to workmen, along with the comparative poverty of the workmen themselves, rendered it advisable that they should be protected, as far as possible from hardship arising from accidents.

An additional advantage of legislation of this type is that by increasing the importance for the employer of adequate safety devices, it reduces the number of accidents to workmen in a manner that cannot be achieved by official inspections.

It is an Act to provide for payment by certain classes of employers to their workmen of compensation for injury by accident. Thus this Act protects the workers, as far as possible, from hardship arising from accidents. The object of awarding compensation is to replace the actual loss suffered by the workmen. It came into force from 1st July, 1924.

9.4.2. Definitions

Following are some definitions given in this Act:

Dependent. Dependent means any of the following relatives of a deceased workman namely:

(i) a wife, a minor legitimate or adopted son, an unmarried legitimate or adopted daughter, or a widowed mother

(ii) if wholly or in part dependent on the earnings of the workman at the time of his death, a husband, a parent other than a widowed mother, a minor illegitimate son, and unmarried illegitimate daughter a daughter illegitimate or illegitimate of married and a minor or if widowed a minor brother, an unmarried or widowed sister, a widowed daughter-in-law, a minor child of deceased son.

Partial Disablement. This disablement is of temporary nature and the earning capacity is reduced due to disablement is of permanent nature. List of injuries resulting permanent partial disablement is given in Schedule I.

Total Disablement. It means such disablement whether of a temporary or permanent nature which incapacitates a workman from all work which he was capable of performing at the time of accident resulting in such disablement. Permanent total disablement shall be deemed to result from injuries where the aggregate percentage loss of earning capacity (as specified in Schedule I) amounts to one hundred percent or more.

Wages. It includes any privilege or benefit which is capable of being estimated in money other than a travelling allowance or any other contributions paid towards pension etc.

Workman. It means any person who is employed in any such capacity specified in Schedule II on monthly wages.

9.4.3. Employer's Liability for Compensation

If a personal injury is caused to a workman by accident arising out of and in the course of his employment, his employer shall be liable to pay compensation in accordance with the provisions of this Act.

Provided that the employer shall not be liable :

(*a*) in respect of any injury which disables the workman for a period less than three days;

(*b*) in respect of any injury not resulting in death caused by an accident which is directly attributed to :

- (*i*) the workman was under the influence of drink or drugs ;
- (*ii*) wilful disobedience of the Worker to an order issued for the purpose of securing safety of the worker ;
- (*iii*) wilful removal or disregard of any safety guard.

But if the worker dies of an accident due to the above reasons the employers have to pay compensation.

9.4.4. Amount of Compensation

(1) Subject to the provisions of this Act the amount of compensation shall be as follows namely:

(*a*) Where death results from the injury	an amount equal to fifty per cent of the monthly wages of the deceased workman multiplied by the relevant factor; or an amount of eighty thousand rupees whichever is more ;
(*b*) Where permanent total disablement results from the injury	an amount equal to sixty per cent of monthly wages of the injured workman multiplied by the relevant factor;

or

an amount of ninety thousand rupees ; whichever is more ;

Explanation I. For the purposes of clause (*a*) and clause (*b*) "relevant factor" in relation to a workman means the factor specified in the second column of Schedule IV against the entry in the first column of the schedule specifying the number of years which are the same as the completed years of the age of the workman on his last birthday immediately preceding the date on which the compensation fell due.

Explanation II. Where the monthly wages of a workman exceed four thousand rupees, his monthly wages for the purposes of clause (*a*) and clause (*b*) shall be deemed to be one thousand rupees only.

(*c*) **Where permanent partial disablement results from the injury.** (*i*) in the case of the injury specified in Part II of Schedule I, such percentage of the compensation which would have been payable in the case of permanent total disablement as is specified therein as being the percentage of the loss of earning capacity caused by that injury and (*ii*) in the case of an injury not specified in Schedule I ; such percentage of the compensa-tion payable in the case of permanent total disablement as in proportionate to the loss of earn-ing capacity (as assessed by the qualified medical practitioner) permanently caused by the injury.

Explanation I. Where more injuries than one are caused by the same accident, the amount of compensation payable under this head shall be aggregated but not so in any case as to exceed the amount which would have been payable if permanent total disablement had resulted from the injuries;

Explanation II. In assessing the loss of earning capacity for the purposes of sub-clause (*ii*) the qualified medical practitioner shall have due regard to the percentages of loss of earning capacity in relation to different injuries specified in Schedule I;

(*d*) **Where temporary disablement, whether total or partial, results from the injury** a half-monthly payment of the sum equivalent to twenty-five percent, of monthly wages of the workman to be paid in accordance with the provisions of sub-section 2.

2. The half-monthly payment referred to in clause (*d*) of subsection (1) shall be payable on the sixteenth day :
   (*i*) from the date, of disablement where such disablement lasts for a period of twenty-eight days or more ; or
   (*ii*) after the expiry of a waiting period of three days from the date of disablement where such disablement lasts for a period of less than twenty-eight days; and thereafter half-monthly during the disablement or during a period of five years whichever period is shorter :

Provided that:

(*a*) there shall be deducted from any lump sum or half monthly payments to which the workman is entitled the amount of any payment or allowance which the workman has received from the employer by way of compensation during the period of disablement prior to the receipt of such lump sum or of the first half-monthly payment, as the case may be; and

(b) no half-monthly payment shall in any case exceed the amount, if any, by which half the amount of the monthly wages of the workman before the accident exceeds half the amount of such wages which he is earning after the accident.

Explanation. Any payment or allowance which the workman has received from the employer towards his medical treatment shall not be a payment or allowance received by him by way of compensation within the meaning of clause (*a*) of the provision.

3. On the ceasing of the disablement before the date on which any half-monthly payment falls due there shall be payable in respect of that half-month a sum proportionate to the duration of the disablement in that half-month.

Compensation to be paid when due and penalty for default:

1. Compensation shall be paid as soon as it falls due.
2. In cases where the employer does not accept the liability for compensation to the extent claimed he shall be bound to make provisional payment based on the extent of liability which he accepts and such payment shall be deposited with the Commissioner or made to the workman, as the case may be, without prejudice to the right of the workman to make any further claim.
3. Where any employer is in default in paying the compensation due under this Act within one month from the date it fell due, the Commissioner may direct that, in addition to the amount of the arrears, simple interest at the rate of 12 percent per annum on the amount due together with, if in the opinion of the Commissioner, there is no justification for the delay, a further sum not exceeding fifty percent, of such amount, shall be recovered from the employer by way of penalty.

SCHEDULE I PART I

LIST OF INJURIES DEEMED TO RESULT IN PERMANENT TOTAL DISABLEMENT

Serial No.	*Description of Injury*	*Percentage of loss of earning capacity*
1.	Loss of both hands or amputation at higher sites	100
2.	Loss of a hand and a foot	100
3.	Double amputation through leg or thighs or amputation through leg or thigh on one side and loss of other foot	100
4.	Loss of sight to such extent as to render the claimant unable to perform any work for which eye-sight is essential	100
5.	Very severe facial disfigurement	100
6.	Absolute deafness	100

PART II

LIST OF INJUREES DEEMED TO RESULT IN PERMANENT PARTIAL DISABLEMENT

Serial No.	*Description of Injury*	*Percentage of loss of earning capacity*
	Amputation cases—Upper limbs (either arm)	
1.	Amputation through shoulder joint	... 90
2.	Amputation below shoulder with stump less than (20.32 cms) from tip of acromion	... 80
3.	Amputation from (20.32 cms) from tip of acromion to less than 11.43 cms below tip of olecranon	... 70
4.	Loss of a hand or of thumb and four fingers of one hand or amputation 11.43 cms below tip of olecranon	... 60
5.	Loss of thumb	... 30
6.	Loss of thumb and its metacarpal bone	... 40
7.	Loss of four fingers of one hand	... 50
8.	Loss of three fingers of one hand	... 30
9.	Loss of two fingers of one hand	... 20
10.	Loss of terminal phalanx of thumb	... 20
	Amputation cases—Upper limbs (either arm)	
11.	Amputation of both feet-resulting in end-bearing stumps	... 90
12.	Amputation through both feet proximal to the metatarsopha-langeal joint	... 80
13.	Loss of all toes of both feet through the metatarsophalangeal joint	... 40
14.	Loss of all toes of both feet proximal to the proximal interphalangeal Joint	... 30
15.	Loss of all toes of both feet distal to the proximal interphal-angeal joint	... 20
16.	Amputation at hip	... 90
17.	Amputation below hip with stump exceeding 12.70 cms in length measured from tip of great trenchanter	... 80
18.	Amputation below hip with stump exceeding 12.70 cms in length measured from tip of greatstrenchanter but not beyond middle thigh	... 70
19.	Amputation below middle thigh to 8.89 cms below knee	... 60

20.	Amputation below knee with stump exceeding 8.89 cms but not exceeding 12.70 cms	...	50
21.	Amputation below knee with stump exceeding 12.70 cms	...	40
22.	Amputation of one foot resulting in end bearing	...	30
23.	Amputation through one foot proximal to the metatarsopha langeal joint	...	30
24.	Loss of all toes of one foot through the metatarsophalangeal joint	...	20
	Other Injuries		
25.	Loss of one eye, without complication, the other being normal	...	40
26.	Loss of vision of one eye, without complications disfigurement of eye-ball, the other being normal	...	20
26A.	Loss of partial vision of one eye	...	10
	A. Fingers of right or left hand: Index Finger		
27.	Whole Index finger	...	14
28.	Two phalanges	...	11
29.	One Phalanx	...	9
30.	Guillotine amputation of tips without loss of bone	...	5
	Middle finger		
31.	Whole	...	12
32.	Two phalanges	...	9
33.	One phalanx	...	7
34.	Guillotine amputation of tip without loss of bone	...	4
	Ring or little finger		
35.	Whole	...	7
36.	Two phalanges	...	6
37.	One phalanx	...	5
38.	Guillotine amputation of tip without loss of bone	...	2
	B. Toe of right or left foot: Great toe		
39.	Through metatarsophalangeal joint	...	14
40.	Part, with some loss of bone	...	3
	Any other toe		
41.	Through metatarsophalageal joint	...	3
42.	Part, with some loss of bone	...	1
	Two toes of one foot (excluding great one)		
43.	Through metatarsophalangeal joint	...	5
44.	Part, with some loss of bone	...	2
	Three toes of one foot, excluding great one		
45.	Through metatarsophalangeal joint	...	9
46.	Part, with some loss of bone	...	3
	Four toes of one foot excluding great toe		
47.	Through metatarsophalageal joint	...	9
48.	Part, with some loss of bone	...	3

Note : Complete and permanent loss of the use of any limb or member referred to in this. Schedule shall be deemed to be the equivalent of the loss of that limb or member.

SCHEDULE IV

Factors for working out lump sum equivalent of compensation amount in case of permanent disablement and death:

Completed years of age on the last birthday of the workman immediately preceding the Factors date on which the compensation fell due

1		2
Not more than	16...	228.54
	17...	227.49
	18...	226.38
	19...	225.22
	20...	224.00
	21...	222.71
	22...	221.37
	23...	219.95
	24...	218.47
	25...	216.91
	26...	215.28
	27...	213.57
	28...	211.79
	29...	209.92
	30...	207.98
	31...	205.95
	32...	203.85
	33...	201.66
	34...	199.40
	35...	197.06
	36...	194.64
	37...	192.14
	38...	189.56
	39...	186.90
	40...	184.17
	41...	181.37
	42...	178.49
	43...	175.54
	44...	172.52
	45...	169.44

46...	...	...	...	...	166.29
47...	...	...	...	...	163.07
48...	...	...	...	...	159.80
49...	...	...	...	...	156.47
50...	...	...	...	...	153.09
51...	...	...	...	...	149.67
52...	....	...	...	...	146.20
53...	...	...	...	...	142.68
54...	...	...	...	...	139.13
55...	...	...	...	...	135.56
56...	...	...	...	...	131.95
57...	...	...	...	...	128.33
58...	...	...	...	...	124.70
59...	...	...	...	...	121.05
60...	...	...	...	...	117.41
61...	...	...	...	...	113.77
62...	...	...	...	...	110.14
63...	...	...	...	...	106.52
64...	...	...	...	...	102.93
65...or more	...	...	...	...	99.37

9.4.5. Notice of Accident

The worker who suffers an injury, however small it may be, should bring it to the notice of employer either personally or through some responsible person.

Every such notice shall give the name and address of the person injured and shall state the cause of the injury together with the date and should be served to the employer or representative of employer.

9.4.6. Medical Examination

The worker who has given notice of an accident must present himself for the medical examination if employer offers such examination free of charge by a qualified medical practitioner.

If the worker refuses for medical examination and other medical aid (free of charge and by qualified medical practitioner) and that such refusal failure or disregard is found to be unreasonable in the circumstances of the case and the injury resulted disablement, then he shall not have the right for compensation of the disablement. .

9.4.7. Distribution of Compensation

No payment of compensation in respect of workman whose injury has resulted in death and no payment of lump sum as a compensation to a woman or a person under a legal disability, shall be made except through commissioner. If any employer has made the payment directly, it shall not be considered to be a payment of compensation.

However in the case of diseased workman, an employer may make an advance up to 3 months wages to the dependents of the diseased worker for meeting the immediate expenses. This advance shall be deducted by the commissioner from the amount of compensation and repaid to the employer.

9.4.8. Occupational Diseases

If a worker suffers any of the specified occupational disease, (the list of which is given in Schedule III of the Act) and he has worked in factory for at least six months, the employer has to pay compensation. Some of the occupational diseases are compressed air illness, poisoning by lead, phosphorus, mercury, benzene arsenic, radium and other radioactive substances X-rays etc.

9.4.9. Commissioner

State government may, by notification in official gazette, appoint any person for workmen's compensation for a specified area. Commissioner has all the powers of a civil court.

9.5. THE PAYMENT OF WAGES ACT, 1936

9.5.1. Introduction

The Act regulates the payment of wages to certain classes of persons employed in industry. Under the Act, the State Government can extend the provisions of this act to the payment of wages to any class of persons in any industrial establishment. The object of this Act is to ensure timely payment of wages to employed persons without unauthorised deductions.

9.5.2. Definitions

1. "Industrial Establishment" means any :
   - (*a*) Tramway service or motor transport service.
   - (*b*) Air transport service excluding services for defence or Civil Aviation department.
   - (*c*) Dock, wharf or jetty, inland vessels
   - (*d*) Mine, quarry or oil field.
   - (*e*) Plantation .
   - (*f*) Workshop, where articles are produced with a view to their use, transport or sale.
   - (*g*) Establishment, where construction development or maintenance of buildings, roads, bridges or canals or of water or where work relating to the generation, transmission and distribution of electricity is being carried out.
2. "Wages means all remuneration expressed in terms of money payable to persons, while in employment and includes :
   - (*i*) Basic wages.
   - (*ii*) Dearness Allowance.
   - (*iii*) Bonus.
   - (*iv*) Payments under any award or settlement between the parties or order of a court.

(*v*) Overtime allowance.

(*vi*) Leave salary.

It will not include :

(*i*) The value of any house accommodation, supply of light, water, medical facilities and other amenities of life specified by the State Government.

(*ii*) Travelling Allowances.

(*iii*) Employer's contribution to pension or Provident Fund.

(*iv*) Gratuity

(*v*) Bonus etc.

9.5.3. Methods of Payment of Wages

1. **Responsibility for Payment of Wages.** Every employer shall be responsible for the payment to persons employed by him, of all wages required to be paid under this Act. Provided that, in the case of persons employed otherwise than by the contractor.

   (*a*) in factories, if a person has been named as manager of the factory ;

   (*b*) in industrial establishment, if there is a person responsible to the employer for the supervision and control of the industrial establishment;

   (*c*) upon railways, railway administration has nominated a person in this behalf for the local area concerned.

   The person so named, the person so responsible to the employer, shall also be responsible for such payment.

2. **Fixation of Wages Period.** Wages period shall be fixed by the person responsible for **the payment of wages** (as shown above) but this wage period will not be more than **one month.**

3. **Time of Payment of Wages**

   (*a*) Any railways, factory or industrial establishment employing less than 1000 persons must make payment of wages before the expiry of the 7th day after the last day of the wage period.

   (*b*) If there are 1000 or more persons employed, then wages must be paid before the expiry of the 10th day after the last day of the wages period.

   (*c*) Where the employment of any person is terminated, the wages earned by him shall be paid before the expiry of the second working day from the day on which his employment is terminated.

   (*d*) Wages must be paid in current coin and currency notes and not in kind.

4. **Maintenance of Register and Record,**

   (*a*) Every employer shall maintain such registers and records giving such particulars of persons employed, work performed, the wages paid, the deductions made, the receipts given by them and such other particulars and in such forms as may be prescribed.

   (*b*) Every register and record is required to be preserved for a period of 3 years after the date of last entry made therein.

9.5.4. Deductions

1. Every payment made by the employed person to the employer or his agent shall be deemed to be a deduction from wages.
2. Any loss of wages resulting from the imposition, for good and sufficient cause, upto a person employed, of the following penalties, shall not be deemed to be deduction from
   - (*a*) With-holding of increment or promotion (including stoppage of increment at an efficiency bar).
   - (*b*) Reduction to a lower post or to a lower stage,
   - (*c*) Suspension.
3. The wages of an employed person shall be paid to him without deductions of any kind except those authorised by this Act. Following deductions from the wages are permitted by this Act:
   - (*i*) Fines.
   - (*ii*) Deductions for absence from duty.
   - (*iii*) Deductions for damage to or loss of goods expressly entrusted to the employed persons, where such damage or loss is directly attributed to his neglect or default.
   - (*iv*) Deductions for the house accommodation supplied to him.
   - (*v*) Deductions for which amenities and services (not includes the supply of tools and raw material required for the purpose of employment) supplied by the employer.
   - (*vi*) Deductions for recovery of advances of loans (including over payments).
   - (*vii*) Deductions of income-tax, contribution of provident funds, payments to co-operative societies.

9.5.5. Fines

1. No fine shall be imposed on any employed person on any of the acts and omissions which are liable to fine are got approved previously from the State Government or from the prescribed authority.
2. A notice specifying such acts and omissions shall be exhibited in the prescribed manner in the premises on which the employment is carried on.
3. No fine shall be imposed until he has been given an opportunity of showing cause against the fine.
4. The total amount of fine which may be imposed in any one wage period shall not exceed an amount equal to three percent of the wages payable to him.
5. No fine shall be imposed on any employed person who is under the age of fifteen years.
6. Every fine shall be deemed to have been imposed on the day of the act or omission.
7. The recovery of all fines must be entered in a prescribed register to the credit of Fines Fund. The money of the fines fund can be used only for the benefits of the workers subject to the approval of the prescribed authority.

9.5.6 Violation of The Act

1. The administration of this Act is the responsibility of the State Government and is exercised by Factory Inspectors.

2. State Government may appoint a presiding officer of any Labour Court or Industrial Tribunal, constituted under the Industrial Disputes Act, 1937 or any commissioner for workmen's compensation or other officer to hear and decide for any specified area all claims arising out of deductions from the wages, or delay in the payment of wages.
3. Penalty for different provisions may vary from Rs. 1500 to Rs. 7500.
4. Penalty for wilfully obstructing or neglecting the Inspector varies from Rs. 1500 to Rs. 7500.
5. An appeal against the order of the authority can be made within 30 days of the date on which the order or direction was made before the court of Small Causes or before the District Court.
6. Whosoever being required to maintain any records or register or to furnish any information or return :
   - (*a*) fails to maintain such register or record; or
   - (*b*) wilfully refuses or neglects to furnish such information or return: or
   - (*c*) willly refuses to furnish information; or
   - (*d*) refuses to answer or wilfully give a false answer to any questions necessary for obtaining any information required to be furnished under this Act; shall for each such offence, be punishable with a fine between Rs. 1500 to Rs. 7500.
7. Whoever:
   - (a) wilfully obstructs an Inspector in the discharge of his duties under this Act; or
   - (b) refuses or wilfully neglects any reasonable facility for making any entry, inspection, examination, supervision or enquiry authorised by or under this Act; shall be punishable with fine which may extend to Rs. 7500.
8. If any person who has been convicted of any offence punishable under this Act is again guilty of an offence involving contravention of the same provision, he shall be punishable on a subsequent conviction with imprisonment for a term not less than 1 month, but which may extend to 6 months and with a fine not less than Rs 3750 but which may extend to Rs. 22500.

9.6. THE MINIMUM WAGES ACT, 1948

9.6.1. Introduction

The concept of minimum wages first evolved with reference to remuneration of workers in those industries where the level of wages was substantially low as compared to the wages for similar types of labour in other industries. As far back as 1928, the International Labour Conference of International Labour Organisation, at Geneva adopted a draft convention on minimum rates of wages can be fixed for workers employed in industries in which no arrangements exist for the effective regulation of wages and where wages are exceptionally low. The need of a legislation for fixation of minimum wages in India received an impetus and Bill to provide for machinery for fixing and periodical revising of minimum wages was prepared and discussed at the 7th session of the Indian Labour Conference in November, 1945. It was introduced in the Central Legislative Assembly on 11th April, 1946.

The justification for statutory fixation of minimum wage is obvious. Such provisions which exist in more advanced countries are even necessary in India, where workers organizations are yet poorly developed and the workers bargaining power is consequently poor. Thus, the object of this Act is doing social justice to workmen, especially those employed in unorganised employments, in order to protect them from exploitation by capitalist classes.

The Bill provides for fixation by the Provincial Governments of minimum wages for employments covered by Schedule to the Bill. The items in the Schedule are those where there is a big chance of exploitation of labour. After sometime, when some experience is gained, more categories of employment can be added and the Bill provides for addition to the Schedule. A higher period is allowed for fixation of minimum wages for agricultural labour as administrative difficulties in this case will be more than in other employments covered by the Schedule. The Bill provides for periodical revision of wages fixed.

In cases where an employer pays less than the minimum wages fixed by the Provincial Government a summary procedure has been provided for recovery of the balance with penalty and subsequent prosecution of the offending party.

9.6.2. Important Provisons of The Act

1. **Interpretation.** In this Act, unless there is anything repugnant in the subject or context,—

(*a*) "adolescent" means a person who has completed his fourteenth year of age but has not completed his eighteenth year;

(*aa*) "adult" means a person who has completed his eighteenth year of age;

(*b*) "appropriate government" means:

(*i*) in relation to any scheduled employment carried on by or under the authority of the Central Government or a railway administration or in relation to a mine, oil field or major port, or any corporation established by a Central Act, the Central Government, and

(*ii*) in relation to any other scheduled employment, the State Government;

(*bb*) "child" means a person who has not completed his fourteenth year of age

(*e*) "competent authority" means the authority appointed by the appropriate Government by notification in its Official Gazette to ascertain from time to time the cost of living index number applicable to the employees employed in the schedule employments specified in such notification;

(*d*) "employer" means any person who employs, whether directly or through another person, or whether on behalf of himself or any other person, one or more employees in any scheduled employment in respect of which minimum rates of wages have been fixed under this Act, and includes,

(*i*) in a factory where there is carried on any scheduled employment in respect of which minimum rates of wages have been fixed under this Act, any person named as manager of the factory ;

(*ii*) in any scheduled employment under the control of any Government in India in respect of which minimum rates of wages have been fixed under this Act, the person or authority appointed by such Government for the supervision and control of employees or where no person or authority is so appointed, the head of the department.

(*iii*) in any scheduled employment under any local authority in respect of which minimum rates of wages have been fixed under this Act, the person appointed by such authority for the supervision and control of employees or where no person is so appointed, the chief executive officer of the local authority;

(*iv*) in any other case where there is carried on any scheduled employment in respect of which minimum rates of wages have been fixed under this Act, any person responsible to the owner for the supervision and control of the employees or for the payment of wages ;

(*e*) "scheduled employment" means an employment specified in the Schedule, or any process or branch of work forming part of such employment;

(*f*) "wages" means all remuneration, capable of being expressed in terms of money, which would, if the terms of the contract of employment, express or implied, were fulfilled, be payable to a person employed in respect of his employment or of work done in such employment [and includes house rent allowance], but does not include—

(*i*) the value of

(*a*) any house accommodation, supply of light, water, medical attendance, or

(*b*) any other amenity or any service excluded general or special order of the appropriate Government;

(*ii*) any contribution paid by the employer to any Pension Fund or Provident Fund or under any scheme of social insurance;

(*iii*) any travelling allowance or the value of any travelling concession;

(*iv*) any sum paid to the person employed to defray special expenses entailed on him by the nature of his employment; or

(*v*) any gratuity payable on discharge;

(*g*) "employee" means any person who is employed for hire or reward to do any work, skilled or unskilled, manual or clerical, in a scheduled employment in respect of which minimum rates of wages have been fixed; and includes an out-worker to whom any articles or materials are given out by another person to be made up, cleaned, washed, altered, ornamented, finished, repaired, adapted or otherwise processed for sale for the purposes of the trade or business of that other person where the process is to be carried out either in the home of the out-worker or in some other premises not being premises under the control and management of that other person; and also includes an employee, declared to by employee by the appropriate Government; but doe s not include any member of the Armed Forces of the Union.

2. **Fixing of minimum rates of wages.** 1. The appropriate Government shall, in the manner hereinafter provided,-

(*a*) fix the minimum rates of wages payable to employees employed in.an employment specified in Part I or Part II of the Schedule and in an employment added to either Part by notification :

Provided that the appropriate Government may, in respect of employees employed in an employment specified in Part II of the Schedule, instead of fixing minimum rates of wages under this clause for the whole State, fix sach rates for a part of the State or for any specified class or classes of such employment in the whole State or part thereof;

(*b*) review at such intervals, as it may think fit, such intervals not exceeding five years, the minimum rates of wages so fixed and revise the minimum rates, if necessary.

(1A) Notwithstanding anything contained in sub-section (1), the appropriate Government may refrain from fixing minimum rates of wages in respect of any scheduled employment in which there are in the whole State less than one thousand employees engaged in such employment, but if at any time, the appropriate Government comes to a finding after such inquiry, as it may make or cause to be made in this behalf, that the number of employees in any scheduled employment in respect of which it has refrained from fixing minimum rates of wages has risen to one thousand or more, it shall fix minimum rates of wages payable to employees in such employment as soon as may be after such finding.

2. The appropriate Government may fix—
   (*a*) a minimum rate of wages for time work (hereinafter referred to as 'a minimum time rate');
   (*b*) a minimum rate of wages for piece work (hereinafter referred to as 'a minimum piece rate');
   (*c*) a minimum rate of remuneration to apply in the case of employees employed on piece work for the purpose of securing to such employees a minimum rate of wages on a time work basis (hereinafter referred to as 'a guaranteed time rate');
   (*d*) a minimum rate (whether a time rate or a piece rate) to apply in substitution for the minimum rate which would otherwise be applicable, in respect of overtime work done by employees (hereinafter referred to as 'overtime rate').
3. In fixing or revising minimum rates of wages under this section—
   (*a*) different minimum rates of wages may be fixed for—
   (*i*) different scheduled employments ;
   (*ii*) different classes of work in the same scheduled employments
   (*iii*) adults, adolescents, children and apprentices ;
   (*iv*) different localities;
   (*b*) minimum rates of wages may be fixed by any one or more following wage-periods, namely:—
   (*i*) by the hour,
   (*ii*) by the day,
   (*iii*) by the month, or
   (*iv*) by such other larger wage-period as may be prescribed, and where such rates are fixed by the day or by the month, the manner of calculating wages for a month or for a day, as the case may be, may be indicated :"

3. Minimum rates of wages. Any minimum rate of wages fixed or revised by the appropriate Government in respect of scheduled employments may consist of—
   (*i*) a basic rate of wages and a special allowance at a rate to be adjusted, at such intervals and in such manner as the appropriate Government may direct, to accord as nearly as practicable with the variation in the cost of living index number applicable to such workers (hereinafter referred to as the 'cost of living allowance'); or
   (*ii*) a basic rate of wages with or without the cost of living allowance, and the cash value of the concessions in respect of supplies of essential commodities at concession rates, where so authorised; or
   (*iii*) an all-inclusive rate allowing for the basic rate, the cost of living allowance and the cash value of the concessions, if any.

4. Procedure for fixing and revising minimum wages.
   (1) In fixing minimum rates of wages in respect of any scheduled employment for the first time under this Act or in revising minimum rates of wages so fixed, the appropriate Government shall either.

(*a*) appoint as many committees and sub-committees as it considers necessary to hold enquiries and advise it in respect of such fixation or revision, as the case may be, or

(*b*) by notification in the Offical Gazette, publish its proposal for the information of persons likely to be affected thereby and specify a date, not less than two months from the date of the notification, on which the proposals will be taken into consideration.

(2) After considering the advice of the committee or committees apppointed under clause (*a*) of sub-section 1, or as the case may be, all representations received by it before the date specified in the notification under clause (*b*) of that sub-section, the appropriate Government shall, by notification in the Official Gazette, fix, or, as the case may be, revise the minimum rates of wages in respect of each scheduled employment, and unless such notification otherwise provides, it shall come into force on the expiry of three months from the date of its issue.

5. **Advisory Board.** For the purpose of co-ordinating the work of committees and sub-committees and advising the appropriate Government generally in the matter of fixing and revising minimum rates of wages, the appropriate Government shall appoint an Advisory Board.

6. **Central Advisory Board.**

(1) For the purpose of advising the Central and State Governments in the matters of the fixation and revision of minimum rates of wages and other matters under this Act and for co-ordinating the work of the Advisory Board, the Central Government shall appoint a Central Advisory Board.

(2) The Central Advisory Board shall consist of persons to be nominated by the Central Government representing employers and employees in the scheduled employments, who shall be equal in number, and independent persons not exceeding one-third of its total number of members; one of such independent persons shall be appointed the Chairman by the appropriate Government.

7. **Composition of Committees, etc.** Each of the committees, sub-committees and the Advisory Board shall consist of persons to be nominated by the appropriate Government representing employers and employees in the scheduled employments, who shall be equal in number, and independent persons not exceeding one third of its total number of members; one of such independent person shall be appointed the Chairman by the appropriate Government.

8. **Fixing hours for normal working day, etc.**

(1) In regard to any scheduled employment minimum rates of wages in respect of which have been fixed under this Act, the appropriate Government may—

(*a*) fix the number of hours of work which shall constitute a normal working day, inclusive of one or more specified intervals;

(*b*) provide for a day of rest in every period of seven days which shall be allowed to all employees or to any specified class of employees and for the payment of remuneration in respect of such days of rest;

(*c*) provide for payment for work on a day of rest at a rate not less than the overtime rate.

(2) The provisions of sub-section (1) shall, in relation to the following classes of employees, apply only to such extent and subject to such conditions as may be presecribed :

(*a*) employees engaged on urgent work, or in any emergency which could not have been foreseen or prevented;

(*b*) employees engaged in work in the nature of preparatory or complementary work which must necessarily be carried on outside the limits laid down for the general working in the employment concerned;

(*c*) employees whose employment is essentially intermittent;

(*d*) employees engaged in any work which for technical reasons has to be completed before the duty is over;

(*e*) employees engaged in work which could not be carried on except at times dependent on the irregular action of natural forces.

(3) For the purposes of clause (*a*) of sub-section 2, employment of an employee is essentially intermittent when it is declared to be so by the appropriate Government on the ground that the daily hours of duty of the employee, or if there be no daily hours of duty as such for the employee, the hours of duty, normally include periods of inaction during which the employee may be on duty but is not called upon to display either physical activity or sustained attention.

9. **Wages of worker who works for less than normal working day.** If an employee whose minimum rate of wages has been fixed under this Act by day works on any day on which he was employed for a period of less than the requisite number of hours constituting a normal working day, he shall, save as otherwise hereinafter provided, be entitled to receive wages in respect of work done by him on that day as if he had worked for a full normal working day :

Provided, however, that he shall not be entitled to receive wages for a full normal working day

(*i*) in any case where his failure to work is caused by his unwillingness to work and not by the omission of the employer to provide him with work, and

(*ii*) in such other cases and circumstances as may be prescribed.

10. **Wages for two or more classes of work.** Where an employee does two or more classes of work to each of which a different minimum rate of wages is applicable, the employer shall pay to such employee in respect of the time respectively occupied in each such class of work, wages at not less than the minimum rate in force in respect of each such class.

11. **Minimum time rate wages for piece work.** Where an employee is employed on piece work for which minimum time rate and not a minimum piece rate has been fixed under this Act, the employer shall pay to such employee wages at not less than the minimum time rate.

12. **Maintenance of registers and records.**

(1) Every employer shall maintain such registers and records giving such particulars of employees employed by him, the work performed by them, the wages paid to them, the receipts given by them and such other particulars and in such form as may be prescribed.

(2) Every employer shall keep exhibited, in such manner as may be prescribed, in the factory, workshop or place where the employees in the scheduled employment may be employed, or in the case of out-workers, in such factory, workshop or place as may be used for giving out work to them, notices in the prescribed form containing prescribed particulars.

(3) The appropriate Government may, by rules made under this Act, provide for the issue of wage books or wage slips to employees employed in any scheduled employment in respect of which minimum rates of wages have been fixed and prescribed, the manner in which entries shall be made and authenticated in such wage books or wage slips by the employer or his agent.

13. Penalties for certain offences. **Any employer who—**

(*a*) pays to any employee less than the minimum rates of wages fixed for that employee's class of work, or less than the amount due to him under the provisions of this Act; or

(*b*) contravenes any rule or order made regarding fixing of hours of work, shall be punishable with imprisonment for a term which may extend to six months, or with fine which may extend to five hundred rupees, or with both:

Provided that in imposing any fine for an offence under this section, the court shall take into consideration the amount of any compensation already awarded against the accused in any proceedings.

14. Exemption of employer from liability in certain cases. Where an employer is charged with an offence against this Act, he shall be entitled, upon complaint duly made by him, to have any other person whom he charges as the actual offender, brought before the court at the time appointed for hearing the charge; and if, after the commission of the offence has been proved, the employer proves to the satisfaction of the court—

(*a*) that he has used due diligence to enforce the execution of this Act; and

(*b*) that the said other person committed the offence in question without his knowledge, consent or connivance, that other person shall be convicted of the offence and shall be liable to the like punishment as if he were the employer and the employer shall be discharged:

Provided that in seeking to prove, as aforesaid, the employer may be examined on oath, and the evidence of the employer or his witness, if any, shall be subject to cross examination by or on behalf of the person whom the employer charges as the actual offender and by the prosecution.

QUESTIONS

1. Define the following as per Factories Act:
   - (*a*) Manufacturing Process
   - (*b*) Adolescent
   - (*c*) Worker
   - (*d*) Week
   - (*e*) Factory
   - (*f*) Occupier.
2. What is a factory? How can it be registered ?
3. What are different health provisions mentioned in the Factories Act ?
4. Explain the importance of the safety provisions in the Factories Act. Explain them regarding fencing of machinery, hoists, lifts and fire.
5. What are the welfare provisions under Factories Act? Explain, how it will affect the productivity.
6. Write short notes on :
   - (*a*) Hours of work for adults, women and young persons ;

   (*b*) Annual leave with wages ;
   (*c*) Penalties on the workers.
7. With reference to the provisions of the Factories Act, 1948, discuss:
   (*a*) Power Press-Safety measures to be taken while working.
   (*b*) Transmission machinery such as driving belts, gears, pulleys flywheels and shafts-Safety measures to be taken while they are in motion.
   (*c*) Dust and fumes injurious to health—measures to be taken to safeguard the health of the workers.
8. Factories Act helps productivity—Justfy the statement with reference to relevant provisions of the Factories Act.
9. Define the following terms of Factories Act,
   (*a*) Factory
   (*b*) Worker
   (*c*) Manufacturing processes
10. Discuss the role of "Inspector of Factories" under the provisions of 'Factories Act'.
11. Write down the aims of Industrial disputes Act.
12. What is an industrial dispute ?
13. Suppose you want to retrench a workman, explain the procedure which you would like to adopt.
14. Explain the following terms :
   (*a*) Wages
   (*b*) Employer
   (*c*) Industry
   (*d*) Average pay,
15. Differentiate between "closure" and "lock-out". What steps are necessary at the time of closure of an industry?
16. Explain the functions of different authorities under the Industrial Disputes Act.
17. What is the difference between "strike" and "lock-out" and what are the penalties for illegal "strikes" and "lock-outs" and for instigating them?
18. Write an essay on Industrial Disputes Act.
19. What are the obligations of employers under the Industrial Disputes Act. 1947 ?
20. (*a*) Describe the composition of the "Works Committee".
   (*b*) Write short note on "Industrial Tribunal".
21. Explain the implications of "lock-out" and "strike" under the Industrial Disputes Act. What amendments of the rules would you suggest, in view of the present labour crisis?
22. To what extent does the Industrial Disputes Act provide for settlement of disputes between management and Industrial Workers? Discuss.
23. What is collective bargaining? Discuss in detail its impact on the employee-employer relations in the industry.
24. Explain the purpose of "Workmen's Compenstion Act". Where is it applicable?
25. Give complete procedure for payment of compensation to the workers.
26. Write short notes on the following.
   (*a*) Occupational diseases.
   (*b*) Partial and total disablement of workman.
27. What are the employer's liabilities for compensation under the "Workmen's Compensation Act"?

28. What is the aim of "Payment of Wages Act"? Which interest of the workers are safeguarded by this Act?
29. Define the terms according to the "Payment of Wages Act".
    (*a*) Industrial Establishment
    (*b*) Wages
    (*c*) Fines
    (*d*) Deduction
    (*e*) Time period of payment of ways
30. What are the penalties for the violation of different provision under the "Payment of Wages Act"?
31. What are the permissible deductions from the wages under "Payment of Wages Act".
32. What is the concept of 'Minimum Wages'?
33. How minimum wages are fixed under the 'Minimum Wages Act'?
34. What is the procedure adopted for fixing or revising the minimum Wages?
35. What elements are included in the term wages as per minimum Wages Act?
36. What is the penalty for defaulting employer, under Minimum Wages Act?

Part-3 Work Study

10 WORK–STUDY—1 (METHOD STUDY)

10.1. INTRODUCTION TO WORK STUDY (WORKANALYSIS)

Work study is a technique which deals with the problems :

(i) as to how should a job be done; and

(ii) how much time a job should take for completion?

Answer for the question, as to how a job should be done, is found by Motion Study (commonly known as Method Study) or some times termed as "Work Simplification". Answer for the second question is found by the Time Study (now-a-days termed as 'Work Measurement').

Object of Work Study is to determine the best method of performing each operation and to eliminate wastage so that production increases with less fatigue. The work study is also used in determining the standard time, that a qualified worker should take to perform the operation when working at a normal pace.

According to the British Standard Institution, "Work Study is a generic term for those techniques, particularly method study and work measurement, which are used in all its context, and which lead systematically to the investigation of all the factors, which affect the efficiency and economy of the situation being reviewed in order to effect improvement."

Productivity and Work Study

As we know that, productivity is nothing but the reduction in wastage of resources. The resources may be men, machines, material, power, space, time etc.

We have also seen from the definition of work study that it reduces wastage of time, effort, increases the efficiency of man and machine. Thus the work study techniques lead to increase in productivity.

According to V.K.R. Menon, productivity implies development of an attitude of mind and constant urge to find better, cheaper, easier, quicker and safer means of doing a job, manufacturing a product and providing service.

But we see that most of these objects can be achieved by different activities of work study. To improve the economic position of our country in comparison to other countries (for factories in particular), we must improve our productivity and performance.

In recent years, there had been regular pay increases, but we have forgotten that without improving the productivity, prices will be sky rocketing and we will lose competition in the world market. To compensate wage increase, we must increase the productivity.

To fight against inflation, we must increase the productivity. The battle fields of this fight are every place where resources (men, material, equipment, money, time, efforts etc.) are used. The factory and the agriculture are most important places where we must emphasise for productivity improvement. Other places like offices, hospitals, teaching institutions etc., also need productivity improvement if the society and the country is to move forward.

Thus, our aim must be to make people more productivity conscious, if we want to improve their standard of living. Productivity holds the key to the prosperity of the individual, a company and of a nation.

"Work Study is an organised continuous effort to improve productivity, quality and to reduce costs within an organisation". For this purpose, a work study engineer must continue to lead the way in "Resources utilization".

Advantages of Work Study

1. Higher productive efficiency.
2. Reduced manufacturing costs.
3. Higher profits.
4. Higher wages and bonus to workers.
5. Accurate delivery dates.
6. Better employer-employee relations.
7. Job satisfaction to workers.
8. Better working conditions.

Objectives Achieved Through Work Study

1. Improvement in processes and standardisation in procedures.
2. Better working conditions and less fatigue.
3. Effective utilisation of resources.
4. Reduced health hazards.
5. Reduced accident risks.
6. Improvement in productivity.
7. Effective labour control.

10.2. POSITION OF WORK STUDY DEPARTMENT IN THE ORGANISATION

Work Study Department must be given a high position in the factory, so that the persons working in the department may not be influenced by the officers working on the floor and their suggestions should be accepted with respect and acted upon.

Work Study Department generally works as a part of the Industrial Engineering Department. Since the Industrial Engineering Department is for the service of the management of an enterprise, therefore, it must be a staff and not a line activity.

The position of the head of the Industrial Engineering Department in relation to his fellow members of the staff depends upon the following important factors :

(*i*) Size of the organisation.

(*ii*) Type of organisation and whether managed by the owner himself or by professionals.

(*iii*) Nature of work carried out in the factory.

(*iv*) Qualifications, experience and personality etc. of the Chief Industrial Engineer and those of other Departmental Heads.

Looking to the above factors there cannot be any standard chart for organizational structure.

A typical organisation chart showing the position of Industrial Engineering Department is given hereunder.

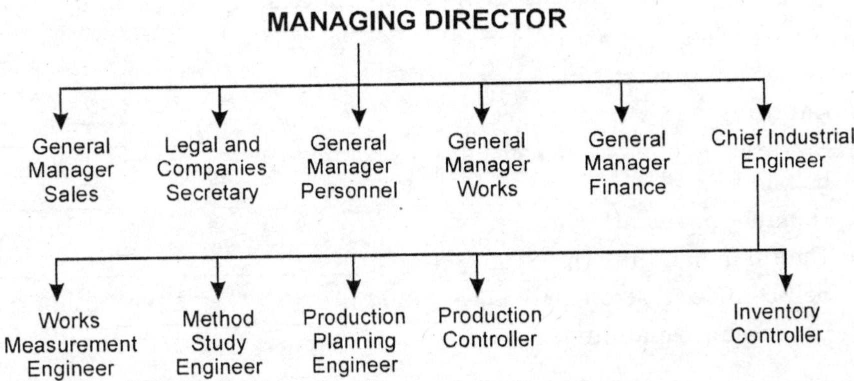

Some times Chief Industrial Engineer is given a place under General Manager Works. It is due to the reason that General Manager Works is responsible to increase the overall productivity and by putting the Industrial Engineering Department under him, he can give more importance to the suggestions or advices placed before him. In such case, the organisational structure will be similar to that shown below :

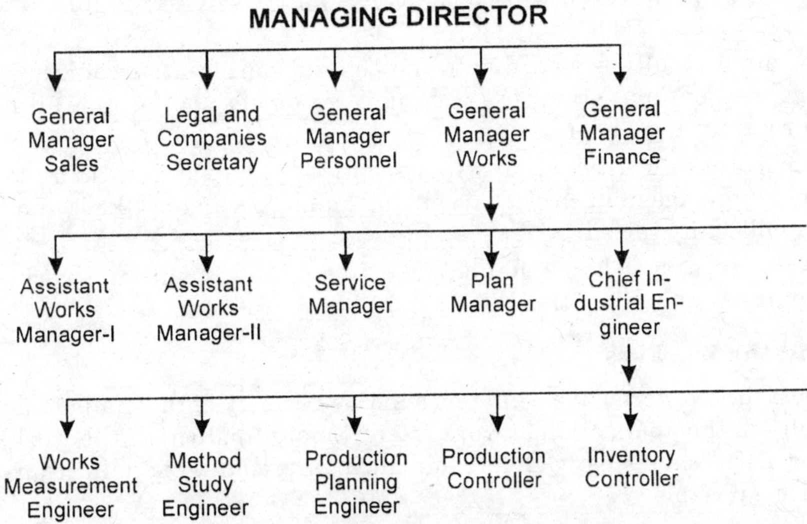

10.3. REQUIREMENTS FOR WORK STUDY (WORK ANALYSIS)

Certain qualities are expected from a work study man, however they vary from work to work. Here some of the requirements or qualities are explained.

Qualities of Work Study Man

(A) **Qualification abilities**

(*i*) Good knowledge of work study techniques.

(*ii*) Good knowledge of different manufacturing processes by which he is conducting the work study.

(*iii*) He must be well qualified and sufficiently trained.

(B) **Mental abilities**

(*i*) Mentally prepared and interested to do that work.

(*ii*) Good observation power, *i.e.*, mental alterness, quick to notice.

(*iii*) A man of clear thoughts.

(*iv*) Power to express things clearly

(C) **Personal qualities**

(*i*) Sincere and honest, so as to gain the confidence and respect of those with whom he had to deal.

(*ii*) He must have enthusiasm.

(*iii*) Tactful in handling the situation.

(*iv*) Self-confident, strong will power and courage.

(*v*) Leadership capabilities.

Good relations before work study is conducted

One of the greatest difficulties in obtaining the active cooperation of the workers is the fear that increasing the productivity will lead to their unemployment. Therefore, before introducing the work study, relations between the management and the workers must be reasonably good and the workers must have confidence in the sincerity of the management towards them. In the absence of good relations, workers will consider it as a trick to get more work out of them without giving any benefit.

The second main difficulty is that due to the general conservatism of human beings, any change in existing methods and practices is an interruption of a comfortable situation in which well established routines have been set up.

The third important difficulty is that when a work study team work in a plant, it appears that it has taken up management's role. The sitting managers do not like it and feel that their position have been illegally seized.

Therefore, it is necessary to know that how the good relations, with the workers on one side and with the management on the other side, can be maintained.

Work Study and the Workers

As stated earlier, if the workers have confidence in the sincerity of the management then there will be no difficulty in the application of work study. Before conducting the work study, all the problems must be discussed honestly. Before and during the course of application of work study, following steps are advisable :

1. Management must take initiative for free and sufficient consultation before the work study is started.
2. If work study is applied, then workers and their representatives are kept fully informed of all that is being done. All the record of work study must also be made available before them to develop a feeling of confidence.
3. Work study improves the flow of work and supply of material. This improves the efficiency of the workers and thereby their earnings. This aspect is liked by the workers very much, specially if they are on piece work.
4. Generally, there is a fear of redundancy arising out of the result of work study. There must be definite policy in respect of their retrenchment or transfer to another department. This is a very important factor and must be discussed by the management with the unions.

5. There may be strong resistance to change in methods of work as a result of method study. The workers must be explained about the new method and its advantages. Sometimes old skilled workers are not satisfied even after this, then as a solution of it, if the output of these old worker is reasonably satisfactory, they will have to be left alone and the changes are taught to the new workers only.
6. Sometimes workers hesitate in being timed, because somebody standing nearby and watching, worries them. In such cases, position of work study man must be such so as to disturb the worker as minimum as possible. Work study man must also see that before attempting to record time, worker becomes accustomed to his presence.
7. Workers representatives should be trained in the techniques of increasing the productivity. This will help in understanding them about the importance of work study and they will also be able to explain it to their fellow workers. This will also help them in ensuring that no steps are being taken which may harm them.

10.4. MOTION-STUDY (METHOD STUDY)

In this field, pioneering work was done by Frank B. Gilbreth and his wife Lillian M. Gilbreth, around 1910, with the name of Motion Study. Frank Gilbreth, the real founder of motion study as science, defined motion study as the "science of eliminating wastefulness resulting from ill-directed and inefficient motions". The aim of motion study is to find the scheme of least wastage of labour.

Later on, the scope of Motion Study was enlarged and it was named as Method Study. Method Study is a technique which analyses each operation of a given piece of work very closely in order to eliminate unnecessary operations and to approach the quickest and easiest method of performing each necessary operation. It includes the standardization of equipment, methods and working conditions, and training of the operator to follow the standard method.

Sometimes method study can also be defined as "systematic recording and critical examination of existing and proposed ways of doing work as a means of developing and applying easier and more effective method and thereby reducing cost."

Aims (Objects) of Motion Study

Some important aims of the motion study are :

1. To eliminate wastage of time and labour.
2. To reduce fatigue and boredom of work by avoiding unnecessary movements.
3. To find the best way of doing a job.
4. To have more effective utilisation of materials, machines and workers.
5. To improve the design of work place layout.
6. To standardise the method, obtained after conducting the motion study.
7. To train the individual worker in its practice as per standardised method.

10.5. PROCEDURE FOR MOTION STUDY

Motion study can be performed in the following steps :

Step I

Break up the operation of the Job. Make a detailed list of all operations in the present method of manufacturing a job. All the material handling, machine work, and hand work are also included in this detail.

Step II

Question each detail of the job. Following questions should be asked on himself by the motion study engineer about the way in which these operations are to be performed, and about the tools and equipments needed. The procedure of this questioning is known as 'Critical Examination'. Questions are asked on the following five points :

(*i*) **Purpose.** What is the purpose of this operation? Does this fulfil the requirements and whether this can be eliminated?

(*ii*) **Place.** Where is the best place to do this operation?

(*iii*) **Sequence.** What is the best time to do this operation and whether it can be done at the same time as before or at any other better time? When will it be more suitable and economical?

(*iv*) **Person.** Who will do this operation? Who can do it in a better way?

(*v*) **Means.** How this operation can be performed, *i.e.*, which machines and tools are to be used? Can we make the work easier and safer for both worker and equipment?

Step III

Develop a new method. After considering the above questions, a new better method is developed. Apart from the above considerations, before finalising the new method, the following facts should also be thought over during the motion study:

Elimination. Every operation or detail of the job should be thought over whether it can be eliminated without any harm.

Combining. In this aspect it is to be observed whether two or more operations can be combined without any adverse effect to save operation time.

Rearrangement. If rearrangement in the sequence of operations help in simplification or in any other aspect then it should be done. For example, in a factory main sequence of operations was :

(*a*) Assembling.

(*b*) Storage.

(*c*) Inspection.

(*d*) Dispatching.

In this sequence, inspection was carried before dispatching and defective components were being sent back to department for correction. After sometimes, it was felt that storage before inspection yields unnecessary more material handling and internal transportation of defective components. It can be avoided if inspection is carried out before sending the products for storage. Then this sequence of operations was rearranged as follows :

(*a*) Assembling.

(*b*) Inspection.

(*c*) Storage.

(*d*) Dispatching.

Simplification. In simplification, it is found that if the operation is possible with any other easy, safe and economical method that should be adopted. The work can also be simplified by :

(*a*) Placing the materials, tools and equipment at proper working area.

(b) Using gravity feed hoppers and other material handling equipment.

(c) Taking useful work by both hands.

(d) Using special jigs and fixtures.

Step IV

Installing the new method. After having developed the method, this is required to be installed. The new method must first be got approved from the supervisors, workers and management. Then the workers must be trained to work according to this new method and their habits must be developed to follow the correct way. For sometime, close contacts must be maintained with the progress of the job until it runs satisfactorily.

Step V

Maintaining new method. Once a method is installed, it should be maintained in its specified form, and should not be allowed to slip back to old form or introduction of any other unauthorised changes. For proper maintenance, following steps are advised :

(i) Copies of the job instruction sheets should be distributed to all concerned. These sheets must supply the details for setting up the job and proper operation.

(ii) Routine checks are necessary to compare what is actually being done against the job instruction sheets.

(iii) Selection and training of persons must be done according to the job specifications for this new method.

10.6. MICRO-MOTION STUDY

Some motions require very small time and it is difficult to measure time for these motions accurately but the time required by these motions cannot be neglected because they are repeated hundreds of time. Therefore, the motions are taken on picture films with the help of picture camera. Very small time upto 0.0005 minute can be measured by this system. When picture camera is used, the procedure is known as "Micromotion Study".

This method gives very accurate analysis of the product but being a costly one, is used when products are likely to continue for a long time. Micromotion study has the following important advantages:

(i) It provides permanent record of motion study with the help of film.

(ii) A large number of workers can see the procedure at any time even after the completion of motion study work.

(iii) Differences in the old and new methods can be demonstrated, if both are filmed.

(iv) Films can be demonstrated at any desired speed.

(v) It gives very accurate time for each motion or operation than that noted by the stopwatch.

10.6.1. Therbligs

Frank Gilbreth developed a set of 17 elementary motions commonly found in manual operations and called them "Therbligs", reverse spellings of his name. We know that motion study is used for deciding the best way of doing work for which present and proposed methods are observed by experts by recording on charts. For the purpose of recording the motions, he splitted up different motions of process into 17 fundamental elements made by various members of human body and each event was allotted a symbol and letter abbreviation. These symbols and abbreviations are used for preparing motion study charts. To maximise the utility of charts sometimes colour codes are also used.

Table showing 17 therbligs with their explanation as given below.

The Seventeen Therbligs

Sl. No.	*Therblig*	*Explanation*	*Abbreviation*	*Symbol*
1.	Search	Attempt to locate an object	*S*	
2.	Hold	Keep an object stationary	*H*	
3.	Select	Choose one object from among a group	*SE*	
4.	Grasp	Gain control or a hold on an object	*G*	
5.	Released loaded	Relinquish hold	*RL*	
6.	Transport loaded	Move object with body number	*TL*	
7.	Transport empty	Research for an object	*TE*	
8.	Position	Orient an object for use at its present location	*P*	
9.	Preposition	Orient an object for easy use at some later time and usually in a different location	*PP*	
10.	Assemble	Put two or more parts together	*A*	
11.	Disassemble	Separate two or more parts	*DA*	
12.	Use	Apply object or tool	*U*	
13.	Inspect	Examine object	*I*	
14.	Avoidable delay	A delay which operator could prevent	*AD*	
15.	Unavoidable delay	A delay which operator could not prevent	*UD*	
16.	Rest to over come fatigue	An attempt to recover from physical or mental work	*R*	
17.	Plan	Mentally chart for future action	*PN*	

Present Symbols of Motion Study. The symbols developed by Gilbreth are much in number and mostly all are not used in motion study. Therefore, motions were further reduced and now-a-days motions and symbols, which are commonly used, are shown in the Table on the next page.

In conclusion, some of the important tools and techniques of method study have been explained and these are found to be very much useful for the quick production and to reduce overhead expenses.

10.6.2. Cyclegraph and Chronocycle Graph

As an aid for micromotion study, Gilbreth also developed (*i*) cyclegraphic, and (*ii*) chronocycle graphic techniques for the study of the motion path of an operator's hand or finger.

Cyclegraph. A small electric bulb is attached to the finger, hand or other part of the body of the operator and it is photographed to record the path of the motion. With a still camera, the path of light so photographed, is called a cyclegraph.

Present Symbols of Motion Study (Process Chart Symbols)

Symbol	*Motion*	*Explanation*
○	Operation	Any operation for making alteration or changing the job is said to be operation
□	Inspection	Checking of the quality correctness and verification is said to be the motions of inspection.
⇒	Transport	Movement or travel of the job or any object.
D	Delay	Any type of delay, *i.e.*, breakdown interference or time required for some adjustment etc.
▽	Storage	Keeping holding and storing the job and other things.
◙	Operation and Inspection	This several time occurs when operation and inspection are combined, *e.g.*, setting of tool.
╪	Change point	These are used before beginning any process or operation and ending or changing the study of process to another process.

Chronocyclegraph. If an interrupter is placed in the electric circuit with the bulb and the light is flashed quickly and off slowly, then the path of bulb in the photograph will appear as a dotted line with pear shaped dots indicating the direction of motion. The space between the dots will be according to the speed of the hand or finger of the body. Size and shape of the pear shaped dot will show whether body part is in acceleration or in retardation. The number of dots will give the time taken by that motion and the technique is called a chronocyclegraph.

10.7. MOTION ECONOMY

Principles

A best method of performing a job is not only with minimum expenditure but certain other rules or principles should be observed for increasing the speed to achieve more economy in production. There are basic 26 principles of motion economy. Although they all are not applied to every operation but form basis or a code for improving the efficiency and reducing fatigue in manual work

(*a*) Principles related to the use of the "Human Body".
(*b*) Principles related to the "arrangement of the work place".
(*c*) Principles related to the "Design of Tools and Equipment".

(A) Principles related to the use of the "Human Body". These are :

1. Both hands should start as well as complete their motions at the same time.
2. Both hands should not be idle at the same time except during rest periods.
3. Use both hands simultaneously and use best motion sequence.
4. Hand motions should be confined to the lowest possible classification in order to reduce fatigue. These are listed in the order of giving least fatigue and maximum economy:
   First–Finger motions.
   Second–Finger and wrist motions.
   Third–Finger, wrist and lower arm motions.
   Fourth–Finger, wrist, lower arm and upper arm motions.
   Fifth–Finger, wrist, lower arm, upper arm and body motions.
5. Utilise momentum to assist the worker, wherever possible.
6. Smooth continuous motions produce less fatigue in comparison to zig-zag or straight line motions involving sudden and sharp change in direction.
7. Ballistic movements are faster, easier and more accurate than controlled movements.
8. Sequence of motions should be arranged to build rhythm and automaticity into the operation. For example, practically every body opens and closes his shirt buttons without thinking, using definite recurring movements. It is performed with positive rhythm and automaticity.
9. Hands should be relieved of all work that can be done by feet or other parts of the body.

(B) Principles related to the Arrangement of the Work Place

1. All tools and materials should be placed at a definite and fixed place with easy reach.
2. All tools, materials and actuating devices should be placed in front of the operator at a distance as near as possible.

3. Provide gravity feed bins and use power or gravity conveyers to transport materials.
4. Wherever possible use drop deliveries. Drop delivery means dropping the article into a chute or on a conveyor as near to the point of assembly as possible so that gravity assists rather than the hands to reach the part to its required place.
5. Tools and material should be located in such a way asto achieve the best sequence of motions.
6. Illuminate the work places properly for adequate seeing and visual perception.
7. Provide proper working tables, stools and chairs, etc., because to work in standing or sitting position on floor consumes more time and energy.
8. The height of the work place and chair etc., should be such that worker can either sit or stand comfortably.
9. Chairs provided should make good posture possible.
10. Keep the shops in good order, neat and clean.

(C) Principles related to the Design of Tools and Equipment

1. The hands should not be used for work that can be done more advantageously with the help of devices. Therefore, following devices should be used to reduce manual work and to free both the hands as far as possible:
   (*a*) use power operated tools and equipment;
   (*b*) use vices, jigs and fixtures, etc.;
   (*c*) use stops, guides etc.;
   (*d*) use foot pedals.
2. Reduced noise increases the speed of work and requires less energy.
3. Wherever practicable, tools and materials should be propositioned to reduce search, find and the select operations.
4. Wherever possible two or more tools should be combined.
5. Handles on tools and cranks should be designed to permit maximum contact with the hands, particularly where force is applied, such as in a screw driver, plier, scrapper etc.
6. When each finger performs some specific movement, such as in type writing, the load should be distributed in accordance with the inherent capacities of the fingers.
7. The location of levers, cross bars and hand wheels, etc. should be so decided that the operator can operate with the least change in body position and with greatest mechanical advantage.

10.8. DESIGN OF WORK PLACE LAYOUT

Bad working condition always affect the productivity adversely. It has been established that comfortable work place will keep workers more satisfied and the more will be the productivity. Hence while designing a work place, its environment and such other factors must also be considered. The science which considers all these factors is known as "Economics". Ergonomics combines the knowledge obtained from the study of anatomy, physiology, psychology etc. to reduce the stresses (like fatigue, eye strain, mental and muscular fatigue) on the workers in their work area.

While designing the machines and equipment, efforts are made to reduce these stresses and thus study on human and machine becomes necessary. Thus the job of machine design is conducted by an ergonomics team which consists of engineers, designers, anatomists, physiologists and psychologists (in small industries, the work is generally carried out by work study team).

Elements Related to Work Place :

Following are some of the important elements which are related to the work place :

1. **Cleanliness.** As cleanliness affects the worker's efficiency hence the working place must be clean. For this purpose, care must be taken to provide a suitable place for every thing connected with the job and worker must be asked to keep everything in its place. Work area must be clean and well painted.
2. **Proper Illumination.** Work place must be properly illuminated (illumination of proper intensity) so as to avoid eye strain. Care must be taken to avoid glaring, flickering. Colour of light selected must be such as to reduce eye fatigue.
3. **Noise.** A work place must be selected so as to have as less noise as possible. Experiments have shown that reduction in noise results in increase in efficiency with lesser fatigue.
4. **Location for Tools and Materials.** All tools and materials required by a worker must be located within the normal grasp area and as far as possible in front of the worker. These tools and materials when placed as near to the worker as possible, he will have to travel lesser distances to take these tools and materials again and again and then put them at their desired places which will avoid the loss of energy and time.

   For the assembly work, it is advisable to provide such arrangement so that the components can slide along the smooth surface and the worker picks them up. It will greatly reduce the time and effort.
5. **Proper Chairs.** Chairs permitting proper posture for the workers may be provided. This is possible when the worker is working on the work bench (e.g., assembly, fitting and inspection etc.). Performing a job on floor in sitting position or on table in standing position requires more energy and time.
6. **Work Bench.** As explained earlier, all the tools and materials must be located within the normal grasp area and as close in front of the operator as possible. Experiments have shown that a semi-circular table having a radius of 20" or 50.8 cm from a point at 4" or 10.16 cm back from the edge or work bench (4" or 10 cm back gives approximately centre line of the operator shoulders and elbow) as shown in Fig.10.1 allows a most comfortable position.

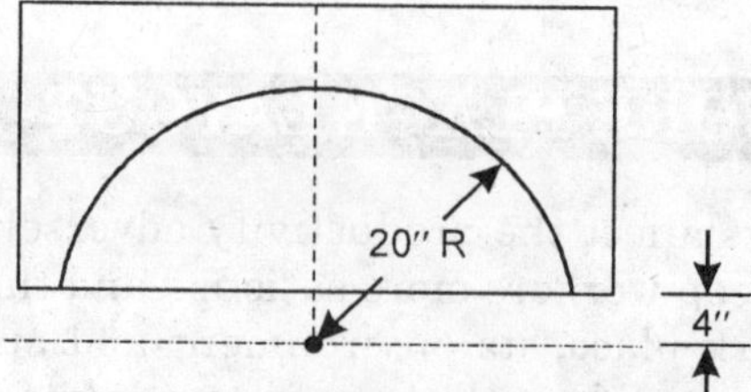

Fig. 10. 1. Shoulder Elbow Centre line.

   The work bench must be so designed that use of both hands can be taken simultaneously.
7. **Designing Machines.** When a worker operates or uses a machine, instrument or tools, it is essential that man-machine must be considered as a single working unit

from the design point of view, as explained above. Machine must be so designed so that worker can use both hands and foot simultaneously for operating it and all the levers, pedals, instruments, handwheels, knobs and buttons must be located within the normal grasp at a suitable height and infront of the operator. Foot pedals must be provided with suitable returning springs. Care must be taken to avoid eye strain, muscular and mental strain.

Fatigue may further be reduced if proper use of jigs or fixtures, stops or guides is taken.

In the end,"work place layout" helps the analyst in determining the required body and eye motions of operators, safety measures and operational difficulties that may occur at a working place.

10.9. ANALYSIS IN THE FORM OF CHARTS

This is a technique by which analysis for developing the methods can be done quickly and easily. Many types of these charts are being used, but the most important among them are given below:

These charts are tools of motion study.

1. Operation process chart.
2. Flow Diagram.
3. Man-Machine Chart.
4. Left-Right Hand Chart.
5. Simo Chart.

Each chart is explained hereunder :

10.9.1. Operation Chart (Fig. 10.2)

This is a graphic representation of the sequence of all operations and inspections involved in the process. In this chart, all components or materials entry points are indicated by the horizontal lines and the processing of these materials are shown vertically. Operation process charts provide a compact overall view of the whole system of operations involved in the manufacture of a product.

For drawing the operation charts, final assembly operations are generally written on the right hand side of the paper. A horizontal line is then drawn at the top of the vertical line denoting the sequence of operations and inspections to represent the starting material. Above this horizontal line, part number (if any) and the name of the item is given, and below the line material size is mentioned.

Standard time for each operation is mentioned on the left hand side of its symbol while a brief description of the operation is given on the right hand side. When another parts is assembled, a horizontal line is drawn into the vertical line just above the operation symbol representing the assembly. The operations and inspections required for the manufacture of this part are then put above this line in the form of column in sequence. Thus additional columns are introduced, for each part assembled, in the left with a horizontal line connecting the main assembly column.

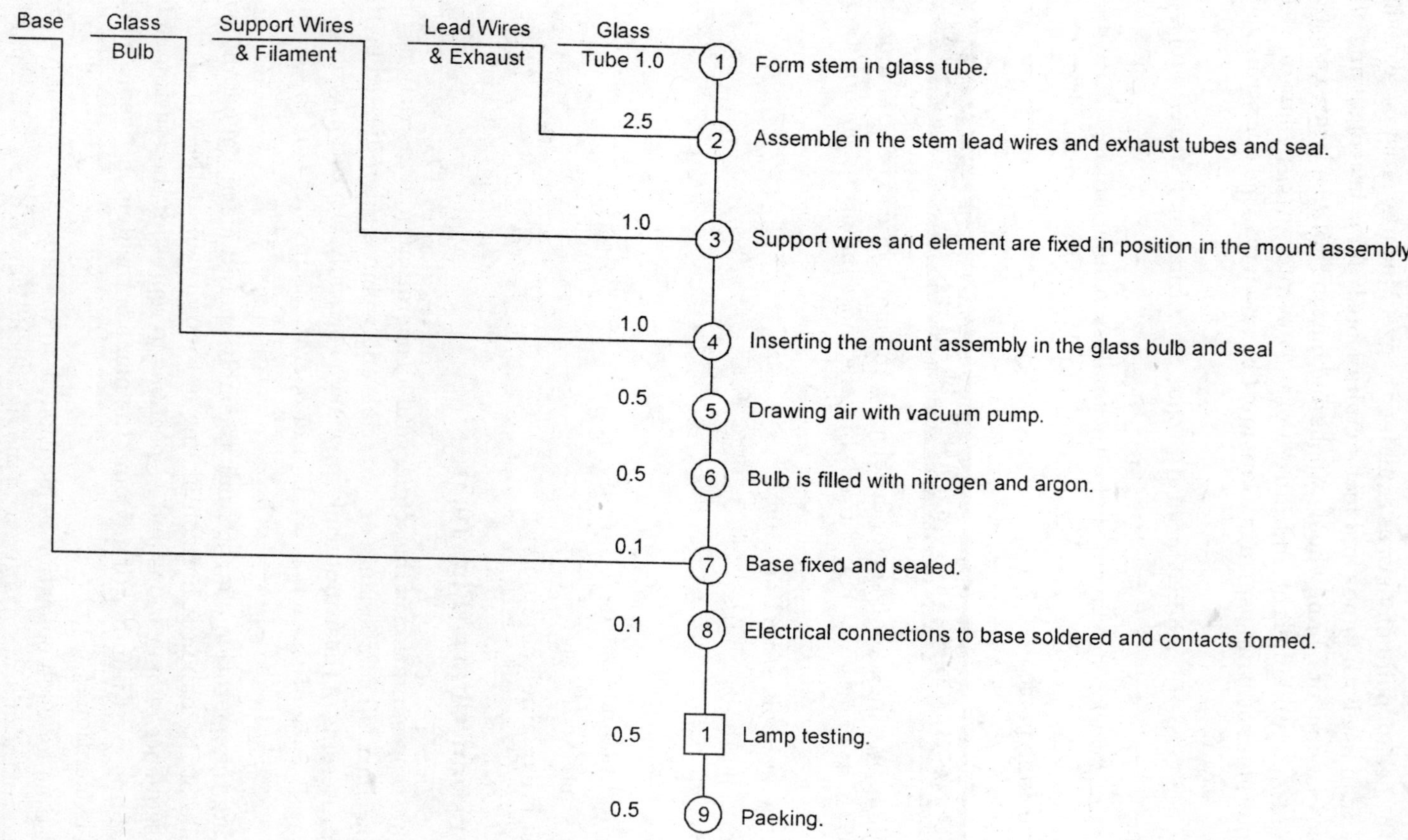

Fig. 10.2 Operation Chart

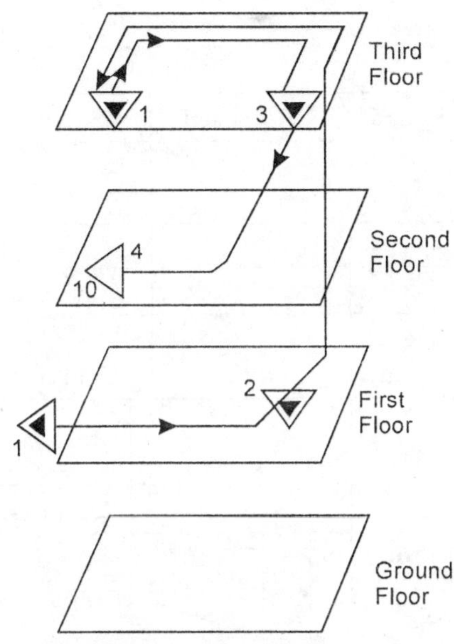

Fig. 10.3 Simplified Flow Diagram

When purchased parts are used in the assembly, a horizontal line is drawn at proper place in the assembly column and parts number and name is given above the line, while the name of the manufacturing company from whom it is procured is given below this line.

After all the operations are given symbols, they must be numbered. Numbering starts at the upper right hand corner of the chart, *i.e.*, from top of the main assembly column and proceed downwards until a horizontal line comes into the column. Then the symbols on this line from top to downwards are measured, this follows till this line joins the main assembly column and so on, and till all the symbols are numbered. Operation process chart for the manufacturing of an electric bulb is given on Fig 10.2.

10.9.2. Flow Process Chart

This is a graphic representation of operation, transportation, inspection, delays and storage occurring during production. This also gives the information regarding distances moved and time required for different items such as transportation, delays and inspection etc. It is usually prepared for one component of an assembly at a time. After preparing this chart, an analyst applies motion study and proposes a new method for doing the same job.

Flow process chart for vulcanizing types is given here. The first step in preparing this chart is filling out of the headings. Each activity is listed in order as the job is following through the plant and notation are made as shown in examples.

The symbols in such charts are short hand tools and serve as sign posts to make critical areas for improvement. In this way, by preparing Flow Process Chart, a process or a job can be analysed step by step. Activities can be eliminated in some cases, combined in others, rearranged for more effective processing or simplified. The proposed new method is also drawn in the chart.

Flow process charts are of following two types:

(*i*) **Flow Process Chart-Product Analysis.** This chart is based on product analysis. This is a graphic representation of different steps involved in performing the work required to convert a product from one stage to another.

Flow Process Chart

Chart No. Sheet No.	Summary				
Subject charted : Tyres	Activity		Present	Proposed	Savings
Activity : Vulcanising of tyres	Operation	O	8		
Method : Present/Proposed	Transport	→	8		
Charted by :	Delay	D	4		
Date :	Inspection	□	2		
Approved by:	Storage	Δ	2		
	Distance		87 m	33 m	44 m
	Time		341.0 min.		

S. No.	Description	Distance in 1 Tyres	Distance in mtrs	Time in min	O	→	D	□	Δ	Remarks
1.	Tyres brought from store for for dismentling of stepney		10	1						
2.	Stepney Dismentled		–	14						
3.	Moved for removing old patches		3	0.5						
4.	Old patches removed			17 5						
5.	Taken for skiving operation		8	0.5						
6.	Skiving			5 0.5						
7.	Taken to flexible buffing		25	1.5						
8.	Buffing of inside surface			20						
9.	Taken for cutting operation		3	0.5						
10.	Cutting			5						
11.	Taken for mounting of new patch		10	1						
12.	New Patch mounted			15						
13.	Patch inspected			5						
14.	Taken to vulcanising m/c		15							
15.	Mounted on vulcanising m/c			2						
16.	Vulcanising			240						
17.	Dismounted			2						
18.	Taken to tyre spreader		3	0.5						
19.	Inspection on spreader			3						
20.	Sent for storage		10	1						

Fig.10.4

(*ii*) **Flow Process Chart-Man Analysis.** This chart is based on man analysis. This is a graphic representation of different steps a person performs when doing a job and his movements from one place to another in performing that job. Until and unless clearly mentioned, flow process chart refers to that of flow process chart based on Product Analysis.

Flow Diagram

It is the plan view of a work to a certain scale and a line diagram indicating the path followed by the object under study. This gives an overall view of an existing or proposed process and is used for making improvement. It shows the path followed by the material, man or equipment. Where more than one floor is involved, an isometric drawing can be used (Fig.10.3).

Normally the "Flow Diagram" should also accompany the Flow Process Chart.

Flow Process Charts and Flow diagrams are very simple and effective tools of method study. They are very useful in establishing the overall sequence of operations and in determining the best layout for an economical and effective flow of materials. They present a clear picture of a process and are very effective tools for studying and improving a complex job. By systematically examining these charts, improvement can be made on the methods of production, sequence of operation and layout etc. Thus, work can be reduced, time can be saved and expenses can be cut.

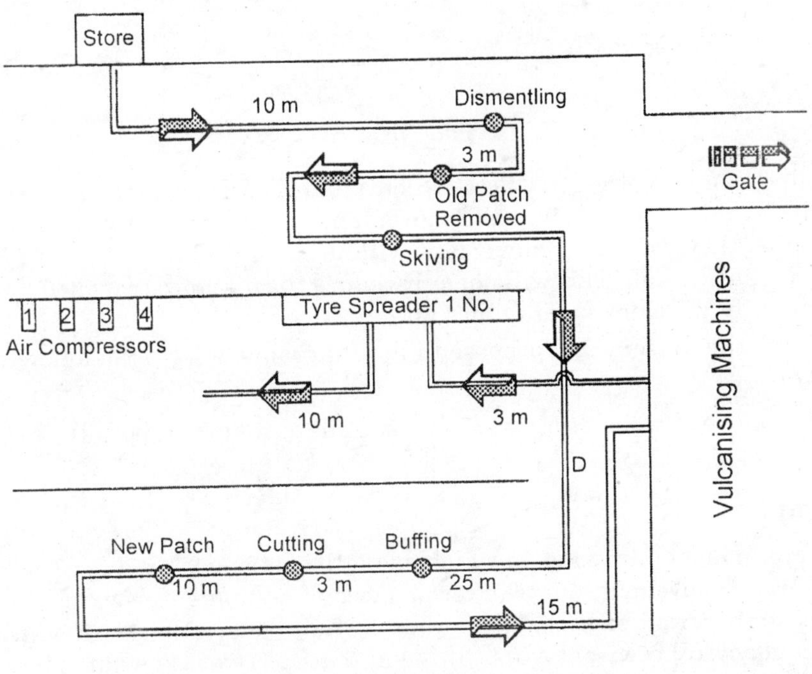

Fig. 10.5.

Fig. 10.4 is a Flow Process chart for vulcanising tyres and Fig. 10.5 is a Flow Diagram of the existing methods. From the study of these two, Fig. 10.6 shows a proposed Flow Diagram. For charting these diagrams, keeping in mind the principles of Motion Economy, the first step is to record the existing method being used for vulcanising of tyres. For this purpose, a Flow Process chart has been charted and flow diagrams have also been made. Now an ideal procedure or process will have maximum number of operations during course of action.

After going through the Flow Process chart, it becomes clear that there is much of transportation between different operations. So to make things more clear, a flow diagram is charted and it clearly shows the distance travelled by a tyre which is being repaired.

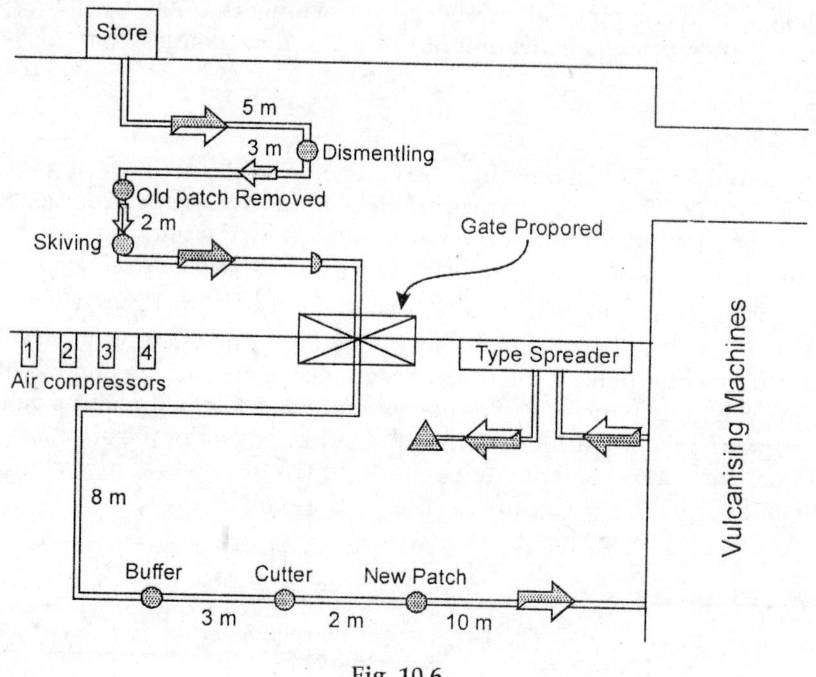

Fig. 10.6.

After critically examining the Flow Process chart and Flow Diagram, an alternative improved layout has been developed. It involves the movement of only two small machines which are flexible and mobile, therefore their movement will not be a problem at all. Further a gate is proposed with the central wall. This will not only reduce the distance travelled by a tyre but will also enable to simplify the things and reduce fatigue.

Now comparing the present and proposed Flow diagrams, we get the following results :

Repairing of tyres

Distance moved by each tyre = 87 m (Existing) = 43 m (Proposed)

Savings = 44 m

String Diagram

This diagram is a layout drawing on which a length of string is used to record the extent as well as the pattern of movement of a worker or piece of equipment working within a limited area during a certain period of time. It is used to study where the journey are irregular in distance and frequency, otherwise it will be difficult to assess exactly what is happening.

It is used to investigate movement in the following situations:

(1) When a group of operator is working.

(2) When a single operator is attending several machines.

(3) In processes, where several sub-assemblies have to be moved to other assembly.

(4) Where processes require the operator to be moved from one work place to another.

(5) For checking the relative values of various layouts.

Construction. To construct a diagram, study is made for the movements in the task concerned and every journey involved in the performance of the work is recorded on the study sheet, the proforma of which is given below :

String Diagram Study

Man/Material/Equipment Studied .... Study No ....
.... Sheet No ....
Department.. Date ....
Section.. Time Started ....
Worker's Name.................................... No .... Time finished ....
Cross Reference .... Study taken by ....

Departure Time	*Arrival Time*	*Time consumed*	*Destination*	*Remarks*

From the study sheet, a scale layout drawing is prepared of the area to which the recorded moves have taken place. The drawing should include building features such as walls and doorways, block plans of machinery and other equipment installed nearby the route, whether or not it is actually concerned with the job or equipment being studied.

This complete drawing should then be attached to a sheet of plywood or composition board and panel pins shown in the String Diagram (Fig. 10.7) driven into it at each of the terminal points observed during the study. It will also be necessary for additional pins to be driven in, where the direction or moves between these points changes.

Now a strong thread is tied to the starting point pin and by reference to the study, taken round of each of the terminal points on the drawing in the sequence in which they were visited. The pins placed at corners along the route enable the thread to follow on the diagram, a path very similar to that actually taken while the study was made. In this way, it is possible to record on the diagram any number of journeys between any number of points.

Fig. 10.7 shows the string diagram recording the journey of a laboratory assistant in performing a day's work.

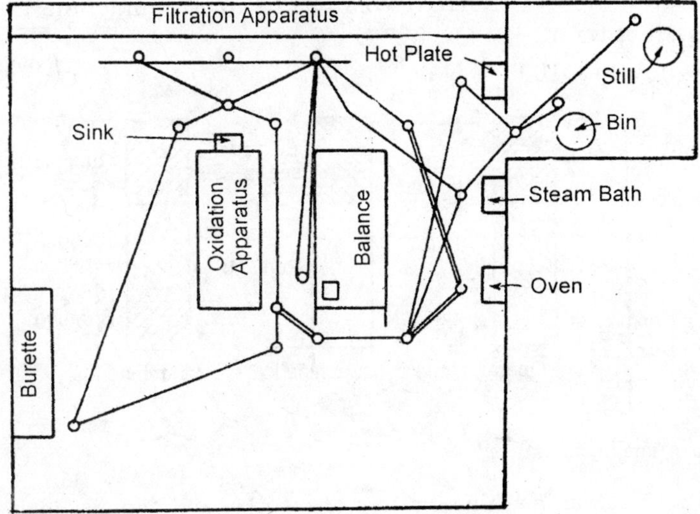

Fig. 10.7. String Diagram (double lines indicate Frequent Journeys).

10.9.3. Man-Machine Chart

This chart describes graphically the activity of a man and machine he is attending against a time scale. When a shop has a number of operators and machines, studies can be made to find what number of machines each worker can operate or how many workers can work on each machine. During the machining cycle of many semi-automatic machines, the operator has time in which he can run one or more other semi-automatic machines. In this way, such charts enable the management to minimise the idle time of the worker and to use the machines to their full capacity.

For example, suppose there are three workers and each worker is doing the same operations on his machine. Suppose that the time to set up a machine cycle is 0.50 minute and machining time taken is 0.75 minute.

Fig. 10.8 shows the case in which one worker one machine.

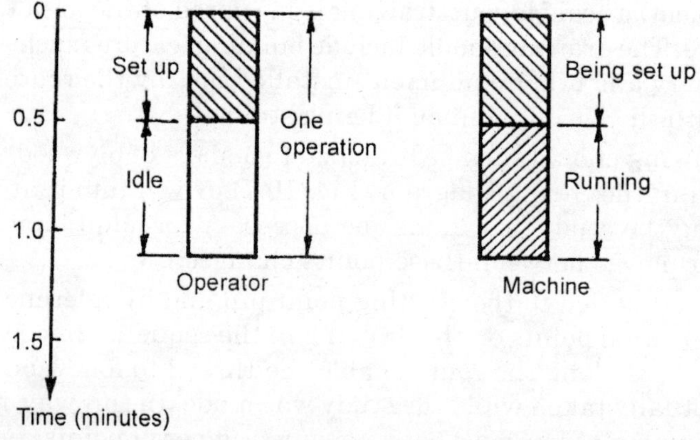

Fig.10.8. Man-machine chart for one operator and one machine.

From Fig. 10.8, it is very clear for each operation that the worker is idle for 0.75 minute, when the machine is running. Its alternative can be to put two machines and let us allow one worker to work on both of them.

This case is shown in Fig. 10.9.

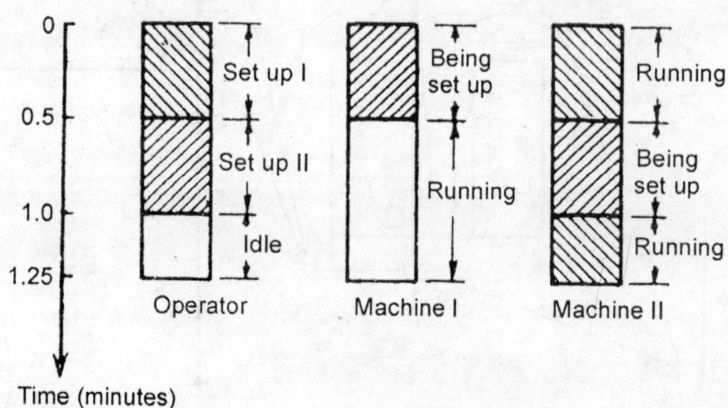

Fig. 10.9. Man-machine chart for one worker and two machines.

Fig. 10.9. Man-machine chart for one worker and two machines. In this case, the worker still remains idle for 0.25 minute in each operation. So in order to minimise this, let us allow one worker to work on three machines. This is shown in Fig. 10.10.

In this case, the worker would have no idle time, except for necessary personal and fatigue allowances, but each machine would be idle for 0.35 minute after each operation. Now, therefore, the problem is which of the alternatives would be economical ? For this purpose, the unit cost of idle time of one worker and the unit cost of idle time of each machine is estimated and then the economical alternative is calculated.

Operation analysis

Where workers do their job independently, management requires to know whether they are doing job in the most efficient way or not.

The purpose of operation analysis is to determine a simpler and more economical way of doing a job, by analysing the job and the individual motions of workers.

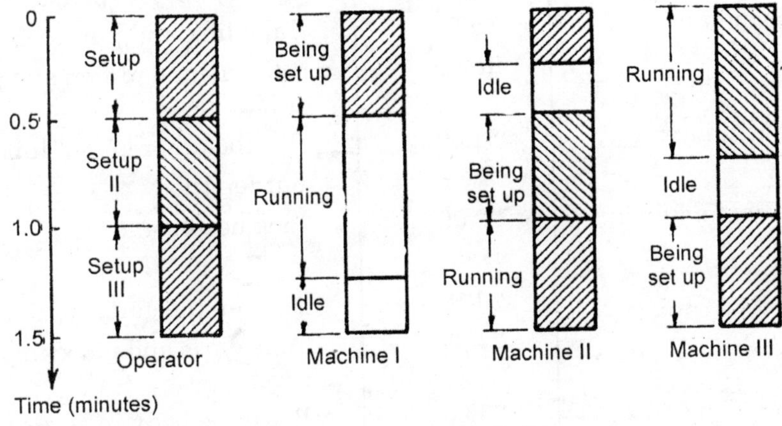

Fig.10.10. Man-machine chart for one worker and three machines.

Here, a close study of the work of individual worker is made to determine a better method of performing his job. To do this, operation anaylsis is applied. In this, the steps in a job and the motions used by the worker to perform these steps are recorded. In this study, principles of Motion Economy are applied. Using these principles as guides, a better and more economical method of performing an operation is developed.

To aid this technique, Left-hand Right-hand chart (Two-hand chart) and Simo Chart are used. These are shown in Figs. 10.11 and 10.12. The purpose of constructing these charts is to point out unbalanced work situations between the two hands so that these situations can be corrected, thereby reducing fatigue and increasing productivity.

After constructing these charts, we question each step. Can a motion be eliminated or simplified? Can we eliminate or reduce transportation? Can we delay ? Can holding be eliminated by using a jig or fixture and so on. Thus questioning each activity and applying the principles of "Motion Economy", manual work can be improved.

10.9.4. Two Hand Chart

This is also known as Left-hand Right-hand Chart and is used to improve the motion sequence of an operator. The chart is used to minimise the necessary motions and to arrange the remaining motions in an economical way. The chart is prepared after studying the working place, arrangement of the worker and of the equipment while he is working.

Two-hand Chart for a Pressure Gauge

Left hand Motions	*Clock* Mts.	*Right hand motions*
Pick up tube having nipple and place at work place	10.00	
	12.00	Pick up the base
	13.50	Take the Screw Driver and tighten the nipple
Pick up sector	14.10	Pick up sector spring
Hold the sector in hand	15.00	Take link and pin to sector
	18.00	Tale pin and pinion and place in position
Place sector in its place	21.00	Pin the other end of link with burden tube
Pick up gauge dial and fix in position	23.00	Pick needle and fix
	23.50	Tighten the gauge dial
Pick the cover	24.00	Take glass and place in position in cover
Take two screws	25.00	Place the body in cover
Place the screw in position	26.00	Tighten both the screws
	26.00	Remove the gauge.

Fig. 10.11.

Some of the operations like assembling of small instruments such as pressure gauge, carburettor, time piece and fuel pump etc. where both hands are used for placing the different components of the article, Left-hand Right-hand Charts are prepared. The study of the chart gives the clear picture of defective arrangement of tools, incorrect motion sequence and unnecessary and defective motive etc.

A Left-hand Right-hand chart for the assembling of pressure gauge is shown in the Table at Fig. 10.11.

10.9.5. SIMO (Simultaneous Motion) Chart

This is similar to Table at Fig. 10.11. "Two-hand Chart" with the difference that the time required for each motion is drawn to scale with the vertical axis and sometimes coloured to represent the particular motion.

Simo Chart

Sketch	*Code*	*Operation: Assembly nut and bolt*
	x = Bolt	Method: Improved
	y = Nuts	Operator: A. Singh
	z = Chairs	Department: Assembly
	L = Finish units	Time Units : 0.001 Min
	M = Assembly area	Prepared by: K. Raj

L.H. Motions	*Time*	*Time Scale*	*Time*	*R.H. Motions*
Reach to x	15	10	15	Reach to y
Grasp bolt	4	20	4	Grasp nut
Return to z	10	30	10	Return to z
Position bolt	21	50	21	Position nut
Hold	15	70	15	Assemble
Carry to L	15	80	15	Idle
Released	4	100	4	Idle

Fig. 10.12.

The procedure to construct this chart is as under.

A camera with high speed clock is placed near the work place and is used to film time and the operator's actions simultaneously. After recording, the film is worked and processed and viewed to determine the motions performed and time taken. From these records, activities and time taken are plotted in the form of Simo Chart as shown in Table at Fig. 10.12.

QUESTIONS

1. Discuss the position of 'Work Study Department' in the organisational structure of a manufacturing concern.
2. How work study is useful for management, labour, society and industrial productivity ?
3. Discuss briefly the role of work study in increasing industrial productivity.
4. Briefly explain the human aspects of work study.
5. Discuss the scope and purpose of work study.
6. Why do the trade unions in India oppose the use of work study in industry ? How the said condition of affair can be improved ?
7. (*a*) Define motion study. State the different charts which are used as tools of motion study.
   (*b*) State the principles of motion economy.

8. Define "Method Study". Example in detail the various steps involved in systematic methods of improvement.
9. Discuss and explain fully, the practice of "critical examination" in Work Study. Prepare an effective list of critical questions aimed at methods improvements.
10. (*a*) Describe various "stage" of Method Study.
    (*b*) Explain the importance of standardisation of methods before taking time study.
11. (*a*) How will you ensured that the improved methods have been properly installed ?
    (*b*) How will you proceed to train workers in the proposed method ?
12. State principles of motion economy as related to human body. What is the significance of these principles for a method study practitioner ?
13. Example the principles of motion economy as related to :
    (*a*) Work place layout; and
    (*b*) Design of tools and equipments.
14. Describe "Micro-Motion Study". Give few suitable examples of its application. Why it has been used as such at accelerated rate in recent years?
15. What are Therbligs ? Example their importance. Give the name, explanation, abbreviation and symbol of each of 17 therbligs.
16. With neat sketches and brief explanation of their utility, clearly distinguish between the following :
    (*i*) Operation process chart and flow process chart.
    (*ii*) Two-hand process chart and activity chart.
17. Make a Left-hand Right-hand operation chart for filling a fountain pen.
18. Write short notes on the following terms :
    (*a*) Symbols of Motion Study.
    (*b*) Motion Picture Camera.
    (*c*) Work Place Layout.
    (*d*) String Diagram.
19. Write short notes on the following :
    (*a*) Simo chart.
    (*b*) Two-hand chart.
    (*c*) Cyclegraph.
    (*d*) Chronocycle graphic study.
    (*e*) Chronocycle graphic study.
20. Discuss the techniques of method study and principles of motion economy which can be utilized to analyse the effectiveness of various aspects of a given plant layout in a larger mechanised caste iron foundry.

WORK–STUDY—2 (TIME STUDY OR WORK MEASUREMENT)

11.1. INTRODUCTION

When a customer wants to purchase some products, then he usually compares the prices with those of similar products, which are being manufactured by other producers. Therefore, to give competitive quotations, estimation of accurate labour cost is very essential as it has got large effect on the price. If the prices are higher, then, the manufacturer may not get supply orders and if these are lower, then losses may occur. Thus exact estimation of time is very essential for correct pricing. As labour cost depends upon time estimation, therefore, time must be estimated as correctly as far as possible.

Secondly, wherever a customer contracts for the purchase of certain products then he desires that the products should reach to him at a promised data which is only possible when manufacturer is aware of the time to be taken by the product during manufacture. Therefore, to find the correct manufacturing time for a product, first time study is performed by the Time Study Engineer.

Definitions

1. **Time study** may be defined as "the art of observing and recording the time required to do each detailed element of an industrial operation". Here, in the definition, the term industrial operation includes manual, mental and machining operations, where,
   (*i*) Manual time is divided into three types of operation, *i.e.*, handling of tools, handling of machines and handling of materials.
   (*ii*) Mental time includes time taken by the worker for thinking over some operations.
   (*iii*) Machining time includes time taken by the machines in doing its share of work.
   Thus time study standardized the time taken by an average worker to perform these operations,
2. It can also be defined in the following words "work measurement is the application of techniques designed to establish the time for a qualified worker to carry-out a specified job at a defined level of performance."

Uses of Time Study

(*i*) It is useful in determining the standard time for various operators, which help in fixing wage rates and incentives.
(*ii*) It is useful to estimate the cost of a product accurately.
(*iii*) It helps in production control.
(*iv*) It helps in predicting accurately as to when the work will be completed and hence customers can be promised to take delivery on a fixed date.

(v) Using the time study techniques, it can be found that how many machines an operator can run.

11.2. PROCEDURE FOR TIME STUDY

For conducting time study, average workers and average machines are selected. This study is conducted by the time Study expert, who should be familiar with all the informations related to the job and the conditions in which it is being done. The location of the expert should be such that he can watch all the operations and movements of the workers without disturbing them from suitable distance.

Time study is performed in the following stages :

(a) **Analysis of Work.** The complete job and its operations are split up into various elements as discussed in the motion study. These elements are finalised after conducting motion study. In the end, time required for job preparation, cleaning of machine, and oiling etc., should also be included. Thus time study includes all the tasks performed by the worker and not only the effective work.

(b) **Standardisation of Methods.** Before conducting time study, all the constituents of the job such as materials, equipment, tools, working condition and methods are standardised. The method should be easy, safe and quickest in the given conditions, so that it can be accepted.

(c) **Making Time Study.** Time study is done on a printed time study record sheet as shown below which is fixed on a board known as Time Study Board. On one corner (generally right-hand top corner) a stop-watch is placed. This stop-watch should have a decimal scale dial so that it can read up to 0.01 minute.

Different time readings of one element are recorded in the corresponding column of the record sheet. Several sets of readings are taken to arrive at an accurate result. After noting all these readings, average time is calculated, neglecting abnormal values, if any. This average time is multiplied by a levelling factor, also called 'Rating Factor', and is generally assumed as 110-120%, to get the time required by a normal worker. This multiple of average time with the rating factor is known as "Normal Time". Some allowance personal (5%), fatigue allowance (20%), preparation allowance (5%) are added to the normal time to obtain the standard time. The standard time is the basis for the calculation of wages and incentives.

Time Study Record Sheet

Element	*Time in Minutes*						*Average observed Time (Neglecting abnormal values)*
	1	*2*	*3*	*4*	5	*6*	
A	3.6	3.4	2.2	3.5	3.8	3.5	3.5 neglecting III reading
B	6.8	7.2	7.0	9.5	6.9	7.1	7.0 neglecting IV reading
C	4.5	4.9	4.8	4.9	4.7	4.4	4.7
Observed Time..........				Personal Allowances..........			
Level or rating factor..........				Fatigue Allowances..........			
Normal time..........				Preparation Allowances..........			
				Standard Time..........			

Thus, Standard time = Average Time x Rating factor + Other allowances

Standard Time

It is the time, which is taken by a normal worker for a specific task or job, working under moderate conditions and including other allowances such as fatigue, setting of tool and job, repairing of tool and checking of job etc.

Rating Factor

The study engineer multiplies actual time with a factor known as 'Rating Factor' or 'Levelling Factor' to get the average time which a normal worker would take. This is expressed as a percentage of the efficiency of representative operator, which indicates how efficient an operator is in comparison to some of his average fellow workers.

11.3. PERFORMANCE RATING

Performance rating is that process, during which the time study engineer compares the performance of the operator under observation with his own concept of normal performance.

In mathematical term,

$$\text{Performance Rating} = \frac{\text{Observed Performance}}{\text{Normal Performance}} \times 100$$

The concept of normal performance, must be such that the time standards set from it, and must be within the capacity of the majority of workers in the enterprise. It would be of no use in setting standard so high that only the best worker would attain them, since programmes or estimates based on them would never be fulfilled. Similarly low standard would result very high earning for some of the workers and consequently, an excessively high labour cost of the product and very large difference in the earnings of the workers.

11.3.1. Methods of Rating

Following are the important methods used for Performance Rating:

1. Speed Rating.
2. Westinghouse System of Rating.
3. Synthetic Rating.
4. Objective Rating.
5. Physiological Evaluation of Performance Rating.

1. **Speed Rating**

   This rating procedure consists of judging the pace or speed of the operator's movement in relation to a normal pace and is noted as a factor. This rating is applied to each element and observed time for each element is multiplied by this factor (The ratio of observed speed to expected speed) so as to get the normal time for the element.

2. **Westinghouse System of Rating**

   A four factor system of Performance Rating was developed at Westinghouse. These factors are :

   1. Skill.
   2. Effort.

3. Conditions.
4. Consistency.

As scale of numerical value for each factor was supplied in the tabular form, the worker was watched while working and given a value from these tables. The time obtained from time study is then levelled by applying the sum of the ratings of all the four factors.

For example, if the observed time for an operator was 1.50 minutes and if the ratings are as follows :

Good skill C_1	+ 0.06
Excellent efforts D_2	+ 0.08
Average conditions D	+ 0.00
Good consistency C	+ 0.01
Total	+ 0.15

The normal time for that operation would be

$$1.50 \times 1.15 = 1.72 \text{ min.}$$

	Skill		*Efforts*
+ 0.15A_1 + 0.13 A_2	Superskill	+ 0.13 A_1 + 0.12 A_2	Excessive
+ 0.11 B_1 + 0.08 B_2	Excellent	+ 0.10 B_1 + 0.08 B_2	Excellent
+ 0.96 C_1 + 0.03 C_2	Good	+ 0.05 C_1 + 0.02 C_2	Good
+ 0.00 D	Average	+ 0.00 D	Average
– 0.05 E_1 – 0.10 E_2	Fair	– 0.04 E_1 – 0.08 E_2	Fair
– 0.16 F_1 – 0.22 F_2	Poor	– 0.12 F_1 – 0.17 F_2	Poor

	Conditions		*Consistency*
+ 0.06 A	Ideal	+ 0.04 A	Perfect
+ 0.04 B	Excellent	+ 0.03 B	Excellent
+ 0.02 C	Good	+ 0.01 C	Good
+ 0.00 D	Average	+ 0.00 D	Average
– 0.03 E	Fair	– 0.02 E	Fair
– 0.07 F	Poor	– 0.04 F	Poor

3. **Synthetic Rating**

In this method, performance of the worker is rated from the values already known by P.M.T.S. (Pre-determined Motion Time System). In this procedure, time study is done in the usual manner and then actual time obtained for certain elements, from this study is compared with that of known standards. The ratio of standard time of a particular element to that of observed time of the same element is the rating factor for the study. The rating factor for the study is the average of rating factors obtained for different elements of the study. Efforts must be obtained to determine the rating factors for as many elements as possible. In this method, it is assumed that performance for the whole of the study will be same as that obtained in these elements.

If R = Performance Rating factor.

P = Predetermined standard for an element.

A = Average of actual time obtained in the time study for that element

Then
$$R = \frac{P}{A}$$

4. **Objective Rating**

In this method, Rating is done in two stages, in first stage, operators speed is rated, by observing speed of movement or rate of activity, and no attention is paid for the job difficulties. After the speed rating is made, in the second stage, an allowance of a secondary adjustment is added to the pace rating by considering the job difficulties. Job difficulties are divided into six classes. A table provides the percentage of adjustments to be made for each of these six factors. These factors are:

(*i*) Amount of body used.

(*ii*) Foot pedals.

(*iii*) Bi-manualness.

(*iv*) Eye-hand co-ordination.

(*v*) Handling requirements.

(*vi*) Weight.

For example, if the selected time for an element is 0.30 minute, the pace rating is 1.10% and if the sum of all secondary adjustments amount to 20%, then the normal time will be

$$= 0.30 \times 1.10 \times 1.20$$
$$= 0.396 \text{ min.}$$

5. **Physiological Evaluation of Performance Rating**

Many studies have recently shown that there is relationship between physical work and the amount of oxygen consumed by the operator. More recently it has also been found that the change in heart rate is also are liable measure of muscular activity. This technique is however not being used now but large number of people in various parts of the world are working on this problem

11.4. ALLOWANCES

To get the standard time, a proper allowance must be added considering the working conditions.

While deciding the quantum (generally in terms of percentage) of allowance to be added to the normal time, following types of allowances are considered :

1. **Relaxation Allowance**

The amount of this allowance depends upon the nature of the job, and includes the following two categories of allowances :

(*A*) **Personal Need Allowance.** It provided for the necessity to go away from the work place to attend the personal needs such as washing, going to lavatory and getting a drink etc. It is commonly taken as 5% for male and 7% for female worker.

(*B*) **Fatigue Allowance.** Fatigue allowance is provided to recover a worker, from the physical and physiological effects of carrying out work. It contains :

(*i*) *A constant portion* : (the minimum or basic fatigue allowance), which must be adequate for a worker who carries out the job while seated, engaged on light work in an ideal working conditions. This is generally considered as 4% for both men and women.

(*ii*) *A variable portion* is added when the working conditions are severe. It is based on factors which vary with the working conditions. These factors are :

(*a*) Standing or other abnormal position,
(*b*) use of force,
(*c*) light,
(*d*) atmospheric condition.
(*e*) visual strain,
(*f*) manual strain,
(*g*) mental strain,
(*h*) other factors,

(*a*) *Standing.* When an operator works in a standing position, he feels more tired. So to overcome this fatigue, an allowance (usually 2%) is given to the workers. However, a seat must be provided wherever possible.

Depending upon the strain involved in working while remaining in the abnormal position, an allowance of 2.5 to 10% is allowed based on the posture.

(*b*) *Use of Force.* For lifting or carrying weights, muscular energy is consumed, for which due allowances are given depending upon the quantum of weight. It requires an allowance of 10% for force upto 2 kg to 20% for loading weights upto 50 kg.

(*c*) *Light.* When lighting is below the prescribed illumination level and it is not possible to improve it, an allowance in proportion to amount of strain is allowed.

(*d*) *Atmospheric Condition.* Air ventilation, temperature, amount of dust or fumes available also affect the working of the workers, hence due allowance varying between 10% and 20% depending upon the atmospheric conditions is allowed.

(*e*) *Visual Strain.* Visual strain is caused by giving very close attention to the work piece or the instrument being used, as in watch making. Maximum visual strain allowance is 4% in good light and 8% under poor light conditions.

(*f*) *Manual Strain.* This is the strain caused by the repeated use of certain members of the body.

(*g*) *Mental Strain.* Mental Strain is caused due to prolonged concentration or due to repeated use of certain mental faculties *viz.*, to attend to a number of machines, as in weaving, or to do mental arithmetic.

(*h*) *Other Factors.* Allowances for fatigue is also required to be allowed in following cases:

(*i*) Loud noise, as in the use of hammers, riveting etc.

(*ii*) Vibration, due to working of certain machines.

How to Reduce Fatigue

The effects of fatigue can be reduced by permitting rest pauses at certain intervals, during which the body recovers from its exertion. During these rest periods, all the employees in a department are not permitted to work. Properly organised rest pauses are beneficial because of the following reasons :

(*i*) Rest pauses increase the production without unduly tiring the workers.

(*ii*) Rest pauses tend to maintain the level of the operator's performance nearer to the optimum and decreases the variation in their performance, which are otherwise caused due to fatigue, when rest pauses are not provided.

(*iii*) Rest pause reduces the quantum of time off taken by the workers for attending personal needs during working hours.

(*iv*) Workers like these rest pauses because they break-up the dullness or monotony.

2. Interference Allowance.

When one worker is attending more than one machine, then interference is the time for which one or more machine units remain idle while attendant is occupied with the work on other machine units. The allowance provided to compensate this idleness due to interference is known as interference allowance.

3. Process Allowance.

This is an allowance provided to compensate for enforced idleness during a process. This includes loss of time due to :

(*i*) no work,

(*ii*) power failure,

(*iii*) faulty material,

(*iv*) faulty tools or equipments.

4. Contingency Allowance.

This is an allowance of time to meet legitimate, irregular and infrequent items of works or delays which cannot economically be measured correctly. It is usually taken as less than 5%.

5. Special Allowance.

These allowances are decided as a policy matter of management. These are allowed for activities which are normally not a part of the operation cycle but are essential for satisfactory performance of work.

These include for the following items :

(*i*) Start up

(*ii*) Cleaning

(*iii*) Shut down

(*iv*) Set up

(*v*) Change over

(*vi*) Tool changing and regrinding.

11.5. METHODS OF TIME STUDY

Time study can be performed by the following methods depending upon the accuracy required :

1. Stop-Watch Method.
2. Time Recording Machine.
3. Motion Picture Camera.

11.5.1. Stop Watch Method

Stop-watch used for time study purpose should be very accurate and preferably be graduated in decimals so that it can record even up to 0.01 minute. It has two hands. Large hand revoloves at a speed of one revolution per minute and its dial is divided in 100 divisions. The small hand revolves at a speed of one revolution in 30 minutes. Dial for this small hand is graduated in such a way that it enables to read upto one minute. The sketch-of stop-watch is shown in Fig. 11.1.

Time Study Board. Time study board is made up of any hard wood. Its shape is such that it rests on the waist line and offers a smooth curvature to support it with the rear arm of left hand as shown in Fig. 11.2.

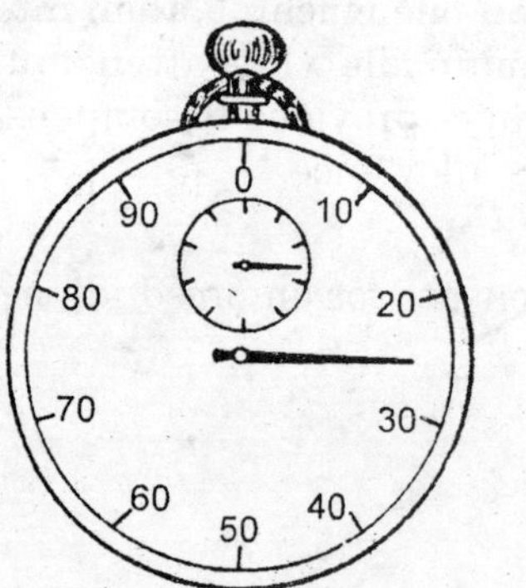

Fig. 11.1. Stop Watch

STOP WATCH

TIME RECORD SHEET

Fig. 11.2. Time Study Board

This board provides a place to keep the stop-watch on the right hand corner.

In addition to the above equipment, a time study expert should keep a pencil, steel tape and calculator etc.

Methods of Timings by Stop-watch

To note the time with the help of stop-watch, following systems are used :

(*a*) **Continuous Method.** In this, the stop-watch is allowed to run continuously and at the end of each operation reading of watch is noted and written in the Time Study Record Sheet. Thus to get the time required for any particular element of operation, the pervious reading is subtracted from the next reading. This method is better as it eliminates the possibilities of delay in noting the readings.

(*b*) **Snap Back Method.** In this method, knob of stop-watch is pressed to stop it at the end of each element of operation and is again started after noting the time required for completing the previous operational element.

This method is generally opposed by workers because it gives lesser time in comparison to actual due to repeated stop and starts of watch.

(c) **Accumulated Method.** With the help of this method, direct reading of each operational element is taken with the help of two watches connected with a lever mechanism so that when one watch is started other automatically stops. The reading of the stop-watch is noted and in the mean time, when next operational element is completed the second watch is started which stops the first one to facilitate in noting the reading.

11.5.2. Time Recording Machine

This type of machine has a paper tape, which rotates on two rollers at uniform speed. This paper tape is graduated in such a way that gives timings in fraction of minutes. Reading can be seen and recorded through a slit provided in the casing of equipment. By using this machine, some errors of the stop-watch method are eliminated.

The Idea of Time Recording machine by a line sketch is shown in Fig. 11.3.

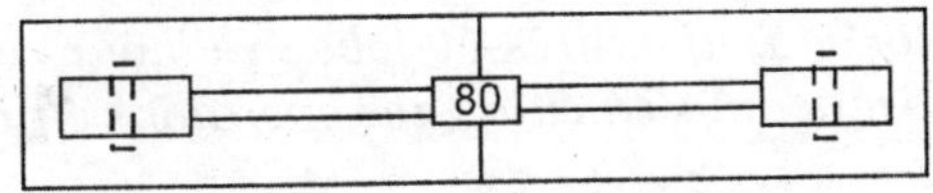

Fig. 11.3. Time Recording Machine

11.5.3. Motion Picture Camera

This camera as already explained is used in micro motion study. The utility of micromotion study has already been described in the 'Motion Study'. This camera is driven at constant speed of several ranges. Because of constant speed, time taken by each film can be calculated. Thus by knowing the number of films covered by operational element, the exact time can be found. For example, if camera was set at 1000 film per minute, *i.e.*, each film takes 0.001 minute and if an operational element covers 68 films, the time required for this operational element would be $0.0001 \times 68 \times 0.068$ minute. Thus, this method is very accurate one but is used for high precision work as this is expensive than other methods.

Following two types of Motion Picture Cameras are in common use:

(*i*) **Spring driven camera.** The speed of this camera is nearly constant and generally remains within ±10%. Normal speed is 16 exposures per second.

(*ii*) **Electric motor driven camera.** These cameras are driven by constant speed electric motors. These are of following types according to speed of motors :

(*a*) **Slow speed camera.** This operates at 50 or 100 frames per minute.

(*b*) **Normal speed camera.** This operates at 960 frames per minute.

11.6. NUMBER OF CYCLES TO BE TIMED

Time required to perform an element of an operation varies slightly from cycle to cycle. However, this variation can be reduced to some extent by using highly standardized raw materials, good tools and equipments, good working conditions and a qualified and well trained operator, but the variation cannot be avoided completely. Time study is a sampling process, therefore, large number of readings should be taken so that the results will be representative of the activity being measured and the desired accuracy may be obtained.

Experiences have shown that 95% confidence level and ±5% accuracy is sufficient for time study. From statistics, for this condition, number of cycles to be timed can be found by the following relation :

$$N' = \left\{ \frac{40\sqrt{N \Sigma X^2 - (\Sigma X)^2}}{\Sigma X} \right\}^2$$

where N' = Required number of observations to predict the operation time within ± 5% accurency and 95% confidence level.

N = Number of readings observed.

X = Eachstop-watchreading.

ΣX = Summation of individual reading.

ΣX^2 = Summation of squares of each reading.

Example 11.1. *An operator manufactures 50 jobs in 6 hours and 30 minutes. If this time includes the time for setting his machine, calculate the operator's efficiency. Standard time allowed for the job was :*

Setting time = *35 min.*

Production time per piece = *8 min.*

Solution.

As standard time = Set up time + Time per piece x No. of pieces produced

∴ Standard time for manufacturing 50 jobs

= 35 + 8 x 50

= 435 min = 7 hours, 15 min.

Efficiency of operator

$$= \frac{\text{Standard time} \times 100}{\text{Actual Time}}$$

$$= \frac{435 \times 100}{390}$$

= **111.5% Ans.**

Example 11.2. *Assuming that the total observed time for an operation of assembling an electric switch is 1.00 min. If the rating is 120%, find the normal time. If an allowance of 10% is allowed for the operation, determine the standard time.*

Solution.

Given

Observed or selected time = 1.00 min.

Rating = 120%

Allowance = 10%

As we know that,

$$\text{Normal time} = \text{Observed time} \times \frac{\text{Rating \%}}{100}$$

$$= 1.00 \times \frac{120}{100} = \textbf{1.20 min. Ans.}$$

Allowance @ $10\% = 1.20 \times \frac{10}{100} = 0.12$ min.

$\therefore$ Standard time = Normal time + Allowances

$$= 1.20 + 0.12 = \textbf{1.32. min. Ans.}$$

Alternative Method

10% allowance means $8 \times 60 \times \frac{10}{100} = 48$ minutes in a day of 8 hours.

$\therefore$ Time available for doing the work = 480 – 48 = 432 min.

Since time taken by one piece $= 1.00 \times \frac{120}{100} = 1.20$ min.

$\therefore$ No. of pieces produced in a day $= \frac{432}{1.20} = 360.$

$$\therefore \quad \text{Standard time/piece} = \frac{\text{Total time available in 8 hrs.}}{\text{No. of pieces produced}}$$

$$= \frac{480}{360} = \textbf{1.33 min. Ans.}$$

This can also be calculated by using the formula.

$$\text{Standard time} = \text{Normal time} \times \frac{100}{100 - \text{Allowance in \%}}$$

$$= 1.20 \times \frac{100}{100 - 10}$$

$$= \frac{1.20}{0.30} = \textbf{1.33 min. Ans.}$$

Thus we see that there is slight difference in the values calculated by both the methods. Second method gives accurate values and is more correct. But sometimes first method is also used being simpler.

Example 11.3. *Following datas were obtained by a work study man from a study conducted by him.*

(*i*) **Maintenance time**

- (*a*) *Get out and put away tools* = 12.0 *min/day.*
- (*b*) *Cleaning of machine* = 5.0 *min/day.*
- (*c*) *Oiling of machine* = 5.0 *min/day.*
- (*d*) *Replenish coolant supply* = 3.0 *min/day.*

(*ii*) **Interruption time**

- (*a*) *Interruption by foremen* = 5.0 *mir/day.*
- (*b*) *Interruption by porter etc.* = 4.0 *min/day.*

(*iii*) *Delay time due to power failure etc.* = 6.0 *min/day.*

(*iv*) *Personal time* = 20.0 *min/day.*

Calculate total allowances, total available cycle time, productive hour, considering a working day of 8 hours.

Solution.

Total allowance (some times also known as station time)

= Total maintenance time + Interruption time + Delay time + Personal time

$= (12.0 + 5 + 5 + 3.0) + (5.0 + 4.0) + 6.0 + 20.0$

$= 25.0 + 9.0 + 6.0 + 20.0$

= **60.0 min per day. Ans.**

∴ Total available cycle time = Total work period - Total allowances

= 480 - 60 = 420 **min/day. Ans.**

$$\text{Productive hour} = -\frac{\text{Time available}}{\text{Number of hours}}$$

$$= \frac{420}{8} = \mathbf{52.5\ min.\ Ans.}$$

Example 11.4. *An observer has taken few observations of an element, as shown below and now he wants to know as to how much readings should be taken for a 95% confidence level and ±5% precision.*

Individual readings in 0.01 min (X) are :

6, 5, 8, 6, 5, 5, 6.

Solution.

Individual readings 0.01 min. min. (X)	6	5	8	6	5	5	6	Total 41
X^2	36	25	64	36	25	25	36	247

Substituting the values of $\sum X$ and $\sum X^2$ in the following formula :

$$N' = \left(40\frac{\sqrt{N\sum X^2 - (\sum X)^2}}{\sum X}\right)$$

where N' = Required Number of observations within ± 5% accuracy and 95% confidence limit.

N = Number of stop-watch readings observed=7

$\sum X$ = Summation of individual readings=41

$\sum X^2$ = Summation of squares of each readings=247

$$\therefore \quad N' = \left[40\frac{\sqrt{7 \times 247 - (41)^2}}{41}\right]^2$$

$$= \left[40\frac{\sqrt{1729 - 1681}}{41}\right]^2$$

$$= \left[\frac{40\sqrt{48}}{41}\right]^2 = (6.76)^2 = 45.70 = 46 \text{ say}$$

Thus 46 observations are required for achieving desired accuracy and confidence level.

Note. This number is only a guiding factor. After taking 46 observations, we should again apply this formula and confirm whether we have taken the sufficient readings.

Example 11.5. *Find out the standard time using the following data :*

Average time for machine elements = 6 min.
Average time for manual elements = 4 min.
Performance rating = 10%
Allowances = 10%

Solution.

As we know that,

$$\text{Normal time} = \text{Machinery time} + \text{Manual time x Rating}$$
$$= 6 + 4 \times 1.1$$
$$= 6 + 4.4 = 10.4 \text{ min.}$$

$$\therefore \quad \text{Standard time} = \text{Normal time} + \text{Allowances}$$
$$= 10.4 + 10.4 \times \frac{10}{100}$$
$$= \mathbf{11.44 \text{ min. Ans.}}$$

11.7. USE OF TIME STUDY DATA

Time study is used to determine the time required to perform the job. With the help of work study, best method of doing a job is decided. The time study is applied to determine the standard time to be taken by an average worker. So with the help of time and motion study, worker's wages can be fixed. Similarly, time study data is utilized to design incentive scheme so that an employee is paid a reward additional to the job hourly rate. The schemes are based on work measurement data which must of course be obtained by proper application of the appropriate techniques.

These incentive schemes increase the output and a sound basis of labour control. They can produce dynamic improvement in labour turnover, absenteeism and industrial relations etc.

For Productivity Bargaining

Productivity bargaining (or agreement) tries to link the basis for calculating wages with work done. For this agreement, the employer and the employees negotiate on the basis of fair wage for the work to be done, thus they link the wages with the work. Following are some of the important aims of productivity bargaining:

1. More efficiency, hence reduced labour cost per unit of production.
2. Better utilization of plant and machinery.
3. Reduction of idle timings.
4. Reduction in restriction practices (*i.e.* delaying tactics in production).
5. Benefits to both the sides (*i.e*) employer and employee), since the bargain is made on a mutual footing.

In present circumstances, a great necessity is being experienced in our country for linking the wages with work done. This can be implemented by mutual agreements between the trade unions and the respective concerns. Hence, as a first step, it is necessary to create and appropriate environment for the productivity bargaining.

The productivity bargaining is a part of **collective bargaining.** Collective bargaining is the process of direct negotiation on a collective or group basis between the representatives of the employees and those of employers for the settlement of disputes. The mutual right and obligations of both parties are agreed between themselves through negotiation in the form of an agreement or contract, which is legal binding on them. Some of the matters which are generally dealt through the collective bargaining are:

1. Recognition of the union.
2. Workers' participation in the management.
3. Wages and other benefits.
4. Procedure for disciplinary action.
5. Accident and safety.
6. Honrs of employment including holidays, leaves, absence, intervals, etc.
7. Pension, sickness and medical facilities.
8. Policy for rotation and transfers etc.

11.8. STANDARD DATA

Generally, large number of man-hours are spent in setting the time standards by using stop-watch time study. Further, management is anxious to have the time standards before the jobs are actually manufactured for cost estimating, scheduling, planning and other decision making purposes. In this, advantage of previous time standards already on hand can be taken.

Every operation consists of number of small work elements which are repeated in various combinations. The time values for these small, work elements are established accurately, and these values are used without further time study, whenever that element occurs. These standardized timings for such elements are known as Standard Data.

For calculations of standard time, using the standard data, first step is to standardize the method (by method study). Then break the operation into small elements and note down their timings from standard data tables and then add the timings of all such elements to get the standard time of the operation.

Uses of Standard Data

1. Standard Data helps in determining in advance that how long it will take to perform an operation in the shop.
2. It helps in comparing two methods and determining best method.
3. Evaluating proposed methods in advance of actual production.
4. Helps in estimating the time required and labour cost.
5. For checking standards established by time study.

Advantages of Standard Data

1. Standard time can be found even when the product is not being manufactured.
2. Provides a basis for decision making, budgeting, estimating etc.
3. Various time study persons can arrive at identical time standards for given method.

4. There can be no dispute about partiality or incorrectness of time study.
5. Economical than the time study by a stop-watch method.
6. Rating or efficiency of the operator can be determined correctly.

11.9. PRE-DETERMINED MOTION TIME SYSTEM (PMTS)

We have earlier discussed that standard data are of two types, namely, macro data and micro data. An element in macro data have its time value of several seconds (*e.g.* pick up the screw driver), whereas in micro data the elements of job are basic human motions with duration of 0.1 second or even less. The micro data is based upon much smaller division of motions (*i.e.* therbligs) as compared to macro data. The PMTS deals with micro data of standard data system.

PMTS can be defined as a work measurement technique where by times established for basic human motions are used to build up the time for a job at a defined level of performance.

Features of PMTS.

1. In this system element time is not measured by a stop watch and thus it avoids the inaccuracies due to human judgement.
2. In this system it is assumed that all manual tasks are made up of certain basic human movements (like, reach, move, turn, release etc.) which are common to almost all jobs.
3. The average time taken by an average worker to perform a basic movement is practically constant.
4. The operations are recorded on a movie film (refer micro-motion study) and analyse the time taken to complete each element.
5. Standard time may be obtained by adding proper allowances.

Methods for Determining PMTS.

Following methods are commonly used for determining the standard data :

1. Work Factor System (W.F.S)
2. Method Time Measurement (MTM)
3. Basic Motion Time

11.10. WORK FACTOR SYSTEM (W.F.S)

In this system, it is assumed that there are four major variables which affect the time required to perform a task. These variables are :

(*i*) **Body members used,** identified by exact definition like Arm, Forearm Swivel, Trunk, Foot and Legs, Fingers or Hand.

(*ii*) **Distance moved,** measured in inches or cms.

(*iii*) **Manual controls required,** measured in Work Factors. These reflect the difficulties involved. These are Definite stop ; Directional control (Steer); Care (Precautions); Change of direction.

(*iv*) **Weight or Resistance**

Work Factor Motion Time Tables

Since basic motion do not involve any work factor, the time required by different body members to move different distances are given first in the tables. Then the time needed by them after considering the work factors (in numbers) is given. Following are the notations used with this system :

When a motion has been identified, according to the four major variables, the correct time value can be selected quickly from the work Factor Motion-Time Table (a part view given below). In this table, value for each body member is given separately and the first column gives the distance moved, the second column gives the time for basic motion. Depending upon the number of work factors involved, time required for the motion can be noted from the corresponding column.

Body Member	*Symbol*	*Work Factors*	*Symbol*
1. Arm	*A*	1. Weight or Resistance	*W*
2. Finger	*F*	2. Directional control (Steer)	*S*
3. Hand	*H*	3. Care (Precaution)	*P*
4. Forearm Swivel	*FS*	4. Change Direction	*U*
5. Trunk	*J*	5. Definite Stop	*D*
6. Foot	*FT*		
7. Leg	*L*		
8. Head turn	*HT*		

Distance Moved	*Time ten thousands of a minute*				
	Basic Time	*Work Factor*			
A (Arm)		*1*	*2*	*3*	*4*
2.54 cm or 1"	18	26	34	40	46
25.4 cm or 10"	42	61	78	93	107
50.8 cm or 20"	58	80	102	124	144
76.2 cm or 30"	70	96	119	142	163

This table shows the values for the motion time when Arm is involved, similarly the values for other body members are also given in the table.

Recording the Analysis

Symbols are used for recording for the motion analysis. In indicating a motion, the body member is indicated first, the distance moved second and the Work Factor third. Few examples are shown here under:

	Description of Motion	*Motion Symbol*	*Time in Min. (From table)*
1.	Toss small part to 10" or 25.4 cm (Basic motion)	A 10	0.0042
2.	Reach 20" or 50.8 cm to nut in the job (definite stop motion *i.e.* one Work Factor)	A 20 D	0.0080
3.	Move 4 lb box 30" or 76.2 cm from pile to place on work table (Weight Definite stop motion *i.e.* 2 Word Factor	A 30 WD	0.0119

11.11. METHODS TIME MEASUREMENT (M.T.M.)

This system of predetermined motion time standards (P.M.T.S.) was developed from motion picture studies. In this system, each manual operation is defined into the basic motion and assigned a predetermined time standard based on nature of the motion and condition under which it is performed.

The motion time data are given in the M.T.M. tables. Unit of time used in the tables is one hundred thousandth of an hour (0.00001 hr.) and is referred to as one Time Measurement Unit (TMU). Thus one T.M.U. = 0.00001 hr. = 0.0006 minute.

In this system motions are classified in following categories :

(*i*) Reach
(*ii*) Move
(*iii*) Turn
(*iv*) Grasp
(*v*) Position
(*vi*) Release load
(*vii*) Disengata
(*viii*) Eye times
(*ix*) Body, leg and foot motions.

1. REACH (R)

Reach is a basic element when hand or finger moves to a destination. This varies with the following factors :

(*i*) **Classes of Reach.** The time to perform a reach motion is affected by the location in which object is lying. Following are the five classes of reach :

Case *A* Reach : Object in fixed location.
Case *B* Reach : Object whose general location is known. Location may vary slightly from cycle to cycle.
Case *C* Reach : Object jumbled with other objects in a group.
Case *D* Reach : Object is very small.
Case *E* Reach : Object is in indefinite position or out of the way.

(*ii*) **The length** of a motion is the length of true path.

(*iii*) **Types of Reach**

(*a*) Hand is neither moving at beginning nor at end.

(*b*) Hand is moving either at beginning or at end.

(*c*) Hand is in motion both at beginning and at end.

2. MOVE (M)

Move is a basic element to transport an object to a destination. Its motion time varies with the following factors :

(*i*) **Class of Move.** It considers the condition of destination.

(*a*) Case A Move : Object to against stop.

(*b*) Case (*B*) Move : Object to approximate location.

(*c*) Case (*C*) Move : Object to exact location.

(*ii*) **Types of Move.** These are the same as those described for reach.

(*iii*) **Length of Motion.** Same as described for reach.

(*iv*) **Weight Factor.** Additional time is needed when an object is moved with weight (above 1.134 kg). The table gives the allowances of time to be added for different weights.

3. TURN (T)

Turn is the motion employed to turn or rotate the hand, wrist and forearm either empty or loaded. The time for a turn depends upon :

(*i*) Weight

(*ii*) Degrees turned.

The table gives the time or different slabs or weights and degrees turned. If pressure is applied while turning, an allowance given in the table is further added.

4. GRASP (G)

Grasp is the basic element employed to secure sufficient control of one or more objects with the fingers or hand to permit the performance of the next basic element required. These elements are classified according to the size of the object and the combination of sizes of objects to be secured (grasped). The time for all such cases are given in the table.

5. POSITION (P)

Position is the basic element employed to align, orient and engage one object with another object. The position time is affected by :

(*i*) **Class of Fit.** (*a*) Loose, (*b*) Close and (*c*) Exact.

(*ii*) **Symmetry,** (*a*) Symmetrical, (*b*) Semi-symmetrical (*c*) Non-symmetrical objects.

(*iii*) **Ease of handling,** (*a*) Easy to handle (*b*) Difficult to handle.

The table shows the time required for all the above cases.

6. RELEASE LOAD (RL)

The release is of following two types :

(*i*) **Normal release.** Simply opening of the fingers.

(*ii*) **Contract release.** The release begins and is completed at the instant. No time is allowed in this case.

7. DISENGAGE (D)

This is the basic element employed to break contract between one object and another object. Time for this element is affected by the following variables :

(*i*) **Class of Fit.** (*a*) Loose (*b*) Close and (*c*) Tight fit.
(*ii*) **Ease of Handling,** (*a*) Easy and (*b*) Difficult to handle.
(*iii*) **Care in Handling.**

8. EYE TIMES

In some cases, when eyes direct the hands or body movements, eye times must be considered. There are two types of eye times.

(*i*) **Eye Travel Time (E.T.)** This varies directly with distance between the point from and to which the eye travels and inversely with the perpendicular distance from the eye to the line of travel.

Eye travel time

$$= 15.2 \times \frac{\text{Distance travelled by eye}}{\text{Perpendicular distance eye to the line of travel}}$$

(*ii*) **Eye Focus Time (EF).** It is the time required to focus the eyes or an object and is equal to 7.3 T.M.U.

9. BODY, LEG AND FOOT MOTIONS

The table gives the time required for the movement of different members of the body, leg and foot.

Recording the Analysis Based on M.T.M. Study

To find out the time required for an operation, break down it into elements. Each element is then identified and recorded in symbols. Then M.T.M. tables are consulted to get the time values for each element. The summation of time values for all the elements of operation gives the time required for performing that operation. Some of the symbols and their description is given hereunder to facilitate the students to understand as to how these are recorded.

Sl. No.	*Symbols*	*Description*
1.	R4A	Reach 4" *i.e.* 10.16 cm case A
2.	R10Bm	Reach 10" *i.e.* 25.4 cm case *B* hand in motion at the end.
3.	M12B 10	Move 12" *i.e.* 30.5 cm case *B* weight 10 lbs (4.54 Kg).
4.	M8B	Move 8" *i.e.* 20.32 cm case *B* object of less than 1 Kg.
5.	mM12B	Move 12" *i.e.* 30.5. cm case *B* hand in motion at beginning object weight less than 1 kg.
6.	T60L	Turn 60° with large load (more than 4.54 kg *i.e.* 10 lbs).
7.	P2NSE	Position class 2 fit non systematical easy to handle
8.	G1A	Grasp case 1*A*
9.	ET $\frac{16}{10}$	Eye travel between 16" *i.e.* 40.6 cm apart line of travel 10" *i.e.* 25.4 cm from eye.
10.	P1SD	Position class 1 fit symmetrical difficult to handle.

11.12. BASIC MOTION TIME STUDY

Following factors are taken into consideration for Basic Motion Time Study :

(i) Classes of motion.

(ii) The distance moved.

(iii) Visual attention.

(iv) Degree of precision.

(v) Amount of force needed in handling the weight.

(vi) Simultaneous performance of two motions.

1. **Class of Motion.** Motions are classified as :

    (a) *Class A Motion* : Stoppage without muscular control, has lowest time values.

    (b) *Class B Motion* : Stoppage by the use of force, needs more time than that of *A*.

    (c) *Class C Motion* : Use of muscular control both to slow down the motion and to end it in a grasping or placing action.

2. **Distance Moved.** In the table, time for each class of motion for different distances are given.

3. **Visual Attention.** The time to perform a motion is also affected by the fact whether or not eye moves with the hand or arm. This requires slightly more time (given in the table for B.M.T.) in the class *B* or *C* motions for travelling the same distances.

4. **Precision Required in Grasping or Positioning.** When a motion ends in grasping a small object or in placing an object in exact location, a certain degree of precision is required depeding upon the tolerance allowed in grasping or positioning. The B.M.T. table gives the time required in moving different distances for different tolerances.

5. **Force Factor.** Whenever a heavy weight is handled, time allowance is added. The allowance of time is given for different distances, depending upon the amount of force. These values are available in B.M.T. tables.

6. **Simultaneous Motions.** The time for reaches and moves are affected by visual attention, eye travel, eye focus etc. The time is to be added for such simultaneous motions (also given in B.M.T. tables).

11.13. WORK SAMPLING

Work sampling also called Activity Sampling or Ratio Delay Study is based on the statistical method first devised by L.H.C. Tippot in 1934. He used this technique firstly, in the British textile industry. Later Morrow carried out several investigations. The results obtained by the all day stop watch time study and such other statistical methods were in most cases, found to be in close agreement with the work sampling method, which places it on a sound reliable basis.

Though stop-watch time study proved to be very useful for repetitive operations but it cannot measure accurately and economically long and irregular work cycles. While most of the indirect activities are of irregular nature and therefore, there must be some way to control the indirect labour activities. For such tasks work sampling has been well established and gained lot of popularity.

Workers have wrong concept that the results of a time study may go against them and reduce their rates, therefore, they oppose the stop-watch method. The technique of Activity sampling though not tried much in our country is gradually coming into use. For this technique, workers have no such feelings.

Objectives

Work sampling is a fact finding tools and has the following two main objectives:

1. To measure activities and delays that a man is working and percentage of that he is not working. It means a fair day's work.
2. Under certain circumstances, to measure manual tasks, that is, to establish time standards for an operation.

Applications of Work Sampling

1. Work sampling can be applied for the estimation of the percentage utilisation of machine tools, cranes and fork trucks etc.
2. Work sampling can also be used to estimate the unavoidable delay time for deciding the delay allowance.
3. To estimate the percentage of the time consumed by various job activities, *i.e.*, supervision, repair, inspection etc.
4. Work sampling is also used to find out time standards, specially where the job is not repetitive and where time study by stop-watch method is not possible, *i.e.*, for maintenance work, office work, repair work and ship building etc. Time standards can be calculated by combining rating with work sampling as illustrated in the following example:

Advantages of Work Sampling Over Time Study

1. Operator is not subjected to long-period stop-watch observations.
2. Group operations can be easily studied by a single analysis.
3. It does not require continuous observation for a long period of time.
4. Many operators or activities which are impractical or costly to be measured by time study can be measured by this.
5. Observations may be taken over a period of days or weeks, thus decreasing the chance of day-to-day or week to week variations affecting the results.
6. The manhours spent by the analyst are much less.
7. A work sampling study can be stopped at any time without affecting the results.
8. In this, random observations are taken thus avoiding prolonged observations, if necessary.
9. This produces less fatigue and are less tedious to observer.
10. It generally requires less time in calculating the results.
11. No stop-watch or any other timing device is needed.
12. Clerical time is minimised.

Disadvantages of work Sampling over "Time Study"

1. It is not economical to study a single operator or machine or for studying operators or machines located over wide areas.
2. It does not permit finer breakdown of activities and delays.
3. Study made of a group represents average while there is no information about the magnitude or individual differences.

4. Management and workers may not be able to understand work sampling as easily as they do time study.
5. Some time no record is kept of the study on the operator, therefore, a new study must be made when a method change occurs in any element.

11.14. THEORY OF WORK SAMPLING

It states that the percentage of observations recorded an operation in any state is a reliable estimate of the percentage time the operation is in any state, provided, "sufficient number of observation are taken at random". Here particular stress should be laid on the words "random" and "sufficient number of observations."

In this method, some error is likely to occur but the error tends to diminish as the number of sample increases.

For example, in following table, there are 36 working observations and four idle observations, *i.e.*, a total of 40 observations.

State	*Total*
Working	36
Idle	4

"Table to show working time and idle time."

In this example, the percentage of idle time is $\frac{4}{40} \times 100 = 10\%$

Working time is $\frac{36}{40} \times 100 = 90\%$

This study is for one operator for an 8 hours a day and indicates that the operator was idle for 10% or 48 minutes of the day, while working for 90% or 432 minutes of the day.

Confidence Level

It is important to decide what level of confidence is desired in the final "Work Sampling" results. The most common confidence level is 95%. The area under the curve at 2 sigma or two standard deviations is 95.45%, which when rounded off gives 95%. This means that the probability is that 95% of the time, the random observations will represent the facts and 5% of the time they will not, Fig. 11.4.

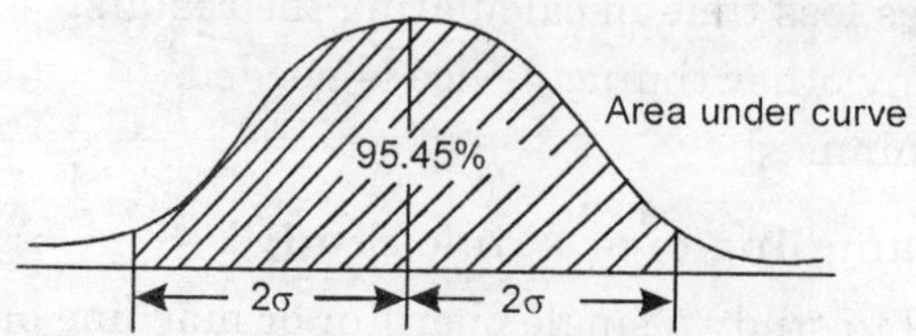

Fig. 11.4. Curve of confidence level.

For many cases, an accuracy of ± 5% is considered satisfactory. This is sometimes referred to as the standard error of the percentage.

Sample Size Determination

To get a desired accuracy, an analyst must take sufficient number of observations. For calculating the number of observations required for achieving the desired accuracy, following formula is used :

$$S \times p = K\sqrt{\frac{p(1-p)}{N}}$$

where,

K = 1, 2 or 3 for confidence level of 68%, 95% and 99.7% respectively.

N = Total number of random observations (sample size).

S = Desired relative accuracy.

p = Percentage occurrence of an activity or delay, expressed as a decimal *e.g.* 15% = 0.15.

Example 11.6. *Determine the percentage of idle time of an automatic screw cutting machine by Work Sampling. Assume that a, confidence level of 95% and an accuracy of ±5% have been considered. Determine how many random observations will be required to give the desired results.*

Solution.

In this example, it is necessary to estimate the value p first. It means a trail study would be made to get a first estimate of the percentage of idle time.

Let us assume that 100 observations were made, out of which 25 observations showed the machines to be idle. The percentage of idle time would be 25%, i.e.=0.25.

The standard formula is

$$S \times p = 2\sqrt{\frac{p(1-p)}{N}} \quad ...(1)$$

Hence

$$S = 0.05$$
$$p = 0.25$$
$$N = ?$$

$$\therefore \quad 0.05 \times 0.25 = 2\sqrt{\frac{0.250(1-0.25)}{N}}$$

or

$$N = \frac{1600(1-0.25)}{0.25} = 4800$$

After the work study is in progress and observations have been taken, a new calculation is to be made in order to recheck the value for N. Suppose the results were as under:

Observations of machine working = 350

Observations of machine idle = 150

Total observations = 500

$$\therefore \text{ Idle time } = \frac{150}{500} \times 100 = 30\% = 0.30.$$

This new information would enable to re-calculate the number of observation required.

Now $p = 0.30$

or $$0.05 \times 0.30 = 2\sqrt{\frac{0.30(1-0.30)}{N}}$$

or $$N = \frac{0.84}{0.000225} = 3733.$$

It is advisable to recalculate N at regular intervals, perhaps at the end of each day, in order to better evaluate the progress of the work study.

Determination of "Accuracy" for a given number of observations

Where the study is over, a calculation is made to find whether the results are within the desired accuracy or not. This can be done by substituting N in the equation (1) instead of S.

Assume that the final results of the study are:

Observations of machines working = 2600

Observations of machine idle = 1400

Total observations = 4000

Then, $$p = \frac{1400}{4000} = 0.35$$

Now $$S \times p = 2\sqrt{\frac{p(1-p)}{N}}$$

or $$0.35 \times S = 2\sqrt{\frac{0.35(1-0.35)}{4000}}$$

$\therefore$ $$S = +\frac{0.01508}{0.35} = +0.043 = +4.3\%$$

As ± 4.3% is below ± 5%, the required accuracy, the number of observations are sufficient.

In this example, it can be said that we are 95% confident that the automatic screw machine is idle 35% of the time. The accuracy or standard error of ± 4.3% means that the results are correct within ± 4.3% of 35% (± 4.3% x 35% = ± 1.5%) or the true value is between 33.5% of 36.5%. The 95% confidence level means that the probability is that 95 cases out of 100 the above results will represent the fact.

11.15. PROCEDURE FOR WORK SAMPLING

The following steps are involved in making a "Work Sampling" study :

1. Define the problem.
   (*a*) State the main objectives or purpose of the problem.
   (*b*) Describe the details of each element to be measured.
2. Obtain the approval of the Foreman of the department in which study is to be made. Obtain the co-operation of the operations to be studied and they should also understand the purpose of study.
3. Determine the desired accuracy of final results in the form of standard error of percentage.
4. State the confidence level.
5. Make a preliminary estimate of the percentage occurrence of the activity or delay to be measured for one day or two days. This may be estimated on the basis of past experience.

6. (*a*) Design the study. Design the number of:
   (*i*) Observations to be made.
   (*ii*) Observers needed. Select and instruct them.
   (*iii*) Days or shifts needed for the study.
   (*b*) Make plans for taking the observations such as time for taking and the route to be followed by the observer.
   (*c*) Design the observations form.
7. Make the observations and record the data.
8. Summarize the data at the end of each day.
9. Check the accuracy or precision of the data at the end of the study.
10. Prepare the report and state results. It required to make recommendations.

Determination of Time Standards by Work Sampling

With work sampling, it is possible to determine the percentage of the day, a worker is idle and the percentage of the day he is working. The average performance index or the speed at which he worked during the working portion of the day can also be determined.

For example, Mohan Singh worked as Drillman and a work sampling study showed that he was idle 15% of the day or 72 minutes and that he worked the remainder of the day or 408 minutes at an average performance index of 110%. He drilled 400 items of acceptable quality during the day. The standard time for the operation he performed can be calculated as shown below :

It is assumed that 15% of the total time is taken as fatigue and other personal allowances.

As standard Time

= Allowance + (total time in minutes) × (Working time in percent)

$$\frac{\text{Performance index in percent}}{\text{Total No. of items produced}}$$

$$= \left(\frac{100}{100-15}\right) \times \frac{480 \times 0.85 \times 1.10}{400} = \textbf{1.32 minutes.}$$

Example 11.7. *A work sampling study showed that 20% of a work week of 48 hours was consumed by avoidable delays. If each time a work sampling observation was made the operator was rated and the average of such ratings was 110%, If 100 units were produced by the operator in that period, calculate standard time.*

Solution.

Duration of work = 48 hours.

Percentage working time = 80%.

∴ Actual time worked by the operator = 48 × 0.80.

$$\therefore \quad \text{Actual time worked by the operator/piece} = \frac{48 \times 0.80}{100}$$

Now, Standard Time = Actual time per piece × Rating

$$= \frac{48 \times 0.80}{100} \times 1.10 = 0.4224 \text{ hours/unit.}$$

∴ Standard Time per unit = **25.34 minutes.**

11.16. ERRORS IN WORK SAMPLING STUDY

While conducting the Work Sampling study some errors are likely to be occurred. Therefore, care must be taken to avoid these errors. Following are some of the errors which generally occur :

(1) Sampling errors. (2) Bias in work sampling.

(3) Non-representatives.

1. Sampling Errors

In sampling study, whole population is represented by a sample. If the size of the sample is small, then there are chance of errors in inferences drawn from this sample. Therefore, while conducting the study care must be taken that sample size must represent the same characteristics as that of the whole population. The sample size can be calculated using the formulae, after a confidence level and level of accuracy is decided. After completing the study, it must be checked, whether sufficient number of observations have been taken or not.

2. Bias in Work Sampling

As a consequence of bias in study, the proportion of an activity (working or idle) shall be different from the actual proportion of time devoted to the activity. Following are the main sources of bias in a study:

(*i*) **Non-random schedule of Observation.** To avoid this error, randomised sampling procedure must be adopted. Before starting the study, actual schedule of observations must be designed. Once the number of observations has been estimated (after deciding the confidence level and accuracy) using the formula and a representative period (number of days over which the study is spread- up) to study has been selected, the number of observations N are distributed over the total number of days selected. Then this number is distributed randomly over the day. For this purpose, any random number table may be used. For example, numbers are taken from the random number table:

3	1	2	5	8
2	5	4	9	1
0	1	3	5	8
6	1	4	4	0

Then using these numbers, we can fix the schedule as—

3rd hour 12th min. 58th sec.

2nd hour 54th min. 10th sec. (leaving Number 9).

1st hour 35th min. 8th sec.

6th hour 14th min. 40 sec.

These times are then chronologically arranged to complete the observation schedule.

As a second way these numbers can also be used to indicate as (leaving last number).

3 hr and 12 min. after the start of the shift.

2 hr and 54 min.—do—

0 hr and 13 min.—do—

6 hr and 14 min.—do—

(*ii*) **Bias on the part of the observer.** Sometimes when the observer observes the worker, who is in transitional state, *i.e.*, he is changing from one state to another state, then the observer can call it either way. In such cases, the observers judgment is required. To avoid any possibility of bias, following precautions must be taken to minimise the judgments:

(*a*) Categories must be defined very clearly.

(*b*) Clearly define the instant at which the observation is to be made. For this purpose, a turn of the corner is preferred so that the category, as the time of first seeing can be noted.

(*c*) If any transitional stage cannot be defined clearly, even then judgement is avoided and tossing of coin must be done.

(*iii*) **Change in the behaviour of the worker.** Sometimes when the observed person knows that he is being observed then he changes his behaviour. To take care of this error, following precautions must be taken :

(*a*) Observation must be randomly spaced.

(*b*) Observation must be taken as soon as the operation is in sightof the observer.

(*c*) Randomise the order in which individual worker is observed when more workers are to be observed.

3. **Non-representativeness in Work Sampling**

Non-representativeness exists when the period studied is not characteristic of the circumstances that prevail in the long run. For example, results taken on any one day cannot represent all the days. On Monday, the worker is fresh while on Friday and Saturday he will be tired. Similarly, the result taken in the day shift, evening shift and in the night shift will be different. Same problem is for seasons, ***i.e.***, results in the summer cannot be applied in the winter and in the rainy seasons.

Therefore, designer of work sampling study must give a careful attention to representativeness of the sample. Periods of abnormal activities and unusual conditions should be avoided.

11.17. MACHINE INTERFERENCE

In the textile industries or wire and cable industries where the product is of continuous length, multi-machine operation is required to be done by a single worker.

In multi-machine operation, a number of machines can be attended by one operator, then some problems arise, such as calculation of machine capacities, production output, number of machine units to be attended by one or group of operators. If too few machines assigned, labour cost will be more, if too many are assigned, the machines will be idle and cost for this excess machine capacity will become burdensome.

Following are the factors which are needed to be defined before proceeding further:

Multi-Machine Operation

It is the simultaneous operation of more than one machine units by one or group of operators. In equation, ***N*** represents the number of identical machine units to be used.

Running Time

It is the time necessary for a machine unit to run without any break to produce one unit of output. This is represented by the word *R*.

Working Time

It is the time an operator must work on the machine units to produce a single unit of output. It is represented by the word W.

Interference

It is the time for which one or more machine units are idle while the attendant is occupied with the work on other machine units. Interference is represented by the word *I*.

To understand how the above mentioned factors used in determining the outputs, let us assume that in a wire insulating line the running time per unit (*R*) is four minutes. Assume also that working time (*W*) per unit of output is one minute. Suppose six machines are assigned to one operator. The operation cycle is shown in Fig. 11.5 from which it is quite clear that one machine unit will be idle while the operator takes care of the others.

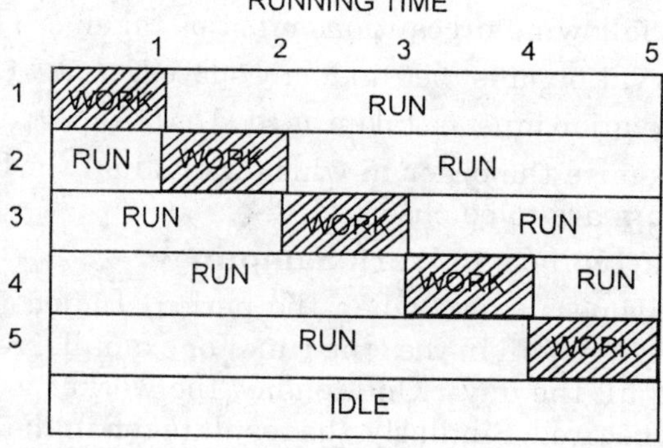

Fig. 11.5. Operating of six machine units.

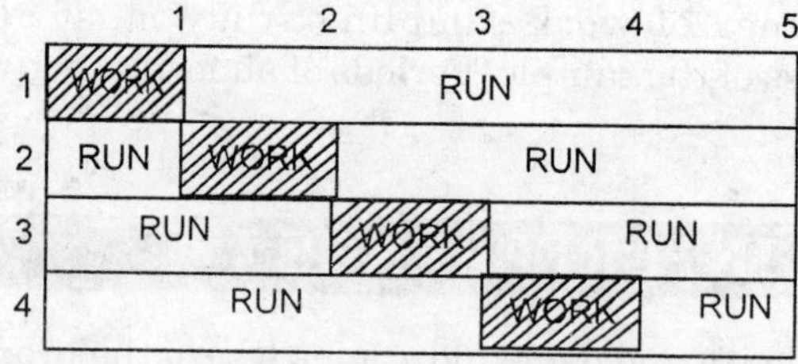

Fig. 11.6. Operation of four machine units.

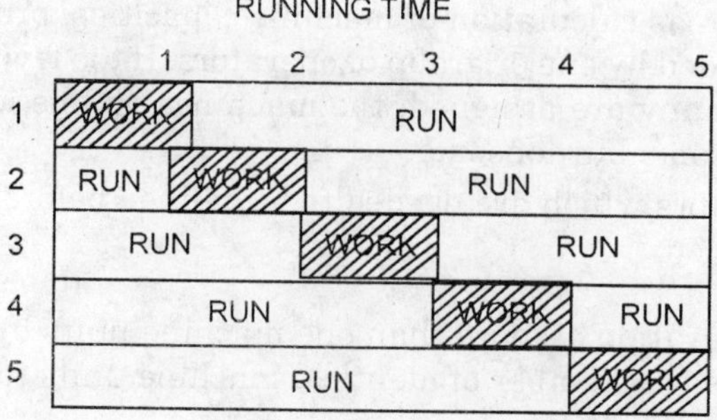

Fig. 11.7. Operation of five machines units.

Now assume that four machine units have been assigned to one operator, the operation cycle is as per Fig. 11.6. In this case, the operator is idle for one minute out of each five minutes, *i.e.* 20% of the time.

Further, let five machine units are assigned to an operator, the operation cycle is as per Fig. 11.7. Here neither operator nor machine unit are idle.

Without considering the factor of interference a good approximation of the proper number of machine units to be assigned to an operator, can be calculated by $\frac{R+W}{W} = N$, in our example

$$N = \frac{4+1}{1} = 5.$$

Machine Interference

The effect of interference occurs when an operator usually attends to several semi-automatic machine units. For a given output, there may be times when all machines are working and the operator is merely waiting for something to happen as in case of alloting four machines to an operator. There may be possible when many of machines are shut down simultaneously though in most cases operator cannot do anything but there is interference idleness.

As per Engineer's point of view, the machine interference is important in two respects. First is to know that how many machines should be assigned to an operator, in which machine interference should be known. The second one, to find out the operator's actual productive efficiency for wage incentive purpose, for which loss of production caused by machine interference has to be evaluated.

Previously much time was spent by time study men in evaluating machine interference by use of stop-watches. But they are not successful due to unpredictable, variable shut down of machine units.

Since machine interference is unpredictable and variable in magnitude, a mathematical technique is evolved which takes into account such uncertainty.

This technique is based on the law of probability, which states "that when an event is based on chance as pertaining to each of several participants acting together, the various possible combinations of occurrence of that event will be disturbed according to the terms of binomial expansion,

$$(d + r)^n = d^n + nd^{n-1} r + \frac{n\left(n-1\right)d^{n-2}r^2}{1\left(2\right)} + \ldots\ldots + r^n$$

where d = probability of occurrence

r = probability of non-occurrence

n = number of machines.

Use of the binomial expansion is quite clear by the following example on interference :

Example. 11.8. *Suppose, at the end of the day, the down time (non-producing time) per machine was 20 per cent of the time for which six percentage interference per machine for the period of operation. Find also the average servicing time per machine.*

Solution.

Here $d = 20\%$, *i.e.* $\frac{1}{5}$

$$r = \frac{4}{5}$$

and $$n = 6$$

Now the binomial expansion is

$$\left(\frac{1}{5}+\frac{4}{5}\right)^6 = \left(\frac{1}{5}\right)^6 + 6\left(\frac{1}{5}\right)^5 \cdot \frac{4}{5} + \frac{6\times 5\left(\frac{1}{5}\right)^4\left(\frac{4}{5}\right)^2}{1.2} + \ldots\ldots + r^n$$

Putting in the form of table

Number of machine down together	*Coefficient Sum*	*d*	*r*	*Wait*	*Interference = multiplication of column 2 3 4 and 5*
(1)	(2)	(3)	(4)	(5)	(6)
6	1	$(1/5)^6$	– –	5	$\frac{5}{15625}$
5	6	$(1/5)^5$	$(4/5)^1$	4	$\frac{96}{15625}$
4	15	$(1/5)^4$	$(4/5)^2$	3	$\frac{720}{15625}$
3	20	$(1/5)^3$	$(4/5)^3$	2	$\frac{2560}{15625}$
2	15	$(1/5)^2$	$(4/5)^4$	1	$\frac{3840}{15625}$
1	6	$(1/5)^1$	$(4/5)^5$	0	0
0	1	– –	$(1/5)^6$	0	0

$$\Sigma \text{ Interference} = \frac{7221}{15625} = 0.462$$

Since there are six machines in the group, the average interference per machine $= \frac{0.462}{6} = 7.7\%$

Further as down time (d) is equal to average servicing time plus average interference time, the average servicing time

$$= 20 - 7.7 = 12.3\%.$$

To ease the evaluation, table charts are compiled showing the relationship between interference, servicing time and down time for a group of any number of machines. These are prepared by assuming various percentages of down time, and calculating as above and then recording the results.

The Economical Number of Machines per Operator

While an operator handles multi-machines to get the output, for an engineer, it is quite important to know the economic number of machines to be allotted per operator.

At the start of this chapter we have discussed that how the number of machines per operator can be found out without considering the factor of machine interference.

The cost of operating number of machines by an operator can be calculated by the formula,

$$\frac{nM + L}{nP}$$

where n = number of machines allotted to an operator.

M = hourly machine rate, *i.e.*, power, depreciation etc.

L = hourly rate of operator's labour.

P = average productive time per machine (or the efficiency in percentage of overall operating time)

For finding the value of P, following factors should also be known:

S = service time machine in percentage of overall operating time, assuming that each machine is allotted to an operator.

D = down time per machine in percentage of total operating time.

I = average interference time per machine in per cent of overall time.

To understand the application of the formula, let us suppose the total average service time per machine in percentage when one machine allotted to one operator is 15% in case when 3, 4, 5,6 machine in actual allotted to one operator. The labour cost is Re. 1 per hour whereas the machine rate is Re. 1 per hour/machine.

It is found out from the machine interference table that for service time of 15%, for machine number 3,4,5,6 the Interference time is equal to 3, 5, 8 and 11 percent. Now applying the data as below :

n	S	I *in* %	P *in* %	nP	nM	L	$nM + L$	$\frac{nM + L}{nP}$
3	15%	3	82.5	2.48	Rs. 3	Rs. 1	Rs. 4	Rs. 1.61
4	15%	5	80.7	3.23	4	1	5	1.55
5	15%	8	78.2	3.91	5	1	6	1.53
6	15%	11	75.7	4.54	6	1	7	1.54

For calculating P, use the following formula

$$P = 100 - I - \frac{S}{100}(100 - I)$$

Put the percentage value *of I, S* in the formula the value of different average productive times is calculated as below :

$$P_3 = 100 - 3 - \frac{15}{100}(100 - 3) = 82.5\%$$

$$P_4 = 100 - 5 - \frac{15}{100}(100 - 5) = 80.7\%$$

$$P_5 = 100 - 8 - \frac{15}{100}(100 - 8) = 78.2\%$$

$$P_6 = 100 - 11 - \frac{15}{100}(100 - 11) = 75.7\%$$

By analysing the table given above, it is seen that an assignment of five machines is the most economical one.

11.18. LINE BALANCING

Line Balancing means balancing the production line and assembly line. The line balancing aims at grouping or distributing the facilities (or tasks) and workmen in an efficient manner so as to obtain optimum result, *i.e.*, the idle time of men and machines are minimised. This results in most promising balance of the capacities of the machines.

It can also be said as "a layout which has equal operating times at the successive operations in the process as a whole".

Product layout requires line balancing and if any production line remains unbalanced, machinery utilisation may be poor, the machine in the line will operate only for a part of the time.

Let us assume that there is a production line with work stations *x*, *y* and z. Also assume that each machine at *x*, *y* and *z* can produce 200 items, 100 items, and 50 items per hour respectively. If each machine were to produce only 50 items per hour then each hour the machines at *x* and *y* would be idle for 45 and 30 minutes respectively. Such a layout will be unbalanced one and the production line needs balancing.

As an another example, a bakery would not be in balance, if the oven continuously baked loaves at the rate of 600 per hour and wrapping machine could only wrap 400 loaves per hour. Hence the production line requires balancing.

Method of Line Balancing

(*i*) The one possibility in the right direction, at least as far as balancing the line is concerned, would be to increase the output.

(*ii*) The second possibility is that another product may be seen close to the first one so that some idle machines may be used jointly.

(*iii*) The third possibility may be to estimate the output of the last work station. This can be taken as the minimum output of all the intermediate work stations.

A balanced layout eliminates bottle-neck operations as well as prevents the unnecessary duplication of equipment capacity. Line balancing is a major consideration in layout because a lack of balance can most easily hinder the production. For balancing it is not essential that output of each operation should be same but the essential is to see that output of fastest machines should be multiple of the output of the remaining other machines.

Example 11.8. *A product requires 4 operations on 4 work stations in line. The operation time per unit is as follows:*

Operation	*Time per unit in minutes*
1	10
2	20
3	10
4	20

The total working hours per month are 150. The required production is of 40 units per month. Suggest how should the time be balanced for maximum utilisation of machines. What percentage of each machine time is idle?

Solution. Working hours/month = 150

= 150 × 60 = 9000 minutes

Production/month = 450 units

$$\text{Time/unit} = \frac{9000}{450} = 20 \text{ minutes}$$

In the question operation time for the last operation, 4 is 20 minutes, on the basis of this last operation work station utilisation can be calculated.

In this question work station 2, *i.e.,* operation 2 also consumes 20 minutes. From the above calculations in a production of 450 units per month, time per unit = 20 minutes.

Therefore, Work station No. 2 and 4 are 100% engaged while work station No. 1 and 3 are 50% engaged.

Heuristic Method

In Heuristic method, simple thumb rules are used to solve the problems, and common sense, logic, and past experiences are applied. Heuristic method breakdown a complex problem into smaller and easily manageable sub-problems, and then each one of them is solved from past experience.

Line balancing problems can also be solved by linear programming model or by dynamic programming.

QUESTIONS

1. What do you understand by "Work Measurement"? What is its relationship with Method Study? What are the objectives of work measurement in an industry?
2. What do you understand by the term"Rating in Time Study? What are the various methods used for Rating ? Describe them.
3. Discuss, how you would select "representative times" in a stopwatch time study.

   Explain how you would decide whether to apply rating to each time representative element time or cycle time.
4. (*a*) What is Standard Time. Describe briefly, how you will calculate "Standard time"from the observed time obtained by time study,

   (*b*) Give a specimen of the "Time Study Sheet".
5. What are the objectives of "Time Study"? Explain, how time study may eliminate the difficulties of the piece work system based on the past records of output.

6. (*a*) Describe briefly the procedure to be followed for "Time Study" by "Stop-watch Method".
   (*b*) Explain the following terms:
   Rating, Standard time, Fatigue allowance.
7. In estimating standard time of job, what different elements of time are considered? Describe how can the fatigue factor be minimised.
8. Describe the procedure of time of study using stop-watch method.
9. Write short notes on:
   (*a*) Standard data. (*b*) Performance rating factor,
   (*c*) Productivity bargaining. (*d*) Collective bargaining.
10. Define the concept of standard time. Explain, clearly the steps involved in arriving at standard time, starting with observed time.
11. Define standard time of an operation. List its various uses.
12. Discuss the need to provide for various allowances in determination of Standard time.
13. What are the relaxation allowances?
14. (*a*) What are the prior preparation needed for successful stop watch time study?
    (*b*) Explain the various methods of reading time of an element by stop-watch time study.
15. Explain the term "rating" with reference to work study.
16. What are the limitations of "rating"?
17. Write a short essay on "Industrial fatigue and Fatigue Allowance".
18. What is the attitude of union towards time study, if it is likely to change on the future?
19. What are the typical errors associated with time study rating? Explain the methods available to minimise these errors.
20. What do you understand by "Standard Data"? What are its advantages ? Also mention the uses of the Standard Data.
21. What are the various systems in use of "Predetermined Motion Time Standards"? Explain one most popular amongst them.
22. Give the list of various advantages of using "Predetermined Motion Time Standard" systems over the ordinary "Time Study".
23. Discuss in details the methods of finding "Standard Time" from M.T.M. data.
24. Explain with examples the following terms used in M.T.M.:
    (*i*) Various classes Reach.
    (*ii*) Various classes of Move.
    (*iii*) Time Measurement Unit.
    (*iv*) Give significance of:

R12C	G4A	M2C
RL1	T30	M16B15
RL12Am	D2E	EP
mM12B	ET16/10P2NSE	

25. Application for Work Sampling Studies is in the determination of fatigue ? Explain.
26. How can the validity of work sampling be left on the management, who is not familiar in the probability and statistical methods ?

27. Where was Work Sampling first used ?
28. What are the advantages of Work Sampling Over Time Study ?
29. Give the applications of Work Sampling.
30. How is it possible to determine the time of day to make the various observations so that biased results should not occur ?
31. What factor be kept in mind while making Work Sampling Studies?
32. To get ±5 per cent precision on work that is estimated to take 80% the worker's time, how many random observations be required at the 95 per cent confidence level?
33. (*a*) Discuss in brief Work Sampling and state some of its applications.
    (*b*) Derive an expression for required number of observations in a work sampling study in relation to precision and level of confidence.
34. Describe the procedure for conducting work sampling in an organisation. Also mention the advantages and disadvantages of this technique.
35. Define :
    (*i*) Multiple machine operation;
    (*ii*) Interference;
    (*iii*) Running time;
    (*iv*) Working time.
36. Describe the formula for the determination of "Economical machine per operator".
37. At the end of the day, the down time per machine was 15% of the time for which 4 machines were operated by an operator. Give the percentage interference per machine for the period of operation. Find also the average servicing time per machine.

12

ERGONOMICS (HUMAN ENGINEERING)

12.1. INTRODUCTION

Ergonomics is the science which deals with the relationship between man and his working environments. It takes care of factors governing the physical and mental strains. Ergonomics consists of words 'Ergo' (which means work), and 'Nomos' (which means 'Natural Laws'). This can also be termed as **'Human Engineering'**.

Ergonomics (or Human Engineering) is defined by I.L.O. (International Labour Organisation) as "the application of human biological sciences in conjunction with engineering sciences to the worker and his working environment so as to obtain maximum satisfaction for the worker which, at the same time, enchances productivity". Thus ergonomics is a multidisciplinary science comprising subjects like anatomy, psychology, physiology, sociology, engineering, anthropologist, physics and medicine.

The task of ergonomics is to develop such conditions for workers, which are necessary to reduce physical workload, to improve working postures, facilitate instrument handling, and thus improves the quality of working life, maximise efficiency of production operators and to minimise human errors.

Objectives

Objective of the study of ergonomics is to optimise the integration of man and machine in order to increase productivity with accuracy. It involves the design of:

1. a work place suitable for the worker,
2. machinery and controls, so as to minimise mental and physical strain on the worker to enable the improvement in efficiency,
3. a favourable environment for performing the task most effectively,
4. task and work organisation,

12.2. DESIGN OF WORKPLACE

Backaches, neckaches and other muscular strains due to bad seating and incorrect working posture are common in industry, where most of the jobs are performed by the operators either in sitting or standing in a fixed posture for a long duration. The interaction of the operator with the immmediate workspace around him is influenced by many factors such as seat design, the working desk and adjacent machine. These factors are responsible for the position and postures of the users and, hence their efficiency.

1. **Location of Tools and Materials.** All tools and materials required must be located within the normal grasp area and as far as possible in front of the worker. This will enable him to travel lesser distances to pick up and put these tools and materials frequently at desired place so as to save time and energy.

   For the assembly work, it is advisable to provide such arrangement so that the components can slide along the smooth surface and the worker picks them up. It will greatly reduce the time and effort.

2. **Proper Chairs.** Chairs permitting proper posture for the workers must be provided. This is possible when the worker is working on the work bench (e.g. assembly, fitting and inspection etc.). Performing a job on floor in sitting position or on table in standing position requires more energy.

   The height of chair and the work bench must be arranged in such a way so that the worker may not feel any difficulty while working. Their height must be such that the top of bench remains at the height of the elbow of the worker. If possible the height of the bench must be such that worker can work both in sitting and standing position. Chairs must be provided with foot rests.

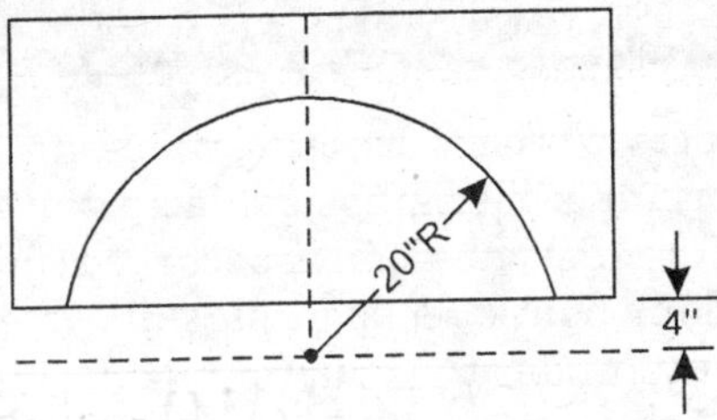

Fig. 12.1. Shoulder Elbow centre line.

3. **Working Desk.** As explained earlier, all the tools and materials must be located within the normal grasp area and as close in front of the operator as possible. Experiment have shown that a semi-circular table having a radius of 20" or 50 cm from a point at 4" or 10 cm back (4" or 10 cm gives approximately centre line of the operator shoulders and elbow) as shown in Fig. 12.1., allows a most comfortable position.

   Working desk must be so designed so that use of both hands can be taken simultaneously.

In the end, "work place layout" helps the analyst in determining the required body and eye motions of operators, safety measures and operational difficulties that may occur at working place.

12.3. DESIGN OF MACHINERY

Most machines today are reasonably well designed for optimum performance, but the capacity of the worker assigned to the machine is generally different. This may result in a job taking longer to complete and the risk of errors increases. To prevent this, user and machinery must be looked as a combined unit. Thus the ergonomics must be involved in fitting the tool and the machine to the worker by designing accordingly.

When a worker operates or uses a machine, instrument or tool, it is essential that man-machine must be considered as a single working unit from the design points of view, as explained above. Machine must be so designed so that worker can use both hands and foot simultaneously for operating it and all the levers, pedals, instruments, handwheels knobs and buttons must be located within the normal grasp at a suitable height and in front of the operator. Foot pedals must be provided with suitably returning springs. Care must be taken to avoid eye, muscular and mental strain.

Fatigue may further be reduced if proper use of jigs or fixtures, stops or guides is taken.

The size of the driver's cab and the placement of gearshift and brake pedals etc. are generally designed to suit common man, resulting transportation operator, if he is a taller or shorter than average, readily succumb to fatigue, through straining to reach the brakes, gears, and other controls. Therefore, modifications to suit the size of the users will result in significant improvement in health and also reduction in accident rates. Generally adjustable chairs are therefore provided.

Design and layout of display panels and instrument should be such that it enable accurate observations. Design and location of various manual controls, knobs, levers, wheels etc. should not cause excessive physical and mental strain to the worker. All control should move in one direction for one kind of action, *e.g.*, acceleration or retardation, energise or de-energise.

12.4. WORK ENVIRONMENT DESIGN

Physical and psychosocial aspects of the work environment are crucial factors which affect comfort of worker and his performance. The physical factors at the workplace include lighting, ventilation, noise and temperature. Psychosocial aspects are concerned with motivational work environment, these include working hours, rest pauses, shiftsystems, health and safety alongwith other factors as described in detail under the chapter on 'Motivation'.

12.5. TASK AND WORK ORGANISATION DESIGN

(*a*) **Task Design.** Task design is based on the nature of job and the design of equipment, machinery and tools in accordance with the ergonomic concepts. This ensures that jobs are within the physical and mental capacities of workers. Efforts be made to include the job with a mixture of repetitive and nonrepetitive work during which recovery from the effects of the former is possible. The task should be designed in such a way that muscles are not required to be used repetitively in a forceful manner.

(*b*) **Work Organization.** Measures such as reducing work rate in paced operations, reducing shift lengths, and provisions for extra rest breaks have proved of greater help. Lifting of heavy objects presents a high risk of overexertion, injuries and cumulative damage to soft tissues around the spin.

12.6. ERGONOMICS AND HEALTH

Ergonomics is helpful in both the prevention of occupational diseases and promotion of health. Studies have suggested that many of the occupational diseases are connected to poor design of tools, machines, work place and work environment. To prevent cumulative/repetitive strain injuries, variety of health problems including visual fatigue, ergonomics play an important role to increase work efficiency and productivity.

12.6.1. Manual handling

Manual handling means a range of activities including lifting, lowering, pushing, pulling, carrying, moving, holding or retaining an object. It also covers activities which require the use of force or effort such as pulling a lever or operating power tools. It has been estimated that about a third of all work injuries occur during manual handling and most of them cause back injury. A risk situation arises when tasks are poorly designed or when handling involves awkward or constrained postures.

Following are the some examples of actions that may cause manual handling injuries:

1. Work involving sudden, Ferky or hard to control movements or which causes discomfort or pain.
2. Work involving too much bending, reaching or twisting.
3. Work where a long time is spent holding the same posture or position.
4. Work that is fast and repetitive.
5. Heavy weights to be lifted and carried manually.
6. Work where a force is needed to carry out a task.
7. The loads to be handled below mid-thigh or above the shoulder.

Preventive Exercises

In order to neutralise the effect of wrong postures for long periods during working it is advisable to perform stretching exercises for neck, back, shoulders, upper body, full body etc. While stretching care should be taken that, move slowly and hold stretches for 5-10 seconds. Right type of exercises can be selected and practised under the guidance of experts.

12.7. INTEGRATING OPERATOR AND OPERATION

Work Place Design:

It deals with the integration of the operator into the operation, with the overall objective of determining how personnel should be integrated into the production process to most effectively contribute to the enterprise objective. Any manufacturing operation includes :

(*i*) Materials - raw, finished and scrap

(*ii*) Tools

(*iii*) Machines and auxiliary equipment

(*iv*) Operator

(*v*) Auxiliary services (utilities etc.)

Before designing a work place, we must know that, what is a work area ? A work area is the space occupied by a machine or a work bench, necessary auxiliary equipment, and the operator; or it may contain a group of similar machines and may require more than one operator. Each work place represents a location along the overall flow pattern.

Planning an Efficient Work Place : In a sense, each work place is a miniature factory, with its own receiving, production and shipping areas. While planning a work place, a care should be taken that each area should be planned for optimum efficiency and it should fit into the overall flow pattern. For this purpose, following guidelines should be followed:

(*a*) From the overall flow pattern, a general direction of material flow should be determined.

(*b*) Then determine direction of flow through the workplace.

(*c*) Decide the items to be contained in the workplace *e.g.* machine, bench, conveyers, containers etc.

(*d*) Sketch of the area indicating the places of major items and their positions in the work place.

(*e*) Sources of material and the direction of material in which it will come and go.

(*f*) Decide method of waste or scrap disposal.

(*g*) Sketch the material handling equipment working in the area.

(*h*) Apply motion economy principles.

(*i*) Indicate distances on the sketch of work place.

Factors Considered in the Work Place Design

1. Purpose of operation.
2. Product design-value analysis.
3. Materials related factors, like:
   - space required, quantity of items, size, etc. for raw, finished and scrap materials.
   - rate of production.
   - inspection requirement.
4. Equipment related factors, like:
   - size.
   - utility, service requirements.
   - auxiliary equipment.
   - number of machines and space required.
   - nature of process.
   - noise, pollution, vibration, safety hazards etc.
5. Material handling methods.
6. Space related factors, like
   - aisles.
   - ceiling height required.
   - space utilisation.
7. Operated related factors:
   - sitting or standing.
   - level of comfort.
   - movement required.
   - number of operators.
   - supervision requirement.
8. Working conditions :
   - Noise, lighting, heating and Ventilation.
   - Dust, Vibration, window location.
9. Method related factors :
   - Direction of flow.
   - Floor levels.
   - Location of items.
   - Material movement.

- Safety requirement.
- Operation sequence.
- Tools and material locations.
- Production rate.
- Economic lot size.
- Auxiliary services.

12.8. FACTORS RELATED TO ENVIRONMENT

12.8.1. Fatigue

It is that state of the worker by which power to work is decreased and pleasure taken in work is reduced. There are so many factors which promote fatigue. Some of them are : repetition of the same work again and again, velocity of fly wheels, whirling of hammers, high speeds at which machines and tools are moving, different types of sounds and vibrations. At the same time, price-rate and financial incentive schemes encourage the worker to work at a faster rate. In such conditions of work, tension is increased and these factors (namely tension, speed, repetition and more strain, etc.) promote fatigue.

Thus, the fatigue is responsible to reduce the power to work with the passing of time. In addition to reduction in the production, continued fatigue also affects adversely the psychology of the worker. When he is tired he can not think clearly, he readily imagines injustice, he becomes angry very quickly and an angry man can do anything without hesitation, which he would have not done in the good state of mind.

It also affects the personal life of the worker because a physically exhausted and completely tired man cannot perform adequately the functions of the head of the family. Thus fatigue not only affects the production but also psychological state of mind, temperament and his personal life.

Contributors to fatigue include stress, worry, sleepiness, insufficient sleep. Generally accepted symptoms of fatigue are:

- Sleepiness.
- Depression
- Irritability
- Headache
- Reduced cognitive ability
- Reduction in alertness.
- Memory and concentration lapses.
- Giddiness.
- Loss of appetite.
- Digestive problems.
- Decreased resistance to illness.

Necessary and Unnecessary Fatigue.

The purpose of 'Fatigue Study' is to reduce its influence in decreasing production and unpleasant feelings. For this purpose, fatigues have been characterised as necessary and unnecessary fatigues. As all the works involve fatigue therefore total elimination is impossible, only it can be reduced. Thus when work is carried out, fatigue will essentially be there.

The fatigue caused by unfavourable working methods and conditions of work is known as "Unnecessary Fatigue". This requires a useless discharge of energy hence capacity of work is decreased unnecessarily. This type of fatigue can be avoided to a large extent.

Elimination of Unnecessary Fatigue.

As explained earlier, unnecessary fatigue can be eliminated. Here some of the considerations in this respect are given as under:

(*i*) **Influence of Hours of Work.** Experiments have shown that average hourly output varies with length of the working day. If the length of working hours in a day is reduced (though upto certain limit) then the average hourly output increases. So many experiments have been conducted by varying the working hours, which shows that hourly output reaches maximum value at about seven hours a day or 40 hours a week.

(*ii*) **Influence of Rest Pauses.** Production and fatigue are influenced considerably by the opportunity provided to the worker for rest during the course of work. Experiments have shown that when number of rest pauses are increased then production is also increased - some-times upto 20%. While setting up the duration and number of rest pauses, it should be considered that most favourable rest pause is that which will conserve all the benefits of incitement or warming and at the same time eliminate fatigue as much as possible. Thus, too long rest pauses are disadvantageous because loss of warming will occur when worker remains away from work for a long time. Research in this regard has shown that 5 minutes rest pause after every 80 minutes work is most desirable.

(*iii*) **Influence of Illumination.** Insufficient illumination causes heavy strain on the eyes of workers and thus resulting unnecessary fatigue. Experiments have shown that illumination of 215 lumens/m^2 is most satisfactory.

(*iv*) **Influence of Atmospheric conditions.** Atmospheric conditions have very important role in determining the efficiency and well being of the worker. An Industrial worker spends most of his time in an environment where heat, moisture, fumes, smokes etc. are constantly evolved in the manufacturing processes. This factor affects the health and comfort of the worker and hence the quality and quantity of production as general efficiency of the worker. Efficiency of the worker is also affected by the temperature, humidity and air circulation.

(*v*) **Influence of Unnecessary Efforts.** Inefficient working methods, bad arrangement of machines and tools are responsible for a waste of human efforts and thus dissatisfaction in work, reduced output and quality.

When methods are selected based on Time and Motion Study and machines arranged systematically then efforts and time of the worker can be saved to a large extent. Work should be carried out at a place and in position of most comfort.

(*vi*) **Influence of Speed.** Speed of the belt, flywheel, gears, coupling etc. may affect the efficiency of workers. These speeds affect the work adversely by increasing the fatigue and discomfort.

(*vii*) **Effect of Noise.** Observations have suggested that excessive noise may adversely affect output and increases fatigue. In the atmosphere of noise and vibrations, workers feel discomfort.

(*viii*) **Humanity.** Variation in humidity play an important role in the productivity of industries. It has been noticed that wet heat and dry cold are more uncomfortable.

Therefore to provide relief from severe dry cold, it is necessary to raise humidity in low temperature. Similarly at higher temperatures, it is necessary to reduce humidity upto certain extent.

(*ix*) **Monotony and Boredom.** The monotony and boredom are the undesirable effects of repetitive work, as the repetitive work destroys such human values as pride in workmanship and individuality. Monotony is described as a desire to have a change due to repetitive work and is a state of mind caused by performance of such tasks, while boredom is a mental fatigue due to routine tasks. Attitude and per-sonality are related with boredom or lack of interest in the job.

Thus, while fatigue is associated with psychological depletion, decreases capacity for work, and is a conscious inability, boredom is a mental dullness, decreased interest in work, and is a feeling of incapacity. Fatigue is due to the work task being temporarily beyond the capacity of a worker, and the worker desires for rest, whereas boredom is due to the consciousness of the uniformity of the work task, the absence of work challenges, and it expresses desire for change.

12.8.2. Lighting

As mentioned above, poor illumination reduces the speed of work and results in strain on eyes and thereby causes more accidents. Light should come from correct direction without producing shadow and should produce the illumination sufficient enough for the work being performed.

In artificial light, glare is most common defect, it is harmful to the eyes. It also produces strain and headache, spoilage of work also increases due to glare.

In order to have sufficient light for all the times, both the natural and artificial lights should be planned and maintained both in the work areas as well as in passages. All the glazed window panels and skylights should be kept clean on both the inner and outer surfaces. Electrical fittings should also be regularly cleaned so that full light is transmitted from them.

12.8.3. Ventilation and Temperature

Proper ventilation provides circulation of fresh air in the work area, which is necessary for comfortable working condition for the workers.

Walls and roofs of the work place should be of such material and so designed that the temperature may not exceed to create uncomfortable working conditions. Effective arrangement should be made to protect the workers from processes producing excessively high temperature. Hot parts of the machinery should be insulated.

12.8.4. Noise and Vibrations

Too much noise and vibrations also produce mental fatigue and reduce the efficiency of the worker. Although noise can not be stopped totally for a running machinery but can be reduced by enclosing the source of noise, use of baffles and sound proof materials in construction etc. Its reduction is very necessary because it is very difficult to concentrate on the work in too much noise. Sometimes too much noise also adversely affects the hearing capacity of the workers. Noise and vibrations can also be controlled to some extent by proper maintenance, checking, lubrication and proper functions etc.

Following are the few examples of noise reduction .

(*i*) Keep noise source away from all reflecting surfaces.

(*ii*) Motors, pumps etc. should be mounted on heavy bases to avoid noise transmission.

(*iii*) All structure borne noise can be significantly reduced by mounting vibration source on flexible supports like springs, corks, foam, rubber etc.

(*iv*) Use conveyers rather than allowing material to fall from a height.

Common causes of vibration in machines are imbalance, misalignment, bearing war or its damage, mechanical looseness, coupling problem, gear problems etc. The solution to these problems is regular inspection, timely removal of defects and proper maintenance.

12.9. GUIDE TO WORK AREA PLANNING

1. Plan for tools, gauges and materials.
2. Use gravity, where possible.
3. Plan the position for each tool and gauge.
4. Plan for delivery of material directly at the point of use.
5. Plan for prompt removal of materials from work place.
6. Provide adequate provision for planned scrap removal.
7. Plan for proper height relationship between material supply, use, and disposal.
8. Eliminate intermediate handling.
9. Place material on pallets etc. and move it alongwith them.
10. Use the same container throughout the system to avoid frequent Changes.
11. Plan each work place in proper relationship with adjacent operations/work places.
12. Use proper containers to prevent damage of materials.
13. Plan for minimum walking.
14. Plan for judicial manual, gravity, and equipment handling.

QUESTIONS

1. Define Ergonomics. Describe the objectives of the study of ergonomics.
2. Explain the factors considered for designing a workplace.
3. Write short notes on :
   (*a*) Design of machinery from ergonomics point of view.
   (*b*) Work-environment design
   (*c*) Task and work organisation design for ergonomics.
4. How will you integrate 'operation' and 'operator'?
5. What factors you would like to consider in the work place design?
6. Discuss various factors related to work environment.
7. Write short notes on following with respect to ergonomics:
   (*a*) Work area planning
   (*b*) Work postures
   (*c*) Noise and Vibrations
   (*d*) Humidity
8. Write an essay on health aspects related to ergonomics.
9. What is fatigue? How unnecessary fatigue can be avoided?

10. What do you understand by "man-machine system"?
11. Discuss various environment factors such as temperature, noise, light, ventilation on the efficiency of workmen.
12. Explain factors considered while designing the workplace.
13. Define fatigue. What are its symptoms? How it can be reduced? Discuss.
14. Discuss various causes of fatigue. What are its effects?

Part–3 Production

13

PRODUCTION AND PRODUCTIVITY

13.1. PRODUCTION

Production is an organised activity of converting raw materials into useful products by organised utilisation of natural resources, men, money, materials and machines. Where as in the input–Conversion–output sequence the smallest unit of productive activity, is termed as operation.

- Production is a sequence of technical processes requiring either directly or indirectly the mental and physical skill of craftsman and consists of changing the shape, size and properties of materials and ultimately converting them into more useful articles.
- In short, we can define the production as "an organised activity of transforming raw materials into finished products."
- Production can also be defined as "producing goods which satisfies some human wants".

Production is a process developed to transform a set of inputs like men, materials, money machinery and energy into a specified set of outputs like finished products and services in desired quantty and quality in order to achieve the objectives of the enterprise.

The production system is a part of larger system–the business system.

The production system can be viewed as a framework of activities or operations within which the creation of value can occur.

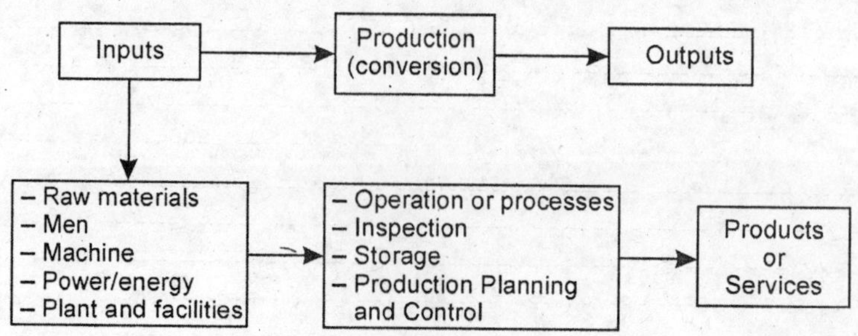

Fig. 13.1 Production system

Production system, as shown in Fig 13.1, consists of inputs at one end and the outputs at the other. The inputs and outputs are connected by a series of operations or processes, storages and inspections.

13.2. TYPES OF PRODUCTION

In general, we have to face two main types of manufacturing situations. Firstly, if manufacturing is done on the customer's order, then one has to wait for the sale order before starting the manufacturing, such as industrial machinery, locomotives, power generating equipment etc. The other situation is when the product is made to stock, the manufacturing is done without any sale order, like televisions, canned foods, electric fitting and appliances. The customer's orders are fulfilled from the stock of finished goods.

For production control, for these two situations, we adopt two types of productions:

1. Intermittent production.
2. Continuous production.

In intermittent production machinery is used for a short duration of time for producing an item, and then changed to produce another item. While in continuous production, set-up of production is fixed and used to produce same item.

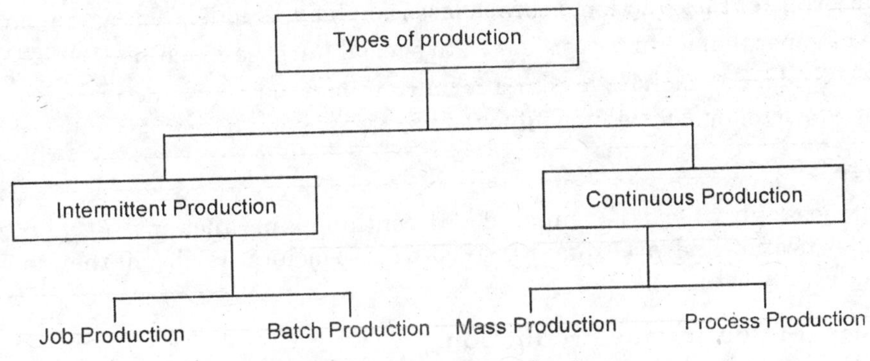

Fig 13.2. Types of production.

Difference between Intermittent and Continuous Production .

If a machinery set up is used for only a short time and then changed for some other different product, this is known as intermittent production method. It consists of variety of products for short runs, on the other hand if the set up of equipment is fixed and used for more time without change, this method is called as continuous method. In this method, a standardized product is required and produced in enormous quantity.

A canning industry is an example of continuous production method whereas an industry manufacturing custom made furniture, requires Intermittent type of production. It must be worthwhile to note that regular working of any industry has no effect on the two types of production methods.

Characteristics of Intermittent Productions

Following are the characteristics of Intermittent method of production :

1. Most of the products adopted are made in small quantities.
2. Similar types of equipments are grouped at one place, *i.e.*, process layout.
3. Work load is different in different departments.
4. General purpose types of machines are used.
5. Machine operators should be highly skilled.

6. Many job instructions are needed.
7. Raw material inventories are high.
8. Methods employed for materials handling are crude and non-smooth.
9. Requires more floor space, storage space etc.

Advantages and Disadvantages of Intermittent Production

Advantages:

1. Best thing of Intermittent Production is its flexibility.
2. Can accept the production of numerous orders of small quantities.
3. The cost of production is little more due to change for new product.
4. The plant layout is flexible.
5. Production delay have no serious effect.
6. Emergency rush order can be pushed more effectively.
7. In intermittent production, there is less risk due to sudden change in market trend.
8. Use of general machines cost less than special purpose machine.
9. The initial investment is less in intermittent method of production.
10. Breakdown of one or two machines never creates much trouble.

Disadvantages:

The disadvantage is only when it is compared with continuous production. But continuous method requires standardization and large quantity. If both these factors are absent then the intermittent production is the only solution.

Characteristics of Continuous Production

1. Large quantity and small variety is essential.
2. Product layout should be adopted.
3. Machine capacity and work loads are balanced.
4. Special purpose machines are required.
5. Highly skilled operators are not needed, few highly skilled operators can manufacture the total output.
6. High skill is needed behind the scenes.
7. Fewer job instructions are needed.
8. Raw material inventories are low.
9. Preventive maintenance is a must.
10. Material movement on floor is quite smooth.
11. Conveyer system can be used for material handling.
12. Requires less floor space, storage space etc.

Advantages and Disadvantages of Continuous Production

Advantages:

1. Low unit cost is the main advantage of this method.
2. Special purpose machine initially cost more but speed up the job and cut labour cost.
3. Continuous process cuts man hours to great extent.

4. Employment of semi-skilled workers further reduce the cost.
5. There is cut in transportation cost.

Disadvantages:

1. Product changing difficulties.
2. Changes of stoppage of work due to one or two machines break-down.
3. Rigidity of output rate.
4. Less flexible in comparison to intermittent method.

(*a*) **Job Production.**

This is the oldest method of production on a very small scale. With this method, individual requirements of the consumers can be met. Each job order stands alone and is not likely to be repeated. This type of production has a lot of flexibility of operation and hence general purpose machines are required.

Factories adopting this type of production, are generally small in size (ship building is an exception). The layout of such factories is made flexible so that maximum varieties of work can be easily and efficiently carried out with slight adjustments.

Even in this age of industrialisation, many things are produced on unit production. This type of production is used for things which cannot be produced on a large scale, things of high artistic nature requiring maximum attention, die work and foundry work etc. Man working in unit production gets an opportunity to produce large type of products, enhance his skills, and can become expert in a very short time.

Advantages

1. It is the only method which can meet the individual requirements.
2. There is no managerial problems, because of very less number of workers, and small size of concern.
3. Such type of production requires less money and is easy to start.
4. There is less risk of loss to the factory adopting this type of production.
5. Because of flexibility, there is no chance of failure of factory due to the reduction of demand in particular field.

Disadvantages:

1. There is no scope of commercial economy.
2. As the purchase of raw materials is less, hence cost of raw materials per unit will be slightly more.
3. For handling different types of jobs, only skilled and intelligent workers are needed, thus labour cost increases.

(*b*) Batch Production.

This type of production is generally adopted in medium size enterprises. Batch production is a stage in between Job production and Mass production.

Batch production is bigger in scale than the Job production while it is smaller than that of Mass production. Batch production requires more machines than Job production and less machines than that of Mass production. In Batch production, some of the machines are one purpose machines and remaining are general purpose machines.

As in this type of production, two or more types of products are manufactured in lots (i.e.batches) at regular interval, therefore this is known as Batch production. Most of the engineering concerns are adopting Batch production. In this type of production, different products are manufactured and stocked and then sold on receipt of orders.

Advantages:

1. While comparing with mass production, it requires less capital.
2. If demand for one product decreases then production for another product may be increased, thus the risk of loss is very less.
3. Comparing with job production, it is more advantageous commercially.

Disadvantages:

1. Comparing with mass production, cost of sales and advertisement per unit is more.
2. Raw material to be purchased are in less quantity than that in mass production. Therefore, it is slightly costlier than that of mass production, because less quantity discount is available.

(c) Mass Production.

This method of production is a large scale production and is a continuous production. In the method of job production, factory works only when orders are received and when orders are not received for some time then for that period work may come to a standstill. But mass production is a continuous production and it does not have any non-producing time.

This type of production requires specially planned layout, one purpose machinery and costly jigs and fixtures etc. In this method, with the use of automatic machines, articles automatically move forward from one stage to the next stage of manufacturing operation.

In mass production, simplification and standardisation of products are made. With the help of specialised (one purpose) machines, articles of standardised nature can easily and economically be produced on a large scale.

Layout of the plant is such that it can be used for only one type of product. Sequence of flow of the product during manufacturing remains same. In this type of production, different machines are assigned a definite nature of work. Throughout the run of the plant, only one type of product can be manufactured.

To avoid the problem of material handling, use of mechanical means such as conveyors of different types, cranes etc. can be used.

Advantages

1. Mass production gives better quality and increased production.
2. Wastage is minimum.
3. As raw materials are purchased on a large scale and hence higher margin of profits can be made while purchasing them.
4. Sales and advertising do not prove to be costly as their expenses are spread over thousands of articles produced, hence cost per unit is low.
5. Only few skilled and rest semi-skilled workers are required hence labour cost is reduced.

Disadvantages

1. During the period of less demand, heavy losses on the invested capital may take place.
2. Because of all the machines used are one purpose machines therefore, this type of production is not changeable to other types of production.
3. Most of the workers handle only particular operations. They may get skill in their job but after some time they feel bored with the repetition of same type of work.
4. As this type of production is on a large scale, therefore it can not fulfil individual

taste. It produces things of standardised form which are demanded on a large scale.

(d) Process Production

In this type of production, the plant and its equipment and layout have been primarily designed to manufacture the desired product. Examples of such production are automobiles, chemical plants, fertilizer plants, cement plants etc. Unlike other production systems, switch over to other product is very difficult and expensive and require change of layout. The change in product becomes extremely difficult and costly affair especially when special purpose machines and complex material handling systems are involved.

One Time Large Projects

Many companies manufacture gigantic size products, such as ships, bridges, special coal handling equipments, turbo electric generator equipments. Many times the final assembly of such projects is done at the installation place and not at the manufacturing company. Heavy and large size equipments are often manufactured in sections in the factory and then moved to the point of installation. These sections are assembled under the guidance of company's engineers.

One time large projects are generally unique, the requirement is only one or very few kind. The size is quite big, and contains thousands of parts, requires months to produce, and involves bigger investment. The method of intermittent manufacturing is always employed. Such large projects are always made on order, lever for stock. The contract negotiations usually take long period and many a time the schedule is behind enough.

For such one time large project, there should be good co-ordination between production control and engineering department. The tremendous number of parts most of which are special and all of which must be completed for the project, makes the scheduling job both difficult and important.

Production control is easier if the project is less complex. One has to plan and schedule only in an overall way but it is impossible to plan minor details in advance. Even one cannot prepare an exact and complete bill of materials, or list of operations to be conducted. Operation times cannot be determined as time study is not possible.

Projects of this type are bread and butter items for some companies. Characteristic of such large projects that only one or two items are to be manufactured, and most orders are one time affairs, one does not get a chance to learn from experience and to avoid mistakes in due course.

13.3. PRODUCTION-FUNCTION

Most important task of the production management is to deal with decision making related to production processes so that the goods manufactured are according to the specifications, in the required quantity, at minimum cost and as per schedule.

In production system, we have materials, parts, ore etc. as inputs. The inputs are processed in a series of operations. The sequence number and type of operations (they may be mechanical, chemical, assembly, inspection, transportation etc.) are specified for each input. The output of the system will be complete parts, products chemicals, etc. A mathematical model of the production system is constructed. This model also has an information system which provides a basis for management decision. These information systems of the model known as "Production Function" provide the equivalent of a "nervous system" for the model.

Production function shows the relationship between the input and output by a firm. By the study of production function, the maximum output which can be achieved with a given inputs (or resources) with a given state of technology is determined. The production function can be represented by the simple mathematical equation,

$$Y = f(X_1, X_2 \text{ etc.})$$

where Y = units of outputs, which is a function of the quantity of two or more inputs with X_1 indicating units of labour and X_2 units of machinery. Some quantities of production are assumed as fixed, *i.e.*, not varying with change of output. Such quantities never enter in the equation.

The method of estimating the production function is the method of least square. The measurement of production function is quite old and the prime studies are made in the agricultural field. A popular production function derived by Mr. Cobb and Mr. Douglas is as follows :

$$P = bL^{a}C^{1-a}$$

where

P = Total output

L = Index of employment of labour in actual manufacturing

C = Index of fixed capital in manufacturing.

a and 1 - a are known as elasticities of production and measured in a percentage. The Cobb-Douglas function in U.S.A. is represented by

$$P = 1.01\ L^{0.75}\ C^{0.26}\ R_2^{0.9409}$$

The above function shows that by 1% change in labour input (L) is associated by 0.75% change in output when capital (C) is fixed. Likewise, by 1% change in capital (C) when labour (L) is constant there is change of 0.25% in output. The coefficient of determination R_2 shows that 94% of the variations on the dependent variable *(P)* were accounted for by the variations in the independent variable *(L* and C).

Utility of Production Function for Managers

Though production function looks very unrealistic but, in fact it is very useful as well as logical.

The usefulness of production function is very easily understandable by the following example:

Dairy economists are very keen in minimizing the cost of feeding cows for milk production. Now take a cow as a single firm, grain and roughage as input, the question arises, in what proportion the grain and roughage would be economical in feeding the cow. Previously, a fixed ratio is always adopted by economical analysis which shows that the ratio depend upon the input prices. As the input prices varies throughout the year, there should always be a change in the ratio. To get the ratios, the production function analysis is adopted. Thus a dairy farmer can use such an analysis for increasing the return from his expenditure on feeds.

Thus the production function is not a useless or theoretical device, but is helpful in making decisions because they can give guidance in two directions:

(*i*) How to obtain maximum output from the given input;

(*ii*) How to obtain a given output from the minimum input.

When complex problems are there, the use of mathematics is quite complicated. But with the development of linear programming, it is possible to handle complicated problems.

Finding of Input Combination from Production Function

From a given production function, for a certain output, one can derive all the combinations of the two factors of production that will produce the same output. For example, the production function is

$$O = .0196H^{0.88}\ N^{1.815}$$

where O = output of transformers in terms of kVA

H = Average hours worked /day

N = Number of labourer employed.

Now, suppose, 1200 kVA is the output then what is the input combinations.

$$1200 = 0.196 H^{0.88} N^{1.815}$$

Now substituting any value for H or N in above equation and by solving we get associated value of N or H. Suppose we want to find the value of average hours H when 38 labourers are employed.

Then $\qquad 1200 = 0.196\ H^{0.88}\ 38^{1.815}$

or $\qquad \log 1200 = \log 0.196 + 0.88 \log H + 1.815 \log 38$

By solving log $\qquad H = 1.045$

or $\qquad H = \text{Antilog } 1.045$

$\qquad = 11.09$

In the same way, we can find the value of H if N is 40, 45, 50 and so on, for the desired output.

13.4. PRODUCTIVITY

"Productivity" is nothing but the reduction in wastage of resources. The resources may be men, machines, material, power, space, time and building etc.

It may also be defined as human endeavour (Effort) to produce more and more with less and less inputs of resources as a result of which the benefits of production may be distributed more equally among maximum number of people.

According to V.K.R. Menon, productivity implies development of an attitude of mind and a constant urge to find better, cheaper, easier, quicker and safer means of doing a job, manufacturing a product and providing a service.

Output is obtained by the combined input of a number of factors such as men, material, money, land, management and production methods etc. The ratio between output and input of these factors is known as "Productivity" of the factor concerned. The most common unit of input is "Man-hour" of working time and productivity due to this factor is known as "Labour Productivity".

It can be represented by

$$P = \frac{O}{M}$$

where $\quad P$ = Labour productivity

O = Unit of output

M = Man-hour or efforts input.

For example, if a manufacturing concern isproducing by using the same materials, machines, workers and number of hours, 150 items now compared with 120 items previously, then its productivity is said to have increased by 25%.

Difference between Production and Productivity

Sometimes, there arises confusion between Production and Productivity. It is, therefore, necessary to differentiate them, so that there may not be any confusion.

"Production" of any commodity or service is the volume of output irrespective of the quantity or quality of resources employed to achieve that level of output. Once we put in it element of efficiency with which the resources are employed, we enter the area of productivity.

Importance of Productivity

In India, there is an autonomous organisation known as National Productivity Council (N.P.C.). It was established in 1958 and has set up 5 regional productivity directorates in the country managed by specialists for organising productivity programmes. It has also established 47 local councils at various industrial centres in the country and they work as the spear head of the productivity movement.

To increase productivity, this organisation supplies publications, utilises audio visual media of films, radio and exhibitions. In collaboration with local productivity councils and various institutions and organisations, it organises and conducts training programmes for various levels of management and provides assistance in other activities and difficulties.

The main reason of our country's poverty is the low level of productivity in practically every sphere of economy and from management to the workers including government. The minimum wages in the United States as established by law is say 3 Dollars/hour. This has to be paid to sweeper, dish-washer or any body else who is asked to work. This works out to be about Rs. 800 per day for an 8 hour day. There are a few people in India who by their labour even at very high position get that much per day. Despite very high wages, their unit cost works out to be a very low figure and inspite of our low wages, our unit costs are high. The main reason is that their productivity is very high and our's is very low. In fact, Indian industries are surviving inspite of low productivity behind the rigid protective wall of exchange control. If this is removed, our economy may be swamped by foreign goods.

Advantages of Productivity:

(*i*) Higher profits
(*ii*) Cheaper products
(*iii*) Higher wages and bonus
(*iv*) Rise in living standard of workers
(*v*) Brings properity in the country
(*vi*) Allows better working conditions.

13.5. FACTORSAFFECTING PRODUCTIVITY

The most important factors affecting productivity can be classified:

(*a*) External Factors.
(*b*) Internal Factors.

(a) **External Factors.** These may be :

(*i*) Natural resources and their mobility.
(*ii*) Availability of capital.
(*iii*) Taxation.
(*iv*) Government laws and restrictions concerning business.
(*v*) Extent of market competition.
(*vi*) Technical and other training facilities.

(*b*) Internal Factors. These may be :

(*i*) Plant layout,

(ii) Material handling.
(iii) Product design.
(iv) Work study.
(v) Method study.
(vi) Quality control.
(vii) Production planning and control.
(viii) Management techniques etc

13.6. HOW TO INCREASE PRODUCTIVITY

To increase productivity, following major items need fullest control and should be minimised :

(a) Wastage of materials
(b) Machine breakdown
(c) Waiting on the part of men and equipment
(d) Excessive handling
(e) Poor management
(f) Poor working conditions
(g) Political effects.

Hence, considering the above factors, the wastage at each stage of production can be reduced which ultimately provides consumers cheaper and better quality products.

In increasing productivity, management plays an important role. There cannot be high productivity without high quality management.

As, (i) It brings the resources together
(ii) It directs and control the workers
(iii) It brings in the latest techniques and puts in the heart and soul to see that the techniques get into the actual position.

The Supervisors, Foremen and Chargemen etc. are in the front line of management *i.e.* they constitute the main line of communication between the top management, middle management and the general body of operatives. Hence, to have high productivity, it is necessary to see their level of education, attitude and technical ability accordingly. In the same way actual operatives are also responsible in increasing the productivity. They are those who keep the shop running. Therefore, it is important that the management should make an investment in their education training and human relations etc.

Productivity can also be raised by mechanisation, rationalisation and computerisation.

13.7. REASONS FOR LOW-PRODUCTIVITY

(i) Frequent machine breakdown
(ii) Lack of managerial control
(iii) Idle men
(iv) Poor quality
(v) Confusion in machine scheduling
(vi) Shortage of materials
(vii) Excess inventory
(viii) Large quantities of reworked material.

13.8. PRODUCTIVITY MEASUREMENT

Productivity must be measured in such a way that it clearly reflects the importance, and there must not be any ambiguities about the measurements of inputs and outputs, as stated earlier.

$$\text{Productivity Index} = \frac{\text{Output}}{\text{Input}}$$

Here the output and input may be of various kinds, *viz.*, cost, man hours etc.

When outputs and inputs measured in term of money, then

$$\text{Productivity} = \frac{\text{Outputs in revenues from production}}{\text{Expenditure on labour, capital or raw material}}$$

It may also be measured as follows:

$$\text{Productivity} = \frac{\text{Profit}}{\text{Investment}}$$

Measurement of Productivity in Various Concerns

1. *In Manufacturing Concerns.* In these concerns, productivity can be measured by any of the above two methods.
2. *In Service Industries.* In these concerns, basic difficulty is to measure outputs and to convert various output to one common denominator. One way to measure can be customers attended per man day or man week. The problem is that different customer require different type of service and the mix of customers changes from day-to-day. Therefore, revenue earned per man-day is more suitable and goal oriented measure.
3. *Office Work.* It is difficult to have any rational basis to measure productivity in the administrative office. However, outputs can be measured in terms of letters replied, pages typed, number of files referred to time spent on them can be measured by work sampling techniques. The problem in the measurement is that letter replied may cover different amount of labour involved in dealing them.
4. *Indirect Labour in Manufacturing.* Productivity of indirect labour may be measured as follows :

$$\text{Productivity} = \frac{\text{No. of indirect labour hour to serve Direct labour}}{\text{Number of direct labour hours}}$$

(*i*) **General Measure of Productivity :**

$$\text{Productivity} = \frac{\text{Output}}{\text{Input}}$$

(*ii*) **Labour Productivity**

(*a*) In terms of Hours :

$$\text{Productivity (i.e. efficiency)} = \frac{\text{Production in Standard hours}}{\text{Actual Man hours}}$$

(*b*) In terms of Money

$$\text{Productivity} = \frac{\text{Total cost (or sales value) of output}}{\text{Number of workers}}$$

The productivity of labour can be increased by increasing efficiency of labour, reducing idle time.

(*iii*) **Material Productivity**

$$\text{Productivity} = \frac{\text{Material cost}}{\text{Number of units produced}}$$

Material productivity can be increased by using minimum materials with the help of skilled workers, adequate machine tools, good design of product.

(*iv*) **Machine Productivity:**

$$\text{Productivity} = \frac{\text{Output in standard hours}}{\text{Actual machine hours}}$$

(*v*) **Selling, Distribution or Administrative Productivity :**

$$\text{Productivity} = \frac{\text{Selling, distribution or Administrative cost}}{\text{Total sales}}$$

(*vi*) **Overall Productivity :**

It is measured by.

$$\text{Return of capital employed} = \frac{\text{Profit}}{\text{Capital employed}}$$

13.9. MAIN CONTRIBUTORS TO PRODUCTIVITY IMPROVEMENT

Following are the main contributors to productivity improvement in large number of industries:

1. *Incentives.* When an incentive scheme is introduced in a concern, it results in a considerable improvement in productivity. However, management must be careful about the correctness of the standards, limitations of the workers, short cut methods developed by workers, quality of work and overburdening of the equipment.
2. *Human Relations.* Good human relations help in cooperative behaviour from workers which results in increase in productivity. Human relations can be improved by labour participation in goal setting, simplification of communication, system of minimising the conflicts, encouragement to get advantage of creative talents of employees and awarding rewards etc.
3. *Cost Control.* Productivity can be increased by reducing the cost of production. This can be done by keeping careful watch over expenditure, minimising wastage of material, reducing machine break-down period, reducing waiting time on the part of men and equipment, avoiding excessive handling, minimising overtime expenses.
4. *Training about Productivity.* Works and supervisors may be trained about the measurement and benefits of productivity, so that the workers may start thinking creatively. The training must include the practice of work simplification, methods study, quality control, raw materials utility, productivity and its socio-economic effects.
5. *Application of New Technology.* In order to remain in field and increase its business in the age of competition, industrialists must regularly adopt new services, new marketing methods more and more automation and application of latest techniques in the field of

material handling ; storekeeping and inventory control, bottlenecks in the flow process and introducing good management information system and feedback reporting system.

6. *Proper Planning and Scheduling.* Help to utilises men, machines and materials to increase productivity.
7. *Design the Product.* A good design of a product helps in minimising wastages of scraps and increase its durability and attraction.
8. *Measurement Skill.* Good supervision and management avoids production inefficiency and inefficient purchasing, maintenance and incorrect specifications for materials and machines. It provides good working conditions and better co-ordinations and good relations.
9. *Standardisation and work simplification* increases production efficiency.

13.10. BENEFITS FROM INCREASED PRODUCTIVITY

Higher productivity results in higher volume of production and hence sales, lower cost and higher profit. It is beneficial to all corners as stated below :

(A) Benefit to Concern :

1. More profit
2. Higher productivity ensures stability of the concern.
3. Higher productivity and higher volume of sales provides opportunity for expansion of the concern and wide spread market.
4. It provides overall prosperity and reputation of the concern.

(B) Benefit to Workers :

1. Higher productivity permits more wages
2. More wages permit better standard of living of workers.
3. Thus more productivity means better working conditions for workers which also help in maintaining better health for workers.
4. Higher productivity yields improved moral and greater satisfaction for workers.

(C) Benefit to the Consumers :

1. More productivity ensures better quality of product.
2. It also enables reduction in prices.
3. It provides more satisfaction to consumers.

(D) Benefit to Nation :

1. It provides greater national wealth.
2. It increases per capita income.
3. It helps expansion of international market with the help of standardised and good quality goods.
4. It improves standard of living.
5. It helps better utilisation of resources of the nation.

13.11. AUTOMATION

The term 'Automation' is relatively new in the language of management and this word was first used at the Ford Motor Company in the late 1940.

'Automation' may be defined "as the moving of a procession of materials and parts in and out of machines, and operating of the machines automatically, all without human control. It requires that the machines, tooling and mechanical handling devices between machines be so integrated so as to become, one continuous machine.

The term 'automation' means different things to different people. Some people consider it to be automatic loading of the machines. While others take it as automatic push button factory.

Automation is something more than just mechanisation. Mechanisation means doing by machine what previously was done by muscles. It also removes human watching, thinking and reacting from fourteen machine operations. But in automation 'Machine Operators' are no longer required to load, put the machine through its cycle, unload, inspect, make any machine corrections found necessary and send the part on its way to the next operation. All these steps are performed by instrument, mechanical and electronic devices or other means of control which feed, operate and link machines together into an automatic process.

Types of Automation

These are of three types :

1. Continuous Automation
2. Segmented Automation
3. Non-manufacturing Automation

1. **Continuous Automation.** This type mostly concerned with homogeneous materials, *i.e.,* liquid, gases and pulverized substances that will flow or conveyorize throughout the whole process, such as chemical plants and oil refineries. They are operated from the control boards and closely approximate the push-button plants. Here the instrument measures, records and controls volumes, weight, flow, pressure, humidity and temperature etc. and in some cases take corrective measures when something starts giving out of control.
2. **Segmented Automation.** It means intermittent automation of section of a process, fabrication or assembly with interval between automated equipment. This type is used where it is not practically possible to automate the whole process, fabrication or assembly.
3. **Non-manufacturing Automation.** This includes office automation and integrated data processing mechanisms and automatic elevators with electronic terms and defectors and transportation ticket selling equipment and 'electronic supervisors', which schedule on and off operations. An electronic computer computes an employee's retirement records in one hour otherwise it would take weeks labour.

Advantages of Automation.

Following are the main advantages :

1. Greater output per rupee of labour.
2. More output per rupee invested in facilities.
3. Lesser floor space is required.
4. Increased safety for operators.
5. Automatic production schedules.
6. Increased uniform quality.
7. It transfers skill, knowledge and efforts from man to machine, therefore, high rate of production.
8. Less scrap.

9. Less inventories.
10. It requires very less expert staff, rest semi-skilled workers.
11. It is beneficial to the general public, as it raises the income of individuals.

Disadvantages

Main disadvantages are:

1. Greater capital investment.
2. Less manufacturing flexibility.
3. During less demand the management cannot use the automated plant for any other purpose.
4. The immediate effect of automation is increase in unemployment.
5. Expensive down time, as the failure of one part may result in the shut down of the whole line *where automation is applicable.*

Applications.

Automated plants are suitably employed in the following cases :

(*i*) Where a product design is stable for such a long period in which the cost of automation can be written off.

(*ii*) Where the volume for continuous manufacture is adequate and steady for a fairly long time so as to make the installation economical, profitable and to permit the use of single purpose equipment.

(*iii*) Where the manufacturing method demands a high degree of manual work, adoption of automation presents attractive cost saving potential.

(*iv*) Where the machines are so complex or work on such a high speed that, it is not possible to work on the efficiency by manual methods.

(*v*) Where the product is hazardous that it cannot possibly be controlled manually e.g. radio–active materials.

Automation is not practically economical if the volume of production is small or where there is a great variety of products are manufactured in the plant or where one operator cannot operate several machines efficiently.

13.11.1. Computer Aided Manufacturing (CAM)

In the Computer aided manufacturing, a computer is added to the conventional manufacturing system so as to perform most of the activities through computers which otherwise would have been done manually.

In this system requisite informations are fed in a proper language or code in right sequence and entered in the memory of the computer of the manufacturing machine. Wherever required, the operations can also be performed manually by the operator.

Such machines can save a considerable time especially on non-machining operations like, setting, adjusting, changing, fitting etc.

QUESTIONS

1. Define Production. What are the types of Production? Explain their advantages and disadvantages.

2. Define 'Productivity'. Distinguish between Production and Productivity.
3. What are the various tools of Productivity? How Productivity can be increased?
4. Define the term 'Automation'. How and where it is applicable.
5. What is the effect of Automation on workers? Discuss.
6. Give the forms of Automation and explain each in short.
7. "Productivity is the economy of means" explain the statement. Describe how productivity of labour and machine are measured.
8. State the difference between production to stock and job order production. Give two typical examples of each.
9. Write pros and cons of the following production methods:
   (*i*) Intermittent method,
   (*ii*) Continuous method.
10. Write a note on one time large projects.
11. Compare continuous and intermittent production systems.
12. Differentiate between job production, batch production and mass production.
13. Explain the term production function. What is the utility of 'production function' for the managers.
14. What is the importance of productivity? Mention various factors which affect productivity.
15. How the productivity can be increased? What are the reasons for low productivity?
16. How the productivity can be measured.
17. Write short notes on :
   (*a*) Productivity index.
   (*b*) Labour productivity.
   (*c*) Material productivity
   (*d*) Machine productivity.
   (*e*) Productivity in terms of money.
18. What are the benefits of increased productivity?
19. Explain the statement, "Productivity is the key to prosperity."
20. Define the term 'Automation.' How and where it is applicable?

14 PRODUCT DESIGN AND DEVELOPMENT

14.1. PRODUCT DESIGN

A product is an article obtained by the transformation of raw material. It may be a consumer product such as a radio, a television, a scooter or an industrial product like, a lathe, a shaping machine etc. Before starting the manufacturing of a product, it is essential to design it. The designer must consider the functional requirement and the aesthetic qualities and keep his eye on the cost of manufacturing. The design department who is responsible for the design of new or modified product, consists of designers, engineers and draughtsmen.

While designing a product, designer must consider the functional requirements and the aesthetic (stylish or that looks good) qualities. Designer must also, at the same time keep his eye on the cost of manufacturing the product. Designer is, therefore, required to give due importance to these two aspects according to their use, *e.g.,* body of the car and its panel board must be good looking, while the engine and transmission system must have good performance, *i.e.,* they need more functional importance. Manufacturing the decorative show pieces, ornaments etc. require more importance for the aesthetic qualities during their designing. In addition, designer must also be cost conscious, and estimates of the cost of the product.

Designer also brought out the procedure for manufacturing the product, how much time it will take for different operations and in complete manufacturing, how much material it will require.

For new or improved product, ideas are originated by (*i*) customers' suggestions, (*ii*) suggestions by production department, (*iii*) other products in the market, or (*iv*) from R&D department. These ideas are given final shape in the form of product design by joint efforts of marketing, R&D, design department and production department.

14.2. REQUIREMENTS OF A GOOD DESIGN

A good product design must fulfil following essential requirements :

(A) Customers satisfaction, and

(B) Earn adequate profit.

(A) **Customers Satisfaction.** The product should satisfy the customers by fulfilling their need and expectations. In order to achieve this object, following points should be kept in view:

(*i*) It should function properly.

(*ii*) It should be of proper quality so as to achieve desired degree of accuracy and reliability.

(*iii*) Easy to use (or operate).

(*iv*) Easy to repair and service.

(*v*) Should be able to withstand rough handling.

(*vi*) Good aesthetic view.

(*vii*) Should have good space utilisation.

(*viii*) It should fulfil the ergonomic requirements of the user.

(B) **Adequate Profit.** The product when manufactured and sold should give adequate profit. For this purpose it should fulfil the following requirements :

(*i*) It should be able to manufacture at reasonable price so that it can compete other products in the market.

(*ii*) A good design has minimum number of parts.

(*iii*) It should adopt latest technology so that manufacturing requires minimum cost per unit of production.

14.2.1. Factors Considered in Designing a Product

While designing a product, several factors are considered, some of them are:

(*i*) *Materials.* Materials should be cheap and should be able to withstand design requirements. During production wastage should be minimised. It should be easily workable and machinable.

(*ii*) *Manufacturing facility.* Product design should commensurate with the facilities available in the factory as regards to equipments, labour and layout,

(*iii*) *Use of Standardisation.* The parts used should be of minimum variety and should either be easily available in the market or can be manufactured easily with the machines available, it should have as many standard (and interchangeable) parts as possible.

(*iv*) *Aesthetic.* The product should be good in appearance and should have attractive colours.

(*v*) *Function.* It should be able to perform its desired function with desired accuracy, reliability and strength.

(*vi*) *Ergonomics.* It should be easy to use, operate and should cause minimum possible fatigue and provide comfort.

(*vii*) *Operating conditions.* The product (industrial product) should operate with minimum of noise, vibration, heat and other hazards. The operators should be able to operate it with available skill.

(*viii*) *Maintenance.* Should be easy to maintain and service.

(*ix*) *Tolerance.* It should have desired tolerances, as tight tolerances will result in increased rejection and thereby adding to the cost of product.

(*x*) *Value engineering.* Factor related to the value engineering should be considered thoroughly to reduce the cost of production.

(*xi*) *Simplification.* The simplification techniques should be adopted to avoid manufacturing complications.

(*xii*) *Economy.* At design stage, it is easy to attach cost than later on when the product is actually being manufactured. All possible ways to reduce the cost should be considered at the design stage.

14.3. FACTORS AFFECTING PRODUCT DESIGN

A. Technical Factors

1. Operating Conditions. Type of workers available, conditions of noise, heat, vibrations etc. generated during manufacturing.
2. Performance. Turning speed, feed etc. of material used, accuracy, type of material required.
3. Maintenance aspects.

B. Industrial Engineering Factors

1. Economy in production. Materials, workstudy, layout, tooling etc.
2. Appearance, *i.e.,* aesthetic look.
3. Ergonomics, *i.e.,* whether the use of the product is comfortable.

C. Production Engineering Factors

1. Standardisation
2. Simplification
3. Tolerance
4. Finish

D. Customers Satisfaction

These factors have already been discussed in the chapter.

Standardization in Design

The production department requires and prefers standardization in design and will be more happy to manufacture according to this. Therefore, the design engineer should take the lead in standardizing the product since it requires:

(*i*) Low investment in plant, equipment and materials resulting in price reduction

(*ii*) Interchangeability of parts.

(*iii*) Possibility of development and good control.

(*iv*) If diversity is preferred, it may meet the desired things and should have good purchasing capacity and satisfactory sales force to meet price competition

Design engineer can achieve standardisation by adopting following steps:

1. The continuous development to technical research is to be taken to the fullest advantage and the management should consider the desire of consumers for quality and style withing a given price range.
2. The manufacture of the product should be within the capacity of the manufacturer both from financial and operating conditions.
3. The methods engineer suggests modification in the operation for the simplification of the product. The purchasing department may find it difficult to get certain specified material and all these conflicts should come to a final decision and co-ordinated.
4. By closely working with the sales department, the reaction of the customer and interest of the salesman should be watched.
5. The purchasing department should be asked to give suggestions regarding economies in procuring the materials.
6. The manufacturing difficulties in highly technical processes can be got removed and improved by the research department.
7. The competitors product should be thoroughly analysed to know their secrets.

14.4. ACTIVITIES IN PRODUCT DESIGN AND DEVELOPMENT

1. Product idea generation
2. Idea screening
3. Concept development and testing.
4. Product design including preparation of drawings and specifications.
5. Business analysis
6. Product development
7. Process planning and development
8. Producing the product
9. Marketing the product

14.5. DESIGN DEPARTMENT

"The design is the problem of anticipating or trying to do what will be required in future and improving what is being already produced." It is one of the important functions in an engineering manufacturing concern.

The quality of an item depends on the efficiency of its design, the quality of material used and the accuracy of workmanship used in the production. The drawings of the product is first prepared on the drawing sheet before the production is started, and the design of the product should be simple and consistent with efficient service.

Responsibilities of Design Department

1. To translate the design into working drawings, specifications and instructions in a way satisfactory to the production department.
2. To translate company's policy in relation to the design of product and interpret the customers' requirement in relation to their orders.
3. To enhance company's reputation by minimising wastage of time in assembling and reducing the cost.
4. To lay down and specify the standard of product quality.
5. To prepare the estimate of purchases, carry out development and research and keep and store files, records of all drawings and specifications.
6. To supervise work done and maintain discipline in the department and to train the design and drafting people.

Co-operation from Other Departments

Having been decided for need of new or improved design of a product, design department starts work of designing with the help of following departments :

(*i*) **Marketing department.** For knowing the exact requirement of the customers and knowing the specialities of the competitor's product.

(*ii*) **Manufacturing Department.** For getting the manufacturing advices and knowing their problems and to collect their ideas and comments for further modifications, if any.

(*iii*) **Accounts department.** For control over cost.

(*iv*) **Personnel department.** For requirement of personnel to be involved in production.

(*v*) **Research and development department.** To develop the product after it is designed. It also takes help of persons engaged in work study and value engineering before finalising the product design.

Qualities of a Design Engineer

If the design of the product is not suitable, the work of production will be either inefficient or waste. Therefore, a "Design Engineer" should have the following essential qualities :

(*i*) He should have ability for commercial success, imagination, vision and inventiveness.

(*ii*) He should have a sense of design from the producer's point of view.

(*iii*) He should keep a balance between the Works Manager and the customer.

(*vi*) He should always keep in mind the effect of designs on the cost and have a sufficient knowledge of the shops in the concern in order to prepare a design requiring the most economic manufacturing process.

(*v*) He should have sufficient knowledge of materials which will enable him to select those most readily and economically available.

(*vi*) He should use standard items in the design.

(*vii*) He should be able to design jigs and fixtures and understand the economies of their implementation.

(*viii*) He should co-operate with sales department and know the needs of prospective customers, receive suggestions for improvements from buyers, learn faults in service.

(*ix*) He should obtain information about the products of competitors.

(*x*) He should co-operate with the purchasing department for low all-round cost and with estimating department on new projects.

(*xi*) He should study the reports of inspection department to find whether the rejections wastage etc. are due to any fundamental weakness in the design.

14.6. PRODUCT ANALYSIS

1. Marketing Aspects
2. Product Characteristics :
   (*i*) Functional aspects
   (*ii*) Operational aspects
   (*iii*) Durability and reliability aspects
   (*iv*) Aesthetic aspects
   (*v*) Ergonomic aspects
   (*vi*) Environmental aspects
   (*vii*) Safety aspects.
3. Economic Analysis :
   (*i*) Cost, sale and profit
   (*ii*) Standardisation
   (*iii*) Simplification
   (*iv*) Break-even analysis
   (*v*) Return on investment.

4. Production Aspects :
   (*i*) Selection of processes
   (*ii*) Selection of materials
   (*iii*) Selection of quality specifications.

14.7. PRODUCT PLANNING

Product planning is the evaluation of range mix, specification and pricing of existing and new products considering the present and future market requirements, competition, company objectives, and satisfying the research design and development support.

Product planning is based on the identification of the needs for a product. These needs may be for the (*a*) removal of the current deficiencies, or (*b*) for anticipated deficiencies. The prod-uct planning function includes :

(*i*) Marketing and its analysis.
(*ii*) Evaluation and selection of product system.
(*iii*) Defining the specifications of : system, performance effectiveness and support characteristics, procurement, process, material.
(*iv*) Planning documentation.
(*v*) Planning strategies.
(*vi*) Preparation and bidding.

14.8. PRODUCT LIFE CYCLE

The demand of a product generally tends to follow a predictable pattern called the 'product life cycles'. Product life cycle indicates the pattern of demand throughout the life of the product. Products go through a series of stages starting with low demand during introduction, proceeding through growth, maturity or saturation, and finally decline.

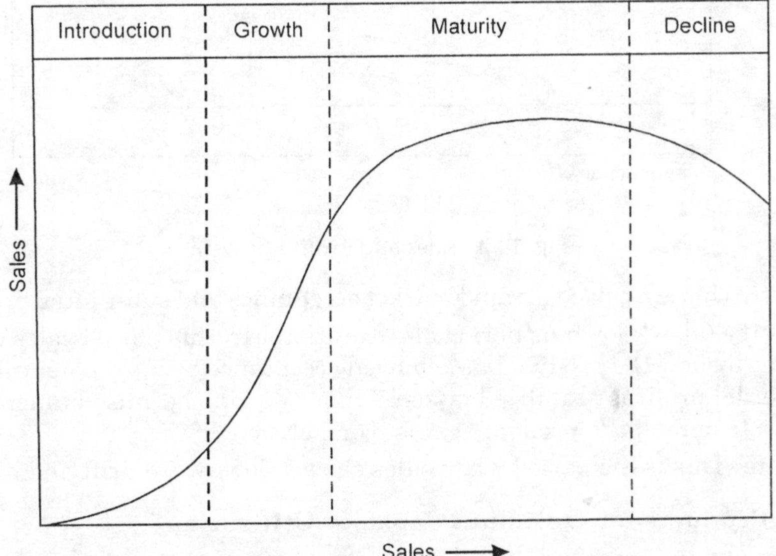

Fig. 14.1. Product life cycle

The time spans of the stages vary considerably from industry to industry. For example, for novelty products total life of the product is generally very short, while for some other products the life cycle may span many years. Each of these stages have different opportunities and problems in respect of market strategy and profit potential. Depending upon the stage of the product, companies can formulate better marketing plans.

Special features of product life cycle are :

(*i*) Products have a limited life.

(*ii*) Product sales pass through distinct stages. Each stage poses different challenges to the company.

(*iii*) Profits rise and fall at different stages of the product life cycle.

(*iv*) In each stage of life cycle, product requires different strategies for marketing, manufacturing, marketing, purchasing, personal and financial matters.

The Product Life Cycle (PLC) concept is used by marketing managers to interpret product and market dynamics and helps in planning, controlling, and forecasting.

Fig. 14.1. indicates the four stages of product life cycle, which are described hereunder :

1. **Introduction.** This is an initial period in which the sales growth is slow as the product is introduced in this period in the market. During this period the profits are nonexistent, since the product introduction requires heavy expenses.

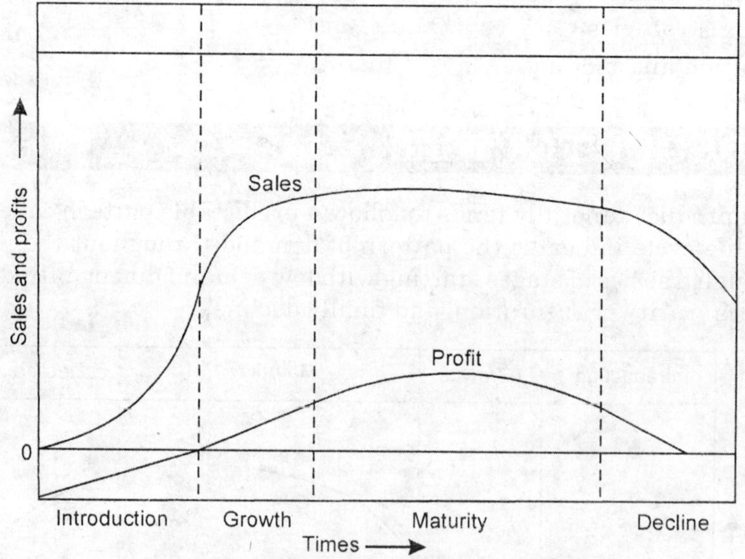

Fig. 14.2. Sales and profit life cycle.

2. **Growth.** This is a period of rapid market acceptance and substantial profit improvement.
3. **Maturity** (also known as period of saturation). In this period sales growth is slowed down as by now the product has achieved acceptance by most potential buyers. During this period profit is stabilized or some times decline because of increased marketing outlays to defend the product against competition.
4. **Decline.** This is the period when sales show a downward drift and profits erode.

Phasing New Products for Optimum Capacity Utilization

As the existing product(s) of a company approaches a decline phase, the company must be prepared to phase in new products, so as to utilize the available productive capacity. This is very necessary for survival and growth of the company. This helps in utilizing the free capacity of existing product due to its decline in demand. In the age of competition and rapidly advancing technologies the company should remain prepared. The ideal timings for introducing the new period is such that when the maturity phase of existing products is complete, the new product's introduction and growth period ends as shown in the Fig. 14.3.

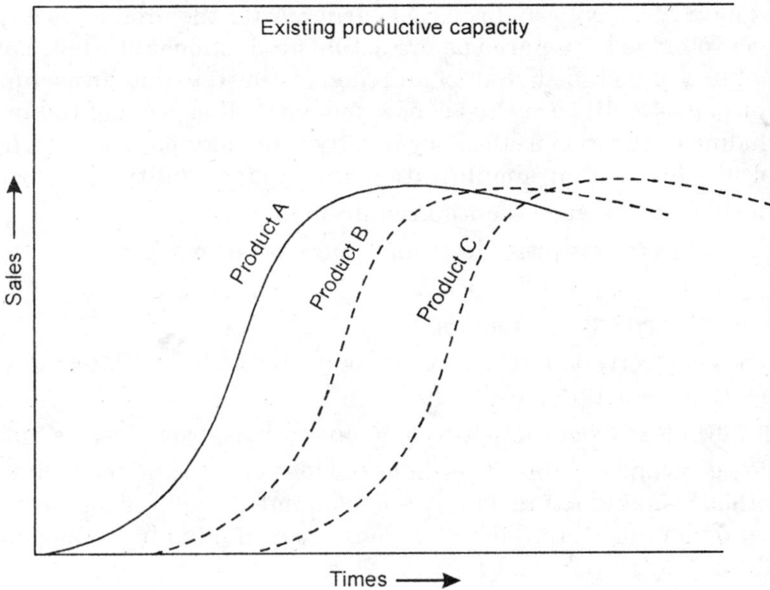

Fig. 14.3. Introduction and growth period of new products.

The aim of all this is smoother transition and faster market penetration to take advantage of early lead over competitors in addition to optimum utilization of plant capacity of the company.

14.9. PRODUCT DEVELOPMENT

Product development is the work contributing towards improvement in the existing knowledge by way of improved ideas, systems, techniques etc. Product development is a specialized activity which may result in creation of new products or modification in the production process to produce the same product. Product development involves design, redesign and fabrication of new or modified product and then testing it to find its usefulness.

Product development is essential in order to:

1. Meet changing needs of the customers,
2. Adjust with the variation in quantity required,
3. Manufacture improved and low cost products,
4. Maintain sales position and net profit.

Following are the steps taken before marketing the product:

(*i*) Market research : to ascertain the need for a new product.

(*ii*) Research to provide base for design.

(*iii*) Design the product.

(iv) *Development:* to develop the design.
(v) *Prototype production:* to prepare a product jointly by the design department and production department for experimental and test purpose.
(vi) *Pre-production:* to produce few items under factory conditions and these samples are tested and supplied to selected customers for inviting their comments.
(vii) Manufacture

First 3 steps have already been discussed earlier. After the product is designed, it needs to be developed and prototype is prepared before actual production is started. Thus development is the fabrications of new or modified product and then testing it to find its usefulness. The research and development departments are thus concerned with all aspects of the product design and applications including its functional efficiency, quality, reliability, possible alternatives for material, wastage, control standardisation, simplification, interchangeability of parts, tolerances etc.

Product is developed keeping essential requirements of

(a) keeping cost as low as possible to have more profit margin
(b) better sales market
(c) changing needs of the customers.

To achieve these objectives, latest inventions in the field, and latest developments in the products of competitors must be considered.

(i) Collect new ideas from competitors, by inventions, from dealers and customers.
(ii) Evaluate good and feasible ideas. Selected ideas are evaluated technically as regards to the method of manufacture, labour and equipment required, performance of the product and cost of manufacture. Then the ideas are evaluated from the point of view of their acceptability by the customer.
(iii) Product is then designed.

Procedure for Product Development

After the design of the product, product development phase is started. Product development is done in the following steps :

(i) Develop the method for production using simplification, standardisation and specialisation techniques.
(ii) Finalise the requirements of the equipments needed for manufacture.
(iii) Finalise the specifications of the material required to be purchased.
(iv) Job requirement of the workers and their training.
(v) System for exercising the control is evolved.
(vi) Prototype is prepared by design department, and method for product developed and is then modified if necessary on the basis of experience.
(vii) Few products are manufactured and their performance is observed. If need arises modifications in the design of the product is done and accordingly method for production is modified.
(viii) Green signal is then given for starting the production in full swing.

14.10. TOOLS FOR PRODUCT DEVELOPMENT

Following are the important tools for product development.

1. Simplification (Variety Reduction)

2. Standardization
3. Rationalisation
4. Specialisation
5. Interchangeability
6. Diversification

These tools have been discussed in the following paragraphs.

14.11. SIMPLIFICATION (VARIETY REDUCTION)

Work simplification means making improvement in methods by eliminating unnecessary parts of the job by combining and rearranging other elements of the job and making them easier and safer to perform. It refers to the elimination of unnecessary varieties, sizes etc. In simplification for scientific methods, superfluous and less important varieties and types are cut down.

Simplification reduces range of products, their types, sizes and also reduces their complexity of manufacturing procedure. Thus, it is helpful in eliminating wastage by avoiding unnecessary variety and unimportant difference in products of daily use.

Due to lack of simplification, some people do not like to purchase foreign products such as automobiles, watches and such other products because their spare parts are not easily available and at the same time it is difficult to repair them when necessity arises.

Simplification is difficult in highly styled items because their styles are changing very rapidly specially for the items used by ladies and children. The consumers, competitors and manufacturers are very much interested to use these changing styles. Therefore, it becomes a difficult problem to use simplification in these items.

Simplification that reduces the number of varieties of finished products is important to both industry and public. The simplification of product involves the reduction of the number and variety of products. Producers often find that 70% to 90% of their sales are concentrated to only 10 to 20% of their products. By eliminating less profitable items and concentrating on the manufacture of the better-selling items, management can reduce costs and increase sales largely.

By simplification, reduction is effected in the number of sizes, shapes, style and types of articles. As for example, in an industry before simplification 683 sizes of folding paper boxes were used but when study was made, it found that 52% of annual consumption was concentrated in 9 sizes, 14 sizes would meet the other needs, with the result sizes were cut down from 683 to 23.

Simplification of a product is not free of possible disadvantages also. For example, suppose manufacturer sells nuts, bolts and washers: Now even washers produced by him are costly, he has to supply washers with bolts and nuts. If he cuts the manufacture of washers then he may not get sufficient order for only bolts and nuts, because customers will prefer to purchase from someone who can offer a complete supply. This will be more easy and less expensive for the customers to order all the three items from one supplier.

Advantages

Simplification is advantageous to all classes of persons, *i.e.*, manufacturers, distributors and consumers. These advantages are summarised below :

(*a*) To manufacturers. By simplification manufacturer can get the following advantages:

(*i*) Use of special purpose machines and tools is possible.

(*ii*) Less capital is blocked in raw materials, finished products, jigs, dies and other special tools.

(*iii*) Less supervision is required.

(*iv*) Less chances of errors.

(*v*) Manufacturing cost decreases because by producing less variety of products, large number of products of same variety are produced.

(*vi*) Correct estimation is possible.

(*vii*) Less chances of obsolescence.

(*viii*) Training to workers becomes easy, quick and economical.

(*ix*) Increased production rate.

(*x*) Lower unit cost.

(*xi*) Investment of capital will be less.

(*xii*) Standardisation is possible, which raises quality of products and products of uniform acceptable quality will be available in the market.

(*xiii*) It reduces wastage of labour and materials.

(*xiv*) Reduction of error in shipment.

(*xv*) Prompt delivery.

(*xvi*) Continuous employment instead of temporary when this or that size or model was needed.

(*b*) To Distributors. Simplification provides the following advantages to distributors :

(*i*) Selling is easy because only few items are to be sold.

(*ii*) Less capital is blocked in keeping the variety of products in hand.

(*iii*) Less depreciation and obsolescence of products in stock.

(*iv*) Selling expenses are reduced because of less handling.

(*v*) Accounting and other clerical work reduced.

(*vi*) Less storage space is required.

(*vii*) Elimination of slow moving stock.

(*c*) To Consumers. By simplification advantages to consumers are :

(*i*) Better quality of products is available.

(*ii*) Better services in delivery and repairs.

(*iii*) Less cost.

(*iv*) Confidence and easiness in purchase.

14.12. STANDARDISATION

It is the setting up of standards for quantity, quality, raw material, sizes, performance etc. of any product. It is done after considering various scientific procedures and is helpful for check-ing the quality performance and value of product. Simplification is the selection of those items which are of greatest demand and elimination of other items, while standardisation is to set the standards for that particular simplified item. The standard fixed should give best method, specification and the type considering all the factors such as availability of equipment and material etc.

It is the best method for achieving interchangeability, manufacture of mass-production and it is a greatest factor in the growth of industry of present day. It has a large scope in the manufacturing of parts and components. Unwise standards cannot be forced on unwilling public or industry. It involves a great deal of technical knowledge and experience. Use of standard parts and interchangeability of components, is very economic and advantageous. A cost reduction sense in design work is a necessity and all efforts must be to reduce the cost of production. Designer should use standard materials, employ standard limits and avoid unnecessary tolerance. He should have good knowledge of standardization..

Standardization can be done in nomenclature, dimension, quality, tools and equipment, process, performance, safety etc. It promotes the manufacture of more regular reliable and improved product at a lower cost. A designer should consider the product from simplification point of view. Simplification is a means of limiting unnecessary variety of products which cannot be justified on economic grounds.

All the tools, equipment, working conditions, materials, quantity etc. shouldbe standardised. Standard of product can only be achieved by standardising tools, equipment, materials etc. A machine should be in good condition to keep the quality of product to be same as was in the beginning. Thus, it is necessary to maintain the machine in good working condition and similarly, if the tools are blunt, the quality of products will not be same and will be impossible to maintain their standard. Therefore, it is most essential to keep the tools and machines both in good condition.

The meaning of standardisation can easily be understood by the following example :

If some manufacturers make 8 threads per inch length and some others 7 to 9 threads per inch length on a stud of 1 inch diameter rod, then it will be very difficult to use them on various machines. To avoid this difficulty, it has been decided to use 8 threads per inch length for one inch diameter by all manufacturers of studs, bolts etc. Thus, if we say a stud on one inch diameter then everyone understands that it will have 8 threads per inch length without explaining. In this way all the products of daily use are standardised which result in the following advantages.

Advantages

(*i*) Interchangeability of products is possible.
(*ii*) Better quality of products.
(*iii*) Use of automatic machines is easily and economically possible.
(*iv*) It is possible to provide guarantee period for the performance of product.
(*v*) It saves large amount of production time and labour, and thus cost of products is reduced.
(*vi*) It helps in reduction of stock, investment and storage space.
(*vii*) It helps in reduction of maintenance spares and thereby reduces maintenance cost.
(*viii*) It provides improved managerial control and better manufacturing efficiency.
(*ix*) Better customer's satisfaction is possible.

Disadvantages

(*i*) Sometimes it results in marginal increase in costs.
(*ii*) Extra cost of changing over to standardisation, sometimes discourage the decision for standardisation.
(*iii*) Restriction to freedom of choice.

Standardisation as a Management Tool

Standardisation should not be restricted to machine, processes or materials but should be extended to administrative procedures, layout of forms etc. which help to improve the efficiency of management functions.

Standardisation programme should be based on the following :

(*i*) Standardisation in administration,

(*ii*) Standardisation in production planning,

(*iii*) Standardisation of materials, and

(*iv*) Design standardisation etc.

Distinction between Simplification and Standardisation

As already explained simplification is concerned with the manufacturing procedures while standardisation is concerned mainly with a particular product or process. Thus simplification is a selective procedure and its purpose is to select the items, sizes and varieties of products, which are most useful and important and to concentrate the complete production on those selected products.

Standardisation is a technical procedure and its purpose is to use and implement best design, size, method, quality or procedure for the performance of the desired work.

For example, if a manufacturer of T.V. reduces its 8 models to 3 models, this is known as simplification of line of products.

When, if the manufacturer decides to use a fix number of components and always use same set procedure and circuit; it is known as standardisation of products.

It will be more clear by another example :

We all know that bolts are generally available in size of $\frac{1''}{4}, \frac{3''}{8}, \frac{1''}{2}, \frac{5''}{8}, \frac{7''}{8}$ and 1", not of the size $\frac{3''}{16}, \frac{7''}{15}, \frac{9''}{16}, \frac{11''}{16}, \frac{18''}{16}, \frac{15''}{19}$, this is the function of simplification, and at the same time it has been standardised that bolts of and $\frac{1''}{4}, \frac{3''}{8}, \frac{1''}{2}, \frac{5''}{8}, \frac{7''}{8}$ and 1" are manufactured at 16, 14, 12, 11, 10 and 8 threads per inch length respectively.

14.13. RATIONALISATION

The process of rationalisation was first started in Germany to rebuild the industries after First World War. Then this rationalisation was used in Japan and England. The utility of rationalisation was felt in other countries also and in 1927 a Geneva World Economic Confer-ence described it as a method or technique for securing minimum waste of effort and material. It includes scientific organisation of labour, simplification of process, improvements in the trans-port system and standardisation of materials and products.

Rationalisation is the removal of all the duplication and overlaps without loss of economy. It eliminates wastage and inefficiency by reforming on scientific basis to all men, material, machine, management and money to ensure maximum output with minimum cost and efforts.

Characteristics of Rationalisation

Rationalisation can be done in several fields as summarised below :

(a) Technical. Technical rationalisation means adopting the following processes :

(i) *Standardisation.* As discussed earlier, it is the process for fixing certain standards of the quality, processes, material etc. to limit the variety so as to eliminate wastage of labour, money and material and to reduce cost of product.

(ii) *Simplification.* To rationalise any industry, simplification is also necessary in which only selected type of products are manufactured so that more attention can be paid.

(iii) *Mechanisation.* It is based on the more use of automatic machines. It is used to speed up the work and thus by increasing turnover, cost of production is reduced to a large extent.

(iv) *Intensification.* It means taking the best use of existing equipment and using the machines at higher speeds and try to increase the production with the available equipment and resources.

(b) Organisation. To rationalise an industry, organisation should be scientifically arranged, because scientific organisation is helpful for running the industries efficiently and to keep cooperation among different departments so as to maintain peaceful working at all levels.

(c) Finance. In this aspect rationalisation is done to see that industries are neither over-capitalised nor under-capitalised. More emphasis should be given on modern equipment through self-financing.

(d) Social. In rationalisation social and human aspects are also taken into consideration. For this, a systematic approach is made to remove causes of labour discontent, to provide adequate incentives, reward to good workers, frame scheme of production and remuneration etc.

Advantages of Rationalisation

From the above discussions, it is clear that rationalisation is very useful. Some of its important advantages are given below :

(i) Better production.

(ii) It improves the quantity and quality of product by utilising men, material and machines in the best way.

(iii) Cost of products can be reduced greatly by using specialised machines and equipments.

(iv) Workers get good wages and incentives.

(v) Prosperity of Community. It helps to improve the prosperity of entire community by adopting rationalisation. Since manufacturers get more profit, workers get more wages, consumers get products at lower prices.

(vi) It helps to bring economic stability in economic field by making improvements all round the industry and trade.

(vii) It promotes industrial cooperation due to scientific knowledge, improved techniques and different industries come closer to make their industries more rationalised.

Limitations

As it has various advantages, it also has some limitations and dangers, some of them are:

(*a*) **Danger to Small and Weak Industries.** When some Industries are rationalised, their quality of products will be better and rates will also be cheaper. While other small and weak industries which could not be.rationalised will be producing poor quality products at higher costs.Thus such industries could not stand in the market for a long time and will be wound up.

(*b*) **Danger of Monopoly.** As rationalised industries produce products at cheaper rates, they will charge higher profits and sell their products at slightly lower rates than unrationalised industries. Thus, rationalisation creates monopoly and others will have to suffer.

(*c*) **Difficulty of finance.** Rationalisation requires big expenditure for modernisation and overall re-organisation of industry. Large capital is therefore needed for this purpose.

(*d*) **Opposition by Workers.** Generally, workers oppose it due to the following reasons:

(*i*) It creates unemployment.

(*ii*) Increase in fatigue and mental strain due to speeding up of work.

(*e*) **Danger of Over-production.** Rationalisation of industries may lead to an increase in production. Therefore, production may increase beyond the consumption capacity of people, which may cause losses.

14.14. SPECIALISATION

Specialisation leads to the break-up of the work into simple process and sub-process which can be formed through machines. Specialisation is a necessity to have economic growth in the industry and to increase the productive power of labour. Every operation or process needs specialisation and this increases the efficiency of the worker, improvement of the tools, invention and application of the machines.

Specialisation means concentrating efforts on a particular field of action or towards a specific attempt. Specialisation means that if a worker instead of completing the full product, performs one small operation on the product and attains proficiency in that one activity, he becomes specialist in that operation.

The specialisation has led to standardisation and interchangeability of parts. The specialisation has increased the automation.

Advantages

1. It reduces the time in learning a trade.
2. It increases the efficiency and permits utilisation of aptitude.
3. The product can be produced more cheaply and better than that under the traditional methods.

Disadvantages

1. It deprives the workmen of all round development.
2. Industrial organisation becomes oversensitive and unemployment may result.
3. The workmen are used as machines and labour becomes a mere commodity.

Limitations

1. Specialisation may result in monotony.
2. Specialised labour and equipment are not flexible, *i.e.*, they cannot be used for other purposes.

Application

1. Specialisation is universal in application,
2. Specialisation applies to :
   (*i*) Products (*ii*) Processes
   (*iii*) Individuals (*iv*) Companies
   (*v*) Jobs (*vi*) Equipments etc.

14.15. INTERCHANGEABILITY

Interchangeability means that any standardised component will assemble correctly with any mating component, both being chosen at random. It plays an important role in the growth of mass production techniques. In this system the parts produced are near identical as possible, because it eliminates the human control of the machines.

Since the task of assembly is simplified, it reduces the cost. It also allows replacement of parts without any problem.

In order to achieve interchangeability appropriate component tolerances must be specified, depending upon the type of fit required. The manufacturing process selected should be able to make components within the specified tolerances. The interchangeable system is also known as system of **limits and fits.**

14.16. PRODUCT DIVERSIFICATION

It is just opposite of variety reduction. Diversification means (*i*) addition of new products, or (*ii*) introduction of established products into new markets. The extent of diversification should be decided based on the market analysis. It adds to the classes of consumers served.

In this more lines of products, more types and sizes are added to satisfy the needs of large number of consumers.

Reasons for diversifications are:

1. Survival of the firm by offsetting declining market.
2. For providing stability by offsetting seasonal slumps.
3. For productive utilisation of resources.
4. To meet the changing needs of customers/group of customers.
5. To take advantage of unusually attractive opportunity for growth.
6. To maintain reputation for industrial leadership.

QUESTIONS

1. Since product design must take into consideration a large number of factors there is always the possibility of error. Draw up a check list which could give a logical approach to checking for design error.
2. What requirements should be fulfilled by a product design ?
3. Which are the departments who are connected with the work of product design, and how? Explain.
4. What factors a design engineer should consider while designing a product ?
5. How design engineer plays an important role in keeping the cost of the product as low?
6. What procedure is followed in product development ?
7. What do you understand by simplification, standardisation, specialisation and rationalisation ?
8. Distinguish between standardisation and simplification. Outline the different techniques of work measurements.
9. State the advantages and disadvantages of rationalisation. Also explain the urgency of introducing rationalism schemes in Indian industries.
10. Why is it necessary to record all the processes before simplification ? What are different recording system ?
11. What can be the limitations for rationalisation ? Explain in detail.
12. Distinguish between standardisation and rationalisation. Outline the different techniques used for work measurement.
13. What is the purpose of standardisation within a plant ? Describe standards which are commonly dealt with towards standardisation in a manufacturing plant.
14. Describe briefly how standardisation is achieved on an international, national and on the factory level.
15. (*i*) Explain fully the difference between "Rationalisation" and 'Standardisation',
    (*ii*) It is feared that 'Rationalisation' in india will increase unemployment. Give your com-ments on it.
16. Discuss the factors relat-ing to the design and development of an engineering product.
17. State advantages of simplification and standardisation to :
    (*i*) Designer. (*ii*) Production Engineer
    (*iii*) Sales Manager. (*iv*) Customer.
18. Write a detailed note on 'Product life cycle?'
19. What is 'Product diversification'? Compare it with variety reduction. Mention the reasons for diversification.

15 PRODUCTION PLANNING AND CONTROL (P.P.C.)

15.1. INTRODUCTION

As we know that production requires the organised utilisation of natural resources, men, money, material and machines. We also know that 'production is an organised activity of converting raw materials into useful products. But before starting that work of actual production, production planning is done in order to anticipate possible difficulties and decide in advance as to how the production should be carried out in a best and economical way. Since only planning of production is not sufficient, hence management takes all possible steps to see that plans chalked by planning department are properly adhered to and the standard set are attained. In order to achieve it, control over production is exercised. The aim of production control is to produce the products of right quality, in right quantity, at the right time by using the best and least expensive methods.

Production planning and control can thus be defined as the process of planning the production in advance, setting the exact route of each item, fixing the starting and finishing dates for each item, to give production orders to shops and lastly to allow up the progress of products according to orders.

The principles of production planning and control lies in the statement "First plan your work, then work your plan."

For performing a job several things are required, *e.g.*, raw materials, machines, cutting tools, gauges, instruments, jigs and fixtures etc. Production Planning and Control (PPC) in such case plan the provision of all the required items in time at different work stations and also remove the material when the job is complete. PPC helps in achieving the highest efficiency by manufacturing the required quantity of the product, or required quality at required time, by the best and most economical method. Some of the important definitions of PPC are given hereunder:

PPC may be defined as the direction and coordination of the firm's material and physical resources towards the attainment of pre-specified production goals in the most efficient available way.

Production Planning and Control comprise the planning, routing, scheduling, dispatching and follow-up functions in the productive process, so organised that the movement of material, performance of machines and operations of labour, however subdivided, are directed and coordinated as to quantity, quality, time place.

Production Planning and Control (P.P.C.) is a set of policies and procedures that are used to manage work flow, inventories backlogs and changes in the level of production rate.

Production planning and control can be defined as the process of planning the production in advance, setting the exact route of each item, fixing the starting and finishing dates for each item, to issue production orders to shops and lastly to follow-up the progress of production according to orders. Production planning and control is one of the basic activities which determines the effectiveness of a production process.

15.1.1. Functions

Production planning and control (PPC) system performs many functions out of which some are performed before the arrival of raw materials and tools, while others are performed when raw material undergoes processing. Following are the major functions of production planning and control.

Phase	*Functions*	*Activities*
1. Planing phase	(*i*) Preplanning (*ii*) Planning (*iii*) Routing and process planning (*iv*) Loading (*v*) Scheduling	These functions involve forecasting product design, process planning, routing, material control, tool control, loading and scheduling.
2. Action phase	Dispatching	In this phase worker is ordered to start the work
3. Control phase	(*i*) Progress reporting (*ii*) Follow-up (expediting) (*iii*) Replanning (*iv*) Inspection	In this phase data for progress is collected, delayed activities are expedited, corrective action is taken and replanning is done, if required. All these activities are considered as control functions.

(A) Planning Phase

(*a*) **Preplanning:**

- *Forecasting:* Estimating the work requirement in future.
- *Estimating* : Estimating the cost of work.
- *Product design* : This includes the preparation of specifications of new product.

(*b*) **Action planning:**

- Process planning and routing : Preparing work details.
- Material requirement planning.
- Tool requirement planning.
- Scheduling.
- Men and Machine loading: Determining men and machine requirements and their control.

(B) Action Phase:

- Despatching : Starting the work.
- Follow-up *i.e.,* carry out work as per action plan.
- Initiate material purchase, receipt, storage etc.

(C) Control Phase :

(*a*) **Progress reporting:**

– Collection of data regarding progress of work, inventory etc.

– Interpreting the data.

(D) Corrective Action:

– Expediting, *i.e.*, making corrections in the work.

– Replanning, *i.e.*, making corrections in the plan and then implement.

Out of the above, some activities have already been discussed in the previous chapters, some are discussed in this chapter, while others will be discussed in next few chapters.

15.1.2. Objectives of P.P.C.

Objectives of production planning and control department are closely linked with the objectives of the enterprise as a whole. Keeping in view, the main aim of customers satisfaction, objectives qf P.P.C. can be summarised as follows :

(*i*) To deliver the product to the customer when he wants it.

(*ii*) To follow-up production schedules to ensure that delivery promises are maintained.

(*iii*) To maintain quality at desired level, *i.e.*, same as that of approved sample.

(*iv*) To maintain adequate level of inventories, as excess or shortage both are harmful.

(*v*) To utilise optimum plant capacities.

(*vi*) To maintain flexibility in manufacturing operation, so that emergency rush can be accommodated.

Production planning and control system which converts the objectives into action is shown in Fig. 15.1.

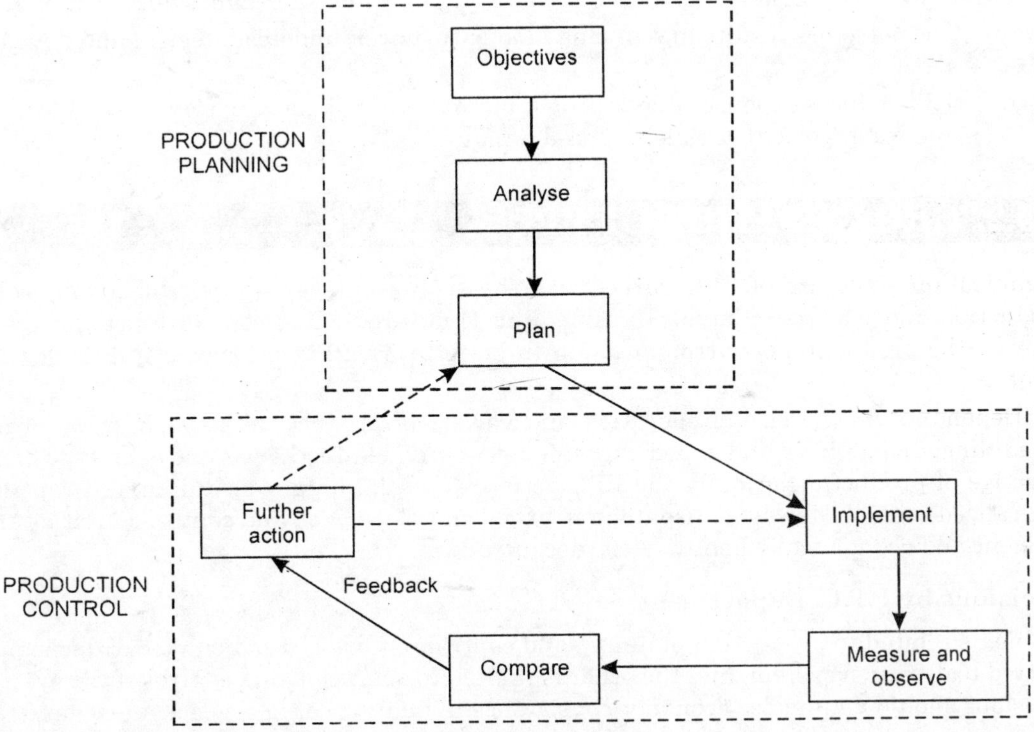

Fig. 15.1. PPC System

15.1.3. Advantages of P.P.C.

Following are the important advantages of Production Planning and Control to the enterprise and to the employees :

(*i*) Improvement in volume of production within quality limits.

(*ii*) To improve the level of quality and maintain consistency in standard.

(*iii*) Optimum utilisation of plant capacity, this enables the utilisation of capital investment.

(*iv*) Optimum utilisation of services and facilities available in the industry. Services and facilities include electricity, water, air, steam, transport, material handling devices etc.

(*v*) *Improved process efficiency*. This enables the enhancement of efficiency of operator (or worker).

(*vi*) *Improves safety*. Since product sequence, routing and all other related aspects are properly planned, high level of safety are achievable.

(*vii*) Overall work cleanliness and no chances of haphazard or hazardous working, if P.P.C. are properly implemented.

(*viii*) Systematic working acts as motivator for a workman. Job satisfaction can also be achieved as workers are engaged for the works best suited for them. This also creates interest for working.

(*ix*) Since the workers take interest and every aspect is planned, very less chances of delays due to materials, tools, equipment, delivery etc.

(*x*) Because of the above reasons, supervision time is also reduced. This allows the supervisors to devote more time towards planning, coordination, feedback informations etc.

(*xi*) Motivated workers can help in generating new ideas for improvement in methods.

(*xii*) These factors results in reducing labour-turnover, and absenteeism and develop team spirit.

(*xiii*) This reduces expenses due to proper maintenance of machinery, reduced level of rejects and wastage of materials, reduced handling.

15.2. ORGANISATION OF PPC

Organisation structure of PPC varies with the size of enterprise, type of layout, volume of production and leadership style. In a medium firm, production control functions are looked after by the production department itself. In large firms, PPC becomes a full fledged department.

Depending on the size of operation and variety of product range each group of routing, scheduling, dispatching and expediting can be sub-divided further as one each type of product or range of products. Normally the PPC activities of planning, scheduling and routing have centralized control. However, dispatching, expediting, feed back and control activities are more efficient and economical when they are decentralized.

Decisions by P.P.C. Department

Problems related to production planning and control require two major type of decision, one is related to design of system, and the other is related to operation and control of the system. The decisions should emphasize economy, consistence in quality, service performance, and delivery commitments. Examples of such problems are :

(a) Decisions related to the design of system :

- Selection of equipment and process
- Job design
- Facility layout.
- Production design of item
- Layout of machineries

(b) Decisions related to the operation and control:

- Production control
- Maintenance of the system
- Labour control
- Improvement decisions.
- Inventory control
- Quality of control
- Cost control

These are the main problems which are required to be solved. Gravity of the problem, however vary from industry to industry, and organisation to organisation depending upon the 'process involved'.

Following Fig. 15.2 shows a chart of functional organisation of P.P.C.

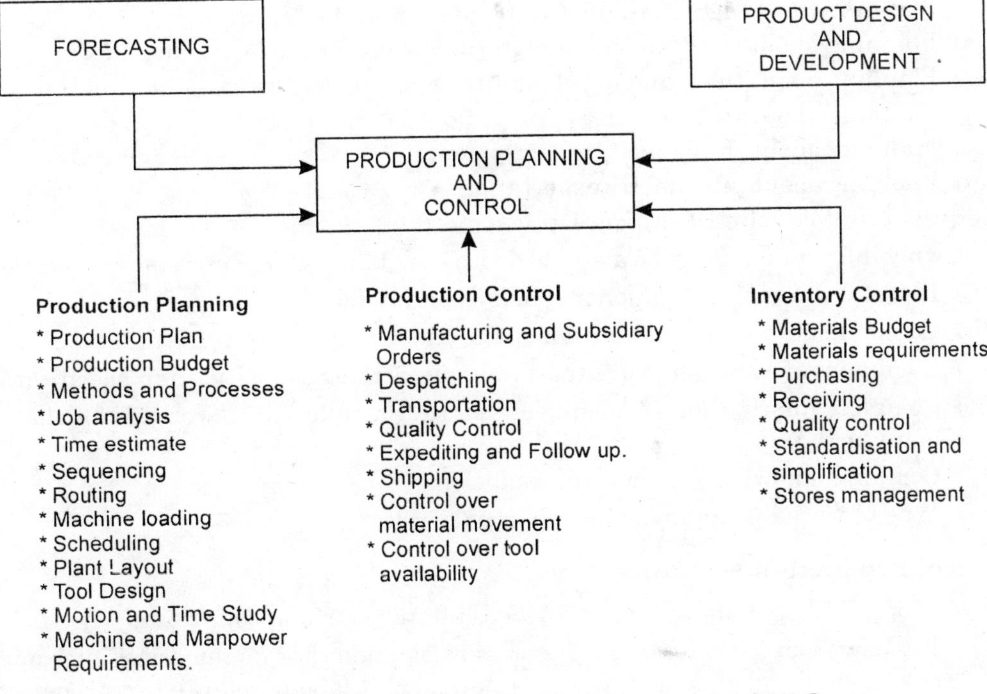

Fig. 15.2. Shows a chart of functional organisation of P.P.C.

Relationship of P.P.C. with other Departments

Production planning and control department is required to coordinate with most of the departments. It has to coordinate with corporate planning for knowing planning objectives, with material management department for knowing purchase schedules and inventory levels, with finance department for financial planning, budget formation and cash flow requirements, with personnel department regarding manpower planning and recruitment, with marketing department regarding sales forecasts, with design department regarding preparation of specifications.

15.3. PRODUCTION PLANNING

Functions of production pre-planning, namely, market reserch and sales forecasting, factory location and layout, equipment policy for purchase and replacement, capacity planning are being discussed at appropriate places in the book.

Here we are discussing the production planning functions.

Before starting any work, it is necessary to plan the things properly for getting best results. Similarly for production, planning in advance is very necessary and if there is no planning then how shall we control? It is the planning department, which decides about each element of the job in anticipation that what work shall be done, where, how and when it shall be done.

The **functions of planning** are grouped as under :

(*i*) Investigation about the complete details and requirements of the product to be manufactured.

(*ii*) Pre-determination of future achievements.

(*iii*) Planning the design of product going to be manufactured.

(*iv*) Planning about the quantity of materials which are to be consumed.

(*v*) Planning about the standard of quality of products to be manufactured.

(*vi*) Planning about the sequence of operations.

(*vii*) Planning about the capacity of equipments.

(*viii*) Planning about internal transportation.

Requirements of the Planning Department.

Following information must be available with the planning department for efficient working:

(*i*) Detailed drawing of components and their assembled.

(*ii*) Complete up-to-date information about the stores and delivery times.

(*iii*) Complete information about the equipments, their capacities and specifications etc.

(*iv*) Complete information regarding standard time allowed to workers for the jobs being manufactured.

(*v*) Complete knowledge of market conditions.

(*vi*) Type of workers employed and their salaries.

Objects of Production Planning

The objects of production planning are divided into two parts as follows :

1. To know from sales forecast, previous sales and other engineering informations, the type of materials, tools, machines, method and labour required in proper quantities and qualities, when and where required for producing the required goods economically.
2. To undertake all preparations required to achieve the production aim established by master schedule, budget and by fluctuating demands of the customers.

Basis of Good Production Planning

Following are the factors which form a basis of good production planning:

1. Organisation

(*a*) Recognition by management of the need for production planning and be prepared to delegate authority as well as responsibility.

(*b*) To have co-operative effort, the supervisor level personnels must recognise that the work schedule is purely an extension of function specialisation. Due to this facility, they devote more time to the activities for which they are best suited.

2. Personnel

(*a*) They must understand the scheduled operations ;

(*b*) They should be trained specially to suit the particular system to be adopted;

(*c*) They must have the interest and aptitude in doing the required work.

3. Standardization

(*a*) Material-purchased or fabricated.

(*b*) Tools and equipments.

(*c*) Method of operation.

(*d*) Method of remuneration for workers.

(*e*) Quality standards and inspection procedures.

(*f*) Set up of organisation.

(*g*) Reporting on progress of manufacture showing comparison with the prepared schedules.

4. Information about Productive Capacities and Requirements

(*a*) Knowledge about the components to be manufactured.

(*b*) Knowledge about production machines with specifications like numbers available, type, feed, speeds and productivity capacities, etc.

(*c*) Knowledge about manufacturing time required, sequence of operation for parts, components and final assembly.

(*d*) Knowledge about material available in stores, total requirement, time required for getting the newly purchased material.

(*e*) Quantity of materials consumed per unit.

(*f*) Knowledge about labour employed and productive capacities for each type of labour.

(*g*) Manufacturing operations of each part.

(*h*) The availability of required tools, jigs and fixtures for each item being manufactured.

5. Planning for Controlled Production

Further, in addition, the following factors also contribute for the good production planning and control:

1. Complete specifications in detail.
2. Advice of job study man for routing of work.
3. Job study data in case of new operation.
4. Getting information for every machine about the amount of work to be allotted on that machine.
5. Determination of alternate machines to achieve flexibility.
6. Layout of the plant, production centres and machines.
7. Equipment and their arrangements for conveying and transporting materials.
8. Methods and facilities for storage and issue of materials.
9. Degree to which product is simplified or standardized.
10. Degree to which operations and processes are simplified.

Advantages.

In view of the above factors, production planning is the answer to greater production on the same investment without unduly speeding up workers. Effective planning always means effective control. The advantages of production planning may be following :

1. Better service to customer in promised delivery dates.
2. Fewer rush orders in the plant and less overtime.
3. Lower inventory of work in process.
4. Less finished stock required to give the same service to customers.
5. Better control of raw materials inventory, which contributes to more effective purchasing.
6. More effective use of equipment.
7. Less loss of time by workers awaiting for materials, which improves plant morale.

Steps in Production Planning

For production planning, following steps are adopted :

(*i*) To decide whether to follow job, batch or mass production system. (For details refer chapter on 'Production Function and Productivity').

(*ii*) Sales Forecasting for estimation of type, quantity and quality of product. For details, refer chapter on 'Market-Research and Sales Forecasting'.

(*iii*) Planning to meet seasonal demands. Many products have seasonal demands, which need to be predicted, and planning is made to meet this demand by timely procurement of material, planning the production and those of sales.

(*iv*) Planning the process. Process planning means the preparation of detailed work plan, *i.e.*, manufacturing plan. Process planning is the systematic determination of the methods by which a product is to be manufactured, economically and competitively.

(*v*) Determine the economic batch quantity for manufacturing the product.

(*vi*) Tools planning. This involves determining tool requirements, plan for procurement, and their maintenance.

(*vii*) Machine loading and scheduling. For details refer chapter on 'Scheduling'.

15.4. PROCESS PLANNING

For manufacturing a product, required process needs to be planned. Process planning is determining the most economical method of performing an activity. Process planning develops the broad plan of manufacturing a product or a component.

For carrying out process planning, following information are required :

(*i*) Quantity of work to be performed.

(*ii*) Details specification of the product

(*iii*) Quality of work.

(*iv*) Availability of equipments, tools, and manpower with period.

(*v*) Sequence of operations to be performed.

(*vi*) Standard time for each operation.

Steps Involved in Process Planning

(*i*) Most economical process is selected depending upon : current production commitments, delivery date, quantity to be produced, quality standards.

(*ii*) Selection of materials, right quality, shape and size of raw material.

(*iii*) Selection of Jigs, fixtures and special attachments.

(*iv*) Selection of cutting tools.

(*v*) Selection of inspection gauges.

(*vi*) Make the process layout indicating sequence of operation.

(*vii*) Documentation of process, *i.e.*, for operation, route sheet etc.

15.5. AGGREGATE PLANNING

Aggregate planning is the essence of intermediate range planning. As we know that intermediate-range planning usually involves from one month to 18 months period, and is usually the function of middle management and involves tectical decisions like quarterly plans, subdividing budgets, and arrangements to meet fluctuations in demand. In intermediate-range planning, management must work within the limitations established in long-range planning, but still has some flexibility in selecting courses of action.

Aggregate planning can be defined as intermediate-range planning in which strategies are devised to economically absorb demand fluctuations.

Aggregate planning can also be defined as the process of determining output levels (in units) of product groups over the coming 6 to 18 months on a weekly or monthly basis, the plan identifies the overall level of outputs in support of the business plan.

It shows the outputs it will produce, expressed in number of units of its product groups or families. Planning at this level ignores such details as how many of each individual product, style, colour option, or model to produce. The plan recognises the existing capacity and the company's overall policies for maintaining inventories and backlogs, employment stability, and subcontracting. Output of aggregate planning should specify values for monthly manpower levels, output levels, overtime commitments, vacation plans, subcontracting needs, and hiring quantities.

As the name implies, aggregate planning involves combining relevant resources into general terms or an overall aggregate.

Successful aggregate planning must consider following aspects :

(*i*) Aggregate planning must be based on forecasting inputs.

(*ii*) Aggregate strategies must fall within the cash-flow constraints set by finance.

(*iii*) Aggregate plans must be translatable into planned production levels for individual products in each month, and assignment of personnel to specific work groups and operations.

(*iv*) Additional productive capacity must be available to accommodate the desired level of production of individual products.

Aggregate Plan v/s Master Schedules

Determination of planned production levels and schedules for individual products is called master production scheduling. The master schedule is derived from the aggregate production plan, and expresses the overall plan in terms of specific items or models that can be assigned priorities. As explained earlier aggregate plan simply expresses the number of end product, and not the model, size, colour etc., whereas master schedule specifies precisely how many of which type (or size) will be produced, and when. This detail is necessary to plan for the material and capacity requirements.

15.6. CAPACITY PLANNING

Capacity is the limiting capability of a productive unit to produce within a stated time period, normally expressed in terms of output units per unit time. This limit can be increased through overtime or by adding a second shift. While specifying capacity, its measure should be selected carefully. For example, number of seats in an airlines is a confusing measure, its effective measure must be 'seat kilometres'.

For a new product, it is difficult to predict capacity requirements, due to uncertainties. Optimistic and pessimistic predictions can have serious effect on capacity requirement.

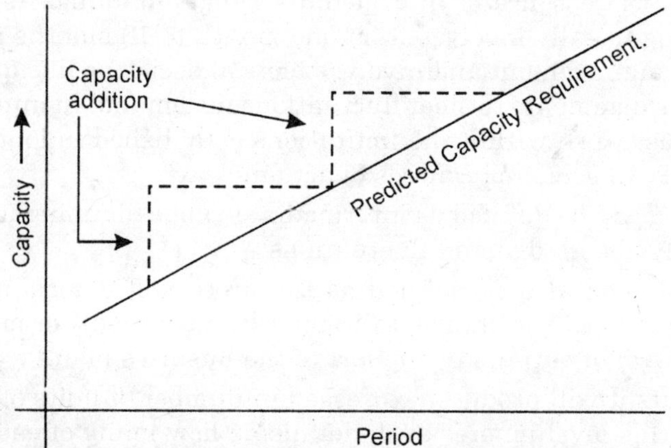

Fig.15.3. Capacity addition to meet requirements.

Capacity is added depending upon the demand growth. Location of new capacity is strategically important and involves assessments of market location, system distribution costs and other factors. When adding the capacity, it is necessary to analyse the cost behaviour at the capacity limits of first and second shifts. It is noted that when new capacity is first added, it is not fully utilised unless the expansion is long overdue. Addition of capacity relieves the stress on existing facilities, making it possible to eliminate overtime and/or multiple shifts.

Definitions

1. **Design Capacity.** Design capacity is the maximum rate of output that might be achieved under ideal conditions.
2. **Effective Capacity.** It is the maximum possible output, given a product mix, scheduiling difficulties, machine maintenance, lunch and tea breaks etc. Effective capacityis less than the design capacity.
3. **Actual Output.**This is the rate of output actually achieved. It is usually less than the effective capacity due to machine break downs, absenteeism, defective outputs, shortage of output and other problems outside the control of production manager.

Measures of Capacity Effectiveness

1. $\text{Efficiency} = \dfrac{\text{Actual Output}}{\text{Effective Capacity}}$

2. $\text{Utilisation} = \dfrac{\text{Actual Output}}{\text{Design Capacity}}$

15.7. ROUTING

Routing may be defined as the selection of path which each part of the product will follow and which is being transformed from raw material to finished products. Path of the product will also give sequence of operations to be adopted while being manufactured.

In other words, routing means determination of most advantageous path to be followed from department to department and machine to machine till raw materials get its final shape.

Thus routing is a technique which involves the analysis of

(*a*) Type of work to be done on product or its parts.

(*b*) Operation required to do the work.

(*c*) Sequence of operation required.

(*d*) Where the work will be done.

(*e*) A proper classification about the personnel required and the machine for doing the work.

For effective production control of a well managed industry with standard conditions, the routing plays an important role, so as to get best results obtained from available plant capacity. Thus routing provides the basis for scheduling, dispatching and follow-up.

While converting raw material into required goods different operations are to be performed and the selection of a particular path of operations for each piece is termed as 'Routing'. This selection of a particular path, *i.e.*, sequence of operations must be the best and cheapest to have the lowest cost of the final product.

Requirements for Proper Routing

(*a*) Process analysis should be done.

(*b*) In case of assembly, product analysis of different components should be done.

(*c*) Analysis of material required should be done.

(*d*) Analysis for the quantity required for each component.

(*e*) Order of preference of various products must be found out.

(*f*) Finding out the place of operation and operations to be performed at different stages of operation.

(*g*) Knowledge of the machines and operations to be used.

(*h*) Knowledge about the quantity of material to be consumed in different stages with regard to the time consumed in different operations and space requirement for material movement.

Product Sequencing

During production, many times, a problem arises when several products are to be manufactured on certain machines according to the determined sequence of operation. In such cases, a problem arises that how to have best machine utilization, *i.e.*, minimum machine idle time, and to satisfy the customers, *i.e.*, to deliver the goods at the right time. Such problems can be solved on the basis of cost ratios.

15.8. MACHINE LOADING

Loading may be defined as the assignment of work to a facility. The facility may be people, equipment, work groups, or an entire plant. Therefore, machine loading is the process of compiling the load or quantity of work assigned to each machine for a given period of time. Machine loading charts can be used to show the availability of machine and production manager can plan it to use for full capacity. If the machine is under loaded, he can plan to put more work, while the machine is overloaded, he can either plan for overtime (for temporary overloading) or providing additional machine and manpower (for permanent overloading).

Main Objectives of Machine Loading

1. To engage the machine continuously at work.
2. To assign dates for producing each part of a product so that the total order can be processed in the shortest possible time.

Further there are two terms generally encountered with the term machines loading.

1. **Overloading.** This may be temporary or permanent. With temporary overloading, the loading can be reduced by over-time work or by diverting the jobs to other machines, if available. While permanent overloading can be met by additional equipments, change in the processing method or by procuring the component by direct purchasing or sub-contracting.
2. **Underloading.** This is due to less work. In mass manufacturing, underloading can be avoided by producing similar components for stock. Many times underloading is due to inefficient management and wrong planning.

15.9. SCHEDULING

Scheduling determines the programme for the operations. In scheduling, order of sequence of each operation and their starting and finishing time is decided so that required materials, machines etc., may be kept ready as per schedule. Thus, scheduling may be defined, as "the fixation of time and date for each operation" as well as it determines the sequence of operations to be followed. This programme is prepared by the planning department and assign timings for various operations or processes.

Routing and scheduling can be easily understood by the examples on railways:

A railway map shows the routes for passengers, which the trains follow and the stations on that route. This is what is known as 'Routing'. Similarly, Railway time table gives the exact timing at which all the trains start and the time they take to reach at various stations and how long they haunt there. It is known as 'Scheduling'.

Types of Schedules

Schedules are of the following types :

(*a*) **Master Schedule.** It shows the dates on which important production items are to be completed. It is a weekly or monthly break-up of the production requirements for each product. Whenever any order is received, it is accommodated first in the master Schedule considering the availability of the machines and labour.

Thus, it helps Production Manager for advance planning and to have check over the production rate and efficiency.

(*b*) **Shop or Manufacturing Schedule.** After preparing master schedule, shops schedules are prepared. It assigns a definite period of time to a particular shop for manufacturing products in required quantity. It shows how much products are to be prepared and on what day or week etc.

Uses of Scheduling

Scheduling informations are useful for different departments for their working. Some of the examples are given below :

(*i*) It helps in planning the manufacturing, purchase and sale, which is also helpful for planning by ancillary and other user industries.

(*ii*) It helps the production department whether production is as per schedule, and if there is any need for coping up the backlog.

(*iii*) It helps in planning the personnel, extra shifts, overtime, machine repair programme etc.

(*iv*) By adhering to schedules, satisfactory relations can be maintained with customers and vendors.

Informations Required for Scheduling

For the purpose of scheduling, following informations are required:

(*i*) Sequence of operations for the manufacture.

(*ii*) Time required for each operation.

(*iii*) Machine capacity and its availability per day.

(*iv*) Availability of material and components.

Aims of Scheduling:

(*i*) Minimum production cost.

(*ii*) Maximum customer satisfaction.

(*iii*) Maximum operator Morale, as he knows his programme in time.

(*iv*) Maximum plant utilisation.

(*v*) Maximum utilisation of manpower.

(*vi*) Minimum storage costs.

Master Schedule and Subsidiary Schedule

It is a key play or a periodic master plan which shows the quantity of each product to be completed each day, week or month, during the period covered. For a new product which appears in the master schedule, a subsidiary schedule is prepared showing the date and time when each of the essential steps in its progress should be completed. The steps in sequence are generally

(*a*) Completion of design ;

(*b*) Completion of bill of material;

(*c*) Completion of operation analysis;

(*d*) Completion of requisition for essential components;

(*e*) Completion of pattern and special tools;

(*f*) Completion of raw material procurement;

(g) Completion of purchase of finished parts procurement;
(h) Completion of component parts;
(i) Completion of sub-assembly;
(j) Completion of assembly;
(k) Completion of final test and inspection;
(l) Completion of packing and shipping.

Scheduling Techniques

Various techniques are used for scheduling purposes. Some common scheduling techniques are:

1. Flow Process Chart
2. Gantt Chart
3. Line of Balance
4. Linear Programming
5. Network techniques

These techniques have been discussed at relevant places in the book.

15.10. DESPATCHING

It is concerned with starting the processes. It gives necessary authority to start a particular work, which has already been planned under routing and scheduling. For starting the work, essential orders and instructions are given. Therefore, the complete definition of despatching is "Release of orders and instructions for starting of production of any item in accordance with the route sheets and schedule charts".

Functions of Despatching.

Following are some of the important functions:

(i) Assignment of work to individual men, machine or work place.
(ii) Release necessary orders and production forms.
(iii) Authorize for issue of materials, tools, jigs, fixtures, gauges, dies for various jobs.
(iv) Required material is authorised to move from stores, or from operation to operation.
(v) Issue machine loading and schedule charts, route sheets and other necessary instructions and forms to be filled up.
(vi) To fix up the responsibility of guiding and controlling materials, and operation process.
(vii) To issue inspection orders stating the type of inspections required at various stages.
(viii) To issue job orders authorising operations, in accordance with the planned schedule.
(ix) Issue of time tickets, drawings, instruction cards and other necessary informations.
(x) Issue necessary formats to exercise production control.

It is realized that a single item on a production schedule can be divided into a requirement for several parts, each having different operations to be performed. Thus it is very difficult to have a standard procedure of Despatching. But depending upon the existing conditions, the Despatch Section or office of a particular industry issues different tickets, forms and cards. Such issue is known as paper work and control through this paper work is termed as "paper work control".

Control Through Paper Work

From the informations of the route sheet, the following documents are prepared:

1. Store issue order for each part.
2. Identity tag for each part.
3. Tool order for each operation on each part.
4. Job card.
5. Inspection order.
6. Move order.

These papers are designed to give all informations contained in route sheet, including specially:

1. The time allowance for each operation and the date scheduled for starting and finishing.
2. Tools and fixtures required.
3. Corresponding blue print data on tolerance and limits for inspection.

Stores Requisition

The main aim of stores requisition is to initiate the movement of material from stores to the shop floor where first process is to be performed, so that it may be available to enable work to start at the scheduled time. Following informations should be mentioned on this requisition:

1. The account to which the values of the material is to be charged when issued.
2. The quantity of material requirement.
3. The description of material.
4. The place where material is to be delivered.
5. Time when delivery is to be made.
6. Approving signature.

These store orders would be made out as soon as the route sheet is available. But it is not possible owing to the facts that sometimes store section requires to acquire the material, further, also it is undersirable to move material on the shop floor too early in advance of the time. In such condition, it is preferred to file the orders and other working papers for the parts and hand over them to despatch section a day or two before. The despatcher then passes this order to the store-keeper to prepare the material ready for issue to the shops when authorized.

Tool Order

It is standard practice to specify the tools, jigs and fixtures and gauges required for each job. The function of a tool order is to ensure that these will be available at the right time when the job is scheduled to be started. Here also, the tool section should be informed in advance to keep them ready for issue to the shop on demand. The authority for collecting these tools is on presentation of the job order for the particular job.

The Job Order

The main function of this is to provide authority for starting an operation. In general, this order is combined with some other forms such as time cards, inspection order and move order. This is, many times, termed as work ticket, job card, production ticket, pay roll card and time ticket.

Generally job orders are prepared in duplicate, one copy is meant for operator and other one for Despatcher's Control Board. When the job order is released, it is date stamped and used as authority to draw any jigs and tools required. When the order is completed, it is again date stamped and after passing through the planning department, to signal the completion of the operation it is now available for costs and pay roll work.

Inspection Order and Move Order

Where inspection orders are not combined with the job order, a separate inspection order is used. It contains the following informations:

1. Order and part number.
2. Operation number.
3. Inspection report, *i.e.*, OK, scrap, bad or repairable.
4. Move order

These inspection reports replace the job card in signalling the completion of an operation to the Planning department, thereby allowing the job card to go immediately to the costs and Pay Roll Department. The planning department can take up the question of replacing defective or repairing the faulty parts.

Another document shown in Fig. 14.10 is Move Order generally combined with job order or inspection order, but when there is transportation which justifies their use, a separate Move Order is issued. This enables a check on the worker during the transportation.

Despatching Boards or Control Boards

The actual assignment of jobs on different production machines is performed through the use of despatching board, which is so designed that shuffling of orders from machine to machine can be done further and at the same time gives a visible picture of the position of shop loading. These boards have space allotted to different machines in the shop and divided into three sections, which are used as follows :

(*a*) To keep a card (*i.e.*, copy of job order) representing the job actually being worked on a machine.

(*b*) Next job in sequence to be carried out on the machine.

(*c*) Several jobs ahead of the particular machine, one behind the other,, in the most possible way in which these are to be worked.

As the work progresses, job in section (*a*) is transferred to the top compartment, and next job held in section (*c*) is moved to compartment (*b*). Thus such control board gives an immediate view of:

(*i*) Whether all machines are engaged, an idle machine can be located, when top compartment is lying vacant.

(*ii*) Whether any machine has to do next job, shown by the absence of a card in (b) compartment.

(*iii*) Whether machine has a fair reserve of work behind it, indicated by the number of cards in the bottom compartment.

Idle Machine Time

In addition to above work, the despatching section has a responsibility for drawing attention to idle machine time, so that remedies may be worked out. Generally, control board enables a report to be made in advance. Such report enables the idle time to be avoided by routing or diverting work from other machines. Idleness due to machine break down can, or course, be reported as it occurs and, treatment for such break down should be urgent.

15.11. PRODUCTION CONTROL

The principle of production control can be defined as "the highest efficiency in production obtained by producing the required quantity of product, of the required quality, at the required time by the best and cheapest method."

As we know that production is an organised activity of converting raw materials into useful products, and production control is the control on organised activities, thus, in other words, we can say that it is the management of production activities.

Production control can also be defined as the process of planning the production in advance, setting the exact route of each item, fixing the starting and finishing dates for each item, to give production orders to shops and lastly to follow up the progress of products according to production orders.

The aim of production control is to produce the products of right quality, in the right quantity, at the right time, by using the best and least expensive methods.

The principle of production control lies in the statement: "first plan your work, then work your plan".

Henri Fayol Defines production control as "the ensuring that all which occurs in accordance with the rules established and the instructions issued".

Objectives

The objectives of production control are as follows :

1. Issuing the necessary orders to the proper personnel through proper channels, so that the production plans may be put into effect.
2. To arrange necessary items likewise materials, machines, tools, equipments, jigs and fixtures, manpower in quantity and quality at a time as planned.
3. To see that personnel should follow the orders so that goods with required quality and quantity may be manufactured and delivered at the promised time.

Corrective Action :

1. Keeping flexibility in schedule.
2. Capacity modification.
3. Changing the number of working hours either by employing additional manpower or by doing overtime.
4. By subcontracting the work or buying the components/items.

Need for Corrective Action: (*i*) Arrival of additional emergency work. (*ii*) Delay in receiving raw material, tools. (*iii*) Industrial relation problems.

Procedure of Production Control

Following are the fields where control is required under production control:

(*a*) **Control of activities** — includes release of manufacturing order and dispatching to start plan at assigned time.

(*b*) **Control of material movement** — includes to get receipt of material from market, issue to shops including movement in shops as per plans.

(*c*) **Control of tools availability** — includes to observe availability of tools to the production shop according to plan.

(*d*) **Control of due date** — includes to observe the reason of delay or stoppage on machine loading which interferes completion of the work on due date.

(*e*) **Control of quality produced** — includes to observe at predetermined stages that right type of materials is processed or not.

(*f*) **Control of replacement** — includes to observe the quantity of raw material and work which fails to pass inspection at each stage of production and issue of necessary replacement orders for such material or work.

(*g*) **Control of labour efficiency** — includes a comparison between the time actually taken by workers for completing the job or work with the time allowed as per plan.

(*h*) **Control of progress of order** — includes the observance of the progress of order by ticking (✓) completed work or the production schedule.

Operation Sheet and Instruction Sheet

As already discussed, operation sheet is prepared, for which, the customer's order is minutely analysed. The first step is to convert the customer order, which is ultimate source of information into detailed forms needed for specifying that how and from what will be made. The information needed includes :

1. Engineering description-includes drawing useful for manufacturing shops with specifications and tolerances, chemical formulation and processing requirements etc.
2. Bill of material-includes an accurate and complete statement of the items to be used in manufacturing, where these are available in stores, this is indicated and the component number and reference number is also shown. Where special materials or components are needed, or the items to be purchased are also indicated.
3. List of Operation-this includes the detailed routing of the order for the items to be processed through each processing stage of completion. The specific type of processing equipment or machine needed at each stage is shown with special tools, if required.
4. Reasonable time estimate. The list of operations must also show the estimated time for completion of each specific operation. This estimate must depend upon the standard time, if available, or by analytical method.

The operation routing, time estimates and bill of material are generally be summed up into a simple document called job layout sheet, operation master, or operation sheet.

Responsibility for preparing this operation sheet may be a part of production control department.

In addition to the operation sheets, an instruction sheet is prepared for the use of the foreman and workers. It describes in detail the method to be followed in performing each operation.

Corrective Action

1. Keeping flexibility in schedule
2. Capacity modification
3. Changing.the number of working hours either by employing additional manpower or by doing overtime work.
4. By subcontracting the work or buying the components/items.

Need for Corrective Action

Corrective action need be taken for:

(*i*) Arrival of additional emergency work

(*ii*) Delay in receiving raw materials, tools etc.

(*iii*) Industrial relation problems.

15.12. PROGRESS CONTROL

It is necessary to watch the progress of work, so that corrective action can be taken, when required. The object of progress control is to achieve the standards set for the efficiency or volume of production. Progress control system should be such that information about the progress of work is furnished timely, adequately and correctly.

Steps in Progress Control

1. Setting up a system to watch and record the progress. The system should enable to compare the progress of work with that of prescribed target. The progress can be recorded and compared on Bar Charts, Gantt Charts, Curves, or other mechanical charts.
2. Making a report on work progress. The report should include the duration of time.
3. Transmission of report. The reports are transmitted to the controlling authority, and the authority analysing the report.
4. Interpretation of the information contained in the progress report.
5. Taking corrective action, if required.

Progress Control Charts

After the work has been scheduled, a progress control system is established. For this, following control charts are necessary :

These charts are used whenever there is discrepancy, these indicate the need for investigation and possible correction.

1. **Project Layout Sheet**

   This is prepared in advance and shows relative importance of process to be done one after the other, *i.e.*, the sequence in which the part should be processed. A typical project layout sheet is shown in Fig. 15.4.

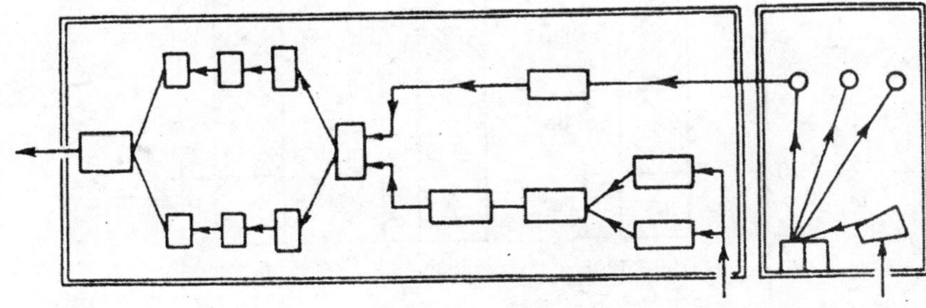

Fig. 15.4. Project layout sheet.

2. **The Load Chart.**

   This shows the work ahead of each machine with respect of time, *i.e.*, in weeks or days. This may be prepared for different departments and also for different machines. This is also known as load chart.

3. **Man-Machine Chart.**

   This chart describes graphically the activity of man and machine he is attending against a time scale. When a shop has a number of operators and machines, studies can be made to find what number of machines each worker can operate or how many workers can work on each machine. During the machining cycle of many semi-automatic machines, the operator has time in which he can run one or more other semi-automatic machines. In this, such charts enable the management to minimise the idle time of the workers and to use the machines to their full capacity.

For example, suppose there are three workers and each worker is doing the same operations on his machine. Suppose the time taken to set up a machine is 0.50 minute and the machining time is 0.75 minute.

Fig. 15.5 (a) shows the case in which one worker operates one machine.

From this Fig., it is very clear that for each operation, the worker is idle for 0.75 minute, when the machine is running. Its alternative can be to put two machines and allow one worker to work on both of them. [Fig. 15.5 (*b*)]

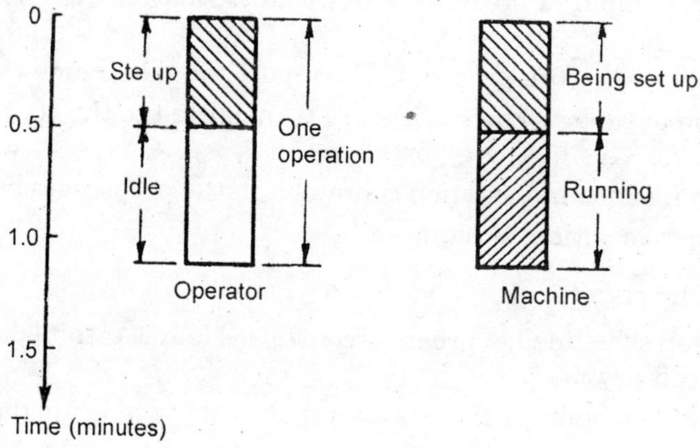

Fig. 15.5. (*a*) Man-machine chart for one operator and one machine.

In this case, the worker still remains idle for 0.25 minute in each operation. In order to minimise this, let us allow one worker to work on three machines. This is shown in Fig. 15.5 (c)

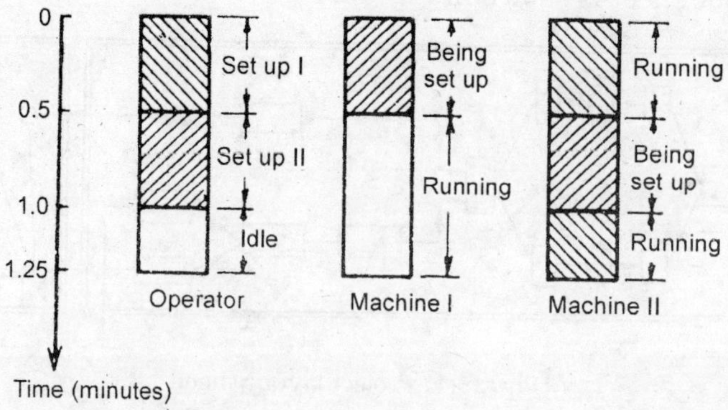

Fig. 15.5. (*b*) Man-machine chart for one worker and two machines.

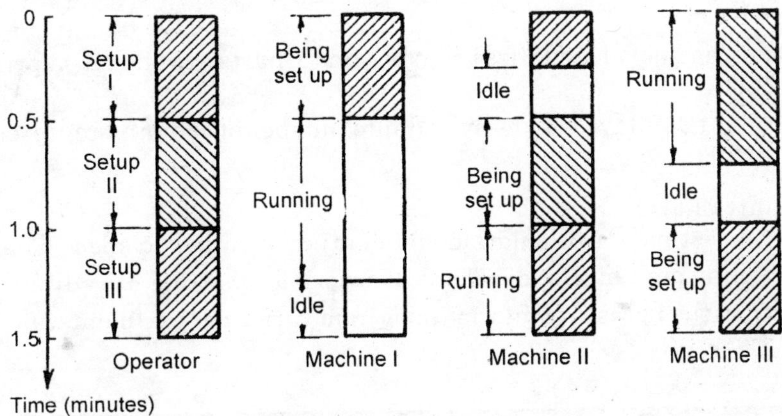

Fig. 15.5. (*c*) Man-machine chart for one worker and three machines.

In this case, the worker would have no idle time, except for necessary personal and fatigue allowances but each machine would be idle for 0.25 minute faster each operation. Now, therefore, the problem is which of the alternatives would be economical. For this purpose, the unit cost of idle time of one worker and the unit cost of idle time of each machine is estimated and then the economical alternative is calculated.

4. **The Progress Card.**

   This card shows the actual processing done on number of parts in respect of time against the scheduled production.

5. **Curve Charts.**

   A graph is plotted between time and quantity produced as shown in Fig. 15.6. showing two lines. The dark line shows scheduled production and the dotted one actual production. This graph indicates whether the scheduled production can be met or not.

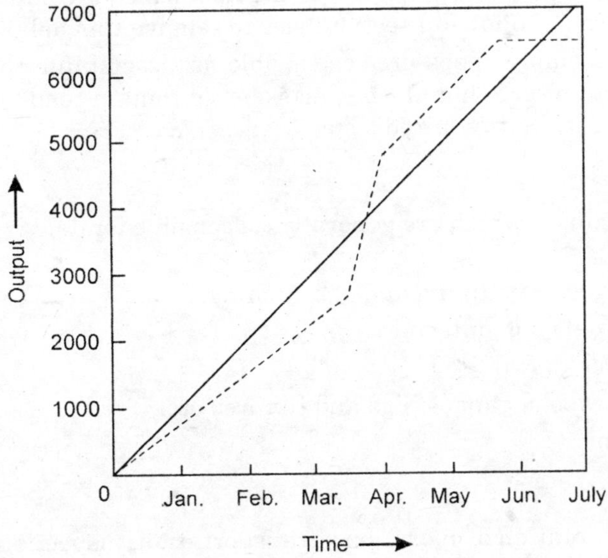

Fig. 15.6. Curve Chart

6. **Gantt Chart.**

   H.L. Gantt had developed these charts. Gant Charts are shown on printed or machine ruled sheets.

   Every column for days is sub-divided into number of columns representing number of hours

Drawbacks of Gantt Charts

1. It takes more time for calculation and plotting of values to keep them upto date.
2. As scheduling man has lot of calculation work for plotting, it is difficult to check.
3. Collection of the necessary informations from various departments may also be a tedious job.

15.13.. FOLLOW-UP (EXPEDITING)

After despatching production orders to various shops, it is necessary to regulate the progress of job through various processes. For this purpose, a follow-up section is formed.

The function of follow-up section is to report daily the progress of work in each shop in a prescribed proforma and to investigate the causes of deviation from the planned performance. This section sees that production is being performed as per schedule and tries to boost it.

Functions.

Follow-up is done for the following purposes :

(*a*) **Material.** Material should reach to shops in required time so that production could be started as per schedule.

(*b*) **Job Progress.** For this follow-up section sees that a particular product is passing through all its operations from raw material to final shape as per schedule.

There are more chances of delay, when one item which is completed in one shop moves to the wrong shop, follow-up section tries to remove this delay.

(*c*) **Assembly.** Assembly shops are responsible for assembling the various components. Follow-up section sees that all the parts should remain ready for assembling purpose in actual quantities at required time.

Causes of Delay

Following are various causes which are generally responsible for delays and should be checked by follow-up section :

(*i*) Errors in routing, scheduling and despatching.

(*ii*) Shortage and delay of material

(*iii*) Equipment breakdown

(*iv*) Lack of proper tools, gauges, jigs and fixtures etc.

(*v*) More rejections.

Flow Process Chart.

This is a graphic representation of operations, transportation, inspection, delays and shortages occurring during production. This also gives the information regarding distance moved and time required for different items such as transportation, delays and inspection etc. Flow processes chart for a gear box casting is drawn below :

Name of the part: Gear Box Casting
Drawing No....
Date of Delivery

Job No ....
Part No ....

Symbol	Description		Time in Minutes			
				Transportation	Delay	Inspection
⊙ → □ D Δ						
⊙ → □ D Δ	Pig Iron Coal and Coke	5 m	—	—	—	—
⊙ → □ D Δ	Charge melted	—	4	—	—	—
⊙ → □ D Δ	Awaited melting	—	—	—	4	—
⊙ → □ D Δ	Molten Metal to Moulding	6 m	—	3	—	—
⊙ → □ D Δ	Pouring	—	2	—	—	—
⊙ → □ D Δ	Cooling	—	—	—	10	—
⊙ → □ D Δ	Transportation Fitling shop	10m	—	5	—	—
⊙ → □ D Δ	Fitling	—	6	—	—	—
⊙ → □ D Δ	Inspection	—	—	—	—	2
⊙ → □ D Δ	Transportation to casting store	10 m	—	5	—	—
⊙ → □ D Δ	Storing	—	—	—	—	—

⊙ = Operation, → = Transportation, □ = Inspection
D = Delay and Δ = Stores.

Flow Process Chart

Reporting

Reporting is a part of management information system, and reports are helpful for the management to take necessary decisions. Reports may be written or verbal. Written reports are treated as formal and authentic. The reports should be clear, concise and well presented. Report should serve following main functions:

(*i*) To help the writer to assess his work.
(*ii*) To convey correct information to others
(*iii*) To provide a record for future reference.

Principles of Reporting

Following are the main principles which determine the effective reporting:

(*i*) Cost of producing the information should be less as compared to the cost of not producing the information.
(*ii*) The information should contribute to decision-making.
(*iii*) Information should be able to provide meaningful conclusion.
(*iv*) Information should be accurate only upto desired degree, as higher degree of accuracy, where not required, may result in avoidable expenditure.

(*v*) Information should be furnished at desired frequency. As too frequent information may result in extra expenditure, while infrequent information may lead to delay in decision and delayed decision may result in avoidable expenditure.

(*vi*) Speed of the information is determined by the importance of decisions and their effect due to delay.

15.14. INSPECTION

Inspection is carried out for confirming that quality is of predetermined standard. During inspection defective parts are rejected so that only products of good quality should reach to the customers. To reduce rejections, inspection is done to various stages starting from raw material to final shape.

To produce products of good quality, tools and machines are also inspected. This topic has already been dealt with in detail in the chapter on 'Inspection and Quality Control'. Readers are advised to go through this chapter.

QUESTIONS

1. Describe the objectives and functions of production planning.
2. What is the main difference between planning and follow-up ?
3. Write and explain principle of production.
4. Why operation and instruction sheets are prepared ?
5. The shorter the time-cycle for production, the smaller is the need for working capital, comment.
6. Write short notes on :
   (*a*) Progress Control. (*b*) Process Planning.
7. What are the informations required by Production Control department.
8. What do you understand by the procedure of production control?
9. What is routing? Explain?
10. Why work sheets are prepared? Give an example.
11. What do you understand by
    (*a*) Product sequencing,
    (*b*) Sequence analysis,
    (*c*) Minimum processing time?
12. Describe clearly the function of routing, scheduling and dispatching?
13. Describe, what is the utility of Gantt chart as a tool of production? Prepare a Gantt chart showing picture of future operation.
14. Describe the progress of an operation with the help of a chart.
15. Describe briefly various charts and diagrams commonly used by production planning of medium size concern.
16. Describe briefly, how you will prepare the master schedule.
17. Show how Gantt chart is used for planning a project.
18. (*a*) What is meant by updating and scheduling of resources ? Explain
    (*b*) Show how a Gantt chart can be used in machine scheduling problem?

19. What is scheduling? Describe various uses of scheduling.
20. What are the objects (aims) of scheduling?
21. Explain how routing, scheduling, despatching and follow-up activities of production control department help in achieving efficient production.
22. Define despatching and follow-up. Explain how they help in controlling production.
23. Write some important functions of a good despatching section. How is this function effectively executed in practice?
24. What is Control Board? Explain.
25. Explain the functions of 'despatching'.
26. 'Reporting is a part of management information system', explain in detail.

16 Market Research and Sales Forecasting

16.1. MARKET RESEARCH (ANALYSIS)

Market research is the analysis of a project to be started, expanded or modified. Broadly speaking market research is the commercial research for the suitability of a business and is a continuous process, *i.e.*, research is always kept continued for the stability of the business. Market research is very essential in mass scale production because volume of production depends upon the continuity of demand. If demand reduces suddenly, production comes to a standstill, which may produce great losses to manufacturer.

Market research includes forecasting, intelligence and statistics. It is an important factor for the sale of products, failure to do this accurately may lead to the production of more goods than the market can absorb. This may mean financial losses to the firm. It may also lead to under production, the results of which are equally unpleasant.

Market research may be defined as a way of finding out facts which must be known before a market policy is to be determined. Before starting a business, planning department makes different investigations affecting the business to maintain good working conditions, better quality and handsome profits. Many new products and firms fail because they start business on a "Guess-estimate" of the goods market but that is never reached. Therefore, investment of small amount of time on careful market analysis is comparatively better instead of bigger loss at a later stage.

Objects of Market Research

The market analysis is a scientific method of determining what to produce, who the purchasers are, where these are located, how much to manufacture, how to sell and when to sell in order to maximise the service rendered, and the profits earned. This is a dynamic world in which the profit opportunities are constantly altering and efficient market research can only enable a manufacturer to earn maximum while giving the customer maximum satisfaction.

Continued success in a business depends on its maintaining a continuous flow of new product ideas. The owner should select only profitable products and leave unprofitable ones. These ideas mainly originate in the sales or research organisations.

Mainly the object of market research is to inform the management as to what the future holds for its products and proposed products.

The market research data can be collected from the internal records of the business, reports obtained by outside sales staff, published sources, investigators in the, field, financial and trade journals and reports of trade associations.

The analysis of the product is made to find out:

(*i*) Sale volume.
(*ii*) Amount of profit and its duration.
(*iii*) Amount of capital needed.
(*iv*) Cost of necessary advertising.
(*v*) Production cost.
(*vi*) Stability of raw materials supply.
(*vii*) Business conditions and trends.
(*viii*) Handling and transportation charges.
(*ix*) Seasonal market characteristics.
(*x*) Any other factors which may be considered relevant to the success of the business.

Necessity of Market Research

The necessity of market research as a technique was felt in the 20th century due to the industrialisation of western society in the 19th century. This necessity improved greatly due to introduction of large scale production and large increase in population.

In the earliest days, there was less gap between the initial manufacturer and the ultimate consumer. Fig. 16.1 shows this relation. The manufacturer knew his customer's demands, desires and habits. They were very close to each other because of few in number. Now modern industry separated customers by complicated organisations, and engaged in mass production for cheap and large scale demands. Therefore, the demands of the customers must be explored, developed and evaluated. The relationship of manufacturer and customer contact is similar to a broken circular chain as shown in Fig. 16.2.

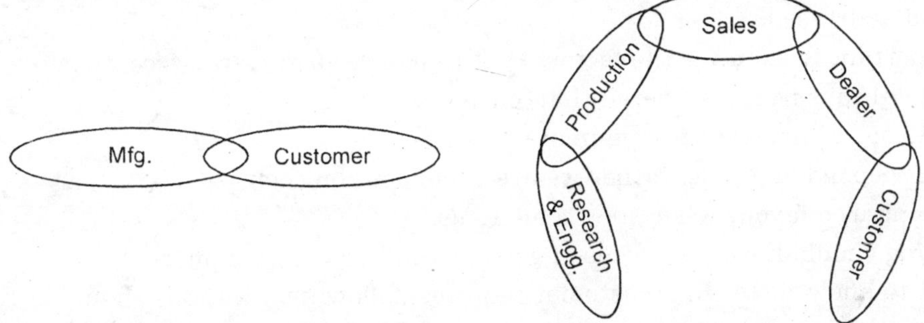

Fig. 16.1. Relation between manufacturer and customer in earlier days.

Fig 16.2. Relation separated between manufacturer and customer in modern industry.

Fig 16.3. shows as to how market research brings manufacturer and customer closer.

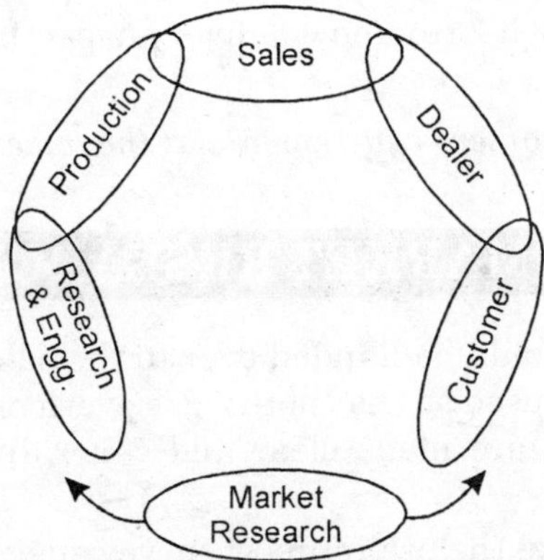

Fig. 16.3. Market research rejoins the broken chain link of manufacturer and customer.

Advantages of Marketing Research

1. Production according to consumer's demand.
2. Acceleration in sales.
3. Reduction in market Expenses.
4. Review of objectives and policies.
5. To know opportunities/new opportunities.

16.2. FOCUS ON CUSTOMERS

Customer is anyone who is impacted by the product or process. The customers can be classified into following three categories :

1. *External Customers.* These may be both current and potential. These are the people outside who are the end users of a firm's products and services.
2. *Internal Customers.* These include all functions impacted by the product at both the managerial and workforce levels. These are the persons within the company who receive the work of another and then add their contribution to the product or service before passing it on to someone else.
3. *Suppliers as Customers.* Suppliers should be considered as extensions of internal customer departments such as manufacturing. Their needs must also be understood and addressed.

It is important to examine the factors that influence customers perception.

It should always be remembered that, customers are :

(*i*) The most important people in any business.
(*ii*) Not dependent on us, rather we are dependent on them.
(*iii*) Doing us a favour when they come to us.

Marketing should have dual focus of getting and keeping customers.

In order to know, as to what customer requires, following questions should be asked :

(*i*) What he expects when he buys your product (to know the *specifications* of the product)
(*ii*) Whether he gets what he expected ? (to know the *conformance* to the specification).
(*iii*) Does it continue to do what he expected ? (to know the *reliability* or conformance through time).
(*iv*) How much he expected to pay ? - (to know the *value* for money aspect).
(*v*) When he wants to have it ? (to know delivery aspect).

The main aim is towards :

"*Fully satisfying agreed customer requirements at the lowest internal cost*".

16.3 UNDERTAKING MARKET RESEARCH

The work of market research should be handed over to the sales department. Throughout the research, scientific methods are used so that nothing is overlooked. The reasons for the various features of the market demand are made clear and generally the maximum information is obtained.

The analyst should first make the preliminary survey suggested by the directors. Since the preliminary survey is the foundation around which a later and more extensive study may be practised, it should be conducted only by an alert and experienced analyst who can make out plans for future operations efficiently. Sometimes a preliminary survey supplies sufficient information that there is no profitable market for the products and hence further analysis is not required.

The collection of several data in survey is generally the most exhausting and frustrating part. The various mediums used can be questionnaire, telephone, personal contacts and interviews. The personal contacts and interviews are the best media as they give compara-tively true and correct information though costly and take more time.

Classification

Market research is sub-divided into four general classifications as described below:

(*a*) Product Analysis.

(*b*) Market Analysis.

(*c*) Distribution Analysis.

(*d*) Competition Analysis.

1. **Product Analysis**

Product analysis is required to find out customer's preferences for the product. This will enable management to make improvements that will meet the requirements of the customers, fulfil the present requirements of the market and will be more acceptable than those of competitor's products.

Product analysis is also carried out to simplify product lines by eliminating those which have a limited demand, or are unprofitable, to determine the method of packing that will bring best sales and to find the suitable prices which may be accepted by the customers and results in handsome profits. It is important to find what characteristics your products have and which other competitor's products have not, in order to know their relative advantages so that customers canbe persuaded to purchase your products only.

A check list of questions to be answered by a product analysis is given below :

1. Whether the product fulfils market requirements.
2. Whether the product is competitive in character, performance and price.
3. Whether the product permits efficient distribution.
4. Whether the product can be sold at handsome profits.
5. Whether the line completes the required sizes.
6. Whether some design improvements are required to fulfil customer's needs and to improve performance.
7. How product can be redesigned to reduce cost of production,packing distribution, transportation and maintenance without affecting quality?
8. Whether reduction of selling price has effects on demand.
9. Whether finished stock can be reduced to minimise investment, warehouse costs and obsolescence.
10. How repairs and replacement methods can be improved ?
11. What is the future trend of change as determined by customer'schanging habits?
12. What new changes and inventions are likely to occur ?
13. What is competition offering ? Whether some better design ideas can be taken from competitor's products.

2. **Market Analysis**

The object of market analysis is to find the location of markets, scope of sales and buying habits of customers that make up the potential market for a product. As the size of industry increases with the consumption of products, therefore, this fact is required for deciding about the capacity of plant and machinery.

A check list of questions to be answered by a market analysis is given below :

1. Who purchases the products?
2. Where are the markets?
3. How many other competitors influence the purchase?
4. What is the volume of sale during a particular time?
5. On what factors buyers pay stress, *e.g.* , quality, price, delivery, safety or service etc.?
6. When customers are mostly in the habit of buying?
7. How often they used to purchase?
8. Do they buy in advance of needs?
9. Whether demand is reasonable?
10. What discount and credit terms are prevailing ?

3. **Distribution Analysis.**

This consists of the study of channels of distribution, methods of pricing, retail price maintenance, selling methods, sales promotion, sales training, ware-housing, distribution cost analysis and other policies and practices required for the product distribution. The economic selection of the best channels of distribution for a product is essential to success in market analysis.

4. **Competition Analysis.**

Competition studies are generally included as a part of marketing analysis. This makes necessary to study the recent or proposed production, sales and pricing policies of the competitors. Most important of these is the analysis of the quality of competitor's products to ascertain how potential customer would compare with one's products.

The sales department should ask its salesmen to report the comment of potential customers about the firm's product or the products of its competitors. It should also study the research and product development work that the competition may be carrying on in order to estimate how these will affect its further sales.

From these studies, plans and policies may be made to guide future activities of concern in order to improve its competitive position.

16.4. MARKET RESEARCH TECHNIQUES

To carry out various analysis as explained above, following techniques are adopted:

1. **Collection of Data.** Since these data are on the table of the organisations, this technique is also known as desk research. In this method, the data are collected from published material (either the company itself or by other agencies, *e.g.*, Journals of the trade, published survey reports, Government publications, international publications, etc.).

   This type of research is carried out for knowing past sales, various factors on sales in the past, fluctuation in the sale.

2. **Interview.** To know the views of salesmen, dealers and consumers interviews are

conducted with a selected sample of people. These interviews can be conducted on telephone, by post or in person depending upon the nature of questions.

3. **Market Survey.** In order to collect specific data or views, a carefully prepared questionnaire is posted to the selected sample of people.
4. **Statistical Methods.** Statistical methods lika Bar chart, frequency polygon, frequency distribution curves and consept of standard deviation are used to serve the purpose.

16.5. FUNCTIONS OF MARKET RESEARCH

Market research (Market analysis) is done to carry out following main functions:

1. To know that who and where the customer is and what he wants.
2. To know the sales trend, marketing potential and its share in the market, which is essential for production planning.
3. To know the defects in the products and reasons of resistance by consumers and then to rectify them in future production.
4. To study the distribution channel and its effectiveness,
5. To exploit new markets and help developing new products.
6. To safeguard the interest of the company against changes in the market in future.
7. To remain in touch with market and help the sales promotion efforts.

16.6. FORECASTING

Forecasting is the estimation of type, quantity and quality of future work, *e.g.*, sale, demand etc. Through forecast of demand, we evaluate the factors in the environment which influence the operation of the firm and formulate annual plans. Based on forecast, we plan for production, material procurement, cash flows, inventory level, manpower, plant capacity etc. Forecasting, therefore, plays a crucial role in the development of plans for the future.

Forecasting is an essential activity to be carried out prior to planning, with the aim to estimate the future work, may it be regarding sales or production or any other aspect of business activity. It starts with the sales forecast and is followed by production forecast and forecasts for costs, purchase, finance, profit or loss etc.

Forecasting is a prediction for future, which by its nature is unknown. The aim of a good forecast is to minimise the uncertainties of the unknown future. Since a more realistic forecast helps in taking more effective decisions. Thus forecast can be defined as, 'a prediction or estimation of a future situation under given conditions'. Forecasts can be both physical as well as financial in nature and are used mainly for planning purposes. Forecasting is the process of using past events to make systematic predictions about future outcomes or trends.

Future predictions are made under two circumstances (*i*) when the firm does not change the course of its action, and (*ii*) when the firm is undergoing some changes. Variable factors like, prices of substitutes and competitors, design, quality etc. are taken into account while forecasting sales.

Steps in Forecasting

For efficient forecasting following steps are necessary:

Step I. Identification of Objective. Purpose of forecasting must be clear, *e.g.*, quantity and composition of demand, inventory control, pricing etc. . .

Step II. Categories of Product. Determine the category of product in which it falls, *e.g.*, capital goods, consumer durables (like T.V., refrigerator, watch, clothes etc.), non-durable consumer goods (like food, beverages etc.).

Step III. Selecting a Proper Method. Method is selected considering the objective of forecasting, type of data available, period for which forecast is to be made (*e.g.*, long term, short term or medium term forecasts).

Step IV. Interpretation of Results. Efficiency of a forecast largely depends upon the interpretation of the results. Whenever there is any change in the assumption, forecast may be revised. Similarly on change of government policy, general business environment, economical and political environment changes, the forecasts must be reviewed.

Purposes of Forecasting for Consumer Goods

- Changes in size and characteristics of population.
- Saturation limit of the market.
- Tastes and preferences of consumers.
- Buying power of the consumers.
- Income level of consumers.
- Replacement/new demand.

16.6.1. Types of Forecasting

There are two types of forecasting :

- Short term forecasting.
- Long term forecasting.

1. **Short Term Forecasting.** This type of forecasting, sometimes also known as near future sales forecasting, covers a period generally from 3 months to one year, depending upon the nature of product. If the demand fluctuates from one month to another, forecasting must be for a very short period.

   Generally this type of forecasting is helpful for short term production planning and for financial planning, inventory control, pricing, setting sales targets etc.

2. **Long Term Forecasting.** This type of forecasting covers for a period of more than one year, generally 5 to 10 years. This type of forecasting is necessary for capital intensive industries like ship building, petroleum refinery, steel plants, power generation etc.

   This type of forecast, supply the framework for corporate investment planning and sourcing of capital. This is also helpful for taking decisions on investment proposals such as modernisation and expansion in the capacity, new unit planning etc.

16.7. SALES FORECASTING

A sales forecast is an estimate of the amount of sales for a specified future period under a proposed marketing plan or programme. Sales forecast has also been defined as, an estimate of sales in terms of money or physical units for a specified future period under a proposed marketing plan or programme and under an assumed set of economic and other forces outside the unit for which the forecast is made.

The management of a firm is required to prepare its forecast of share of the market that it can hope to capture over the period of forecasting. In other words, sales forecast is an estimate of the sales potential of the firm in future. All plants are based on the sales forecasts. This forecast helps the management in determining as to how much revenue can be expected to be realised, how much to manufacture, and what shall be the requirement of men, machine and money.

Thus we can define sales forecasting as, estimation of type, quantity and quality of future sales. Goal for the sales department is decided on the basis of this forecast and these forecasts also help in planning future development of the concern. The sales forecast forms a basis for production targets.

From above, looking to its importance, it is essential that sales forecast must be accurate, simple, easy to understand and economical.

Importance of Sales Forecasting

Sales forecasting is a very important function for a manufacturing concern, since it is useful in following ways:

(*i*) It helps to determine production volumes considering availability of facilities, like equipment, capital, manpower, space etc.

(*ii*) It forms a basis of sales budget, production budget, natural budget etc.

(*iii*) It helps in taking decision about the plant expansion and changes in production mix or should it divert its resource for manufacturing other products.

(*iv*) It helps in deciding policies.

(*v*) It facilitates in deciding the extent of advertising etc.

(*vi*) The sales forecast is a commitment on the part of the sales department and it must be achieved during the given period.

(*vii*) Sales forecast helps in preparing production and purchasing schedules.

(*viii*) Accurate sales forecasting is a very good aid for the purpose of decision making.

(*ix*) It helps in guiding marketing, production and other business activities for achieving these targets.

16.8. APPLICATIONS OF SALES FORECASTS

Sales forecasts can be used for following purposes :

1. It helps the management to decide marketing strategies.
2. It helps in preparing the budget and for setting financial policies.
3. It helps to determine limiting conditions for various departments while taking management decisions.
4. With accurate forecasting, seasonal variations in demand can be stabilized and regulated so as to cut production costs. As with reliable sales forecasts it is possible to produce at an average rate so that plant capacity and manpower is fully utilised during the entire period. Thus forecasting enables to overcome seasonal variations.
5. It helps in material planning and avoids the evils of both the over-stocking and under-stocking. This will also enable to take advantage of favourable prices of raw material during the season.

6. *Product Planning.* From forecasts we find out which product is more profitable and which should be manufactured and which should be dropped.
7. *Planning Expansions.* Long range forecasts can predict future demand trends, which will enable the planning for expansion of the concern.
8. *Financial Planning.* Sales forecast permits an evaluation of expenses and income etc.
9. *Inventory Control.* It facilitates better planning and control over the inventories.
10. *Production Control.* It will help in better production control, *i.e.,* better use of equipments, controls over-time of labour, better deliveries, better control over work-in-progress inventories.
11. *Sales Planning.* It helps in finding out which territory needs more attention. Various sales programmes can be reassessed looking to their achievements.

List of Statistical Data Helpful in Sales Forecasting

(A) **For assessing general economic conditions of the country**

1. *Industrial production index.* This index is based on the physical output of the factories and mines.
2. *Bank debits.* This will give overall financial condition of the business.
3. *Employment.* Increased employment anticipates growth in demand, while decline in employment anticipates decline in production.

(B) **For assessing future price trends**

1. *Money in circulation.* Increase of money in circulation without corresponding increase in goods supply indicates prices will rise.
2. *Crop production.* It indicates the trend of prices for agricultural product.
3. *Price Index.* It is a reliable indicator prepared by the Government.

(C) **For assessing purchasing power of the consumer**

1. *Rate of wages.* Wage rates, bonus etc., indicates workers' purchasing power.
2. *Disposal income.* This shows the actual amount of money the consumer is left to spend.

16.9. FACTORS CONSIDERED FOR SALES FORECASTING

Following factors should be considered while making the sales forecast:

1. **Competition.** To assess demand, it is the main factor to know about the existing and new competitors and their future programme, quality of their product, sales of their product. Opinion of the customers about the products of other competitors with reference to the product manufactured by the firm must also be considered.
2. **Changes in Technology.** With the advancement of technology, new products are coming in the market and the taste and the likings of the consumers changes with the advancement and change of technology.
3. **Government Action.** When the government produces or purchases then depending upon the government policy and rules, the sales of the products are also affected.
4. **Factors Related to the Concern Itself.** These factors are related to the change in the capacity of the plant, change in price due to the change in expenditure, change in product mix etc.

Accurate sales forecasting is essential for a business house to enable it to produce the required quantity at the right time. Further, it makes the arrangement in advance for raw materials, equipments, labour etc. Many firms manufacture on the order basis, but in general, every firm produces the material in advance to meet the future demand.

16.10. TYPES OF FORECASTING

There are two types of forecasting:

1. Short-term forecasting.
2. Long-term forecasting.

1. **Short-term forecasting.** This type of forecasting can be defined when it covers a period of three months, six months or one year. Generally, the last one is most preferred. The period is dependent upon the nature of business, if the demand fluctuates from one month to another, forecasting may be done only for a short period.
2. **Long-term forecasting.** The forecasting that covers a period of 5, 10 and even 20 years. The period here also depends upon the nature of business, but beyond 12 years, the future is assumed as uncertain. But in many industries like ship building, petroleum refinery, paper making industries, a long term forecasting is needed as the total investment cost of equipment is quite high.

Purposes of Short-Term Forecasting

1. To adopt suitable production policy, so that the problem of overproduction and short supply of raw materials, machines etc. can be avoided.
2. To reduce the cost of raw materials, machinery etc.
3. To have proper control of inventory.
4. To set the sales targets.
5. To have proper controls.
6. To arrange the financial requirements in advance to meet the demand.

Purposes of Long-Term Forecasting

1. To plan for the new unit of production or expansion of existing unit to meet the demand.
2. To plan for long-term financial requirements.
3. To train the personnel so that man power requirement can be met in future.

16.11. ELEMENTS OF A GOOD FORECASTING

Following four elements are suggested for adopting a forecasting method:

1. **Accuracy.** The previous method must be checked for accuracy by observing that the predictions made in past are accurate or not.
2. **Simplicity.** The method must be simple and easily understandable, further can satisfy the management.
3. **Economy.** As for an undertaking, cost is a main factor so the method of such type should be adopted which is economical.
4. **Availability.** The technique must be able to produce meaningful results quickly. The technique which takes much time to produce useful information, is of no use. Therefore, the results should be timely available.

Following points must be made clear before making a forecast:

1. Forecast must be made in terms of rupees or sale volume or in units.
2. Forecast must be made on annual basis and then further divided as per requirement, *i.e.*, monthwise, weekwise or so, on the basis of previous years records.
3. Forecast for new product may be done by monthwise, either using other manufacturing concern's data or by survey.
4. Forecast must be made in terms of product groups and broken for individual products, the division may be according to the sizes, brands, cables, colours etc. A typical example shows how the product group is divided.

16.12. METHODS OF FORECASTING

Following are the methods generally employed for forecasting:

1. **Survey of Buyer's Views.**

   This is the most direct method for making forecasting for short-term, in which the customers are asked what they are thinking to buy in near future say, in the coming years. In this method, all the burden is with consumers, which may misjudge or mislead or may be uncertain about the quantity to be purchased by them in near future. The disadvantages of this method are as follows:

   (*i*) Consumer's buying inventions are irregular.

   (*ii*) When consumers have to select between different alternatives, they are unable to foresee their choices.

   (*iii*) Buyers may be anxious for purchasing products but due to certain limitations they may be unable to purchase them.

2. **Collective Opinion or Sales Force Polling.**

   In this method, forecasting depends upon the salesmen's estimation for their respective areas, because the salesmen are closest to the customers, they can estimate more properly about the customer's reaction, about the product and their future requirements. All the estimates of salesmen are consolidated to know the total estimate of the sales. The final estimate then goes through severe checking to avoid undue imagination which is done many times by the salesman.

   The revised estimates are then again examined in the light of factors like expected change in design, change in prices, advertisements, competition, further changes like, purchasing power of local people, employment, population etc.

   The method of collective opinion takes advantages of collective wisdom of salesmen, senior executives like production manager, sales manager, marketing officials and managers.

   Advantages

   1. This method is simple, and requires no statistical technique.
   2. The forecasts are based on the knowledge of salesmen, who are directly responsible for the sales.
   3. In practice, this method is very much useful in the case of new products.

   Disadvantages

   1. This method is useful only for short-term forecasting, *i.e.*, maximum for one year.

2. As the forecasting is dependent upon salesmen estimation and if sales quotas are fixed then they, in general, underestimate the forecast.
3. As salesmen have no knowledge about the economic changes, their estimates are not so correct many times.
4. As the estimation is full time job, the quality to look into the future must be with the salesmen.

3. **Trends Projections**

A well established firm has considerable datas on sales. These datas are arranged in a chronological order, which is known as 'time series'. Thus time series are analysed before making the forecasts. There is a common method which is generally employed and is known as "project the trend". In this method, the trend line is projected by some statistical method generally, by least square method. The method is well-understood by the example given below.

A real challenge for the forecaster comes when there is turning point, *i.e.*, when management will change or revise its sales and production all together. Many analysts have thus, given much thought before making forecasting to these turning points. There are four factors generally responsible for turning points, *viz.*,

1. Trend
2. Seasonal variations
3. Cyclical fluctuations
4. Irregular or random forces.

4. **Economic Indicators**

In this method, the forecasting is dependent upon certain economic indicators, which are generally published by Central Statistical Organization under the national income estimates. Some of these indicators are:

1. Personal income for the demand of consumer goods.
2. Agricultural income for the demand of agricultural inputs, implements etc.
3. Construction contracts sanctioned for demand of building materials.
4. Registration of automobiles for the demand of accessories, petrols etc.

The forecasting is done with the help of least square equations. The example illustrated below will give an idea, as to how the forecasting is done.

This method has some limitations, likewise.

(*i*) Appropriate economic indicators is defective to find out.

(*ii*) For newer products no past data are available.

16.13. FORECASTING FOR NEW PRODUCTS

This is comparatively a difficult task, as there is no past data, trend or past information available on which future can be predicted. However, following methods are used for forecasting for new products:

1. *Direct Survey Method.* A survey by sampling technique from prospective customers is conducted to know as to how the consumers will respond to this product. After survey other aspects, like economical changes, fashion changes, social requirements, political changes, habits of people etc., are incorporated.

2. *Collection Opinion or Indirect Survey Methods.* In this method, the response of consumers will be predicted through the opinion of distributors, salesmen, selling agents, shop-keepers *(i.e.* retailers) etc.
3. *Comparison with Established Product.* Sales figures can be compared, if the product under consideration is comparable to an existing product. In case the new product is a substitute for a competitor's product, its acceptance by public will largely depend upon the customers' liking to the present product and on advertising programme.
4. *Limited market trial.* In this method, opinion of potential customers is collected to predict the forecasts.

16.14. FORECASTING FOR ESTABLISHED PRODUCTS

1. *Following a past trend.* In this method, a graph of past trends is plotted and is extended by free hand to predict future.
2. *Moving average method.* A moving average forecast is obtained by taking average of datas of desired number of past periods. For example forecasts of year 1993 will be the average sales of 1990, 1991 and 1992 ; whereas for 1994 it will be the average of 1991, 1992 and 1993. For short term forecasts, the period for past data will bc months in place of years.
3. *Least square method.* This is mathematical device which places a line through a series of plotted points in such a way that the sum of the squares of deviations of the actual points above and below the trend line is at the minimum. This gives a line which is most fit.
4. *Economic Indicators.* In this method, the forecasting is dependent upon certain economic indicators, which are generally published by Central Statistical Organization as national income estimates. Some of these indicators are :
   - Personal income for the demand of consumers' goods.
   - Agricultural income for the demand of agricultural inputs, implements etc.
   - Construction contracts sanctioned for demand of building materials.
   - Registration of automobiles for the demand of accessories, petrols etc.

   This method has some limitations, likewise :

   (i) Appropriate economic indicator is difficult to find out.

   (ii) For newer products, no past data are available.
5. *Correlation analysis of sales forecasting.* This is a statistical method used for expressing the relationships between two or more variables.
6. *Market research.* In this method of forecasting, future demands of the product can be predicted through critical analysis of the marketing forces, changing pattern of socio-economic pressures, political changes etc.
7. *Sales force opinion.* Views of salesmen, distributors, selling agents, traders, etc., are grouped to forecast sales.

16.15 TIME SERIES FORECASTING

These are the demand characteristics over time. In this, time series analysis is done by an analyst who plots demand data on a time scale, studies the plots, and looks for consistent shapes or patterns. These time series data are analysed for forecasting future activity levels Time series data refer to a set of values of some variables measured at the equally spaced time intervals such as monthly inventory levels, quarterly sales or monthly production levels etc. The demand have following patterns:

1. **Constant Pattern.** Refer Fig. 16.4. In this pattern demand remains constant throughout the period.

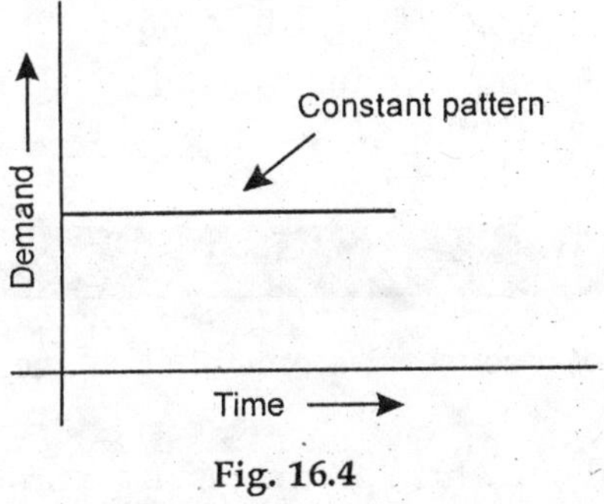

Fig. 16.4

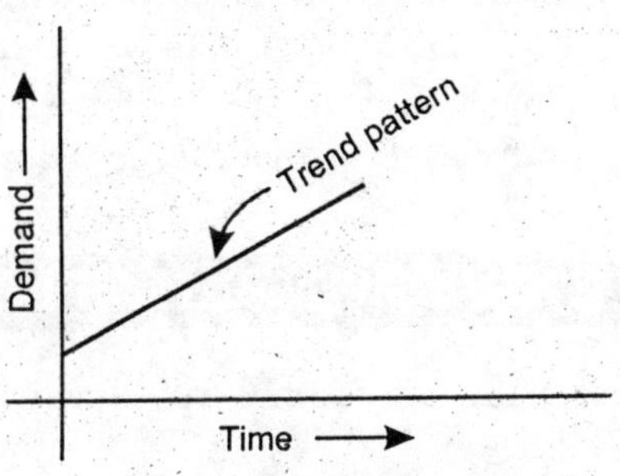

Fig. 16.5

2. **Trend Pattern.** It refers to the long-term growth or decline in the average level of demand, as shown in the Fig. 16.5.
3. **Seasonal Pattern.** It refers to the annually repetitive demand fluctuation that may be caused by weather, tradition or other factors.

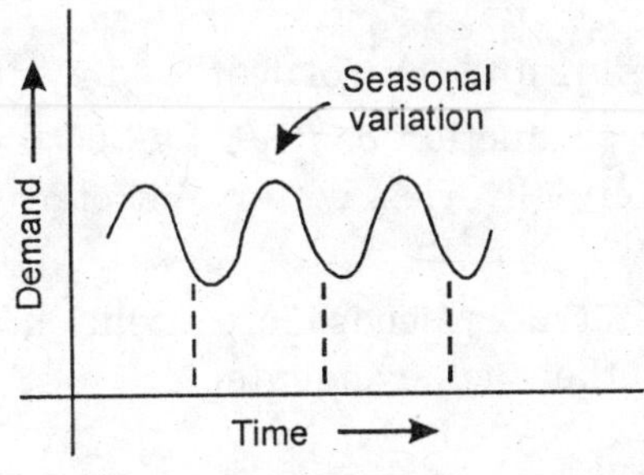

Fig. 16.6.

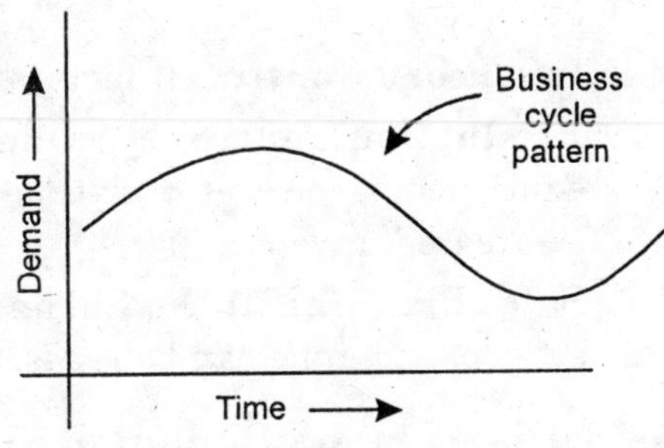

Fig. 16.7

4. **Cycle Pattern.** Business cycle refers to the large deviation to actual demand values due to complex environmental influences. Refer Fig. 16.7. These are similar to the seasonable components except that seasonality occurs at regular intervals and is of constant durations whereas it varies in both time and duration of occurance.

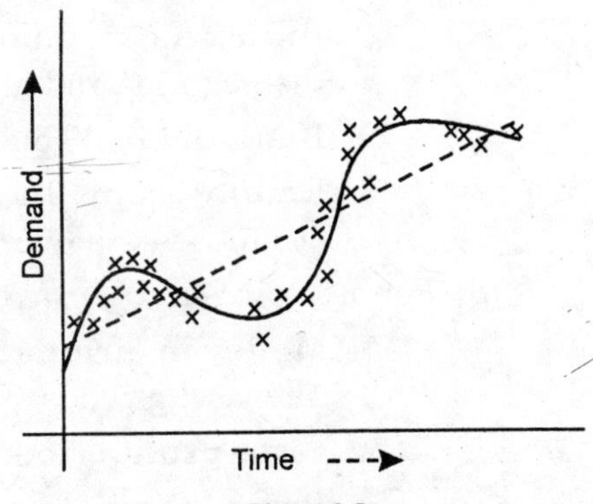

Fig. 16.8

16.16. SELECTION OF FORECAST

There are several guide lines for selecting a forecast from available forecasts, one of them is as follows:

1. Prefer those forecasts which have reasonings underlying the forecasts.
2. Prefer only those forecasts which are prepared by qualified personnels, as the future is uncertain, qualified forecaster must tell his assumptions on which forecast is based.
3. Look into the previous years' forecasts, surveys should be examined as to whether the forecasts were right or wrong.
4. Use only those forecasts which are reliable for records. Keep in mind to prefer only those of the forecasts which are prepared by using different techniques.
5. Reject that particular forecast in which forecaster injected himself too strongly as an individual into his forecast, as it will be a biased one.

16.17. USES OF SALES FORECASTS

The sales forecasts are helpful for various divisions of a concern. Some of such uses are given hereunder:

1. **Product Planning.** From forecasts we find out which product is more profitable and which should be manufactured and which should be dropped.
2. **Planning Expansions.** Long range forecasts can predict future demand trends, which will enable the planning before expansion of the concern.
3. **Financial Planning.** Sales forecast permits an evaluation of expenses and income etc.
4. **Inventory Control.** It facilitates better planning and control over the inventories.
5. **Production control.** It will help in better production control, *i.e.,* better use of equipments, controls over-time of labour, better deliveries, better control over work-in-progress inventories.
6. **Sales Planning.** It helps in finding out which territory needs more attention. Various sales programme can be reassessed looking to their achievements.

List of Statistical Data Helpful in Sales Forecasting

(A) For *assessing general economic conditions* of the country

1. **Industrial production Index.** This index is based on the physical output of the factories and mines.
2. **Bank debits.** This will give overall financial condition of the business.
3. **Employment.** Increased employment anticipates growth in demand, while decline in employment anticipates decline in production.

(B) For *assessing future price trends*

1. **Money in circulation:** Increase of money in circulation without corresponding increase in goods supply indicates prices will rise.
2. **Crop production:** It indicates the trend of prices for agricultural products.
3. **Price Index:** It is reliable Indicator prepared by the government.

(C) For *assessing purchasing power of the consumer*

1. **Rate of wages:** Wage rates, bonus etc., indicates worker's purchasing power.
2. **Disposal Income:** This shows the actual amount of money the consumer is left with to spend.

Solved Examples

Example 16.1. *The actual sales of a company are as follows:*

Year	1968	1969	1970	1971	1972
Sales in Rupees	45,000	56,000	78,000	46,000	75,000

By the method of least squares, find the trend values for each of the five years. Also estimate the annual sales for ***1973****.*

Solution.

Year	*Sales ('000 Rs.)*			
	Y	*X*	X^2	*XY*
1968	45	1	1	45
1969	56	2	4	112
1970	78	3	9	234
1971	46	4	16	184
1972	75	5	25	375
$n = 5$	$\Sigma Y = 300$	$\Sigma X = 15$	$\Sigma X^2 = 55$	$\Sigma XY = 950$

Substituting the values in the least square equation.

$$\Sigma Y = n.a + b\Sigma X \quad \text{... } (i)$$

$$\Sigma XY = a\Sigma X + b\Sigma X^2 \quad \text{... } (ii)$$

Putting values from above table in equations (*i*) and (*ii*)

$$300 = 5a + 15b \quad \text{... } (iii)$$

$$950 = 15a + 55b \quad \text{... } (iv)$$

Solving equations (*iii*) and (*iv*), we get

$$a = 45, b = 5$$

This is trend equation

$$Y = 45 + 5x$$

Now trend values are

$$Y\ 1968 = 45 + 5\ (1) = \text{Rs. } 50{,}000$$

$$Y\ 1969 = 45 + 5\ (2) = \text{Rs. } 55{,}000$$

$$Y\ 1970 = 45 + 5\ (3) = \text{Rs. } 60{,}000$$

$$Y\ 1971 = 45 + 5\ (4) = \text{Rs. } 65{,}000$$

$$Y\ 1972 = 45 + 5\ (5) = \text{Rs. } 70{,}000$$

The forecasting for 1973 will be

(Y) 1973 = 45 + 5 (6) = Rs. 75,000

Example 16.2. *With least square method.*

Suppose a firm is manufacturing automobiles and finds a relationship between sale of automobile and the Index of demand for cars. The sales for the last five years are:

Year	1970	1971	1972	1973	1974
Sales	110	130	150	160	180
Demand Index	100	110	140	150	200

Find the relation between the demand Index and the sale of automobile, further, make a forecast for the year 1975 supposing the demand Index rises to 210.

Solution.

Year	*Index X in '0*	*(Sales) Y in '0*	X^2	*XY*
1970	10	11	100	110
1971	11	13	121	143
1972	14	15	196	210
1973	15	16	225	240
1974	20	18	400	360
$n = 5$	$\Sigma X = 70$	$\Sigma Y = 73$	$\Sigma X^2 = 1042$	$\Sigma XY = 1063$

Now putting values from table in the least square equations.

$$\Sigma Y = n.a + b\Sigma X \quad \ldots (i)$$

$$\Sigma XY = a\Sigma X + b\Sigma X^2 \quad \ldots (ii)$$

Now, we get

$$73 = 5a + 70\,b \quad \ldots (iii)$$

$$1063 = 70a + 1042b \quad \ldots (iv)$$

Solving equations (*iii*) and (*iv*), we get

$$a = 5.36,\ b = 0.66$$

Now the trend equation will be

$$y = 5.36 + 0.66x$$

The y and x in equation (v) are one-tenth of actual (Y, X).

Then equation (v) will be

$$\frac{Y}{10} = 5.36 + 0.66\left(\frac{X}{10}\right)$$

Then ,

$$Y = 53.6 + 0.66\,X$$

Then equation (vi) is the relation between the demand Index and sales.

Forecasting for year 1975 with the demand Index 210.

$$Y = 53.6 + 0.66\,(210) = 192 \text{ automobiles.}$$

Example 16.3. *In the table below, some previous years' records are shown. Now if the forecast for product group for 1975 is Rs. 150,000, then divide this product group and find the forecast for product X.*

Year	Product Group Sales	Product X	Sales product X(in percentage)
1972	80000	16000	20%
1973	120000	26400	22%
1974	100000	24000	24%

Solution.

Now the forecast can be broken under two conditions:

(*i*) According to trend, supposing the sales increase as per trend, then in this year, the percentage of product *X* will be 26%.

(*ii*) According to average, the average of the percentage of the last three years is 22%.

Thus the forecast for product *X* according to trend is Rs. 39,000 and according to average Rs. 33,000.

QUESTIONS

1. What are the benefits of "Market Research" and under whose control should this be done?
2. Write an essay on "Market Research".
3. Explain the necessity of market research in the "Modern Industry". How market research is conducted?
4. What are the objects of market analysis ? Explain in detail.
5. Enumerate the factors involved in forecasting. State the purpose of forecasting, both short term and long term.
6. Discuss briefly the various methods of forecasting demand and point out their limitations.
7. Write down the procedure of making a sales forecast. What is the criteria of a good sales forecasting method?
8. What are the possible approaches for forecasting demand for new products ?
9. Explain various market research techniques.
10. Explain functions of 'market research'.
11. What is forecasting? Discuss various steps for forecasting.
12. Discuss short term and long term forecasts.
13. Mention statistical data which are helpful in sales forecasting.
14. Describe different types of sales forecasting.
15. List various elements of good forecasting.
16. Discuss methods adopted for forecasting new products.
17. Discuss methods used for forecasting of already established products.
18. Mention different applications of sales forecasts.

17

VALUE ENGINEERING (VALUE ANALYSIS)

17.1. INTRODUCTION

Value Engineering, also known as value-analysis, is a systematic application of recognised techniques, which:

1. identifies the function of a product or service,
2. establishes a value for that function, and
3. achieving that function at the lowest total cost without degradation.

In other words, value engineering is the conscious, systematic application of a set of techniques that identify needed functions, establish values for them, and develop alternatives to perform these functions for minimum cost. The other attributes which are affected by value engineering are reliability, maintainability, reduction in weight, and logistics.

Here the important point is not the saving, but the approach. Using the normal cost reduction techniques we try to reduce the cost of product. But by using the value engineering techniques, we get an entirely different product. The value engineering approach aims to find the lowest cost way to perform the desired *functions* rather than lowest cost way producing the *product*.

Value Engineering is a tool of management which attempts the question of saving cost from the point of view of 'Value' or in other words the main aim is to study the relationship between the design function and cost of a part, keeping in view to reduce part and cost through change in design, modification in specification of the material used by changing the source of supply and so on.

Value engineering identifies the areas of excessive or unnecessary expenses and attempts to improve the value of the product. It provides the base for better performance at a lower cost while reducing neither necessary quality reliability nor maintainability.

In general terms value engineering is also called as value analysis. But theoretically, value engineering is the application of the concepts of value analysis at the design or premanufacture stage of the components with a view to cut down the unnecessary costs, without impairing the function or utility of the product.

Value analysis is a technique of cost reduction based on systematic and organised examination of every item of cost which goes into the manufacture of the product in terms of the value or customer satisfaction it adds to the product.

Value analysis can also be defined as 'the systematic examination of all factors which contribute to the cost of a product, part or a material with the object of uncovering those possibilities of cost reduction which will not in any way reduce the quality, performance or any other attribute of the product which is sought by the customer'.

Thus value analysis means the organised and exhaustively critical study of a product in terms of the design, functions, and costs with the object of cost reduction.

The value of a product can be increased either by increasing its utility with the same cost or by decreasing its cost for the same utility. Users have different concepts of value depending upon time, place and availability of substitute items.

Value Engineering can also be defined as, conscious, systematic application of a set of techniques that identify needed functions, establish values for them, and develop alternatives to perform these functions for minimum cost.

Necessity for value engineering arises because, technology is changing rapidly and previously unavailable solutions can be developed.

Objects of Value Analysis

(*i*) to simplify the product
(*ii*) to use cheaper and better material
(*iii*) to use efficient and economical process
(*iv*) to reduce the cost of the product
(*v*) to improve the product design
(*vi*) to increase the utility of the product
(*vii*) to increase the profits.

17.2. VALUE

Value differs both from price and cost. It can be defined as the cost proportionate to the utility, i.e.

$$\text{Value} = \frac{Utility}{Cost}$$

Thus the value of a product can be increased either by increasing its utility with the same cost or by decreasing its cost for the same utility. Users have different concepts of value depending upon time, place and availability of substitute items. Value is adjudged by cost value, use value, esteem value and exchange (re-sale) value.

Value and Cost

In the manufacture of industrial products, cost is incurred to create value, costs and values have an input output relationships. The scope to optimise the input of costs in order to produce a given set of values is always there. Value is what the product is worth to the customer or user.

The price at which the product sells or can sell on the market is a measure of its value to the customer or user. Cost comprises of the (*i*) money value represented by the material used to make the product, (*ii*) wages of the workers, and (*iii*) other indirect costs attributable to its manufacture. The excess of value or market price over the costs incurred in producing the product represents the margin of profit of the manufacturer. In order to make his product more profitable, the manufacturer should be making a constant search for reducing the manufacturing costs. Reduced manufacturing costs means one or more of the following advantages:

(*i*) Increase the margin of profit.

(*ii*) Reduce the loss.

(*iii*) Enable a reduction in selling price and thus achieve a greater demand for the product.

Customer or user pays the assigned price for the product because he considers the satisfaction derived from its use worth that price; he is generally unconcerned about what it costs the manufacturer to produce the product.

Normally selling price depends upon the benefit which the customers expect to drive by using the product. This benefit is translated by the customer in terms of money which he can pay or in other words, this is the value which the customer places on the article for its purchase. This amount is entirely based on the wishes of the customer and has nothing to do with the money spent on producing the article. In some products, we usually observe that, price paid by the customer is very high even if the cost of production is small. The reason behind this is that he is very anxious to purchase it and has rated its value very high.

Thus it is necessary for the manufacturer to incur costs in such a way so as to get good response from the customers and the product will be appreciated by them. So to ascertain the value of the product, the businessman makes the systematic efforts. The process of making the systematic efforts to evaluate the value of the product is known as 'value analysis'.

Types of Values

(*a*) **Cost Value.** It is the cost of manufacturing a product or component.

(*b*) **Use Value.** It considers workdone, functions performed or service rendered and efficiency/effectiveness of product.

(*c*) **Esteem Value.** It involves the qualities and appearance of the product which attracts persons and creates a desire in them to possess the product.

(*d*) **Exchange Value.** It considers the properties or qualities which will remain attractive enough to other people to permit market resale in the future.

Maximum value is obtained when essential function is achieved for minimum cost.

This statement can be expressed mathematically as follows:

$$V_{max} = \frac{F}{C_{min}}$$

where,

V_{max} = Maximum value

F = Function

C_{min} = Minimum cost

Functions of a Product

Functions can be classified into following two categories :

1. **Basic Functions (or Primary Functions).** These are the functions without which the product would virtually lose all of its value, and in some cases even its identity, For example, if lead is removed from an ordinary wooden lead pencil, it would not only eliminate the basic function of pencil but will leave us with not more than a stick.
2. **Secondary Functions.** These functions support the basic functions, although they may or may not be essential functions. For example, pencil without lead may still retain the esteem value by just being seen in the pocket.

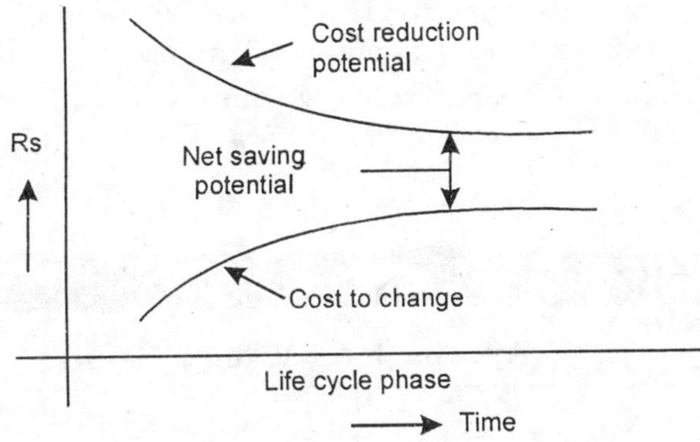

Fig. 19.7. Potential savings in money through Value Engineering.

Requirements of a Product.

Generally there are two requirements, *i.e.*, functional or aesthetic, *i.e.*, a product should be useful and should be pleasing in appearance. Thus Value Engineers look them in the following ways:

1. **Use.** It is the function for which the part is manufactured. For example, what a pen is supposed to do ? The answer is that it should write and hold ink.
2. **Esteem.** Actually this is something wider than the aesthetic side of design. The fact that a product is pleasing to look at, may induce people to buy but there are other factors. In short, the esteem aspect is concerned with getting the customer to buy.

As example before, the pen having gold plated body or other features cause the customer to purchase more readily.

When value analysis is done, then it is clear that the 'use' function cannot be avoided because it is main function. But it is not necessary in the case of Esteem function. Any benefit added to a product, over and above those required to meet the use function, must add to the cost causing a higher price.

When analysing, it is essential to consider how much be added in order to sale the part. The esteem function cannot be eliminated altogether, but it should not be over-emphasised. Now suppose the cost of gold plated pen is Rs. 1000. This cost further be divided as

Use = Rs. 150

Esteem = Rs. 850

Now the question is whether Rs. 850 is justified for esteem purpose? Do the additional features add to the value? This matter is closely related with the profit making.

The reasonable price of a product can be obtained by comparing with a comparative product. When this comparison is done, the possibility of substitution is examined. Such as whether a pen with a plastic body? Can the method of filling be simplified? Does the cap has to be made of expensive material and so on?

17.3. STAGES IN VALUE ANALYSIS

Value analysis is carried out in the following stages:

1. **What the customer wants, *i.e.*, to recognise the customer's needs or wants.**
2. **Finding out the best method of performing the work to be done.** Full use should be made of modern knowledge relating to production standardisation, simplification, work study, operation research, network analysis and other techniques to determine the most economic methods.

3. **To have the 'appropriate cost' for the 'appropriate performance'**, *i.e.*, to have the correct relationship between cost and performance.
4. **Search for better ways of performing work and consider the functional use of each part of a product.** The vital part of value analysis is to eliminate the unnecessary function.

17.4. APPROACH FOR VALUE ANALYSIS

Table. Approach for Value analysis

Subject	*Basic Question*	*Analysis*	*Answer*
Function	What functions are performed	1. Is there any possibility of elimination ? 2. What alternative methods are available ?	
Material	What is the material specification?	1. Can alternative material be used? 2. Can the specification be amended ?	
	What quality of material should be used?	1. Is the size or weight of material excessive. 2. Can the quality be reduced? 3. Will a cheaper material serve the same purpose? 4. Is the cutting done economically without waste ?	
Labour	Which are the direct labour costs?	1. Are all the operations necessary? 2. Will alternative operation be cheaper? 3. Can certain assembly operations be modified?	
Process	Are the best process being used?	1. Are all the operations necessary? 2. Will alternative operations be cheaper? 3. Can certain assembly operations be modified ?	
Stand–ardisation	Are the materials or components standard?	1. Can the materials be standardised ? 2. Can a number of product use Standard (common) parts? 3. Can methods be standardised?	

There is no standard approach, but a small idea can be formed by the following discussions.

Value analysis is essentially a job for a team. Much discussion is required. Any suggestions which are obtained during discussion are recorded and a proper investigation is done.

A standard form of questions as shown on previous page is developed and the analysis is made on the basis of proforma.

Another questionnaire given below may cover the following:

1. Does the function or part contribute value?
2. Is the cost reasonable having regard to the product usefulness?
3. Are the features essential?
4. Are there any alternative products?
5. Whether additional facility are accessory or any other feature that add to the value of the product as compared to the expenses required for this additional facility or accessory or factor?
6. Whether a component of the product should be made or purchased?
7. Whether it is more profitable to reduce number of varieties?
8. Whether materials which are being used at present should be substituted by other materials and what shall be the reaction of the customers?
9. Whether workers of lesser skill can be employed to reduce labour cost.

This questionnaire will help to reduce the cost of the product without affecting usefulness, and the sales adversely. This must be a continuous feature for the management to bring the product to the lowest possible cost, and simultaneously to keep a watch about the image of the product in the eyes of the customers and the price which they are willing to pay.

The answer of the above three questions give a useful product with lowest possible cost:

17.5. ADVANTAGES OF VALUE ENGINEERING

There are many advantages beside the normal advantages of cost reduction lower cost, lower prices and higher profits. Further, the following advantages may be possible whether value analysis is employed in the business:

1. The most suitable products are manufactured because a careful study is made to determine the desirable feature of each product in terms of customer's requirement.
2. Each product should be manufactured at the lowest possible cost because special attention is paid for simplfication, standardisation and improved methods of production.
3. Quality is maintained at desired level because there is no question to reduce cost at the expense of quality.
4. Value Engineering is based on the principle that management effectiveness can be measured in terms of cost saving. Any saving in cost is treated as increased efficiency.
5. The constant search for improvement will lead to greater all-round efficiency.
6. Suggestion box method may be employed and any idea can be looked into by the Value Engineers.

17.6. THE METHOD OF ANALYSIS

Value Analysis team must keep an open mind to any suggestion, and all the suggestions should be noted down in writing and should not be rejected without consideration even if they appear *prima facie* unworkable. Subcontractors and suppliers of material can come forward with reliable suggestions as regards alternative materials and their advice must be explored. Representatives of other deptts. like those from the inspection, packing and shipping and store-keeping can be associated with the discussion when points pertaining to their specialised areas are being discussed.

The actual explorations in cost reduction are based on the familiar method of questioning. Following are these questions:

1. Can the part be eliminated?
2. Can you combine it with other parts?
3. Can you separate it into simpler parts?
4. Can you use a standard part? Generally standard parts are economical.
5. Can you use standard materials?
6. Can you use cheap materials? Cheaper materials need not always mean inferior materials.
7. Can you use less materials? There is scope for considerable saving in materials, particularly in sheet and plate work by preplanning the jobs.
8. Can you buy more cheaply?
9. Can you reduce rejects?
10. Can you ease limits? Unnecessary tight tolerances are costly to obtain and many times, they serve no useful purpose.
11. Can you save on finish? Critical examination often reveals possibilities of saving on surface finish, which includes paintings, electroplating etc.
12. Can you use better methods? This question is particularly important for parts having high labour cost content.
13. Can you reduce the risk of error? Could the reliability of the process be improved?
14. Can you do anything else? Any other possibility of cost reduction in the peculiar circumstances of the best-usage may occur to the team.

Suggestion Scheme

Good suggestion scheme really facilitates the work of a value analysis team. Such a scheme invites the participation of the whole body of employees in cost reduction effort and suggestions which come from men on the job are generally very sound as regards practicability. The scheme also ensures a proper receptive atmosphere for the changes brought in the wake of Value Analysis work and to that extent makes the implementation easier.

17.7. TEAM APPROACH IN VALUE ANALYSIS

Value Analysis requires the cooperation of all the functional deptts. in an enterprise. As all deliberations must be based on the ultimate satisfaction which the customer wants from the product, the sales and market research deptt. should be intimately connected with value analysis exercises. The design deptt. and engg. deptt. which translates the customer requirements into the physical embodiment of the product must also be intimately concerned as they alone would be in a position to know as to why certain parts with certain properties must be assembled to make the product. As a major portion of the product cost is accountable by materials, the purchase deptt. should also be closely connected with exercise. The manufacturing deptt. which translates the design into reality and the costing deptt. possesses the factual data about the different cost elements as also their interaction are the others which must necessarily be associated with Value Analysis.

This organised exercise is unlikely to succeed without the enlightened cooperation from the the functional areas. The team must be consisting of senior representatives of the above 5 functional deptts. and they should possess special expertise in their own area which they represent so as to enable to influence the changes consequent to the recommendations of the Value Analysis team.

In large enterprises, Value Analysis should be a full time job for the team member. The Value Analysis team must have a position directly reporting to the top management. It is only when an enlightened support from the top is assured then only the Value Analysis team will be able to implement its suggestions to the advantage of the enterprise.

17.8. STEPS IN VALUE ANALYSIS APPROACH

Sequence of steps for systematic approach of value engineering are :

1. **Orientation.** Familiarization with needs, specifications, customer desires.
2. **Information.** All those facts which have bearing on the problem should be gathered. A typical list of information gathered is given hereunder :
   - Engineering information
   - Manufacturing information
   - Procurement information
   - Quality Control-rejections, tolerance
   - Reliability
   - Customer's experience
   - Cost information- Materials information
   - Packaging and preservation
   - Planning
   - Shipping
   - Scheduling
   - Testing
   - Tooling.
3. **Creativity.** Use of imagination and brainstorming. Adopt the process of 'blast, create and then refine'.
4. **Evaluation (Analysis).** Estimate value of ideas and explore best.
5. **Planning.** After selecting few alternatives or combination of alternatives, each of them be investigated thoroughly. For this purpose specialists, and vendors are also consulted. If necessary, go back to previous phase for more information, to further amplify the creative ideas and to make further evaluations. Refinement process must be carried out to its conclusion. On the basis of final outcome, detailed planning is carried out and a report is prepared for approval.
6. **Execution (Implementation).** The recommendations are followed till the decision is taken and then it is implemented. Since it is not necessary that implementation will continue smoothly and expeditiously, after decision is taken. Value engineers are therefore expected to see that the approved recommendations are implemented and hindrances, if any, can be sorted out.

17.9. WASTE CONTROL

Industrial waste may be defined as resources rendered unusable. The resources may be men, machines, materials, money and time. Wastage is mainly due to the failure in utilising given resources effectively for the benefit of the organisation. **Wastage control** is the process of identifying and quantifying the wastages, and initiating the activities for preventing, controlling, and salvaging the wastage.

Wastage can be classified as follows:

1. **By Nature.** Avoidable or unavoidable waste.
2. **By Resource.** these include wastage of man-hours, machine-hours, production facilities etc.
3. **By their causes.** These are:
   - Poor planning and design wastage.
   - Transportation wastage.
   - Wastage due to defective purchasing practices,
   - Storage wastage.
   - Conversion wastage.
4. **By Outputs.** These may be reusable wastage or unusable wastage.

Cost of Wastage

1. **Direct Cost Wastage:**
   (*a*) Loss of manpower.
   (*b*) Loss of machine hour
   (*c*) Loss of materials
2. **Indirect Cost Wastage:**
   (*a*) Loss of plant Capacity
   (*b*) Loss of sales due to production shortfall
   (*c*) Loss of production due to unused capacity.
   (*d*) Loss of goodwill.

Definitions:

Following definitions are important to consider wastage control in the industry:

Obsolete: These are those materials and equipments which are not damaged and which have economic worth but are no longer useful for the company's operation due to several reasons such as changes in product line, process, materials and so on.

Surplus: These are materials and equipments which have no immediate use but have accumulated due to faulty planning, forecasting and purchasing. However, these may have usage value in future.

Scrap: It is the process wastage such as turnings, borings, sprues and flashes etc. These may have an end use within the plant.

The unnecessary accumulation of obsolete surplus and scrap items is said to be waste and enough capital is blocked in it.

The increase in all such items will increase the product cost, which in turn will reduce the profits. Therefore, efforts shall be made to minimise such causes by means of intelligent planning and effective production control.

Major Causes of Obsolete/Surplus

The reasons for the accumulation of these items are:

(a) *Change in product design.* Due to change in the design of product, some items become obsolete.

(b) *Rationalisation.* Sometimes raw materials and equipments etc. are rationalised for want of simplification. This render some items as surplus or obsolete.

(c) When a machine breakdown occurs, sometimes it is rectified by using components of an identical machine which is already not functioning due to one reason or the other. This is called "Cannibalisation". By continued removing parts from the identical machine renders obsolete or scrap items.

(d) *Faulty Planning and forecasting.* Materials planning is based on sales forecast and this may result in surplus items, if not properly planned.

(e) *Faulty Purchase Practices.* If purchases are made in bulk then technological changes, storage space requirements etc. lead to the generation of surplus and obsolete items.

(f) *Other Reasons.* Faulty storekeeping and recording, poor materials handling, improper codification and inadequate manufacturing methods also cause obsolete surplus and scrap items.

Reasons for Scrap. These are

(i) Due to men:

1. Carelessness on the part of the operator.
2. Operator not trained properly.
3. Lack of attention on the part of the setter, inspector or supervisor.
4. Faulty instructions.
5. Written instructions and drawings misread.

(ii) *Due to machines:*

1. Plant and equipment in poor condition.
2. Design of plant and equipment may be poor.
3. Tools and gauges not standard one.

(iii) Due to materials:

1. Materials not upto the specifications.
2. Improper solution of materials.

(iv) Due to methods:

1. Improper techniques.
2. Poor works organisation.

We cannot totally avoid the scraps but these can be minimised by controlling the above reasons for scrap.

Disposal of Surplus Materials

A periodical study is essential for finding out the obsolete or suplus items. These items should then be re-examined for their alternative use. If they could not be used anywhere in the concern, they must be disposed of.

Mode of disposal should be decided in the following priority:

(a) Send it back on resale to the original supplier, if they are interested or otherwise,

(b) Sell them at the best possible price. If it is not possible then, (*c*) Sell it at any available price even at scrap value. In case, if it could not be sold at scrap value or at any other rate then,

(*d*) give away free, as there is no use of preserving it year after year and blocking the space.

Disposal of Scrap

When the scrap cannot be utilised within the organisation then it should be disposed of at regular intervals. It is profitable to dispose the scrap direct to the end-users rather than to a middleman who normally pays lower returns. Before disposal action is taken, it should be segregated according to metal and sizes to fetch good return. Following two methods are commonly adopted for scrap disposal:

1. Disposal by auction.
2. Disposal by tender.

Buyers in both the cases are required to inspect the scrap in the scrapyard and they are also required to deposit earnest money.

Salvage Operations

Salvage is defined as an act of saving. Salvage operations discussed here are confined to wastage of materials. Waste materials can be salvaged under two methods, namely, (*i*) reuse, or (*ii*) resale.

1. **Reuse of Wastage.**

   Following are the 3 methods of reuse of wastage

   (*a*) Reuse without rework for alternate uses

   (*b*) Reuse after rework.

   (*c*) Reuse after value addition, *e.g.*, recyeling.

2. **Resale of Wastage**

   When wastage is not reusable or if it is uneconomical for reuse, it is resold as scrap, as discussed earlier.

Role of Management in Waste Control Programme.

1. Stock records should be checked and items which have not been consumed (non-moving) for a period of one year should be isolated. A list of such items and their value in terms of money and time should be prepared. Similarly, such lists should be prepared for items which have not been used for more than one year say 2, 3, 4 years and so on. These lists are then forwarded to the top management for disposal action. A separate list should be prepared for imported parts and insurance parts. This analysis should be done atleast once in a year.

2. Whenever there is change in production programme, design and product lines are undertaken. Material manager must be kept in the picture. This will help in several ways as under :

   (*i*) He is in a position to inform top management of the amount of stock of materials on hand that are likely to be rendered obsolete if and when the changes are introduced.

   (*ii*) He could guide the top management as to when the changes should be made so that the existing stock can be consumed in full.

   (*iii*) Materials manager should freeze further orders for such materials and negotiate with the suppliers to take back the stock. For sometimes, he can introduce the buy-back clause.

3. Many organisations have introduced "Effective Point Advice" Scheme, known as EPA. Under this scheme, the proposed changes, details of new materials and products required, details of previous materials and products which will be invalid/obsolete when the change occurs and the probable data when the change is expected to be introduced are detailed and circulated to concerned departments.

   This scheme helps in taking off the stocks of "Invalid" items, cancellation of orders for such items, placing orders for new items etc. This system thus helps in better coordination of changes with minimum "side effects" such as the accumulation of obsolete items.
4. If it is possible in some cases to salvage scrap for usage within the organisation, management should see that it is profitable.

QUESTIONS

1. Define Value Engineering. What are its advantages?
2. "Value analysis is nothing but a new fangled phrase to describe the old fashioned device of cost reduction". State with arguments whether you agree with this statement.
3. What are the objects of value Engineering?
4. What are the stages in which value analysis is carried out?
5. Explain the procedure for "value analysis" carried out for value engineering.
6. What is the role of management in waste control?
7. Write short notes on:
   (*a*) Objectives of value analysis
   (*b*) Value
   (*c*) Team approach in value analysis
   (*d*) Functions of a product from 'value' point of view.
8. Discuss requirements of a product from value engineering point of view.
9. Discuss 'approach for value analysis'.
10. Enumerate the advantages of value engineering.
11. Discuss various steps in value engineering approach.
12. Define waste control. How wastage can be classified?
13. Write short notes on:
    (*a*) Value and cost
    (*b*) Cost of wastage
    (*c*) Salvage
    (*d*) Role of management in wastage control.

18

Plant Location and Layout

18.1. PLANT LOCATION

Location of an industry is an important operation management decision. It isa two-step decision: first, choice of the region and second, the choice of site within the region. Location decision is based on the organisation's long-term strategies such as technological, marketing, resource availability and financial strategies.

The objective of plant location decision-making is to minimise the sum of all costs affected by location.

When it has been decided to start a factory, it is most important to select a suitable site or location to house the factory. The location has great effect on the success or failure for the operation of a plant. Therefore, it should be based upon a careful consideration of all factors that are essentially needed in efficient running of a particular industry.

The necessary factors in the selection of plant location vary among industries and with changing technical and economical conditions. Some industries have tended to follow their markets in the location of their plants such as plastic industries, textile industries of Bombay, Nangal Fertilizer near Bhakra Dam and Chitranjan Locomotives near Maithan Dam, are located around the source of power. Iron and Steel industries in Orissa and Bihar have tended to seek the source of their raw materials. In recent years, the danger of air attacks on highly industrialized areas in a future war, has become a great consideration.

Site selection is not an easy problem because if the selection is not proper then all money spent on factory building, machinery and their installation etc. will go as waste and the owner has to suffer a great loss. Therefore, while selecting a site, owner must consider technical, commercial, financial aspects which may provide maximum advantages. It is sometimes possible that all the requirements and features of suitable site may not be available at one particular location but then it will be advantageous to find out suitable site with combinations of all essential requirements of the particular industry to be established as explained in following paras:

18.2. SITE SELECTION

The problem of the selection of a factory site can be solved in the following two stages :

(*a*) The general location of the factory.

(*b*) The selection of a particular site.

1. **General location of the Factory.**

   Following factors must be considered in this respect:

   1. Availability of raw materials.
   2. Proximity to markets.
   3. Availability of transport facilities.
   4. Availability of efficient and cheap labour.
   5. Availability of power and fuel.
   6. Climatic and atmospheric conditions.
   7. Availability of power.
   8. Availability of capital.
   9. Social and recreational facilities.
   10. Business and commercial facilities.
   11. Existence of related industries.
   12. Other factors like local bye-laws, taxes, fire protection facilities, banks, railway station etc.

2. **Selection of Actual Site**

   After selecting a general area for the plant, next step is to select a suitable site in that area. This is most important decision. Sometimes all the requirements and features of suitable site may not be available at one particular location and in such cases it will be advantageous to find out a suitable site with a combination of maximum essential requirements of the particular industry from maximum overall economy point of view.

   Important points which should be considered while selecting a specific site are discussed hereunder:

   1. **Community Attitude.** Most communities usually welcome setting up of a new industry as it would provide direct and indirect employment opportunities to the local people. However, in case of polluting or adversely affecting industries, the local population provide resistance and tries its best that such industries stay as far away as possible. This resistance sometimes create law and order situation. Thus the attitude of the people and that of state government influences the location of the industry.
   2. **Community Facilities.** These are the facilities which affect the quality of life such as schools, hospitals, housing, banking, communication, police, fire protection, cultural, social, recreational, and other facilities.
   3. **Topography.** This includes subsoil conditions suitable for taking bearing loads of the building foundation. The cost of levelling and developing the area, laying the water supply lines, electricity, drainage and sewage should remain within reasonable limits.
   4. **Transportation Facilities.** The plant site should be accessible by road and rail, so that the transportation cost is minimum and movement is easy and quick.
   5. **Waste Disposal.** The process waste including solid, liquid and gaseous effluents are required to be disposed of. The plant should be positioned so that prevailing winds carry out fumes away from populated areas, and that waste may be disposed of properly and at reasonable expenses.

6. **Ecology and Pollution.** Because of growing awareness towards maintenance of natural ecological balance, this aspect is gaining importance. Before selection of final area, it should be checked, if there is any restriction imposed in the area.
7. **Size of Land.** The plot of land must be sufficient in size to meet the needs of the proposed plant including parking areas and other facilities, and also space for future expansion. It should also be ensured that available land is free from any dispute.
8. **Supporting Industries.** The supporting industries and other services should be available in the nearby area.

18.3. SELECTION OF SITE IN AN URBAN AREA

Advantages

1. It is sometimes possible to find an existing building which can be used to house the factory.
2. It is easier to sell the building, if it is desired, at a later stage.
3. Power and water is easily available.
4. If other factories are also situated in a big city, there will be good opportunity for discussing and having exchange of knowledge.
5. Good market for small manufacturers.
6. It is well served by railways and roads from various parts of the country so that transportation of incoming and outgoing materials is convenient and cheap.
7. It is a good labour market, where all types of labour is available. Seasonal labour is also easily obtained than that in a smaller centre of population, especially when unskilled labour is required.
8. Services for repairs and maintenance etc. can be available with existing industries.
9. Large number of government facilities like-Post office, Banks, Railways, Police and Fire protection will be easily available.
10. Houses for workers are easily available.
11. Education for the children of the employees is not a problem.

Disadvantages

1. Often sites are limited as sufficient land is not available and being congested climate will not be healthy,
2. The cost of land is high and rates are liable to increase further. Land for expansion is not available at reasonable rates. The larger the city, the higher the land rate.
3. Because of high standard of living, higher wages of labour will have to be paid.
4. More problems about labour and employer relations.
5. Cost of building will be high.
6. High taxes.

18.4 SELECTION OF SITE IN A RURAL AREA

Advantages

1. The cost of land is less than in a city area and usually easier to get space for future expansion.
2. The cheap land enables a more efficient layout of works to be made and gives greater freedom in selecting the most economic design for the buildings.
3. Rail and road connections can be arranged easily.
4. Labour supply may be arranged from the nearby areas by transport from where the labour is cheaply available.
5. Healthy surrounding and pleasant atmosphere.
6. Less labour trouble,
7. Lesser taxes and restrictions.

Disadvantages

1. Sufficient power and water facilities may not be available.
2. Repairing work may become difficult, because of less industries in the area.
3. Skilled workers are not easily available.
4. No recreational facilities.
5. Facilities for education to children and adults (part time courses) may not be available.
6. Government facilities may not be sufficient.
7. Transport and housing facilities may not be satisfactory.

18.5. PLANT LAYOUT

After the site has been selected, the next step is to make a suitable layout. Best planning of a factory layout for constant operating efficiency is a difficult work and needs a good deal of experience. Some of the plans which appear quite all right from the drawing often fail when put in actual practice.

The layout of factory building should be such that the handling time is minimised to a great extent. A best layout will show that it saves the floor space, shortens the travel of materials, increases production and reduces cost by utilizing labour more efficiently. If the layout is hazardous the products will not be economical and the costs may be very high resulting in losses.

Apart from technical considerations, the factory building should have good appearance, look neat and clean. Such a plant will have a good effect on the moral of workers and the people in its surroundings will also be proud of it.

Plant layout is "an arrangement of machines within a factory, so that each operation is performed at the point of greatest convenience."

Plant layout may also be defined as "a technique of locating different machines and plant services within the factor so that the greatest possible output of high quality at the lowest possible total cost can be available."

Proper plant layout is one of keys of success in factory management. It signifies arrangement of machines, work area, transport, storing of material and processing of different parts.

The layout for the same product may be numerous but which costs less to process is the best. These vary with the size and type of plant.

Main Objects of Scientific Layout

(*i*) To produce better quality products.
(*ii*) Maximum utilisation of floor area.
(*iii*) To reduce internal transport from one operation to the next as much as possible.
(*iv*) Lighting and ventilating of areas.
(*v*) Lower cost of scrap and waste.
(*vi*) Fewer accidents.
(*vii*) Minimising production delays.
(*viii*) Space for future expansion.
(*ix*) Safety of equipment and personnel.
(*x*) Better working conditions for both executive and operative employees
(*xi*) Avoidance of unnecessary changes.
(*xii*) Savings of costs.
(*xiii*) Easy supervision.
(*xiv*) Proper production control.
(*xv*) To estimate waste effort and speeding of production.

Advantages of Scientific Layout

A scientific layout has got the following important advantages :

1. It reduces internal transport to a minimum.
2. It minimises accidents and makes supervision easy and quick.
3. It makes repairs and maintenance easy.
4. It yields higher profits. Therefore, higher wages can be paid to workers.
5. It reduces labour turn-over.
6. It reduces production delays to a large extent.
7. It keeps the shops neat and clean.
8. It minimises changes in the layout to large extent every time.
9. It keeps control over the production.
10. It eliminates waste efforts and thus speed of production increases.
11. Back tracking is reduced.
12. Less capital is spent on machinery.
13. It reduces set-up and total operation time.
14. It reduces wastage and spoiled work.
15. Time and motion study can be easily and accurately performed.
16. Better utilisation of manpower.
17. Improvement in method of production can be made.

18.6. FACTORS AFFECTING LAYOUT

Following are the major considerations which should be followed while making layout of any kind of factory:

1. **Organisation of Departments.**

   It means, where various production departments such as machine shop, welding shop and assembly shop etc. should be located in the building? What should be their size etc.? For this purpose, the process or operations are studied and product analysis should be made. This will show:

   (*i*) What is to be produced?

   (*ii*) How much is to be produced ?

   (*iii*) What will be the sequence of operations?

   (*iv*) How much time each operation will take ?

   (*v*) How the machines can be best grouped ?

   (*vi*) What will be the capacity of machines and their production etc.?

   (*vii*) The amount of space needed and necessity of special provisions, if any.,

2. **Location of Production Departments in the Building.**

   The various production departments should be located in such a way that the traffic or movement of workers should be easy. Flow of materials within the department and also between one department and another department should be economically and neatly managed. In the diagram given below, "Layout of a Chemical Factory" is shown,where material flows from Raw-material Stores (R. S.) to production plants (1 to 5), then after processing, it reaches Finished Store (F. S.). The layout shows that it shortens the travel of materials and movement of persons. Loading and unloading is done nearby. Such a layout of building is proved to be economical.

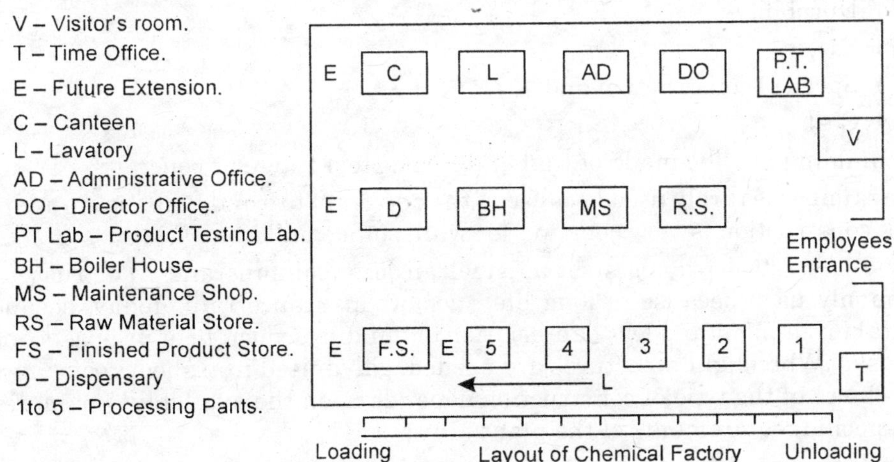

Fig. 18.1

3. **Position of Service Departments.**

   Service departments mean canteen, stores, toilets, first-aid, water, schooling and conveyance etc. These should be properly positioned after making and should be suitably allotted for all these services. These should be located from factory as well as workers' point of value. For this, factory Act must be followed.

4. **Premises.**

   The various sections of departments of the factory can be arranged into three main groups, *i.e.*, Administrative, Services and Production Departments.

As far as possible, administrative departments should be located in a separate wing, where there should be no noise and disturbances due to movement and vibrations of machines etc.

General service departments such as finished parts store, tool rooms, toilet should be as central as possible. Safety provisions for the empolyees should be as central as possible. Raw material stores and heavy machinery stores should be near the production department.

The various shops of production departments such as foundry, welding, machine shop, smithy shop etc., should be properly arranged.

5. **Size and Local Conditions of Site.**

If the site is of small size and the manufacturing methods involve the gravity flow of products, *e.g.*, chemicals and paints, a multi-storey building must be designed. In this case the flow of material will be much easier:

When heavy machinery is used and bulky work tackled, *e.g.*, locomotives or aircraft etc., a single storey building is preferred.

Usually single-storey building is preferred, if land is cheap. It involves lighter foundations, less vibrations, better supervision, flexibility with regard to layout, more effective floor area, better natural lighting and no necessity of lifts and elevators etc.

6. **Type of Construction.**

The main points concerning structural materials are as below:

(*a*) Strength

(*b*) Durability

(*c*) Safety

(*d*) Speed of construction and

(*e*) Cost.

The building may be made of timber, bricks, steel frame or concrete.

Today timber is rarely used because of the danger of fire and high insurance rates. The brick construction is very common for walls, office building.

Now-a-days steel frames such as steel girders, columns and roof trusses etc., are commonly used because of long life and low insurance rate. Today, because of low capital investment and less depreciation of building, concrete or pre-cast construction are used. When light structures are needed, galvanised iron sheet roofs may be used. The choice of the type of construction depends upon the availability of materials and the specific requirements of the plant.

7. **Ventilation and Air Conditioning.**

This factor is of extreme importance, as heat, dust, moisture, fumes and smoke etc., are greatly produced in manufacturing process. These reduce the percentage of oxygen and increase the percentage of carbon dioxide etc. in the factory environment, which makes breathing difficult and develop certain diseases. Hence proper ventilation and air conditioning is very essential. These are conducive to health and efficiency and will create lively and healthy atmosphere in the factory,

Great care was taken in past that clerks on small salaries were comfortably housed and they would not have been expected to do good work unless so cared for, but high priced machines were only too often expected to produce good results in spite of all sorts of physical discomfort and inconvenience to workers. There is no difference between the psychology of the office and that of shop. Workmen can naturally produce more and better in well-ventilated and air conditioned rooms.

For comfortable environment, employee requires 0.03 cu.m of fresh air per minute at a temperature of about 27°C. In this respect, the Factories Act has made some provisions and those must be followed while making the layout of the building.

8. **Lighting.**

Good lighting provides safe working place and helps in increasing vision. This increases the efficiency of workers and also reduces accidents. While installation of light points, the factors, given below should be considered:

(*i*) The light should be cool or give off less heat.

(*ii*) There should be sufficient visibility of the complete job.

(*iii*) There should not be any glare.

(*iv*) Shadows should be avoided.

(*v*) Brightness must be uniform throughout the area.

(*vi*) Light must not be dazzling.

The amount of light required for any job will depend on the nature and type of job. For precision job, even hundred lumens/m^2 of light may be used.

9. **Appearance.**

A huge capital is invested on the purchase of machinery, building construction and other equipments. The appearance of the factory also plays important role in raising productive efficiency and reduces labour turnover. Therefore, this factor should not be neglected. With a small additional expense, it can be made beautiful. The windows, doors and colouring scheme should be properly planned. Just as a well-designed machine is pleasing to look at, so a well designed factory building must be pleasing to look. Therefore, it should be kept and coloured in such a way that the atmosphere created is bright, cheerful and restful.

10. **Plant Protection.**

The factory should be surrounded by boundary walls all around and boundary walls must be covered with broken glass, pieces of fencing wire should be laid over it.

To prevent theft, strict security guards should be employed. There should be only one main gate and it should always be kept under the control of safety guard. Unauthorised persons should not be permitted to enter inside without permission and photography should be strictly prohibited.

Provisions for storing inflammable materials should be made far away from the main building. For this, Factories Act must be followed.

11. **Provisions for Future Expansion.**

Enough space in shops must be allowed for future expansion. The usual practice to layout buildings corresponding to shapes of such letters as U, H, E, T, L, and F shown in the figure depending upon departmental problems and flow of materials through the plant is adopted. All the plans shown in the fig. 18.2 lend themselves to expand in several directions from end walls. Dotted line shows space for future expansion.

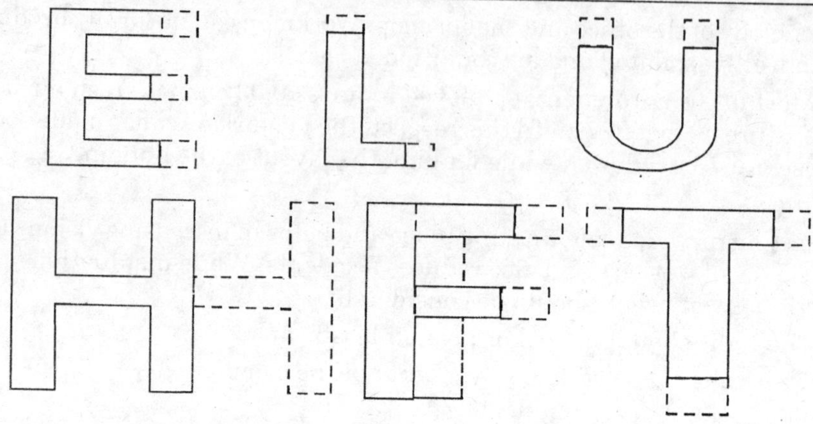

Fig. 18.2

12. **Sanitary Convenience**

    Provisions for good lavatories, washing and dressing facilities must be made in the layout at different central places. Care should be taken to keep the equipment as simple as possible and of a quality consistent with the workers' social status. This will inspire health and efficient atmosphere.

    All the above factors must be taken into account while planning a general factory layout. Various departmental heads should sit and consult together and an attempt be made to arrange a best possible layout, which may produce maximum efficiency with minimum expense.

18.7. FACTORS INFLUENCING LAYOUT

These are:

1. **Type of Industry.** Industries are generally classified according to their processes of manufacture. The process of manufacture can be classified into four categories:
   (*a*) **Synthetic Process.** When two or more materials are mixed to get a product, the process is known as synthetic process. The example of such a process is to produce the cement by mixing limestone and clay.
   (*b*) **Analytical Process.** This is opposite of synthetic process. It is the breaking up of a material into several parts. The refining of petroleum is the example of this case.
   (*c*) **Conditioning Process.** In the conditioning process, the form of raw materials is changed into desired product as in jute industry.
   (*d*) **Extractive Process.** In this type, by applying heat, desired product is extracted from the original raw material, *e.g.*, manufacture of aluminium from bauxite.
2. **Type of Products.** Type of product means whether the product is heavy or light, large or small, liquid or solid. It is also a consideration in plant layout.
3. **Volume of Production.** According to this point, while plant layout is being due, it should be kept in mind that, what volume is required to be produced. In this case, it should be seen that which type of production is adopted :-
   (*a*) Job Production, (*b*) Batch Production or
   (*c*) Mass Production

4. **Influence of Processes.** Last but not the least factor to consider, is the process through which the material passes in the concern. Much care should be given to the material handling problem, position of store room and tool room.

Keeping in view of the type of industry and volume of production, there can be following methods of layout:

18.8. PRINCIPLES OF PLANT LAYOUT

According to Muther, there are six basic principles of best layout. These are:

1. **Principle of Over-all Integration.** According to this principle, the best layout is one which integrates the men, materials, machinery, supporting activities and any other such factors that results in the best compromise.
2. **Principle of Minimum Distance.** According to this principle, other things being equal, the best layout is one in which men and materials have to move the minimum distance between operations.
3. **Principle of Flow.** Muther said that, other things being equal, the best layout is one which arranges the work area for each operation or process in the same order or sequence that forms, treats or assembles the materials.
4. **Principle of Cubic Space.** According to this, the best layout is one in which all the available space both vertical and horizontal is most economically and effectively used.
5. **Principle of Satisfaction and Safety.** According to this, other things being equal, the best layout is one which makes work satisfying, pleasant and safer for workers.
6. **Principle of Flexibility.** It means the best layout is one which can be adopted and re-arranged at a minimum cost and with least inconvenience.

18.9. SYMPTOMS OF A BAD LAYOUT

A poor or badly planned layout will generally show the following symptoms:

1. Congestion of machines, materials, parts, assemblies and even workers.
2. Excessive amount of work in process.
3. Poor utilization of available space.
4. Long material flow lines.
5. Some machines heavily loaded and some remain idle for long periods.
6. Long production cycles.
7. Delays in delivery.
8. Excessive mental or physical strain on workers.
9. Difficult to supervise and control properly.

18.10. SPACE PLANNING

For a proper layout, it is necessary to analyse space available, required, or to be allocated to each activity or function of the enterprise. Production activities are necessary for every enterprise, but vary with the type of industry, however a number of supporting services are also required in each enterprise but in varying degree.

Main acrtivity centres for various facilities are:

1. **Production.**
   - Production control.
   - Industrial engineering.
   - Quality control.
   - Maintenance.
   - Receiving storage
   - Warehousing and shipping
   - Tool room and Tool crib.
   - Scrap and waste disposal.
2. **Administrative**
   - General Manager.
   - Sales and Marketing.
   - Purchasing.
   - Personnel Management.
   - Finance and Accounting.
   - Library
   - Reception, conference room etc.
   - Fire fighting
3. **Welfare**
   - Medical
   - Guest house
   - Recreation
   - Parking
   - Canteen
   - Education facilities etc.
4. **Colony**
   - Residences.
   - Community halls.
   - Parks, landscaping etc.
   - Shopping complex.
   - Power Generation.

Factors Considered in Space Planning

In adding to the above, Layout planner must consider the following factors for determining the space requirement for the enterprise:

- Equipment sizes and numbers.
- Expansion plans.
- Business trends and Long term planning.
- Flexibility desired.
- Material flow pattern.
- Manufacturing methods.
- Material handling system and equipment

- Transportation
- Production capacity.
- Services.
- Safety aspects.
- Organisational set-up.
- Type of product.
- Possible changes in product or line.
- Number of shifts.
- Product size.
- Storage methods.
- Inventory policy.
- Aisels.
- Stairs, lifts, elevators and ramps.
- Number of floors.

Flexibility of Layout

As far as possible certain amount of flexibility of arrangement and operation is essentially desired in a plant layout. Economy should be the prime consideration in layout. When changes are affected in the product design, methods of operation, the type of the product or the production quantities then the machines or departments may also have to be arranged. Therefore, it is necessary to design layouts in such a way so as to minimise the affect of subsequent alterations on the production process. Flexibility in layout can be secured in several ways:

(*i*) Keep enough unobstructed floor areas.

(*ii*) Separate electric motors to be allowed on individual machines.

(*iii*) Mobile machinery should be used.

(*iv*) Equipment can be placed on rubber footings instead of being mounted permanently.

(*v*) As far as possible small tools should be used.

(*vi*) Portable conveyer units may be employed.

(*vii*) Overhead electrical lighting arrangement which are easily detachable be used instead of permanent fittings.

(*viii*) Make use of portable jigs and fixtures.

Machine Requirements

In order to layout a plant, the number of machines required should be known. This information can be calculated by the following way :

No. of items for which material is required

$$= \frac{\text{No. of satisfactory items required}}{\frac{100 - \text{per cent scrap loss}}{100}}$$

Total machine time

$$= \frac{\text{No. of items for which materials is required}}{\text{Standard time per item} \times \frac{1}{\text{Expected efficiency}}}$$

∴ No. of machines required.

$$= \frac{\text{Total machine time}}{\text{No. of hours available per machine}}$$

Work Station Design

"Work station" or "Work place" may be defined as the floor space occupied by the worker and the machine or group of machines. In the design of work station layout generally following space requirements are taken into consideration:

(*i*) The rectangular space occupied by the length and width of the machine or group of machines. This should include the space needed for covers, wheels, shafts, levers, doors, pulleys and handles etc.

(*ii*) Floor space for the power source or say electric motor when placed on the floor or within the working area.

(*iii*) Floor space required by the workers to perform work.

(*iv*) Clearance space for feeding the work on and off the machine.

(*v*) Space for racks, convey or stations, bins etc., which either contain the work to be processed or receive the work after it has been processed on the machine.

(*vi*) Space for tool racks, work benches and auxiliary equipment etc. required by the individual machine, if any.

In addition, the work station needs much more space than the machine indicates. Hence enough floor space for individual machine should be left aside while making plant layout.

Storage Space Requirement

In plant layout, while allotting space for work stations provision must be made for materials storage space essentially required inside the plants. For awaiting processing or moving from one area to the next area, every area or department must have a space required for such purpose.

The space requirement depends on various factors, such as :

(*i*) The quantity of raw materials required to be used per hour.

(*ii*) Volume and weight of partially processed parts awaiting moving from one machine to the next machine.

(*iii*) Volume and weight of parts on the move from one department to the next department.

(*iv*) Volume and weight of scrap.

(*v*) The ceiling height of the plant building.

(*vi*) The floor load bearing capacity.

(*vii*) Total production per assembly.

(*viii*) The raised ground required for storage.

(*ix*) Methods to be adopted for storage purpose.

When the total space required for all machines has been estimated, provision must be made for employee's service facilities such as canteen, first aid, drinking water, rest room, waiting room, washing places, urinals, sales department, personnel department, office and store-keepers enclosure etc.

18.11. METHODS OF LAYOUT

Keeping in view the type of industry and volume of production, there can be following methods of layout.

(*a*) Line or Product Layout.

(*b*) Functional or Process Layout.

(*c*) Fixed Position Layout.

(*d*) Combination.

1. Line or Product Layout

This type of layout is very popular in mass production. In this layout, only one product or one type of product is an operating area. In order to justify the line layout, the product must be standardised and manufactured in huge quantities. The machines in such a layout are arranged in the order in which they are to be used. The operations are performed in sequence. All parts, sub-assemblies etc. are started at right time to be ready at the required time and are kept moving until the finished product is available at the end of the assembly line. This arrangement is also known as the "Synthetic system" or manufacture.

For example, suppose a factory manufactures tapes, drills, reamers and cutters. Production of each of these, articles may be made in separate department and in each department machines will be laid out in that sequence in which the operations have to be performed on the product. For example, in the reamer department, there will be group of lathes to turn the reamer blanks, the lathes will be followed by the milling

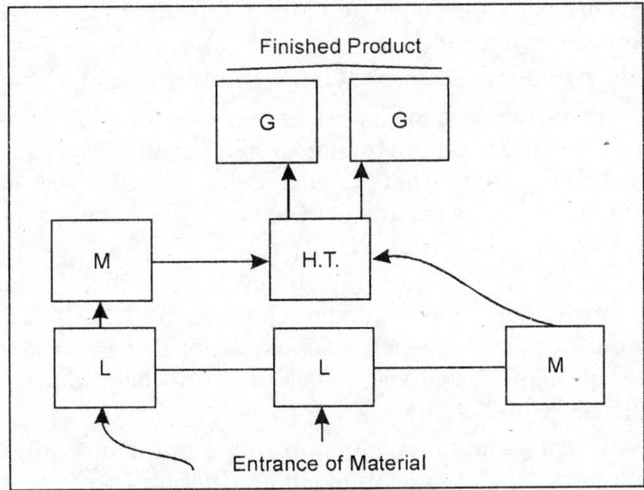

Fig. 18.3. Product Layout

machines which square the shank and mill the flutes, next to the milling machines will be furnaced for heat treating the reamers and last will come the grinding machines to do the finishing. Fig. 18.3 shows an arrangement of this type.

Suitability. This is suitable for continuous process industries such as car or automobile manufacturing and chemical industries.

Advantages.

1. It lowers the overall manufacturing time as product under this system proceeds rapidly from operation to operation without any handling.
2. Less space is needed for placing machines.
3. There is minimum of handling or transportation.
4. There is less work-in-process.
5. Better utilisation of machines and labour.
6. It minimises counting, inspecting and clerical work etc.
7. There is smooth flow of materials.
8. Promises for supply of products to customers are more reliable.
9. Use of gravity and power conveyers for material handling reduce the necessity of large aisles.
10. Production control is simplified greatly.

Disadvantages.

1. When the model or type changes, the layout of machinery also requires a change.
2. All machines in the arrangement cannot be used to their maximum capacity.
3. The manufacturing cost rises with a fall in the volume of production.
4. If one or more lines are running light, there is great machine idleness.
5. Specialised and strict supervision is needed.
6. If any one of the machines in the shop breaks down the other machines have to remain idle till that machine becomes again ready to commence operation.
7. For expansion purpose, it is not possible to add more machines.
8. Each worker performs job at a particular machine, so he is not skilled for other machines or operation.

2. Functional or Process Layout (Group Technology).

Under this arrangement each 'department or section is responsible' for carrying out a particular process and not a particular product as under in line type of layout. There is assembling of similar operations in each department or section. Therefore, machines in this type of layout are generally arranged on functional basis. This type is also called analytical layout.

Thus for example, in a factory manufacturing tapes, drills, reamers and cutters mentioned above there may be four departments, the lathe, the milling, the heat treatment and the grinding, each responsible for a specific operation. All the products manufacture in this factory have to pass through these four principle operations. Fig. 18.4 shows this arrangement.

Suitability. In this, similar equipment and similar machines are grouped together. This is very useful where low volume of production is required.

Advantages

1. Similar jobs are manufactured on similar machines, hence supervision is simple.
2. Less machines are required.
3. This offers areas of incentive for each worker to raise the level of performance.
4. There will be better control on precision or complicated processes.

5. The layout is flexible, hence it can easily be managed to change in the rate of production, in the raw materials used.

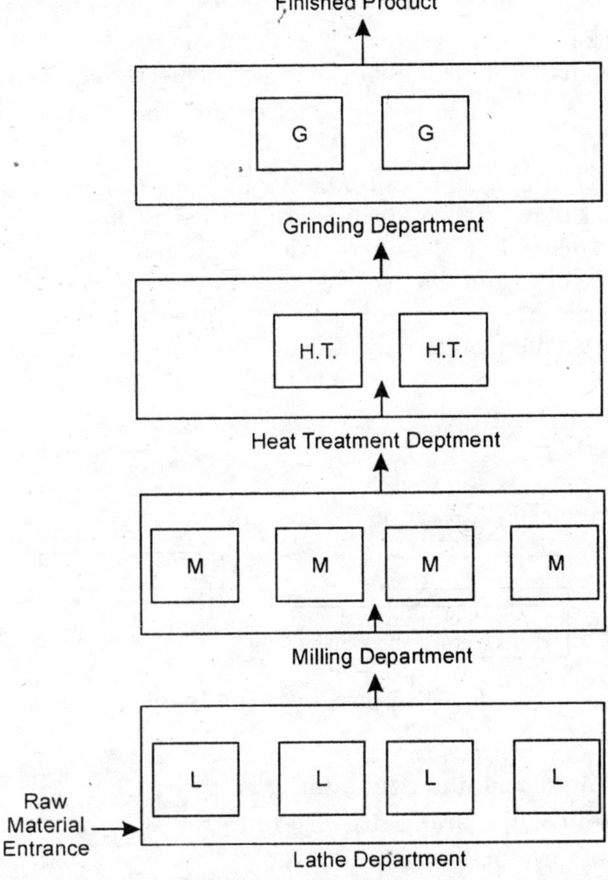

Fig 18.4. Process Layout

6. Any break-down of one machine does not affect production as it can be done on a standby machine.
7. Capital outlay for machines is minimum.
8. New workers have better training facilities on the job. Workers know, how to run various machines in the group and also to set up work.
9. Foremen become specialised in the performance of the job and know all about the equipments and their operations.

Disadvantages

1. Handling and back-tracking of materials is too much.
2. It makes necessary to plan and supervise the work of each department, each worker and machine. This makes production control more difficult and more costly.
3. Generally more floor area is required.
4. Specialization creates monotony and there will be difficulty for the workers to find jobs in other industries.
5. Total production cycle time is more, due to long distances and waiting.

6. Routing and scheduling is more difficult, as the work does not flow through any definite mechanical channels.
7. There are no cheaper and automatic devices for internal transportation.
8. Inspection of work for each operation is necessary as the material passes to the next department. This result in more inspection and causes delays.
9. More training will be required to prepare the workers for the jobs.

3. Fixed Position Layout.

This type of layout is used in manufacturing huge aircraft, ship vessels and pressure vessels etc. as the product materials are too heavy. For these types of products, it is convenient and economical to bring the tools, machines and men etc. to the work place. This type of layout was very common before the Industrial Revolution but the present industries have grown much in size and complexity, therefore, now-a-days it is easy and more economical to move the materials to the equipment and macnines. Fig. 18.5 shows a simple arrangement of this type of layout. This type is also known as "Static Product Layout".

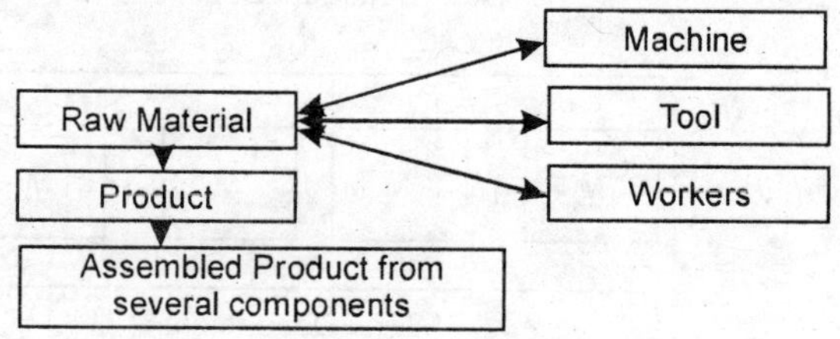

Fig. 18.5. Fixed position Layout.

Advantages.

1. Capital investment is minimum.
2. Continuity of operations are ensured.
3. Less total production cost.
4. Less material movement.

Disadvantages.

1. Machines and tools etc. take more time to reach at the work place.
2. Highly skilled workers are required.
3. Complicated jigs and fixtures may be required in fixing jobs and tools etc.

4. Combination.

Now-a-days in pure state, any one form of layout is very rarely found. Therefore, a combination of either of the three methods is formed according to the requirement of industry. In factories, where first the products are manufactured and then assembled, this method is mostly used.

18.12. FLOW PATTERN

"Flow Pattern" means the system to be adopted for the movement of raw materials from the beginning and upto the end of manufacturing. The overall-objectives of the 'Flow Pattern' is to plan for the economical movement of the raw materials throughout the plant. The Flow Pattern affects the cost of:

(*i*) Material handling
(*ii*) Amount of work in process.
(*iii*) Capital and space tied up by work-in-process.
(*iv*) Length of total production time.
(*v*) The rate of performance and co-ordination of operations.
(*vi*) Amount of physical and mental strain on the operators.
(*vii*) Supervision and control mechanisms.

Quite often a plant layout design starts with the flow system around which services and other facilities are added and buildings designed and modified accordingly but sometimes the flow must be adopted to existing buildings.

Factors Governing Flow Pattern

(*i*) External transport facilities.
(*ii*) Number of products to be handled.
(*iii*) Number of operations on each product.
(*iv*) Number of units to be processed.
(*v*) Number of sub-assemblies made up ahead of assembly line.
(*vi*) Size and shape of available land.
(*vii*) Necessary flow between work areas.

The flow system can be classified into horizontal and vertical. The horizontal flow system is adopted on a shop floor while vertical flow is adopted where material has to move in a multi-storey building.

Horizontal Flow Lines

There are five basic types of horizontal flow lines :

(*i*) I-Flow or Line-Flow
(*ii*) L-Flow
(*iii*) U-Flow
(*iv*) S-Flow
(*v*) O-Flow

(*i*) **I-Flow or Line Flow.** It is the simplest form of flow. In this, materials are fed at one end, the components leave the line at the other. This type is economical in space and convenient in I-shaped buildings, I-Flow is preferred for building automobile Industries (Fig. 18.6)

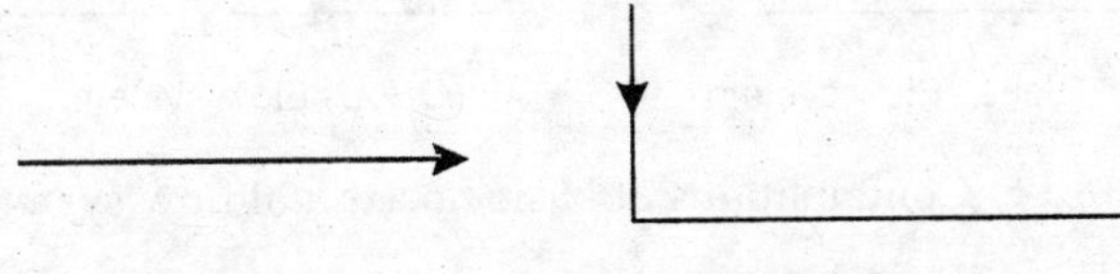

Fig. 18.6 **Fig.18.7**

(*ii*) **L-Flow.** It is similar to the I-Flow and is used where I-line cannot be accommodated in the available space (Fig. 18.7)

(*iii*) **U-Flow.** In this, both feeding and output take place at the same end, *i.e.*, it allows both receiving and dispatching of goods to be done at one side. In comparison to I or L-flow, this method is easier for supervision. This type of flow can be adopted in the manufacture of Electric Motor Industry (Fig, 18.8).

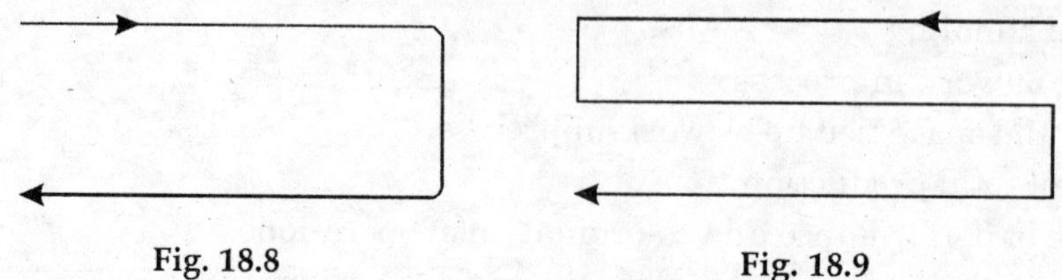

Fig. 18.8 Fig. 18.9

(*iv*) **S-Flow.** If the production line is so long that zig-zagging on the plant floor is necessary than S-flow is adopted. This type provides efficient utilization of space and is compact enough to allow effective supervision (Fig. 18.9 and 18.10)

Fig 18.10 Fig 18.11

(*v*) **O-Flow.** This type is used where process or operations are performed on a rotary table or a rotary handling system. The components are moved from one working station to the other and when they leave the O-line, a complete set of process or operations has been performed. The components are inspected before they are moved on to a second line of an additional series of processes or operations or to an assembly line. O-flow can be adopted by industries manufacturing electric bulbs (Fig. 18.11)

These above mentioned 5 basic flow lines are mostly used by industries in various combinations. Examples of combinations of a basic horizontal flow systems are shown in Fig. 18.12

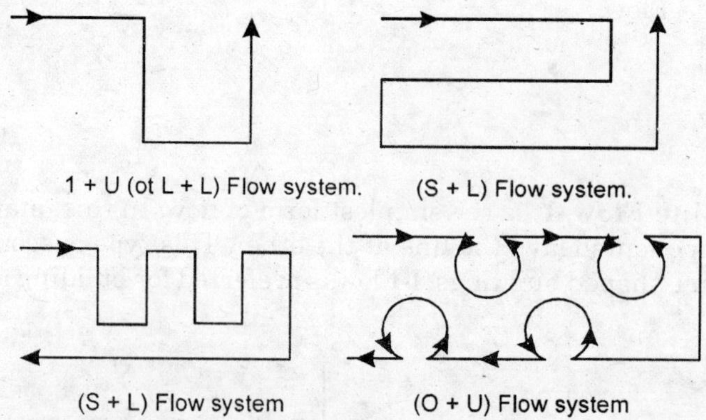

Fig. 18.12. Combinations of basic horizontal flow systems.

Undirectional and Retractional flow

(*a*) **Undirectional flow.** The flow is said to be Undirectional when the material is passed from one to another without passing along the same path (Fig. 18.13). The flow methods explained above are unidirectional flow type.

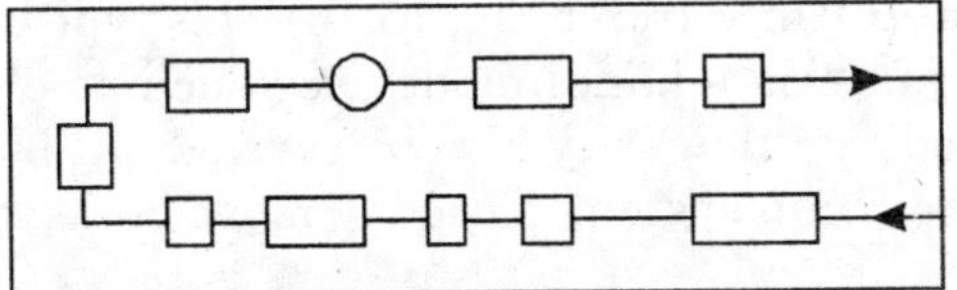

Fig. 18.13. Undirectional flow.

(*b*) **Retractional Flow.** In this, the flow is repeated, i.e., two or more non-consecutive operations are performed on the same machine. This aspect of flow is decided by consideration of machine utilizations. In this flow, the available machine time is fully utilized but schedules have to allow for repeated machine setting and for the fact that intermittent localized halts occur in the production line, *i.e.,* each time a machine is switched over from one operation to another. This flow is also known as "Repeated flow" (Fig.18.14).

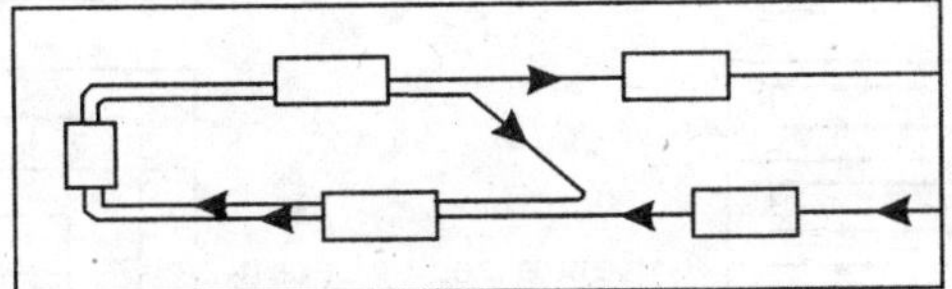

Fig. 18.14. Repeated flow.

Vertical Flow Lines

This type of flow is for multi-storey buildings, so that the materials handling systems and control mechanism to operate effectively, following six basic aspects of vertical flow systems are in use (Fig.18.15):

(*i*) Processing downward or upward.

(*ii*) Centralized or decentralised elevation.

(*iii*) Undirectional or Retractional flow.

(*iv*) Vertical or Inclined flow.

(*v*) Single or multi-flow.

(*vi*) Flow between buildings.

1. **Processing Downwards or Upwards.** In downward processing, the materials are fed from the top and in upward processing, the materials are fed from the bottom floor while the finished product is received at the top floor.

   In processing downward, many gravity handling system such as roller lines, chutes, pipes, buckets, hand operated lifts etc. can be used. These are economical in installation, operation and maintenance etc.

2. **Centralized or Decentralized Elevation.** In a centralized elevation, all the material handling devices are installed at one central place of the buildings. Therefore, this system is economical in supervision and maintenance. It sometimes reduce installation costs also. This method is usefully employed when the flow on each floor is a U-flow.

   A decentralized elevation method is more costly in installation, maintenance and space, but by this method, handling on each floor can be greatly reduced and more flexibility in design of the flow lines is possible.

3. **Undirectional or Retractional Flow.** In this type of flow, material has to come back on the floor which it had already passed previously. This is done purposely to achieve better utilisation of available space and machines.

4. **Vertical or Inclined Flow.** (refer Fig. 15.13) This type of flow is more economical and is carried on with materials handling devices such as elevators, chutes, and buckets etc. In addition, inclined flow may also be carried out by convey or belts used in coal handling plants and chain system is used to move boiler greates etc. and similar other tasks.
5. **Single or Multi-flow.** In a single flow, there is only one-flow line of materials while in multi-flow, there will be several flow lines and all these feed one assembly line.

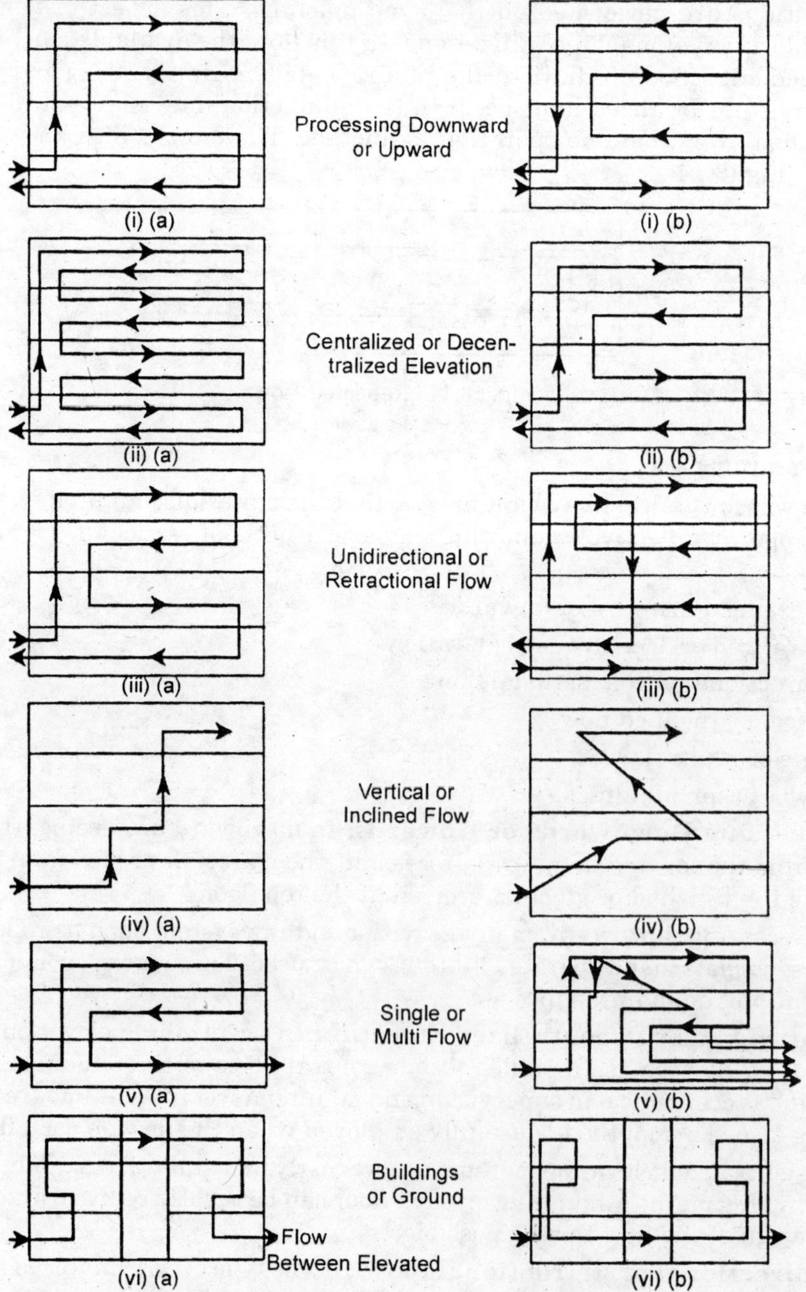

Fig. 18.15. Six basic aspects of vertical flow systems

6. **Flow between Buildings.** When one production is executed in several adjacent buildings the flow of goods achieved may be either on elevated flow or on ground flow. Ground flow is cheaper but requires more handling than an elevated flow. Elevated flow allows the ground for traffic and storage purposes.

18.13. TRAVEL CHART

The chart which gives an estimate about the amount of material handlings between various work stations is known as " Travel Chart". The aim in the construction of Travel Chart is to decide such a layout so that overall materials handling function performed is minimum.

(*i*) The first step in the construction of this chart is to make the list of work stations along the heading and down the stub of the table as shown in Table 15.14 *(b)*.

(*ii*) The next step is to establish a basic measure to indicate the amount of materials handling to be done between each work station. If all the parts are nearly of the same size, then number of parts to be moved from one work station to the next may be a satisfactory measure of the materials handling task. In other cases, we may use the physical volume of parts.

As an example of Travel Chart, suppose there are three parts to be manufactured in four different shops. The required information for these parts is given in Table below:

Part No.	*No. of load*	*Sequence of operations.*
I	200	*ABCBD*
II	100	*ACD*
III	300	*CBD*

Operation Summary Table 18.1

The information in the Table 18.1 such as "Number of loads" is collected from an analysis of the annual or monthly production. The processing sequences such as *A, B, C, D* etc. is collected through various route sheets.

		From			
		A	B	C	D
To	B	200		200 300	
	C	100	200		
	D		200 300	100	

Travel Chart Table 18.2

From Table 18.1, one finds that 200 loads of Product I are moved from machine Group A to machine Group B. The figure 200 is entered in the square representing movement from Group *A* to Group *B* as shown in Table 18.2. Similarly figure 200 is entered in the square *C* to represent movement from Group *B* to Group *C*. Again, figure 200 is entered in square *B* to represent its movement from Group *C* to Group *B*. Then figure 200 is entered in square *D* to represent movement from *BD to D*.

In the similar way, Table 18.2 is completed for part number II and III. So in this way this travel chart shows that total movement for the load from *B* is 700. This 700 shows that 200 load moved from *B* to *C* and 500 moved from *B* to *D*. Further it gives that 200 loads moved from *A* to *B*, 100 from *A* to C, 500 from C to *B* and 100 from *C* to *D*. From this, it can be concluded that from materials handling point of view shop *B* and *C* be adjacent. Also shop *D* should be located close to shop *B*. It is less important that shops A and *B*, *A* and C and *C* and *D* be adjacent. With this information, the planning department can begin blocking in rough area sketches and proceed to locate individual work stations on the drawing. Much planning and rearranging still may be needed at the final state to layout planning. So in this case, the desired economical layout will be as shown in Fig 18.16.

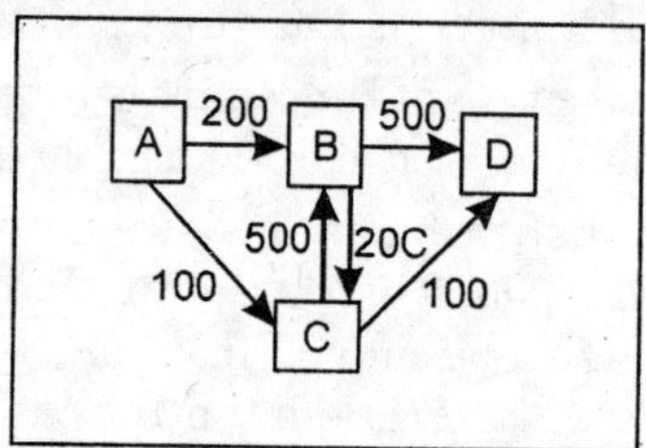

Fig 18.16 An economical layout plotted from the study of Travel chart. It shows amount of handling at various individual work stations.

Use of Travel Chart

1. To analyse material handling and plan department locations.
2. To compare layouts and to determine their efficiency.
3. To plan materials handling procedure and routes.
4. To shorten manufacturing cycles.
5. To reduce work in progress.
6. To reduce work labour costs.
7. To assist improving materials handling procedure.
8. To determine relative self-sufficiency of various areas and to decide end use of components.
9. To determine inventory control difficulties.
10. To make economical use of available areas.

18.14. ANALYTICAL TOOLS OF PLANT LAYOUT

This is a procedure of making the layout of the plant or making improvement in the existing layout with the help of a number of tools and techniques. In this a plan showing the position of machines, flow of work and materials handling devices etc. is prepared to a scale on a drawing sheet or floor.

The various tools and techniques used for preparation of plant layout are described in short below—

(*a*) Flow process chart.

(*b*) Process flow diagram,

(*c*) Machine data card.

(d) Templates

(e) Scale models.

(a) **Flow Process Chart.** This is a graphic representation of sequence of operations, transportation, inspection, delays and storage occurring during manufacture. This gives the information regarding distance moved and time required for various activities such as transportation, delays and inspection etc. This chart helps in determining hidden efficiencies in the process and may suggest rearrangement of layout.

This also points out elimination of unnecessary movements and processes.

(b) **Process Flow Diagram.** It is the diagram of the building plant representing graphically the movement of materials on the layout drawing. With its help proper material handling arrangements can be made and it indicates long material hauls and back tracking of present layout, which thereby helps in improving the layout.

(c) **Machine Data Cards.** These cards give complete specification of each machine to be installed such as output capacity, foundations, space needed, methods of operation, maintenance and handling devices of machines etc.

(d) **Templates.** After studying the flow process chart, process flow diagram and machines data cards a floor plan is prepared by fixing the area occupied by each item to be erected in the shops. This floor plan is prepared at certain scale, say 1 $cm^2 = 1\ m^2$. Now from thick sheets of paper or card board on the same scale, pieces of sheet are cut (known as templates) to represent various items which are to be housed in the plant and are placed on the floor plan at suitable places. These templates are so arranged as to give best layout.

These make the layout visual before actually drawn and is carefully examined. The changes, if any, required are made before making the actual layout drawing.

(e) **Scale Models.** It is an improvement over the template methods. In this tools, instead of templates, use of three dimensional scale model is made. These models may be of wood or metal and when used on a layout, series of additional informations about the height and of the projected parts of the machines are obtained. This is similar to a child's doll house.

This technique is useful for complex layout, requiring huge initial investment.

In conclusion, plant layout is an important consideration. Hence various experts such as production engineer, material handling engineer safety engineer and work study engineer etc. should all sit together to arrive for final best layout.

18.15. LAYOUT OF SERVICES

The tool rooms, store rooms, water, power, transportations, cafeteria, wash rooms and lavatories etc., include the service centre of a plant. The shorter the distance from the operations to these centres the less time will be consumed by workers in using these services. Generally the service centers are located where the space is available after planning for manufacturing. The exact location is determined by its nature, number of persons to avail such a service and how much any service is made use of.

The factors affecting the labour of most important service centres such as store room, transportation, water, power and fire protection are as under :

1. **Store Room.** Store room layout as far as possible should satisfy the following essential requirements :

(*i*) It should provide an easy receipt, storage, issue and inspection of materials.

(*ii*) It should have enough storage capacity and facilities.

(*iii*) It should have proper protection against wastage, damage,deterioration and thefts etc.

(*iv*) It should permit easy and clear identification and location of materials.

(*v*) It should be simple and servicable.

(*vi*) It should have bins of proper width for handling the materials.

2. **Transportation.** Transportation required in the factory premises is for different purposes, such as transportation of materials and equipment, transportation of labourers and other employees and transportation of products, proper consideration is essential so that the layout is economical and convenient. For more details, chapter on material handling may be consulted.

3. **Water.** The layout of the water service is very necessary consideration. For this purpose, certain provisions are given in the FACTORY ACT, those must strictly be followed. According to Factory Act, in every factory in which more than 250 workers are employed water coolers should be installed at suitable places. The water centres should be marked by the work DRINKING WATER. Water centres should be located at least 6 m from latrines, urinals and washrooms. There should be one water centre for every 150 workers upto 500 workers and one centre for every additional 500 workers.

4. **Power.** The electrical energy required for running the plants may be purchased from an outside source or generated itself. The electric energy is transformed into mechanical power and is supplied to the machines and equipments in the following two ways :

   (*a*) Group Drive

   (*b*) Individual Drive.

   Today individual drive is generally adopted. So in the layout, it is to be seen that from where electrical cables will pass and where protecting devices, switches, starters and control panels are to be fixed.

5. **Fire Protection.** For this, suitable places must be allotted in the shop for locating water buckets, sand buckets and fire extinguishers. Inflammable materials must be kept in separate store at a safe distance, minimum 15 m from the general storage.

   In the layout, provision to escape, in case of fire, must be kept. A factory employing more than 20 persons and storing inflammable materials and explosives must arrange for training of persons regarding the routine to be adopted in case of fire.

QUESTIONS

1. What are the factors that are considered for selecting a site for a factory?
2. Discuss how site of a factory would influence the production cost.
3. Give the comparative advantages and disadvantages of big city and small city in plant location.
4. For what type of factory single storey building is preferred to the multi-storey building? Discuss.
5. Name and discuss the factors which you need for the selection of a plant site.
6. It is generally felt that "rural areas are good for locating large plants, semi-urban areas for locating medium sized plants and urban areas for small scale plants". Comment.

7. Discuss how plant layout and materials handling method depends on the nature product and the quantity of manufacture, give examples.
8. Distinguish fully between the product layout and the process layout of shop.
9. What is the difference between functional and product layout of machines ? State advantages of functional layout and product layout of machines.
10. Explain the importance of "Travel chart" in effective layout of a production plant.
11. Discuss the different principles of plant layout in the industry.
12. With suitable sketches of the travel chart, explain how it can be used for reorienting the existing layout of a plant and subsequent mechanisation of its handling system.
13. (*a*) Explain with the help of an example, how a "Process flow chart" could be used to prepare the layout of any factory.
    (*b*) State any other techniques which could be used for the above purpose.
    (*c*) State the advantages of a well-designed factory layout.
14. Identify of tools and techniques of plant layout. Explain how manufacturing plant handling equipment and type of buildings are inter-related in the development of the factory layout.
15. Sketch the "layout" you will recommend for the "foundry shop" of an automobile manufacturing concern, showing locations of important installations in the foundry. Make any assumptions required for the layout and suggest how you will justify your recommendation.
16. Explain "Product Layout" and "Process Layout". Discuss factors which influence the selection of one or the other.
17. Discuss the factors which influence the layout of a plant manufacturing nuts and bolts. on a mass production basis.
18. Discuss the relative merits of analytical and synthetic systems of layout. What system of layout will you recommend for the following and why?
    (*i*) Bicycle manufacturing unit,
    (*ii*) Ordinance unit manufacturing tanks, and
    (*iii*) Ship building unit.
19. Explain briefly the basic principles involved in preparing the layout of an industrial plant, indicating the important techniques available for the purpose.
20. (*a*) What information is necessary for determining a suitable layout for a plant?
    (*b*) Discuss the advantage and limitations of the process layout.
21. (*a*) What information is necessary for planning a plant layout or revising an existing one? How will you proceed to prepare a plan for such a layout or revising an existing one? How will you proceed to prepare a plan for such a layout ?
    (*b*) What are steps in designing such a layout ?
22. State the principles governing the layout of
    (*i*) storage facilities, (*ii*) fire protection and (*iii*) power in a large factory.
23. (*a*) What information is necessary for planning a plant layout or revising an existing one?
    (*b*) What are steps in designing such a layout?
24. Define "Plant layout" Explain the important objects of specific plant layout.
25. Explain different methods of plant layout. Which type of layout should be used in a cotton mill? Explain.
26. What are the possible advantages of scientific layout.

19

DECISION—MAKING

19.1. INTRODUCTION

Decision making is the most important job of management and we can say that good decision making ability is the key to a successful career in management. As managers are required to take decisions very frequently, and efficiency of concern, loss or profit, environment is affected by these decisions, great amount of attention is being paid to this process now-a-days.

In general, decisions are the output of the following inputs:

1. Knowledge and information.
2. Ability and skill regarding,
   (*a*) Communication,
   (*b*) Analytical, and
   (*c*) Conceptual.
3. Value System:
   (*a*) Opinions,
   (*b*) Attitudes,
   (*c*) Habits, and
   (*d*) Belief

The task of management involves large number of decisions. For example, in starting a factory some of the decisions which are to be taken by the management are: what is to be produced ? How much to produce? What must be the organisation set up ? Where to install this factory? How and which type of workers to be employed ? How the raw material is to be procured? What must be the specifications and the quality of the raw material ? From where this raw material is to be procured? Where to sell the final product ? What should be the selling price of the product ? Number of varieties of the products to be produced, and so many other decisions are to be taken by the manager. List of these questions itself shows that how much these decisions may affect the working of whole of the factory.

Decision Making Defined

Thus we see that main function of the administration and management is to make decisions and to see that these are being carried out, not only in the starting of a concern but also in the course of running a plant, large number of decisions are required to be taken. Such problems may arise due to the changes in the situations and due to other unforeseen circumstances during the course of production. These problems can be solved through decision making for proper running of the concern. Such problem may be related to organisational structure, procedure, coordination, division of work and responsibility, deviation of quality standard, reduction in output etc.

"Decision-Making" implies commitment of something—a point of a view, a principle and course of action etc.

In other words, a decision is a course of action or inaction selected to meet the requirements of a solution of problem.

"Decision-making" is an intellectual activity, because it calls for both judgement and imagination to select one from among many alternatives.

A "Decision" is something that takes place prior to the actual performance of the action that has been decided upon.

Decision-making can also be defined as, an act of choice, wherein a manager forms a conclusion about what must be done under a given situation. A decision represents a course of behaviour chosen from a mumber of possible alternatives.

Decision-Making and Management

As explained above, it is the power of decision which affects the efficiency, working and profitability of the concern. Thus management should take correct decisions at correct time. Sometimes this work becomes more complicated when there are more than one alternative solutions of a problem. Manager must be able to select one best alternative.

Some persons are of the opinion that capacity for making decision is a God gift and training cannot develop it in him, if he is not having this capacity originally. But others are of opinion that of course, good decision makers must be intelligent from the beginning but with practice, experience and training he can improve his decision making ability and can become a very good manager.

Fig. 19.1 explains the Management System using "Decision Making" as its central focus. The various sub systems are involved in different types of decisions but they do not act independently.

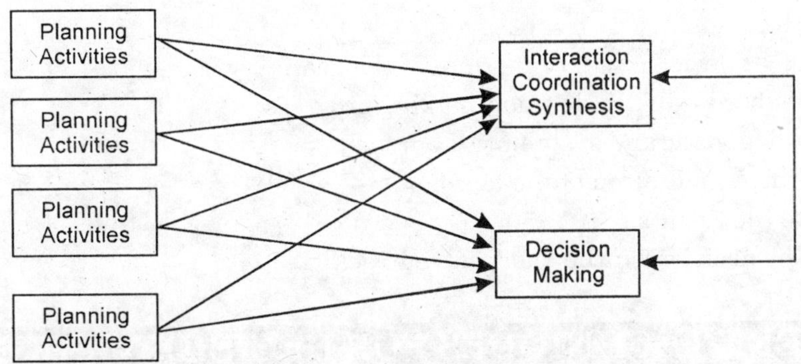

Fig. 19.1. Management system using Decision Making as its central focus.

Characteristics of Good Decisions

The main characteristics of decision-making are:

(*i*) It is the choice of the best course among the alternatives.

(*ii*) It is the end process proceeded by deliberation and reasonings.
(*iii*) It is associated with commitment.
(*iv*) It is rational.
(*v*) These relate the means to the end.
(*vi*) Evaluation process exists in every course of decision making.
(*vii*) These may be negative and may just be not to decide.

Problem and Opportunity Finding

(A) **Problem Finding.** A problem arises when an actual state of affairs differ from a desired state of affairs. The problems may be of following types :
  (*i*) Deviation from past experience
  (*ii*) Deviation from plan
  (*iii*) Performance of competitors
  (*iv*) Other people creating a problem.

(B) **Opportunity Finding.** Opportunities are the situations that occur when circumstances offer the chance to the stated goals and objectives.

Biases in Decision-Making

In human decision-making most times, managers use 'heuristics', *i.e.*, the rules of thumb and use intuitive sense. But this leads to a number of biases. Some of the most common biases are:
(*i*) Easy recall.
(*ii*) Easy search.
(*iii*) Overrating the importance of representative information.
(*iv*) Smaller size of the sample.
(*v*) Arriving at decisions by adjusting some initial values.
(*vi*) Over-confidence.

Guidelines for Effective Decision-Making

Following guidelines must be followed for effective decision-making:
- Define the goals.
- Ensure that decision will contribute to the goal.
- Involve subordinates in decision-making progress.
- Adopt a diagnostic and systematic approach.
- Ensure implementation of the decision.
- Evaluate the results.
- Revise the decision on the basis of feed back.

19.2. MODERN TECHNIQUES FOR DECISION-MAKING

In actual practice, all the Non-programmed decisions are made with some amount of uncertainty. However, its degree may vary depending upon its extent of certainty and uncertainty. Thus there are certain risks involved in decision making.

There are number of modern techniques which can be used to improve the quality of decision making under the normal conditions of uncertainty. Among them most important are:

(*i*) risk analysis,

(*ii*) decision trees, and

(*iii*) preference theory.

1. **Risk Analysis**

   In risk analysis, decision-maker wants to know the size and nature of risk involved in the decision and degree of probability of success. Decision tree technique depicts the decision points, chance events, and probabilities involved in various courses that might be undertaken. In preference or utility theory, preferences are decided on the basis of attitude towards risk, personal risk and probability that the risk of decision being wrong.

2. **Decision Tree**

   Decision tree is one of the best way to analyze a decision. These are a useful way of modelling decisions that involve a progression of decisions, each with outcomes that include uncertainty. Decision trees, in the form of a tree, depict:

   (*a*) the decision points

   (*b*) chance events, and

   (*c*) probabilities involved in various courses that might be undertaken.

   Decision tree approach makes it possible to analyze atleast the major alternatives and the fact that subsequent decisions may depend on events in the future. By assigning the probabilities of various events in the tree, managers can also comprehend the true probability of decision leading to the desired results.

3. **Preference Theory (or Utility Theory)**

   This theory is based on the notion that individual attitude varies towards risk. Some persons are willing to take only smaller risks and avoid major risks, while others are willing to take greater risks. According to the preference theory, purely statistical probabilities, as applied to decision-making, rest on the assumption that decision makers will follow them.

   Managers avoid risk if the penalty of being wrong is severe (monetary loss, job security or reputation). Decision-maker's aversion or acceptance of risk depends upon the probability of risk and his attitude toward risk. Higher-level managers are accustomed to take larger risks. Most managers are risk averters and hence miss opportunities.

19.3. CURRENT TRENDS IN DECISION-MAKING

1. Increasing use of tools and models in decision making.
2. Increasing use of behavioural science to the problems of administrative decisions.
3. Greater use of computer applications and advancement in management information systems, which is the backbone of decision making process.
4. Conceptualisation of administration decision as a complex system of processes, activities and sub-system under dynamic conditions.
5. Development of theories, analytical concepts, and models based upon research findings.

19.4. CLASSIFICATION OF DECISIONS

Decisions can be classified in the following ways:

1. Major and Minor decisions.
2. Routine and strategic decisions.
3. Policy and oprating decisions.
4. Programmed and unprogrammed decisions.
5. Departmental and non-economic decisions.
6. Organisational and personal decisions.

1. **Major and Minor Decisions.** These can be categorised on the basis of their intensity. For example. purchase of a new precision machine of worth Rs. 5 lacs is categorised as major decision, while purchase of stationery (pencil, papers. pens etc.) for office use will be the minor decision.
2. **Routine and Strategic Decisions.** The decisions which arise during the course of production and are settled on the basis of past practice termed as "Routine decision". For example, deputing a worker in a particular shift is a routine decision while "Lock out" of the factory or stopping the production of one item in the factory are "strategic decision".
3. **Policy and Operating Decisions.** Whether the piece rate system or time rate system to be followed in the factory for calculating the wages of the workers is the "policy decision" and is required to be taken at high level. While the calculation of the wages is the example of "operating decision".
4. **Programmed and Unprogrammed Decisions.** These are classified on the basis of procedure adopted. Programmed decisions are those which are repetitive and of routine nature for which definite procedures have to be worked out, *e.g.*, granting of earned leave to the workers, allowing overtime work to a certain worker, allowing annual increment to workers etc. Unprogrammed decisions are those, which are taken at the time when they arise because this or similar problems have not arisen earlier. Example of such decision is whether to stop or to start manufacturing any particular product.
5. **Departmental and Non-Economic Decisions.** These are taken by the departmental heads and relate to the individual departments only. Decisions relating to the non-economic factors such as technical values, normal behaviour etc. may be known as non-economic decisions.
6. **Organisational and Personal Decisions.** When the managers take decisions in their official capacity, it is termed that they have taken on organisational decision. On the other hand, personal decisions relate to the manager as an individual and not as member of the organisation.

19.5. PROCEDURE OF DECISION MAKING

Good decisions can only be made if following steps are taken before making decisions:

1. Recognising and analysing the problems.
2. Finding relevant facts.
3. Determining possible alternatives.
4. Evaluating the impact of alternatives.

5. Selecting the best solutions.
6. Implementation of the decisions.

1. **Recognising and Analysing the Problems.** The main job of a manager is to find out the real problem before arriving at a decision. There may be a large number of symptoms that could indicate real issue. Hence first step is to recognise and identify the real problem, and not simply the symptoms. It is just like a job of Physician analysing all the symptoms before identifying the cause of illness. For example, a manager notices a symptom of reduction in production. The problem is to find out why production is declining, whether it is due to reduction in the availability of raw material, power, labour crisis, rising inefficiency in the plant or in employees.

   To solve the difficult problems many managers normally break a problem into its parts for easier diagnosis and solution. For this, generally different factors responsible for each part are found and seen whether it is controllable and, who will control and how it is to be controlled.

2. **Finding Relevant Facts.** After recognising and analysing the problems, next step is to collect all the relevant data. A decision must always be based on facts instead of guesses and random thinking. As, such decisions, taken on the basis of facts, reduce the degree of uncertainty and risk, this also helps the manager to know the probable results of the decision.

3. **Determining Possible Alternatives.** Generally, problems have more than one alternative and it is very rare that a problem has only one solution. To find out possible solution, manager has to keep an open mind because he must not consider only one solution which he wants to implement, he must consider all the possible solutions including competitor's solutions or those used in the past.

   After developing different alternatives next step in decision making is to evaluate the consequences of each proposed alternatives.

4. **Evaluating the Impact of Alternatives.** This is a very important function of decision maker, as decision depends very much on the skill and care used in evaluating each alternative. After listing alternative solutions, decision maker must mentally put it into effect and visualise the impact of the alternatives and thus he forecasts what will happen if a certain alternative is adopted. While evaluating the impact of alternatives, manager must keep in mind all the limitations of the concern.

5. **Selecting the Best Solution.** Best solution is then selected by comparing the merits and demerits, gains and losses etc. of each alternative. Decision maker must also consider degree of risk, availability of resources, limitations and time required for implementation.

6. **Implementation of Decisions.** After selecting a best solution, it is required to be converted into effective action. Actually manager makes the decision but he himself does not apply it. Hence the decision must be communicated to the persons applying it in a simple, clear and easily understandable language. For better implementation it is necessary that subordinates must feel sense of participation, for which they may be associated at some stage in decision making process. In the beginning manager himself must take personal interest in implementing the decision.

19.6. DECISION UNDER CERTAINTY

The decisions may be taken as discussed before when the problems are under certainty, *i.e.*, where a complete knowledge about the nature of future conditions is known. Let us take a simple example:

Example 19.1. *In a firm having a contract to build a dam across a river requiring 300,000 cubic meters of gravel, found two feasible sources whose characteristics are given below:*

	Source A	*Source B*
Distance between source and dam site	*1.8 km*	*0.6 km*
Cost of gravel per cubic meter at source	...	*Rs. 80*
Purchase price of pit	*Rs. 7,200,000*	...
Road construction necessary	*Rs. 2,400,000*	*None*
Overburden to be removed at Rs. 240/- per cubic meter	...	*60,000 cu m.*
Hauling cost per meter per km as tendered by hauling contractor	*Rs. 72*	*Rs. 84.*

Solution. To make decision on the basis of economy, the cost of securing the required gravel from either source should be determined.

Source A

For 300,000 cubic meters of gravel

Purchase price of pit	= Rs. 7,200,000
Road construction	= Rs. 2,400,000
Hauling cost 300,000 × 1.8 @ Rs. 72 per cubic meter per/km.	= Rs. 39,900,000
Total	= Rs. 48,500,000

Source B

Cost of gravel at pit 300,000 cubic meters	= Rs. 24,000,000
Removal of overburden 60,000 cubic meters	= Rs. 14,400,000
Hauling cost 300,000 × 0.6 km × 84 per cu. metre/km	= Rs. 15, 100,000
Total	= Rs. 53,500,000

Thus the decision must be in favour of Source *A* on the basis of economic analysis.

As every body knows that now-a-days a businessman or manager is unable to have a complete idea about the future conditions which may arise in near future, such problems when exist, the decision making by manager is known as decision making under uncertainty.

19.7. DECISION UNDER UNCERTAINTY

When such condition of uncertainty is there then, to make decision, a businessman or a manager has two alternatives. First one is to apply some short cut method such as thumb rules etc. When it is found that the future is so unpredictable that no refined analysis is possible; the other alternative is to deal systematically with uncertainty itself, with careful use of probabilities in addition to the application of statistics whenever possible. In general, it is always better to have an intermediate position between the above two alternatives, to avoid the minute analysis of every element of uncertainty. Now it is very clear that theory of probability plays an important role while making decision under the condition of uncertainty. The condition of uncertainty can easily by understood by following example:

Example 19.2. *A classical example of seasonal articles is very useful for understanding. If a seller is selling crackers in the Deepawali season, the uncertainty is about the demand, the seller does not know how many packets of crackers he will be able to sell during the Deepawali season. This problem is of inventory decision.*

Following assumptions are made:

1. *No additional packet should be ordered after the selling season starts.*
2. *Unsold crackers will involve a total loss.*
3. *The cost of each packet to the seller is Rs. 10.00 and profit earned by him on each packet is Rs. 10.00*

The seller's estimate of sales are as follows:

100 per cent chance if he has 1000 packets.

75 per cent chance if he has 1300 packets.

50 per cent chance if he has 1500 packets.

25 per cent chance if he has 1800 packets.

0 per cent chance if he has 2400 packets.

Now the problem is that how many packets the seller should stock.

Solution. Now, by analysing the problem it is clear that if the seller stocks too few packets, he loses the profit of Rs. 10 per packet, if he stocks too many, then he must suffer Rs. 10 on each unsold packet. Thus it is quite reasonable that he should keep stock of packets upto the point at which the probability of having too many packets is equal to the probability of having too few. This is the point of 50 per cent probability, at which 1500 packets are to be stocked.

Suppose the margin of profit is higher, in that case, the seller should take more risk, because now the reward for having packets on hand is potentially greater per packet than the penalty for having too many. If in our example, the profit is Rs. 30.00 per packet, it would be desirable to stock 1800 packets. It is true that at this level, the chances of having too many crackers (75%) and it is three times as great as those of having too few (25%), but this is in proportion to the relative reward and penalties.

The probability can easily be found by the use of following formula:

$$p = \frac{x}{x+y}$$

where p = Probability that this quantity will be sold

x = Loss per unit on quantity unsold

y = Profit per unit.

From the above example we have seen that a table of probabilities has to be made, which causes the main difficulty. Though past experience may help the seller to formulate his probabilities, but the past is often a misleading guide to the future. If the past sales were irregular, fluctuating from year to year then a statistical problem is developed for formulating the probabilities table.

It is desirable to point out here that most inventory problems do not involve as great uncertainty as that of above problem. In most of cases, the companies will have some fairly continuous experience, so that probabilities can be established more firmly.

As already said that in most of the cases, uncertainty always occur, this fact can easily be understandable by the MIN-MAX INVENTORY CONTROL, in which the company uses the stocked items continuously but wishes to know how much it should stock.

Min-Max Inventory Control

This problem is more typical than previous one, because there is continuous consumption of inventory, with uncertainty about how much to keep on hand to meet the needs with minimum cost. As discussed before, the cost of keeping too small quantity is the loss of sales that will cause shortage of stock from time to time. The cost of too large quantity consists of storage cost, interest on the money involved, and the risk of obsolescence. The lot size (the economical lot size or the economical ordering quantity dealt in the chapter 'Materials Management and Inventory Control') will help in determining the quantity required at particular moment, since it will indicate the quantity added to the inventory.

Now in min-max inventory control two points are to be known, *i.e.*, reorder point and the quantity to be ordered. If there is no uncertainty, the graph between the time and the balance in hand is as shown in Fig. 19.2

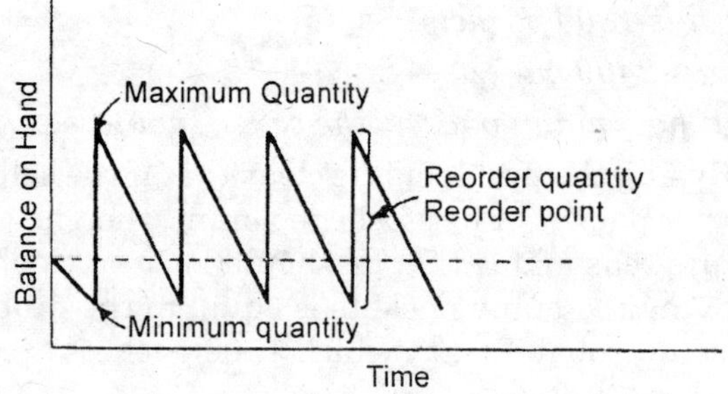

Fig. 19.2: Graph between the balance in hand and time under the condition of certainty

In this case, when the quantity in hand falls to the reorder point, an order must be placed for the ordered quantity. Since there is no uncertainty, this ordered quantity will arrive just as the stock at hand falls to minimum. Then with the new arrival, the stock position reaches to maximum (*i.e.*, minimum + order quantity = maximum). As consumption continues, the stock will again fall towards the reorder point.

But under uncertainty, this is not the situation. As if no uncertainty is there, there is no need to maintain the minimum quantity, *i.e.*, safe reserve at all, because the new order would arrive exactly on time, when inventory falls to zero. Now under uncertainty there are two types of uncertainty: uncertainty about the rate of consumption of inventory and uncertainty about the amount of time required for delivering the new order. The consumption increases with the demand and slows down in period of decline in sales. The time required for supplying depends upon the supplier and on the transportation of facilities ~ these are subjected to uncertainty. Further if the parts stored are manufactured by the company itself, there is uncertainty due to the bottleneck in production, breakdown in machines and so on.

This is clear that min-max inventory control involved uncertainty, thus to solve such problem the theory of probability is used. Now the pattern of graph (Fig.19.2 changes to graph shown in Fig. 19.3

The graph shown in Fig. 19.3 shows that inventory will fall below the minimum, even down to the zero, because of rapid consumption or delay in the delivery of ordered quantity. Many times the inventory will reach above the maximum, because the slower consumption after the order was placed, or because of rapid delivery.

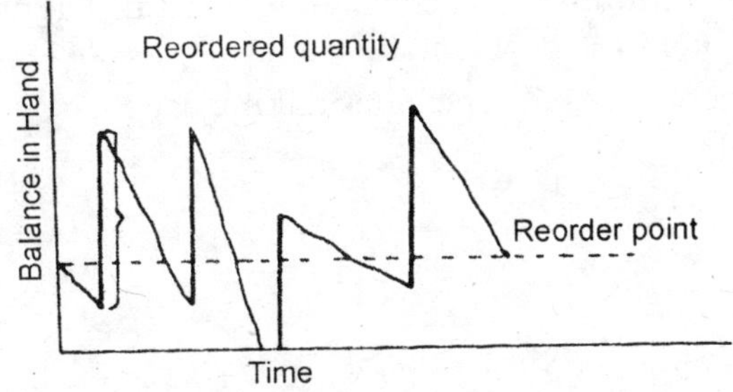

Fig. 19.3: Graph between the balance in hand and the time under the condition of uncertainty.

The computation required for reordering point and ordered quantity is quite tedious and complicated, which requires lengthy statistical procedures and is beyond the scope of this book.

19.8. GROUP DECISION–MAKING

Group decision-making is the decision-making with the active participation by involving subordinates. It helps in introducing a change, enhances their sense of belongingness, and improves the environment in the organisation. As this is an urge of the employees working in an organisation for their involvement in decision-making, therefore group decision- making unfreezes the fixed and formed attitude and creates a good and healthy work culture. The group develops certain standards and norms of conduct and those individuals who fail to live up to these standards are subject to pressure to conform to these standards.

Participative Management in the form of Quality circles, shop floor Councils etc. are also sort of group (collective) decision-making. For details, readers may refer the chapter on "Participative Management".

19.9. TOOLS FOR DECISION-MAKING

Following tools or techniques are common for decision-making:

1. Break-even Analysis.
2. Value Analysis.
3. Locational Analysis.
4. Make or Buy.
5. Equipment Replacement Analysis.
6. Linear Programming.
7. Transportational Problems.
8. Waiting line or Queuing Theory
9. Simulation.
10. Dynamic Programming

(Items 6–10:) *Dealt under heading "Operation Research"* .

11. Inventory Management–Dealt in chapter on "Materials Management".
12. Capital Investment Analysis Dealt in chapter on Financial Management".

Quantitative Techniques for Decision-Making:

Application of quantitative techniques to management decision-making reduces the risk and uncertainty the manager confronts. These techniques have been discussed in the book. These techniques when used with computer, help the manager to take right decisions, being scientific methods to the solution of business problems.

Various quantitative techniques for decision-making are :

(*i*) Inventory Control.
(*ii*) Break-Even Analysis
(*iii*) Linear Programming
(*iv*) Budgeting
(*v*) Waiting line theory
(*vi*) Game Models
(*vii*) Transportation Models
(*viii*) Decision Tree
(*ix*) Simulation.

19.10. OPERATION-RESEARCH

It is the method of analysis by which management receives aid for their decisions. Though the name of the method, Operation Research (O.R.) is relatively new, but the method used for this is not a new one. Operation Research is concerned with the application of the principles and the methods of science to the problems of strategy. The subject of operation research was born during second World War in U.K. and was used for military strategy. During World War II a group of scientists, having representatives from mathematics, statistics, physical and social sciences were entrusted the study of various military operations. This team was very successful and greatly contributed to the meticulous handling of entire operation and related problems of the operation. The need for assigning such studies for operations had arisen because military strategies and their decisions became so important and costly that the best scientists, under the sponsorship of military organs were grouped together to provide quantitative informations by adopting scientific techniques and methods for facilitating in taking decisions.

After the World War II, it was started applying in the fields of industry, trade, agriculture, planning and various other fields of economy. The operation research can be defined as:

Definitions

(*i*) It is the application of scientitic methods, techniques and tools to problems involving the operations of a system so as to provide those in the control of the system with optimum solutions to the problems.

(*ii*) Operation Research is a tool for taking decisions which searches the optimum in parity with the overall objectives and constraints of the organisation.

(*iii*) It is the application of the scientific methods by scientists and subject specialists to the study of the given operation. Its purpose is to give administration, a basis for predicting quantitatively the most effective results of an operation under given set of variable conditions and thereby to provide a sound basis for decision making.

(*iv*) Operation Research is a scientific method of providing executive department with a quantitative basis of decisions regarding the operations under their control.

(*v*) Operation Research is a scientific approach to problem solving for executing management.

(*vi*) Operation Research is the application of modern methods of mathematical science to complex problems involving management of large systems of men, machines, materials, and money in industry, business, government and defence. The distinctive approach is to develop a scientific model of the system incorporating measurement of factors such as chance and risk, to predict and compare the outcome of alternative decisions, strategies or controls.

(*vii*) Operation Research is an aid for executive in making his decisions by providing him with the needed quantitative informations based on the scientific method of analysis.

In fact in Operation Research, research technique and scientific methods are employed for the analysis and also for studying the current or future problems. Thus Operation Research offers alternative plans for a problem to the management for decision. Although it is very clear that Operation Research never makes decisions for the management. Instead, the method presents management with a careful scientific and quantitative analysis of problem so that the management will be in a better position to make sounder decision.

Operation Research can be used for solving different types of problems, such as:

1. Problems dealing with the waiting line, the arrival of units or persons requiring service.
2. Problems dealing with the allocation of material or activities among limited facilities.
3. Equipment replacement problems.
4. Problems dealing with production processing, *i.e.*, production control, balance and material shipment.

But it may be remembered that *O.R.* never replaces a manager as decision maker. The ultimate and full responsibility for analysing all factors and making decision will be with the manager.

In the more wider sense, *O.R.* does not solve the every day problems such as output by one worker or machine capacity, instead it is concerned with the overall aspect of business operation- such as the relationship between inventory, sales, production and scheduling. It may also deal with the overall flow of goods and services from plants to consumers.

The team doing operation research may have statistician, psychologist, labour specialists, mathematician and others depending upon the requirement for the problems.

Various Phases in Operation Research Study

The main objective of operation research is to provide better quantitative information for making decision. Now our aim is to learn how we can have better decision. The procedure for making decision with the OR study generally involves the following phases:

1. **Judgement Phase:**
   (*i*) Determination of operation
   (*ii*) Determination of objectives.
   (*iii*) Determination of effectiveness of measures
   (*iv*) Determination of type of problem, its origin and causes.
2. **Research Phase:**
   (*i*) Observation and data collection for better understanding of the problem.
   (*ii*) Formulation of relevant hypothesis and models.
   (*iii*) Analysis of available information and verification of hypothesis.
   (*iv*) Production and generation of results and consideration of alternatives.
3. **Action Phase:**
   (*i*) Recommendations for remedial action to those who first, posed the problem, this includes the assumptions made, scope and limitations, alternative courses of action and their effect.
   (*ii*) Putting the solution to work: implementation.

In many cases, we follow these points in full, but in other cases we leave of important steps out. Judgement and subjective decision making can be all right, but they often are not good enough. Thus industries look to operation research for more objective way to make decision. It is found that method used should consider the emotional and subjective factors also. For example, the skill and creative labour are important factors in our business and if management wants to have a new location, the management has to consider the personal feeling of the employees for the location which it chooses. A location problem solved under chapter 'Locational Economics' shows how such factors are considered in their economic light.

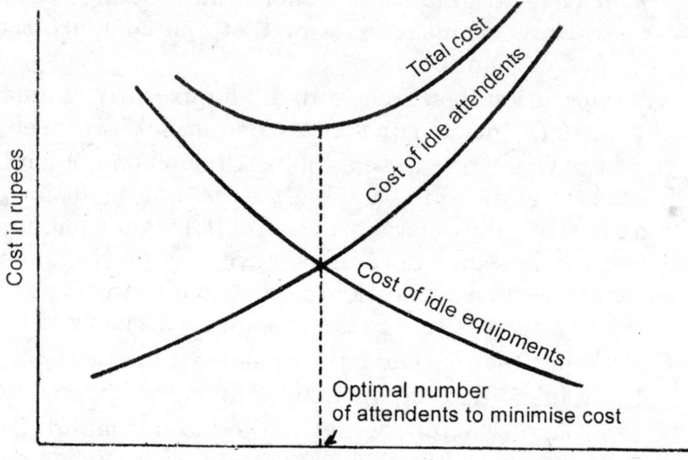

Fig. 19.4

To have a more clear idea as to how the *O.R.* methods are utilised in making decisions let us take a waiting line problem. The main problem of waiting line generally occurs in maintenance department where there is always a formation of queues because by nature the maintenance operation is an inefficient operation. To avoid the waiting line if we employ many attendants, then cost of keeping them is expensive, if we have few, then cost of idle equipments is again considerable.

This can easily be judged from Fig. 19.4

If in a firm, from the past record it is found that 50 machines are to be repaired per day. Now the problem is that how many attendants must be employed in the maintenance department economically. An analysis is done by finding the cost and the idle time when, 1, 2, 3, 4 attendants are employed, the computation is as follows :

Number of maintenance men	*1*	*2*	*3*	*4*
Average number of m/cs needing repair/day	50	50	50	50
Average idle time of each machine waiting for repair	30 min	20 min	10 min	6 min
Total idle time for all m/cs per day	25 hrs	16 2/3 hrs.	8 1/3 hrs	5 hrs
Let average down time cost per hr per m/c	Rs. 20	Rs. 20	Rs. 20	Rs. 20
Total down time cost for all machines per day	Rs. 500	Rs. 333.33	Rs. 166.67	Rs. 100
Average wages paid to maintenance man per day @ Rs. 10 per hour with day of 8 working hours	Rs. 80	Rs. 160	Rs. 240	Rs. 320
Total cost per day for repair and machine idle time	Rs. 580	Rs. 493.33	Rs. 406.67	Rs. 420

Now looking at the above solution with all cost considerations, it will be most economical for the firm to employ three maintenance men.

Scope of Operation Research

In its recent years of organised development O.R. has emerged successfully for different cases of research for military, the government and industry. The basic problem in most of the developing countries in Asia and Africa is to remove poverty and hunger as quickly as possible, so there is a great scope for economics, statistics, administrators, politicians and technicians working in a team to solve this problem by an O.R. approach.

On the other hand, with the explosion of population and consequent shortage of food, every country is facing the problem of optimum allocation of land for various crops in accordance with climatic conditions and available facilities. The problem of optimal distribution of water from a resource like a canal for irrigation purposes is faced by developing country. Hence a good amount of scientific work can be done in this direction.

In the field of Industrial Engineering there is a chain of problems, starting from the procurement of material to the dispatch of finished products. Management is always interested on optimizing profits. Hence in order to provide decision on scientific basis, *O.R.* study team considers various alternative methods and their effects on existing system, the *O.R.* approach is equally useful for the economists, administrators, planners, irrigation or agricultural experts and statisticians etc.

O.R. study is complete only when we consider human factors to the alternatives made available. Operations Research is done by a team of scientists or experts from different related disciplines. For example, for solving a problem related to the inventory management, O.R. team must include an engineer who knows about stores and material management, a cost accountant, and mathematician-cum-statistician. For large and complicated problems the team must include, a mathematician, a statistician, one or two engineers, economists, computer programmer and psychologist etc.

Limitations of Operation Research

(*i*) These do not take into account qualitative and emotional factors.

(*ii*) These are applicable to only specific categories of decisions making problems.

(*iii*) These are required to be interpreted correctly.

(*iv*) Due to conventional thinking, changes face lot of resistance from workers and sometimes even from employer.

(*v*) Models are only idealised representation of reality and not be regarded as absolute.

Application of Operation Research

Important fields where operation Research can be applied are being described hereunder:

(*i*) **Inventory Control Models.** Operation Research study involves balancing Inventory costs against one or more of the following costs:

1. Shortage costs
2. Ordering costs

This study helps in taking decision about—

(*a*) How much to purchase

(*b*) When to order

(*c*) Whether to manufacture or to purchase, *i.e.*, make and buy decisions.

The most well known use is in the form of Economic Order Quantity operations for finding economic lot size.

(*ii*) **Waiting Line Models.** These models are used for minimising the waiting time and idle time together with the costs associated therewith. Waiting line models are of two types

(*a*) Queuing theory, which is applicable for determining the number of service facilities and/or the timing for arrivals for servicing

(*b*) Sequencing thereby which is applicable for determining the sequence of the servicing.

(*iii*) **Replacement Models.** These models are used for determining the time of replacement or maintenance of item, which may either

(*i*) become obsolete, or

(*ii*) become inefficient for use, or

(*iii*) become beyond economical to repair or maintain.

(*iv*) **Allocation Models.** These models are used to solve the problems arising when (*a*) there are number of activities which are to be performed and there are number of alternative ways of doing them (*b*) the resources or facilities are limited which do not allow each activity to be performed in best possible way. Thus these models help to combine activities and available resources so as to optimise and get a solution to obtain an overall effectiveness.

(*v*) **Competitive Strategies.** Such type of strategies are adopted where efficiency of decision of one agency is dependent on the decision of another agency. Examples of such strategies are game of cards or chess,where these strategies are termed as "Theory".

(*vi*) **Linear Programming Techniques.** These techniques are used for solving operation problems having many variables subjected to certain restrictions. In such problems objectives are-profit, costs, quantities manufactured etc. whereas restrictions may be *e.g.,*: policies of government, capacity of the plant, demand of the product, availability of raw material, water or power and storage capacity etc.

These techniques are applied to a very wide range of problems. Here only some of the common applications are being mentioned :

(*a*) **Distribution or Transportation Problems.** In such problems various centres with their demand are given and various ware houses with their stock position are also known, then by using linear programming technique we can find out most economical distribution of the products to various centres from various ware houses.

(*b*) **Product Mix.** These techniques can be applied to determine best mix of the products for a plant with available resources, so as to get maximum profit or minimum cost of production.

(*c*) **Production Planning.** These techniques can also be applied to allocate various jobs to different machines so as to get maximum profit or to maximise production or to minimise total production time.

(*d*) **Assignment of Personnel.** Similarly this technique can be applied for assignment of different personnel with different aptitude to different jobs so as to complete the task within a minimum time.

(*e*) **Agricultural Production.** We can also apply this technique to minimise cultivator's profit, involving cultivation of number of items with different returns and cropping time in different type of land having variable fertility.

(*f*) **Financial Applications.** Many financial decision making problems can be solved by using linear programming techniques. Some of them are :

(*i*) To select best portfolio in order to maximise return on investment out of alternative investment opportunities like bonds, stocks etc. Such problems are generally faced by the managers of mutual funds, banks and insurance companies etc.

(*ii*) In deciding financial mix strategies, involving the selection of means for financing firms, projects, inventories etc.

QUESTIONS

1. How does decision making differ under conditions of uncertainty than those of certainty or risk ? Explain with an example.
2. "Decision making is said to be primary function of management". Discuss the process of decision making in the management of an enterprise
3. (*a*) Discuss the role and process of decision in the management of an enterprise.
   (*b*) Explain (*i*) Decision under risk and (ii) Decision under uncertainty.
4. Describe any one method adopted to collect data for decision making.
5. Explain how the operation research help in decision making problems.
6. What is Operation Research?
7. Explain "Decision making" and describe its impact in administration.
8. Define 'Decision Making' and give its characteristics.
9. Write short notes on:
   (*i*) Current trends in decision making.
   (*ii*) Decision making and administration.
10. Distinguish the following:
    (*a*) Major and minor decisions.
    (*b*) Policy and operating decisions.
    (*c*) Routine and strategic decisions.
    (*d*) Organisational and personal decisions.
11. Describe in detail procedure of "Decision-Making".
12. Give examples of decision Making under:
    (*i*) Certainty
    (*ii*) Uncertainty.
13. If a seller is dealing in wax candles in Deepawali season. The uncertainty is about the demand, the seller does not know how many packets he will be able to sell during this season. This problem is of inventory decision.
    Following assumptions are made:
    (*i*) No additional packets should be ordered after the selling season starts.
    (*ii*) Unsold candles will involve 50% loss.
    (*iii*) The cost of each packet to the seller is Rs. 3.00 and profit earned by him on each packet is Re. 1. The seller's estimate of sales are as follows
    100% Chance, if he has 10,000 Packets.

75% Chance if he has 16,000 Packets .
50% Chance, if he has 18,000 Packets.
25% Chance, if he has 25,000 Packets.
0% Chance, if he has 28,000 Packets.
Now the question is, how many packets the seller should stock?

14. Define decision making. How it is different from policy?

15. How will you classify the decisions? Describibe each one of them

16. What are the important decision making techniques? Describe each in brief.

17. (*a*) Mention guidelines for effective decision-making.
(*b*) Describe current trends in decision–making.

20

NETWORK ANALYSIS (TECHNIQUES)

20.1. INTRODUCTION

Network techniques were developed from the 'Milestone Chart' and 'Bar Chart'. These conventional planning methods, because of their inherent limitations could not be used for planning large and complex projects.

The network analysis helps designing, planning, coordinating, scheduling, and in decision - making in order to accomplish the project economically in the minimum available time with the limited available resources.

Network analysis is a system which plans projects by analysing the project activities. Projects are broken down to individual tasks or activities, which are arranged in logical sequence. It is also decided as to which tasks will be performed simultaneously and which others sequentially. A network diagram is then constructed which presents the relationship between all the activities involved. Time, costs and other resoures are allocated to the different activities.

Project work-breakdown methodology enables splitting of project work into hierarchical work-breakdown levels of sub-projects, tasks, work packages and activities. Each activity represents an identifiable lower-level job which consumes time, and resources.

As discussed above, a project consists of a number of activities involving the consumption of labour, time, material and money etc. Many of these activities will be interdependent and the rest can be carried out independently in order to achieve the desired objectives. The project management should not only plan, schedule, co-ordinate and optimize the activities of the various participants in the project effectively but should also identify and watch closely those critical activities which must be completed within their allotted duration, otherwise, the total project completion time will require extension. On the other hand, management should take advantage of those activities which have some spare time and allow flexibility of planning and economic utilization of the resources.

These techniques were developed m 1957 and is suitable for the construction of engineering projects and for scheduling plant maintenance etc. CPM. technique is useful to determine how best to reduce the time required to perform routine production, maintenance and construction and to minimise the direct and indirect expenses. CPM was first used by the research team lead by Morgan R. Walker to determine how best to reduce the time required to perform routme plant overhauling, maintenance and construction work.

With the help of CPM., a manager can know which operation should be started after completing a particular operation and what is the status of the work as related to the scheduled timings. Although, an experienced person may know it but this information, available from the network, helps all concerned. It also tells that at what moment and in which operations time schedules are adhered strictly so that future programme is not affected and where it can be delayed and to what extent, without affecting the last date of completion of project.

Objectives of Network Analysis

Network analysis entails a group of techniques for presenting information relating to time and resources so as to assist in the planning, scheduling, and controlling of projects. The information usually represented by a network includes the sequences, interdependencies, interrelationship, and criticality of various activities of the project. A network analysis has following objectives:

1. Powerful tool of planning, scheduling and control.
2. Shows the inter-relationships of the activities of a project or a programme,
3. Minimise total cost where the cost of delays and cost of resources required to carry out the tasks can be measured.
4. Minimise total time where required, *e.g.*, in maintenance of production line machinery in a factory.
5. Minimisation of idle resources.
6. Minimise production delays.
7. To provide systematic approach in planning and scheduling.
8. Follow an integrated approach and bring about better coordination between the departments.
9. Focuses attention on critical activities of the project.
10. Provides up-to-date status information.
11. Suggests areas for increasing efficiency, reduction of cost.

Applications of Network Techniques

As explained earlier, network analysis the systematic application for planning, scheduling, monitoring and controlling projects or programmes.

Network techniques can be applied to chain of events involving the use of time, labour and physical resources.

Some of other important applications are :

(*a*) Construction/Industrial Projects
(*b*) Planning
(*c*) Assembly line scheduling
(*d*) Budget and auditing
(*e*) Programmes involving several activities
(*f*) Installation of a complex new plant/equipment
(*g*) Research and development
(*h*) Market penetration programmes
(*i*) Strategic and tactical planning
(*j*) Maintenance and overhauling complicated equipment in the plants/factories.
(*k*) Organising of large functions etc.

Unless the project happens to be a very small one, the number of activities involved will be so large that it will be very difficult for the management to keep effective control. Therefore, to deal with large and complex projects or works, a number of management techniques called as 'Network Techniques' have been developed.

A few of the more popular techniques are:

(*a*) Critical Path Method (C.P.M.)

(*b*) Programme Evaluation and Review Technique. (P.E.R.T.)

(*c*) Resource Allocation and Multi-Project Scheduling (R.A.M.P.S.)

Among these, C.P.M. and P.E.R.T. are considered to be most convenient for application to various engineering projects. Their common features are that they make use of the network model for depicting the time plan of the project, apply the critical path concept for determining project duration and identifying critical activities, and employ network analysis techniques for controlling the project time objectives.

Experience has shown the following:

1. C.P.M. is best suited for developing the sub-network of sub-groups and task having activities with deterministic single-time duration.
2. PERT is useful for project feasibility reports and sub-projects or tasks involving uncertainties. In such cases, probabilistic approach of three-times is used for assessing the activity duration.

Scheduling Through Network

A schedule is a work programme, set date-wise in a logical sequence; it is a time table for action. Time scheduling is the process of developing a work programme. It implies programming of the chosen work plan on a calender basis and provides the base against which all progress is measured. Scheduling methodology varies with the planning teachnique and the nature of task to be performed. Simple projects can be scheduled using the 'bar chart methodology'. The 'Line-of-Balance' (LOB) technique is widely accepted for scheduling the repetitive work projects, while network scheduling is suitable for all types of projects.

The method of presentation of a sechedule depends upon the scheduling technique used. Generally, all these techniques use time scale along the horizontal axis. The time scale mostly uses as a 'week' as the unit of time. Each scheduling technique has its own merits and demerits. The sechdules are presented in the bar chart form for ease of comprehension and communication. These charts are supplemented with the appropriate planning technique for monitoring the progress of the projects.

20.2. GANTT CHARTS (BAR CHARTS)

A pictorial chart, also known as the "Bar Chart" was for the first time developed by Henry Gantt around 1900 and is used to deal with complex activities. The bar chart consists of two coordinates, the horizontal represents the time elapsed and the vertical represents the jobs or activities performed. The jobs or activities are shown in the form of bars as shown in Fig. 20.1.

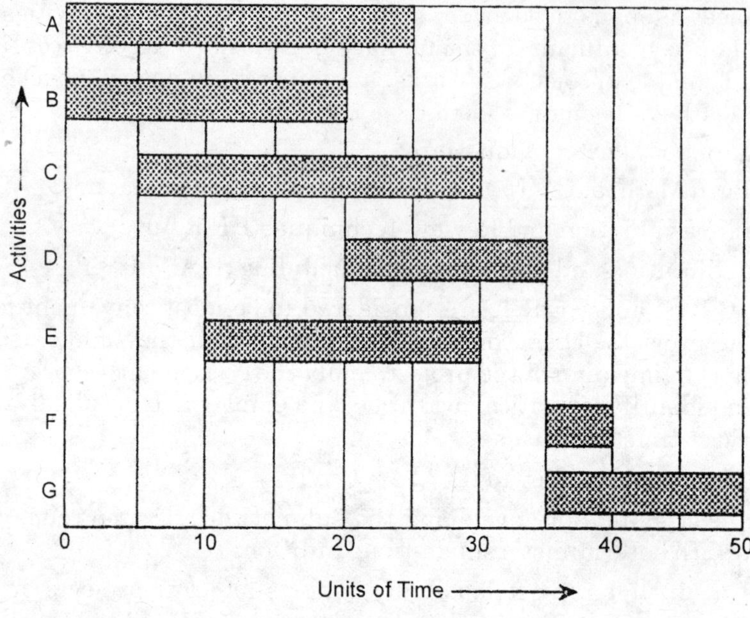

Fig. 20.1.

The length of the bar shows the time a job or that activity takes for completion. In every project some jobs are taken up concurrently and some are to be completed before others begin. Hence in a bar chart, some of the bars run parallel or overlap each other timewise and some run serially with one bar beginning after another bar ends.

In Fig. 20.1 for example, activities *A* and *B* can start at the same time and proceed concurrently or in parallel, though they take different time intervals for their completion. Activity C begins 5 days after the start of activity A and *B*. Activity *D* cannot be started until activity *B* is over. The bars representing *B* and *D*, therefore, run serially.

Limitations of a Bar Chart.

A bar chart may appear to be an excellent pictorial representation of the project, but in actual practice, these have serious limitations. A few of the limitations are :

1. In any project, there are large number of activities which can be started with a certain degree of concurrency, the bar chart cannot indicate clearly the interdependences among the various activities. This is a major limitation. The mere fact that two or more activities are scheduled for simultaneous or overlapping times do not always make them related or inter-dependent or completely independent.

   Suppose a project requires digging foundation, erecting shuttering and concreting activities as follows:

   Digging foundation = 20 days

   Erecting shuttering = 10 days

   Concreting = 12 days

   If the activities are not allowed to run in parallel but in strict sequence, the total time to complete the project will be 42 days. But here, it can be seen that erection of shuttering of side boards can be started after the 12 days work of foundation digging. In the same way, pouring of concrete can begin say, 5 days after the erection of side boards. The bar chart for this is shown in Fig.20.2. According to this plan, the side board erectors will have only 2 days of work after the digging work is over.

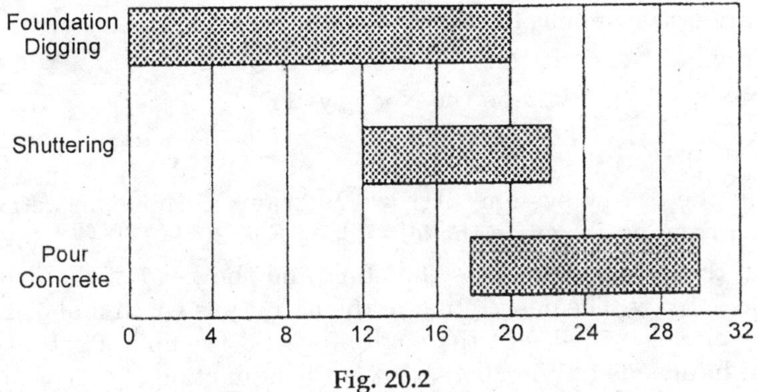

Fig. 20.2

If due to some unexpected difficulties, the digging work is delayed by 8–10 days, how will this reflect on the shuttering or concrete pouring jobs ? This is not indicated by the bar chart.

2. The bar chart does not indicate the progress of work, hence it cannot be used as control device. In a dynamic programme, the knowledge of the amount of work in progress or work completed is very essential. Usual changes in plans are a necessary part of a large project and a bar chart does not give much information under such circumstances.

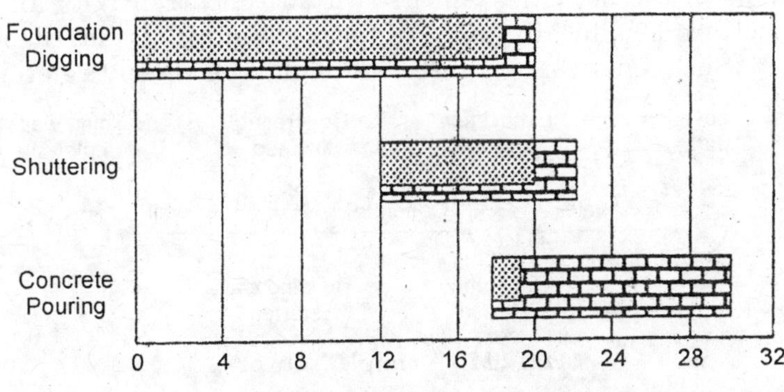

Fig. 20.3 Progress chart

20.3. CRITICAL PATH METHOD

Activity and Events

Activity. A project consists of several activities or operations, and the project is said to be completed when all such activities are completed. Activity is the actual performance of a task. This consumes resources, *i.e.*, time, manpower, space, material, money etc.

Event. It is a start or completion of a task. In other words, an event is an instantaneous point of time at which activity or activities start or finish. This does not consume time or resources.

Following example will clarify the differences between an event and activity:

Start Machine Installation: An event

Machine Installation: An activity

Completion of Machine Installation : An event

Mainly there are two systems of network construction:

1. AOA system, *i.e.*, 'Activity on the Arrow system'.
2. AON system, *i.e.*, 'Activity on the Node system'.

20.3.1. A.O.A. System

In the 'Activity on the Arrow system' (Arrow Diagram Method) an activity is graphically represented by an 'arrow' as shown on the left-side of Fig. 20.4.

The tail end of the arrow represents the start and the head of the arrow represents the finish or end of the activity. The description of the activity is written above the arrow. Events are represented by circles or nodes at the beginning and the end of activity arrow/arrows as shown on the right hand side of Fig. 20.4. An event is a junction of two or more activities.

Fig. 20.4. Representation of activity and event in AOA system.

The simple network shown in Fig. 20.5 clarifies the representation of activities and events In any project, certain activities have to be completed before the commencement of certain other activities. Some of the activities can be started concurrently. If all the activities and events in the project are graphically represented showing their interdependencies, then a Network is obtained. Such a network represents the plan for the entire project.

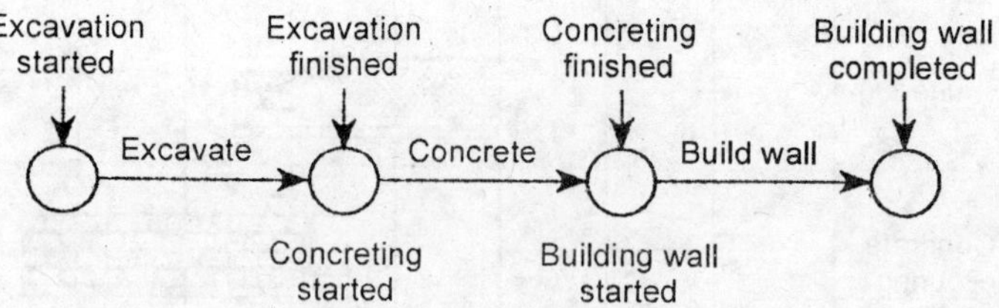

Fig. 20.5. A simple Network.

Rules for Network Construction

- The length of the arrow bears no relationship to the time which the activity takes or the resources which the activity consumes.
- The arrow in a network identifies the logical conditions of dependency. The geometry of arrow diagram is of no significance except that it should be aesthetically pleasing.
- The direction of the arrow indicates the direction of work flow. The normal convention is to go from left to right.
- All networks are constructed logically on the principle of dependency.
- No event can be reached in a project before the activity which immediately precedes is completed. Similarly no activity can be started until the event which immediately precedes it, has been reached.

- Every activity in the network should be completed to reach the objective or the end event.
- No set of activities can form a circular loop.

Numbering the Events and Activity Identification

Rules for numbering events and identification of activities are as follows :

- All events must be numbered.
- The same number cannot be used for more than one event. This is necessary in order to identify each activity.
- Events can be numbered in any order but usually forward numbering system is more familiar. In this method, first event in the network is numbered 1 (or zero) and the second 2 and so on. In such a way the event number at the tail of each activity arrow is always smaller than the event number at the head of that activity arrow. This implies that the final event of the network will have the largest number and will be equal to the number of the nodes in the network.

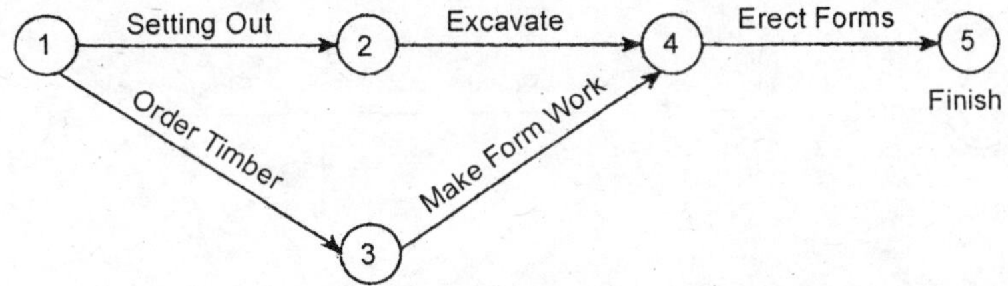

Fig. 20.6. Numbering of events and activity Identification.

Fig. 20.6 illustrates the forward numbering of events and activities identification in a network.

Activity Description	*Activity Identification*
Setting out	1-2
Order timber	1-3
Excavate	2-4
Make Form Work	3-4
Erect Forms	4-5

Use of Dummy Activities

A dummy is an artificial activity introduced in a network to:

- Maintain a unique numbering system for the different activities.
- Keep the logical sequence of activities and their interrelationships correct. A dummy is shown by a dotted arrow as indicated in Fig.20.7.

-----------→

Fig. 20.7

Dummy does not consume Time or Resources.

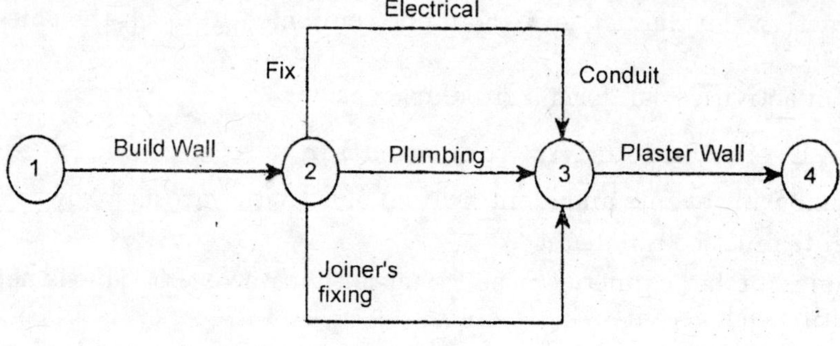

Fig. 20.8.

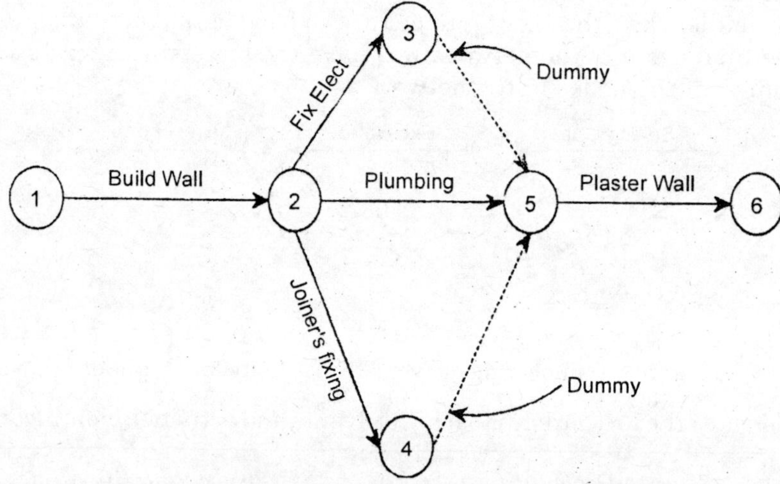

Fig. 20.9. Use of dummies to identify activities.

Consider the network shown in Fig 20.8. Three of the activities in the network, *i.e.*, fixing of electrical conduits, plumbing and joiner's fixing bear the same number 2-3. Thus the identification of activities is not unique. This situation can be corrected by using dummy arrows as shown in Fig.20.9. Now fixing electrical conduits is identified by 2-3, plumbirg by 2-5 and joiner's fixing by 2-4. Activities 3-5 and 4-5 are dummies.

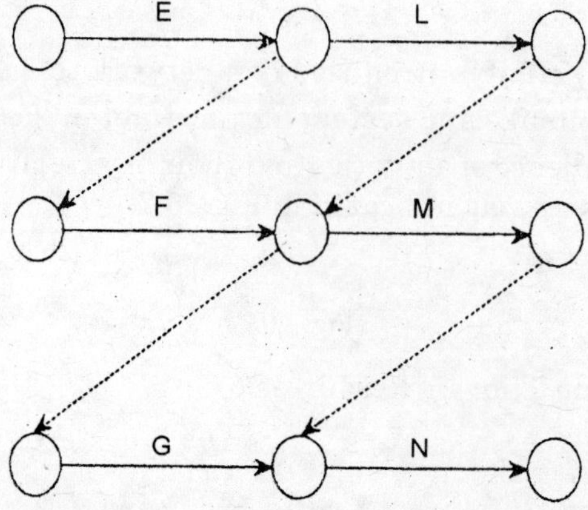

Fig. 22.10. Use of Dummies to show dependents.

Consider the network shown in Fig. 20.10. Let *EFG* represent the shuttering on three bays of a retaining wall and *L, M* and *N,* the corresponding concreting operations. In view of the nature of the activities, it is reasonable to presuppose that in each case, the shuttering has to precede concreting. As regards the labour, only one forward crew and one concreting crew are available. Dummies are used here to represent the restraint and consequent interdependency.

Network Development

In developing a network diagram, the following questions must be asked for each operation:

- What activity must immediately precede this operation ?
- What activity should immediately follow this operation ?
- What activities can take place concurrently with this operation ?

Based on these questions, each activity is connected with one or several of the ways as shown in Figs. 20.11 to 20.14.

Network Representation	*Interpretation*
(*a*) Sequential	Activity *B* cannot start before activity A is completed or activity *B* follows activity A, or activity *A* precedes B.  A B **Fig. 20.11**
(*b*) Diverging	Activity *Q* and *R* cannot start before the completion of activity *P*. Activity *Q* and *R* could begin at the same time. 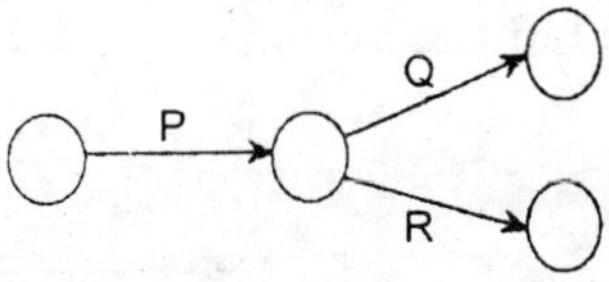 Q P R **Fig. 20.12**
(*c*) Converging	Activity N cannot start before both the activities L and M are completed. 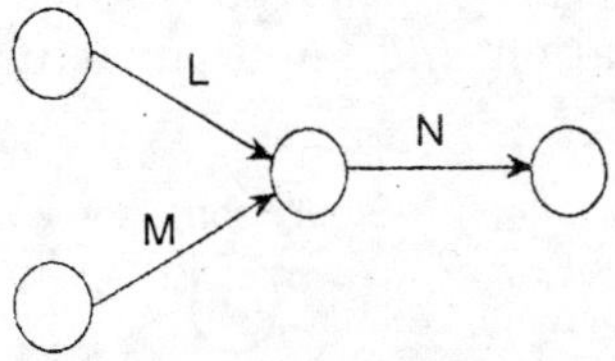 L N M **Fig. 20.13**
(*d*) Parallel	In these activity chains, B follows A and F follows E but the activity chains are completely independent of each other. 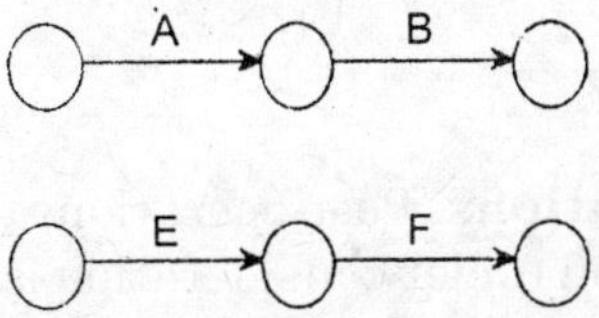 A B E F **Fig. 20.14**

In the first instance, it is important to prepare a network that represents the time logical dependency of activities on one another, assuming availability of unlimited resources.

It is useful to show each arrow with a horizontal portion being used for activity description that should always be included, in every network. This layout with horizontal lines imparts not only nearness but also permits the network to be separated into a series of horizontal zones; presenting either separate sections of the project or perhaps different types of work such as design, contracting, civil works, etc

20.3.2. AON System

Terms used in AON system are:

(*i*) **Operation or Activity.** A project consists of several activities or operations and the project is known to be completed when all such activities are completed. In AON system, operations are represented by the circles. Different operations are numbered and these numbers are posted inside the circles representing that operation. The schedule time is written on the left top corner of the circle. Fig. 20.15 shows that the operation number 4 has its schedule time of 6 days.

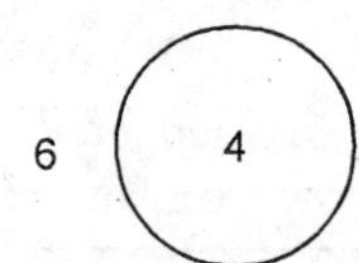

Fig. 20.15

(*ii*) **Pre-operation.** Pre-operations (PRE-OPR) are the operations which precede the operation under consideration, *e.g.*, machine installation can only be done after machine foundation is completed, thus machine foundation is the pre-operation of machine installation and is written on the left as shown in Fig. 20.16. The arrow connecting these two circles shows the relation between them and indicates that the operation on the left end of the arrow should be completed before the beginning of the operation on the right end of the arrow.

Fig. 20.16

Sometimes an operation has more than one pre-operation, *e.g.*, roofing of a workshop can only be started when super-structure and the steel fabrication is completed. Thus 'steel fabrication' and 'super-structure' are the "Pre-operations" of the roofing as shown in Fig.20.17.

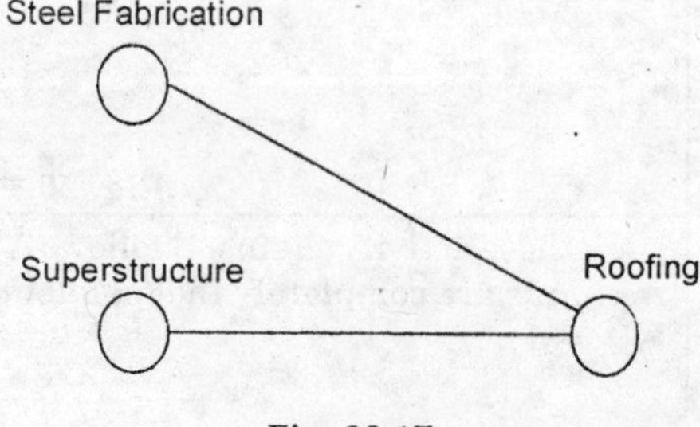

Fig. 20.17

(*iii*) **Post-operations.** Post-operations (POST-OPR) are the operations which follow after the operation under consideration is completed. In the previous example of Fig. 20.16,

'Machine Installation' is the 'POST-OPR' of the 'machine foundation'. In the example shown in Fig.20.17, 'roofing' is the 'POST-OPR' of 'Steel fabrication' and 'super structure'.

(*iv*) **Concurrent Operations.** These are the independent operations and do not have any 'PRE-OPR' and these can be started separately at the same time. In Fig. 20.17 steel fabrication and super-structure are the concurrent operations.

(*v*) **Earliest Finish.** It is the earliest possible time in which the particular operation can be completed. This is given on the top right corner outside the operation circle and is enclosed in a rectangle. It will be clear from the example shown in Fig. 20.18. in which machine foundation has its schedule time of 15 days and it does not have any PRE-OPR, hence its 'earliest finish' is 15 days. Operation 'Machine installation' has 10 days schedule time and its PRE-OPR will take 15 days, thus the 'earliest finish' of this is 15 +10 = 25 days, *i.e.*, this operation can be completed after 25 days of starting of the work.

When any operation has more than one PRE-OPR then earliest finish time = Largest earliest finish of PRE-OPRS + schedule time for the operation under consideration. In the example shown in Fig. 20.19, earliest finish times for operations A and *B* are 10 and 15 days respectively (as they have no PRE-OPRS, their earliest finish = schedule time) and the earliest finish for C = Largest earliest finish of PRE-OPRS + schedule time for operation C. = 15 + 20 = 35 days. (15 is the largest earliest finish among operations *A* and B

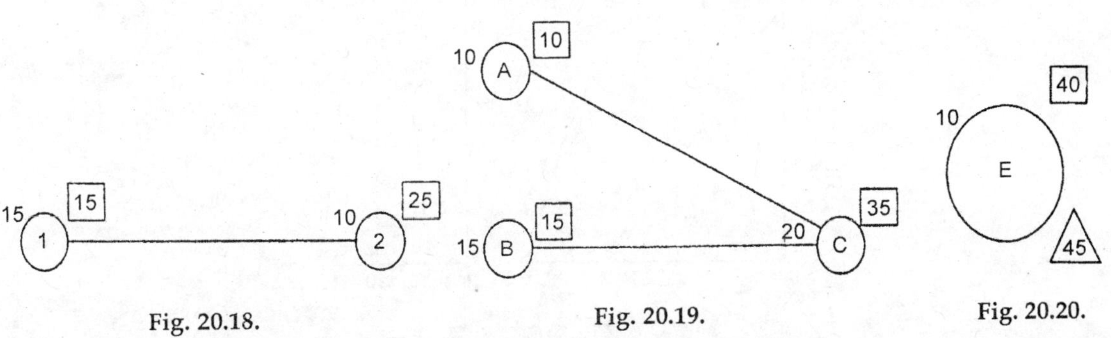

Fig. 20.18. Fig. 20.19. Fig. 20.20.

(*vi*) **Latest Finish Time.** It is the latest time by which the operation must be completed so that scheduled date for the completion of the project may not be delayed.

For the last operation:

Latest finish = Earliest finish

For other operations :

Latest finish = Latest finish of the post-operation-Time required for post operation.

Note that if any operation has more than one post operations then use smallest among them. It is written in a triangle below the operation circle. Fig.20.20 shows that operation time for *E* is 10 days and its earliest finish is 40 days while its latest finish time is 45 days.

(*vii*) **Critical Path.** A path along the network in which 'Earliest Finish' and 'Latest Finish' are equal is known as "Critical Path" and is represented by double or thick arrow line to distinguish clearly. More stress is given on this path, because a slight delay on this path will effect adversely on the completion time of the whole project.

(*viii*) **Slack.** It gives the range of time available at an event for accomplishing an activity without delaying the project completion date. On critical paths, slack is zero. Slack is the difference between the latest finish time and the earliest finish time, *i.e.*, in the event shown in Fig. 32.20 slack is (45-40) = 5 days.

(*ix*) **Earliest Start.** It is the earliest possible time by which the work can be started. Earliest Start = Earliest finish time-Operation time.

(*x*) **Latest Start.** It is the latest possible time by which the work can be started. ∴ Latest start = Latest finish time–Operation time.

(*xi*) **Positive Slack.** If $T_L - T_E$ is positive, then this represents, a situation where extra resources, *i.e.*, men, material and machines are available.

(*xii*) **Negative Slack.** If $T_L - T_E$ is negative, then this represents that the programme is falling behind schedule.

(*xiii*) **Zero Slack.** If $T_L - T_E$ is zero then this represents an ideal situation which falls on the **'Critical path'**.

Due to slack conditions, there may be more than one critical path. In such a case, all the paths should be analysed to evaluate the resulting actions by changing one or more events or activities along the path as a means of improving the schedule.

20.3.3. Time Estimates

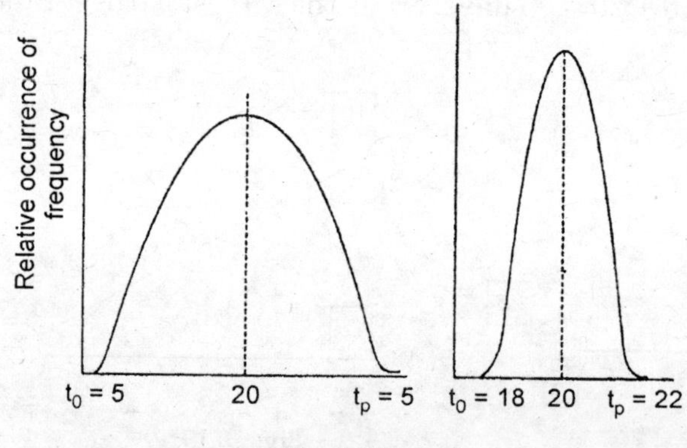

Fig. 20.21

Once the network has been decided by the planner, the next point is to estimate the time required for the execution of each activity or job. In C.P.M., there exists only one time estimate for each activity and no uncertainties are taken into consideration. Therefore in C.P.M. we deal with a more deterministic system as compared to that in P.E.R.T. This point has been explained in the figure. The range and hence the uncertainty in Fig.20.21 (*a*) is more whereas in Fig.20.21 (*b*), the range is small, and the system tends to be a more deterministic model.

20.3.4. How to Draw the Network Diagram

Before starting to draw the network, following measures should be taken serially:

1. Prepare a list of the activities included in the project and their dependencies on other activities.
2. Draft the network roughly, usually by soft pencil and an eraser on a large piece of paper.
3. The estimate of time required for each activity is made considering manpower and equipments available and in certain cases assumptions are based on statistical approach and experience.
4. These time estimates are then written on each activity.

5. Then scheduling computations are done to get earliest and latest allowable start and finish times for each activity, to identify critical path and to indicate the amount of slack on non-critical paths.
6. Now this is prepared in final form for use in the field. Project is controlled by checking the progress against the schedule.

Big Size Networks

Several network charts contain thousands of operations. Such charts require considerable time and efforts and require more than one man to prepare them. For simplicity, a group of operations is shown as a single operation in general chart but the details of each such operation is given separately. For example, in the construction of workshop, main operations are :

- Construction of building.
- Installation of machines
- Electric wiring for light and power
- Flooring
- Plastering and
- Painting on walls etc.

Among these, each of the operation contains several activities, *i.e.*, construction of building itself contains several activities like excavation, foundation, procurement of building materials and steel, construction of walls, roofs, floors etc. In big projects, different persons are made responsible for different types of work, who will make their own detailed network considering scheduled time and will execute the work accordingly, *i.e.*, the person deputed for construction of building will look after only this work and will try to complete the work as per schedule shown in general chart.

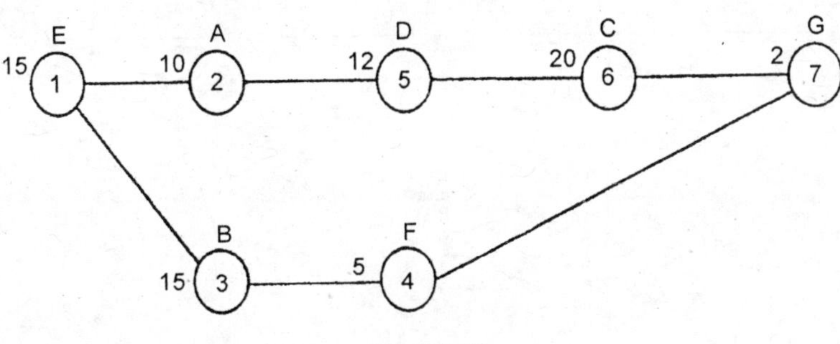

Fig. 20.22

20.3.5. Advantages of Critical Path Method

Some of the important advantages are summarised here: — It helps in ascertaining time schedules.

- With its help, control by the management becomes easy.
- It makes better and detailed planning possible.
- It encourages discipline.
- It provides a standard method for communicating project plans, schedules and cost performance.
- It identifies most critical activities and thus more attention can be paid on these activities.

The CPM technique requires greater planning than required otherwise. Thus, this method increases the planning cost but this cost can easily be justified by concentrating attention on critical paths only and avoiding unnecessary expenses on the strict supervision over the whole programme.

Example 20.1. *Following Table shows the operation time in working days for different activities. Draw the critical path on the diagram.*

Activity	*Particulars*	*Time in days*
A	Machine Foundation	10
B	Electric Fitting	15
C	Repair of floor	20
D	Installation of Machine	12
E	Procure Workshop Building	15
F	Whitewash	5
G	Clean up	2

Solution. The above activities are drawn in the network as shown in Fig. 20.22. Each activity is represented by the numerals in the circle. Number of days are mentioned on the left corner of circle representing the operation.

After drawing the network diagram, Earliest Finish time for each operation is calculated and noted on the top right corner of the circle and inscribed in the rectangles as shown in the Fig. 20.23.

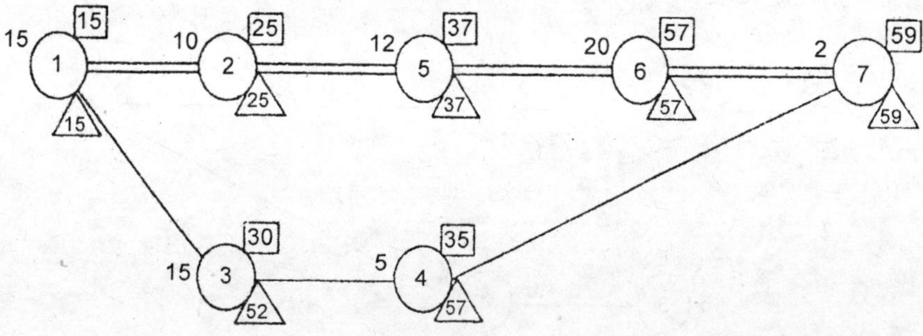

Fig. 20.23

For the last operation 7, latest finish time = Earliest finish time, *i.e.,* 59 days in this case. From this value, Latest Finish time for other operations is calculated and written on the right bottom corner of the circle and inscribed in a triangle. For operations 2,3,4,5 and 6 latest finish time is calculated by subtracting the working days required from the latest of post-operation. For operation 1, Latest Finish time calculated by considering operation 2 is 25-10 = 15 days and by considering operation 3 is 52-15 = 37 days. In such cases, lower value is considered as the Latest Finish time. Hence for operation 1, Latest Finish time = 15 days.

Operations which are having Earliest Finish = Latest Finish are joined with double line and represent the critical path as shown in Fig. 20.23.

20.4. PROGRAMME EVALUATION REVIEW TECHNIQUE (PERT)

P.E.R.T. (Programme Evaluation and Review Technique) is a technique used for scheduling and controlling the projects. It is helpful in the programmes, where activities are subject to considerable degree of uncertainty in performance time. It is very essential for timely execution of the projects. Originally, it was used in designing and producing major Weapon Systems for the U.S. Military Establishments. Then, it was used in large concerns, which due to their size were using computers. After its becoming public property in 1959, producers also thought it to use due to the advantage that it has disciplined approach to planning, scheduling, controlling and monitoring the progress of variety of projects.

C.P.M. uses only one-time estimate for each activity while P.E.R.T. uses three times estimates. But one time estimate is sufficient for small projects.

Difference between C.P.M. and P.E.R.T.

P.E.R.T. is a technique used for scheduling and controlling the projects, where activities are subject to considerable degree of uncertainty in the performance time. The methods of calculating time of start, finish, critical path and project time of P.E.R.T. and C.P.M. are similar, still there are some differences between the two. These differences are:

(*i*) C.P.M. is the activity oriented technique while P.E.R.T. is the event oriented technique. Event means the beginning or ending of one or more activities. P.E.R.T. network diagram uses the line and arrow to connect the events (shown by circles) which are related to each other.

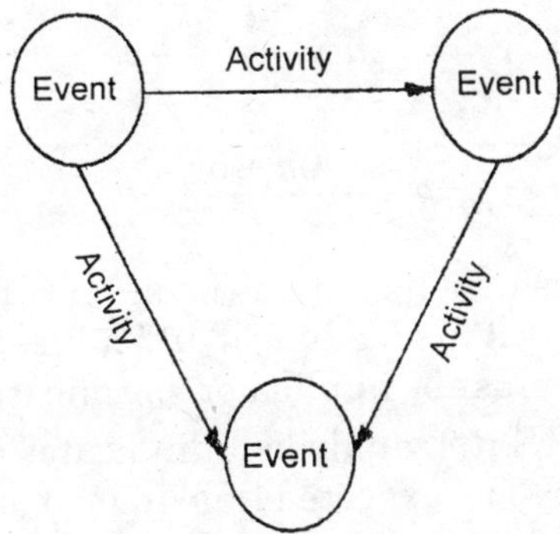

Fig. 20.24. Relation between event and activity.

(*ii*) C.P.M. has one time estimate while P.E.R.T. has three time estimates.

(*iii*) P.E.R.T. requires use of dummies for showing proper sequencing. C.P.M. does not require use of dummy activity.

(*iv*) PERT is a probabilistic model with uncertainty in duration. C.P.M. has well known activity duration.

(*v*) P.E.R.T. does not show critical path. C.P.M. marks the critical activity.

(*vi*) C.P.M. requires better utilisation of resources. In P.E.R.T. resources are always available.

Three-time Estimates for P.E.R.T.

P.E.R.T. is based on the assumption that operation time cannot be estimated accurately, because of the various uncertainties involved in the working. To take these uncertainties into account, the P.E.R.T. uses the following three time estimates:

- Optimistic time (a)
- Most Likely time (m)
- Pessimistic time (b)

Optimistic time. In this, it is assumed that every thing will go well, therefore it is the estimate of the minimum possible time, which an activity takes for completion under ideal conditions. In this, no provision is made for delays or breakdowns etc. Always conditions better than normal are assumed. This estimate of time is denoted by "a".

Most likely time. It is the value, which will probably be the actual time. In this, it is assumed that things go in the normal way, with a few delays or set backs etc. This estimate of time, lies between the optimistic and pessimistic time. It is denoted by "m".

Pessimistic time. This time is based on the assumption that every thing will go badly. Thus, it is the maximum possible time taken for the completion of an activity. This does not include major catastrophes like labour strikes, acts of God and unrest etc. This is denoted by "b".

Expected Time or Average Time

According to β distribution, we can get the expected time (t_e) by adding together $\frac{1}{6}$ th of the optimistic, $\frac{2}{3}$ rd of the most likely and $\frac{1}{6}$ th of the pessimistic time estimates. Thus :

$$t_e = \frac{1}{6}a + \frac{2}{3}m + \frac{1}{6}b$$

or

$$t_e = \frac{a + 4m + b}{6}$$

Performance of these activities depends upon the several factors like weather, equipment and other personnel problems. To stick to schedule, if difficulties are experienced in any particular activity then additional resources must be applied or specifications can also be relaxed.

Equation (1) is important for P.E.R.T. analysis. It indicates as how to calculate the expected time from the three-time estimates. The expected time indicates that there is a fifty-fifty chance of getting the job done within that time.

Some Definitions used in P.E.R.T.

1. **Event.** It is the start or completion of a task. It is represented by a circle and do not consume time or resources.
2. **Activity.** It is the actual performance of a task. It consumes time and resources, such as manpower, space, material etc. It is represented by the line and arrow.
3. **Successor Event.** It is the event or events that immediately follow another event.
4. **Predecessor Event.** It is an event which comes immediately before another event.
5. **Earliest Expected Time (T_E).** It is the earliest expected completion time of the project and is equal to the sum of expected time (t_e) of all the activities along the longest path of the project.
6. **Latest Allowable Time (T_L).** It is the largest possible time an event can take without delaying the final completion date.

   T_L for an event = Total expected time for the end event of the project from longest path. Total expected time for the event under consideration from longest path.
7. **Slack.** It is the difference of Latest Allowable Time (T_L) and Earliest Expected Time (T_E) *i.e.*, Slack = $T_L - T_E$. It is the range of time available for the performance of an activity without delaying the completion date of the project. This value of slack indicates

that how much critical that event is and how much stress have to be given on that activity.

8. **Critical Path.** This is a path on the network along which no slippage is allowed. In this path, slack is either negative or zero.

9. **Variance.** Variance = $\sigma^2 = \left\{\frac{b-a}{6}\right\}^2$ or $\sigma^2 =$ or $\sigma^2 = \left\{\frac{t_p - t_0}{6}\right\}^2$

where, $a = t_0$ = Optimistic time; $b = t_p$ = Pessimistic time ; σ = Standard deviation

Example 20.2. *Show the Earliest and Latest expected times on the following network and also indicate the critical path on it. Fig. 20.25.*

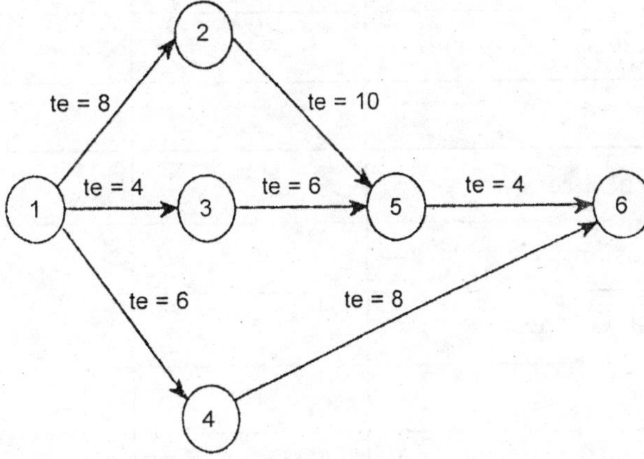

Fig. 20.25

Solution. Earliest and Latest times are shown on the network given in Fig.20.26. In this network, critical path will be the path along the events, 1, 2, 5 and 6, because on this whole path, $T_E = T_L$ *i.e.*, slack is always equal to zero. Hence more stress should be given for the execution of the activities falling on this path.

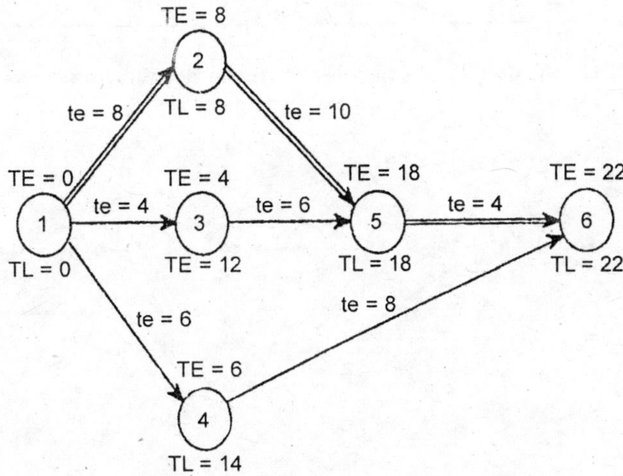

Fig. 20.26

Example 20.3. *Draw a network diagram for the construction of single storey house.*

Solution. Before drawing network, a list of activities with their pre-event and successive events should be prepared as in the Table below:

Activity	*Pre-Event*	*Successive Event*
A. Acquire land	1	2
B. Drawing and design	1	3
C. Estimation	3	4
D. Procure building material	4	5
E. Procure electric material	4	6
F. Foundation	5	7
G. Super-structure	7	8
H. Electrification	6	9
I. Doors and windows	5	10
J. Roofing	8	11
K. Plaster work	10, 11	12
L. Painting and white wash	9, 12	13
M. Clearing	13	14
N. Furniture work	14	15

Now on the basis of the above Table network can be drawn as shown in Fig.20.27:

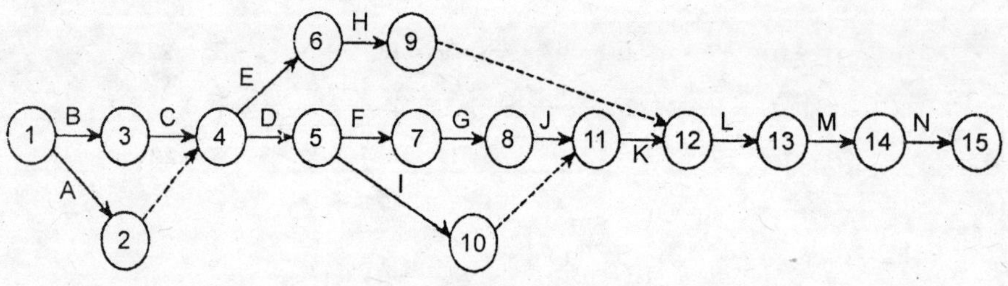

Fig. 20.27

Example 20.4. *Show the Earliest Expected Time (TE) and Latest Allowable Time (TL) for each activity, on the chart of previous example. Also indicate the critical path. Time for each event is given hereunder. Calculate the schedule completion time (TL) of the project.*

Activity	Time in working days		
	a	***m***	***b***
A	5	10	15
B	2	3	4
C	2	4	6
D	8	10	18
E	3	4	5
F	7	8	12
G	18	22	29
H	6	8	10
I	8	9	16
J	20	25	30
K	12	16	20
L	8	14	20
M	3	4	8
N	5	7	12

Solution. Such network can be drawn in the following steps:

Step I. First calculate expected time t_e from the given values of a, *m* and ***b*** using the relation

$$t_e = \frac{a + 4m + b}{6}$$

These values of t_e are calculated in the form of Table as below:

Activity	*a*	*m*	*b*	$t_e = \frac{a + 4m + b}{6}$
A	5	10	15	$\frac{5 + 40 + 15}{6} = 10$
B	2	3	4	$\frac{2 + 12 + 4}{6} = 3$
C	2	4	6	$\frac{2 + 16 + 6}{6} = 4$

D	8	10	18	$\frac{8+40+18}{6} = 11$
E	3	4	5	$\frac{3+16+5}{6} = 4$
F	7	8	12	$\frac{7+32+12}{6} = 8.5$
G	18	22	29	$\frac{18+88+29}{6} = 22.5$
H	6	8	10	$\frac{6+32+10}{6} = 8$
I	8	9	16	$\frac{8+36+16}{6} = 10$
J	20	25	30	$\frac{20+100+30}{6} = 25$
K	12	16	20	$\frac{12+64+20}{6} = 16$
L	8	14	20	$\frac{8+56+20}{6} = 14$
M	3	4	8	$\frac{3+16+8}{6} = 4.5$
N	5	7	12	$\frac{5+28+12}{6} = 7.5$

Step II. Earliest Expected Time (T_E) for each event is the sum of the expected time (t_e) of all activities, upto that event along the longest path. T_E for each activity is indicated on the network shown in Fig. 32.28. in which T_E for last event = T_L = 119 days.

Step III. As latest allowable time (T_L) is the latest time by which an event must be completed so that project proceeds as per schedule. To calculate it, start from the last event and proceed towards left.

T_L for an event = T_L for its successor event $-t_e$ for activity linking two events.

e.g. T_L for event 13 = T_L for event *14*-t_e for activity 13-14.

T_L calculated from this way are indicated on the network shown in Fig. 20.28.

Step IV. Mark the critical path. It is the path along which slack is zero, *i.e.*, $T_E = T_L$. It is shown by the double line in the diagram. In this example critical path is the path along the events 1, 2, 4, 5,7, 8, 11, 12,13,14 and 15.

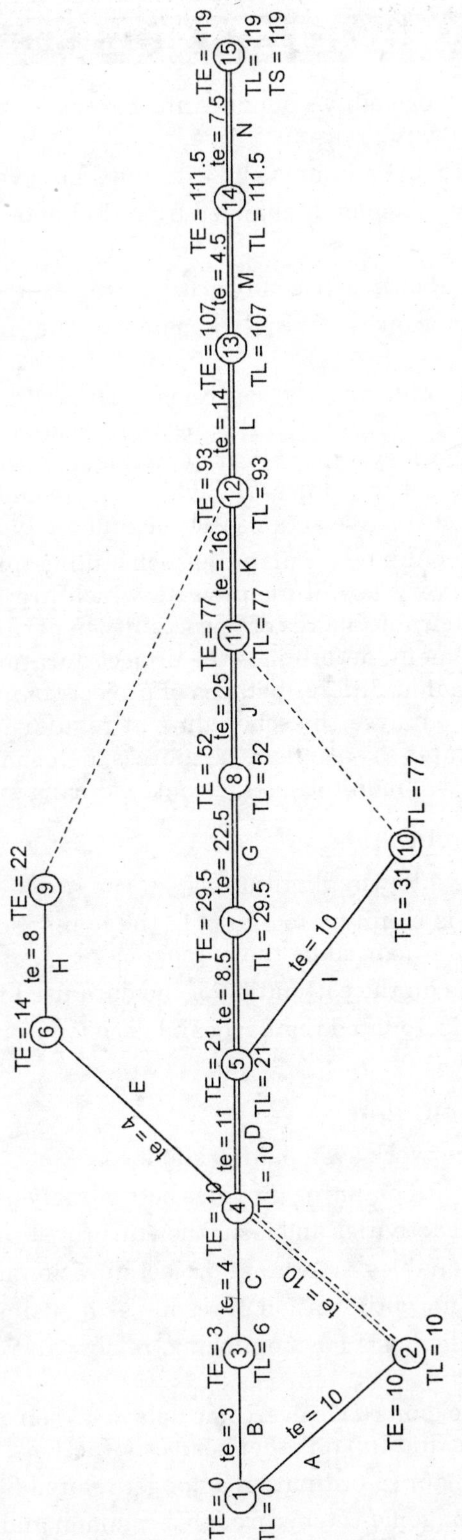

TE = 0
TL = 0
1
te = 3
B
te = 10
A
TE = 3
TL = 6
3
TE = 10
TL = 10
2
te = 4
C
te = 10
TE = 10
TL = 10
4
te = 11
D
te = 4
E
TE = 14
6
te = 8
H
TE = 22
9
TE = 21
TL = 21
5
te = 8.5
F
te = 10
I
TE = 29.5
TL = 29.5
7
te = 22.5
G
TE = 52
TL = 52
8
TE = 31
TL = 77
10
te = 25
J
TE = 77
TL = 77
11
te = 16
K
TE = 93
TL = 93
12
te = 14
L
TE = 107
TL = 107
13
te = 4.5
M
TE = 111.5
TL = 111.5
14
te = 7.5
N
TE = 119
TL = 119
TS = 119
15

Fig. 20.28

20.5. USES OF NETWORK TECHNIQUES

Even if the planning is done thoroughly, slippages and cost over-runs are not uncommon. These may occur because of the following reasons :

- As planning is based on estimates and estimates may vary at the time of execution.
- Availability of resources may be changed from that of originally planned.
- Poor supervision.
- Unexpected technical difficulties may arise during execution.
- Unforeseen circumstances, like strike, power cut, non-availability of material, equipments etc.

Therefore, a continuous monitoring and control is necessary during execution of the project. For continuous monitoring and control, P.E.R.T. network system is adopted for executing the project as per plan. The network system helps the management for taking timely actions and decisions so as to achieve project schedules. Delays are overcome by updating the network at regular intervals and taking corrective actions in time and analysing future work.

Network technique is a technique for planning, scheduling (programming) and controlling progress of projects. This is very useful for projects which are complex in nature or where activities are subject to considerable degree of uncertainty in performance time. This technique provides an effective management, determines the project duration more accurately, identifies the activities which are critical at different stages of project completion to enable to pay more attention on these activities, analyse the scheduling at regular interval for taking corrective action well in advance, facilitates in optimising resources, helps management for taking timely and better decisions for effective monitoring and control during execution of the project.

Limitations of Network Techniques

Network techniques have following limitations:

- Network technique is simply a tool to help the management, hence its effectiveness depends on how well it is used by the management.
- Its accuracy depends on the estimation of the data used in the network.
- It is useful only if it is updated regularly and decisions for corrective actions are taken timely.

Advantages of Network Technique

Main advantages of the network system are as follows :

1. Detailed and thoughtful planning provides better analysis and logical thinking.
2. Identifies the critical activities and focus them to provide greater managerial attention.
3. Network technique enables to forecast project duration more accurately.
4. It is a powerful tool for optimisation of resources by using the concept of slack.
5. It provides a scientific basis for monitoring, review and control, to evaluate effect of slippages.
6. It helps in taking decisions (*i*) to overcome delays, (*ii*) on crashing programme, (*iii*) for optimising resources and (*iv*) on other corrective actions.
7. It helps in getting better co-ordination amongst related fields.
8. It is an effective management tool through a common and simple language, providing common understanding.

In this chapter, efforts have been made to show following applications of network through solved examples, for the help of readers:

1. Estimating activity time (duration).
2. Crashing of Network.
3. Optimising the Cost.
4. Updating the Network.
5. Smoothing the resources.
6. Levelling the resources.

20.6. CRASHING OF NETWORK

Time aspect is the main and significant aspect in a network. It is primary object to complete the project at the earliest to get quicker realisation of benefits of the project. As discussed earlier, activities on critical path and sub-critical path needs special attention either to complete the project as per schedule or to reduce the completion time. To reduce the schedule time, non-critical activities can be considered as potential pools of resources for diverting to critical or near critical activities.

In some projects, it is desirable to cut down the total project time, even if it leads to increase in cost. It is generally desired where cost considerations are unimportant or less important then completing the project in absolute minimum time, *e.g.*, defence works in emergency. Generally it is possible to reduce the project duration by changing the resources allocated to it. The increase or decrease in the project duration results in decrease or increase in the cost of the project. For this purpose, time and costs are analysed in a systematic way. This analysis also helps in determining optimum duration of the project.

For studying the project time and cost analysis, we shall first discuss about project costs and time-cost relationships.

Project Costs

There are two types of costs associated with a project:

(*i*) *Direct costs.* It represents the expenditure which can be directly allocated to different activities in a project, like manpower, materials etc.

(*ii*) *Indirect costs.* It represents the expenditure on those items which are shared by more than one activities and cannot be directly allocated to individual activity of a project, *e.g.*, overhead, depreciation, establishment charges etc. Thus longer the project takes to complete, the higher is the indirect costs.

Conducting a crash programme usually results in an increase in the cost of those activities that are constructed under the crash programme. In order to keep the total increase in cost to a minimum, it is necessary to crash those activities which permit reduction in construction time at the least total increase in cost. The reduction in time for a project can be achieved by reducing the duration of one or more activities lying on the critical path.

Total cost of a project is the sum of the direct and the indirect costs. These costs are plotted in Fig. 20.29.

With the help of this curve, we can determine optimum duration, which is also referred as target duration. If the critical path is equal or shorter than this optimum duration, there is no need to reduce the network, *i.e.*, crashing the duration of any activity. If, however, the critical path is longer than the project's optimum duration, then there is need to reduce the duration of some activities, so that the critical path is equal to the optimum duration.

These curves help the management to determine following aspects - for taking further decisions about deciding the project duration and resource allocation:

(*a*) Determining the project duration, for which the cost is least, *i.e.*, optimum duration of the project at which the cost is optimum as shown in Fig. 20.30.

(*b*) Determining the least cost of a reduction in project duration to a stipulated date. This is done when the stipulated date is earlier than the optimum time for the project.

(*c*) Determining the time-cost-risk relationship. In this, risk involved in eliminating any activity is calculated. This time-cost risk helps the management to take a decision about most economical solution, based on the circumstances and the objective of a particular situation.

This shows that the network technique is an analytical tool for better planning, scheduling, monitoring and decision-making.

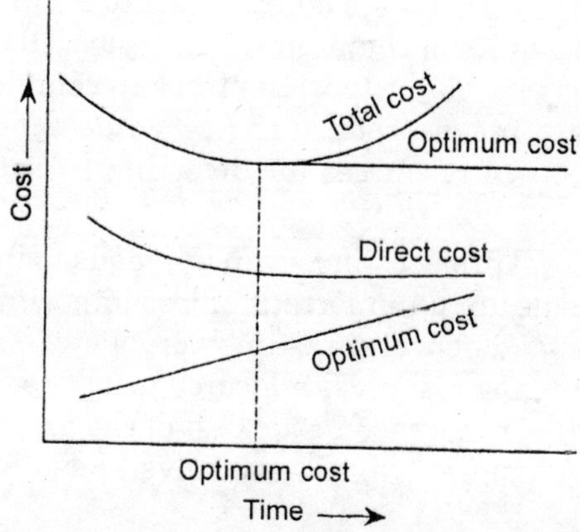

Fig. 20.29. Project cost curves.

C$_C$ A, Crash point
C$_N$ B, Normal point
Cost
T$_C$ T$_N$
Time

Fig. 20.30. Time cost relationship for an activity

Crash Point and Normal Point

Fig. 32.30 shows variation in the cost of an activity with time. The figure also indicates that there is critical point in time beyond which it will become expensive to try to shorten the time schedule of an activity. It also indicates that lengthening an activity more than a certain time duration results in negligible cost savings. First such point is "Crash Point" while second such points is known as "Normal Point", as shown in the Fig. 20.30.

Cost Slope

In actual practice, we assume the time-cost curve to be linear between two points, Crash point A and Normal point B. The curve shown in Fig. 20.30 shows that, there is a change in cost for change in time. The term 'cost-slope' is defined as the "increase in the cost of the activity per unit decrease in the time". Mathematically, we can say,

$$\text{Cost slope} = \frac{\text{Crash cost} - \text{Normal cost}}{\text{Normal time} - \text{Crash time}}$$

In simple words, we can say that cost slope of an activity is the "increase in cost of an activity by reducing the duration by one unit".

Crashing Procedure

The cost slope concept helps in finding lowest cost solution by sequential compressing the activities having lowest cost slope, i.e., having lowest incremental cost on critical path. Sometimes by crashing one activity, critical path is shifted, therefore, at each shift of the critical path, it will be necessary to calculate the cost slopes of the activities on new critical path. Then the activity having the lowest cost slope, needs to be compressed on this new critical path. This process is repeated until the project crash point is reached.

Procedure for crashing a project is explained hereunder :

(*i*) The ratio of increase in cost to decrease in time for each activity that can be crashed on the critical path is calculated and compared.

(*ii*) The activity having the lowest ratio is reduced to the next lower time value.

(*iii*) The critical path for the network is again calculated using the new time for the crashed activity.

(*iv*) Repeat steps (*ii*) and (*iii*) until the critical path is equal to optimum project duration or equal to prescribed project duration.

Example 20.5. *For a Network shown below, Normal time, Crash time, Normal cost and Crash costs are given in the table. Contract the network by crashing it to optimum value and calculate the optimum project cost. Indirect cost is given as Rs. 100 per day.*

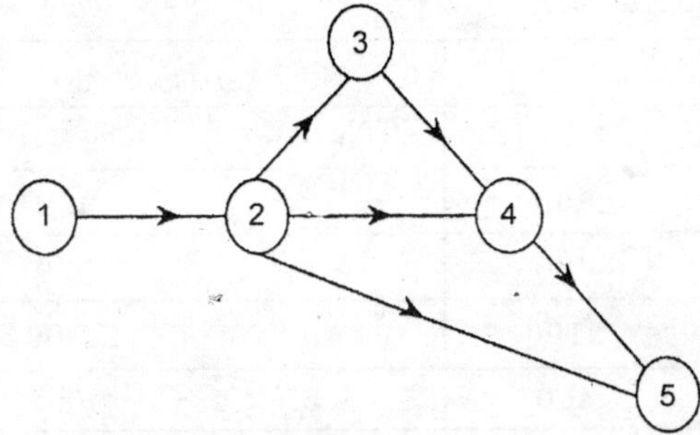

Fig. 20.31.

Activity	*Normal*		*Crash*	
	Time in days	*Cost in Rs.*	*Time in days*	*Cost in Rs.*
1 – 2	3	300	2	400
2 – 3	6	480	4	520
2 – 4	7	2100	5	2500
2 – 5	8	400	6	600
3 – 4	4	320	3	360
4 – 5	5	500	4	520

Solution. By drawing the network with normal duration, we see (from Fig. 20.32) that critical path is 1 – 2 – 3 – 4 – 5.

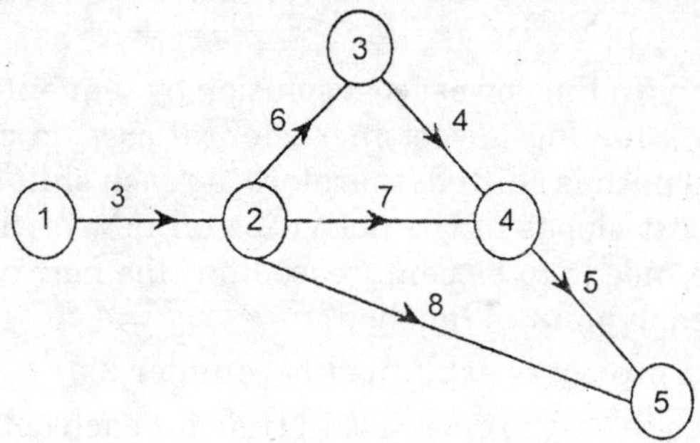

Fig. 20.32.

The project duration is, therefore, equal to 18 days. On this path,

Crash time = 13 days (from given data)

By adding values of all the activities,

Normal cost = Rs. 4100 (from given table)

and Crash cost = Rs. 4900 (from given table).

To construct the network, in first stage we should identify those activities on critical path, which have cost-slopes less than the indirect cost. For this purpose cost-slopes are calculated hereunder:

Activity	*Normal*		*Crash Cost*			*Cost-slope*	
	Time in days	*Cost in Rs.*	*Time in days*	*Cost in Rs.*	*ΔC*	*ΔT*	*ΔC/ΔT*
1-2	3	300	2	400	100	1	100
2-3	6	480	4	520	40	2	20
2-4	7	2100	5	2500	400	2	200
2-5	8	400	6	600	200	2	100
3-4	4	320	3	360	40	1	40
4-5	5	500	4	520	20	1	20

Critical path activities 2–3 and 4–5 have least cost slopes. Therefore, these activities are first crashed and network is again drawn (Refer Fig. 20.33).

This network shows that, after crashing activities 2–3 by 2 days and 4–5 by 1 day, the critical path is same, *i.e.* 1-2-3-4-5 and has 15 days duration.

Now in second stage, the least cost slope in remaining activities is for activity 3-4 on the critical path. By crashing this activity, we see that now two paths become critical path, 1-2-3-4-5 and 1-2-4-5 as shown below:

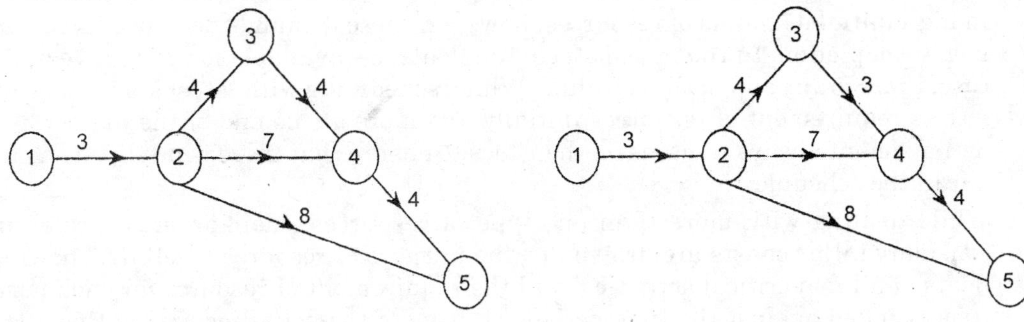

Fig. 20.33. Fig. 20.34.

Now we see that after crashing activities 2-3, 4-5 and 3-4, there is no other activity on both the critical paths which have cost-slopes less than indirect cost. This shows that, this is the optimum network and hence optimum project duration = 14 days.

Total direct project cost for this optimum duration

= Direct cost for all activities on the network

= Cost on activities 1-2; 2-3; 2-4; 2-5 ; 3-4 ; 4-5

= 300 + 520 + 2100 + 400 + 360 + 520 = Rs. 4200.

And indirect cost for 14 days @ Rs. 100 per day = Rs. 1400

Total project cost after crashing (*i.e.* optimum project cost) = 4200 +1400 = **Rs. 5600**

Whereas total cost with all normal activities was (*i.e.*, without crashing)

= Normal cost + Indirect cost for 18 days

= 4100 +1800 = **Rs. 5900.**

Thus the optimum cost of the project is Rs. *5600*. By crashing to optimum value we could save Rs. 300. If we further crash the project beyond optimum value, the project shall become costlier.

20.7. RESOURCE SMOOTHING AND RESOURCE LEVELLING

A resource is the physical variable like, labour crew, finance, equipment etc. available at the disposal of the management for completion of the project. The completion of a project on the scheduled date depends upon the availability of resources at desired time.

Resources may affect the project in two ways:

(*i*) When resources are limited, activities may be delayed due to non-availability of the resources. Therefore, in such circumstances, main constraint is resources and maximum demand of any resource is not to exceed a certain limit. In such circumstances, activities are to be rescheduled so that the total demand of resource at any time remains within the limit, which may even increase the project duration. This is known as "Resource levelling".

Levelling of resources is based on delaying the starting of non-critical activities to make use of their floats for cutting down the peak requirement of resources. There are two limits of resequencing these activities, *i.e.*, between the earliest start times and latest start times. In resequencing, it is assumed that an activity cannot be split, and once started will continue till its completion. Earliest start of non-critical activity results in high initial demands of resources, however, these demands decrease as the project nears completion. In the initial stage, the floats are available for corrective action, in case, there is any slip in the schedule. While, scheduling with latest start times results in less requirement of resources initially and more at the end of the project, but the management always remains on their toes to ensure that there is no slip, as no float is left in the schedule.

While dealing with more than one type of resources, their order of preference is considered. Bar charts are drawn, for the purpose of resource levelling, showing the floats of all non-critical activities, and the requirement of resource for each period of time is noted against the time period. Shifting of the activities within their floats is then started, beginning from the last non-critical activity and continuing upto the first activity. One activity is moved at a time and the effect of shifting is studied, till a limiting position is reached and when a further shifting starts increasing the resource demand.

(*ii*) When main constraint is projects duration time, it is kept unchanged. This means activities on critical path remains unchanged, so that total project duration is maintained. For this purpose, activities having slack are shifted, so that a uniform demand of resource is maintained. This process is known as "Resource Smoothing" or "Load Smoothing". The process of distributing the resources is called as "Resource Allocation".

Resource Smoothing and Resource Allocation problems are solved by plotting the resource (also known as load) on "histogram', which is compared with the available resources prior to smoothing of this load. In this smoothing, load is shifted from peaks to the valley by shifting the activities having slack.

Same procedure is adopted for all types of resources, *i.e.,* men or crew size, finance, equipment etc. If the labour employed are of different types then smoothing is required to be done separately for various categories of skilled men like, turners, welders, carpenters, designers, masons, electricians etc.

Resource allocation is helpful to rearrange activities on the network in such a way that project can be completed with available resources and without increase in duration. In case, it is not possible to get the work completed within schedule period and within available resources, the activities are rescheduled in such a way that minimum additional time for project completion is taken with available resources.

Example 20.6. *Consider a project shown in the network given below. Duration of each activity is shown in the table below. Labourers required for each activity are also shown in the table. Carry out resource smoothing of the project.*

Activity	*Duration in days*	*Labourers required*
1 – 2	3	2
2 – 3	4	2
2 – 4	4	4
3 – 7	4	6
4 – 5	2	2
4 – 7	2	4
5 – 6	3	2
6 – 7	2	2

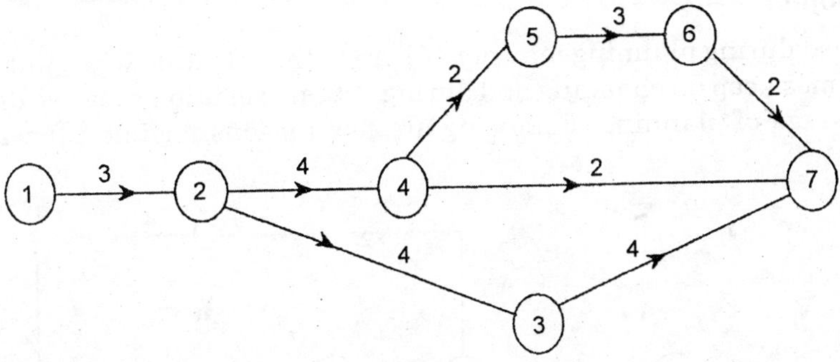

Fig. 20.35

Solution. Critical path in the network is found to be 1-2-4-5-6-7. The time scale version of this network is drawn here under, and number of labourers required for each activity is mentioned on them. Load histogram is also drawn below time version of the network.

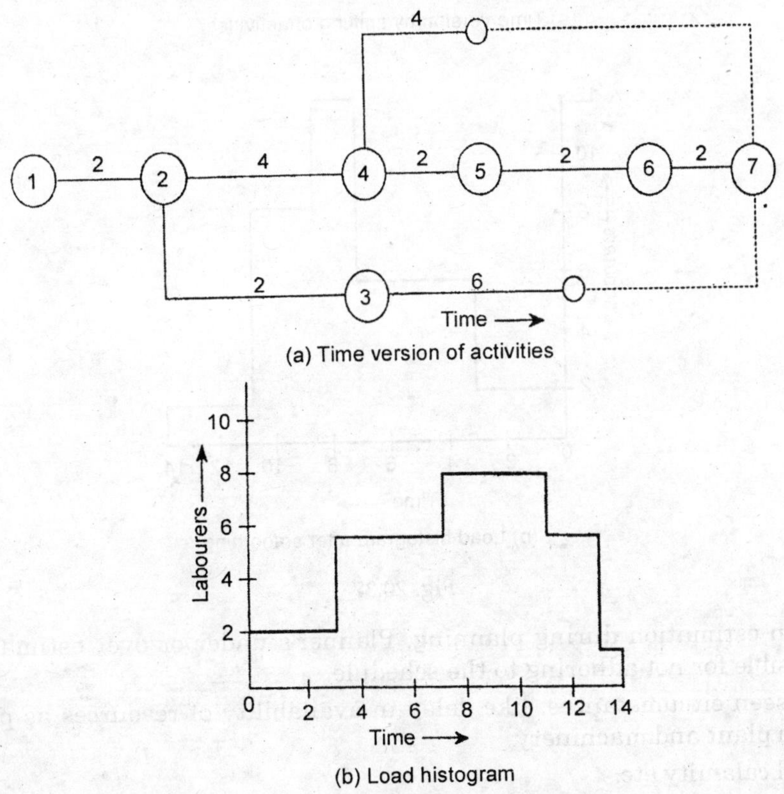

Fig. 20.36.

The Fig. 20.36 (*b*) shows that maximum number of labourers are required on 8th and 9th day. If the activity 4-7 is shifted from this place to 12th and 13th day, we get more uniform load. In this case, it is not possible to shift any other activities for smoothing the load. Hence the diagram shown in Fig. 20.37 (*a*) and 20.37 (*b*), has the least overloading and hence it is the optimum arrangement.

Up-Dating a Project

A network designed during planning may not adhere to the schedule when put to work, because situations sometimes keep on changing and during actual execution they are different than that assumed at the stage of planning. Following are few reasons for not following the designed schedule-exactly:

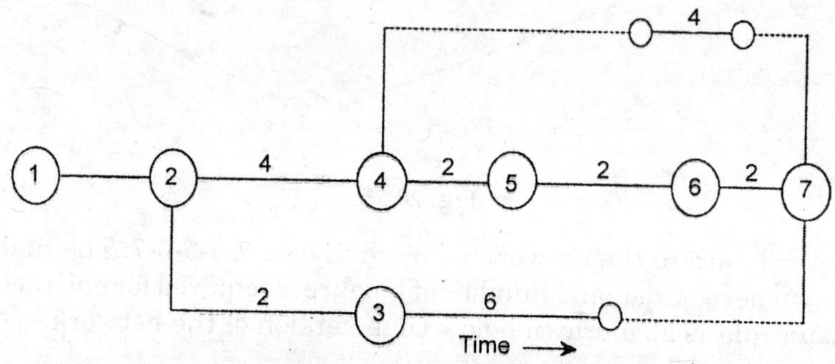

(a) Time version by shifting of activities

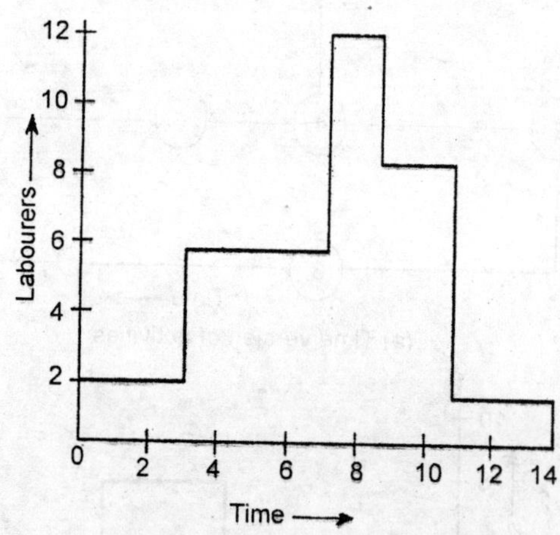

(b) Load histogram after smoothing

Fig. 20.37

(i) Error in estimation during planning. Planner's under or over estimation is mainly responsible for not adhering to the schedule.

(ii) Unforeseen circumstances, like delay in availability of resources as planned, break down in plant and machinery.

(iii) Natural calamity etc.

It has been observed that, inspite of best efforts, some activities need more time in completion than originally planned, or some new activities crop up. To ensure that scheduled time is maintained, it is necessary to review the progress of project and redraft the network according to latest requirements. During redrafting scheduled dates are revised, but if it is not possible to delay the project, then activities on new critical path are accelerated by allocating extra resources, in order to adhere to committed date.

The process of reviewing the progress of the project execution, is known as "updating".

Example. 20.7. *Network shown below indicates time in weeks required for completion of each activity.*

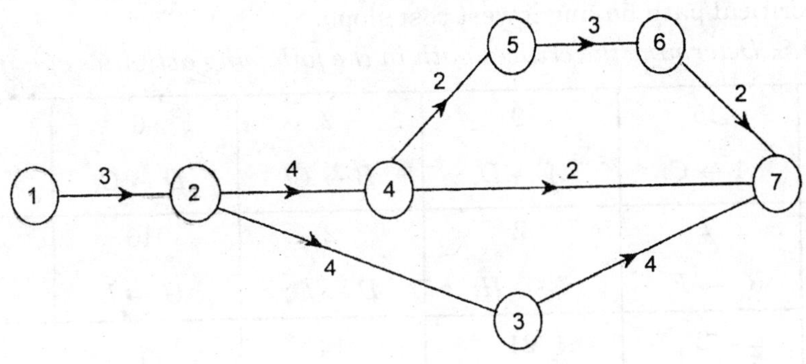

Fig. 20.38.

The network is reviewed after 8 weeks and found that activities have progressed as under:

Activity	*Time required for balance work*	*Remarks*
1 – 2	0	Completed
2 – 3	0	Completed
2 – 4	0	Completed
3 – 7	3	Partially done
4 – 5	2	Not started
4 – 7	2	Not started
5 – 6	3	Not started
6 – 7	2	Not started

Solution. To know the exact progress of the activities, a revised network is drawn, indicating required times as on the date of review, *i.e.*, after 8 weeks. (Refer Fig. 20.39.)

All the completed activities are indicated in Fig.20.39 by one arrow called "elapsed time arrow" showing already consumed times and having new event numbers.

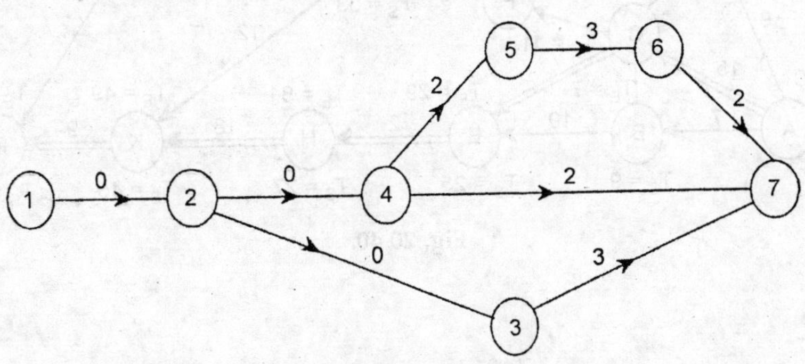

Fig. 20.39.

This means the project shall be delayed by one week. If it is necessary to adhere to schedule even at the cost of extra expenditure, then crashing is desired to be done to keep the earlier scheduled time. Therefore, in order to crash the network, one week must be taken of from the activities on the critical path having lowest cost slope.

Example 20.8. *Determine the critical path in the following activities of a project:*

7 $A \to B;$	15 $A \to C;$	9 $A \to D;$	2 $B \to C;$	6 $D \to C;$	10 $B \to E;$
14 $C \to E;$	7 $C \to F;$	2 $E \to H;$	2 $D \to G;$	16 $G \to I;$	9 $F \to I;$
18 $H \to K;$	12 $I \to K;$	21 $G \to J;$	14 $J \to L;$	1 $K \to M;$	6 and $R \to M;$

Also indicate the slack periods and slack paths, when the project is to be completed in 54 days. The earliest finish time of each activity has been indicated on arrow.

Solution. Network for activities, given in the problem is drawn at Fig.20.40, and Earliest expected time (T_E) and the latest allowable time T_S is also calculated for each event and indicated on the diagram.

Slacks for each activity is indicated on the network diagram to show slack ($T_S - T_L$) on each activity which indicates the path ACEHKM is a critical path because events on this path indicate minimum slack.

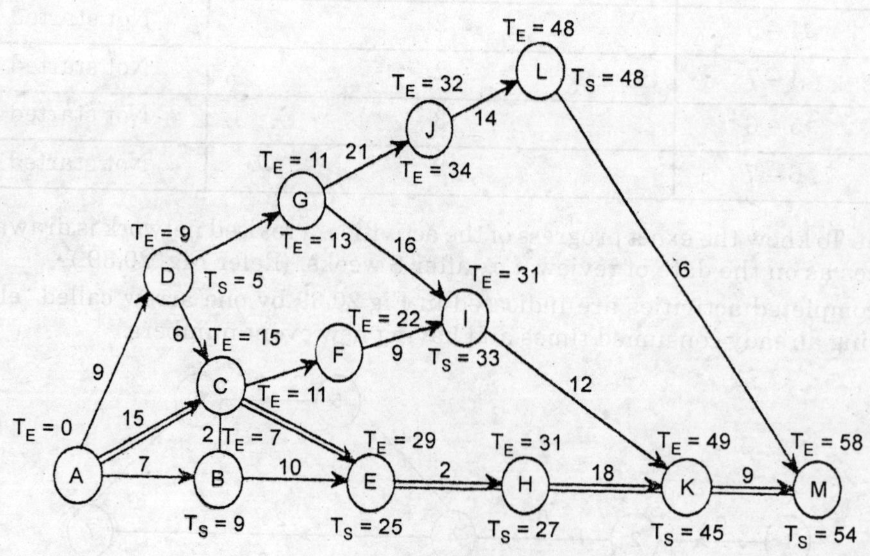

Fig. 20.40.

Example. 20.9. *For a project, following information is given:*

	Duration in days		
Job i – j	*Optimistic t_o*	*Most likely t_L*	*Pessimistic tp*
7 – 5	3	5	13
7 – 6	1	2	15
5 – 4	6	7	8
5 – 3	2	4	12
6 – 4	2	5	14
4 – 2	4	6	8
4 – 3	5	9	13
2 – 1	1	2	3
3 – 1	1	4	7

(*a*) Draw project network.

(*b*) Calculate length and variance of critical path.

(*c*) With what probability, the critical path calculated in (*b*) will be achieved.

Solution. Project network is drawn hereunder (Fig.20.41).

Average or expected time required for each activity is calculated as follows:

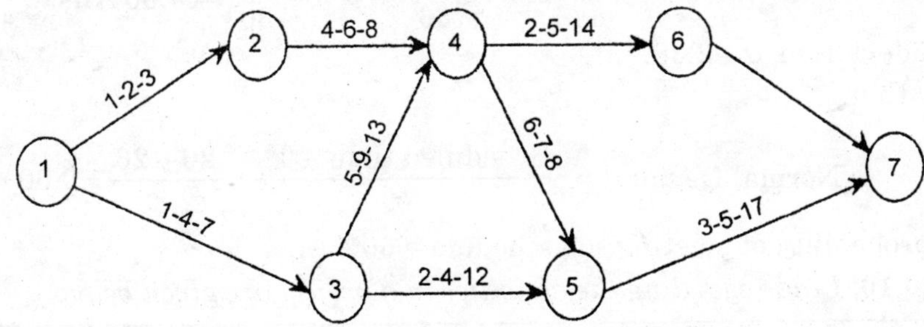

Fig. 20. 41

Activity i – j	t_o	t_L	t_P	$t_e = \dfrac{t_o + 4t_L + t_p}{6}$	$\sigma^2 = \left(\dfrac{t_p - t_o}{6}\right)^2$
1 – 2	1	2	3	2.00	$(2/6)^2$
1 – 3	1	4	7	4.00	1
2 – 4	4	6	8	6.00	$(4/6)^2$
3 – 4	5	9	13	9.00	$(8/6)^2$
3 – 5	2	4	12	5.00	$(10/6)^2$
4 – 5	6	7	8	7.00	$(2/6)^2$
4 – 6	2	5	14	6.00	4
5 – 7	3	5	13	6.00	$(10/6)^2$
6 – 7	1	2	15	4.00	$(14/6)^2$

By knowing the values of t_e for each activity, we calculate the values T_E and T_L for each event and indicate it on the network drawn at Fig.20.42.

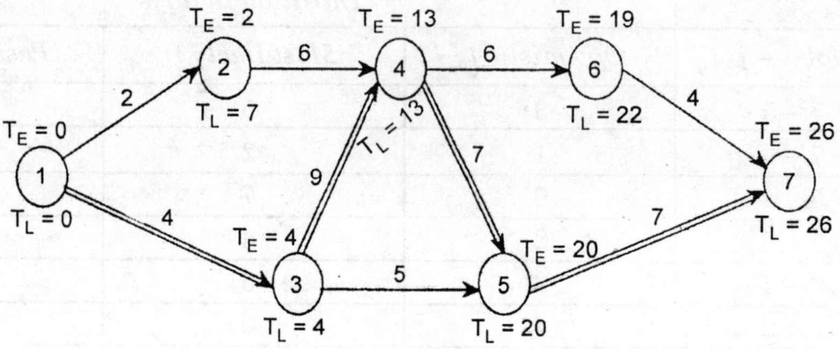

Fig. 20.42

From the values of T_E and T_L, it is seen that critical path in this network is 1–3–4–5–7 and length of the project is **26 days.**

Variance along the critical path = $\Sigma\sigma^2$

$$= 1 + \left(\frac{8}{6}\right)^2 + \left(\frac{2}{6}\right)^2 + \left(\frac{10}{6}\right)^2$$

$$= \frac{36 + 64 + 4 + 100}{36} = \frac{204}{36} = \mathbf{5.66\ Ans.}$$

$\therefore$ Standard deviation, $\sigma = 2.38$.

As we know that,

$$\text{Normal Deviate} = \frac{\text{Scheduled time} - T_E}{\sigma} = \frac{26 - 26}{2.38} = 0.00$$

Therefore, probability of meeting the schedule = 50% Ans.

Example 20.10. *Data regarding the activities in a project are given below*

Activity	*Immediate predecessor*	*Time in days*		*Increase in cost for decreasing the duration by one day (in units of money)*
		Normal duration	*Minimum duration*	
A	–	5	4	1
B	–	8	7	2
C	A	2	2	-
D	A	6	4	3
E	B,C	4	4	-
F	B, C, D	4	3	1

(*a*) Draw the project network.

(*b*) Using normal duration, determine the critical path and the project duration.

(*c*) If there is a saving of 2 units of money for every day saved in the project duration, find the optimal schedule.

Solution. Network is drawn by using the given data. (Fig.20.43*a*)

From the values T_E and T_L indicated on the above network, we see that critical path is 1–2–5–6, *i.e.* A–D–F and the project duration is 15 days.

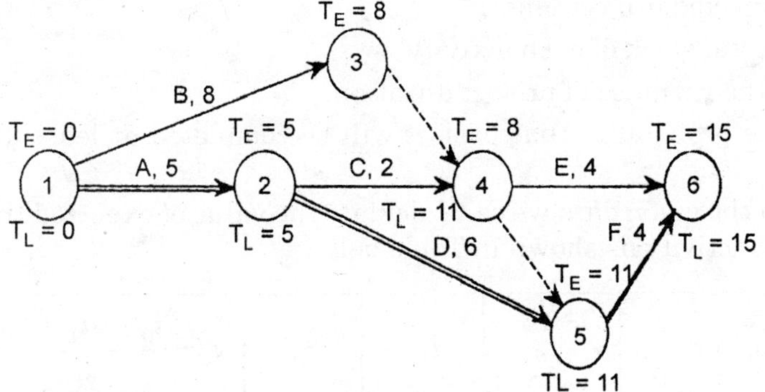

Fig. 20.43 (*a*)

As we know that optimum duration is achieved by crashing those activities which has cost slopes less than indirect expenditure per day.

To crash the project, first of all crashing is done on the activity having least cost slope on the critical path. Therefore, first we should crash activity *A* and *F* by one day each. The network is again drawn after crashing these activities *A* and *F*.

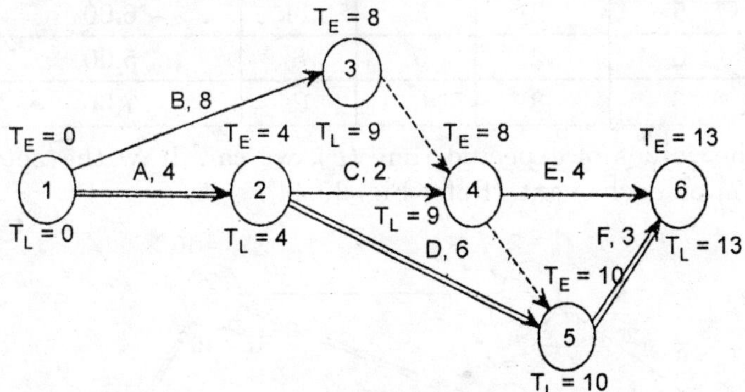

Fig. 20.43. (*b*)

Still the critical path remains same, *i.e., ADF.* In II stage, only activity *D* is left on critical path for crashing. But, since by crashing this activity, the cost increases by 3 units whereas saving is only 2 units from indirect expenses, hence further crashing is not economical. Therefore, optimal schedule is 13 days.

Example 20.11. *A small project is composed of seven activities, as given below:*

Activity		*Estimated duration (week)*		
i	*j*	*Optimistic*	*Most likely*	*Pessimistic*
1	2	1	1	7
1	3	1	4	7
1	4	2	2	8
2	5	1	1	1
3	5	2	5	14
4	6	2	5	8
5	6	3	6	15

- Draw project network.
- Find the expected duration and variance of all activities.
- What is expected project length ?
- Calculate total slack of each activity.
- Calculate the variance of project duration.
- What is the probability that project will be completed at least 3 weeks earlier than expected?

Solution. From the given data we can calculate the value of expected time (t_e) required and variance (σ^2) of each activity as shown in Table below:

Activity		t_0	t_L	t_p	$t_e = \dfrac{t_0 + 4t_L + t_p}{6}$	$\sigma^2 = \left(\dfrac{t_p - t_0}{6}\right)^2$
i	j					
1	2	1	1	7	2.00	1
1	3	1	4	7	4.00	1
1	4	2	2	8	3.00	1
2	5	1	1	1	1.00	0
3	5	2	5	14	6.00	4
4	6	2	5	8	5.00	1
5	6	3	6	15	7.00	4

Now by using the values of expected time (t_e), we can draw the network as below and indicate the T_E and T_L on each event. (Refer Fig. 20.44).

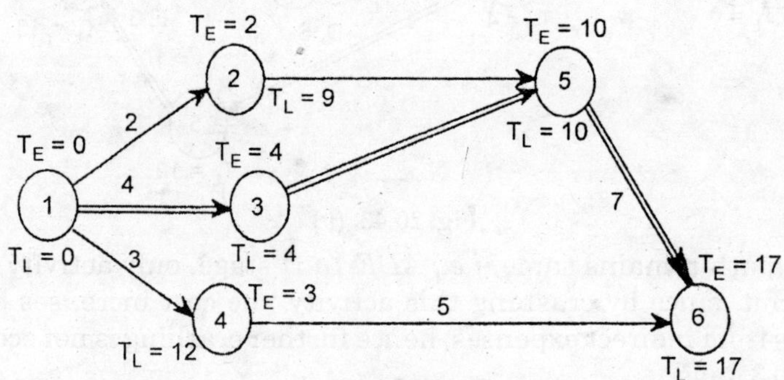

Fig. 20.44.

By knowing the values of T_E and T_L, we see that critical path is 1–3–5–6, *i.e.*, the path having minimum slack, and the expected project length is 17 weeks, slacks on all the activities are given below:

Activity	*Slack*	*Activity*	*Slack*
1-2	7	2 – 5	7
1-3	0	3 – 5	0
1-4	9	4 – 6	9
		5 – 6	0

To calculate probability, we first calculate variance along critical path,

$\Sigma\sigma^2$ along critical path = 1 + 4 + 4 = 9

$\therefore$ Standard deviation, $\sigma = 3$.

$$\text{Normal deviation} = \frac{\text{Scheduled time} - \text{Expected time}}{\sigma} = -\frac{3}{3} = -1$$

Hence the probability that project will be completed 3 weeks earlier than expected is 15.9%. [As we know that probability, at – 1 normal deviation is 15.9%]. **Ans.**

Example 20.12. *A small maintenance project consisting of jobs given in the Table below. With each job. normal time and crash time are given in days. The cost of crashing a job in rupees per day is also given :*

Job i – j	*Normal duration in days*	*Crash duration in days*	*Cost of crashing Rs. / day*
1 – 2	9	6	20
1 – 3	8	5	25
1 – 4	15	10	30
2 – 4	5	3	10
3 – 4	10	6	15
4 – 5	2	1	40

– What is the normal length and the minimum project length ?

– Determine the minimum crashing cost schedule from normal length, by each day for 7 days.

– If overhead costs total Rs. 60 day, what is the optimal length schedule in terms of both crashing and overhead costs ?

Solution. Network with given values of normal duration is drawn hereunder. (Fig.20.45a).

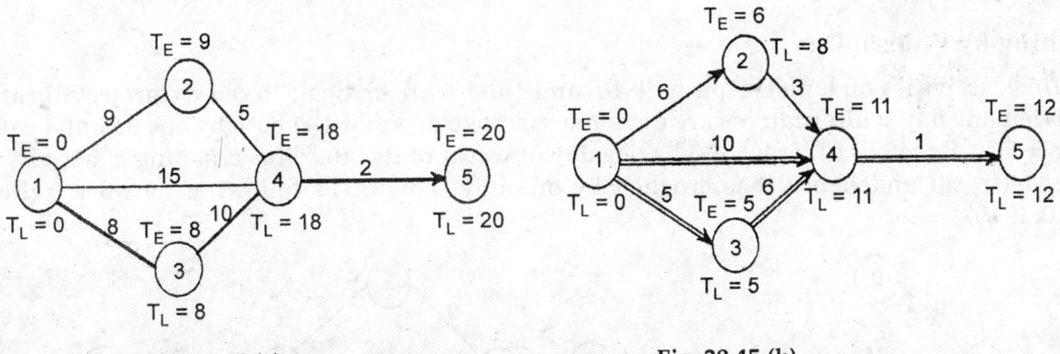

Fig. 20.45 (a) **Fig. 20.45 (b)**

Now the network is again drawn with crash duration of each activity. (Fig. 20.45*b*).

By drawing the project network we have calculated that expected time with normal duration is 20 days, whereas it is 12 days with crash duration (can also be termed as minimum project length).

Now we crash the project, starting from that with normal duration, for determining minimum crashing cost.

Crashing by One Day

With normal duration, critical path is 1–3–4–5 and the least expensive activity to crash on critical path is 3–4. It is crashed from 10 days to 9 days at a cost of Rs. 15. [Refer Fig.20.45 (c)].

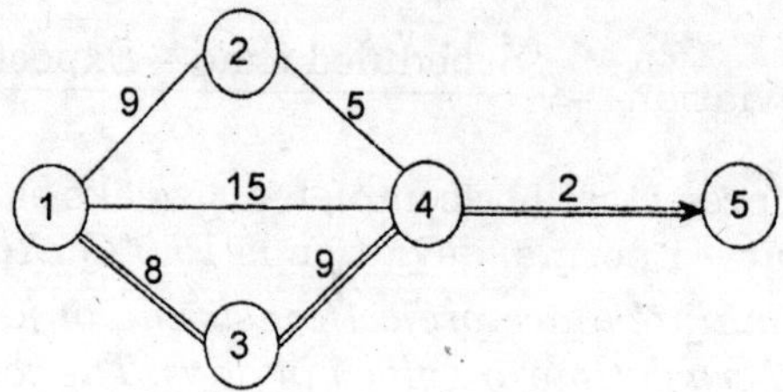

Fig. 20.45 (c)

Crashing by Second Day

Again the critical path is same and the activity 3-4 is crashed again by one day at a cost of Rs. 15. [Refer Fig. 20.45 (*d*)].

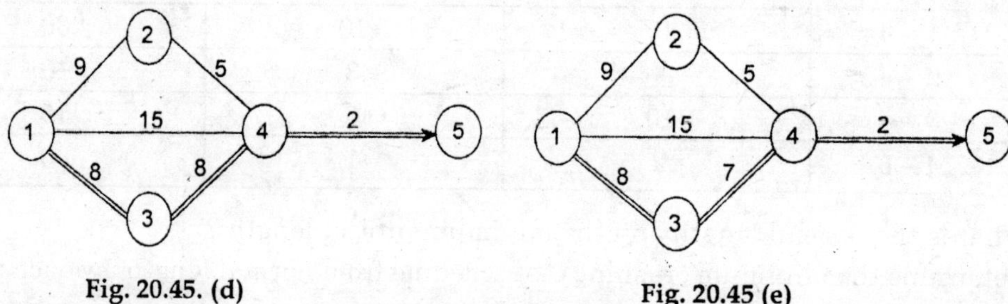

Fig. 20.45. (d) Fig. 20.45 (e)

Crashing by Third Day

Still critical path is same and activity 3–4 is crashed by one more day at a cost of Rs. 15. (Refer Fig.20.45 (*e*))

Crashing by Fourth Day

This time, activities on both the paths 1-4-5 and 1-3-4-5 are critical. To reduce project duration by further one day, 2 alternatives are available (*i*) crash 3–4 and 1–4 both by one day at a cost of Rs. 15 + 30 = Rs. 45 or (*ii*) crash 4-5 by one day at a cost of Rs. 40. Thus crashing of activity 4 – 5 is economical and hence it is crashed by one day. This gives following network : (Refer Fig. 20.45 (*f*))

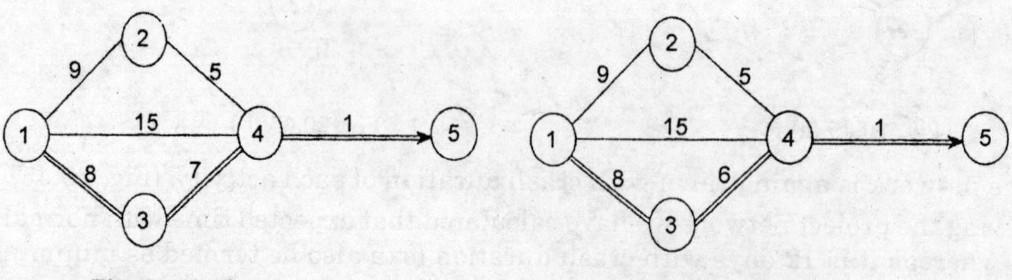

Fig. 20.45 (*f*) Fig. 20.45 (*g*)

Crashing by Fifth Day

This time we have left with only one alternative, *i.e.,* to reduce both activities 1—4 and 3—4 both by one day at a cost of Rs. 45. Then new network shall be as shown in Fig.20.45 *(g).*

Crashing by Sixth Day

After having crashed the activities 1–4, 3–4 and 4–5 completely, all the paths become critical. Thus now to reduce duration by one day, activities 1-3, 1-4 and 2-4 are to be crashed by one day each (since crashing of activity 2-4 is less costly than that of 1-2, hence activity 2-4 is being crashed) at a cost of Rs. 25 + 30 +10 = Rs. 65. The new network shall be as shown in Fig. 20.45 *(h):*

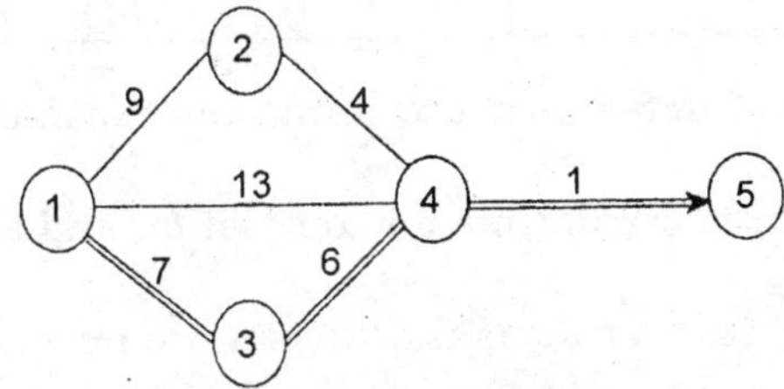

Fig. 20. 45 (*h*)

Crashing by Seventh Day

Now these activities 1-3, 1-4 and 2-4 are again crashed by one day each at a cost of Rs. 65.

Optimal Length Schedule

Since we know that crashing is optimal when all activities on critical path having cost slopes less than that indirect expenses are crashed. In this case, indirect expenses are Rs. 60 per day hence crashing upto the stage of 5th day, i.e., 15 day project length is optimum. Because after this, the cost for crashing per day is Rs. 65, i.e., more than the overhead cost of Rs. 60 per day.

In Table below, we calculate the crashing and overhead costs for each day of crashing:

Completion time in days	*Network*	*Overhead cost Rs. 60 per day*	*Crash cost For one day*	*Progressive*	*Overhead Crash cost in Rs.*
20	All Normal	1200	–	–	1200
19	Crash 3–4	1140	15	15	1155
18	Crash 3–4	1080	15	30	1110
17	Crash 3–4	1020	15	45	1065
16	Crash 4–5	960	40	85	1045
15	Crash 3–4 and 1–4	900	45	130	1030
14	Crash 1–3,1–4 & 2–4	840	65	195	1035
13	Crash 1–3,1–4 & 2–4	780	65	260	1040

The value of total cost shown in the Table also confirms that the optimal project length is **15 days.**

Example 20.13. *Nine tasks A,B...I are to be completed in a sequence such that the task A must be completed before D or E, tasks B or D before F, task C before G or H and the task F or G before the task I. Normal completion time for each of the task in days, minimum completion time and the increase in cost for each day less than the normal, in rupees are shown below:*

Task	*A*	*B*	*C*	*D*	*E*	*F*	*G*	*H*	*I*
Normal time in days	9	11	8	10	17	8	9	15	10
Minimum time in days	7	8	8	9	14	7	9	12	9
Increase in cost for each day less in Rs.	1	2	—	3	4	1	—	6	4

(*i*) Draw the network and determine the minimum normal time for completion of the network.

(*ii*) Determine the minimum crash time for completion and the additional minimum cost to achieve it.

Solution. From the given data for normal duration, we now draw the network.

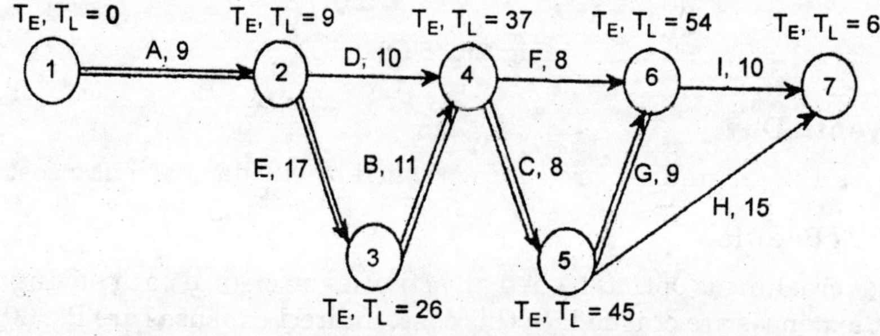

Fig. 20. 46 (*a*)

As indicated in the above network, minimum normal time of completion of the project is 64 days.

Minimum crash time for completion of the project is determined by drawing the network and putting the given crash time on each activity.

Crashing

Since critical path is *AEBCGI* and minimum increase in crash cost is on activity A, therefore, additional cost for **2 days** saved is Rs. 2. Next minimum cost slope is for activity *B*. To crash *B* by 3 days, increase in cost shall be Rs. 6. For third crashing, next activity having minimum cost slope is *E*. Therefore, to crash *E*, we can save 3 days at an additional expenditure of Rs. 12. In the end, activity *I* is crashed by one day at a cost of Rs. 4.

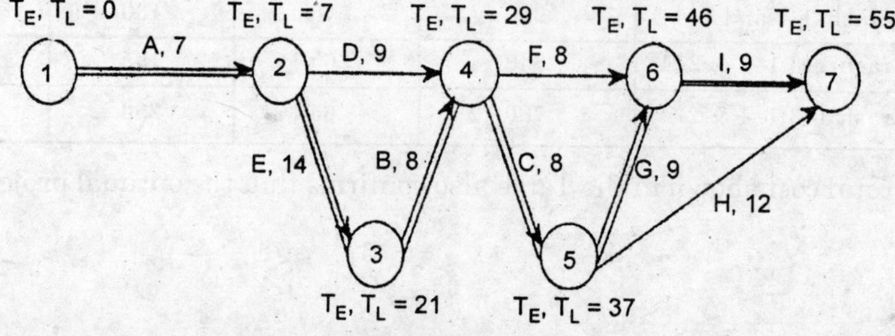

Fig. 20. 46 (*b*)

Thus total increase in cost shall be 2 + 6 + 12 + 4 = **Rs. 24.** Ans.

Example 20.14. A *project has following activities:*

Activity	*Immediate Predecessors*	*Time in days*	*Manpower needed every day*
A	—	4	9
B	—	2	3
C	—	2	6
D	—	4	4
E	*B*	3	8
F	*C*	2	1
G	*D, F*	3	2
H	*E, F*	4	1

(*a*) Draw the project network.

(*b*) Find the critical path and the project duration.

(*c*) Find a schedule which minimises the day-today variation in manpower requirement (resource levelling).

Solution. The network is drawn from the given data. Number of days required for completion of each activity are also indicated in the diagram. The project network drawn in the Fig.20.47 (*a*) shows that the critical path is *CFGH* and the project duration is 11 days.

The time scale version of this network is drawn in the Fig.20.47 (*b*) and manpower needed for each activity is mentioned on them. Load histogram is also shown below the time version diagram.

Figure 20.47 (*c*) shows that maximum numbers are required during first 4 days. Therefore, to level the manpower requirement, the activities A, *B* and *E* (non-critical activities) are to be shifted

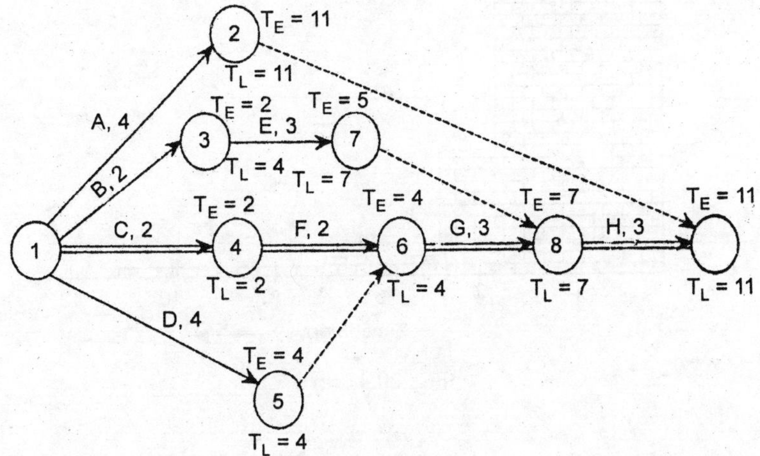

Fig. 20.47 (*a*)

within slack period, as shown in Fig. 20.47 (*d*), in order to get uniform manpower requirement.

Figure shown above below the time scale version and histogram after resource levelling. (Refer Fig.20.47 (*d*) and 20.47 (*e*).

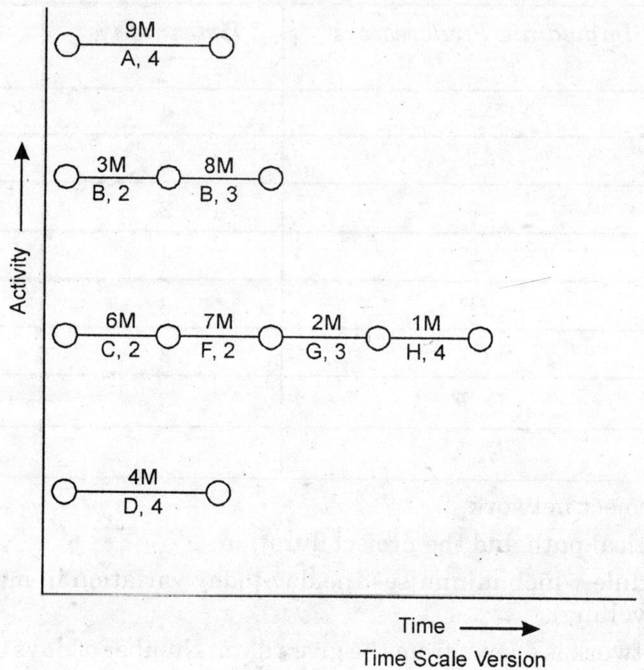

Fig. 20.47 (*b*)

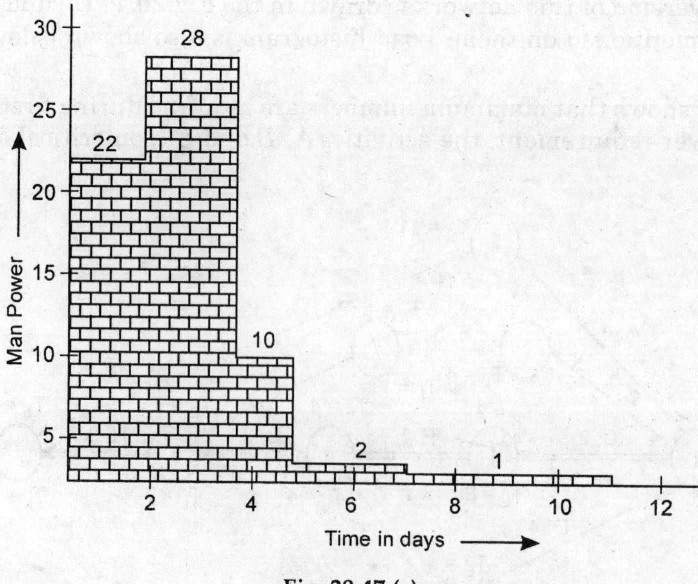

Fig. 20.47 (*c*)

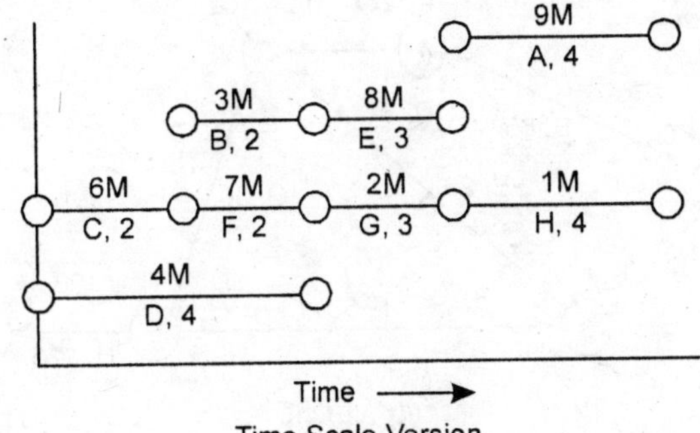

Fig. 20.47 (*d*)

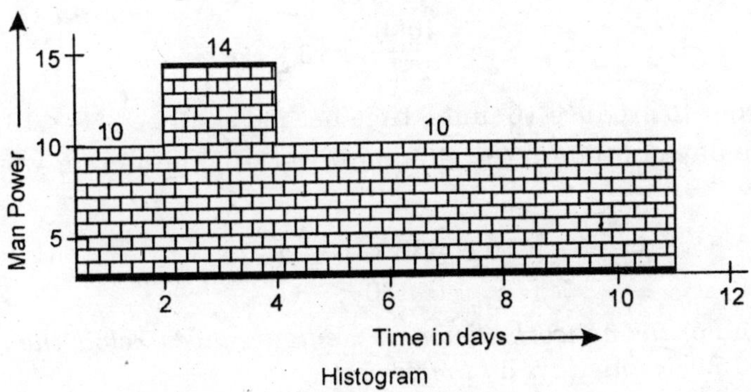

Fig. 20.47 (*e*) Histogram

Example 20.15. *An assembly consists of a different operations as shown below :*

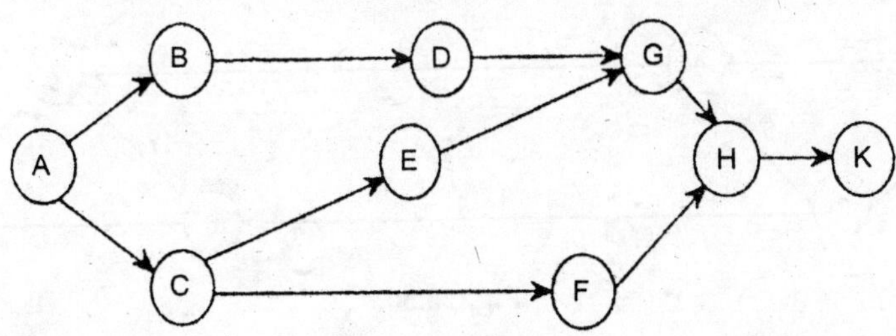

Fig. 20.48.

Standard time for the operations are:

Operation	*A*	*B*	*C*	*D*	*E*	*F*	*G*	*H*	*K*
Standard time, minutes	60	65	29	37	28	63	36	126	64

Determine the most efficient number of work stations to produce 4000 units in a year. Assume that there are 250 working days in a year.

Solution. The network given in the problem is event oriented, now it is converted into activity oriented as follows. The values of expected time T_E are indicated on it.

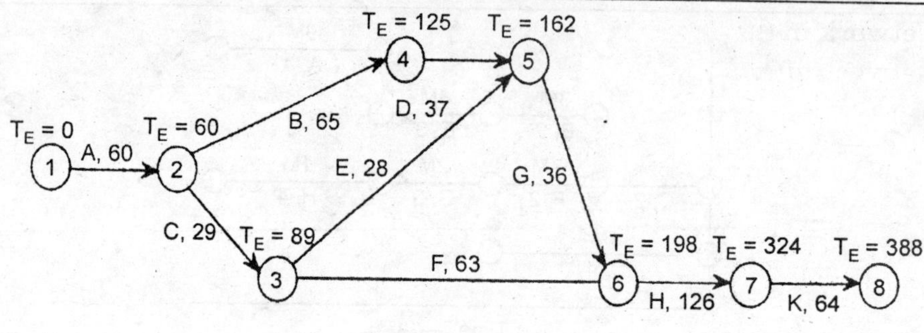

Fig. 20.49.

From this network we see that time required to produce one unit is 388 min. Since, number of units to be produced in one day.

$$= \frac{4000}{250} = 16.$$

Therefore, in order to produce 16 units, time needed shall be 388 × 16 min.

Considering one day of 8 hours (*i.e.* 480 min) working, minimum work stations required shall be

$$= \frac{388 \times 16}{480} = 13 \text{ No. } \textbf{Ans.}$$

Example 20.16. *For the network shown in the figure given below the following conditions were observed after 15 working days on the project:*

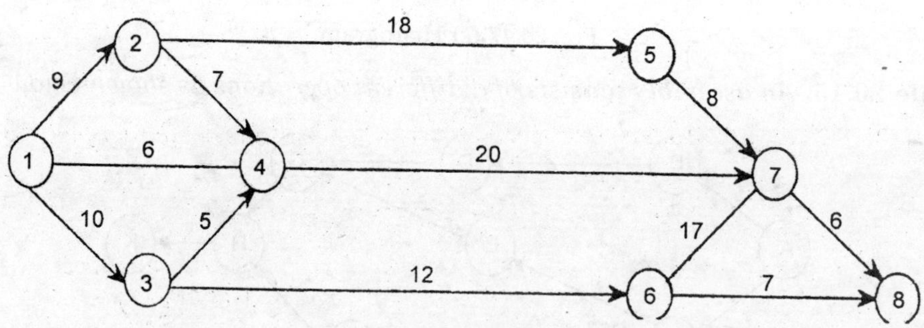

Fig. 20.50.

(*a*) Activities 1-2,1-3, and 1-4 are completed as originally planned.

(*b*) Activity 2-4 in process and will be completed in 3 more days.

(*c*) Activity 3-6 is in process and will need 18 days more for completion.

(*d*) Activity 6-7 appears to present some problem and its new estimated time of completion is 12 days,

(*e*) Activity 6-8 can be completed in 5 days instead of originally planned 7 days.

(*i*) Formulate a new project based on the assessment at the end of 15 days. Include all activities in the new project.

(*ii*) Compare the critical paths for the old and new network.

Solution. We now draw the network for the position in the beginning and after 15 working days respectively.

(*a*) Network in the beginning: (Fig.20.51)

(*b*) Network after 15 days (Fig.20.52)

New Network

If we indicate all the completed activities by one arrow called 'Elapsed time arrow', showing already consumed time and the diagram is given a new event number, then the new project indicating required time at the end of 15 days shall be

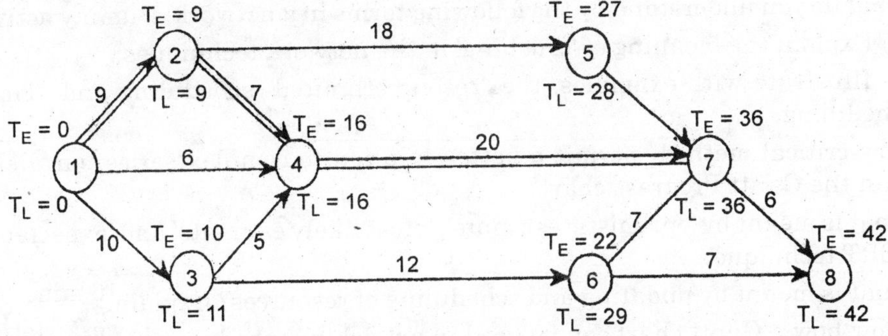

Fig. 20.51.

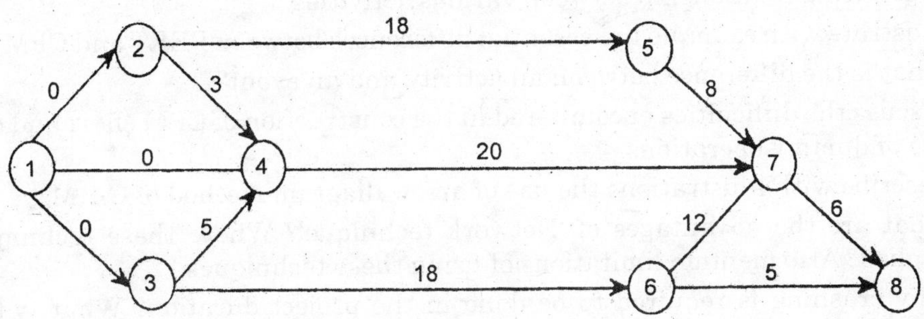

Fig. 20.52.

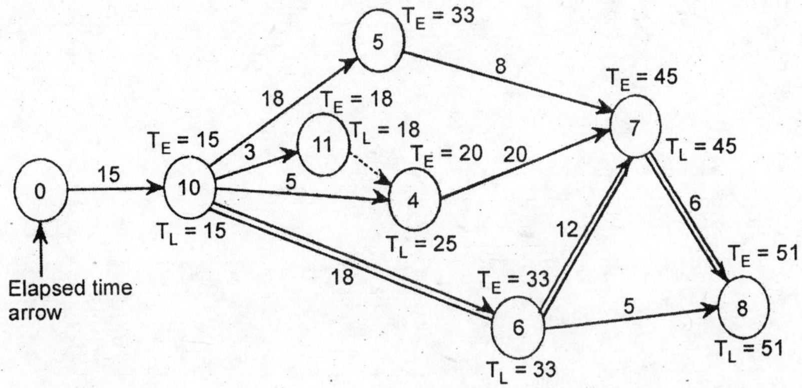

Fig. 20.53.

The above networks show the critical path in the (*i*) old, *i.e.*, beginning of network is 1-2-4-7-8 and (*ii*) new network is 0-10-6-7-8.

QUESTIONS

1. List the limitation of bar chart in production planning. Give one example to explain each limitation.
2. Describe various kinds of floats. Explain significance of each kind of float.
3. Discuss in what aspects, C.P.M. and PERT techniques differ from each other.
4. What do you understand by the following terms in a network; Dummy activity, Loping?
5. (*a*) Explain the meaning of 'crushing' in the network techniques;

   (*b*) Illustrate with examples, the "resource limited" scheduling and "Times limited" scheduling.
6. How critical method permit a better solution to complex series parallel operations than the Gantt Progress chart?
7. What is meant by 'optimistic estimate', 'most likely estimate' and 'expected time' in the PERT technique?
8. What is meant by updating and scheduling of resources? Explain.
9. Show how a Gantt chart can be used in a machine scheduling problem?
10. Explain the following with reference to CPM and PERT: (*a*) Activity slack or float; (*b*) Sequencing relationship between various activities.
11. Illustrate with example the essential differences between PERT and CPM techniques.
12. What is the difference between an activity and an event?
13. Discuss the difficulties encountered in the construction of CPM chart and describe the use of dummy operations.
14. Describe with illustrations the use of arrow diagram method of C.P.M.
15. What are the advantages of 'Network technique'? Where these techniques can be applied? Also mention limitations of using these techniques.
16. Why crashing is required to be done in the project duration? What is the optimal crashing?
17. Define cost-slopes. What is the difference between 'Resource smoothing' and 'Resource levelling?

Part–5 Inspection and Quality Control

21 INSPECTION AND ACCEPTANCE SAMPLING

21.1. INTRODUCTION

A worker manufactures products according to his skill and ability. During manufacturing, he inspects his assigned job whether he is doing it as per laid specifications or not. In mass and inter-changeable production, mostly semi-skilled workers are engaged to produce goods, hence separate inspecting staff is deputed to inspect jobs to ensure that products manufactured are according to established standards and to stop doing further work on spoiled products.

The reputation and success of any industry largely depends upon quality of his products. Inspection does not create quality but it helps to control it. The aim is to prevent defects by finding and eliminating the causes of trouble. Inspection sorts out below standard materials and products and stops their manufacturing.

Definitions

Inspection is the function to judge the quality of a product. According to Dr. W. R. Springle, "Inspection is the process of measuring the quality of a product or service in terms of established standards".

A broad definition given by Kimball, "Inspection is the art of comparing materials, products or performance, with established standards". Whenever products are manufactured, some will be in the limits of errors and some will be outside the allowances provided. With the help of inspection, such products are selected which will be satisfactory in all conditions of work.

Definition given by Alford and Beatly, "Inspection is the art of applying tests, preferably by the aid of measuring appliances to observe whether a given item of product is within the specified limit of variability.

Inspection is an important aspect ofproduction control. Products should be checked at various stages for the size, shape and quality. It stops the wrong production and thus wastage can be checked. Defective parts cannot reach the assembly points. To maintain the desired accuracy and quickness, special gauges and other measuring devices must be used. So inspection is a tool for controlling the quality of product.

Inspection controls the quality of the product and is a must in a production shop, inspite of its adding to the expenditure. It is true that inspection controls the quality of product and is a must in a production shop. This statement can be justified, if we first study the objects of inspection.

Objects of Inspection.

The main objects are :

1. To collect information regarding the performance of the product with established standards for the use of engineering, production, purchasing and quality control etc.
2. To sort out poor quality manufactured products and thus to maintain the standard.
3. To establish and increase the reputation by protecting consumers from receiving poor quality products.

So, for achieving these objectives, there is inspection in every organisation and its cost has to be borne by the employer but if there is no inspection, the products of poor quality may reach to the consumers. Material wastage and spoilage will be more, machining time will be more. So products of poor quality and high cost will reduce the reputation of the concern and demand of their products will gradually go on reducing and the business may come to standstill.

So, with the little additional cost inspection system can be organised which provides large benefits or we can say it is impossible to run any organisation whatever its size may be, without proper inspection, economically and efficiently.

Principles of Inspection

The two most important principles of Inspection are :

(*a*) Inspection function for maximum efficiency must be independent but co-ordinate with the functions of production, planning and sales department.

(*b*) Improvement in quality performance is achieved as a result of changes in engineering specifications or manufacturing procedures and by inspection techniques.

21.2. ORGANISATION OF INSPECTION DEPARTMENT

Inspection department should not be attached directly under those who are engaged in increasing the quantity of production, unless the quantity of the products is of much importance.

If the production foreman will be the incharge of inspection work, then quality of product will receive less attention and he will simply try to increase to quantity of production. If the quality is of average importance then inspection department may be kept as a staff department under the works superintendent. In this system, production and inspection both work under the supervision of superintendent.

If quality is of maximum importance, the inspection should be a major manufacturing function directly under the control of works manager. In this way, inspection department holds a similar position as that of purchasing department and the engineering department.

Qualifications of Inspectors

In order to carry out the full responsibilities, Inspector must possess certain special qualifications. Following qualities are necessary in any Inspector:

1. He should know his job thoroughly. For this purpose, technical .knowledge and skill in the art of inspection is essential.
2. He should be intelligent, capable and of good grasping power.
3. He should understand his responsibility and be able to work with patience. Any negligence of his part may lead to serious loss in product quality.
4. He must know statistical quality control technique well.

5. He should be cost conscious and, therefore, do not set unnecessary strict and narrow limits.
6. He should be able to minimise or present wastage by using a substitute to the material already in use.
7. He should have the working knowledge of the general quality standards.
8. He should know the reasons for standard through and understanding of material and processes.

Duties and Responsibilities of Chief Inspector

Chief Inspector is the head of inspection department. The inspection is the responsibility of the chief inspector who organises this Work and supervises the work of the inspector.

To maintain the standard of quality, the inspection department prevents the defective products from passing forward to next operation or to the stores. Inspectors should point out the faulty operations and should inform the way to prevent them. Following are the main responsibilities of the Chief Inspector :

1. To organise and supervise the work of the inspecting staff.
2. To train the staff to carry out their duties effectively
3. To reject the products which are below standard.
4. To send reports on inspected work and to suggest the ways to minimise faulty production.
5. To see that proper care of costly equipments in inspection department, is being taken.

Functions of Inspection Department

1. **To inspect Raw Materials.** This is done to see that raw materials received are physically and chemically in accordance with specifications. This is done to eliminate the loss of labour and machining time on the defective materials.

   For some materials, visual examination may be sufficient while for others inspection may be necessary to test the electrical, mechanical and chemical properties etc.
2. **Metallurgical and Metallographical Inspection.** To be sure to see that the metallic structure, hardness and other properties, after the various processes or operations have been performed, are according to specifications.
3. **Purchase Parts Inspection.** The aim of such inspection is to see that all the purchase parts, *i.e.*, tools, spares, jigs and fixtures, general supplies etc. are according to laid specifications. This is to make sure that there is no loss, inferior quality or short counts or damages in accepted quality.
4. **Work in Process Inspection.** To see that product is correctly formed and dimensioned in accordance with specifications during the process of their manufacture at various stages. This has the advantages of
   (*i*) preventing wastage of time and money on defective units and
   (*ii*) preventing delays in assemblies.
5. **Tool Inspection.** To inspect the different tools, which are purchased or made to see that whether they are capable of producing the items in accordance with specifications.
6. **Periodic Gauge and other Measuring Instruments Inspection.** To make sure that these equipment are capable of giving the desired results, whenever used.
7. To collect errors in design or manufacturing methods that results in more assembly time or poor performance.

8. **Finished Products Inspection.** To inspect finished products before they are marketed to see that product of poor quality may be either rejected or in certain industries may be sold out as 'seconds' at a low price.
9. **Salvaging.** This is the function of inspection in which poor quality work is reworked to eliminate the defects or used for some other purpose or converted to scrap material etc.
10. **Complaints Division.** It is the function of inspection which receives reports on defective material or workmanship, design, shape etc. from the sales and service decision. This then investigates and makes recommendations to the manufacturing department to prevent future occurrences.

21.3. INSPECTION STANDARDS

To meet the requirement of quality control certain inspection standards are to be formed. The most important may be:

(*i*) Inspection standards for raw materials.
(*ii*) Inspection standards for work in process.
(*iii*) Working inspection standards.
(*iv*) Inspection standards for finished product.
(*v*) Inspection standards of the completed mechanism.

1. **Inspection Standards of Raw Materials.** The inspection standards for raw materials are based upon purchase specifications. These have been dealt in detail on the chapter of "Purchase Organisation".
2. **Inspection Standards for Work in Process.** These may be classified in five heads:
   (*a*) *Relating to physical condition or properties of materials.* Inspection of the condition of the product after any given process or may have reference to the result or to the fitness for the process or operation.
   (*b*) *Relating to shape and size.* Inter-changeable manufacture is based on such standards. To maintain control over quality, shape and size largely forms the basis for most of the machine shops, engineering and machanical industries.
   (*c*) *Relating to degree of finish.* Standards are to be fixed for smoothness, shade, polish, matt, tint and burnish etc. Formerly standards were not available but today with the help of profilometer, we can compare surface irregularities so that variations as fine as 0.0000025 mm are comparable.
   (*d*) *Chemical.* In chemical industries such as food, soap, cosmetic, drug etc. samples are selected for inspection and products are tested in accordance with statistical quality control techniques.
   (*e*) *Functional or Performance.* This standard vary with the industry, for example in food industry, the product is tested to see if it has the desired flavour or not. In the same way, in a diesel engine assembly, fuel pump and injectors are properly calibrated on specially developed testing equipment before delivery to the assembly department.
3. **Working Inspection Standards.** After limits and tolerance have been determined and they are then given on working drawings. Precision in dimension is transferred to working drawings whose blue prints are given to operators and the work is carried out

by them on specially designed machines for economical production. The work is simply inspected by the use of "GO" and "NO GO" gauges.

4. **Inspection Standards for Finished Products.** The standards for finished machine parts, sub-assemblies and assemblies allow :
   (*a*) for components that will assemble with those which they must fit to make a sub-assembly.
   (*b*) for sub-assemblies that will group into a final assembly; and
   (*c*) for final assemblies that will enter a completed mechanism. Complex and elaborate gauges and fixtures are used for the inspection of such finished products.
   The standards for other finished products are such as will ensure that the product will satisfy the customer.
5. **Inspection Standards of the Complete Mechanism.** After the components of a mechanism have been assembled, a final test or series of tests are conducted. For example, a life is tested to carry a specified overload without permanent set. A gun barrel will stand a heavy proof charge without bursting or bulging.

21.4. KINDS OF INSPECTION

Because of the varieties of manufactured products and the wide differences in comparative qualities, it is reasonable to expect various kinds of inspection.

The most important of these are :

1. Tool Inspection (Trail-run-Inspection).
2. First Piece Inspection.
3. Working Inspection.
4. Sample Inspection.
5. Operation Inspection.
6. Final Inspection.
7. Pilot Piece Inspection.
8. Key Operation Inspection.
9. Functional Inspection.
10. Endurance Inspection.

    The above kinds are based on methods. To this list two other kinds which are concerned with the location of the work of inspection are also added. These are :
11. Floor or patrolling Inspection.
12. Centralized Inspection.

1. **Tool Inspection.** According to this method tools, fixtures, jigs and gauges are inspected in advance to the work of production. In this method, it has been assumed that when tools are proper, the products manufactured by them will be satisfactory. This method can give good results in automatic production work. Then, the trial run of a single piece is made to see that product is within tolerances.
2. **First Piece Inspection.** In automatic machines, if first 3 or 4 products are inspected and are found to be satisfactory then it is assumed that product manufactured afterwards will also be satisfactory. It assures that work has begun correctly.
3. **Working Inspection.** According to this type of inspection, the products should be

inspected while they are in process, that they are being produced according to specifications.

Inspectors should check products at definite intervals to make sure that they are being produced as per requirements.

4. **Sample Inspection.** In this, certain percentage from a lot is inspected and the entire lot is judged by the result of these samples.
5. **Operation Inspection.** It is the inspection at the completion of operation before the work in process passed to another operation or machine or department.
6. **Final Inspection.** In this type of inspection, articles are inspected when they are completely manufactured before sending them to the store.
7. **Pilot Piece Inspection.** This is used in product layout. The product is passed through its entire sequence of operations on a series of machines installed for producing that product. After one piece is manufactured, each tool, each machine is tested so that all defective tools are replaced and all incorrect adjustments are made allright. When a good product starts coming, the production line is allowed for actual production.
8. **Key Operation Inspection.** There are certain operations which are quite costly or difficult, *i.e.*, operators usually do mistake at such places. Such operations are known as 'key operations'. Inspection is done prior to and immediately after the completion of each of these operations.
9. **Functional Inspection.** This inspection is carried out after the completion of assembly to check the accuracy of assembly to ensure it will function as required.
10. **Endurance Inspection.** This inspection is carried out to estimate how much time an assembly will withstand its use and to determine weakness for correction.
11. **Floor or Patrolling Inspection.** According to this, inspection is done at or near the machine. In this inspection, work ranges from general patrolling-supervision, *i.e.*, keeping an eye on work at machines, to careful measurement of product at its place of production.

Advantages

1. Errors caught in time prevent spoilage of large amount of work.
2. This inspection can help in removing the troubles or difficulties in the doing of work.
3. This requires less handling of job because work does not have to be moved from the place of production. Thus indirect labour cost will be less.
4. Delays at inspection room and thus wastage of time is minimised.
5. Product layout and mass production can well be achieved.
6. The work of routing, scheduling, despatching is simplified.
7. It reduces labour cost.
8. Reduction of work in process is possible.

Disadvantages

1. Inspector has to move from one area to another and thus his time is wasted.
2. Advance machines for inspection purpose cannot be used.
3. Keeping a track of good or bad products is slightly difficult.
4. Sometimes work may pile up at work stations. The worker has completed his work but awaiting for inspection.
5. Presence of large quantities of work on the floor complicates to keep work moving.
6. The Inspector may be influenced by some of the workers and start favouritism.

7. Highly skilled inspectors to be engaged.
8. There can be delay in deciding doubtful cases.

12. **Centralised Inspection.** In this kind, inspection is carried out in the inspection rooms. The parts to be checked are moved to special rooms where precision measuring devices are located. Main idea in this is to separate inspection from manufacturing.

    Centralised inspection does not mean one inspection room but a number of such rooms or cribs may be installed, each located centrally in respect to the machine. The usual practice is to locate cribs/rooms parallel to the flow of work through the shop.

    Advantages

    1. Inspectors of less skill can perform the job well.
    2. Better quality can be achieved because of no or little understanding between workers and inspectors.
    3. With the aid of fixed and automatic inspection, devices mass inspection at lower cost is possible.
    4. Because of better working conditions and less interferences, inspector can check the products with higher speed.
    5. Accurate inspection with delicate instruments can be done under controlled atmosphere.
    6. To avoid displacement or theft, work can be stored in self-counting trays.
    7. Less number of gauges, instruments etc. are required.
    8. Decision on doubtful cases can be taken at once by authority.
    9. The shops mostly remain neat and clean as there is no accumulation of finished parts. They are collected and sent to inspection room.

    Disadvantages

    1. Workers will come to know their weak points after the completion of jobs.
    2. Materials handling is more.
    3. Delay at inspection room causes wastage of time.
    4. Here routing, scheduling and despatching includes the inspection room, so the work of production control increases.
    5. If the inspection room is not built in the line of flow, there may be break in the plan of product layout for straight line manufacture.
    6. Due to non-detection of machining errors in time, there may be more spoilage of work.

13. **Combined Method.** This is combination of Floor and Centralised Inspection systems. Large and heavy jobs usually require patrolling inspection. This is essential to keep operations running and clear up troubles on the spot resulting in the reduction of spoiled materials and machining costs.

    The necessity for more accurate inspection of certain parts or sub-assemblies cannot be denied and they may require to move them to the central inspection room.

    Therefore, for introducing any kind of inspection, the situation must be studied thoroughly before taking the decision.

21.5. INSPECTION PROCEDURE FOR MASS PRODUCTION

Methods of Inspection

To control the quality of manufactured products, following three methods of inspection are usually adopted in mass scale production. In big industries, all these methods are used together.

1. Screening or 100% Inspection.
2. Lot by Lot Inspection.
3. Process Inspection.

Each method has been explained as under :

1. **Screening.** It is that method of inspection, in which each and every unit manufactured is inspected to meet the desired specifications. The aim is to catch all the defective products produced. But experience has shown that screening or 100% inspection does not guarantee a perfect product due to monotony. Monotony creates fatigue and lowers attention. If cent per cent correct products are required then at least 200 per cent inspection is necessary.

   Further, there are many types of'destructive' testing where 100 per cent inspection would result in 100 per cent destruction of products. For example, sharpness testing of razor blades, tensile strength tests of wire, chip test of enamel, filament test of electric bulb and firing tests of ammunition etc. With such products, other methods of quality control are necessary.

   Hundred per cent inspection is necessary for : (*i*) Important components upon which the functioning of the whole assembly depends, (*ii*) Where a process normally yields a high percentage of defective products. For example, production of high precision ball bearings in which generally 20% defective products may come.

2. **Lot by Lot Inspection.** This method is also known as Sampling Inspection. This method was developed to eliminate the high cost of Screening Inspection. In this method, small number of samples are drawn from the lot and the inspector judges from them the acceptability of the whole lot.

   Here modern statistics of mathematical probability helps the inspector by furnishing him with ready made sampling plans.

   Lot by Lot Inspecting method has been dealt in details in the chapter on 'Acceptance Sampling'.

3. **Process Inspection.** The purpose of this method of inspection is to search out defective products where and when they occur, so that an immediate corrective action can be taken. This inspection deals with all causes of defective work; be it operator, operation, raw material, tool or machine etc. So, in process inspection, inspector patrols on assigned areas and checks machines, methods of operations, and occasional pieces of products from raw material to finished products.

   The limitations of this method are that inspectors cannot be stationed at all machines at all times. As a result, large quantities of defective materials may slip from the knowledge of inspectors.

   This method is used for inspecting precision machining, intricate casting, certain type of spot and resistance welding and in many chemical, mechanical and electrical measurements.

When and Where, How and How much to inspect

Following are the problems of inspection, which should be decided before the inspection starts, *i.e.,* while planning the inspection activity :

1. Where to inspect?
2. When to inspect?
3. How to inspect?
4. How much to inspect?

1. **Where to Inspect.** Inspection may be done either at the machine itself or in a central inspection room separated from actual production. Floor inspection saves the cost of transportation of the material from the place of production to the inspection room. Floor inspection provides quicker inspection service. Floor inspection is very useful specially when the product is very bulky and when it becomes very difficult to carry the products from production site to inspection room. In continuous industries where subsequent operations are linked together by moving belts or other mechanical handling devices, it is out of question to carry the product off into separate inspection room.

   On the other hand, a separate inspection room provides accurate and rapid inspection than that provided at production site. At central inspection room, inspection condition will be better, and proper precision instruments may be provided. In the case of central inspection room, there are less chances of the inspector being influenced. Therefore, one of the above mentioned way is selected after considering all the factors.

2. **When to Inspect.** This problem of 'when to inspect' depends upon the nature of products and the procedure employed for manufacture. No general rule can be given about whether inspection should be done after each operation in the process or only at the final stage of completion. Generally a compromise between the two methods is adopted.

   Usually a product is inspected when it is transferred from one production department to another, so that responsibility may be fixed for any defective work. Inspection is necessary after that operation in which there are more chances of defects, so that main aim of inspection (to control the quality with minimum possible cost) can be achieved.

3. **How to Inspect.** Different methods of inspection have already been discussed in this chapter. One of them should be adopted after considering all the factors like type of products, operations involved etc.

   'GO and NOT GO' gauges are preferred for inspection because this system requires very less time and even a semi-skilled worker can perform the inspection work. These gauges have replaced the micrometers which require more time and a skilled worker. Therefore, the use of 'GO and NOT GO' gauges is economical and simple hence being used widely.

4. **How Much to Inspect.** This factor is decided in the light of the product and accuracy desired. In some cases, sample inspection is employed. In this, defective products may reach to the customers. Therefore, this system is not advisable where accuracy is required. Although this system is cheaper and is adopted for ordinary articles and where automatic machines are used.

   The products, in which accuracy is important consideration, should be inspected through a thorough 100 per cent inspeciton.

21.6. TOOLS FOR INSPECTION

As already discussed, inspection is "The function of comparing or determining the confirmance of product to specification". The specifications provide necessary details as to what is required, then inspection is done to see what is actually produced. This work of inspection requires equipments. These equipments help to speed up inspection and precision. Following are the important methods of inspection :

(*i*) **Inspection by Measurement.** Exact measurements are determined with the help of micrometer, vernier callipers, torque indicating spanners.

(*ii*) **Limit Gauges.** These can be used even by an unskilled operator to know quickly whether the dimensions of the product are within the limits of the specifications

(*iii*) **Multiple Gauging.** These consists of electric contacts operating coloured signal lamps to indicate whether the dimension is correct, oversize or under-size.

(*iv*) **Air Gauges.** This equipment is very useful for inspection in mass production work.

(*v*) **Optical Comparators.** The object is magnified 10 to 50 times and projected on a screen to enable to compare with known standards.

(*vi*) **Non-destructive Testing.** For detecting defects in materials, these testing methods are employed. The test methods are visual, pressure and leak penetration, thermal, radiography, acoustic, magnetic, electrical and elecro-magnetic induction etc.

In order that parts produced are of consistent and of acceptable quality, the inspection gauges and test equipments are always kept in accurate condition. Adequate past inspection records should always be kept, because it provides valuable information as to recurring troubles and their remedies.

21.7. SAMPLING INSPECTION

To understand 'sampling inspection' properly, we must first discuss the two words 'sampling' and 'inspection'.

Sampling. A sampling may be defined as the number of items or component parts drawn from a lot, batch or population. Sampling is an act of drawing samples from a batch on random basis. Since sampling depends upon statistical probability, samples must be drawn from all sides and different depths of the box containing the batch of the component parts, for inspection, so that every part has an equal chance of being selected. The samples should be collected at regular intervals from entire population run so as to obtain a sample truly representative of the lot.

Inspection. Every manufactured item or component is expected to perform certain functions. The act of checking whether the item or component will be able to perform its function is known as inspection. The act of inspection separates defective items from non-defective ones to ensure the adequate quality of the product. It also locates defects in raw materials and flaws in the processes which otherwise cause problems at final stage.

Inspection decides conformance or non-conformance of the product.

(*a*) **Conformance** means judging whether the product conforms to specification.

(*b*) **Non-Conformance** Non-Conforming products may be fit or unfit for use. A non-conforming lot is further investigated as to whether every piece is inspected and defectives are considered for (*i*) repairing, (*ii*) downgrading the item and sold as 'seconds' (*iii*) corrective action is taken, and (*iv*) scrapped.

Advantages of Sampling Inspection

Advantages of sampling inspection as compared to 100 percent inspection are :

1. Less amount of inspection for achieving a predecided degree of certainty about the quality.
2. It is less expensive.
3. Since less fatigue and boredom is experienced by inspectors, hence their operating efficiency is high.
4. Since fewer parts are inspected, no damage to remaining pieces (in case of destructive testing).
5. Fear of rejection of entire lot, pressurises for improvement in quality.

Applications of Sampling Inspection

The following are important places where sampling inspection is widely used :

(*i*) At all the places where destructive testing of product is not avoidable, hence inspection is prohibited.
(*ii*) Where inspection caused lot of 'Fatigue'.
(*iii*) Where inspection cost is too high.
(*iv*) This is widely suitable in mass production.

Uses of Sampling Inspection in Industry

(*a*) To determine the acceptability and quality of incoming raw materials, component parts and finished products.
(*b*) To determine the acceptability and quality of outgoing product.
(*c*) To determine the acceptability of work in process for further processing with the plant.
(*d*) To improve and control the quality of product.

21.8. ACCEPTANCE SAMPLING

For the purpose of acceptance, inspection is carried out at many stages in the process of manufacturing. These stages may be: inspection of incoming materials and parts, process inspection at various points in the manufacturing operations, final inspection by a manufacturer of his own product, and finally inspection of the finished product by the purchaser.

Inspection for acceptance is generally carried out on a sampling basis. The use of sampling inspection to decide whether or not to accept the lot is known as Acceptance Sampling. A sample from the inspection lot is inspected and if the number of defective items is more than the stated number (the number is decided using statistics after a decision about confidence level depending upon the place of application of the product and its critically) known as *Acceptance Number*, the whole lot is rejected.

The purpose of Acceptance Sampling is, therefore, to decide whether to accept or reject the lot. It does not control the quality during the process of manufacturing.

Role of Acceptance Sampling

Acceptance Sampling is very widely used in practice due to the following merits:

1. Acceptance Sampling is much less expensive than 100 per cent inspection.
2. It is general experience that 100 per cent inspection removes only 82 to 95 percent of

defective material. Very good 100 per cent inspection may remove at the most 99 percent of the defectives, but still cannot reach the level of 100 percent. Due to the effect of inspection fatigue involved in 100 percent inspection, a good sampling plan therefore, may actually give better results than that achieved by 100 per cent inspection.

3. Because of its economy, it is possible to carry out sample inspection at various stages. Acceptance number is evaluated using sampling plan and confidence level.
4. The 100 per cent inspection is not possible, where quality can be tested only by destroying the items. In such cases, sampling inspection is the only solution.

Producer's and Consumer's Risks (Sampling Risks)

Sampling inspection plan helps to decide whether to accept a lot or reject it on the basis of the sampling. But there is a possibility, of (*a*) rejecting a lot as unsatisfactory when as of acceptable quality, and (*b*) accepting a lot as satisfactory when it is below the quality level. Hence in any acceptance sampling plan, the producers and the consumers, the sellers and the buyers are exposed to some risks, which are called producer's and consumer's risks.

Probability Concept

The basic idea in the theory of Probability is the law of large numbers. Probability concept states that 'certain mass phenomena have a tendency towards regularity in behaviour, *i.e.*, a sample is drawn from the mass or universe (population) without any bias, the sample is quite likely to display those characteristics that are found in the whole mass.' Therefore, inferences drawn from the study of such a sample can be relied upon as being representative of the whole mass.

Universe. It means a group of items from which a sample is drawn.

Sampling. So in this way, sampling enables us to draw conclusion about a mass of items based upon the careful study of a small number of items. These number of items in known as 'sample'. The chief application of the theory of probability is in Statistical Quality Control. Inspection of each individual item of production to determine whether it meets specifications or not may be too expensive and monotonous. Therefore, samples are regularly taken at random from a lot and information from the study of samples tells us the extent to which specifications are being met. Sampling is the tool or technique of statistical quality control. *Webster* defined a sample as a product to represent the quality of the whole lot.

Acceptance Sampling Illustration. Frequently, we in our daily life come in contact with sampling. For example, if we purchase a bag of potatoes, only a few potatoes can be observed from the whole bag. Therefore, we draw an inference about the whole bag by only inspecting a few. If these look allright, it is assumed that all the potatoes in that bag will be allright.

The basic concept of sampling lies in testing the samples for acceptance or rejection. Some products such as electric bulbs, radio valves, razor blades, bolts etc. require to be subjected to destructive tests so as to ascertain their life. A cent per cent inspection and destructive testing of such type of products cannot be possible and also sometimes the cost of cent per cent inspection is extremely high. So for such problems acceptance sampling can be widely used.

In this method, samples are collected at regular intervals and subjected for inspection.

The various methods of sampling depend upon the way of their collection and means of inspection.

21.9. BASIS OF SAMPLING INSPECTION

(*i*) Variables basis, and

(*ii*) Attributes basis.

1. *Variable basis.* In this, inspection of samples is conducted on measurement (variable) basis, *i.e.,* on the basis of actual reading taken. Examples of variables are dimensions in mm ; hardness in units ; operating temperature in Fahrenheit ; tensile strength in kg/cm^2 ; percentage of a particular item in a chemical compound ; weight in kg of the contents of any packet, time in seconds of the blow of a fuse, life in hours of an electric bulb and so on. Variables are dealt *in X (x-bar)* and *R* Shewhart control charts.

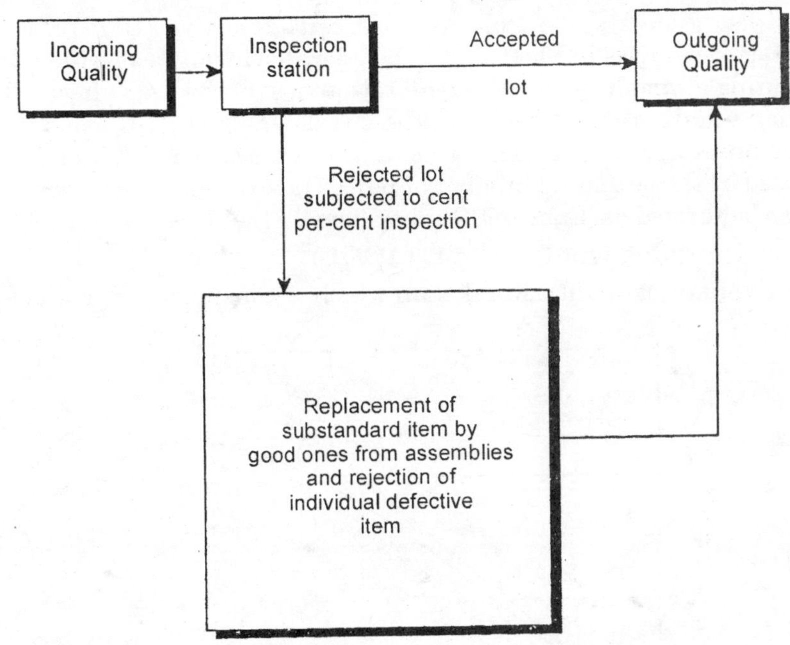

Fig. 21.1. Dealing with lot rejected in Sampling Inspection.

2. *Attributes basis.* In this, inspection of samples is conducted on 'GO' and 'NOT GO' basis, *i.e.,* determining whether or not the product in the sample conforms to the specified tolerances.

   Many requirements are necessarily stated in terms of attributes rather than variables. For example, the glass cover of a pressure gauge either is not cracked or is cracked. A lithographic paper either has a certain desired colour or it has not. Similarly, a spot weld in sheet metal either has not caused cracked edges of the sheets or it has. The surface finish of the top of dinning table presents a satisfactory appearance or it does not.

   Since, majority of acceptance sampling is conducted on attributes basis, therefore, acceptance tables are formed for ' GO' and ' NOT GO' datas.

21.10. QUALITY INDICES

Quality indices for acceptance sampling plan are :

1. **Acceptance Quality Level (AQL)**

   It is a fraction defective that can be tolerated without serious effect on further processing operation or customer reaction. In other words AQL is the maximum percent defective that, for the purpose of sampling inspection, can be considered satisfactory as a process average. AQL can also be termed as maximum number or percentage of defective pieces in a 'good' lot.

2. **Rejectable Quality Level (RQL)**

   This is also known as 'lot tolerance percent defective (LTPD)'. It represents the percentage defectives in a lot that can be tolerated in only a specified proportion of lots. By adopting a sampling plan that will reject most of the losts offered that would cause too much unfavourable reaction of the customer. This RQL helps in real protection against unsatisfacory material, reaching the customer. RQL or LTPD can also be expressed by the minimum number or percentage of defective pieces in a 'bad' lot. This can also be termed as 'Limiting Quality Level'. (LQL).

3. **Average Outgoing Quality Limit (AOQL)**

   This is the limit of quality, worst than which, a consumer will not get any lot.

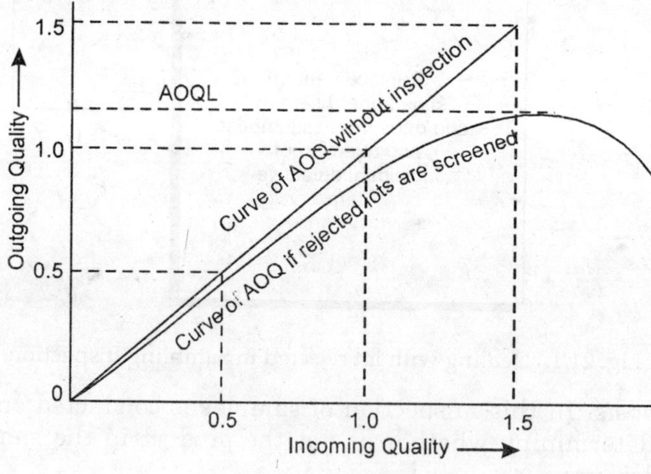

Fig. 21.2. A.O.Q.L.

Process Average (Average percent Defective)

It determines that before removal of any rejects whether or not the product is being manufactured under satisfactory control : It also determines whether normal reduced or tightened sampling inspection is necessary to ensure the desired quality level.

21.11. PROCEDURE OF SAMPLING INSPECTION

Following four steps are essential in setting up acceptance sampling inspection :

1. Setting of inspection lots ;
2. Arranging for rational lots ;

3. Establishing an allowable per cent defective ;
4. Selecting a Sampling Plan.

1. **Setting of Inspection Lots.**

Under sampling inspection, the lot size varies from about 300 products upto any number. Theoretically, there is no upper limit for the lot size but in practice lots should be kept small enough so that they are easy to move and do not move and do not require special handling. For lots smaller than 300 either process inspection or screening is economical and, therefore, preferable.

Another factor influencing lot size is how frequently you wish to inspect the work from one machine or process.

2. **Arranging for Rational Lots.**

A 'rational lot' is one whose units have been produced from the same sources. As far as possible, a lot should consist of products manufactured from one batch of raw materials, one production line, known pattern, mould or die and in one and the same shift. Often it is not possible in practice to separate product strictly in this manner but it should adhere to the rule of arranging rational lots as closely as possible. If we mix up products from different sources and find a bad lot, we cannot put out finger immediately upon the source of trouble which can be pointed out if there are rational lots.

3. **Establishing an Allowable Per Cent Defective.**

In mass production, it is often not possible to continually produce hundred per cent satisfactory products. It can be assumed that certain percentage of defectives will always present on certain processes ; however if the percentage does not exceed a certain limit, it is more economical to allow the defectives to go through rather than to sort out each lot. This limit is called the Allowable Per Cent Defective'.

But how to establish the Allowable Percent Defective ? To do this, watch the product for some time while it is under regular operation. Collect sufficient data over a period of one to two weeks to determine the percentage of defective normally occurring in the product from certain equipment or process.

4. **Selecting a Sampling Plan.**

Now-a-days, three important plans are in use :

(*a*) Single Sampling Plan (*b*) Double Sampling Plan
(*c*) Sequential or Multiple Sampling Plan.

21.12. SAMPLING PLANS

1. **Single Sampling Plan.**

In inspection, defective product is one that fails to conform to the specifications. The most common system in this plan is to take a single sample from the lot at random. Single sample does not mean unit, it may have number of units. The acceptance and rejection of the lot depends on the number of defective in the sample. For designing a sampling plan, the following symbols may be used :

N = Number of products in a given lot

n = Number of samples drawn from the lot (N) at random

A = Acceptance number. It means the maximum allowable number of defectives in a samples size, n.

R = Rejection number.

Selection of N and n. The selection of the values of N and n can be done in an industry by two ways :

(*i*) Sample inspected may have some fix percentage of the lot, *i.e.*, $\frac{n}{N} \times 100 =$ *constant. In such method, percentage varies from* ***10 to 20%.***

This method is used when lot size is comparatively small.

(*ii*) In this method, the value of *n, i.e.*, sample size is obtained from Master Table for Single Sampling Plan. See Table 27.1.

The procedure of single sampling plan is explained as under :

(*i*) Inspect a sample of *n* pieces.

(*ii*) If the number of defects found in the sampling does not exceed (*A*) accept the lot.

(*iii*) If the number of defects found in the sample exceeds (A) inspect all the pieces in remainder of the lot.

(*iv*) Correct or replace all the defective pieces found.

For example let us take that the allowable per cent defective for a certain item is 1 per cent. Lot size is 400. From the master Table 27.1, the sample size is found to be 75. Acceptance number is 1 and Rejection number 2. (Refer Table 27.1 on page 194).

Now from the lot size of 400 units, take 75 units at random. Inspect and if not more than one defective piece is found, accept the lot, since the acceptance number is 1. If two or more defectives are found, reject the lot, since rejection number is 2.

2. Double Sampling plan.

In the single sampling plan, if the sample on inspection is found defective then the lot is rejected. To overcome this, double sampling plan is a sort of modification on single sampling plan. In this method, the lot is not rejected but again a second sample is drawn to judge the quality. The procedure outlined is explained as under :

Let, n_1 = Number of products in the first sample

A_1 = Acceptance number for first sample

n_2 = Number of products in the second sample

A_2 = Acceptance number for both samples.

Procedure

(*i*) Inspect first a sample of n_1 pieces.

(*ii*) If the number of defects found in the first sample does not exceed A_1, accept the lot.

(*iii*) If the number of defects in the first sample exceeds A_2, inspect all the products in the remainder of the lot.

(*iv*) If the number of defects in the first sample exceeds A_1 but does not exceed A_2 inspect a second sample of n_2 pieces.

(*v*) If the total number of defects in the first and the second sample combined does not exceed A_2 accept the lot.

(*vi*) If the total number of defects found in the first and second sample combined exceeds A_2 inspect the pieces in the remainder of the lot.

(*vii*) Correct or replace all defective products found.

In double sampling plan, less inspection is required as compared to single sampling plan. The number of samples drawn from a lot in case of double sampling plan for first sample is comparatively quite small. In general, when the products are good enough, the very few second samples need to be taken. This causes, therefore, less inspection, *i.e.,* less inspection cost.

3. **Sequential Sampling Plan.**

The third form of the sampling plan is the sequential one. In this plan- one, two, three or more samples are drawn before it is possible to reach a decision to accept or reject the lot.

To illustrate, let us assume that the Allowable percent defective, for a certain product is 2 per cent. Lot size 755 pieces each.

Now from the master Table 21.2 of sequential sampling plan, the following information is collected (Refer Table 21.2 on page 472):

Sample size n	*Acceptance No. A*	*Rejection No. R*
40	0	3
60	1	4
80	1	5
100	2	5
120	4	5

Now start using the plan. Begin by selection of 40 sample pieces at random from the lot. If there is no defective, accept the lot, since acceptance number is 0. If there are three or more defectives, reject the lot, as the rejection number is 3. But what is to be done, if there are 1 or 2 defectives ? The defectives, found between the acceptance and rejection number, the lot can neither be accepted nor rejected. Now collect additional information by taking another sample of 20 from the lot. This brings the total sample size up to 60 (40 +20).

Again compare the total number of defectives found upto the point to determine whether to accept or reject the lot or to continue sampling. This process may go on until the highest sample size 120 is reached at which the gap between the acceptance and rejection number disappear and the problem of acceptability is finally solved.

The following table shows the comparative size of samples with their acceptance and rejection numbers developed for single, double and sequential sampling plans.

From the table, it is found that sequential sampling requires comparatively much less inspection than single and double sampling hence widely adopted. Still there are some plants where single sampling is preferred. The reason being their material handling problems. For example, if the product is heavy and difficult to transport, such as heavy coil, large castings, heavy large machine parts etc., it will be less costly to move a large number of sample articles to a place of inspection once instead of transport much smaller number of articles several times.

Type of sampling	Sample	Sample size	Combined Samples, +		
			Size	Acceptance number	Rejection
Single	First	225	225	14	15
Double	First	150	150	9	24
	Second	300	450	23	24
Sequential	First	50	50	1	6
	Second	50	100	3	9
	Third	50	150	7	13
	Fourth	50	200	10	16
	Fifth	50	250	13	19
	Sixth	50	300	16	22
	Seventh	50	350	19	25
	Eighth	50	400	24	25

Sampling Continuous Products

Continuous products like chains, belts ropes, metal coil, yarn wires, cloth and cord etc. often require a considerable amount of visual examination for defects. For such products, Master sampling Tables are also given. In this, size is considered as the basis of units of length. For example, for such a product, if 2% defectives are allowed, then in a single sampling plan for a lot size 9999 or less, sample size is 675, A=22, R=23. It means inspect 675 meters length of product, if 22 metre length or less is found to be defective, accept the lot but if 23 or more is found to be defective, reject the lot.

Disposition of Defective Products

If a lot consisting of work-in-process or complete product is rejected, it can be subjected to 100% inspection to take out all the defectives or it can be sent directly to repair or sold as second hand or be scrapped entirely, whichever procedure involves the least loss.

Secondly, as soon as any lot is rejected, the shop foreman must be informed immediately so that he can check the trouble and correct the faulty worker, process or equipment that may be responsible for the defective lot. Thus sampling inspection provides a most important service to the shops. It immediately stops the flow of defective products and permits remedy before materials and time are needlessly wasted.

Selection of Random Numbers

Appendix A (see at the end of the chapter) contains digits (from 0 to 9) arranged randomly. For convenience of reading, the digits are grouped into sets of 3 and are arranged in 12 rows on each page..

For obtaining random numbers, any one of the page may be used. After choosing a page of random numbers, a pencil may be dropped blindly and the starting point for reading of the numbers shall be random digit nearest to the starting point may then be read up or down, right or left but it may perhaps be more convenient to read them vertically downward till the bottom of the page is reached and thereafter the numbers in the adjacent column to the right are read starting from the top of the page and moving downward as earlier as possible. The systematic method of reading the numbers may be carried on to the succeeding pages, if necessary.

If the random numbers to be chosen consist of single digits (as would be the case when lot size does not exceed 10) then the digit of any single column may be used, taking 0 to represent10.

If the random numbers to be chosen consist of two digits (as would be the case when lot size does not exceed 100) then any two adjoining columns may be used taping to represent 100. If the random numbers to be chosen consist of three or more digits then a similar method as explained above may be followed.

Example. *Suppose it is required to obtain a sample of 10 components from a lot of 200. If components in the lot are assigned serial numbers upto 200, the problem then becomes to obtain 10 random numbers in the range 1 to 200. Taking the 3 digited random numbers from Appendix A and starting from any numbers. Say 242, occurring in the eleventh row and proceeding downwards, the numbers so obtained are 24, 82, 70, 90, 33, 78, 32, 28, 20 and 27. When proceeding upwards the magnitude, of the numbers becomes 24, 26, 25, 22, 44, 40, 93, 32, 72, and 62. The components in the lot corresponding to these numbers shall then be selected to constitute the required random sample of size 10.*

APPENDIX–A

Three-Digits Random Number Table

	110	450	961	514	031	264	177	264	492	084	119	481
	439	112	626	718	311	581	076	362	024	540	309	115
	397	266	725	966	552	259	256	965	170	280	809	292
	062	101	326	207	318	266	501	990	915	519	317	542
	919	719	933	233	214	316	392	849	807	246	216	400
	689	312	404	509	529	744	132	958	965	107	905	590
	726	072	444	217	002	249	831	216	639	301	867	291
	344	277	229	261	945	017	356	671	289	394	219	479
	172	898	252	847	310	221	382	816	409	015	150	053
	110	139	266	686	065	691	669	708	031	140	552	237
	052	645	242	806	204	274	044	036	715	266	712	726
	403	146	822	667	521	426	548	006	229	062	465	722
	340	212	706	311	335	577	716	187	113	424	253	296
	300	019	901	180	515	549	666	508	736	292	904	118
	765	618	335	759	816	906	291	158	331	362	546	017
	999	138	780	930	442	889	628	124	314	562	192	612
	101	468	329	411	197	026	371	710	012	383	045	273
	954	456	282	668	853	969	760	201	362	816	918	614
	152	791	207	281	786	641	013	878	381	251	356	117
	165	197	271	213	865	646	107	409	445	220	207	301
	312	080	695	409	746	310	809	703	439	928	098	711

	744	829	902	398	891	619	723	219	106	342	254	918
	597	579	007	858	431	328	745	585	702	365	252	187
	595	353	531	298	179	762	308	302	710	541	597	118
	031	008	258	194	352	121	269	291	456	919	009	966
	581	957	231	920	310	959	855	774	237	220	124	459
	059	478	006	904	694	241	191	292	417	756	010	006
	352	121	235	760	396	343	469	629	743	939	695	735
	022	491	692	026	827	391	492	216	082	772	149	049
	292	504	956	299	838	176	562	380	064	563	491	002
	016	289	315	597	597	211	332	212	129	526	614	383
	406	115	574	159	518	977	400	604	211	437	982	589
	844	121	426	815	715	847	218	280	162	417	582	445
	793	146	875	122	171	927	486	094	582	168	152	009
	022	491	692	026	827	391	492	216	082	772	149	049
	292	504	956	299	838	176	562	380	064	563		
	016	289	315	597	597	211	332	212	129	526	614	383
	406	115	574	159	518	977	400	604	211	437	982	589
	844	121	426	815	715	847	218	280	162	417	582	445
	793	146	875	122	171	927	486	094	582	168	152	009
	533	660	803	937	042	294	627	988	807	901	234	576
	243	739	606	517	055	840	006	081	570	891	833	702
	006	899	597	434	709	546	019	186	414	342	934	229
	906	393	507	277	728	920	509	026	728	203	656	343
	732	983	880	180	212	816	278	052	231	795	660	093
	396	623	173	008	325	853	045	233	437	016	195	855
	504	990	163	061	390	896	320	139	589	116	332	302
	016	289	315	597	597	211	332	212	129	526	614	383
	406	115	574	159	518	977	400	604	211	437	982	589
	844	121	426	815	715	847	218	280	162	417	582	445
	793	146	875	122	171	927	486	094	582	168	152	009
	533	660	803	937	042	294	627	988	807	901	234	576
	243	739	606	517	055	840	006	081	570	891	833	702
	006	899	597	434	709	546	019	186	414	342	934	229
	906	393	507	277	728	920	509	026	728	203	656	343
	732	983	880	180	212	816	278	052	231	795	660	093
	396	623	173	008	325	853	045	233	437	016	195	855
	504	990	163	061	390	896	320	139	589	116	332	302

Table 21.1. *Master Table of Single Sampling Plan*

Lot size	*Sample Size*	*Allowable per cent Defective*																					
		0.25		0.50		0.75		1		2		3		4		5		6-7		8		9-12	
		A	R	A	R	A	R	A	R	A	R	A	R	A	R	A	R	A	R	A	R	A	R
499 or less	75							1	2	2	3	3	4	4	5	5	6	6	7	8	9	10	11
500 to 799	115					↓		2	3	3	4	4	5	6	7	8	9	9	10	11	12	14	15
800 to 1299	150			↓		1	2	3	4	4	5	5	6	8	9	10	11	12	13	15	16	20	21
1300 to 3199	225			1	2	2	3	4	5	5	6	8	9	11	12	14	15	17	18	21	22	29	30
3200 to 7999	300	↓		2	3	3	4	5	6	7	8	10	11	14	15	18	19	22	23	26	27	↑	
8000 to 21999	450	1	2	3	4	4	5	6	7	9	10	14	15	20	21	26	27	↑		↑			
22,000 to 99,999	750	2	3	4	5	5	6	8	9	13	14	23	24	↑		↑							
10,000 and up	1500	3	4	6	7	8	9	13	14	23	24												

A = Acceptance Number; *R* = Rejection number.

Arrow →: When there is an arrow below given, i.e., allowable percent defective use first sampling data below arrows in upper left-hand corner (forming large lots if possible) or first sampling data above arrows in lower right hand corner as the case may be.

Table 21.2 *Master Sampling Table of Sequential Plan*

Lot size	*Sample Size*	*Allowable per cent Defective*																											
		0.26		0.50		0.75		1		1.5		2		3		4		5		6		7		8		9		10		12	
		A	R	A	R	A	R	A	R	A	R	A	R	A	R	A	R	A	R	A	R	A	R	A	R	A	R	A	R	A	R
(1)	(2)	(3)		(4)		(5)		(6)		(7)		(8)		(9)		(10)		(11)		(12)		(13)		(14)		(15)		(16)		(17)	
499	40							0	1	0	2	0	3	1	4	1	6	2	6	2	6	2	7	4	7	3	8	9	4	4	9
to	50							0	2	0	3	1	3	1	4	2	5	2	6	3	7	2	8	4	9	4	9	5	10	5	11
less	60							0	3	1	3	1	3	2	4	2	6	3	7	4	8	4	9	5	10	5	11	7	12	8	11
	70							1	3	1	4	1	4	2	5	3	6	4	8	5	9	5	9	6	10	7	11	8	13	7	13
	80	↓		↓		↓		2	3	3	4	3	4	4	5	5	6	7	8	8	9	8	9	9	10	10	11	12	13	8	13
500	40					+	1	+	2	0	3	0	3	0	4	1	5	1		1	6	1	7	2	8	2	8	2	9	4	10
to 799	60					+	1	0	2	0	3	1	4	1	5	2	6	1	7	3	8	3	8	4	10	5	11	5	11	6	12
	80					0	2	1	3	1	4	1	0	1	6	3	7	3	8	4	10	5	11	6	12	7	13	8	14	9	15
	100					0	2	1	3	2	4	2	5	2	6	4	8	5	9	5	11	7	13	8	14	9	16	10	17	11	18
	120	↓		↓		1	2	2	3	3	4	4	5	5	6	7	4	8	9	10	11	12	13	13	14	15	16	16	17	18	16

(1)	(2)	(3)	(4)	(5)	(6)	(7)	(8)	(9)	(10)	(11)	(12)	(13)	(14)	(15)	(16)	(17)
	40	↓	+ 1	+ 1	+ 2	+ 3	0 3	0 4	0 4	0 6	1 5	1 7	1 1	2 8	2 9	2 10
800	60		+ 2	0 2	0 2	0 3	0 4	1 5	1 6	2 7	2 8	3 9	3 10	4 11	4 12	5 12
to	80		0 2	0 2	0 3	1 4	1 4	2 6	2 7	3 8	4 10	5 11	5 12	6 13	8 15	8 15
1299	100		0 2	0 2	0 3	1 4	1 5	2 6	3 8	5 10	5 11	7 13	7 14	9 15	10 17	10 18
	120		0 2	1 3	1 3	2 5	2 6	3 7	9 9	6 11	7 13	8 14	9 16	11 18	12 19	22 18
	160		1 2	2 3	3 4	4 5	5 6	7 8	9 10	11 13	13 14	15 16	16 17	18 19	19 20	22 18
	50	+ 1	+ 1	+ 2	+ 3	+ 3	0 4	0 4	0 6	0 6	1 7	1 1	2 8	2 10	3 10	3 11
1300	75	+ 1	+ 1	0 2	0 3	0 4	0 5	1 5	2 7	2 8	3 9	4 12	4 12	5 12	6 14	6 15
to	100	+ 1	+ 2	1 2	1 4	1 4	1 5	2 6	3 8	3 8	5 11	6 12	6 14	8 15	9 17	10 18
3199	125	0 2	0 2	1 3	1 4	2 5	6 7	3 7	4 9	5 11	7 13	8 15	9 16	11 18	12 20	13 21
	150	0 2	0 2	2 3	2 5	2 5	3 7	4 8	9 10	7 13	9 15	10 17	11 19	14 21	15 23	16 25
	200	1 2	1 2	4 3	4 5	5 6	6 5	8 9	10 11	13 14	17 18	17 18	20 21	22 23	25 26	27 28

(1)	(2)	(3)	(4)	(5)	(6)	(7)	(8)	(9)	(10)	(11)	(12)	(13)	(14)	(15)	(16)	(17)
	50	+ 1	+ 2	+ 2	0 4	+ 3	+ 4	+ 5	9 6	0 7	0 8	3 14	1 10	1 11	2 11	2 12
3200	100	+ 1	+ 2	0 3	1 5	1 4	1 5	1 7	2 8	3 10	4 12	5 15	5 15	6 16	8 17	9 19
to	150	0 2	0 3	2 4	2 5	1 5	2 7	2 8	5 11	5 13	8 15	9 17	10 19	11 21	13 23	15 25
7999	200	0 2	0 3	2 4	2 6	3 6	3 8	4 10	7 13	8 16	12 19	13 21	15 24	16 26	19 29	21 33
	250	0 2	1 4	2 5	2 7	4 8	5 9	6 11	9 15	11 18	15 22	17 25	19 28	22 32	25 35	28 31
	300	1 2	3 4	4 5	5 6	7 8	8 9	10 11	15 16	7 18	22 23	35 26	22 30	32 33	36 37	39 43
	100	+ 2	+ 3	+ 3	+ 5	0 5	0 5	0 7	1 9	1 11	3 11	3 14	4 16	5 17	↑	↑
	150	+ 2	+ 3	0 4	0 5	1 6	2 7	2 9	3 11	4 14	6 16	7 17	9 20	10 22		
8000	200	0 2	0 3	0 5	1 6	2 7	3 8	3 10	6 13	7 17	10 19	11 12	13 24	16 27		
to	250	0 2	0 4	1 5	2 6	2 8	4 9	5 12	8 16	10 10	13 22	15 25	18 29	19 32		
9999	300	0 3	1 4	2 6	3 7	2 8	5 11	6 13	10 18	12 22	16 26	19 29	22 23	24 37		
	400	1 3	1 4	3 7	3 8	3 10	8 14	10 16	14 22	18 27	23 33	29 37	31 42	34 47		
	500	2 3	3 4	6 7	7 7	9 10	13 14	16 17	22 23	28 29	34 35	40 41	45 46	50 51		

(1)	(2)	(3)	(4)	(5)	(6)	(7)	(8)	(9)	(10)	(11)	(12)	(13)	(14)	(15)	(16)	(17)
	100	+ 2	+ 3	+ 4	+ 5	+ 6	+ 8	0 8	0 11	2 19	2 16	↑	↑	↑	↑	↑
22000	200	+ 3	+ 4	0 5	0 6	1 7	1 10	3 11	3 15	6 18	8 20					
to	300	0 3	0 4	1 6	1 8	2 9	3 12	5 14	7 19	11 23	14 26					
99999	440	0 3	1 5	2 7	3 9	4 11	5 14	8 17	11 23	16 28	21 23					
	600	1 4	2 6	3 9	5 11	7 14	10 18	14 23	19 31	27 28	34 46					
	800	1 4	3 7	5 11	8 14	11 11	14 23	20 28	27 28	37 49	46 58					
	1000	3 4	6 7	10 11	13 14	17 18	22 23	30 31	40 41	53 54	65 66					
	200	+ 5	+ 5	+ 7	+ 8	0 9	0 13	2 13	2 18	↑	↑	↑	↑	↑	↑	↑
100000	400	+ 4	0 6	8 8	0 10	3 12	3 17	7 18	9 25							
to	600	0 4	1 7	2 10	2 12	5 15	7 20	12 22	17 23							
and up	800	1 5	1 8	4 11	5 14	8 18	11 24	18 19	24 40							
	1000	1 5	3 9	5 13	7 17	11 21	15 28	23 35	32 47							
	1000	2 5	3 9	7 15	9 19	14 24	19 32	28 40	39 55							
	1600	4 5	8 9	14 15	19 20	24 25	33 34	45 46	61 62							

+ = No. of Acceptance at this sample size. A = Acceptance No. R = Rejection No.

Arrow → When there is an arrow below given 'Allowable percent Defective' use first sampling data below arrows in upper left hand corner (forming large lots, if possible) or first sampling data above arrows in lower right hand corner as the case may be.

21.13. OPERATING CHARACTERISTIC (OC) CURVE

All practical sampling plans have an operating characteristic curve. Following points need emphasis regarding O.C. Curves:

(*i*) There is some chance that good lots will be rejected (known as manufacturer's risk).

(*ii*) There is some chance that bad lots will be accepted (known as consumer's risk).

(*iii*) These risks can be calculated by the theory of probability and depend on the number of samples inspected, the acceptance number, and the precent defective in the lots offered for sample inspection. Given the amount of risk which can be tolerated, a sampling plan can be divided to meet the requirements.

(*iv*) The larger the sample used for inspection, the nearer the OC Curve approaches the ideal. However beyond certain point, the added cost in inspecting a large number of parts far exceeds the benefit derived.

Parameters for O.C. Curves

The two parameters of an O.C. Curve are the sample size and acceptance number. The desired quality levels (p) and the probability of acceptance (P_2) must be selected so that the proper sampling plan can be designed.

Following factors should be decided for a sampling plan:

(*i*) Accpetance Quality Level (A.Q.L.): To measure the producer's risk, a minimum percent of defective items in a lot is decided, below which the lot should be accepted. This is known as A.Q.L.

(*ii*) Rejectable Quality Level (R.Q.L.), P_1: To measure the customer's risk, we must decide maximum per cent of defective items in a lot whih he can accept. This is called R.Q.L. or Lot Tolerance Per cent Defective (L.T.P.D).

(*iii*) Producer's Risk. This is the probability of rejecting a good lot.

(*iv*) Consumer's Risk. This is the probability of accepting a poor lot.

In any acceptance sampling plan, three parameters are specified. The first parameter is number of articles N in the lot from which sample is to be drawn. The second parameter is the number of articles n in the random sample drawn from the lot and the third is the acceptance number C. This acceptance number C is the maximum allowable number of defective articles in the sample. If more than C defectives are found in the sample, the lot is liable to be rejected. Since the lot size has little affect on the probability of acceptance, therefore lot size is generally ignored in deriving a sampling plan.

Operating Characteristic Curves:

O.C. Curve of an acceptance sampling plan (*i.e.* for a particular combination of n and c) shows how well the sampling plan discriminates between good and bad lots. In order to examine the suitability of an acceptance sampling plan, it is necessary to compare their performance over a range of possible quality levels of the product. The graph of this performance is known as operating characteristic curve. Fig. 21.3 below shows an ideal O.C. Curve where it is desired to accept all lots having 3% or less defectives, and to reject all lots having more than 3%. In this curve, all lots with less than 3% defectives have a probability of acceptane of 100%, while all lots with morethan 3% defectives have a probability of acceptance as 0%. However such a plan does not exist in reality.

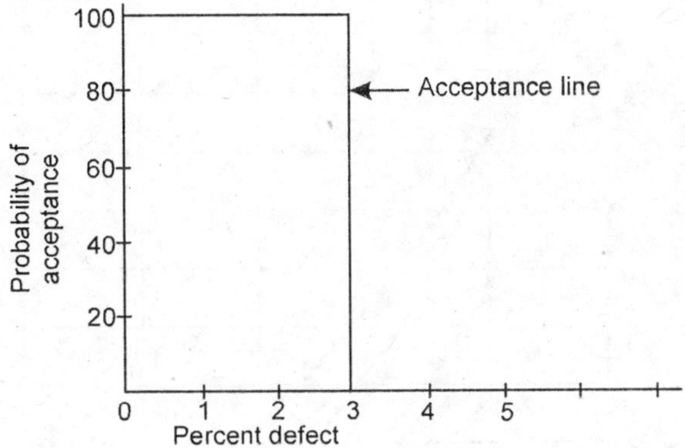

Fig. 21.3. An ideal sampling plan performance

Graph 21.4 is an OC curve for a sampling plan with $n = 50$ and $C = 1$. Graph 21.4 shows the probability of acceptance of lot for various values of percent defective in the lot. Suppose if the actual lot quality were 1 per cent, samples of $n = 50$ would accept the lot as satisfactory about 94 percent of time and reject it about 6 per cent of the time.

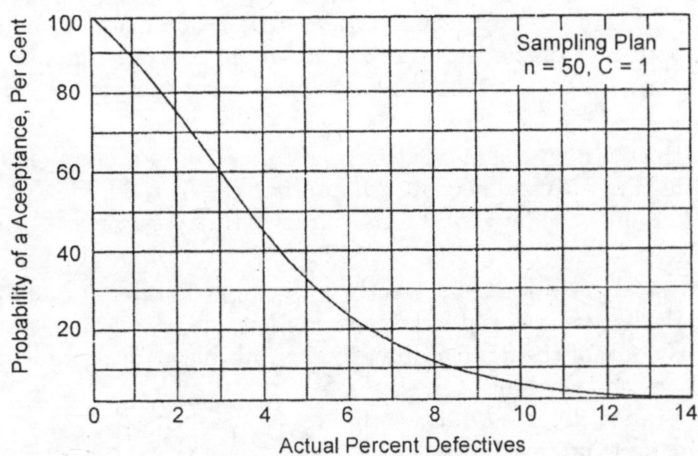

Fig. 21.4. OC cirve for a sampling plan with $n = 50$ and C = 1

Note however that if the actual quality of the lot were some what worse than 1% defective, say 6% the probability of accepting, there lots fall drastically to about 20%. This is the situation, we would like in a sampling plan. If the actual quality is good, then there should be a high probability of acceptance, but if the actual quality is poor, then the probability acceptance should be low. Thus, in this way, the OC curve shows how well a given sampling plan discriminates.

Affect of Sample Size on the Sampling Plan. The discriminating power of any sampling plan depends largely on the size of the sample. Graph 21.5 shows the OC curves for sample sizes of 100, 200 and 300 with the accetance number remaining in proportion to the sample size. Graph 21.5 shows that the OC curve becomes steeper as the sample size goes up. If the discrimination power of all the three plans shown in graph 21.5 compared, it is found that these

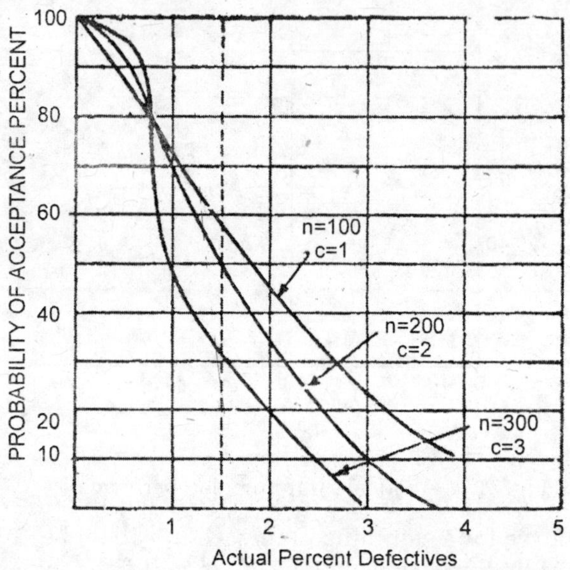

Fig. 21.5. OC curves for different samples size with acceptance numbers in proportion to sample sizes

would accept lots of about 0.7% defectives about 80% of the time (the approximate cross over points of the three curves). However, if actual quality falls to 3 per cent defectives, the plan with $n = 100$ accepts lots about 25% of the time, $n = 200$ about 10% of the time, and $n = 300$ less than 1% of the time. Therefore, it shows that the plans with larger sample sizes are definitely more effective.

What happens to the OC curve, if any of the acceptance number changes? Graph 21.6 shows OC curves for a sample of $n = 50$ and acceptance number $C = 0$, 1, 2 and 3. Graph indicates that the effect is mainly to change the level of the OC curve so that lower acceptance numbers make the plan "tighter".

A sampling plan that discriminates perfectly between good and bad lots would have an OC curve that was vertical; that is, it would follow the dashed line of Graph 21.5. For all lots having percent defectives to the left of the dashed line, the probability of acceptance is 100. For all lots having percent defectives to the right of the line, the probability of acceptance to zero. But the only plan which could achieve this discrimination is one requiring cent percent inspection. Therefore, the proper justification for the selection of a sampling plan is the balance between inspection costs and the probable cost of rejected parts. By making sampling plans, more discrimination (increasing sample sizes) or tighter (decreasing acceptance numbers) we can approach any desired level of outgoing quality that we please, but at increasing inspection costs. These increased inspection efforts would result in lower probable costs of passing defectives and at some point the combination of these incremental costs will be minimum. This minumum point defines the most economical sampling plan for a given situation.

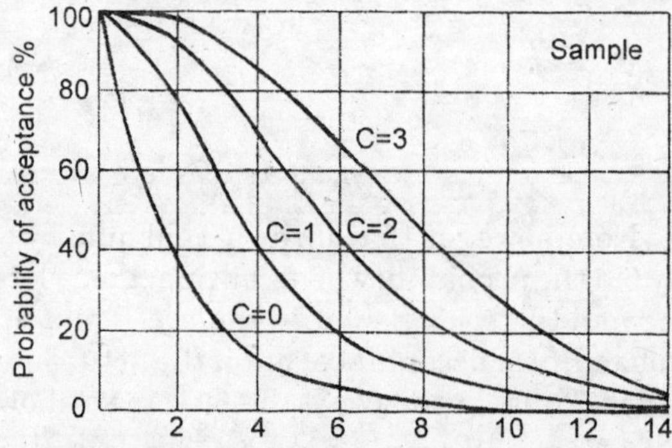

Fig. 21.6. OC curve with different acceptance

O.C. Curves for Double Sampling Plan

As discussed previously, double sampling plans are generally specified by following:

n_1 = Number of items in the first sample,

c_1 = acceptance number for the first sample (*i.e.* maximum number of defectives that will permit the acceptance of the lot on the basis of first sample).

n_2 = number of items in the second lot

c_2 = acceptance number for the two samples combined(*i.e.* maximum number of defectives that will permit the acceptance of the lot on the basis of two samples).

For example, interpretation of following sampling plan is given hereunder:

$$n_1 = 30$$
$$c_1 = 0$$
$$n_2 = 60$$
$$c_2 = 3$$

1. Inspect a first sample of thirty terms from a lot.
2. Accept the lot on the basis of first sample; if the sample contains O defectives.
3. Reject the lot on the basis of first sample, if the sample contains more than 3 defectives.
4. Inspect a second sample of 60 items, if the first sample contains 1, 2, or 3 defectives.
5. Accept the lot on the basis of both the samples combined togther (30 + 60 = 90 items); if the defectives are 3 or less.
6. Reject the entire lot on the basis of combined sample, if the defectives are more than 3 items.

Fig. 21.7 shows three O.C. Curves involved in the analysis of this double sampling plan. Three curves divide the figure in four zones indicating following possiblities for acceptance or selection:

1. **I zone (lowest zone)** – Acceptance after first sample.
2. **II zone (highest zone)** – Rejection after the first sample.

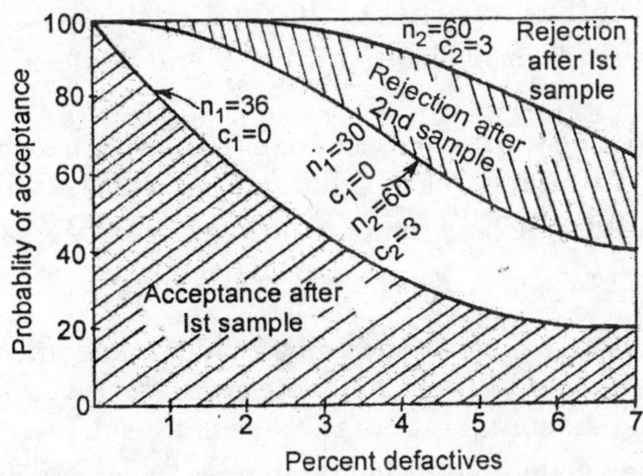

Fig. 21.7. Characteristics of a double sampling plan

3. **III zone (lower without hatching zone)** – Acceptance after second sample.
4. **IV zone (higher with hatching zone)** – Rejection after second sample.

Characteristics of the lowest curve is $n = 30$ and $c = 0$. Characteristics of the highest curve is $m = 60$ and $c = 3$. Characteristics of the middle curve is the actual O.C. Curve of the double sampling plan.

Zones of O.C. Curve:

O.C. curve can be divided into following 3 zones:

(*a*) **Acceptance Zone.** In this zone, all the batches are accepted. Therefore, the O.C. curve should be so selected that its acceptance zone accepts what is considered to be satisfactory lot.

(*b*) **Rejection Zone.** In this zone, all the batches are rejected. Hence the O.C. curve selected should be such that it rejects what is considered to be an unsatisfactory lot.

(*c*) **Zone of Indecision.** This is the zone where there is no surety that whether any particular batch or lot will be accepted or rejected this problem can be solved either by adopting 100% inspection or by taking larger sample, but these will increase the inspection costs. A batch or lot in this zone is worse than acceptable lot, and better than those what is considered as unacceptable. Thus its quality is borderline, and practically does not matter much whether a lot is finally accepted or rejected from this zone.

Conflicting Interests of Producer and Consumer

In the selection of a sampling plan, there are always two affected parties; the party submitting the items for acceptance, and the party for whom the decision is made regarding acceptance or rejection. These parties are referred as "producer" and "consumer". Both these have completely opposite viewpoint, as consumer wants to protect against the acceptance of too many defective items, whereas on the other hand, producer wants to be protected against the rejection of too much good items or products.

21.14. MACHINE OR PROCESS CAPABILITY

Every production engineer knows that repetitive production cycles result in products that are not identical in their characteristics. The reason for this is simply that the production cycles are not really identical in every respect. The causes for variations in the production process may be:

(*i*) The raw materials vary slightly in their properties from batch to batch and these variations may affect the properties of the final product.

(*ii*) Operators are different from each other in their skill, performance, aptitude and interest in work.

(*iii*) The parameter of the operators may change from cycle to cycle as may be the speeds, the motions of the operators and the characteristic of the tools and machines.

(*iv*) The external conditions such as temperature, pressure, light and humidity may vary.

Machine Capabilities

Since machines do not always give exactly the same results, machine capabilities change with time. Machine capability is affected due to machine wear, tool wear, lubrication and coolant conditions, the operators, and machinability of the raw material.

Machine capability is the variation obtained under stable and controlled conditions, and is equal to 6 times the standard deviation (σ). Actual variation from a machine is expected to be larger than the machine capability due to instabilities and other causes that may creep in from time to time.

For estimating the machine capability, standard deviation is determined by collecting sufficient number of observations under stable conditions.

Process Capabilities

Process capability is the variation obtained under stable or controlled process conditions and is equal to 6. The word 'process' here includes variation more than that expected due to inferior batch of material, change in machine setting, tool wear, change of operator etc. This change in variation is controlled and brought as close to process capability as possible. This process capability for a process is estimated after collecting sufficient number of observations under stable conditions.

Variation in a Process

In specifying specification, an ideal quantity of physical dimensions: strength, density, composition etc. are indicated but it is also pointed out that deviation from this ideal figure will be allowed, provided they remain within predetermined limits. One of the functions of quality control is to decide whether these tolerances are compatible with the inherent variabilities of the process or not. In short, there are following two types of variations in a process:

1. Chance variation.
2. Assignable cause variation.

1. **Chance Variation.** This is also known as usual variations. There is always a constant cause system which is operating in a production cycle. As long as constant cause system continues to operate, some percentage of the varying results continue to fall between any given pair of limits. It is distribution of results which is suitable and constant. The deviation is expected in the system.
2. **Assignable Cause Variation.** This is also known as unusual variation. It is the amount of deviation greater than the specified specification limits. This deviation may be due to the difference in operators, difference in materials or difference in working conditions etc. It has already been explained above that variation is inevitable in any production cycle and there are definite reasons for it. It is found that some of the reasons can be investigated easily and economically while others require thorough investigation and hence are uneconomical. Uneconomical causes are designated as chance variation while economical causes as assignable cause variation. Hence the aim is to put demarcation lines between economical and uneconomical causes. These demarcation lines are known as control lines.

QUESTIONS

1. (*a*) Define Inspection and give its objectives.
   (*b*) What type of function is that of inspection ?
2. Explain how an inspection department might be organised.
3. Describe the place of inspection function in the manufacturing organisation.
4. Why is Inspection so necessary in manufacturing under present day conditions ?
5. (*a*) What is tool inspection ?
   (*b*) Why is first piece inspection important ?
   (*c*) What is accomplished through working inspection ?
6. Discuss the importance of the inspection department in a manufacturing concern. What is its effect on 'Quality Control' and 'Cost Control' ?
7. Define Inspection. Analyse the essential elements of an inspection plan.
8. Why is inspection important in an industry ? Describe the various types of inspection methods.

9. What are the two most commonly used types of inspection ? Explain them in detail.
10. Describe differences between floor and centralised inspection and the conditions that indicate one better than the other.
11. Name and discuss the inspection practices used for controlling quality of products.
12. A reputed company suddenly observes a drop in the market sales of its products due to deterioration on product quality.

    Assuming yourself to be an incharge of the inspection department, discuss in some details and with reference to the products in questions the procedure you would like to adopt for reorienting the quality control programme.
13. Write short notes on :
    (*i*) Cage inspection *vs.* Floor inspection.
    (*ii*) Inspection procedure for mass scale production.
    (*iii*) Qualifications of Inspector.
14. 'Inspection is a tool for Controlling the Quality', comment.
15. 'Inspection controls the quality of the product and is a must in a production Shop, in spite of its adding to the Expenditure. Justify the statement.
16. What is acceptance sampling? Describe in detail. Why it is widely used in practice.
17. Write short notes on :
    (*a*) Role of accceptance sampling
    (*b*) Characteristics of acceptance sampling.
18. What are the basis for sampling inspection? Explain each of them.
19. Where do you prefer to use sampling inspection for quality control?
20. Describe the procedure for sampling inspection.
21. Write short notes on the following :
    (*a*) Random Numbers.
    (*b*) Sampling Plan.
    (*c*) Advantages and disadvantages of sampling inspections.
    (*d*) Producer's risk and consumer's risk in acceptance sampling.
22. What is the use of O.C. curves in inspection?
23. Plot the O.C. curves for different value of n and c and make the inferences from the plot drawn.
24. Write short note on the objectives of operating characteristic curves.
25. Define O.C. curves and explain its significance.
26. Describe O.C. Curves for double sampling plan. Draw an O.C. Curve indicating various zones.

22

Quality Control and Quality Assurance

22.1. INTRODUCTION

Quality control in its simplest term, is the control of quality during manufacturing. Both quality control and inspection are used to ensure quality. Inspection is a determining function which determines raw materials, supplies, parts or finished products etc. As acceptable or unacceptable, as control becomes effective, the need for inspection decreases. Quality control determines the causes for variation in the characteristics of products and gives solutions by which these variations can be controlled. It is economic in its purpose, objective in its procedure, dynamic in its operation and helpful in its treatment.

Since variations in raw materials have large effect on the quality of in-process materials, quality control includes statistical sampling and testing before acceptance. It also includes the examination of quality characteristics in finished products so as to assure satisfactory outgoing quality.

Co-operation between the quality control group and other departments such as production, planning and inspection is of vital importance. With proper managerial support and co-operation, the quality control programme will be more successful.

Definition of Quality

In current quality control theory and practice, the meaning of "Quality" is closely allied to cost and customer needs. "Quality" may simply be defined as fitness for purpose at lowest cost.

"Quality" of any product is regarded as the degree to which it fulfills the requirements of the customer. "Quality" means degree of perfection. Quality is not absolute but it can only be judged or realized by comparing with some standards. It can be determined by some characteristics, namely, design, size, material, chemical composition, mechanical functioning, workmanship, finishing and other properties.

Meaning of Quality Control

Quality of product depends upon the application of materials, men, machines and manufacturing conditions. The systematic control of these factors is the quality control. The quality of a product differs greatly due to these factors. For example, a skilled worker will produce products of better quality and a less skilled worker will produce poor quality products, similarly better machines and better material with satisfactory manufacturing conditions produce a better quality product. Thus it is clear that to control the quality of product, the factors which are responsible for quality are required to be controlled properly.

In the words of Alford and Beatly, "quality control" may be broadly defined as that "Industrial management technique by means of which products of uniform acceptable quality are manufactured". Quality control concern with making things right rather than discovering and rejecting those made wrong.

"It may also be defined as the function or collection of duties which must be performed throughout the organisation in order to achieve its quality objectives" or in other words "Quality is everybody's business and not only the duty of the persons on the Inspection Staff."

In short, we can say that quality control is a technique of management for achieving required standard of products.

Objectives of Quality Control

(*i*) To set up standards of quality acceptable to the customer and economical to achieve and maintain.

(*ii*) To locate and identify the process faults so as to control defectives, scrap and waste.

(*iii*) To take necessary corrective measures so as to maintain the quality of the products.

(*iv*) To ensure that sub-standard products do not reach the customers.

Factors Affecting Quality

In addition to men, materials, machines and manufacturing conditions, there are some other factors which affect the product quality. These are :

(*i*) Market Research, *i.e.*, demand of purchasers.

(*ii*) Money, *i.e.*, capability to invest.

(*iii*) Management, *i,e.*, management policies for quality level.

(*iv*) Production methods and product design.

Apart from these, poor packing, appropriate transportation and after sales services are the areas which can cause damage to a company's quality image. There are cases where goods of acceptable quality before transportation were downgraded on receipt by the retailer just because they had been damaged in transportation.

Modern quality control begins with an evaluation of the customer's requirements and has a part to play at every stage from goods manufactured right through sales to a customer who remains satisfied.

To be more effective, quality should be every body's business and not merely the activity of the person's in the laboratory or in the Inspection Staff.

Advantage of Quality Control

There are many advantages by controlling the product quality. Some of them are listed below :

1. Quality of product is improved which in turn increases sales.
2. Scrap rejection and rework are minimised thus reducing wastage, so the cost of manufacturing reduces.
3. Good quality product improves reputation.
4. Inspection cost reduces to a great extent.
5. Uniformity in quality can be achieved.
6. Improvement in manufacturer and consumer relations.
7. Improvement in technical knowledge and engineering data for process development and manufacturing design.

Indian Standard Institution (I.S.I.) -Now known as, Bureau of Standard

To protect the interest of the consumers, Indian Standard Institution is serving in India. In most of the western countries, consumers have formed their own associations to protect their interests. In some countries, these associations receive official support and guidance.

I.S.I, serves consumers through certification Marks Scheme. Under this scheme, I.S.I, has been vested with the authority to grant licences to manufacturers to apply the I.S.I mark on their products in token of their conformity to the desired Indian standards.

To control the quality, I.S.I inspectors carry out surprise inspec-tions of the factories of the licencee. Inspectors may check the incoming raw materials, outgoing finished product and may carry out necessary tests at different levels of control during production.

Thus I.S.I mark gives guarantee to the purchaser that the goods with this mark have been manufactured under a well-defined system of quality control.

Inspection, Quality Control and Quality Assurance

Inspection is a process of sorting good from a lot. Whereas Quality Control is aimed at prevention of defects at the very source, relies on effective feed back system, and procedure for corrective action. In Quality control programme, inspection data are used to take prompt corrective action to check the defects. For this purpose, detailed studies are conducted to find out that from where the defect is originated, and how to prevent it, may it be at manufacturing, design, purchase of raw materials, despatch, or storage stage.

Quality Assurance means to provide the necessary confidence to the customer as well as to top management that all concerned are carrying out their job effectively and that the product quality is as per customer's satisfaction with economy. Quality products can be produced only when all the departments fully participate and co-operate.

Now-a-days customers demand for higher quality and reliability. It has also been felt that even a single defect, whatever may be the reasons, result in economic loss. These reasons have necessitated the need for total quality and reliability programmes to cover wide spectrum of functions and various areas of product design, production system design through various stages of material, manufacture and commitment to efficient maintenance and operation of the system as a whole. This is necessary of quality assurance and reliability of the product. This assures the continuous failure free system to the customers.

22.2. QUALITY CONTROL ORGANISATION

Over the years, the status of the quality control organisation changed from a function merely responsible for detecting inferior or standard material to a function that establishes what are termed preventive programmes. These programmes are designed to detect quality problems in the design stage or at any point in the manufacturing process and to follow up on corrective action. Immediate responsibility for quality products rest with the manufacturing departments. All the activities concerning product quality are usually brought together in the organisation which may be known as inspection, quality control, quality assurance department or any other similar name.

Quality control is a staff activity since it serves the line or production department by assisting them in managing quality. Since the quality control function has authority delegated by management to evaluate material produced by the manufacturing department, it should not be in a position to control or dictate to the quality activity.

The quality control organisation depending upon the type of product, method of quality is sufficient enough to carry out following activities :

1. Inspection of raw material, product or processes.
2. Salvage inspection to determine rejected part and assembly disposition.
3. Records-and-reports maintenance
4. Statistical quality control
5. Gauges for inspection.
6. Design for quality control and inspection
7. Quality control system maintenance and development.

Functions of Quality Control Department

Quality control department has the following important functions to perform :

1. Only the products of uniform and standard quality are allowed to be sold.
2. To suggest methods and ways to prevent the manufacturing defects.
3. To reject the defective goods so that the products of poor quality may not reach to the customers.
4. To find out the points where the control is breaking down and investigate the causes of it.
5. To correct the rejected goods, if it is possible. This procedure is known as 'Rehabilitation of defective goods'.

Product Quality Analysis

It includes :

(*i*) The various functions to be performed by the manufactured product.
(*ii*) Life and durability of product.
(*iii*) Working conditions required during manufacturing.
(*iv*) Product specifications.
(*v*) Manufacturing processes and methods.
(*vi*) Maintenance and installation of policies.

Responsibilities of Quality Assurance Department

- To plan, develop and establish quality policies.
- To assure that products of described specification reaches to the customers.
- Regularly evaluate the effectiveness of the Quality programmes.
- Conduct studies and investigations related to the quality problems.
- Liaise with different departments, in and outside the organisation.
- Organise training programmes on quality.
- Plan and coordinate vendor quality surveys and evaluate their results.
- Develop Quality assurance system and regularly evaluate its effectiveness.

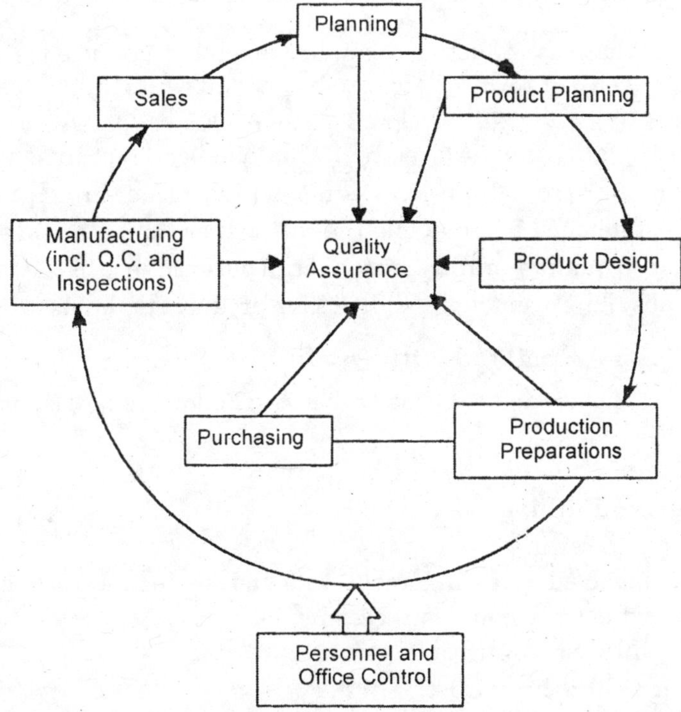

Fin. 22.1. Concept of Gross Functions for Quality Management.

Quality Assurance System

Quality assurance System should be developed incorporating the following aspects :

- Formulate the quality control and manufacturing procedures.
- Percentage checking be decided.
- Procedure and norms for plant performance as regards to quality be developed.
- Rejection analysis and immediate feed back system for corrective action.
- Prepare a manual for quality assurance.
- Formulate plans for quality improvement, quality motivation and quality awareness in the entire organisation.

22.3. ECONOMICS OF QUALITY

The good economic performance is most essential for survival and growth of any organisation in the highly competitive environment. Therefore, one of the most common objectives of every organisation is to attain excellence in its economic performance. The single most important factor which leads to good economic performance is the 'quality' of its products or services.

Therefore, in order to achieve economy, quality management system must contribute towards the establishment of customer oriented quality discipline in the marketing, design, engineering, procurement, production, inspection, testing and other related servicing functions. Every body in the organisation must be involved in the production and delivery of quality product or services, consistently to meet the customer needs and satisfaction.

Quality and Cost

Studies have indicated that any reduction in quality results in a reduced level of satisfaction and decrease in customer goodwill towards the producer. This will lead to reduction in return on investment in the long run. Following are the general principles of quality and cost relationship:

(*i*) Costs of poor quality are far large than that had been recognised.
(*ii*) Appraisal costs are reduced by focussing on preventing errors at the source.
(*iii*) System be established for reducing the cost rather than reducing the quality.
(*iv*) By focussing on quality improvement overall performance of the firm can be improved.
(*v*) Focus of quality improvement be shifted from product attributes to operational procedure.

Quality Cost (or Costs Associated with Quality)

Quality cost means cost of poor quality goods or services. Following are the main quality associated costs :

1. Failure Costs.

(*A*) Internal Failure Costs :

(*i*) Scrap and rework cost.
(*ii*) Costs involved in testing, inspecting and sorting for down-gradation.
(*iii*) Losses due to avoidable processing.
(*iv*) Expenditure in failure analysis.

(*B*) External Failure Cost:

(*i*) Warranty charges
(*ii*) Redressal of complaints
(*iii*) Loss of future sales
(*iv*) Other expenses on return of materials, failure analysis outside the factory.

2. Appraisal/Detection Costs

(*i*) Incoming test and inspection including materials in-process and final quality sampling.
(*ii*) Quality audits.
(*iii*) Equipment calibration.
(*iv*) Evaluation of performance.
(*vi*) Evaluation of customer satisfaction.

3. Prevention Costs:

(*i*) Quality planning.
(*ii*) New product review.
(*iii*) Process control.
(*iv*) Training and education.
(*v*) Process quality planning.

Quality Cost Control

For the purpose of reducing the cost, when internal and external failure costs are cut down, the appraisal cost and preventive cost may slightly go up. Therefore, it is necessary for optimum balance to reduce failure cost with slight increase in appraisal and preventive cost, with the aim of substantial reduction in total quality cost without compromising with the quality.

Efforts for reducing quality cost must be continuous. The cost reduction programme must be followed in following stages :

1. Identification of quality cost items.
2. Structuring of quality cost reporting, including related analysis and control, and
3. Maintenance of programme to ensure the objectives of higher quality at lower cost.

Quality control and quality cost must be directed in such a way so as to provide the firm with major added business value.

The Cost Balance

It means the problem of balancing the value of a given result against the cost of a given result. Usually, it becomes progressively more expensive as the quality specifications narrow the limits. This expense increases very greatly as we approach closer and closer to perfection. This is shown in Fig. 22.2. The Quality Control Engineer has always before him the problem of demanding great precisions to fulfil the requirements to which *the* goods will be used and yet keeping this precision within justified cost limits.

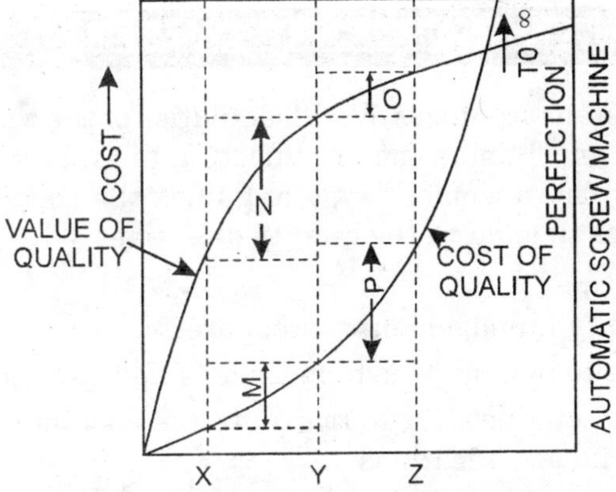

Fig. 22.2. Relation of costs and quality.

(Quality at level Y is the most economical. *A* drop to level *X* reduces the cost by M and reduces the value by *N* which is greater than *M*. *A* rise to level *Z* increased the value by *O* but increase the cost by *P*, which is greater than O.)

22.4. CAUSES OF QUALITY FAILURES

Quality failures occur due to various causes, most of them are because of lack of involvement of men concerned with the quality. Studies have indicated that more than 50% of quality failures are due to human errors at various levels, such as understanding of customers' requirements, manufacturing, inspection, testing, packaging, design etc.

Errors effecting quality can be classified into following categories :

(*a*) **Errors due to Inadvertence.** These are due to lack of knowledge of the product, and continues due to lack of information about quality deficiency. Such mistakes can be controlled, if a system for feed back is developed in which quality performance results are analysed in a regular and timely manner.

(*b*) **Errors due to Lack of Technique.** These errors are due to lack of knowledge, skill, technique etc. In such cases, performance of'better' operation are compared with those of'poor' or 'defect prone' operators, and the process adopted by them are studied and reasons for errors are investigated.

(c) **Wilful Errors.** Sometimes quality is compromised due to early delivery schedules, reduction in cost, safety etc.

Reduction of Errors by Improved Motivation

Quality motivational programmes are developed for getting quality product from the line staff so that they take interest in improving the quality. Motivational programmes are designed after identifying the sources/reasons of failures. Operators are motivated by designing a campaign to secure alertness, awareness and new actions, and by observing the managers for their behaviour or reaction on any quality problem. Campaign can be launched through mass meetings, quality posters, exhibition of quality deficiencies etc. Campaign may also invite operators to participate in analysing the causes of defects or the failure on the part of operation and/or systems. Trainings are very helpful in making the operators aware of the technological do's and don'ts and the purpose behind each operation.

22.5. QUALITY MANAGEMENT SYSTEM

A quality management system organizes overall activities of the company in such a way that the technical, administrative and human factors affecting the quality of products or services are under control. The quality management system guides the cooperated actions of the people, machines and informations to achieve the quality objectives.

1. Activities :

Activities of quality management system are :

1. Marketing to evaluate customer needs and use requirements.
2. Design and engineering to translate the customer needs into product, process and material specifications.
3. Purchasing to select the competent vendors who can supply materials, components, sub assemblies as per specifications.
4. Production to ensure that product is produced under controlled conditions in conformity with standards.
5. Quality assurance to identify appropriate test methods and exercise quality control techniques.
6. Shipping to ensure proper packaging, transportation and distribution of material.
7. Documentation to maintain system and progress documents at each stage of operation.
8. Product development for innovation and improvement based on customer's feed back.
9. Auditing to identify the non-conformity of the system and product, and follow up the corrective actions.

2. Benefits

1. To meet the customer requirements by providing quality products or services to satisfy the customer needs.
2. Good reputation helps in better marketability of the company's products and services.
3. Confidence is created.
4. Consistency in quality.

5. Productivity improvement.
6. Better financial performance.
7. Brings clarity in working.
8. Better documentation.
9. Better monitoring.
10. Increases export potential.
11. Human resource development.

3. Quality Function.

1. Marketing and market research.
2. Design and product development.
3. Procurement.
4. Process planning and development.
5. Production.
6. Inspection, testing and examination.
7. Packaging and storage.
8. Sales and distribution.
9. Installation and operation
10. Technical assistance and maintenance
11. Disposal after use

4. Quality and Top Management

Responsibility for and commitment to quality always belong to the highest level of management. Following action points are necessary to be adopted by top management to achieve quality objectives of the company:

1. Define and state quality policy
2. Appoint a management representative
3. Define responsibility and authority
4. Establish an internal verification system
5. Establish a quality system
6. Review the functioning of quality system at regular intervals.

5. Installing the Quality System

(*A*) Preparations

1. Analyse the existing status and identify what needs to be done? Prepare an action-plan.
2. Develop an organisation structure.
3. Develop quality system documentation.
4. Prepare the material and machinery resoucres.

(*B*) Implementation

1. Implement the documented quality system.
2. Establish internal quality audit system.
3. Monitor, control and stabilize the quality system.
4. Hormonise the practices with the standards

22.6. CUSTOMER SATISFACTION

Quality management is focussed on the requirements of the customer, who have a set of expectations and requirements that must be met to win repeat business. From quality point of view, requirements of the customers are related to the following elements:

(a) *Specification :* to meet the expected requirement from the product.

(b) *Conformance:* Whether the product meets the expectation for which he wants to purchase.

(c) *Reliability :* Whether it can meet the requirement through out the expected life.

(d) *Value (cost) :* Whether it fulfils its value.

(e) *Delivery :* Whether it will be available, when desired.

In order to achieve the objective of customer satisfaction, following duties should strictly be performed by every individual/department:

1. To monitor performance and customer satisfaction levels.
2. To identify improvements necessary in the customer interface,
3. To assess and agree the customer's requirements.
4. To tailor output to the customers' demand.

Care of External Customers

It is most important to give top most priority to long-term total satisfaction of the customer. This satisfaction can only come with a quality product that fully conforms to the customer's expectations, and with a proper after-sales service. Customer's complaints must be viewed as an opportunity for improvement.

Care of Internal Customers

The persons within the company which receives the work of another individual/department and then adds his contribution to the product or service before passing it on to some one else, is known as *internal customer.* If the internal customers' requirements are agreed and met, a chain of quality is made that reaches to the external customer. This concept of internal customer is a start of a total quality process.

22.7. PRODUCTION PLANNING FOR QUALITY

Quality in production can be achieved by planning and implementing the production operations under controlled conditions. These controlled conditions include control of:

1. Materials.
2. Production Equipments.
3. Processes.
4. Personnel.
5. Utilities and environment.
6. Supplies.
7. Measurement control.
8. Control of non-conformance.
9. Documentation.

To ensure right quality of material and product, the product verification is conducted at three main stages of production process, namely:

(*a*) Incoming materials and parts.

(*b*) In-process inspection, and

(*c*) Completed product verification.

Appropriate methods for inspection and testing of incoming material, semi-finished, and finished products should be applied to verify conformity.

The production activity involves the use of manufacturing processes to change the physical raw material into product. A quality product can be produced only when the 'process is capable' and production operations are performed under 'controlled conditions'.

Under *process capability,* production process should be verified as capable of producing in accordance with product specifications. The critical operations of the process which are of significant importance from quality point of view should be identified, and if required, suitably modified to ensure that these characteristics remain within specifications.

Integrate Quality in Manufacture Planning

Integrate quality in manufacture planning with following objectives :

1. to prevent defects
2. to minimise variability.

For the purpose of preventing the defects, product design as well as process design should be reviewed. The concept of designing the process to be error free through 'error-proofing'. The idea is the design of machines and tools so as to make human error improbable. In error-proofing, care is taken for redundancy, *i.e.,* requiring multiple improbable events to occur simultaneously before a defect can be created or can escape. The objectives *of 'error-proofing'* are :

1. Eliminating the possibility of error
2. Substituting a more reliable process for the worker
3. Making the work easier to perform
4. Selecting the error before further processing
5. Minimising the effect of the error.

Controllability Concept:

(*a*) *Worker-controllable defects:*

- Failure to check work.
- Improper operation of machine.

(*b*) *Management-controllable defects :*

- Inadequate training
- Inadequate machine
- Inadequate machine maintenance
- Problems related to process
- Material handling problems
- Wrong material
- Tool, fixture and gauge maintenance problems.

An ideal objective for manufacturing planning is to place human beings in a state of self-control, for which people must be provided with :

1. Knowledge of what they are supposed to do

2. Knowledge of what they are actually doing
3. A process that is capable of regulating to meet specifications.

1. *Knowledge of what people are supposed to do :*

   This knowledge consists of: .

   (*a*) Written specifications of product, a product sample, and other definition of the end result to be attained.

   (*b*) Written specification and instructions for process.

   (*c*) What decisions to make and what actions to take.

   For above aspects, all necessary informations must be provided.

2. *Knowledge of what people are actually doing :*

   The people must have means for knowing whether their performance conforms to standard. This conformance applies to:

   (*a*) Product characteristics in the form of product specifications.

   (*b*) Process variables in the form of process specifications.

   This knowledge is secured from measurements taken (*i*) during the process, (*ii*) by production workers, and (*c*) by inspection. This is possible though proper feed back.

3. *A process that is capable of regulating to meet specification :*

   Regulating the process depends on a number of management- controllable factors, such as:

   (*a*) The process must be capable of meeting the tolerances.

   (*b*) The worker must be trained as to how to use the regulating mechanisms and procedures:

   (*c*) The process must be maintained sufficiently to retain its inherent capability.

   Self Inspection

   Under this concept, all inspection and conformance decisions, both on the process and on the product, are made by the production worker. However, independent audit of these decisions is also required. Quality department inspects a random sample to ensure that the decision-making process used by production workers regarding to accept or reject a product is valid.

   The self-inspection system should be instituted in a well planned manner, and for this a quality culture should be developed in the production department.

22.8. QUALITY POLICY

Quality policy is the overall quality intention and direction of an organisation as regards quality as formally expressed by top management. The quality policy should be expressed in an easily understandable language and should be relevant to organisational policies. The quality objectives should be both ambitious and achievable. The management should be committed to implement its quality policy. Quality policy should be developed and documented related to the following :

(*i*) level of clientele constitutes the company's market.

(*ii*) whether the company strives for quality leadership, competitiveness, or adequacy.

(*iii*) grade of quality to be provided.

(*iv*) objective for quality.

(*v*) approach to be adopted to achieve quality objectives

(*vi*) role to company personal responsible for implementation of quality policy.

(*vii*) whether the company to market its products on the basis of high reliability at higher price or lower reliability at lower price.

(*viii*) should the reliability, maintainability etc. be quantified?

(*ix*) should top management actively participate in quality planning and assurance or should it delegate this to someone else?

Quality Goals. A goal is a statement of the desired result to be achieved within a specified time, these goals form the basis of detailed planning of quality activities. Tactical goals are short range (say 1 year), and strategic goals are long range (say 5 years).

22.9. QUALITY IMPROVEMENT

Quality Management is accomplished by the use of three managerial processes : quality planning, quality control, and quality improvement. These three quality processes provide a methodological approach to addressing quality.

It is a general experience that management controllable defects are much more than operator controllable defects. According to J.M. Juran, about 80 percent of the defects are management controllable. Lack of awareness on the part of many industrial managers regarding the fact that majority of defects are management controllable compels them to believe that most defects are the result of operator carelessness, indifference and sabotage.

Quality Problems

Before studying the 'Quality Improvement', we must know different types of quality problems. Quality problems are of following two types :

1. **Sporadic Quality Problems**

   These are detected and acted by the process of quality control (during operation). A sporadic problem is a sudden, adverse change in the status quo, which requires remedy through restoring status quo. The variations due to sporadic problems are so significant that they trigger the alarm signals of the control systems. The significant variations are a form of sporadic departure from standard which call for quick diagnosis of the cause and removal of the cause to restore status quo. The sequence of events used to restore the status quo is known as trouble shooting or fire fighting. These problems are dramatic and must receive immediate attention.

2. **Chronic Quality Problems**

   Chronic problem is a long-standing adverse situation which requires remedy through changing the status quo. For chronic problems, by adopting continuous improvement concept better and better levels of performance can be achieved. These problems occur for a long time and are often difficult to solve, as they are accepted as inevitable.

   In chronic problems, the same problem comes up over and over again, suggesting that the cause is not a reported error but a basic deficiency in the design, process, system etc. Being continuous in nature, these problems are accepted as unavoidable. The solution calls for extensive and complex data collection over long periods, analysis of data by Statistical Quality Control personnel. The solution of these problems, when implemented, provide superior of performance as compared to that of previous level.

22.10. STEPS IN QUALITY IMPROVEMENT

1. **Proving the Need.** In this step management is convinced that the quality issue is significant and companywide improvement efforts are necessary. For getting approval of the management following actions are necessary :
   (*a*) Collection of factual information and necessary data to show the gravity of quality problem.
   (*b*) Benefit expected from this improvement to justify requested resources.
2. **Identify Projects.** This step of project identification consists of nominating, screening and selecting the project.
3. **Organising Project Teams.** A project team consisting of about six to eight persons drawn from different departments is assigned the task of addressing the "problem selected as above.
4. **Verifying the Project Need.** The selected project should be of importance. The scope of project and size of the problem should again be reviewed after the team has met once or twice to be sure that whether the mission assigned to the team can be accomplished within about 6 months time. If the project is likely to take more time, it should be divided into number of projects.
5. **Diagnosing the Causes.** Since the diagnosis is the "process of studying the symptoms of a problem and determining their cause (*s*), it begins with collection of data on the symptoms and ends with the agreement on the causes. A *cause* is a proven reason for the existence of the defect. In cases causes are too many, only vital few are tackled first.
6. **Providing a Remedy and Proving its Effectiveness** : After determining the cause of the problem, the next step is to choose a remedy. Generaly problems have more than one alternative solution. Each of these alternatives are then evaluated to find an optimum solution.

   Before finally adopting a remedy, its effectiveness must be proved. This can be done in two stages, in first stage reliability is proved through theoretical prediction, run in a pilot plant, of the testing of a prototype. In second stage, final evalution under real-world conditions is carried out.
7. **Dealing with Resistance to Change.** It is a general tendency that change is resisted by the managers, supervisors, workforce or the union. The change consists of two parts, namely a technological change, and a social consequences of the technological change. The people generally voice objections on the ground of technological change, but in reality their objection or the social effect. Therefore, while proposing a change, we must (*i*) be aware that we are dealing with a pattern of human habits, beliefs and traditions, and (*ii*) find out the social effect of the proposed changes.

   For introducing a change, following suggestions are kept in view :
   1. Provide participation of those who are likely to be affected by change.
   2. Establish the need for the change.
   3. Enough time be provided, so as to avoid surprises.
   4. Working with the recognised leadership of the culture.
   5. Tearing the people with dignity.

   Thereafter, while implementing the change, the resistance, if still felt may be dealt directly through:
   (*a*) Persuasion

(b) Offering something for something.

(c) Make some changes in the proposals to meet the specific objections.

(d) Drop the proposal, if not possible to implement.

The task of dealing with resistance to change is an art and should be done in a methodical way.

8. **Instituting Controls to Hold the Gains.** It is essential to hold the gains so that benefits continue on and on. For this purpose following steps are taken :

(a) A process capable of holding the gains under operating conditions be provided to the operating forces.

(b) Establish the new operating procedure and train the operating forces.

(c) Controls should be exercised through feed back mechanisms, measuring the actual performance and comparing with the standards.

22.11. STATISTICAL QUALITY CONTROL (S.Q.C)

These days, the Statistical Quality Control is used more or less in every kind of industry. It is now becoming an integral part of Management Control. Statistical Quality Control involves the statistical analysis of the inspection data obtained from the samples. Statistical Quality Control technique was introduced during II World War by Dr. WALTER A. Shewartan American Scientist. The quality in statistical quality control is usually related to measurement made of the items manufactured, a good quality item is an item which conforms to specified standard, and is not mean to have highest standards of manufacture. Most desirable situation represents consistency in quality standards rather than the absolute standards.

Before understanding S.Q.C, we must just know the meaning of each word in the term:

Statistics: Statistics means data, sufficient enough to obtain reliable results.

Quality. Quality is a relative term, and can be defined as fitness for the purpose.

Control. Control is a system for measuring and checking. It suggests when to inspect, how often to inspect and how much to inspect, this also incorporates a feed back mechanism to explore the cause of poor quality and takes corrective steps.

Advantages

Statistical Quality control is one of the tool for scientific management, and has following main advantages over 100 per cent inspection:

(i) **Reduction in Costs.** Since only a fractional output is inspected, hence cost of inspection is greatly reduced.

(ii) **Greater Efficiency.** It requires a lesser time and boredom as compared to the 100 per cent inspection and hence the efficiency increases.

(iii) **Easy to Apply.** Once the statistical quality control plan is established, it is easy to apply even by a man who does not have extensive specialised training.

(iv) **Accurate Prediction.** Specifications can easily be predicted for the future, which is not possible even with 100 per cent inspection.

(v) **Can be used where inspection needs destruction of items.** In case where destruction of product is necessary for inspection, 100 percent inspection is not possible (which will spoil all the products), sampling inspection is resorted to.

(vi) **Early Detection of Faults.** The moment a sample point falls outside the control limits, it is taken as a danger signal and necessary corrective measures are taken. Whereas in 100 per cent inspection, unwanted variations in quality may be detected after large number of defective items have already been produced. Thus, by using the Control charts, we can know from graphic picture that how the production is proceeding and where corrective action is required and where it is not required.

22.12. TECHNIQUES USED IN S.Q.C.

Following are the techniques commonly used in S.Q.C.

1. Acceptance Sampling. (already discussed)
2. Control Charts.
3. Analysis of data.

Acceptance sampling have already been discussed in detail in previous in chapter.

22.13. CONTROL CHARTS

Since variations in manufacturing process are unavoidable, the control chart tells when to leave a process alone and prevent unnecessary frequent adjustments. Control charts are graphical representation and are based on statistical sampling theory, according to which an adequate sized random sample is drawn from each lot. A control chart detects variations in the processing and warns if there is any departure from the specified tolerance limits. These control charts immediately tell the undesired variations and help in detecting the cause and its removal.

In control charts, where both upper and lower values are specified for a quality characteristic, as soon as some products show a variation outside the tolerances, a review of situation is taken and corrective step is immediately taken.

Advantages

Control charts are advantageous from following reasons:-

(*i*) It indicates whether the process is in control or out of control at a particular point of time.

(*ii*) It ensures level of quality, and hence also builds up the reputation of the organisation due to customers satisfaction.

(*iii*) It detects unusual variations taking place in a process.

(*iv*) It helps in reducing the rejection, as it warns in time so as to rectify the process in time.

(*v*) It helps in setting of tolerance limits.

Causes of Variation in Quality

(*a*) **Chance Causes.** These vary at random and are independent of each other. It is difficult and also uneconomical to detect and eliminate these causes. These are natural and are beyond human control.

(*b*) **Assignable Causes.** These are non-random and can be identified. These causes may creep in at any stage of the process. The variations due to these can be detected and eliminated and hence are also known as preventive or controllable variations.

Types of Control Charts

(a) **Control Charts for Variables.** These are used to achieve and maintain an acceptable quality level for a process whose product can be subjected to quantitative measurements, such as length of stud, dia of a stud etc.

(b) **Control Charts for Attributes.** These are used to achieve and maintain an acceptable quality level for a process whose product can not be subjected to quantitative measurements but can be classified as 'good' or 'bad' such as 'go' and 'no go' gauges etc.

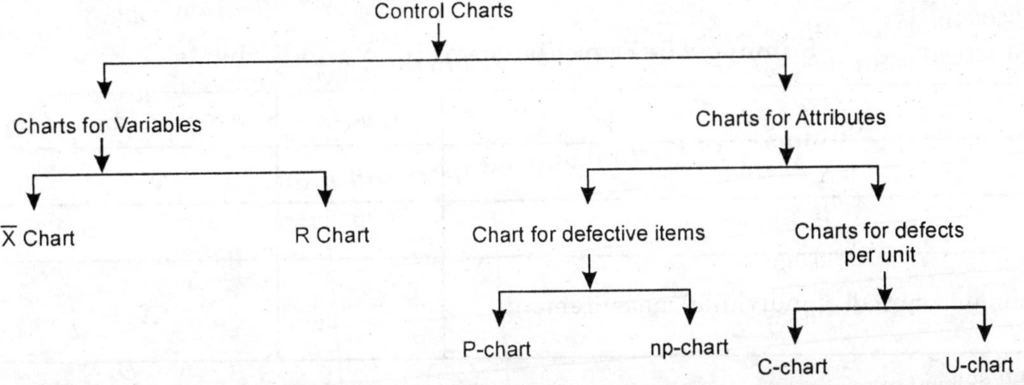

22.14. CONTROL CHARTS FOR VARIABLES

The $\bar{X}$ and R-Charts

This chart is used for the quality characteristics which are specified as variables, *i.e.*, on the basis of actual readings taken. The purpose or objective of this chart is:

(a) To establish whether the process is in statistical control or not.

(b) To determine whether the process capability is compatible with the specifications.

(c) To detect trends in the process so as to assist in planning, adjustment and resetting of the process.

(d) To show when the process is likely to be out of control.

Procedure. A number of samples of component coming out of the process are taken over a period of time. Each sample must be taken at random and the size of sample is generally kept 5 but 10-15 units can be taken for sensitive control charts. For each sample, the average value ($\bar{X}$) of all the measurements and the range R are calculated. The grand average ($\bar{X}$) is equal to the average value of all the average, ($\bar{X}$) and ($\bar{R}$) ($\bar{R}$ is equal to the average of all the ranges) are then found and from these we can calculate the control limits for the ($\bar{X}$) and R charts. Therefore,

For $\bar{X}$ charts:

Upper Control Limit, UCL $\bar{X} = \bar{X} + A_2 \bar{R}$

Lower Control Limit, LCL $\bar{X} = \bar{X} - A_2 \bar{R}$.

$\bar{X}$ and Rare also called centre line values.

For R chart:

$UCL_R = D_4 R$

$LCL_R = D_3 \bar{R}$

Here the factors A_2, D_3 and D_4 depend on the number of units per sample. The larger this number, the closer the limits. The value of the factors A_2, D_4 and D_3 can be obtained from Statistical Quality Control tables. However, for ready reference these are given below in tabular form.

As long as the $\bar{X}$, R values for each sample are within the control limits, the process is said to be in statistical control.

Summary of Formulae used in $\bar{X}$ and R charts

Chart	*Centre*	*3 Sigma Control limits*
$\bar{X}$ Average	$\bar{X}$	$\bar{X} \pm A_2 \bar{R}$
R, Range	R	$D_3 R$ and $D_4 \bar{R}$
Estimated spread of individual measurements		$\bar{X} \pm \dfrac{3\bar{R}}{d_2}$

Where d_2 is a factor, whose value depends on number of units in a sample. Its value is seen from *S.Q.C.* Table given below.

Process Out of Control

After computing the control limits the next step is to determine whether the process is in statistical control or not. If it is not, means there is some external cause that throws the process out of control. This cause must be traced and removed so that the process may return to operate under stable statistical conditions.

Factors used in the $\bar{X}$ and R Quality Control Charts

No.of unit in a sample	A_2	D_3	D_4	d_2
2	1.88	0	3.17	1.13
3	1.02	0	2.57	1.69
4	0.73	0	2.28	2.06
5	0.58	0	2.11	2.33
6	0.48	0	2.00	2.53
7	0.42	0.08	1.92	2.70
8	0.37	0.14	1.86	2.85
9	0.34	0.18	1.82	2.97
10	0.31	0.22	1.78	3.08
11	0.29	0.26	1.74	3.17
12	0.27	0.28	1.72	3,26
13	0.25	0.31	1.69	3.34
14	0.24	0.33	1.67	3.41
15	0.22	0.35	1.65	3.47

The various reasons for the process being out of control may be:

(i) Faulty tools

(ii) Sudden significant change in properties of new materials in a new consignment

(iii) Breakdown of lubrication system

(iv) Faults in timing or speed mechanism etc.

Tracing of these causes is sometimes simple and straight forward but when the process is subject to the combined effect of several external causes simultaneously then it may be lengthy and complicated business.

Process in Control

If the process is found to be in statistical control, a comparison between the required specifications and the process capability may be carried out to determine whether the two are compatible. Should the specified tolerances prove to be too tight for the process capability?

There are three possible alternatives:

(a) Re-evaluate the specifications. Whether the tight tolerances are actually needed or they can be relaxed without affecting quality.

(b) If relaxation in specifications is not allowed then a more accurate process is required to be selected.

(c) If both the above alternatives are not acceptable than 100% inspection is carried out to trace out the defectives.

Conclusions. When the process is not in control then the points will fall outside the control limits on either ($\bar{X}$) or R charts. It means assignable causes (Human controlled causes) are present in the process. When all the points fall inside the control limits even then we cannot definitely say that no assignable cause is present but it is not economical to trace the causes. Even in the best manufacturing process, certain errors may develop and that constitute the assignable causes but no statistical action can be taken. This leads to many practical difficulties regarding what relationship shows satisfactory control.

One of the most common causes of lack of control is shift in the mean $\bar{X}$. $\bar{X}$ chart is also useful for the purpose of detecting shift in production. Tool wear and resetting of machines often account for such a shift. It is necessary to find out when machine resetting becomes desirable, bearing in mind that too frequent adjustments are a serious set back to production output.

Fig. No. 22.2. shows four examples of $\bar{X}$ charts. The charts a, b and c show the relation between the process variability and the specifications. The fourth illustrates that there is an adequate process from the point of view of the specifications but there is constant shift in $\bar{X}$. It means periodic resetting of machine is needed to bring down the value of $\bar{X}$ to the control limits, if the original conditions are to be regained.

Therefore, it can be said that the problem of resetting is closely associated with the relationship between process capability and the specifications. Case (a) in Fig. no. 22.2 would require a smaller number of machine resets than case (b)

This can further be illustrated in Fig. no. 22.3. In case (a), the mean $\bar{X}$ can shift a great on either side without causing a remarkable increase in the amount of defective items. In case (b), the process capability is compatible with specified limits. In case (c), the process $\pm 3\sigma$ is slightly wider than the specified tolerance so that the amount of defectives (scrap) becomes quite large whenever there is even a small shift in X. This needs frequent adjustments.

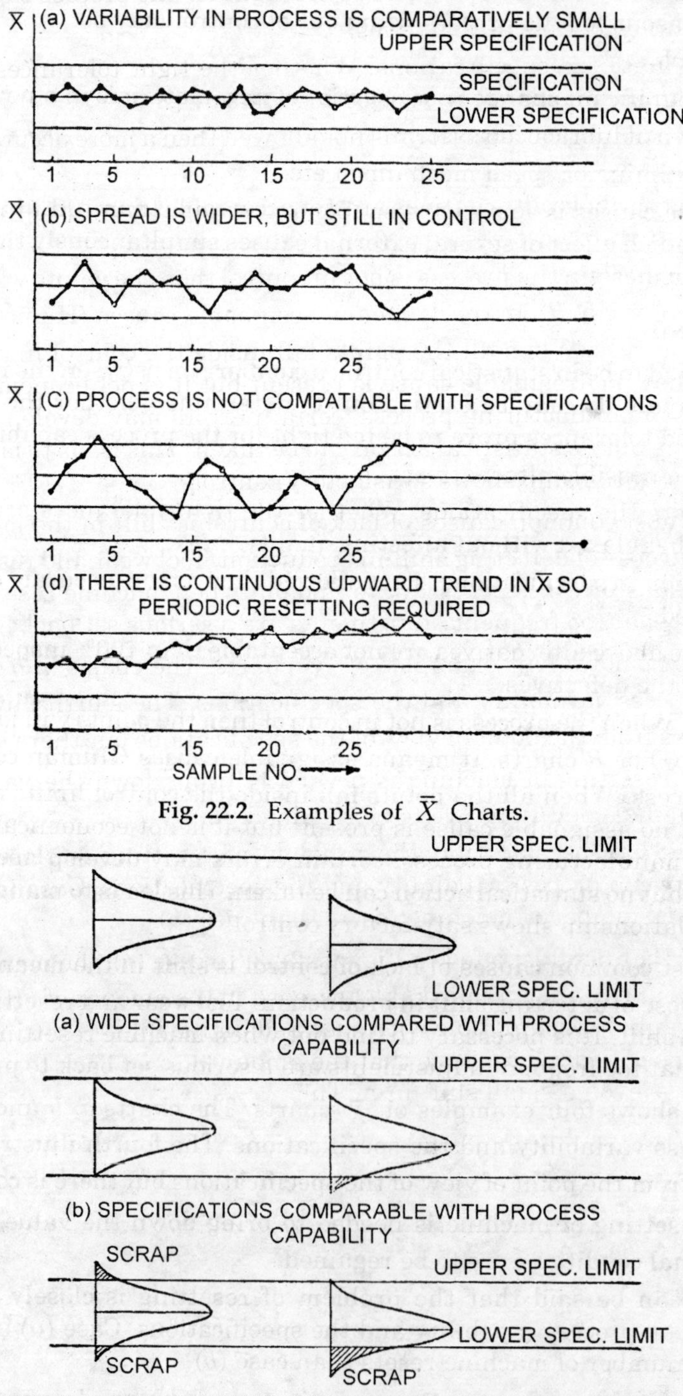

Fig. 22.2. Examples of $\bar{X}$ Charts.

Fig. 22.3. Charts on the left side show that the mean is half way between the upper and lower specification limits while charts on the right side show downward shift of the mean.

To illustrate how $\bar{X}$ and R charts are used in process control few examples are worked out as under :

Example 22.1 *The following table gives record of 5 measurements per sample from the lot size of 50 for the critical dimensions of jeep valve stem diameter taken every hour,*

(i) Compute the control limits, make plot and explain procedure.

(ii) Interpret plot make decision regarding quality of product, process control and cost of inspection.

Solution: It is given that specifications are (9.642 φ + 0.002 – 0.02 mm)

	Five measurements per sample						
Sample	*a*	*b*	c	*d*	e	$\bar{X}$	R
1	9.484	9.483	9.485	9.485	9.491	9.4876	0.009
2	9.483	9.494	9.490	9.484	9.485	9.4850	0.007
3	9.485	9.492	9.483	9.486	9.490	9.4872	0.009
4	9.486	9.481	9.487	9.490	9.490	9.4868	0.009
5	9.486	9.491	9.484	9.487	9.490	9.4876	0.008
6	9.490	9.491	9.489	9.491	9.483	9.4886	0.008
7	9.482	9.486	9.483	9.484	9.486	9.4842	0.004
8	9.484	9.487	9.487	9.485	9.496	9.4838	0.003
9	9.485	9.488	9.486	9.484	9.487	9.4860	0.002
10	9.484	9.481	9.482	9.485	9.483	9.4830	0.004
11	9.485	9.482	9.490	9.487	9.484	9.4856	0.008
12	9.485	9.487	9.481	9.482	9.478	9.4826	0.009
13	9.488	9.477	9.482	9.485	9.484	9.4832	0.014
14	9.485	9.491	9.477	9.490	9.478	9.4860	0.014
15	9.474	9.483	9.487	9.488	9.490	9.4822	0.016

$$UCL\,\bar{X} = \bar{X} + A_2\,\bar{R}$$

$$LCL\,\bar{X} = \bar{X} - A_2\,\bar{R}$$

$$UCR_R = D_4\,\bar{R}$$

$$LCL_R = D_3\,\bar{R}$$

Here $\bar{X} = \dfrac{\text{Sum of all } \bar{X}}{\text{Total No. of samples}} = 9.485$

$$\bar{R} = \frac{\text{Sum of all } R}{\text{Total No. of samples}} = 0.008$$

From *S.Q.C.* table, the values of A_2, D_4 and D_3 can be recorded from the 5 measurement sample coloumns.

$$A_2 = 0.58$$

$$D_3 = 0$$

and $D_4 = 2.11$

Therefore
$$UCL\ \bar{X} = 9.485 + 0.58 \times 0.008$$
$$= 9.4896 \text{ say } 9.490$$
$$LCLX = 9.485 - 0.58 \times 0.008 = 9.480$$
$$UCL_R = D_4\bar{R} = 2.11 \times 0.008 = 0.0169$$
$$UCL_R = D_3 R = 0 \times 0.008 = 0$$

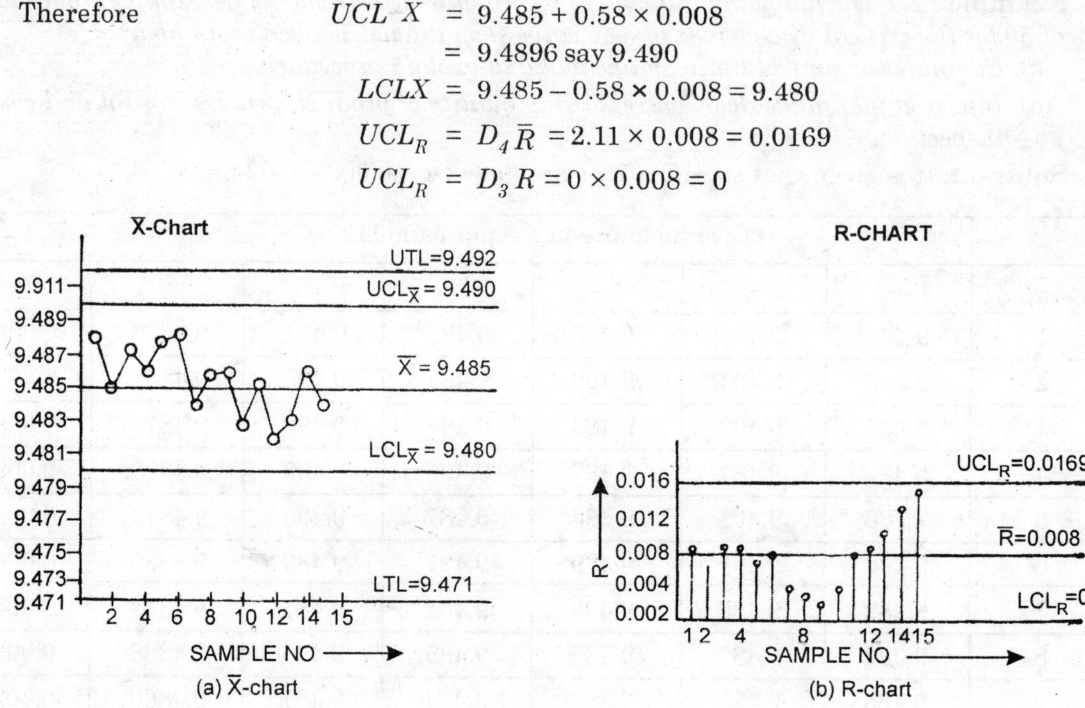

(a) $\bar{X}$-chart (b) R-chart

Fig. 22.4. $\bar{X}$ and R chart.

Now charts for $\bar{X}$ and R plotted as shown in plot no. 22.4 taking abscissa as sample no. and ordinate as $\bar{X}$ and R. $\bar{X}$ and R charts must be drawn one over the other as shown, *i.e.*, R chart must be exactly under $\bar{X}$ chart.

What the $\bar{X}$ and R Charts tell?

Sometimes $\bar{X}$ chart does not give satisfactory results, this may occur due to old machine, or worn out parts or misalignment or where processing is inherently quite variable. Here the 'Range' chart is used as additional tool to control. The purpose of this chart is to have constant check over the variability of the process. Process variability demonstrated in Fig. 31.3 shows that though the mean or average of the process may be perfectly centred about the specified dimension, excessive variability will result in poor quality products.

The use of R-chart is called for, if after using the $\bar{X}$ chart for some time it is found that it frequently fails to indicate trouble promptly.

The R-chart does not replace the $\bar{X}$-chart but simply supplements with additional information about the production process.

The R-chart is also used for high precision process whose variability must be carefully held within prescribed limits. Similarly many electro-chemical processes such as plating, and micro-chemical-biological production, such as fermentation of yeast and penicillin require the use of R-chart because unusual variability is quite inherent in such processes.

Example 22.2. *The following record taken for a sample of 5 pieces from* a process each hour for a period of 24 hours.

Design control limits, make plot and draw Inferences regarding quality.

S.No.	*Time*	*Measurements*					$\bar{X}$	*R*
1	8 am.	995	997	1002	995	1000	0.998	0.097
2	9 a.m.	990	1002	997	1003	1005	0.999	0.015
3	10 a.m.	1003	1005	993	1004	995	1.001	0.009
4	11 a.m.	1002	999	1003	995	1001	1.000	0.006
5	12 a.m.	100	996	999	1006	1001	1.000	0:006
6	1 p.m.	1004	1001	998	1004	997	1.000	0.007
7	2 p.m.	1002	1002	999	1003	1004	1.002	0.006
8	3 p.m.	1001	1007	1006	999	998	1.002	0.009
9	4 p.m.	999	995	994	991	996	0.995	0.009
10	5 p.m.	994	993	991	993	996	0.993	0.005
11	6 p.m.	994	996	995	995	994	0.994	0.005
12	7 p.m.	994	995	998	999	1001	0.997	0.007
13	8 p.m.	1002	1004	1000	994	1005	1.000	0.010
14	9 p.m.	1003	1000	996	1000	1005	1.000	0.009
15	10 p.m.	996	1001	1006	1001	1008	1.003	0.012
16	11 p.m.	925	1003	1004	1006	1001	1.003	0.023
17	12 p.m.	1006	1005	1006	1009	1008	1.006	0.007
18	1 a.m.	996	999	1001	1008	996	0.999	0.012
19	2 a.m.	1001	1004	995	1001	1008	1.002	0.013
20	3 a.m.	1003	995	1002	921	996	0.997	0.012
21	4 a.m.	1000	991	993	997	1003	0.997	0.013
22	5 a.m.	1003	997	998	1008	1001	0.999	0.006
23	6 a.m.	1006	1001	999	996	997	0.999	0.010
24	7 a.m.	1005	1000	1001	998	1000	1.001	0.007
	Total						23.976	0.216
	Average						0.99	0.009

So,

$$X = 0.999$$

$$\bar{R} = 0.009$$

From *S.Q.C.* tables for sample size 5

$$A_2 = 0.58,\ D_4 = 2.11 \text{ and } D_3 = 0.$$

$$UCL_{\bar{X}} = \bar{\bar{X}} + A_2 \bar{R}$$

$$= 0.999 + (0.58) \times 0.009 = 1.004$$

$$LCL_{\bar{X}} = \bar{\bar{X}} - A_2 \bar{R} = 0.999 - 0.00522 = 0.994$$

$$UCL_R = D_4 \bar{R} = (2.11 \times 0.009) = 0.019$$

$$LCL_R = D_3 \bar{R} = 0 \times 0.009 = 0.$$

Now $\bar{X}$ and R charts are plotted on the plot as shown in Fig. 22.5 taking abscissa as sample No. and ordinates as $(\bar{X})$ and R respectively.

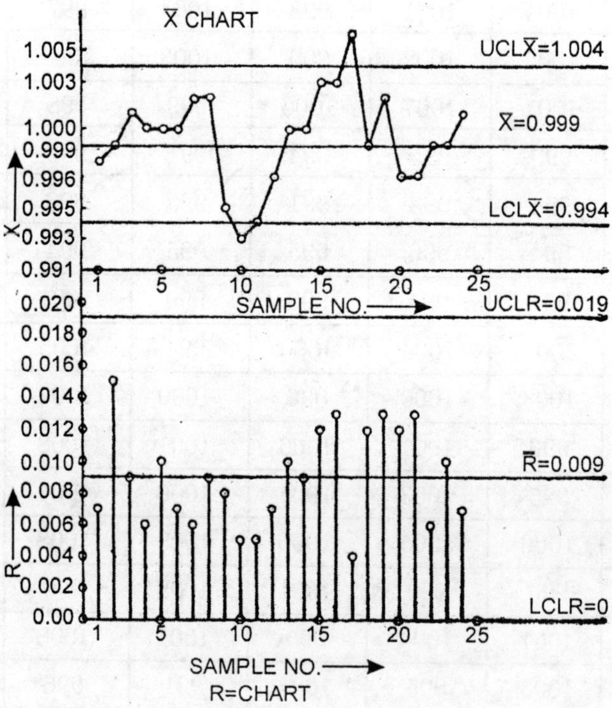

Fig. 22.5

Inference

Let us look at the Fig. 22.4.

In the $\bar{X}$ chart, most of the time the plotted points representing averages are well within the control limits but in Sample No. 10 and 17, the plotted points fall outside the control limits.

It means something has probably gone wrong or is about to go wrong with the process and check is needed to prevent the appearance of defective products.

If the cause has been eliminated, the following plotted points will stay well within the control limits, but if more points fall outside the control limits then a very thorough investigation should be made, even, if it is necessary to shut down production temporarily until every thing is adjusted again and no more points fall outside.

22.15. CONTROL CHARTS FOR ATTRIBUTES

The $\bar{X}$ and R control charts are applicable for quality characteristics which are measured directly, *i. e.*, for variables. There are instances in industrial practice where direct measurement are not required or possible. Under such circumstances, the inspection results are based on the classification of products as being defective, acceptable as good or bad according as that product conforms or fails to conform to the specified specifications.

In manufacturing, sometime it is required to control burns, cracks, voids, tends, scratches, missing and wrong components, rust etc. Here we inspect products only as good or bad but not how much good or how much bad. Furthermore, there are many quality characteristics that come under the category of measurable variables but direct measurement is not taken for reasons of economy. These products are inspected with'go' and 'not go' gauges. Again under this type our aim is to tell that whether product conforms or does not confirm to the specified values. Quality characteristics expressed in this way are known as attributes.

The various control charts for attribute are explained as under:

22.15.1. THE P-CHART

This is the control chart for per cent defectives or for fraction defectives. This is used whenever the quality characteristics are expressed as the number of units conforming or not conforming to the specified specifications either by visual inspection or by "go' and "not go' gauges.

The Central Line Value

It is denoted by P and may be defined as the ratio between the total number of defective products observed in all the samples combined and the total number of products inspected. For example, if 15 products are found to be defectives in a sample of 200, then $\frac{15}{200}$ is the value of $\bar{P}$

Fraction and Per cent Defectives.

The fraction defective value is represented in decimals proportion of defectives out of one product and per cent defective is the fraction defective value expressed as percentage. As in the above example, fraction defective of 15/200 = 0.075 and per cent defective will be 0.075/100 = 7.5%.

Standard Deviation

The standard deviation for fraction defective denoted by σp is

calculated by the formula $\sigma p = \sqrt{\frac{\bar{P}(1-\bar{p})}{n}}$

Where, n = sample size

$\bar{p}$ = function effective

Trial Control Limits

Just as the control limits for the $\bar{X}$ and R- chart are obtained as $\pm$ 3 σ values above the average. The two control limits, upper and lower for this chart are also calculated by simple adding or subtracting 3 σ values from central line value. These trail limits are computed to determine whether a process is in statistical control or not.

So, $$UCLP = E\,\bar{p} + 3\sigma p$$

$$= \bar{P} + \sqrt{\frac{\bar{P}(1-\bar{P})}{n}}$$

Similarly $$LCL_P = \bar{P} - 3\sqrt{\frac{\bar{P}(1-\bar{P})}{n}}$$

Mostly the control limits are obtained on the basis of about 10 to 25 samples to pick up the problem and standard deviation from the samples is calculated for future production control.

Constant Sample Size

The preliminary data for the construction of P-chart is by inspection of samples of constant sizes.

Example 22.3. *The table shows that the successive lots of spindle are coming out of the machine. The spindles are subjected to inspection for burrs. The spindles are inspected in samples of 100 each. Presence of a single or more burrs discriminated the value to be as defective. Compute and construct the chart.*

Sample No.	*Sample Size*	*Defectives*	*Percentage*
1	100	1	1
2	100	1	1
3	100	2	2
4	100	1	1
5	100	1	1
6	100	0	0
7	100	1	1
8	100	0	1
9	100	1	1
10	100	2	2
11	100	3	3
12	100	2	2
13	100	1	2
14	100	2	2
15	100	2	2
16	100	7	7
17	100	1	1
18	100	2	2
19	100	0	0

Computation and Construction

Here the maximum percent defective is 7% and the total number of samples inspected are 20. On graph paper, make abscissa for sample numbers of 1, 2, 3, upto 20. Make ordinate as percent defective so as to accommodate 7%. Next go on marking various points as shown by the table as sample *vs.* percent defective.

Draw three firm horizontal lines, one each for central line value, upper limit and lower limit after obtaining by calculations.

Estimated fraction defective

$$\bar{P} = \frac{\textit{Sum of defective values}}{\textit{Total number of products inspected}}$$

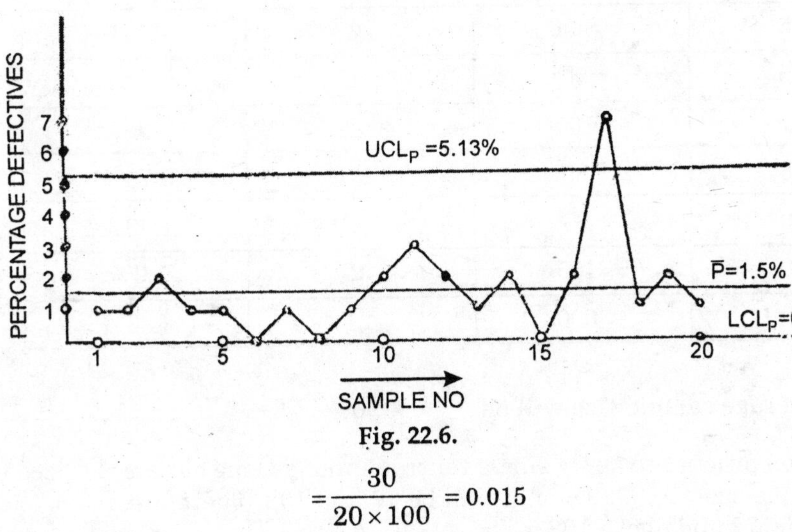

Fig. 22.6.

$$= \frac{30}{20 \times 100} = 0.015$$

Per cent defective of

$$\bar{P} = 100\ \bar{P} = 100 \times 0.015 = 1.5\%$$

Standard deviation $= \sigma P = \sqrt{\dfrac{\bar{P}(1-\bar{P})}{n}}$

$$= \sqrt{\frac{0.015(1-0.015)}{100}} = 0.0121$$

Then uppercontrol limit $= \bar{P} + 3\sigma_P$

$$UCL_P = 0.015 + 3 \times 0.0121 = 0.0513$$

Lower control limit $= \bar{P} - 3\ \sigma_P$

$$= 0.015 - 3 \times 0.0121 = 0.015 - 0.0363$$

= – ve value, but - ve value is not possible.

Therefore, $LCL_P = 0.$

Variable Sample Size

Now consider an example of a P-chart for variable sample size. This is because, hourly, daily or weekly production somewhat varies. Therefore, it is not always feasible to take the samples of constant sizes all the time under these conditions, such problems can be solved as under:

Example 22.4

Date	*Sample*	*Defectives*	*Per cent*
11	φ120	3	2.5%
12	100	1	1%
13	φ45	2	4.44%
14	φ60	2	3.33%
15	φ130	2	1.54%
16	90	1	1.1%
17	105	4	3.8%
18	80	3	3.75%
19	75	1	1.33%
20	105	2	1.9%
Total	900	21	2.33%

Here, the average sample size will be $\frac{900}{10} = 90$

It is a common practice to apply single control limits as long as sample sizes varies ± 20% of the average sample size, i.e. ± 20% of 90 will be 72 and 108. Therefore, mark the samples with @ which are below 72 and above 108.

Calculations. $\bar{P}$ the fraction defective $\frac{21}{900} = 0.023$

As the samples on dates 12,17,18,19 and 20 are covered within ± 20%of averages, we have now the following sample sizes for which control limits are to be calculated separately.

1	2	3	4	5
90	120	45	60	130

For this purpose, let us frame a table as follows : Go on calculating and filling the values.

Sample Size	σp	$3\sigma_P$	$UCL_P(\bar{P}+3\sigma_P)$	$LCL_P(\bar{P}-3\sigma_P)$
90	0.011	0.033	0.056	0
120	0.013	0.039	0.062	0
45	0.022	0.066	0.089	0
60	0.019	0.057	0.080	0
130	0.013	0.039	0.062	0

22.15.2. THE C-CHART

This is another method of plotting attribute characteristics. In this case, the sample size taken is a single unit, such as length, breadth and area or a fixed time etc. In some cases, it is required to find the number of defects per unit rather than the per cent defective. For example take a case in which a larger number of small components form a large unit, say a car or a transistor. The transistor set may have defects at various points. In this case, it seems natural to count the number of defects per set, rather than to determine all points at which the unit is defective. This attempt to use P-chart to locate all the points at which transistor is defective seems to be wrong, impossible to some extent and impracticable way as approach to the problems. Such a condition warrants the necessity for the use of a *C*- chart.

Examples on C-chart

The distribution of the variable in *C-chart* very closely follows the Poisson's distribution. The examples given below show some of representative types of defects, following Poisson's distribution where *C-chart* technique can be effectively applied:

(*i*) Number of blemishes per 100 square metres
(*ii*) Typing mistakes on the part of typist
(*iii*) Number of spots on a distempered wall
(*iv*) Air gap between two matching parts of a joint
(*v*) Welding defect in a truss.
(*vi*) Unweaven points on a piece of textile cloth.
(*vii*) Leakage in water-tight joints of radiator.

(*i*) *The average number of defects.* It is denoted by $\bar{C}$ and is the ratio between the total number of defects found in all samples and the total number of samples inspected.

(*ii*) *Standard Deviation. T* sigma or standard deviation for number of defects per unit production is calculated from the formula

$$\sigma = \sqrt{C}$$

Trial Control Limits

The control limits can be calculated by $\pm\, 3\sqrt{C}$ from the central line value $\bar{C}$.

$$UCL_C = \bar{C} + 3\sqrt{C} \qquad LCL = \bar{C} - 3\sqrt{C}$$

Illustrative Examples

The following table shows the number of point defects on the surface of bus body on Sept. 21,2016.

Computation

(*i*) Compute the average number of defect $\bar{C}$

$$\therefore \bar{C} = \frac{110}{20} = 5.5$$

Date	*Body No.*	*No. of defects*
21/9/16	1	2
	2	4
	3	7
	4	5
	5	5
	6	6
	7	8
	8	14
	9	2
	10	9
	11	3
	12	0
	13	5
	14	1
	15	3
	16	12
	17	4
	18	6
	19	12
	20	6

(*ii*) Compute the trial control limits

$$UCL_C = 5.5 + 3\sqrt{5.5} = 12.54$$

$$LCL_C = 5.5 - 3\sqrt{5.5} = -1.74$$

$$= 0, \text{ as } -\text{ve defects are not possible.}$$

Construction

1. Mark abscissa as the body number to a suitable scale (1 to 20).

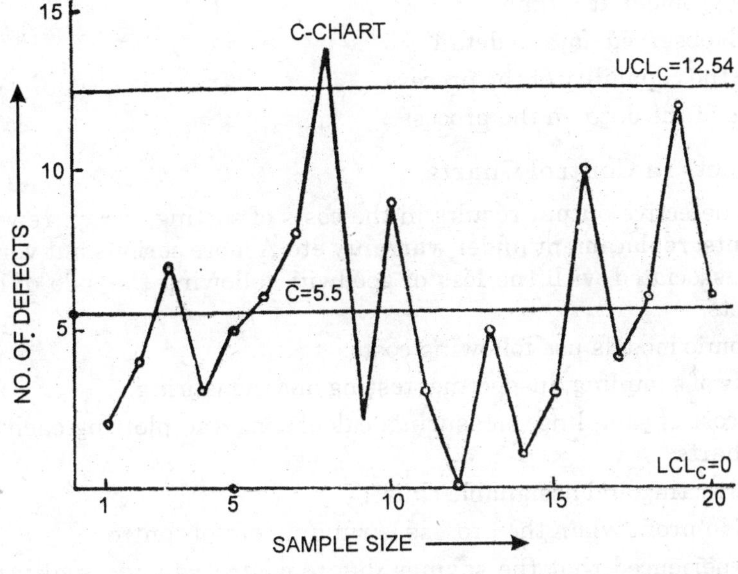

Fig. 22.7.

2. Mark ordinate as number of defects say upto 15. Looking to the table, the maximum number of 14 defects are in body No.8.
3. Mark various points for the body number and the number of defects in that body.
4. Join all the 20 points with straight lines.
5. Mark three horizontal lines in thick, one each for control line value, upper control limit and lower control limit. The data relate to the production on 21/9/16, the C value requires recalculation which will be $\frac{110-14}{19} = 5.03$.The value 5.03. will be the standard value of $\overline{C}$ for the next day's production. Consequently the control limits are also revised if it is decided to apply the data in next day's production, *i.e.* 22/9/16.

22.16. STATISTICAL PROCESS CONTROL (S.P.C.)

Application of statistical methods at the process control stage is known as Statistical Process Control. Customer quality assurance schemes now pushing the manufacturers towards the use of process controls. The greater degree of process control allows an overall reduction in inspection and test effort. This helps in areas other than lowering total quality related costs such as vendor rating, efficient management of non-production areas like purchasing, design and even marketing.

Implementation of S.P.C. Programmes

Essential steps in the process are:

1. Formalize the procedures
2. Check the specification
3. Emphasize the need for process quality control.
4. Plan for quality training.
5. Follow up.

6. Take one problem at a timé.
7. Record all observed data in detail.
8. Measure the capability of the process
9. Make use of the data on the process.

Economical Aspects In Control Charts

The production of defective output results in the costs of sorting, scrap, rework, dealing with customer complaints, replacement under warranty etc. A more serious but very difficult cost to ascertain is that associated with the loss of goodwill, following the sale of defective or non-conforming products.

Designers of economic models use following costs:

- fixed costs of sampling, inspecting, testing and measuring.
- variable cost of sampling, measuring, calculating and plotting each sample value on control charts.
- cost of correcting and assignable cause.
- total loss in profit when the procėss is running out of control.

It has been experienced that the savings due to control of poor quality products, better control over the quality of purchased products, use of more economical materials or methods due to their greater reliability, are some times spectacular.

Quality is a dynamic phenomena and is being improved continuously with the new developments in technology and management technique.

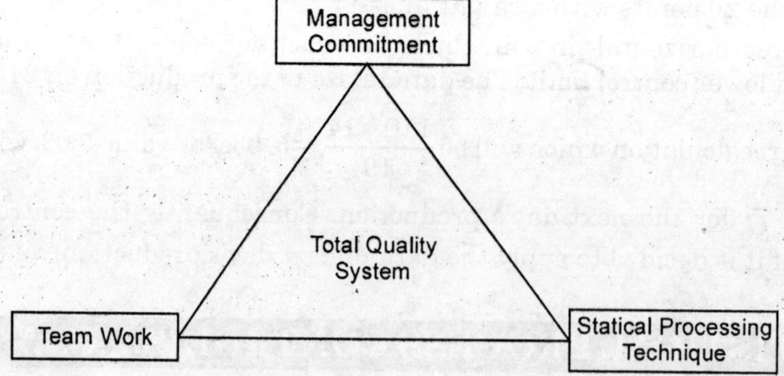

Fig. 22.8. The T. Q. M. Model.

QUESTIONS

1. Explain why control over the quality of product is essential.
2. How the quality of the product can be controlled? Explain each method in detail.
3. State the principles and purposes of quality control.
4. What are the objectives and basis of quality control in factories? Suggest a scheme for the evaluation of quality control in a mass production organisation.
5. Define quality control. State in brief the Objectives and Principles of quality control
6. Define quality. State the functions of the quality control department.

7. State the important objectives of "Quality control". Explain briefly how these objectives are achieved in Engineering Industry.
8. What factors should be considered in determining the place of quality control department in a manufacturing organisation? List of important items of equipment and methods to be used in the quality control department of any manufacturing organisation with which you are familiar.
9. "Quality Control is at system of inspection analysis and action applies to a manufacturing Process?" Discuss this with examples from manufacturing Industry.
10. Should the quality control manager be responsible to the Production Manager or to the Works Manager? Give reason for your answer.
11. Illustrate with the help of suitable examples how quality control methods to be used are dependent on the quality specifications.
12. Explain the working of a quality control division attached to a steel plant.
13. (*a*) Explain the difference between Inspection and Quality Control.
    (*b*) What general types of inspection equipment and gauges might be found in a small factory making cycle or sewing machines parts ?
14. Describe the methods of quality control.
15. State the advantages of Quality control. Show clearly, how it can reduce the cost of production.
16. (*a*) Define "Quality control". Give the objectives.
    (*b*) How does it relate to Inspection?
17. Quality can be pegged to production, comment on this statement.
18. (*a*) Differentiate Inspection, Quality Control and Quality assurance.
    (*b*) What are the causes of quality failures
19. (*a*) Describe in detail about 'economics of quality.' What are the costs associated with quality.
    (*b*) What should be the organisational set up for quality control.
20. Discuss 'Quality Management System'.
21. (*a*) What are the objectives and basis of quality control in factories ?
    (*b*) Define attribute and variables inspections.
    (*c*) What are the control charts ? How they are advantageous in S.Q.C.
22. (*a*) Detail the steps necessary to maintain the quality of a mass manufactured product.
    (*b*) State the advantages of using statistical methods of quality control.
23. Define statistical quality control. Discuss practical devices used as tools of statistical quality control in factories.
24. Discuss frequency distribution charts to use as devices of quality control.
25. (*a*) Define quality. State the functions of the quality control department.
    (*b*) Name the different methods of inspection which are used in industry. Describe sampling inspection.
26. Write short notes on the following:
    (*a*) Sampling Plan
    (*b*) Statistical techniques used for process control,
    (*c*) Statistical quality control.
    (*d*) Single sampling Plan and Double Sampling Plan,

(e) Limits and limitations of Control Charts.

(f) Schewhart Control Charts.

27. Describe the methods of statistical quality control and state their advantages in relation to inspection.

28. State the objectives of quality control and show how statistical quality control helps in achieving them.

29. (a) Describe statistical quality control as a technique of management.

(b) Show by illustrative examples, range of application of statistical quality control techniques in manufacturing concern.

30. (a) What is meant by assignable causes? When is a process said to be under control?

(b) Explain how to introduce statistical quality control in a manufacturing concern.

31. Name and describe the purpose of the following methods:

(a) Least squares

(b) Correlation

(c) Significance

(d) Analysis of Variance.

32. What are chance causes? What are assignable causes? What are indicated by statistical methods?

33. When is sampling desired in place of 100 per cent inspection. Name three classes of sampling plans and compare cost and difficulty of each.

34. Describe three methods of plotting a frequency diagram. What type of information may they indicate?

35. How does a control chart for average and ranges differ one for per cent defectives? Describe how these might be useful in production of some component.

36. (a) How far does the reliability of a random sample vary with

(i) the size of the sample

(ii) the degree of variation in the universe?

(b) In a locality containing 18,000 families, a sample of 840 families was selected at random. Of these 840 families, 206 families were found to have a monthly income of Rs. 500 or less. It is desired to estimate how many out of 18,000 families have a monthly income of Rs. 500 or less. Within what limits would you place your estimates?

37. A normal curve has an average of 140.6 and standard deviation of 3.70. What percentage of the area under the curve will fall between limits of 135.50 and 142.50?

38. Assume the specification given in example 19 is 10= 0.001 mm.

(a) How many items would be rejected?

(b) Assume the products to be normally distributed.
What will be percentage of the items rejected?

Problems on Process Capability

39. (*a*) Define Process Capability.

Cell mid -point	*Frequency*	*Cell mid-point*	*Frequency*
0.516	1	0.508	18
0.515	0	0.507	22
0.514	1	0.506	12
0.513	3	0.505	4
0.512	2	0.504	2
0.511	8	0.503	0
0.510	11	0.502	0
0.509	15	0.501	1

(*b*) The frequency tally sheet shows a process capability study run in conjunction with a rough turn operation on a simple component parts. The rough turn requirement for outside diameter is = 0.005 *cm*.

(*i*) Calculate the process capability for the machine under study.

(*ii*) Is machine capable of producing a quality component ?

Illustrate

Control Chart for Attribute 20. Data

Sample no.	*Sample size*	*No. of defective*	*Sample No.*	*Sample size*	*No.of Defective*
1	200	13	12	200	3
2	200	1	13	200	6
3	200	0	14	200	8
4	200	2	15	200	5
5	200	4	16	200	9
6	200	1	17	200	3
7	200	2	18	200	1
8	200	0	19	200	1
9	200	3	20	200	2
10	200	2	21	200	3
11	200	1	22	200	1

Construct the appropriate control chart for the process represented by the following data collected in the past month:

What can be concluded about the behaviour of the process during the past month ? What limits are appropriate for controlling next month's production?

40. A *p–chart* is to be used to analyse the September record for 100% inspection of certain radio transmitting tubes. The total number cited during the months was 2196 and the total number of defectives was 158. Compute p.Compute also individual 3-sigma control limits for the following three days and state whether the fraction defective fall within control limits for each day.

Date,	number inspected,	Number defectives
Sept. 14,	54,	8
15,	161,	24
16,	213,	3

41. The following table gives the number of missing rivets noted at aircraft final inspection:-
See Table on page No. 249.

Aircraft number	*Number of missing rivets*	*Aircraft number*	*Number of missing rivets*	*Aircraft number*	*Number of misssing rivets*
201	8	210	12	218	14
202	16	211	28	219	11
203	10	212	20	220	9
204	12	213	29	221	10
205	11	214	25	222	22
206	15	215	15	223	7
207	8	216	9	224	28
208	1	217	9	225	9
209	21				

Find $\bar{C}$ compute trial control limits and plot a control chart for *C*. What value of *C*, would you suggest for the subsequent period?

42. (*a*) What do you mean by revised control limits for Chart?

(*b*) The following details collected from 100 metre pieces of woollen cloth:

Purchaser's insp. number	*Number of defects*	*Purchaser's insp. number*	*Number of defects*
1	15	11	1
2	5	12	3
3	1	13	5
4	4	14	7
5	3	15	4
6	0	16	10
7	3	17	5
8	1	18	0
9	6	18	1

(*a*) Compute the value of C and its control limits.

(*b*) Draw *C-chart*.

(*c*) Compute values of C for the future production if you deem it necessary.

43. (*a*) Describe briefly, any two types of sampling inspection used in practice and mention where each are applicable.

(*b*) A purchased item is received in lot sizes of 5000 each. After receiving inspection, the following single sampling plan is applied to each of these lots:

Sample size, $n = 100$

Acceptance number, $c = 2$

If the lots coming into inspection are 2% defective, rejected lots, are 100 per cent inspected and all observed defectives are replaced, what is the average outgoing quality after inspection?

23

TOTAL QUALITY MANAGEMENT

23.1. INTRODUCTION

In order to capture increased market share, quality had been the main concern of every manufacturer since old days. Started with the inspection concept moved to the quality control concept, when it was realised that making the inspection department only responsible for quality of the product would be counter productive. Concept of quality control emphasises self inspection and appropriate system to ensure quality by identifying defectives and eliminating them. Help of statistical quality control and sample analysis were also undertaken.

Then arose the concept of quality assurance. But the quality movement did not stop with this, and the attempt is to continuously improve the quality and assure higher and higher standards of quality, offer better products to the consumer, ensure better and longer service, and improve the utility of the product. It was felt that quality is not the job of quality control department only but other departments like sales, procurement, material handling, accounting, industrial relations, design, production, forecasting, marketing, stores, after sales service have also to contribute substantially. Thus quality is the responsibility of all the employees. The workers should run the system, managers should design, and improve the systems, while top management should provide leadership and team spirit.

In a Total Quality Management concept, the word quality has a wider meaning, it means quality of output of every department and by every employee, cleanliness, orderliness, punctuality, customer service, standardization of works and continuous efforts for their improvement are also part of T.Q.M. In this, needs of the customer are constantly monitored to improve the products and processes to meet their requirements.

In Total Quality Management programme, voluntary participation of work people is sought for the quality of the task.

Effective T.Q.M. results in greater customer satisfaction, fewer defects, less waste, reduced costs, improved profitability and increased productivity. For the effectiveness of T.Q.M. programme a careful analysis of the customers' needs, and an assessment of the extent to which these needs are currently met, and a suitable plan to fill up the gap between the current level and the expectation is necessary.

For the success of T.Q.M., top managers must provide vision, reinforce values emphasizing quality, set quality goals and deploy necessary resources for these quality programmes. For this purpose, training and development, and free flow of information is essential. The top managers must continuously monitor, evaluate, get feed back about the T.Q.M. programme and take necessary steps for its improvement.

Customer satisfaction is the most important aspect of T.Q.M. The customer may be external to the organisation or may be inside the organisation. Meeting the needs of outside customers depend on meeting the needs of the inside customers. Inside customer is an individual or department receiving the output of another individual or department of the concern.

From the above, we can say that, the T.Q.M. involves effective decision making, problem solving and integration of Quality Planning, Quality Implementation and Quality improvement strategies of all the departments of an organisation, committed and involved employees, lower costs, higher revenue and high profits for the organisation.

Definitions

Definitions related to the various terms used in Quality Systems have been standardised by International Organisation for Standardization (I.S.O.) vide their I.S.O. 8402 : 1986 Quality-Vocabulary. Bureau of Indian Standards has adopted the same vide its I.S. 13999 : 1988. Here some definitions are being given for various terms used in the field of quality as applied to products, and services.

1. **Product or Service.** may be either (*a*) the result of activities or processes (tangible product : intangible product, such as a service, a computer programme, a design, direction for use) or (*b*) an activity or process (such as the provision of a service or the execution of a production process).
2. **Quality.** The totality of features and characteristics of a product or service that on its ability to satisfy stated or implied needs.
3. **Quality Policy.** The overall quality intentions and direction of an organisation as regards quality, as formally expressed by top management.
4. **Quality Management.** It is that aspect of the overall management function that determines and implements the quality policy.
5. **Quality Assurance.** All those planned and systematic actions necessary to provide adequate confidence that a product or service will satisfy given requirements for quality.
6. **Quality Control.** The operational techniques and activities that are used to fulfil requirements for quality. The quality control involves operational techniques and activities aimed both at monitoring a process and at eliminating causes of unsatisfactory performance at relevant stages in order to result in economic effectiveness.
7. **Quality System.** The organisational structure, responsibilities, procedures, processes and resources for implementing quality management. The quality system should only be as comprehensive as needed to meet the quality objectives.
8. **Quality Plan.** A document setting out the specific quality practices, resources and sequence of activities relevant to a particular product, service, contract or project.
9. **Quality Audit.** A systematic and independent examination to determine whether quality activities and related results comply with planned arrangements and whether these arrangements are implemented effectively and are suitable to achieve objectives. The purpose of a quality audit is to evaluate the need for improvement or corrective action.
10. **Quality System Review.** A formal evaluation by top management of the status and adequacy of the quality system in relation to quality policy and new objectives resulting from changing circumstances.
11. **Design Review** : A formal documented, comprehensive and systematic examination of a design to evaluate the design requirements and the capacity of the design to meet these requirements and to identify problems and propose solutions.

12. **Inspection.** Activities such as measuring, examining, testing, gauging one or more characteristics of a product or service and comparing these with specified requirements to determine conformity.
13. **Reliability** : The ability of an item to perform a required function under stated conditions for a stated period of time.

    The term reliability is also used as a reliability characteristic denoting a probability of success or a success ratio.
14. **Non-conformity** : The non fulfilment of specified requirements, and covers the departure or absence of one or more quality characteristics or quality system elements from specified requirements.
15. **Defect**: The non-fulfilment of intended usage requirements, and covers the departure or absence of one or more quality characteristics from intended usage requirements.
16. **Specification** : The document that prescribes the requirements with which the product or service has to conform.

A specification should refer to or include drawings, patterns or other relevant documents and should also indicate the means and the criteria whereby conformity can be checked.

Requirements of T.Q.M.:

1. **Sound Foundation.** Philosophy, Policy, Culture, Leadership and Commitment.
2. **Sound Infrastructure.** Organisation, Systems, Procedures, Manuals, Customer involvement, Suppliers involvement, Training and Education and Total Employees Involvement.
3. **Use of Specific Tools and Techniques**

Aims of T.Q.M.

1. Conformance to customer requirements.
2. Prevention of producing bad quality.
3. Ideal of Zero Defect as the performance standard.
4. Measurement of cost of quality.

Ways for T.Q.M.

In order to implement T.Q.M., following actions are necessary :

1. Adopt new philosophy of refusing to allow defects.
2. Create consistency of purpose for improvement.
3. Improving production and service quality should be a continuous process.
4. Cease dependance on mass inspection and adopt Statistical Quality Control.
5. Insist quantifiable evidence from the suppliers about their products.
6. All employees should be trained, retrained and refresher courses be arranged.
7. Provide proper tools to all the employees.
8. Adopt proper communication system.
9. Encourage productivity.
10. Encourage coordination between departments.
11. Permanent commitment of top management to quality.
12. Respect towards work and humanity.
13. Adopt consumer orientation and not the product orientation.

14. Objective should be, Quality first, and not the short term profits.
15. Use facts and data.

23.2. ELEMENTS OF TOTAL QUALITY MANAGEMENT

1. Customers Satisfaction.
2. Employees involvement.
3. Morale of employees.
4. Quality Control Circles and suggestion system.
5. Higher revenue.
6. Lower cost.
7. Quality control.
8. Control of Production.
9. Quality planning.
10. Quality Improvement.
11. Quality implementation.
12. Quality Assurance System.
13. Vendor control and quality in procurement.
14. Customer relationship management.
15. Total organisation involvement.
16. Measurement information analysis.
17. Quality education and training.
18. Strategic quality management.
19. Leadership.

23.3. TOTAL QUALITY CONTROL (T.Q.C.)

Total Quality Control is an effective system for integrating the quality development, quality maintenance and quality improvement efforts of various groups in an organisation so as to enable production and service at the most economical levels which allow for full customer satisfaction. T.Q.C. requires participation of all divisions and by all employees. It calls for teamwork. This is an integrated quality control, which means quality control with cost control (*i.e.*, price control and profit control), quantity control (amount of production, amount of sales, amount of stock) and control of delivery date.

Quality Planning:

Quality planning is a systematic process for:

(*i*) identifying customers.
(*ii*) discovering the customers needs.
(*iii*) designing responsive products.
(*iv*) developing the process for creating and delivering the products.
(*v*) transferring the process and its contents to those who will perform the product or service.

Integrated quality planning helps in

(*i*) reducing the overall time, effort and cost for entire product cycle,
(*ii*) higher customer satisfaction,
(*iii*) lower the deficiencies in the product and processes.

Quality Implementation

Quality Implementation ensures that a process continuously produces the quality which was planned. For effective implementation:

(*i*) Resources like men and material are deployed on specific tasks,
(*ii*) *Self* control is necessary for all those who run the process, as it increases the effectiveness of quality implementation.
(*iii*) Personal leadership qualities are expected from managers for motivating and training his people and for creating healthy culture.
(*iv*) Total organisational involvement.
(*v*) Effective information system regarding customers needs, satisfaction and opinion about products.
(*vi*) Set measurable standards.
(*vii*) Effective feed back system is necessary.
(*viii*) Use of statistical quality control and control charts.

Characteristics of Total Quality Control Concept

1. Quality Control is the responsibility of all the workers and all the divisions.
2. Total Quality Control is a group activity and can not be done by individuals.
3. It calls for team work.
4. Quality Control Circle activities are part of the T.Q.C.
5. It adopts the philosophy of refusing to allow any defect.
6. It relies on Sampling (S.Q.C.) rather than cent-percent inspection.
7. Continuous process for improving quality of products and services.
8. All employees are provided with proper tools and proper training to do the quality job.
9. It clearly defines top management's permanent commitment to quality.

Integrated Quality Control

In affecting integrated quality control, control of quality is central, but at the same time cost control (profit control and price control), quantity control (amount of production, of sales, of stock) and control of delivery date are to be promoted. This method is based on the fundamental assumption of QC that a manufacturer must develop, produce and sell commodities that satisfy the needs of consumers. This extends the term quality to the quality of work in the offices, in the service related industries and in the banks etc.

23.4. EFFECTIVE TOTAL QUALITY IMPLEMENTATION

1. Quality Implementation ensures that a process continuously produce the quality that was planned into it. **Effective Implementation includes :**

   (*i*) A clearly stated policy.

(ii) Development of resources of men, machine and others to specific tasks involved, identifying the departments/ individuals to do the specific tasks.

(iii) Proper selection of control factors, with details of when, where, who, what, how and why they are to be done.

(iv) Establishing self control for all those who run the process.

(v) Personnel leadership from the Manager in motivating, training and recognising the work of his people. Creation of a healthy culture.

(vi) Existence of an established Quality Assurance System.

(vii) Total Organisational Involvement, both formal and informal, such as Quality Circles.

(viii) Informations needed about deficiencies in the goods and processes, and cost of poor quality, with analysis of their causes.

(ix) Measurable standards are to be established for having a benchmark for Quality Implementation purposes.

2. **A feedback loop** measures on output from a process, compares them with the established standards and takes the necessary action. Control standards are established based on the actual performance of the process. CONTROL CHARTS are the tools for establishing control standards and testing the actuals against standards.

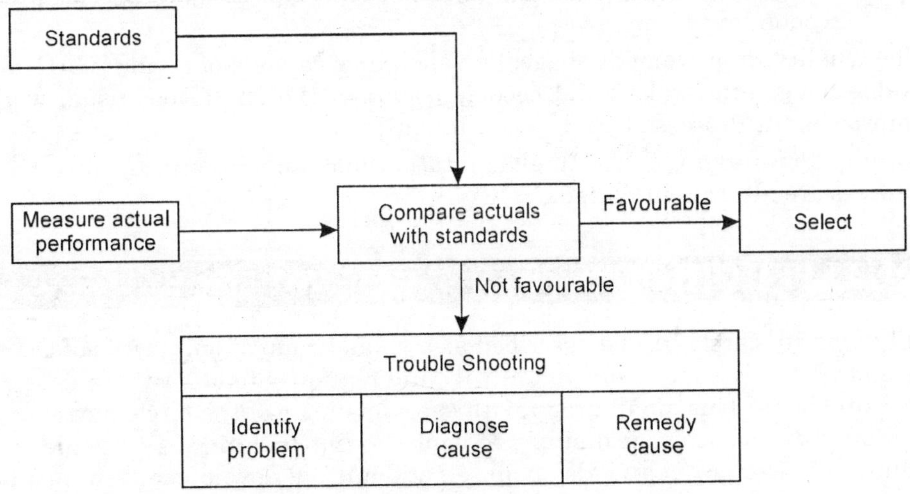

Fig 23.1. Quality control Feed-back loop.

23.5. TOTAL QUALITY IMPROVEMENT

1. Total Quality Improvement is a structured process for reducing the deficiencies that are present in products, processes and services and/or improving performance whenever there is an opportunity to improve.
2. Improvements take place in following steps:
   (i) A clear understanding of the SYMPTOMS
   (ii) A diagnosis to find the CAUSES
   (iii) To find REMEDY/REMEDIES for the causes :

(a) For achieving Quality Improvement specific problems are to be identified and well defined such as : reducing energy consumption, improving capacity, reducing lead time and reducing failure rates.

(b) Diagnosing the root cause is a structured process. The team must analyze the symptoms to identify and clearly define the problem or problems. Then they must formulate assumptions, hypothesis and theories which might be causing the symptoms. Lastly, they test the theories systematically until the data and the analysis establish the causes. Brain storming, Pareto Analysis, Flow diagrams, Data Analysis, Data Collection, Lshikawa Diagrams, Histograms are all helpful in this exercise.

(c) Once the root cause/causes is/are known, the team should deliberate in great detail by considering all aspects such as managerial, technical, personnel, financial and other aspects before formulating any remedies. Control charts, Motivational Techniques, Training Methods are very helpful in this connection.

3. To overcome resistance to change, some of the things that a manager must do are :
   (i) providing enough participation
   (ii) giving time to adjust and accommodate
   (iii) being flexible instead of being rigid
   (iv) being capable of practising what he says, recognizing, respecting and positively responding to employees.
4. The Quality Improvement suggestion should be capable of giving "GAINS' which are stable, long term and should become a part of the employees usual work. Quality Improvement Process should be continuous.
5. Quality Planning, Quality Implementation and Control and Quality Improvement Process are all "Inter-Related".

23.6. QUALITY CIRCLES

Conceptually, Quality Circle can be described as a small group of employees of the same work area, doing similar work, that meets voluntarily and regularly to identify, analyse and resolve work related problems. This small group with every member of the circle participating to the full, carries on the activities, utilising problem solving techniques to achieve control or improvement in the work area and also help self and mutual development in the process.

The concept of the Quality Circle is based on 'respect for the human individual' as against the traditional assumption based on suspicion and mistrust between management and its employees. Quality circles built mutual trust and create greater understanding between the management and the workers. Cooperation and not confrontation is the key element in its operation. Quality Circles aim at building people, developing them, arousing genuine interest and dedication to their work to improve quality, productivity, cost reduction etc.

Objectives

Some of the broad objectives of the Quality Circle are :

(i) To improve quality, productivity, safety and cost reduction.
(ii) To give chance to the employees to use their wisdom and creativity.
(iii) To encourage team spirit, cohesive culture among different levels and sections of the employees.

(*iv*) To promote self and mutual development including leadership quality.

(*v*) To fulfil the self esteem and motivational needs of employees.

(*vi*) To improve the quality of work-life of employees.

Implementation of Quality Circles in an Organisation

For the success of Quality Circle programme, following actions are necessary in the Organisation:

(*a*) Few managers representing production, quality control, design, process planning form the Quality Circle (Q.C.) and steering committee. This acts as a policy making body and will monitor the Q.C. in the Organisation.

(*b*) Top management must attend the orientation courses designed for them.

(*c*) A committed top and middle management is necessary.

(*d*) A facilitator must be appointed, who serves as a link between top management, Q.C, steering committee, middle management circle leaders and circle members. Facilitator will coordinate regarding training courses, get the support from all concerned including top management, Q.C, steering committee, circle leader and circle members to help the circle leader in conducting the meetings and to provide necessary resources.

Benefits of Quality Circles (Q.C.)

1. Through the forum of Q.C, the chronic problems of organisations which really create hurdles in work get resolved by the grass root employees of organisation, whose knowledge and experience otherwise is not fully utilized.
2. With such a capable work force any organisation can easily undertake more difficult and challenging assignments for its growth and profit.
3. As the employees gain experience they take more challenging projects, in due course they undertake projects on cost reduction, material handling, quality improvement, preventing wastage, improving delivery schedule, improving customer service, improving inspection and test methods, preventing accidents, improving design and process etc.

Organisation and Working

Q.C. was conceived in Japan in 1962 as a forum for training its work force for improving the quality of products. Q.C. is a voluntary one. Employees are free to join or not to join. In it, 8 to 10 employees including the supervisor from same workshop doing similar work join together as a group. The supervisor can become leader of the group, if the members of Q.C. so desire.

It is a part time activity, members of Q.C. are allowed to meet for an hour every week. During the various meetings, this group progressively identify, select, analyse and solve the problems. Later they offer their proposed solutions to management for consideration, approval and implementation.

Additionally a senior officer from same workshop is nominated as facilitator who guides the activities of the group.

A Management Committee at senior level is also formed, which overviews the progress of Quality Circles.

Training of members, leaders and facilitators is very important for the success of programme.

Launching of Quality Circle Programme

The typical steps for launching programme are as under :

(*i*) Orientation Programme for Senior Management Personnel.

(*ii*) Orientation Programme for Managers and Executives.
(*iii*) Orientation Programme for Selected Supervisors.
(*iv*) Orientation Programme for Workers (selected area).
(*v*) Formation of Circles (Minimum 2 and Maximum 4).
(*vi*) Training of Facilitators,
(*vii*) Training of Leaders,
(*viii*) Q.C. meetings for projects.

Brain Storming

1. **What is Brain Storming.** It is a technique for stimulating a group of people to come out with ideas on a specific topic and collectively seek the solution of a problem.
2. **When Brain Storming can be Used.** It can be used in all fields, whether the subject is at one's home or work area.
3. **What happens during Brain Storming.** A group of people meet and generate ideas. The session may be used to identify, analyse and solve the problems.

Flow Diagram of Activities in Brain Storming

Fig 23.2 Shows the flow diagram of activities in Brain-storming.

(*i*) A group of people having 8–10 members is formed. The group members should have some background, information or previous experience with the work area.
(*ii*) One of the member can be nominated/chosen as a leader of the group and another member as recorder. The leader must have all the skills of a good conference leader.
(*iii*) The recorder puts down all ideas on a big sheet of paper even the ones which seem to overlap. He is also free to contribute his own ideas at his turn.

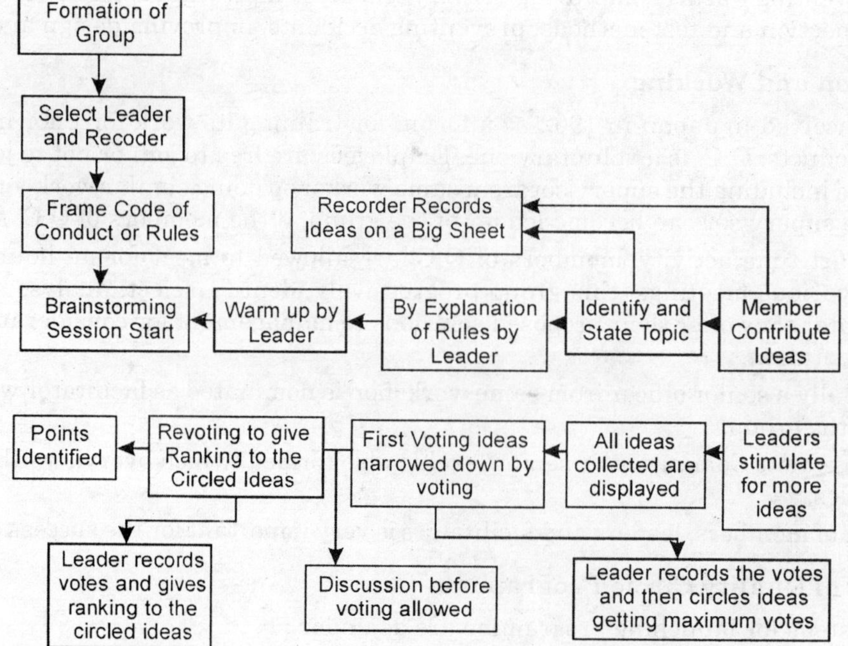

Fig. 23.2. Flow diagram of activities in Brain-storming.

(*iv*) At the start of Brain-storming session, the leader warms up the group to get the group attention and interest.

(*v*) The leader explains the rules to the members and states the topic. The rules generally followed are as under:

Rules for Quality Circles

(*a*) Each member can contribute an idea on his turn in rotation.

(*b*) Each member offers only one idea per turn regardless of how many he or she has in mind.

(*c*) Not every one has an idea during each rotation, when this occurs just say "Pass".

(*d*) No criticism or comments should be passed on the ideas being contributed by the member, however odd it may look, be patient and welcome their ideas.

(*e*) During brain-storming, no evolution of suggested idea should occur. This applies equally to leader, phrases such as "We have tried it before", "Impractical", "Well may be it would work", "Doubtful", "Very good", etc. should not be uttered.

(*f*) Members can vote by raising their hands. —

(*g*) Only supporting votes are taken. Votes against the ideas are not allowed.

(*h*) The time allotted for brain-storming session should be variable. The length of time that can be spent profitably will vary widely with nature of problem and the group itself. As a general practice one hour is probably the minimum.

(*i*) While members given their ideas, they are recorded by the Recorder on a large sheet.

(*j*) It is often helpful to set a goal originally, *i.e.*, let us start for 30 ideas.

(*k*) When all members say "pass" then the first phase of brain-storming session is over. This means all ideas have been exhausted.

(*l*) Now all the ideas recorded on the sheet are displayed.

(*m*) These massive number of ideas are then narrowed down by the process of voting. The voting technique works because the members are experts in their areas.

(*n*) Members vote on each idea. The leader records each vote next to the idea. Members can vote for as many ideas as they feel have value. Only supporting votes are taken.

(*o*) Leader draws a circle around those ideas that receive the most votes. The members decide as to how many of the top ideas are to be identified.

(*p*) Now the members can focus on a few important ideas instead of being somewhat confused by a large number of them. These few important ideas are voted on to give ranking to the circle ideas. Leader writes the ranking number beside each idea that has been circled.

(*q*) A member can halt the voting on any idea and argue for or against it. Others can join, if they wish. Only when the discussion has finished, the volting take place.

Idea ranked in the session can then be taken up for analysis or solution later on.

Duties of Circle Leader

For the success of Quality Circles, circle leader must have following duties:

(*i*) He must assume the responsibility of guiding the members.

(*ii*) He must make his members sure about what is going on.

(*iii*) He must channelise the discussions.

(*iv*) Every member be allowed equal opportunity.

(*v*) Specific task be assigned to each member.

(*vi*) He must work in coordination with facilitator.

Steps for Setting up Quality Circles

For starting Quality Circles in an organisation, following steps should be taken:

(*i*) First of all managers, supervisors and foremen must be made to understand the concept and activities of Q.C. circles.

(*ii*) Management's total support and commitment should be made known to every one in the organisation.

(*iii*) Steering committee is formed with the top management personnel to give direction to Quality Control Circle activities.

(*iv*) A facilitator (or some times known as promoter) is selected fromthe senior management level, who will serve as coordinator and advisor to the circle.

(*v*) Supervisor and foremen are then trained to act as Q.C. circle leaders.

(*vi*) Members of each circle must be selected from the persons who are doing similar type of work or belong to the same department or section.

(*vii*) Membership to the circle is voluntary.

(*viii*) First few meetings of the circle are held with a view to train them.

(*ix*) To start with only one or two circles should be formed in an organisation, and then increase the number gradually as more and more experience is gained.

(*x*) Meetings must be held-regularly, may be once a week initially and once a month on completion of basic training of members.

(*xi*) Everyone's suggestion or problem matching with the circles objectives be discussed.

(*xii*) Total participation of team members must be encouraged.

(*xiii*) Recommendations of the circle must be considered and decisions should be taken without delay.

23.7. MAIN CONCEPTS OF TQM

1. Quality for Profit.

Quality improvement in product and services, business processes and people is profitable. Quality is the single largest factor in achieving market success for any company. Actual quality improvement also increases sales by generating customer demand.

Fig 23.3 indicates that, to gain increase in profit *P* through increased sales would require a significant increase *A* in operating costs (sales, personnel, promotion, inventories etc.), while the same profit *P* can be increased through quality improvement by increasing operating costs *B*, which also diminishes through time.

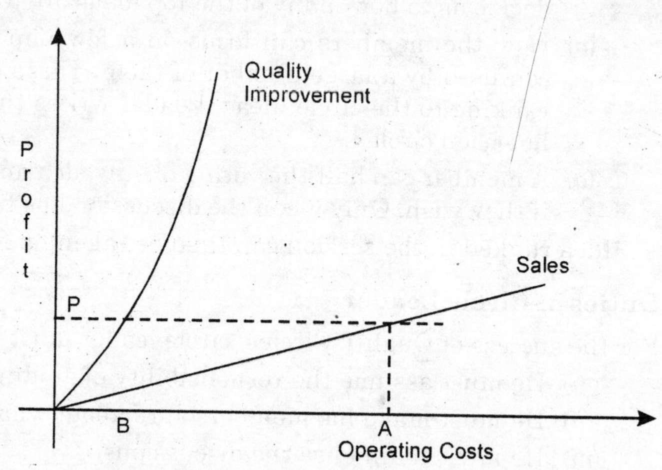

Fig 23.3. Quality improvement reduces cost.

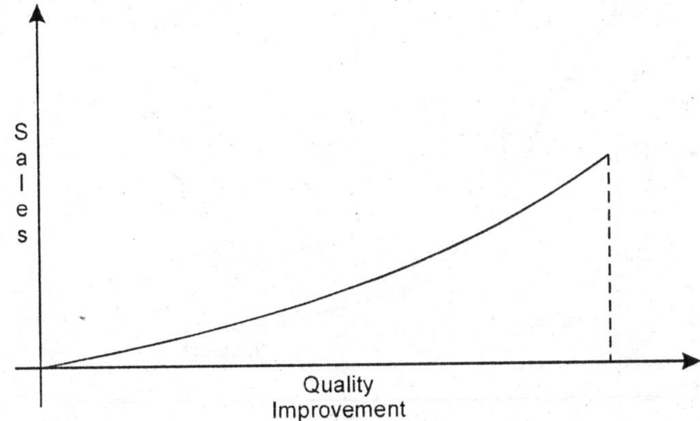

Fig 23.4. Quality itself increases sales.

Fig. 23.4 indicates, more quality improves, faster will be increase in sales because customer satisfaction carries its own acceleration. 'Quality reputation' when grows, it acts as a major element in advertising and reduces the money required on advertisement.

2. Right First Time or Zero Defect.

Main aim of TQM is the conviction that it is possible to achieve defect-free work most of time. This can be phrased as : right first time or zero defects. The idea is to strive for perfection in the work. Right first time is the result of an emphasis on prevention, and the use of measurement, process control and the data-driven elimination of waste and error, continuous improvement. Planned and systematic action such as documentation, work processes, quality audits, quality assurance etc. prevents quality problems.

Importance of zero defect can be visualised from the fact that, if one sets an acceptable quality level of 99 percent, the results will be: 10000 wrong prescriptions in a hospital treating 1 million patients in a year, no electricity, telephone and television transmission for about 15 minutes each day, no newspaper for 4 days in a year, one misspelled word on every page of a book. It means 1 percent goods were waste or scrap.

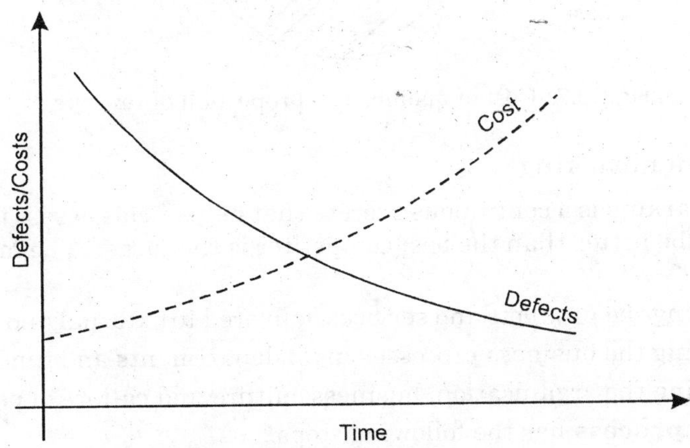

Fig 23.5. 'Traditional' quality

Fig 23.5 indicates defects/cost as per traditional culture. In this culture, achieving quality is expensive-defects are reduced over time only by increasing cost through extensive inspection, checking and progress chasing. In this, most effort is concentrated on correcting failure.

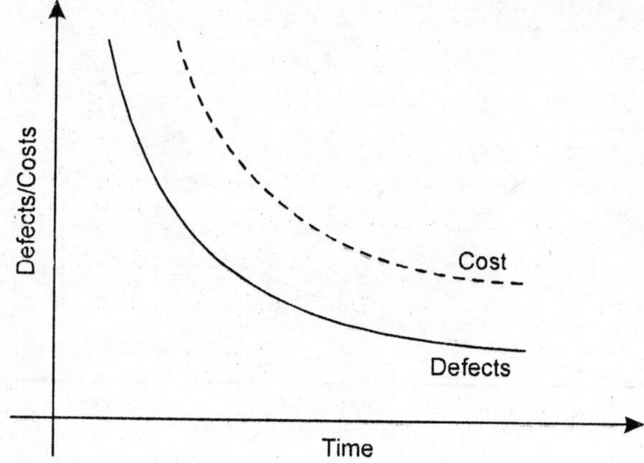

Fig 23.6. 'Total quality' Concept

Fig 23.6 Indicates that by adopting TQM management, after certain time defects and costs both will be minimal.

3. Cost of Quality.

As discussed in earlier chapters, cost of quality includes prevention costs, appraisal costs, internal failure costs, external failure costs, the cost of exceeding customer requirements and the cost of lost opporunities. Taken together these costs amount to 20-30 percent of its revenue.

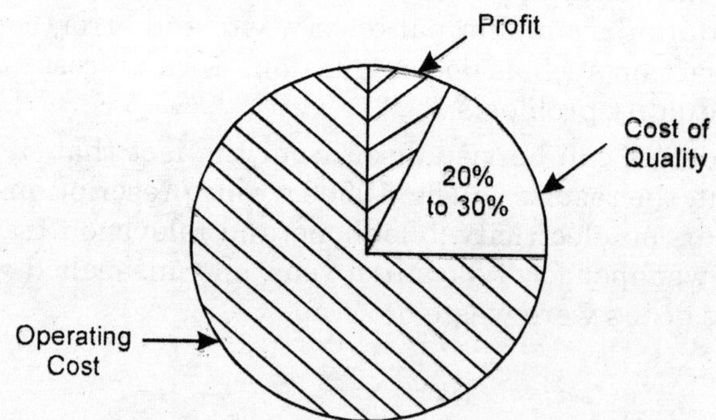

Fig. 23.7. Cost of quaility as a proportion of revenue.

4. Competitive Benchmarking.

Competitive benchmarking is a continuous process that helps firms assess their competition: In this case, to strive to be better than the best competitor is the target. The means to achieve this aim are :

(*a*) benchmarking the products and services delivered to external and internal customers,

(*b*) benchmarking the business processes in all departments and functions, and

(*c*) benchmarking the organisation, business culture and calibre of people.

Benchmarking process has the following steps :

1. Decide what is going to be benchmarked.
2. Select the competitors who are the best in terms of products and services, business processes, and people and aspects that one's firm wants to measure.
3. Decide the most appropriate measurements.

4. Determine competitor's strengths against own company.
5. Develop an action plan.

5. Involving Everybody.

This aspect has already been discussed in this chapter.

6. Synergy in Team Work.

Synergy means harmony in working, and is the result of team work in which output is greater than each of the inputs taken separately and also greater than the sum total of the inputs. As theoretical knowledge of engineers as well as practical knowledge of workers are essential for progress, both of them act as partners for effective management.

Main points for the success of team work are :

(i) Team members be valued as individual.
(*ii*) Individuals feel integrated within a team.
(*iii*) Team in-charges be fair to all team members.
(*iv*) Team must be confident.
(*v*) Individuals must enjoy themselves.

7. Self-management.

This aspect has already been discussed in the book.

8. Managers as Role Models.

Managers need to be conscious that they are role models for total quality. It is very important that what they say and do about total quality. The best TQM programme has a system of management feedback so that managers get some idea on how they are doing as role models for quality. Performance feedback is most important to enable managers at all levels to improve their contribution.

Feedback should be on general management areas: leadership , team work, motivating, people development and commitment to the total quality process.

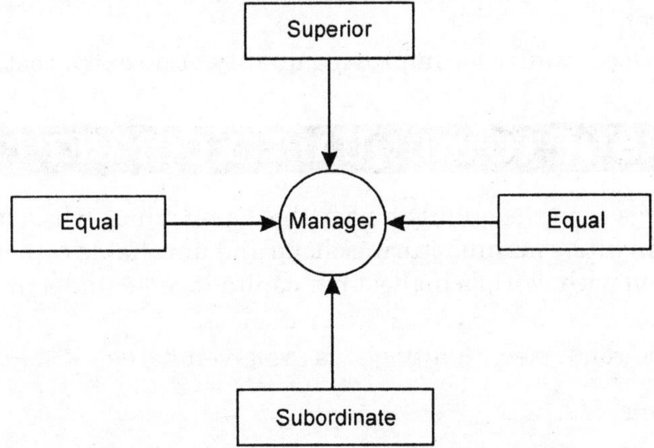

Fig 23.8. Directions of managerial feedback.

9. Recognition and Rewards.

This concept has already been discussed in the preceding chapters.

10. Quality Delivery Process.

It is the name given to the implementation of new systems. This is necessary for quality improvement which is a continuous process. Following steps are taken for quality delivery process.

(*i*) Create mission statement.
(*ii*) Determine the outputs of the workgroup.
(*iii*) Identify both internal and external customers.
(*iv*) Define agreed customer requirements for each output.
(*v*) Develop specifications for each output of work group.
(*vi*) Determine the group's work processes.
(*vii*) Identify the measurements of each output.
(*viii*) Identify any problem/opportunity for achieving target.
(*ix*) Establish a project team to solve the identified problem.
(*x*) Measure customer satisfaction against the agreed customer requirements.

The ways in which the quality of outputs can be measured are :

1. Defects
2. Rework
3. Scrap
4. Lost items
5. Work behind schedule
6. Late deliveries
7. Surplus items.

Key measurements for each output are :

1. *Target:* budget or level of performance.
2. *Forecast:* level of performance.
3. *Actuals:* level of performance.
4. *Problem*: difference between the actual and target level of performance where actual is less than target.
5. *Opportunity*: Opportunity for improving quality at no extra cost.

23.8. PIONEERS OF TOTAL QUALITY CONCEPT

By adopting the learnings from the quality gurus, the Japan which was a largely illiterate, semi-industrialized country in fifties manufacturing cheap and unreliable copies of Western products, has now became a nation with world's highest per capita income and a producer of best quality goods.

Views of some of the renowned quality gurus are given here :

1. W. Edwards Deming

Dr. Deming was the first American quality expert to reach Japan in 1947 to teach Japanese managers methodically about quality.

According to Deming, interpreting quality in terms of reliability, dependability, predictability and consistency of product and service, it is clear that quality improvement is analogous to reduction of variation, *i.e.*,

"Quality and productivity increase as variability decreases".

Deming's points on promoting product or service quality are :

1. Be constant and purposeful in improving products and services. Aim is to be competitive, to stay in business, to meet long-term needs.
2. Adopt new philosophy. Commonly accepted delays, mistakes, defective workmanship can no longer be tolerated.
3. Stop depending on mass inspection, demand statistical evidence of quality being built into manufacturing and purchasing functions.
4. Work to minimise total cost not just initial cost. Move towards a single supplier for any one item on a long-term relationship of loyalty and trust.
5. Improve the system continually. Make better every process for planning, production and service to improve quality, increase productivity and decrease costs.
6. Institute modern methods of on-the-job training. New skills are required to keep up with changes in material, methods, product design, machinery, techniques and service.
7. Set up new ways of supervising production workers. Improvement of quality will automatically improve productivity. Management should initiate action in response to reports of inherited defects, maintenance needs, bad tools, confused operational definitions and other things that lead to poor quality.
8. Drive out fear, so that everyone may work effectively for the company.
9. People in research, design, sales and production should work as a team-to deal effectively with problems of products and service.
10. Eliminate numerical goals, slogans, exhortations (like zero defects).
11. Use statistical methods for continuous improvement of quality and productivity.
12. Abolish performance appraised and management by objectives.
13. Institute a vigorous programme of education and retraining. Competitive advantage is always rooted in knowledge.
14. Push every day to progress the thirteen preceding points and take action to make the total transformation happen.

According to Deming, following are the **major obstacles in implementing** his philosophy.

1. Preoccupation with short-term profits.
2. Lack of consistency.
3. Reliance on only visible figures.
4. Performance appraisal.
5. Managerial job mobility.

2. Dr. Joseph M. Juran

Juran developed his TQM message around the following ten steps:

1. Create awareness of the need and opportunity for quality improvement.
2. Set goals for continuous improvement.
3. Build an organisation to achieve goals for establishing a quality council, identifying problems, selecting a project, appointing teams and choosing facilitators.
4. Give training to everyone
5. Carry out projects to solve problems
6. Report progress

7. Show recognition
8. Communicate results
9. Keep a record of successes
10. Incorporate annual improvements into the company's regular systems and processes and thereby maintain momentum.

Juran expresses his essential message to managers through the three basic quality related processes : quality planning, quality control and quality improvement which has become known as the Juran trilogy.

3. Kaoru Ishikawa

He is known as 'Father of Quality Circles' and is known for his role in launching Japan's quality movement in the 1960s.

According to him, **seven basic tools** were 'indispensable for quality control'. These tools are:

(*i*) Pareto analysis.
(*ii*) Fishbone diagrams.
(*iii*) Stratification.
(*iv*) Tally charts.
(*v*) Histograms.
(*vi*) Scatter diagrams.
(*vii*) Control charts.

With these tools , Ishikawa argued, managers and staff could tackle and solve the quality problems facing them.

4. Philip B. Crosby

Crosby prefers to target his training on managers rather than on quality control people. He cited his zero defects goal as something practical, reasonable and achievable. He listed following four essentials of quality management. He calls them 'The absolutes':

1. Quality is defined as conformance to requirements, not as goodness.
2. Quality is achieved by prevention not appraisal.
3. The quality performance standard is zero defects.
4. Quality is measured by the price of non-conformance not by indexes.

5. William E. Conway

Conway defines quality as a result of quality management which is 'the development, manufacture, administration and distribution of consistent low-cost products and services that customers want and need'. He targets three categories of waste in a company : time, capital and material, with time being his priority, excessive inventory comes second which requires space with all the associated costs.

Conway recommended following **six tools for continuous improvement**:

1. *Human relations skills:* Motivate and train all empolyess at all levels of the company.
2. *Statistical surveys:* Collection of data about internal and external customers, employees, technology and equipment.
3. *Simple statistical techniques:* Charts and diagrams should be used to identify problems.
4. *Statistical Process Control:* These are used to reduce variation
5. *Imagining for problem Solving:* Technique encourages creativity when linked to 'vision statements' and brainstorming.

6. *Industrial Engineering:* To use workstudy including pacing, work simplification, method analysis, plant layout and material handling to make improvement.

6. Genichi Taguchi

Taguchi devised a quality improvement technique that uses experimental design methods for efficient characterisation of a product or process, combined with a statistical analysis of its variability. He divided the behaviour of a product or process in terms of factors (parameters or variables) as follows :

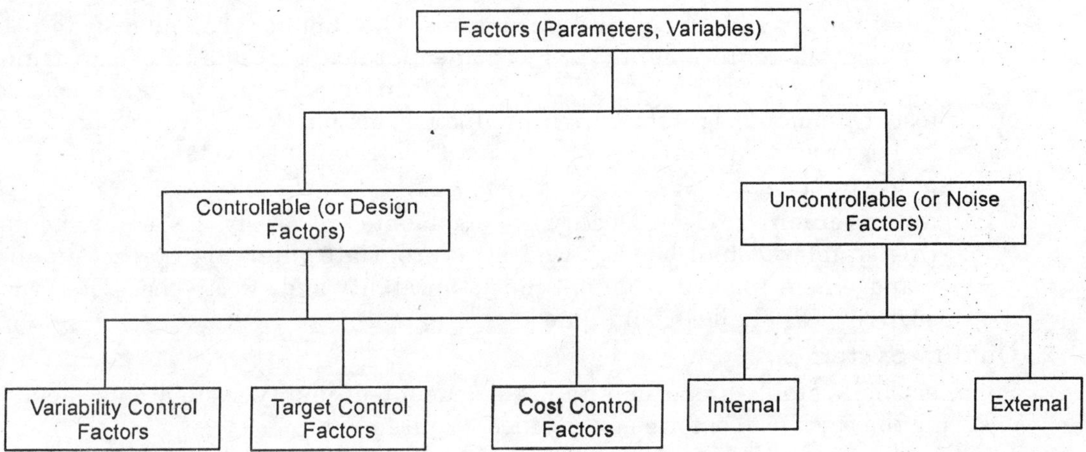

Principal idea in the Taguchi philosophy is that statistical testing of a product should be carried out at the design stage in order to make the product and the process robust to variations in the manufacturing and use environment.

Taguchi suggested that following steps should be taken in carrying out statistical studies:

1. Define the problem.
2. Determine the objectives.
3. Conduct a brainstorming session.
4. Design the experiment.
5. Conduct the experiment.
6. Analyse the data.
7. Interpret the results.
8. Run a confirmatory experiment.

Taguchi defines quality in a negative way as, the loss imparted to society from the time the product is shipped." This loss include

(*a*) the cost of customer dissatisfaction which may lead to a loss of reputation and goodwill for the company,

(*b*) direct loss to the company arising from .warranty and service costs,

(*c*) indirect loss due to market share loss, and

(*d*) increased marketing efforts needed to overcome lack of competitiveness.

23.9. QUALITY SYSTEM REQUIREMENTS

1. **Management Responsibility**

   1.1. **Quality policy.** Suppliers management shall define and document its policy and objectives for, and commitment to quality. This policy must be understood, implemented, and maintained at all levels in the organisation.

   1.2. **Responsibility and authority.** The responsibility, authority and the inter-relation of all personnel who manage, perform, and verify work affecting quality shall be defined.

   1.3. **Verification resources and personnel.** The supplier shall identify in-house verification requirements, provide adequate resources and assign trained personnel for verification activities. Verification activities include inspection, test and monitoring of the design, production, installation and servicing processes and or product, design reviews and audits of the quality system, processes and/or product.

   1.4. **Management review.** Quality system adopted to satisfy the requirements of this standard shall be reviewed at appropriate intervals by the suppliers management to ensure its continuity, suitability and effectiveness. Records of such reviews shall be maintained.

2. **Quality System**

   Supplier shall establish and maintain a documented quality system as a means of ensuring that product conforms to specified requirement.

3. **Design Control**

   3.1. **General.** The supplier shall establish and maintain procedures to control and verify the design of the product in order to ensure that the specified requirements are met with.

   3.2. **Design and development planning-** The supplier shall draw up plans that identify the responsibility for each design and development activity.

   The design and verification activities shall be planned and assigned to qualified personnel, equipped with adequate resources.

   Organisational and technical interfaces between different groups shall be identified and the necessary information documented, transmitted and regularly reviewed.

   3.3. **Design input.** Design input reqirements relating to the product shall be identified, documented, and their selection reviewed by the supplier for adequacy.

   3.4. **Design output.** This shall be documented and expressed in terms of requirements, calculations and analysis.

   3.5. **Design verification.** The supplier shall plan, establish, document and assign to competent personnel functions for verifying the design.

4. **Document Control**

   The supplier shall assure and maintain procedures to control all documents and data that relate to the requirements of this International Standard. These documents shall be reviewed and approved for adequacy by authorised personnel prior to issue.

5. **Purchasing**

   5.1. **General.** The supplier shall ensure that purchased product conforms to specified requirements.

5.2. **Assessment of sub-contractors.** The supplier shall select sub-contractors on the basis of their abilities to meet subcontract requirements, including quality requirements. The supplier shall establish and maintain records of acceptable sub-contractors. Supplier shall ensure that quality system controls are effective.

5.3. **Purchasing data.** Purchasing documents shall contain data clearly describing the product ordered, including the type, class, style, grade or other precise identification, specifications, drawings, process requirements, inspection instructions and other relevant technical data, including requirements for approval or qualification of product, procedures, process-equipment and personnel. The supplier shall review and approve purchasing documents for adequacy of specified requirements prior to release.

6. Purchaser Supplied Product

The supplier shall establish and maintain procedures for verification, storage and maintenance of purchaser supplied product provided for incorporation into the supplies.

7. Process Control

The supplier shall identify and plan the production and, where applicable, installation processes which directly affect quality and shall ensure that these processes are carried out under controlled conditions.

8. Inspection and Testing

8.1. **Receiving inspection and testing.** The supplier shall ensure that incoming product is not used or processed until it has been inspected or otherwise verified as conforming to specified requirements.

8.2. **In process inspection and testing.** The supplier shall:

(*a*) inspect, test and identify product as required by the quality plan or documented procedures ;

(*b*) establish product conforming to specified requirements by use of process monitoring and control methods ;

(*c*) hold product until the required inspection and tests have been completed ; and

(*d*) identify non-conforming product.

8.3. **Final inspection and testing.** The supplier shall carry out all final inspection and testing in accordance with the quality plan or documented procedures to complete the evidence of conformance of the finished product to the specified requirements. No product shall be despatched until all the activities specified in the quality plan or documented procedures have been satisfactorily completed.

8.4. **Inspection and test records.** The supplier shall establish and maintain records which give evidence that the product has passed inspection and/or test with defined acceptance criteria.

9. Inspection, Measuring and Test Equipment

The supplier shall control, calibrate and maintain inspection, measuring and test equipment. Equipment shall be used in a manner which ensures that measurement uncertainty is known and is consistent with the required capability.

10. Inspection and Test Status

The inspection and test status of product shall be identified by using markings, authorised stamps, tags, labels, routing cards, inspection records, test software, physical location which indicate the conformance or non-conformance of product with regard to inspection and tests performed.

11. Control of Non-conforming Product

The supplier shall establish and maintain procedure to ensure that product that does not conform to specified requirements is prevented from inadvertant use or installation. The responsibility for review and authority for the disposition of non-conforming product shall be defined. Non-conforming product shall be reviewed in accordance with documented procedures. It may be :

(*a*) reworked to meet the specified requirements, or
(*b*) accepted with or without concession, or
(*c*) re-graded for alternative applications, or
(*d*) rejected or scrapped.

12. Corrective Action

The supplier shall establish, document, and maintain procedures for:

(*a*) investigating the cause of non-conforming product and corrective action needed to prevent recurrence;
(*b*) analysing all processes, work operations, concessions, quality records, service reports and customer complaints to detect and eliminate potential causes of non-conforming product;
(*c*) initiating preventive actions ;
(*d*) implementing and recording changes in procedures resulting from corrective action.

13. Handling, Storage, Packaging and Delivery

13.1. General. Supplier shall establish, document and maintain procedures for handling, storage, packaging and delivery of product.

13.2. Handling. The supplier shall provide methods and means of handling that prevent damage or deterioration.

13.3. Storage. The supplier shall provide secure storage areas or stock rooms to prevent damage or deterioration of product, pending use or delivery. In order to detect deterioration, the condition of product in stock shall be assessed at appropriate intervals.

13.4. Packaging. The supplier shall control packing, preservation and making processes to the extent necessary to ensure conformance to specified requirements and shall identify, preserve and segregate all products from the time of receipt until the suppliers responsibility ceases.

13.5. Delivery. The supplier shall arrange for the protection of the quality of product after final inspection and test. This protection shall be extended to include delivery to destination.

14. Quality Records

The supplier shall establish and maintain procedures for identification, collection, indexing, filing storage, maintenance and disposition of quality records.

Quality records shall be maintained to demonstrate achievement of the required quality and the effective operation of the quality system.

15. Internal Quality Audits

The supplier shall carry out a comprehensive system of planned and documented internal quality audits to verify whether quality activities comply with planned arrangement and to determine the effectiveness of the quality system.

Audits and follow up actions shall be carried out in accordace with documented procedures. The results of the audits shall be brought to the attention of the personnel having responsibility in the area audited, who shall take timely corrective action on the deficiencies found by the audit.

16. **Training**

The supplier shall establish and maintain procedures for identifying the training needs and provide for the training of all personnel performing activities affecting quality.

23.10. QUALITY SYSTEM PRINCIPLES

1. **Quality loop**. The quality system typically applies to, and interacts with, all activities pertinent to the quality of a product or service. It involves all phases from initial identification to the final satisfaction of requirements and customer expectations. These phases and activities are indicated in the quality loop shown in Fig. 23.9
2. **Resources and Personnel.** Management should provide sufficient and appropriate resources essential to the implementation of quality policies and the achievement of quality objectives. These resources may include; (*a*) human resources and specialized skills, (*b*) design and development equipment, (*c*) production equipment, (*d*) inspection, test and examination equipment, and (*e*) instrumentation and computer software.

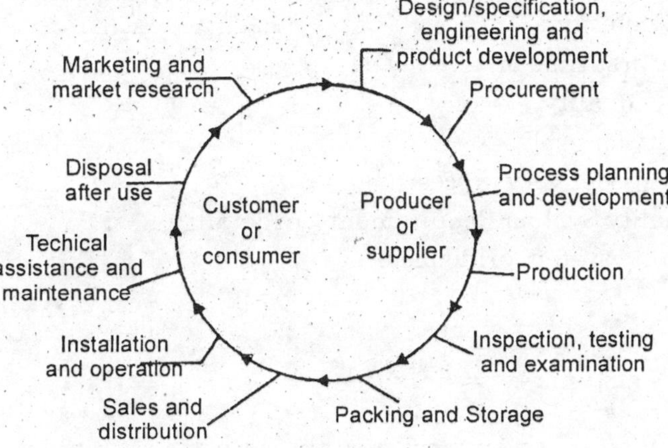

Fig 23.9. Quality loop.

3. **Documentation of the System**

   3.1. **Quality policies and procedures.** All the elements, requirements, and provisions adopted by a company for its quality management system should be documented in a systematic and orderly manner in the form of written policies and procedures.

   3.2. **Quality manual.** Main document used in drawing up andimplementing a quality system is a 'Quality Manual'.

   3.3. **Quality records.** Quality records and charts pertaining to design, inspection, testing, survey, audit, review or related results are important constituents of a quality management system.

4. **Auditing the Quality Systems**

All elements, aspects and components pertainingto a quality system should be internally audited and evaluated on a regular basis. Provision should be made by company management for independent review and evaluation of the quality system.

QUESTIONS

1. Explain the term "Total Quality Management".
2. What are the characteristics of total quality manegement concept?
3. How total quality can be improved? explain in detail.
4. How total quality can be implemented effectively?
5. Explain different concepts of total quality management.
6. Name the pioneers of total quality concepts. Explain their contribution.
7. Enumerate the elements of TQM.
8. Explain the aims of TQM.
9. Enumerate the ways for TQM.
10. Write a note on 'focous on costomers' with reference to TQM.
11. Discuss the term 'Total Quality Control'.
12. Write an essay on "Total Quality improvement".
13. What is 'Quality Circle'? What are its objectives?
14. Discuss, how a quality circle programme can be launched.
15. List out the rules for quality circle.
16. Write short notes on:
    (*a*) Right first time or zero defect.
    (*b*) Cost of quality.
    (*c*) Quality for profit.
17. Discuss quality delivery process.
18. Discuss 'Quality System Requirements' in detail.
19. Explain quality system principles.

Part–6 **Materials Management and Inventory Control**

24 Purchasing and Store-Keeping

24.1. INTRODUCTION

In any workshop or industry purchase means buying of equipments, materials, tools, parts, stores etc. required for industry. As one of the first act of manufacturing business is to purchase materials, hence purchasing is a primary function. Competitive sales cannot be made unless the materials used for manufacturing or for resales, are purchased at ultimate cost which is commensurate with that available to competitors.

The importance of the purchasing function varies with the nature and size of industry. In small factories, this function is performed by Works Manager but in large manufacturing concerns, where large quantities of materials are consumed, the buying function is given to a separate department under a highly competent executive designated as Chief Buyer or Purchase Manager or Purchasing Officer.

The costs of direct and indirect materials form a part of the prime cost of the product. Careful buying helps in reducing the cost of materials and thereby increasing profits.

Hence purchasing is one of the delicate activities and the persons employed for this job should be sincere, honest and intelligent.

Definition

Purchasing is an activity responsible for getting the right materials to the right place at right time in right quantity at the right price.

For an organisation, purchasing (procurement) is that function which is responsible for that phase of the material cycle, from the time an item is requisitioned until it is delivered to the user. This includes the selection of vendors, deciding the price and negotiating the quality and delivery. It also coordinates for transportation, receiving, inspection and inventory control.

Objects

The main objects of purchasing department are:

(*a*) "What to purchase", *i.e.*, to purchase required products of right quality.

(*b*) "When to purchase", *i.e.*, to purchase at right time,

(*c*) "Where to purchase", *i.e.*, to purchase from a reliable supplier or right source.

(*d*) "How much to purchase", *i.e.*, to purchase in right quantity.

(*e*) "What rate to purchase", *i.e.*, to purchase economically or at right price.

To achieve these five objectives, certain functions are to be performed by the purchasing department, which are described ahead.

24.2. ORGANISATION OF PURCHASE DEPARTMENT

Organisation of purchase department depends upon the size of the concern, type of production or service, purchase policy, availability of materials in the market, quantum of money involved in purchases, types of materials purchased, percentage of product cost represented by materials, and delegation of powers. The department is headed by a Purchase Manager, or Chief Purchase Manager.

Functions of Purchasing Department

1. To purchase materials on properly authorised requisitions.
2. To place orders of the requisitioned goods with height suppliers.
3. To obtain right type and quality of goods at cheapest price.
4. To purchase right quantities at right time.
5. To see that deliveries of all goods are received within time.
6. To check and see that the goods are received in accordance with the orders placed in respect of quality, quantity and specifications.
7. To advise the management regarding possible economies to be maintained by manufacturing an item instead of purchasing or *vice-versa*.
8. To study the market conditions and enter into rate contract with he large suppliers to ensure availability of materials all the time.
9. To study the various sources of supply and decide upon the most convenient as well as alternate supplies.
10. To keep the list of available and reliable suppliers.
11. To keep the list of articles needed in the organisation upto date with their quantities for placing orders.
12. To prepare specifications, to obtain quotations and compare these quotations for placing orders.
13. To look that suppliers' payments are made promptly so that public relations are maintained.
14. To purchase directly all small items, which do not require quotations.
15. To consider first the interest of the enterprise.
16. To assist purchasing agents, co-operate all, raise the purchasing standards.

Duties of Purchase Manager

The most important and essential duties of a purchasing officer are:

1. To maintain the standard of quality of product by selecting right quality of materials during purchases.
2. To organise and direct the purchasing department for efficient working.
3. To represent his concern with other concerns during purchasing contacts.
4. He should maintain the reputation of the concern for integrity and fair dealings with others while negotiating.
5. Shops should not await for materials.

6. To make a final check on all the requisitioned goods from different shops in the interest of economy as regards quality, quantity and specifications.
7. To act as a representative of the firm in the preparation of purchasing budget.
8. To spend money on purchases very carefully and wisely.
9. To suggest, the materials which can economically be produced in the concern instead of purchasing and *vice-versa*.

Relations with Other Departments

Purchase department, in order to efficiently discharge its functions, has to interact with various departments as shown in Fig. 24.1.

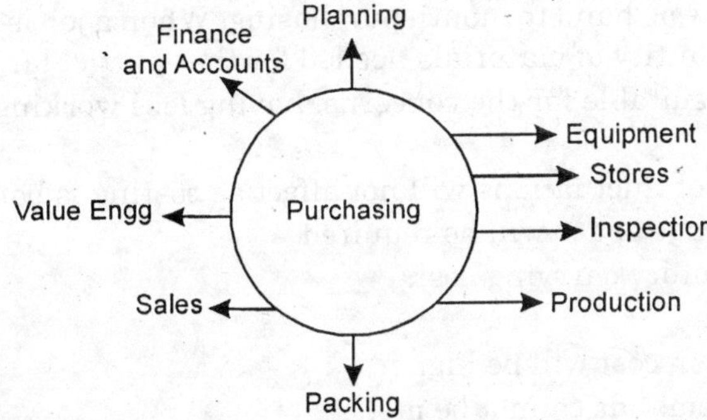

Fig. 24.1. Interaction of purchasing with other deptts

1. **Relations with Engineering Department.** Purchase and production departments help design/engineering department in selection of material, as the quality, the prices paid for them, manufacturability and cost of manufacture mainly related to their specifications.
2. **Relations with Production/Operations Department.** Relationship of purchasing and production departments starts as soon as the production department sends its manufacturing schedule or materials requisition to purchasing department. Purchasing, immediately on receipt of manufacturing sechdule, translates these documents into a procurement schedule. In case of any problem regarding such schedule, they have to coordinate and settle it down.

   Purchase department in consultation with production department also helps in taking 'make or buy' decisions.
3. **Relations with Marketing Department.** Purchasing–production–sales cycle is based on sales forecast. The forecasts are the basis for the production schedule, which in turn is the basis for the purchasing schedule. Immediate communication about any change in the sales forecast is necessary, to the purchasing and production for modifying their schedules.
4. **Relations with Finance Department.** Accurate sales forcast and procurement schedule are the most important data for planning of working capital and cash flow planning. In case of any change in schedule, finance department must be informed, alongwith production and sales department.

24.3. METHODS OF PURCHASING

(*a*) Purchasing strictly by requirement
(*b*) Purchasing for a specified period
(*c*) Market purchasing
(*d*) Contract Purchasing
(*e*) Central Purchase Organisation
(*f*) Through Directorate General of Supplies and Disposals.

All these methods of purchasing are described in brief as below :

(*a*) Purchasing Strictly by Requirement

This is also know as hand to mouth purchasing. When a job is taken in hand, only then the required quantity of materials needed for that particular job is purchased.

Therefore, it is suitable for the concerns, having less working capital.

Advantages

(*i*) The market fluctuations will not affect as costing is based on the market rates.
(*ii*) small storage space will be required
(*iii*) Less inventory carrying cost.

Disadvantages

(*i*) Distribution cost will be higher.
(*ii*) Sudden demands cannot be met.
(*iii*) Bargaining cannot be had due to the small amount involved.

(*b*) Purchasing for a Specified Period

Generally, the standard items, which are regularly used are purchased in quantities that will be sufficient for a particular future period.

Advantages

(*i*) As the order is received, production can, at once, be started.
(*ii*) The market fluctuations will not affect to a small size.
(*iii*) The involved working capital will be less.
(*iv*) Less storage space is needed.
(*v*) Cost analysis is easier.

(*c*) Market Purchasing

The reasonable requirements based on production planning are calculated. Market trends are analysed and then purchasing is done.

Generally, raw materials in process of manufacturing are purchased by this method.

Advantage

As purchasing is done in lot, distribution cost is less.

Disadvantages

(*i*) If the market topples, there is big loss.
(*ii*) Large space is required.

(*d*) Rate Contract Purchasing

Contracts are given to suppliers for large amounts of future requirements, for a certain period (say 2, 3 years), subject to review and cancellation with an appropriate period of notice. While calling quotations, the approximate quantity and time etc. are specified. Many concerns that use large quantities of basic materials such as pig iron, coal, coke, etc. have found it very desirable to contract for the entire supply of such materials for a considerable period of time.

Contract purchasing can be classified in the following two classes:-

(*i*) Rate Contract.

(*ii*) Running contract.

(*i*) **Rate Contract.** Under this system, rates are fixed for certain items of stock or component part of product for certain period. In this system, no tenders are invited but rates are fixed by analysing the market trends by the purchaser. Any firm whosoever is interested in supplying the material at these fixed rates for that duration can make the supply.

Products like fans, paints, cables, tyres etc. can be purchased under this method. This is simple and convenient method. Now-a-days most of the government departments such as P.W.D., Irrigation and Housing Board etc. adopt this method. In this method, they are not bound to purchase from one supplier but they can receive the materials from any reliable source.

(*ii*) **Running Contract.** In this, the rate as well as quantity for certain period is fixed. As soon as the desired quantity is supplied by the suppliers, the contract is automatically terminated.

Advantages

(*i*) It avoids necessity for keeping stocks.

(*ii*) It gives a measure of safety to suppliers.

(*iii*) The purchase is not affected by market fluctuations and the supply ensured.

(*iv*) As fewer purchase orders are required to be placed, it therefore, reduces to a great extent clerical work, accounting and receiving work etc.

(*v*) The purchase department is relieved from the routine work and hence can pay more attention on the major works.

(*vi*) No time is needed to be wasted in calling quotations and finalising the purchases. It ensures quick purchase.

(*vii*) The maintenance of records is improved as the items are standardised.

(*viii*) Normally during the period of contract, there is no change in price rate.

Disadvantage.

The supply may not be regular, as it is out of control of production department.

(*e*) Central Purchase Organisation.

Large concerns or certain big government concerns may have section-wise stores at different places and each section may have a separate store. In such case, there arises a problem as to whether each store should make its own purchases or whether purchases should be made by the Central Stores that would go on supplying material to section-wise stores.

If the local sectional stores is allowed to make its own purchases, there would be delay and the shops can get materials very soon after they have sent their requisitions. But local purchases may sometimes lead to malpractice. The purchase officer may have some kind of understanding with the local dealers and this may result in purchases at higher rates.

Advantages

(*i*) When the Central Stores make a purchase, it is on a large scale, naturally, it can obtain a good bargain and the things will be cheaper.

(*ii*) A strict control and check is possible. Therefore, there will be a little chance of malpractices.

(*iii*) It can have a direct contract with the manufacturer and can get things as per specifications.

(*iv*) Suitable arrangements for storage can be made.

The only difficulty in this system is that sometimes, there may be delay in getting materials from the Central Store but this can be minimized by supplying sectional stores with sufficient quantities in advance.

(*f*) **Directorate General of Supplies and Disposals.**

To avoid unpleasant situations in the various government departments for purchasing materials and equipment, there is a Central Purchase Organisation which provides the supplies at very cheap rates. This relieves a lot of botheration to the individual departments. This department enters into contract with various firms for supply of certain materials to government departments during the year at agreed rates. These firms have to certify that they are not supplying to others the same materials at rate lesser than that mentioned in the rate contract.

The various government departments as and when required place orders on the firms for the supply of material at the rate contract prices.

For the Central Government, Directorate General of Supplies and Disposal with various branches in the country and the Central Purchases Department for State Government Departments are the organisations.

24.4. PURCHASING PROCEDURE

For a medium industry, following purchasing procedure is generally adopted, although slight variation can be there depending upon the circumstances:

1. After receiving the purchase requisition form, exact quantity of material to be purchased and its specification is decided.
2. Prepare a list of suppliers who deal with the business of the articles to be purchased and are reliable.
3. If the material to be purchased is of small amount and required urgently, it may be purchased locally.
4. If necessary, prepare and issue N.I.T. (Notice Inviting Tenders) to the concerning supplier, mentioning different terms, conditions, date and time of opening of tenders.
5. Open the tenders at prescribed time on the prescribed date.
6. Prepare a comparative statement of the rates, terms and conditions mentioned in the tenders and then study them.
7. If required, samples may be received from the firm who have quoted the lowest rates.
8. Place the purchase order, to the firm selected after the study of sample, rates, terms and other conditions, mentioning the date by which the material must be received.
9. Copy of the purchase order must be sent to the stores, the department who has sent the requisition, Accounts Section and to Inspection Department.
10. A detailed inspection is carried out after the material is received. If the material is found to be satisfactory, the bill of the supplier is passed and the payment is made to the firm.

Steps in Purchasing

Following steps are commonly used in purchasing:

1. Purchase requisition (Indenting).
2. Tender/enquiry, evaluation of tenders, select the supplier.
3. Placing of orders on suppliers.

4. Follow-up of purchase orders.
5. Receipt of materials.
6. Inspection of materials.
7. Close the order.

24.5. PURCHASE REQUISITION (INDENTING)

Actual work of purchase starts from the time purchase department receives purchase requisition (Generally known as Indent) from the indentor. Indentor may be either (*i*) user department (for non-stock items) or (*ii*) material planning section (for replenishing the stock items). User department sends his requisition (indent) in the preseribed form (varies from organisation to organisation). Purchase department should be given sufficient time to procure material.

Purchase Requistion Form (Indent)

In any workshop or industry, the purschasing department places orders for materials according to the requisitions received from:

(*a*) Store-keeper for the standard items, the stocks of which require restocking again and again.

(*b*) Production shops, for special materials, which are not stocked in stores.

Whenever any special materials is rquired in the shops, the production department prepares atleast three copies of purchase requisition.

This form is in three parts as shown below:

Requisition No........................ Date..................

Shop ....

Required for:

1. (a) Work Order No.............
   (*b*) Department use...................
   (*c*) To stock.......................

S.N.	*Description of material*	*Specification*	*Quantity*	*Approx. cost*	*Remarks*

Delivery required up to Signature...........
(Indentor)

Addresses of probable suppliers...
....

2. Report of Storekeeper..
....

Signature...........
(Storekeeper)

3. (For the use of purchase section)
Supplier.................
Purchase Order No..............
Dater of Delivery Promised............... Signature...........
(Chief buyer)

Part I is completed by the indentor (Production Department). For quick purchasing and minimising the work of purchase section, he should mention the addresses of probable suppliers, who can supply these special materials.

Out of three copies one copy is retained by the Indentor and other two copies are sent to the storekeeper for onward transmission.

Part II is filled by the storekeeper in remaining two copies and he reports on it whether the required material is available in the store or not. If storekeeper also wants this material for stocking in store, he adds his demand also.

Now both the copies are passed on the purchase section and part III of form is filled by them later making necessary arrangement for purchases. Out of these two copies, one is kept by purchase section for records and other sent back to the requisitioner, so that he may come to know that arrangement for the required purchases has been made.

However, this form varies slightly from organisation to organisation.

24.6. TENDERS

A tender or a quotation is a written offer to do a work or to provide a material at a given price within a prescribed period and under certain specific conditions.

Types of Tenders

Following are the three types of tenders :

1. Single Tender
2. Closed Tender
3. Open Tender.

1. **Single Tender.** When the quality is of extreme importance, only a reliable firm will be asked to supply and rates are fixed by mutual acceptance.
2. **Closed Tender.** When material is required, firms which are registered will be invited to tender their rates and the most economic offer will be considered for placing the order.

   In this system, the tenders are invited only from some limited firms. Hence this system is also called "Limited Tender System".

   The last date to tender, the terms and conditions of supply and payments are mentioned in the tender notice. If the rate quoted by more than one firm are same, the order is placed on a known reliable firm.
3. **Open Tender.** This type of tender system is adopted when quantities to be purchased involved large amount. Here this system is also known as 'unlimited tender system'. A tender notice in trade journals is published, so that wide publicity can be given.

   All the interested firms will apply for the tender form available at certain price. These tender forms contain dates of receiving and opening the tenders, the approximate quantity required, period and place of delivery, specifications and other terms and conditions etc., for supply.

   A certain amount will have to be deposited by the supplier, as earnest money at the time of tendering to ensure that the supplier does not back-out after his rates are approved.

Notice Inviting Tenders

Tenders are invited by an industry when some materials are required to be purchased. The tenders are invited from the firms dealing with the supply of the items to be purchased. The notice should contain the following:

1. Name of material to be purchased with detailed specification and if necessary drawing must also be enclosed.
2. Quantity to be purchased.
3. If the material required is of particular make, it must also be mentioned.
4. Whether the sample is to be sent with the tenders.
5. Period of delivery.
6. Earnest money to be deposited.
7. Purchasing terms and conditions.
8. Date, time and place for receiving and opening of the tenders.

A specimen of Tender Notice is being given below :

TENDER NOTICE

Sealed quotations are invited for the supply of 20 numbers of 4 H.P. Centrifugal Bore Hole Submersible Electrical Pumping sets, which will be received by the undersigned upto 3 P.M. on 20th May 1985.

The pumping set should be complete with all fittings, *viz.*, starter; cable etc. Full specifications and other details including drawing and model of the pumping set, should accompany the tender.

Rates must be inclusive of packing and forwarding charges and must be F.O.R. Patna. An earnest money of Rs. 2000 must accompany the tender in the form of treasury challan or bank drafts.

Pumps will have to be supplied within 30 days of the issue of the supply order. 90% payment will be made after the completion of satisfactory supply and remaining 10% after the satisfactory working of the pumps for 3 months.

Sd...........

Name and Address of the
authority inviting tenders

After seeing this Tender Notice, suppliers must send the tenders or quotations so that it may reach before the time of opening. While filling up the tenders, conditions mentioned in the notice must be fulfilled. Other conditions, if any, must also be mentioned so that no dispute arises afterwards. Following should also be clearly mentioned in the tenders:

1. Whether the rates are F.O.R. or ex-godown.
2. If rates for items having different specifications are quoted, it must be clearly mentioned.
3. Guarantee period, if any.
4. If necessary, drawing must be enclosed.
5. Whether rates are inclusive of sales tax or not.

6. Percentage of advance payment, if desired.
7. Whether packing and forwarding charges are extra or included in the rates.

Opening of Tenders

The tenders are sent by the suppliers in sealed envelope (the word 'tender' or 'quotation' and its date of opening must be written on the top of the envelope). On the date of opening, at the prescribed time, purchase officer opens all the tenders or quotations received till that time, in the presence of the representatives of the suppliers, if present. At the time of opening the tenders or quotations, the purchase officer writes on each tenders – S. No. of tender/Total No. of tenders received/No. of pages in that particular tender, *e.g.*, when he writes on any tender IV/ 13/3, it means, this tender is *IV* out of 13 tenders received and it has 3 pages, he also attests the corrections and over-writings if any, at the time of opening the tender.

Comparative Statement

After opening and numbering all the tenders or quotations, a comparative statement is prepared. This helps to study the proposals in one sight. Following proforma is generally used for preparing the comparative statement:

Comparative Statement				+
Date of Issue of N.I.T.......................			**Date of receipt of tenders**	
S. No.	Name of article with specifications	Quantity required	Firm No. 1 Rate in Rs. Terms & Con-ditions (1) (2) (3)	Firm No. 2 Rate in Rs. (1) (2) (3)

This statement gives all the details including alternative offers, terms and conditions of delivery, if differs than that required. This statement should be perfectly correct. On this basis, Purchase Officer studies the statement thoroughly and takes the advice of the experts, if required. It is not always necessary to purchase the items only from the firms quoting lowest rates. For this purpose, sample, specifications, make, guarantee period, period of supply, other expenses like freight, sales tax, packing and forwarding charges etc. are considered.

Evaluation of Tenders

Tenders are evaluated to determine the 'lowest evaluated tender' or 'lowest acceptable tender?' This indicates that order may be awarded to the tenderer who is not only low in price but also provide advantages in respect of other evaluated criteria, and fulfils the purchasing parameters.

Negotiations.

Negotiation is essentially a discussion on a business transaction leading to finalisation of purchase and sale contract of goods and services. The factors which are considered for discussions include quality, conditions of supply, price, payment terms, freight, insurance, mode of packing, transport, delivery schedule, inspection, legal terms etc. While purchasing capital equipment, buyer have to consider after-sales service, availability of spares, supply of spares, guarantee, warranty and buy-back clauses.

Most organisations prefer negotiations as a policy where full advantages of competition could not be explored. Negotiations are not only carried out for getting prices reduced, but also for getting favourable conditions.

24.7. PLACEMENT OF PURCHASE ORDER

It is a letter sent to the supplier asking to supply the said material. At least six copies of purchase order are prepared by the purchase section and each copy is separately signed by the Purchase Officer.

Out of these copies, one copy each is sent to store-keeper, supplier, Accounts section, Inspection department and to the department placing the requisition and one copy is retained by the purchase department for record.

The contract is concluded with the posting of the purchase order to the successful bidder. The purchase order must be posted within the validity period of the offer. It becomes legally binding only on its acceptance by the other party. Acknowledgement of purchase order should be closely watched and disputes, if any, on any of the terms or other stipulations must be settled immediately so as to bring a legally enforceable contract into existence.

Purchase order must contain:

1. Complete description of material/equipment.
2. Item wise quantity, unit rate, and value
3. Date of delivery.
4. Terms of delivery.
5. Prices (firm or variable), provision of taxes and duties.
6. Clauses for liquidated damages.
7. Payment terms and paying authority.
8. Security deposit and performance guarantee.
9. Warranty.
10. Consignee address and despatch instructions including insurance and freight payment.
11. Instructions governing supply, inspection and testing criteria and drawing of samples.
12. Place of inspection.
13. General purchase conditions.
14. Arbitration and jurisdiction clause.
15. *Force Majeure* clause.
16. Provisions of cancellation, removal of rejects, penalty, bonus etc.

Purchase Order Form

A proforma of purchase order is given below :

Factory Code No...................... Purchase Order No.............

Telephone No............................ Date..................

Telegraphic Address Requisition No....................

To

M/s.......................

....

....

From

M/s..........................

....

....

Refer Your Tender/quotation No..........Dated.............................

Please supply the following in accordance with the terms and conditions mentioned as under :

S.No.	*Description of material*	*Quantity*	*Rate*	*Amount*	*Delivery date promised*

Terms and Conditions

....

....

....

Signature
(Purchase Officer)

Specifications for Ordering Machinery

Purchase of materials for manufacturing concern calls for great skill and knowledge of the particular type of manufacture. This problem has to be looked at from three points of view. These points are :

(*a*) Quantity,

(*b*) Quality, and

(*c*) Price.

It is from the point of view of quality that specifications have to be laid down before ordering machinery. There are many forms of giving specifications. The important among them are as under :

1. **Brand or Trade Name.** The buyer depends entirely on the producer's reputation for quality when he specifies materials by brand or trade name.
2. **Blue Print or Dimension Sheet.** This is prepared by production engineering

department to meet the special requirements of the concern. This form of specification is useful in the purchase of tools and fixtures.

3. **Chemical Analysis or Physical Characteristics.** Specification by chemical analysis or physical characteristics is considered to be ideal for raw-material in the metallic class. It is essential to conduct laboratory tests to check such specifications.
4. **Description of Purpose or Use.** It is very advantageous to the buyer. Here it would be the responsibility of the supplier or seller to meet the requirements of specifications. For example, when tools or machines are to be bought, the buyer generally does not process complete technical knowledge about them. It would be desirable to specify performance along with physical and mechanical requirements.
5. **Samples.** The use of samples as a form of specification has its limitations. Sometimes disputes may arise and, therefore, samples should be used in a form of specification. Samples should only be used when more reliable firms are not available.
6. **Identification with Standard Specification.** This is the most satisfactory method, of course, the standard must be such that the buyer requirements must be met. Standards for certain materials are fixed by reputed institutions and they may be accepted by all. This facilitates trade and commerce considerably.

   The specifications given must have the following essential features:

   1. It should be as simple as possible.
   2. It should be exact.
   3. It should be capable of verification.
   4. It should be such that a number of suppliers can meet it.

Standard Specifications

These are published in our country by Indian Standard Institution. Standard specifications published by Indian Standard Institution are called 'Indian Standards'. ISI have now been named as Bureau of Standards.

These are written in a very clear and concise manner. Wherever necessary, they are supplemented by tables, schedules and diagrams.

Their study will give the reader some idea how specifications are to be written. Indian standards are constantly being revised and amended so as to keep them up-to-date and so it is desirable to refer always to the latest version.

Earnest Money

It is the amount of money, which is demanded along with the tenders, so that the supplier should not back out at the time of accepting the rates. If the supplier does not agree to supply the material at the quoted rates, this earnest money will be forfeited.

24.8. FOLLOW-UP

Function of purchase department does not cease with the placement of purchase order. There should be a regular follow-up of purchase order placed. A register for this purpose is maintained for all the orders placesd. Supplying firms should be regularly contacted so as to ensure timely supply of materials.

Critical items need vigorous follow-up, while others need routine follow-up.

Important functions of follow-up section are:

1. To secure an acceptance of order from the seller.
2. To secure a commitment for delivery schedule.
3. To chase various activities from placement of orders till final payment after receipt of satisfactory and timely supply of material.

24.9. RECEIPT AND INSPECTION OF MATERIAL

All incoming materials on receipt are physically checked, counted and then referred to inspection and quality control department, to ensure whether it meets the purchase order requirements. The rejected items are returned to the supplier, while accepted items are sent to storage for recording and keeping them properly at their locations.

Sometimes inspection are carried out at supplier's place, known as pre-delivery inspection. On receipt of such item it must be got ensured from the same team which carried out pre-delivery inspection, that the material is same.

The purchase department then verifies the bills and ensures timely payment.

Supplier Certification

When supplier has an ISO certification and when buying organisation has had a fairly lengthy positive experience with the supplier, the quality system of both firms can be integrated to reduce the total cost associated with quality. The objective, in addition to maintaining desired quality levels, is to reduce duplicate efforts in inspection and related quality control activities. Such supplier firms may have certification agreements in the form of supplier's guarantee of quality specifying the reponsibilites of both the parties for specifications, statistical process control applications, corrective procedures etc.

24.10. PURCHASING PARAMETERS (PRINCIPLES OF PURCHASE)

Following are the main purchasing parameters :

1. **Right Time.** This parameter is most critical one due to the consequences of stock out. To determine the right time, information about all the elements of total lead time should be available, *i.e.*, internal administrative lead time of non-vibrating indents into an order, manufacturing and transportation time and inspection lead time.
2. **Right Source.** Following are the main sources for the procurement of spare parts :
   (*i*) Manufacturers
   (*ii*) Authorised dealers of Manufacturers.
   (*iii*) Local dealers (Holding quality materials only).
   (*iv*) By getting them manufactured.

   While selecting a source of supply, timely supply, reliability, price and service facilities offered should be considered.
3. **Right Price.** Lowest acceptable price consistent with quality, timely supply etc., should be considered.
4. **Right Quantity.** While inviting the tenders or placing the enquiries, quality specifications mentioning tolerances should be clearly spelled out.

5. **Right Quantity.** The problem of determining the right quantity is interlinked with the right time. The quantity will be different for each category for different durations. Broad guidelines are given by the concept of Economic Order Quantity and Economic Batch Size as described in the chapter in 'Inventory Control'.
6. **Right Place of Delivery / Transportation.** In most of the cases, items have to be supplied directly to the consuming plants, which may be located at far distant places from the head-quarter. The place of delivery should be clearly mentioned in the supply order.
7. **Right Procedure.** Right procedure to be adopted has to be formally developed for the pre-purchase, ordering and post purchase systems. Pre-purchase system means initiating the purchase through indents requirement, planning, selection of suppliers, obtaining quotations, and evaluating them. With purchase order, generally an acknowledgement copy is also sent to the supplier, who then return it as a written acceptance of supply order and to abide by the terms and conditions mentioned in the order. Post purchase system includes follow up with the suppliers.
8. **Right Contract.** Purchase order is a legal document that binds selling company with the buying company. Various terms and conditions about insurance, sales tax, octroi, customs, excise, breach of contract, settlement of dispute, F.O.B., F.I.R., C.I.F. etc. are clearly mentioned in the contract.

24.11. STORES AND STOREKEEPING

Generally unworked material is known as store and the place where it is housed called "Store Room"

Types of stores:

Stores are generally of the following categories :

1. Raw materials.
2. Consumable Stores.
3. Inflammable Stores like Petrol, Kerosene oil etc.
4. Chemicals like Carbide, Sulphuric Acid etc.
5. Machinery and Equipment.
6. Hand Tools.
7. Furniture.
8. Finished Products.
9. Scrap.
10. Unserviceable Stores.
11. Empties and Packages etc.

Finished products ready for sale are called stock and the place where they are kept called "Stock Room".

In small factories or concerns, the store room and stock room may be one and under the control of one officer but in a big organisation both are separate and separately controlled.

Purpose of Store-keeping

1. To see that the stock of no item at any time falls below the prescribed minimum or goes in excess of fixed maximum quantity.

2. To examine carefully all goods and materials on receipt.
3. To arrange for a systematic and efficient storing of materials.
4. To maintain accurate and prompt distribution of items to departments as and when required under Issue Requisition Notes.
5. To maintain efficient quantity records of movement of stock and to account for all goods that have come under their charge.
6. To prevent any theft, wastage or deterioration of stock.

Duties of Store-keeper

The store-keeper is very important figure in this organisation and he is as much responsible for the articles in his charge as a cashier for the cash. He should, therefore, take steps to reduce thefts and wastage of materials to a minimum.

1. The first most important duty is to plan the stores. He has some space at his disposal and has to put the space to the maximum use.
2. To keep record of materials and their cost.
3. Whenever requisitions are received from shops, they are checked and if found correct, material issued and entries made in the required registers.
4. He has to check the balance of items from time to time and see that desired quantities are available.
5. Whenever the existing stock of any item is likely to be exhausted he should send its information to Store Officer, who in turn will inform to purchase section for its purchase.
6. He has to prevent leakage, theft, wastage and deterioration.
7. He has to see that material is issued only against written requisition.
8. He should not permit everybody to go inside and issued material must be handed over outside the store, so as to prevent theft and disturbances.

24.12. LOCATION AND LAYOUT OF STORES

Store Location

(*a*) *Centralised* Srore(Fig.37.1). In small factories, it is desirable to centralise the materials so that these may be brought under the control of one Store-keeper and the Store-room should as far as possible be near the place, where material is to be used. If there are several manufacturing departments, the Store-room will be most conveniently situated, where it is near to all the departments. This will reduce handling and a lot of manual work is eliminated. This type is called Centralised Store.

(*b*) *Decentralised Store* (Fig. 37.2). In large factories, where there are several departments, each using a different type of materials, it becomes beneficial to separate the stores.

For example, near the welding department, store the materials required for welding; near the foundry department store the parts which are used there; near assembly department store the parts that are required there and so on.

Some stores that are common to several or all departments as for example, soap, stationery, printed forms, cotton waste, etc. should be kept at a central place.

This type is known as Decentralised Store.

Examples of both the types are shown with the help of sketches below :

Moulding & Casting	Smithy or Forging	Heat Treatment	Machine Shop
Foundry		Stores	
Pattern Making			
Fitting Shop		Office	Packing & storing

Fig. 24.1. Centralised Store-Keeping

	S	Smithy of Forging	S
Moulding & Casting	S		Machine Shop
Pattern making		Office	S
S S Fitting Shop		Cycle Stand	Packing & Storing

Fig. 24.2. Decentralised Store-Keeping. ('S' indicates stores).

System of Location of Material

In small factories, where there is one small store, the Store-keeper may remember the location of material but in large factory where several thousand items are handled by him, memory would become unreliable. Hence to facilitate the work of Store-keeper, it is, therefore, necessary to set up a system of numbering the locations. Under this system, all locations, in a Store-room are numbered and these numbers are entered in the Index register against the items which are located.

Suppose code number for any item is 28-18E-35. This means the location is in store-room 28, Rack 18, Shelf *E* and Bin 35. By this system, man approaches at the correct place and correct material and issuing becomes quick and easy.

Layout of Stores.

It depends on the following factors:

1. **Flow of Materials.** According to this factor, materials should move minimum possible distances.
2. **Character of Materials.** The materials that are not damaged by weather can be stored out of doors in shed.

   Materials like cement, plaster etc., must be placed in dry place.

   Tools and machines etc. should also be placed in dry places and coated to prevent rusting.
3. **Quantity, Weight etc. of Materials.** It is necessary to find the space required for different quantities of material.
4. **Frequency of Handling.** Handling consists of the following four stages : (*a*) Receipt (*b*) Inspection (*c*) Storage and (*d*) Issue of Materials.

The following are general hints to carry out these stages of handling smoothly and correctly :

1. Layout is such that inward material may be quickly received.
2. Unloading platforms are built of suitable height.
3. All round the stores there is thorough siding. If trucks are used for transporting the material, sufficient parking space is provided.
4. For heavy material suitable equipment for internal transport is provided.
5. It is to be seen that each section of the store has sufficient allotting space. The material is to be arranged in such a way that inward and outward movement of supplies can be carried out smoothly.

Placement of Material in Stores.

Whatever may be the type of location, materials are now-a-days placed in racks and bins as shown in Fig. 37.3 (*a*). This arrangement is an old method and is obsolete now-a-days. Fig. 37.3 (*b*) is present modified method and under this, the storekeeper has an advantage that he can search out the material immediately with less labour and fatigue. At the entrace of the store flag "A" represents the type of materials placed in a particular row while flag "B" shows a particular material in a particular bin. The speciality of this modified arrangement is that as soon as the storekeeper enters the store, every bin is properly visible even from a distance. This was not the case in the old method. In the old method issuing was inconvenient as well as involved more movements. This new arrangement also looks better.

24.13. METHODS OF STORING

Storing method depends upon the type of item to be stored. Store department must ensure that the things are stored in such a way so that it may not be spoiled by errors in, rusting and deterioration. Sufficient precautions and inspection should be observed for this purpose. For this purpose items of stores can be classified into the following categories :

(*a*) **Raw Materials.** These are used in the making of products, like pig iron in a steel plant, raw cotton in a textile mill. These are stored as per the type of material

X = Store Rack Y = Open Way

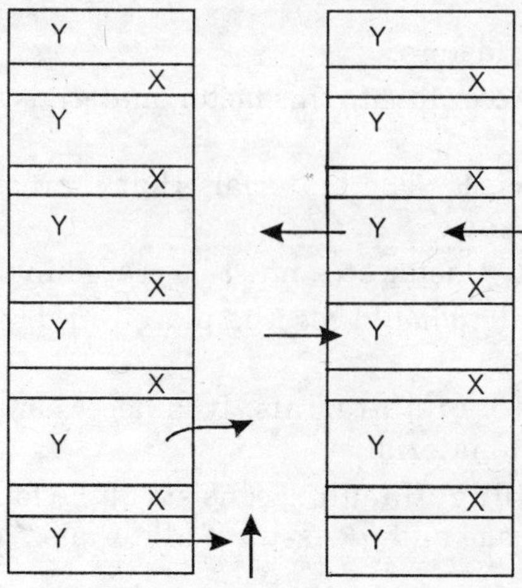

Fig. 37.3 (*a*)

(*b*) **Spare Parts.** These are the parts which are purchased from outside source and are used in the assembly of final products or for the repair of the production equipments. These are placed in bins and racks separately. Each bin is allotted to one item. Rust prevention is done by coating materials when necessary with oil grease etc. Some of the items need special attention while they are in stores. The method to preserve them is explained hereunder.

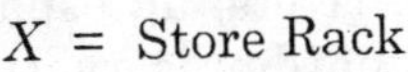

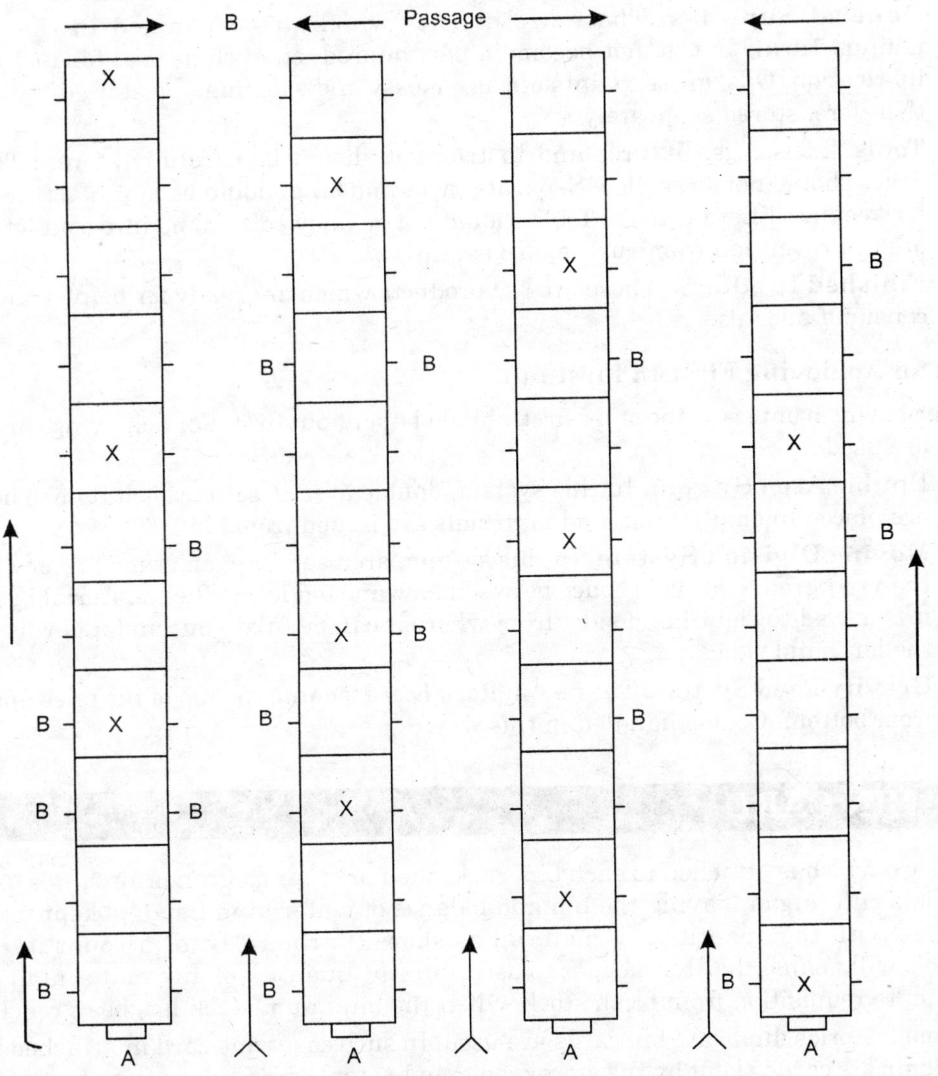

Fig. 37.3. (*b*)

(*i*) Rubber parts, such as belts, mounting pads, tyres, tubes etc., should be stored in dark room. Talc powder can also be used.

(*ii*) Instruments, electronic items and their parts should be stored in dust free conditions, preferably in an air-conditioned store room. Wherever possible antirust oil compound can also be used.

(*iii*) Welding rods should be stored in moisture-free conditions.

(*iv*) Bearings should be cleaned in solvent oil and after inspection should be repacked with grease and kept in plastic covers/bags.

(*v*) Shafts, gears etc. should be stored after complete painting with de-watering protective film.

(*vi*) Fastners, screws, washers, rivets, autospares etc. are stored in shelves after treating with hard tacky or hard preservative film.

(*c*) **General Supplies.** These are articles which are consumed in the process of manufacturing but do not become a part of product, such as coal for fuel and oil for lubrication. Oils, grass, paints etc. are messy and soon make a store dirty. These are, therefore, stored separately.

(*d*) **Tools.** Tools, jigs, fixtures and instrument should be carefully stored. The cutting edges should not be spoiled. Separate racks and bins should be manufactured specially for keeping different tools. Tools should not be allowed to come into contact with each other. Prevention from rust is also essential.

(*e*) **Finished Products.** These are the products which are ready for being transported to consumers for use.

Method for Achieving First-in First-out.

The material which enters in the store first, should be sent out first. For achieving this, following methods are used :

1. **Double Area System.** In this system, double area is set for each item. The new lots are placed in empty area, and materials are issued from old lot.
2. **Moving Division System.** In this system, area set for each item is somewhat larger than required to provide space between new and old lots. When material becomes old, it is moved to right hand side, from where it can be taken out and a new is placed on the left hand side.
3. **Gravity Feed System.** The new materials are fed into the top of the piles and removed from bottom. Coal is handled in this way.

24.14. BIN CARD

This is a card which is attached to each bin, rack, shelf or other container for stores. A record of all materials entering or leaving the bin and balance of material in hand, is kept in this card. These agree with the quantities of material as shown in the relevant account in the stores ledger. This will enable the storekeeper to ascertain the quantity of any material in stock and remind him to requisition from fresh stock, when the minimum stock has been reached.

In some factories duplicate bin cards are used. In such cases one card in attached to the bin and the duplicate card is kept by the storekeeper on his table for ready reference. Bin cards are checked from time to time by the Inspectors and they put their initials on these cards and note down the discrepancies.

Now-a-days, to avoid delay in production, an ordering level or safety level is also introduced between the maximum quantity and minimum quantity. At this ordering level, orders are placed for the purchase of material and if by chance material is not received and minimum quantity level is reached in the stores, some alternative arrangements are urgently made.

A sample of bin card proforma is given below :

BIN CARD			
Bin No.............. Article...............		Minimum Quantity.............. Ordering Level.............. Maximum Quantity..............	
Date	Quantity Received	Quantity Issued	Balance
Checked Initials..........			

24.15. INDENT ON STORE

It is also called material issue requisition. An important rule, which should be strictly followed is, not to allow any material to pass from the stores department into the works except upon the authority of written requisitions. These Indents on stores are the demands upon the store-keeper signed by authorised persons to issue to bearer, and to be charged to a particular job or department mentioned therein.

Such indent on stores are made out in triplicate from bound books supplied to each department. They contain the date, the necessary particulars of the stores requisitioned, such as quantity and description, and job number to which the material is to be charged ; department number, signature of the party making it, space for the initial of the issuing store-keeper and the signature of the persons receiving the material.

As it is in triplicate, the original copy is sent to the cost department for costing, duplicate is retained by the store-keeper and triplicate in the bound book by the Indentor as a permanent record. This can also be used in duplicate. In such cases, the original copy is sent to the cost department by the store-keeper after making the necessary entries.

A sample of indent on store is given below:

MATERIAL ISSUE REQUISITION

Book No................	Indent No................
Shop/Deptt...........	Date..........................
To The Store-keeper,	
Please issue the under-mentioned goods for job No.......................	

S.No.	Material with specifi-cations	Quantity		Store ledger page No. page where posted	Initials of store-keeper	Rate	Cost	Remarks
		Demanded	Supplied					
No. of items .... Received								
								.... Indentor

24.16. MATERIAL RETURNED NOTE

Materials issued for departmental use, sometimes not utilised and returned to the store-keeper, must be properly recorded and their values may be duly entered in the store records and these values may be credited to the account of the departments concerned by cost depart ment. For this purpose Material Returned Notes are written out in triplicate. Two copies being sent to the store-keeper along with the returned material, one of these is returned to the foreman with the storekeeper's acknowledgement. The copy retained by store-keeper is entered by him on the bin cards and ledgers and then passed on to the stores accountant to be priced and entered by him in the relative stores card. It will then be dealt with by the cost department, the account of the department concerned being given credit in respect thereof. This can also be used in duplicate.

Material Returned Note

From Job No. Serial No. ....

Please recieve the under mentioned materials: Date ....

Description of material	*Reason for returning*	*Quantity*	*Rate*	*Value*	*Store Ledger page No.*
Bin Card No.				Received No..........	
				Signature...... (Store Keeper)	

Note. The last three columns will be filled-in by the costing department.

24.17. STORE ACCOUNTING

Mostly store accounts are referred to in the details pertaining to the material which is not for re-sale. A better stores procedure is a safeguard against waste of material and theft etc.

In order to maintain an efficient record of stores, the following books and records will be required and these are maintained separately for different types of materials.

1. **Inward and Outward Register.** When the material is despatched by the supplier through rail, he will send its receipt issued by the Railway Authority called 'RR'. On the production of that receipt to railways, material can be received. A separate register is maintained by store-keeper, in which daily entries of R.R. received are made and known as Inward Register.

   In the same way, when some material goes out of the store to other place, entries of R.R. are made by store-keeper in outward Register and that R.R. is sent to the customer, on the production of which, he can take the material from railways.

2. **Stock Register.** These are :

   (*i*) Dead Stock or Non-Consumable Register.

   (*ii*) Consumable register.

   (*i*) *Dead Stock or Non-consumable Register.* This is maintained by store-keeper, in which entries of non-consumable articles such as all machinery, equipment and furniture etc. are made. The register shows complete details of articles together with accessories. The different items are entered on different pages. All transactions about a particular item are entered on one page.

   (*ii*) *Consumable Register.* In this, store-keeper maintains record of consumable stores received, such as coke, diesel, oil, kerosene, petrol, lubricants, cotton waste, paints etc. The different items are entered on different pages. All the transactions about a particular item are entered on one page.

3. **Daily Receipt Register.** This may be in a register or loose leaf form. Whenever any material comes in the store, it is entered datewise in the daily receipt register. Material is then inspected and if found suitable is entered in Stock Register.

   If the material is found defective, it will be rejected and either the material or its report will be sent to the supplier. The incidental charges that are incurred will also be noted in daily receipt register.

4. **Issue Register.** This may be in register or loose leaf form. All stores issued are entered date wise in it by store-keeper. From the Receipt and Issue registers, store ledger is prepared by accounts section.

5. **Surplus Stock Register.** Sometimes such purchases are made, which do not come in use for long time, say 3 years. Such materials are then declared surplus and recorded in a separate register called "Surplus Stock Register".

   Thus unnecessary material is removed from the Stock Register to facilitate easy handling.

6. **Suspense Register.** The defective item or items received in excess should not be placed in the bins but in "Suspense cell". A separate register is maintained by store-keeper for all such items placed in suspense and known as Suspense register.
7. **Condemned Article Register.** Unserviceable material after use or obsolete material, which is authorised to be condemned by authorised persons, is entered in this register and will be shown as stock until disposed of. The balance of condemned article will be taken out from store ledger and will be shown condemned.
8. **Loan register.** Sometimes non-consumable materials are is used from store on loan for temporary period by producing a slip of authority. Before issuing, material is entered in this register and signature of the bearer are taken in the register and slip of authority is kept safe.

   When the material comes back, slip is returned and entry of material received back is made in loan register.
9. **Empty Containers and Package Register.** The record of empty containers and packages is kept in this register by the storekeeper. They should be disposed of at convenient intervals by auction or otherwise to the best of advantage.

   The above mentioned are the various records, which must be kept by any storekeeper for easy and smooth handling of stores.

Advantages of Good Store-keeping and Store-recording.

1. Ready record of all materials and store purchases may be obtained.
2. As the materials are arranged in a systematic way in racks and bins, handling of stores becomes very easy.
3. Unnecessary confusion and delays in issue of material is avoided.
4. It helps to operate shops efficiently.
5. Overstocking is avoided and delays due to lack of materials are prevented.
6. Wastage of time and labour, leakage, thefts and pilferages of stores are reduced to their minimum.
7. Classification of receipts and issues are made easy.
8. Each item issued can be traced to its repective department, so as to ensure correct costing.
9. To safeguard the materials which are lying in stores.

Store Ledger

Name of Article   Bin No.........

			Quality					Physical Verification				Remarks
Date of transac tion	Source of receipt with bill no. etc.	Specfi-cation	Received	Issued	Balance after each transaction	Rate	Amount	Sig. of S.K.	Rate	Result	Sig. of verifying officer	Indicating obsolete surplus or/and unserviceable etc.

Store Ledger : It is detailed record of the receipt and issue of materials with respect to quality, quantity and value of all the items kept in store. A separate Sheet or Card is maintained for each article. It contains the name, description, bin number etc. It records the receipts, issues and balance in hand of each and every article. At the time of physical verification Verifying Officer after, inspection, gives his recommendations in the remarks column.

24.18. VALUATION OF MATERIALS ISSUED FROM STORES

To find out the cost of material issued from stores, several methods are used. The choice of method should be based on the nature of material and the type of business. Following are some important methods, which are commonly used :

1. "First-in-first-out" method.
2, "Last-in-first-out" method.
3. Average price method.
4. Fixed price method.
5. Actual value method.
6. Current value method.
7. Inflated price method.

These methods are now discussed in detail below :

1. "First-in First-out" Method.

This is also known as original cost method. In this system goods received are entered in the stores record at actual cost plus other charges such as freight, taxes and insurance etc. In this system, the materials first received are issued first. Materials from second lot are issued only when first lot is exhausted. The price is charged at the cost at which that lot was purchased.

Application

This method is suitable,

(*i*) where size and cost of material is large;

(*ii*) where at any time more than 2 or 3 lots are not likely to remain in stock ;

(*iii*) where the production is rapid.

Advantages

(*i*) In this method actual cost of material consumed is considered.

(*ii*) it is simple in use and do not require lengthy calculations.

Disadvantage

In this method there is no consideration of the current market prices.

Table 1 shows that how this method is applied.

2. "Last-in First-out" Method

As the name suggests, in this system, the material of the last lot of a particular item is first issued and hence the price of material issued is charged at the rate of material received in the last lot (the newest lot price). If the last lot is exhausted than the price of the remaining last lot is considered.

Application. This system is applicable, where production is rapid.

Advantage. With this method current cost is charged.

Disadvantage. Old stock is not exhausted first, which always remains in stock and hence liable to deteriorate or to become out of date. This method can easily be understood with the help of Table 2.

3. Average Price Method

In this method average cost of material is charged for the product, there are several ways of determining the average price but generally following two methods are in use:

(*a*) Simple average method.

(*b*) Month end average method.

(*a*) *Simple Average Method.* It means the average cost of material in hand on the date of issue from stores. Each time, when the material is issued average cost is calculated. Therefore, new calculations are necessary after every entry to obtain the mean price.

(*b*) *Month End Average Method.* In this method average cost of each type of material is calculated at the end of each month and is charged for all the issues during the following month.

Tables 3 and 4 will explain the correct procedure of charging the cost by these two methods.

e.g., average cost of the material during January will be

$$= \frac{\text{Amount spent} = 460}{\text{Units availabe} = 400} = \text{Rs. } 1.15$$

Now this rate, *i.e.*, Rs. 1.15 /unit will be charged during the month of February.

4. Fixed Price Method

In this method, issued material is charged at a predetermined estimated price, for a fixed period. Mostly for one year one rate is charged. Therefore, receipts and issues are recorded in quantities only which make store-keeping easy. This method is also known as "Standard Price" method. Price is generally fixed on the basis of past experience and future trends.

Application. This system is mostly used, where fluctuations in the market prices are very less and few.

5. Actual Cost Method.

In this method actual cost is charged for the material to be issued from the store.

Application. This system is generally used, where purchasing is done only for the specific purpose, such as special Dies, Jigs and Fixtures and other special item etc.

6. Current Value Method

This method charges current market price for the materials irrespective of the purchased price. This helps in estimating the actual cost of product by which tenders can stand market competition.

This system involves a great difficulty in finding out actual market price at every issue from the stores and, therefore, not so common.

7. Inflated Price Method

In this system, the charged cost of the material is slightly raised (inflated) by small percentage of the actual purchase price. All the other methods have not been taken into account, the wastage of material in stores, which is unavoidable. Therefore, certain percentage is charged for normal wastage on the purchase price. Thus cost of material issued is raised by some percentage to recover the wastage.

Table 1.

Description of material .... Bin No. ....

Date	*Receipts*			*Issues*			*Balance*		
	Quantity	*Rate Rs.*	*Amount Rs.*	*Quantity*	*Rate Rs.*	*Amount Rs.*	*Quantity*	*Rate Rs.*	*Amount Rs.*
Jan. 1	—	—	—	—	—	—	20	1.00	20.00
Jan. 9	100	1.00	100.00	—	—	—	120	1.00	120.00
Jan. 13	—	—	—	80	1.00	80.00	40	1.00	40.00
							40	1.00	40.00
Jan. 14	300	1.10	330	—	—	—			
				40	1.00	40.00	300	1.10	330.00
Jan. 18	—	—	—	40	1.10	40.00	140	1.10	154.00
							140	1.00	154.00
Jan. 20	200	0.90	180.00	—	—	—			
							200	0.90	180.00
				140	1.10	154.00			
Jan 24	—						90	0.90	81.00
				110	0.90	99.00			

"First-in First-out" Method

Table 2.

Description of material .... Bin No. ....

Date	Receipts			Issues			Balance		
	Quantity	*Rate Rs.*	*Amount Rs.*	*Quantity*	*Rate Rs.*	*Amount Rs.*	*Quantity*	*Rate Rs.*	*Amount Rs.*
Jan. 1	—	—	—	—	—	—	40	1.00	40.00
Jan. 6	300	1.20	360.00	—	—	—	40 300	1.00 1.20	40.00 360.00
Jan. 8	—	—	—	200	1.20	240.00	40 100	1.00 1.20	40.00 120.00
Jan. 11	—	—	—	60	1.20	72.00	40 40	1.00 1.20	40.00 48.00
Jan. 12	200	1.10	220.00	—	—	—	40 40 200	1.00 1.20 1.10	40.00 48.00 220.00
Jan. 16	—	—	—	200 25	1.10 1.20	220 30	40 15	1.00 1.20	40.00 18.00

"Last-in First-out" Method

Table 3.

Description of material .... Bin No. ....

Date	*Receipts*			*Issues*			*Balance*		
	Quantity	*Rate Rs.*	*Amount Rs.*	*Quantity*	*Rate Rs.*	*Amount Rs.*	*Quantity*	*Rate Rs.*	*Amount Rs.*
Jan. 1	—	—	—	—	—	—	100	1.00	100
Jan. 3	200	1.00	200.00	—	—	—	300	1.00	300
Jan. 6	—	—	—	250	1.00	250	50	1.00	50
Jan. 9	200	1.25	250.00	—	—	—	250	1.20	300
Jan. 22	—	—	—	150	1.20	1.80	100	1.20	120

"Simple-average price" Method

Table 4.

Description of material .... Bin No. ....

Date	Receipts			Issues			Balance		
	Quantity	*Rate Rs.*	*Amount Rs.*	*Quantity*	*Rate Rs.*	*Amount Rs.*	*Quantity*	*Rate Rs.*	*Amount Rs.*
Jan. 1	—	—	—	—	—	—	50	1.50	55
Jan. 6	100	1.00	100	—	—	—	150	—	155
Jan. 10	—	—	—	100	1.00	110	50	—	45
Jan. 14	—	—	—	30	1.10	33	20	—	12
Jan. 19	300	1.20	360	—	—	—	320	—	372
Jan. 23	—	—	—	220	1.10	220	120	—	152
Jan. 26	—	—	—	70	1.10	77	50	—	75

"Month End Average" Method

24.19. STORAGE AND HANDLING EQUIPMENTS

A good amount of labour and money can be saved by using right method of storing and by employing proper handling equipments for the movement of material 'into and from' stores.

1. **Storage Equipments**

   Various types of equipments are used in stores for storage of materials. Basic commonly used storage equipments—Racks (Steel or wooden, open or closed types), Bins of various sizes, Tote boxes (pans), Pallets, Stands of various sizes.

   (*i*) **Racks.** Open racks are used for packed or bottled materials, while closed rocks are used for loose material and nuts, bolts, spares etc.

   (*ii*) **Tote Pans.** These are suitable for storing small items.

   (*iii*) **Pallets.** Flat pallets are used for bags, boxed and regular shaped heavy items. Box pallets or Post pallets (provided with 4 posts) are suitable for all types of irregular shaped items.

   (*iv*) **Stands.** 'A' type stands are suitable for storing bars and tubes, sheets or plates etc. Other design of stands are fabricated depending upon the type of material.

   (*v*) **Steel Almirah Cabinets.** These are suggested for expensive items or items which are affected by dust or open air.

   (*vi*) **Bins.** These are commonly used for storing items of general nature.

2. **Store Handling Equipments.**

   Unnecessary handling should be avoided and all manual handling requiring too much physical strain must be mechanised. Such material handling equipments are two tier trollies, four wheel trollies, two wheel hand trucks, lift trucks, small mobile jib cranes, roller conveyor, chutes etc., which do not use automotive power are adopted for transporting smaller stores.

   In large stores, equipments with automotive powers are commonly used. Some of the commonly used such equipments are—fork lift trucks, mobile crane, gantry cranes, powered belt, roller or chain conveyers, elevators etc.

24.20. PROTECTION OF STORES

The protection of stores from fire, rust and corrosion, dust, theft, weather, heat, cold and moisture is an important aspect of the store-keeping function. Each kind of material such as textiles, rubber goods, leather goods and metals require its own kind of care. The following points should be remembered in this connection :

1. **To Protect Goods from Fire.** It is essential to store them in fire-proof buildings and bins with adequate automatic sprinkler provision. Adequate fire-fighting equipment such as high pressure water lines, modern sprinkler system, suitable chemical extinguishers, fire pails, sand etc. should be provided. A clean, orderly store-room is less likely to contain oil range and other substances susceptible to spontaneous combustion.

   For certain classes of goods as oils etc. foamite sprinklers should be supplied. Gasoline and fuel oil should be stored in under-ground tanks. Explosives, such as blasting powder and dynamite, should be stored at a distance from all other buildings in store houses used for other purpose.

2. **To Protect Goods from Damage by Dust.** Storage should be in boxes or in closed

cabinets. In city areas, where there is considerable dust in the atmosphere, air conditioned storage areas may prove advisable for such materials. Writing paper, electronic goods and finished textile goods are samples of goods requiring special protection from dust.

3. **Protection Against Weather Conditions.** Materials whose bulk and nature require that they be stored out of doors, can be protected by open sheds or by textiles or by plastic coverings.
4. **Protection Against Deterioration.** Some materials deteriorate with age. Such materials should not be over-stocked and a first in first out storage system should be adopted. Another form of deterioration is the damage which may result from improper materials handling, the adoption of most suitable containers, handling equipment and methods can do much *to* reduce this source of damage.
5. **Protection Against Theft.** Protection against theft can be insured by locking the store room and excluding all persons not directly concerned with the receipt and issue of stores. Stores should be issued only on the authority of proper signed requisitions.

24.21. INTER-RELATIONSHIP

The main function of the stores department is to fulfil the requirements of manufacturing shops in the most effective and economical way. In order to achieve these objects it has to perform the following main functions :

1. To see that the stock of no item at any time falls below the / prescribed minimum or goes in excess of fixed maximum quantity.
2. To examine carefully all goods and materials on receipt.
3. To arrange for a systematic and efficient storing of materials. ,
4. To maintain accurate and prompt distribution of all items to departments as and when required under Issue Requisition Notes.
5. To maintain efficient quantity records of movement of stock and to account for all goods that have come under their charge.
6. To prevent any theft, wastage or deterioration of stock.

Mostly all the shop's requirements are sent to purchase department through stores department, where it is firstly checked, that the same materials are in the stock or not. If purchases are to be made, the quantity required to be purchased is decided by the experience of previous records, and demand initimate to purchase department. Thus with the help of stores, purchases are made economically.

In order to keep effective and smooth supply to the manufacturing shops, following facts must be noted to control stores :

1. Ready record of all materials and store purchases should be made.
2. A best system of pricing the materials for the purpose of cost accounting should be introduced.
3. Material should be arranged in a systematic way in racks and bins and materials may be known by symbols, to make handling very easy.
4. To safeguard the materials lying in stores.
5. Each section of the store has sufficient allotting space. The material is to be arranged in such a way that inward and outward movement of supplies can be carried out smoothly.

Thus, a store department helps the costing department by maintaining the proper record for the receipt and issue of material and noting the price to be charged for the material issued.

24.22. PHYSICAL VERIFICATION (STOCK-TAKING)

Various records are kept for maintaining the receipt and issue of materials such as store receipt book, store issue register, bin cards, store ledger and issue indents etc. So as to avoid theft or errors in accounts of stores, a set procedure known as stack taking or physical verification is adopted.

The various common errors which can be found in stores are :

1. Clerical mistakes.
2. Improper storage
3. Pilferage.
4. Leakage, losses etc.
5. Careless handling.
6. Loss in handling.

Generally, the following two methods are used to check these above mentioned errors :

(a) Annual Physical Verification
(*b*) Perpetual Inventory Control.

1. **Annual Physical Verification.** In this, an independent person of a high rank known as verifying officer checks the stock lying in a store once in a year, so as to see that the quantities as shown in store-ledger, bin cards and actually available in bins tally each other. After verification, verifying officer submits a list of shortages, excess and comments about damaged, surplus, obsolete and unserviceable stores.

   In this method checking is started at one part of the store-room and make the round of all the stores, checking all the items in a certain number of bins each day and comparing them with the balance shown on the bin bards and in the stores ledger. In the larger companies one or two men or as many as may be required by the particular business to be engaged continuously in counting materials on hand. In this method at the end of the year, the plant is shut down and in a few days complete chekcing is done. The advantage of this method is that a thorough check of all the work is performed at a time and all the discrepancies are known as collectively.

2. **Perpetual Inventory Control.** This is a perpetual of continous check throughout the year in such a way that each item is checked at least once. In this system, the material is checked as it reaches to its minimum level. This can be performed by the store-keeper or somebody else specially engaged for this task as he notices, that the balance on the bin card has reached the minimum. Special provision is made for checking items which have not reached their minimum during a period.

   The advantage of this method is that the production need not to be shut down for some time. Only minimum quantities are counted, weighed etc., therefore, less labour and time is taken. This method is comparatively more accurate.

   This method is very suitable for larger firms having huge quantities of different materials. If annual physical verfication is done in such plants, complete shut down of the plant may produce large losses to the owner. Therefore, for small plants which takes hardly few days for complete checking, 'Annual Physical Verification' is done. In such plants necessity of shuting down the plant also does not arise, as daily issues and receipts are not much.

QUESTIONS

1. What are the functions of purchase organisation?
2. Explain the different methods of purchasing.
3. Describe purchasing procedure to be adopted for a medium size industry.
4. Describe the system of purchase of equipment and stores in an industry. How would you ensure the supplies to be of good quality at competitive rates?
5. Write short notes on :
   (*i*) Earned Money,
   (*ii*) Security Deposit,
   (*iii*) Specifications,
   (*iv*) Tender and Quotations,
   (*v*) Bill of Material,
   (*vi*) Purchase contracts.
6. Outline a system of stock control and purchasing suitable for a concern engaged on mass manufacture of a light engineering product.
7. What are the different methods of purchasing generally followed by industrial firms ? What are the different steps in the procurement cycle?
8. How should the Purchase department arrange the supply of items from
   (*i*) foreign market and
   (*ii*) Home market ?
9. (*i*) Explain the functions of the purchase department in a light engineering concern.
   (*ii*) Explain in detail the procedure of purchasing a machine tool from a foreign supplier.
10. (*i*) What important policy decisions a purchase manager must make in planning his purchases?
    (*ii*) Formulate a model procedure of purchase to achieve timely delivery, economy and satisfaction to the vendor.
11. Distinguish between
    (*i*) Purchase requisition and
    (*ii*) Purchase by tender.
12. Explain how specification and standards contribute to product quality.
13. What are the main functions of the store organisation? What are the advantages of good store-keeping and how do they effect the ultimate production cost?
14. Write the duties of store-keeper in a medium size general purpose workshop ?
15. What is the importance of good store-keeping ?
16. What are the different types of stores and where they are to be located
17. What are the various records maintained in the stores ? Explain them briefly.
18. How the material should be stored in stores ?
19. Describe the procedure for the receipt of materials into the stores and their issue from there.
20. How fuels, lubricants, machine parts and tools are kept and handled in stores ?
21. Write short notes on the following :

(*i*) Material Returned Note (*ii*) Indent on Stores
(*iii*) Protection of Stores (*iv*) Stock Register
(*v*) Store Ledger (*vi*) Bin Card.

22. Assuming yourself to be an incharge of stores of a manufacturing organisation, discuss what remedial measure you will adopt to minimise the cases of stores run-outs and production hold-ups ?
23. State the duties of the controller of stores and outing a system for effective control of stores. Show the use of any significant ratios for this control.
24. Write short note on :

    Double bin of inventory control.
25. Explain briefly the different types of stores and discuss the advantages of centralised and decentralised stores?
26. What are the different methods of store verification and their advantages and disadvantages?
27. Explain different types of storage equipments.
28. Write brief note on "The 5 R's of purchasing".

    (Note. 5 R's means to procure materials of right quality, in right quantity, from right source, at right time and at right price.)
29. What are the different ways of valuing the material issued from stores? Explain them in brief.
30. Write short notes on :
    (*a*) Receiving inspection.
    (*b*) Inter-relationship of stores department.
    (*c*) Methods of ahieving 'first-in first-out'.
31. What action would you like to take for the protection of stores?

25

MATERIALS MANAGEMENT (M.M.)

25.1. INTRODUCTION

Materials Management is a function, which aims for integrated approach towards the management of materials in an industrial undertaking. Its main object is cost reduction and efficient handling of materials at all stages and in all sections of the undertaking.

Materials Managements functions include several important aspects connected with materials, such as purchasing, storage, inventory control, materials handling, standardisation etc. Hence this subject has become very important and gaining more and more importance.

Even two decades ago the term materials management was little known and understood in the sense in which it is used today. Many terms, like purchasing, store-keeping, material handling etc. were used to denote more or less same meaning as that of materials management, but these terms were unable to give complete idea of materials management.

Materials management covers a very wide field and deals with material costs, its supply, utilisation and handling. It is concerned with the planning and programming of materials and equipment, market research for purchase, procurements of materials (capital goods, raw material, components and semi-finished items), packaging, storage and inventory control, transportation of materials, salvage, material handling, disposal of scrap and surplus etc.

Materials management can also be defined as the functions responsible for the coordination of planning, purchasing, transporting, storing and controlling the materials in an optimum manner, so as to provide a pre-decided service to the customer at a minimum cost.

Thus materials management is a concept that integrates all the activities of planning, scheduling and controlling materials from design through production and including delivery to the customer. Thus it establishes full responsibility over the material flow system with full accountability for quantity, delivery and cost.

25.2. EVOLUTION

25.2.1. Supply Management

The term "purchasing" or "procurement" were originally used, later on this term was replaced by **"supply management"**. While purchasing dealt only purchasing functions, supply management dealt starting from participating in deciding materials specification, value analysis, supplier selection etc. including purchasing activities. Supply managers participate in new product development and are responsible for selecting sources, managing costs, developing and nurturing supplier partnerships and strategic alliances and issuing long-term agreements with carefully selected suppliers.

Supply management has major focus on :

1. To deal with activities that have great potential for impacting the success of the firm, and
2. To be inter-disciplinary in nature and integrate supply actions with those of other important sections of the firm.

Till 1950s, purchase department used to be clerically oriented order-placing unit. Later on, progressive firms started giving managerial emphasis, specialisation and professionalism on purchasing operations. The purchasing function comprises the activities associated with the acquisition of the materials, services and equipment used in operations. In 1970s, it was augmented by an emphasis on longer-range strategic planning for materials.

Since early 1990s, the strategic emphasis has been enhanced by purchasing participation in various cross-functional terms for various activities such as product design, supplier qualification and selection, quality, commodity management. By further accelerating the strategic emphasis, more progressive firms have led to the development of the **Supply management** concept. The supply management is a process responsible for the development and management of a firm's total supply system–both the internal and external.

25.2.2. Materials Management

Now-a-days, "materials management" concept which is different from purchasing/procurement/supply management concepts has emerged and has become popular. This materials management concept is designed to enhance coordination and control of various materials activities.

Materials management provides an integrated systems approach to the coordination of materials activities and the control of total materials cost. All those major activities which contribute to the cost of materials are assigned to the materials management department. The objective of this is to optimise performance of the materials system. Here the materials means raw materials, spare parts, components, factory suppliers, packing materials etc.

25.3. SCOPE (FUNCTIONS) OF MATERIALS MANAGEMENT

Following functions are included under the direction and control of Materials Manager, incharge of materials management department:

1. Materials planning and programming.
2. Purchasing and supply management.
3. Receiving, storekeeping and ware housing.
4. Inventory control.
5. Simplification, codification and standardisation in stores.
6. Transportation.
7. Inspection and Quality control.
8. Materials handling.
9. Value engineering and absolute materials.
10. Disposal of scrap, surplus and obsolete materials.

Looking to the above functions it is clear that Materials Manager has to work in close co-operation with different heads of departments. For example he must co-operate with:

(i) *Production Department for*:

(a) knowing, in how much quantity and at what times materials are required.

(b) inventory control;

(ii) *Sales Department,* for transportation of outgoing material;

(iii) Almost *all the Departments,* for material handling operations throughout the undertaking;

(iv) *Sales and Production Departments,* for the disposal of scrap and surplus;

(v) *Inspection and Quality Control Department,* for getting the incoming materials inspected.

25.4. IMPORTANCE OF MATERIALS MANAGEMENT

A survey conducted by the Directorate of Industrial Statistics during 1954-57 showed that the average materials cost is 64 per cent of the sales value. Thus only 36 per cent costs is for wages and salaries, overhead and profit etc. In some industries it costs upto 70 per cent. These figures themselves show the importance of materials management.

In addition to the cost of material (being 64 per cent), inventory carrying costs, come out to be 20 per cent of the material costs. Inventory carrying cost comprises interest charges on the cost of inventory, storage and material handling costs, costs of insurance, physical deterioration and obsolescence. Thus total material cost will amount to 76.8 or 77 per cent (64 per cent plus 20 per cent of 64 per cent) of the sales revenue.

In countries like Japan, inventory consciousness has proved to reduce materials cost substantially. In the year of application of scientific methods and techniques of materials management, *i.e.,* 1958-a saving of more than 3 per cent could be achieved in a period of merely 18 months. Thus in our country, it is very essential to develop inventory consciousness.

In addition to reduce material costs, efficient materials management is useful for following purposes:

(a) For reducing foreign exchange, by utilising the imported items to their maximum value and thus helps in reducing the imports.

(b) By reducing the cost of finished goods and maintaining the quality, it is possible for Indian manufacturers to compete better in foreign market and earn more foreign exchange.

Uptil now efforts have been made for saving in the wages (wages are about 16 per cent of sales value), which was not liked by the labour class and such steps created the labour problems. But the above facts show that more efforts must be made for the saving in materials cost (about 77 per cent) by utilising the techniques of materials management and that too without creating any labour problem.

Materials management resulted in increased productivity of capital by preventing large amount of capital being locked up for long periods in inventories.

25.5. OBJECTIVES OF MATERIALS MANAGEMENT

Materials management aims at reducing the cost of production so as to help the organisation in maximizing its profit. As objectives of materials management are many, they can be classified into two categories, viz., primary objectives and secondary objectives.

Primary Objectives include :

1. Provisioning of materials in specified quality and quantity at economic cost at specified time.
2. Minimizing investments and costs of inventories and assurance of a high inventory turn-over.

Secondary Objectives mainly include :

1. To reduce materials cost by adopting various techniques such as variety reduction, simplification, standardization, value analysis, inventory control etc.
2. Coordination of such functions as planning and scheduling, storage, upkeep and maintenance of materials, materials handling etc.
3. Ensure uniform flow of materials for production.
4. Ensure right quality at right price.
5. Establish and maintain good relations with suppliers.
6. Economy in using the imported items and to find their substitutes.

25.6. MATERIALS MANAGEMENT AS A SCIENCE

Best of materials should always be available in time to avoid idleness of machines and men. Materials management, therefore, form the key to the productivity of machines and other capital assets and labour, and can contribute considerably towards achieving efficiency, effectiveness and cost reduction. Materials management is responsible for coordination of materials requirement planning, sourcing, purchasing, handling, storing and controlling materials in an optimum manner so as to achieve its objectives.

Materials management is a science in the sense that it adopts a systematic and scientific approach integrated for improving the management process, by adopting :

(*i*) management Science techniques ; like network, quantitative and simulation approach *e.g.* linear, and dynamic programming, queing theory, break-even point theory, Monto Carlo probability theory, equipment replacement theory etc.

(*ii*) scientific Management Information System and electronic computers.

(*iii*) scientific methods of decision making.

(*iv*) Information feed back system for better controlling,

(*v*) Human behavioural Science approaches.

Materials Management is an art also, as it is an application of human skills to utilize the talent of the people, and because it manages human beings to achieve the desired results.

Materials management department, if not managed scientifically and systematically *e.g.* by scientific purchasing, inventory control, entire organisation may lead to losses. Therefore in order to achieve optimum results, this department must adopt scientific, rational and logical approach.

25.7. INTEGRATED MATERIALS MANAGEMENT APPROACH

As explained earlier materials management is a very wide term and covers a wide range of activities. Various functions performed by materials management must be well integrated, otherwise a conflict of interest might arise, in case they function independently. In such a **situation :**

(*a*) Purchase department, in order to avail the discount may buy large quantities without taking into account its impact in inventory carrying costs and warehousing costs.

(*b*) Marketing department may be interested to have a high level of finished goods inventory to satisfy his customer needs.

(*c*) Production department may be interested to have high raw material inventory to achieve an optimum level of machine utilization.

(*d*) Purchase department may be interested to have the materials well in advance to avoid the chance of stockout.

These invidividual interests on inventory level create a lot of problems in the non-liquidity of money and sometimes lead to bankruptcy of financial resources.

In order to sort out these problems "Integrated Materials Management" concept is adopted to take care of needs of all functions, and a close control of inventory is ensured to make use of resources in an optimum way. Inventory carry costs are as high as 25% which means idle resources without any productive use, and an avoidable burden on finances of the enterprise.

An ideal situation of inventory level is 'Just in Time', which is practised in Japan, where only 6 hours inventories are kept. In integrated approach all the departments make efforts to optimize the inventories.

Advantages of Integrated Approach

Integrated materials management approach has following advantages :

1. It ensures better support and cooperation in the accomplishment of materials functions.
2. It creates an atmosphere of trust and better relations between different sections/ departments.
3. This ensures faster and accurate communication.
4. It establishes clear accountability.
5. This helps in evaluating the performance of materials management in an objective manner.
6. This develops team spirit, resulting in better morale and cooperation.
7. This ensures better opportunities for growth and development of the organisation.

25.8. ORGANISATION OF MATERIALS MANAGEMENT

In order to fulfil the objectives laid down for the materials management department by following the organizational principles and the corporate objectives, an appropriate organisation structure is necessary. The organisation aims at better division of work, reasonable authority and responsibility, span of control and favourable working environment.

The position of the materials management department in any organisation depends upon type of industry, variety and volume of materials. Present trend is to have an integrated materials management department, or some times simply known as materials department, headed by General Manager Materials with the purchase manager, stores manager inventory control manager, materials planning manager, cost reduction and value engineering manager etc. Integrated materials management concept helps in coordination of interrelated activities.

Aims : Aims of the materials management organisations are :

1. To help in effective functioning of the enterprise by providing smooth materials flow.
2. To provide coordination between different functionaries in the department itself as well as with other departments of the enterprise.

3. To avoid all types of delays, wastages and spoilages.
4. Reduction in operational costs.

Types of Organizational Structures

Organizational structure of materials management department may be based on :

(*i*) Commodities

(*ii*) Functions

(*iii*) Locations.

1. **Organisation Based on Commodities.**

In this type, materials are generally classified as; raw materials, consumables, fuels, imported items, spare parts, bought-out components etc. or as electrical items, cement, steel, chemical items, spare parts, consumables, machine tools, fuels. These classes of materials can further be sub classified, *e.g.*, raw materials as ferrous items, non-ferrous items or consumables as greases, lubricants etc.

2. **Organisation Based on Functions**

In this type of organisation, materials management department is divided into sections based on functions like; purchase, stores, inventory control, materials planning, materials handling (or transport),.value engineering and cost reduction etc. These sections are further sub divided into sub-sections based on functions like, purchase section into source development, vendor evaluation, tendering, evaluation and issue of orders, follow-up, importation, procurement of capital equipment, spares procurement etc. whereas stores section can be subdivided into receipts, issues, and custody.

3. **Organisation Based on Locations**

When an enterprise has more than one plant located in different locations, they can have either centralized materials management department at the headquarters or decentralized set-up at each location.

(*a*) **Centralized Set-up**

By establishing a centralized materials management department the enterprise can have the advantage of specialized expertise, bulk supply order to get quantity discount. This also enables the proper use of resources, standardization of policies, uniformity of procedures. In such a set-up, however materials are stored only at the user plant. This can be done by making the specific plant as consignee in the purchase order itself to avoid rehandling of the materials.

However this system may have following **draw backs:**

(*i*) delay in procurement

(*ii*) large efforts required by user unit in follow-up

(*iii*) more stock—out chances resulting in emergency procurement.

(*iv*) requires lot of efforts by user departments to interact with the purchase department at headquarters.

In this type of set-up more attention should be given on following points :

(*i*) complete specifications of materials should be given in the requisition by user department.

(*ii*) planned indents should be given well in time to avoid emergency/urgent indents.

(*iii*) all instructions related to supply be mentioned at the time of placing the indent, so as to avoid last minute changes, cancellations and postponements.

Generally this type of set-up is preferred in multi-product, multi-unit enterprises, where centralized purchasing is done in respect of key items, referred as 'A' items (refer ABC analysis in the chapter on 'Inventory Management' in the book) and those for capital equipment.

(*b*) **Decentralized Set-Up**

In this set-up each unit is made responsible for purchases for its own use. Some enterprises may even make each department responsible for purchases of their own requirements. The advantages of this system are :

(*i*) Materials manager of local unit, being at the local spot shall be more committed and have better knowledge of the needs of his unit.

(*ii*) Local materials manager will have better knowledge of local suppliers, transport facilities and warehousing facilities.

(*iii*) It reduces time lost in communication.

(*iv*) Better liaison, coordination and interrelationship.

Since the advantages of one system are the disadvantages of another and *vice-versa,* hence a combination of both is adopted in practice. As pointed out earlier, generally 'A' category items and capital equipments are purchased centrally while other items are left to the local units.

ORGANIZATIONAL CHART

Organizational chart for materials management department is drawn after the organisation set-up for it is designed considering all the relevant factors. It indicates the structural relationship among different functions, and the positions of the personnel. This also indicates the lines of command, *i.e.,* authority and responsibility.

An example of organisation chart of materials management department is shown here, however this can vary depending upon the circumstances.

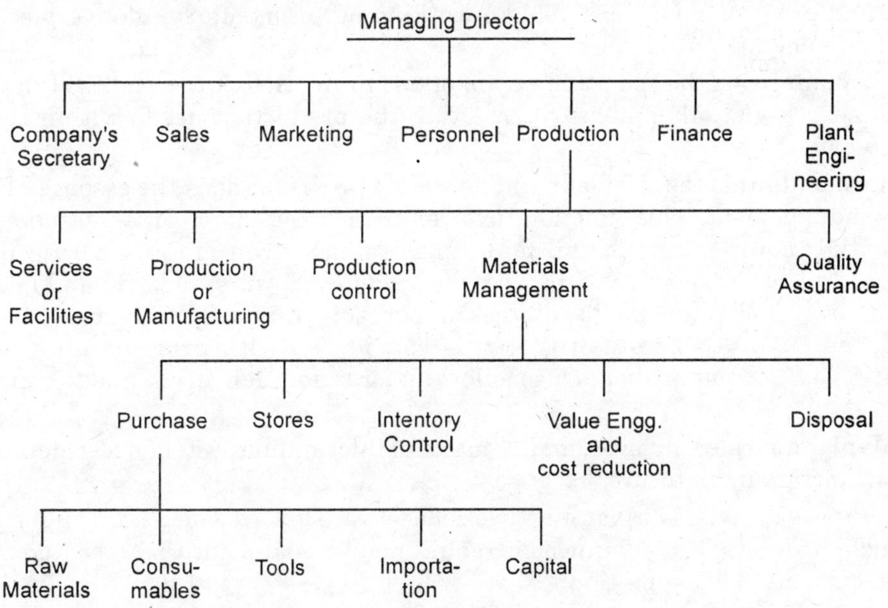

Fig. 25.1.

Inter-Relationship

In any organizational structure designing inter-relationship or interactions has to be considered, whether it may be (*a*) amongst the constituents within the department, and (*b*) with outsiders, may it be within the enterprise or outside the enterprise.

25.9. MATERIALS PLANNING

As planning and controlling are the main functions of a manager, materials planning and budgeting is given a prominent place in the integrated materials management set-up. Planning for materials and working out a realistic budget not only help motivate people but also serve as a control device. As we know that in an enterprise planning is done at all levels of the organisation, as illustrated in the following diagram :

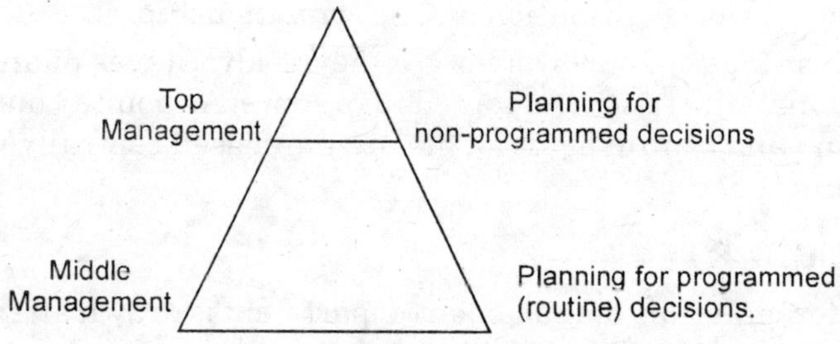

Fig. 25.2.

There are large number of non-programmed decisions in materials planning, such as import policy, foreign exchange availability, credit squeeze etc., which are taken by top management. For routine and programmed decisions like working out economic lot, delivery schedule etc., middle level management are involved.

Materials planning is the scientific way of determining the requirements of raw materials, components, spares and other items for meeting the production needs within the economic investment policies.

Planning of materials requirement and its timely provisioning is the essence of the success of materials management. This function involves the setting up of consumption standards of working out the requirements for all materials for any given manufacturing programme, considering all relevant factors, *i.e.,* make or buy, laying down standards and specifications, sources of supply available, availability of stock, import substitution etc. Lead time, manufacturing schedule, economic ordering quantity etc. is considered with programming for material requirement. The department should also follow-up for timely deliveries, and to expedite in case of emergencies.

Materials planning also involves, maintenance of information system*to* feed details necessary for its better functioning in future.

For the purpose of materials planning two concepts are followed depending upon the category. Direct production materials are planned on 'requirement basis', while the stock items are planned on the basis of norms of consumption.

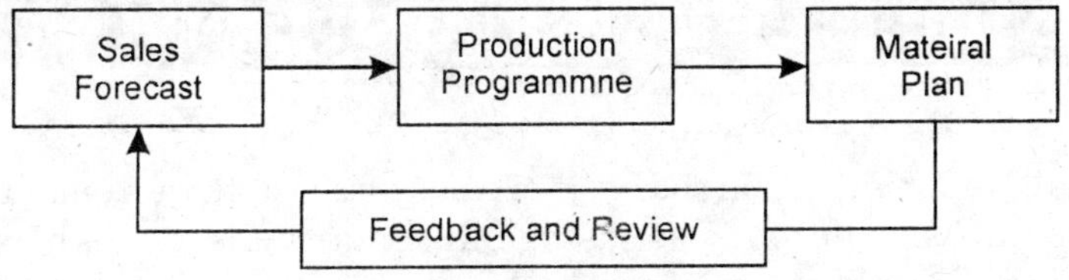

Fig. 25.3. Materials planning.

Thus materials planning function is a sub-system in the overall planning activity of the organisation. Purchase section initiates purchase activities only when they are informed by planning cell about the quantity required, procurement programme, and financial provisioning. Materials requirement and its programming is based on lead time so that delivery is ensured at the right time. Materials planning cell prepares its plan based on the production schedules and bill of materials received from the production control department. Consumable items are planned considering the consumption pattern, minimum and maximum level of inventories. For project works, network techniques are used to arrive at the latest date by which the materials should be received.

Considering the quantum, period of consumption, lead time etc. the purchase section can decide about the procedure for their purchase, *i.e.*, contract buying, or bulk purchase etc.

Factors Governing the Materials Planning

(*A*) **External Factors :** These cover the factors which are related to the overall business activity affecting the internal policy of the organisation towards the materials management.

1. Price trends of the materials in the market.
2. Import policy of the government, for imported materials
3. Prevailing credit policy of the banks.

(*B*) **Internal Factors :** These factors are related to the internal business activities of the firm :

1. Objectives of the organisation on which entire planning including materials planning depends.
2. Production programme and scheduling.
3. Lead time decides the inventory level, in turn which help in planning materials requirement and its programming.
4. Working capital requirements and its availability.
5. Purchasing policy of the enterprise.

Benefits of Materials Planning

(*i*) To ensure that materials and components are available in right quantity at right time.

(*ii*) Reduction in inventory.

(*iii*) Improved customer service because of the adherence to the production schedules.

(*iv*) Quicker response to the change in demand.

(*v*) Better machine utilisation, hence greater productivity and economy.

25.10. TECHNIQUES OF MATERIALS PLANNING

1. **Bill of Materials Explosion.**

   Materials planning is done on the basis of sales forecast. Requirement of various materials are arrived at from sales forecast using bill of materials through explosion charts. Bill of materials indicate materials required for a given component. It also indicates bought-out items and shop made items. Explosion chart is then made by combining all the bills of materials, so as to give the exact materials requirement. Thus materials requirement is determined with the help of explosion charts. Delivery schedules of materials are then prepared considering the production, scheduling and inventory level in the stock and organisation policies for maximum and minimum inventory level. For details about 'bill of materials', refer chapter on 'purchasing'.

2. **Past Consumption Analysis**

   The materials which are consumed continuously and for which no bill of materials are made, like maintenance items, lubricants, fuel etc., past consumption data is analysed and then future projections are made.

25.11. MATERIALS REQUIREMENT PLANNING (M.R.P.)

As we have already discussed, planning of materials requirement and its timely provisioning is the essence of the success of materials management. Before the start of manufacturing process or a service facility, it is necessary to have required materials in hand. If the material is not available in time, entire efforts of starting the manufacturing will go waste. Therefore, materials management department should make prior estimation of materials requirement and proper planning is done, so that right material is available at right time.

M.R.P. can be defined as a computational technique that converts the master schedule for end products into detailed schedule for raw materials and components required for the end product. The detailed schedule identifies the quantities of each raw materials and components. M.R.P. also tells as to when each of these items must be ordered and delivered so as to meet the target of master schedule of the final product.

Materials requirement planning is the scientific way of determining the requirements of raw materials, components, spares and other items required for meeting production needs within the economic investment policies of a productive system.

In manufacturing concerns, the demand for raw materials, components, subassemblies etc. is dependent on the production plan for the final product. Therefore, once we know the production requirements of the final product, it is possible to determine as to how manyparts or components will be needed in each future time period. The production requirements for the final product are determined by the sales forecasts.

The materials requirements are derived directly from the production schedules. Requirement plans normally indicate the production lead time, a planned stock record, and the timing of production order releases phased to take account of production lead times.

Several options are available to satisfy net requirements of the material. It can vary from one extreme when we can manufacture the quantity sufficient to satisfy the requirement for entire planning horizon (season, year or manufacturing order) in single batch, to other extreme when we can manufacture the quantity sufficient to meet only a requirement for a week or so. The cost of holding inventory and cost of set-up must be considered in determining a decision policy. Different options available depend upon the policy which we adopt. These may be :

(*i*) **Lot-for-lot.** In this policy, lot size for a batch is chosen to satisfy the net requirement for a single period.

(*ii*) **Economic Ordering Quantity (EOQ).** In this policy, EOQ is calculated based on expected requirement.

(*iii*) **Period Order Quantity.** In this policy, the lot size is equal to the actual requirements for a predetermined fixed period.

(*iv*) **Part-period Total Cost Balancing.** In this policy, holding costs and set-up costs are balanced as closely as possible for each lot size decision.

Objectives

The objectives of materials requirement planning are :

(*i*) To avoid inventory stockouts so that production runs smoothly, according to plans,

(*ii*) To reduce investment in raw materials and work in process inventories,

(*iii*) Reduction in production and delivery lead times, as it identifies materials and components' quantities, timings, availability and procurement and production actions required to meet delivery deadlines, and by coordinating these actions delay in production can be avoided, and

(*iv*) Realistic delivery promises which can enchance customer satisfaction.

Reactive System of Inventory

Reactive or traditional systems of inventory control is simple to manage, but have serious drawbacks, in particular, high inventory costs and unreliable delivery performance. This planning system is a newer way and is more complex to manage, but it offers several advantages, like reduction in inventory and their associated cost, items are available when needed, carries only those items and components that are needed, reduces order processing delays, setting up realistic job completion dates, completion of jobs on time, order promises are kept and production lead times are shortened.

Therefore M.R.P., being an inventory planning system is more beneficial than reactive systems of inventory control (such as the order quantity, reorder point system). MRP reduces the need for large safety stocks, because we know that how many items will exactly be needed and we do not need to accumulate excessive stocks in advance. Thus MRP is a system of planning and scheduling the time-phased materials requirements for production operations.

Capacity Requirement Planning

Each time the MRP system is updated, it is necessary to ensure that shop capacity is sufficient to implement the current plan. Capacity requirements planning (also known as detailed capacity planning) is a technique that answers this problem.

Thus capacity requirements planning is a process of modifying the Master Production Schedule or planned resources to make capacity consistent with the production schedule.

Earlier inventory control techniques were used for material control, but recently emphasis has been shifted to Material Requirements Planning (M.R.P.) based systems. Conventional techniques of inventory control were not very effective to produce the desired reduction in inventory investments while maintaining high service levels including better capacity utilisation and higher productivity.

Because of not following proper M.R.P., following symptoms are indicated :

(*i*) High incidence of shortages.

(*ii*) Insufficient lead time for procurement.

(*iii*) Receipts have no relationship with actual requirements.

(*iv*) Extremely large inventory investments.

(*v*) Poor inventory turnover.

(*vi*) Last minute adhoc decisions and too much follow-ups at nick of time.

(*vii*) Buck passing and finger pointing.

In these circumstances only solution is to follow proper M.R.P. and develop systems based on more realistic assumption of the prevailing conditions. Some preparations are necessary before starting M.R.P., and good manufacturing support systems should be developed first, for which proper documentation is the first requirement. Based on Master schedule of the manufacturing system, requirement for all the items to be manufactured is determined, and net requirement is calculated considering inventory available, orders in hand for each item and their delivery schedule. Based on these inputs of the master schedule, M.R.P. establishes, maintains and drives priorities for planning, expediting, retarding or cancelling orders.

Guidelines (Pre-requisites) for Launching M.R.P.

For launching M.R.P. in any organisation following pre-requisites are necessary :

(*i*) All inventory items are identified.

(*ii*) Inventory reports containing data on the inventory status of every item is prepared.

(*iii*) A bill of materials, and product manufacturing details are available.

(*iv*) Master schedule of the manufacturing of different products indicating number of end products to be manufactured.

(*v*) Lead times for all inventory items are known or at least estimated considering market position.

Information Sharing

Effective functioning of the M.R.P. system also demands an effective sharing of the information between related departments. Prompt and correct informations sharing with manufacturing, production control, marketing, inventory control departments are necessary.

Top management should take interest in M.R.P. system, as its efficiency or failure both effects the entire organisation's working, increases the avoidable expenses in idle time for man, machine or purchase of items at higher rates at nick of time for fulfilment of delivery schedules thereby affecting the reputation of the organisation.

25.11.1. SPARE PARTS PLANNING

Although spare parts management is a part of material management, but since it requires special attention due to its typical problems, this is being discussed separately in these paragraphs.

Machines worth crores of Rupees are generally idle, for want of spares, while crores of rupees are locked in obsolete items. This emphasizes the need of paying more attention on management of spares. Improvement in the capacity utilisation and cost reduction can be achieved by better spare parts management.

Objective of Spare Parts Management is to provide right parts in right quantity, in right place at the right time and at the right cost.

A spare part can be defined as parts identical to the parts of a machine which needs replacement due to wear and tear during the operating life of equipment.

Spare parts management is discussed separately.

SOLVED EXAMPLES

Example 25.1. *Product structure of an end-product P is shown in following figure. What are the requirements of various lower level items for producing 100 units of P.*

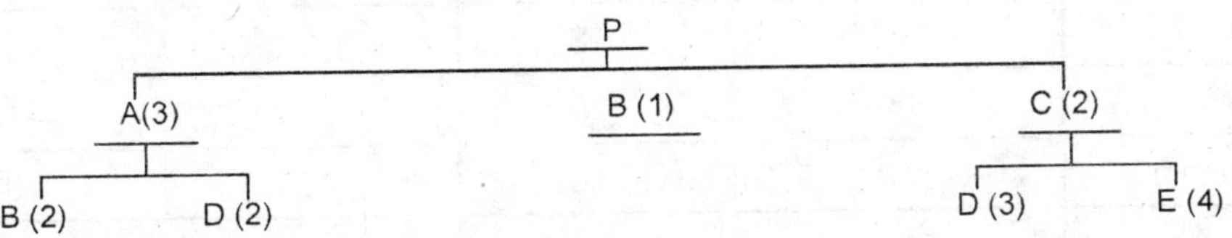

Solution :

Above diagram shows that :

(i) For producing each unit of end product *P*, we require 3 numbers of A, 1 number of *B*, and 2 numbers of *C*.

(ii) For producing each unit of *A*, we require 2 numbers of *B* and 2 numbers of *D*.

(iii) Each unit of *C* requires 3 units of *D* and 4 units of *E*.

Therefore, for producing one unit of *P*, we require

(a) $A = 3$ numbers.

(b) $B = 1 + (3 \times 2) = 7$ numbers

(c) $C = 2$ numbers

(d) $D = (3 \times 2) + (2 \times 3) = 12$ numbers

(e) $E = (2 \times 4) = 8$ numbers.

For producing 100 numbers of *P* ; requirements of various lower level items are as under.

$A = 100 \times 3 = 300$

$B = 100 \times 7 = 700$,

$C = 100 \times 2 = 200$

$D = 100 \times 12 = 1200$

$E = 100 \times 8 = 800$.

Example 25.2. *If the lead time for various items in previous example are illustrated as shown below, find out the time schedule of the requirement of these items for shipping out the 100 units of product P on day 8. Specially as to when an item is required and when an order for its production procurement is to be placed and in what quantities.*

P. Lead Time (LT) = 2

A (3), LT = 1 B (1), LT = 3 C (2), LT = 2

B (2), LT = 3 D (2), LT = 3 D (3), LT = 3 E (4), LT = 1

Solution. If 100 units *P* are to be shipped out on day 8, considering its lead time of 2 days needed for assembling (or producing) it from *A*, *B* and C, the order for assembling of *P* should therefore be placed two days prior to day 8, *i.e.*, on day 6.

Similarly, other calculations are done in the tabular form as shown below :

Item	*Requirement*		*Lead Time*	*Release of order on day*
	Quantity	*On day*		
P	100	8	2	8 – 2 = 6
A	300	6	1	6 – 1 = 5
B (for P)	100	6	3	6 – 3 = 3
(for A)	600	5	3	5 – 3 = 2
C	200	6	2	6 – 2 = 4
D (for A)	600	5	3	5 – 3 = 2
(for C)	600	4	3	4 – 3 = 1
E	800	4	1	4 – 1 = 3

Above table shows summarised production plans. In this problem it was assumed that the items were produced as and when required. This type of production plan is called lot-for-lot production.

25.12. MANUFACTURING RESOURCE PLANNING (MRP II)

Manufacturing resource planning, also known as MRP II or closed loop MRP is an integrated information system that steps beyond first generation MRP to synchronize all aspects of the business. It (MRP II system) coordinates sales, purchasing, manufacturing, finance and engineering by adopting a focal production plan and by using one unified data base to plan and update the activities in all the systems of business.

This means, the MRP II involves developing a production plan from the business to specify monthly production levels. Since the production is then expected to produce this committed level, sales department to sell at these levels, and the finance department to ensure adequate financial resources for these levels, all these functional departments develop these production levels by consensus.

Marketing manager, production manager and finance manager may meet monthly to update sales forecasts and revise the master schedule. Top managers of all these three departments decide the product mix, aggregate production plans, financial requirements, and pricing strategies.

Therefore, MRP II provides help for coordinating the efforts of manufacturing, finance, marketing, engineering and personal departments towards the common business plan. Managers of these departments also analyse the problems, determine the alternative solutions, and take a final decision, they also evaluate the implications of their decisions.

25.13. JUST-IN-TIME (JIT) PHILOSOPHY

JIT means a structural approach in a manufacturing organisation focussed on improving timeliness, quality, productivity and flexibility utilising various methods of work simplification and waste elimination. The company following the JIT philosophy want to do work systematically, remove excess work, eliminate waste, unevenness and unreasonableness and thereby raise their productivity.

JIT concept when applied results in smaller set-up costs which justifies smaller lot sizes and provide greater flexibility for changeovers from one product to another. Companies adopting JIT concept found improvement in productivity, reducing set–up–time, reducing inventory, improving quality, saving space and reducing lead times. Reduction in economical batch sizes lead to reduction in-process inventory.

Importance of JIT

Just-in-time is not just an inventory reduction programe or **kanban**, or material requirement planning, or a production control technique. It is a corporate strategic philosophy and aims at **elimination of waste.**

NOTE : Kanban is a Japanese word meaning signal. A kanban is a card or a tag usually attached to work-in-process parts, and it is used to facilitate the proper movement of these parts. This movement may be within the same manufacturing plant or between plants.

It is based on following factors :

1. Unnecessary complexity in the design of products should be removed for producing it at least cost.
2. Plant layout should be changed to eliminate or shorten material movement and reduce time loss.
3. Provide incentives to workers to tap their knowledge to develop methods of eliminating waste of all forms.
4. People should be accountable for accuracy and institute programmes to measure it.
5. Reduce paper work. Use of on-line, real-time data update and retrievel and interaction decision making is important.
6. Scrap should be completely avoided, as scrap is more costly than mere material.
7. Reduce inventories by eliminating large queues and many kinds of safety stocks. When ordering purchase of parts from vendors, negotiate prices based on long term commitments and then schedule frequent releases to support the flow of production with minimal inventory.
8. In order to strive for continuous improvement, set goals and when they are achieved, set them higher.

Benefits

JIT leads to productivity improvement in the following ways :

— Smaller lot size inventories.

— Smaller buffer inventories.

— Less indirect cost in inventories.

— Less space for inventories.

— Less equipment to handle inventories.

— Less inventory accounting

— Less physical inventory control effort

— Less scrap

— Less direct labour wasted on rework.

— Reduction in delays and scrap also improve market response.

— Because of speedy changeover, reduces production lead times, better delivery dates can be promised, as the product mix and quantities can be changed quickly as demand and forecasts of demand change.

For reduction in in-process inventories use of *Kanban* is very helpful.

Applications

JIT Purchasing. : JIT purchasing emphasises on supplying materials just in time for use on factory floor, equally important are the close relationships with suppliers on long-term basis who are geographically close for frequent deliveries of small and exact quantities. For the success of JIT, cooperation from the company's vendors is essential. In this concept vendors are virtually an extension of the company. JIT vendors have to deliver goods to production line at the required time ; which may be quite frequent — say every 3 or 4 hours. In view of this JIT purchase agreements need be simple, specifying price, specifications, and an overall quantity to be delivered in accordance with long-term production schedules. The specifications are focused on product performance rather than being highly detailed.

The objective of this system alongwith*Kanban* is to have right number of parts or components at the right place at the right time.

JIT Production System. In this concept, factory produces the required goods only at the times when they are needed in the quantity that is needed, and in this situation the inventory of the finished goods and work in progress would be almost zero. If we make raw material suppliers also agree to deliver their goods only at a time in quantities we need them, then we are almost eliminating raw materials as well. In such a situation we shall have near zero inventories.

In this system, workers go to the preceding process to withdraw the required parts or components for their operations using the *Kanban* system. If there are fluctuations in the rates of which these materials are withdrawn, then the preceding process must hold buffer in-process inventories to give off the shelf service. This require minimising production fluctuations on the final assembly line by scheduling small lots of individual models.

In JIT production processes are so designed that it need less specialisation of workers, and the physical layout is so arranged that a worker can operate two or three different machines for providing flexibility in processes. The organisation of multi functional workers have following benefits :

(*i*) A decrease in the number of workers required, resulting in increase in productivity.

(*ii*) Increased worker satisfaction because of more broadly defined jobs.

JIT Implementation Methods

1. **Autonomation.** This means "autonomous defects control" or worker controlled quality control. Although **JIT** systems control production quantities, the production flow would be interrupted if the items delivered were defective. The **autonomation** system is designed to ensure that, theoretically 100 percent good units flow to subsequent operations.
2. **Self Discipline.** For the success of **JIT** systems, positive human relations is most essential. Here each worker is his own boss, as he produces and checks his own work and ensures zero defectives in his output that is sent to the next process in line.
3. **Waste and its Elimination.** Anything other than the minimum amount of plant, material, parts, energy, space, and people's time which are absolutely essential to add value to the product or service, is *waste.* Cost reduction can be achieved through eliniination of wasteful operations. There are many types of wastes which need elimination are : storage, material handling, set-up time,inspection, expediting, machine

breakdowns, paper work, over-production, queuing (or waiting), unnecessary stock, idle time, idle cash, motion without work, talent misuse etc. All these add cost, without adding value.

4. **Good Housekeeping.** Workplace should be organised with a purpose and to attain unidirectional flow of process. "5-S" principles as discussed earlier should be followed.
5. **Poka-Yoke (Fool proofing):** As discussed earlier **Poka-Yoke** is designing the work process to eliminate human mistakes.

25.14. SUPPLY CHAIN

We have discussed in the beginning of this chapter about "supply management". The main task of supply management is to develop and manage the "supply chain".**Supply chain** is responsible for ensuring that the right materials, services and technology are purchased from the right source, at the right time, in the right quality.

This supply chain is the upstream portion of the organisation's **value chain.** The value chain is a series of organizations extending to the firms which extract materials from mother earth performing a series of value-adding activities and fabricate the finished good or service puchased by the ultimate consumer.

Once a service or comodity is identified as critical for the organisation's operations, a strategic supply plan must be developed.

A cross-functional team, under the leadership of a supply professional is involved in the selection of the desired supplier, negotiation of applicable terms and conditions. This supply professional must be both technically and commercially competent.

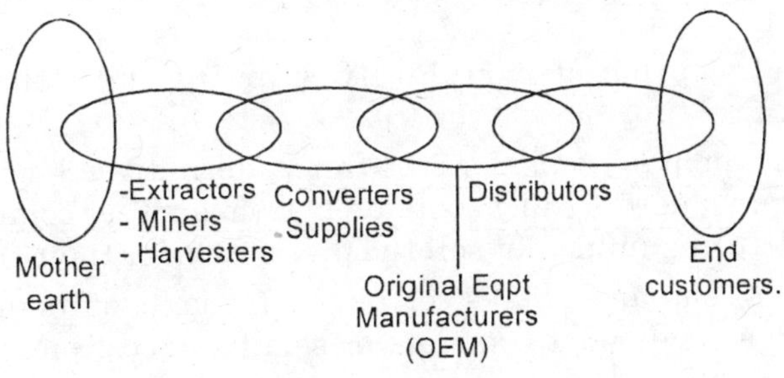

Fig. 25.4. Supply chain.

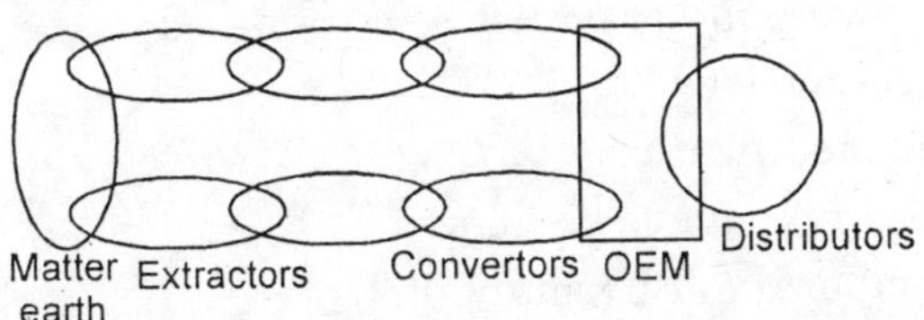

Fig. 25.5. Supply chain network (with value chain).

Vendors	Traditional Suppliers	Certified Suppliers	Partnership type suppliers	Strategic alliance with suppliers

Fig. 25.6. Stages in supply relationship

25.15. MAKE OR BUY DECISIONS

Make or buy is a valid consideration in any cost reduction or product improvement programme. Advantages and disadvantages of possible alternatives should be evaluated and the choice that identifies the minimum cost makes for the final decision.

Make. It requires appropriate production equipment, suitable personnel, material, adequate space, supervisions, design standards and overheads, maintenance, taxes, insurances, management attention and other indirect and hidden costs.

It also provide work for idle equipment and personnel, utilise scrap material specification and experimentation. It ensures continuity of supply, may cost less than purchase and keep design and research information secret.

Buy. Permits lower investment in facilities, smaller labour force, less handling, lower plant cost for building and upkeep, less overhead or taxes, insurance and supervision and less problems of man-management relations.

Buy permits specialisation, allows manufacture by most efficient equipment, lowers inventories, change of design without loss of investment in equipment or inventory, obtaining best price and product by supplies more varied experience and encourages growth of ancillaries.

Whether to make or buy is sometimes referred as a purchasing function. Though the decision whether to make components in ones own factory or to buy them from market is a top management policy matter.

Theoretically, a company has a choice of three alternatives before starting for a new product.

1. Purchase the product complete from a contracted manufacturer.
2. Purchase some components and materials, and manufacture and assemble the balance in its own plant.
3. Manufacture the product completely, starting with the extraction of basic raw-materials.

In practice, almost no company considers the third alternative. Some companies choose the first alternative and obtain a new product completely from another company. These companies usually have no manufacturing units, but sell the product under their trade marks.

But generally, most of companies make certain components of its product and buy others. The companies may buy a component complete or semifinished from outside or buy the raw material.

Before taking a decision to purchase from outside, in case, the product was being manufactured at the company's works, following factors must be considered :

1. What quantities are involved ?
2. Will drawings need modification ?
3. Whether jigs, tools, and gauges be loaned ?
4. Will demand be temporary or permanent ?
5. Will demand fluctuate ?
6. Are special manufacturing techniques involved ?
7. Is there any question of secrecy ?
8. Is there a likely market elsewhere ?
9. Are frequent design changes likely ?
10. Arrangement for inspection, sampling etc.
11. Retention of own production personnel.

12. Whether notice of termination is required ?

If it is decided that the part must be manufactured in company's own plant, in case the part is previously purchased from outside, following factors must be considered :

1. Are patents or copy rights involved ?
2. If so, what are the royalties ?
3. Have the best prices been obtained ?
4. Are the quantities optimized ?
5. Is the previously contracted firm already making something similar which could be added to the new item, thus reducing production costs ?
6. Techniques of production may be special.
7. Is raw material readily available ?
8. Is free issue material to be provided ?
9. Will any tax be involved ?

Criteria For Make or Buy Decision

As already discussed that companies prefer own manufacturing, and buying only raw material or semifinished parts in case of new product. Such decision is made in the following cases :

1. Finished product can be made cheaper by the firm than by outside suppliers.
2. Finished product is manufactured by limited number of outside firms, which are unable to meet the demand.
3. The part has an importance for the firm, and requires extremely close quality control.
4. The part can readily be manufactured with the existing facilities and the company have manufacturing experience.
5. Requires high investment on facilities, which are not already available at supplier's plant.
6. Has a demand that is both stable and relatively large.

Companies will usually buy a finished part from an outside supplier when :

1. They do not have facilities to make it and there are other profitable opportunities for investing company's capital.
2. Existing facilities can be used more economically to make other parts.
3. The skill of personnel employed by the company is not readily adopted to make the part.
4. Patent or other legal barriers prevent the company for making the part.
5. Demand for the part is either temporary or seasonal.

Analysis For Make-Buy Decisions

There are three types of analysis :

1. Simple cost analysis
2. Economic analysis
3. Break-even-point analysis.

1. **Simple Cost Analysis**

   A make or buy cost analysis involves a determination and comparison of the cost to make the part and the cost to buy it. The final make or buy decision must be based on a careful weighing of the cost considerations and various qualitative considerations. The most difficult make-buy factors to assess are those that will significantly be affected by changes in economic conditions, technological advancement, growth of the firm, or changes in the labour-management in the near future. Studies show that more mistakes are made in making what could be more profitable to buy than in buying what could more profitable to be made.

The other two methods of analysis are being discussed in the chapter on "Inventory Management".

QUESTIONS

1. Explain the importance of Material Management.
2. Explain the different functions of Material Management department.
3. What is material handling? Suggest some steps to reduce the material handling cost.
4. To make or Buy decision, what factors are involved? Explain.
5. Explain the criteria for Make or Buy decision.
6. Explain two analysis for making a decision regarding Make or Buy.
7. Describe in detail the procedure and personnel involved in Make or Buy decision.
8. What is materials management? Write an essay on "evolution of materials management".
9. What are the objectives of materials management? Explain.
10. Write short notes on
    (*a*) Integrated materials management approach.
    (*b*) Characteristics of good materials management.
    (*c*) Materials management as a science.
11. Compare and contrast "supply management" and "materials management".
12. Write short notes on
    (*a*) Scope of materials management.
    (*b*) Advantages of integrated materials management approach.
13. What is materials planning? Explain the different techniques of materials planning.
14. Explain the factors governing materials planning.
15. What is MRP? Explain. What are the pre-requisites for launching MRP?
16. Explain the term.
    (*a*) Manufacturing resource planning (MRP II).
    (*b*) Capacity requirement planning.
17. What is 'Just-in-time philosophy'? Explain JIT production planning.
18. What is 'supply chain'? Explain in detail.

26

INVENTORY MANAGEMENT

26.1. INTRODUCTION

An effective management is necessary to ensure adequate supplies at optimum cost. The study of all the categories of inventory is carried out in detail with regard to its size and frequency of the various orders that must be placed. Additional controls must be exercised on higher value stocks.

Since inventory is money, and makes a heavy demand of working capital, it requires special attention to inventory control.

Inventory

Inventory can be defined as follows:

(*i*) Inventory is a detailed list of movable goods.

(*ii*) Inventory is a physical stock of items that a business or production enterprise keeps in hand for efficient running of affairs or its production.

(*iii*) Inventory is the quantity of goods, raw materials or other resources that are idle at any given point of time.

(*iv*) Usable but idle resource.

Inventories consist of raw materials, component parts, supplies or finished assemblies etc. which are purchased from an outside source, and the goods manufactured in the enterprise itself. In simple words, 'inventories' refer to stocks held by the firm.

When the demand for commodities increases, the inventory level decreases, while with the replenishment the inventory level increases. However changes in the demand for a commodity are not under the control of the firm, but the amount and time of replenishment is controllable.

Inventories are of following **types:**

1. **Production Inventories.** Raw materials, parts and components which enter the firm's product in the production process.
2. Maintenance, repair, and operating supplies which are consumed but do not become part of the product.
3. **In-process Inventories.** Semi-finished products found at various stages of the production operation.
4. **Finished Goods Inventories.** Completed products ready for shipment.

Inventory v/s Stores

The words, inventory and stores are some times confused, these must therefore be clearly understood. Stores means all those articles which are kept in store, while inventory comprises stores as well as materials in transit, materials in process, finished products and stock lying at company's show rooms and at distribution centres which have not been sold out.

Need for Inventory

Inventories in a business serve as the suspension system of an automobile. Ups and downs in sales are absorbed by inventory of finished goods. It enables a constant rate of production for the firm, even if the source of supply are not too reliable, may be due to power shortage, transport problem, labour unrest etc.

There are five reasons why a firm carries inventories :

(*i*) To gain economies in purchasing beyond current requirements.
(*ii*) To level out production cycles by producing to inventory.
(*iii*) To carry a reserve in order to prevent stock-out or lost sales.
(*iv*) To maintain service stocks while replacement stocks are in transit.
(*v*) Protection against variations in demand.

Thus an inventory helps in maintaining production rate and lowering manufacturing costs. A company can have substantial savings by using a rational procedure for inventory management. These savings are realised in several forms, depending on the particular situation. Some of the common sources of such savings are :

(*i*) lower purchase cost,
(*ii*) lower interest expenses,
(*iii*) increase in the availability of internal funds.
(*iv*) lower operating costs (clerical, expediting, transportation, receiving etc.),
(*v*) dependable delivery schedules, and
(*vi*) better customer service in the supply of goods.

But keeping inventory also leads to :

(*a*) Blocking working capital.
(*b*) Occupying space.
(*c*) Increasing risks of obsolescence, spoilage, theft, pilferage etc.
(*d*) Increasing maintenance and preservation costs.
(*e*) Increasing insurance premium etc.

26.2. TYPES OF INVENTORIES

Inventories can be classified in two ways, namely : (*i*) according to needs, (*ii*) according to the functions.

1. **Classification According to Needs**

(*a*) *Economic lot Inventories:* Since there is a fixed cost in ordering, hence it is economical to order beyond the immediate needs and divide the fixed ordering costs among a larger number of units. In addition, the manufacturer, from whom purchases are made, gains from producing and shipping in large quantities, and a portion of this gain can be passed on to the purchaser through quantity discount.

(*b*) *Fluctuation or Stabilizing Inventories:* Since it is not always possible to match the timing of production and sales, some inventories are accumulated due to the time lag between production and sales. Since demand is also not accurately predicted, some reserve stocks are necessary. These safety stocks are fluctuation or stabiliz-ing inventories.

(c) *Anticipation Inventories:* These inventories are required to meet (*i*) seasonal demand and are produced and stocked throughout the year in order to meet high demand during the season, (*ii*) the high demand during promotion programmes launched by the firm, and (*iii*) the demand during temporary shut down of the plant for repair or maintenance.

(d) *Transportation Inventories:* These are also known as transit inventories. These are (*i*) raw materials and supply inventories which are in transit and have already been paid for, and (*ii*) finished goods despatched to buyer and payments of which not received.

2. Classification As Per Functions

(a) *Production Inventories:* Raw materials, parts, and components required during the production process are called production inventories.

(b) *Maintenance, Repair, and Operation (M.R.O.) Inventories:* These items are consumed in production process and do not become a part of product, *e.g.*, lubricating oils, fuels, spare parts etc.

(c) *Inprocess Inventories:* These are the items which are semi-finished and are waiting for their turn at work place for further processing.

(d) *Finished Product Inventories:* These are the finished goods and are completed products ready for sale.

(e) *Materials in transit Inventories:* As discussed at 1 (*d*) above.

26.3. SYMPTOMS OF POOR INVENTORY MANAGEMENT

Following are the symptoms of poor inventory management

1. High rate of order cancellations.
2. Excessive machine down-time due to materials shortages.
3. Periodic lack of adequate storage space.
4. Large scale inventories written-down because of price declines, distress sales, disposal of obsolete or slow moving items.
5. Widely varying rate of inventory losses.
6. Large written-downs at the time of physical inventory taking.
7. Continuous growing inventory quantities.
8. Inability to meet delivery schedules.
9. Uneven production rate.

26.4. A SYTEMS APPROACH FOR INVENTORY MANAGEMENT

This approach emphasises that inventory should be managed by developing and then following proper systems. The inventories should be viewed in terms of the total system of production and marketing. The aim of the systems approach is to reduce the size of inventories without destroying their effectiveness .

Following are some of the steps in this regard.

1. Better forecasting/material planning.
2. Fewer varieties.
3. Centralised inventories.
4. Developing a batch of reliable vendors to cater to the needs of a variety of items ensuring the right quantity, in right place and particularly at right time.
5. Effective follow up.
6. Control through reports at a regular frequency.
7. Effective budgetary control.
8. Following the scientific tools, like "Economic Order Quantity", "Selective Control Techniques" etc.

26.5. INVENTORY CONTROL

Inventory control is the means by which material of the corrent quantity and quality is made available as and when required with due regard to economy in storage and ordering costs, and working capital.

It may also be defined "as the systematic location, storage and recording of goods in such a way that desired degree of service can be made to the operating shops at minimum ultimate cost".

The Need of Inventory Control. The necessity of inventory control is to maintain a reserve (store) of goods that will ensure manufacturing according to the production plan based on sales requirements and the lowest possible ultimate cost. Losses from improper inventory control include purchases in excess than what needed, the cost of slowed up production resulting from material not being available when wanted. Each time a machine is shut down for lack of materials or each time sale is postponed or cancelled for lack of finished goods a factory loses money.

To promote smooth factory operation and to prevent piling up or idle machine time proper quantity of material must be on hand when it is wanted. Proper inventory control can reduce such losses to a great extent.

Functions of Inventory Control

Following are the most important functions of Inventory Control:

(*a*) To *run the stores effectively*. This includes layout, storing media (bins, shelves and open space etc.), utilization of storage space, receiving and issuing procedures etc.

(*b*) To ensure timely availability of material and avoid built up of stock levels.

(*c*) *Technical responsibility for the state of materials.* This includes methods of storing, maintenance procedures, studies of deterioration and obsolescence.

(*d*) *Stock Control System.* Physical verification (stock-taking), records, ordering policies and procedures for the purchase of goods.

(*e*) Maintenance of specified raw materials; general supplies, work in-process and component parts in sufficient quantities to meet the demand of production.

(*f*) Protecting the Inventory from losses due to improper handling or storing of goods and unauthorised removal from stores.

(*g*) Pricing all materials supplied to the shops so as to estimate material cost.

Essential Steps in Inventory Control

It is essential that the necessary materials shall be on hand when required and it is just as essential that no more stores shall be carried than is necessary. The maximum and minimum quantities of all stores should, therefore, be fixed with much care. In several cases, these limits can be set only by experience and careful observation. It is found that this results in a great reduction of inventory.

Advantage of Inventory Control

1. It creates buffer between input and output.
2. It ensures against delays in deliveries.
3. It allows for possible increase in output.
4. It allows advantage of quantity discounts.
5. It ensures against scarcity of materials in the market.
6. It utilizes the benefit of price fluctuations.

Hence, in conclusion with a good Inventory Control, a firm is able to make purchase in economic lots, maintain continuity of operations, avoid time consuming small orders, and guarantee prompt delivery of finished goods.

Objectives of Inventory Planning and Control

The objectives of Inventory Planning and Control are to ensure

1. Timely availability of required materials or acceptable quality (Planning)
2. To avoid build-up stock levels by inflow of materials much inadvance of requirements or accumulation of unwanted items which though ordered earlier, but not required now.

It is the duty of the Production Department to intimate Materials Management Department about the changes. In case, such information are not passed on to the material management department, the inventory build-up is unavoidable and it is difficult to take up preventive action in advance.

26.6. INVENTORY BUILD-UP

Inventory build-up starts because of the reasons, either (*i*) items get ordered in excess of the requirement or (*ii*) they do not get used at the same rate at which they are received.

To overcome the first possibility, orders should be placed after consulting the production department. Production and Materials Management departments must together work out the delivery schedules, which must be decided after considering the past performances of the suppliers. Sometimes inventories, get build-up because excessive quantities are received at a particular time. For example, receiving the years requirement spread over 4 quarterly deliveries, is different from receiving in one lot. In the second case the organisation isforced to carry inventory of 12 months at a time. The other danger is that such material deteriorates in storage or pilferred or damaged.

Now coming to the second aspect, stores inventory is consumed by the production department by drawing materials from stores and converting it into finished goods. If the consumption rate falls down, then inventory build-up takes place. The consumption rate may fall down because of any of the following reasons:

(*i*) Due to change in production plans.
(*ii*) Due to discontinuance of manufacture of a product.
(*iii*) Due to change in design for a particular assembly or set of components.

In such cases rescheduling of the deliveries or reducing the quantities of the pending order must be assorted to. In case the item is not required at all, the further supplies must be stopped and pending ordersbe cancelled.

Delivery Schedule

In order to control build-ups this aspect is most important. Production and material management departments must, together, workout delivery schedules. This must be done considering the past experiences. Inventories get build-up not only because excess quantities are ordered and received but also because excessive quantities are received at a particular time. For example, receiving the year's requirement spread over 6 bi-monthly deliveries is different from receiving a six-monthly lots. In second case 6 months inventory has to be carried at a time.

Next stage, while ordering and accepting the supplies is to ensure that material received only as per requirement. For this purpose following precautions are taken:

1. Availability of material into stock and material awaiting inspection from the past supply should also be taken into account.
2. Care should be taken to accept the supplies only as per delivery schedule since, the natural tendency on the part of suppliers is to take deliveries as early as possible and in as few lots as he can. Further, there is general belief in personnel, that timely supply means, it should not be late, may be early, whereas it should not be too early, i.e., much before its requirement.

Actions to be taken for Avoiding Inventory Build-up

1. Items with no issues and receipts in last one year should be identified in the beginning of the financial year. In consultation with production control and research and designs department, all the pending open purchase orders, if any, items should be cancelled.
2. In the cases where, items have been received without any issues in the past, matter should be investigated. These investigations may reveal either of the following:
   (*a*) Items are for new project and utilisation is expected to be started in near future.
   (*b*) Items are received for the production planned a few months later.
   (*c*) The item is a replacement for an obsolete item, but will be issued only after existing stock of the obsolete item is exhausted.
   (*d*) The item is for a product whose production has been suspended or delayed due to a temporary slump in the demand.
   (*e*) Item is supplied much ahead of the requirement.
   (*f*) The item is not required.

   No action is required in the cases of (*a*), (*b*) and (*c*), whereas immediate action is called for in the case of (*d*) and (*e*), rescheduling the deliveries and reducing the total order quantities. In case of (*f*), immediate stoppage of further supplies and cancellation of pending purchase order has to be done.
3. A list of items which are in excess of predetermined levels should be prepared and investigation is to be done as to why the level has gone up and whether their supplies need to be slowed down.
4. Do not accept the following reasons for early supplies:
   (*a*) We need the material any way.
   (*b*) What difference does it make if we have a little extra stock.
   (*c*) Let us not harass the poor supplier. Taking back the material will mean a lot of extra expenditure to him.

(*d*) If we return the material today, he may not supply in time on the next occasion etc.

Therefore, at the risk of causing some inconvenience to the supplier, goods if received in advance of intimated delivery schedules should be returned back.

Disposal of Surplus Materials

A periodical study is necessary for finding obsolete or surplus (not being used from a considerable period) items. These items must then be re-examined for their alternative use. If they could not be used anywhere in the concern they must be disposed of. Mode of disposal must be decided in follewing priority.:

(*a*) Send it back on resale to the original supplier, if they are, interested, or otherwise.

(*b*) Sell them at the best possible price. If it is not possible then.

(*c*) Sell it at any available price even at scrap value. In case, if it could not be sold at scrap value or at any other rate, then.

(*d*) Give away free, as there is no use of preserving it year after year and blocking the space.

26.7. QUANTITY STANDARDS IN INVENTORY CONTROL

There are five important quantity standards used as tool to control Inventory. These are as follows (see Fig. 26.1)

1. The Maximum Stores.
2. The Minimum Stores.
3. The Standard Order.
4. The Ordering Point.
5. Lead or Procurement Time.

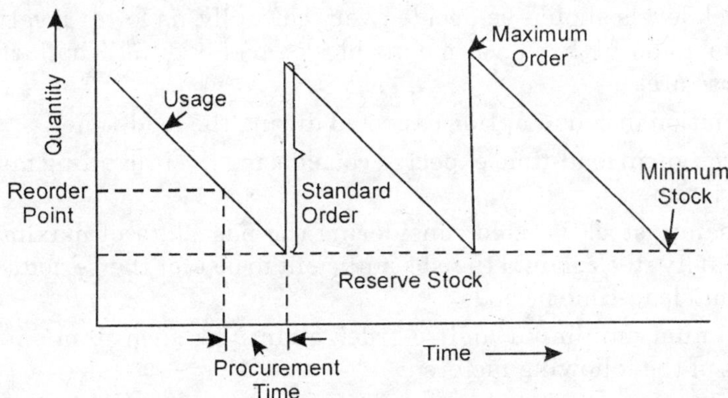

Fig 26.1

1. **The Maximum Stores.** This term is applied to designate the upper limit of the Inventory and represents the largest quantity which in the interest of economy should generally be kept in stores.
2. **The Minimum Stores.** This term is applied to designate the lower limit of the Inventory and represents a reserve or margin of safety to be used in case of emergency. When requirements have been abnormal it is intended that there must always be atleast this quantity available in stores.

3. **The Standard Order.** It is the quantity to be purchased at any time. Repeat order for a given product are always for this quantity until this is revised.
4. **The Ordering Point.** This represents the quantity required to ensure against exhaustion of the supply during the interval between the placement of an order and delivery. When the balance falls to this level, it is an indication that a new purchase order must be placed.
5. **Lead Time.** It is the time which takes the stock to reach from Re-order point to Minimum Stock level. It may also be defined as the time that elapses between the voicing of a need for anything and the time taken to satisfy the need. If one order is palced today and after 40 days it is fulfilled, then 40 days period is lead time. Hence, it shows that the order should be placed 40 days earlier. Load time determines the amount of material to be kept in reserve. As the lead time decreases, the reserve stock also decreases and *vice versa*. Therefore, the lead time analysis is very necessary, and the attempts should be made to reduce this period.

   Lead Time Includes:
   1. Requisitioning of materials.
   2. Time to process the enquiries and to place the order.
   3. Time to deliver the order to supplier.
   4. Time for the supplier to fulfil the order.
   5. Transportation time to reach the purchaser, inspection etc.
6. **Reserve (Safety or Buffer Stock).** If every thing goes as per programme, i.e., order is placed exactly at Reorder level, consumption rate remains same and material is received within lead time then there is no need for reserve or safety stock. But this seldom happens. Therefore to safeguard the production against uncertainties in consumption rate and lead-time, an extra stock is maintained all along and this is called as safety stock, reserve stock or buffer stock.

   Safety stock levels should be decided very carefully, as lower level may lead to stock-out positions and higher level means blockage of capital. The factors considered for this purpose are:
   1. Variation in consumption expected during the lead-time.
   2. Variation in lead-time expected considering the prevailing market conditions for that item.

Generally the safety stock is fixed considering the past data of maximum lead-time and normal lead-time. Safety stock should then be sufficient to last for the periodic difference between maximum and normal lead-time periods.

In setting maximum, minimum and re-order quantities each item should be considered separately in terms of the following factors :

(*a*) Economic size of each purchase order.
(*b*) Increased lock-up of capital.
(*c*) The time required to receive the goods after requisitioning.
(*d*) The probable depreciation and obsolescence.
(*e*) The rate of demand etc.

26.8. SELECTIVE CONTROL TECHNIQUES

'Selective Inventory Management' or 'Selective Control Techniques' are based on the priniciple that it is inpossible to manage and control every item in inventory holdings in the same way and skill so as to meet the two broad objectives of inventory control, *i.e.*, to reduce investment in inventories, and also to avoid stock-outs and shortages. This technique, therefore, concentrates on those items where it is justified either due to essentiality or amount of money involved.

Therefore, in other words the approach is to evaluate a trade off between the cost of inventories as against cost of control. For example, the inventory of high value items (in terms of annual usage) is to be controlled carefully, because a small percentage decrease in inventory can save a lot, while in case of low value items, the cost of control may be more than the possible savings.

Some of the common techniques used for exercising selective control are being described here under.

(1) A-B-C Control Policy

It is difficult and very costly to give equal attention to all the items of inventory. A-B-C analysis is meant for relative inventory control in which maximum attention can be given to items which consume more money and a fair attention can be given to medium value items, while the attention for low value items can be reduced to routine procedure only. This policy can also be applied in various other aspects of materials management.

If all the store items of an undertaking are analysed in terms of annual consumption of each item in rupees, it will be found that nearly 10 percent (sometimes even less) of the items are responsible for about 70 percent of total annual consumption cost, about 20 percent items will require about 25 percent of total consumption cost and rest 70 percent of the items require only 5 percent of the total annual consumption cost. The first category, small number of high consumption cost items, are called A items ; second category of medium consumption value items are known as *B* items, while the third category, *i.e.*, large number of items with small annual consumption cost are *C* items.

It is necessary to clear that *A-B-C* analysis does not depend on the unit cost of the items but on its annual consumption. Further it is also clarified that it does not indicate importance of any item or category, and every item is equally important. For example while installing a big machine of lacs of rupees, some foundation bolts (cost may be nearly Rs. 100 or 200 only) are not available in stores then this machine cannot be erected. Thus those bolts are equally important as that of machine although one is in category *A* and another in category *C*.

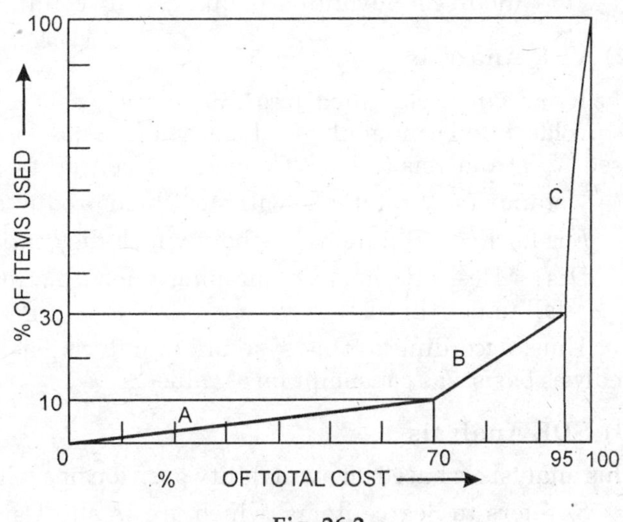

Fig. 26.2

A-B-C analysis is a basic technique of materials management and can be applied over almost all the aspects of materials management such as purchase, sales, inspection, inventory control, store-keeping etc.

Thus we see that control policies for *A*, *B* and *C* items are based on two principles, namely (*i*) to keep capital tied up inventories as low as practicable, (*ii*) to ensure that all the materials would be available when required. Control policies based on these two principles are described hereunder:

Policies for A items

(*i*) Since these items account for 70% of the total value hence they should be ordered more frequently, but in small quantities in order to reduce capital locked up at any time.

(*ii*) The requirement of such items must be planned in advance for expected future consumption, so that only the required quantities arrive a little before they are required for consumption.

(*iii*) Purchase of *A* items should be looked into by the top executives in purchasing department.

(*iv*) Since *A* items should be stocked as minimum as possible, maximum efforts should be made to expedite the delivery. Deliveries within a specified period of order must be adhered to.

(*v*) Two or more suppliers for each item may be engaged, so that dependence on one supplier is eliminated to safeguard against failure by one supplier.

(*vi*) Ordering quantities, re-order point and minimum stock level should be revised frequently.

Policies for B items

(*i*) The policies for *B* items, in general, are in between those for *A* and *C* items.

(*ii*) Order for those items must be placed less frequently than for *A* items. Generally 3 to 6 orders per year are placed for *B* items.

Policies for C items

(*i*) Since C items do not involve much capital tie up, the stock for such items may be kept liberally (*i.e.*, stock for 6 months to one year).

(*ii*) Annual or 6 monthly orders should be placed to reduce paper work and ordering costs and to get advantage of quantity discounts for bulk purchases.

(2) VED Analysis

The items can be classified according to their use, consumption, values etc. *A-B-C* classification is an oldest and commonly used method, but now-a-days *VED* and *SDE* analysis are also being used. *VED* analysis is done to consider essentiality of stocking spares.

V stands for Vital items, without which production would come to halt.

E is for Essential items, without which dislocation of production work occurs.

D is for Desirable items. Remaining items which do not cause any immediate loss in production fall under this category.

Thus, according to this system of analysis basis is criticality of items, whereas in *A-B-C* analysis basis was consumption of values.

(3) SDE Analysis

This analysis is based on availability position of each item. In this analysis,

S- refers to Scarce items, which are in short supply and their availability is scarce. This includes imported items.

D - refers to Difficult items, which cannot be procured easily.

E - refers to Easily available items.

(4) MNG Analysis

In this analysis,

M - refers to Moving items. These items are consumed from time to time.

N - refers to Non-moving items. These items are those items which are not consumed in last one year.

G - refers to Ghost items. These are those items which had nil balance, both at the beginning and at the end of the last financial year and there were no transactions (receipt or issues) during the year. These are non-existing items for which the store-keeper keeps bin-cards showing nil balance.

Above mentioned 4 control techniques are commonly used. However, following are some other methods which help the materials management to selectively control the large number of items and effectively channelise his energy to problem areas resulting in optimal use of his efforts.

S. *No.*	*Title*	*Basis*	*Application*
1.	F.S.N. (Fast, Slow, Non-moving)	Issues from stores	Obsolescence control
2.	H.M.L. (High, Medium, Low)	Unit price of material	To delegate purchasing powers
3.	V.E.I.N. (Vital, Essential, Important, Normal)	Equipment criticality	Maintenance
4.	F.A.N. (Failure Analysis)	Design and Issue of spares	Reliability Engineer-ing
5.	G.O.L.F. (Govt. Ordinary, Local, Foreign)	Source of origin of material	Purchase strategy
6.	S.O.S. (Seasonal Off-seasonal)	Nature of supply	To decide stock level

26.8. CODIFICATION

It is an effective tool of inventory control. Today it is used to properly classify equipments, raw materials, components and spares to suit the particular needs of any organisation. Codification is helpful to prevent duplication and multiplicity of stores and the mistakes which are caused by the normal practice of describing the material.

The main features of rationalised code are:

(*i*) It describes an article objectively

(*ii*) It is an all-numeric 8-digit code and

(*iii*) It describes an article progressively from general to particular.

For example :

(1) 03 01 15 15 — Radian 12 SWg (size)

First two digits 03 indicate — Arc Welding electrodes

Second two digits 01 Indicate — Manual electrodes (local-M.S.)

Third two digits 15 indicate — Radian

Last two digits 15 indicate — 12 SWg (size)

The code has got enough flexibility to absorb all the materials of the concern and has the provisions for unforeseen contingencies also.

First two digits indicate the main group, that is all the materials are divided into 100 main groups, say for instance 10 gases, 20 chemicals, 42 screws, 64 hand tools etc.

Third and fourth digit indicate the type of article. For example

21	XX	Iron and Steel
21	10	Steel-Mild
21	01	Steel- Alloy WJQ

Fifth and sixth digits indicate the shape and metallurgical conditions.

For example:

21	10	10	XX	Wire, Mild, steel
21	10	10	10	Wire, Mild, steel 0.116"

Thus, last two digits indicate the size.

In this way with the help of codification materials are specified at every stage that is in the main groups, types, shapes and metallurgical conditions and sizes. For all the materials, the code length is constant and is useful for the use of punched cards and computers.

Now codification is applied to all purchased items, *i.e.*, raw materials, semi-finished and finished products, saleable products and components.

26.10. ECONOMIC ORDERING QUANTITY (E.O.Q.)

The evaluation of the most economic quantity to bepurchased involves calculation of the following two costs:

(*a*) Procurement cost or buying cost. Set up cost in case of manufacturing.

(*b*) Inventory carrying cost.

A. Procurement Cost or Buying Cost:

This cost includes the expenditure made on :

(*i*) Calling quotations.

(*ii*) Processing quotations,

(*iii*) Placing purchase orders.

(*iv*) Receiving and inspecting.

(*v*) Verifying and payment of bills.

(*vi*) Other incidental charges etc.

Set-up cost in case of manufacturing:

It includes :

(*i*) Cost of setting up the process or equipment etc.

(*ii*) Cost of scrap which may occur at the beginning of new operation.

(*iii*) Cost of planning production and controlling.

(*iv*) Cost of machine idle time during set up etc.

(b) Inventory Carrying Cost

This consists of expenditure made for:

(*i*) Insurance.

(*ii*) Storage and handling.

(iii) Obsolescence and Depreciation.

(iv) Deterioration.

(v) Taxes.

(vi) Interest etc.

For manufacturing it will include, unit material, unit direct labour, all the unit burden excepting items affected by lot size.

This cost varies between 10 to 20% of the product cost.

The economic ordering quantity is obtained by the quantity whose procurement cost is equal to inventory carrying cost.

Let A = Total items consumed per year.

P = Procurement cost per order.

e = Annual Inventory carrying cost per unit.

= Unit cost × Inventory carrying charges = C × I

and Q = Economic order quantity.

Let y = Total cost of one year's requirement

Then, Total cost

= (number of lots) × procurement cost + (consumption quantity × variable cost per unit) + (average inventory cost × Inventory carrying charges).

$$\therefore \quad y = \frac{A}{Q} P + A \times C + \frac{Q}{2} \times C \times 1 \quad \text{... (1)}$$

This equation can be used to determine the total cost.

By differentiating w.r.t Q and equating equation (1) to zero, the economic purchase order is obtained.

Thus $$-\frac{AP}{Q^2} + \frac{C \times I}{2} = 0 \text{ or } \frac{AP}{Q^2} = \frac{C \times I}{2}$$

Therefore, $$C \times I = e$$

or $$Q^2 = \frac{2AP}{e}$$

or $$Q = \sqrt{\frac{2AP}{e}} = \sqrt{\frac{2AP}{C \times 1}} \quad \text{... (2)}$$

This formula was developed by Mr. F.W. Harris in 1915.

Thus using Equations (1) and (2), the most economical purchase order size and the minimum total cost for a given set of conditions can be obtained.

The Economic Ordering Quantity can be obtained by plotting the relevant cost against the order quantity, as below (Refer Fig 26.3)

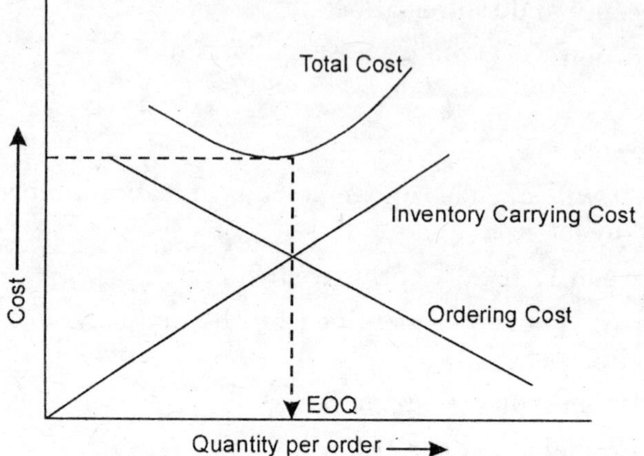

Fig. 26.3. Economic ordering quantity

Since the total cost curve is flat at the bottom we can deviate upto 25 percent on either side of the economic ordering quantity, without any significant extra cost, depending upon the circumstances. Therefore, for perishable items order can be reduced by 25 percent from E.O.Q, where quantity discount is available, we can enhance the order by 25 percent over the E.O.Q.

Important assumptions in applying the E.O.Q. model:

1. Demand is continuous and constant, and does not change with time.
2. Lead-time is constant.
3. Delivery of all the items is instantaneous.
4. Replenishment of one item has no effect on the replenishment of any other item of inventory.
5. Purchase price and their cost parameters, *i.e.*, P and C are constant.

Problem 26.1 *A plant producing a line of hydraulic valves can supply the factory warehouse at the rate of 750/ month. The warehouse ship, 3000 valves per year at a unit selling price of Rs. 250. Considering the plant's ordering and set up cost of Rs. 300 and the inventory carrying cost rate of 20%. What quantities should the warehouse order from the plant?*

Solution.

Let Q = the quantity, the warehouse should order from the plant.

A = No. of items consumed/year = 3000

P = Ordering and set up cost/order = Rs. 300

C = Annual inventory carrying cost/item

$$= \frac{\text{Total inventory carrying cost}}{\text{Total No. of items consumed}}$$

$$= \frac{3000 \times 250 \times 20}{3000 \times 100} = \text{Rs. } 50$$

Now

$$Q = \sqrt{\frac{2AP}{C}} = \sqrt{\frac{2 \times 3000 \times 300}{50}}$$

$$= \sqrt{30{,}000}$$

$$Q = 189.7 \text{ say } \mathbf{190 \text{ units Ans.}}$$

Problem 26.2 *The rate of a particular raw material from stores is 20 units per year. The cost of placing and receiving an order is Rs. 40. The cost of each unit is Rs. 100. The cost of carrying inventory in percent/year is 0.16 and it depends on the average stock.*

Determine : (i) The economic ordering quantity (ii) If the lead time is 3 months, calculate order point.

Solution. Let

Q = Economic ordering quantity = ?

A = No.of units consumed/year = 20

P = Ordering and set up cost = Rs. 40

C = Annual inventory carrying cost per unit

$$= \frac{\text{Total annual inventory carrying cost}}{\text{Total items consumed in a year}}$$

$$= \frac{20 \times 100 \times 0.16}{20} = \text{Rs. } 16$$

$$\therefore \quad Q = \sqrt{\frac{2AP}{C}} = \sqrt{\frac{2 \times 20 \times 40}{16}}$$

$$= \textbf{10 items. Ans.}$$

(*ii*) To determine re-order point

Let Q_0 = Stock level at reorder point

a = Consumption rate

t_0 = Lead time

Them $Q_0 = a \times t_0$

Hence $$a = \frac{20}{12} \text{ items/month}$$

$$t_0 = 3 \text{ months}$$

$$Q_0 = a \times t_0$$

$$= \frac{20}{12} \times 3 = 5 \text{ units.}$$

That is, when stock level reaches to 5 units, Reorder should be sent.

Problem 26.3 *A company producing motors, decides to make a particular item in batches. The following information is available.*

Cost of setting–up machine and tools = Rs. 800

Annual rate of depreciation, interest etc. = 15%

Consumption of parts in assembly shop = 100/month

Processing of each item takes 8 hours on the machine

Labour rate = Rs. 10 per day (Assume 8 hours in a day)

Material cost = Rs. 3 per kg Weight of each item = 15 kg.

Overhead expenses on each part is allocated at 100% of the duration of machine run, assuming that machine loading factor is about 80%.

Solution.

Material cost of each part $= 3 \times 15 =$ Rs. 45

Labour cost of each part $= \frac{10}{8} \times 8 =$ Rs. 10

Prime cost of each part $= 45 + 10 =$ Rs. 55

Overhead = 100% of 55 = Rs. 55

$\therefore$ Manufacturing cost = Rs. 45 + 10 + 55 = Rs. 110

Now Economic lot size, $Q = \sqrt{\frac{2AP}{C}}$

A = Annual items to be consumed

$= 100 \times 12 = 1200$

P = Set up cost = Rs. 800

C = Inventory carrying cost/unit

$= 110 \times 0.15$

$$= Q = \sqrt{\frac{2 \times 1200 \times 800}{110 \times 0.15}}$$

= **341 Ans.**

Running hours of machine $= \frac{341 \times 8}{0.80} =$ **3410 hours. Ans.**

Problem 26.4. *A factory is manufacturing Hubs in batches. The following details are available.*

Cost of setting–up machine and tools = Rs. 1400

Annual rate of depreciation, interest etc. = 18%

Consumption of parts in assembly shop = 120/month

Processing of each item takes 6 hours on the machine

Labour rate = Rs. 20/ day for 8 hours

Material cost = Rs. 5/ kg

Weight of each item = 4 kg.

Overhead on each item is allocated at 120% of the prime cost. Find out:

(*i*) Economic batch size for machining and

(*ii*) *Duration of machine run, assuming that the machine loading factor is about 90%.*

Solution.

Material cost $= 5 \times 4 =$ Rs. 20

Labour cost = Time for producton of each unit × hourly rate

$= 6 \times \frac{20}{8} =$ Rs. 15.

$\therefore$ Prime cost = Rs. 20 + 15 = Rs. 35

Now overheads = 120% of prime cost

$= 1.20 \times 35 =$ Rs. 42

$\therefore$ Unit cost = Prime cost + Overheads

$$= \text{Rs. } 35 + 42 = \text{Rs. } 77/\text{ unit}$$

$\therefore$ $$N = 120 \times 12 = 1440$$

As, $$C = 77 \text{ Rs./unit, A} = \text{Rs. } 1440, \text{ I} = 0.18$$

$\therefore$ $$Q = \sqrt{\frac{2 \times 1440 \times 1400}{77 \times 0.18}}$$

$\therefore$ $$Q = \sqrt{\frac{144 \times 4000 \times 100}{11 \times 18}}$$

$\therefore$ $$= \sqrt{\frac{144 \times 40 \times 10^4}{11 \times 18}}$$

$$= 534 \text{ (say)}$$

Runnig hours of the machine

$$= \frac{534 \times 6}{0.90} = \textbf{3560 hours Ans.}$$

Problem 26.5. *Determine the economic order quantity for a product whose average daily consumption rate is 80 units. The cost of each unit is Re. 0.50 and the inventory carrying charges is 0.20. The cost of placing and receiving the order is Rs. 10. Assuming total working days in a year as 300, obtain the annual inventory capital also.*

Solution.

(*i*) No. of units consumed/year,

$$A = 80 \times 300$$
$$= 24{,}000 \text{ units}$$

Ordering cost, $$P = \text{Rs. } 10$$

Annual Inventory carrying charge/unit,

$$C = \text{Re. } 0.20$$

$\therefore$ Economic ordering quantity,

$$Q = \sqrt{\frac{2AP}{C}}$$

$$= \sqrt{\frac{2 \times 24{,}000 \times 10}{0.20}} = 1549.2$$

$$= \textbf{say 1550 units. Ans.}$$

(*ii*) Annual Inventory capital = Cost of units consumed per year + Procurement cost/year + Inventory carrying cost per year.

$$= 24{,}000 + 0.50 + \frac{A \times P}{Q} + \frac{Q \times C}{2}$$

$$= 12{,}000 + \frac{24{,}000 \times 10}{1550} + \frac{1550 \times 0.20}{2}$$

$$= 12{,}000 + 155 + 155 = \textbf{Rs. 12,310 Ans.}$$

Problem 26.6.

(*a*) *Explain the term economic order quantity.*

(*b*) *The total annual demand for an Inventory item is 2,000 units. The Inventory carrying cost per rupee purchase value of Inventory per year is 10 paise. The order cost per order is Rs. 5. The purchase price of the unit consists of two elements Rs. 2 per unit and Rs. 40 as fixed charges per order.*

(*i*) *Determine the economic order quantity and the order quantity per year.*

(*ii*) *If 100 more units are ordered over and above the economic order quantity per order, what is the difference in total annual costs?*

Solution. (*i*) Here

$$Q = \sqrt{\frac{2AP}{C}}$$

Q = Economic ordering quantity

A = 2000 units

P = Order cost per order = Rs. 5

C = Inventory carrying cost

$$= \text{Rs. } \left(2 + \frac{40}{Q}\right) \times 0.1 \text{ (given in the question)}$$

n = No. of orders placed per year

$$Q = \sqrt{\frac{2 \times 2000 \times 5}{\left(2 + \frac{40}{Q}\right)0.1}}$$

or

$$Q = \sqrt{\frac{2 \times 10^5 Q}{2Q + 40}}$$

Squaring both the sides,

$$Q^2 = \frac{2 \times 10^5 Q}{(2Q + 40)}$$

or $$2Q^2 + 40Q - 2 \times 10^5 = 0$$

or $$Q^2 + 20Q - 10^5 = 0$$

This is a quadratic equation

$\therefore$ Q = 306. 5 or – 326.5

Taking Q = 306.5 say 307

$$\therefore \quad n = \frac{2000}{307} = 6.5 \text{ say } 7$$

$\therefore$ Economic ordering quantity, Q = 307 **Units Ans.**

$\therefore$ No. of units ordered 307×7 = **2149. Ans.**

(*ii*) Total annual cost in first case,

Cost of units + Procurement cost + Inventory carrying cost.

$$= 2149\left(2+\frac{40}{307}\right)+5\times 7+0.1\left(2+\frac{40}{307}\right)\times 2149$$

$$= 4578 + 35 + 457.80 = \text{Rs. } 5070.80$$

Total annual cost in 2nd case

Here $Q_1 = 307 + 100 = 407$

$n = 7$

$\therefore$ Annual demand $= 407 \times 7 = 2849$

$\therefore$ Procurement cost $= 5 \times n = 5 \times 7 = 35$

and Inventory carrying cost

$$= 0.1\left(2+\frac{40}{407}\right)\times 2849 = 597.\ 80$$

$$\text{Cost of units} = \text{Rs. } 2849\left(2+\frac{40}{407}\right)$$

$$= \text{Rs. } 5978$$

$$\therefore \quad \text{Total cost} = 5978 + 35 + 597.80$$

$$= \text{Rs. } 6610.80$$

$\therefore$ Difference in the total annual cost

$= 6610.80 - 5070.80 =$ **Rs. 1540 Ans.**

26.11. INVENTORY MODELS

The inventory models identify the relationship to quantify the order size which minimises the total cost. Before going into details of inventory models, we shall first discuss, the meaning of models.

Models

Models aim at creating a set of relationship which approximate the real world situation. These are simple from the point of view of computation and gives satisfactory results. Models are very helpful in decision-making. "Models are structures involving relationships among- concept."

Economic theory deals with the scientific approach for selecting a best alternative, and constructs a simplified model of reality on the basis of which laws describing regularities in economic behaviour are derived. A model deals with the relationship of a given dependent variable with one or more independent variables.

Examples of models are : Quantitative models, Allocation models, Queuing or waiting line models, Simulation models, Inventory models. Network or scheduling models.

Complex problems of the practical world thus can be solved by concentrating only on some key features insted of every detail. This approximation of reality, which we may construct in various forms are called as 'model'. Models exist in many forms, and the particular form selected depends upon the purpose. The decision-making through models is (*a*) economical to construct as compared to actual situation and its modification, if required, (*b*) Convenient to analyse and experiment as compared to those with complex situations, and (*c*) decision-making with these models is quick.

Types of Models

Models are of different types, some of them are:

(*i*) Predicitive
(*ii*) Descriptive
(*iii*) Nominative
(*iv*) Inconic
(*v*) Analog
(*vi*) Symbolic
(*vii*) Deterministic
(*viii*) Probabilistic

(*i*) **Predictive Models.** This indicate that "If this occurs, then that will follow".

(*ii*) **Descriptive Models.** These provide descriptive picture of a situation and do not predict or recommend e.g. organisation chart.

(*iii*) **Nominative Models.** These provide the best answer to a problem, e.g. economic lot size model.

(*iv*) **Inconic Models.** These retain some of the physical characteristics of the things they represent, *e.g.*, Three dimension scale models.

(*v*) **Analog Model.** These employ one set of properties to represent some other set of properties which the system being studied possesses, e.g., frequency distribution charts, flow charts etc.

(*vi*) **Symoblic Model.** These use symbols to descibe the real world, e.g., quantitative models, allocation models, queuing models, inventory models, simulation models and network or scheduling models.

(*vii*) **Deterministic Models.** These determine the output (representing the solution) from a set of input values, e.g., Profit = Revenue – Costs.

(*viii*) **Probabilistic Models.** These involve probability distributions for inputs and provide a range of values of atleast one output variables with a probability associated with each value. These models assist decision-making under conditions of risk (uncertainty).

Inventory Models

Inventory models mainly deal with two decisions, namely :

1. How much to order at one time, and
2. When to order this quantity to minimise total cost.

These models are suitable both for (*a*) buying items for production purposes from outside, and (*b*) producing them with in the firm to meet the demand of customers. It is extremely difficult to formulate one common model which takes into account all variations in real systems. Even if such a model is developed, it will be difficult to solve it. Therefore, inventory models are developed for specific purposes only. Inventory models, some times known as 'Economic Ordering Quantity Models', are of following two types:

(1) Deterministic models.
(2) Probabilistic (Stochastic) models.

26.12. DETERMINISTIC MODELS (MODELS ASSUMING CERTAINTY)

These models while determining 'Economic Ordering Quantity', which some times known as 'Economic Lot Size' or 'Optimum Lot Size' make following assumptions:

(i) Exact demand is known for given period.

(ii) Demand is uniform and constant (finite) over a period of time.

(iii) Cost of order is same regardless of size.

(iv) Price of raw materials are stable.

(v) Holding cost is proportional to the amount of inventory as well as the time for which inventory is held. E.O.Q. models under different situations are explained hereunder :

Fig. 26.4

26.13. INSTANTANEOUS REPLENISHMENT MODELS

In this situation supply is received instantaneously. All other assumptions as mentioned above hold good.

26.13.1. No Shortage Situation

In this type of instantaneous replenishment model, no shortages are allowed.

Let A = Annual consumption rate.

P = Procurement cost per order.

C = Annual Inventory carrying cost per item.

and Q = Economic ordering quantity.

Then,

Procurement cost/year = No. of orders placed in a year × Cost per order

$$= \frac{A \times P}{Q} \quad \ldots (1)$$

and Inventory carrying cost/year

= Average value of Inventory in a year × Annual inventory carrying cost/item

$$= \frac{Q}{2} \times \text{C} \quad \ldots (2)$$

$$\therefore \quad \text{Total cost} = \frac{A \times P}{Q} + \frac{Q \times C}{2} \quad \ldots (3)$$

This total cost will be minimum, when

$$\frac{A \times P}{Q} = \frac{Q \times C}{2}$$

or $$Q^2 = \frac{2AP}{C}$$

or $$Q = \left(\frac{2AP}{C}\right)^{1/2}$$

Hence most economic ordering quantity

$$= \sqrt{\frac{2AP}{C}} \quad \text{... (4)}$$

Note1 : Some times, C is given as $H + ip$.

Where, H = Holding cost.

i = Interest rate.

p = price per unit of item.

Note 2 : If

L = Lead-time in days.

R = Inventory consumption rate in units per day.

$\therefore$ Reorder Point = LR.

Note 3 :

If B is the buffer stock which is required to be maintained,

$\therefore$ Reorder point = B + LR

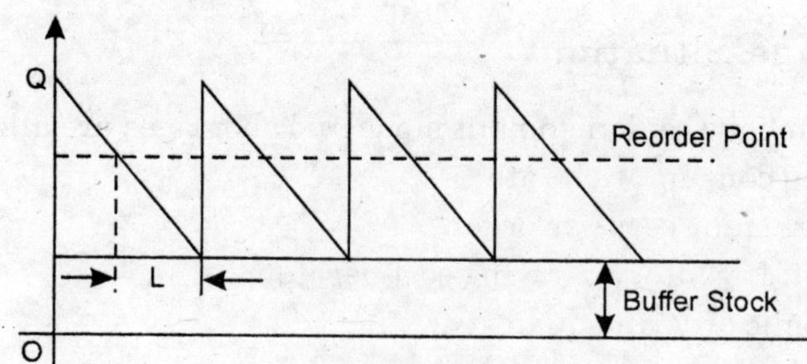

Fig. 26.5.

Example 26.7. *Calculate E.O.Q. for an item, if its annual usage rate is 600 units, procurement cost is Rs. 20 per order, cost per piece is Rs. 100, and inventory carrying cost is 10%.*

Solution. As we know that,

$$Q = \sqrt{\frac{2AP}{C}}$$

where, $A = 600$

$P = 20$

and $C = 10\%$ of $100 = 10$.

$$\therefore \qquad Q = \sqrt{\frac{2 \times 600 \times 20}{10}} = 48.98$$

Since the size of order is preferred to be same, each time therefore, first we calculate the number of orders per year

$$= \frac{600}{48.98} = 12 \text{ (Say) (rounded)}$$

$$\text{Hence E.O.Q} = \frac{600}{12} = \textbf{50 units. Ans.}$$

Example 26.8. *Requirement of an item in a manufacturing concern is 250,000 per year, the price of which is Rs. 20 per thousand, the cost of holding stock is 10% per annum, and the cost of ordering is Rs. 12 per order. Determine E.O.Q.*

Solution. Since E.O.Q $= \sqrt{\frac{2AP}{C}}$

where, considering one unit of material as 1000 pieces for simplifying the calculations;

$A = 250$

$p =$ Rs. 12

$C =$ 10 % of 20 = Rs.2

$$\therefore \qquad \text{E.O.Q.} = \sqrt{\frac{2 \times 250 \times 12}{2}}$$

$$= 54.77 \text{ or } 54770 \text{ items}$$

$$\text{Therefore number of orders} = \frac{250{,}000}{54770} = 4.56$$

$$= \text{Say 5 (rounded).}$$

$$\therefore \qquad \text{E.O.Q.} = \frac{250{,}000}{5} = \textbf{50,000. Ans.}$$

Example 26.9. *A manufacturer is required to purchase 2500 pieces of an item per year. The price of each item is Rs. 10. Ordering cost is Rs. 60 and inventory carrying cost is 20% per year, find out*

(*a*) *What should be ordering quantity?*

(*b*) *Number of orders issued per year.*

(*c*) *Order interval, considering 300 working days in a year.*

Solution. Since E.O.Q $= \sqrt{\frac{2AP}{C}}$

where, $A = 2500$

$P =$ Rs. 60

$C =$ 20 % of Rs. 10 = Rs. 2

$$\therefore \qquad \text{E.O.Q.} = \sqrt{\frac{2 \times 2500 \times 60}{2}}$$

$= 387.2$. **Ans.**

(*b*) Number of orders/year = 2500/387.2 = 6.46

$=$ say **6 Ans.**

(*c*) Ordering interval $= \dfrac{300}{6} =$ **50 days. Ans.**

Note : Quantity to be ordered/order $= \dfrac{2500}{6}$

$= 416.6$ or between **410 to 420** (rounded)

Example 26.10. *A manufacturing concern buys 60,000 items each year. The cost of each item is Re 1.00 and the ordering cost is Rs. 80 per-order. Holding cost per year is Re 0.20. Taxes, insurance and interest togather are charged at the rate of 15%. Determine*

(*a*) *Order quantity*

(*b*) *Number of orders placed in a year*

(*c*) *Time between orders if working days per year are 300.*

Solution. Since, $\text{E.O.Q} = \sqrt{\dfrac{2AP}{C}}$

where

$$A = 60{,}000 \text{ items}$$
$$P = 80$$
$$C = H + ip$$
$$= 0.20 + .15 \times 1 = 0.35.$$

$$\therefore \quad \text{E.O.Q.} = \sqrt{\frac{2 \times 60{,}000 \times 80}{0.35}} = 5237$$

In order to have full number of orders $\dfrac{60{,}000}{5237}$

$= 11.46$; i.e. 12

(*a*) Order quantity $= \dfrac{60{,}000}{12} =$ **5000 items Ans.**

(*b*) Number of orders $=$ **12 Ans.**

(*c*) Order interval $= \dfrac{300}{12} =$ **25 days Ans.**

Example 26.11. *A manufacturing concern has a demand of 10,000 pieces of a particular item. Each item costs Rs. 2, ordering % cost is Rs. 80 per order and inventory carrying cost is 25%. Past lead times are 15 days, 13 days, 25 days, 12 days and 10 days. Calculate*

(*a*) *E.O.Q.*

(*b*) *Safety stock.*

(*c*) *Normal lead-time consumption.*

(*d*) *Average inventory.*

(*e*) *Reorder level.*

Solution. As we know that,

$$E.O.Q = \sqrt{\frac{2AP}{C}}$$

Where, $A =$ 10,000 items

$P =$ Rs .80

$C = 0.25 \times 2 = 0.50$

(a) $\therefore$ $$E.O.Q = \sqrt{\frac{2 \times 10{,}000 \times 80}{0.50}} = 1788$$

say **2000** considering full number of orders (5) in a year **Ans.**

(b) Safety stock = (Maximum lead time – Normal lead-time) × monthly consumption.

$$\text{Normal lead–time} = \frac{15 + 13 + 25 + 12 + 10}{5} \times \frac{1}{30}$$

$$= \frac{15}{30} \text{ months.}$$

$$\therefore \quad \text{Safety stock} = \left(\frac{25}{30} - \frac{15}{30}\right) \times \frac{10{,}000}{12}$$

$$= 278$$

say = **280 to 300 units Ans.**

(c) Normal lead-time consumption

$$= \frac{15}{30} \times \frac{10{,}000}{12}$$

= **417 units Ans.**

(d) Average inventory

$$= \frac{\text{Maximum} + \text{Minimum}}{2}$$

$$= \frac{(2000 + 300) + 300}{2}$$

= **1300** units **Ans.**

(e) Reorder level

= Normal lead time consumption + safety stock

= 417 + 300 = 717 **unit ans.**

Example 26.12. *A particular item in a factory has a demand of 10,000 units per year. Cost of one order is Rs. 150 and the holding cost is Rs. 2 per unit per year. If replacement is instantaneous and no shortages are allowed, determine :*

(a) *E.O.Q.*

(b) *Total cost per year if the cost of one unit is Re 1.*

Solution. Since,

$$\text{E.O.Q.} = \sqrt{\frac{2AP}{C}}$$

where, A = 10, 000 units/year

P = Rs. 150

C = Rs. 2 per unit per year

$$\therefore \qquad \text{E.O.Q} = \sqrt{\frac{2 \times 10{,}000 \times 150}{2.00}}$$

$$= \textbf{1225 units Ans.}$$

Total cost per year = (cost of material consumed) + (Procurement cost + Inventory carrying cost)

$$= (10{,}000 \times 1) + \left(\frac{10{,}000}{1225} \times 150 + 2 \times \frac{1225}{2}\right)$$

$$= 10{,}000 + 1225 + 1225$$

$$= \textbf{Rs. 12450. Ans.}$$

Here, Procurement cost = No of orders × ordering cost and

Inventory carrying cost = Holding cost/unit/year × Average inventory.

26.13.2. Instantaneous Replenishment Model with Shortages:

In this type of model shortages are allowed, some times the temporary stock out positions are allowed, if the customer/user is willing to wait until it is replenished. In such situations, extra expenditure is incurred on expediting and extra communication. In some cases it is economical to wait rather than keeping in stock, *e.g.*, in high value irregularly required items. The stock out situations become serious when sales are lost. Therefore, as a policy and on economical reasons management can allow shortages in limited items and for limited periods.

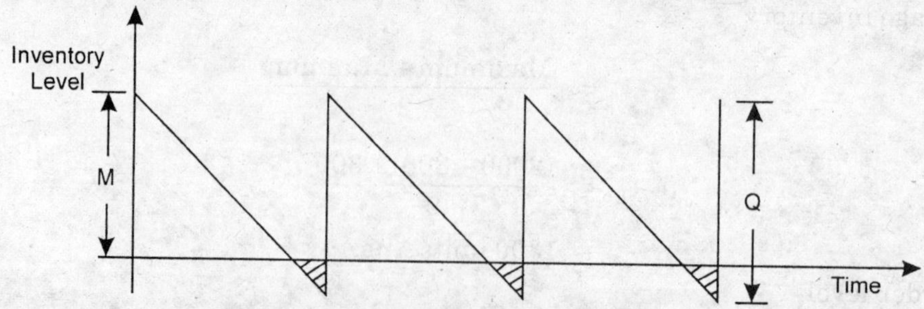

Fig. 26.6. E.O.Q model with shortage allowed.

In the cases when shortages are allowed, Economic Ordering Quantity.

$$Q = \sqrt{\frac{2AP}{C}} \times \sqrt{\frac{C+S}{S}}$$

and Maximum Inventory, $$M = \frac{Q.S}{C+S}$$

where, S = Shortage cost and M = Maximum inventory all other terms remain same.

Example 26.13. *In a factory having annual demand of 10,000 units of a particular item, ordering cost is Rs. 100 per order, cost of item is Rs. 10.00 per unit, inventory carrying cost is 15% of the cost of product for an year, and shortage cost is Rs. 20 per unit per year.*

Determine Economic Ordering Quantity and Maximum inventory.

Solution. Since, Economic Ordering Quantity,

$$Q = \sqrt{\frac{2AP}{C}} \cdot \sqrt{\frac{C+S}{S}}$$

Where,

$$A = 10{,}000 \text{ units}$$
$$P = \text{Rs. } 100 \text{ per order}$$
$$C = 15\% \text{ of } 10 = \text{Rs. } 1.5.$$
$$S = \text{Rs. } 20.$$

$$\therefore \quad Q = \sqrt{\frac{2 \times 10000 \times 100}{1.5}} \sqrt{\frac{1.5+20}{20}}$$
$$= 1155 \times 1.037 = 1197.5$$

Say **1250** (with 8 orders per year) **Ans.**

Maximum Inventory, $M = \frac{Q.S}{C+S} = \frac{1197.5 \times 20}{1.5+20} = 1114$ Ans.

26.14. REPLENISHMENT OF STOCK WITH FINITE RATE

26.14.1. Shortages not allowed

When a particular item of supply is manufactured on order rather than purchasing them from market in lots, these models are applicable. In this case items are despatched continuously as being manufactured. Therefore, during replenishment periods, the items are received, as well as consumed, but when maximum inventory level is reached, production is stopped temporarily. This inventory is then used. Such a model is shown in Fig. 26.7. This shows that in the beginning, inventory increases at a constant rate of (K-A) during replenishment period, until it reaches maximum level. During no replenishment it decreases at a constant rate of A. In this case, Economic Ordering Quantity,

$$Q = \sqrt{\frac{2AP}{C}} \cdot \sqrt{\frac{K}{K-A}}$$

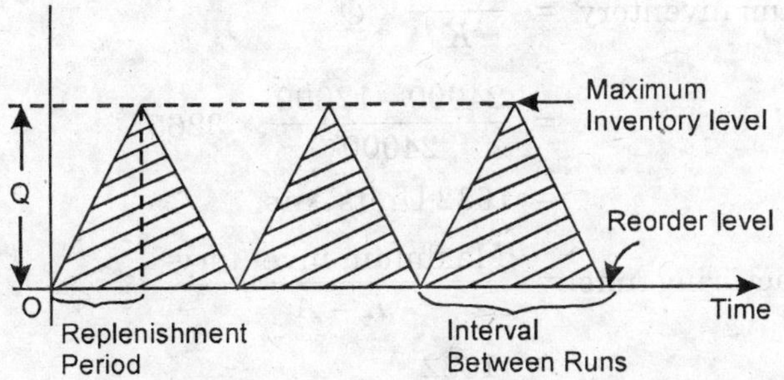

Fig. 26.7.

Where,

K = Number of items produced in a unit time.

P = Set-up cost per run.

Rest all other abbreviations remain same.

Example 26.14. *A manufacturing company has a demand of 12000 units of a particular item in a year, and can manufacture this item at the rate of 2000 units per month. If cost of each set-up is Rs. 400, holding cost per unit per month is Re. 0.15. Determine*

(a) *Optimum lot size*

(b) Total cost per year, assuming cost of each unit as Rs. 4.

(c) *Maximum inventory*

(d) Manufacturing time

(e) Number of cycles in a year

(f) *Total cycle time*

Solution, (a) Since,

$$E.O.Q, Q = \sqrt{\frac{2AP}{C}} \cdot \sqrt{\frac{K}{K-A}}$$

where,

A = 12000 units per year

P = Rs. 400/set up

$C = 0.15 \times 12$ = Re. 1.8/ unit/year.

$K = 2000 \times 12 = 24000$ unit/year.

$$\therefore \quad Q = \sqrt{\frac{2 \times 12000 \times 400}{1.8}} \cdot \sqrt{\frac{24000}{24000-12000}}$$

$$= \textbf{3265 units Ans.}$$

(b) Since, Total cost per year = cost of items consumed + cost of set up/year+ inventory carrying cost.

For Optimum value of Q,

Set up cost/year = Inventory carrying cost.

$$\therefore \quad \text{Total cost} = 12000 \times 4 + 2 \times \frac{12000}{3265} \times 400$$

$$= 48000 + 2940 = \textbf{Rs. 50940 per year Ans.}$$

(c)
$$\text{Maximum inventory} = \frac{K-A}{K} \times Q$$

$$= \frac{24000-12000}{24000} \times 3265$$

$$= \textbf{1632 Units Ans.}$$

(d)
$$\text{Manufacturing time} = \frac{\text{Maximum inventory}}{K-A}$$

$$= \frac{1632}{12000} = \textbf{0.136 year Ans.}$$

(e) Number of cycles/year

$$= \frac{12000}{3265} = \textbf{3.675 Ans.}$$

(f) Total cycle time

$$= \frac{1}{3.675} = \textbf{0.272} \text{ year Ans.}$$

26.14.2. Replenishment of stock with finite rate–shortages allowed:

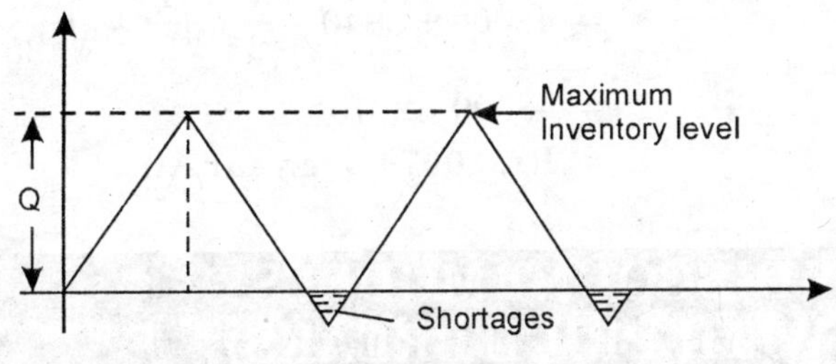

Fig. 26.8

Similar to previous model replenishment is done at finite rate in this model, except that in this model shortages are also permitted. In this model, Economic Ordering Quantity,

$$Q = \sqrt{\frac{2AP}{C}}\sqrt{\frac{K}{K-A}}\cdot\sqrt{\frac{C+S}{S}}$$

with abreviations as mentioned in earlier formulae.

Example 26.15. *Let us take data of example 26.14, except that shortage cost of one unit is Rs. 25 per year.*

Solution.

(a) Since, economic ordering quantity

$$Q = \sqrt{\frac{2AP}{C}}\cdot\sqrt{\frac{K}{K-A}}\sqrt{\frac{C+S}{S}}$$

$$= \sqrt{\frac{2 \times 12000 \times 400}{1.8}} \times \sqrt{\frac{24000}{24000-12000}} \times \sqrt{\frac{1.8+25}{25}}$$

$$= \textbf{3880 units Ans.}$$

(b) Maximum Inventory

$$= \sqrt{\frac{2 \times 12000 \times 400}{1.8}} \times \sqrt{\frac{12000}{24000}} \times \sqrt{\frac{25}{26.8}}$$

$$= \textbf{1577 units Ans.}$$

(c) Manufacturing time $= \dfrac{3380}{24000} = \textbf{0.1408 year Ans.}$

(*d*) Number of Cycles in a year $= \dfrac{12000}{3380}$

$= \mathbf{3.55\ Ans.}$

(*e*) Total cycle time $= \dfrac{1}{3.55} = \mathbf{0.2817\ year\ Ans.}$

(*f*) Total cost per year $= 12000 \times 4 + 2 \times \dfrac{12000}{3380} \times 400 \times \sqrt{\dfrac{K-A}{K}} \cdot \sqrt{\dfrac{C+S}{S}}$

$$= 48000 + 2840 \times \frac{1}{2} \cdot \sqrt{\frac{1}{2}} \times \sqrt{\frac{26.8}{25}}$$

$$= 48000 + 2079$$

$$= \textbf{Rs. 50079 per year Ans.}$$

26.15. QUANTITY DISCOUNT MODELS (MODELS WITH PRICE BREAKS)

In the inventory models described so far, production or purchase cost per unit was assumed as constant. Some times the cost depends upon the quantity manufactured or purchased. Usually suppliers offer discount for the purchase of large quantities. This price discount factor is being considered in this model.

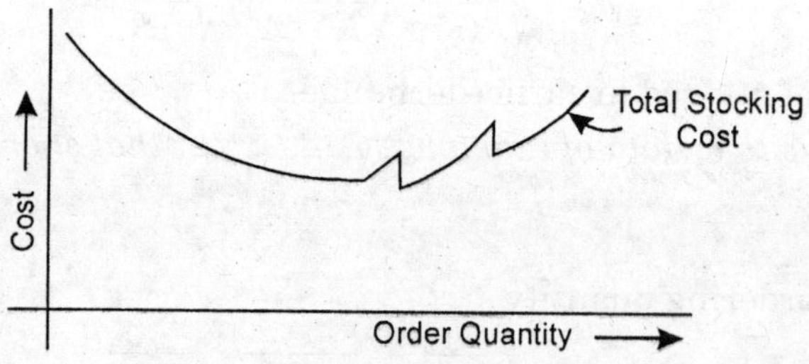

Fig. 26.9.

In these models, quantities are calculated considering the normal model, then it is confirmed whether it is really optimum. This process starts with the maximum discounted price. This will be clear from the following example :

Example 26.16. *A manufacturing concern consumes 200 items per month working for 30 days in a month. The cost of item is Rs. 1000. For a lot of more than 50, the price is Rs. 950. Find out optimum purchase quantity, if ordering cost is Rs. 10,000 and handling charges are 1% of unit cost/month.*

Solution. As a first step, let us calculate quantity considering rate of Rs. 950.

$$Q = \sqrt{\frac{2AP}{C}}$$

$$= \sqrt{\frac{2 \times 200 \times 10{,}000}{950 \times 1}}$$

$= 64.9 = \mathbf{65}$ **say.**

Since for 65 items the price is least, hence this is optimal quantity ∴ E.O.Q. = **65 Ans.**

QUESTIONS

1. What is A-B-C control policy? Describe it in detail.
2. What is material handling? Suggest some steps to reduce the material handling cost.
3. Describe the procedure for disposing the surplus and obsolete items.
4. What is Inventory control? Explain its importance in an industrial undertaking.
5. Describe various functons of Inventory control.
6. What are the quantity standards and how they can be used as a tool to Inventory control?
7. What is the purpose of stock-taking? How stock taking of a large concern is done?
8. Discuss any difference in inventory planning for jobing and mass production industries.
9. Explain how the standard order quantity is determined and point out how it helps in inventory control?
10. Write short notes on :
    (*i*) Economic lot size,
    (*ii*) *ABC* analysis in inventory control and
    (*iii*) Perpetual inventory control.
11. Describe briefly the different elements of inventory carrying costs.
12. The rate of use of a particular raw material from stores is 20 units per year. The cost of placing and receiving an order is Rs. 40. The cost of each unit is Rs. 100. The cost of carrying inventory in per cent per year in 0.16 and it depends upon the average stock. Determine the economic order quantity. If the lead time is 3 months, calculate the reorder point. [10.5 units]
13. Find economic order quantity from the following data :
    Average annual demand = 30,000
    Inventory carrying cost = 12% of the unit value per year 7.
    Cost of placing an order = Rs. 70
    Cost/unit = Rs.2 [4, 834,500 (Rounded of)]
14. A factory uses two pieces per of a rod 6 mm dia and 150 mm length in one of their manufacturing processes. The rod costs Rs. 3 each and the total expenses involved in purchasing and receiving them are Rs. 50 per order. The annual inventory carrying cost per item is Re. 1. The procurement period is 3 days and minimum stock kept is 8 pieces. Find out:
    (*i*) Standard ordering quantity
    (*ii*) Reorder point and
    (*iii*) Maximum stock [(*i*) 245, 200, (*ii*) 14, (*iii*) 280]
15. Determine the economic order quantity from the following data :
    Average annual demand = 10,000 units.
    Inventory carrying cost = 20% per rupee value/year
    Cost of placing order = Rs. 100
    Cost per unit = Rs. 5

Determine the most economical lot size for the following conditions :

Fixed cost per lot = Rs. 75

Various costs per unit = Rs. 0.25

Peicentage charge for interest, taxes, insurance and storage etc. 40%

Production rate = 80,000 units/year.

Demand rate = 15,000 units/year.

16. (*a*) What are the four basic components of the inventory system? Discuss the significance of each component.
   (*b*) In what ways can inventories serve to reduce the cost and to increase the cost?
   (*c*) Determine the economic order quantity for a prouct whose average daily consumption rate is 8 units. The cost of each unit is Rs. 0.50 and the inventory carrying charge is Rs. 0.20. The cost of placing and receiving the order is Rs. 10.00. Assuming total working days in year as 300, obtain the annual inventory capital also.
17. Machine parts are produced at the rate of 200 units per day. The cost of each unit is Rs. 15 and the storage cost Re 0.0005 per unit per day. If preparation and set up cost is Rs. 500 for the production run and assembly by using 50 units per day, determine the minimum cost, batch size and length of production run assuming 10% interest charges and 300 days per year.
18. Deduce an expression for 'economic order quantity' assuming that the cost of managing inventory is composed of two parts (*i*) ordering cost and (*ii*) carrying cost. The rate of use of a particular raw material from stores is 20 units per year. The cost of placing and receiving an order is Rs. 4000. The cost of each unit is Rs. 100.00. The cost of carrying inventory in percent per year is 0.16 and it depends on the average stock. Determine the Economic Order Quantity. If the lead time is 3 months, calculate the order point.
19. What functions do inventories serve in a manufacturing concern? Discuss both the advantages and disadvantages.
20. "Inventories are necessary evil." What is your view? Discuss.
21. How will you classify different types of inventories?
22. Explain what is meant by the terms (*a*) "inventory carrying costs" and (*b*) "inventory acquisition cost"?
23. List and discuss the main limitations of E.O.Q theory.
24. Write down symptoms of poor inventory management.
25. What are the quantity standards, and how they can be used as a tool to inventory control.
26. Explain how the standard order quantity is determined, and point out how it helps in inventory control?
27. What is inventory built-up? How it can be avoided? How codification help in reducing inventory build-up?
28. What do you understand by a model? Name various types of models. Explain how deterministic type of models are used in inventory control?
29. Explain the following terms relating to materials, and state on what basis they are fixed?
   (*a*) Minimum stock level.
   (*b*) Maximum stock level.
   (*c*) Reorder level
   (*d*) Buffer stock
   (*e*) Lead-time

Part–7 Financial Management, Engineering Economics and Costing

27 FINANCIAL MANAGEMENT

27.1. INTRODUCTION

The business organisations seek to achieve their objectives by obtaining funds from various sources and then investing them in different types of assets such as plant, buildings, machines etc. Financial management is managing the finances through scientific decision-making

Financial management is concerned with the acquisition (investment), financing (arranging funds) and management of assets with some overall goal in mind.

Success of a firm depends on the ability to raise funds invest in assets and manage wisely.

Money is required in a business to (*i*) start it; (*ii*) keep it going on; and (*iii*) expand the business. Every business concern requires capital for the following purposes:

1. To finance the fixed assets or for block expenditure on land, building, machinery, tools and equipment. This capital is known as Fixed or Block Capital.
2. To finance the current assets, *i.e.*, to meet current working expenses known as working or revolving or circulating capital. This capital supplies the funds necessary to run the business.
3. To finance for improvement and expansions.

Social Goals

While profit maximisation is the primary goal for any business organisation, social responsibility is also important for them. In case of Government organisations and public sector organisations, social responsibility is the primary goal and profit is secondary. Social responsibility includes service to the people, protecting the consumer, paying fare wages to the employees, upliftment of the weaker sections, welfare facilities like medical education, environment improvement programmes etc.

Financial Objectives

In making financial decisions, it is important to set out clear objectives. Following are the basic financial objectives:

(*a*) Profit maximisation.

(*b*) Maximisation of shareholders' /owners' wealth.

(*c*) Reduction in cost.

(*d*) Minimising risks.

(e) Sustained increase in the value of firm
(f) Wealth maximisation.

27.2. FUNCTIONS OF FINANCIAL MANAGEMENT

Financial manager is concerned with the following aspects :

1. Identifying the present strengths and weaknesses of the organisation and the scope for improvement, by conducting the financial analysis.
2. Planning the financial strategies. This involves the consideration of methods and levels of funds raising, profitability and the financing of expansion plan of the organisation.
3. Arranging the funds when required, in the form needed in the most economical way.
4. Conducting financial appraisal of the possible courses of action. The appraisals are needed in respect of possible take overs and mergers, analysis of capital projects, or alternative methods of funding.
5. Advising about capital structure.
6. Consideration of an appropriate level for drawings by dividends to the owners/ share holders.
7. Ensuring that assets are controlled and used in an efficient manner.
8. Cash management. Preparation of detailed cash budgets and/or forecast funds flow statement so that future problems can be foreseen and remedial measures taken in advance. These take care of both shortage and excess of cash. Finance managers must find ways of raising more funds needed, or investing excess funds for an appropriate length of time.
9. Finance managers are likely to draw attention on other disciplines also, like accounting and budgeting.

In order to enable financial managers to perform above functions satisfactorily, he must have good knowledge of accounting, economics, mathematics, statistics, law especially taxation, financial market etc.

The functions of finance thus involve three major decisions the firm must make :

(a) The investment decisions,
(b) The financing decisions, and
(c) The dividend decisions.

Each of these decisions are taken in relation to the objective of the firm, an optimal combination of these three will maximise the value of the firm to its shareholders. Since the decisions are interrelated, their joint impact on the market price of the firm's stock must be considered

1. **Investment Decisions.**

   This is the most important decision. Capital investment, i.e., allocation of capital to investment proposals is the most important aspect, whose benefits are to be realised in future. As future benefits are not known with certainty, the Investment proposals involve risk. These should, therefore, be evaluated in relation to expected return and risk. Considerable attention is paid to determine the appropriate required rate of return on the investment. In addition to taking capital investment decisions, finance managers are concerned with the management of current assets efficiently in order to maximise profitability relative to the amount of funds tied up in asset. Investment decisions also include the decisions about mergers and acquisition of another company.

2. **Financing Decisions.**

   Finance manager is required to determine the best financing mix or capital structure. An optimal financing mix is one in which market price per share could be maximised. Financing decision are taken in relation to the overall valuation of the firm. Various methods of obtaining short, intermediate, and long term financing are also explored, examined, analysed and a decision is taken. While taking financing decisions, the influence of inflamination on financial market and on the cost of funds to the firm is also considered.

3. **Dividend Decision.**

   The dividend decision includes the percentage of earnings paid to stockholders in cash dividends, stock dividends and splits, and the repurchase of stock.

27.3. FUNDS REQUIREMENT

Funds requirement is assessed for different purposes, namely for feasibility study of a project, detailed planning of a project, and for operation and expansion of the business. For feasibility study, only broad estimates are sufficient and are generally obtained from the past experience of the similar works by interpolating the present trends and the condition of the proposed project in comparison to the one whose figures are being adopted. While during detailed planning, estimated requirement is comparatively more realistic and prepared after going into details more thoroughly.

Here we are discussing the funds requirement for a running business including its long term planning for expansion.

The main function of financial management is to ensure that the firm must have sufficient funds to meet financial obligations when they are needed and to take advantage of investment opportunities. To achieve this objective, a thorough study is conducted about 'flow of funds' *i.e.*, statement of funds requirement indicating the amount of fund needed and at what time. This 'statement of funds' is a summary of a firm's changes in financial position from one period to another. This indicates that how the funds will be used and how it will be financed over specific period of time. This includes the cash as well as non-cash transactions.

Forecast, financial statements are prepared for selected future dates, generally for middle term and long term plans of the firm. Budgets are used for one year and are prepared only to fulfil the firms' objectives envisaged in the forecast for that particular year. These forecast financial statements are based on the sales forecast and future strategies for expanding the business and includes forecast income statements, forecast assets, liabilities, shareholders, equity etc.

Capital Requirement Determination

Total capital requirement can be determined by the following two methods:

(*a*) **Estimating method.** In this method an estimate is prepared on the basis of various costs of investment—fixed assets, working capital and expansion requirement.

(*b*) **Comparison method.** In this method an attempt is made to find concerns of similar size and conditions to that of proposed company. From the statistics of these concerns the probable requirement of capital is estimated.

Sometimes both the methods are used to find the correct capital requirement.

27.4. TYPES OF CAPITAL

As discussed earlier, capital is necessary for an enterprise to keep it dynamic and covers money, land, building, machinery materials etc, develop products, keeps workers and machines at work and is necessary for the firm's progress and creating value. For the operation of any firm, two types of capital are required,

(*a*) one for purchasing fixed assets like land, building, machinery etc. and is known as **fixed capital,**

(*b*) another to meet day-to-day needs and is known as **working capital.**

Fixed capital is associated with long term assets and whereas working capital is related to current operation.

27.4.1. Fixed or Block Capital

To start an industry, large amount of money is to be invested for more or less permanently fixed assets and this cannot be got back at will. The 'fixed capital' is invested in the plant, equipment, land and buildings etc. which cannot be disposed of without breaking up the business. Concerns engaged in commerce, trade, merchandise banking etc. need very little fixed investments. But manufacturers of heavy and capital goods need major parts of their funds in fixed assets. Fixed or block capital is required for the following important items :

1. Land.
2. Building and other installations.
3. Power and electric supply.
4. Water supply and drainage.
5. Machinery and their installations.
6. Tools
7. Administrative office and equipment.
8. Furniture.
9. Patents, etc.

27.4.2. Working Capital

Working capital is that part of capital which is required to meet the day-to-day needs in running the business. It is required for the purchase of raw material, for meeting the day to day expenses such as salaries, rent, stationery etc. Some capital is also required to keep the stock of partly finished products, some cash is also required for emergency work.

Working capital generally involves the use of short-term funds in business and is regularly converted to cash. Materials are changed into finished products, products are sold out to realise cash and the cash is utilized in purchasing the materials etc. Thus, this working capital is also known as revolving or circulating capital.

At any time working capital can be calculated by deducting current liabilities from working assets of the concern as shown in the following equations:

Working assets – Current Liabilities = Working Capital.

Working capital is required to meet the following important items:

1. Purchase of raw material and supplies, and their storage costs.
2. Payment of wages.

3. Maintenance costs.
4. Advertisement and selling expenses.
5. Transportation costs.
6. Expenditure on production during time lag between sale of product and receipt of their payment, and also during the production cycle.

Classification of Working capital

Working capital can be classified in following two heads:

1. **Regular or Permanent or Fixed Working Capital.** Working capital invested in starting the circulation of current assets and keeping it moving is permanently locked up. For example, every manufacturing concern has to maintain a minimum stock of raw materials for work in progress, finished products, loose tools and equipments. It also requires money for the payment of wages throughout the year.
2. **Seasonal, Variable or Special Working Capital.** Requirement of working capital varies with the seasonal changes in many industries. Additional working capital may also be required on account of certain abnormal conditions. For example, for strikes, lockout and to face cut-throat competition additional capital is required. Similarly, special advertisement campaigns or execution of special orders of the government will have to be financed by additional working capital.

Factors Affecting Working Capital

It is very difficult to determine the amount of working capital required, as there is no formula for calculating it. Working capital requirement depends upon several factors. Following are some of the factors which should be considered while determining the working capital:

1. Length of period of manufacture.
2. Turnover of working capital.
3. Terms of purchase and sales.
4. Nature and volume of business.
5. Business cycle (seasonal variations in business).
6. Converting working assets into cash.

1. **Length of Period of Manufacture.** Value of output and the average length of the period of manufacture is important in determining how much working capital a company will need. A factory manufacturing a product requiring a long period of manufacture will need large amount of money for the large amount of raw material, pay for labour and other incidental expenses and wait for a long period till the finished product is ready for sale. Thus large amount of capital is tied up in the process of manufacture. Ship-building is an example of it, as manufacture of a ship requires 3 to 4 years, hence the raw material, wages, labour and other expenses for such a long time have to be borne by the manufacturers. In the mean time there is risk of getting the prices down.
2. **Turnover of Working Capital.** 'Turnover' is the ratio of annual gross sales to average working assets. Thus, this ratio shows how many times the amount invested in working assets have been traded. The ratio is more when demand is more and products are sold quickly *e.g.*, a retail store deals with a product which has great demand and which can be sold almost as quickly as it is stocked, with large gross sales and investment in stock will be small. If, on the other hand, store deals with the products having an irregular and slow demand, the amount of working capital invested in stock will necessarily be heavy.

3. **Terms of Purchase and Sales.** A firm purchasing its requirement on cash will need large working capital than that purchasing on credit. Similarly a firm selling the product on cash will require less working capital than that of selling the product on credit.
4. **Nature of the Business.** Requirement of working capital depends upon the nature of the business. There are certain business which require large amount of fixed capital and need a lesser amount of working capital like railways etc., while there are some business like trading companies which require little in fixed capital and large amount of working capital.
5. **Business Cycle.** In most of the business there are variations of prices. Manufacturers psychologically like to take advantage of it and stop the sale of their products during the low rates and sell during high rates. In both the cases large amount of money is required for working capital.
6. **Converting Working Assets into Cash.** A concern having a good amount of quick or liquid working assets requires less working capital. Quick assets mean the bills receivable that mature within few days and the merchandise which is already sold or readily salable in cash. The current assets which require some time to convert into cash cannot be considered as quick assets. Hence a working capital required in a concern depends upon the quick or liquid working assets. A concern having a little quick assets requires large amount of working capital and *vice-versa.*

27.5. CAPITALISATION

'Capitalisation' means the process of determining the capital structure of a company. It is one of the most difficult task for the promoter, since the estimate of capital requirement is dependent upon many uncertain factors and unforeseen contingencies of a concern (that has not even yet started functioning). The success or failure of the concern is largely dependent on the financial planning. Thus the total amount of all shares, bonds, debentures represent the capitalisation. There are large chances of the concern being over-capitalised or under-capitalised.

Over-Capitalisation

This state of affair for a concern occurs where the amount of the shares issued is much in excess of actual requirement, and thus the rate of profit, *i.e.,* the dividend rate and also premium will be too low to allow the shares to sell at par value. This means the funds invested in the concern are not profitably employed and the enterprise can not pay fair return on its capital investment.

Over-capitalisation is resulted because of following reasons :

(*i*) Concern may raise more money by issue of shares and debentures than it can use fully and profitably.

(*ii*) Concern may borrow large sum of money than desired and hence a major part of the earnings may be given away to the creditors and left very little for the share holders.

(*iii*) Some times company purchases plant, machinery or building etc. during its peak of prosperity. But when slumps set-in, the books show the assets and capital at high value, even when large amount of working capital is lost. Thus the value of assets falls, whereas the capital stands at its original figure.

(*iv*) If a company does not make sufficient reserves for depreciation and equipment replacement, then after some time although capital value as per book is sufficient but the company is not having money for equipment replacement.

Disadvantages. Following are the disadvantages of over-capitalisation:

1. When shares sell below par value, company suffers a fall in its credit, hence it becomes difficult to raise further capital for extension and improvement.
2. To cover up the lack of profit other methods have to be adopted, which will lead to poor quality, rise in products price.
3. It is a wastage (or misapplication) of country's resources.
4. There will be loss of capital and loss of income to the shareholders. Because if the shareholders sell their shares then they have to suffer a heavy loss (as these shares cannot give full return) and if they continue to hold these shares, there will hardly be any dividend.
5. Due to low profit, welfare facilities and good wages can not be given to the workers which will further increase inefficiency.
6. Because of the higher rates, poor quality and low share value, company will have poor reputation in the public.

Under -Capitalisation

Under-capitalisation means insufficiency of the capital required to meet the total needs of the concern. Thus due to financial weakness, under-capitalisation is resulted. This results a condition when unusually large return is earned on total investment. Main reason for the under-capitalisation is wrong estimation of capital needs and the failure of promoters to raise the required capital. It faces the danger of going out of business.

For removing under-capitalisation, capital has to be borrowed at high rates from other sources. The money borrowed at high rate of interest is always a source of trouble, as it effects adversely on industrial growth, it tends to increase the price of the product and reduces profit. Generally experienced and highly qualified persons when start their business without their own capital, face the trouble of under-capitalisation and ultimately face the liquidation. Hence as remedy to it precautions should be taken are:- purchase the materials on long term credit, sell the product quickly and collect their money promptly, keep minimum stock, and small dividends are paid. It means every efforts must be taken to increase the working capital.

Thus it has been observed that under-capitalisation is a lesser evil as it can be corrected in an easier way by increasing the amount of debentures or shares.

Fair Capitalisation

As discussed above both the stages of over-capitalisation and under-capitalisation are dangerous for the concerns. The concern must not use more capital than needed, as idle money reduces the profit by an amount equal to its interest, nor the concern must have less capital than that is needed, as it creates the danger of the concerns going out of business. Thus, the work of estimation of capital requirement, its raising and proper handling requires good experience and ability. It is therefore necessary to discourage both the under and the over capitalisation and the concern should be of "Fair capitalisation".

Reserve foe Working Capital

Setting of reserve for working capital is necessary for sound financial administration, in order to cover credit losses, liquidate debts, provide for improvement and expansion, for obsolescence and taxes, offset price fluctuations and inventories.

The reserve may be revenue reserve or capital reserve.

27.6. RAISING OF FINANCE (METHODS OF FINANCING)

Selecting the Sources of Funds

The capital required for concern can be raised by various ways. The amount collected by each way depends upon the conditions of the money market and the type of work for which capital is required.

In an individual ownership and partnership enterprises, individual investment is the main source of finance, however they can take loans from banks and financial corporations. As these are small concerns and hence these have little problem of finance as compared to that for large scale industries. The large scale industries are mainly run by joint stock companies and as such they feel large problems of financing and the funds are to be raised from various sources.

Main sources of finance are the following:

1. Shares.
2. Debentures.
3. Public deposits.
4. Managing Agents.
5. Loans from Banks.
6. Ploughing back of earnings.
7. Other financial institutions.

Financing of Fixed Capital

Fixed capital of large scale industries are financed through (*i*) Shares (*ii*) Debentures (*iii*) Public deposits (*iv*) Managing Agents (*v*) Loans from financial institutions like Industrial Financial Corporation, State Financial Corporations, Industrial Development Corporation etc.

Financing of Working Capital

Working capital is generally financed from :

(A) For Regular Works. (*i*) Shares (*ii*) Debentures (*iii*) Ploughing back of earnings.

(B) For Seasonal Working Capital. Through (*i*) Loan from Banks (*ii*) Managing agents (*iii*) Public deposits (*iv*) Financial institutions.

Each of the methods for raising the capital is described hereunder:

1. Shares.

A big amount of capital required is collected through the shares issued to public. Shares can be issued at any time, generally these are issued at the time of starting of new business, expanding or reorganizing the existing concern. Amount to be collected by shares is first decided, and then ensure that the value of shares issued to the public should not exceed this predetermined decision.

Shares issued by the company may be of following types :

(*a*) Preference shares.
(*b*) Ordinary shares.
(*c*) Deferred shares.

(*a*) Preference Shares. A person holding these shares is entitled to get fixed rate of dividend. He gets his rate of dividend before any amount paid to the ordinary shareholders. Thus, as its name suggests, it gets preference over other shares for getting dividend. Similarly these shares get preference over other shares, if repayment of capital is done. When these shareholders get above mentioned facility, these have limitation that they will not get more than the fixed rate of dividend even when profit is very large. These preference shares are of the following two types:

(i) *Cumulative preference shares.* In these snares, if the profits are not sufficient to pay the fixed dividend in any year then the deficit is paid up from the profits of the next year.

(ii) *Non-cumulative preference shares.*In these shares the dividend is not transferred to the next year, if the profits of any year are insufficient to pay the fixed dividend.

(b) **Ordinary Shares.** These shares get their dividend only after payment of the fixed dividend on preference shares. The advantage for the holders of the ordinary shares is that there is no limit of dividend, and thus they may get higher dividend if the profits are large. If there is a loss, then ordinary shareholders do not get any dividend.

(c) **Deferred Shares.** As the name suggests, these shares have their claim last of all. Holders of these shares get their dividend only after the payment of the dividend on all other classes of shares. Generally these shares are issued to the promoters and to the persons who have helped in the formation of the company.

2. Debentures

When company desires to raise the required finance through loans instead of sale of shares, then debentures are issued. In this way it is advantageous because debenture holder cannot claim for ownership and he is to be paid interest only. Debentures may be issued either for initial needs of the enterprise or for the development and extensions. Debenture holders has no liabilities. Debenture provides finance for a specified period and the company can adjust its financial plan accordingly.

3. Public Deposits

Some of the concerns raise their capital by accepting the deposits direct from the public for fixed terms generally, 6 months to 7 years. Fixed capital is generally raised through long term deposits while working capital by short period deposits. In India this method was initially employed by cotton mills specially those located at Ahmedabad, Bombay and Sholapur. The deposits are taken for 6 months in the purchasing season when cotton has to be purchased and are repaid after 6 months when the clothes are sold. However, this method has started gaining importance now in other fields also.

This method has the advantage of enabling a company to keep its share capital low and to borrow at cheap rates. This facilitates payment of higher dividends than that would be possible if the entire money is taken in the shape of share capital. This system is also helpful where the banking assistance/facilities are not adequate for industries.

This method cannot be relied upon, specially during the period of depression when the industry is on the downgrade. During such period industry requires more money but the depositors get panic and withdraw their funds, which creates an embrassive position for a concern.

4. Managing Agents

This source has played a very important role in early days of industrial development in India for setting up and development of industries. Managing agents have provided fixed and working capital themselves and also arranged through other sources like inducing their friends and relatives to purchase the shares and debentures, arranging loans from banks and public deposits.

Managing agents had played an important role in promotion, financing and management of industrial concerns. The malpractices in management by some of the managing agents have come to light in recent years and the public have become very distrustful of managing agents as a class. Hence the financing of Indian Industries has become less dependent on them than before.

5. **Loans from Banks**

   Upto some years ago commercial banks were providing finance only for the working capital requirement of industries and were avoiding long-term advance against fixed assets. This system was followed due to security reasons, but from this policy small entrepreneur was most sufferer.

   But now-a-days State Bank of India and other nationalised banks provide financial assistance also to the small scale industries under liberalised scheme. The loans are granted to these industries for fixed as well as working capital requirements. State Bank of India has a special scheme to assist engineers, craftsman and other qualified persons who are in need of money for starting an industry.

6. **Ploughing Back of Earnings**

   Every developing industry requires capital for extension and improvement. Ideal method for financing for expansion and improvement of an industry is reinvestment of a part of the profits, which is also known as ploughing back of earnings. The reserve of capital built-up during a continuous spell of prosperous period, can be used as working capital. This system provides sound financial management. This helps in the depression period in addition to that for expansion and improvement of concern.

7. **Leasing.** Fixed assets like land, machinery etc. can be obtained on lease for a number of years on rental basis.
8. **Profit Flowback.** The profit is not distributed to the shareholders or owners and is retained for financial expansion and growth of the concern.
9. **Credit Facilities.** This is an important source of short term financing. In this system, goods and services are obtained on credit. However, in case cash discount is offered, discount forgone becomes a cost of trade credit.
10. **Trade Credit.** These are the financial assistance available from other firms from whom the business has dealings. Most important of them are suppliers of inventory.
11. **Short Term Loans.** These are commercial bank loans as creditor revolving credit agreement. Accounts receivable and inventory are the principal assets used to secure short-term business loans.

Other Financial Institutions

(*A*) **Industrial Finance Corporation.** This corporation was established in 1948 with the object of making long term and medium term credits to the industrial concerns, by providing the loans for the period upto 25 years, after examining the technical, financial and economical soundness of the concern. It sanctions loans only for the fixed capital like purchase of land for factory site and construction of factory buildings to the large industrial concerns.

(*B*) **State Financial Corporations.** These financial corporations are working in most of the states, which grant loans to medium and small industries. Its scope of activities is wider than that of the Industrial Finance Corporation of India as it can also grant accommodation to industrial concerns. It grants loans and advances for a period not exceeding 20 years.

(*C*) **Industrial Development Banks.** This bank is owned by the Reserve Bank of India. It coordinates and supplements the needs of other financing bodies. This bank provides financial assistance to the industries in the form of loans, shares and bonds. It also provides technical assistance to desirous industries.

(*D*) **Unit Trust of India.** This trust was established in 1964 with the idea to provide opportunities for the investment of low income group by acquiring shares in industries. This trust can invest on an industry upto the extent of 5 percent of its investible funds.

(*E*) **Insurance Corporations.** Mutual Funds etc.

Holding of Cash

An organisation must hold cash for following purposes:

(*a*) **For transaction purposes.** In this category, the cash is required to meet payments for carrying out normal functions of business, such as purchases, wages, taxes, dividends etc.

(*b*) **For speculative purposes.** The cash is also required to take advantage of temporary opportunities such as a sudden decline in the price of a raw material.

(*c*) **For precautionary purposes.** Cash is also needed to maintain a safety cushion or buffer to meet unexpected cash needs.

Most firms establish a target level of cash balances to maintain, as excess cash balance results in loss of interest. Optimal level of cash is determined with the help of cash management models and sources available for taking loans at short notice.

27.7. CAPITAL INVESTMENT DECISIONS

Investment means laying out the money (also known as outlay) on an activity or a project with the expectation of some benefit. In an enterprise, expenditure may be either (*a*) to carry out normal operational transactions or (*b*) to plan for the acquisition of assets which will increase production and wealth. Former is generally termed as 'current' expenditure, and is expected to result in benefits in a short period of less than a year. The latter is termed as 'capital' expenditure, and is expected to result in benefits in future period of one or more years and is also known as capital budgeting decisions.

An investment proposal should be judged in relation to whether or not it provides a return equal to, or greater than, that required by investors. Capital budgeting is involved in generating investment proposals consistent with the firm's strategic objectives.

Capital budgeting can be defined as the process of identifying, analysing, and selecting investment projects whose returns are expected to extend beyond one year. Capital expenditure proposals include:

- Purchase of equipment, land or building in order to expand or to diversify into a new line of business.
- Replacement of an existing capital asset.
- Expenditure on research and development programme.
- Lease or buy analysis.

Capital expenditure proposals may be aimed at:

(*a*) acquisition of a new plant to increase the production capacity, or to improve the product through adopting changed technology.

(*b*) minimizing the cost of production arising due to a decision relating to the choice of production processes and plant replacement decisions.

(*c*) non-economic developments like pollution control, fire protection etc.

It is difficult to estimate future benefits accurately from new investment due to uncertainty and risk. Therefore, investment proposals should be evaluated in terms of both expected return and risk. This requires a careful assessment of alternative proposals so as to ensure safety, profitability and liquidity of the enterprise.

For making investment acceptable practice is to prepare a comparative statement of current rate of interest and profit. The profit in any case should be higher than current rate of interest. This is because if we take capital/money for investment on loan, we are required to pay interest on it. Therefore, the yield should be greater than the rate of interest so that enterprise could expect profit.

Significance of Capital Investment Decisions:

Capital investment decisions are basically the examination as to how well the expected future returns justify the related present investments. Capital investment decisions are highly significant due to number of reasons, some of them are :

(*a*) **Investment linked with objectives.** An enterprise with an objective of survival and growth, incurs capital expenditure every year and takes investment decisions, e.g., investment in fixed assets and inventory.

(*b*) **Long term commitments.** A capital project, like hydroelectric project is expected to bring benefits in future years. Such projects require the commitment of funds for future years, and draws the future direction by determining its product, markets, production facilities and technology.

(*c*) **No-going back.** It is difficult to reverse a capital project decision.

27.7.1. Techniques Used In Capital Investment Decisions

For taking capital investment decisions, following techniques are used to evaluate and select the alternative methods:

1. **Payback Period.** This technique determines as to how long it will take (in years) to payback invested capital.

   This period can be determined using the following formula :

$$P = \frac{C}{R}$$

where, P = Pay back period in year
C = Original capital investment
R = Annual return expected, *i.e.*, total annual earings after deducting taxes.

   This method is not much reliable as it does not take into account its insurance, interest and maintenance. Further, in the beginning, the return is generally less, which increases gradually, but here we consider it as constant. This method also does not consider depreciation and obsolescence.

2. **Present Worth Method.** This method is more accurate and reasonable and is used to evaluate the present value of new equipment. For the purpose of comparison, future costs are translated into today's money.

   A 'present-worth rupee' is today's value of money invested (at certain interest rate) after given number of years from today. This can be clearly understood by the following example :

   If we have Rs. 5000 to invest and want to know what will be its worth in ten years at 10 percent interest, using the formula

$$F = P(1+i)^n$$

where, F = Worth of money in future

P = Present amount of money

i = Interest rate

n = Number of years.

Substituting in this formula, we have

$$F = 5000\,(1 + 0.10)^{10} = 5000\,(2.594) = \text{Rs. } 12{,}970$$

Thus, Rs. 5,000 today is worth Rs. 12,970 after ten years from now or in other words Rs. 12,970 after ten years from now has a present worth of Rs. 5,000.

While comparing two alternatives, all the costs must be translated into present-worth and they must be compared for equal length of services, *e.g.*, if machine A has its life of 3 years and *B* has 6 years, then to compare two machines, we must compare the present worth value of 6 years service of two A machines and one *B* machine.

3. **Rate of Return Method.** In this method, average annual net income (after tax and depreciation deductions) is expressed as percentage of capital investment. The formula used for this purpose is:

$$\text{Percentage rate of return} = \frac{\text{Earning per year}}{\text{Net investment}} \times 100\}>$$

Discounted Rate of Return. In this case, following formula is used :

$$C = \frac{R}{(1+r)^n}$$

where, C = Investment cost

R = Expected earning in nth year

r = Rate of return.

If we have to find out the rate of return when a machine has worked for n years and earnings in each year is R_1 (in first year), R_2 (in second year), R_3 (in third year) and so on, then following formula is used for calculating r, by trial and error method :

$$C = \frac{R_1}{(1+r)} + \frac{R_2}{(1+r)^2} + \frac{R_3}{(1+r)^3} + \ldots + \frac{R_n}{(1+r)^n} + \frac{S}{(1+r)^n}$$

S = Salvage value of machine after n years.

4. **MAPI Method.** The term MAPI stands for Machinery and Allied Products Institute of Washington, which has developed this method. This is a new method and was developed by George Teborgh, the director of this institute. The reasoning behind this method is described as follows :

Almost all the equipments are subjected to deterioration and obsolescene in varying degree with the passage of time. Thus with the passage of time, operating inferiority increases. Hence the old machine has this operating inferiority high and book value as low. While a new machine to be purchased will have operating inferiority minimum and cost as a maximum. Hence the problem before manager is to choose between more capital cost and less imperfection on one hand and less capital cost and more imperfection on the other.

The MAPI has developed a new approach which helps in deciding this problem. The existing equipment which is to be replaced is known as *Defender* and the new which will replace the old one is known as the Challenger.

For estimating as to whether the proposed replacement is profitable, the adverse minimum of the defender and the challenger are found and compared. 'Adverse minimum' of the defender or the challenger is the lowest sum of the time adjusted average of capital cost and operating inferiority (expressed in terms of money) obtainable from a machine. The calculations can easily be done with the help of MAPI charts.

27.8. MANAGEMENT OF ASSETS

Decisions regarding management of assets must be made in accordance with the objectives of the firm to maximise shareholder's wealth. We explore ways of efficiently managing the current assets like cash, marketable securities, receivable accounts and inventories in order to maximise profitability. Quite a large amount of attention is required to be paid on managing the current assets, *i.e.*, working capital, but sufficient attention should also be paid to the maintenance of longer-term assets and liabilities.

If an industry is to operate efficiently, receivables and inventories must be tightly monitored and controlled. This is more important particularly for a fast growing concern because the investment in such assets quickly mushroom out of control.

In order to determine appropriate level of current assets, management must consider that, with greater level of current assets, the greater is the liquidity of firm. With greater liquidity, risk becomes less, but profitability is also less.

In order to manage receivables, a proper credit and collection policy and procedure should be followed. This needs decisions on :

- The length of credit period.
- The size of the cash discount.
- The level of collection expenditure etc.

27.9. FINANCIAL ANALYSIS

Most decisions are based on estimate of future events, their associated returns and likely risks involved. Analysis of current performance and financial position is a prerequisite to most important decision. Information on past and present performance can be obtained from different sources.

Financial analysis includes comparisons of changing economic conditions in the country, the industries, the organisations, and within industry. The use of ratios are extremely helpful in financial analysis.

Main areas for which ratios are calculated are :

1. Profitability and Asset Utility

(*a*) Rate of return on investment

(*i*) Return on operating assets

$$= \frac{\text{Operating profit before interest and taxes}}{\text{Average operating assets}} \times 100$$

(*ii*) Return to ordinary shareholders

$$= \frac{\text{No profit after tax and preference dividend}}{\text{Average equity of ordinary shareholders}} \times 100$$

(*b*) Net profit margin $= \dfrac{\text{Operating profit}}{\text{Sales}} \times 100$

(*c*) Asset turnover $= \dfrac{\text{Sales}}{\text{Average operating assets}}$

2. Long Term Capital Structure and Capital Intensity

(*a*) Debt/equity ratio $= \dfrac{\text{Long term debt}}{\text{Long term debt plus equity}} \times 100$

(*b*) Capital/Intensity $= \dfrac{\text{Fixed assets}}{\text{Total assets}}$

3. Liquidity and Working Capital

(*a*) Current ratio $= \dfrac{\text{Current assets}}{\text{Current liability}}$

(*b*) Liquid assets ratio or acid test ratio $= \dfrac{\text{Current assets less stock/inventories}}{\text{Current liability}}$

(*c*) Debtor's turn over $= \dfrac{\text{Sales}}{\text{Average debtors}}$

(*d*) Stock turnover $= \dfrac{\text{Cost of goods sold}}{\text{Average stock}}$

(*e*) Average period of stock holding $= \dfrac{\text{Average stock}}{\text{Cost of goods sold}} \times 365$

(*f*) Creditor turnover $= \dfrac{\text{Credit purchases}}{\text{Average creditors}}$

4. Security

(*a*) Security of current liabilities $= \dfrac{\text{Net worth}}{\text{Current liabilities}}$

(*b*) Debt coverage $= \dfrac{\text{Net profit before interest and taxes}}{\text{Debt interest}}$

(*c*) Preference dividend coverage $= \dfrac{\text{Net profit after taxes}}{\text{Preference dividend requirement}}$

5. Ordinary Shares

(*a*) Earning per share $= \dfrac{\text{Net profit less preference dividends}}{\text{Number of shares outstanding}}$

(*b*) Price earning ratio $= \dfrac{\text{Market price per share}}{\text{Earning per share}}$

(*c*) Dividend per share $= \dfrac{\text{Dividends}}{\text{Number of shares issued}}$

(*d*) Dividend yield $= \dfrac{\text{Dividends per share}}{\text{Market price per share}} \times 100$

(*e*) Book value per share $= \dfrac{\text{Ordinary shareholder's equity}}{\text{Number of shares issued}}$

6. Balance Sheet Ratios

(*a*) **Liquidity Ratios.** Liquidity is the ability of an asset to be converted into cash without a significant price concession. Liquidity ratios measure a firms ability to meet short-term obligations.

(*i*) Current ratio $= \dfrac{\text{Current assets}}{\text{Current liabilities}}$

(*ii*) Acid test, or quick ratio $= \dfrac{\text{Current assets} - \text{Inventories}}{\text{Current liabilities}}$

(*b*) **Debt (Financial Leverage) Ratios.** Debt ratios show the extent to which the firm is using borrowed money.

(*i*) Debt to Equity ratio $= \dfrac{\text{Total debt}}{\text{Share holder's equity}}$

(*ii*) Debt-to-Total asset ratio $= \dfrac{\text{Total debt}}{\text{Total assets}}$

(*iii*) Long term debt to Long term Financing (capitalisation) ratio

$$= \frac{\text{Long term debt}}{\text{Total capitalisation}}$$

(c) Coverage Ratios. These relate the financial changes of a firm to its ability to service or cover them.

$$\text{Interest coverage ratio} = \frac{\text{Earnings before interest and taxes}}{\text{Interest expense}}$$

This ratio indicate the firms ability to meet its interest payments and avoid bankruptcy.

(*d*) Activity Ratios. These are also known as efficiency or turnover ratio, and measure how effectively the firm is using its assets.

(*i*) Receivable activity $= \dfrac{\text{Annual net credit sales}}{\text{Receivables}}$

(*ii*) Receivable turnover in days $= \dfrac{\text{Days in the year}}{\text{Receivable turnover}}$

$$= \frac{\text{Receivable} \times \text{Days in the year}}{\text{Annual credit sales}}$$

(*iii*) Payable turnover in days or average payable period

$$= \frac{\text{Days in the year}}{\text{Payable turnover}}$$

(*iv*) Inventory activity $= \frac{\text{Cost of goods sold}}{\text{Inventory}}$

$$= \frac{\text{Accounts payable} \times \text{Days in the year}}{\text{Annual credit purchases}}$$

(*v*) Inventory turnover in days $= \frac{\text{Days in the year}}{\text{Inventory turnover}}$

$$= \frac{\text{Inventory} \times \text{Days in the year}}{\text{Cost of goods sold}}$$

(*vi*) *Firm's operating cycle.* This is the length of time from the commitment of cash for purchases until the collection of receivables resulting from the sale of goods or services.

Operating cycle = Inventory turnover in days + Receivable turnover in days.

(*vii*) *Firm's cash cycle.* This is the length of time from the actual outlay of cash for purchases until the collection of receivables resulting from the sale of goods or services. Cash cycle = Operating cycle – Payable turnover in days.

QUESTIONS

1. What is financial management ? Describe the role of financial management in a Business.
2. What are financial goals ? Explain various financial objectives.
3. Describe functions of the financial management.
4. What for funds are required in an industrial concern? Explain different types of capital.
5. What is working capital? Explain in detail.
6. Explain the term capitalisation. Compare over-capitalisation and under-capitalisation.
7. Explain different methods of raising finance.
8. Write a note on capital investment decisions.
9. Explain the techniques used in capital investment decisions.
10. How will you manage the assets in an enterprise?
11. What is financial analysis? How it is done?
12. What is "Ratio analysis" and how it is useful in judging the financial performance of a firm?
13. Enumerate the various sources of finance for large scale industries.
14. Describe how capital shares are raised by a public limited company.
15. Differentiate between fixed and working capitals. Explain both the terms in detail.
16. What factors must be considered while deciding working capital? What is capitalisation? Enumerate the effects of over–capitalisation and under–capitalisation.

28

INDIRECT EXPENSES AND DEPRECIATION

28.1. INTRODUCTION

In the chapter on "costing", we shall discuss that, apart from direct labour cost and direct material cost, there are several other expenditures in every factory, e.g., cost of advertisement, building rent, depreciation charges of plant, building, cost of packing, cost of transportation, salaries, commission to salesmen etc. All other expenses, except direct material and direct labour cost, which occur in the firm are known as expenses. These expenses are of two types, namely;

(*i*) Direct expenses

(*ii*) Indirect expenses.

The indirect expenses are also known as 'Overhead Expenses' or 'Oncost'. These overhead expenses are further classified into following three groups :

1. Factory expenses.
2. Administrative expenses.
3. Sales and Distribution expenses.

In the chapter on 'costing' different expenses made on a product manufactured in an industry had already been discussed. Direct labour and direct material costs can be calculated with the help of work order, material requisition slip, wage sheets etc.

As regards to oncosts, some of them can easily be known from various records, example of such oncosts are: power charges, insurance, building rent, water charges, fuel charges, etc. But some other charges require good knowledge and experiences of the estimator. These charges are discussed in this chapter :

1. Depreciation
2. Obsolescence
3. Interest on capital
4. Idleness
5. Repairs and maintenance.

28.2. DEPRECIATION

Whenever any machine or equipment performs useful work, its wear and tear is bound to occur. This can be minimised upto some extent by proper care and maintenance but can't be totally prevented. Its efficiency also reduces with the lapse of time and at one time it becomes uneconomical to be used further and needs replacement by another new unit.

Therefore, we can say that efficiency and value of machine or asset constantly reduces with the lapse of time during its use, which is known as "Depreciation". Some money must be set aside yearly from the profits, so that when the equipment becomes uneconomical, it can be replaced by the new one. Therefore, the initial cost of machine plus installation charges + repair charges—scrape value is charged against overheads and is spread over the machine's useful life.

For this purpose depreciation account for the complete plant or individual equipment is opened in the company's Books and is known as "Depreciation Fund" or "Sinking Fund". This amount is deducted yearly from the profits and kept separately to have sufficient money for replacement at the end of useful life.

Types of Depreciation

For further understanding depreciation can classified as under :

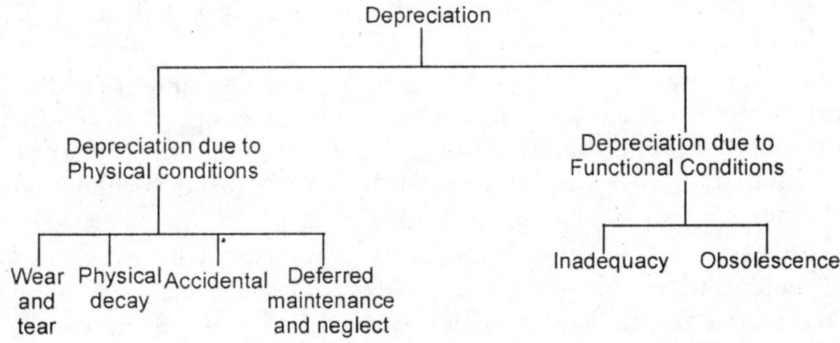

Fig. 28.1.

Now, each type of depreciation is explained in short below :

(*a*) **Depreciation due to "Wear and Tear".** Everybody knows that when any machinery performs work, wear and tear of certain components takes place, although sufficient precautions are taken, *i.e.*, proper lubrication and cooling is done, which minimise wear and tear but it cannot be totally prevented. However, the cost of replacement because of this cause is the value of depreciation due to wear and tear.

(*b*) **Depreciation due to "Physical Decay".** There are certain items in a factory such as insulation of material, furniture, electric cables, poles, buildings, chemicals and vessels etc., which get decay, because of climatic and atmospheric effect, with the result the value of these articles goes on reducing with the lapse of time. Although every effort is made by the owner to keep them in serviceable condition, even then because of climatic and atmospheric effect, there will be reduction in their costs. This reduction in cost is depreciation due to physical decay.

(*c*) **"Accidental" Depreciation.** Although, the machine might have been installed only few days back and sufficient care is taken to prevent accident, even then, accident may occur due to some wrong operation, or some loose component or some other cause, which may result in a heavy damage. The depreciation in a machine caused due to this reason is called accidental depreciation.

Now-a-days, to overcome this problem, most of the owners get their equipment insured with the insurance companies. For that, owners have to pay certain yearly premium. The amount of premium depends upon the estimated cost and life of equipment.

(*d*) **Depreciation due to "Deferred Maintenance and Neglect".** Every manufacturer provides certain instructions for the smooth and efficient running of an equipment. For example, in the case of a vehicle, a manufacturer gave the following instructions:

(*i*) Lubricating oil of particular grade should be used in engine.

(*ii*) Oil should be drained and new oil should be refilled after first 1000 km running and then every 5000 km.

(*iii*) All the bolts and nuts should be re-tightened after every 5000 km running.

(*iv*) Decarbonising after 30,000 km running and so on.

If these instructions are not properly followed because of neglect and proper maintenance is not done as recommended by manufacturer; then the value of the vehicle may reduce and depreciation in value because of this, is called depreciation due to deferred maintenance and neglect.

(*e*) **Inadequacy.** This is the form of functional depreciation. Inadequacy means reduction in efficiency of an asset. This may result even if any equipment is servicing under proper precautions and sufficient maintenance is provided, there is fall in efficiency with the lapse of time.

Secondly, suppose after 2-3 years of running, the demand of products manufactured by certain plant is increased, but the plant cannot cope with the increased demand. This needs additional money either to replace it with the bigger size machinery or installation of another similar size plants. This is, what is called depreciation due to inadequacy.

(*f*) **Depreciation by "Obsolescence".** Now-a-days because of faster scientific advancement, there are changes every day. If a new machinery comes in the market, which is more efficient because of new invention or better design and product produced by the new equipment are cheaper and better than the existing one, then the existing machinery has to be replaced to withstand market competition.

This is called depreciation by obsolescence and is of functional type.

28.3. METHODS OF CALCULATING DEPRECIATION

The following are the various methods of providing depreciation with solved examples for clear understanding :

1. Straight Line Method
2. Diminishing Balance Method
3. Sinking Fund Method
4. Annuity Charging Method
5. The Insurance Policy Method
6. The Revaluation or Regular Valuation Method
7. Machine Hour Basis Method
8. The Sum of the Year's Digits Method.

1. Straight Line Method

This method assumes that the loss in value of machine is directly proportional to its age. It means one should deduct the scrap value from the original value and divide the remaining value by the number of years of useful life.

Let C be the initial cost of a machine.

S be the scrap value.

N be the number of years of life of machine.

and D be the depreciation amount per year.

Then, $$D = \frac{C - S}{N}$$

This method of calculating depreciation fund is also known as "Fixed Instalment" method, because every year same (fixed) amount is deducted and no consideration is made about the maintenance and repair charges, which gradually increase as the machine is getting old.

This will be clear by the following example :

Example 28.1.

(a) *A boiler was purchased for Rs. 45,000 on 1st January, 1996, the erection and installation work costs Rs. 7000. The boiler was replaced by a new one on 31st Dec. 2015. If the Scrap Value was estimated as Rs. 15,000, what should be the rate of depreciation and depreciation fund on 15th June, 2005.*

(b) *If after 12 years of running, some boiler tubes are replaced and the replacement cost is Rs. 1500, what will be the new rate of depreciation?*

Solution.

(a) Total cost = Boiler cost + Erection and installation charges

C = Rs. 45,000 + Rs. 7,000 = Rs. 52,000

Scrap value S = Rs. 15,000

Life of boiler = From 1st January, 1996 to 31st Dec. 2015 = 20 years.

∴ Rate of depreciation. $$D = \frac{C - S}{N}$$

$$= \frac{52{,}000 - 15{,}000}{20} = \frac{37{,}000}{20} = \text{Rs. } 1{,}850$$

∴ Depreciation in value of boiler per year = **Rs. 1850** only. Ans.

Now, depreciation fund on 15th June 2015, *i.e.*, 9 Instalments (from 1st January, 1996 to 15th June, 2005) could be accumulated.

∴ Depreciation fund collected up to 15 June 2005

= Rs. 9 × 1850 = **Rs. 16,650** only. Ans.

(b) As after 12 years tubes have been replaced and cost of replacement is Rs. 1500.

Now, book value in 12 years will be Rs. 52,000 – 12 × 1850

Rs. 29,800

and replacement cost = Rs. 1500.

Hence, new book value = Rs. 29,800 + Rs. 1500

= Rs. 31,300

As, scrap value is same Rs. 15,000, hence the depreciation

= Rs. 16,300 in 8 years

∴ Now rate of depreciation

$$= \text{Rs. } \frac{16{,}300}{8} = \text{Rs. } 2037.50$$

∴ New rate of depreciation per year = **Rs. 2037.50** only. **Ans.**

2. Diminishing Balance Method

This is also called "Reducing Balance" method. The diminishing value of machine is much greater in the early years. It depreciates rapidly in the early years and later on slowly. Therefore, it is better to depreciate more during the early years, when the repairs and renewals are not costly.

So under this method, the book value of the machine goes on decreasing as its existence continues. A certain percentage of the current book value is taken as the depreciation. Therefore, this is also called "Percentage on Book Value" method.

In this, let x be the fixed percentage taken to calculate the yearly depreciation on the book value.

Then $$x = 1 - \left(\frac{S}{C}\right)^{1/N}$$

where, C = Initial cost, S = Scrap value, N = No. of the years of life.

It will be more clear by the following solved example.

Example 28.2 *A lathe is purchased forRs. 8,000 and the assumed life is 10 years and scrap value Rs. 2,000. If the depreciation is charged by Diminishing Balance method, calculate the percentage by which value of the lathe is reducing every year and depreciation fund after 2 years.*

Solution.
$$C = 8{,}000$$
$$S = 2{,}000$$
$$N = 10.$$

We know that $$x = 1 - \left(\frac{S}{C}\right)^{1/N}$$

Substituting the given values in the above formula,

$$x = 1 - \left(\frac{2000}{8000}\right)^{1/10}$$
$$= 1 - (0.25)^{1/10}$$
$$\therefore \quad x = (1 - 0.8706) = 0.1294 = 12.9\%$$
$$\therefore \quad \text{Required \%} = \mathbf{12.94.\ Ans.}$$
$$\therefore \quad \text{Value of lathe after 1 year} = 8000\ (1 - 0.1294) = 8000 \times 0.8706$$
$$= \text{Rs. } 6964.80$$
$$\therefore \text{ Depreciation fund after 1 year} = 8000 - 6964.80$$
$$= \text{Rs. } 1035.20$$
$$\text{Now value of lathe after 2 years} = (6964.80)\ (0.8706)$$
$$= \text{Rs. } 6063.55$$
$$\therefore \quad \text{Depreciation of 2nd year} = 6964.80 - 6063.55$$
$$= \text{Rs. } 901.25$$
$$\therefore \text{ Depreciation fund after 2 years} = 1035.20 + 901.25$$
$$= \mathbf{Rs.1936.54.\ Ans.}$$

3. Sinking Fund Method

In this system, a depreciation fund equal to the actual loss in the value of the asset or machine is estimated, taking into account the interest on the so accumulated fund. The rate of depreciation will be constant throughout the life of machine.

Let D = Rate of depreciation per year.

R = Rate of interest on accumulated fund in fraction number.

C = Total cost of machine.

S = Scrap value.

N = No. of years of life of machine.

$$D = \frac{R(C-S)}{(1+R)^N - 1}$$

This will be clear by the following solved example.

Example 28.3. *A machine is purchased for Rs. 40,000. The estimated life of machine is 15 years and scrap value Rs. 15,000. If the rate of interest on the depreciation fund is charged at 5%, calculate the rate of depreciation by sinking fund method.*

Solution.

The required formula is $D = \frac{R(C-S)}{(1+R)^{N-1}}$

Hence by substitution,

$$D = 0.05\frac{(40,000-15,000)}{(1+0.05)^{15}-1} = \frac{0.05 \times 25,000}{(1.05)^{15}-1}$$

$$= \frac{1250}{(2.080-1)} = \frac{1250}{1.08} = \text{Rs. } 1157.40$$

Hence required depreciation is **Rs. 1157.40 per year. Ans.**

Example 28.4. *An industrial plant with initial value of Rs. 200,000, and the salvage value of Rs. 20,000 at the end of 20 years, is sold for Rs. 145,000 at the end of 10 years. What is the profit or loss if sinking fund depreciation method at 8% compounded annually was adopted.*

Solution. $D = \frac{R(C-S)}{(1+R)^N - 1}$

Here, $D = ?$

$R = 0.08$

C = Rs. 200,000

S = Rs. 20,000

$N = 20$

So $D = \frac{0.08(200,000-20,000)}{(1+0.08)^{20}-1}$ = Rs. 4342

∴ The rate of depreciation = Rs. 4342 per year.

But as per the question, he sold the plant for Rs. 145,000 at the end of 10 years. Thus, we are required to calculate the value of plant at the end of 10 years, which can be obtained as under:

The depreciation amount will be collected each year for 10 years, on which 8% compound interest will be earned. So the amount of depreciation plus compound interest collected in 10 years = Rs. 62,900.

This can be calculated as follows :

Let C_1 be the amount collected for 10 years as depreciation fund along with 8% compound interest. From the formula

$$D = \frac{R(C - S)}{[(1+R)^N - 1]}$$

Converting it in the form of C_1

$$D = \frac{R \times C_1}{[(1+R)^n - 1]}$$

or $$C_1 = \frac{D[(1+R)^N - 1]}{R}.$$

Here D = Rs. 4342, $R = 0.08$

N = 10 years

$\therefore$ $$C_1 = \frac{4342[(1+0.08)^{10} - 1]}{0.08}$$

= Rs. 62,900

Thus the value of plant received at the end of 10 years

= Rs. 145,000 + 62,900 = Rs. 207,900

But Initial value of plant = Rs. 200,000

Hence profit to owner = 207,900 – 200,000

= **Rs. 7900. Ans.**

4. The Annuity Charging Method

In this, interest is charged on the cost of machine or assets every year on the book value, but the rate of depreciation is constant every year.

Let C = Cost of machine.

S = Scrap value.

N = No. of years of machine life.

R = Rate of interest in fraction.

D = Rate of depreciation.

If the value of machine after 1 year becomes C_1, then

$$D = CR + C - C_1 = C(1+R) - C_1.$$

In the same way, the value of machine after 2 years will be say, C_2.

Then $$D = C_1R + C_1 - C_2 = C_1(1+R) - C_2.$$

Hence, the standard formula will be

$$D = \frac{[C(1+R)^N - S]\ [1 - (1+R)]}{[1 - (1+R)^N]}$$

Hence, by substituting the different values in the above formula the rate of depreciation can be calculated.

It will be more clear by the following example.

Example 28.5. *Find the depreciation annually be the annuity charging method after 3 years, when the cost of machine is Rs. 8000 and scrap value is Rs. 4000. Rate of interest is 5%.*

Solution. $R = 5\% = 0.05$

$C =$ Rs. 8000

$S =$ Rs. 4000

$N =$ 3 years.

Hence, by substituting the given values in the formula :

$$D = \frac{[C(1+R)^N - S]\ [1-(1+R)]}{[1-(1+R)^N]}$$

$$= \frac{[8000\,(1+0.05)^3 - 4000]\ [1-(1+0.05)]}{[1-(1+0.05)^3]}$$

$$= \frac{(8000 \times 1.16 - 4000)\,(-0.05)}{1-1.16}$$

$$= \frac{5280 \times 0.05}{0.16} = 1650.$$

Hence, depreciation annuity = **Rs. 1650.**

Now, suppose we have to calculate the reduced value of asset after two years, it can be done in this way :

$$= \frac{[C(1+R)^N - S]\ [1-(1+R)]}{[1-(1+R)^N]}$$

Hence, now S will become C_2, where C_2 is the reduced value of asset after two years and, therefore, $N = 2$ years.

Hence by substitution

$$1650 = \frac{[8000(1+0.05)^2 - C_2]\ [1-(1+0.05)]}{[1-(1+0.05)^2]}$$

or $$1650 = \frac{(8000 \times 1.1 - C_2) \times (-0.05)}{-0.1}$$

or $$1650 \times 2 = 8800 - C_2$$

or $$C_2 = 8800 - 3300 = \text{Rs. } 5500 \text{ only}$$

∴ The reduced value of asset after two years

= **Rs. 5500 only. Ans.**

5. The Insurance Policy Method

This method covers the risk of the machine becoming unserviceable before its estimated life. In this, machine is insured with the insurance company and premiums are paid on the insurance policy. When the policy matures, the insurance company provides sufficient sum to replace the machine.

6. Revaluation or Regular Valuation Method

This is not a standard method. In this, every year the value of machine is ravalued and the difference between the book value and revalued value is charged as a depreciation fund.

7. Machine Hour Basis Method

In this, rate of depreciation is calculated considering the total number of hours a machine runs in a year and, therefore, a work hour chart of every machine is maintained to know the total number of hours the machine run in a year,

This will be clear by the following example :

Example 28.6. *What are Depreciation Charges ?*

A machine is costing Rs. 11,000 and expected to run for 10 years at the end of which its scrap value is likely to be Rs. 1000. Machine is expected to run 2000 hours/year on an average. Estimate the depreciation charges per hour of the machine.

Solution.

Cost of machine = Rs. 11,000

Scrap value = Rs. 1000

∴ Depreciation fund

= 11,000- 1000 = Rs. 10,000

Life of machine = 10 years

$= 10 \times 2000$

= 20,000 hours.

∴ Depreciation charges/hour

$$= \frac{10{,}000}{20{,}000}$$

= **50 paise hr. Ans.**

Example 28.7. *The estimated life of a lathe is 10 years and it works 16 hours a day. The initial cost of lathe is Rs. 8000 and scrap value after 10 years is Rs. 2500. If the machine works for 5840 hours in a year, calculate the rate of depreciation charged annually under machine hour basis method.*

Solution. Here

N = 10 years

C = Rs. 8000

S = Rs. 2500

$C - S = 8000 - 2500$ = Rs. 5500.

Therefore, loss in the cost of lathe in 10 years = Rs. 5500.

Now, life of machine in hours

$= 10 \times 365 \times 16$

∴ Depreciation/hour $= \dfrac{5500}{10 \times 365 \times 16} = \dfrac{55}{584}$

∴ Depreciation in one year (In one year lathe works for 5840 hours)

$$= \frac{55}{584} \times 5840 = 550.$$

∴ Rate of depreciation/year = **Rs. 550. Ans.**

8. The Sum of the Year's Digits Method

In this, as the new equipment is installed, the reduction in value will be faster initially and it will go on decreasing gradually. This fact is taken into account and, therefore, greater amount of depreciation is made during the early years of life and it goes on reducing as the life of equipment decreases. Therefore, for calculating depreciation, the net amount (total cost-scrap value) is spread over whole life in a decreasing proportion.

It will be more clear by the following example :

Examples 28.8. *The cost of a machine is Rs. 16,000 and its scrap value is Rs. 4000. Determine depreciation charges for each year, if the estimated life of machine is 4 years.*

Solution. Here

$$C = \text{Rs. } 16{,}000$$
$$S = \text{Rs. } 4000$$
$$N = 4 \text{ years.}$$

Then

$$C - S = 16{,}000 - 4000 = \text{Rs. } 12{,}000$$

Now, sum of the digits of the years will be

$$(1 + 2 + 3 + 4) = 10$$

Now, depreciation charges for each year can be calculated as follows:

Depreciation charges for the 1st year = $\frac{4}{10} \times 12{,}000 =$ **Rs. 4800.**

Depreciation charges for the 2nd year = $\frac{3}{10} \times 12{,}000 =$ **3600.**

Depreciation charges for the 3rd year = $\frac{2}{10} \times 12{,}000 =$ **Rs. 2400.**

Depreciation charges for the 4th year = $\frac{1}{10} \times 12{,}000 =$ **Rs. 1200.**

Therefore, from above it is clear that higher depreciation charges are made during the early years and this is the advantage of this method.

Example 28.9. *Expenses for the following three machines have been allocated as under :*

Machine A	*Rs.* 370
Machine B	*Rs.* 663
Machine C	*Rs.* 930

One overhead have also been used for bringing the materials to these machines. The utilisation of these 3 machines and the crane is as follows:

Machine	A	B	C
Hrs used with crane	200	150	500
Hrs without crane	540	630	–

If expenses on crane are Rs. 595, calculate machine-hour rate for each machine and rate for machines when used with crane.

Solution.

Machine	*Total Expenses in Rs.*	*Total hrs. used*	*Hourly rate in Rs. without crane i.e. 2/3*	*Hourly rate with crane 4 + 0.70 in Rs.*
1	2	3	4	5
A	370	740	0.50	1.20
B	663	780	0.85	1.55
C	930	500	1.86	2.56
Crane	595	850	0.70	--

Example 28.10. *A company has been set up for the manufacture of a specially designed pump approved by the government. The company has a capacity of producing 50,000 units per year. Government placed an order of only 10,000 units and the company failed to get any other order from other sources. The company charged the entire depreciation of the year over 10,000 units, but the government objected to it. Give your opinion on this point of dispute.*

Please also give your opinion about the rate of depreciation if government places an order of 80,000 units for manufacturing in one year.

Solution. The act of the company for charging the depreciation of the whole year on 10,000 units instead of 50,000 units is not justified, because the government did not take any guarantee for placing the order for full capacity of 50,000 units. In these circumstances, the government is liable to pay depreciation for 10,000 units only. Suppose the depreciation for full year is Rs. 100,000. Thus depreciation for each unit is $\left(\frac{100,000}{50,000} = \text{Rs. } 2.00\right)$. Thus the government must pay Rs. 2 × 10,000 = Rs. 20,000 and rest Rs, 80,000 is treated as a case of indirect expenses due to idleness of the factory.

Similarly, if the government places an order of 80,000 units and the same is executed in the same one year then also depreciation at the rate of Rs. 2.00 per unit should be charged. Since this is a good luck of the company and also good efforts made by them to produce more than the capacity, the company has full right to get more amount on account of depreciation.

28.4. OBSOLESCENCE

Suppose a factory owner purchases a machine for his production shop but after some duration a better machine comes in the market, whose production rate is very high and is much economical. Although the old machine is efficient but becomes out of fashion and uneconomical due to new better machine which has come in the market. This is known as 'Obsolescence'. Consideration of this factor is of much importance and some money should also be set aside from the profit for this cause.

Hence "Obsolescence" is the depreciation of existing machinery or asset due to new and better invention, design, equipment or process etc.

It is very difficult problem for the estimator to provide for the on-cost for obsolescence, because no body can say when a revolutionary change in the machine is coming in the market. But it is a general practice to reduce the life of a machine so as to account for the effect of obsolescence. Now the depreciation and obsolescence charges are calculated on this reduced life.

Suppose an estimator expects the life of machines as 20 years, then the depreciation rate will be 100/20 = 5%. By considering obsolescence also, its life may be taken as 15 years. Then the combined depreciation and obsolescence charges will be 100/15 = 6.66% instead of 5%. Therefore, the difference 6.66 - 5.00 = 1.66% will be obsolescence charges.

28.5. INTEREST ON CAPITAL

While preparing cost account, interest on capital invested is also considered. The rate of interest is that, which would have been available if that capital is deposited in some bank. By charging the interest, cost of product increases and the profit seems to be lesser.

Interest should be charged on the products produced, because :

(*i*) Real profit is not received until interest on capital is charged. Because manufacturer gets an amount equal to interest even if he does not work.

(*ii*) The stocks of raw and finished products cost more, because of the rent and interest on the blocked money.

(*iii*) If the capital is borrowed for business, then the interest has to be paid. Similarly, if manufacturer himself provides capital, he should be credited by a sum equal to the interest.

Some manufacturers do not charge the interest on the invested capital. They have the following points to advocate their views :

(*i*) As interest is also a part of the profit, it should not be charged separately.

(*ii*) It is charged to show less profit to deceive the consumers and to increase the cost of product.

(*iii*) It complicates clerical work.

28.5.1 Amortization

This refers to the process of reducing the principal on a loan by a series of periodic payments to the lender. If the entire loan is paid off by the periodic payments, we say the loan is "fully amortising".

The setting aside of money at intervals for the gradual payment of a debt is called "amortisation".

28.6. IDLENESS

Idleness in an industry may be of following two kinds :

(*i*) Idleness of machines. (*ii*) Idleness of workers :

These idlenesses are discussed as under :

1. **Idleness of Machines.** This is the time, when machines remain without doing any useful work. Idleness of machine may be due to the several reasons. Following are some of them :

   (*a*) *Mechanical reasons.* Examples of such reasons are breakdown of machines, power failure, accidents etc.

   (*b*) *Bad planning.* Machine may remain idle due to bad planning. Reasons for such idleness are : not engaging the machines to their full capacity, providing more machines or lack of supervision.

2. **Idleness of Workers.** In this category worker remains idle but he is paid for this duration also. The idleness of the worker may be due to some of the following important reasons :

   (*a*) *Labour.* In this category workers do not perform useful work due to their personal reasons, *e.g.*, due to lockout, strikes, accidents and natural calls etc.

   (*b*) *Mechanical.* Examples of mechanical reasons when worker remains free are : power failure, breakdown of machines etc.

   (*c*) *Supervisory.* Due to poor supervision, sometimes worker wastes his time for waiting to receive the instructions from supervisor. Sometimes workers waste their time in gossiping or wandering here and there unnecessarily because of poor supervision.

28.7. REPAIRS AND MAINTENANCE

Every machine requires maintenance for increasing its life and to keep the machine in good condition to remove unnecessary delays in the production. For maintenance, machines are cleaned, lubricated and checked thoroughly from time to time to replace the worn out parts. Manufacturer's instructions for machine maintenance should be carried out properly.

Repair is the process of bringing the defective machine into efficient working condition. Every machine has to be repaired sometimes or the other during the course of its useful life. Some money has to be spent on the maintenance and repairs. For determining overheads, this expenditure should also be considered. Repairs and maintenance charges can be determined with the help of 'diminishing balance' method, which has already been discussed in the chapter.

28.8. INTEREST CONCEPT

The term "Interest" means periodic payment for the use of "Capital". It can be seen both from the borrowers' as well as lenders point of view. The borrower receives money which forms the capital for production of goods and services. Thus he earns profit by the borrowed capital and it is, therefore, fair that he should pay a part of this profit to the lender in the nature of interest.

It may be defined as 'the paid money for the.use of borrowed capital'.

It may also be defined as 'the income produced by money which has been loaned'.

This can be explained by the following example :

Suppose Mr. A comes to Mr. *B* and desires to borrow Rs. 1000 saying he will return it after one year. Mr. *B* has Rs. 1000 in his pocket, in which he had planned to purchase a few luxuries which he does not now possess. He decides that it would not be too bad to go without these luxuries, if Mr. A would promise to pay him something extra for his doing without these personal pleasures for a year. He thinks that Rs. 100 would be a fair price for this year of sacrifice on his part.

He quickly remembers that although he has known Mr. A for some time and believes he is entirely honest. Human nature has its weakness and there is some possibility that Mr. A might run off and not repay what he has borrowed. Also he remembers how many innocent people are killed by accident each year and realizes that this might happen to his friend so that he would not get back his money. He feels that he should also be paid some money for this risk. He thinks an additional Rs. 50 to be paid for this risk. He tells to Mr. A, he will be glad to let him use Rs. 1000 for a year, if Mr. A will promise to give him back Rs. 1150 at the end of the year. Mr. A agrees to do this, and the deal is made. The extra Rs. 150 which Mr. *B* receives at the end of the year is said to be the interest which is earned from his Rs. 1000 investment.

Interest may be divided into two categories :

(*A*) Pure interest or net interest or general interest.

(*B*) Gross interest or commercial interest.

(*A*) Pure Interest

It is one which is same for all exchanges of loans and which involves:

(*i*) No risk of non-payment

(ii) No inconveniences and

(iii) No additional work.

Suppose a person lends Rs. 100 and gets backRs. 106at the end of one year without involving risk of loss, any inconvenience or additional work, then Rs. 6 is the pure interest and Rs. 6 per hundred per annum is the rate of pure interest or the general rate of interest.

(B) Gross Interest or Commercial Interest

It is gross or the total interest earned on the capital under the actual commercial conditions, *i.e.*, conditions involving risk of loss, inconvenience and additional work. Suppose, a person lends Rs. 100 and gets back Rs. 115 at the end of one year, he has earned gross interest of Rs. 15 per hundred per annum. This gross interest includes the pure interest and the money cost of risk, inconveniences and additional work involved in the transaction. Thus, the rate of gross interest varies with nature of securities, persons involved in deal, time and place.

The following questions arise in the study of rate of interest:

(a) Why should pure interest be paid at all ?

(b) Why are there different rates of gross interest ?

(c) Why does the rate of gross interest vary ?

(d) How is interest related with rent ?

(a) Reason for Paying Interest. This question should be seen from the borrower's points of view and from the lender's point of view. Thus borrower receives money which forms the capital for production of goods and services. Production brings wealth to the borrower resulting from the capital borrowed and it is, therefore, fair that he should pay a part of this benefit to the lender on capital in the nature of interest.

The lender of money has accumulated money through abstinence from immediate consumption. It is then justified that this sacrifice be rewarded in the form of interest on capital so accumulated.

(b) Reasons for Different Rates of Gross Interest. The rates of gross interest vary with the nature of securities, persons involved in the deal, time, place etc. The reasons for these different rates are as below :

(i) Differences in risk involved.

(ii) Differences for inconveniences.

(iii) Differences in additional work involved.

(iv) Differences in cost of investment.

(v) Differences in period of investment.

(vi) Possibility of changes in the value of money.

(c) Reasons for Variations in the Rate of Interest. The important reasons may be :

(i) New inventions and better methods and techniques of production increase the level of productivity of capital goods. The demand for capital increases and hence the rate of interest increases.

(ii) Due to certain changes, the durability of capital goods may reduce or the capital goods may become obsolete. Then the demand for replacement increases resulting in increased rate of interest.

(iii) Changes in the general rate of real wages may change the rate of interest. In this case, people can afford to save some more money. If saving is more, rate of interest will fall.

(*iv*) Changes in saving habits of people may cause corresponding variations in the rate of interest. Thus, if people start saving more money, the rate of interest may fall.

(*v*) Variation in the rate of interest may take place due to variations in rate at which price index is changing. It has been found that the rate of gross interest is more, if the rate of increase of price index is higher.

Interest in Relation to Rent

Once the capital has been invested in capital goods the return from the capital goods replaces the interest on the capital. Now this return from capital goods is closely related to the return or the rent on the land. Thus the rent is the surplus earnings on the land, the quantity of land being fixed. Similarly the return on the durable capital goods is in the same nature of surplus earnings and hence is termed as "Quasi rent".

Thus corresponding to rent on land we have quasi rent on capital goods.

28.9. THEORIES OF INTEREST

Any theory of interest should be able to answer the following two factors:

(*a*) Why interest should be charged, and

(*b*) Why the rate of interest at any time or any place is? What it is?

The various theories of interest are:

1. Productivity theories of interest.
2. Abstinence theory of interest.
3. The Austrian theory or Bohm-Bawerle's theory of interest.
4. Time Preference theory of interest or Fisher's theory of interest.
5. The Neo-classical theory of interest, and
6. The Liquid Preference theory of interest.

1. Productivity Theory of Interest. This theory states that

(*a*) Interest on capital is justifiable because of the productivity of capital, and

(*b*) The rate of interest is proportional to the productivity of capital.

Suppose a person borrows money, invests it on machinery, process goods and earns profits. It means, the borrower is in a position to pay interest on the borrowed capital because he earns through the borrowed money. What should be the rate of interest? This theory states that the rate of interest should be proportional to the productivity of the capital.

2. Abstinence Theory. This theory suggests that in order to lend capital to borrowers, the creditors shall have to undergo a sacrifice. They abstain from consumption. The rate of interest is a reward to the capitalists for abstaining from the unproductive consumption for wealth to make it available for production. This abstinence from consumption is regarded as a real sacrifice or cost which deserves a reward in the form of rate of interest. If the lenders consume goods and services, they get pleasure. If they do not, they feel pain of not having that pleasure and, therefore, interest is to be paid.

3. The Austrian Theory. An Austrian economist, Mr. Bohm Bawerle is the main person to develop this theory. This theory has three main statements.

(*a*) Mostly people prefer present consumption of future. A bird in hand is worth two in the bush. People see future needs as something rather vague and unimportant and present needs as something very urgent and definite, they discount the future. According to this theory, interest is the price paid in order to overcome this unreasonable preference for present over future needs.

(*b*) The capital is productive and the more round-about method of production is adopted, the higher is the productivity of capital. Productivity explains as the willingness to pay interest.

(*c*) At any time, supply of capital arises from the savings through postponing present consumption while the demand for capital due to greater productivity of round-about process of production involving greater time.

Regarding the rate of interest the theory states that it is determined by the force of demand and supply of capital.

4. **Time-Preference Theory.** Prof. Fisher has stated his theory in terms of time perference. According to him interest is the price of time. He says that there is a time-preference for all individuals. They will save different amounts for different periods and for different rates of interest. Similarly, there will be people who will demand different amounts for different periods for investment. There will be a market of supply of savings and demand for savings but time-preference will alone determine the rate of interest because demand for investment is infinite and, therefore, it is always there. The determining factor is supply of saving which depends on the time-preference of the people.

5. **The Neo-Classical Theory.** According to this theory the rate of interest brings demand and supply of money for investment into equilibrium with one another. This condition is analogous to the condition that at any price of a commodity, the demand for the commodity equals the supply. The interaction of these two forces determines the rate of interest. It can be represented graphically.

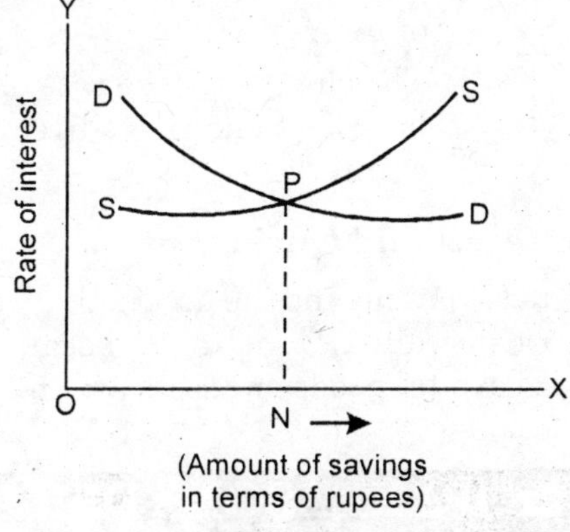

Fig. 28.2.

Let *DD* is the demand curve and *SS* the supply curve saving. *P* is the point of interaction of both the curves. Therefore, *PN* is the rate of interest and *ON* is the quantity of saving supplied and demanded in the market.

6. **Liquidity Preference Theory.** Keynes developed this theory which deals with the following three factors :

(*i*) The nature of interest,

(*ii*) The necessity of interest and

(*iii*) Determination of the rate of interest.

(*i*) **The Nature of Interest.** Keynes says that there is the "real rate" of interest. He defined various commodity rates of interest and the money rate of interest is treated as a particular case of commodity rate. For example, if 5 kg of sugar today may be exchanged for 6 kg of sugar after one year, then the sugar rate of interest is 20%. Different commodities have different commodity rate of interest.

(*ii*) **The Necessity of Interest.** Keynes disagree that the rate of interest determines the amount of savings. According to him, the savings depend on the general level of income of people and their marginal requirement to consume. Having saved some money, an individual has the alternative of either keeping this money which is readily available whenever required or investing it for a definite duration and earning interest. The interest earned is a reward on his savings.

(*iii*) **Rate of Interest.** Keynes states that the rate of interest is determined by the supply and demand for money itself. According to him, if the rate of interest increases, the amount of cash intended to be hoarded by public would fall below the available supply of hoards. A new equilibrium is then reached and the amount of hoards gets reduced. Reverse action takes place, if the rate of interest falls.

Why Interest Varies

There are several reasons of interest variations.

1. If the productivity as capital goods is the reason for demand for liquid capital, then the demand will increase or decrease according to the changes in productivity. New invention will change the level of productivity and hence rate of interest.
2. Some technical reasons connected with the nature of the capital goods may change the rate of interest. The more rapidly the capital goods wear out or become obsolete, the greater will be the demand for fresh capital to replace them.
3. The changes in the habits of the people to hard capital will affect the rate of interest.
4. The secular changes in the normal expectation of life may cause the rate of interest to vary over long periods. The longer the expectation of life, the lower becomes the rate of interest.
5. The changes in the rate of interest will depend on the level of income of people. If they have just enough to live, they cannot save any thing at all, whatever may be the rate of interest.

Interest and Quasi-rent

Quasi-rent means the productivity of the capital goods. Whatever return we get from the capital goods is called 'Quasi-rent', because it is in the form of surplus. In other words, the returns of real capital goods or assets are called quasi-rent.

28.10. REASONS FOR INTEREST

From the above explanation, it is clear that the interest represents payment for the use of borrowed money, and it represents payment to the lender for several things

(*i*) It pays him for foregoing the use of his money during the time the borrower has promised to pay it.

(*ii*) It is payment for the risk he took in permitting another person to use his money.

He can get interest by loaning money acts as an incentive for him to accumulate capital to lend. Thus interest usually represents payment for several reasons.

In the transaction between Mr. *A* and Mr. *B*, Mr. *A* promised to repay Mr. *B* the amount he borrowed and in addition agreed to pay a specified rate of interest. Thus, the amount of principal to be repaid and the rate of interest were guaranteed by the borrower. These are fundamental conditions where interest is involved. Repayment of the principal is guaranteed by the borrower, and the rate of pay for the use of the borrowed funds is specified. In this way there is a clear distinction between interest and profits, since profit arises from the investment of capital in business ventures where there is no guarantee of return of the capital and no assurance as to what, if any, the rate of return will be.

The Productivity of Capital

Some people are afraid as how a person can afford to borrow money to undertake business, when not only the capital but interest must also be repaid. This capital is productive,*i.e.*, equipment which is purchased with the borrowed capital enables the borrower to produce more income than he could without it. He can thus repay the borrowed money plus interest and still have a net profit which he otherwise would have not been able to earn. The following example explains this:

Suppose a gardener earns his living by mowing and otherwise taking care of lawns. Using an ordinary lawn mower and trimming shovers, he takes care of 12 lawns at a fee of Rs. 40 per lawn per month. His annual income is

$$40 \times 12 \times 12 = \textbf{Rs. 5760}$$

He purchases a gasoline-powered lawn mower and some electric trimming shovers. These cost a total of Rs. 1500.

He borrowed Rs. 1500 at 12% interest. Now with the help of this new equipment he can take care of 20 lawns. His annual income now is

$$20 \times 40 \times 12 = \text{Rs. } 9600$$

His expenses are as follows :

Lawn mower and shovers	Rs. 1500
Interest	Rs. 180
Gasoline	Rs. 500
	Rs. 2180

His net annual earnings are as follows :

Income	Rs. 9600
Expenses .	Rs. 2180
Net Income	Rs. 7420

While in the first case his earning was Rs. 5760. Thus, by borrowing money, he earned Rs. 7420 – 5760 = Rs. 1660, extra.

The productivity of capital explains why there is a constant interchange of money in business activity. In order to increase our productivity and thereby our standard of living, there has to be a constant flow of capital into business enterprise. Interest and profit are, therefore, essential factors in making an adequate supply of capital available so that the economy of this country can expand and provide jobs. Unless interest and profit rates are adequate, the necessary capital will not be available from public.

28.11. KINDS OF INTERESTS

Interest is of two kinds :

(*i*) Simple Interest and

(*ii*) Compound Interest.

28.11.1. Simple Interest

Simple interest is directly proportional to time and the total interest is payable at the end of the specified period usually one year. For example, if Rs. 2000 are borrowed for 2 years at 9% interest rate, the interest earned will be

$$\text{Rs. } (2000 \times 0.09 \times 2) = \text{Rs. } 360$$

The interest I is found by the formula,

$$I = P \times n \times i$$

where I = Simple interest amount, P = Principal amount.
i = Rate of Interest and n = No. of years in the period

If one wishes to know the entire amount due *i.e.* (principal + interest).

$$S = P + I = P(1 + ni)$$

Interest computed in this way is known as simple interest and the factor $(1 + ni)$ is called the interest factor.

Ordinary Simple Interest. Usually the unit of time for the interest period is taken as one year and the resulting interest rate is the rate per year. When it is required to compute the interest due for a fraction of one year, it is often the practice to consider 360 days in a year.

Thus, 50 days are equal to $\frac{50}{360}$ of one year. Interest calculated on this basis is called "Ordinary simple interest"

Exact Simple Interest. If the interest is calculated on the basis of 365 days in a year, the result is called "Exact simple interest."

28.11.2. Compound Interest

When the interest due at the end of the period becomes a part of the principal and itself earns interest along with the principal, it is called "Compound interest". Depending upon the length of the interest period, quarterly or so, the formula for compound interest is

$$S = P(1 + i)^n$$

where S = compound amount.

Here the factor $(1 + i)^n$ is called compound amount factor or CAF.

If interest is paid more than once in a year say semi-annually, quarterly or monthly etc. the formula for compound amount factor is

$$\text{CAF} = \left(1 + \frac{i}{m}\right)^n$$

where i = interest rate per year
n = no. of years in the period
m = no. of periods per year.

Example 28.11. *Calculate the compound amount when Rs. 2000 are lent at 9% interest rate for 3 years, being compounded semi-annually.*

Solution. No. of periods per year = 2

$$S = P\left(1 + \frac{i}{m}\right)^n = 2000\left(1 + \frac{0.09}{2}\right)^{3 \times 2} = 2000\,(1.045)^6$$

$$= \textbf{Rs. 2660 only.}$$ **Ans.**

28.12. PRESENT WORTH

People wish to determine the value at the present time of a sum of money which will be available at some time in the future. For example, suppose a person purchased a Rs. 100 saving bond. The bond states that 10 years from the date of purchase, the government would pay the holder of the bond Rs. 100. How much would the bond be worth, at the time of receipt. Naturally, it would be worth just what was paid in it, say Rs. 30. Thus Rs. 30 could said to be "present value" of Rs. 100 which was to be received 10 years later.

Compound Amount Factor (CAF) is used to determine the future value of present capital. For example, the future value of present capital of Rs. 2450. The same thing expressed in the reverse way, it means that the present value of Rs. 2450 at 7% interest 3 years back is Rs. 2000. Therefore, the formula in Present Worth Factor (PWF) is written as

$$PWF = \frac{1}{(1+i)^n}$$

$$P = \left[\frac{1}{(1+i)^n - 1}\right]$$

Here, S = Future capital and
P = Present worth.

PWF can be expressed in the form of hyphens like (*PWF*-7% – 3). The value of *PWF* can be seen from the standard interest table.

Example 28.12. *Determine the present value of Rs. 5000 due after 5 years at 9% compound interest rate.*

Solution.

$$P = \frac{S}{(1+i)^n} = \frac{5000}{(1+0.09)^5} = \frac{5000}{(1.09)^5} = \mathbf{3249.66\ Ans.}$$

The above explained CAF and PWF refer to amounts payable in one single payment (SP), it should, therefore, be called as CAF (SP) and PWF (SP) standing for $(1+i)^n$, $\frac{1}{(1+i)^n}$ respectively.

In most of the cases payments are made in series of periodical "equal payments". These are called "Annuities".

28.13. ANNUITIES

An annuity is a series of equal payments occurring at equal periods of time. It may also be said as "Equal payment or uniform payment series". In certain business dealings, equal payments are made at the end of equal periods of time and all such accumulated payments are allowed to earn compound interest. Periods of time may be of any length, say a year and month etc. but periods should be of equal length. Interest is expressed in yearly terms but the actual interest is paid at the end of each equal period. Hire purchase payments, instalment buying, L.I.C. premium payments etc. are made by this method.

Features. These have the following common features :

(*i*) These involve series of payments.

(*ii*) All payments are of equal amount.

(*iii*) Payments occur at equal time intervals.

(*iv*) All payments are made at the end of periods.

(*v*) Compound interest is earned on all accumulated payments.

28.13.1. Kinds of Annuities

1. Capital Recovery Annuity,
2. Present Worth Annuity,
3. Sinking Fund Annuity,
4. Compound Annuity.

1. **Capital Recovery Annuity.**

This is applied in case of debt payments where this initial debt or capital is recovered in uniform or equal periodical payments. It is commonly seen in deferred payments, instalment purchase etc., in all such cases the seller recovers his capital along with accumulated compensating interest not in open single lump sum payment but in "Periodical equal payments". The desired formula for this is :

$$D = P\left[\frac{i(1+i)^n}{(1+i)^n - 1}\right]$$

Where D = Equal payment amount,
P = Initial capital
i = Compound interest rate and
n = No. of interest periods.

and $\frac{i(1+i)^n}{(1+i)^n - 1}$ is called *CRF* (*EP*)

where *CRF* (*EP*) is known as Capital Recovery Factor (Equal Payments).

The values of CRF (EP), can be seen from standard interest tables. These can be expressed through hyphens as [CRF (EP)-8%-7] where 8% means interest rate is 8% per year and the money is borrowed for 7 years.

Example 28.13. *A person took a loan of Rs. 10,000 from a bank for 5 years at 15% compound interest. The person wants to pay-off the amount in 5 equal annual instalments. Determine the amount of each equal payment.*

Solution.

$$D = P\left[\frac{i(1+i)^n}{(1+i)^n - 1}\right] = 10{,}000\left[\frac{0.15(1.15)^5}{(1.15)^5 - 1}\right]$$

$$= \frac{10{,}000 \times 0.317}{1.01135} = \textbf{Rs. 2983 Ans.}$$

2. **Present Worth Annuity.**

This is applied in cases of L.I.C. premiums and all other retirement plans. These are usually known as premium annuities, income annuities and other future provisions. The desired formula is

$$PW = D\left[\frac{(1+i)^n - 1}{i(1+i)^n}\right]$$

where PW = Present worth of entire annuity

D = Periodical payment amount

and $\frac{(1+i)^n - 1}{i(1+i)^n}$ = PWF (EP) called present worth factor equal payments.

This can be expressed in the form of hyphens as [PWF (eP) 5%-6] means interest rate is 5% on 6 years. The value of PWF-(eP) at different interest rates corresponding to different periods are found in standard interest tables.

Example 28.14. A person wants that his daughter should get a fixed amount of Rs. 500 at the end of every year for the coming 7 years, so that they may put today itself in the bank total present worth capital which is earning a 7% interest, compounded annuity.

Here
$$PW = D\left[\frac{(1+i)^n - 1}{i(1+i)^n}\right] = \left[\frac{(1+0.07)^7 - 1}{0.07\,(1+0.07)^7}\right]$$
$$= 500\left[\frac{(1+0.07)^7 - 1}{0.07\,(0.07)^7}\right] = 500\left[\frac{1.606 - 1}{0.07 \times 1.606}\right]$$
$$= \frac{500 \times 0.606}{0.07 \times 1.606} = \textbf{Rs. 2695.25. Ans.}$$

3. Sinking Fund Annuity.

This is applied when a definite sum requires to be collected at a future date by setting aside at equal intervals of time equal amounts ; so that these equal period payments while earning compound interest total up to the desired amount at the desired future date. Suppose a manufacturing concern wants to open a depreciation reserve fund for machinery replacement by setting apart equal depreciation amounts in the sinking fund.

The desired formula is :
$$D = S\left[\frac{i}{(1+i)^n}\right]$$

where D = periodical equal payment amount and

S = Desired future total

$$\frac{i}{(1+i)^n - 1} = \text{Sinking fund factor or SFF (EP)}$$

Example 28.15. *A manufacturing concern desires at the end of 5 years a sinking fund of Rs. 30,000. What equal amount should it deposit every year and, earning 10% interest.*

Solution. Here,
$$D = S\left[\frac{i}{(1+i)^n - 1}\right]$$
$$= 30{,}000\left[\frac{0.10}{(1+0.1)^5 - 1}\right] = \frac{3000}{(1+0.1)^5 - 1}$$
$$= \textbf{Rs. 4914. Ans}$$

4. Compound Amount Annuity.

In this a person deposits equal amounts at the end of a number of periods and each amount is allowed to earn compound interest per period. This is used in savings deposit schemes and commulative time deposit schemes.

The desired formula is : $CA = D\left[\dfrac{(1+i)^n - 1}{i}\right]$

where CA = compound amount and

D = periodical payment amounts

and $\dfrac{(1+i)^n - 1}{i}$ = CAE (eP) called compound amount factor equal payment.

Example 28.16. *Calculate the total compound amount for a 5 years annuity paying Rs. 500 at every year end, earning interest rate of 9% per year.*

$$CA = D\left[\frac{(1+i)^n - 1}{i}\right] = 500\left[\frac{(1+0.09)^5 - 1}{0.09}\right]$$

$$= \frac{500 \times 0.539}{0.09} = \textbf{Rs. 2994.45 Ans.}$$

28.14. PROFIT

The profit of a firm equals the total sale proceeds minus the cost of production. It is the residual part of the total sale proceeds left over after paying off all the items of expenditure in the cost of production including rent on land, wages for labour, interest on borrowed capital, salaries of management and organisation etc. But, out of this profit, later on certain adjustment is to be made. We have to subtract not only actual cost but also certain imputed cost in order to obtain "gross profit". Owner's capital and owner's labour is to be paid although they have not been actually paid. These cost should be added to the actual costs. In addition, certain tax obligations might have arisen during that year. These can be paid next year also, but to arrive at a correct figure of gross profits we should add those tax payments on the cost side. The value of the existing stock is also obtained and this should also be deducted to obtain the true value of "Gross Profits".

To obtain "Net Profits", we are required to make still certain adjustments. From the gross profit, deduct depreciation charges and the cost of new investment during that period. The final position is called as "Net Profits". It can be summarised in the following ways :

1. Residue = Actual Receipts during a period—Actual payments made during that period.
2. Gross Profit = Residue-Imputed charges of owner's labour and capital—Tax obligations—Value of balance stock.
3. Net Profit = Gross Profit—Value of capital equipment added during the period—Depreciation charges.

28.14.1. Theories of Profit

Various theories of profit have been put forth by different economists to explain the profits. The important among these are :

1. Risk and Uncertainty theory
2. Dynamic Approach to the profit theory
3. Residual theory of Profits.

1. **Risk and Uncertainty Theory.**

   This theory was introduced by Howley and according to him net profit is the residual income of the owner after making payments for all factors of production and is the reward for the risk taken by him. It concludes that profits are due to the risk taken by the owner. The owner has to bear the risk of losing capital, there are certain risks which can not be insured. They are known as uninsurable risks. We cannot predict when fashion will change or when new invention will come or when will war outbreak etc. There are unforeseeable changes and hence in value risks which cannot be insured payments made for these uninsurable risks are called 'profits'.

2. **Dynamic Theory of Profits.**

   Mr. J.B. Clark introduced this theory. According to Clark, the pure profit in a dynamic society is the residual income of the owner after making all payments including rent, wages interest and salary of management. Such pure profit in the form of residual earning result only in a dynamic society where the changes in population, stock of capital, tastes or fashion, production techniques, managment principles etc. occur dynamically. In a static society since there are no such changes, no pure profit may result. Thus pure profit is a sign of progress. Thus to increase profit an owner may produce a new commodity, popularise it and earn large profit and soon competition sets in, the profit decline. Thus in maintaining pure profits high continuous progress is essential.

3. **Rent Theory of Profits.**

   This theory was introduced by Walker, who considered profit as a form of rent. He says that owner earns profit in the same way as land earns rent. Marshall has criticized this theory for the following reasons :

   (*a*) Where as rent on land is in the form of surplus earnings, profit is not.

   (*b*) Land may produce zero or positive rent but never negative rent whereas net profit may be positive, zero or negative.

QUESTIONS

1. What is depreciation ? Discuss the various methods of calculating it.
2. What are the various Indirect Expenses which are essential in estimating total cost? Explain.
3. (*a*) Describe the basic concepts of depreciation.

   (*b*) What does the, "Reserve of depreciation" account indicate ?
4. What are the situations in which replacement of an equipment, generating unit on a machine tool becomes essential ? Describe any one method of depreciation accounting.

5. An Industrial Plant with initial value of Rs. 220,000 and the salvage value of Rs. 40,000 at the end of 20 years is sold for Rs. 195,000 at the end of 1 year. What is the profit or loss if sinking fund depreciation method at 8% compounded annually was adopted?
6. Define overhead ? Describe various types of overhead.
7. Mention the principles on which overheads are apportioned? Describe the basis upon which following expenses are allocated :
   (i) Lighting
   (ii) Depreciation of plant and machinery
   (iii) Time-keeping
   (iv) Fire insurance of the factory
   (v) Insurance for transportation of finished products
   (vi) Expenses of small tools
   (vii) Audit fees
   (viii) Overhead crane service.
8. Define fixed and variable overheads. Give five examples to illustrate each.
9. Factory *A* has a lower rate of overhead absorption than factory*B*. Both factories produce the same type of goods. Discuss whether this can be taken as a sign that factory A is more efficient than factory *B*.
10. Describe the necessary for controlling of selling and distribution cost. Give example of two products for which marketing costs are very high as compared to manufacturing costs.
11. *(a)* Define "Selling overhead" and "Distribution overhead" and give examples. Explain how the selling overheads are allocated to products?
    (b) What are the main differences between Selling and Distribution expenses?
12. How following expenses are generally treated in the cost accounts:
    (i) Expenses on warehouse,
    (ii) Expenses on design and development,
    (iii) Bad debts,
    (iv) Computer,
    (v) Moving and refining the existing plant,
    (vi) Dismantling and selling one of the existing plant,
    (vii) Rectification of product after sales during warranty period,
    (viii) Expenses on trade fair and exhibition and,
    (ix) Market Research.
13. Explain the various elements which exist in the actual rate of interests.
14. Why does an actual rate of interest differ from person to person and place to place and industry to industry ?
15. Name the various theories of interest and explain any two of them.
16. Discuss and explain the neo-classical theory of interest.
17. Define :
    (i) Gross profit
    (ii) Net profit
    (iii) Pure profit

(iv) Pure interest

(v) Gross interest.

18. Write short notes on :

(i) Rent and quasi-rent

(ii) Dynamic theory of profits

(iii) Rent theory of profits.

19. If Rs. 1000 loan earns Rs. 45 interest in six months. What is the ordinary simple interest rate?

20. How long will it take Rs. 10 to double if interest at rate of 5% compounded semiannuity?

21. What interest rate compounded quarterly will have to be earned in order to Rs. 500 to amount to Rs. 1200 in 10 years?

22. Find the present value of Rs. 900 due in 5 years, if interest is at the rate of 9% compounded semi-annually. A large concern has made two offers to the owner of a small company for the purchase of his business. Offer *A* is Rs. 100,000 in cash. Offer *B* is Rs. 10,000 in cash, Rs. 50,000 at the end of the one year and Rs. 100,000 at the end of 3 years. If money is worth 6%, which is better offer from the view point of the owner or the small company.

23. How much will have to be deposited at the end of each year for 12 years in order to amount Rs. 12,000, if interest is earned at the rate of 15%.

24. A loan company advertises that they borrow Rs. 5,000 and repay in monthly instalments of Rs. 280 each. What rate of interest is the loan company receiving as its money ?

25. A sum of money is accumulated by depositing Rs. 1,200 annually, in monthly instalments for 10 years. Interest is paid at the annual rate of 6%. What amount will be accumulated at the end of the 10 years period ?

29 Elements of Economics (Economic Concepts)

29.1. TERMS USED IN ECONOMICS.

29.1.1. Economics

Economics is the science which studies human behaviour and aims at meeting maximum objectives with the help of limited resources.

Economics is the art and science which deals with the economic problems of the people living in a society.

Economics as applied to industrial undertakings has two main divisions:

1. Micro Economics
2. Macro Economics.

Micro–Economics can be defined as, "the branch of economics where the unit of study is a firm or an individual." It is the main concept and a numerical tool for economics concerning with industries. The Micro–Economics deals with smaller units of the economy like behaviour of individual customer, plant or industrial undertaking.

Macro–Economics deals with whole economy, and studies the growth of national income and economical environment as a whole. It plays an important role in forecasting and other factors related to marketing.

Economics is a subject of interest to the engineers, as they are to deal with the economic problems related to increasing the production, reducing the efforts, increasing the wealth, improving the living standard, reduction in cost of the products etc.

29.1.2. Income

Income (personal) is defined as those incomings which are in the form of money and payment in kind. Whereas income from business is found by deducting the outgoings (expenditure on material, labour and other overheads etc.) from gross income. Income can be derived either from personal services or from property.

National income is either

(*i*) the money value of all goods and services produced during a particular period, generally one year, or

(*ii*) the sum of all personal incomes derived from economic activity during this time.

29.1.3. Investment

In a business, investments are made on :

- Land and buildings
- Procurement of raw materials, tools, instruments etc.
- Purchase and installations of machinery.
- Internal services like material handling devices, transport vehicles, light, water, gas, power etc.
- Administrative and selling services.
- Works related to productivity improvement, cost–reduction etc.
- Payment of wages to the employees.
- Other works related to running the business and its development.

29.1.4. Reserve

Reserves for working capital are very necessary for sound financial management. It ensures stability and financial soundness of the enterprise. This helps, to cover credit, losses, to liquidate debts, to expand, for replacement of machinery, for taxes, to meet contingencies like fire, theft, strikes etc.

Reserves are of two types, namely revenue reserves and capital reserves. Revenue reserves are required to meet future commitments such as, distribution of dividends, research and developments etc. Whereas capital reserves are made for increasing the capital.

29.1.5. Assets and Liabilities

Assets. These are the resources of the business concern. Examples of assets are : cash, properties, machinery, stocks etc.

Liabilities. Liabilities are the claims of the creditors against the business enterprise. The examples of the liabilities are :

(a) *Current Liabilities.* Bank overdraft, short term loans, trade credit, wages etc.

(b) *Fixed Liabilities.* Amount owed, long term debts etc.

(c) *Contingent Liabilities.* Guarantees and when principal debtors fail to pay etc.

29.1.6. Utility

Utility may be defined as the power of things and services to satisfy some human wants. It can also be defined as the satisfaction which we actually obtain from the things or services we consume.

Economic utilities are of five types :

1. *Form Utility.* A person is said to create form utility when he changes the form of matter in order to make it more serviceable. For example, table out of a log of wood.
2. *Place Utility.* When a person transports a commodity from a place where it is wanted less to a place where it is wanted more, he creates place utility, *e.g.*, bringing timber from mountains to plains.
3. *Time Utility.* When an article is stored till the time it will be needed and valued more, time utility is added to it, *e.g.*, storing of articles by shopkeepers, storing of vegetables and fruits in cold storage for sale when they are not available.

4. *Possession Utility.* Possession or ownership utility is created by transfer or change of ownership of an article from a person who has little use for it to a person who has greater use for the same, *e.g.*, selling of a table by carpenter to an office.
5. *Service Utility.* Those who render direct or personal service to the consumers create service utility, *e.g.*, doctors, lawyers, teachers, domestic servants etc.

29.1.7. Market

In ordinary sense, a market is a place where things are brought and sold. But in economic sense, a market is a place or region, where buyers and sellers have free competition with one another. The buyers and sellers may not be at one place, they may have free intercourses by means of post, telegraph, telephones etc. Therefore, in the economic sense, the term market is applied to commodities, and buyers and sellers or the same who are in direct competition with one market to another.

Essentials of Market.

The following are the essentials of a market:

1. A commodity.
2. A large number of buyers and sellers.
3. An area or region which may be a village, a city, a country or the whole world.
4. Competition between buyers and sellers.

When there is perfect competition between buyers and sellers, there can be only one price for the commodity at any given time. Some allowance may be made for cost of transportation from one part of the market to another.

Classification of Markets.

Markets may be classified in respect of (a) Space and (b) Time.

Under space, we may have,

1. Local Markets,
2. National Markets and.
3. International Markets.

Under time, we may have,

1. Short period markets.
2. Moderately long period markets.
3. Long period markets.
4. Secular markets or very long period markets.

(*a*) **Space Market.** When commodity is brought and sold only within or near its place of production, it has local market, *e.g.*, fresh vegetables, milk etc.

When the area of the market covers a whole country the commodity is said to have National Market.

When competition in the case of a commodity is world-wide, the market is said to be International.

(*b*) **Time Market.** This division of market refers to the period for which the market for any commodity exists.

Market Price.

Market price of a commodity is the price that prevails in the market at any time. It can change at any time. The market price of a commodity at a certain time is determined by the interaction of the forces of demand and supply. No buyer will be prepared to pay anything more than the marginal utility of the commodity to him. He would rather pay less. On the other hand, no seller is prepared to accept anything less than the cost of production of the commodity to him. He would like to charge as high a price as possible. Marginal utility and marginal cost of production are the two limits. The price fluctuates between them. It is fixed at a point where it is equal to supply. Competition between buyers raise the price, and between sellers lower the price.

Normal Price. Normal price is the price which is likely to prevail in the long run if sufficient time is allowed for adjustment between demand and supply. Normal Price is neither abnormally high nor abnormally low. It is more or less a constant price and the market price fluctuates above and below. The governing factor for the normal price is the cost of production or supply of a commodity. It, therefore, tends to be equal to its marginal cost of production.

Monopoly Markets

Under conditions of perfect competition value is determined as a result of interaction of the forces of demand and supply. Under monopoly, the supply is under the control of the monopolist. Therefore, the law of demand and supply does not work freely. The aim of the monopolist is to get maximum net profit from the monopoly. In order to achieve this aim, he has to study the conditions of demand and supply.

In determining the price policy, the monopolist has two possibilities before him :

1. He may fix a particular price for his product when he puts the quantity on the market according to the demand.
2. He may fix quantity of product in the market and sell it for whatever price he gets. The monopolist will go on producing so long as the marginal revenue is greater than the marginal cost. He will stop producing the commodity where marginal revenue is equal to marginal cost.

At this point, his net profit is maximum. In order to reach this point, he follows the method of trial and error in fixing the price.

29.1.8. Money

Money is all that serves as a medium of exchange. It includes metallic coins, currency notes, cheques, bills of exchange, hundies and drafts.

Functions of Money

1. It serves as a medium of exchange. All buying and selling is done through the medium of money.
2. Money is used as a common measure of value. The values of all commodities are measured in terms of money.
3. It serves as a standard of deferred payment. All borrowing and lending is done in money.
4. It serves as a store of value. We store value in the form of money, not in the form of any other commodity.

Kinds of Money

1. **Standard Money.** It is that form of money in terms of which all values are measured and the face value of which is equal to its intrinsic value, *e.g.*, gold coins.

2. **Token Money.** It is that form of money the intrinsic value of which is less than its face value, *e.g.*, small coins and paper notes.
3. **Paper Money.** It is made of paper and issued by the government of a country. It is of two kinds (a) Convertible (*b*) Inconvertible.
   (*a*) Paper money is convertible when it can be converted into standard money at the option of the holder.
   (*b*) It is said to be inconvertible when it cannot be redeemed into gold or silver on presentation. Such notes are issued by the government of a country in times of emergency.
4. **Legal Tender Money.** Money which can be legally tendered for payment of debts or other obligations is said to be legal tender money.
   There are two kinds of legal tenders :
   (*a*) *Limited Legal Tender.* It is that form of legal tender money which can be paid in discharge of an obligation upto a certain limit. Small coins other than 50 paise bits are legal tender upto Rs. 10
   (*b*) *Unlimited Legal Tender.* It is the form of legal tender money which can be paid in discharge of debt to any amount.

29.1.9. Trade Cycle

Trade in any commodity does not always remain in the same state of activity. Sometimes it improves, at other times it deteriorates. It is seen that these changes follow one another. That is, a period of good trade is followed by a period of depression. The cycle of these changes is called the Trade Cycle.

During period of good trade, the prices rise, the unemployment percentage goes low, productive activities and orders increase, profit goes up. The wages of workers increase.

During bad trade or "Slump" prices drop and profits decrease, unemployment increases, productive activities are curtailed and wages are cut. Lower standard of living is forced on majority of population. The wholesale prices fall much in excess of the retail prices. The rate of interest falls.

All these factors, force the management to introduce economic measures like stoppage of waste, introduction of greater efficiency or even retrenchment of staff. Thus the cost of production per unit is reduced below its price and a narrow margin of profit starts being earned. The fluctuations like the swing of a pendulum automatically generate movement in other direction with equal momentum. Periods of prosperity contain in themselves seeds of depression. There is a regular time interval in the occurrence of boom and slump in trade, which varies from 7 to 10 years from peak to peak. These changes do not occur only in India but affect the whole world.

Characteristics of Trade Cycle

1. The trade cycle is synchronous. That is, the upward and downward movements occur at approximately the same period in all industries. A good business in one industry stimulates business in other industries.
2. Trade cycle is an international feature. Through International trade and foreign exchange, the prosperity or depression spreads to other countries.
3. Boom and slump affect all industries, but not to the same extent. The industries manufacturing capital goods such as engineering, ship building, aircraft etc., experience the heaviest fluctuations.

4. The cycles exhibit a wave-like movement and the different recorded cycles are members of the same family, but no two cycles are exactly similar.

Causes of Trade Cycle

Following theories have been formulated in regard to the causes of the cycle.

1. Climate Theory
2. Theory of Under-consumption.
3. Monetary Theory
4. Psychological Theory.

1. **Climate Theory.** According to 'Jevons' trade cycles are caused by sun spots, which occur at an interval of 10-45 years. They adversely affect the crops, decrease the purchasing power of cultivator and cause depression.
2. **Theory of Under-consumption.** When inequality of income exist, that is, large portion of total wealth is owned by a few, and greater portion of this income is saved, the savings are invested in productive enterprises which add more and more of consumption goods. But on the other hand, the equivalent income to buy these goods is not available. Thus the supply of goods increases in relation to demand. There is a glut (circulation of money) of market which cannot be sold at a profit. So the profits decrease further, investment stops, more income is received than spent and depression sets in.
3. **Monetary Theory.** According to this theory, the trade cycle is a purely monetary phenomenon. The upward movement of the trade cycle is brought about by the expansion of credit, when rates of interest are low, the investors borrow more and expand their business activities. The process continues, income increases and the prices also increase. The demand for loans rises. Bank reserves get depleted owing to increased cash circulation. The banks increase rates of interest and hesitate to advance loans. From this point the trend of trade takes a turn.
4. **Psychological Theory.** According to this theory, the cause of the cycle is business confidence or rather over confidence. During boom, people expect more profits and expand their business and carry production beyond profitable sale. At some point, business has to be curtailed and conditions of depression start.

29.1.10. Profit

The profit of a firm equals the total sale proceeds minus the cost of production. If the residual part of the total sale proceeds left over after paying off all the items of expenditure in the cost of production including rent on land, wages for labour, interest on borrowed capital, salaries of management and organisation etc. But, out of this profit, later on certain adjustment is to be made. We have to subtract not only actual cost but also certain imputed cost in order to obtain "gross profit". Owner's capital and owner's labour is to be paid although they have not been actually paid. These costs should be added to the actual costs. In addition, certain tax obligations might have arisen during the course of the year but it is not essential for us to pay them up during that year. These can be paid next year, but to arrive at a correct figure of gross profits we should add those tax payments on the cost side. The value of the existing stock is also obtained and this should also be deducted to obtain the true value of "Gross Profits".

To obtain "Net Profits", we are required to make still certain adjustments. From the gross profit, deduct depreciation charges and the cost of new investment during that period. The final position is called as "Net Profits". It can be summarised in the following ways :

1. Residue = Actual receipts during a period – Actual payments made during the period.
2. Gross Profit = Residue – Imputed charges of owner's labour and capital Tax obligations – Value of balance stock.

3. Net Profit = Gross Profit – Value of capital equipment added during the period – Depreciation charges.

29.1.11. Theories of Profit

As already discussed in previous chapter, various theories of profit have been put forth by different economists to explain the profits. The important among these are :

1. Risks and Uncertainty theory
2. Dynamic Approach to the Profit theory
3. Residual or Rent theory of Profits.

1. **Risk and Uncertainty Theory.** This theory was introduced by Howley and according to him net profit is the residual income of the owner after making payments for all factors of production and is the reward for the risk taken by him. It concludes that profits are due to the risk taken by the owner. The owner has to bear the risk of losing capital, there are certain risks which can not be insured. They are known as uninsurable risks. We cannot predict when fashion will change or when new invention will come or when will war outbreak etc. There are unforeseeable changes and hence in value risks which cannot be insured, payments made for these uninsurable risks are called 'profits'.
2. **Dynamic Theory of Profits.** Mr. J.B. Clark introduced this theory. According to Clark, the pure profit in a dynamic society is the residual income of the owner after making all payments including rent, wages, interest and salary. Such pure profit in the form of residual earning result only in a dynamic society where the changes in population, changes in the stock of capital, changes in tastes or fashions, changes in production techniques and changes in management principles, occur dynamically. In a static society since there are no such changes, no pure profit may result. Thus pure profit is a sign of progress. Thus to increase profit an owner may produce a new commodity, popularise it and earn large profit and soon competition sets in ; the profit decline. Thus in maintaining pure profits high continuous progress is essential.
3. **Rent Theory of Profit.** This theory was introduced by Walker, who considered profit as a form of rent. He says that owner earns profit in the same way as land earns rent. Marshall has criticized theory for the following reasons :
   (*a*) Whereas rent on land is in the form of surplus earnings, profit is not.
   (*b*) Land may produce zero or positive rent whereas net profit may be positive, zero or negative.

29.1.12. Price and Pricing

Value of an item expressed in terms of money is called price. The price of everything falls and rises from time to time and place to place, and with every such change the purchasing power of money changes for that item. Price of everything is the rate at which it can be exchanged for anything else. Price is determined by the interaction of two sets of influences, namely, demand and supply.

A 'price' for a product or service refers to the amount of money needed to acquire that product or service. In a competitive business environment, Marketing Managers strive to establish pricing policies for goods or services to meet certain objectives such as:

(*i*) To enable the firm to earn a fair percentage of profit.
(*ii*) To meet or stay ahead of competition.
(*iii*) To maintain or increase the firm's share of market.
(*iv*) To stabilize its prices.

Pricing is the most important decision-making process because this is the factor which brings revenues and profits to the concern. Mistake in pricing decision may adversely affect the firm, its growth, profit and future.

Factors Influencing Pricing.

(*A*) *Internal Factors.*

(*i*) Corporate and marketing objectives of the firm.
(*ii*) Basic characteristics of the product.
(*iii*) Stage of the product on product life cycle.
(*iv*) Electricity of demand of the product.
(*v*) Image sought by the firm through pricing.
(*vi*) Costs of manufacturing and marketing.

(*B*) *External Factors.*

(*i*) Buyer behaviour regarding the particular product.
(*ii*) Market characteristics.
(*iii*) Extent of bargaining power of customers.
(*iv*) Competitors' pricing policy.
(*v*) Government controls/regulations on pricing.
(*vi*) Social considerations.

Pricing Strategies

A number of pricing strategies may be adopted to sell the product. When introducing a new product following policies may be used:

(*i*) Skim the cream pricing.
(*ii*) Penetration pricing.
(*iii*) Old pricing or psychological pricing.
(*iv*) One price system or variable price system.
(*v*) Leader pricing.
(*vi*) Follow the market pricing.

Pricing Methods

There are several methods of pricing, each of them is suitable for achieving a particular pricing objective. Some of the commonly used methods of pricing are as under:

1. Cost based pricing.
2. Demand based pricing.
3. Competition based pricing.
4. Product-line based pricing.
5. Tender pricing.
6. Rebate and discounts (differentiated) pricing.

29.1.13. Demand

Demand means an effective desire, that is the desire coupled with purchasing power in order to become demand. Demand varies with the price, there are many other factors which have influence over demand.

Law of Demand. The relation of price and demand is known as "law of demand", which states that, "higher the price, lower the demand and *vice-versa,* other things remain the same".

The 'law of demand' is also shown graphically in the form of a chart which is called 'Demand Curve' (Fig. 29.1). *DD* is the demand curve for an article or commodity. The curve slopes down towards right side indicates that when price rises, less is the demand and when price falls more is the demand. Such types of slopes are called 'Negative slopes'.

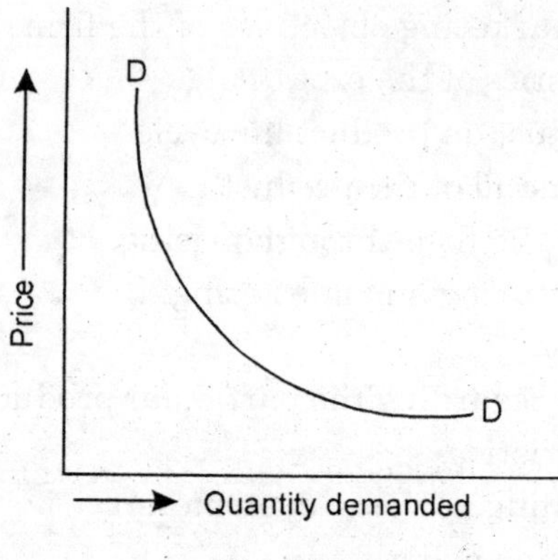

Fig. 29.1

Elasticity of Demand

Law of demand states that higher the price, lower the demand and *vice-versa.* But definition is not clear about range of change, it only guides the direction of change. This means that it is not clear that how much increase in price lowers how much demand. For knowing the range, we should know the elasticity of demand. The elasticity of demand can be defined as "the degree of responsiveness of quantity demanded to a change in price". This means that it represents the rate of change in quantity demanded due to the change in the price. Strictly speaking, elasticity of demand refers to the way in which the demand for a good response to a change in its price, whether a rise or a fall.

Factors Affecting the Elasticity of Demand

(*a*) **Type of Commodity.** The demand of necessities like wheat, sugar or salt never changes with the change of price. Such demand is inelastic, whereas, the demand of luxuries like television, cosmetics changes with the price, called elastic demand.

(*b*) **Customer's Income.** People with high income are less affected by price change, whereas the low income group suffers more. A rich man never cuts his consumption of milk or fruit with the price rise, whereas lower income people certainly cut their demand.

(*c*) **Part of Income Spent on the Commodity.** If any one spends a definite small amount of the income on a commodity then there is no effect by the price rise.

(*d*) **Use of Commodity.** Demand of a commodity having many uses, is elastic, such as steel, where, by price change the demand may be changed. If the commodity having limited uses, the demand may be inelastic.

(*e*) **Durability of Commodity.** If a commodity can be repaired, and the expenses are less, in comparison with the price of new commodity like foot wears etc. In such cases by the price rise, one would like to use the commodity even after repair. Thus more demand for such goods, causes higher elasticity of demand.

(f) **Substitute for the Commodity.** If a commodity has a number of substitutes, the demand is relatively elastic. Such as if petrol prices rise then people leave the cars, and like to use scooters, buses or cycles.

(g) **Urgency of Demand.** If the price of an essential commodity rises, such as sugar, wheat or salt, one would like to give up something else than giving up the sugar or salt. If one has the habit of smoking, the demand is elastic, because with price rise in cigarettes one would like to give up smoking or reduce number of the same.

Relative Elastic Demand. When a reduction in price leads to less than proportional increase in demand. Here the shape of demand curve is steep.

In actual practice, we generally meet cases mentioned at *b, d* and *e* above.

Change in Demand. The change in demand means 'an increase or decrease in demand'. An increase in demand means that at the same previous prices there is an increase in demand.

If so then demand curve will lie to the right of the original curve (Fig. 29.1). The increase in demand may be due to increase in people's income, discovery of new use of the product, an improvement in customer's taste etc.

Likewise the decrease in demand would mean that at the same previous level of prices, less quantity would be sold. The demand curve will then lie towards left of the original curve.

The increase or decrease in demand is also termed as 'shift in demand schedule'. This is because the demand curve shifts towards left or right with decrease or increase in demand.

29.1.14. Supply

Supply of a commodity refers to the various quantities of a commodity which a seller is willing and able to sell at different prices in a given market, at a point of time, other things being constant. Price of a commodity is affected by the demand and the supply.

Law of Supply. "As the price of a commodity rises, its supply increases and as the price falls, its supply declines". Thus the quantity offered for sale is directly proportional to price, *i.e.*, larger the supply, higher the price or *vice-versa* (Fig. 29.2), other things remain same.

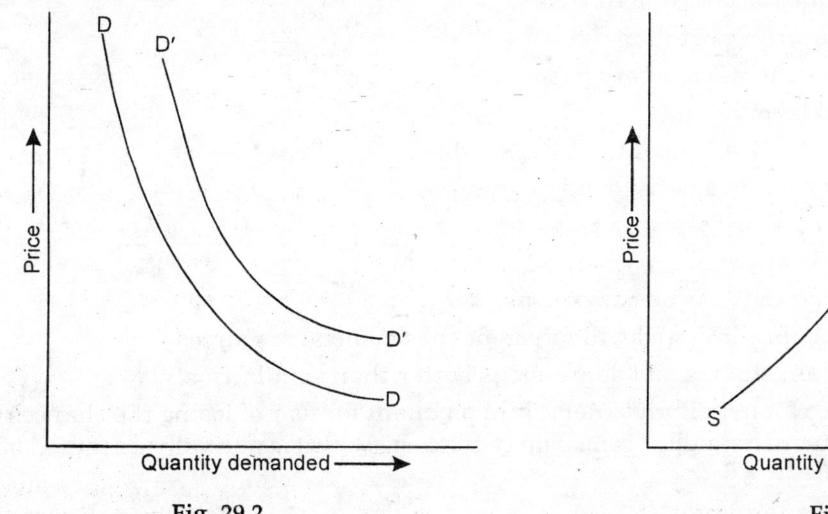

Fig. 29.2.

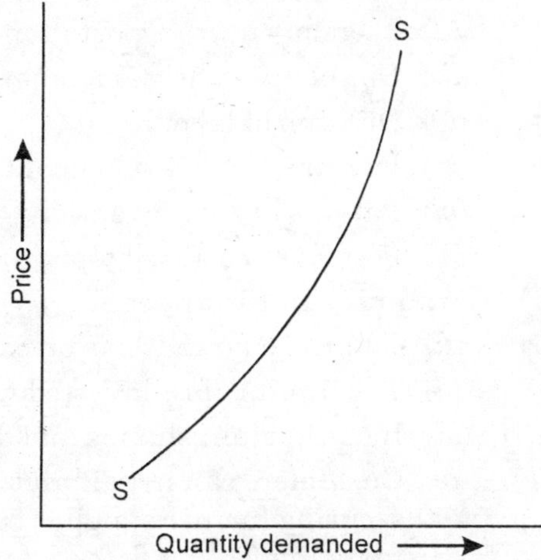

Fig. 29.3.

Increase and Decrease in Supply. This means a change in quantity supplied without any change in price. This, therefore indicates a shift in supply schedules to the right with increase in supply and to the left with decrease in supply.

Determination of Price. Prices under perfect competition are determined by the laws of demand and supply. Prices will be fixed at a point where the supply and demand are at an equilibrium. The equilibrium will change by changes in forces of demand and supplv.

29.1.15. Economies of Size

Since the efficiency and profitability of a concern depends, among other things, on its size also, one of the first decisions made by an entrepreneur establishing a new enterprise is on the size. He will first decide the size, keeping the finances and other things in his mind. He may also study the opportunities for expansion in future. Size of a concern can be measured in following ways:

(*A*) *Input,*

- (*i*) Net worth
- (*ii*) Size of total assets
- (*iii*) Employment
- (*iv*) Amount of power and
- (*v*) Materials used.

(*B*) Output,

- (*i*) Volume of output
- (*ii*) Value of output.

Out of these, output seems to be the best way to indicate the size, whatsoever may be the combination of men and machines.

Large Size v/s Small Size.

New inventions and other developments made it profitable to produce the goods on mass scale. Concerns can be grouped into following economies.

(*A*) **Economies in Production.** Large production is economical, *i.e.*, cost of production per unit is less because of following reasons.

- (*i*) Bulk purchasing of raw materials.
- (*ii*) Economy in transportation.
- (*iii*) Use of automatic machinery is possible,
- (*iv*) Division of labour.
- (*v*) Research and development can be possible.
- (*vi*) Patents of new inventions can be acquired.
- (*vii*) Possible to utilise by-products.

(*B*) **Economies in Finance**

- (*i*) Can raise large funds on easy terms.
- (*ii*) The profits, if re-invested will augment the financial resources.
- (*iii*) It can sustain slumps and depressions better than small firms.
- (*iv*) Customers can not afford to default in payment for fear of losing the chances of securing further supplies from a large concern (which is normally a reputed one in its line).

(*C*) **Economies in Management**

- (*i*) Expert advice is available,
- (*ii*) Lower overheads.
- (*iii*) Modern management techniques can be employed.

(*D*) **Economies in Marketing**

(*i*) Better advertising.

(*ii*) Lesser overheads, since volume is too large.

(*iii*) Prompt service is possible.

Large firms not necessarily have all the advantages, it has certain weaknesses also. Some of the **weaknesses of large firms** are:

1. Coordination between different departments is difficult.
2. Top Management should be very efficient and capable of exercising adequate control and harmony among various departments.
3. Any mistake, may lead to very costly and difficult to rectify.
4. Difficult to maintain good human relations. .
5. Social evils, like monopoly, exploitation of labour, concentration of economic power, exploitation of consumers.

Some of the important **advantages of small firms** are :

(*i*) Owner can pay more attention to the working and can avoid wastages etc. immediately. Thus efficiency is higher.

(*ii*) Can pay more attention to the quality and variety.

(*iii*) Can take care of customers' individual tastes and requirements.

(*iv*) Can change without much problem to take care of changes in fashions.

Looking to the advantages and weaknesses of both the large and small firms, generally entrepreneur wants to start on a small scale and expand gradually till it reaches to the optimum size. Optimum size of the firm is that size when the cost per unit of production is minimum.

In short following are the **main factors which influence the size of a concern.**

1. **Technical.** The more complicated the process or automatic the machinery, the larger will be the size.
2. **Managerial.** Managerial ability available.
3. **Finance.** Financial resources available.
4. **Marketing.** Marketing staff and technique employed. Risks and fluctuations in demand.

29.2. ECONOMICS APPLIED TO INDUSTRIES

Economics which is applied to industrial undertaking has two main divisions.

1. Micro Economics
2. Macro Economics

Micro economics can be defined as the branch of economics where the unit of study is a firm or an individual. Whereas Macro economics, is more aggregative and has unit of study as whole of the economy.

Micro economics, also known as price theory is the main concept and a numerical tool for economics concerning with industries.

Some of the concepts of micro economics are,

(*i*) Elasticity of Demand

(*ii*) Marginal Revenue

(*iii*) Short and Long run Demands

(*iv*) Various Market Forms.

These all concepts of micro economics have great significance to economics concerning with the industries. Whereas the macro economics plays an important significance in the area of forecasting such as input analysis (see chapter 24).

29.3. PRICE, DEMAND AND SUPPLY

29.3.1. Price and Demand

For an economist the relation between Price and Sale is quite important. The demand varies with the price though there are many other factors which have influence over demand.

Law of Demand

The relation between price and supply is known as 'law of demand' which states that 'higher the price, lower the demand and *vice versa,* other things remain the same'.

Demand Schedule

The relationship of price to demand or supply is shown in tabular form below. This is also termed as 'Price-Quantity relationships'.

Demand Schedule

Quantity	*Price*
100 units	Rs. 10
150 units	Rs. 8
200 units	Rs. 6
250 units	Rs. 4

Such types of tables are known as 'Demand Schedules'.

Demand Curve. The 'law of demand' is also shown graphically in the form of a chart which is called 'Demand Curve' (Fig. 29.4) *DD* is the demand curve for an article or commodity. The curve slopes down towards right side indicates that when price rises, less is the demand and when price falls more is the demand. Such types of slopes are called 'Negative slopes'.

Elasticity of Demand

Law of demand states that higher the price, lower the demand and *vice versa*. But definition is not clear about range of change, it only guides the direction of change. This means that it is not clear that how much increase in price lowers how much demand. For knowing the range, we should know the elasticity of demand. The elasticity of demand can be defined as "the degree of responsiveness of quantity demanded to a change in price". This means that it represents the rate of change in quantity demanded due to the change in the price.

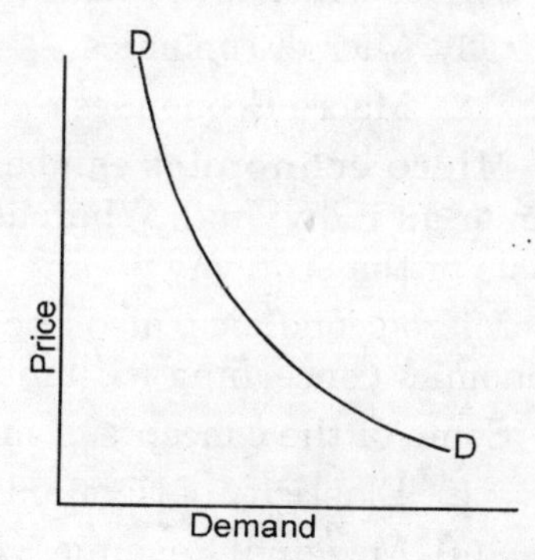

Fig. 29.4

Thus if elasticity of demand is represented by E_P, then

$$E_P = \frac{Q_2 - Q_1}{Q_1} / \frac{P_2 - P_1}{P_1}$$

where Q_1 = quantity demanded before price rise
Q_2 = quantity demanded after price rise
P_1 = price before price rise
P_2 = price after price rise

Suppose Q_1 = 2000,
Q_2 = 2500,
P_1 = 10 and
P_2 = 9

$$E_p = \frac{(2,500-2,000)}{2000} / \frac{9-10}{10} = -2.50$$

the negative sign represents that there is an inverse relationship between price and demand, generally this negative sign is omitted.

There is a modification in the above formula

$$E_p = \frac{Q_2 - Q_1}{\frac{Q_2 + Q_1}{2}} / \frac{P_2 - P_1}{\frac{P_2 + P_1}{2}} = \frac{Q_2 - Q_1}{Q_2 + Q_1} / \frac{P_2 - P_1}{P_2 + P_1}$$

Putting the above example values in this modified formula, then

$$E_p = \frac{500}{4500} / \frac{-1}{19} = -2.11$$

Thus the conclusion of above calculation is that by one per cent reduction in price causes 2.5 per cent rise in demand by first formula whereas by modified formula the rise in demand is 2.1 per cent.

The elasticity of demand depends upon the following factors :

(a) **Type of Commodity.** The demand of necessities like wheat, sugar or salt never changes with the change of price. Such demand is inelastic, whereas, the demand of luxuries like Television, Sarees, Cosmetics changes with the price, called elastic.

(b) **Customer's Income.** People with high income are less affected by price change, whereas the low income group suffers more. Such as a rich man never cuts his consumption of milk or fruit with the price rise whereas lower income people certainly cut their demand.

(c) **Part of income spent on the commodity.** If any one spends a definite small amount of the income on a commodity then there is no effect by the price rise.

(d) **Use of Commodity.** A commodity having many uses, then demand is elastic, such as steel, having different uses, by price change the demand may be changed. If the commodity having limited uses the demand may be inelastic.

(e) **Durability of Commodity.** If a commodity can be repaired, and the expenses are less, in comparison with the price of new commodity like foot wears etc., in such cases by the price rise, one would like to use the commodity even after repair. Thus more demand for such goods, causes higher elasticity of demand.

(f) **Substitute for the Commodity.** If a commodity have number of substitutes, the demand is relatively elastic. Such as if petrol prices are high then people leave the cars, and like to use scooters, buses or cycles.

(g) **Urgency of Demand.** If the price of an essential commodity rises, such as sugar, wheat or salt, one would like to give up something else than giving up the sugar or salt. If one has the habit of smoking, the demand is elastic, because with price rise in cigarettes, one would like to give up smoking or reduce number of the same.

Types of Price Elasticity

There are five types of price elasticity.

(a) **Perfect Elastic Demand.** When no reduction in price is needed to cause an increase in demand. If such case is there, a firm can sell any required quantity at the prevailing price but more at all at even slightly higher price. Here the shape of demand curve is horizontal.

(b) **Perfect Inelastic Demand.** When with a change in price, even large, causes no change in demand. Here the shape of demand curve is vertical.

(c) **Demand with Unit Elasticity.** When with proportionate change in price causes an equal proportional change in demand. The shape of demand curve is rectangular hyperbola.

(d) **Relative Inelastic Demand.** When a reduction in price leads to more than proportional increase in demand. Here the shape of demand curve is flat.

(e) **Relative Inelastic Demand.** When a reduction in price leads to less than proportional increase in demand. Here the shape of demand curve is steep.

In actual practice, we generally meet cases *b, d* and *e* above.

Change in Demand

The change in demand means 'an increase or decrease in demand'. An increase in demand means that at the same previous prices there is an increase in demand. If so, then demand curve will lie to the right of the original curve (Fig. 29.5). The increase in demand may be due to increase in people's income, discovery of new use of the product, an improvement in customers' taste etc.

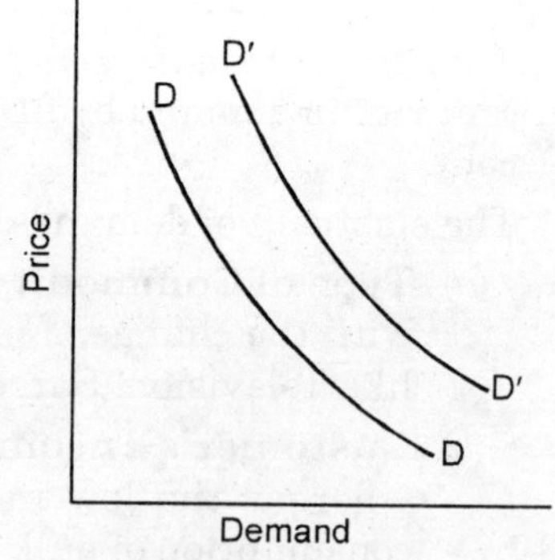

Fig. 29.5.

Likewise the decrease in demand would mean that at the same previous level of prices, less quantity would be sold. The demand curve will then lie towards left of the original curve.

The increase or decrease in demand is also termed as 'shift in demand schedules'. This is because the demand curve shifts towards left or right with decrease or increase in demand.

29.3.2. Law of Supply

As the price of a commodity rises, its supply increases and as the price falls, its supply declines. Thus the quantity offered for sale is directly proportional to price, *i.e.*, larger the supply, higher the price or *vice versa* (Fig. 29.6).

Increase and Decrease in Supply. This means a change in quantity supplied without any change in price. This therefore, indicates a shift in supply schedules to the right with increase in supply and to the left with decrease in supply.

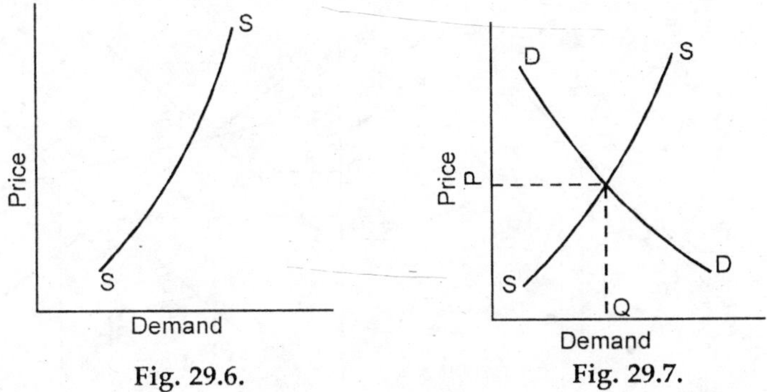

Fig. 29.6. Fig. 29.7.

Determination of Price. Prices under perfect competition are determined by the laws'of demand and supply. Prices will be fixed at a point where the supply and demand are at an equilibrium (as shown in Fig. 29.7). The equilibrium will change by changes in forces of demand and supply.

Micro Economics Analysis of Price and Quantity

There may be following conditions due to change in demand or supply :

(*a*) If demand increases, prices will go up and *vice versa*. As per Fig. 29.8 the demand curve shifts towards right side from *DD* to D_1D_1 whereas the supply curve *SS* remains the same. Due to this, the prices go up from *OP* to OP_1. However, the sales will also increase from *OQ* to OQ_1.

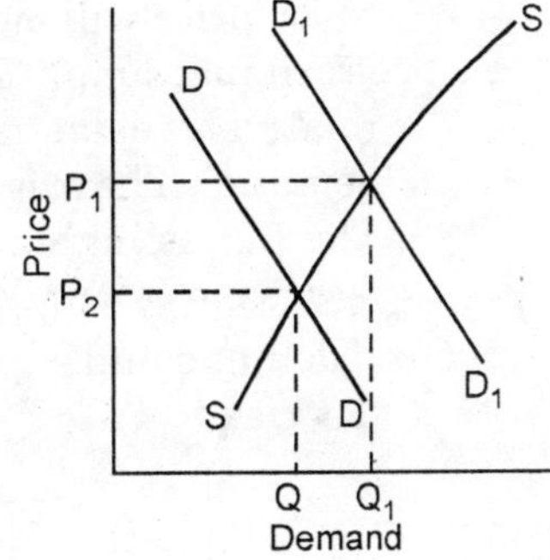

Fig. 29.8.

(*b*) When supply increases, price goes down and *vice versa*. As per Fig. 29.9. the supply curve shifts towards right, *i.e.*, from *SS* to S_1 S_1 while demand curve remains unchanged. The analysis shows that price falls from *OP* to OP_1, but the sales increase from *OQ* to OQ_1.

(*c*) With a shift in the demand curve, price will rise less or fall less if supply curve is elastic (flat); price will rise or fall more if the supply curve is inelastic (steep). If rise in price is more, rise in sale will be less; if rise in price is less, rise in sales will be more.

In Fig. 29.10. demand curve shifts from DD to D_1 D_1. The supply curve S_1S_1 is steep. Another supply curve S_2S_2 is a flat one. Both supply curves cut demand curve *DD* at point *E*. This indicates that before shift in demand the price is *OP*. S_1S_1 curve cuts D_1D_1 at E_1, this price

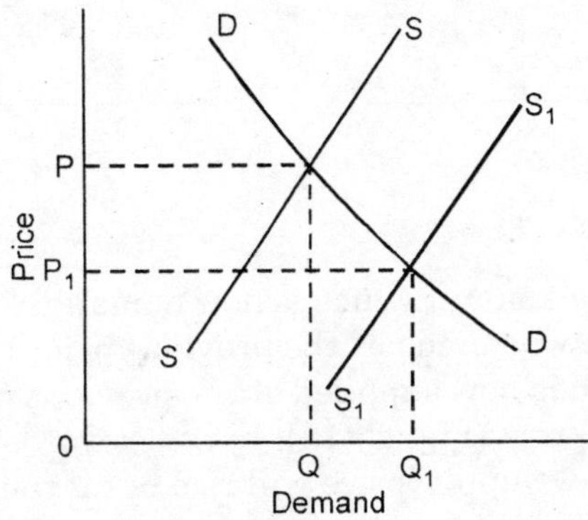

Fig. 29.9.

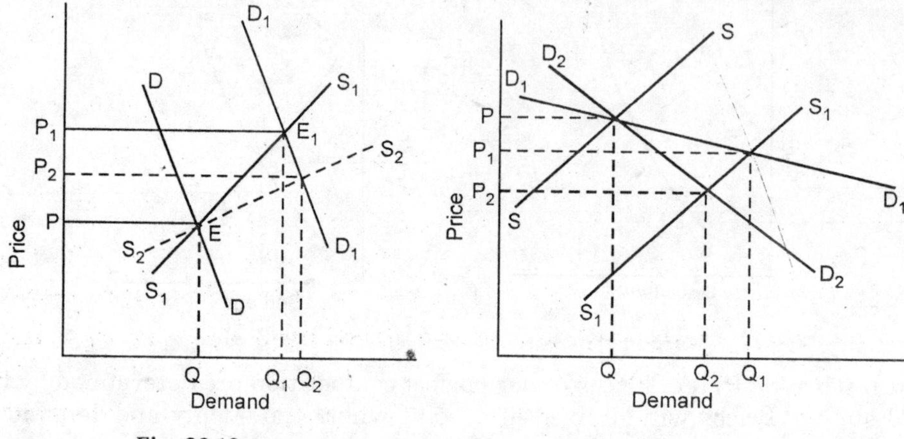

Fig. 29.10. Fig. 29.11.

changes to OP_1 and for flat supply curve the change in price is OP_2, which is less than OP_1. But with price OP_2 the quantity is OQ_2 which is more than the OQ_1 which is a quantity with price OP_1.

(*d*) With a shift in the supply curve, price will rise less or fall less if demand curve is elastic (flat), price will more or fall more if demand curve is inelastic (steep). In Fig. 29.11, *SS* is original supply curve, S_1S_1 is the new supply curve, D_1D_1 is steep demand curve (*i.e.*, relatively inelastic demand and D_2D_2 is the flat demand curve (*i.e.*, relatively inelastic demand). The original price *OP* then changes to OP_1 (steep curve) and OP_2 (flat curve). The OP_1 is higher than OP_2. In the same way quantity demand OQ_2 changes to OQ_1 (steep curve) and OQ_2 (flat curve) OQ_1 is more than OQ_2.

(*e*) If demand and supply shift (increase), sales are bound to increase but price may or may not rise.

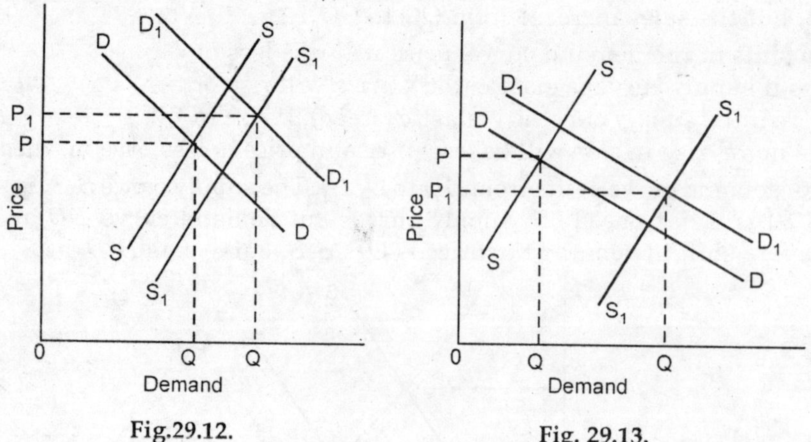

Fig.29.12. Fig. 29.13.

The price will rise if the amount which is now demanded at previous price exceeds the supply which would now be made at the previous price (Fig. 29.12). But the price will fall if the amount which is now supplied at the previous price is more than the amount now demanded at the price (Fig. 29.13). In other words if at the previous price, new demand exceeds the new supply, price will rise but if the new demand is less than the new supply, price will fall.

(*f*) An increase in demand with a simultaneous decrease in supply will rise price and increase sales if the new demand price for the old equilibrium amount is higher than its new supply price. Similarly, price will rise and sale will diminish if the new supply price for the old amount is higher than its new demand price.

Price Fixing and Government Intervention

For many essential commodities government interferes in price fixing by keeping the price above or below the level of equilibrium. While doing so, following difficulties arise :

Difficulties in Price Fixing.

1. Government attempt to fix the price of a commodity above equilibrium price is generally termed as 'support price'. Suppose during year 1977-78 government fixed minimum price Rs. 110 per quintal for wheat much above the equilibrium price (say Rs. 80 per quintal), consumers limit their consumption of commodity by postponing their purchase at all levels. But on other side farmers are encouraged to produce more under the incentive of higher reward. Thus there is no equilibrium between demand and supply.

   In this case to maintain higher price level only two courses of action are left:

   (*a*) The government through their agencies can buy large quantity of commodity to maintain the difference in supply and demand of commodity.

   (*b*) The government can ask the producers to curtail their output as the same is going on in U.S.A. to support the price of wheat.

2. If Government fixes maximum price below equilibrium price, (for eample as in the case of sugar or such commodity). Suppose equilibrium price of sugar is Rs. 3.00 per kilogram but the price has been controlled at Rs. 2.15 per kilogram. Under this condition the manufacturers of commodity would reduce their supply and causing a large number of unsatisfied consumers. Then further the problem would arise as to whom should get the commodity and thus causing a long queues for the available supply. In addition to this, the dealers would like to keep some quantity in reserve for specially forward customers which increases the black marketing and tendency of holding the commodity. Under these circumstances government may adopt the following measures :

   (*a*) Introduce rationing

   (*b*) Payment of subsidy to the manufacturers to neutralise the effect of low prices and encourage them to produce more.

Market Period : Short run and Long run period and their effect on supply and demand

For economist it is important to have analysis regarding change in supply and demand over time. The reason may be to take time to make those adjustments in the size and organisation of a concern which are necessary for greater production. The price theory is developed by Marshall. According to Marshall three periods of time, *i.e.*, market period, short run period and long run period are defined.

Market Period. According to Marshall market period is a single day or few days. The fundamental feature of the market period is that it will be so short that supplies or demands of the commodity will be limited to the present stocks or at the most to the supplies and demands insight.

Short Run Period. Marshall defined short run period as period long enough for the supplies or demand of a commodity to be altered but increases or decreases in current output but not long enough for the fixed equipment to be changed to produce a large or a smaller output.

Long Run Period. As defined by Marshall, there is enough time to build additional plants, or clear more land for crops, or alternatively old equipment and factories can be closed down. A firm producing at overtime rates or by using stand-by equipment will usually plan to increase output by buying new equipment. The firm will do this provided there is assurance that increased demand will be maintained.

29.3.3. Effect of Time

1. **Effect of Time on Demand.**

   Suppose electricity rates are reduced in the short run, present users of electric appliances will make greater use of their appliances, but in the long run, more and more people might be induced to use these appliances, causing a still greater demand of electricity. From above example, the difference or say effect of short run and long run on demand is quite clear. The distinction between short run and long run is important in a competitive situation. In short run, the question is whether competitors will follow suit, whereas in long run, due to competition finding of the different substitutes and other complex effect may follow.

   There are two categories which cause difference between long run and short run demands:

   1. There may be delay in imparting knowledge about relative change in the price of substitute. Many a time a consumer's tendency to stick to old method, causes delay on the part of consumer's response to the price change.
   2. Many a time, to have the advantage of a price change, an additional equipment is required to use the commodity. For example, frozen vegetables are cheaper than canned vegetables. But to use the frozen vegetables, an additional equipment like refrigerator is required which reduces the advantage of lower price of frozen vegetables.

   Thus it is quite clear that long run demand not wholly depends on price cut. But price cut may accelerate the rate of demand.

2. **Effect of Time on Supply.**

   The supply curve for market period will be vertical, *i.e.*, supply remains fixed whatever the price. The market period supply curve is not applicable in all cases. It is particularly important in the case of perishable goods which are difficult or say impossible to store and the demand for which is subject to short run fluctuations. For example, in a place, the supply of ice in summer on any given morning is fixed. A sudden shift in the demand due to unexpected hot day cannot influence the supply of ice on that particular day.

   In case of short run period the supply curve would be sloping line, moving upward from left to the right thereby indicating that with price increase, supply also increases.

   In long period supply curve will tend to have a flatter slope than the short period supply curve indicating that with a price increase the supply tend to be larger than in the short run period.

3. **Effect of Time on Price Fixation.**

   Now let us see that how price can be determined in different time periods, given a change in demand. In the market period, an upward shift (towards right) in the demand curve would result in an immediate rise in price as there will be no increase in supply. But under short run period the production is more causing a fall in the price due to increased out put. Further, under long run period, with more equipment installed, the output would increase still further and thus the price would further drop.

On the other hand, a downward shift (towards left side) in demand curve would not immediately affect the quantity applied but the price would drop sharply, followed by some recovery as reduced output in the short period. In the long period firms would see more profitable use for their plants. They would decide not to replace equipment as it wears out. This will reduce output still further and permit some recovery in price.

Fig. 29.14. shows the demand of a commodity where SS, $S_1 S_1$, S_2S_2 represent the market period, short run period and long run period supply curve. Suppose the demand for the commodity in the market shifts to D_1D_1. Now, immediately, supply of commodity cannot be increased and hence market or momentary equilibrium is established at price OP_1

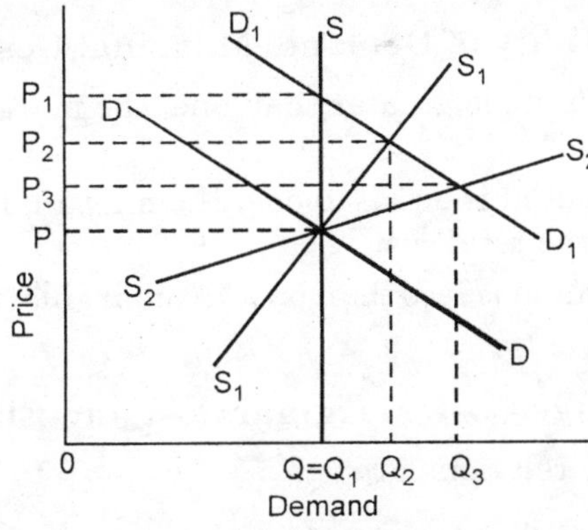

Fig. 29.14.

In short run, the supply of commodity can be increased by using more intensively the existing equipment for longer hours. As a result the price drops to OP_2.

In case of long run, supply can be fully adjusted to meet the changed demand conditions. Now firms would come for additional manufacture with additional equipment. Thus supply increases further, and the price is still lower OP_3.

29.4. MARGINAL PRICING

Let us define some related terms. An average cost means total amount received from sales divided by the number of units sold, *i.e.*, A.C. = $\frac{T.C.}{Q}$.

Total cost means total amount received. It can be obtained by multiplying number of units with price *i.e.* $T.R. = Q \times P$.

Increment Cost. It is difference between the total cost after price rise and total cost before price rise,

$$I.C. = R_2 - R_1$$

Marginal Cost. This is the additional cost earned by selling an additional (marginal) unit of production. This means that it is the total cost when one more or less unit is sold.

In actual practice, it is rare that output increased by one unit. The extra cost earned on additional output which is due to additional input can be determined by finding out the change in total cost as a result of this output.

Thus

$$M.C. = \frac{R_2 - R_1}{Q_2 - Q_1}$$

where R_1 and R_2 are the total cost before and after price Q_1 and Q_2 is the quantity before and after.

Example 29.1. *Suppose the price of a product is reduced from Rs. 10 to Rs. 9, due to this sale increases from 1000 to 1500 units. Calculate incremental cost and marginal cost.*

Solution.

$$= I.C.\ R_2 - R_1$$

$$= 9 \times 1500 - 10 \times 1000. = \text{Rs. } 3500.$$

$$M.C. = \frac{R_2 - R_1}{Q_2 - Q_1}$$

$$= \frac{3500}{1500 - 1000} = \text{Rs.}7.$$

Relationship Between Elasticity of Demand, Marginal Cost and Total Cost

1. When elasticity of demand is greater than one, the marginal cost is positive and total cost rises as price falls.
2. When elasticity of demand is equal to one, the marginal, cost is zero and a change in price will not change the total cost.
3. When elasticity of demand is less than one, the marginal cost is negative and total cost falls as price falls.

Relationship Between Average Cost, Marginal Cost and Elasticity of Demand

As for Mrs. *J.* Robinson the relations are :

At any output.

1. Average cost $= \text{Marginal} \times \frac{e}{e-1}$

$$\text{A.C.} = \text{M.C.} \times \frac{e}{e-1}$$

2. Marginal cost $= \text{Average cost} \times \frac{e-1}{e}$

$$\text{M.C.} = \text{A.C.} \times e - \frac{1}{e}$$

where

$$e = \frac{A.C.}{A.C. - M.C.}$$

A relationship between Total cost, Average cost and Marginal cost is shown in the following table :

Units of Output	*Fixed cost Rs.*	*Variable cost Rs.*	*Total cost Rs.*	*Marginal cost Rs.*	*Average cost 4 + 1 Rs.*	*Average fixed cost 2 + 1 Rs.*	*Average variable cost 3 + 1 Rs.*
(1)	(2)	(3)	(4)	(5)	(6)	(7)	(8)
0	176	0	176	—	—		
1	176	75	251	75	251	176	75
2	176	130	306	55	153	88	65
3	176	175	351	45	117	59	58

4	176	209	385	34	96	44	52
5	176	238	414	29	83	35	48
6	176	265	441	27	74	29	44
7	176	289	465	24	66	25	41
8	176	312	488	23	61	22	39
9	176	328	504	16	56	20	36
10	176	344	520	16	52	18	34
11	176	367	543	23	49	16	33
12	176	400	576	33	48	15	33
13	176	448	624	48	48	14	34
14	176	510	686	62	49	13	36
15	176	600	776	90	52	12	40

Values in the above table are arbitrary. On studying the above table, following points are note-worthy :

1. Average cost is equal to total cost divided by number of units produced. For example, at output of 10 units, the total cost is Rs. 520. Hence average cost is Rs. 52.
2. The total cost is equal to the sum of fixed cost and all the marginal cost is 176 + 75 + 55 + 45 + 34 = 385. It may also be remembered that the fixed cost is the initial cost which the concern committed irrespective of quantity produced.
3. Where marginal cost is falling, total cost will be rising at a declining rate, but on other side, where marginal cost is rising, total cost will be rising at an increasing rate.
4. When marginal cost is lower than the average cost, average cost would be falling, for example upto the 12 units of output. This will be so irrespective of the fact whether the marginal cost is rising or falling. For example, for an output of 11 and 12 units, the marginal cost is rising, but the average cost is falling.
5. When the marginal cost is greater than the average cost, the average cost would be rising, for example, for output of 14 and 15 units.
6. If the marginal cost first falls and then rises, *i.e.*, the marginal cost curve is U-shaped, the marginal cost will be equal to the average cost at a point where the average cost is the minimum. For example, at an output of 13 units, the cost is lowest at Rs. 48 where the marginal cost is also Rs. 48
7. If the marginal cost is below the average variable cost, latter must be falling. This can be verified for 11 units of output.
8. If the marginal cost is higher than the average variable cost, the latter must be rising. This can be verified at output level of 13,14 and 15 units.
9. If marginal cost first falls and then rises, it will be equal to the average variable cost at a point, where the average variable cost is minimum. This is so at an output level of 12 units where marginal cost and average variable cost are equal to Rs. 33.

The above analysis can easily be given graphically as follows :

1. When *M.C.* Falls, *A.C.* also falls. For example as from 1 unit to 10 units of output.

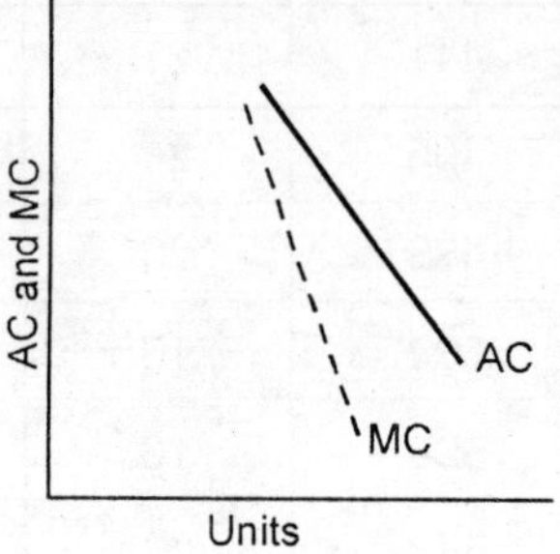

Fig. 29.15.

2. When *M.C.* and *A.C.* are constant. For example at production of 13 units.
3. When *A.C.* increases *M.C.* also increases. For example from 13 units to 15 units of production.

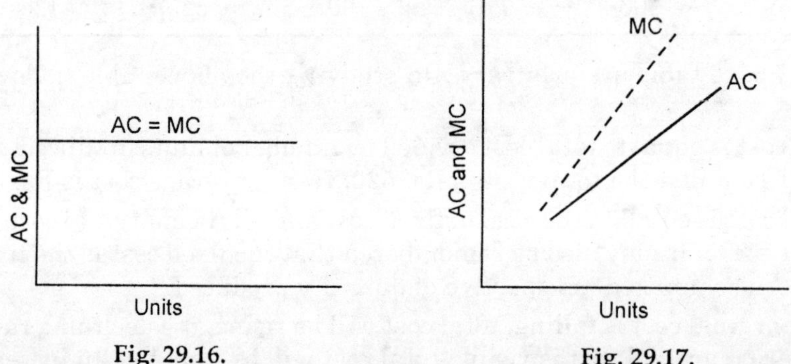

Fig. 29.16. Fig. 29.17.

4. If we plot a graph between units and *A.C.* and *M.C*, we get a U-shaped curve, both curves interchanging at the lower *A.C.* value and the value for *M.C.* must be equal to *A.C.* at this point. 0 point is the point of intersection and *M.C.* is equal to *A.C.* at this point.

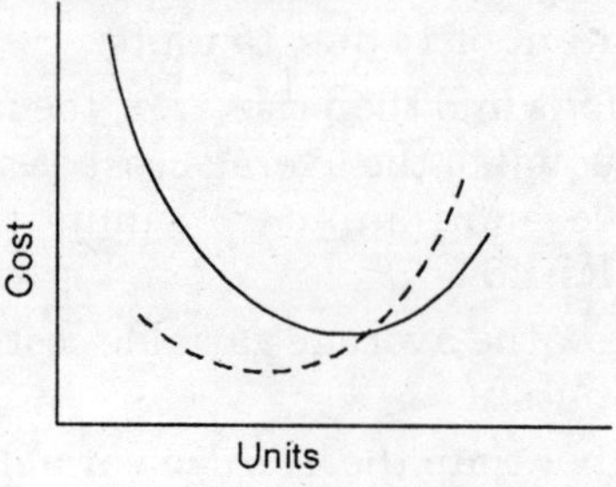

Fig. 29.18.

29.5. FORMS OF MARKET

According to the rate of commpetition the market can be of three types;

1. Perfect competition market
2. Monopoly market
3. Imperfect competition market.

1. **Perfect Competition Market.**

   For a perfect competition market following conditions are necessary:

   1. Large number of retailers, producers and customers.
   2. Production of 'identical goods'.
   3. Free entry in market.
   4. Perfect mobility of factors of production.
   5. Perfect knowledge about the prices to the customers.
   6. It is assumed that there are no transport charges in perfect competition.

   But it is a fact that above mentioned six conditions never prevail practically in the market, thus truly there is no perfect competition market, but there is always some imperfect competition called as pure competition, free competition or fair competition. Thus if the first three conditions are satisfied then that is a pure or fair or free competition, and this exists in markets like food grain, fruits and vegetables.

   In pure competition, there is only one price in the market. Prices cannot be changed by individual relation as he is selling only a small quantity of total supply. If he changes the price, no effect may be there in the market. The change in price can only be brought about by a change in the total supply. Thus in pure competition, seller or retailer accepts the prices which have been given by the industry.

2. **Monopoly Market.**

   Monopoly market is that market where there is only one supplier in whole of the market. A true monopoly means that the total income of the consumers is taken away by one supplier, but in fact, this is not possible. Of course, it is possible that supply of one commodity is controlled by one producer which has no close substitutes. This is called 'impure or imperfect monopoly'.

   A monopolist has control on the supply and the price. There may be many reasons of monopoly likewise government sanction, nature of plant or the industry which requires highly special and rare technique of production,*e.g.*, production of Coca-Cola concentrate by a single firm.

3. **Imperfect Competition Market.**

   It is more practical case. This means the competition never follow any of condition for perfect competition. There are two types of Imperfect Competition :

   1. Monopolistic competition
   2. Obligopoly.

   Of the two, monopolistic is more important. In this case, there are many customers and sellers, but they are not manufacturing identical goods, though they are producing same goods. In this type of market, a specific quality of the goods will separate it from other producer's goods. Due to this there are different prices as each manufacturer quotes his own price, such as soap, tooth paste etc.

   Due to special quality in the goods a particular group of customers patronises that product and continues to purchase that same even if there is price hike. This is called 'monopolistic element'. But the price hike is also upto a level, after that level the customers may switch over to another producers' goods, providing a substitute. Due to this, it is known as monopolistic competition.

Obligopoly means that only few producers are in market. If producers are selling identical goods we call it a case of pure obligopoly but if they are selling different goods, it will be a case of imperfect obligopoly.

The Concept of Revenue

Revenue of firm is the receipt or sale proceeds. Like *A.C.*, average revenue is the total revenue divided by the number of units sold. Similarly there is marginal revenue and total revenue. The relationship between *A.R.* and *M.R.* is just the same as of *A.C.* and *M.C.* as discussed before.

But *A.R.* is generally greater than *AC*.

$$AR. = AC. + AP.$$

$$A.P. = \text{Average profit.}$$

All the competition prices are determined with the reference of *M.C.* and *M.R.* They are settled where the two are equal.

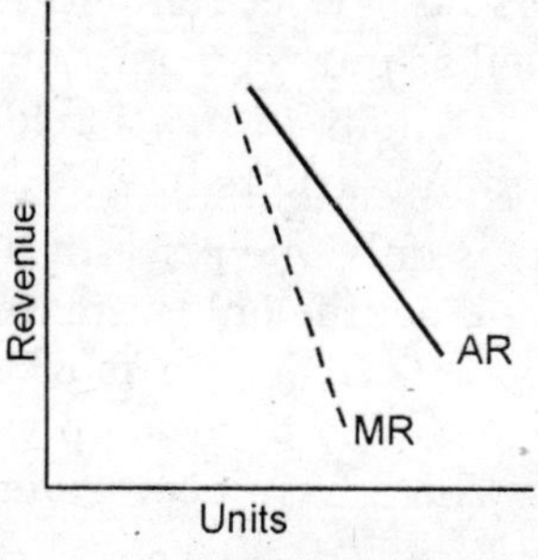

Fig. 29.19

Example 29.2. Suppose a firm in monopolistic competition produces tooth pastes. Their *A.R.* curve is going downward showing that tooth paste can be sold in large quantity at lower price (Fig.29.19).

Now on plotting of two U-curves of *A.C* and *M.C*, we see that at *O* the *MC* and *M.R.* curve cut each other, *i.e.,* at *O* both are equal. Passing a vertical line through *O* cutting, A.R. and *A.C.* curve at *P′* and *C′* then *OP* is the price of the commodity per unit and *CP* is the profit per unit.

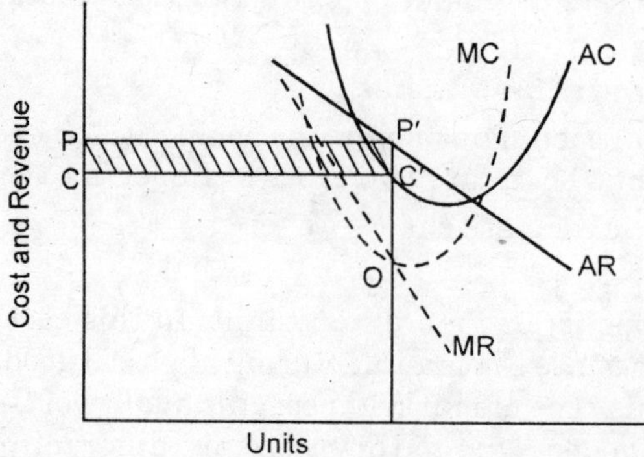

Fig. 29.20.

In the same way for rising and constant cost (this is mainly applied to monopoly market) is shown in Figs 29.21. and 29.22.

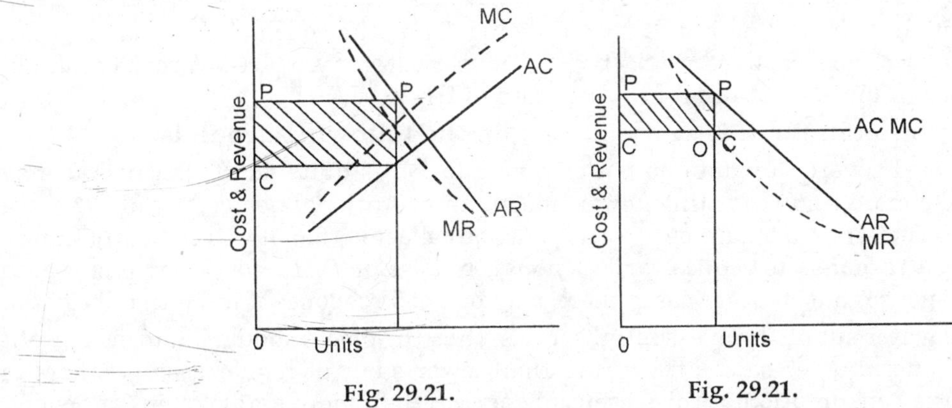

Fig. 29.21. **Fig. 29.21.**

In the above Fig. *OP* is price per unit and *PC* is the profit per unit.

Example Relating to Micro analysis. A water supply board of a city has excess water and decided to reduce the tariff. The table below gives data on water consumption by seven users and total revenue received from them before and after the rate reduction for a year.

Users	*Total Revenue in Rupees*		*Total consumption in kiloliters*	
	Before	**After**	**Before**	**After**
I	156450	164900	582880	1538800
II	32400	39050	101580	319820
III	171800	142480	463980	1385700
IV	73200	82753	265890	796760
V	77650	51400	228960	430210
VI	56600	34000	179950	254570
VII	68500	49550	235810	444310

Now

1. What conclusion would be drawn from the data on total revenue regarding elasticity of demand for water supply?
2. Is it profitable for the board to reduce the tariff ?
3. Can it still justify rate reduction by the board?

Solution.

(*i*) By observing the total revenue column one may be able to know that demand is elastic or inelastic. If due to price fall, the revenue increases than demand is elastic, and if revenue decreases then the demand is inelastic. By observing the table we can say that in case of *I, II* and *IV* the total revenue increases then demand is elastic whereas in rest of the cases the total revenue decreases which means that the demand is inelastic.

(*ii*) By studying the table it is seen that water consumption by all the users increased manifold, *i.e.*, about $2\frac{1}{2}$ times but the total revenue shows a decline, *i.e.*, from Rs. 636,600 to Rs. 564,100. This means due to reduction in tariff there is a rise in consumption of water but there is decline in the total revenue. Thus the conclusion is that it is not profitable for the board to reduce the tariff. But userwise rate reduction proved profitable in case of *I*, *II* and *IV* but unprofitable in case of III, V, VI, VII.

(*iii*) **The reduction in tariff is still justified on the following grounds:**

1. Period covered by data on water consumption is quite short. Because it may take more time for fitting new connection in additional homes, installing extra taps etc. If for a longer period data may be collected then it will certainly show a good response to reduce tariff. Though in case of *I*, *II* and *IV* there is a good response, but in other cases there may be good response if more time is given.
2. As water supply is an essential service, thus the object should be "to earn profit through higher sales at low rate than lower sales at higher cost". If there is large consumption of this essential service, then more employment of people, benefit to public, causing a satisfaction to social welfare.
3. The increase in consumption by $2\frac{1}{2}$ times of consumption at pre-reduction rates shows that previously the board was working at below capacity level. The unutilised capacity of such an extent in a public utility undertaking is a social wastage and thus creating adverse effects to the social welfare. Thus reduction of rate helps in utilizing more capacity.

QUESTIONS

1. Define utility. Explain different types of utility.
2. Explain the terms "money" and "market" in detail.
3. Write short notes on:
   (*a*) Value of money
   (*b*) Trade cycle, and
   (*c*) Monopoly markets.
4. Describe different theories of Trade Cycle in brief.
5. State classification of market and explain each in brief.
6. Define following terms:
   (*a*) Economics
   (*b*) Income
   (*c*) Investment
   (*d*) Assets and Liability.
   (*e*) Capital
7. What is profit? Describe theories of profit.
8. Explain Economies of size in detail.
9. What is Profit? What are its functions? How do you measure it?
10. Describe different factors considered for price determination.
11. Explain the effect of demand and supply on price.
12. Write short notes on:
    (*a*) Effect of time on demand
    (*b*) Marginal pricing

(c) Marginal cost

(d) Rate of return on investment.

13. Distinguish between macro economics and micro economics. How is micro economics useful in managerial decision making?
14. What is meant by 'demand'? Calculate the price elasticity of demand if $Q_1 = 4000, Q_2 = 5000$, P_1 = Rs. 20, P_2 = Rs. 19.
15. State and explain the law of demand.
16. Define price elasticity of demand.
17. State the relationship between price elasticity of demand average revenue, marginal revenue, marginal revenue and total revenue.
18. Define elasticity of demand and discuss the factors affecting it.
19. What is difference between:

    (i) Short run period and long run period?

    (ii) Types of market?

30 ENGINEERING AND MANAGERIAL ECONOMICS

30.1. INTRODUCTION TO ENGINEERING ECONOMICS

Engineering economics is the economics applied to engineering problems. It is based on economic analysis for identifying engineering problems, and evaluating various alternatives utilising the economic concepts. It is, therefore, concerned with the economic problems of the engineering firm. Economic aspects have already been discussed in detail in the previous chapters.

Importance of Engineering Economics

Engineers are required to use economic concepts in following major fields:

(*i*) Increasing production

(*ii*) Improving productivity

(*iii*) Reducing human efforts

(*iv*) Increasing wealth by maximising profit

(*v*) Controlling cost

(*vi*) Reducing cost

(*vii*) Economics has very important role to play in all engineering decisions. Economics plays a major role in manufacturing, construction, mining and other engineering industries, starting from selection of site to production planning and control, selection of equipment and their replacement analysis, to material handling system selection, and to wage structure of the workers.

(*viii*) It provides a number of tools and techniques to solve engineering problems may it be related to product-mix, output level, pricing the product, investment, quantum of advertisement etc.

(*ix*) It helps in understanding the market conditions, general economic environment in which the firm is working.

(*x*) It provides the basis for resource allocation problem.

(*xi*) Engineering economics deals with identification of economic choices, and is concerned with the decision making of engineering problems of economic nature.

It provides an analytical and scientific approach resulting in qualitative decisions.

Definitions

Engineering economics is a collection of mathematical techniques which simplifies economic comparisons. With these techniques, a rational, meaningful approach to evaluate the economic aspects of different methods (alternatives) of accomplishing a given objective can be developed.

Engineering economy is about determining the economic factors and the economic criteria utilised when one or more alternatives are considered for selection.

The techniques and models of engineering economy assist people in making decisions. Since decisions affect the future, numbers used in an engineering economic analysis are best estimates of what is expected to occur. Engineering economic method analyse the past (outcome analysis) and also future alternative decisions.

Steps to Problem Solving

Steps involved in the problem solving approach or the decision-making process are :

1. Understand the problem and goal.
2. Collect relevant information.
3. Define the alternative solutions.
4. Evaluate each alternative.
5. Select the best alternative using some criteria.
6. Implement the solution and monitor the results.

For details refer chapter *"Decision-making"* in the book.

Engineering economy has a mojor role in steps 2 to 5.

30.2 TIME VALUE OF MONEY

It is true that money makes money, if we decide to invest money today, we expect to have more money in the future. This change in the amount of money over a given time period is called the *time value of money.* This concept is very important in engineering economy, and is equally important while we invest either in bank, or business or in stock mutual fund. If a person or company borrows money today, by tomorrow more than the original loan principal will be owed.

Equivalence

The concept *of equivalence,* is the combination of time value of money and interest rate, and means the different sums of money at different times are equal in economic value. For example, if the interest rate is 10% per year, Rs. 100 today would be equivalent to Rs. 110 one year from today. Therefore, if someone offers you a gift of Rs. 100 today or Rs. 110 one year from today, it would make no difference. The two sums of money are equivalent to each other when the interest rate is 10% per year.

As in future equivalence, same principle can be applied to determine equivalence for the past years. Therefore, if you have Rs. 100 now, it is equivalent to Rs. $\frac{100}{1.10}$ = Rs. 90.91 last year.

Example 30.1. *If interest rate is 5% per year, make necessary calculations to show which of the following statements are true and which are false.*

1. *Rs. 99 now is equal to Rs. 105.4 one year from now.*
2. *Rs. 200 one year ago is equivalent to Rs. 205 now.*
3. *Rs. 2000 now is equivalent to Rs. 1900 one year ago.*
4. *Rs. 3000 now is equivalent to Rs. 3150 one year from now.*
5. *Interest accumulated in 1 year on an investment of Rs. 5000 is Rs. 250.*

Solution

1. Total amount accrued in 1 year = Rs. 99 × 1.05 = Rs. 103.45 ≠ Rs. 105.4. Therefore the statement is false.
2. Required investment 1 year ago = Rs. 205/1.05 = Rs. 195.24 ≠ Rs. 200. Therefore, the statement is false.
3. Total amount accrued in 1 year = Rs. 1900 × 1.05 = Rs. 1995 ≠ Rs. 2000 . Therefore, the statement is false.
4. Total amount accrued in 1 year = Rs. 3000 × 1.05 = Rs. 3150 . True.
5. Interest in 1 year = Rs. 5000 × 0.05 = Rs. 250, True.

For details on *'Interest'* readers may refer the chapter *"Interest, Annuities and Profit'* in the book.

30.3. CASH FLOWS

The actual inflows and outflows of money are called cash flows. Without cash-flow estimates over a stated time period, no engineering economy study can be conducted. To perform economic analysis, estimates may be needed on financing, interest rates, life of assets, revenues, costs, tax effects etc. Every company has cash receipts-revenue and income (inflows); and cash disbursements - expenses, and costs (outflows). These receipts and disbursement are the cash flows with a positive sign representing cash inflows and a negative sign representing cash outflows.

Cash inflows or receipts, may comprise of the following, depending upon the nature of the activities and type of business:

- Revenues.
- Operating cost reductions.
- Receipt of loan principal.
- Asset salvage value
- Income tax savings
- Receipts from stock and bond sales.
- Construction and facility cost savings.
- Savings or return of corporate capital funds.

Cash outflows or disbursements, may comprise of the following, again depending upon the nature of the activity and type of business:

- First cost of assets
- Operating costs
- Periodic maintenance and rebuild cost
- Loan interest and principal payments
- Major, expected upgradation costs
- Income taxes
- Bond dividends and bond payment
- Expenditure of corporate capital funds.

Once the cash inflows and outflow estimates are developed, the net cash flow over a stated period of time is represented as

$$\text{Net cash flow} = \text{receipts} - \text{disbursements}$$
$$= \text{Cash inflow} - \text{Cash outflows.}$$

Cash–flow Diagram

A cashflow diagram is simply a graphical representation of cash flows drawn on a time scale. In cash flow diagram time $t = 0$ represents the present, and $t = 1$ represents the end of time period 1, and so on. Figure 30.1 shows the cash flow diagram both time and cash-flow magnitude.

The direction of the arrows on the cash-flow diagram is important. Vertical arrow pointing up indicates a positive cash flow, while pointing down indicates a negative cash flow. The diagram drawn in the Fig. 30.1. illustrates a receipt (cash inflow) at the end of year 1 and a disbursement (cash outflow) at the end of year 2.

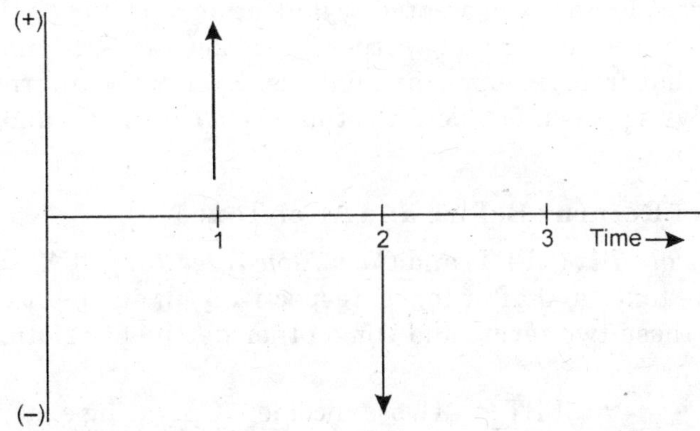

Fig. 30.1. Cash-flow diagram indicating positive and negative cash flows.

30.4. TAXATION CONCEPT

Indian tax structure, as it has evolved over the years, consists of large number of taxes ; both direct and indirect *e.g.*, income tax, corporate tax, wealth tax, excise duty, sales tax etc. Major objectives of taxation are :

(*i*) to raise resources for development,

(*ii*) to reduce inequalities of income and wealth, and

(*iii*) to restrict consumption so as to check inflationary pressures.

Taxation can be classified as direct taxes, and indirect taxes. Direct taxes include taxes on income and property, whereas indirect taxes cover taxes on commodities and services. Important direct taxes are income tax, corporate tax, estate duty and wealth tax. Important examples of indirect taxes are sales tax, excise duties etc.

Through their taxing power, central and state governments can exercise influence on the behaviour of business and their owners. Therefore, most business decisions are affected either directly or indirectly by taxes.

A corporation's taxable income is found by deducting all expenses, including depreciation and interest from revenue. This taxable income is then subjected to the graduated tax structure, which is announced by the government from time to time.

Depreciation, as discussed in a separate chapter, is the systematic allocation of the cost of a capital asset over a period of time. Depreciation deductions taken on a firm's tax return are treated as expense items. Thus, depreciation lowers taxable income.

Interest paid on outstanding corporate department is treated as an expense and is tax deductible. However, dividends paid to preferred or common stockholders are not tax deductible. Thus, for a profitable, tax-paying company, the use of debt in its financing mix results in a significant tax advantage relative to the use of preferred or common stock.

When a capital asset is sold, a *capital gain or loss* is generally incurred. The capital gain is the amount by which the proceeds from the sale of a capital asset exceeds the asset's original cost. There has been a differential tax treatment of capital gains income and operating income, with the capital gains being treated more favourably.

Any income reported by a sole proprietorship or a partnership becomes income of the owners, and is taxed at the personal rate.

When economic analysis is performed, it is reasonable to ask if the analysis should be on a *before tax* or *after-tax basis*. For a tax-exempted organisation, aftertax analysis is not necessary. For taxed organisations (corporations and partnerships) the after-tax analysis may result in a different decision than that from a before-tax analysis. Even if the alternative chosen may be the same, after tax analysis gives much better estimates of cash flows and the anticipated rate of return for an alternative.

Cash Flow and Rate of Return : Before and After Taxes

The terms *Cash Flow Before Tax* (CFBT) and *Cash Flow After Tax* (CFAT) are used to represent annual cash flows before taxes and after taxes, respectively, in an engineering economy study. Relationships between these two terms and some other pertinent relations directly affecting corporate income taxes are

$$\begin{aligned}
\text{CFBT} &= \text{Gross income} - \text{Operating expenses} \\
\text{Taxable Income} &= \text{CFBT} - \text{Depreciation} + \text{Net capital gains} - \\
&\quad \text{Net capital losses} + \text{depreciation recapture.} \\
\text{Taxes} &= \text{Taxable Income} \times \text{Tax rate.} \\
\text{CFAT} &= \text{CFBT} - \text{Taxes.} \\
\text{After tax Rate of Return} &= \text{After tax ROR} \\
&= \text{(Before tax ROR) (1–tax rate).}
\end{aligned}$$

The net cash flow (NCF) for an after tax engineering economy analysis, is :

$$\begin{aligned}
\text{NCF} &= \text{Gross Income} - \text{Capital expenses} - \\
&\quad \text{Operating expenses} + \text{Salvage Value} - \text{Taxes.}
\end{aligned}$$

In practice, the considerations made for the after tax computations give the analyst a much clearer estimate of the monetary impact of Taxes.

30.5. TOOLS OF ENGINEERING ECONOMICS

Following are the important tools of engineering economics which are used for solving economic problems of engineering concerns :

1. Models.
2. Operation Research.
3. Break–Even–Analysis–Discussed separately in the book.
4. Value Engineering.
5. Make–Buy.
6. Economic Ordering Quantity-Already discussed in this book.

7. Economic Batch (or Lot) Quantity.
8. Equipment Replacement Analysis–Discussed separately in the book.
9. Economic Theories.
10. Location Analysis
11. Cost Control.
12. Cost Reduction.

These tools have been discussed in the book at relevant places.

30.6. FINANCIAL OR ACCOUNTING RATIO ANALYSIS

Financial or Accounting ratio may be defined as relating one accounting figure to another to provide better comparison.

Most commonly used financial ratios are:

A. Activity Ratio

1. $\text{Inventory Turnover} = \dfrac{\text{Cost of material}}{\text{Average inventory}}$

2. $\text{Average inventory period (months)} = \dfrac{\text{Average inventory}}{\text{Consumption per month}}$.

B. Cost Ratio (Per cent)

1. Employee expenses as percentage of production.
2. Fixed costs as percentage of production.
3. Variable costs as percentage of production.

C. Profitability Ratios (Percentage)

1. Gross Operating Margins

$$= \frac{\text{Gross operating profit before depreciation, interest and tax}}{\text{Turn over}} \times 100$$

2. $\text{Return on Equity} = \dfrac{\text{Net operating profit after tax and dividend}}{\text{Equity paid up and free reserves}} \times 100$

D. Return on Investment (*R.O.I.*)

$$R.O.I. = \frac{\text{Net profit}}{\text{Capital employed}} = \frac{\text{Net profit}}{\text{Turn over}} \times \frac{\text{Turn over}}{\text{Capital employed}}$$

$$= \text{Net profit ratio} \times \text{Capital Turn over ratio}$$

Uses of Financial Ratio Analysis

Financial ratios provide useful indictations to appraise financial health of a concern and overall efficiency of the project. Computation of ratios often leads to a further enquiry into various aspects of project, and which enables to bring out some important facts, which ultimately helps in:

- Planning : short, medium and long range.
- Diagnosis of financial ills or industrial sickness.
- Decision making of all types.
- Keeping a continuous watch on the financial trends and taking corrective actions well in advance.

30.7. BENEFIT/COST RATIO

The benefit/cost method of analysis is based on the ratio of the benefits to costs associated with a particular project. A project is considered to be attractive when the benefits derived from its implementation, as reduced by expected disbenefits, exceed its associated costs.

Therefore, first step in benefit/cost analysis is to determine which of the elements are benefits, disbenefits and costs. These terms can be expressed as follows :

Benefits. Advantages experienced by the owner

Disbenefits. Disadvantages to the owner during the implementation of the project.

Costs. Anticipated expenditures for construction, operation, maintenance etc., less salvage values.

Conventional Benefit/cost/B/C ratio is calculated as follows:

$$\text{B/C ratio} = \frac{\text{Benefit} - \text{Disbenefit}}{\text{Cost}}$$

If B/C ratio is greater than or equal to 1.0, it indicates that the project evaluated is economically advantageous.

The modified benefit/cost ratio, which now-a-days is gaining support, includes maintenance and operation (M&O) costs in the numerator and treated similar to disbenefits. The denominator, in this case, includes only the initial investment cost. The modified B/C cost ratio is calculated as :

$$\text{Modified B/C} = \frac{\text{Benefit} - \text{Disbenefit} - \text{M\&O Costs}}{\text{Initial investment}}$$

The salvage value, in this case also, is included in the denominator as a negative cost, as previously treated.

The steps for the B/C analysis are summarized below:

1. Calculate the total cost of each alternative.
2. Subtract the costs of the lower-investment alternative from those of the largercost alternative, which we consider the alternative to be justified. Use this value as *C* in the B/C ratio.
3. Calculate the total benefits of each alternative.
4. Subtract the benefits for the lower-cost alternative from the benefits for the largercost alternative, paying attention to algebraic signs. Use this value as *B*. Calculate the B/C ratio.
5. If B/C $\geq$ 1. The incremental investment is justified ; select the larger investment alternative. Otherwise, select the lower-cost alternative.

30.8. MANAGERIAL ECONOMICS

Managerial Economics is economics applied to decision-making. It is based on economic analysis for identifying problems, organising information, and evaluating alternatives. Managerial economics serve as a link between economic theories and managerial practice.

Managerial Economics is the integration of economic theory with business practice for the purpose of facilitating decision-making and forward planning by management.

Features of Managerial Economics

- It is concerned with decision-making of economic nature.
- It deals with identification of economic choices and allocation of resources.
- It deals, as to how decisions should be taken to achieve the organisational goals.
- It provides a link between traditional economics and the decision sciences for managerial decision-making.
- It is concerned with those analytical tools which are helpful in improving the decision-making.

Nature of Managerial Economics

Managerial economics is concerned with the business firms and their economic problems. To understand the nature of managerial economics better, let us study the nature of economic theory relevant for managerial decision-making.

(*a*) **Macro-economic Conditions.** The decisions of the firm are generally made within the broad framework of economic environment within which the firm operates. These are known as macroeconomic conditions. From this point of view, these conditions are: working of the market, pace of economic change, economic policies of the government.

(*b*) **Micro-economic Analysis.** This deals with the problems of an individual firm, industry etc. This helps in studying as to what is going on within the firm, how best to allocate scarce sources for various activities of the firm. Some of the popular microeconomic concepts are the elasticity of demand, marginal cost, opportunity cost, market structure. Some of the common models used in microeconomic theory are model for monopoly price, model for price determination and the behaviour and managerial models.

Managerial Economics and Traditional Economics

Managerial Economics is an applied field, whereas economics provide certain basic concepts and analytical tools. Both of them are concerned with problems of scarcity and resource allocation, generally labour and capital in order to find the best way to utilize them for achieving the set goals.

Main contributions of economics to managerial economics are :

(*a*) To help in understanding the market conditions and the general economic environment in which the firm is working.

(*b*) To provide philosophy for understanding and analysing resource allocation problems.

Success of any business depends upon technical and economic efficiency. Technical efficiency means production with best technological specifications, while economic efficiency means maximisation of its goals, *i.e.*, sales, profit etc. Managerial economics is concerned with both kinds of efficiencies and takes the help of economic analysis for achieving both these efficiencies.

30.8.1. Importance of Managerial Economics

Managerial economics helps the decision-making process in the following ways :

(*i*) It provides a number of tools and techniques. These techniques are in the form of models, which helps the manager to establish essential relationships that represent the actual situation.

(*ii*) It provides most of the concepts that are required for the analysis of the problems, concepts of elasticity of demand, fixed and variable costs, short and long-run costs etc. help in understanding and then solving the decision problems.

(*iii*) It helps in taking decisions about product-mix, level of output and price of the product, investment, how much to advertise, etc.

(*iv*) Managerial economics helps in taking decision on following subjects:

- Objectives of a business firm
- Production and cost
- Profit
- Pricing and output
- Demand forecasting
- Competition
- Investment
- Sales promotion and market strategy.

30.9. MANAGERIAL ECONOMICS AND RELATED DISCIPLINES

Managerial economics has relation to number of disciplines. Relationship with some of the important disciplines is described hereunder :

1. **Statistics.** Managerial economics use statistically arrived functional relationships for decision making. It also uses theory of probability to deal with the uncertainty of future events. It also employs statistical methods for empirical testing of economic generalisations.
2. **Mathematics.** Most of economic concepts, *e.g.*, demand, price, cost, product, wages, interest, capital etc. are quantitative in nature. In economic analysis various mathematical tools and concepts like, vectors, algebra, calculus, exponentials etc. are used.
3. **Accounting.** Accounting informations are the principal sources of data required by managerial economics for its decision-making. These accounting data are provided in a form so as to fit easily into the concepts and analysis of managerial economics.
4. **Psychology and Organisation Behaviour.** Managerial economics analyses the individual behaviour of microeconomic units, like a buyer, seller, an investor, a worker and an employer. Psychology helps in understanding the behavioural aspects.
5. **Operation Research.** Object of both Operation Research and Managerial economics is to take effective decisions for adopting best way of achieving firm's objectives. The difference in both of them is that, managerial economics is a fundamental academic subject to make one understand and analyse the problems, while operation research is a functional activity carried out to help the manager to carry out his job of solving decision problems.

Operation Research is concerned with model building. Economic theory is also concerned with model building. Economic models are general and confined to broad economic decisions only, while operation research models can solve problems of various disciplines. O.R. Models, like linear programming and queuing etc. are widely used in managerial economics.

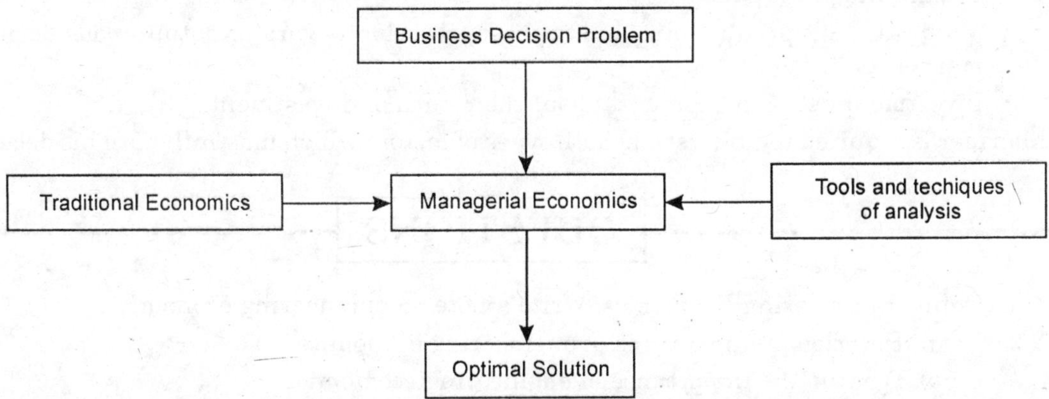

Fig. 30.2. Managerial Economics and Decision-making

30.10. ROLE OF MANAGERIAL ECONOMICS IN DECISION-MAKING.

Main tasks of a manager, are making decisions and processing informations. For making intelligent decisions, managers must be able to obtain, process and use information. The knowledge of economic theories to a manager helps him in these functions. Manager is required to take two types of decisions : specific decisions or general task decisions based on the informations obtained and processed by him.

1. ***Specific Decisions.***

   These are not likely to be frequently repeated and are very important decisions and require the use of basic economics. Some of such decisions are–whether install a costly plant or get the work done from outside, whether or not to close down a branch of the firm that has recently been profitable. These include decisions related to pricing, demand forecasting, economic analysis of the industry etc.

2. ***General Task Decisions.***

   Decisions are influenced by external factors as well as internal factors. Internal factors are within control, while external factors are beyond control, but timely adjustments can be done to these external factors. The managerial economics help in understanding these external factors.

   Important external factors are :

   - General economic conditions like level and rate of growth of national economy, influence of international factors.
   - Prospects of demand for the product. For example, change occurring in the purchasing power of public in general, changes undergoing in fashions, tastes and preferences.
   - Factors influencing input cost.
   - Market conditions for raw material and for finished product.

- Firms share in the market.
- Government's economic policies.

Internal factors are :

- Production, sales, inventory schedules, their present positions and forecasts for future.
- Pricing and profit policies.
- Most profitable product-mix, and the best prices for its various outputs considering the market conditions.
- Investment decisions, forecast about the return on investment.

Manager is required to understand both types of factors which may influence his decisions.

QUESTIONS

1. Define Engineering Economics. Write a note on engineering economics.
2. (*a*) Describe main features of engineering economics.
   (*b*) What is the importance of engineering ecomomics.
3. Describe role of managerial economics in decision-making.
4. Define 'models'. Name different types of models. Explain any three of them.
5. Write a note on 'Market' with reference to Managerial Economics.
6. Discuss the difference between fixed cost, variable cost and semivariable cost.
7. Write a note on 'production models'.
8. Explain different tools of engineering economics in brief.
9. Write short notes on:
   (*a*) Models (*b*) Operation Research
   (*c*) Value engineering (d) Economic lot size,
   (*e*) Benefit/cost ratio
10. Explain different measures exercised for cost control.
11. Define the term value engineering. How it is useful from engineering economics point of view?
12. Define Managerial Economics. Describe its main features.
13. Write a note on "Managerial Economics".
14. What is the importance of managerial economics?
15. Describe role of managerial economics in decision making.
16. Discuss nature and scope of managerial economics.
17. How is managerial economics different from traditional economics?

31

BREAK-EVEN ANALYSIS

31.1. BREAK-EVEN POINT (B.E.P)

The break-even point means the level of output or sales at which no profit or loss is achieved. It indicates the position at which marginal profit or contribution is just sufficient to cover fixed overheads. In other words, a business is said to be break-even when its income equals its expenditure. When production exceeds the "Break-even point", the business makes a profit and when it is below the "Break-even point", the business makes loss. This is shown in Fig. 31.1.

Some Important Definitions

(*i*) **Angle of Incidence.** It is the angle at which income line or sales line cuts the total cost line. If the angle is large, it is an indication that profits are being made at a high rate, on the other hand, if the angle is small it indicates that less profits are being made and are achieved under less favourable conditions.

(*ii*) **Margin of Safety.** It is the output at full capacity minus the output at "Break Even Point". It is expressed as percentage of output at full capacity. If the margin of safety is small, a small drop in production capacity will reduce the profit greatly. It can also be expressed as:

$$\text{Margin of safety} = \left(\frac{\text{Sales at full capacity} - \text{Sales at B.E.P.}}{\text{Sales at full Capacity}}\right) \times 100$$

(*iii*) **Contribution.** It is the difference between sales and variable cost (marginal cost). It is also called as Marginal Profit or Gross Marginal. The marginal profit provides the contribution towards fixed cost and profit.

Contribution = (Sales-Variable cost) which in turn will be equal to Fixed cost + Profit.

Position of Break-Even Point

If B.E.P. is over to the left of the chart with a large angle of incidence, it shows that output can be based considerably. If B.E.P. is over to the right of the chart, the margin of safety is low, which means.

(*i*) the fixed overheads are too great for the amount of sales being done, and

(*ii*) the fixed and variable costs are high while the profit is small.

If the production volume is below B.E.P., the company will be running in loss and beyond it profit can be had.

Determination of B.E.P.

Break-evenpoint may be determined in terms of physical units or in money terms.

1. **B.E.P. in terms of physical units.** This is convenient for the single product firm. It represents the number of units of a product which must be sold to earn enough revenue just to cover all expenses.
2. **B.E.P. in terms of sales value.** Multi-product firms are not in a position to measure the B.E.P. in terms of any common unit of product. In these firms it is covenient to determine the B.E.P. in terms of total rupee sales.

Break-Even Point Calculations

Let
$$S = \text{Sales price}$$
$$V = \text{Variable cost}$$
$$F = \text{Fixed cost}$$
$$P = \text{Profit}$$

Now $S = F + V + P$

or $S - V = F + P$ ...(*i*)

At break-even point, $P = 0$.

$\therefore$ $S - V = F$ ...(*ii*)

Multiplying both sides of Eq. (*ii*) by S.

$\therefore$ $S(S - V) = F \times S$

or
$$S = \frac{F \times S}{(S-V)} = \frac{F}{\left(\frac{S-V}{S}\right)}$$
$$= \frac{\text{Fixed cost}}{\text{Contribution per unit}}$$

and Sales at B.E.P. $= \text{Rs. } \dfrac{F \times S}{(S-V)}$ ...(*iii*)

and No. of units at B.E.P. $\dfrac{\text{Fixed cost}}{\text{contribution/unit}}$

$$= \frac{\text{Fixed cost}}{\text{Marginal Profit unit}}$$ ...(*iv*)

31.2. BREAK-EVEN POINT THEORY

The break-even point of any two variable situations is the point or the value at which they become equal as the result of a common variable.

There are following two methods to obtain break-even point:

(*a*) Mathematical method.

(*b*) Graphical method.

(*a*) **Mathematical Method.**

Let cost be the common variable in two situations 1 and 2, then cost equations will be

$C_1 = f_1(x)$... a function of (x) ...(1)

$C_2 = f_2(x)$...another function of (x) ...(2)

C_1 – may be as total cost, annual cost, cost per item or cost per day etc. for situation 1.

C_2 – same as C_1 but application to situation 2.

x – variable effecting C_1 and C_2.

To solve for the value of x, let

$$C_1 = C_2$$

i.e $$f_{1(x)} = f_{2(x)} \quad \text{...(3)}$$

Equation (3) can be solved for obtaining the value of x. The value of x making the cost equal in both the situations, is called "Break Even Value". Below this value of x one situation will be economical while above it another situation will be economical.

Example. 31.1. *A 25 H.P. unit is required to drive a pump to remove water from a tunnel. The number of hours for which the power unit will run per year is dependent on weather conditions. The power unit is to be used for 4 years.*

For the supply of power following two plans are under consideration.

Plan I. *This plan requires the construction of power line and purchase of electric motor at a total cost of Rs.* ***16,000***. *The salvage value of which is Rs.* ***4000*** *after 4 years of working. Cost of electricity per hour of operation is Rs. 6.80. Equipment being automatic, no attendant is needed. Maintenance is estimated to Rs. 2400 per annum.*

Plan II. *This plan needs a gasoline engine, which costs Rs.* ***11,000***. *The engine will be condemned at the end of 4 years. The cost of fuel and oil per hour of operation is estimated as Rs. 8.40. Hourly wages of operator is Rs. 2.00. Maintenance is estimated at Rs. 3 per hour of operation.*

Solve by "Break-even point" theory, which of the plan will be economical ?

Solution.

Plan I. Let, N = No. of hours of operation per year

Then, total annual cost

$$= \left\{\frac{16{,}000 - 4{,}000}{4}\right\} + 6.8N + 2400$$

$$= 5400 + 6.8\text{ N} \quad \text{...(1)}$$

Plan II. Similarly, total annual cost

$$= \frac{11{,}000}{4} + 8.4\text{N} + 2\text{N} + 3\text{N}$$

$$= 2750 + 13.4\text{ N} \quad \text{...(2)}$$

There is one value of N for which the cost of Plans I and II will be equal. Hence N may be determined by equating equations (1) and (2).

$$5400 + 6.8\,N = 2750 + 13.4\,N$$

$$13.4\,N - 6.8\,N = 5400 - 2750$$

$$6.6\,N = 2650$$

$$N = 401 \text{ hours.}$$

For given conditions, annual costs of the two alternatives are calculated to be equal for 401 hours of usage per annum. If usage comes to be less than 401 hours per annum, selection of plan II is economical. For more than 401 hours, the selection for automatic equipment, *i.e.*, plan I will be more economical.

(b) Graphical Method

Although the break-even point may be calculated mathematically, but it is usually represented graphically because it enables manager to see more clearly the break-even point and the possibilities for profits and losses. By using these charts one can predict probable profits at various levels of output.

A break-even chart given in Fig. 31.1 is used to determine break-even point and amount of profit or loss under varying conditions of output and costs. Sales or expenditure in rupees is represented on vertical axis, while output (either in quantity or in percentage capacity) is represented on horizontal axis. Line A represents the "fixed cost", line *B* represents total cost or total expenses, while line *C* represents sales revenue and indicates income at various levels of output. The point where lines *B* and *C* intersect each other, is "Break Even Point. The space between lines *B* and *C* to the right of the "Break Even Point" represents potential profit, whereas to the left of the "Break Even Point" potential loss. The amount of loss or profit can be measured on vertical scale.

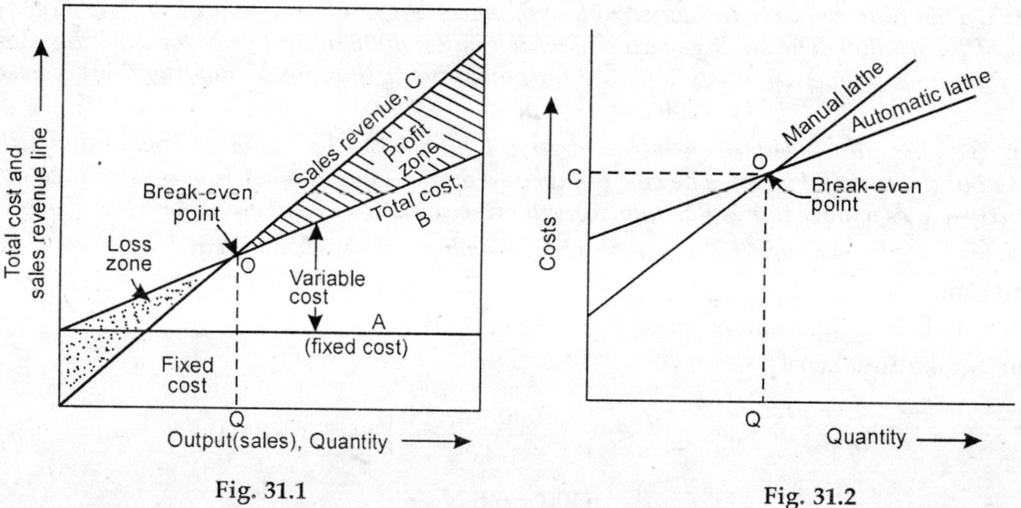

Fig. 31.1

Fig. 31.2

This method can be applied to various management problems. For example, suppose a manager wants to replace an old lathe machine being used for manufacturing screws by automatic screw machine. Then he must first know whether it will be profitable or not, for which he must adopt break-even point theory and construct the chart as shown in Fig. 31.2. The figure shows that for a production less than *Q*, it must not be changed whereas for production more than *Q*, automatic machine or new machine will be economical or in other words below *Q* manual lathe is cheaper; beyond *Q*, automatic machine is cheaper. This break-even point is also known as "cut even point".

31.3. BREAK-EVEN ANALYSIS (COST ANLYSIS)

Break-Even Chart

A break-even chart is a graphical representation of the relationship between costs and revenue at a given time, and determine the break-even point and profit potential under varying conditions of output and cost.

Functions of Break-Even Chart

1. To represent economical position of production on graph.
2. To tell for likely profits or losses at various levels of output.
3. To help the management to decide the production level.
4. To indicate margin of safety.

Assumption in Break-Even Analysis

The various assumptions that underline in this technique are given as under:

(*i*) It is assumed that over the entire range of volume of production 'all costs are perfectly variable.

(*ii*) It is assumed that over the entire range of volume of production all costs are absolutely fixed.

(*iii*) It is assumed that with the physical volume of production all revenue is perfectly variable.

(*iv*) The volume of sales and volume of production are equal.

(*v*) It is assumed that for multi products firms, the product mix should be stable.

31.4. APPLICATIONS (USES)

Break-even analysis not only highlights the areas of economic strength and weaknesses in the firm but also helps in finding out the ways which can enhance its profitability. With the help of this analysis management of a production firm can take decisions related to the following:

(*i*) Safety margin with proposed volume.

(*ii*) Quantity needed to have desired profit.

(*iii*) Effect of change in price.

(*iv*) Effect of change in costs.

(*v*) Whether to accept an order or not.

(*vi*) Whether to make or buy.

1. **Safety Margin**

   It refers the extent to which the concern can afford to decline in sales upto the break-even point. It can be represented by the percentage ratio of sales over break-even point volume to the sales volume.

$$\therefore \qquad \text{Safety margin} = \frac{\text{Sales volume} - \text{Sales at B.E.P.}}{\text{Sales volume}} \times 100$$

2. **Quantity Needed to have Desired Profit**

   This is the most common application of break-even analysis and the desired quantity is given by

$$\text{Target quantity} = \frac{\text{Fixed cost} + \text{Target profit}}{\text{Contribution per unit}}$$

3. **The Effect of Change in Price**

   Sometimes management is required to consider whether to reduce price of a product or not. Management has to consider the following facts in this regard:

If the sales price is reduced then contribution margin will reduce and this will increase the sales volume. But this increased volume may or may not receive increase in demand because it depends on elasticity of demand.

The change in break-even point due to rate variation in sales price is drawn below (Fig 31.3). At different price levels total revenue line can be plotted and the chart shows that as the price of a product is reduced the break-even point shifts towards right side and *vice versa.* From the chart, one can then estimate the volume that will be sold and profit at each price level.

From the chart

At B.E.P., $Q = \dfrac{F+P}{S-V}$

$\therefore$ $Q_1 = \dfrac{F+P}{S_1-V}$

where S_1 = New changed sales price

Q_1 = New changed B.E.P. in units

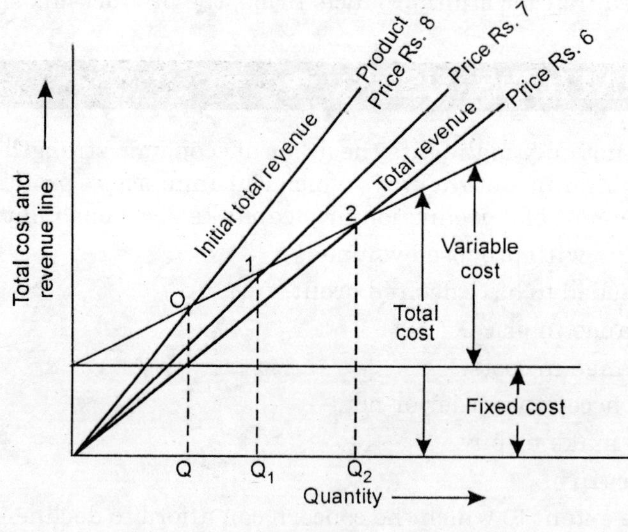

Fig. 31.3.

4. Effects of Change in Costs

There are two types of costs :

(*a*) Variable cost.

(*b*) Fixed cost.

(*a*) **Variable Cost Change.** An increase in variable cost leads to reduction in the contribution margin. This increase in variable cost will reduce the profit. Therefore, what should be the new price to maintain the present profit without any change in sales volume.

As there is reduction in contribution margin, it will cause increase in sales volume. Therefore, what should be the sales volume to maintain the present profit without change in the price (Fig. 31.4).

$$Q = \frac{F+P}{S-V}$$

$$Q_1 = \frac{F+P}{S_1 - V_1}$$

where Q_1 = New Break-even point

V_1 = New Variable cost.

If sales volume is same, then $Q = Q_1$

$\therefore \quad S_1 - V_1 = S - V$

or $\quad S_1 = S + (V_1 - V)$ ...(1)

where S_1 is the new selling price to maintain present profit.

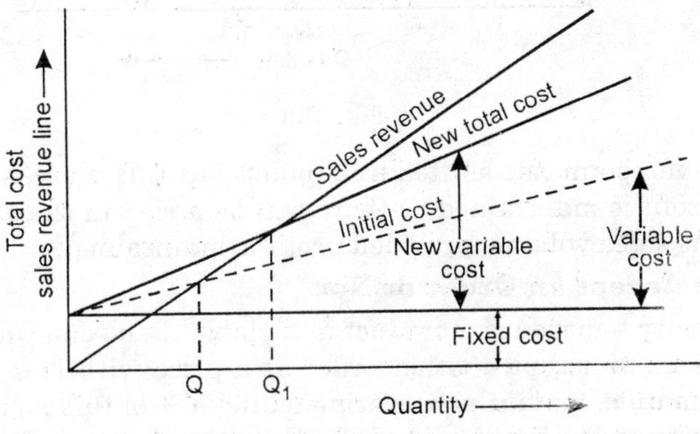

Fig. 31.4

Due to increase in the variable cost, Break-even point has shifted from point Q to point Q_1. Thus higher quantity is to be sold to maintain the present profit assuming no change in the price of the product.

(b) **Change in Fixed Cost.** The fixed cost may change due to an increase in executive salaries, taxes, insurances and building rent etc. This is turn will bring change in the break-even point, assuming no change in product price.

Here, $$Q = \frac{F+P}{S-V} \quad ...(1)$$

$$Q_1 = \frac{F_1+P}{S-V} \quad ...(2)$$

Solving Eqs. (1) and (2), we have $Q_1 = Q + \dfrac{F_1 - F}{S-V}$ ...(3)

and if Q is same and there is change in sales price, then

$$S_1 = S + \frac{F_1 - F}{Q}$$

Here, F_1 = New fixed cost. ...(4)

This is shown graphically in Fig. 31.5

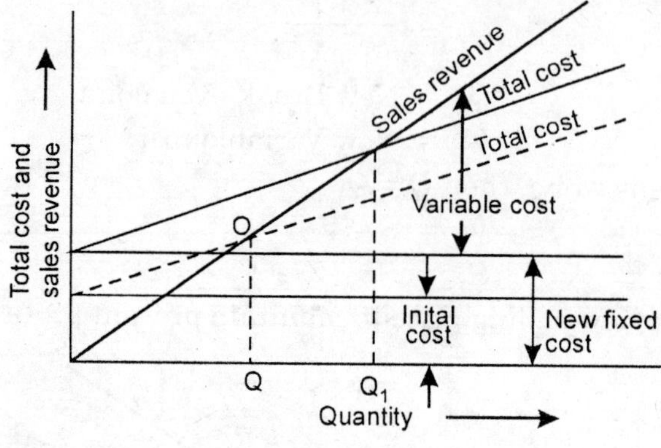

Fig. 31.5

The Break-even point has shifted from point 0 to 1. If there is no change in price and volume of profit is maintained or there will be a rise in the sales price, if there is no change in the sales volume, provided profit is maintained.

5. **Whether to Accept an Order or Not**

If extra capacity to produce a product is variable then sometimes management has to decide whether to accept another order at a price with less than the initial selling price. For example, a plant is operating on its 50% of full capacity. A buyer offered to buy 4000 units at Rs. 5 per unit while the average cost is Rs. 6. Now the problem is whether to accept this order or not. The other details of the product are :

Total capacity = 20,000 units
Present output = 10,000 units
Direct material cost = Rs. 10,000
Direct labour cost = Rs. 10,000
Fixed costs = Rs. 40,000

In this question, one can find that additional cost of making these 4000 units is Rs. 4000 for material cost and Rs. 4000 for labour cost (total Rs. 8000) and the revenue from sales would be

$$\text{Rs. } 4000 \times 5 = \text{Rs. } 20{,}000$$

Thus the concern will save

$$\text{Rs. } 20{,}000 - \text{Rs. } 8{,}000 = \text{Rs. } 12{,}000$$

So, it would be profitable to accept anything more than Rs. 2 per unit which is the direct cost per unit. There is only danger that, if other consumers come to know that this product is being sold at a lower price, they may also then demand supply at the lower price or otherwise they may not be further interested to buy from this concern. Therefore, in such cases acceptance should be kept secret.

6. **Whether to Add or Drop a Product Line**

In this case, following two situations arise :

(*a*) Should a new product be added in view of the estimated revenue and cost ?

(*b*) If the product is dropped from the line, what would be consequent effects on revenue and costs?

Example 31.2. *The following data from a plant is available:*

Product	*Price Rs.*	*Variable cost Rs.*	*Percentage sales units*
A	10	6	20
B	6	4	30
C	20	12	50

Fixed cost per year = Rs. 7500

Total sales of three products = 25,000

It is decided by the management to drop the product *A* and add product *D*. To find whether this decision is profitable or not ? Assume sales for products *B*, *C* and *D* as Rs. 26,000.

Product	*Price Rs.*	*Variable cost Rs.*	*Percentage sales units*
D	16	6	10
B	6	4	50
C	20	12	40

Solution. Total fixed cost per year = Rs. 7500.

Sales for the current year = 26,000

Product A contribution is Rs. (10 – 6) = Rs. 4

∴ Contribution for 20 percent sales of product A

$$= \frac{10-6}{10} \times 0.20 = 0.08$$

Similarly for product *B*, $= \dfrac{6-4}{6} \times 0.30 = 0.10$

and *Product C*, $\dfrac{20-12}{20} \times 0.50 = 0.20$

Thus contribution ratio for product, *A*, *B* and *C*

$$= 0.08 + 0.10 + 0.20 = 0.38$$

∴ Total contribution of sales

$$= 0.38 \times 25{,}000 = \text{Rs. } 9500$$

∴ Profit = Contribution – Fixed costs

$$= 9500 - 7500 = \text{Rs. } 2000.$$

Similarly, the profit or contribution of new product line of products *D*,*B*,*C*

$$D = \frac{16-6}{16} \times 10\% = 0.06$$

$$B = \frac{6-4}{6} \times 0.50 = 0.17$$

$$C = \frac{20-12}{20} \times 0.40 = 0.16$$

∴ Total contribution ratio

$$= 0.06 + 0.17 + 0.16 = 0.39$$

∴ Total contribution from sales = 26,000 × 0.39 = Rs. 10,140

∴ Profit = 10,140 – 7500 = **Rs. 2640.**

Hence proposed decision is profitable to drop *A* and add *D*.

7. Whether to Make or Buy

Assuming the cost to purchase is in direct proportion with the quantity purchased, the Break-even point can be plotted as shown in Fig. 31.6.

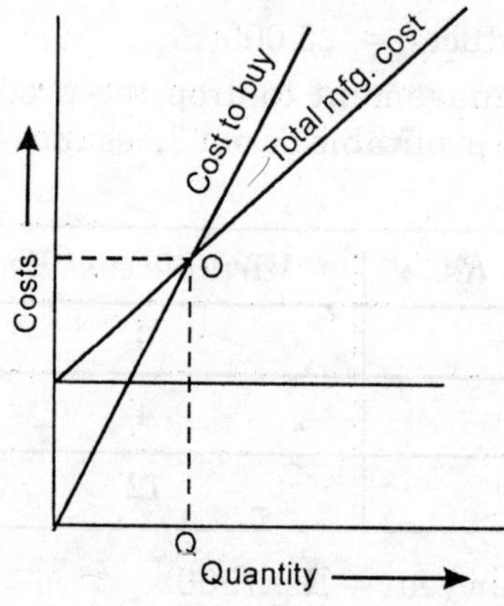

Fig. 31.6.

Let *Q* be the quantity at Break-even point, for less than *Q* it is cheaper to buy; and for more than *Q* it is cheaper to make.

It can also be written as

$$Q = \frac{\text{Fixed cost}}{\text{Purchase price} - \text{Variable cost}}$$

Thus in this way Break Even Point theory can be applied to solve several problems of an industry such as minimum quantity to be manufactured to avoid losses, which machine will be profitable for a particular production etc. This theory is used as a tool by management to aid in making decisions.

Example.31.3. (*a*) *What is break-even analysis ? What information does it provide to the management ?*

(*b*) *The fixed costs of a company are Rs. 350,000. The net sales amount to Rs. 600,000 annually. The direct costs are 35% of sales in rupees. Determine the following:*

(*i*) The "break-even point" in terms of sales rupees.

(*ii*) The sales required to earn a profit of Rs. 80,000.

Solution. (*a*) Break-even analysis. Equipments are used to produce products at profitable rate, so that the products can stand competition, replacement decision is not an easy job, it requires several considerations. As it involves large capital investment, hence a wrong decision may adversely affect the profitability of whole concern. Therefore, a scientific approach to solve this problem is essential. For this purpose the theory of Break Even Point is very helpful. The break-even point of any two variable situations is the point or the value at which they become equal as the result of a common variable.

Let cost be the common variable in two situations 1 and 2, then cost equations will be

$$c_1 = f_1 (x) \text{...a function of } (x) \quad \text{...(1)}$$

$$c_2 = f_2 (x) \text{...another function of } (x) \quad \text{...(2)}$$

To solve for the value of x, let $c_1 = c_2$

i.e. $$f_1(x) = f_2(x) \quad \text{...(3)}$$

Equation (3) can be solved for obtaining the value of (x). The value of x making the cost equal in both the situations is called "Break Even Value" (Fig. 31.1) Below the value of x, one situation will be economical while above it another situation will be economical.

Information to Management

This analysis is used as a tool by management to aid in making decisions.

1. It can be applied to solve several problems of an industry such as minimum quantity to manufacture to avoid losses, which machine will be profitable for a particular production etc.
2. It helps to determine the unit cost of a product, corresponding to any particular quantity of production.
3. It suggests about the selling price fixation.
4. It informs about the percentage financial yield for a project.
5. It informs about the fact that industry must run at its scheduled target capacity to get advantage of the optimal cost of production per unit

(*b*) Break Even Point, B.E.P.

$$= \frac{F}{1 - V/S}$$

(*i*) where, F = Fixed cost

V = Variable cost per unit or total variable cost also known as direct cost and

S = Selling price.

Hence in question,

F = Rs. 350,000

V = 0.35 × S

S = 600,000

Hence B.E.P $$= \frac{350{,}000}{1 - \dfrac{0.35 \times 600{,}000}{600{,}000}} = \frac{350{,}000}{0.65}$$

= **Rs. 538,461.53 Ans.**

(*ii*) Profit = 80,000

Sales = ?

Now, Sales $$= \frac{\text{Fixed cost + Profit}}{1\text{–V/S}}$$

∴ Sales $$= \frac{350{,}000 + 80{,}000}{1 - 0.35} = \frac{4{,}30{,}000}{0.65}$$

= **Rs. 661,538.46 Ans.**

Example 31.4. *An engine lathe costing Rs. 10,000 can produce components at the rate of 6 pieces per hour and another automatic lathe costing Rs. 20,000 can produce 20 pieces per hour. The operator on either of the machine is to be paid at the rate of Rs. 1.50 per hour. Determine the minimum number of pieces which will change the cost situation in favour of the automatic lathe.*

Solution. *First situation :*

Cost of engine lathe = Rs. 10,000.

Production = 6 pieces/hr.

Operator rate = Rs. 1.50/hr.

Second situation :

Cost of automatic lathe = Rs. 20,000.

Production = 20 pieces/hr.

Operator rate = 1.50/hr.

Let N be the production pieces at which cost equations are equal

$$\text{Then, } 10{,}000 + \frac{N}{6} \times 1.50 = 20{,}000 + \frac{N}{20} \times 1.50$$

$$\text{or} \qquad \frac{N}{6} \times \frac{3}{2} - \frac{N}{20} \times \frac{3}{2} = 10{,}000$$

$$\text{or} \qquad 7N = 10{,}000 \times 40$$

$$\text{or} \qquad N = \frac{10{,}000 \times 40}{7} = 57{,}142.86 \text{ say } \mathbf{57{,}143 \text{ pieces.}} \qquad \textbf{Ans.}$$

It means if production is more than 57,143 pieces then automatic machine will be economical.

Example. 31.5. *The fixed costs for the year 2009-10 are Rs. 500,000 variable cost per unit is Rs. 25. The estimated sales for the period are valued at Rs. 1,500,000. Each unit sells at Rs. 150. Determine :*

(*i*) Break-even point

(*ii*) Rs. 1,200,000 will be the likely sales turnover for the next budget period, calculate the estimated contribution and profit.

(*iii*) If a profit target of Rs. 650,000 has been budgeted, compute the turnover required.

Solution, (*i*) Break-even point

$$= \frac{F}{1-(V/S)}$$

where F = Fixed cost = 500,000

V = Variable cost = Rs. 25/unit

S = Selling cost = Rs. 150/unit

$$\therefore \qquad \text{B.E.P.} = \frac{500{,}000}{1-\frac{25}{150}} = \frac{500{,}000 \times 6}{5}$$

$$= \textbf{Rs. 600,000. Ans.}$$

$$(ii) \qquad \text{Sales} = \frac{\text{Fixed cost} + \text{Profit}}{1\text{–V/S}}$$

or $$\text{Profit} = 1{,}200{,}0000 \times \frac{5}{6} - 500{,}000$$

$$= 1{,}000{,}000 - 500{,}000$$

$$= \textbf{Rs. 500,000. Ans.}$$

Now, estimated contribution

$$= \text{Fixed cost} + \text{Profit}$$

$$= 500{,}000 + 500{,}000$$

$$= \textbf{Rs. 1,000,000. Ans.}$$

(*iii*) If profit is 650,000 then sales = ?

Now sales $$\text{Sales} = \frac{\text{Fixed cost} + \text{Profit}}{1\text{–V/S}} = \frac{500{,}000 + 650{,}000}{1 - 1/6}$$

$$= \frac{1{,}150{,}000 \times 6}{5}$$

$$= \textbf{Rs. 1,380,000. Ans.}$$

Example. 31.6. *The fixed costs for the financial year 2010-11 are Rs. 40,000. The sales for this period are of Rs. 100,000. The variable cost per unit is Rs. 2. Selling price of each product is Rs. 10 and the number of units involved coincides with the expected volume of output. Construct the Break-even chart and determine :*

(*a*) *Break-even point*

(*b*) *How many minimum product should be sold to earn profit.*

(*c*) *Profit earned at a turnover of Rs. 80,000*

(*d*) *Margin of safety.*

(*e*) *Angle of incidence.*

Solution. Here

Fixed cost	F =	Rs. 40,000
Variable cost	V =	Rs. 2 per unit
Selling price	S =	Rs. 10 per unit
Total Sales	=	Rs. 100,000

$$\text{No. of products sold} = \frac{\text{Total sales}}{\text{Selling price of one product}}$$

$$\frac{100{,}000}{10} = 10{,}000 \text{ units}$$

Now draw the break-even chart, as described under :

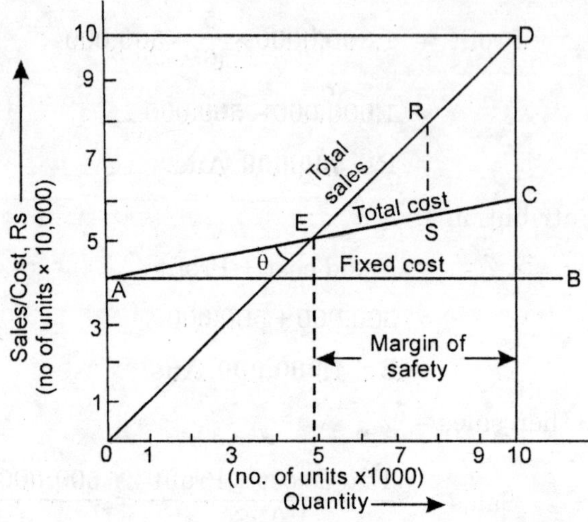

Fig. 31.7

1. Draw on the graph paper fixed cost line *AB* at Rs. 40,000.
2. Variable cost = No. of products x Variable cost/product = 10,000 x 2 = 20,000.
3. Variable cost varies from zero at 0 unit sale to Rs. 20,000 at 10,000 units sale. Thus draw the variable cost line *AC* above the fixed cost line, as shown in the graph. Thus total cost = Fixed cost + Variable cost.
4. Sales is zero at 0 unit and is Rs. 100,000 at 10,000 units sales. Thus draw the sales line *OD*. Total cost line and total sales line intersect at point *E*, which is known as Break-even point on the break-even chart.
   (*a*) Break-even point is at 5,000 units or Rs. 50,000 sales.
   (*b*) The firm should sell more than 5,000 units to receive profit.
   (*c*) Profit at sales of Rs. 80,000. This is denoted by *RS* in the chart and is equal to Rs. 24,000.
   (*d*) Margin of safety.
   It is marked at 10,000 units and is equal to
   Total sales – Sales at Break-even point

$$100,000\text{-}50,000 = \text{Rs. } 50,000$$

$$\text{Percentage} = \frac{50,000}{100,000} \times 100 = 50\%$$

   (*e*) **Angle of incidence**

$$\theta = 34° \text{ by measurement.}$$

Example 31.7. *A company is planning to launch a new product. For any volume of production below 400 unit, the fixed cost is Rs. 6,000 and the variable cost is Rs. 20 per unit. If the volume is to be more than 400, larger equipment will be needed and the fixed cost will be Rs. 10,000. However, the variable cost will reduce to Rs. 10 per unit. At any volume the selling price is Rs. 30 per unit*

(*a*) What is the break-even point ?
(*b*) What is the profit or loss if the volume is fixed at 500 units ?
(*c*) What are the assumptions made in your analysis ?

Solution, (*a*) Here

Q = Quantity at Break-even point

F = Fixed costs = Rs. 6000

V = Variable costs = Rs. 20/unit

S = Selling price = Rs. 30/unit.

Now $$Q(S-V) = F + P$$

where P = Profit, but at Break-even point,

$$P = O$$

$\therefore$ $$Q(S-V) = F \quad ...(1)$$

Hence by substitution $$Q = \frac{6000}{(30-20)} = 600 \text{ units}$$

It means Break Even Point will be at the production of 600 **units.** **Ans.**

(*b*) Here

$$Q_1 = 500 \text{ units}$$
$$F_1 = 10{,}000$$
$$V_1 = \text{Rs. } 10 \text{ /unit}$$
$$S_1 = S = \text{Rs. } 30\text{/unit}$$
$$P = ?$$

NOW $$Q_1(S_1 - V_1) = F_1 + P$$

or $$500\,(30-10) = 10{,}000 + P$$

or $$P = 0$$

i.e., at 500 units production, neither there is any profit nor loss. That means with these changed conditions, break-even point has shifted to 500 units while initially it was at 600 units.

(c) Assumption

1. The selling price in both the situations is assumed to be constant.
2. The volume of sales and the volume of production is assumed to be equal.

Example 31.8. *A tooth-paste company sold 250,000 packets for which the variable cost of manufacture was Rs. 4.20 per packet. Each packet contributes 30% of its revenue to fixed costs and profit. This year the company decided to give a price reduction of 5%.*

How many more packets will the company have to sell at the ***5%*** *price reduction in order to earn the same profit.*

Solution. Total Revenue

= Fixed cost + profit + Variable cost

$\therefore$ Selling price = Fixed cost unit + Profit/unit + Variable cost/unit

Let Selling price = Rs. S. ...(1)

It is given that 30% of contribution = (Fixed cost + Profit) per unit

$\therefore$ $0.3\,S$ = (Fixed cost + profit)/unit ...(2)

Putting the value of Eq. (2) in Eq. (1)

$\therefore$ Selling price = $0.3\,S + 4.20$

where 4.20 is variable cost.

Now $$S = 0.3\,S + 4.20$$
$$S = \textbf{Rs. 6.}$$

Putting this value of S in Eq. (2)

$$0.3 \times 6 = \text{(Fixed cost + Profit)/unit}$$

or $\quad$ (Fixed cost + Profit)/unit = 1.8.

Now if price reduction is 5%, then

$$S_1 = 6 - \frac{6 \times 5}{100} = 5.70$$

$$\therefore \quad Q_1 = Q \times \frac{F + P}{S_1 - V}$$

$$= \frac{1.8}{5.70 - 4.20} \times \frac{250,000}{1} = 300,000$$

$\therefore$ Additional production = 300,000 – 250,000 = **50,000 Ans.**

Example 31.9. (*a*) *What is meant by break-even analysis ? Discuss the assumptions that underline the technique and its uses.*

(*b*) *In the past two years it is observed in metal working industry that the material cost has risen by 20% whereas other costs have risen by 10%. Assuming that the selling prices have advanced by 10% and that material costs represents* $33\frac{1}{3}\%$ *of the total cost. Indicate the effect on the break-even point of typical break-even chart.*

Solution.

(*a*) **Break-even analysis. A** business is said to be break-even when its income equals expenditure. The break-even point means the level of output or sales at which no profit or loss is made. Below the Break even point, the loss occurs and above this point profit is earned.

The various assumptions that underline in this technique are given as under :

(*i*) It is assumed that over the entire range of volume of production all costs are perfectly variable.

(*ii*) It is assumed that over the entire range of volume of production all costs are absolutely fixed.

(*iii*) It is assumed that with the physical volume of production all revenue is perfectly variable.

(*iv*) The volume of sales and volume of production are equal,

(*v*) It is assumed that for multi-product firms, the product mix should be stable.

(*b*) Suppose initial total variable cost = Rs. 300 Fixed cost will be same in all the conditions. Thus variable cost will be proportional to total cost. Now according to question after two years, material cost increases by 20% and other cost by 10% and material cost is $\frac{1}{3}$ of total cost. It means if material cost is 100, other cost will be Rs. 200. Thus total cost is Rs. 100 + 200 $\quad$ =Rs. 300.

$$\text{New Material Cost} = 100 \times 1.20 = 120$$

$$\text{New labour cost} = 200 \times 1.1 = 220$$

$$\therefore \quad \text{New total variable cost} = \text{Rs. } 340$$

Let initial selling price = Rs. 350 (we can assume any value)

After 2 years, new selling price = Rs. 350 × 1.1 = Rs. 385. Output in both the situations is assumed to be any fixed quantity. Now plot is drawn between total cost and selling price for the initial situation and new changed situation. The firm lines on the plot indicate the initial situation while dotted lines changed situations. From the plot, it is found that the Break Even Point has shifted from right to left. It means new break-even point will be at lower output and angle of incidence also large, which shows that profit margin is also more in the changed situation.

Example 31.10. *A plant is manufacturing 3000 heavy duty lathes per year and is operating at 75% of its capacity. The annual sales return is Rs. 10,500,000. The fixed cost of the plant is Rs. 4,000,000 and variable cost Rs. 4150.00 per unit. There is a proposal to utilise spare capacity by manufacturing precision lathes which would increase the fixed cost by Rs. 800,000 but reduce the variable cost by Rs. 750 per unit.*

(i) *Is the proposal economical ? Given reasons for answer.*

(ii) *If reduction in selling price by Rs. 500 per unit requires the plant to be run at 90% of its capacity to break-even, would this be a better proposal than the earlier one.*

Solution. Plant output = 3000 lathes/year = Q

Operation at = 75% of capacity

$$\therefore \quad \text{Capacity of plant} = \frac{3000}{0.75}$$

$$= 400 \text{ lathes/year}$$

$$\text{Annual sales} = \text{Rs. } 10{,}500{,}000$$

$$F = \text{Fixed cost} = 4{,}000{,}000$$

$$V = \text{Variable cost} = \text{Rs. } 4150/\text{unit}$$

$$S = \text{Selling price of lathe} = \frac{10{,}500{,}000}{3000} = 3500$$

Now $\quad Q(S-V) = F + P$

or $\quad 3000\,(3500-4150) = 4{,}000{,}000 + P$

or $\quad P = 3000 \times 3500 - 3000 \times 4150 - 4{,}000{,}000$

or $\quad P = -$ **Rs. 5,950,000 Ans.**

Minus sign indicates that the firm is making **a** loss of Rs. 5,950,000 Ans.

First proposal

Plant will use spare capacity in the manufacture of precision lathes.

$\therefore$ Space capacity = 1000 units

Here, Fixed cost $\quad F_1 = 4{,}000{,}000 + 800{,}000$

$$= 4{,}800{,}000$$

Variable cost $\quad V_1 = 4150 - 750 = \text{Rs. } 3400$

$$Q_1 = 3000 + 1000 = 4000 \text{ units.}$$

Assuming sales price same, then

$$Q_1(S - V_1) = F_1 + P$$

or $\quad 4000(3500 - 3400) = 4{,}800{,}000 + P$

or $\quad P = -4{,}400{,}000$

Here again there is loss but this loss is less than the initial loss and this can be recovered by increasing the price of precision lathes (1000 lathes produced by utilising spare capacity). In calculations we assumed Rs. 3500 per unit but being precision lathes, its selling price can be much higher.

Second proposal:

Here we have to utilise 90% of the capacity at B.E.P.

$$\therefore Q \text{ at B.E.P.} = \frac{F}{S-V} = \frac{4,000,000}{(3500-500)-4150}$$

$$= 3478 \text{ units}$$

$$\therefore 90\% \text{ of } 3478 = 3130 \text{ units}$$

In this proposal the loss will be extremely high. Therefore, it is not possible to accept this proposal. Hence first proposal should be accepted and loss may be recovered by keeping higher selling price of 1000 units of precision lathes.

QUESTIONS

1. The following cost figures are taken from the budget of a company producing consumer goods (budget period is one year)

Direct material Rs. 1,800,000

Direct labour = Rs. 1,600,000

Factory overhead = Rs. 900,000 (Fixed) + Rs. 400,000 (Variable)

Administrative overhead = Rs. 200,000 (Variable) + Rs. 600,000 (Fixed)

Selling and distribution overhead = Rs. 500,000 (Variable) + Rs. 300,000 (Fixed)

In the sales budget the sales amount for the budgeted period is estimated at Rs. 6,100,000.

(*a*) Draw the break-even chart.

(*b*) What is the estimated profit ?

(*c*) What is the sales amount at the break-even point ?

(*d*) Show in the chart the result of a 10% increase in the product selling price without any change in the cost.

2. A concern sells 3000 cycles every year the price of each is Rs. 600. The available cost data are shown below :

Material cost = Rs. 400,000

Labour cost = Rs. 300,000

Factory cost = Rs. 250,000 (Fixed)

Rs. 350,000 (Variable)

Administration and distribution overhead

Rs. 150,000 (Fixed)

Rs. 100,000 (Variable)

Draw the break-even chart to scale and mention the minimum economic production. What will be the profit, if the selling price is reduced by 5% without any reduction in the production cost ? Also show the new Break-even point and plot the new unit cost curve.

3. The annual sales of a company is Rs. 120,000. Fixed costs including insurance, depreciation etc. is Rs. 15,000. Variable costs Rs. 3 per unit. Plant capacity was 40,000 units and the selling price is Rs. 4 per unit. Total investment in plant and equipment was Rs. 110,000.

(*a*) Draw a break-even for the company.

(*b*) Find and show the profit before taxes, if any, and compute the rate of return on the investment.

4. Explain the term Break-Even Point theory. How does it help in equipment replacement decisions ?

5. A ceiling fan manufacturer buys a component at Rs. 10 each. If he decides to make it himself, his fixed and variable cost will be Rs. 10,000 and Rs. 5 per component respectively. To decide whether to make or buy the component, calculate B.E.P.

6. Explain the term 'break-even point' Define 'angle of incidence' and 'margin of safety'.

7. Explain and illustrate some of the applications of 'break-event point'.

8. Write short notes on:

(*a*) Information provided by 'break-even analysis' to the management.

(*b*) Break-even analysis, a tool for decision-making.

32

EQUIPMENT REPLACEMENT ANALYSIS

32.1. INTRODUCTION

Equipment replacement decision plays an important role in the economic running of any concern for years or decades. A firm has to face three types of replacement decisions:

(a) The replacement of capital equipment, as it wears out or becomes obsolete.

(b) The capital equipment required for expansion.

(c) The displacement of old technology by the new, *i.e.*, the introduction of an improved equipment in the market which may produce cheaper products. It is also known as replacement of obsolete equipments.

Equipments are used to produce products at profitable rate, so that the products can stand competition. Replacement decision is not an easy job, it requires several considerations. As it involves large capital investment, hence a wrong decision may adversely affect the profitability of whole concern. Therefore, a scientific approach to solve such problems is essential.

32.2. REASONS FOR REPLACEMENT OF EQUIPMENT

The main reasons are :

(a) Deterioration (b) Obsolescence

(c) Inadequacy (d) Working conditions

(a) **Deterioration.** It becomes necessary to replace the machine when it wears out and does not function properly. Such machinery start lowering the quality of product, decreasing the production and increase in labour and maintenance costs.

(b) **Obsolescence.** Whenever new equipment comes in the market, which is capable of producting more products of good quality with less labour and has more efficiency, the existing machine is to be replaced with this machine, although it was functioning well.

Generally this is necessitated because the products manufactured by new machine will be cheaper.

(c) **Inadequacy.** With the change of product design to meet the customers demand or quantity to be manufactured, old machinery becomes inadequate and, therefore, call for different manufacturing equipment.

(*d*) **Working Conditions.** To take replacement decision, working conditions are also responsible. Machinery yielding more smoke or noise (unpleasant conditions) and hazardous to work may cause pollution and accidents. Similarly, worker may not like to work on an old machinery because of hazardous nature of a particular process. Such machinery needs replacement.

32.3. EQUIPMENT REPLACEMENT POLICY

Sometimes a manufacturer has to face a problem of replacing the equipment, since this is a continuous process and, therefore, a set system for this must be evolved. The main consideration is "when to replace" but this when requires many considerations to reach at suitable conclusion. Large number of factors are responsible to replace the equipment before the expiry of the estimated life, some of them are:

(*i*) To reduce production cost
(*ii*) To reduce fatigue
(*iii*) To raise quality
(*iv*) To increase output
(*v*) To secure greater convenience, safety and reliability.

32.4. GUIDELINES FOR REPLACEMENTANALYSIS

There are certain rules which may be used as guidelines for replacement analysis :

1. **For Equipment in Use.**
   (*a*) *Do consider* :
   (*i*) Operating cost
   (*ii*) Repair and maintenance cost
   (*iii*) Down time cost
   (*iv*) Salvage value
   (*v*) Rebuilding cost
   (*b*) Do not consider :
   (*i*) Original cost
   (*ii*) Money already spent on repairs and maintenance
   (*iii*) Unrealistic book value.
2. **For New Equipment**
   (*a*) *Do consider* :
   (*i*) Initial cost
   (*ii*) Interest on capital investment
   (*iii*) Salvage value at the end of useful life
   (*iv*) Cost advantage of improved product
   (*v*) Labour savings.
   (*b*) *Do not consider* :
   (*i*) Any savings not clearly assessable
   (*ii*) Overhead charges

Capital Recovery

Capital recovery of an equipment is the paying for itself.

"Capital recovery period", is the time for the "pay off" period during which time any investment in the new equipment must "pay for itself".

In replacement studies, the matter of equivalence should be considered. Because of the "interest", a rupee today is not a rupee next year. Hence, Rupees must be converted into their value at particular time before they are truly comparable.

32.5. METHODS FOR REPLACEMENT STUDIES

Following are some of the important methods which are used for equipment replacement studies :

1. Pay back period method.
2. Total life average method.
3. Annual cost method
4. Present worth method.
5. Rate of return method.
6. M.A.P.I. method.

32.5.1. Pay-Back Period Method

This method determines as to how long it will take (in years) to pay back invested capital.

Let,

P = Pay back period in years.

C = Original capital investment.

R = Annual return expected (*i.e.*, total annual earning after deducting taxes).

Then

$$P = \frac{C}{R}$$

This method is not much reliable as it does not take into account its insurance, interest and maintenance. Further, in the beginning the return is generally less, which increases gradually but here it is considered to be constant. This method does not consider depreciation and obsolescence.

32.5.2. Total Life Average Method

In this method, all the costs involved in buying, operating and maintaining an equipment or asset are added together into one total figure and this sum is divided by the total estimated life to get an average annual cost.

Example 32.1. *An existing piece of equipment has its market value of Rs. 10,000, maintenance cost is Rs. 1000 per year and has a life of 10 years and no salvage value. The interst rate is 10%. The proposed equipment has an installed cost of Rs. 100,000, maintenance cost of Rs. 800 per year, a life of 50 years and salvage value of Rs. 15,000. Suggest, whether proposed equipment should be purchased or not.*

Solution

Factor	*Existing Equipment*	*Proposed Equipment*
1. Depreciation	Rs. 10000	Rs. (100000 – 15000) = Rs. 85000
2. Maintenance	Rs. 1000 × 10 = Rs. 10000	Rs. 800 × 50 = 40000
3. Interest 10%	= Rs. 5500	= Rs. 216750 (see calculations below)
4. Total life cost	Rs. 25,500	Rs. 341750.
5. Average cost/year	25,500 ÷ 10 = Rs. 2550	341750 ÷ 50 = Rs. 6835.

Interest is calculated by the following method :

Interest for existing equipment.

Total life = 10 years

Hence yearly reduction in cost

$$= \frac{10{,}000}{10} = \text{Rs. } 1000.$$

Interest for the first year @ 10%

$$= \frac{10{,}000 \times 10}{100} = \text{Rs. } 1000.$$

Now cost of equipment in second year is equal to

Total cost – Yearly reduction in cost i.e. (10,000 – 1000)

= Rs. 9000.

∴ Interest for 2nd year @ 10%

$$= \frac{9000 \times 10}{100} = \text{Rs. } 900.$$

Similarly, cost of equipment in 3rd year

= Rs. 9000 – 1000

= Rs. 8000.

∴ Interest in 3rd year @ 10%

$$= \frac{8000 \times 10}{100} = \text{Rs. } 800.$$

and so on.

Total interest of 10 years life can be calculated by the following formula :

$$\text{Total interest} = \frac{n}{2}\{2a - (n-1)d\}$$

where n = Total life of equipment = 10 years

a = First years interest = Rs. 1000.

d = Difference between the two consecutive years interest, i.e., (1000 – 900) or (900 – 800)

= Rs. 100.

$$\text{Hence total interest} = \frac{10}{2}\{2 \times 1000 - (10-1)100\}$$

$$= 5 \times 1100 = \text{Rs. } 5500.$$

Similarly, interest for the proposed equipment :

Total life = 50 years

$$\text{Yearly cost reduction} = \frac{85000}{50} = \text{Rs. } 1700$$

$$\text{Interest for the first year @ 10\%} = \frac{85000 \times 10}{100} = \text{Rs. } 8500.$$

Now cost of equipment in second year

= Rs. (85,000 – 1700) = Rs. 83,300.

∴ Interest for second year @ 10%

$$= \frac{83,300 \times 10}{100} = \text{Rs. } 8330.$$

Similarly cost of equipment for the 3rd year

$$= (83,000 - 1700)$$
$$= \text{Rs. } 81,600$$

$$\text{Interest for 3rd year} = \frac{81,600 \times 10}{100} = \text{Rs. } 8160.$$

∴ Total interest for 50 years

$$= \frac{n}{2}\{2a - (n-1)d\}$$

Here

$$n = 50$$
$$a = 8500$$
$$d = (8500 - 8330) = \text{Rs. } 170$$

$$\therefore \text{ Total interest } \frac{50}{2}\{2 \times 8500 - (50-1)170\}$$

$$= 25 \times 8670 = \text{Rs. } 216,750$$

Since average cost per year of existing equipment is much lower than the proposed equipment, hence new equipment should not be puchased.

32.5.3. Annual Cost Method

This method is to compare the annual costs of obtaining service from different equipments.

Annual cost = Capital recovery + Operating costs ...(1)

In equation (1) capital recovery is denoted by C.R.

C.R. = (*P* – *L*) × Capital recovery factor + $L \times i$

$$= (P - L)\left[\frac{i(1+i)^n}{(1+i)^n - 1}\right] + L \times i$$

where P = Cost of equipment

n = Life of equipment in years

i = Interest rate.

Here, $\left[\frac{i(1+i)^n}{(1+i)^n - 1}\right]$ is called capital recovery factor, denoted by C.R.F.

The following table gives the values of C.R.F. at different values of annual compound interest.

Table

5% Interest factors for annual compounding.

In n years	*Single Payment* $(PWF)_1$	*Equal Payment Series*	
		$(PWF)_2$	*C.R.F.*
1	0.9524	0.9524	1.0500
2	0.9070	1.8594	0.5378
4	0.8227	3.5460	0.2820
6	0.7462	5.0756	0.1970
8	0.6768	6.4632	0.1540
10	0.6139	7.7217	0.1295
15	0.4810	10.3796	0.0963
20	0.3768	12.4622	0.0802

Tables for other values of rate of interest for different values of machine life in years are also available.

Example 32.2. *The cost details of two equipments are given below, find out the most economical one.*

S.No.	*Factor*	*Equipment I*	*Equipment II*
1.	Initial cost (P)	Rs. 15000	Rs. 25000
2.	Annual operating cost	Rs. 800	Rs. 500
3.	Life n	6 years	6 years
4.	Interest rate i	5%	5%
5.	Salvage value (L)	1000	4000

Solution. Capital Recovery,

$$C.R. = (P - L) \times C.R.F. + L \times i$$

The value of C.R.F. for $i = 5\%$ and $n = 6$ years can be seen from tables which is 0.1970.

Equipment 1

$C.R. = (15000 - 1000) \times 0.1970$

$+ 1000 \times \dfrac{5}{100}$

$= 14,000 \times 0.1970 + 50$

= Rs. 2808

Total annual cost

= C.R. + Operating costs

= 2808 + 800 = Rs. 3608

Equipment 2

$C.R. = (25,000 - 4000) \times 0.1970$

$+ 4000 \times \dfrac{5}{100}$

$= 21,000 \times 0.1970 + 200$

= Rs. 4337

Total annual cost

= C.R. + Operating cost

= 4337 + 500 = Rs. 4837

Total annual cost of equipment 1 is less, therefore, equipment 1 should be chosen.

Example. 32.3. *The following are the data for two equipments, suggest whether to purchase the equipment or not*

Existing Equipment	*Proposed Equipment*
(*i*) Market value = Rs. 40000	(*i*) Installed cost = Rs. 90000
(*ii*) *Overhauling charges to make it work for next 5 years* = Rs. 20000	(*ii*) Expected life = 15 years
(*iii*) Resale value = Rs. 30000	(*iii*) Resale value = Rs. 10000
(*iv*) Maintenance cost = Rs. 200 per year more than the proposed equipment	(*iv*) Maintenance cost/year = Rs. 100
(*v*) Interest 10%	(*v*) Interest 10%
(*vi*) For $n = 5$ and $i = 10\%$ C.R.F. = 0.2638	(*vi*) For $n = 15$, $i = 10\%$ C.R.F. 0.13147

Solution.

Existing Equipment	*Proposed Equipment*
$C.R. = (40{,}000 + 20{,}000 - 30{,}000) \times 0.2638 + 30{,}000 \times \frac{10}{100}$	$C.R. + (90{,}000 - 10{,}000) \times 0.13147 + 10{,}000 \times \frac{10}{100}$
$= 30{,}000 \times 0.2638 + 3000$	$= 80{,}000 \times 0.13147 + 1000$
= Rs. 10,914	= Rs. 11,517.60
Total annual cost	Total annual cost
= C.R. + Maintenance cost	= C.R. + Maintenance cost
= 10914 + (200+ 100)	= 11517.60 + 100
Rs. 11,214	**Rs. 11,617.60**

An existing equipment involves lower total annual cost, the proposed equipment should not be purchased.

32.5.4. Present Worth Method.

This method is accurate and reasonable and used to evaluate the present value of new equipment. For the purpose of comparison, future costs are translated into today's value of money.

A "present worth of rupee" is today's value of money invested (at certain interest rate) after given number of years from today. This can be clearly understood by the following examples :

If we have Rs. 5000 to invest and want to know what will be its worth in 10 years at 10% interest, using the formula

$$F = p(1 + i)^n \quad \ldots(1)$$

where F = Worth of money in future

P = Present amount of money

i = Interest rate

n = Number of years.

Substituting in equation (1), we have

$$F = 5000(1+0.10)^{10}$$
$$= 5000\,(2.594) = \text{Rs. } 12{,}970.$$

Thus Rs. 5000 today is worth Rs. 12,970 after 10 years from now or in other words Rs. 12,970 after 10 years from now has a present worth of Rs. 5000.

While comparing two alternatives all the costs must be translated into present worth and they must be compared for equal length of services, *e.g.*, if machine A has life of 3 years and B has 6 years then to compare the two machines we must compare the present worth value of 6 years service of two A machines and one B machine.

In equation (1), $(1 + i)^n$ is called "compound amount factor". The values of $(1 + i)^n$ can be seen from tables for equal payment series, Present Worth Factor (P.W.F.) can be calculated by putting the values of n and i in equation (1).

Similarly, we can solve for P, to determine the present worth of a sum to be paid in n years hence that is

$$P = \frac{F}{(1+i)^n} \qquad \text{...(2)}$$

where, $\frac{1}{(1+i)^n}$ = Present value of a single payment F to be made in n years with interest i.

Therefore, if we were to receive a payment of Rs. 10,000 in 10 years, we should be willing to accept a smaller but equivalent sum now. If interest at the rate of 10% is charged then smaller but equivalent sum would be

$$P = 10{,}000 \times 0.3855 = \text{Rs. } 3855$$

Since $\frac{1}{(1+0.10)^{10}} = 0.3855$ is known as single payment present worth factor (P.W.F.)

The value of (PWF) can be seen from the tables or can be calculated by the above formula.

Example 32.4. *Initial cost of an equipment is Rs. 10,000, annual operating cost is Rs. 1000 and life of equipment is 8 years. If the salvage value is 1000 and interest rate is 5%. Find the present worth of the equipment :*

PWF_2 for n = 8 and i = 5% is 6.4632

PWF_1 for n = 8 and i = 5% is 0.6768.

Solution. Initial cost = Rs. 10,000.

Present worth of annual Operating costs = 1,000 × $(PWF)_2$ (for 8-years and 5%).

= 1000 × 6.4632 = Rs. 6463.20

Present worth of salvage value = 1000 × $(PWF)_1$ for 8 years and $i = 5\%$

= 1000 × 0.6768 = Rs. 676.8

∴ Present worth of equipment = 10,000 + 6463.20–676.80

= **Rs. 15,786.40 Ans.**

The net total Rs. 15,786.40 is the present value of the expenditure over the 8 years expected life of the equipment. The initial investment is already at present value, *i.e.*, the present value factor $(PWF)_2$ is 1.00. The annual costs of operation are on 8 year annuity, so the entire stream of annual costs can be adjusted to present value by the multiplication of $(PWF)_2$. Finally the present value of salvage is deducted.

Example 32.5. *Describe the present-worth for the purpose of depreciation.*

A machine costing Rs. 10,000 has yearly operating charges of Rs. 200. If it has a 10 year life and money is worth 6%, what is the present worth of the cost for service provided by the machine? Given that (SPWF – 6% – 10) = 7.2965.

Solution. (*i*) Initial cost of machine

= Rs. 10,000.

(*ii*) Present worth of operating charges

= Rs. 200 × $(PWF)_2$ for 10 years and $i = 6\%$

= Rs. 200 × 7.2965

= 1459.30

∴ Total present worth of machine

= Rs. 10,000 + Rs. 1459.30

= **Rs. 11,459.30 Ans.**

Example 32.6. *A manufacturing firm has an old machine, which is overhauled after every 3 years, can give service upto a total period of 9 years. Assuming the expenditure data given below, suggest whether new machine which also has a life of 9 years should be purchased or not.*

Old Machine

1. Cost of present repair = Rs. 1000.
2. Cost of repair after 3 years = Rs. 1800.
3. Cost of repair after next 3 years = Rs. 2200.
4. Resale value after 9 years = Rs. 1200.
5. Operating costs = Rs. 2000/year for 9 years.
6. Old machine at present can be sold for Rs. 1200.

New Machine

1. Installed cost = Rs. 10,000.
2. Resale value after 9 years = Rs. 2000
3. Operating costs Rs. 1500/year for 9 years.

Assume interest @ 10%

Given that for $i = 10\%$ and

$n = 3$, single payment present worth factor = 0.75131

$n = 6$, S.P.P.W.F. = 0.56447

$n = 9$, S.P.P.W.F. = 0.42410

and equal payment series present worth factor for $i = 10\%$ and $n = 9$ years is 5.7590.

Solution.

Old Machine

Present worth of repair expenditure of	
Rs. 1000 (present repair)	= Rs. 1000.00
Rs. 1800 (3 years) Rs. 1800 × 0.75131	= Rs. 1352.358
Rs. 2200 (6 years) Rs. 2200 × 0.56447	= Rs. 1241.834
Rs. 1200 (Resale value) Rs. 1200 × 0.42410	= Rs. – 508.920
Present worth of operating cost of	= Rs. 2000 × 5.7590
Rs. 2000 per year for 9 years	= Rs. 11,518.00
Total	Rs. 14,603.27

New Machine

Present worth of New Machine

(*i*) Installed cost of new machine – Present cost of Old machine, *i.e.* (Rs. 10,000–Rs. 1200) = Rs. 8800.00

(*ii*) Present worth or resale value after 9 years Rs. 2000 × 0.4241 = Rs. 848.20

(*iii*) Present worth of operating cost Rs. 1500 × 5.759 = Rs. 8638.50

Total present worth Rs. 15,590.30

As the present worth of old machine is less than present worth of new machine, therefore, new machine should not be purchased.

Example 32.7. *Machine A, operated manually costs Rs. 2000, has a life of 2 years. While an automatic machine B costs Rs. 3000 but has a life of 4 years. Operating cost for machine A is Rs. 4000 per year, while that of machine B is Rs. 3000 only. Which of the machines should be purchased? Consider 10% interest.*

Solution. For comparing the two machines for equal period we must consider two machines *A* against one machine *B*. Expenses of each is to be converted into present worth.

Machine A

Expenses converted in terms of present worth :

(*i*) Present worth of cost of first piece = Rs. 2000 of machine *A*.

(*ii*) Present worth of operating cost of first piece,

(*a*) In first year

$$P = F\left[\frac{1}{(1+i)^n}\right] = \frac{4000}{(1+0.10)}$$

$$= 4000 \times 0.909 = \text{Rs. } 3636$$

(*b*) In second year

$$= \frac{4000}{(1+0.10)^2} = 4000 \times 0.8264 = \text{Rs. } 3306$$

(*iii*) Present worth of operating cost of second piece of machine *A*, purchased after the expiry of life of first piece, *i.e.*, 2 years.

$$= \frac{2000}{(1+0.10)^2} = 2000 \times 0.8264 = \text{Rs. } 1652$$

(*iv*) Present worth of operating cost of second piece

(*a*) In third year $= \dfrac{4000}{(1+0.10)^3} = 4000 \times 0.7523 =$ **Rs. 3005**

(*b*) In fourth year $= \dfrac{4000}{(1+0.10)^4} = 4000 \times 0.6830 =$ **Rs. 2732**

Thus total expenditure in terms of present worth required if machine *A* is used = 2000 + 3636 + 3306 + 1652 + 3005 + 2732 = **Rs. 16,331.**

Machine B

Expenses converted in terms of present worth :

(*i*) Present worth of cost of machine *B* = **Rs. 3000**

(*ii*) Present worth of operating cost

(*a*) In first year $= \dfrac{3000}{(1+0.10)} = 3000 \times 0.909 =$ Rs. 2727

(*b*) In second year $= \dfrac{3000}{(1+0.10)^2} = 3000 \times 0.8264 =$ **Rs. 2479**

(*c*) In third year $= \dfrac{3000}{(1+0.10)^3} = 3000 \times 0.7513 =$ **Rs. 2254**

(*d*) In fourth year $= \dfrac{3000}{(1+0.10)^4} = 3000 \times 0.6830 =$ **Rs. 2049**

Total expendure on machine B in terms of present worth = **Rs. 12,509**

Thus the machine *B* is economical as its expenses are less and hence machine *B* must be purchased.

Example 32.8. *A company is considering to purchase a machine for a job. Two alternative machines are available in the market, one a standard machine and the other a semi-automatic one. The comparative data of them are given below :*

Item	*Machine A*	*Machine B*
Purchase price	*Rs.* 20,000	Rs. 30,000
Estimated economic life (years)	4	4
Salvage value at the end of 4 years	Rs. 4000	Rs. 10000
Labour cost per year	Rs. 12000	Rs. 6000
Maintenance cost during first year	Rs. 1000	Rs. 2000
Increase in maintenance cost per year after the first year	Nil	Rs. 200

All the costs incurred during a year can be assumed to occur at the end of the year. The prevailing interest rate for money is 10% using the present value method, determine which machine is to be preferred.

(*Management Science, Sec. B, Summer 1978*)

Solution.

Machine A

This problem is required to be solved by the present worth method, therefore, all the expenditure will be converted in terms of present worth.

(*i*) Purchase price of machine = **Rs. 20,000**

(*ii*) Present worth of labour cost :

First year, $P = F \dfrac{1}{(1+i)^n}$

$= 12{,}000 \times \dfrac{1}{(1+0.10)^1} = \text{Rs. } 10{,}909.09$

2nd year $= 12{,}000 \times \dfrac{1}{(1+0.10)^2} = \text{Rs. } 9917.35$

3rd year $= 12{,}000 \times \dfrac{1}{(1+0.10)^3} = \text{Rs. } 9015.78$

4th year $= 12{,}000 \times \dfrac{1}{(1+0.10)^4} = \text{Rs. } 8196.16$

Total = **Rs. 38,112.38.**

(*iii*) Present worth of maintenance cost

1st year $= 1000 \times \dfrac{1}{(1+0.10)} = \text{Rs. } 909.09$

2nd year $= 1000 \times \dfrac{1}{(1+0.10)^2} = \text{Rs. } 826.45$

3rd year $= 1000 \times \dfrac{1}{(1+0.10)^3} = \text{Rs. } 751.31$

4th year $= 1000 \times \dfrac{1}{(1+0.10)^4} = \text{Rs. } 683.01$

Total = **Rs. 3169.86**

(*iv*) present worth of salvage value

$= 4000 \times \dfrac{1}{(1+0.1)^4} = \textbf{Rs. 2732.05}$

∴ Total present worth of machine *A*

$= 20{,}000 + 38{,}112.38 + 3169.86 - 2732.05$

= **Rs. 58,580.19**

Machine B

(*i*) Purchase price of machine = Rs. 30,000

(*ii*) Present worth of labour cost

1st year $= 6000 \times \dfrac{1}{(1+0.01)} = \text{Rs. } 5454.55$

2nd year $= 6000 \times \dfrac{1}{(1+0.01)^2} = \text{Rs. } 4958.68$

3rd year $= 6000 \times \dfrac{1}{(1+0.01)^3} = \text{Rs. } 4507.86$

4th year $= 6000 \times \dfrac{1}{(1+0.01)^4} = \text{Rs. } 4098.10$

Total = **Rs. 19,019.22**

(*iii*) Present worth of maintenance cost :

1st year $= 2000 \times \dfrac{1}{(1+0.01)} = \text{Rs. } 1818.19$

2nd year $= 2200 \times \dfrac{1}{(1+0.01)^2} = \text{Rs. } 1818.18$

3rd year $= 2400 \times \dfrac{1}{(1+0.01)^3} = \text{Rs. } 1803.15$

4th year $= 2600 \times \dfrac{1}{(1+0.01)^4} = \text{Rs. } 1775.83$

Total = **Rs. 7215.35**

(*iv*) Present worth of salvage value

$$= 10{,}000 \times \frac{1}{(1+0.01)^4} = \textbf{Rs. 6830.13}$$

∴ Total present worth of machine

$$= 30{,}000 + 19{,}019.22 + 7215.35 - 6830.13$$

$$= \textbf{Rs. 49,404.44}$$

As present worth of machine *B* is less, therefore, machine *B* should be preferred.

Example 32.9. *For a specific work, two machine tools are available in the market with the following operating data :*

Description	*Machine tool A*	*Machine tool B*
Initial investment	Rs. 5000	Rs. 8000
Annual p.c. of fixed charges	12%	18%
Hourly wages	Rs. 1.25	Rs. 1.10
Hourly service charges	Rs. 1.00	Rs. 1.00
Pieces produced per hour	6	9
Annual shop hours	2000	2000

(*i*) *If both the machines are assumed to be operating continuously throughout the year, which of the machine tools should you recommend for purchase, basing your decision on the "lower cost per unit of output"?*

(*ii*) *If both the machines cannot be used on any other kind of work and the annual production is limited to 6,000 parts, instead, which of the two machine tools shall provide lower cost per piece ?*

Solution.

Description	*Machine A*	*Machine B*
(*i*) Initial investment	Rs. 5000	Rs. 8000
(*ii*) Annual fixed charges	$5000 \times 0.12 =$ Rs. 600	$8000 \times 0.18 =$ Rs. 1440
(*iii*) Labour charges	$2000 \times 1.25 =$ Rs. 2500	$2000 \times 1.10 =$ Rs. 2200
(*iv*) Service charges	$2000 \times 1 =$ Rs. 2000	$2000 \times 1 =$ Rs. 2000
(*v*) Total cost (*i*) to (*iv*)	Rs. 10100	Rs. 13640
(*vi*) Annual production	$2000 \times 6 = 12000$	$2000 \times 9 = 18000$ pieces
(*vii*) Cost per piece	$\frac{10100}{12000} = 0.84$	$\frac{13640}{18000} = 0.76$

Thus, production cost per piece by machine *B* is less.

Therefore, machine *B* is recommended for purchase.

(*ii*) If production is limited to 6000 pieces on each machine.

Then, cost per piece for machine *A*

$$= \frac{10100}{6000} = \text{Rs. } 1.68$$

Cost per piece for machine *B*

$$\frac{13640}{6000} = \text{Rs. } 2.27$$

In this condition, machine A should be purchased being lower unit cost.

Example 32.10.

(*a*) *Cost patterns for two machines A and B are shown below:*

(Cost in rupee at beginning of the year)

Year	*Machine A*	*Machine B*
1	900	1400
2	600	100
3	700	700

If cost of money is 10%, which machine is costly and by how much?

(*b*) *Yearly outlays for machine 1, which is to be replaced every 3 years and for machine 2, which is to be replaced every 6 years are given below:*

Year	*Machine 1 (Rs.)*	*Machine B (Rs.)*
1	1000	1700
2	200	100
3	400	200
4		300
5		400
6		500

If cost of money is 10% which machine is advantageous and by how much ?

Solution. (*a*)

Year	*Machine A*		*Machine B*	
	Cost	*Interest*	*Cost*	*Interest*
1st	900	90	1400	140
2nd	900 + 600	150	1400 + 100	150
3rd	900 + 600 + 700	220	1400 + 100 + 700	220
Total	2200	460	2200	510
Total Cost with interest	2200 + 460 = Rs. 2660		2200 + 510 = 2710	

Machine *B* is costly by Rs. 50 only.

Solution (*b*)

Year	*Machine A*		*Machine B*	
	Cost	*Interest*	*Cost*	*Interest*
1	1000	100	1700	170
2	1000 + 200	120	1700 + 100	180
3	1000 + 200 + 400	160	1700 + 100 + 200	200
4	Machine will be replaced after 3 years $\therefore$ 1600	160	1700 + 100 + 200 + 300	230
5	1600 + 200	180	1700 + 100 + 200 + 300 + 400	270
6	1600 + 200 + 400	220	1700 + 100 + 200 + 300 + 400 + 500	320
Total	2200	940	3200	1370
Total cost with interest	2200 + 940 = Rs. 3190		3200 + 1370 = Rs. 4570	

Thus machine A is cheaper by

$$4570 - 3140 = \textbf{Rs. 1430.} \quad \textbf{Ans.}$$

Example 32.11. *Machine A, operated manually, costs Rs. 4000 has a life of 2 years. While an automatic machine B costs Rs. 5000 but has a life of 4 years. Operating costs for machine A is Rs. 4000 per year while of machine B is Rs. 3000 only. Which should be purchased ? Consider 10% interest.*

Solution. For comparing the two machines for equal period we must consider 2 machines A against one machine B. Each of the expense is to be converted into present worth.

Machine A

Expenses converted in terms of present worth :

(*i*) Present worth of cost of first piece = Rs. 4000 of machine A

(*ii*) Present worth of operating cost of first piece.

(*a*) In first year

$$P = F\left[\frac{1}{(1+i)^n}\right] = \frac{4000}{(1+0.10)}$$

$$= 4000 \times 0.909 = \text{Rs. } 3636$$

(*b*) In second year

$$= \frac{4000}{(1+0.10)^2} = 4000 \times 0.8264 = \text{Rs. } 3306$$

(*iii*) Present worth of cost of second piece of machine A, purchased after the expiry of life of first piece, *i.e.*, 2 years

$$= \frac{2000}{(1+0.10)^2} = 2000 \times 0.8264 = \text{Rs. } 1652$$

(*iv*) Present worth of operating cost of second piece

(*a*) In third year $= \dfrac{4000}{(1+0.10)^3} = 4000 \times 0.7513 = \text{Rs. } 3005$

(*b*) In fourth year $= \dfrac{4000}{(1+0.10)^4} = 4000 \times 0.6830 = \text{Rs. } 2732.$

Thus total expenditure in terms of present worth if machine A is used = 4000 + 3636 + 3306 +1652 + 3005 + 2732

$$= \textbf{Rs. 18,331}$$

Machine B

Expenses converted in terms of present worth :

(*i*) Present worth of cost of machine B = Rs. 5000.

(*ii*) Present worth of operating cost.

(*a*) In first year $= \dfrac{3000}{(1+0.10)} = 3000 \times 0.909 = \text{Rs. } 2727$

(*b*) In second year $= \dfrac{3000}{(1+0.10)^2} = 3000 \times 0.8264 = \text{Rs. } 2479$

(c) In third year $= \dfrac{3000}{(1+0.10)^3} = 3000 \times 0.7513 = \text{Rs. } 2254$

(d) In fourth year $= \dfrac{3000}{(1+0.10)^4} = 3000 \times 0.6830 = \text{Rs. } 2049$

Total expenditure on machine B in terms of present worth = **Rs. 14,509**

Thus the machine B is economical as its expenses are less and hence machine B must be purchased.

32.5.5. Rate of Return Method

In this method average annual net income (after tax and depreciation deductions) is expressed as percentage of capital investment. The formula used for this purpose is :

Percentage rate of return

$$= \frac{\text{Earnings per year}}{\text{Net investment}} \times 100$$

For example a new equipment with net investment of Rs. 20,000 gives an average earning of Rs. 4000 per annum after deducting taxes and depreciation, then

Percentage rate of return

$$= \frac{4000 \times 100}{20000} = 20\%$$

But this method has a drawback that earnings of all the years cannot have the value equal to that of today (present worth). Hence the method will be more useful and practical if the earnings of all years are first converted to present worth and then calculations are made for rate of return. Following method is an improvement over this method.

Discounted Rate of Return. In this case following formula is used:

$$C = \frac{R}{(1+r)^n}$$

where C = Investment cost

R = Expected earning in the nth year

r = Rate of return.

If we have to find out the rate of return when a machine has worked for n years and earnings in each year is R_1 (in first year), R_2 (in second year), R_3 (in third year) etc., then following formula is used (it is calculated for r, by trial and error method):

$$C = \frac{R_1}{(1+r)} + \frac{R_2}{(1+r)^2} + \frac{R_3}{(1+r)^3} + \dots + \frac{R_n}{(1+r)^n} + \frac{S}{(1+r)^n}$$

where S = Salvage value of machine after n years.

Example 32.12. *Whether a machine having following particulars must be purchased or not:*

Cost of machine = Rs. 4000

Expected return in first year = Rs. 2400

Expected return in second year = Rs. 1600

Expected return in third year = Rs. 1400

Salvage value at the end of third year = Rs. 400

Solution. Substituting the above data in the formula,

$$C = \frac{R_1}{(1+r)} + \frac{R_2}{(1+r)^2} + \ldots + \frac{R_n}{(1+r)^n} + \frac{S}{(1+r)^n}$$

or

$$4000 = \frac{2400}{(1+r)} + \frac{1600}{(1+r)^2} + \frac{1400}{(1+r)^3} + \frac{400}{(1+r)^4}$$

By trial and error method of substitution, we get

$$r = 0.21, \qquad i.e.\ 21\%.$$

Now the question is whether this 21% return is high enough to justify the investment. If the rate of interest is 10% this return of 21% on the investment is worthwhile and the machine can be purchased.

32.5.6. MAPI Method.

The term MAPI stands for Machinery and Allied Products Institute of Washington, who has developed this method. This is a method developed by George Terborgh, the Director of this institute. The method is described as follows :

Almost all the equipments are subjected to deterioration and obsolescence in varying degree with the passage of time. Thus with the passage of time operating inferiority increases. Hence the old machine has his operating inferiority high and book value as low. While a new machine will have operating inferiority minimum and cost at a minimum. Hence the problem before manager is to choose between more capital cost and less imperfection, on one hand and less capital cost and more imperfection, on the other.

The MAPI has developed a new approach which helps in deciding this problem. The existing equipment which is to be replaced is known as DEFENDER and the new which will replace the old one is known as the CHALLENGER.

For estimating as to whether the proposed replacement is profitable, the "adverse minimum" of the defender and the challenger are found and compared. "Adverse minimum" of the defender or the challenger is the lowest sum of the time adjusted average of capital cost and operating inferiority (expressed in terms of money) obtainable from a machine. The calculations can easily be done with the help of MAPI charts.

Advantage of MAPI Method

Following are some of the advantages of MAPI method :

1. Calculations are simple.
2. Management knows as to when a machine is to be replaced.
3. This method can be applied to a single as well as a combination of several machines for replacement.
4. It aids in budgeting equipment expenditure.
5. There is full provision for future deterioration and obsolescence on the new machines.

32.6. HIRE-PURCHASING

Machines can be procured either by purchasing (*i.e.* paying full cost in cash) or on hire-purchase basis. In this second method (*i.e.* hire-purchasing) rental payments are adjusted towards the purchased price. In this way purchaser does not lose the money he has paid out in rent. This system is now-a-days being preferred by small entrepreneur, who wants to start a small scale industry and does not have much money. Example of such system is that National Industries Corporation supplying machinery on hire-purchase basis to Small Scale Industries. Although some interest is charged on this.

Advantages

Following are some of the important advantages of the hire purchase system :

1. Small entrepreneur can expand his production facilities without increasing his financial burden.
2. Purchaser can use the equipment without paying the full purchase price at the time of procurement, thereby avoiding any loans or other debt.
3. This system allows the owner to use his funds for other important works like research, design, inventory, better wages etc.

Disadvantages

Following are some of the disadvantages of hirepurchase system :

1. Some owners feel prestige in owning their machinery and they directly purchase the machines. Thus psychological aspect is a disadvantage.
2. Generally the firms charge high amount of interest (or profit) on the machines sold on hire-purchase system. Thus purchaser has to pay more price in this system.
3. Highly technical and specialised equipments are generally not available on hire-purchase system.

QUESTIONS

1. What are the different factors which are responsible to replace the equipment although it may be running?
2. Explain the 'Present Worth Method' for equipment replacement studies.
3. What is the 'hire-purchase system' ? Explain its advantages and disadvantages over direct purchasing.
4. What is 'Discounted Rate of Return' method ? How is this method used for equipment study?
5. A new material loading system costs Rs. 30,000 including the cost of relay out. This decreases the number of workers by 5. After adding increased maintenance and power costs, the net monetary operating advantage is estimated as Rs. 1200 per year. If estimated economic life is 5 years, calculate the rate of return 'before tax' and 'after tax'. Assume depreciation term of 10 years.
6. Write short notes on :
   (*a*) Replacement analysis.
   (*b*) Present worth analysis applied to equipment replacement.
7. Discuss the importance and scope of 'equipment annual cost method' and 'Present value of method' in machine replacement analysis.
8. The present cost of a pneumatic machine tool is Rs. 1.8 lakhs. The salvage value at the end of life is nil. The present operating cost is 50,000 per year. The operating and maintenance cost are not expected to increase significantly during its operating life

but new technical improvements are expected each year at the rate of 3% per year. It indirectly implies an increase in operating cost. Determine the expected economic service life of machine tool.

(*a*) Neglecting the time value of money and

(*b*) When the interest rate is 10% per annum

(*c*) Present worth method should be used.

9. The following data are available for the existing equipment and for the proposed equipment. Find by 'Total life average method', whether the firm should make replacement or not.

	Existing Equipment	*Proposed Equipment*
1. Cost	Rs. 2000 (Market value)	Rs. 10000 (Installed)
2. Annual operating cost	Rs. 5000	Rs. 4000
3. Scrap value	Rs. 500	Rs. 1000
4. Interest	10%	10%
5. Life	1 year	9 years

10. Make a choice between purchasing a new machine, life 15 years or keeping an old machine which requires a major overhaul now, again at the end of 5 years and another at the end of 10 years to give 14 years of the service. Data are :

Old Machine

(*i*) Repair now for Rs. 1000

(*ii*) Repair after 5 years for Rs. 1600

(*iii*) Repair again after 5 years for Rs. 2200

(*iv*) Sell at the end of 15 years for Rs. 600

(*v*) Spend an average of Rs. 2600 per year for 15 years of maintenance, direct labour and all other operating costs.

New Machine

(*i*) Sell the machine for Rs. 700

(*ii*) Purchase new machine for Rs. 9000

(*iii*) Sell the new machine after 15 years for Rs. 1200

(*iv*) Spend an average of Rs. 1200 per year for 15 years of maintenance and operating expenses.

Single payment P.W. factor for i = 10%

$n = 5$ single P.P.W. factor = 0.6209

$n = 10$ single P.P.W. factor = 0.3855

$n = 15$ single P.P.W. factor = 0.2394

Equal payment series P.W. factor for $n = 15$ and $i = 10\% = 7.606$. Take the decision whether to buy the new machine or not.

11. The following are the data for the two machines. Using the 'Annual cost method', find out which machine will be preferred.

Factor	*Machine A*	*Machine B*
Initial cost (P)	Rs. 15000	Rs. 10000
Annual operating cost	Rs. 800	Rs. 1000
Life (n)	8 years	8 years
Salvage value (L)	Rs. 3000	Rs. 1000
Interest Rate (i)	5%	5%

33

Elements of Costs, Costing and Cost Control

33.1. ELEMENTS OF COST

In any factory, the cost of the products manufactured is calculated so that the exact idea about the amount of profit can be made. We know that there are hundreds of different items of expenditure, which are made in the factory and all these are charged on the product manufactured. The total cost is divided into the different headings known as "Elements of Cost".

For easy and accurate calculations, the total cost of a product can be divided into three main 'Elements'. These are :

1. Materials
2. Labour
3. Expenses

1. Materials Cost

These can be further classified into :

(*i*) Direct materials, and

(*ii*) Indirect materials

(*i*) *Direct Materials.* These are those materials which when operated or processed in the factory shops through various stages form the final useful shape of the main product or component part of the main product. These are also known as 'Productive Materials'.

(*ii*) *Indirect Materials.* These are those materials which are essentially needed in various shops for helping the materials to be converted into the final useful shapes. Difference between direct and indirect forms of materials can be easily understood by the following example :

Suppose a person continuously working in Milling Machine Shop is cutting gear teeth on cast iron blanks. Now the cast iron blank, of which the gear is made, will be the direct material while the coolant required for cooling the cutter, grease and lubricating oil needed for lubricating the machine, kerosene oil and cotton waste etc., needed for cleaning the machine are known as 'Indirect Materials'.

2. Labour Cost

Labour employed in any factory may be of following two classes :

(*i*) Direct labour, and (*ii*) Indirect labour.

(i) *Direct Labour.* The workers, who actually work or process different material manually or with the aid of machines is known as 'Direct Labour'. This is also called 'productive Labour'. The nature of their duties is such that their wages can be directly charged to the job, which they are manufacturing.

Workers engaged for operating on various production machines in machine shop, welding shop, pattern making shop, electric winding shop and assembly shop etc. is known as 'Direct Labour'.

(ii) *Indirect Labour.* Any other labour, who helps the productive labour in performing their duties is known as 'indirect Labour'. The nature of their duties is such that their wages cannot be charged directly to a particular job but are charged on the total number of products produced in the plant during a particular period.

Foreman, Supervisors, Inspectors, Chowkidars, Gate-keepers, Store-keepers, Crane Driver and Gangmen etc., are classified as Indirect Labour.

Now again consider the above example of Milling machine shop. The worker who is producing gears continuously on the milling machine is known as Direct Labour, while the foremen, supervising in the milling machine shop, the inspector checking the accuracy of gears and helper, who is bringing blanks and taking away the gear from the worker are examples of Indirect Labour.

3. Expenses

We have discussed, direct material cost and direct labour cost but apart from those, you will find that, in each factory there are several other expenditure, such as cost of advertisement, building, cost of packing, cost of transportation, salaries and commission to salesmen etc. All these expenditure are known as 'Expenses'. So, we can say that except direct material and direct labour cost, all other expenses, which are incurred in the factory are known as 'Expenses'.

The cost of Indirect material and Indirect labour is also included in the expenses.

Expenses may be of two classes :

(i) Direct or chargeable Expenses, and

(ii) Indirect Expenses

(i) *Direct Expenses.* These are those expenses, which can be charged directly to a particular job and are incurred for that specific job only. For example, cost of special jigs and fixtures, cost of some special patterns and cost of experimental work on a particular job etc.

(ii) *Indirect Expenses.* These are also known as overhead charged, on cost, burden or indirect charges. These can be further classified as:

(a) Factory expenses

(b) Administrative expenses

(c) Selling expenses and

(d) Distribution expenses.

(a) Factory Expenses. These overheads include all the expenditure made on the actual operation of the product in the plant, such as Indirect material and Indirect labour. It is also named as works on cost.

(b) Administrative Expenses. These overheads include all the expenditure made on the salaries of general offfice staff and executive staff, telegraph telex, computer and telephone charges, depreciation of office building and equipment etc.

This is also known as establishment on-cost or office expenses.

(c) **Selling Expenses.** These overheads include all the expenditure made on the salaries of persons working in sales department, advertising expenses and agency expenses etc.

(d) **Distribution Expenses.** These overheads include all the expenses made on holding finished stock, despatching them to the customer and packing cost etc.

33.2. FIXED AND VARIABLE OVERHEADS

All the overheads described above can be classified into following two forms :

1. Fixed overheads
2. Variable overheads

1. **Fixed Overheads.**

These are those indirect expenses, which remain constant whatever may be the volume of production. Examples of the overheads are :

(a) **Salaries of officers.** These charges are for the salaries and allowances paid to the Supervisors and other Engineers, Officers, etc. These are known as supervisory charges and are generally calculated in terms of expenses per machine hour.

(b) **Depreciation of machines and equipment.** This is the diminition in value due to the age, wear and tear. Various methods of calculating depreciation have been described in detail in next chapter.

(c) **Interest on capital invested.** The interest on capital invested is calculated assuming, if the capital is deposited in some bank.

(d) **Rent of building and insurance.**

2. **Variable Overheads**

These are those indirect expenses, which vary with the volume of production. Examples of these overheads are :

(a) **Power or fuel consumed.** These are expenses on power

(i) if generated in the factory includes expenditure on fuel, salary of power-house staff, expenditure on running and maintenance, and depreciation of power-house building, plants etc.

(ii) if brought from other agency, includes charges paid to them.

(b) **Repairs and maintenance.** This includes the expenditure incurred on the repairs and maintenance of machines in the factory. This expenditure is converted into expenditure per machine hour and then charged to various departments of the factory.

(c) **Consumable store supplies.** The expenditure made on the salary of store staff, stationery etc. required in stores, lighting charge for stores and other similar expenses are included in this category.

(d) **Expenses on tools.** Generally the tools have very short life and are required to be purchased frequently. Hence they are charged in two ways. Firstly, the expenditure incurred on the purchase of such tools are directly charged. Secondly, these are depreciated.

Now, from above we can see that variable overhead increase proportionately with the rate of production, but fixed overheads remain almost constant. So by increasing the amount of production, the total cost of the product can be reduced. It is also essential that there should at least some minimum amount of production which can cover the fixed overheads.

Thus large profits can be earned by increasing the production and lowering fixed overheads.

33.3. COMPONENTS OF COST

The various components of cost are :

1. Prime cost.
2. Factory cost.
3. Office cost.
4. Total cost.

1. *Prime cost.* It consists of direct material cost, direct labour cost and direct expenses, *i.e.*, Prime cost = Direct material cost + Direct labour cost + Direct expenses. Prime cost is also named as 'Direct cost'.
2. *Factory cost.* It consists of prime cost and factory expenses. Factory cost = Prime cost + Factory expenses. Factory cost is also named as 'Works Cost'.
3. *Office cost.* It consists of factory cost and administrative expenses. Office cost = Factory cost + Administrative expenses. Office cost is also named as manufacturing cost or cost of production.
4. *Total cost.* It includes office cost and selling and distribution expenses, *i.e.*, Total cost = Office cost + Selling expenses + Distribution expenses.

Selling Price

If the profit is added in the total cost of the product it is called 'selling price'. The customers get the articles by paying the price which is named as selling price.

The relation between the elements of cost and components of cost can be best illustrated by the chart given below :

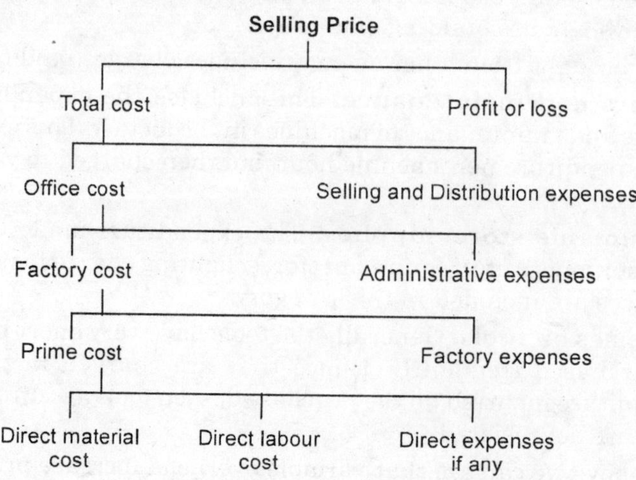

This can also be illustrated by the block diagram.

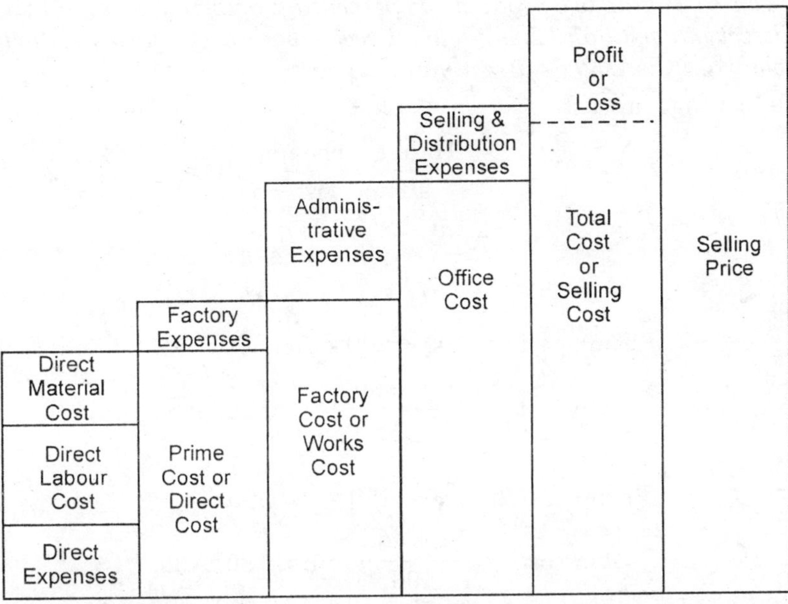

Fig. 33.1. Block diagram to illustrate the relation between 'Elements of Cost' and 'Components of Cost'.

33.4. ALLOCATION OF ON-COST (OVERHEAD-EXPENSES)

It has been discussed above about the various forms of on-cost. After estimating the total on cost, next step is the allocation of this on cost over the production. To run the business in utmost economical way, it is necessary to know, the variation of on-cost with the variation of production. In this chapter several methods of allocation of on-cost are being discussed but the choice of a particular method depends upon the nature of work, type of organisation and types of machines used etc. Following are the different methods of on-cost allocation :

1. Percentage on Prime cost.
2. Percentage on Direct Labour cost.
3. Percentage on Direct Material cost.
4. Man Hour Rate.
5. Machine Hour Rate.
6. Combination of Man Hour and Machine Hour Rate.
7. Unit Rate Method.

1. Percentage on Prime Cost

This is very simple method and hence has gained popularity. This method is suitable, where labour and material both play equal role. In this, prime cost is the basis of allocation of on-cost and total on-cost of the factory is expressed as the percentage of the prime cost and the percentage is charged on each job being manufactured. The required formula will be:

$$\text{Percentage on prime cost} = \frac{\text{Total overheads}}{\text{Prime cost}} \times 100$$

The method of allocation can be best understood by the following solved examples:

Example 33.1. *A factory has total overheads of Rs. 6 lacs, while the prime cost is Rs. 10.0 lacs. Find out the on-cost of the two products by percentage on prime cost method. If product first has Rs. 100 as direct material and Rs. 200 as direct labour cost, while product second has Rs. 150 as direct labour and Rs. 150 as direct material cost.*

Solution. Percentage on-cost

$$= \frac{\text{Total overheads}}{\text{Prime cost}} \times 100$$

$$= \frac{6}{10} \times 100 = 60\% \text{ of prime cost.}$$

1st Product

$$\text{Prime cost} = 100 + 200 = \text{Rs. } 300$$

$$\therefore \quad \text{On-cost} = 300 \times \frac{60}{100} = \textbf{Rs. 180 Ans}$$

2nd Product

$$\text{Prime cost} = 150 + 150 = \text{Rs. } 300$$

$$\therefore \quad \text{On-cost} = \frac{300 \times 60}{100} = \textbf{Rs. 180. Ans.}$$

From the above example, it can be seen that both the products will be charged equally for on-cost, while product first has labour cost as Rs. 200 and product second has labour cost Rs. 150. Actually material cost has to do nothing with the overheads and products which require large manufacturing time should have more overheads. This fact has not been considered in this method. Therefore, this method is a faulty one and is only suitable in the following two cases :

(*a*) Where only one type of product is being manufactured.

(*b*) Where direct labour and direct material cost are nearly same.

2. **Percentage on Direct Labour Cost.**

In this method, allocation of on cost depends upon the wages paid to the direct labour. This method is very reasonable and simple in calculation and, therefore, very popular. This is very suitable where production is mainly carried out by hand and is the ratio of the total on-cost to the direct labour cost for a particular period.

$$\therefore \quad \text{Percentage on cost} = \frac{\text{Total overheads}}{\text{Direct labour cost}} \times 100$$

This will be more clear by the following solved example:

Example. 33.2. *Factory overheads of a certain concern for the year 1970-71 were Rs. 8.0 lacs and total direct wages paid to the labour during the above period were Rs. 32.0 lacs, find out the percentage on cost by percentage on direct labour cost method.*

Solution. Percentage on-cost

$$= \frac{\text{Total over heads}}{\text{Direct labour cost}} \times 100 = \frac{8}{32} \times 100$$

$$= \textbf{25\% of the direct labour cost Ans.}$$

3. **Percentage on Direct Material Cost.**

In this method, allocation of on-cost depends upon the total direct materials cost. This method is generally used where the major part of the cost is material like foundries and mines etc. It is the percentage ratio of the total on-cost to the direct material cost for a particular period. This is explained by the solved example :

Example 33.3. *A foundry department of a factory producing water meter body had Rs. 5.0 lacs as total overheads while the material cost was Rs. 25.0 lacs, calculate the percentage on-cost.*

Solution. Percentage on-cost.

$$= \frac{\text{Total overheads}}{\text{Total direct material cost}} \times 100 = \frac{5000}{25000} \times 100$$

$$= \textbf{20\% of direct material cost}$$

4. **Man-Hour Rate.**

This method is very similar to the percentage on direct labour cost method. The difference in the two methods is that, it is an improvement over the previous method, in which the basis of allocation was the total direct labour cost, whereas in this, basis of the total hours spent by the direct labour and not the wages paid to them.

This method is generally used where most of the work is performed by manual labour and where labour employed is of different categories and is paid different rates. Man-hour rate is the ratio of overheads to the direct man hours spent on the job, *i.e.*,

$$\text{Man-hour rate} = \frac{\text{Total overheads}}{\text{Total direct man hour spent}}$$

It will be more clear by the following solved example:

Example 33.4. *A factory produces two components A and B. Component A requires 20 hours and is manufactured by the workers paid at the rate of Rs. 10.00 per hour, while component B also requires 20 hours but the workers producing it are paid at the rate of Rs. 7.5 per hour. Find out the on-cost of each component, if (i) it is 40% of the direct labour cost, (ii) Rs. 2.00 per man-hour.*

Solution. Component A

$$\text{Labour charges} = 20 \times 10 = \text{Rs. } 200.$$

(*i*) On-cost @ 40% of direct labour cost

$$= 200 \times \frac{40}{100} = \text{Rs. } 80.00$$

(*ii*) On-cost @ Rs. 2.00 per man hour

$$= 20 \times 2 = \text{Rs.}40.00$$

Component B

$$\text{Labour Charges } 20 \times 7.5 = 150.00$$

(*i*) On-cost @ 40% of direct labour cost

$$= 150 \times \frac{40}{100} = \text{Rs. } 60.00$$

(*ii*) On-cost @ Rs. 2.00 per man hour

$$= 20 \times 2 = \text{Rs. } 40.00$$

It is clear from the example that by considering percentage on direct labour cost method, the component A's on cost is Rs. 8.00 while component *B's* on cost is Rs. 6.00. Actually both the components take same time, therefore, indirect expenses should also be equal but this is not the case and therefore, percentage on direct labour cost method is not very accurate one. This gives less on-cost where labour is cheap and gives high on-cost, while labour is costly and, therefore, this method increases the cost of component, which has already higher labour cost, irrespective of the time needed for the completion of the job.

From the above example, it is clear, that on-costs by man hour method for both the components are same. Man hour method has removed the drawbacks of direct labour cost method and hence is comparatively more accurate method of on-cost allocation.

5. Machine-Hour Rate.

The method generally used where work is done mostly by machines and not by hand. The indirect expenses increased in each shop during a particular period are distributed over a group of similar machines. These expenses are then distributed on the basis of total productive machine hours. Machine hour rate is the rate of the total overheads to the total productive machine hour, *i.e.*

$$\text{Machine-hour rate} = \frac{\text{Total over heads}}{\text{Total productive machine hour}}$$

Total overheads in this system are distributed over the group of similar machines in the following ways:

(*i*) Power consumption is metered separately.

(*ii*) Depreciation charges are calculated separately.

(*iii*) Building rents, insurance, taxes, light charges and indirect labour and indirect materials are distributed on the basis of the floor area occupied by the machines.

(*iv*) The expenditure of wages paid for the ideal period of machines is not considered in these overheads but is separately charged from the profit and loss accounts.

This method will be clear by the following solved example :

Example 33.5. *A factory has 15 lathes of same make and capacity and 5 shapers of same make and capacity. Lathes occupy 30 m^2 area while shapers occupy 15 m^2. During one calendar year, factory expenses for this section area are as follows :*

		Rs.
(*i*)	Building rent and depreciation	5,000
(*ii*)	Indirect labour and material	15,000
(*iii*)	Insurance	2,000
(*iv*)	Depreciation charges of lathes	5,000
(*v*)	Depreciation charges of shapers	3,000
(*vi*)	Power consumption for the lathes	2,000
(*vii*)	Power consumption for the shapers	1,000

Find out the machine hour rate for lathes and shapers, if all the lathes and shapers work for 25,000 hours and 8,000 hours respectively.

Solution. (*a*) **Lathe Section.** Total overheads for the lathe section will be as follows :

(*i*) Building rent and depreciation (charged on the basis of floor area occupied)

$$= \frac{5000 \times 30}{(30+15)} = \text{Rs}.\ 3333.33$$

(*ii*) Indirect labour and material

$$= \frac{15{,}000 \times 30}{(30 + 15)} = \text{Rs. } 10{,}000$$

(*iii*) Insurance $= \frac{2000 \times 30}{(30 + 15)} = \text{Rs. } 1333.33$

(*iv*) Depreciation = Rs. 5,000

(*v*) Power = Rs. 2,000

∴ Total overheads = Rs. 21,666.66

∴ Machine hour rate for lathes

$$= \frac{21{,}666.66}{25{,}000} = \textbf{Rs. 0.87 Ans.}$$

(*b*) Shaper section. Total overhead for the shaper section will be as follows:

(*i*) Building rent and depreciation

$$= \frac{5{,}000 \times 15}{(15 + 30)} = \text{Rs. } 1666.66$$

(*ii*) Indirect labour and material

$$= \frac{15{,}000 \times 15}{(15 + 30)} = \text{Rs. } 5000$$

(*iii*) Insurance $= \frac{2000 \times 15}{(15 + 30)} = \text{Rs. } 666.66$

(*iv*) Power consumption Rs. 1000.00

(*v*) Depreciation Rs. 3000.00

∴ Total overheads = 1666.66 + 5000 + 666.66 + 1000 + 3000

= Rs. 11333.32

∴ Machine hour rate for shapers

$$= \frac{11333.32}{8000} = \textbf{Rs. 1.42. Ans.}$$

6. **Combination of Man-hour and Machine-hour Rate.**

   As the name indicates, this method is simply a combination of man-hour rate and machine-hour rate methods. As it has already been discussed, the Man-Hour rate method is suitable only where work is done by hand, for example, in fitting and assembly shops etc. Similarly machine hour rate method is suitable where almost all the work is done by machines. Shops, where work is done by hand, man-hour rate method is applied, and in shops where work is done by machines, machine hour rate method is applied. Thus, in this way, both the methods can be applied in one factory and the method is known as 'combination of man-hour and machine hour rate method of allocation'

7. **Unit Rate Method.**

   This is also known as "Production Unit Basis" method. In this, on cost is allocated on the basis of unit of production. Unit of production is generally piece, kilogram, tonne, litres, meter etc. This method is mostly used where only one type of production is carried out. This method cannot be used in factories, where different kinds of products are manufactured.

Unit rate is the overheads for one unit and can be calculated as the ratio of total overheads to the quantity of production during a particular period *i.e.*

$$\text{Overhead/unit} = \frac{\text{Total overheads}}{\text{Quantity of production}}$$

This will be more clear by the following solved example:

Example 33.6. *A manufacturing concern produces 5000 machines per year. If the overheads during that year are Rs. 800,000, calculate the overhead cost on each machine.*

Solution. Overhead cost per unit can be estimated by unit rate method.

$$\text{Overhead/unit} = \frac{\text{Total overheads}}{\text{Quantity of production}}$$

Here, total overheads = Rs. 800,000

Quantity of production = 5,000

∴ Over heads on each machine

$$= \frac{800{,}000}{5{,}000} = \text{Rs. } 160.00$$

Therefore, overheads on each machine will be **Rs. 160.00 Ans.**

33.5. SOME EXAMPLES OF ALLOCATION OF ON-COSTS

There are certain facilities which are used by more than one department. The expenses on such facilities are estimated for whole factory and then allocated to departments as follows. When there is clear cut and exact estimation of cost for each department, it is known as allocation, and if it is only an estimation, then it is termed as "apportion".

(*i*) *Factory Lighting.* It is allocated in proportion to the number of points in each department. If metres are provided separately, then the charges are according to these metre readings.

(*ii*) *Factory Rent.* It is allocated in proportion to the floor space occupied by each department.

(*iii*) *Insurance to Factory.* Criteria are same as for factory rent.

(*iv*) *Depreciation and Repairs to factory building.* Criteria are same as for factory rent.

(*v*) *Fuel and Power.* These are allocated in proportion to the horse power of machineries installed in the various departments.

(*vi*) *Works Canteen.* The expenditure is allocated in proportion to the number of workers benefitted.

(*vii*) *Welfare Expenses.* The expenditure is allocated in proportion to the number of workers benefitted.

(*viii*) *Any other item.* Expenses incurred on any item other than those mentioned above, the criteria can be fixed by the Works Manager/General Manager on the basis of his judgement based on the circumstances.

(*ix*) *Inspection.* If these charges can be identified then can be charged directly to specific product, otherwise it can be treated as factory overhead.

(*x*) *Transport Charges.* The expenditure incurred on movement of material from stores to production shops, from one shop to another shop, is a part of factory overhead and is distributed in proportion to distance traveled or weight of stores handled.

(*xi*) *Cost of Containers and Packing Cases.* Where containers are exhausted or sold with the product then it forms a part of production costs. Where containers can be roused and packing cases which are returnable and capable of alternative use, the expenses form a part of selling and distribution overhead.

(*xii*) *Insurance of products in transit.* These expenses form a part of the distribution and an average is charged to each product.

(*xiii*) *Waste or loss of finished stock.* Such losses are written off and loss is taken into profit and loss account.

(*xiv*) *Expenses of Costing Department.* These form a part of administration overhead.

(*xv*) *Cost of small tools.* The cost of small tools, the account of which is difficult to maintain cannot be taken as capital expenditure, because the account of depreciation cannot be maintained. Therefore, such expenses are charged to the individual departments of the factory on the basis of actual issues.

(*xvi*) *Bonus.* Bonus is paid out of profit of the undertaking. But when minimum bonus is paid (being obligatory), it is charged to production overheads and is apportioned to different departments on the basis of wages of each department.

(*xvii*) *Overtime.* The overtime premium is charged (*a*) directly to the job, if the overtime work is done due to pressure of the work (*b*) to the department concerned if due to the fault of the department (c) to profit and loss account if the overtime work is done due to the reasons beyond the control, *e.g.* flood, fire etc.

(*xviii*) *Wages to apprentices.* Since the speed of work is less for apprentices than that of skilled workers, and more spoilage of work by them, generally a portion of their wages, say 50% is charged direct to the job and rest to production overhead.

(*xix*) *Wages paid during the training period.* These are charged to production overhead.

(*xx*) *Wages for the idle time.* Such expenses are treated depending upon the type of idle time *i.e.* normal or abnormal ; controllable or uncontrollable.

(*a*) *Normal and controllable idle time costs.* These are allocated to the department concerned and charged to the departmental overhead and absorbed in production cost.

(*b*) *Normal and uncontrollable.* Charged directly to the job.

(c) *Abnormal and uncontrollable.* These are written off to the profit and loss account. Examples of such idle time are strikes, lockouts, fire, flood major breakdown etc.

(*xxi*) *Allowances paid to the workers.* Dearness allowances being part of the wages are included in direct wages. Whereas other allowances being part of the wages are included in direct wages. Whereas other allowances are considered as part of welfare activities and then apportioned to different departments on some suitable basis.

(*xxii*) *Leave with pay.* The burden of leave pay is calculated at one place are treated as factory overhead.

(*xxiii*) *Re-operation of defective*. For small works this is treated as direct wages and charged to good output. But for heavier expenses and large works, such expenses are collected at one place and treated as departmental overhead.

Example 33.7 *During 2011, following expenditure was incurred in a concern:*

		Rs.
Direct Material		200, 000
Direct Wages		80,000
Factory expenses:		
(a) Fixed expenses	50,000	
(b) Variable expenses	40,000	90,000
		370,000

It was expected that following charges will take place in 2012:

(i) *Output will be raised by employing 50% additional workers.*
(ii) *Efficiency will decline by 10% because of new workers.*
(iii) *Fixed expenses will increase by 10%; and*
(iv) *Direct material will be purchased at the rate of 5% lower than 2011 prices.*
(v) *Draw the budget for 2012, assuming that variable expenses vary with number of person employed.*

Solution.

Assuming output in 2011	100%
Increased labour	50%
	150%
Decline in efficiency @ 10 % on 150%	15%
	135%

∴ Total output shall increase by 35% only.

Budget for 2012

		Rs.	Rs.
(i) Material costs			
Direct Materials		200, 000	
Add 35 % due to increase in output		70,000	
Less 5 % reduction in price		(–) 13,500	
		256,500	256, 500
(ii) Labour costs			
Direct wages		80,000	
Add 50% for additional labour		40,000	
		120, 000	120,000
(iii) Factory expenses			
Fixed expenses	50,000		
Add 10% increase	5,000		
	55,000	55,000	
Variable expenses	40,000		
Add 50 % increase	20, 000		
	60,000	60,000	115, 000
Total			491, 500

Example 33.8. *A machine costing Rs. 20,000 will have a scrap value of Rs. 2,000 after its life of 10 years. Repairs expected during whole life cost Rs. 4,000. Machine is expected to run 2400 hours per year on an average. Its electric consumption is 15 units per hour, available at the rate of 10 paise per unit. Machine occupies one fourth area of the department which has been taken on monthly rent of Rs. 400 and two points have been provided out of ten for lighting on the machine. Lighting charges are Rs. 150 per month. Foreman employed at the salary of Rs. 800 per month devotes one-fourth of his time on the machine. Find out the machine hour rate assuming insurance @ 1% per annum.*

Solution. *Fixed expenses per month.*

	Rs.
Rent (one-fourth)	100.00
Lighting (one-fifth of the total)	30.00
Foreman's salary (one-fourth)	200.00
Insurance (1% of the cost of machine per year)	16.67
	346.67

Since number of working hours per year = 2400 hours

Hence number of working hour per month = 200

Therefore, fixed expenses per hour

$$= \frac{346.67}{200} = 1.734.$$

Variable Expenses

(*i*) Depreciation

$$\text{Depreciation per year} = \frac{20,000 - 2,000}{10} = 1800$$

$$\therefore \quad \text{Depreciation per hour} = \frac{1800}{2400} = 0.75$$

$$(ii) \quad \text{Repairs per hour} = \frac{4000}{10 \times 2400} = 0.16$$

(*iii*) Electric Charges per hour 15 units @ 10 paise = 1.50

∴ Machnie- hour rate = 4.15

Hence machine-hour rate of this machine is **Rs. 4.15 Ans.**

Example 33.9 *Suppose following informations are given for the year 2010*:

	Rs.
Expenditure on Material	250,000
Expenditure on Direct Labour	100,000
Factory expenses	120,000
Office and administrative expenses	47,000

Determine the cost of a product which is likely to require material for Rs. 10,000 and wages for Rs. 5,000.

Solution. The product shall have the indirect expenses in the same ratio as that of whole concern. *For the concern,* it is given that –

		Rs.
	Materials	250,000
	Direct labour	100,000
∴	Prime cost	350,000
	Factory expenses	120,000
∴	Factory cost	470,000
	Office and administrative expenses	47,000
∴	Total cost	517,000

Here % ratio of factory expenses to direct labour

$$= \frac{120,000}{100,000} \times 100 = 120\ \%$$

Similarly % ratio of office and adm. expenses to factory cost

$$= \frac{47,000}{470,000} \times 100 = 10\%$$

Hence for the product

		Rs.
	Materials	10,000
	Direct labour	5,000
	Prime cost	15,000
∴	Factory overhead - 120% of labour cost	6,000
∴	Factory cost	21,000
	Office and Admn. expenses = 10% of factory cost	2,100
∴	Total cost	23,100

∴ Total cost of the product shall be Rs. **23,100. Ans.**

33.6. SOME EXAMPLES OF OVERHEADS

Items	*Head to which charged*
(*i*) Wages paid to indirect workers *e.g.* Repair gangs ; Foremen; Watch and Ward staff etc.	Factory over-head
(*ii*) Work's Canteen and Welfare expenses	"
(*iii*) Employee's State Insurance contribution	"
(*iv*) Factory rent,	"
(*v*) Factory lighting	"
(*vi*) Water, power and fuel (coal gas and furnace oil)	
(*vii*) Insurance of plant, factory etc.	"
(*viii*) Depreciation of plant, machinery, tools and their repairs.	"
(*ix*) Consumable stores in factory such as cotton waste, grease etc.,	"

(*x*) Charges for telephones installed in the factory and stationery consumed in the factory.	"
(*xi*) Material transportation expenses for bringing materials from stores.	"
(*xii*) Cost of idle time of workers which cannot be charged on any product.	"
(*xiii*) Cost for any material which cannot be directly charged.	"
(*xiv*) Salaries of General Manager, Finance Manager, Secretary and their staff	Administrative overheads
(*xv*) Office rent (if rented) or Repair and depreciation of office premises	"
(*xvi*) Light and power required for office	"
(*xvii*) Bank charges	"
(*xviii*) Telephone, telegram and postal charges.	"
(*xix*) Insurance of office premises and equipments.	"
(*xx*) Printing and stationery for office.	"
(*xxi*) Expenditure incurred on legal section	"
(*xxii*) Expenditure incurred on audit.	"
(*xxiii*) Salaries of the Sales manager, his staff, salesmen etc.	Selling Expenses
(*xxiv*) Travelling expenses, commission and other facilities to salesmen.	"
(*xxv*) Advertising expenses	"
(*xxvi*) Showroom expenses	"
(*xxvii*) Printing of catalogue price list etc.	"
(*xxviii*) Packing and carriage charges.	"
(*xxix*) Insurance on finished goods, showrooms goods and transit goods in godowns	"
(*xxx*) Expenses on delivery van including operation, maintenance, running and depreciation and repairs.	" "
(*xxxi*) Telephone and postal expenditure of sales.	"
(*xxxii*) Entertainment expenses.	"
(*xxxiii*) Legal charges incurred for recovery for debts etc.	"
(*xxxiv*) Rebate to customers	"

Some Typical Cases

(*a*) **Income Tax.** Since that is a part of profits, it will be ignored in costing.

(*b*) **Construction of playing fields and equipments for them and other welfare activities of permanent nature.** The expenditure incurred on these activities is a capital expenditure and hence only depreciation should be included in the proportion of number of persons getting benefits from the facility.

(*c*) **Pay for Holidays.** Pay for office staff is a part of office expenses where pay for factory workers

(*i*) for direct workers, the direct wages are taken after inflation of pay taking care of holidays

(*ii*) for indirect workers, it is charged to factory overheads.

(*d*) **Shifting an equipment or plant.** Since this is not a capital expenditure, but still requires abnormal expenditure, hence it cannot be charged to any head, but should be debited to profit and loss account.

(*e*) **Installing new plant.** This is a capital expenditure and hence depreciation is credited every year into it.

(*f*) **Dismantling of plant.** The final gain or loss on realisation of sale proceeds, should be transferred to profit and loss account.

(*g*) **Drawing offices costs.** Where works related to the drawing office is heavy, the time taken by the draughtsman is booked to the job concerned directly. But where drawing office provides general service to the whole concern, the expenditure is treated as production overhead.

(*h*) **Market Research.** This is an item of selling overhead. Where market research is carried out for a particular product, the expenses are directly charged to product.

(*i*) **After sales service.** The expenditure of after sales service includes salary of the staff employed for the purpose, expenditure on rectification during the warranty period. The expenses are treated as a part of product cost. However, in some undertakings after sales service expenses are treated as a part of selling overheads and are proportioned to different products on the basis of sales.

Example 33.10. *A certain piece of work is produced by a firm in batches of 100. The direct material cost for that 100 piece work is Rs.160.00 and the direct labour cost is Rs. 200.00. Factory on cost is 35% of the total material and labour cost. Overhead charges are 20% of the factory cost. Calculate prime cost and factory cost. If the management wants to make a profit of 10% on the gross cost, determine the selling price of each article.*

Solution. No. of products to be manufactured = 100

Direct material cost = Rs. 160.00

Direct labour cost = Rs. 200.00

Hence, Prime cost = Direct material cost + Direct labour cost

= Rs. 160.00 + Rs. 200.00

= Rs. 360.00 **Ans.**

As factory on-cost is 35% of the Prime cost.

$$\text{Factory on-cost} = \frac{360 \times 35}{100} = \text{Rs. } 126.00$$

Factory cost = Prime cost + Factory on-cost

= Rs. 360 + Rs. 126 = **Rs. 486.00 Ans.**

As overhead charges are 20% of the factory cost.

$$\therefore \quad \text{Overhead cost} = \frac{20 \times 486}{100} \text{ Rs. } 97.20$$

$$\therefore \quad \text{Total cost} = \text{Prime cost + Factory on cost + Overhead}$$

$$= \text{Rs. } 360 + \text{Rs. } 126 + \text{Rs. } 97.20$$

$$= \text{Rs. } 583.20$$

Now, management wants profit of 10% on the gross, *i.e.*, total cost.

Hence,

$$\text{Selling price of 100 pieces} = \frac{110 \times 583.20}{100} \text{ Rs. } 641.52$$

Hence, Selling price of each work piece $= \frac{641.52}{100} =$ **Rs. 6.4152** **Say Rs. 6.42 Ans.**

Example 33.11. *The market price of a lathe is Rs. 50000 and the discount allowed to the distributor is 20% of the market price. It is found that the selling expense cost is 1/4 th the factory cost and if the material cost, labour cost and factory overhead charges are in the ratio of 1: 4 : 2; what profit is made by the factory on each other, if the material cost is Rs. 4000? Neglect other overheads.*

Solution. Market price of a lathe

$$= \text{Rs. } 50000$$

$$\text{Discount allowed} = 20\% \text{ on market price}$$

$$= \frac{50000 \times 20}{100} \text{ Rs. } 10000$$

Hence, Selling price at factory $= \text{Rs. } (50{,}000 - 10{,}000) = \text{Rs. } 40{,}000$ ... (1)

Now, Selling price at factory $=$ Factory cost + Selling expenses + Profit

But, Selling expenses $= \frac{1}{4}$ (Factory cost)

$$\text{Selling price} = \frac{5}{4} \text{ Factory cost + Profit} \quad \text{... (2)}$$

Now, Factory cost = Material cost + Labour cost + Overheads

$$\text{Here Material cost} = \text{Rs. } 4000$$

$$\text{Labour cost} = 4 \times 4000 = \text{Rs. } 16000$$

and Overhead expenses $= 2 \times 4000 = \text{Rs. } 8000$

$$\therefore \quad \text{Factory cost} = 4000 + 16000 + 8000 = \text{Rs. } 28000 \quad \text{... (3)}$$

Substituting value in Eq. (2) from Eqs. (1) and (3)

Then, $40000 = \frac{5}{4} \times 28000 + \text{Profit}$

$$\therefore \quad \text{Profit} = \text{Rs. } 40000 - 35000 \text{ or Rs. } 5000$$

Hence profit on each lathe is **Rs. 5000. Ans.**

Example 33.12. *Two workmen engaged on a forging. Hammer complete 20 connecting rods, each weighing 4 kg. The workmen are paid at the rate of Rs. 100 and Rs. 60 per day and material cost is Rs. 20 per kg. If 140% of direct labour is charged to compensate for both factory overheads and administrative expenses, what will be per unit cost of production of these units.?*

Solution. Rate of first worker = Rs. 100/day

Rate of second worker = Rs. 60/day

No. of connecting rods = 20.

Weight of each connecting rod = 4 kg.

and overhead charges = 40% of direct labour charges

First find the total cost of 20 pieces.

Total cost consists of Labour cost + Material cost + Factory over-heads + Administrative overheads

Labour cost for 20 pieces = Rs. 100 + Rs. 60 = Rs. 160

Material weight = $20 \times 4 = 80$ Kg.

Material cost = $80 \times 20 =$ Rs. 1600

Factory and administrative overheads

$$= 160 \times \frac{140}{100} \text{ Rs. } 224$$

∴ Total cost of 20 pieces = $160 + 1600 + 224 = 1984$

$$\text{Total cost per unit of Production} = \frac{\text{Total cost}}{\text{No. of pieces}} = \frac{1984}{20}$$

= Rs . 99.20

Hence the production cost of each connecting rod will be

= **Rs. 99.20 Ans.**

Example 33.13. *A factory is producing 1000 bolts and nuts per hour on a machine. Its material cost is Rs. 375, labour cost Rs. 245 and the direct expense is Rs. 80. The factory on cost is 150% of the total labour cost and office on cost is 30% of the total factory cost. If the selling price of each bolt and nut is Rs. 1.30, calculate whether the management is going in loss or gain and by what amount?*

Solution. Material cost = Rs. 375

Labour cost = Rs. 245

Direct expenses = Rs. 80

Overhead charges. Factory on-cost

= 150% of total labour cost

$$= \frac{150 \times 245}{100} = \text{Rs. } 367.50$$

Hence total factory cost = $375 + 245 + 80 + 367.50$

= Rs. 1067.50

Now, office on-cost is 30% of total factory cost

$$= \frac{1067.50 \times 30}{100} = \text{Rs. } 320.25$$

Hence, total cost of production per 1000 bolts and nuts

= Factory cost + Office on cost

= Rs. 1067.50 + Rs. 320.25

= Rs. 1387.75

∴ Production cost per piece = 1.38775, say Rs. 1.39 per piece.

But selling price is Rs. 1.30 per piece.

Hence the management is undergoing a loss of Rs. 1.39 – 1.30

= **Rs. 0.09 per piece. Ans.**

Example. 33.14. *A small firm is producing 100 pens per day. The direct material cost is found to be Rs. 160, direct labour cost Rs. 200 and factory overheads chargeable to it Rs. 250. If the selling on-cost is 40% of the factory cost, what must be the selling price of each pen to realise a profit of 14.6% of the selling price ?*

Solution. No of pens to be manufactured = 100

Direct material cost = Rs. 160

Direct labour cost = Rs. 200

Factory overhead charges = Rs. 250

Selling on-cost = 40% of factory cost

Profit = 14.6% of selling price

Let selling price of 100 pens is Rs. R

Hence, profit on selling price of Rs. R

$$= \frac{14.6 \times R}{100}$$

Total cost = Selling price – Profit

$$= R - \frac{14.6\,R}{100} \qquad \text{...(1)}$$

New, factory cost = Material cost + Labour cost + Overheads

= Rs. 160 + 200 + 250 = Rs. 610.

Total cost = Factory cost + Selling on-cost

But selling on-cost = 40% of factory cost

$$= \frac{610 \times 40}{100} = \text{Rs. } 244$$

Total cost = 610 + 244 = Rs. 854

Hence, substituting in Eq. (1)

$$854 = R - \frac{14.6\,R}{100}$$

or R = 1000.

Hence selling price of each pen

$$= \text{Rs. } \frac{1000}{100} = \textbf{Rs. 10 Ans.}$$

33.7. COST CONCEPT

Since there are large number of determinants which influence the cost, these determinants vary from situation to situation, and enterprise to enterprise. Therefore, for taking a decision about any such determinants, we must analyse them thoroughly. In order to take right decisions, it is necessary to understand different costs. Some of them are explained here under:

1. **Actual Costs.** These are the costs which the firm incurs while producing or acquiring

a good or a service. The actual costs are also known as acquisition cost or outlay cost. The examples of such costs are material costs, labour costs, rent etc.

2. **Opportunity Cost.** Opportunity cost represents the benefits or revenue forgone by pursuing one course of action rather than other. This means, when best alternative is adopted, it is obvious that second best alternative can not be implemented and its benefits are for gone. Thus the benefit of this second best alternative which has been sacrificed due to the selection of best alternative is known as the opportunity cost of the best alternative.

   Opportunity costs can also be defined as, the return from the second best use of the firm's resources which the firm forgoes in order to avail of the return from the best use of the resources.

   Some examples of opportunity cost are:

   (*a*) opportunity cost of the funds employed in the firm is the amount of interest which otherwise could have been earned.

   (*b*) opportunity cost of labour in own business is the income which he would have earned by accepting a job outside.

   (*c*) opportunity cost of space used in expansion of the business is the amount of rent which could be fetched if it is rented out to some body else.

3. **Marginal Cost.** Marginal cost is the increase in cost as a result of a unit change in output.

   Marginal cost can also be defined as, the additional costs incurred when there is a unit change in the existing output of goods and services.

   In mathematical term, marginal cost of nth unit $M.\ C_n$ is the difference between the total cost of nth unit $T.\ C_n$ and the total cost of $(n-1)^{th}$ unit $(T.\ C_{n-1})$

$$MC_n = TC_n - TC_{n-1}$$

   In other words, marginal cost is the rate at which total cost changes with the change in output.

4. **Incremental Costs.** Incremental costs may be defined as,

   (*a*) The difference in total costs resulting from a contemplated change in policy or

   (*b*) The addition to costs resulting from a change in the nature and the level of business activity.

   The examples of the change are change in output level, product line, or product mix; adding or replacing a machine or distribution channel; advertising policy or level of investment.

   While taking a decision, it may be ascertained that incremental revenue should exceed incremental cost. Incremental revenue is a change in total revenue resulting from a change. The difference between incremental revenue and incremental cost is known as incremental income.

5. **Sunk Costs.** Sunk costs are the costs that are not altered by a change in quantity and can not be recovered, *e.g.*, depreciation. This may also be defined as the cost for which the expenditure has been incurred in the past and which will not be affected by the particular decision. These are the parts of the outlay (actual) costs.

6. **Fixed and Variable Costs.** Fixed costs are the part of the total cost of the firm which do not vary with the variation in the output. Examples of the fixed costs are rent of land or building, property tax etc. The fixed cost are also known as overhead costs or

indirect costs. If the production increases the fixed cost per unit decreases, as the total fixed cost is divided between large number of units.

Variable costs, are directly dependent on the volume of production or service. Examples of variable costs are material costs, labour costs etc.

7. **Short Run and Long Run Costs.** To understand short run cost and long run cost, we must first discuss 'short run' and 'long run'. Short run is a period in which the firm is free to vary its output but does not have the time to change its scale of plant. As inputs, like machinery, buildings etc., can not be changed by the firm at any moment, since it takes time to replace, add or dismantle them. To meet increased demand, in such circumstances, only way is to increase output by intensive working of existing capital equipment. Whereas if demand decreases, the output can be reduced by keeping equipment idle for proportionate period of time.

   Long run is a period in which all inputs can be varied as desired. This is a period long enough to enable to adjust its supply and output completely to changes in demand.

   Short run costs are the costs that vary with the degree of plant utilisation (*i.e.* output) and other fixed factors. It is the short run while fixed costs remain unchanged, variable costs fluctuate with the output.

   Long run costs, on the other hand, are the costs that vary with the size of plant. 'Short run' and 'long run' costs are used for predicting the effect of temporary, and permanent output decisions on costs, prices, and hence profits.

8. **Cost-Output Relationship.** Cost-output relationship for short and long are described here-under :

   (A) For Short Run : For short run, the total Cost (*TC*) to a firm for a given level of output is the sum of the total variable cost (*TVC*) and the total fixed cost (*TFC*).

$$TC = TFC + TVC$$

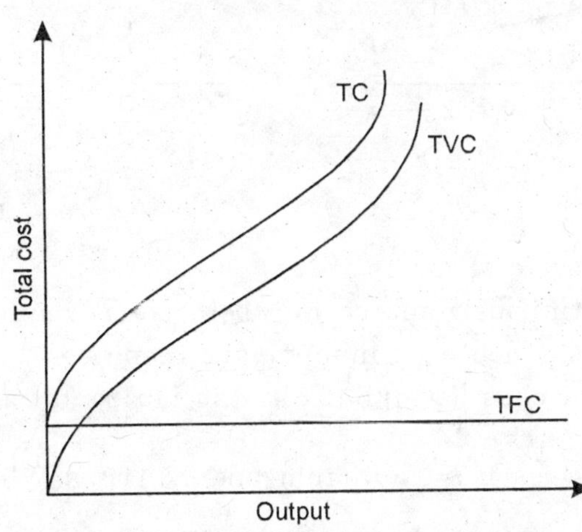

Fig. 33.1. Short run total cost curves.

The shape of these costs can graphically be shown a follows:

Average costs for short run can be expressed as follows:

(*i*) Average fixed cost (AFC) is the fixed cost per unit of output

i.e., $$AFCT = \frac{TFC}{Q}$$

where, Q = output

Since TFC is constant, AFC therefore continuously decline.

(*ii*) Average variable cost (AVC) is similarly the variable cost per unit.

i.e.,
$$AVC = \frac{TVC}{Q}$$

AVC curve first declines and then rises.

(*iii*) Therefore, average total cost,

$$\text{ATC} = \frac{TC}{Q} = \frac{TFC}{Q} + \frac{TVC}{Q} = AFC + AVC$$

These, average costs can be represented, graphically as shown below:

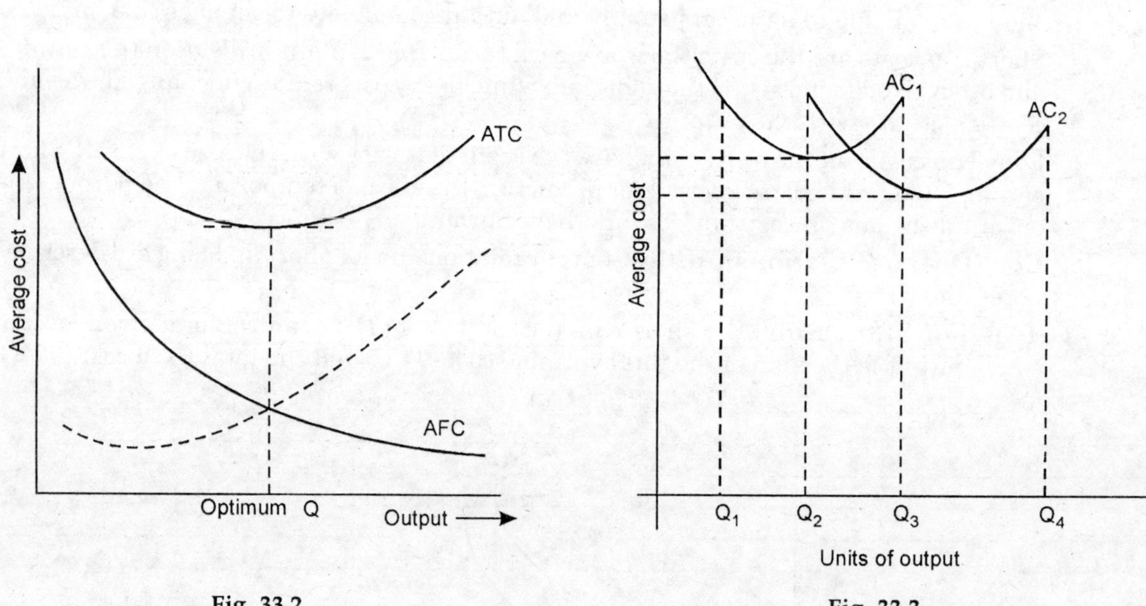

Fig. 33.2. **Fig. 33.3.**

The properties of average cost curves are :

(*i*) AFC declines continuously, approaching both axes asymptotically.

(*ii*) AVC first declines, reaches a minimum, and then rises.

(*iii*) When AFC approaches asymptotically the horizontal axis, AVC approaches ATC asymptotically.

(*iv*) ATC first declines, reaches a minimum, and then rises. When it is minimum, output is at optimum level.

B. For Long Run. As already discussed under heading 'long run costs', in the long run, all factors are variable and the firm has number of alternatives. For example, a firm has two choices for production, *i.e.*, small or medium size plant. These plants operate with average costs of AC_1 and AC_2 respectively.

Here, for production between Q_1 and Q_2 only one option, *i.e.*, with small plant, is available, whereas for production between Q_2 and Q_3 both the options, *i.e.*, either to use small plant or medium size plant are available. Again for production between Q_3 and Q_4 only medium size plant can be used. These curves help to find out which option is economical for a particular level of output.

Here we have discussed only two options, but in practice large number of options are available. In such circumstances curves can be drawn for each alternative and then best is selected for a particular level of output.

33.8. STANDARD COST

It is the pre-determined cost of a product. After compiling different expenses, an estimated cost of product is forecasted, which is known as "Standard cost". It is used as a device to check and lower overhead expenses and improving efficiency. Generally, standard costs are not flexible but when sudden variation in the material costs or any change in the production methods occur, standard cost should be modified.

Advantages of Standard Cost

(*i*) It provides a check on various expenses

(*ii*) It helps in deciding the budget

(*iii*) It helps in budgetary control

(*iv*) It helps reduction in wastage of material and labour

(*v*) It helps in price determination

(*vi*) It is a measure of arriving at the efficiency of the whole concern.

Standard Costing

Standard costing is "the preparation and use of standard costs, their comparison with actual costs and the analysis of variances to find out their causes and points of incidence". In other words, Standard costing is a system which controls the cost of each unit through determination before hand of what should be the cost and then comparing it with the actual costs.

Thus "standard cost is a predetermined or budgeted costs of a unit of a product and helps in comparing with actual costs".

Thus we see that Standard costing is complementary to budgetary control, since a system of budgetary control cannot function unless cost of each unit is strictly controlled.

Determination of Standard Costs

As we know that standards are used for comparing the efficiency, hence, as a general rule, standards must be such that they can be attained with some efforts. The standards should neither be unattainable nor should be such that which can be attained without any effort.

The standards are decided by using past experience and by taking the help of experiments or previously fixed norms (*e.g.*, using time and motion study or by adopting standard data for work study). As far as possible standards for indirect expenses should also be fixed in quantitative terms, which can be converted into money afterwards.

How to Exercise Control Over Cost

As we have discussed that there are three components of cost: namely materials cost, labour cost and overheads. Hence to exercise full control, Cost Accountant must exercise full control over all these three costs, as explained below.

Saving Material Cost

Material cost is a main component in the total cost of the product (varying from 25 to 70%). Therefore, in order to control the cost, it is necessary to pay maximum attention for controlling material cost in following way :

1. **Control over abnormal losses.** These are avoidable losses and are wastage which should be controlled. These losses arise due to mischief or inefficiency. These may occur due to theft, fire or damage, careless handling etc. However, there are some normal losses which are unavoidable, *e.g.*, loss of weight due to evaporation.
2. **Material handling charges.** Material must be handled through economical means *i.e.*, after examining various methods like using crane, manual labour or other devices. Bulky materials must be stored, transported and handled in a planned way so as to minimise handling charges.
3. **Control over inventory.** Inventory must be kept in a scientific way and only in required quantities. For proper inventory control modern techniques must be adopted.
4. **Control over Indirect material.** Indirect material is controlled by using past experiences and each type of indirect material decided by way of rational thinking, *e.g.*,
   (*a*) Past history of record should be kept for repairs and maintenance of machines which shall give quantity and frequency of lubricants, spares and repairs needed.
   (*b*) For special jobs, bill of materials be prepared, which gives full details of parts required.
   (*c*) Deciding the norms for consumption of fuels and lubricating oils etc. for the furnaces, cranes, trucks, dumpers and other machines.
5. **Reclamation of loss from defective products.** Defective products must be dismantled in the reclamation room, from where
   (*i*) good and serviceable parts should be sent for use again; while
   (*ii*) the parts which are defective but can be made serviceable with some extra efforts are sent to the workshop for correction; whereas
   (*iii*) the parts which are completely spoiled are either used in the foundry or sold as scrap.
6. **Control over consumption in the workshop.** To check whether the consumption of material is justified or not, two methods are employed
   (*i*) to compare with that of past years record of consumption and
   (*ii*) to compare with that of standards set for the purpose.

33.9. COSTING

Costing has been defined by the Institute of Cost and Works Accountants, England as : "The technique and process of ascertaining costs". Whereas, Wheldon has defined the costing as : "Costing is the classifying and recording the appropriate allocation of expenditure for the determination of the costs of products or services, and for presentation of suitably arranged data for the purposes of control, and guidance of management".

It is the determination of an actual cost of an article, after adding different expenses incurred in various departments.

It may also be defined as the system, which systematically records all the expenditure to determine the cost of manufactured products.

It differs from estimating that costing is a determination of cost after knowing the expenditure incurred in various departments on the product, while estimating is the pre-determination of cost based on the assumptions and previous experiences.

Aims of Costing

Main aims of costing are:

1. To determine the exact cost of each article.
2. To determine the cost incurred during each operation to keep control over workers' wages.
3. To provide information to ascertain the selling price of the product.
4. To supply information for detection of wastage.
5. It helps in reducing the total cost of manufacture.
6. It suggests changes in design when the cost is higher.
7. To help in formulating the policies for charging the prices of the product.
8. To facilitate preparation of estimate for submitting the rates in tenders or quotations.
9. To compare the actual cost with the estimated cost of the component.

Advantages of Efficient Costing

Efficient costing has got the following advantages:

(*i*) It helps in tracing wastage, leakage and spoiled material.
(*ii*) It gives information regarding profitable and unprofitable activities.
(*iii*) It provides an effective check on wage systems.
(*iv*) Actual causes of reduction in profits can be easily found.
(*v*) It gives information, regarding component parts, whether it is profitable to manufacture them in the factory or to purchase from outside market.
(*vi*) It also helps in the settlement of wage rates with trade unions at the time of dispute.
(*vii*) It provides data for comparison between actual cost and estimated cost of an article.
(*viii*) It provides data for overhead charges etc. to assist in the preparation of estimates for future work.
(*ix*) It helps the management in forming the policies of price determination.
(*x*) It provides information of detailed expenditure, so. that it can be checked when it is tending to exceed.
(*xi*) It keeps control over selling price.
(*xii*) The main advantages of costing is to compare the output of the persons of same trade and working on same type of machines.
(*xiii*) It helps in determining the efficiency of administrative and operative functions and decides the weak points, where wastage and expenses need check.
(*xiv*) It helps the planning department in deciding about the quantity of material required and the sequence of operations on the job.

33.10. METHODS OF COSTING

1. Multiple costs.
2. Job costs.

3. Departmental costing.
4. Unit costs.
5. Process costs.
6. Operating costs.

Each method is explained in short below :

1. **Multiple Cost.** Concerns manufacturing a variety of standardised products, having no relation to one another in cost, quality and the types of process etc., such as type-writer, gramophones and cycle etc., use this costing method.
2. **Job Costs.** This method is also known as "order costs" or "terminal costs" In this method, all the items are charged to a specific order. This method is also adopted by builders, contractors etc., as it helps in showing the cost of each separate contract or job or order of a work.

   Daily record of direct material, direct labour and estimated overhead cost for each order is recorded in production order or cost sheet and thus the total cost of the job is obtained from the cost sheet.

   This method is useful when products are produced in distinguishable lots and it is also desirable to keep a separate record of each lot.
3. **Departmental Costing.** This method is adopted in determining the cost of the output of each department separately for the manufacture of the standardised products. For example, in a steel mill there are three separate departments such as blast furnace, open hearth and rolling mill department. The cost of all the three is determined separately.
4. **Unit Costs.** This method is adopted by the firms, which supply a uniform product rather than a variety of products such as mines, quarries etc.
5. **Process Costs.** This method is applied to industries such as oil refining, chemical, paint and other similar industries, where the raw material passes through a number of processes or operations before it is converted into a final product. By-products should be taken into account while calculating the cost of each process of manufacture in this method of costing.

   This method indicates the cost of a product at different stages as it passes through various processes or operations or departments and, therefore, a comparison of cost of various processes is also possible. This method is adopted for mass scale production. For example, in garment making, cutting and sewing are two different operations. In this system, the cost of the two operations is determined separately.
6. **Operating Costs.** Firms providing utility services find this method useful. For example, in railways, transport service, water works, electricity boards etc., cost is determined on the basis of operating expenses and charges are made as tonne-km or passenger per km, per 1000 litres or kilowatt-hour etc.

33.11. COST CONTROL

Cost control means the procedures and measures by which the cost of carrying out an activity is kept under check. The aim of cost control is two-fold, *viz.*

(*i*) to see that cost does not exceed beyond a certain level.

(*ii*) thereafter, as a further step, it must adopt such measures and procedures by which the cost is further reduced.

Cost control is a technique which involves, the determination of standards in respect of each item of cost and determining the actual cost of those very items, detections of variations of actuals from the standards laid down, analysing these variances in order to find out the real cause and then taking necessary corrective steps for future.

How to Control Costs

As we know that elements of cost are material, labour and expenses, if we make complete systematic check on each and every element, the cost can be kept in control. If a businessman does not have any check and a scientific way of calculating the total cost of the products produced, then he may not earn exact profits, and even he may run into losses. Therefore, to earn good profits, it is essential to keep control over each and every element of cost, such as :

(*i*) Control on prime cost,

(*ii*) Control on overheads, and

(*iii*) Control on indirect materials and tools.

1. **Control on Prime Cost.**

Prime cost of a product has got great role over the total cost. It consists of Direct Material cost and Direct Labour cost.

Since **direct material cost** is the most important item of expenditure, following factors must be considered to keep control on it:

(*i*) To purchase right material at right time at right price.

(*ii*) Efficient system of store-keeping.

(*iii*) To ensure that always right quantities of materials are consumed with less wastage.

(*iv*) Over-stocking must be avoided.

(*v*) As far as possible minimum handling should be there with economy.

(*vi*) Try to utilise waste and scrap for some other works.

Direct labour cost is also a part of the prime cost. In this respect, following steps may be useful:

(*i*) It is necessary to express labour charges in terms of time.

(*ii*) Labour rate should be fixed accurately with the help of Time and Motion Study.

(*iii*) A right system of time recording can be introduced to calculate the time taken by each worker.

(*iv*) Suitable inspection and supervision methods should be introduced.

(*v*) A suitable method of wage payment should be selected and introduced.

(*vi*) Proper tools, jigs and fixtures be used to reduce production time.

2. **Control on Overheads.**

To run the business efficiently, it is very essential to have strict control on the overheads. Prime cost of product does not vary much from industry to industry for the same product, it is the overhead charges which are much responsible. If these are minimised, cost can be controlled to a large extent. For this purpose, following steps must be taken:

(*i*) A set procedure for determining the total overhead charges of different departments should be followed and charges of each department should be compared whether they are in excess or not.

(*ii*) Keep control on the indirect labour force.

(*iii*) Simplification and set procedure for accounts and all administrative work is required to be done.

(*iv*) As far as possible less work should be got done during extra hours.

3. **Control on Indirect Material and Tools.**

This can be kept under control by allowing a fixed amount for each shop and should be revised at regular intervals according to the needs.

As standard cost is a tool to keep control over the total cost, therefore, total cost should always be compared with it and short-comings and defects are to be found out.

To determine the total cost, each of the above head is added. For detailed description, 'Elements of Cost' should be consulted.

33.12. HOW TO CONTROL MATERIAL COSTS

Material cost is a main component in the total cost of the product (varying from 25 to 65%). Therefore, in order to control the cost, it is necessary to pay maximum attention for controlling material cost in following ways :

1. **Control over abnormal losses.** These are avoidable losses and wastages which should be controlled. These arise either due to mischief or inefficiency and may occur due to theft, fire, or damage because of careless handling etc. These can be controlled by training the store staff, keeping strict vigil and control, adopting the policy of incentives for efficient and punishment for careless staff.

2. **Material handling.** Material handling is an art and science involving movement, packaging, and storing of materials in any form, *i.e.*, by means of gravity, manual effort or by power driven machines. Materials are received from market and stored in stores, moved to processing departments, moved from machine to machine during the process of manufacturing, semi processed parts are moved from one department to another and then to final assembly section, and then through inspection department to dispatch and packing section.

   Material must be handled through economical means, *i.e.*, after examining various methods like using conveyers, gravity feed, cranes, fork-lift trucks, manual labour or other devices. Special care must be taken for bulky material and they must be stored, transported and handled in a planned way so as to minimise handling charges.

   Material handling expenses can be reduced to a great extent if the layout is according to the handling requirement. Layout should be made after considering flow process charts, travel charts etc.

3. **Control over Inventory.** Inventory must be kept in a scientific way and only in required quantities. Inventory control is a systematic location, storage, and recording of goods in such a way that desired degree of service can be made to the operating shops at minimum ultimate cost. There is a need for inventory control to maintain a desired level of stores based on requirements and economical aspects. All out efforts may be made to avoid inventory build ups. Inventory build up starts because either (*i*) items are purchased in excess of requirements, or (*ii*) they do not get consumed at the rate at which they are received. As a remedial measure, the position of Inventory build up is renewed at frequent intervals and corrective actions should be taken.

4. **Reclamation from defective products.** Defective products must be dismantled in the reclamation room, from where

(i) goods and serviceable parts are sent for use again ; while

(ii) the defective parts can be made serviceable with some extra efforts, whereas

(iii) the parts which are completely spoiled are either used in the foundry or sold as scrap.

5. **Control over consumption.** To check whether the consumption of material is justified or not, two steps are taken,

(i) to compare with that of the past years record of consumption,

(ii) to compare with that of standards set for the purpose.

6. **Protection of stores.** Protection of stores from fire, rust and corrosion, dust, theft, weather, heat, cold and moisture (depending upon the nature of material) is an important aspect. Each type of material such as textiles, rubber goods, leather goods, cement, petroleum products, tools, and metals require its own kind of care. Each category of item should therefore be stored in the conditions where they can be maintained in good conditions without any harm.

7. **Procurement of material.** While purchasing, following parameters should be considered :

(a) **Purchase at right time**–Neither too early to avoid inventory build-up, nor too late to avoid loss of production or loss due to emergency purchases. Lead time plays an important role.

(b) **Right Source**–reliability of supplier, nearness to enable to pursue for timely supply, quality.

(c) **Right Quality**–quality of material should not be sacrificed to maintain quality of finished product and hence reputation of the concern.

(d) **Right Quantity**–concept of Economic ordering Quantity, be kept in view.

(e) **Right Contract**–while purchasing, proper contract agreement must be signed to avoid future complicacies and delay arising due to them.

(f) **Right place of Delivery**–to avoid necessary handling.

33.13. WASTE CONTROL

Following definitions are important to consider wastage control in the industry:

Obsolete: These are those materials and equipments which are not damaged and which have economic worth but are no longer useful for the company's operation due to several reasons such as changes in product line, process, materials and so on.

Surplus: These are materials and equipments which have no immediate use but have accumulated due to faulty planning, forecasting and purchasing. However, these may have usage value in future.

Scrap: It is the process wastage such as turnings, boring, sprues and flashes etc. These may have an end use within the plant.

The unnecessary accumulation of obsolete surplus and scrap items is said to be waste and enough capital is blocked in it.

The increase in all such items will increase the product cost, which in turn will reduce the profits. Therefore, efforts shall be made tominimise such causes by means of intelligent planning and effective production control.

Major Causes of Obsolete/Surplus

The reasons for the accumulation of these items are :

(a) *Changes in product design.* Due to change in the design of product, some items become obsolete.

(b) *Rationalisation.* Sometimes raw materials and equipments etc. are rationalised for want of simplification. This renders some items as surplus or obsolete.

(c) When a machine breakdown occurs, sometimes it is rectified by using components of an identical machine which is already not functioning due to one reason or the other. This is called "Cannibalisation". By continued removing parts from the identical machine renders obsolete or scrap items.

(d) *Faulty Planning and Forecasting.* Material planning is based on sales forecast and this may result in surplus items, if not properly planned.

(e) *Faulty Purchase Practices.* If purchased are made in bulk then technological changes, storage space requirements etc. lead to the generation of surplus and obsolete items.

(f) *Other Reasons.* Faulty storekeeping and recording, poor materials handling, improper codification and inadequate manufacturing methods also cause obsolete surplus and scrap items.

Reasons for Scrap

(i) Due to men :

1. Carelessness on the part of the operator.
2. Opertor not trained properly.
3. Lack of attention on the part of the setter, inspector or supervisor.
4. Faulty instructions.
5. Written instructions and drawings misread.

(ii) Due to machines :

1. Plant and equipment in poor conditions
2. Design of plant and requirement may be poor
3. Tools and gauges not standard one.

(iii) Due to materials :

1. Materials not up to the specifications.
2. Improper selection of materials.

(iv) Due to methods :

1. Improper techniques.
2. Poor works organisation.

We cannot totally avoid the scraps but these can be minimised by controlling the above reasons for scrap.

Disposal of Surplus Materials. A periodical study is essential for finding out the obsolete or surplus items. These items should then be re-examined for their alternative use. If they could not be used anywhere in the concern, they must be disposed of.

Mode of disposal should be decided in the following priority :

(a) Send it back on resale to the original supplier, if they are interested or otherwise,

(b) Sell them at the best possible price. If it is not possible then,

(c) Sell it at any available price even at scrap value. In case, if it could not be sold at scrap value or at any other rate then,

(d) Give away free, as there is no use of preserving it year after year and blocking the space.

Disposal of Scrap. When the scrap cannot be utilised within the organisation then it should be disposed of at regular intervals. It is profitable to dispose the scrap direct to the end users rather than to a middleman who normally pays lower returns. Before disposal action is taken, it should be segregated according to metal and sizes to fetch good return. Following two methods are commonly adopted for scrap disposal:

1. Disposal by auction.
2. Disposal by tender.

Buyers in both the cases are required to inspect the scrap in the scrapyard and they are also required to deposit earnest money.

Role of Management in Waste Control Programme

1. Stock records should be checked and items which have not been consumed (non-moving) for a period of one year should be isolated. A list of such items and their value in terms of money and time should be prepared. Similarly, such lists should be prepared for items which have not been used for more than one year say 2, 3, 4 years and so on. These lists are then forwarded to the top management for disposal action. A separate list should be prepared for imported parts and insurance parts. This analysis should be done atleast once in a year.
2. Whenever there is change in production programme, design and product lines are undertaken. Materials Manager must be kept in the picture. This will help in several ways as under :
   (*i*) He is in a position to inform top management of the amount of stock of materials on hand that are likely to be rendered obsolete if and when the changes are introduced.
   (*ii*) He could guide the top management as to when the changes should be made so that the existing stock can be consumed in full.
   (*iii*) Materials Manager should freeze further order for such materials and to negotiate with the suppliers to take back the stock. For sometimes he can introduce the buy-back clause.

33.14. COST SAVING AREAS

As we know that cost of the product consists of (*i*) material cost (*ii*) labour cost (*iii*) overheads. Therefore, to reduce the cost, it is necessary to bring down the expenditure on these elements. Following are some of the areas, in which saving can be done as discussed below :

(*i*) Materials
(*ii*) Machinability
(*iii*) Tolerances
(*iv*) Fewer parts
(*v*) Tool design
(*vi*) Make or Buy
(*vii*) Increase productivity
(*viii*) Distribution system

1. **Materials.** In order to reduce the cost of the product, materials of lower or different quality which will not affect the utility of the product are selected. Common examples of such substitution of material are use of steel window frames instead of timber frames,

use of aluminium instead of copper in electric transmission lines. This process of substitution is based on the principle that if a cheaper material can work satisfactorily then there is no use in using costly material. Sometimes another alternative is desired to be found, *e.g.*, in the radio valve industry, many parts made from expensive nickel can be manufactured with nickel plated mild steel, similarly copper plated mild steel can be used in place of pure copper.

2. **Machinability.** Some materials are easier to machine and allow faster cutting speeds and less tool wear and breakage. Though such material might be slightly costly but can be adopted if saves more in machining and gives overall saving in the cost.
3. **Tolerances.** When more exact the measurement and more insistent on more perfectness (*i.e.* very close limits), although the parts shall be much better but it costs more. Therefore a permissible variation (which may not affect the quality of the product) is allowed so that parts will cost less to manufacture. The tolerance is, therefore, kept as fairly close, as to less tolerance would mean unnecessary large number of rejects, frequent machine setting, more inspections, more skilled operators, etc. Hence the tolerance is decided looking to the importance and the place where the part is to be used.
4. **Fewer Parts.** If extra facilities, features or parts can be reduced without effective much in use of the product but saves lot of money, then we can reduce the parts. This is known as simplification of the product. It is also better to keep minimum possible components in a product. A large number of components will reduce the reliability of product and there are much chances of failure of the production due to the failure of one or other component.
5. **Tool Design.** A compromise is made between the use of the new tool and the cost of the element of tool in the total cost of the product. That is, if the new tool is expensive then the products are manufactured with the help of existing tools and equipments whereas if we find that the purchase of new equipments will reduce the manufacturing cost, then we should definitely use the new tool or equipment.

   Here it is also pointed out that use of standard tools is better instead of special tools unless extraordinary circumstances arise.
6. **Make or Buy.** If any part of the product is found to be uneconomical to manufacture, it must be purchased from some other manufacturer producing it on large scale.
7. **Increase Productivity.** Main factor to reduce the process is 'by increasing the productivity, we must adopt
   (*a*) Work study techniques
   (*b*) Effective Production Planning and Control
   (*c*) Simplification and Standardisation
   (*d*) Develop good industrial relations etc.

Cost of Delays

Generally, we neglect the cost of delays, and we adopt measures for reduction in material cost, labour cost etc. Since time is money, saving in time not only increases productivity but also reduces delays in production schedules, commissioning of projects, availability of equipment for production etc., besides image and reputation of the company. Delays, can however be controlled bv adopting techniques like PERT/CPM.

33.15. TECHNIQUES OF COST CONTROL

1. Standard Costing
2. Inventory Control
3. Quality Control
4. Production Control
5. Reports and Return
6. Work-Study
7. Budget and Budgetary Control

1. **Standard Costing.** Standard costing is the preparation and use of standard costs, their comparison with actual costs and the measurements and analysis of variances to their causes and points of incidence. Standard costs are the costs that are obtained under efficient operations. They are predetermined costs and represents targets to control costs. The extent of success is measured by comparison of actual performance and standard performance.

   A standard cost must

   (*a*) be able to establish meaningful standard (may be in physical and monetary terms),

   (*b*) have a system for measuring actual quantities and costs, and

   (*c*) facilitate for corrective action.

2. **Inventory Control.** Inventory control may be defined as the systematic location, storage and recording of goods in such a way that desired degree of services can be made at the minimum cost. The necessity of inventory control is to maintain a reserve (store) of goods that will ensure manufacturing according to a production plan with the lowest possible ultimate cost. For details, topic on "Inventory Control" may be referred.

3. **Quality Control.** In simplest term, quality control is the control of quality during manufacturing. Whereas quality of any product is regarded as the degree to which it fulfils the requirements of the customer. Quality can be determined by some characteristics namely, design, size, material, chemical composition, mechanical functioning, workmanship, finishing and other properties. Quality of a product depends upon the application of materials, men, machine and manufacturing conditions. Systematic control of all these factors is the quality control.

   In the words of Alford and Beatly, "quality control" may be broadly defined as that industrial management technique by means of which products of uniform acceptable quality are manufactured. Quality control is concerned with the making things right rather than discovering and rejecting those made wrong.

   Now-a-days Statistical Quality Control technique is used as a means for quality control in the industries. Statistical quality control involves the statistical analysis of the inspection data obtained from samples. The quality in statistical quality control is usually related to measurements made of the items manufactured. A good quality item is an item which conforms to specified standard, and does not mean having highest standards of manufacture. Most desirable situation represents consistency in quality standards rather than the absolute standards.

4. **Production Control.** Production control is the design and use of a systematic procedure for established plan and controlling all the elements of an activity. Production control can also be defined as the process of planning the production in advance, setting the

exact route of each item, fixing the starting and finishing dates for each item, to give production orders to shops and lastly to follow-up the progress according to the production orders. The aim of production control is to produce the products of right quality, in the right quantity, at the right time, by using the best and least expensive methods.

Henri Fayol defines production as, "ensuring that all which occurs is in accordance with the rules established and the instructions issued". Production control rests on mechanism by means of which observations of current happenings are recorded and continuously compared with the planned production programme. Production control includes the control of activities, control over material movement, control over time, control of tool availability, control of quantity produced, control over workers efficiency.

For the purpose of effective production control, it is necessary to properly implement, routing, scheduling, despatching and followup.

5. **Reports and Returns.** As we know that during the process of production, delays may creep up either in material receipts, work in progress, assembly or erection etc. In order to know the point of delay and time of delay so that the follow-up can be done, certain reporting system should be introduced. The reporting system and returns should be so designed that the manager must not only take corrective action after a delay has occurred, but also anticipate and prevent before it actually develops, as we all know that, 'prevention is better than cure', and also that, 'a stitch in time saves nine'.

   A report in the form of tabular statements, charts comparing side by side is always preferred. Columns of the statement, charts and other factors to be reported alongwith the frequency should be designed considering the purpose for which reports are required. The speed with which information is produced is important where short-term decisions have to be made.

   The task of monitoring and control is simplified, if suitable formats are designed for each purpose. Principle of designing a format is that, it should be related to time, cost and other resources like manpower, equipment, and material, and should be properly presented so that it can be understood properly and quick decisions can be taken.

   Generally the reports are obtained for monitoring and control with following objects :

   (*i*) Comparing progress achieved with targets.

   (*ii*) Cost, incurred on each unit of production is to be compared with that of budget.

   (*iii*) To review the targets and time schedules for future, if necessary.

   (*vi*) Identify the deviations and short fall and determining the causes for initiating corrective action.

   (*v*) Record keeping. Information so received are recorded so as to use them in future, if so required.

6. **Work Study.** This technique consists of standardisation of method for performing a job on the basis of scientific study after critical evaluation of the existing and proposed methods. Certain standards are then developed and installed to compare the performance.

7. **Budget and Budgetary Control.** Budget is a tool of management for planning its future activities including estimate of sales, production, expenditure etc. Budget estimates are based on past experiences, present business conditions and expected future trends. Expected results are projected in financial terms or in numerical terms, like units of products, man hours, machine hours etc.

Budget provides predetermined standards of performance for the guidance of the efforts and activities in the business. As budgets provide standards of performance, they become the basis for control. Control used for the execution of budgets is what is called "Budgetary controls".

Budgetary control means application of control in relation to budgets. This is process of comparing the actual results with the corresponding budget data to know the actual as "the process which keeps the actual standard as nearly as possible to the predetermined standard by strict supervision and control".

33.16. COST REDUCTION TECHNIQUES

Cost reduction may be defined as, the real and permanent reduction in unit cost of goods manufactured or services rendered without affecting their suitability for the intended use.

Cost can be reduced in two ways firstly by enhancing management effectiveness, especially in the field of Material Planning, Inventory Control, Purchasing, Warehousing, Quality Control, Timely inspection and issue of materials, Packaging, Transporation of raw materials as well as finished product etc. Second way of reducing the cost is by following cost-reduction techniques.

Some of the most common cost-reduction techniques are.

1. Standardization.
2. Simplification (Variety reduction)
3. Value analysis (Values engineering)
4. Codification

These techniques have been discussed in the book at relevant places.

Steps for Cost Control and Cost-Reduction

Following essential steps are required to be taken for effective cost control and cost-redcution.

1. Inculcating an all round cost consciousness in the organisation.
2. Setting objectives and targets.
3. While setting standards and norms, scope of cost reduction is to be explored.
4. Decide priorities for attack to achieve quick results.
5. Control on consumptio as well as on block-up of capital is to be exercised.
6. Provide right climate to encourage creativity.
7. Reporting and monitoring system should be strengthened.

QUESTIONS

1. Explain in detail the various elements which go to make up the total cost of any product.
2. How would you calculate the cost of a finished product in a factory? Define and explain factory cost, manufacturing cost and selling cost.
3. How the total cost of product can be divided into different groups?
4. What are the different factors which affect the sales price?
5. State the principal elements of cost of a product and define each of them. Explain how you would collect cost figures in respect of each element.
6. How is the sale price of any product fixed?

7. Differentiate between fixed and variable costs. Mention whether following are either fixed or variable overheads, justify your answer.
   (*a*) Depreciation
   (*b*) Interest on capital
   (*c*) Operators charges
   (*d*) Fuel and lubricants
   (*e*) Supervisory charges
   (*f*) Salary of sweepers.
8. What do you understand by:
   (*a*) Primary cost
   (*b*) Factory cost
   (*c*) Sales price
   (*d*) Production cost
   (*e*) Total cost
9. Describe briefly with examples, the following terms:
   (*a*) Over heads
   (*b*) Direct material cost, and
   (*c*) Direct labour cost
10. What are the various 'Indirect Expenses' which are essential in estimating the total cost? Explain.
11. What is meant by a machine-hour rate for allocation of total cost? Explain how it is ascertained and point out how it differs from a labour-hour rate?
12. What is costing? What is use of standard cost? Give its advantages.
13. Describe various costing methods.
14. How the cost of a product is controlled?
15. Give the procedure of costing.
16. "Cost control and cost reduction are thoroughly inter-related". Discuss this statement.

Part–8 Miscellaneous

34 ENVIRONMENTAL POLLUTION AND CONTROL

34.1. INTRODUCTION

The word **'environment'** is taken from the Greek word 'Environ' which means surroundings or outside. In simple words 'Environment' refers to surroundings in which man lives and works.

F.J. Monkhouse defined environment as, "the whole sum of the surrounding external conditions within which an organism, a community or an object exists." Thus in simple words, we can say that environment is a surrounding external condition influencing development or growth of the people, animals or plants, living or working conditions etc.

Environment supplies required food, nutrient and energy, and other living conditions that may influence the organisms directly or indirectly. Environment is a complex of several things (air, water, light, soil, temperature etc.).

Our immediate concern is the quality of space we live in, the air we breathe, the food we eat, the water we drink and resources we draw from the environment to support our economy.

The types of plants and animals living in a particular region depend on the physical environment in that region. A change in physical environment brings about a change in biological environment or *vice-versa*.

Environmental Pollution

Here, environment comprises air, water and land. While, 'Pollution' means the act of destroying the purity or sanctity or making it foul or filthy. Therefore, in environmental pollution, we shall study the causes and acts of destroying the purity of air, water and land and their effect on ecology, *i.e.*, plants, animals, and human beings and measures to control their effects.

In short, environmental pollution may be described as the unfavourable alterations of our surroundings because of the acts and omission of men. Man's greed for quick economic gains has led to imbalance of this planet earth, thereby threatening the very survival of mankind. In our large and industrial towns, we are already experiencing the effects of air, water, soil and noise pollution which has already crossed the human tolerance.

34.2. ENVIRONMENTAL PROBLEMS

Environmental problems are innumerable and are divided into following categories:

1. Local Problems

   (*i*) Unsafe water

(ii) Accumulating urban garbage

(iii) Untreated sewage

(iv) Polluted urban air due to vehicular transport.

(v) Polluted indoor air due to smoke of fuelwoods, stove, smoking etc.

(vi) Noise pollution

2. Regional and National Environmental Problems.

(i) Polluting industries.

(ii) River pollution.

(iii) Deforestation.

(iv) Acid rain

3. Global Environmental Problems

(i) Accumulation of green house gases.

(ii) Dumping of chemical and nuclear waste into sea.

(iii) Ozone depletion.

Indian Environmental Problems

Indian environmental problems can be divided in following three categories:

1. **Problems arising out of lack of development.** Examples of these problems are deforestation due to fuelwood extraction, unhygienic slums, soil erosion, lack of sanitation and protected water supply. These problems intensify if the tempo of development is slow.
2. **Problems due to lack of environmental safeguards in development projects.** Examples of such problems are air and water pollution, hazardous waste disposal, waterlogging in irrigation projects, pesticide pollution, fertilizer runoff into streams etc. Sufficient investments are necessary in developing projects to compensate for environmental degradation.
3. **Problems related to global environment.** Examples of such problems are global warming, ozone depletion, marine pollution, loss of genetic diversity, automobile pollution etc

From the first two categories of problems, we observe that first is arising out of lack of development, and if we do not develop rapidly, these problems will overtake us. If we do not care for the environment, second category of problems will overwhelm us. Issues related to environment management must therefore be seen in this context.

For Indian scenerio after globalisation, only option with us is to have high levels of economic growth and a high degree of environmental protection. This is necessary to raise the income levels of the poor and protect our environmental resources.

34.3. ENVIRONMENTAL POLICIES

India is one of the few developing countries to have comprehensive environmental regulations, but the implementation of pollution control measures has been rather weak. After the Bhopal incident, Ministry of Environment and Forests (MOEF) reviewed the environmental regulations. The focus of regulatory changes were threefold, namely :

(a) Making the regulations more stringent.

(*b*) Enacting new statutes in areas where shortcomings existed.

(*c*) Reviewing existing laws.

Government of India brought out a comprehensive act in 1986, the environmental Protection Act. Government of India has also imposed restrictions and prohibitions on the expansion and modernisation of any activity or new projects being undertaken unless environmental clearance had been accorded. The Government has recently started emphasising the improving environmental quality. Following approach would help in reducing the discharges, emission and wastes and induce industrial units to inter nationalise the environmental improvement costs, namely:

1. A system of compensation for damages.
2. Improving the environmental monitoring system.
3. Reducing the enforcement cost.
4. Relaxation of industrial relocation policies to non-polluted areas.
5. Introducing emission or discharge analysis system.
6. Enforcement of reduction of pollutants at the source.
7. Introducing pollution based taxes.

Thus there is a need for harmonising of economic and environment policies so that enforcement of environmental quality norms are achieved. In this respect following suggestions are hereby recommended:

(*a*) Every project proposal must include Environmental Impact Assessment.

(*b*) For industrial self-regulation, industries could be asked to prepare detailed environmental audits or statements. These reports should be submitted on monthly basis.

(*c*) Pollution Control Boards, Industries Deptts and other major deptts should prepare area Environmental Plans to indicate perspective industrial location sites from long term point of view.

(*d*) Environmental health analysis.

(*e*) Inventory of pollution sources be prepared.

(*f*) More stress be given by Pollution Control Boards on environmental education.

34.4. AIR POLLUTION

Air pollution may be defined as the presence in the outdoor atmosphere of one or more contaminants or combination thereof in such quantities and of such duration as may be, or may tend to be injurious to human, plant or animal life, or property, or which unreasonably interfere with the comfortable enjoyment of life or property, or the conduct of business.

Atmosphere is a dynamic system, and absorbs various pollutants from natural as well as manmade sources, thus acting as a natural sink. Gases like CO, CO_2, H_2S, SO_2 and NO_2 as well as particulate matter such as sand and dust, are continously released into the atmosphere through natural activities such as forest fires, decaying of vegetation, winds and sand or dust-storms. Man-made pollutants, *e.g.*, CO, NO_2, CO_2, hydrocarbons, particulates are also released into atmosphere. Now a days the problem of airpollution has alarmingly increased due to population and other human activities. The pollutants are now-a-days enter the atmosphere at a faster rate than are absorbed by natural sink, thus accumulating in the air, and disturbing the equilibrium in the atmosphere, green house effect on global warming is outcome of excessive pollution.

The United Nations Conference on the Human Environment held at Stockholm in 1972, in which India also was a participant, and in that conference firm decisions were taken by various countries to take appropriate step for the preservation of the natural resources of the earth which, among other things, include the preservation of the quality of air and control of air pollution. In this background, the Air (Preservation and Control of Pollution) Act, 1981 was enacted by Government of India. The object of the Act is to provide for the prevention, control and abetment of air pollution. As per this act, "air pollution" means the presence in the atmosphere of any air pollutant, and "air pollutant" means any solid, liquid or gaseous substance including noise present in the atmosphere in such concentration as may be or tend to be injurious to human beings or other living creatures or plants or property or environement.

Common Air Pollutants

Following are the common air pollutants :

1. **Carbon Monoxide (CO)**: The atmospheric air contains 0.1 to 0.12 p.p.m. of *CO*. Major part of CO in the atmosphere is due to
   (*i*) Automobile exhausts (60%),
   (*ii*) Forest fires and agricultural burning (17%) and
   (*iii*) Industrial operations (10%).

   In cities, due to pollution, level of CO in atmosphere reaches even upto 55 ppm. Although soil microorganisms act as a major sink of CO from ambient atmosphere, still it exists significantly in the atmoshpere. Large CO producing areas have now very less soil sink available around them.
2. **Oxides of Nitrogen**: There are 8 possible oxides of nitrogen, but only N_2O, NO and NO_2 are common. These are 0.25 ppm, 0.1 to 2 ppm and 0.5 to 4 ppm respectively. NO and NO_2 are significant from air pollution point of view. These are formed in the combustion process at high temperatures and are converted to HNO. Level of these oxides is more in urban areas as compared to those of rural areas, and varies with the traffic intensity. Use of catalytic converters can minimize the level of these oxides. In industries also the level can be reduced by using a two stage combustion process.
3. **Sulphur Dioxide (SO_2)** : Combustion of any sulphur bearing material produces SO_2. 33% SO_2 emission is due to combustion of fuels, coal fired power houses, transport, refinery and metallurgical industries. The concentration of man-made SO_2 is in urban and industrial areas. SO_2 reacts with water vapour to produce droplets of H_2SO_4. This may cause extensive damage to materials, water, vegetation, stone, steel, paint, fishes etc. Reduction of SO_2 emission can be done by removing the sulphur content either before the fuel is burnt or during combustion or after combustion.
4. **Hydrocarbons**: These are emitted by natural biological activities, automobile exhaust, burning of coal, oil, wood refuse etc.
5. **Particulates**: Atmosphere contains several types of particles in varying sizes from 0.1 μ to 10 μ. These particles include dust, smoke, fog, ash etc. Dusts, mist, smoke, smog and fumes are the result of these. Particulates may also result due to combustion of coal, fuel etc. and from automobile exhausts. The particulates may enter the respiratory track and cause serious health hazards. The size and chemical characteristics of the particles are significant than their concentration. These are also capable of scattering light and.reducing the visibility.

34.5. SOURCES OF AIR POLLUTION

As explained earlier man made activities are mainly responsible for the air pollution. The main sources of air pollution are described hereunder :

(*A*) Fuel burning

(*B*) Industrial processes

(*C*) Automobile exhaust

Each of these sources are described here :

(*A*) Fuel Burning

These operations are performed for heat and power generation. The fuel burnt may be coal, gases, oil, refuse, wood etc. These are responsible for generating air pollution of the following types:

(*i*) **Smoke.** This is a product of incomplete combustion of coal, carbon monoxide, carbon dioxide etc.

(*ii*) **Dust.** It is finely divided powder and remains in atmosphere in floating condition. These are generated in large quantity in mining, quarrying, construction, cement industries etc.

(*iii*) **Fumes.** Solid particles generated by condensation from gaseous state, and often accompanied by a chemical reaction such as oxidation, are known as fumes.

(*iv*) **Gases.** These are formless fluids.

(*v*) **Smog.** This is a formation of heavy, cloudy, hazy, floating layer formed by the mixture of smoke, dust, fog, mist etc.

(*B*) Industrial Process

As mentioned earlier industries like cement, chemical, textile, thermal power stations, steel plants, oil refineries, fertilizers etc. are main contributors to air pollution. These are responsible for emitting harmful gases, fly ash, dust, soot.

With the proliferation of lead, mercury, oxides of nitrogen, ozone, cyanides, sulphur compounds etc. are responsible for health hazards and are increasing regularly. The workers working in mining, construction and cement industries have to inhale lot of dust and suffer from Asthama, Tuberculosis, Silicosia, Byssionosis etc.

(*C*) Automobile Exhaust

Most of the vehicles and construction equipment are operated by diesel engines and their exhaust is responsible for major air-pollution. The construction equipment may be either stationary equipment without prime mover like air compressors, diesel generating sets, concrete mixers, dewatering pumps or may be with prime movers, *e.g.*, dumpers, transit mixers, compactors, shovels, excavators, graders, loaders, pavers etc.

Automobile exhausts has following main constituents :

1. **Gases:** Carbon monoxide, nitric oxides, unburnt hydrocarbons, partial oxidation products.
2. **Particulates:** These include lead compounds, carbon and various other inorganic or organic materials.

Further more, additional hydrocarbons and fuel additives are contributed by the evaporation of gasoline from automobile tanks.

Emission from Diesel Engines.

Emission from diesel engine powered automobiles may be as follows :

Hydrocarbons	200-500 p.p.m.
Carbon monoxide	0.1 to 0.3%
Oxides of Nitrogen	2000 to 3000 p.p.m.

Pollutants and their Sources.

Pollutants and their sources of emission are :

Carbon Monoxide	→	Automobile exhaust
Sulphur dioxide	→	Oil burners
Nitric Oxide	→	Combustion
Nitrogen dioxide	→	Combustion
Ozone	→	Atmospheric photochemical reactions
Methane	→	Natural gas, decaying organic matter
Ethylene	→	Auto exhaust
Acetylene	→	Auto exhaust
Ammonia	→	Decaying organic matter
Hydrogen Sulphide	→	Decaying organic matter

Diesel Engine Combustion and Smoke

Complete mixing of air and diesel in the combustion chamber is virtually impossible due to variation in the engine load and the quantity of the injected fuel. Some overrich mixture is burnt in the deficiency of the oxygen, which results production of CO, hydrocarbons and NO_2. These are the pollutants emitted from automobiles in the form of smoke. Some fuel molecules undergo thermal decomposition and dehydrogenation and produce soot formation, which also effects the density of the exhaust smoke.

The diesel engines emit less amount of CO, hydrocarbons and NO_2 when well maintained. The engine exhaust:

(*a*) develops smog, reducing visibility and constituting a traffic hazard.

(*b*) irritates the eyes, throat and the lungs.

(*c*) is harmful for the food crops. The soot particles in the smoke spoil the building appearance.

(*d*) has a disagreeable odour.

Production of hydrocarbons, CO and NO_2 in combustion are explained hereunder :

(*i*) **Hydrocarbons.** These are the unburnt gasoline vapour coming out with the exhaust from the tail pipe. The main reason of these is the incomplete combustion of the fuel. They also occur due to fuel evaporation and crank case blow by. These depend upon combustion chamber design, air fuel ratio, load and mode of operation of the engine.

(*ii*) **Carbon Monoxide (CO).** Main reasons for carbon monoxide emission in the exhaust gases are the insufficient amount of air in the air fuel mixture and insufficient time available for complete combustion. Maximum amount of carbon monoxide is produced at the time of start, when supply of air is minimum.

(*iii*) **Oxides of Nitrogen NO_2** They are the combination of nitric oxide (NO) and nitrogen dioxide (NO_2). Increased combustion of fuel raises the temperature, and this increased temperature produces more nitrogen dioxide (NO_2). The NO_2 creates pollution problem when released in the atmosphere. The main factors which affect the formation of NO_2 are : combustion temperature, presence of oxygen spark advance and airfuel ratio. Increased spark advance produces high NO_2 concentration in the exhaust, where as the lean and rich mixtures produce low NO_2 concentration.

Noxious Gas Pollution

Combustion of fuel, may be in diesel engines or burners etc. produces carbon monoxide, oxides of nitrogen, sulphur dioxide. Sulphur dioxide is most harmful amongst them. If its intensity is more, it may cause choking sensation, affect respiratory system and damage the vegetation. Nitrogen dioxide is a Colourless gas and is highly irritating to eyes and lungs.

34.6. EFFECTS OF AIR POLLUTION

Air pollution has many adverse effects. It damages the building structures, materials, vegetations, causes health hazards and obstructs vision. The effects of air pollution can be categorised as:

(*a*) Effects on human health

(*b*) Effects on animals

(c) Effects on plants

(*d*) Effects on materials

(*e*) Effects on atmosphere.

(*A*) Effects on Human Health. Air pollution seriously affects the respiratory system. Carbon monoxide when absorbed into the lungs and reduces the haemoglobin availabe to carry oxygen to the body. This may cause injury to vital organs. Sulphur dioxide also causes cough, shortens breath and can cause irritation to the eyes. It when converted to sulphuric acid damages the lungs. It also helps in severe infections and allergic response. Even very low concentration of ozone can cause damage to the lungs. Hydrogen sulphide and other organic oxides can create odour problems. Hydrocarbons are believed to cause cancer in lung, whereas lead emitted by automobile exhausts is a cumulative poison and can cause brain damage.

Some of the chronic diseases due to exposure to polluted air are lung cancer, bronchitis, emphysema and asthma.

(*B*) Effects on Animals. The effects of air pollution due to its inhaling on animals are similar to those on human. Air pollutants also enter the animal body through ingestion of contaminated plant materials. Among the metallic contaminants, arsenic, lead and molybdenum are important. Air contaminated with ozone, floride effects the forage crops, which when eaten continuously by the animals, affects the animals adversely.

(*C*) Effects on Plants. As we know that leaf veins function as the transport system for water, minerals and food. The leaf tissues form cells in between them. Air pollution damages these leaf veins and tissues. The damage can be in the form of Necrosis (refers to dead areas on a leaf structure), Chlorosis (resulting in yellowing of the leaf), Abscission (dropping of leaves). When the absorption of sulphur dioxide exceeds a particular level, the cells become inactive and are killed, resulting in tissue collapse and drying of plants adversely. Chlorine, ammonia, hydrogen sulphide, and ethylene also affect the vegetations adversely. Smog also causes injuries to the plants and certain species are injured even with very small concentration of smog.

(*D*) Effects on Materials. Air pollution also adversely affects building structures and materials. Smoke, dust and oxides of sulphur are most destructive pollutants. Sulphur dioxide changes with moisture and air to sulphuric acid which is corrosive. Moisture, temperature, sunlight and air movement decide the rate of attack of pollutants. Aluminium, copper, iron and steel are corroded when exposed to contaminated air. Building structures are damaged/disfigured due to polluted air, sooty deposits, normal weathering.

(*E*) **Effects on Atmosphere.** Increased combustion of fossil fuels and oil, enchances the carbon dioxide concentration of the atmosphere. Carbon dioxide absorbs heat and the radiative cooling effect of the earth is thus decreased. CO_2 is the single culprit responsible for half of global warming. This is known as "greenhouse effect" and is expected to raise the planet's temperature between 1.5 and 4.5°*C* in about 60 years.

'Greenhouse' is a shield that keeps our planet warm enough to sustain life, but is now becoming a heat trap threatening to disrupt the global environment. A thin layer of certain gases, about 25 km like a greenhouse glass letting heat through but stopping enough radiation back into space to warm our world. But now "Greenhouse" layer is becoming denser; keeping in more heat.

34.6.1. Ozone Layer

Ozone layer is about 50-70 km above the earth's surface. The ozone shell acts as a fence protecting from the incoming harmful ultraviolet rays. It screens out about 99% of ultraviolet radiations from reaching the earth's surface. Chloroflouro carbons (CFCs) which are mainly used in air conditioning, refrigeration and jet propellsion are mainly responsible for depleting the ozone. Excessive ultravoilet light are harmful for skin causing skin cancers and genetic composition of man as well as plants.

34.7. PREVENTING AIR POLLUTON

In order to prevent air pollution following steps must be taken:

1. Every one of us must feel responsibility and take initiative immediately to prevent air pollution.
2. We should start planting trees, as they purify the air, and thus keep the sky clean. Trees breathe carbon dioxide and release oxygen. Forests act as vast sinks for carbon dioxide and tend to reduce global warming.
3. Curtail vehicular emission by using them to minimum possible, using fuel efficient engines, keeping vehicles in maintained condition. Conserve fuel, encourage mass transport, use cars in pools, monitor the fuel emission.
4. Polythene, plastic containers, polyurethane foams and P.V.C are eco-non-friendly items, therefore their use should be avoided, disposal of these plastics is not an easy task, as burning produces soot, corrosive gases and highly offensive odour.
5. Avoid using aerosol products (airconditioners, refrigerators etc.) as these have chloroflourocarbons (CFCs) which depletes the ozone umbrella.
6. Maximise use of solar energy and solar heaters, solar energy electric plants be encouraged.
7. Air pollution monitoring should be carried out regularly.
8. While preparing a project, environment management plan should be prepared for formation, implementation and monitoring of environmental protection measures during and after commissioning of projects.

9. Emission levels of pollutants from chimneys should conform to the pollution control standards prescribed by the central or state pollution control boards, for which necessary arrangements must be made. Generally used air cleaning devices are :
   (*a*) Electrostatic precipitators
   (*b*) Cyclone separators
   (*c*) Wet collectors
   (*d*) Gravity settlers
   (*e*) Bag filters
   (*f*) Cyclone filters
   (*g*) Wet scrubbers
   (*h*) Absorbers or Adsorbers
10. For indoor pollution, use proper ventilation so that used air or vitiated air gets removed by fresh air.

34.8. CONTROL OF AIR POLLUTION

A. **Control of Pollutants.** For the purpose of air pollution control, the pollution can be divided into following categories:
   1. Particulate control in chimnies.
   2. Particulate control in atmosphere.
   3. Dust control.

1. **Particulate control in chimnies.** Plants used in construction, cement industries, thermal powerplants etc. emit particulates through chimnies. These emit dusts of coal, stone, cement, lime sand etc. and combustion gases. The persons engaged on these plants and in nearby areas are badly affected by this type of pollution. These also adversely affect the nearby residential areas, and cultivated farm etc. Dust collectors are required to be installed with such plants to remove suspended particles from the chimney emission. The Dust Collectors are of several types, and their suitability is required to be decided depending upon the characteristics of the particulate.
2. **Particulate control in atmosphere.** In construction, cement, and mining industries thermal plant areas, coal, stone aggregates, ore, sand etc. are stored at site or plant areas. These should be maintained in such a condition so as to prevent dust from becoming wind borne while in storage or being handled, loaded or transported. Following steps may help in this respect:
   (*i*) Wetting of material to prevent dust becoming wind borne.
   (*ii*) Location of stock piles in an area, protected from prevailing winds.
   (*iii*) Installation of windbreaks, *i.e.*, trees, walls etc. to protect stockpiles from direct exposure to the prevailing winds.
   (*iv*) Storage of materials in bins, silos or any other type of enclosures.
   (*v*) Plant and plant areas should be cleaned regularly of accumulated dust, dirt etc.
3. **Dust Control.** Dust emitted due to haulage, working of heavy earth moving equipment etc. are needed to be controlled by adopting following measures:
   (*i*) Maintaining haul roads, moving the vehicles at reasonable speed, sprinkling water on unpaved haul roads.

(ii) Heavy earth moving equipments should be provided with cabins so as to protect the operators.

B. **Site Selection.** For installing an industry, it is necessory to select the site which will have minimum adverse effects on people, animals, agriculture etc.

C. **Control of Motor Vehicles Emission.** In order to control emission from motor vehicles proper maintenance including engine tuning, use of catalytic reactors etc. are necessary.

D. **Use of Latest Technology.** Equipments with latest technology, fuel efficient engines, plants with dust collectors etc, should be used so as to have better control over air pollution.

34.9. WATER POLLUTION

India is a country blessed with both perennial rivers and rivers with seasonal flow of water besides water sources in the form of lakes, ponds, sea inlets as well as a vast seashore which provide a source of livelihood for many. Over the years, the growth of industrial activity has tended to pollute the water courses making the water unsuitable for both drinking as well as for irrigation, besides rendering water unfit for the survival of fish and other aquatic living beings. Due to increasing tendency of urbanisation; it is essential to ensure that the domestic and industrial effluents are not allowed to be discharged into the water courses without adequate treatment.

The water (Prevention and Control of Pollution) Act 1974 enacted to provide for the prevention and control of water pollution and the maintaining or restoring of wholesomeness of water. As per this act, "water pollution" means such contamination of water or such alteration of the physical, chemical or biological properties of water or such discharge of any sewage or trade effluent or of any other liquid, gaseous or solid substance into water as may, or is likely to, create a nuisance or render such water harmful or injurious to public health or safety, or to domestic, commercial, industrial, agricultural or other legitimate uses, or to the life and health of animals or plants or of aquatic organisms.

In short, "Water Pollution" can be defined as the adverse change in composition or condition of water so that it becomes less suitable for the purposes for which it would be suitable in its natural state. These changes may be physical, chemical, biological or radioactive. Thus water pollution means addition of any thing to water which changes the natural quality of water so that people residing in downstream do not receive the natural water of the stream.

Sources of Water Pollution

There are large number of sources which pollute the water, but following are the main sources of water pollution:

1. **Sewage.** Raw or ill treated municipal or domestic sewage is generally poured into the rivers or canals. This may cause the water borne diseases like typhoid, cholera, dysentery, infections etc. sewage may seep into the empty water pipe due to which fungi, colonial bacteria etc. may flock in.
2. **Industrial Effluents.** Most industries pour their toxic and obnoxious effluents into rivers. These industrial effluents contain both organic and inorganic hazardous materials and nonbiodegradable materials. These when discharged into rivers, are injurious to public health and destroy many fishes and water birds in downstream. Mineral oil floats from the petroleum and natural gas drilling units into the rivers and oceans. Mine water also takes acidic water, ores etc.

3. **Agriculture and Fertilizers.** Fertilizers, insecticides, pesticides, herbicides used in agricultural practices leach into the rivers and canals. Fungicides employed in treating seeds have mercury compounds. Phosphates, nitrates and ammonium groups enter the water flow through the inorganic fertilizers, which are very harmful to human beings.
4. **Refuse and spoil heaps.** Underground water pollution occurs by the substances leached from refuse, spoil heaps and fertilizers spread over the land. This type of pollution is more serious due to difficulty in treatment of the polluted water.
5. **Pollution in Ocean.** Discharge of sewage and industrial effluents, discharge of sewage and rubbish from ships, transportation of oil and exploration of the sea bed also pollute the sea. Tons of plastic trash is dumped over board which is adversely affecting the life of sea animals. Apart from ship wrecks the offshore oil production is a major cause of spillage. These kill large number of sea birds or fishes etc.

Nature and Effects of Water Pollution

Water may have following contaminants:

(*i*) **Acids.** These can cause damage to metals or concrete structures pumps etc. due to their corrosive property. These also adversely affect the fishes and other aquatic animals.

(*ii*) **Alkalis.** Like acids, these also adversely affect the fishes and other aquatic animals.

(*iii*) **Dyes.** These are found from the discharge of effluents from dyeing and printing industries, textile industries, paper and ink manufacturing industries etc. these impart colours and create aesthetic problems.

(*iv*) **Fats, Soaps and Waxes.** These produce unpleasant odours.

(*v*) **Gaseous pollutants.** Presence of excess amount of free chlorine in rivers as,

(*a*) It is a powerful irritant

(*b*) It causes a disease of the lungs of man

(*c*) It destroys the aquatic life

(*d*) It is corrosive.

Presence of hydrogen sulphide causes odour nuisance, respiratory problems, irritation, and is lethal to fishes. Presence of ozone is highly toxic to fish. Carbon dioxide and carbon monoxide are also harmful to the fishes.

(*vi*) **Pesticides.** These are harmful for men as well as fishes.

(*vii*) **Toxic Metals.** Lead, arsenic, copper, cadmium, mercury, nickel etc. are toxic to living organisms. These kill the aquatic plants and animals. These prevent the use of water for drinking purposes.

(*viii*) **Oils.** Fuel oils create the aesthetic problems, reaeration of water is affected. The oil coat the gills of fish and thus affect respiration of fish. This spoils the beaches making bathing impossible in such places.

34.10. SEWAGE TREATMENT

The object of sewage treatment is to remove Biochemical Oxygen Demand (*BOD*), phosphorus, nitrogen, solids and bacteria. It is necesary for converting a raw and harmful sewage into an acceptable. effluent.

The treatment processes are divided into following three groups :

1. **Primary Treatment.**

This has a mechanical process and includes screening, grinding, flocculation and sedimentation. Screening removes larger suspended and floating materials. Grinders have cutting teeth used to chop the solid material into smaller pieces. Flocculation is an agitation process which makes the smaller suspended particles to form flocks so that they can settle out rapidly. In sedimentation, the suspended solids are removed by gravitational settling. The primary treatment reduces 60 percent of the total suspended solids, 35 percent BOD, 20 percent Chemical Oxygen Demand (COD) and 10 percent of nitrogen and phosphorous.

2. **Secondary Treatment.**

   This is a biological process when the wastes are fed onto trickling filter beds, they trickle or percolate over the stones (or other filling materials of the beds). In activated sludge process, biologically active growth are continuously circulated through organic waste in the presence of oxygen. Aeration activates the sludge particles. Secondary treatment reduces 90 percent BOD, 80 percent *COD*, 50 percent of total nitrogen, 30 percent of total phosphorous and 90 percent of suspended matter.

3. **Tertiary Treatment.**

   These are the advanced biological, chemical and physical processes. This method is used for purification of waste water, and also in the recycling of waste water. This method is more efficient for removal of pollutants. This treatment is carried out in following steps:

   (*a*) **Chemical Coagulation and Filtration.** In this, chemical coagulants like alum and ferrous sulphate react with suspended matter to form flocks which settle out rapidly. Thereafter filtration is done.

   (*b*) **Adsorption.** This process is used for removing odours. Activated carbon (porous carbon) is used as adsorbing material.

   (*c*) **Chemical Oxidation.** In order to get pure water, waste water is oxidised by using ozone or hydrogen peroxide.

   (*d*) **Desalination.** This process removes the dissolved substances. For this purpose ion exchange, reverse osmosis and electro dialysis techniques may be employed.

   (*e*) **Oxidation Ponds.** In this process, organic matters are decomposed by bacteria and are consumed by algae.

34.11. TREATMENT OF WATER

Water whether from underground or from surface source found in nature are polluted. This water can not be supplied directly for drinking purposes due to aesthetic, physiological, transmission of water borne diseases etc. Natural water may also have decaying leaves, vegetations or animals, minerals in soluble or suspended state. For all these reasons water requires treatment. It must be free from germs of diseases, unpleasant tastes and odours. Degree and methods of treatment depend on the nature of source, quality of water and purpose for which it is required.

Various treatment methods and the impurities removed by them are given hereunder :

Process	*Impurity Removed*
1. Screening	Floating matter
2. Plain sedimentation	Large suspended solids
3. Coagulation	Fine particles
4. Aeration	Tastes, odour, oxygen defficiency
5. Filtration	Colloidal particles, micro organisms
6. Activated carbon	Elements causing tastes and odours

7. Softening	Hardness
8. Disinfection	Living organisms

It is not necessary to adopt all the above mentioned processes. Selection of treatment process depend on the quality of water available at the source and that required for the purpose. Ground water is free from suspended solids, but often cause problems due to hardness.

34.12. PREVENTION OF WATER POLLUTION

Water pollution can be prevented by adopting following actions:

(*i*) Each drop of water is precious, save it.

(*ii*) Use kitchen wastes to make organic fertilizers, as these are more beneficial compared to the inorganic ones.

(*iii*) Recycle the effluents. Heavy metals could be recovered from the industrial effluents.

(*iv*) Keep away spraying pesticides. Use of neem leaves be encouraged.

(*v*) Use biomass for generating electricity.

(*vi*) Waste water treatment processes, should be adopted.

(*vii*) Garbage should be dumped in selected areas and use garbage compactors. Solid wastes should be sent for recycling.

(*viii*) Avoid using polybags, encourage use of cloth or canvas bags.

34.13. WASTE MANAGEMENT

Waste is defined as every substance or object arising from human or animal activities, that has to be discarded as useless or unwanted. Waste can be any trash, rubbish (combustible or noncombustible), garbage, refuse, filth, bottles, glass crockery, cans, cartons, scrap metal, junked vehicles, appliances or hardware, waste soil, rock, construction material, animal carcasses, sludge from a waste treatment plant or discarded matter or any industrial, commerical, mining, agricultural or other waste.

Waste matter is classified as solid, liquid or sludge based on its consistency, and hazardous or nonhazardous based on whether or not they have properties as ignitability, reactivity and leachable toxic components or are bio-hazards.

Category	*Source of generation*
1. Municipal solid waste	– Residential – *Commercial*: Hotel restaurants, market, shoping complexes etc – *Open area:* Recreation areas, parks, playgrounds etc.
2. Industrial waste	– Chemicals, textile by-products etc.
3. Agriculture waste	– Agriculture by-products, residues etc.
4. Hazardous waste	– Chemicals, oil from refineries waste from ordnance and fire work – *Hospitals* : Bio-medical waste.

Waste Management is the collection, transportation, processing, and disposal of waste material in an effort to reduce their effect on human health or local aesthetics. A subfocus in recent decades has been to reduce waste materials' effect on the natural world and the environment.

Managing domestic, industrial and commercial waste has traditionally consisted of collection, followed by disposal. Some of the common methods for effective waste management are:

1. Sanitary landfills.
2. Composting.
3. Incineration.
4. Reduction in wastage.
5. Reusing.
6. Recycling.

The Municipal Solid Waste (Management and Handling) Rules, 2000 framed under Environmental (Protection) Act, 1986 by the Ministry of Environment and Forests, Government of India provides requirements for solid waste management.

34.13.1. Municipal Wastes

These wastes can be classified as :

1. **Rubbish :** These include both combustible and noncombustible substances, such as paper, scrap material, broken glass, wood, cardboard, cans etc. Scattered rubbish creates nuisance.
2. **Garbage :** These are the wastes resulted from food products, such as cooked and uncooked vegetables, rotten fruits etc. These give rise to flies and other insect problems besides unpleasant odour.
3. **Refuse :** These are the all sorts of solid wastes from a community. Such wastes include garbage, rubbish, ashes, dead animals, industrial wastes, etc.

Removal and disposal of refuse is a very important aspect and becoming a challenging problem. This aspect should be well planned.

Collection and Disposal of Refuse

Refuse collection is generally divided into two categories, namely primary collection and secondary collection.

Primary collection involves delivery of the wastes by the house holders to community storage. Dust bins kept at each house are unloaded to wheel barrows or rickshaws, from where it is taken to community storage bins of 1 to 2 m^3 capacities at intervals of 50 to 100 metres.

Secondary collection and transportation to the disposal sites is often done by heavy motor vehicles. Heavy motor vehicles may be flat body trucks, tipping trucks, container carrier system, dumper placer etc. The refuse should be dumped into sanitary refills to avoid making it a breeding ground of mosquitoes, flies etc. These refuse are placed in trenches or low lying areas in layers of about 1.5 metres, covering each layer by about 20 cms of earth. The area till covered, should be sprayed with solution of creosote or paraffin.

34.13.2. Industrial Wastes

The waste from industry to industry vary and hence require different method of treatment. Characteristics and type of treatment required for waste of different industries are given below:-

Type of Industry	*Pollution characteristics*	*Method of treatment suggested*
Paper and Pulp	High BOD, Alkaline and Sodium contents	Biological treatment chemical and lime treatment.
Tannery	High BOD, salt, lime, sulphide solids and colour	Biological and chemical treatment.
Sugar cane	High BOD, volatile solids, low pH	Biological treatment.
Petrochemical/oil, refinery	Oil, High BOD, Solids, oil greases	Chemical and Biological treatment, Oil separative grease trapping.
Fertilizer	High Nitrogen	Biological treatment.

34.14. ODOUR CONTROL

Use of high sulphur content fuels produce unpleasant odour. In addition to diesel engines, such fuels are used in hot-mix asphalt plant either (*i*) in coating of asphalt mix carrying vehicle bodies by kerosene, which would be avoided by using other compounds, or (*ii*) as burner fuel, where low sulphur content fuels should be used. The odour can also be controlled by (*i*) producing asphalt mix of temperature, as low as possible, and (*ii*) by getting effective combustion of fuel.

Types of Odours

Odours can be classified into following groups :

(*i*) Spicy e.g. cloves
(*ii*) Flowery e.g. geranium, rose
(*iii*) Fruity e.g. oil of orange
(*iv*) Resinous e.g. turpentine or eucalyptus oil
(*v*) Burnt e.g. tar
(*vi*) Foul e.g. sulphuretted hydrogen.

Odour Control Methods

Odour can be controlled in two ways :

1. Reducing the source, diluting the odour by greater dispersal, removing the odour from a gas stream by absorption, adsorption, or by oxidation, or chemically converting the odourous product to one less odorous.
2. Hiding the original odour by introducing a more powerful pleasing odour, or by modifying the original odour.

34.15. NOISE POLLUTION

Noise may be defined as unwanted sound at a wrong time and at wrong place. Generally prolonged and loud sound is considered as noise. Meaningful sound is generally meant for inviting attention or expecting a consequent response, such as the cry of a baby. Sounds when soft, rhythmic and for short duration are acceptable, but they are unacceptable when loud, random or prolonged. Excessive noise can result in loss of hearing, increase in accidents decrease productivity.

It is, therefore, necessary to reduce noise pollution particularly in urban and industrial areas. Level of sound from certain sources is indicated hereunder :

Source	*Sound level, decibal, dB*
Launching space rocket	170
Jet plane take off	150
Pneumatic riveter	130
Running motor cycle	118
Farm tractor	98
Heavy city traffic	85
Average city traffic	70
Normal conversation	60
Business office	50
Library	35
Rustling of leaves	10

Effects of Sound at Different Levels are :

135 dB	Painful
110 dB	Discomfortable
88 dB	Hearing impairment on prolonged exposure
65 dB	Intrusive

(*a*) **Physiological Effects.** Immediate permanent hearing impairment may be caused at high levels of about 150 dB. Sound levels in the range of 120-150dB, effects on respiratory system, dizziness, loss of physical control, and other changes due to stress, nausea, and vomiting may be caused. Even sounds of the level of 70 dB may have measurable physiological effects.

(*b*) **Psychological and Other Effects.** Deterioration in concentration and even mental disorientation have been noticed at high noise levels, though temporarily. Loud continous noise reduces the working efficiency, interferes with communication, increases the frequency of errors in working which may even cause accidents.

Noise Pollution in Construction Industry

High level noises are created in the plants due to collision or friction of metal against metal, aggregate against aggregate, and metal against aggregate, movement of compressed air into the atmosphere, and the combustion of fuel in the burner. Areas of high level noises are:crushers, burners, blowers, exhaust fans, pug mills. Operators in most plants are, therefore, housed in cabin, where exposure level to noise is reduced. If an employee is required to work near plant area without cabin, it should be for shorter durations, as prolonged exposure in excessive noise is irritating, produce mental fatigue and reduce the efficiency of persons around the plants, especially asphalt plants where noise level is too high.

Approaches for Noise Control

Following are the main approaches which are used for noise control

1. Modify the present practices and procedure so as to minimise the noise level, *e.g.*, use of welding instead of riveting,
2. Shielding the source of noise generation, *e.g.*, use of sound absorbing motor mountings, better installations, better design, use of enclosures for motors, use of vibration damping etc. Regular maintenance also help in reducing the noise level. Sound absorption, sound insulation and vibration control also help in transmitting the noise from the source. The paths of noise transmission may be through structure of machinery; surface and panels attached to the source; cables, conduits, wires, pipes, ducts, belts etc.
3. Shielding the noise receiver, *e.g.*, using carefully earplug, earmuff, helmets, control cabins etc. Wherever noise level can not be reduced, the persons working in high noise level are need be protected.

Methods of Noise Control

As discussed above, depending upon the circumstances noise can be reduced upto some extent by using baffles, sound proof materials, by doing proper maintenance and lubrication, mounting the noise and vibration source on flexible supports, providing conveyors to avoid fall of material on metals from height.

Industrial noise control methods include following steps :

(*i*) replacing noise producing machinery with quiet alternatives,

(*ii*) interrupting the path with insulating material,

(*iii*) follow the noise control approaches as described above and

(*iv*) protecting the workers by providing earmuffs.

Community noise is mainly due to air traffic, highway traffic and construction activities. To control these noises flight paths are diverted from populated areas to other areas. The highway traffic causes noise due to noise of exhaust, engine, tire, gears and transmission and aerodynamic (wind) noise. Modern cars are being made to produce less noise, but heavy vehicles still produce too much noise. The solution to this problem is only to have highways away from populated areas, designing non stop operations, smooth traffic flow.

Now-a-days noise is also produced by sources responsible for luxuries like TVs, stereos, orchestra, loudspeakers, fireworks, generators, coolers, airconditioners, mixers and grinders, washing machines etc. These noises can only be controlled or contained by public awareness.

Trees are supposed to be the best for noise control. More and more trees should be planted along the roads, rail tracks and around the aerodromes. These should be planted in plenty in colonies, hospitals, school campuses etc. to protect the people from noise pollution from outside.

34.16. FUNCTIONS OF POLLUTION CONTROL BOARDS

Pollution Control Boards are constituted as per powers delegated under the provisions of Air (Prevention and Control of Pollution) Act, 1981. Refer section 34.17.1.

(*i*) Developing, regulating, guiding and leading the environmental movement.

(*ii*) Encourage polluting industries to set up pollution control equipment.

(*iii*) Framing of rules for waste management.

(*iv*) To create awareness for automobile pollution control.

(v) River cleanup action plans.

(vi) Setting and enforcing standards for air quality.

Other functions of pollution control boards have been mentioned in article 3.17.1.

34.17. LEGISLATION ON POLLUTION

Government of India has adopted various legislations related to various environmental aspects, from time to time, some of the main legislations are :

1. Water (Prevention and Control of Pollution) Act passed in 1974.
2. Air (Prevention and Control of Pollution) Act passed in 1981.
3. Establishment of Pollution Control Boards through Water Act.
4. Environment (Protection) Act. A comprehensive legislation passed in 1986, is meant for total protection of the environment.
5. Forest (Conservation) Act 1980.
6. The Wild life (Protection) Act,1972.

Government of India has also issued following policy statements with an idea of'integrated natural resource management' and 'ecological units of planning' for land use :

1. National Conservation Strategy.
2. Policy Statement on Environment and Development.
3. Policy Statement for Abetement of Pollution.
4. National Forest Policy, 1988.

Because of handful of polluters, the entire humanity is suffering and people are being deprived of their legitimate right of clean environment. Environmental problems like polluted water, dirty air, too much noise, are the major cause of millions of deaths and illnesses across the globe.

Today, it is unfortunate that man has forgotten that he is a product of his environement and all his social, moral, spiritual, health and economic wellbeing depends on his harmony with nature only. Despite greater awareness and debate about the disastrous consequences of environmental destruction, people all over the world continue to plunder the global environment.

Therefore, realising the need for strict enforcement of environment and human rights laws to protect and preserve the basic rights of the people; and also to save the present and succeeding generations from the scourage of pollution and to protect their dignity, the above mentioned Acts have been enacted by the Government.

The objective of these Acts is the improvement of environment and the prevention of hazards to human beings, other living creatures, plants and property.

In order to achieve the desired objective and to have better enforcement of laws, the knowledge based on environmental law has to be broadened and all the environmental protection laws should be brought under one umbrella and laws for deterrent punishment need to be enacted for criminals destroying the environment for their personal gains. Further, the laws need simplification which will encourage compliance.

34.17.1. Air (Prevention and Control of Pollution) Act, 1981.

The origin of the Act lies in the United Nations Conference on the Human Environment held in Stockholm in 1972, in which India also was a participant, in which decisions were taken to take appropriate steps for the preservation of the natural resources of earth including the preservation of the quality of air and control of air pollution.

The object of the Act is to provide for the prevention, control and abatement of air pollution, for the establishment of Pollution Control Boards. The Boards are established with a view to carry out the aforesaid purposes. The Act confers and assign to such Boards powers and functions relating there to and for matters connected there with.

Central Pollution Control Board, and State Pollution Control Boards have been constituted under Section 3 and Section 4 respectively of the Act.

Functions of Central Pollution Control Board.

Main funtions are:

1. To improve the quality of air and to prevent, control or abete air pollution in the country.
2. Advise the Central Government on any matter concerning the improvement of the quality of air and the prevention, control or abatement of air pollution.
3. Plan and cause to be executed through a nation-wide programme for the prevention, control or abatement of air pollution.
4. Coordinate the activities of the State Boards and resolve disputes among them.
5. Provide technical assistance and guidance etc. to the State Boards.
6. Plan and organise the training of persons engaged or to be engaged in programmes.
7. To perform other functions as mentioned in para 34.16.

Functions of State Boards

Main Funtions of State Pollution Control Boards:

1. To plan a comprehensive programme for the prevention, control or abatement of air pollution and to secure the execution thereof.
2. To advise the State Government on any related matter.
3. To collect and disseminate information relating to air pollution.
4. To collaborate with the Central Board in organising the training.
5. To inspect air pollution control areas at such intervals as it may think necessary.

34.17.2. Water (Prevention and Control of Pollution) Act, 1974.

India is a country blessed with both perennial rivers and rivers with seasonal flow of water besides water sources in the form of lakes, ponds, sea inlets as well as a vast sea-shore which provide a source of livelihood for many. Over the years, the growth of industrial activity has tended to pollute the water courses making the water unsuitable for both drinking as well as for irrigation, besides rendering water unfit for the survival of fish and other aquatic living beings. Consequently it was decided to enact a law on the subject.

The water (Prevention and Control of Pollution) Act, 1974 is an Act to provide for the prevention and control of water pollution and the maintaining or restoring of wholesomeness of water, for the establishment of Boards for the prevention and control of water pollution. The Pollution Control Boards were established with a view to carrying out the purposes aforesaid. The Act confers on and assign to such Boards powers and functions relating thereto and matters connected therewith.

Functions of Central Pollution Control Board

Main functions are:

1. To promote cleanliness of streams and wells in the different areas of the States.
2. Advise the Central Government on any matter concerning the prevention and control of water pollution.
3. Coordinate the activites of the State Boards and resolve disputes among them.
4. Provide technical assistance and guidance etc to the State Boards on the subject.
5. Plan and oragnise the training of persons engaged or to be engaged in programmes.

Functions of State Pollution Control Boards.

As per Act, these boards have following main functions.

1. To plan a comprehensive programme for the prevention, control or abatement of pollution of the streams and wells in the State and to secure the execution thereof.
2. To advise the State Government on any concerned matter.
3. To collect and disseminate information relating to water pollution.
4. To encourage, conduct and participate in investigations and research relating to this aspect.
5. To collaborate with the Central Board in organising the training of persons engaged or to be engaged in related programmes.

QUESTIONS

1. What do you understand by "environmental pollution"? Explain in detail.
2. Write an essay on "Ecology and Industrial Development".
3. (*a*) What are the major environmental problems?
   (*b*) What is ecology?
4. Define Air Pollution. Explain in detail about common air pollutants.
5. What are major sources of air pollution? Explain them in brief.
6. What are the effects of air pollution? Explain each of them.
7. Describe ozone layer. Explain steps to be taken for preventing air pollution.
8. How the air pollution can be controlled? Explain in detail.
9. Define water pollution. What are the sources of water pollution? What are the major contaminants of water?
10. Write an essay on "Treatment of Water".
11. What are municipal wastes? How they can be collected and disposed of?
12. Explain in detail about Industrial Wastes.
13. Explain "Noise Pollution" in detail.
14. Write short notes on:
    (*a*) Odour Control
    (*b*) Methods of noise control
    (*c*) Major Legislations related to various environmental aspects.

APPENDIX:
ISO-9000 : A QUALITY MANAGEMENT SYSTEM

1.1. INTRODUCTION

ISO is the **International Organisation for Standardization**. It is located is Switzerland and was established in 1947 to develop common international standards in many areas. Its members come from over 130 national standards bodies. ISO first published its quality standards in 1987, revised then in 1994, and then re-published an updated version in 2000. Standards presently applicable are known as **"ISO-9000 : 2008 Standards"**, and facilitate international trade by providing a single set of standards that people everywhere would recognise and respect.

ISO-9000 refers to a set of standards and is the only available internationally accepted standard for quality management system in the world. It is rapidly becoming the most important quality standard and hundreds of thousands companies in over 100 countries have already adopted it. ISO-9000 is applicable to all types of organisations in manufacturing or service sectors. It is a documentation-oriented system which allows complete freedom on selection and use of process and framing of operating procedures and work instructions. This is a widely recognised quality management tool and meet the quality requirements of every kind of products or services. Production of consistently good quality product or service is very important for customer confidence and higher positioning of buyer perception. Every conscious company who wants to survive and grow, have either adopted this standard or in the process of adopting it.

A properly established quality management system will help to reduce cost, improve quality, develop confidence and a good image in the minds of customers and public. This requires consistent implementation, careful auditing and total commitment of the whole organisation.

The second revision of ISO-9000 series, known as ISO-9000 : 2000 does not include the term 'Quality Assurance'. This reflects the fact that the quality management system requirements specified in this edition, in addition to quality assurance of product, also aim to enhance customer satisfaction.

The ISO-9000:2000 have been adopted as Indian standard without deviations by the Bureau of Indian Standards (BIS)., and this is referred as "IS/ISO. 9000 : 2000 Quality management systems". BIS has now adopted the latest version ISO-9000:2008 (discussed in the end of this chapter).

The adoption of quality management system by any organisation should be a strategic decision. The design and implementation of an organisation's quality management system is influenced by varying needs. The quality management principles stated in ISO-9000 and ISO-9004 of 1994 have been taken into consideration during the development of this International standard.

This International standard promotes the adoption of a process approach when developing, implementing, and improving the effectiveness of a quality management system, to enhance customer satisfaction by meeting customer requirements.

An activity using resources, and managed in order to enable the transformation of inputs into outputs, can be considered as a process. Often the output from one process directly forms the input to the next. The application of a system of processes within an organisation, together with the identification and interactions of these processes, and their management, can be referred to as the "process approach".

ISO-9000 set of standards are **"generic management system standards"**. This means that the same standards can be applied:

- to any organisation, large or small, whatever its product;
- including whether its "product" is actually a service;
- in any sector of activity; and
- whether it is a business enterprise, a public administration, or a government department.

The "ISO-9000 quality management system" adopting organisations fulfill:

- the customer's quality requirements ;
- applicable regulatory requirements ;
- enhance customer satisfaction ; and
- achieve continual improvement of its performance.

Many companies require their suppliers to adopt ISO-9000 and get registered. Registered companies find that their market opportunities have increased, as it ensures a sound quality management system. Registered companies had reduction in customer complaints, significant reductions in operating costs and increased demand for their products and services. Other benefits can include better working conditions, increased market share, and increased profits.

Aims of ISO - 9000

To provide for development of quality system to achieve:

(d) Quality for products or services, and

(e) Customer satisfaction.

Areas of Application

1. Marketing
2. Design and development
3. Procurement
4. Production
5. Quality Assurance
6. Packaging and storage
7. Sales and distribution
8. Servicing

Who Can Adopt ISO-9000?

1. Manufacturing organisations:

    (d) Product manufacturing industries

    (e) Processing industries.

2. Service Organisations :
   (d) Technical - Consultancy, design, engineering, testing etc.
   (e) Professional - Legal, security, training, management etc.
   (f) Hospitability - Catering, hotels, tourism etc.
   (g) Banking - Insurance, banking, portfolio management etc.
   (h) Transportation - Airlines, rail, road, sea travels.
   (i) Health - Hospitals, nursing homes, laboratories etc.
   (j) Communication - Postal, Telecommunication.
   (k) Government - Police, Taxation, public administration, public services etc.

1.2. HISTORY AND ORIGIN OF ISO-9000

After issuing several inspection system documents in the 1950's, the U.S military later integrated them into a set of requirements documents and issued them in December, 1963 with the names of Lqvshfwlrq#V|vwhp#Uhtxluhphqwv#dqg#Txdolw|#Surjudpph#Uhtxluhphqwv1 Thereafter, documents issued were on standard clauses in procurement, contracts, required control over final inspection and testing; and then on Fdoleudwlrq#V|vwhp#Uhtxluhphqwv. Similarly, Canadian series of standards were issued in four levels in the mid 1970's ; and the British standard was issued in three levels in 1979 as quality management systems.

In the meantime, in December, 1979, the United States issued Generic Guidelines for quality systems. This was a menu of quality management elements, and each organisation could choose the elements they felt were helpful, allowing them for almost infinite degree of tailoring.

Since different standards for different countries were creating problems to international trade, necessity was felt for developing internationally recognised quality management standards. The ISO Technical Committee (TC -176) was, therefore, constituted, which had its first meeting in 1980, and issued its first standard ISO 8402 regarding "Quality System - Vocabulary". Thereafter, in 1987, they issued ISO-900.1, 9002 9003 and 9004. These standards were later on revised in 1994, and then extensively revised in the year 2000. This was then modified in 2008.

Before going into the details of ISO-9000 series of standards, we shall first discuss the term "standard" and "standardisation".

Standard. A standard is defined as a document, established by consensus and approved by a recognised body, that provides ; for common and repeated use, rules, guidelines or characteristics for activities or their results, aimed at the achievement of the optimum degree of order in a given context.

Standardization. A standardisation is an activity consisting of the process of formulating, issuing and implementing standards.

1.3. ADVANTAGES (NEEDS) OF ISO-9000

It is widely acknowledged that proper quality management improves business, often having a positive effect on investment, market share, sales, sales growth, sales margins, competitive advantage, and avoidance of litigation. The quality principles in ISO 9000:2000 are also sound,and

ISO 9000 guidelines provide a comprehensive model for quality management systems that can make any company competitive. Implementing ISO often gives the following advantages:

1. Creates a more efficient, effective operation
2. Increase customer satisfaction and relation
3. Reduces audits
4. Improves marketing
5. Improves employee motivation, awareness, and morale
6. Promotes international trade
7. Increases profit
8. Reduces waste and increases productivity
9. Common tools for standardization.
10. Reduction in Scrap, re-work, and non-conformities.
11. Reduction in breakdowns and downtimes.
12. Reduction in claims of nonconforming product, and returned product.
13. Improvements in on-time deliveries

Against above benefits, there is only one negative side, i.e., increase in the prevention and appraisal costs.

1.4. ISO-9000:2000 SET OF STANDARDS

ISO-9000 currently includes three quantity standards : ISO-9000 : 2000, ISO-9001 : 2000 and ISO-9004: 2000. In these standards ISO-9001 : 2000 presents requirements, while ISO-9000 : 2000 and ISO-9004 : 2000 presents guidelines. All of these are process standards (not product standards). The certificate is awarded to an organisation in respect of compliance of standards ISO-9001 : 2000.

Following standards currently make up the ISO-9000 family :

Standards and Guidelines	*Purpose*
ISO-9000 : 2000, Quality Management Systems – Fundamentals and Vocabulary.	For understanding the standards and defines the fundamental terms and definitions used in the ISO-9000 family.
ISO-9001 : 2000, Quality Management Systems – Requirements	This is the requirement standard used to assess the ability to meet the customer and applicable regulatory requirements and thereby, address customer satisfaction. It is now the only standard in the ISO-9000 family against which third-party certification can be granted.
ISO-9004 : 2000, Quality Management Systems - Guidelines for performance improvements	This guideline standard provides guidance for continual improvement of quality management system to benefit all parties

From the given table, it is clear that in order to develop a quality management system, you are required to only meet the requirements specified by ISO - 9001:2000. You can consult the ISO-9000 : 2000 and ISO - 9004 : 2000 guidelines only when you need clarification. Your quality management system must simply meet requirements, as specified in ISO-9001: 2000. When your quality system has been fully developed and implemented, you carry out an internal assessment to ensure that you have met every single ISO-9001 : 2000 requirement. When you are ready, you ask an external auditor to audit the effectiveness of your quality management system. If your auditors find that you have introduced and implemented the ISO-9001: 2000 standard, they will certify that your quality system has met ISO's requirements, will then issue an official certificate to you and will record your achievement in their registry. You can then announce to the world that the quality of your products and services is managed, controlled, and assured by a registered ISO-9001: 2000 Quality Management System.

1.5. QUALITY MANAGEMENT PRINCIPLES–ISO - 9000 : 2000

ISO - 9000:2000 standards are based on eight quality management principles. ISO choose these principle because they can be used to improve organisational performance and achieve success. These principles can be used by senior management as a framework to guide their organisation towards improved performance. The eight quality management principles, as given in the ISO -9000: 2000, Quality management systems – Fundamentals and Vocabulary; and in ISO -9004: 2000, Quality management systems – Guidelines for performance improvements are:

Principle 1 : Focus on your Customers

Organisations depend on their customers. Therefore:

- Organisations must understand customer needs.
- Organisations must meet customer requirements.
- Organisations must exceed customer expectations.

Principle 2 : Provide Leadership

Organisations rely on leaders. Therefore :

- Leaders must establish a unity of purpose and set the direction the organisation should take.
- Leaders must create an environmental that encourages people to achieve the organisation's objectives.

Principle 3 : Involvement of People.

People at all levels are the essence of an organisation and therefore:

- Organisations must encourage the involvement of people at all levels.
- Organisations must help people to develop and use their abilities.

Principle 4 : Use a Process Approach

Organisations are more efficient and effective, when they use a process. Therefore:

- Organisations must use a process approach to manage activities and related resources.

Principle 5 : Take a System Approach

Organisations are more efficient and effective, when they use a systems approach. Therefore:

- Organisations must identify inter-related processes and treat them as a system.
- Organisations must use a systems approach to manage their inter-related processes.

Principle 6 : Encourage Continual Improvement

Organisations are more efficient and effective, when they continually try to improve. Therefore:

- Organisations must make a permanent commitment to continually improve their overall performance.

Principle 7 : Get the Facts Before taking a Decision

Organisations perform better, when their decisions are based on facts. Therefore:

- Organisations must base decisions on the analysis of factual information and data.

Principle 8 : Mutually Beneficial Supplier Relationship

Organisations depend on their suppliers to help them create value. Therefore:

- Organisations must maintain a mutually beneficial relationship with their suppliers.

1.6. ISO-9001 : 2000 - REQUIREMENTS

ISO - 9001: 2000 is the standard intended for quality management system assessment and registration. This apply uniformly to organisations of any size or description. ISO presents its requirements in section 4 to 8 of ISO - 9001 : 2000 standard. Broad features of these sections and requirement thereof, which have to be built in the documentation and then implemented, are given hereunder :

Section 4 : System Requirements

4.1. Establish your Quality System

Your organisation needs to document and use a quality system. Then, there is a need to continually improve it. For this, the organisation must:

- Identify Key processes to meet customer requirements.
- Establish the order of these processed and how they fit together.
- Establish how you will control these processes.
- Make resources available to support these processes.
- Measure these processes to not only ensure that they do what you wanted to put that you plan for them to improve.
- Where any process has been outsourced, it must be ensured that control over them is retained.
- Implement your quality management system.
- Manage and monitor process performance.
- Improve the quality management system.

4.2. Documentation Requirements

- Develop documents that reflect what organisation does.
- Develop documents to implement quality system including quality policy and objectives.
- Document procedures.
- Describe as to how processes interact.
- Prepare Quality Manual including the scope of quality system.

- Approve documents before their distribution.
- Provide the correct version of documents at points of use.
- Review and re-approve documents, whenever they are updated.
- Monitor documents that come from external sources.
- Quality records (working forms/registers or other records) are used and kept to prove the system is functioning properly.
- Develop a procedure to control records.

Section 5 : Management Requirements

5.1. Management Commitment

Top management should support the Quality Management System and should involve in its continual improvement:

- Promote the importance of quality.
- Promote the need to meet customer requirements, regulatory requirements, and satisfactory requirements.
- Develop a quality management system.
- Establish quality policies.
- Ensure quality objectives are established.
- Provide quality resources.
- Implement quality management systems.
- Perform quality management reviews.
- Improve quality management system.

5.2. Customer Focus

- Understand and identify customer requirements.
- Meet customers requirements
- Enhance customer satisfaction.

5.3. Establish a Quality Policy

- Define the organisation's quality policy and ensure that it serves the organisations purpose.
- Ensure that it emphasises the need to meet requirements.
- Ensure that it facilitates the development of quality objectives.
- Ensure that it makes a commitment to continuous improvement.
- Review the policy to ensure that it is still suitable.

5.4. Quality Planning

- Formulate quality objectives by ensuring that objectives are set for functional areas.
- Ensure that objectives support the quality policy.
- Ensure that objectives are measurable.

- Plan the development and implementation of quality management system.
- Plan the improvement of quality management system.

5.5. Authority and Responsibility of Quality System

- Define and communicate responsibilities and authorities.
- Appoint management representative who should oversee the quality management system and report the status regularly.
- Ensure sufficient communication processes are established.
- Ensure responsibilities and authorities are defined and communicated within the organisation.

5.6. Management Review

- Evaluate the performance of quality system and whether it should be improved.
- Inputs to management review shall include: results of audits, customer feedback, process performance and product conformity; any preventive and corrective actions; previous actions and their outcomes and recommendations for improvement.
- Generate actions to improve quality system and products.

Section 6. Resource Management Requirements

6.1. Provision of Resources

- Provide resources needed for implementing the quality management system (QMS) and make sure that customer requirements are being met.

6.2. Providing Human Resources

- Provide competent personnel for which ensure that they have the right experience, education, training and skills.
- Maintain a record of competence.

6.3. Providing Infrastructure

- Provide and maintain the infrastructure needed to achieve product/service conformity to requirements.

6.4. Providing Work Environment

- Identify needed work environment.
- Manage needed work environment.

Section 7. Realisation Requirements

7.1. Planning of Product Realisation

- Plan and develop processes needed to realise (make/generate) the product in line with QMS.
- Develop methods to control quality during product realisation.

7.2. Customer Related Processes

- Identify customer requirements and other requirements imposed by external agencies (including statutory requirements) and the requirements that organisation wishes to meet.
- Review customers' product requirement before you agree to sell it.
- Handle any changed requirements.
- Communicate with customers by developing a process to control communications with customers and implement it.

7.3. Product Design and Development

- Define your product design and development stages.
- Clarify design and development responsibilities and authorities.
- Manage interaction between design and development groups.
- Update design and development plans, as changes occur.
- Define design and development inputs.
- Create product design and development outputs.
- Approve design and development outputs prior to release.
- Use design and development outputs to control product quality.
- Carry out design and development reviews.
- Perform design and development verifications.
- Conduct design and development validations.
- Manage design and development changes.

7.4. Control Purchasing Function

- Control purchasing process - For this ensure that suppliers as well as purchased product meet requirements.
- Describe the products which are being purchased.
- Specify the requirements that must be met.
- Verify purchased products at suppliers premises and also at your own premises.

7.5. Control Production and Service Provisions

- Control production and service provisions 1h. processes informations, instructions, equipment, measurements and other activities.
- Validate production and service provision 1h, prove that processes, personnel and equipment can produce planned outputs.
- Identify and track the products 1h. establish and maintain the indentity of the products and their status.
- Protect the property (drawings, data, personnel, environment etc.) supplied by the customers.
- Preserve the products and components during internal processing as well as during final delivery.

7.6. Control of Monitoring and Measuring Devices

- Calibrate the equipment and verify them at specified intervals or prior to use against any relevant standards.
- Caliberation must be adjusted, as necessary.
- It must be identified to establish, when the equipment will require re-calibration.
- Calibrated equipment must be stored and used in such a way as to prevent its mis-alignment.

Section 8. Remedial Requirements (Measure, Analysis and Improvement).

8.1. Perform Remedial Processes

- Plan and implement remedial processes to demonstrate that a process is capable of producing desired results.
- Use remedial processes to improve QMS.

8.2. Monitor and Measure Quality

- Monitor and measure customer satisfaction.
- Plan and perform regular internal audits.
- Monitor and measure quality processes.
- Take action, when processes fail to achieve planned results.
- Monitor and measure product/service characteristics.
- Keep a record of product/service monitoring and measuring activities.

8.3. Control Non-Conforming Products

- Ensure that products/services/processes not conforming to requirements/plans are suitably identified and controlled to prevent misuse.
- Controls and responsibilities must be identified within a documented procedure.
- Re-verify non-conforming products that were corrected, meet the requirements.
- Maintain records of such products and describe the actions taken to deal with non-conformities.

8.4. Analyse Quality Information/Data

- Demonstrate the effectiveness of the quality system and then evaluate where continual improvement can be achieved. Standard indicators are usually : customer satisfaction ; conformance to requirements ; characteristics and trends of processes and products ; and supplier performance.

8.5. Make Quality Improvements

- Improve quality management system through the use of quality policy, objectives, audits, analysis of data, corrective and preventive actions and management review.
- Corrective action be taken after analysing cause of problems and a documented procedure be written to this effect.

- Record the results that corrective actions achieve.
- Examine the effectiveness of corrective actions.
- Develop preventive actions to eliminate potential problems. For this, a documented procedure should be established.

1.7. ISO-9000:2008 VERSION

ISO-9001:2008 basically re-narrates ISO-9000:2000. The 2008 version only introduced clarifications to the requirements of ISO-9001:2000 and some changes intended to improve consistency with ISO-14001: 2004. There were no new requirements.

This fourth edition (first edition ISO-9000:1987 version, second edition ISO-9000:1994 version; third edition ISO-9000:2000 version, and fourth edition ISO-9000:2008 version) cancels and replaces the third editions, which has been **amended** to clarify points in the text and to enhance compatibility with ISO-14001: 2004.

This version states that the design and implementation of an organisation's quality management system is influenced by:

(d) its organisational environment, changes in that environment, and the risks associated with that environment,

(e) its verying needs,

(f) its particular objectives,

(g) the products provided,

(h) the process employed,

(i) its size and organisational structure.

It is not the idea of this standard to imply uniformity in the structure of quality management systems or uniformity of documentation.

This International Standard promotes the adoption of a process approach when developing, implementing, and improving the effectiveness of a quality management system, to enhance customer satisfaction by meeting customer requirements. According to this new version, ensuring control over oustcourced processes does not absolve the organisation of the responsibility of conformity to all customer, statutory and regulatory requirements. The type and extent of control to be applied to the outsourced processes shall be defined within the quality management system.

This new version also defines the term 'work environment' which relates to those conditions under which work is performed including physical, environmental and other factors (such as noise, temperature, humidity, lighting or weather).

This version also include the post-delivery activities under the heading "customer-related processes" which include actions under warranty provisions, contractual obligations, such as maintenance services, and supplementary services, such as re-cycling or final disposal.

1.8. EFFECTIVENESS OF ISO-9000

Effectiveness of the ISO system being implemented depends on a number of factors, the most significant of which are:

1. **Commitment of senior management to monitor, control and improve quality.** Organizations that implement an ISO system without this desire and commitment

often take the cheapest road to get a certificate and ignore problem areas uncovered in the audits.

2. **How well the ISO system integrates into current business practices.**

   Many organisations that implement ISO try to make their system fit into a readymade quality manual instead of creating a manual that documents existing practices and only adds new processes to meet the ISO standard, when necessary.

3. **How well the ISO system focuses on improving the customer experience.**

   The broadest definition of quality is "Whatever the customer perceives good quality to be." This means that a company doesn't necessarily have to make a product that never fails; some customers will have a higher tolerance for product failures, if they always receive shipments on-time or have a positive experience in some other dimension of customer service. An ISO system should take into account all areas of the customer experience and the industry expectations, and seek to improve them on a continual basis. This means taking into account all processes that deal with the three stakeholders (customers, suppliers, and organization); only then will a company be able to sustain improvements in the customer's experience.

4. **How well the auditor finds and communicates areas of improvement.**

   Many auditors simply rely on submitting reports that indicate compliance or non-compliance or non-compliance with the appropriate section of the standard. Auditors that can clearly identify and communicate areas of improvement in language and terms executive management understands facilitate action on improvement initiatives by the companies, they audit. When management doesn't understand why they were non-compliant and the business implications associated with non-compliance, they simply ignore the reports and focus on what they do understand.

1.9. INSTALLATION OF QUALITY SYSTEM

The installation process of a quality system can be broadly divided into following three phases :

1. Preparations for ISO-9000 quality system.
2. Implementation of ISO-9000 quality system.
3. Registration and Certification of quality system.

Time required for installing the quality system may vary from 6 months to even 5 to 7 years, depending upon the following factors :

(i) Existing level of quality management.
(ii) The will of management and personnel to adopt the quality system.
(iii) Complexity of the process.
(iv) Characteristics of product.
(v) Competence and skill of the employees.
(vi) Size of the organisation.
(vii) Promptness in taking corrective actions.

1. Preparations for Quality System

Preparations for ISO-9000 quality system is done in following steps:

Step 1 : Pdqdjhphqw Ãv#frpplwphqw#wr#LVR#0<333. It can be demonstrated by:

(d) Making the organization's people to understand and implement the quality policy.

(e) Taking appropriate action for establishment and implementation of a quality system.

(f) Not permitting any deviation in quality activities.

(g) Involvement of top management in planning implementation and review activities of quality system.

Step 2: Vhw#xs#dq#lpsohphqwdwlrq#frpplwwhh. This committee may have 4 to 6 members selected from various disciplines. One ISO-9000 co-ordinator is also appointed to co-ordinate all quality system activities under the leadership of top management.

Step 3 : Vwduw#LVR0dzduhqhvv#fdpsdljq. Awareness programmes are conducted to communicate the employees of all levels to make them understand the purpose of introduction of ISO-9000 quality system, its advantages to the employees and customers.

Step 4 : Frqgxfw#Vwdwxv#Uhylhz#dqg#suhsduh#dq#Dfwlrq#Sodq. This includes the following:

(d) List out as to what is needed to install the quality system ?

(e) Review the existing set up against, what is needed,

(f) What actions are to be taken to meet the requirements of quality system ? It should be clarified :

What is to be done ?

Who will do it ?

By what time it shall be done ?

Step 5: Ghyhors#dq#rujdqlvdwlrq#vwuxfwxuh#iru#txdolw|#pdqdjhphqw. This aspect have already been discussed in detail in the chapter on 'organising the quality'.

Step 6: Ghyhors#Txdolw|#V|vwhp#Grfxphqwdwlrq. Quality system is normally documented by means of:

Quality Manuals.

Quality Procedures.

Work instructions, and

Quality records.

Step 7 : Suhsduh#wkh#uhvrxufh#v|vwhp#wr#phhw#wkh#uhtxluhphqwv#ri#vwdqgdugv. For design, development, production and supply of the products or services, various resources, such as machineries, facilities, know-how, testing and measuring equipments, material handling equipments etc. are required. Right type of process technology, and right type of processing and control equipments are required for effective implementation of quality system.

2. Implementation of ISO-9000 Quality System

ISO-9000 quality system can be implemented only after preparation phase, as explained above, is complete. Main steps involved in the implementation phase are:

Step 8 : Lpsohphqw#wkh#grfxphqwhg#txdolw|#v|vwhp: In this step, quality related activities are performed as per the quality policies, procedures, work instructions, as defined in quality manual and other quality system documentation.

Step 9 : Hvwdeolvk#lqwhuqdo#txdolw|#dxglw#v|vwhp. An internal auditors team is formed, who are trained with professional agency. They should conduct a planned and documented periodical audit of all quality related activities of the quality system. In initial stages, it helps various departments to continuously improve their performance.

Step 10: Prqlwru#dqg#vwdelol}h#wkh#txdolw|#v|vwhp. Implementation of quality system should be continuously monitored to ensure that all activities are being performed as planned, any deviation found is corrected. The observations of monitoring should be reported to the management and concerned persons.

Step 11: Frqgxfw#Suh0uhjlvwudwlrq#lqwhuqdo#dxglw. After stabilization of the system, an internal audit should be conducted to determine whether all the requirements are being met to qualify for certification. For this purpose, a detailed check list is prepared and then used during pre-registration assessment of quality system. Only when the system is found satisfactory, certification body should be approached for registration.

3. Registration and Certification

The organisation after having established and operating the quality system, now it need to be verified and certified by an independent certification body to meet the contractual requirements with their customers.

Step 12 : Dsso|#iru#uhjlvwudwlrq. Registration process starts with the submission of an application in the prescribed proforma alongwith a questionnaire, quality system documentation, and registration fees, to the nationally/internationally recognised and accredited certification agencies. Every country has one or more recognised certification agencies. In India Bureau of Indian Standards (BIS) is a qualified certification body. In addition to BIS, some other international accredited certification bodies are also operating in India.

Step 13: Dghtxdf|#dxglw#e|#fhuwlilfdwlrq#erg|. This is basically an office exercise by the auditors to determine the extent to which the documented quality system is meeting the requirements of the quality system standards with quality manual, quality procedures and other quality documents. The adequacy audit is done in two phases : (d) examination of quality system documentation, and (e) preaudit visit of the organisation.

Step 14 : Frpsoldqfh#dxglw#e|#wkh#fhuwlilfdwlrq#erg|. This audit is carried out to determine the extent to which the documented quality system is implemented and observed by the personnel of the organisation. In this audit, data gathering and collection of evidences is done through interviews, discussions, examination of records and physical observation of the processes. The non-conformities identified during the audit are substantiated by evidences. These non-conformities (if any) are to be corrected by the organisation within a specific time frame, and got to be re-verified from the auditors.

Afterall, the corrective actions are taken, and requirements of ISO quality standards are met, the auditors recommend the certification body for quality system certification.

Step 15: Fhuwlilfdwlrq:- Based on the final recommendations of the auditors, ISO-9000 quality system certificate is issued by the certification agency. This certificate is valid for specific period, generally three years. During this validity period, the certification body conducts unannounced surveillance visits to verify the effective implementation and maintenance of the quality system established by the firm. If the firm fails to maintain the quality system, the certificate may be withdrawn or suspended.

The licence granted by the certification body automatically expires at the end of the validity period, which is required to be got renewed by the firm. The licence can be renewed, after satisfactory compliance audit of the firm is re-conducted by the certification body.

1.10. QUALITY AUDITS

Quality audits are performed to find whether the end product satisfies the desired quality specifications, proper functioning of all equipment and machinery, and operators are carrying out their duties as per specified quality plans. Special care must be given for auditing of tools, gauges and testing equipments, specifications and drawings. Audits should be carried out by unbiased persons and without prior intimation, it should cover each and every person involved in the process.

'Quality audit' can be defined as "a systematic and independent examination to determine whether quality activities and related results comply with planned arrangements and whether these arrangements are implemented effectively and are suitable to achieve objectives".

The purpose of a quality audit is to evaluate the need for improvement or corrective action. The quality audit is an independent review conducted to compare some aspects of quality performance with a standard for that performance.

The purpose of quality audits is also to provide independent assurance that:

(i) plans for attaining quality are such that when followed, intended quality can be attained,
(ii) products are fit for use and safe for the user,
(iii) standards and regulations defined by government agencies and other bodies are being followed,
(iv) there is conformance to specification,
(v) the data system provides correct and adequate information on quality to all concerned,
(vi) deficiencies are identified and corrective actions are taken in time, and
(vii) improvement opportunities are identified and concerned personnel are informed.

The quality audits are scheduled on the basis of the status and importance of the activity to be audited and shall be carried out by personnel independent of those having direct responsibility for the activity being audited. The results of the audits are recorded and brought to the notice of personnel, having responsibility in the area audited. The management personnel responsible for the area shall take timely corrective action on deficiencies found during the audit. The results of these quality audits form an integral part of the input to management review activities. Management needs to establish a system for correcting deficiencies or non-conformities revealed during the audit.

In the initial stages, quality audits should be carried out frequently, say once a quarter. Once the system is well-established, an annual audit may be adequate. Similarly, departments critical to the successful operation of the quality system like manufacturing may be audited more frequently than others like marketing and training.

Follow-up of quality audit activities shall verify and record the implementation of the corrective action taken.

Quality audits are of three kinds ; namely: (d) first party audit i.e. internal audit, carried out by the organisation itself and used for internal quality management purpose, (e) second party audit i.e. Customer audit and is carried out by the customer and (f) third party audit i.e. external audit and is carried out by an independent organisation usually a qualified national or international agency.

1.10.1. Types of Audits

1. **System Audit:** It includes evaluation of any activity that can affect final product quality. Quality systems audit, reviews the quality aspects of various segments of the overall quality system, such as marketing, design and development, production, quality assurance, process control, final inspection and testing, internal audit etc.
2. **Product Audit:** It involves the re-inspection of product to verify the adequacy of acceptance or rejection decisions made by inspection and testing department. Product audit is an independent evaluation of product quality to determine its fitness for use and conformance to specification. This takes place after completion of inspection, and is conducted for:
   (d) estimating the quality level of the products delivered to the customers,
   (e) evaluating the effectiveness of the inspection decisions, and
   (f) providing information useful in improving the outgoing product quality level and improving effectiveness of inspection.
3. **Adequacy Audit:** It is a management audit to determine the extent to which the documented system represented by the quality manual and procedures adequately meets the requirements of the applicable standard.

1.10.2. Structuring the Audit Programmes

Audit programmes are usually structured i.e. they are designed to carry out agreed purposes, and are conducted under agreed rules of conduct. The audit programmes are structured collectively by heads of activities which are to be the subject of audit, heads of auditing department, and upper management.

Audits are generally conducted by full time auditors, who are skilled in both, technical and human relations aspects. Sometimes, auditors relationships with those whose work is being audited become quite strained. Deficiencies found in the audit may be resented because of the implied criticism therein. In order to avoid such a situation, an extensive discussions is warranted with respect to the following :

(i) Reasons behind the audit,
(ii) Avoiding an atmosphere of blame.
(iii) Balance in reporting.
(iv) Depersonalising the report.
(v) Post audit meeting.

Steps in Structuring an Audit Programme are:

1. Discussion on purposes to be achieved by audit.
2. Approach for conducting the audit.
3. Study of policies,procedures and other applicable rules.

4. Scheduling of audit.
5. Conducting the audit.
6. Verification of factual findings.
7. Preparation of report with facts and recommendations
8. Discussion of reports.
9. Decisions on action to be taken.
10. Follow-up.

Planning and Performing Audits

Main steps in performing quality audits are initiation, planning, implementation, reporting and completing. Steps for planning and performing in detail are:

1. Request for audit programme.
2. Determination of scope, objective and timing.
3. Selection of audit team including its leader.
4. Determination of audit elements.
5. Assignment elements to auditors.
6. Preparation of audit plan.
7. Distribution of audit plan and audit notification.
8. Audit commencement meeting.
9. Data/evidence gathering and evaluation.
10. Audit supervision and co-ordination.
11. Post audit meeting.
12. Drafting of report
13. Review and submit report finding.
14. Finalizing the audit report
15. Distribution of the audit report.
16. Decision on follow-up of finding.
17. Follow-up.

Use of Reference Standards in the Audit.

The reference standards normally available include:

1. Policies of the company applicable to quality.
2. Customer and company quality specifications.
3. Pertinent government specification.
4. Company, industry, and other pertinent quality standards on products and processes
5. Published guides for conduct of quality audits.
6. Pertinent quality departmental instructions.

Discoveries of Causes and Recommendations of Audit

In many companies, the auditor is expected to investigate major deficiencies in an effort to determine their causes, This investigation then becomes the basis of the auditor's recommendation.

Auditors are also expected to make recommendations with a view of reducing deficiencies and improving performance.

1.10.3. Audit Reporting

Audit results are documented in the audit report, the draft of which should be discussed and reviewed in a post-audit meeting held with the management of the activity that was audited. The report should include the following items :

(i) Purpose and scope of the audit.
(ii) Details of the audit plan, including audit personnel, dates, activities audited, personnel contacted, material or documents reviewed, number of observations made etc.
(iii) Standards, check-list, or other documents used during the audit.
(iv) Audit observations, supported with evidences, conclusions, and recommendations.
(v) Recommendations about improvement opportunities.
(vi) Recommendations for follow-up the proposed corrective actions.

QUESTIONS

1. What is quality management system? What are its benefits?
2. Explain the term 'ISO-9000 Quality System' ? Illustrate various ISO-9000 standards.
3. What are the aims of ISO-9000 ? Mention their areas of application.
4. (d) Who can adopt ISO-9000?
   (e) Explain the benefits of ISO-9000.
5. How will you do planning for installation of quality system?
6. Explain ISO-9000 : 2000 in detail.
7. Explain the history and origin of ISO-9000.
8. Explain the quality management principles of ISO-9000 : 2000 standards.
9. Explain the various requirements for ISO-9001 : 2000
10. Explain about ISO-9000:2008 version in detail.
11. Explain in detail about 'quality audit ?
12. Explain different types of quality audits.

A

B

C

G

H

I

J

K

L

M

Q

R

S

T

U

V

W

X

Y

Z

INDUSTRIAL ENGINEERING AND MANAGEMENT

S.C. Sharma, T.R. Banga

FEEDBACK FORM

1. Which topics from your examination point of view are inadequately or not covered in this book?

___

___

2. Is there any misprints/ mistakes/ factual inaccuracy in this book? If so, please specify.

___

___

3. What is your assessment of this book as regards the presentation of the subject-matter, expression, precision and price in relation to the other recommended books available on this subject?

___

___

4. Which competing books you regard as better than this? Please mention their author and publishers.

___

___

5. Any further suggestions/comments you would like to make for the improvement of the book?

___

___

PS: If needed, please attach a separate sheet.

Name : ____________________

College : ____________________

Address : ____________________

Email : ____________________

Mobile : ____________________

Please mail the feedback form at:

KHANNA BOOK PUBLISHING CO. (P) LTD.

4C/4344, Ansari Road, Daryaganj, New Delhi-110002

You can also email this feedback form at contact@khannabooks.com or Whatsapp at +91 – 99109 09320

BEST FEEDBACK WILL BE REWARDED SUITABLY